SOCIOLOGY IN OUR TIMES

SOCIOLOGY IN OUR TIMES

SIXTH CANADIAN EDITION

Jane Lothian Murray
University of Winnipeg

Rick Linden
University of Manitoba

Diana Kendall
Baylor University

NELSON EDUCATION

NELSON EDUCATION

Sociology in Our Times, Sixth Canadian Edition

by Jane Lothian Murray, Rick Linden, and Diana Kendall

Vice President, Editorial Higher Education:
Anne Williams

Acquisitions Editor:
Maya Castle

Marketing Manager:
Terry Fedorkiw

Developmental Editor:
Liisa Kelly

Photo Researcher and Permissions Coordinator:
Carrie McGregor

Senior Content Production Manager:
Natalia Denesiuk Harris

Production Service:
Cenveo Publisher Services

Copy Editor:
Sheila Wawanash

Proofreader:
Erin Moore

Indexer:
BIM Indexing Services

Senior Production Coordinator:
Ferial Suleman

Design Director:
Ken Phipps

Managing Designer:
Franca Amore

Interior Design:
Sharon Lucas

Cover Image and Design:
Trinh Truong

Compositor:
Cenveo Publisher Services

Printer:
RR Donnelley

Printed and bound in the United States of America
3 4 5 6 17 16 15 14

For more information contact Nelson Education Ltd., 1120 Birchmount Road, Toronto, Ontario, M1K 5G4. Or you can visit our Internet site at http://www.nelson.com

Library and Archives Canada Cataloguing in Publication Data

Lothian Murray, Jane, 1960–
Sociology in our times / Jane Lothian Murray, Rick Linden, Diana Kendall. — 6th Canadian ed.

Prev. eds. by Diana Kendall, Rick Linden and Jane Lothian Murray.
Includes bibliographical references and index.
ISBN-13: 978-0-17-664874-9

1. Sociology—Textbooks. 2. Sociology—Canada—Textbooks. I. Linden, Rick II. Kendall, Diana Elizabeth III. Title.

HM586.K45 2013 301 C2012-907790-9

PKG ISBN-13: 978-0-17-664874-9
PKG ISBN-10: 0-17-664874-7

To the memory of my mother-in-law, Mildred Cormack. She was a great friend who taught me the value of storytelling as a way of understanding the world (as well as keeping her grandchildren amused).

—Rick Linden

For my buddy, my love, Douglas William Nanton

—Jane Lothian Murray

BRIEF CONTENTS

CONTENTS

PART III ▪ SOCIAL DIFFERENCES AND SOCIAL INEQUALITY

BOXES

SOCIOLOGY AND EVERYDAY LIFE

POINT/COUNTERPOINT

SOCIOLOGY IN GLOBAL PERSPECTIVE

SOCIOLOGY AND NEW MEDIA

(online at http://www.nelson.com/sociologyinourtimes6e)

PREFACE

Welcome to the sixth Canadian edition of *Sociology in Our Times*. As this edition was being written, we became acutely aware of how our country and the world have changed in recent years. Even as some things change, however, others remain the same. One thing that has not changed is the significance of education and the profound importance of understanding how and why people act the way they do, how societies grapple with issues and major problems, and why many of us are reassured by social institutions—including family, religion, education, government, and the media—even at times when we might like to see certain changes occur in these institutions.

Like previous editions of this widely read text, this sixth Canadian edition is a cutting-edge book in at least two ways: (1) by including a diversity of classical and contemporary theory, interesting and relevant research, and lived experiences that accurately mirror the diversity in society itself, and (2) by showing students that sociology involves important questions and issues that they confront both personally and vicariously (for example, through the media). Speaking to a wide variety of Canadian students, this text captures their interest by taking into account their concerns and perspectives. The research within it includes the best work of classical and established contemporary sociologists, and an inclusive treatment of all people is woven throughout the text's examination of sociology.

By using the latest theory and research, *Sociology in Our Times* not only provides students with the most relevant information about sociological thinking, but also helps students consider the significance of the interlocking nature of class, race, and gender in all aspects of life.

We have sought to make the research accessible and engaging for both students and instructors. Concepts and theories are presented in a straightforward and understandable way, and the wealth of concrete examples and lived experiences woven throughout the chapters makes the relevance of sociological theory and research abundantly clear to students.

NEW FEATURES

Changes in the Sixth Canadian Edition

The sixth Canadian edition of *Sociology in Our Times* provides us with the opportunity to further improve a text that has been well received by students and educators. We have added several hundred new references that incorporate the most recent new developments in sociological research, including the latest census data from Statistics Canada. In response to reviewers' comments, we have once again reduced the length of most of the chapters while retaining the features that have made it attractive to students and to instructors. We have also added two new chapters, "Sex, Sexualities, and Intimate Relationships" and "Mass Media," because of the importance of these topics to today's educators and students.

- Chapter 1 ("The Sociological Perspective") introduces students to the main theoretical perspectives used in sociology and includes a revised discussion of postmodernism. Students are also introduced to the importance of having a global sociological imagination. The opening narrative introduces students to the new chapter theme of consumerism and student debt.
- Chapter 2 ("Sociological Research") describes how social scientists conduct their research and the links between research and theory. The chapter includes a new example of field research that involves a study of how Sri Lankans responded to the 2004 tsunami. The study focused on the relief effort and how the money donated by people in Canada and other countries might best help those who have been affected by natural disasters. A box ("Social Research Methods and New Media") has been added outlining how researchers can use the new social media both as a research area and as a method for doing research (available online at **http://www.nelson.com/sociologyinourtimes6e**).
- Chapter 3 ("Culture") has the most recent census data on language diversity, ethnicity, and Aboriginal peoples in Canada. This chapter has a new opening narrative and Sociology and Everyday Life box ("How Much Do You Know About Multiculturalism in Canada?" on page 63).
- Chapter 4 ("Socialization") has shifted focus somewhat to examine the effects of positive socialization and interesting new issues relating to early childhood and adolescent socialization that are particularly relevant to students attending university for the first time. A new Sociology and Everyday Life box (page 93) tests students on their knowledge on socialization and university life.
- Chapter 5 ("Society, Social Structure, and Interaction") includes recent research on homelessness in Canada and provides an update on the debate about panhandling.
- Chapter 6 ("Groups and Organizations") examines how organizations affect our behaviour.
- Chapter 7 ("Crime and Deviance") features some new material on computer hacking and a new box on cybercrime ("The Growth of Cybercrime," available online). A Point/Counterpoint box ("'If It Bleeds, It Leads': Fear of Crime and the Media," page 195) now discusses the failure of the media to adequately cover the disappearances of marginalized women who were eventually found to have been murdered by Robert Pickton. Finally, a new Point/Counterpoint box ("Do Tougher Prison Sentences Reduce Crime?" page 201) discusses the issue of whether longer prison sentences have an impact on crime rates.

- Chapter 8 ("Social Class and Stratification in Canada") has incorporated the most recent data on the distribution of wealth and income, as well as poverty, in today's society.
- Chapter 9 ("Global Stratification") has an updated discussion of the progress that has been made in improving the lives of the world's poorest people. The new Human Development Index (HDI) rankings are included, along with a new version of the HDI rankings adjusted for each country's level of inequality. A new Point/Counterpoint box ("The Foxconn Suicides," page 264) examines the reasons behind the suicides at China's Foxconn factory, which produces Apple products.
- Chapter 10 ("Ethnic Relations and Race") takes a closer look at the significance of ethnic diversity with an emphasis on various forms of racism. This chapter also includes the newest census data on ethnic origins, language diversity, and visible minorities.
- Chapter 11 ("Gender") provides a more balanced discussion of gender by presenting both male and female perspectives on the challenges associated with "being gendered." Also highlighted in this chapter are the gains made by women in terms of gender equity—including those made in educational institutions—and women's remaining challenges, such as the wage gap and inequalities in the distribution of unpaid labour in the home.
- Chapter 12 ("Sex, Sexualities, and Intimate Relationships") is a new chapter that examines a range of issues related to sexuality today. Topics such as sexual health, diverse sexualities, sexual double standards, and "hookup cultures" were selected on the basis of their relevance to young adults.
- Chapter 13 ("Families") has the most recent data on changes in Canadian families, including an increase in the number of singles, stepfamilies, and common-law families, while maintaining its focus on family diversity and change.
- Chapter 14 ("Education") examines the positive changes in recent decades in terms of gender bias in education and the gap in educational attainment between men and women. The chapter also includes an examination of bullying and school violence.
- Chapter 15 ("Religion") has not been extensively revised for this edition. While some material has been updated, data on religious affiliation from the 2011 census was not available at the time of publication.
- Chapter 16 ("Health, Healthcare, and Disability") contains updated statistics on health and healthcare. One area of particular interest are new statistics showing that the global HIV/AIDS situation has been improving because of awareness programs and the availability of better treatment for those with HIV/AIDS. A new Point/Counterpoint box ("Pink Ribbons, Inc.: The Corporatization of Medical Charities," page 453) examines the issue of the corporatization of medical charities using the example of the pink ribbon fundraising campaign for breast cancer.
- Chapter 17 ("Mass Media") is a new chapter that deals with the mass media but focuses particularly on new media. New social and digital media have had a huge impact on people around the world and are changing almost daily. Students' lives have changed because of the new media, and it is important that this text discuss some of the new and exciting research being done in this area.
- Chapter 18 ("Aging") offers a fresh discussion on the impact on older people, particularly women, of negative attitudes toward aging. The chapter also has a new box ("Seniors and New Media," available online at **http://www.nelson.com/sociologyinourtimes6e**) on the ways in which seniors are using new media to stay in contact with family and friends. Statistics in the chapter have been extensively updated to reflect the aging of Canadian society.
- Chapter 19 ("The Economy and Work") has new material on the impact of new technology in the workplace and updated statistics on employment and the economy.
- Chapter 20 ("Power, Politics, and Government") includes updated information on the Canadian political scene and a new box ("The Political Impact of Social Media," available online at **http://www.nelson.com/sociologyinourtimes6e**) on how the new media are affecting politics.
- Chapter 21 ("Population and Urbanization") examines population patterns and also looks at urban life. This edition includes updated statistics on Canada's population and urbanization (available online at **http://www.nelson.com/sociologyinourtimes6e**).
- Chapter 22 ("Collective Behaviour, Social Movements, and Social Change") includes interesting new examples of protest movements in Canada and elsewhere, such as the 2011 Occupy movement (available online at **http://www.nelson.com/sociologyinourtimes6e**).

UNIQUE FEATURES

The following special features are specifically designed to reflect the themes of relevance and diversity in *Sociology in Our Times*, as well as to support student learning. The enhanced pedagogical framework new to this edition aims to respect diverse learning preferences and engage today's students. While we have retained the hallmark features of the text, such as the Lived Experiences that open each chapter, we have introduced new elements—such as the Time to Review feature—to support better student outcomes.

Providing Interesting and Engaging Lived Experiences Throughout

Authentic first-person accounts are used as opening vignettes and throughout each chapter to create interest and give concrete meaning to the topics being discussed. Lived experiences, including racism, child abuse, environmental activism, eating disorders, disability, and homelessness, provide opportunities for students to consider social life beyond their own experiences and to examine class, ethnicity, gender, and age from diverse perspectives. An unusually wide range of diverse experiences—both positive and negative—is systematically incorporated to expose students to a multiplicity of viewpoints. The lived experiences have been selected for their ability to speak to students, to assist them in learning concepts and theories, and to illustrate how they can be applied to other situations. New Lived Experiences for the sixth Canadian edition explore topics such as debt (Chapter 1, "The Sociological Perspective"); the student experiences of socialization, racism, and casual relationships (respectively, Chapter 4, "Socialization"; Chapter 10, "Ethnic Relations and Race"; and Chapter 12, "Sex, Sexualities, and Intimate Relationships"); the impact of social media on politics (Chapter 17, "Mass Media"); and a journalist's educated analysis of the anti-capitalist Occupy protests (Chapter 22, "Collective Behaviour, Social Movements, and Social Change").

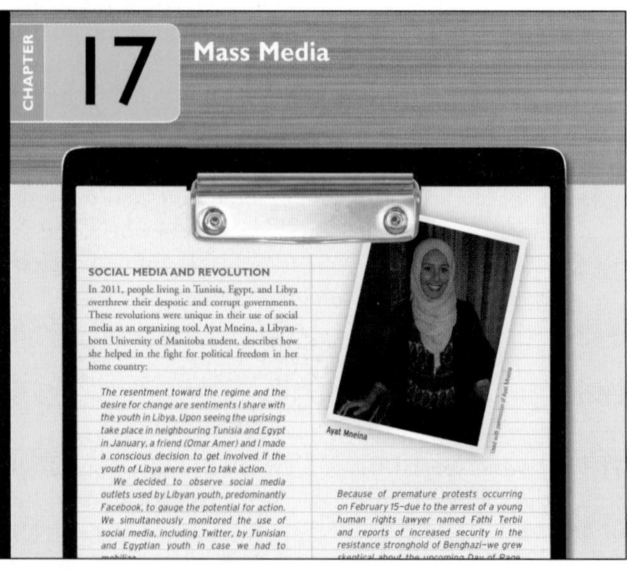

CHAPTER 17 Mass Media

SOCIAL MEDIA AND REVOLUTION

In 2011, people living in Tunisia, Egypt, and Libya overthrew their despotic and corrupt governments. These revolutions were unique in their use of social media as an organizing tool. Ayat Mneina, a Libyan-born University of Manitoba student, describes how she helped in the fight for political freedom in her home country:

The resentment toward the regime and the desire for change are sentiments I share with the youth in Libya. Upon seeing the uprisings take place in neighbouring Tunisia and Egypt in January, a friend (Omar Amer) and I made a conscious decision to get involved if the youth of Libya were ever to take action.

We decided to observe social media outlets used by Libyan youth, predominantly Facebook, to gauge the potential for action. We simultaneously monitored the use of social media, including Twitter, by Tunisian and Egyptian youth in case we had to

Ayat Mneina

Used with permission of Ayat Mneina

Because of premature protests occurring on February 15—due to the arrest of a young human rights lawyer named Fathi Terbil and reports of increased security in the resistance stronghold of Benghazi—we grew

Focusing on the Relationship Between Sociology and Everyday Life

Each chapter has a brief Sociology and Everyday Life quiz that relates the sociological perspective to the pressing social issues presented in the opening vignette. (Answers are provided online at **http://www.nelson.com/sociologyinourtimes6e.**) Do official statistics accurately reflect crime rates in Canada? Does increasing cultural diversity lead to an increasing incidence of hate crimes and racism? Do individuals over the age of 65 have the highest rate of poverty? Topics such as these will pique the interest of students.

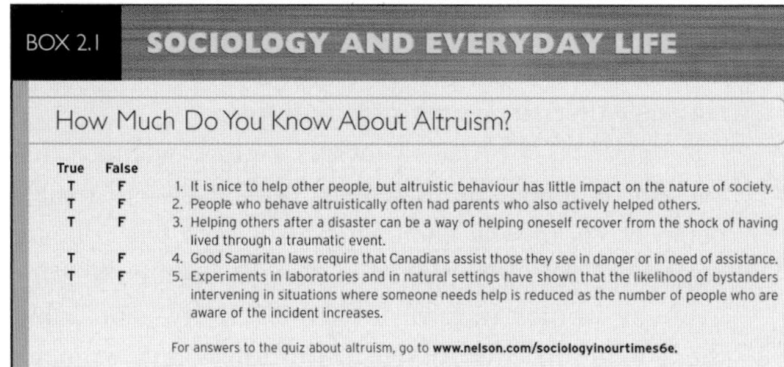

BOX 2.1 SOCIOLOGY AND EVERYDAY LIFE

How Much Do You Know About Altruism?

True	False	
T	F	1. It is nice to help other people, but altruistic behaviour has little impact on the nature of society.
T	F	2. People who behave altruistically often had parents who also actively helped others.
T	F	3. Helping others after a disaster can be a way of helping oneself recover from the shock of having lived through a traumatic event.
T	F	4. Good Samaritan laws require that Canadians assist those they see in danger or in need of assistance.
T	F	5. Experiments in laboratories and in natural settings have shown that the likelihood of bystanders intervening in situations where someone needs help is reduced as the number of people who are aware of the incident increases.

For answers to the quiz about altruism, go to **www.nelson.com/sociologyinourtimes6e.**

Emphasizing the Importance of a Global Perspective

In our interconnected world, the sociological imagination must extend beyond national borders. The global implications of topics are examined throughout each chapter and in Sociology in Global Perspective boxes. Topics include extended families in the global economy; global advertising; and wealth, poverty, and aging in Russia.

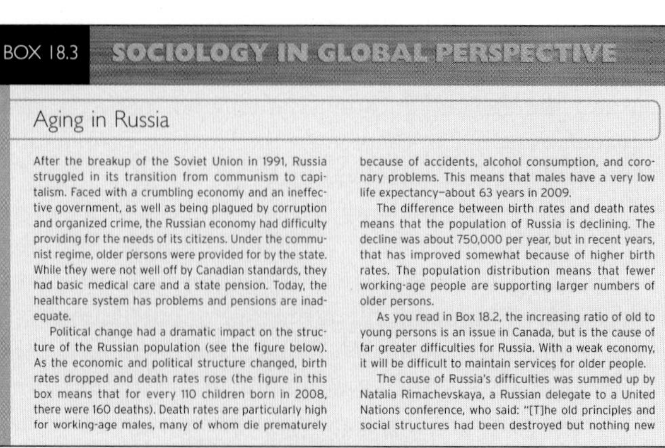

BOX 18.3 SOCIOLOGY IN GLOBAL PERSPECTIVE

Aging in Russia

After the breakup of the Soviet Union in 1991, Russia struggled in its transition from communism to capitalism. Faced with a crumbling economy and an ineffective government, as well as being plagued by corruption and organized crime, the Russian economy had difficulty providing for the needs of its citizens. Under the communist regime, older persons were provided for by the state. While they were not well off by Canadian standards, they had basic medical care and a state pension. Today, the healthcare system has problems and pensions are inadequate.

Political change had a dramatic impact on the structure of the Russian population (see the figure below). As the economic and political structure changed, birth rates dropped and death rates rose (the figure in this box means that for every 110 children born in 2008, there were 160 deaths). Death rates are particularly high for working-age males, many of whom die prematurely because of accidents, alcohol consumption, and coronary problems. This means that males have a very low life expectancy—about 63 years in 2009.

The difference between birth rates and death rates means that the population of Russia is declining. The decline was about 750,000 per year, but in recent years, that has improved somewhat because of higher birth rates. The population distribution means that fewer working-age people are supporting larger numbers of older persons.

As you read in Box 18.2, the increasing ratio of old to young persons is an issue in Canada, but is the cause of far greater difficulties for Russia. With a weak economy, it will be difficult to maintain services for older people.

The cause of Russia's difficulties was summed up by Natalia Rimachevskaya, a Russian delegate to a United Nations conference, who said: "[T]he old principles and social structures had been destroyed but nothing new

NEW to this Edition: Encouraging Students to Use Their Sociological Knowledge to Think Critically Through Point/ Counterpoint Boxes

Point/Counterpoint boxes encourage students to use their sociological knowledge to grapple with some of today's most hotly contested issues, such as the deterrent effects of increased prison sentences; the practice of corporations, such as Apple, of using offshore factories where working conditions may be very harsh; and the corporatization of medical charities. The topics covered can be used as springboards for in-class debate or online discussion forums.

BOX 13.3 POINT/COUNTERPOINT

Baby by Stealth: Reproduction Law Forcing "Dangerous Alternatives"

At the same time as reproductive technologies stretch the notion of the family beyond the nuclear, and just as Canada bends to accommodate that evolution, a prevailing piece of federal legislation is being accused of inadvertently forcing a slew of prospective parents underground.

At the root of this underworld, some argue, is the 2004 *Assisted Human Reproduction Act*—the Canadian government's most comprehensive attempt to regulate reproductive technologies. Some onlookers fear that the legislation has created a secretive black market, where couples seek sperm and egg donors on Craigslist or in university libraries.

Where those couples quietly compensate donors for their gametes, despite the legislation that criminalizes doing so. Where lesbian couples lie to doctors about their sexual orientation to avoid paying to quarantine a friend's sperm for six months. And where doctors and counsellors sometimes adopt the credo of "Don't ask, don't tell."

The act—which is a result of the Royal Commission on New Reproductive Technologies in 1993—has triggered condemnation from the right and left, and was the focal point of an International Women's Day conference in Toronto last week. There, at the Law Society of Upper Canada, panellists argued that some of the legislation

Census Profile

The Census Profiles provide information highlighting changes in Canadian society based on census data. Each unique box uses recent statistics, ensuring students are up-to-date and informed about the topics discussed.

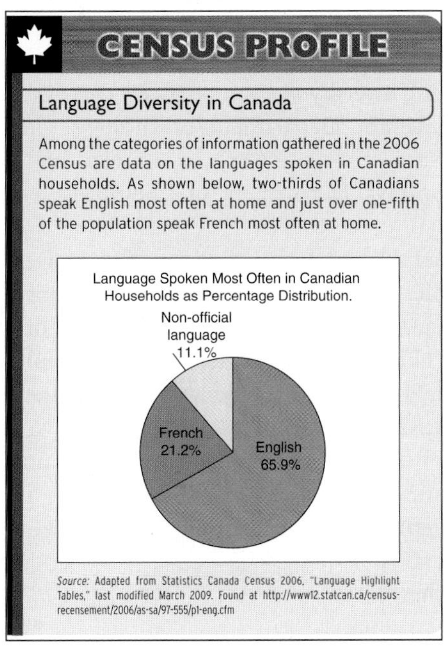

CENSUS PROFILE

Language Diversity in Canada

Among the categories of information gathered in the 2006 Census are data on the languages spoken in Canadian households. As shown below, two-thirds of Canadians speak English most often at home and just over one-fifth of the population speak French most often at home.

Source: Adapted from Statistics Canada Census 2006, "Language Highlight Tables," last modified March 2009. Found at http://www12.statcan.ca/census-recensement/2006/as-sa/97-555/pl-eng.cfm

Looking Ahead to Sociology in the Future

Beyond highlighting the contemporary relevance of sociology, this text encourages students to consider the sociological perspective as it might be in the future. The concluding section of a number of chapters considers the future and suggests how our social lives may look in the years to come. Environmental issues, homelessness, technology, population, deviance and crime, and the economy and work are among the topics discussed.

In-Text Learning Aids

Sociology in Our Times includes a number of pedagogical aids to promote students' mastery of sociological concepts and terminology.

NEW to this edition: Learning Objectives. A list of key themes at the beginning of each chapter gives students an overview of major topics and a convenient aid for review.

NEW to this edition: Critical Thinking Questions. After each chapter's opening lived experience, a series of introductory questions invites students to think about the major topics discussed in the vignette and the chapter.

NEW to this edition: Concept Snapshot. A brief summary of all major perspectives covered in the chapter and the key people connected to those theories are presented in a table format that is efficient for studying.

NEW to this edition: Integrated Running Glossary. Major concepts and key terms are highlighted in bold print within the text flow and defined in the margin and again at the end of the chapters and in the glossary at the back of the book.

NEW to this edition: Time to Review Questions. Time to Review questions provoke students to review and retain key information from the preceding paragraphs.

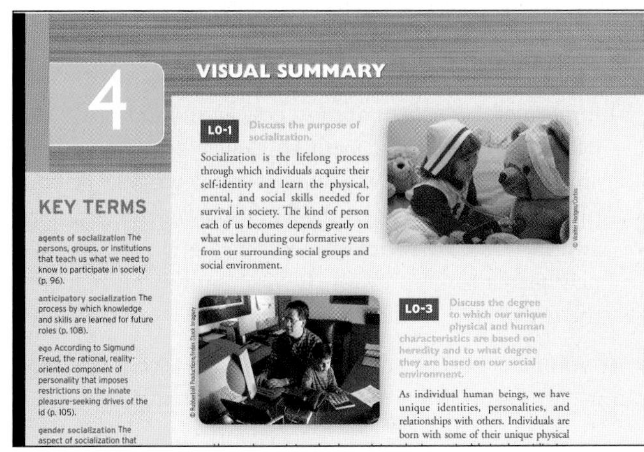

4 VISUAL SUMMARY

KEY TERMS

agents of socialization The persons, groups, or institutions that teach us what we need to know to participate in society (p. 96).

anticipatory socialization The process by which knowledge and skills are learned for future roles (p. 108).

ego According to Sigmund Freud, the rational, reality-oriented component of personality that imposes restrictions on the innate pleasure-seeking drives of the id (p. 105).

gender socialization The aspect of socialization that

LO-1 Discuss the purpose of socialization.

Socialization is the lifelong process through which individuals acquire their self-identity and learn the physical, mental, and social skills needed for survival in society. The kind of person each of us becomes depends greatly on what we learn during our formative years from our surrounding social groups and social environment.

© Walter Hodges/Corbis

© Rubberball Productions/Index Stock Imagery

LO-3 Discuss the degree to which our unique physical and human characteristics are based on heredity and to what degree they are based on our social environment.

As individual human beings, we have unique identities, personalities, and relationships with others. Individuals are born with some of their unique physical

NEW to this edition: Visual Summary. The Visual Summary provides a concise summary of key points and theoretical perspectives and includes several features that are new to this edition. Summarized learning objectives are illustrated by a relevant image from the chapter, and a Key Figures feature reintroduces students to the major players in each chapter with a few important points and a portrait. Additionally, Application Questions encourage students to assess their knowledge of the chapter and apply insights they have gained to other issues, while a list of Key Terms with page references provides a helpful study aid.

FOR STUDENTS

CourseMate NEW to this edition: Nelson Education's **CourseMate websites** bring course concepts to life with interactive learning and exam preparation tools that integrate with the printed textbook. Students activate their knowledge through quizzes, games, and flashcards, among many other tools.

The **CourseMate websites** provide immediate feedback that enables students to connect results to the work they have just produced, increasing their learning efficiency. Watch student comprehension and engagement soar as your class engages with these student-focused sites.

The **CourseMate website** for *Sociology in Our Times*, Sixth Canadian Edition, provides students with interactive learning tools, including

- interactive quizzes (including true-false, multiple-choice, and essay questions)
- flashcards, crosswords, and concentration games
- online chapters (Ch. 21, "Population and Urbanization"; Ch. 22, "Collective Behaviour, Social Movements, and Social Change")
- "You Can Make a Difference" boxes
- video clips and exercises
- a final exam
- "Sociology and New Media" boxes: Social media are very important in the lives of most college and university students. A significant benefit of a sociology course is its ability to encourage students to think critically about phenomena such as new media. Topics in the Sociology and New Media boxes range from the way seniors use new media to keep in touch with family and friends to the use of new media by politicians.

If you have purchased a new copy of this textbook, you can access CourseMate by using the Printed Access Card located in the inside front cover of your copy. If you have purchased a second-hand copy of the textbook, you can access CourseMate by logging onto **http://www.nelson.com/sociologyinourtimes6e**.

FOR INSTRUCTORS

neta The **Nelson Education Teaching Advantage (NETA)** program delivers research-based instructor resources that promote student engagement and higher-order thinking to enable the success of Canadian students and educators.

Instructors today face many challenges. Resources are limited, time is scarce, and a new kind of student has emerged: one who is juggling school with work, has gaps in his or her basic knowledge, and is immersed in technology in a way that has led to a completely new style of learning. In response, Nelson Education has gathered a group of dedicated instructors to advise us on the creation of richer and more flexible ancillaries and online learning platforms that respond to the needs of today's teaching environments. Whether your course is offered in-class, online, or both, Nelson is pleased to provide pedagogically-driven, research-based resources to support you.

The members of our editorial advisory board have experience across a variety of disciplines and are recognized for their commitment to teaching. They include

Norman Althouse, Haskayne School of Business, University of Calgary
Brenda Chant-Smith, Department of Psychology, Trent University
Scott Follows, Manning School of Business Administration, Acadia University
Jon Houseman, Department of Biology, University of Ottawa
Glen Loppnow, Department of Chemistry, University of Alberta
Tanya Noel, Department of Biology, York University
Gary Poole, Senior Scholar, Centre for Health Education Scholarship, and Associate Director, School of Population and Public Health, University of British Columbia
Dan Pratt, Department of Educational Studies, University of British Columbia
Mercedes Rowinsky-Geurts, Department of Languages and Literatures, Wilfrid Laurier University
David DiBattista, Department of Psychology, Brock University
Roger Fisher, PhD

In consultation with the editorial advisory board, Nelson Education has completely rethought the structure, approaches, and formats of our key textbook ancillaries and online learning platforms. We've also increased our investment in editorial support for our ancillary and digital authors. The result is the Nelson Education Teaching Advantage and its key components: ***NETA Engagement, NETA Assessment, NETA Presentation,*** and ***NETA Digital***. Each component includes one or more ancillaries prepared according to our best practices and may also be accompanied by documentation explaining the theory behind the practices.

NETA Engagement presents materials that help instructors deliver engaging content and activities to their classes. Instead of Instructor's Manuals that regurgitate chapter outlines and key terms from the text, NETA Enriched Instructor's Manuals (EIMs) provide genuine assistance to teachers. The EIMs answer questions like *What should students learn?, Why should students care?,* and *What are some common student misconceptions and stumbling blocks?* EIMs not only identify the topics that cause students the most difficulty, but also describe techniques and resources to help students master these concepts. Dr. Roger Fisher's *Instructor's Guide to Classroom Engagement (IGCE)* accompanies every Enriched Instructor's Manual. (Information about the NETA Enriched Instructor's Manual prepared for *Sociology in Our Times*, Sixth Canadian Edition, is included in the description of the IRCD below.)

NETA Assessment relates to testing materials. Under NETA Assessment, Nelson's authors create multiple-choice questions that reflect research-based best practices for constructing effective questions and testing not just recall but also higher-order thinking. Our guidelines were developed by David DiBattista, a 3M National Teaching Fellow whose recent research as a professor of psychology at Brock University has focused on multiple-choice testing. All Test Bank authors receive training at workshops conducted by Prof. DiBattista, as do the copyeditors assigned to each Test Bank. A copy of *Multiple Choice Tests: Getting Beyond Remembering*, Prof. DiBattista's guide to writing effective tests, is included with every Nelson Test Bank/Computerized Test Bank package. (Information about the NETA Test Bank prepared for *Sociology in Our Times*, Sixth Canadian Edition, is included in the description of the IRCD below.)

NETA Presentation has been developed to help instructors make the best use of PowerPoint® in their classrooms. With a clean and uncluttered design developed by Maureen Stone of StoneSoup Consulting, NETA Presentation features slides with improved readability, more multi-media and graphic materials, activities to use in class, and tips for instructors on the Notes page. A copy of *NETA Guidelines for Classroom Presentations* by Maureen Stone is included with each set of PowerPoint slides. (Information about the NETA PowerPoint® prepared for *Sociology in Our Times*, Sixth Canadian Edition, is included in the description of the IRCD below.)

NETA Digital is a framework based on Arthur Chickering and Zelda Gamson's seminal work "Seven Principles of Good Practice In Undergraduate Education" (*AAHE Bulletin*, 1987) and the follow-up work by Chickering and Stephen C. Ehrmann, "Implementing the Seven Principles: Technology as Lever"(*AAHE Bulletin*, 1996). This aspect of the NETA program guides the writing and development of our digital products to ensure that they appropriately reflect the core goals of contact, collaboration, multimodal learning, time on task, prompt feedback, active learning, and high expectations. The resulting focus on pedagogical utility, rather than technological wizardry, ensures that all of our technology supports better outcomes for students.

IRCD

Key instructor ancillaries are provided on the *Instructor's Resource CD* (ISBN 978-0-17-664866-4), giving instructors the ultimate tool for customizing lectures and presentations. (Downloadable web versions are also available at **http://www.nelson.com/sociologyinourtimes6e**.) The IRCD includes

- **NETA Engagement:** The Enriched Instructor's Manual was written by Tamy Superle of Carleton University. It is organized according to the textbook chapters and addresses eight key educational concerns, such as typical stumbling blocks student face and how to address them. Other features include engagement strategies for in-class and online activities, chapter summaries, and lists of suggested additional resources.
- **NETA Assessment:** The Test Bank was written by Caitlin Forsey of the University of British Columbia. It includes over 2500 multiple-choice questions written according to NETA guidelines for effective construction and development of higher-order questions. Also included are approximately 650 true/false questions and more than 250 short-answer and essay questions. Test Bank files are provided in Word format for easy editing and in PDF format for convenient printing whatever your system.

  The Computerized Test Bank by ExamView® includes all the questions from the Test Bank. The easy-to-use ExamView software is compatible with Microsoft Windows and Mac OS. Create tests by selecting questions from the question bank, modifying these questions as desired, and adding new questions you write yourself. You can administer quizzes online and export tests to WebCT, Blackboard, and other formats.

- **NETA Presentation:** Microsoft® PowerPoint® lecture slides for every chapter have also been created by Tamy Superle of Carleton University. There is an average of sixty slides per chapter, many featuring key figures, tables, and photographs from *Sociology in Our Times*, Sixth Canadian Edition. NETA principles of clear design and engaging content have been incorporated throughout.
- **Image Library:** This resource consists of digital copies of figures, short tables, and photographs used in the book. Instructors may use these jpegs to create their own PowerPoint presentations.
- **DayOne:** Day One—Prof InClass is a PowerPoint presentation that you can customize to orient your students to the class and their text at the beginning of the course.

Fostering Conversations
About Teaching Sociology in Canada
Join the conversation!

- **Fostering Conversations about Teaching Sociology in Canada:** We invite you to join Fostering Conversations about Teaching Sociology in Canada, a virtual community site built by Sociology educators for Sociology educators. A dynamic, continually-evolving blog that houses dozens of self-reflexive pieces about various aspects of teaching—including student engagement, assessment, course preparation, and teaching with technology—Fostering Conversations is an educator's toolkit and a virtual home for sharing teaching ideas, practices, and complexities. Housing contributions by educators from across the country, including universities and colleges, large and small, Fostering Conversations provides a framework for cross-institutional conversations about the craft of teaching in the 21st century. Join the conversation today! Visit **http://community.cengage.com/Site/fosteringconversations/**

ACKNOWLEDGMENTS

This edition of *Sociology in Our Times* would not have been possible without the insightful critiques of these colleagues, who have reviewed some or all of this book or its previous editions. Our profound thanks to each reviewer for engaging in this time-consuming process:

Kate Anderson, Humber College

Elizabeth Bishop, Confederation College

William Boetang, University of Saskatchewan

Catherine Chiappetta-Swanson, McMaster University

Cathy Fillmore, University of Winnipeg

Mark Ihnat, Humber College

Ron Joudrey, Red Deer College

Ellen McBride, Medicine Hat College

Alice Propper, York University

Harry Rosenbaum, University of Winnipeg

Deborah White, Trent University

Kevin Willison, Lakehead University at Orillia

We express our deep appreciation to Krista Robson of Red Deer College and Anthony Iafrate of Lambton College and the University of Windsor, who coordinated feedback from their students and whose feedback has greatly informed the pedagogical enhancements to the textbook and CourseMate platform.

We would also like to express our appreciation to the many individuals at Nelson Education involved in the development and production of *Sociology in Our Times*. Among them, Joanna Cotton gave us encouragement and sound advice for the first three editions and Cara Yarzab acted as a mentor and friend throughout work on several earlier editions. Laura Macleod and Mark Grzeskowiak helped us through the fifth edition. The sixth edition has seen many changes, including two new chapters and a new design. We have very much enjoyed the friendship and guidance given throughout this process by Maya Castle, our Acquisitions Editor, and Developmental Editor Liisa Kelly, who have worked closely with us from the beginning of the project. Sheila Wawanash has helped keep our prose legible and facts straight as the copy editor, and Natalia Denesiuk Harris has overseen the production process. We also thank Terry Fedorkiw and the sales and marketing staff for their great work in ensuring that there would be a sixth edition of this book, and Carrie McGregor and Debbie Yea, who managed the permissions research and clearances for this edition. As always, the commitment, good humour, and hard work of the Nelson team have made this a rewarding and enjoyable experience.

Jane would like to thank her friend and former student Caitlin Forsey for her contribution to the new "Sex, Sexualities, and Intimate Relationships" chapter. Jane would also like to thank her colleague Richard Jochelson for providing a detailed discussion of changes in law pertaining to sexuality.

We would both like to thank our families for their encouragement, patience, and support (even when we were really miserable), for making sure that we were still enjoying life, and for encouraging us—mostly in the form of nurturance, sustenance, and love—when we spent too much time away from them working on this project.

LETTER TO INSTRUCTORS

Dear Instructor,

CourseMate, Nelson Education's online engagement and assessment platform, is built with you and your students in mind.

CourseMate is designed to support your wonderful efforts to create an interactive, engaging online course, whether it accounts for 5 percent or 100 percent of your students' course experience. The digital assets found in this platform were selected for their pedagogical utility. Each digital asset contributes to the creation of an enriching online learning experience that respects diverse learning preferences and supports better student outcomes.

Our development of this learning tool has been guided by Arthur Chickering and Zelda Gamson's seminal work, "Seven Principles of Good Practice In Undergraduate Education" (*AAHE Bulletin*, 1987), and the follow-up work by Chickering and Stephen C. Ehrmann, "Implementing the Seven Principles: Technology as Lever"(*AAHE Bulletin*, 1996). Our attention to these principles ensures CourseMate appropriately reflects the core goals of contact, collaboration, multimodal learning, time on task, prompt feedback, active learning, and high expectations.

You can use CourseMate in several ways, including the following:

- **To help students prepare for class:**
  Instructors can assign pre-test questions before class. Students receive immediate feedback to the pre-test, including e-book excerpts covering the concepts they have yet to master. To confirm whether students have completed their pre-class assignment, instructors consult the Engagement Tracker for immediate insight into each student's time on task and achievement. The Engagement Tracker helps instructors identify at-risk students early so they can intervene as needed.
- **To engage students:**
  Students can watch the video clips for each chapter and answer critical thinking questions. They practise comprehension by adding notes to the embedded e-book and highlighting important passages, as well as by using interactive flashcards and answering quiz questions.
- **To help students develop their critical thinking skills:**
  Students can challenge their higher-order thinking skills with the critical thinking questions that conclude almost all of the digital assets—including Applying Sociology to My Life boxes, Focus on Social Policy boxes, Video Clips, Sociology in the Media boxes, and Internet Activities. Their responses are captured within the Engagement Tracker.
- **To assess students:**
  Instructors can attach grades to student responses to the pre-test, post-test, and critical thinking questions. Instructors might also choose to load the text's test bank to their learning management system (LMS).
- **To create an online learning community:**
  Instructors can ask students to watch a video clip or read one of the boxed assets (such as the Sociology in the Media boxes). Rather than have each student respond to the culminating critical thinking question, some instructors post the critical thinking question to the discussion board on their LMS. Yet others assign the question for in-class discussion or a small group response via email.

However you choose to incorporate CourseMate into your course, we sincerely hope it supports the construction of an online community of engaged learners. To access CourseMate, please contact your Nelson representative.

Should you wish to contact me, please feel free to do so by emailing Maya.Castle@nelson.com.

Warmest wishes,

Maya Castle
Acquisitions Editor
Nelson Education
Canada's Learning Advantage

Social Movements
Education
Religion
Parsons
Families
Looking-Glass Self
Parsons
Race
Politics
Ethics
Crime
nants
heory
ology Work
Religion
Critical Approach
lism Dramaturgy
Cooley
Structural Functionalism
Symbolic Interact

CHAPTER 1

The Sociological Perspective

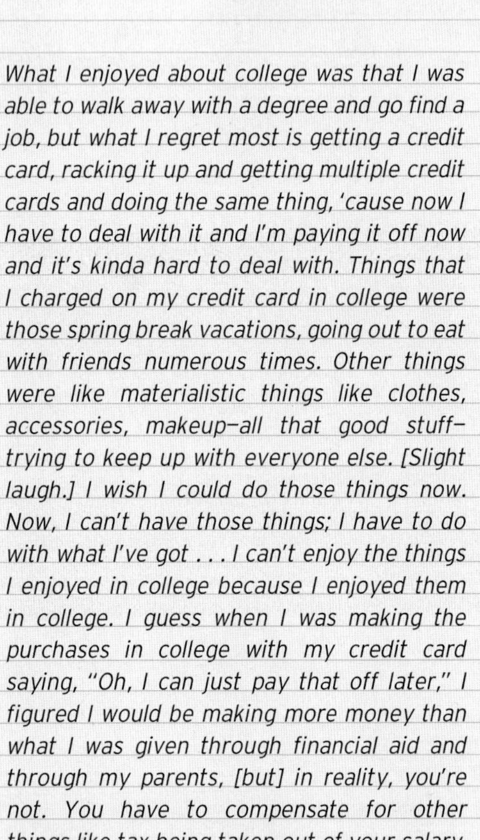

What I enjoyed about college was that I was able to walk away with a degree and go find a job, but what I regret most is getting a credit card, racking it up and getting multiple credit cards and doing the same thing, 'cause now I have to deal with it and I'm paying it off now and it's kinda hard to deal with. Things that I charged on my credit card in college were those spring break vacations, going out to eat with friends numerous times. Other things were like materialistic things like clothes, accessories, makeup—all that good stuff—trying to keep up with everyone else. [Slight laugh.] I wish I could do those things now. Now, I can't have those things; I have to do with what I've got . . . I can't enjoy the things I enjoyed in college because I enjoyed them in college. I guess when I was making the purchases in college with my credit card saying, "Oh, I can just pay that off later," I figured I would be making more money than what I was given through financial aid and through my parents, [but] in reality, you're not. You have to compensate for other things like tax being taken out of your salary, groceries, gas is something I didn't even think about because my parents always paid it. I mean, all those little things: They will add up!

—A college graduate who is struggling to pay off $7000 in credit card debt with high interest rates, explains why she must use 20 percent of her postgraduation take-home salary to try to reduce this debt.

Personal troubles for students around the world these days: student loan debt in an age of poor job prospects and diminishing returns on university degrees.

Like millions of university students, this college graduate quickly learned both the liberating and constraining aspects of living in a "consumer society" where many of us rely on our credit cards to pay for items we want to purchase or services we need. Many university students continue to increase their credit card purchases to pay for expenses and online shopping, which has become more popular than going to the mall. For many years companies targeted college students, trying to get them to apply for a credit card regardless of whether they had the ability to pay off their balances or not.

Why are sociologists interested in studying consumerism? Sociologists study the *consumer society*—a society in which discretionary consumption is a mass phenomenon among people across diverse income categories—because it provides interesting and important insights into many aspects of social life and our world. In the consumer society, for example, purchasing goods and services is not limited to the wealthy or even the middle class; people in all but the lowest income brackets spend time, energy, and money on shopping, and some amass large debts in the process (see Baudrillard, 1998/1970; Ritzer, 1995; Schor, 1999). According to sociologists, shopping and consumption—in this instance, the money that people spend on goods and services—are processes that extend beyond our individual choices and are rooted in larger structural conditions in the social, political, and economic order in which we live. In the 2000s, many people have had financial problems not only because of their own consumerism but also because of national and global economic instability.

In this chapter, we will see how the sociological perspective helps us examine social issues such as debt accumulation and overspending and wrestle with some of the difficulties of attempting to study human behaviour. Throughout this text, you will be invited to use the sociological perspective and to apply your sociological imagination to reexamine your social world and explore important social issues and problems you may not have considered before. Before reading on, take the quiz in Box 1.1 on page 6, which lists a number of commonsense notions about consumption and credit card debt.

Critical Thinking Questions

1. Why have shopping, spending, credit card debt, and bankruptcy become major problems for some people?
2. How are social relations and social meanings shaped by what people in a given society produce and how they consume?
3. The millenial generation (those born after 1982) has often been described as the "entitlement generation." Is credit card debt an example of this entitlement or of other social factors? How do you respond to this label?

CHAPTER FOCUS QUESTION How does sociology add to our knowledge of human societies and of social issues such as consumerism?

LEARNING OBJECTIVES

AFTER READING THIS CHAPTER, YOU SHOULD BE ABLE TO

LO-1 Define *sociology* and explain how it can help us understand ourselves and others.

LO-2 Explain why the sociological imagination is important for studying society.

LO-3 Discuss the major contributions of early sociologists.

LO-4 Describe the key assumptions behind each of the contemporary theoretical perspectives.

LO-1 PUTTING SOCIAL LIFE INTO PERSPECTIVE

sociology The systematic study of human society and social interaction.

Sociology is the systematic study of human society and social interaction. It is a *systematic* study because sociologists apply both theoretical perspectives and research methods (or orderly approaches) to examinations of social behaviour. Sociologists study human societies and their social interactions in order to develop theories of how human behaviour is shaped by group life and how, in turn, group life is affected by individuals.

Why Study Sociology?

society A large social grouping that shares the same geographical territory and is subject to the same political authority and dominant cultural expectations.

global interdependence A relationship in which the lives of all people are intertwined closely and any one nation's problems are part of a larger global problem.

commonsense knowledge A form of knowing that guides ordinary conduct in everyday life.

Sociology helps us gain a better understanding of ourselves and our social world. It enables us to see how behaviour is largely shaped by the groups to which we belong and the society in which we live.

Most of us take our social world for granted and view our lives in personal terms. Because of our culture's emphasis on individualism, we often do not consider the complex connections between our own lives and the larger, recurring patterns of the society and world in which we live. Sociology helps us look beyond our personal experiences and gain insights into society and the larger world order. A **society** is a large social grouping that shares the same geographical territory and is subject to the same political authority and dominant cultural expectations, such as Canada, the United States, or Mexico. Examining the world order helps us understand that each of us is affected by **global interdependence**—a relationship in which the lives of all people are closely intertwined and any one nation's problems are part of a larger global problem.

Individuals can make use of sociology on a more personal level. Sociology enables us to move beyond established ways of thinking, thus allowing us to gain new insights into ourselves and to develop a greater awareness of the connection between our own "world" and that of other people. According to sociologist Peter Berger (1963:23), sociological inquiry helps us see that "things are not what they seem." Sociology provides new ways of approaching problems and making decisions in everyday life. It promotes understanding and tolerance by enabling each of us to look beyond our personal experiences (see Figure 1.1).

Many of us rely on intuition or common sense gained from personal experience to help us understand our daily lives and other people's behaviour. **Commonsense knowledge** guides ordinary conduct in everyday life. We often rely on common sense—or "what everybody knows"—to answer key questions about behaviour: Why do people behave the way they do? Who makes the rules? Why do some people break rules and why do others follow them?

Many commonsense notions are myths. A *myth* is a popular but false notion that may be used, either intentionally or unintentionally, to perpetuate certain beliefs or "theories" even in the light of conclusive evidence to the contrary.

The media are the source of much of our commonsense knowledge. Television talk show hosts and news anchors, journalists for magazines and newspapers, authors of the many books in print, bloggers—even Facebook and Twitter—all provide us with information about family life, sexual assault, homelessness, AIDS, violence, and thousands of related sociological topics. With all of this information readily available, why should we study sociology? What can we learn that is better than relying on common sense or information from an alleged expert on a talk show?

The answer is that sociologists strive to use scientific standards, not popular myths or hearsay, in studying society and social interaction. They use systematic research techniques and are accountable to the scientific community for their methods and the presentation of their findings. Although some sociologists argue that sociology must be completely value free—without distorting subjective (personal or emotional) bias—others do not think that total objectivity is an attainable or desirable goal when studying human behaviour. This issue will be discussed in Chapter 2.

Sociologists attempt to discover patterns or commonalities in human behaviour. For example, when they study suicide, they look for patterns of behaviour even though *individuals* usually

FIGURE 1.1 FIELDS THAT USE SOCIAL SCIENCE RESEARCH

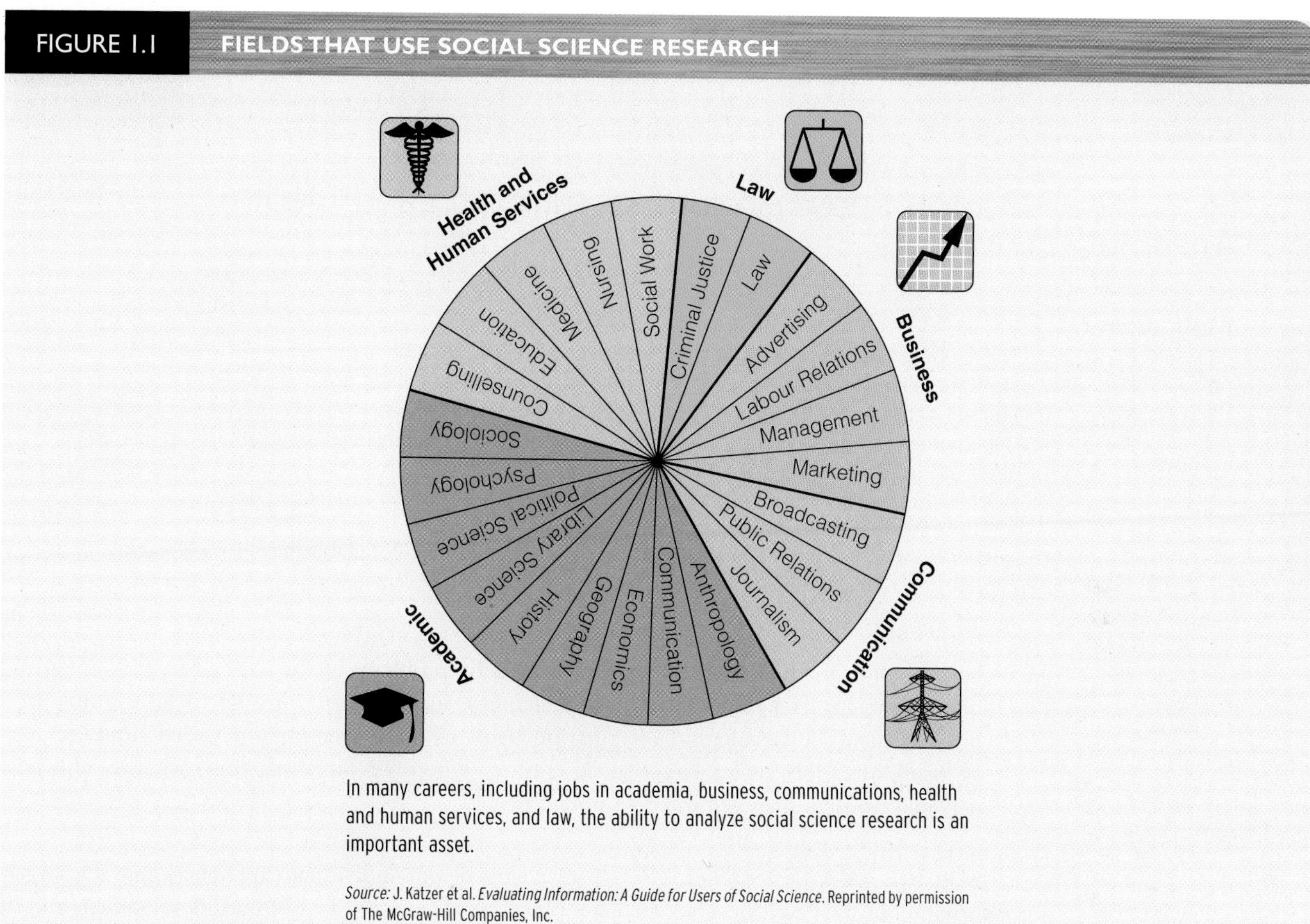

In many careers, including jobs in academia, business, communications, health and human services, and law, the ability to analyze social science research is an important asset.

Source: J. Katzer et al. *Evaluating Information: A Guide for Users of Social Science*. Reprinted by permission of The McGraw-Hill Companies, Inc.

commit suicide and other *individuals* suffer as a result of these actions. Consequently, sociologists seek out the multiple causes and effects of suicide and other social problems. They analyze the impact of the problem not only from the standpoint of the people directly involved, but also from the standpoint of the effects of such behaviour on others in society.

TIME TO REVIEW

- What commonsense understandings do you take for granted in everyday life?
- Which of these (if any) are myths?

THE SOCIOLOGICAL IMAGINATION LO-2

Sociologist C. Wright Mills (1959b) described sociological reasoning as the **sociological imagination**—the ability to see the relationship between individual experiences and the larger society. This awareness enables us to understand the link between our personal experiences and the social contexts in which they occur. The sociological imagination helps us distinguish between personal troubles and social (or public) issues. *Personal troubles* are private problems of individuals and the networks of people with whom they associate regularly. As a result, those problems must be solved by individuals within their immediate social settings—for example, one person being unemployed may be a personal trouble. *Public issues* are matters

sociological imagination C. Wright Mills's term for the ability to see the relationship between individual experiences and the larger society.

BOX 1.1 **SOCIOLOGY AND EVERYDAY LIFE**

How Much Do You Know About Consumption and Debt Accumulation?

True	False	
T	F	1. The average Canadian household has just over $100,000 in debt
T	F	2. Most students need student loans to pay for their university education.
T	F	3. Student debt in Canada has declined in recent years.
T	F	4. Overspending is primarily a problem for people in the higher-income brackets in Canada and other affluent nations.
T	F	5. College students spend more money online than people in any other age category.

For answers to quiz on consumption and credit cards, go to **www.nelson.com/sociologyinourtimes6e.**

beyond an individual's control that are caused by problems at the societal level. Widespread unemployment as a result of economic changes, such as plant closings, is an example of a public issue. The sociological imagination helps us place seemingly personal troubles, such as losing one's job, into a larger social context, where we can distinguish whether and how personal troubles may be related to public issues.

SUICIDE AS A PERSONAL TROUBLE Many of our individual experiences may be largely beyond our own control. They are determined by society—by its historical development and its organization. In everyday life, we do not define personal experiences in these terms. If a person commits suicide, many people consider it the result of the individual's personal problems. Historical explanations of suicide focused on suicide as personal trouble, viewing the act as sinful or criminal (Evans and Farberow, 1988). Suicide was believed to be part of an evolutionary process whereby "weak-brained individuals were sorted by insanity and voluntary death" (Morselli, 1975/1881).

SUICIDE AS A PUBLIC ISSUE We can use the sociological imagination to look at the problem of suicide as a public issue—a societal problem. For example, we may use our sociological imagination to understand why suicide rates are so high in some Aboriginal communities in Canada. Early sociologist Émile Durkheim refused to accept commonsense explanations of suicide. In what was probably the first sociological study to use scientific research methods, he related suicide to the issue of cohesiveness (or lack of it) in society instead of viewing suicide as an isolated act that could be understood only by studying individual personalities or inherited tendencies. Contemporary societies often deal with suicide as a public issue by enacting legislation related to matters such as assisted suicide.

THE IMPORTANCE OF A GLOBAL SOCIOLOGICAL IMAGINATION Although existing sociological theory and research provide the foundation for sociological thinking, we must reach beyond past studies that have focused primarily on North America to develop a more comprehensive *global* approach for the future. In the 21st century, we face important challenges in a rapidly changing nation and world. The world's **high-income countries** are nations with highly industrialized economies; technologically advanced industrial, administrative, and service occupations; and relatively high levels of national and personal income. Examples include the United States, Canada, Australia, New Zealand, Japan, and the countries of Western Europe.

high-income countries Nations with highly industrialized economies; technologically advanced industrial, administrative, and service occupations; and relatively high levels of national and personal income.

As compared with other nations of the world, many high-income nations have a high standard of living and a lower death rate due to advances in nutrition and medical technology.

However, everyone living in a so-called high-income country does not necessarily have a high income or an outstanding quality of life. Even among middle- and upper-income people, problems such as personal debt may threaten economic and social stability. This may increasingly be the case as the effects of the recent global economic crisis take hold.

In contrast, **middle-income countries** are nations with industrializing economies, particularly in urban areas, and moderate levels of national and personal income. Examples of middle-income countries include Brazil and Mexico, which are experiencing rapid industrialization. **Low-income countries** are primarily agrarian, with little industrialization and low levels of national and personal income. Examples of low-income countries include many of the nations of Africa and Asia, where people typically work the land and are among the poorest in the world (see Chapter 9).

middle-income countries Nations with industrializing economies, particularly in urban areas, and moderate levels of national and personal income.

low-income countries Countries that are primarily agrarian, with little industrialization and low levels of national and personal income.

Throughout this text, we will continue to develop our sociological imaginations by examining social life in Canada and other nations. The future of this country is deeply intertwined with the future of all other nations of the world on economic, political, environmental, and humanitarian levels. We buy many goods and services that were produced in other nations, and we sell much of what we produce to the people of other nations. Peace in other nations is important if we are to ensure peace within our borders. Famine, unrest, and brutality in other regions of the world must be of concern to people in Canada. Moreover, fires, earthquakes, famine, or environmental pollution in one nation typically has an adverse influence on other nations as well. Global problems contribute to the large influx of immigrants who arrive in Canada annually. These immigrants bring with them a rich diversity of language, customs, religions, and previous life experiences; they also contribute to dramatic population changes that will have a long-term effect on this country.

Whatever your race or ethnicity, class, sex, or age, are you able to include in your thinking the perspectives of people who are quite different from you in experiences and points of view? Before you answer this question, a few definitions are in order. *Race* is a term used by many people to specify groups of people distinguished by physical characteristics such as skin colour, but no "pure" racial types exist and most sociologists consider the concept of race to be a social construction used to justify existing social inequalities. *Ethnicity* refers to a group's cultural heritage or identity; it is based on factors such as language or country of origin. *Class* is the relative location of a person or group within the larger society; it is based on wealth, power, prestige, or other valued resources. *Sex* refers to the biological and anatomical differences between females and males. By contrast, *gender* refers to the meanings, beliefs, and practices associated with sex differences, referred to as *femininity* and *masculinity* (see Box 1.2 on page 16).

In forming your own global sociological imagination and in seeing the possibilities for sociology in the 21st century, it will be helpful for you to understand the development of the discipline.

THE DEVELOPMENT OF SOCIOLOGICAL THINKING LO-3

Throughout history, social philosophers and religious authorities have made countless observations about human behaviour. However, early thinkers focused their thoughts on what they believed society *ought* to be like, rather than describing how society *was.*

Several revolutions that took place in the 18th century had a profound influence on the origins of sociology. The Enlightenment produced an intellectual revolution in how people thought about social change, progress, and critical thinking. The optimistic views of the *philosophes* and other social thinkers regarding progress and equal opportunity (at least for some people) became part of the impetus for political and economic revolutions, first in America and then in France. The Enlightenment thinkers had emphasized a sense of common purpose and hope for human progress; the French Revolution and its aftermath replaced these ideals with discord and overt conflict (see Arendt, 1973a; Schama, 1989).

industrialization The process by which societies are transformed from dependence on agriculture and handmade products to an emphasis on manufacturing and related industries.

urbanization The process by which an increasing proportion of a population lives in cities rather than in rural areas.

During the 19th and early 20th centuries, another form of revolution also occurred: the Industrial Revolution. **Industrialization** is the process by which societies are transformed from dependence on agriculture and handmade products to an emphasis on manufacturing and related industries. This process first occurred during the Industrial Revolution in Britain between 1760 and 1850, and was soon repeated throughout Western Europe. By the mid-19th century, industrialization was well under way in Canada and the United States. Massive economic, technological, and social changes occurred as machine technology and the factory system shifted the economic base of these nations from agriculture to manufacturing. A new social class of industrialists emerged in textiles, iron smelting, and related industries. Many people who had laboured on the land were forced to leave their tightly knit rural communities and sacrifice well-defined social relationships to seek employment as factory workers in the emerging cities, which became the centres of industrial work.

Urbanization accompanied modernization and the rapid process of industrialization. **Urbanization** is the process by which an increasing proportion of a population lives in cities rather than in rural areas. Although cities existed long before the Industrial Revolution, the development of the factory system led to a rapid increase in both the number of cities and the size of their populations. People from diverse backgrounds worked together in the same factory. At the same time, many people shifted from being *producers* to being *consumers*. For example, families living in the cities had to buy food with their wages because they could no longer grow their own crops to consume or to barter for other resources. Similarly, people had to pay rent for their lodging because they could no longer exchange their services for shelter.

These living and working conditions led to the development of new social problems: inadequate housing, crowding, unsanitary conditions, poverty, pollution, and crime. Wages were

© fStop/Alamy

As Canada continues to become increasingly diverse, sociologists need to recognize the importance of taking all people's experiences into account as we confront public issues.

so low that entire families—including young children—were forced to work, often under hazardous conditions and with no job security. As these conditions became more visible, a new breed of social thinkers turned its attention to trying to understand why and how society was changing.

TIME TO REVIEW

- What were the primary social factors that contributed to the development of sociological thinking?

Early Thinkers: A Concern with Social Order and Stability

At the same time that urban problems were worsening, natural scientists had been using reason, or rational thinking, to discover the laws of physics and the movement of the planets. Social thinkers began to believe that by applying the methods developed by the natural sciences, they might discover the laws of human behaviour and apply these laws to solve social problems. Historically, the time was ripe for such thoughts because the Age of Enlightenment had produced a belief in reason and humanity's ability to perfect itself.

Early social thinkers—such as Auguste Comte, Harriet Martineau, Herbert Spencer, and Émile Durkheim—were interested in analyzing social order and stability, and many of their ideas had a dramatic influence on modern sociology.

positivism A belief that the world can best be understood through scientific inquiry.

AUGUSTE COMTE French philosopher Auguste Comte (1798–1857) coined the term *sociology* from the Latin *socius* ("social, being with others") and the Greek *logos* ("study of") to describe a new science that would engage in the study of society. Even though he never conducted sociological research, Comte is considered by some to be the "founder of sociology." His theory that societies contain *social statics* (forces for social order and stability) and *social dynamics* (forces for conflict and change) continues to be used, although not in these exact terms, in contemporary sociology.

Drawing heavily on the ideas of his mentor, Count Henri de Saint-Simon, Comte stressed that the methods of the natural sciences should be applied to the objective study of society. Comte's philosophy became known as **positivism**—a belief that the world can best be understood through scientific inquiry. Comte believed that objective, bias-free knowledge was attainable only through the use of science rather than religion.

The ideas of Saint-Simon and Comte regarding the objective, scientific study of society are deeply embedded in the discipline of sociology. Of particular importance is Comte's idea that the nature of human thinking and knowledge passed through several stages as societies evolved from simple to more complex. Comte described how the idea systems and their corresponding social structural arrangements changed according to what he termed the *law of the three stages:* the theological, metaphysical, and scientific (or positivistic) stages. Comte believed that knowledge began in the *theological stage*—explanations were based on religion and the supernatural. Next, knowledge moved to the *metaphysical stage*—explanations were based on abstract philosophical speculation. Finally, knowledge would reach the *scientific*, or *positive, stage*—explanations are based on systematic observation,

Auguste Comte

experimentation, comparison, and historical analysis. Shifts in the forms of knowledge in societies were linked to changes in the structural systems of society. In the theological stage, kinship was the most prominent unit of society; however, in the metaphysical stage, the state became the prominent unit and control shifted from small groups to the state, military, and law. In the scientific, or positive, stage, industry became the prominent structural unit in society and scientists became the spiritual leaders, replacing in importance the priests and philosophers of the previous stages of knowledge. For Comte, this progression through the three stages constituted the basic law of social dynamics, and, when coupled with the laws of statics (which emphasized social order and stability), constituted the new science of sociology, which could bring about positive social change.

HARRIET MARTINEAU As a woman in a male-dominated discipline and society, Harriet Martineau (1802–1876) received no recognition in the field of sociology until recently; however, the British sociologist made Comte's works more accessible for a wide variety of scholars. Not only did she translate and condense Comte's work, but she was also an active sociologist in her own right. Martineau studied the social customs of Britain and the United States, and analyzed the consequences of industrialization and capitalism. In *Society in America* (1962/1837), she examined religion, politics, child rearing, slavery, and immigration in the United States, paying special attention to social distinctions based on class, race, and gender. Her works explore the status of women, children, and "sufferers" (persons who were considered to be criminal, mentally ill, handicapped, poor, or alcoholic).

Based on her reading of Mary Wollstonecraft's *A Vindication of the Rights of Women* (1974/1797), Martineau advocated racial and gender equality. She was also committed to creating a science of society that would be grounded in empirical observations and widely accessible to people. She argued that sociologists should be impartial in their assessment of society, but that comparing the existing state of society with the principles on which it was founded is entirely appropriate (Lengermann and Niebrugge-Brantley, 1998).

Some scholars have argued that Martineau's place in the history of sociology should be as a founding member of this field of study, not just as the translator of Auguste Comte's work (Hoecker-Drysdale, 1992; Lengermann and Niebrugge-Brantley, 1998). Others have highlighted her influence in spreading the idea that societal progress could be brought about by the spread of democracy and the growth of industrial capitalism (Polanyi, 1944). Martineau believed that a better society would emerge if women and men were treated equally, enlightened reform occurred, and cooperation existed among people in all social classes (but led by the middle class).

In keeping with the sociological imagination, Martineau not only analyzed large-scale social structures in society but also explored how these factors influenced the lives of people, particularly women, children, and those who were marginalized by virtue of being criminal, mentally ill, disabled, poor, or alcoholic (Lengermann and Niebrugge-Brantley, 1998). She remained convinced that sociology, the "true science of human nature," could bring about new knowledge and understanding, enlarging people's capacity to create a just society and live heroic lives (Hoecker-Drysdale, 1992).

Harriet Martineau

HERBERT SPENCER Unlike Comte, who was strongly influenced by the upheavals of the French Revolution, British social theorist Herbert Spencer (1820–1903) was born in a more peaceful and optimistic period in his country's history. Spencer's major contribution to sociology was an evolutionary perspective on social order and social change. Although the term *evolution* has various meanings, evolutionary theory should be taken to mean "a theory to explain the mechanisms of organic/social change" (Haines, 1997:81). According to Spencer's theory of general evolution, society, like a biological organism, has various interdependent parts (such as the family, the economy, and the government) that work to ensure the stability and survival of the entire society.

social Darwinism The belief that those species of animals (including human beings) best adapted to their environment survive and prosper, whereas those poorly adapted die out.

Spencer believed that societies developed through a process of "struggle" (for existence) and "fitness" (for survival), which he referred to as the "survival of the fittest." Because this phrase is often attributed to Charles Darwin, Spencer's view of society is known as **social Darwinism**—the belief that those species of animals (including human beings) best adapted to their environment survive and prosper, whereas those poorly adapted die out. Spencer equated this process of *natural selection* with progress, because only the "fittest" members of society would survive the competition; the "unfit" would be filtered out of society. Based on this belief, he strongly opposed any social reform that might interfere with the natural selection process and, thus, damage society by favouring its least worthy members.

social facts Émile Durkheim's term for patterned ways of acting, thinking, and feeling that exist outside any one individual.

Critics have suggested that many of Spencer's ideas had serious flaws. For one thing, societies are not the same as biological systems; people are able to create and transform the environment in which they live. Moreover, the notion of the survival of the fittest can easily be used to justify class, racial–ethnic, and gender inequalities and to rationalize the lack of action to eliminate harmful practices that contribute to such inequalities. Not surprisingly, Spencer's hands-off view was applauded by wealthy industrialists of his day. John D. Rockefeller, who gained monopolistic control of much of the U.S. oil industry early in the 20th century, maintained that the growth of giant businesses was merely the "survival of the fittest" (Feagin, Baker, and Feagin, 2006).

Social Darwinism served as a rationalization for some people's assertion of the superiority of the white race. After the American Civil War, it was used to justify the repression and neglect of African Americans as well as the policies that resulted in the annihilation of Native American populations. Although some social reformers spoke out against these justifications, "scientific" racism continued to exist (Turner, Singleton, and Musick, 1984). In both positive and negative ways, many of Spencer's ideas and concepts have been deeply embedded in social thinking and public policy for more than a century.

ÉMILE DURKHEIM French sociologist Émile Durkheim (1858–1917) criticized some of Spencer's views while incorporating others into his own writing. Durkheim stressed that people are the product of their social environment and that behaviour cannot be fully understood in terms of *individual* biological and psychological traits. He believed that the limits of human potential are *socially,* not *biologically,* based. As Durkheim saw religious traditions evaporating in his society, he searched for a scientific, rational way to provide for societal integration and stability (Hadden, 1997).

In *The Rules of Sociological Method* (1964a/1895), Durkheim set forth one of his most important contributions to sociology: the idea that societies are built on social facts. **Social facts** are patterned ways of acting, thinking, and feeling that exist outside any one individual but that exert social control over each person. Durkheim believed that social facts must be explained by other social facts—by reference to the social structure rather than to individual attributes.

Émile Durkheim

Durkheim was concerned with social order and social stability because he lived during the period of rapid social changes in Europe resulting from industrialization and urbanization. His recurring question was this: How do societies manage to hold together? In *The Division of Labor in Society* (1933/1893), Durkheim concluded that preindustrial societies were held together by strong traditions and by members' shared moral beliefs and values. As societies industrialized, more specialized economic activity became the basis of the social bond because people became interdependent.

Durkheim observed that rapid social change and a more specialized division of labour produce *strains* in society. These strains lead to a breakdown in traditional organization, values, and authority and to a dramatic increase in **anomie**—a condition in which social control becomes ineffective as a result of the loss of shared values and of a sense of purpose in society. According to Durkheim, anomie is most likely to occur during a period of rapid social change. In *Suicide* (1964b/1897), he explored the relationship between anomic social conditions and suicide, as discussed in Chapter 2.

anomie Émile Durkheim's term for a condition in which social control becomes ineffective as a result of the loss of shared values and a sense of purpose in society.

Durkheim's contributions to sociology are so significant that he has been referred to as "*the* crucial figure in the development of sociology as an academic discipline [and as] one of the deepest roots of the sociological imagination" (Tiryakian, 1978:187). He has long been viewed as a proponent of the scientific approach to examining social facts that lie outside individuals. He is also described as the founding figure of the functionalist theoretical tradition. Scholars have acknowledged Durkheim's influence on contemporary social theory, including the structuralist and postmodernist schools of thought. Like Comte, Martineau, and Spencer, Durkheim emphasized that sociology should be a science based on observation and the systematic study of social facts rather than on individual characteristics or traits.

Although they acknowledge Durkheim's important contributions, some critics note that his emphasis on societal stability, or the "problem of order"—how society can establish and maintain social stability and cohesiveness—obscures the *subjective meaning* that individuals give to social phenomena, such as religion, work, and suicide. In this view, overemphasis on *structure* and the determining power of "society" resulted in a corresponding neglect of *agency,* the beliefs and actions of the actors involved, in much of Durkheim's theorizing (Zeitlin, 1997).

TIME TO REVIEW

- Why were early thinkers concerned with social order and stability?

Differing Views on the Status Quo: Stability versus Change

Together with Karl Marx, Max Weber, and Georg Simmel, Durkheim established the course for modern sociology. We will look first at Marx's and Weber's divergent thoughts about conflict and social change in societies, and then at Simmel's analysis of society.

class conflict Karl Marx's term for the struggle between the capitalist class and the working class.

KARL MARX In sharp contrast to Durkheim's focus on the stability of society, German economist and philosopher Karl Marx (1818–1883) stressed that history is a continuous clash between conflicting ideas and forces. He believed that conflict—especially class conflict—is necessary to produce social change and a better society. For Marx, the most important changes were economic. He concluded that the capitalist economic system was responsible for the overwhelming poverty that he observed in London at the beginning of the Industrial Revolution (Marx and Engels, 1967/1848).

bourgeoisie Karl Marx's term for the class comprised of those who own and control the means of production.

In the Marxian framework, **class conflict** is the struggle between the capitalist class and the working class. The capitalist class, or **bourgeoisie**, comprises those who own and control the

means of production—the tools, land, factories, and money for investment that form the economic basis of a society. The working class, or **proletariat**, is composed of those who must sell their labour because they have no other means to earn a livelihood. From Marx's viewpoint, the capitalist class controls and exploits the masses of struggling workers by paying less than the value of their labour. This exploitation results in workers' **alienation**—a feeling of powerlessness and estrangement from other people and from oneself. Marx predicted that the working class would become aware of its exploitation, overthrow the capitalists, and establish a free and classless society.

Marx's theories provide a springboard for neo-Marxist analysts and other scholars to examine the economic, political, and social relations embedded in production and consumption in historical and contemporary societies. But what is Marx's place in the history of sociology? Marx is regarded as one of the most profound sociological thinkers, one who combined ideas derived from philosophy, history, and the social sciences into a new theoretical configuration. However, his social and economic analyses have also inspired heated debates among generations of social scientists. Central to his views was the belief that society should not just be studied but should also be changed because the *status quo* (the existing state of society) involved the oppression of most of the population by a small group of wealthy people. Those who believe that sociology should be value free are uncomfortable with Marx's advocacy of what some perceive to be radical social change. Scholars who examine society through the lens of race, gender, and class believe that his analysis places too much emphasis on class relations, often to the exclusion of issues regarding race/ethnicity and gender. In recent decades, scholars have shown renewed interest in Marx's *social theory*, as opposed to his radical ideology (see Lewis, 1998; Postone, 1997). Throughout this text, we will continue to explore Marx's various contributions to sociological thinking.

© Henry Guttmann/Getty Images

Karl Marx

means of production Karl Marx's term for tools, land, factories, and money for investment that form the economic basis of a society.

proletariat Karl Marx's term for those who must sell their labour because they have no other means to earn a livelihood.

alienation A feeling of powerlessness and estrangement from other people and from oneself.

MAX WEBER German social scientist Max Weber (pronounced VAY-ber) (1864–1920) was also concerned about the changes brought about by the Industrial Revolution. Although he disagreed with Marx's idea that economics is *the* central force in social change, Weber acknowledged that economic interests are important in shaping human action. Even so, he thought that economic systems are heavily influenced by other factors in a society. As we will see in Chapter 15, one of Weber's most important works, *The Protestant Ethic and the Spirit of Capitalism* (1976/1904–1905), evaluated the role of the Protestant Reformation in producing a social climate in which capitalism could exist and flourish.

Unlike many early analysts who believed that values could not be separated from the research process, Weber emphasized that sociology should be *value free*—that is, research should be conducted in a scientific manner and should exclude the researcher's personal values and economic interests (Turner, Beeghley, and Powers, 1998). Weber realized, however, that social behaviour cannot be analyzed by the objective criteria that we use to measure such things as temperature or weight. Although he recognized that sociologists cannot be totally value free, Weber stressed that they should employ *verstehen* (German for "understanding" or "insight") to gain the ability to see the world as others see it. In contemporary sociology, Weber's idea has been incorporated into the concept of the sociological imagination (discussed earlier in this chapter).

Weber was also concerned that large-scale organizations (bureaucracies) were becoming increasingly oriented toward routine administration and a specialized division of labour, which he believed were destructive to human vitality and freedom. According to Weber, rational

© Mondadori Portfolio/Getty Images

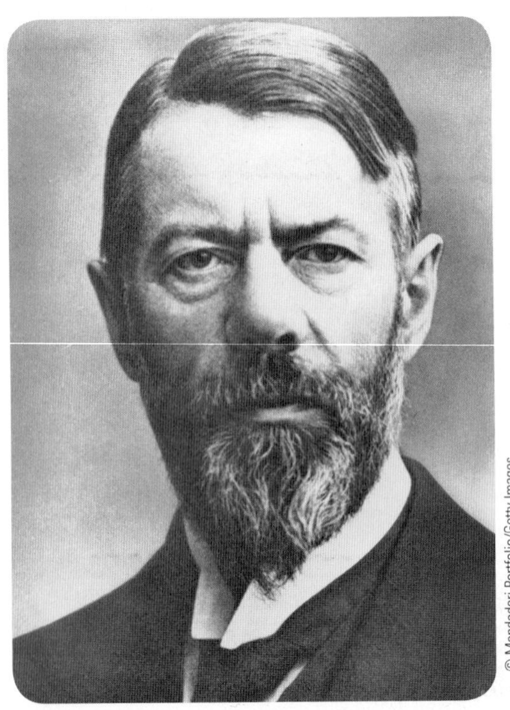

Max Weber

bureaucracy, rather than class struggle, was the most significant factor in determining the social relations among people in industrial societies. In this view, bureaucratic domination can be used to maintain powerful (capitalist) interests in society. As we will see in Chapter 6, Weber's work on bureaucracy has had a far-reaching impact.

Weber made significant contributions to modern sociology by emphasizing the goal of value-free inquiry and the necessity of understanding how others see the world. He also provided important insights on the process of rationalization, bureaucracy, religion, and many other topics. In his writings, Weber was more aware of women's issues than were many of the scholars of his day. Perhaps his awareness at least partially resulted from the fact that his wife, Marianne Weber, was an important figure in the women's movement in Germany in the early 20th century (Roth, 1988).

GEORG SIMMEL At about the same time that Durkheim was developing the field of sociology in France, the German sociologist Georg Simmel (pronounced ZIM-mel) (1858–1918) was theorizing about society as a web of patterned interactions among people. The main purpose of sociology, according to Simmel, should be to examine these social interaction processes within groups. In *The Sociology of Georg Simmel* (1950/1902–1917), he analyzed how social interactions vary depending on the size of the social group. He concluded that interaction patterns differed between a *dyad,* a social group with two members,

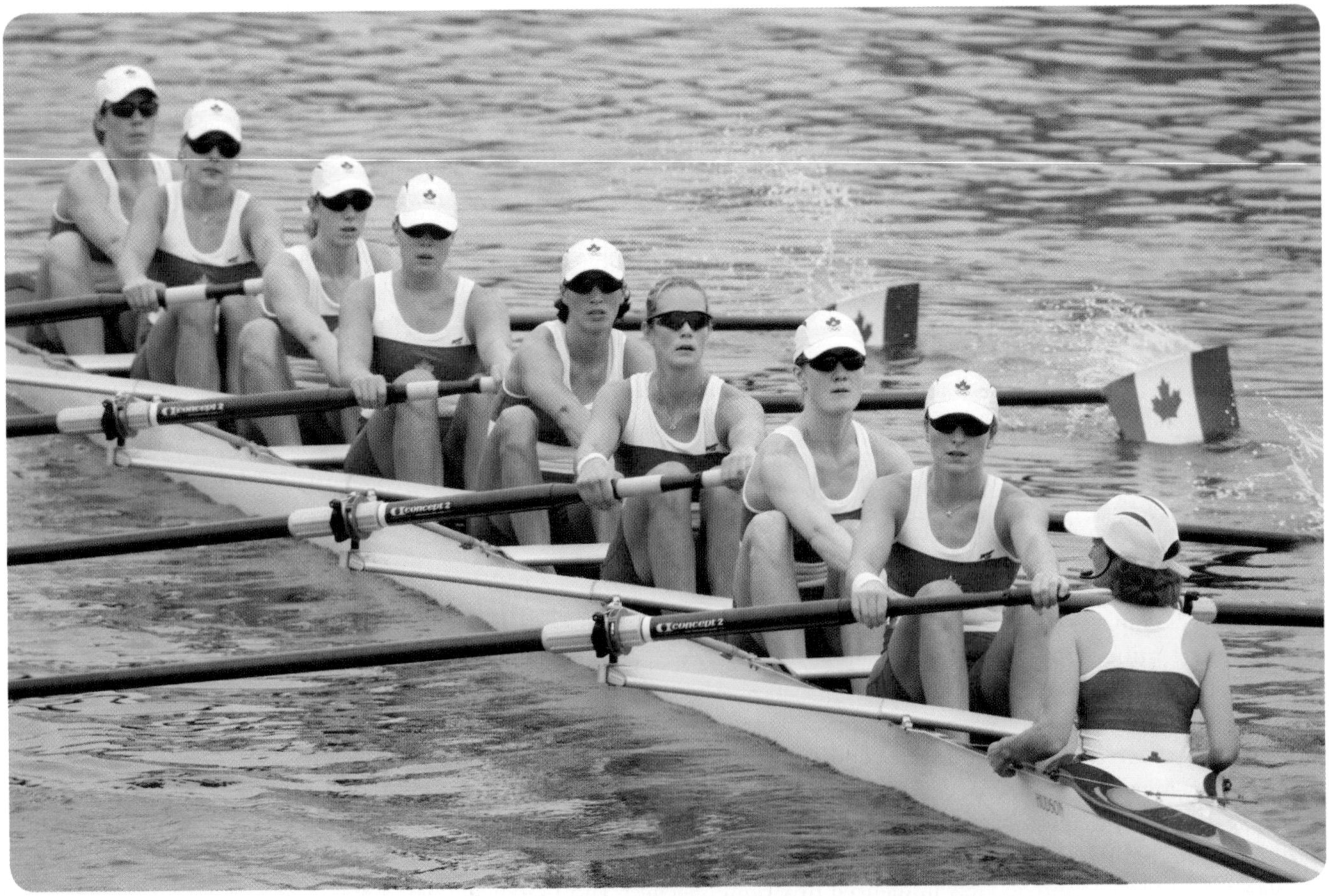
© THE CANADIAN PRESS/Jonathan Hayward

According to the sociologist Georg Simmel, society is a web of patterned interactions among people. If we focus on the behaviour of individuals in isolation, such as any one of the members of this women's rowing team, we may miss the underlying forms that make up the "geometry of social life."

and a *triad*, a social group with three members. He developed *formal sociology*, an approach that focuses attention on the universal, recurring social forms that underlie the varying content of social interaction. Simmel referred to these forms as the "geometry of social life." He also distinguished between the *forms* of social interaction (such as cooperation or conflict) and the *content* of social interaction in different contexts (for example, between leaders and followers).

Like the other social thinkers of his day, Simmel analyzed the impact of industrialization and urbanization on people's lives. He concluded that class conflict was becoming more pronounced in modern industrial societies. He also linked the increase in individualism, as opposed to concern for the group, to the fact that people now had many cross-cutting "social spheres"—membership in a number of organizations and voluntary associations—rather than the singular community ties of the past. Simmel assessed the costs of "progress" on the upper-class city dweller who, he believed, had to develop certain techniques to survive the overwhelming stimulation of the city. Simmel's ultimate concern was to protect the autonomy of the individual in society.

TIME TO REVIEW

- Marx, Weber, and Simmel focused their analysis primarily on social change. Why?

CONTEMPORARY THEORETICAL PERSPECTIVES LO-4

Given the many and varied ideas and trends that influenced the development of sociology, how do contemporary sociologists view society? Some see it as basically a stable and ongoing entity; others view it in terms of many groups competing for scarce resources; still others describe it as based on the everyday, routine interactions among individuals. Each of these views represents a method of examining the same phenomena. Each is based on general ideas as to how social life is organized and represents an effort to link specific observations in a meaningful way. Each utilizes **theory**—a set of logically interrelated statements that attempts to describe, explain, and (occasionally) predict social events. Each theory helps interpret reality in a distinct way by providing a framework in which observations may be logically ordered. Sociologists refer to this theoretical framework as a **perspective**—an overall approach to or viewpoint on some subject. The major theoretical perspectives that have emerged in sociology include the functionalist, conflict, feminist, and interactionist perspectives. Other perspectives, such as postmodernism, have emerged and gained acceptance among some social thinkers more recently. Before turning to the specifics of these perspectives, we should note that some theorists and theories do not fit neatly into any of these perspectives. Nevertheless, these perspectives will be used throughout this book to show you how sociologists try to understand many of the issues affecting Canadian society.

theory A set of logically interrelated statements that attempts to describe, explain, and (occasionally) predict social events.

perspective An overall approach to or viewpoint on some subject.

Functionalist Perspectives

Also known as *functionalism* and *structural functionalism*, **functionalist perspectives** are based on the assumption that society is a stable, orderly system. This stable system is characterized by **societal consensus**, whereby the majority of members share a common set of values, beliefs, and behavioural expectations. According to this perspective, a society is composed of interrelated parts, each of which serves a function and (ideally) contributes to the overall stability of the society. Since this approach was influenced by Comte, Spencer, and Durkheim, who often drew on the work of natural scientists, early functionalists compared society to a living, evolving organism. Societies develop social structures, or institutions, and these persist because they play

functionalist perspectives The sociological approach that views society as a stable, orderly system.

societal consensus A situation whereby the majority of members share a common set of values, beliefs, and behavioural expectations.

BOX 1.2 **POINT/COUNTERPOINT**

From Sociological Illiteracy to Sociological Imagination

What follows is an excerpt from an article written by Dr. Judith Shapiro, professor of anthropology and former president of Barnard College:

> At one point in the mid-1980s, when I was teaching, I started paying attention to a common phrase, repeated like a mantra by students there and elsewhere: "racism, sexism, and classism." I had heard the phrase so often that I had become quite used to it, but it suddenly struck me as odd.
>
> The terms *racism* and *sexism* seemed unproblematic enough, referring to discrimination based on what we take to be physical differences of one kind of another. But what did *classism* really mean? Although my 1960s ears were expecting to hear students talk about class, instead I was hearing about classism. Had the students been talking about class, they would have discussed the structure of our society, and how socioeconomic inequalities were built into it. In fact, talk of that kind was relatively rare in students' political conversations. Rather, they seemed to be concerned about individuals—prejudice against individuals belonging to less-privileged socioeconomic groups.
>
> That discovery led me to wonder how the students saw race and gender. Were they also viewing racism and sexism exclusively in terms of individual identities and interpersonal relationships? If so, what did that say about the students' chances for improving the world? Had the goal of creating a more just society dwindled down into a matter of sensitivity training?
>
> I realized, however, that I was being unfair to the students. For one thing, they were living in a far more diverse community than I had known in my undergraduate days; navigating a culturally complex universe of fellow students was for them a significant task. Although some were retreating from that project, and spending most of their time with those who were most like them, others were reaching out, realizing that the reason a college assembles a diverse group of students is to extend their horizons.
>
> And yet, those students of the 1980s were missing something important, something we should have given them during their college years. Too many of them were deficient in the skills needed for analyzing society in economic, political, and structural terms. They seemed unable to move beyond their immediate experience to see how that experience was shaped by larger social and historical forces. They were suffering from a lack of what the eminent sociologist C. Wright Mills called "the sociological imagination"—which is in short supply among today's students as well.
>
> I have come to refer to that condition as sociological illiteracy. Just as a person may be illiterate in the most literal sense (unable to read or write), or scientifically illiterate, or innumerate (as we have come to call someone who lacks quantitative skills), so a person may be uneducated in the social sciences, and thus unable to make use of the insights and tools that those disciplines provide.
>
> Many undergraduates today demonstrate impressive levels of civic engagement in the form of community service. They serve meals in soup kitchens, work in homeless shelters, and staff AIDS hot lines. They work as interns in a variety of social agencies. Too few of them, however, are able to raise their eyes to the level of policy and social structure. They need the sociological imagination to see how their on-the-ground activities fit into a bigger picture, so that more of them can cross the bridge from serious moral commitment to effective political participation.
>
> As teachers, we must admit our share of responsibility for that state of affairs. We need to adjust the focus between what we want to teach and what our students need to learn. Those of us who are faculty members in the social sciences must be sure that we are providing to all of our students, majors and nonmajors alike, basic tools of social and cultural understanding, as they have evolved over time in our various disciplines.
>
> As faculty members, we must remember that our responsibilities extend beyond the academy. Sociologists such as Mills wrote with a force and grace that enabled them to reach a wide audience. We have not seen their like in years—too many years. More of us must follow their example and write for the general reader. And we should encourage our students—so full of energy, intelligence, and commitment—to move beyond the *personal* to the political.

Source: "From Sociological Illiteracy to Sociological Imagination," by Judith Shapiro, *The Chronicle of Higher Education*, March 31, 2000, p. A68. Reprinted by permission of the author.

a part in helping society survive. These institutions include the family, education, government, religion, and the economy. If anything adverse happens to one of these institutions, or parts, all other parts are affected and the system no longer functions properly. As Durkheim noted, rapid social change and a more specialized division of labour produce *strains* in society that lead to a breakdown in these traditional institutions and may result in social problems, such as increased rates of crime and suicide.

TALCOTT PARSONS AND ROBERT MERTON Talcott Parsons (1902–1979), a founder of the sociology department at Harvard University, was perhaps the most influential advocate of the functionalist perspective. He stressed that, to survive, all societies must make provisions for meeting social needs (Parsons, 1951; Parsons and Shils, 1951). For example, Parsons (1955) suggested that a division of labour (distinct, specialized functions) between husband and wife is essential for family stability and social order. The husband/father performs the *instrumental tasks,* which involve leadership and decision-making responsibilities in the home and employment outside the home to support the family. The wife/mother is responsible for the *expressive tasks,* including housework, caring for the children, and providing emotional support for the entire family. Parsons believed that other institutions, including school, church, and government, must function to assist the family and that all institutions must work together to preserve the system over time (Parsons, 1955). Although his analysis has been criticized for its conservative bias, his work still influences sociological thinking about gender roles and the family.

Functionalism was refined further by a student of Parsons, Robert K. Merton (1910–2003), who distinguished between manifest and latent functions of social institutions. **Manifest functions** are intended and/or overtly recognized by the participants in a social unit. In contrast, **latent functions** are unintended functions that are hidden and remain unacknowledged by participants. For example, a manifest function of education is the transmission of knowledge and skills from one generation to the next; a latent function is the establishment of social relations and networks. Merton noted that all features of a social system may not be functional at all times; **dysfunctions** are the undesirable consequences of any element of a society. A dysfunction of education can be the perpetuation of gender, racial, and class inequalities. Such dysfunctions may threaten the capacity of a society to adapt and survive (Merton, 1968).

manifest functions Open, stated, and intended goals or consequences of activities within an organization or institution.

latent functions Unintended functions that are hidden and remain unacknowledged by participants.

APPLYING A FUNCTIONALIST PERSPECTIVE TO SUICIDE How might functionalists analyze the problem of suicide, which we examined at the beginning of this chapter? Although a number of possible functionalist explanations exist, we will look briefly at only one. Most functionalists emphasize the importance to a society of shared moral values and strong social bonds. When rapid social change or other disruptive conditions occur, moral values may erode, people may become more uncertain about how to act, and suicide rates may therefore increase.

In his classic study of suicide, functionalist Émile Durkheim (1964b/1897) argued that suicide rates are a reflection of a society's degree of **social solidarity**—that is, the state of having shared beliefs and values among members of a social group, along with intense and frequent interaction among group members. According to Durkheim, people are most likely to kill themselves when social solidarity is either very weak or very strong.

Durkheim collected data from vital statistics for approximately 26,000 suicides and classified them according to variables such as age, sex, marital status, family size, religion, geographic location, and method of suicide. From this analysis, he was able to identify four distinct categories of suicide: egoistic, altruistic, anomic, and fatalistic. *Egoistic suicide* occurs among people who are isolated from any social group. For example, Durkheim concluded that suicide rates were relatively high in Protestant countries in Europe because Protestants were more loosely tied to the church than were Catholics. Similarly, single people had proportionately higher suicide rates than married persons because they had a low degree of social integration, which contributed to their loneliness. In contrast, *altruistic suicide* occurs among individuals who are excessively integrated into

dysfunctions A term referring to the undesirable consequences of any element of a society.

social solidarity The state of having shared beliefs and values among members of a social group, along with intense and frequent interaction among group members.

society. An example is soldiers who kill themselves after defeat in battle because they have so strongly identified with their cause that they believe they cannot live with the shame of defeat.

Durkheim recognized that the degree of social integration is not the only variable that influences the suicide rate. In keeping with the functionalist perspective, Durkheim emphasized the importance of social stability and social consensus. Rapid social change and shifts in moral values make it difficult for people to know what is right and wrong. *Anomic suicide* results from a lack of shared values or purpose and from the absence of social regulation. In contrast, excessive regulation and oppressive discipline may contribute to *fatalistic suicide,* as in the suicide of slaves.

Although Durkheim's analysis of suicide was developed in the 19th century, it can be used to understand suicide rates among categories of people in Canada today. For example, the rate of suicide among Aboriginal people in Canada is two to three times higher than that of non-Aboriginal people (Kirmayer et al., 2007). (See Figure 1.2.) Centuries of attempts to assimilate Aboriginal people have resulted in a weakening of traditional Aboriginal cultures. Government intervention in the form of such policies as relocating First Nations people to reserves, prohibiting traditional religious or spiritual practices, sending Aboriginal children to residential schools, and destroying Aboriginal people's economic base have resulted in social breakdown and disorganization in many Aboriginal communities.

Choosing Life: Special Report on Suicide Among Aboriginal Peoples, prepared by the Royal Commission on Aboriginal Peoples, includes the following comments:

> We believe that suicide is a special issue. It is first and foremost a matter of life and death for that minority of Aboriginal people whose inner despair threatens daily to overwhelm them. But, like other forms of violence and self-destructive behaviour in Aboriginal communities, it is also the expression of a kind of collective anguish—part grief, part anger—tearing at the minds and hearts of many people. This anguish is the cumulative effect of 300 years of colonial history: lands occupied, resources seized, beliefs and cultures ridiculed, children taken away, power concentrated in distant capitals, hopes for honourable co-existence dashed over and over again. (1995:x)

Today, suicide rates are epidemic in some Aboriginal communities. Suicides due to social breakdown and normlessness are an example of what Durkheim defined as anomic suicides (Kirmayer et al., 2007). Using Durkheim's theoretical framework, these suicides can be best understood as indicative of social, rather than personal, problems.

Conflict Perspectives

conflict perspectives The sociological approach that views groups in society as engaged in a continuous power struggle for control of scarce resources.

According to **conflict perspectives**, groups in society are engaged in a continuous power struggle for control of scarce resources. Conflict may take the form of politics, litigation, negotiations, or family discussions about financial matters. Simmel, Marx, and Weber contributed significantly to this perspective by focusing on the inevitability of clashes between social groups. Today, advocates of conflict perspectives view social life as a continuous power struggle among competing social groups.

MAX WEBER AND RALF DAHRENDORF As previously discussed, Marx focused on the exploitation and oppression of the proletariat (the workers) by the bourgeoisie (the owners, or capitalist class). Weber recognized the importance of economic conditions in producing inequality and conflict in society but added *power* and *prestige* as other sources of inequality. He defined power as the ability of a person within a social relationship to carry out his or her own will despite resistance from others. Prestige—"status group" to Weber—is a positive or negative social estimation of honour (Weber, 1968/1922).

FIGURE 1.2 COMPARISON OF SUICIDE RATES OF FIRST NATIONS AND GENERAL POPULATION IN CANADA, 1979–2000

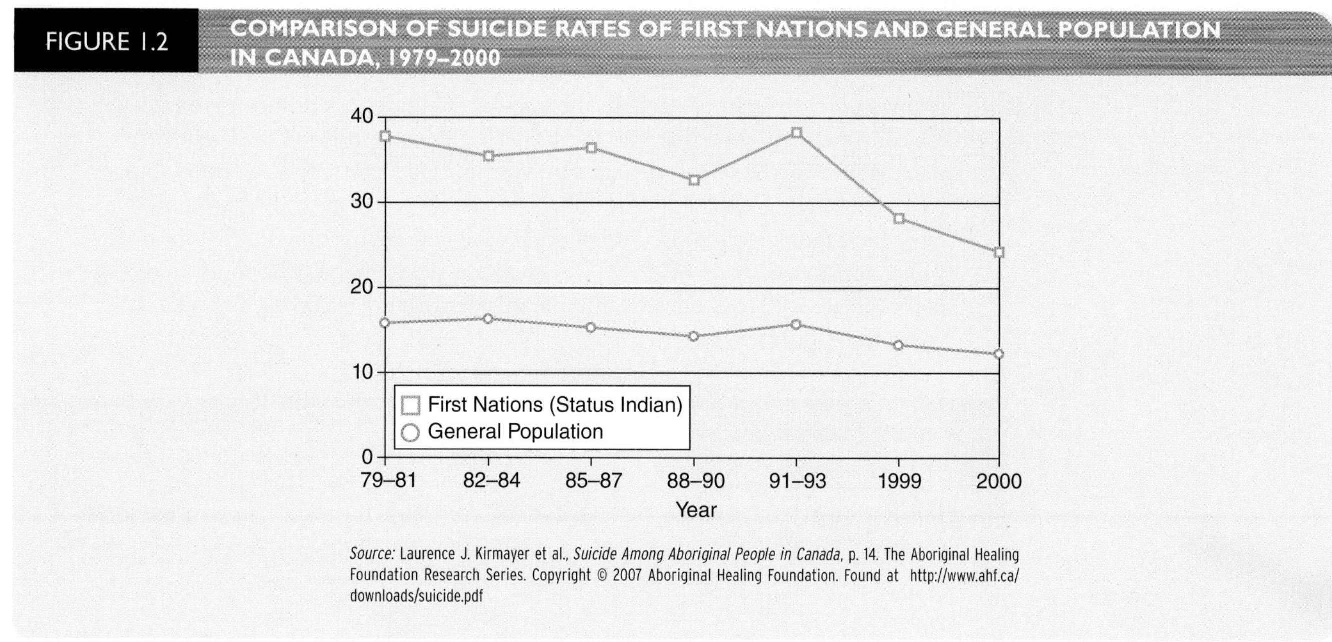

Source: Laurence J. Kirmayer et al., *Suicide Among Aboriginal People in Canada*, p. 14. The Aboriginal Healing Foundation Research Series. Copyright © 2007 Aboriginal Healing Foundation. Found at http://www.ahf.ca/downloads/suicide.pdf

Other theorists have looked at conflict among many groups and interests (such as employers and employees) as a part of everyday life in any society. Ralf Dahrendorf (1959), for example, observed that conflict is inherent in *all* authority relationships, not just that between the capitalist class and the working class. To Dahrendorf, *power* is the critical variable in explaining human behaviour. People in positions of authority benefit from the conformity of others; those who are forced to conform feel resentment and demonstrate resistance, much as a child may resent parental authority. The advantaged group that possesses authority attempts to preserve the status quo—the existing set of social arrangements—and may use coercion to do so.

APPLYING CONFLICT PERSPECTIVES TO SUICIDE How might advocates of a conflict approach explain patterns of suicide among young people in Canada?

Social Class Although many other factors may be present, social class pressures can affect rates of suicide among young people. According to some conflict theorists, North American teenagers are confronted with a capitalist economy predicated on consumption and waste and on the need to achieve high levels of economic success. Some young people may perceive that they have no future because they see few educational or employment opportunities in our technologically oriented society. Some researchers suggest that young people from low-income or working-class backgrounds are among the most powerless people in society. Low levels of family income and education and financial uncertainty associated with unemployment are known risk factors associated with suicide among Canadian youth (Kutcher and Szumilas, 2008).

Racial Oppression Racial oppression may explain the high suicide rates of some minority groups. This fact is more glaringly reflected in the extremely high rate of suicide among some Aboriginal communities. Canadian children and youth living in Aboriginal reserve communities have a suicide rate almost five times that of children and youth in the general population (Chandler and Lalonde, 2008).

Most research has focused on individualistic reasons why some young Aboriginal people commit suicide. However, analysts using a conflict framework focus on the effects of social inequality and racial discrimination on suicidal behaviour. The *Special Report on Suicide Among Aboriginal Peoples* (Royal Commission on Aboriginal Peoples, 1995) makes frequent references to oppression as a significant factor in Aboriginal suicide. For example, Sarah MacKay of the Shibogama First Nations Council comments:

> Many reports written today about the suicides of youth . . . outline in great detail the contributing factors that lead to suicide. Yet these reports fail to clearly identify the reasons why the suicides occur. The contributing factors, such as sexual abuse, family violence, alcohol and drug abuse, solvent abuse . . . are only symptoms of a bigger and more devastating cycle of oppression and deprivation . . . first initiated with colonial contact in 1492 . . . We must stop the immoral behaviours caused by oppressions . . . [That's how] to stop the suicides that are occurring amongst our youth today (1995:19).

TIME TO REVIEW

- Evaluate the extent to which you live in a society characterized by consensus, social cohesion, and shared values or by conflict and unequal division of power and wealth.

Feminist Perspectives

In the past several decades, feminists have radically transformed the discipline of sociology. Feminist theory first emerged as a critique of traditional sociological theory and methodology. The primary criticism was that sociology did not acknowledge the experiences of women. Written by men, sociology involved the study of men and not humankind, much less women; sociology examined only half of social reality (Fox, 1989). Feminist scholar Dorothy Smith (1974) argued that sociological methods, concepts, and analyses were products of the "male social universe." If women appeared at all, it was as men saw them and not as they saw themselves. In this way, feminist sociologists argued, sociology furthered the subordination and exploitation of women (Anderson, 1996). The first task of feminist sociology was to provide the missing half of social reality by generating research and theory "by, for, and about women" (Smith, 1987). In doing so, feminist sociology brought the personal problems of women, including violence against women, the poverty of women, and the invisibility of women's reproductive labour, into the public forum.

feminist perspectives The sociological approach that focuses on the significance of gender in understanding and explaining inequalities that exist between men and women in the household, in the paid labour force, and in the realms of politics, law, and culture.

Feminist perspectives focus on the significance of gender in understanding and explaining inequalities that exist between men and women in the household, in the paid labour force, and in the realms of politics, law, and culture (Armstrong and Armstrong, 1994; Luxton, 1995; Marshall, 1995). Feminism is not one single unified approach. Rather, it is characterized by a variety of perspectives, debates, and approaches among feminist writers—namely, the liberal, radical, and socialist strains (discussed in Chapter 11, "Gender"). Feminist sociology incorporates both microlevel and macrolevel analyses in studying the experiences of women. For example, some feminist theorists, such as Margrit Eichler, have used a structural approach to explain how gender inequality is created and maintained in a society dominated by men (Armstrong and Armstrong, 1994; Eichler, 1988b). Other feminist research has focused on the interpersonal relationships between men and women in terms of verbal and nonverbal communication styles, attitudes, and values in explaining the dynamics of power and social control in the private sphere (Mackie, 1995). For example, "Who eats first, sits last, or talks back reflects the micro-politics of gender" (Coltrane, 1992:104).

All of these approaches share the belief that "women and men are equal and should be equally valued as well as have equal rights" (Basow, 1992). According to feminists (including many men as well as women), we live in a *patriarchy,* a hierarchical system of power in which males possess greater economic and social privilege than females (Saunders, 1999). Feminist perspectives emphasize that gender roles are socially created, rather than determined by one's biological inheritance, and that change is essential for people to achieve their human potential without limits based on gender. Feminism views society as reinforcing social expectations through social learning: What we learn is a social product of the political and economic structure of the society in which we live (Renzetti and Curran, 1995). Feminists argue that women's subordination can end only after the patriarchal system of male dominance is replaced with a more egalitarian system.

Photographer: Karyn Gorra. Used with permission of Margrit Eichler.

Margrit Eichler

APPLYING FEMINIST PERSPECTIVES TO SUICIDE Feminist research on suicide has examined the role of gender on attitudes toward suicide. Specifically, feminist analysts have found that gender plays a significant role in a person's risk for suicidal behaviour and how the suicidal behaviour is evaluated. In North America, nonfatal suicidal behaviour is more common in women and fatal suicides are more common among men (Canetto and Sakinofsky, 1998:1). Feminists describe this phenomenon as the "gender paradox" in suicide. Researchers utilizing a feminist perspective focus on differences in gender socialization to explain this pattern. For example, Canetto explains that cultural expectations about gender and suicidal behaviour are like scripts that individuals refer to as a model for their behaviour. She argues that in North American culture, suicide is viewed as a masculine behaviour. Killing oneself may be perceived as a powerful act for a male in response to particular life circumstances, such as a debilitating illness or a serious setback in achievement (such as a job loss). In contrast, "attempting suicide" is regarded as feminine. Although this behaviour is viewed negatively, it may be expected in females in some circumstances. Nonfatal suicidal behaviour may be viewed as an understandable "feminine" response to relationship problems, such as the loss of a boyfriend, lover, or husband. Some analysts suggest that the gender paradox in suicidal behaviour reflects the fact that women and men will tend to adopt the self-destructive behaviours that are congruent with the gender scripts of their culture (Canetto and Sakinofsky, 1998:17).

Other feminist theorists have emphasized that we must examine social–structural pressures that are brought to bear on young women—for example, cultural assumptions about women and what their multiple roles should be in the family, in education, and in the workplace—and look at how these may contribute to their behaviour. Women also experience unequal educational and employment opportunities that may contribute to feelings of powerlessness and alienation. Recent research shows that persistent gender gaps in employment, politics, education, and other areas of social life tend to adversely affect women more than men. Feminist theorists would suggest that the higher rate of attempted suicide among women of all age groups may be an expression of their sense of powerlessness in a male-dominated society.

macrolevel analysis Sociological theory and research that focus on whole societies, large-scale social structures, and social systems.

Symbolic Interactionist Perspectives

The functionalist and conflict perspectives have been criticized for focusing primarily on macrolevel analysis. A **macrolevel analysis** examines whole societies, large-scale social structures, and social systems instead of looking at important social dynamics in individuals' lives. Our final perspective, symbolic interactionism, fills this void by examining people's day-to-day interactions and their behaviour in groups. Thus, symbolic interactionist approaches are based on a **microlevel analysis**, which focuses on small groups rather than large-scale social structures.

microlevel analysis Sociological theory and research that focus on small groups rather than on large-scale social structures.

symbolic interactionist perspectives The sociological approach that views society as the sum of the interactions of individuals and groups.

symbol Anything that meaningfully represents something else.

We can trace the origins of this perspective to the Chicago School, especially George Herbert Mead (1863–1931), and Herbert Blumer (1900–1987), who is credited with coining the term *symbolic interactionism.* According to **symbolic interactionist perspectives**, society is the sum of the interactions of individuals and groups. Theorists using this perspective focus on the process of *interaction*—defined as immediate, reciprocally oriented communication between two or more people—and the part that *symbols* play in giving meaning to human communication. A **symbol** is anything that meaningfully represents something else. Examples of symbols include signs, gestures, written language, and shared values. Symbolic interaction occurs when people communicate through the use of symbols; for example, a gift of food—a cake or a casserole—to a newcomer in a neighbourhood is a symbol of welcome and friendship. Symbols are instrumental in helping people derive meanings from social situations. In social encounters, each person's interpretation or definition of a given situation becomes a *subjective reality* from that person's viewpoint. We often assume that what we consider to be "reality" is shared; however, this assumption is often incorrect. Subjective reality is acquired and shared through agreed-upon symbols, especially language. If a person shouts, "Fire!" in a crowded movie theatre, for example, that language produces the same response (attempting to escape) in all of those who hear and understand it. When people in a group do not share the same meaning for a given symbol, however, confusion results; for example, people who did not know the meaning of the word *fire* would not know what the commotion was about. How people *interpret* the messages they receive and the situations they encounter becomes their subjective reality and may strongly influence their behaviour.

APPLYING SYMBOLIC INTERACTIONIST PERSPECTIVES TO SUICIDE Sociologists applying a symbolic interactionist framework to the study of suicide would primarily focus on a microlevel analysis of suicidal persons' face-to-face interactions with others and the roles that people play in society. In our efforts to interact with others, we define particular situations according to our own subjective reality. This theoretical viewpoint applies to suicide just as it does to other types of conduct. In studying suicide, the interactionist focuses on the various meanings that are attributed to the act of suicide.

Around the world, there is much variation among different cultures regarding the meaning of suicide. In Japan, for example, where suicide has traditionally been accepted, the words used to describe it reflect tolerance toward suicide. In English, the word *suicide* is derived from a Latin word meaning "murder." In contrast, the Japanese have 35 different expressions for suicide, but none meaning self-murder (Fuse, 1997). The meaning attached to suicide in Japan is closely related to Japanese views of death. These include that death is something to be welcomed and that it allows one to have a continuing life through one's children and their children (Leenaars et al., 1998).

How might a symbolic interactionist perspective be applied to understand the pattern of suicide among youth in some Aboriginal communities? Once again, the symbolic interactionist perspective focuses on the meaning of suicide in attempting to understand patterns or variations in suicide rates. These patterns may be an indication of the redefinition among Aboriginal youth of the meaning of suicide. A young Aboriginal student from New Brunswick discusses how suicide is viewed by some of his peers:

> Too many [North] American Indian youths find this life devoid of meaning and worth little, whereas death is a way of finding peace and reunion with glorified ancestors. Suicide is often viewed as a brave, heroic act. Self-destructive behaviour becomes a learned and rewarded pattern. Those who die by suicide become idols of their peer group. (Royal Commission on Aboriginal Peoples, 1995:10)

From this point of view, suicide is seen as a way of gaining peer approval and acceptance. When suicide becomes defined as a brave or heroic act, we can expect an increase in suicide rates.

This definition helps to explain why clusters of suicide have become more common among Aboriginal Canadian youth in recent years. For example, the Inuit of the east coast of Hudson

Bay experienced a dramatic increase in suicide between 1987 and 1991. Most of this increase was the result of a cluster of suicides in 1991. Furthermore, more than 90 percent of these suicides occurred in the 15 to 25 age group (Kirmayer, 1994:10). The symbolic interactionist perspective would view this as learned behaviour. Suicide becomes viewed by some youth as a socially acceptable solution to life's problems. As this symbolic interactionist analysis of suicide makes clear, social learning is important in how we define ourselves and our relationships to others. Because symbolic interactionist perspectives focus on the microlevel of society, they help us see how individuals interact in their daily lives and interpret their experiences; however, this approach is limited in that it basically ignores the larger social context in which behaviour takes place. If we focus primarily on the individual and small-group context of behaviour, we may overlook important macrolevel societal forces that are beyond the control of individuals. These include the effects of socially imposed definitions of race and ethnicity, gender, class, and age on people's lives.

Postmodern Perspectives

According to **postmodern perspectives**, cultural and social changes characteristic of postmodernity are closely linked to post-industrialization, consumerism, and global communications. It is useful to begin by distinguishing between postmodernity, postmodern social theory, and postmodernism.

postmodern perspectives The sociological approach that attempts to explain social life in modern societies that are characterized by post-industrialization, consumerism, and global communications.

Postmodernity is often used to describe a *historical era* subsequent to modernity, which began with the Enlightenment and ended in the mid-19th century. Just as functionalist, conflict, and symbolic interactionist perspectives emerged in the aftermath of the Industrial Revolution, postmodernity emerged after World War II (late 1940s); it reflected a belief that some nations were entering a period of post-industrialization.

Under postmodernism, the general belief systems, or "metanarratives," that characterize modern thinking are rejected. These include science and reason, world religion (e.g., Christianity, Islam, and Buddhism), and political ideology (e.g., communism, liberalism, and socialism).

According to important postmodern thinker Jean-François Lyotard (1984), postmodern knowledge involves a rejection of the grand narratives of science, politics, religion, and others; this, in turn, creates a crisis, or "break," in the status of knowledge in Western societies—"the postmodern condition," he calls it. Lyotard opposes the grand narratives that seek to tell the Truth about the world in which we live; he believes that boundaries should not be placed on academic disciplines, such as philosophy, literature, art, and the social sciences, where much could be learned by sharing ideas (Forsey, 2009).

This approach opens up broad new avenues of inquiry by challenging existing foundations and explores how certain perspectives have the power to privilege some groups while downgrading others and how some people are designated as "normal" or "right" while others are considered "wrong" or "abnormal." In this sense, one of the central political motivations of postmodernism is to demonstrate how power works *through* issues of race, class, gender, sexuality, age, and ability and to question how dominant narratives structure these differences.

Postmodernism can also refer to *cultural products*—for example, art, movies, and architecture—that are different from modern cultural products. These cultural products blur the boundaries between high and mass culture by bringing together different genres of music, literature, and art. Andy Warhol's pictures, for example, draw on both popular cultural forms (Coke cans and images of Marilyn Monroe) and high cultural forms (images of Mona Lisa) to create a collage of existing artistic styles. Postmodernism is also used more broadly to describe societies characterized by an *information explosion* and an economy in which large numbers of people either provide or apply information or are employed in service jobs (such as fast-food servers or healthcare workers). There is also a corresponding *rise of a consumer society* and the emergence of a *global village,* in which people around the world communicate with one another by electronic technologies, such as television, telephone, fax, email, and on a variety of social media sources such as Facebook and Twitter.

According to Jean Baudrillard (1983), the postmodern world is also characterized by *simulations* to the extent that it is becoming increasingly difficult to distinguish between the "real" and those things that simulate the real. Have you ever complimented someone on her designer jeans or purse, only to have her admit they are "knockoffs" purchased online? Could you tell the difference?

Baudrillard talks, too, about "the dissolution of TV into life, the dissolution of life into TV" (1983:55), describing how the medium ceases to serve as a mirror of reality. Instead, it becomes that reality, or, in some cases, even more real than that reality. Reality TV shows such as *Jersey Shore, The Bachelor,* and the *Real Housewives* franchise are good examples of what Baudrillard terms "hyperreality": Rather than portraying how people live and behave, they distort the boundary between real life and acting, which in turn leads to the subordination and ultimate dissolution of "the real." In the postmodern world, there is no more reality—only hyperreality (Forsey, 2009).

APPLYING POSTMODERN PERSPECTIVES TO SUICIDE Do information technologies, such as computers and the Internet, bind people together, or do they create a world where people feel only tenuously involved in the collective life and interpersonal relations? Such questions might be asked by postmodern analysts in a study of people's suicidal behaviour.

According to some postmodern thinkers, we face a high-tech world in which images, ideas, and identity-forming material pass before our eyes at an accelerated pace. As a result, we are required to develop our own coherent narrative order by which we understand ourselves and the social events that take place around us (Gergen, 1991; Harvey, 1989.) Consider the tragic case of the 13-year-old girl who committed suicide after she received cruel messages on MySpace. Weeks later, her family learned that a boy she had been communicating with did not exist but had been fabricated by a neighbourhood mother in an attempt to bully the child (World NewsMaker, 2007). From a postmodern approach, representations such as this reflect a world in which individuals and the media may establish "fake" realities and pseudo-explanations in the absence of *real* knowledge about events or their causes. In future chapters, we use a postmodern framework to examine topics such as cultural ideas; language use; issues of race, class, and gender; the political economy; and individual self-conceptions.

Each of the sociological perspectives we have examined involves different assumptions. Consequently, each leads us to ask different questions and to view the world somewhat differently. Different aspects of reality are the focus of each approach. While functionalism emphasizes social cohesion and order, conflict and feminist approaches focus primarily on social conflict and change. In contrast, symbolic interactionism primarily examines people's interactions and shared meanings in everyday life. The Concept Snapshot reviews the major perspectives. Throughout this book, we will be using these perspectives as lenses through which to view our social world. You can also use each approach to help in developing your own sociological imagination.

CONCEPT SNAPSHOT

FUNCTIONALIST PERSPECTIVES **Key thinkers:** Émile Durkheim, Talcott Parsons, Robert Merton	Society is composed of interrelated parts that work together to maintain stability within society. This stability is threatened by dysfunctional acts and institutions.
CONFLICT PERSPECTIVES **Key thinkers:** Karl Marx, Max Weber, Ralf Dahrendorf	Society is characterized by social inequality; social life is a struggle for scarce resources. Social arrangements benefit some groups at the expense of others.
FEMINIST PERSPECTIVES **Key thinkers:** Dorothy Smith, Margrit Eichler, Meg Luxton	Society is based on patriarchy—a hierarchical system of power in which males possess greater economic and social privilege than females.
SYMBOLIC INTERACTIONIST PERSPECTIVES **Key thinkers:** George Herbert Mead, Herbert Blumer	Society is the sum of the interactions of people and groups. Behaviour is learned in interaction with other people; how people define a situation becomes the foundation for how they behave.
POSTMODERNIST PERSPECTIVES **Key thinkers:** Jean-François Lyotard, Jean Baudrillard	Societies characterized by post-industrialization, consumerism, and global communications bring into question existing assumptions about social life and the nature of reality.

VISUAL SUMMARY

KEY TERMS

alienation A feeling of powerlessness and estrangement from other people and from oneself (p. 13).

anomie Émile Durkheim's term for a condition in which social control becomes ineffective as a result of the loss of shared values and a sense of purpose in society (p. 12).

bourgeoisie Karl Marx's term for the class comprised of those who own and control the means of production (p. 12).

class conflict Karl Marx's term for the struggle between the capitalist class and the working class (p. 12).

commonsense knowledge A form of knowing that guides ordinary conduct in everyday life. (p. 4).

conflict perspectives The sociological approach that views groups in society as engaged in a continuous power struggle for control of scarce resources (p. 18).

dysfunctions A term referring to the undesirable consequences of any element of a society (p. 17).

feminist perspectives The sociological approach that focuses on the significance of gender in understanding and explaining inequalities that exist between men and women in the household, in the paid labour force, and in the realms of politics, law, and culture (p. 20).

functionalist perspectives The sociological approach that views society as a stable, orderly system (p. 15).

LO-1 Define *sociology* and explain how can it help us understand ourselves and others.

© fStop/Alamy

Sociology is the systematic study of human society and social interaction. We study sociology to understand how human behaviour is shaped by group life and, in turn, how group life is affected by individuals. Our culture tends to emphasize individualism, and sociology pushes us to consider more complex connections between our personal lives and the larger world.

LO-2 Explain why the sociological imagination is important for studying society.

According to C. Wright Mills, the sociological imagination helps us understand how seemingly personal troubles, such as student debt are related to larger social forces. It allows us to see the relationship between individual experiences and the larger society. It is important to have a global sociological imagination because the future of this country is deeply intertwined with the future of all nations of the world on economic, political, environmental, and humanitarian levels.

© THE CANADIAN PRESS/Nathan Denette

LO-3 Discuss the major contributions of early sociologists.

© Prisma/UIG/Getty Images

Comte, considered by many the founder of sociology, coined the term *sociology* to describe the new science engaging in the study of society. Others have argued that Harriet Martineau should be viewed as a founding member of sociology due to her enlightened perspective that social progress must involve gender and social equality. The ideas of Émile Durkheim, Karl Marx, and Max Weber helped lead the way to contemporary sociology. Durkheim argued that societies are built on social facts, that rapid social change produces strains in society, and that the loss of shared values and purpose can lead to a condition of anomie. Marx stressed that within society there is a continuous clash between the owners of the means of production and the workers, who have no choice but to sell their labour to others. According to Weber, it is necessary to acknowledge the meanings that individuals attach to their own actions.

LO-4 Describe the key assumptions behind each of the major contemporary sociological perspectives.

Photographer: Karyn Gorra. Used with permission of Margrit Eichler.

Functionalist perspectives assume that society is a stable, orderly system characterized by societal consensus; however, this perspective has been criticized for overlooking the importance of change in societies. Conflict perspectives argue that society is a continuous power struggle among competing groups, often based on class, race, ethnicity, or gender. Critics of conflict theory note that it minimizes the importance of social stability and shared values in society. Feminist perspectives focus on the significance of gender in understanding and explaining inequalities that exist between men and women in the household, in the paid labour force, and in politics, law, and culture. Symbolic interactionist perspectives focus on how people make sense of their everyday social interactions, which are made possible by the use of mutually understood symbols. However, this approach focuses on the microlevel of society and tends to ignore the macrolevel social context. From an alternative perspective, postmodern theorists believe that entirely new ways of examining social life are needed and that it is time to move beyond functionalist, conflict, and interactionist perspectives.

APPLICATION QUESTIONS

1. What does C. Wright Mills mean when he says the sociological imagination helps us "grasp history and biography and the relations between the two within society" (Mills, 1959b:6)? How might this idea be applied to various trends in suicide in today's society?
2. As a sociologist, how would you remain objective and yet see the world as others see it? Would you make subjective decisions when trying to understand the perspectives of others?
3. Early social thinkers were concerned about stability in times of rapid change. In our more global world, is stability still a primary goal? Or is constant conflict important for the well-being of all humans? Use the conflict and feminist perspectives to support your analysis.
4. According to the functionalist perspective, what would happen to society if one of its institutions—say, the education system—were to break down?

global interdependence A relationship in which the lives of all people are intertwined closely and any one nation's problems are part of a larger global problem (p. 4).

high-income countries Nations with highly industrialized economies; technologically advanced industrial, administrative, and service occupations; and relatively high levels of national and personal income (p. 6).

industrialization The process by which societies are transformed from dependence on agriculture and handmade products to an emphasis on manufacturing and related industries (p. 8).

latent functions Unintended functions that are hidden and remain unacknowledged by participants (p. 17).

low-income countries Countries that are primarily agrarian, with little industrialization and low levels of national and personal income (p. 7).

macrolevel analysis Sociological theory and research that focus on whole societies, large-scale social structures, and social systems (p. 21).

manifest functions Open, stated, and intended goals or consequences of activities within an organization or institution (p. 17).

means of production Karl Marx's term for tools, land, factories, and money for investment that form the economic basis of a society (p. 13).

microlevel analysis Sociological theory and research that focus on small groups rather than on large-scale social structures (p. 21).

middle-income countries Nations with industrializing economies, particularly in urban areas, and moderate levels of national and personal income (p. 7).

perspective An overall approach to or viewpoint on some subject (p. 15).

positivism A belief that the world can best be understood through scientific inquiry (p. 9).

postmodern perspectives The sociological approach that attempts to explain social life in modern societies that are characterized by post-industrialization, consumerism, and global communications (p. 23).

proletariat Karl Marx's term for those who must sell their labour because they have no other means to earn a livelihood (p. 13).

social Darwinism The belief that those species of animals (including human beings) best adapted to their environment survive and prosper, whereas those poorly adapted die out (p. 11).

social facts Émile Durkheim's term for patterned ways of acting, thinking, and feeling that exist outside any one individual (p. 11).

social solidarity The state of having shared beliefs and values among members of a social group, along with intense and frequent interaction among group members (p. 17).

societal consensus A situation whereby the majority of members share a common set of values, beliefs, and behavioural expectations (p. 15).

society A large social grouping that shares the same geographical territory and is subject to the same political authority and dominant cultural expectations (p. 4).

sociological imagination C. Wright Mills's term for the ability to see the relationship between individual experiences and the larger society (p. 5).

sociology The systematic study of human society and social interaction (p. 4).

symbol Anything that meaningfully represents something else (p. 22).

symbolic interactionist perspectives The sociological approach that views society as the sum of the interactions of individuals and groups (p. 22).

theory A set of logically interrelated statements that attempts to describe, explain, and (occasionally) predict social events (p. 15).

urbanization The process by which an increasing proportion of a population lives in cities rather than in rural areas (p. 8).

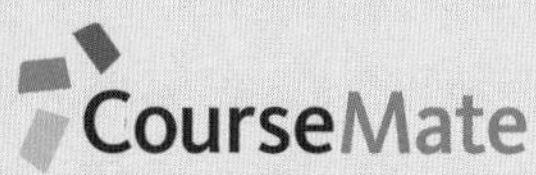

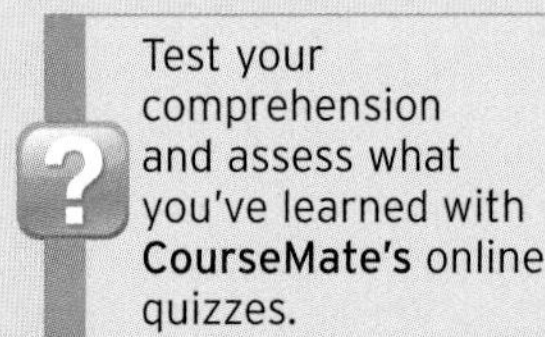

Test your comprehension and assess what you've learned with **CourseMate's** online quizzes.

For other interesting Lived Experiences, watch the video clips on **CourseMate.**

Practise what you've learned with flashcards containing key terms and definitions on **CourseMate.**

CHAPTER

2 Sociological Research

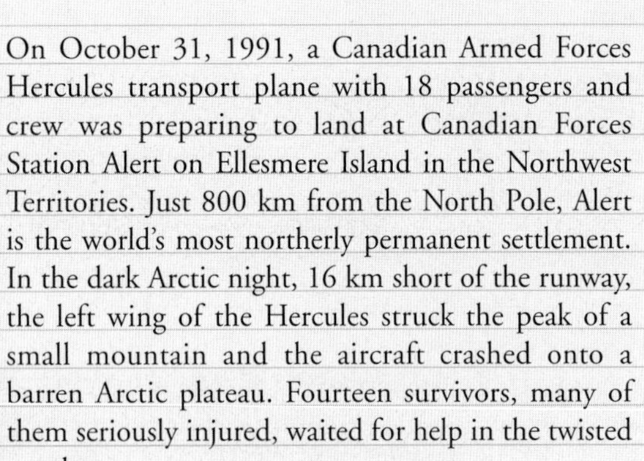

On October 31, 1991, a Canadian Armed Forces Hercules transport plane with 18 passengers and crew was preparing to land at Canadian Forces Station Alert on Ellesmere Island in the Northwest Territories. Just 800 km from the North Pole, Alert is the world's most northerly permanent settlement. In the dark Arctic night, 16 km short of the runway, the left wing of the Hercules struck the peak of a small mountain and the aircraft crashed onto a barren Arctic plateau. Fourteen survivors, many of them seriously injured, waited for help in the twisted wreckage.

Thirty-two hours later, another Hercules, with a team of search and rescue technicians (SARtechs) on board, was circling the crash site. The SARtechs were hoping conditions would allow them to parachute into the site to help the survivors. The temperature was −66°C, visibility on the ground was limited, and the winds of 35 to 40 knots were more than three times the permissible limit for parachuting. Because of the terrible weather conditions, a U.S. Air Force crew had just cancelled their attempt at a jump onto the crash site. In the back of the Canadian Hercules, Warrant Officer Arnie Macauley, the SARtech team leader, addressed his men:

> *Okay, guys, you know the situation. The winds are pretty stiff. They've blown away all our marker lights . . . It looks like a snowfield down there, but ground conditions are unknown. We'll be landing at a good clip. We'll try for flare illumination, but I can't promise you anything.*
>
> *One more thing. Once we're down there, we're down for good. Marv will try for a supply drop, but we can expect the survival gear to be blown away. We'll have no way of extracting ourselves or the survivors . . .*
>
> *That's the situation, men. We can expect casualties. I have to inform you that the jump involves a knowing risk of life. I can't ask any of you to do this.*
>
> *Some of the SARtechs studied their boots; others looked out the open door into the howling void. One by one, they looked back at him. "Arnie," one said, "you know how we feel."*
>
> *Good guys, Arnie thought. I hope like hell I'm doing the right thing.*
>
> *Arnie checked the closures on his padded orange jumpsuit and the fasteners of his parachute harness. He pulled on his gloves. The jumpmaster clipped their static lines to the overhead cable, and the men crowded around the open door. There were six of them. They squeezed into the opening and grabbed one another by the legs, arms, waist. They would go together.* (Mason Lee, 1991:229–231)

Image IS2012-1018-11, http://www.combatcamera.forces.gc.ca. Department of National Defence, 2012. Reproduced with permission of the Minister of Public Works and Government Services Canada, 2012.

The rescuers completed their harrowing jump with relatively minor injuries and immediately began caring for the survivors.

Thirteen people are alive today because of the heroism of the SARtechs and the rest of the crew involved in this rescue. Why do people like Warrant Officer Macauley and his men risk their lives in order to save others? This question has been asked by sociologists who have studied **altruism**—behaviour intended to help others and done without any expectation of personal benefit.

In this chapter, you will learn how sociological research methods help us understand social phenomena such as altruism. How do sociologists determine what to study? How do they conduct their research? What factors determine the best method to use in social research? These questions address the process of doing sociological research—an exciting process that challenges us to go as "strangers" into a familiar world.

Several researchers have conducted studies that try to help us understand altruistic behaviour, and their work will be used to illustrate the different research methods used by sociologists. Before reading on, test your knowledge of altruism by answering the questions in Box 2.1 on page 33.

Source: From *Death and Deliverance*, by Robert Mason Lee (Macfarlane Walter & Ross, Toronto, 1992), pp. 229–231.

Critical Thinking Questions

1. In this chapter, we will discuss several studies of altruism. Which aspects of this topic will you be most interested in studying?
2. Can you think of ways in which your fellow students are behaving altruistically by helping others? Do students typically help others by donating time or by contributing money?
3. Why do you think sociologists have spent much more time studying negative behaviours, such as criminality, than studying positive behaviours like altruism?

CHAPTER FOCUS QUESTION

How does social research add to our knowledge of human societies?

LEARNING OBJECTIVES

AFTER READING THIS CHAPTER, YOU SHOULD BE ABLE TO

LO-1 Understand the relationship between theory and research.

LO-2 Identify the main steps in the sociological research process.

LO-3 Explain why it is important to have different methods of conducting social research and know something about each of these methods.

LO-4 Discuss how research has contributed to our understanding of altruism.

LO-5 Explain why a code of ethics for sociological research is necessary.

LO-1 WHY IS SOCIOLOGICAL RESEARCH NECESSARY?

altruism Behaviour intended to help others and done without any expectation of personal benefit.

Sociological research results in a body of information that helps us move beyond guesswork and common sense in understanding society. During this course, you will learn that commonsense beliefs about society are often wrong. The sociological perspective incorporates theory and research to arrive at an informed understanding of the "hows" and "whys" of human social interaction.

Five Ways of Knowing the World

Sociologists seek to understand social behaviour. People have always tried to bring order to the chaotic world of experience by trying to understand the social and physical worlds in which they live. Understanding is the major goal of science, but this goal is shared by other fields, including philosophy, religion, the media, and the arts. We have several ways of knowing the world:

1. *Personal experience.* We discover for ourselves many of the things we know. If we put our tongue on a frozen doorknob, we learn that removing it can be painful.
2. *Tradition.* People may hold a belief because "everyone knows" it to be true. Tradition tells us that something is right because it has always been done that way. We accept what has always been believed rather than finding the answers by ourselves.
3. *Authority.* Experts tell us that something is true. We do not all need to go to the moon to discover its mineral composition, but instead accept the judgment of space scientists. Much of what we know about medicine, crime, and many other phenomena is based on what authorities have told us.
4. *Religion.* Religious authority gives us truths based on our particular scriptures. Beliefs about factors as diverse as morality, diet, dress, and hair styles are based on religious authority.
5. *Science.* The scientific way of knowing involves controlled, systematic observation. Scientists insist that all statements be tested and that testing procedures be open to public inspection.

CP PHOTO 1998 (stf/Andrew Vaughan)

Many Nova Scotians contributed their time to help search for bodies and debris after the crash of Swissair Flight 111 off the Nova Scotia coast.

Personal experience, tradition, authority, and religion are all valid sources of understanding. However, there is no way to resolve disagreements between those who have had different experiences, or who believe in different religions, traditions, or authorities. For example, if two religious groups have different views concerning the activities that are permissible on the Sabbath or the role that women should play in society, there is no institutionalized way of reconciling these contrary positions.

Scientific explanations differ from the other ways of knowing in several fundamental ways that allow scientists to resolve differences in their understanding of the world.

First, science is *empirical.* Science is based on the assumption that knowledge is best gained by direct, systematic observation.

Second, scientific knowledge is *systematic* and *public.* The procedures used by scientists are organized, public, and recognized by other scientists. The scientific community will not accept claims that cannot be publicly verified.

Third, science has a built-in mechanism for *self-correction.* Scientists do not claim that their findings represent eternal truths,

BOX 2.1 **SOCIOLOGY AND EVERYDAY LIFE**

How Much Do You Know About Altruism?

True	False	
T	F	1. It is nice to help other people, but altruistic behaviour has little impact on the nature of society.
T	F	2. People who behave altruistically often had parents who also actively helped others.
T	F	3. Helping others after a disaster can be a way of helping oneself recover from the shock of having lived through a traumatic event.
T	F	4. Good Samaritan laws require that Canadians assist those they see in danger or in need of assistance.
T	F	5. Experiments in laboratories and in natural settings have shown that the likelihood of bystanders intervening in situations where someone needs help is reduced as the number of people who are aware of the incident increases.

For answers to the quiz about altruism, go to **www.nelson.com/sociologyinourtimes6e.**

but rather they present **hypotheses**—tentative statements of the relationship between two or more concepts or variables—that are subject to verification by themselves and by others. What is accepted as scientific truth changes over time as more evidence accumulates. By contrast, making changes in understandings based on tradition, authority, or religious belief can be difficult.

hypotheses Tentative statements of the relationship between two or more concepts or variables.

Fourth, science is ***objective.*** Scientists try to ensure that their biases and values do not affect their research. In some situations, this criterion is easily met. Two scientists measuring the time it takes for a ball to fall 300 metres should arrive at the same answer despite having different backgrounds and values. However, complete objectivity is not possible in the social sciences. Weber pointed out long ago that the researchers' values even influence their selection of research problems. Weber also believed that sociology was fundamentally concerned with the subjective meaning of social action. This means that "the primary task of the sociologist is to understand the meaning an act has for the actor himself, not for the observer" (Natanson, 1963:278). Kirby and McKenna tell us that "our interaction with the social world is affected by such variables as gender, race, class, sexuality, age, physical ability" and conclude that "this does not mean that facts about the social world do not exist, but that what we see and how we go about constructing meaning is a matter of interpretation" (1989:25). For example, marriage may mean different things for men and for women, and people with disabilities may experience the world differently than those without disabilities. The point is not that the observers lack objectivity, but rather that they experience social life in different ways. Researchers must always carefully describe the methods they have used in their research so that others can decide for themselves how the researchers' subjectivity has affected their conclusions.

objective Free from distorted subjective (personal or emotional) bias.

descriptive study Research that attempts to describe social reality or provide facts about some group, practice, or event.

Descriptive and Explanatory Studies

Sociological studies can be descriptive or explanatory. **Descriptive studies** describe social reality or provide facts about some group, practice, or event. Descriptive studies are designed to find out what is happening to whom, where, and when. For example, the census provides a wealth of descriptive information about the people of Canada, including age, marital status, and place of residence. A descriptive study of altruism might try to determine what percentage of people would return a lost wallet or help a stranger in distress. **Explanatory studies** try to explain relationships and to provide information on why certain events do or do not occur.

explanatory study Research that attempts to explain relationships and to provide information on why certain events do or do not occur.

An explanatory study of altruism might ask, "Why are some people more likely than others to offer help?" or "Why do some countries rely on volunteer blood donations while others pay donors?"

The Theory and Research Cycle

deductive approach Research in which the investigator begins with a theory and then collects information and data to test the theory.

inductive approach Research in which the investigator collects information or data (facts or evidence) and then generates theories from the analysis of that data.

The relationship between theory and research has been described as a continuous cycle, (see Figure 2.1). The theory and research cycle consists of deductive and inductive approaches. In the **deductive approach**, the researcher begins with a theory and uses research to test the theory: (1) Theories generate hypotheses; (2) hypotheses lead to observations; (3) observations lead to generalizations; and (4) generalizations are used to support the theory, to suggest modifications to it, or to refute it. Consider the question "Why do people help others?" Using the deductive method, we would start by formulating a theory about the "causes" of altruism and then test our theory by collecting and analyzing data. We might conduct experiments on helping behaviour or do surveys that ask why some people help and others don't.

In the **inductive approach**, the researcher collects data and then generates theories from the analysis of those data: (1) Specific observations suggest generalizations; (2) generalizations produce a tentative theory; (3) the theory is tested through the formation of hypotheses; and (4) hypotheses may provide suggestions for additional observations. Using the inductive approach to study altruism, we might start by collecting and analyzing data related to helping behaviour and then generating a theory (see Glaser and Strauss, 1967; Reinharz, 1992).

The process of inquiry is rarely as tidy as the diagram in Figure 2.1 suggests. Instead, sociologists typically move back and forth from theory to research throughout the course of their inquiry. In fact, investigators rarely, if ever, begin with either just a theory or with research data.

FIGURE 2.1 THE THEORY AND RESEARCH CYCLE

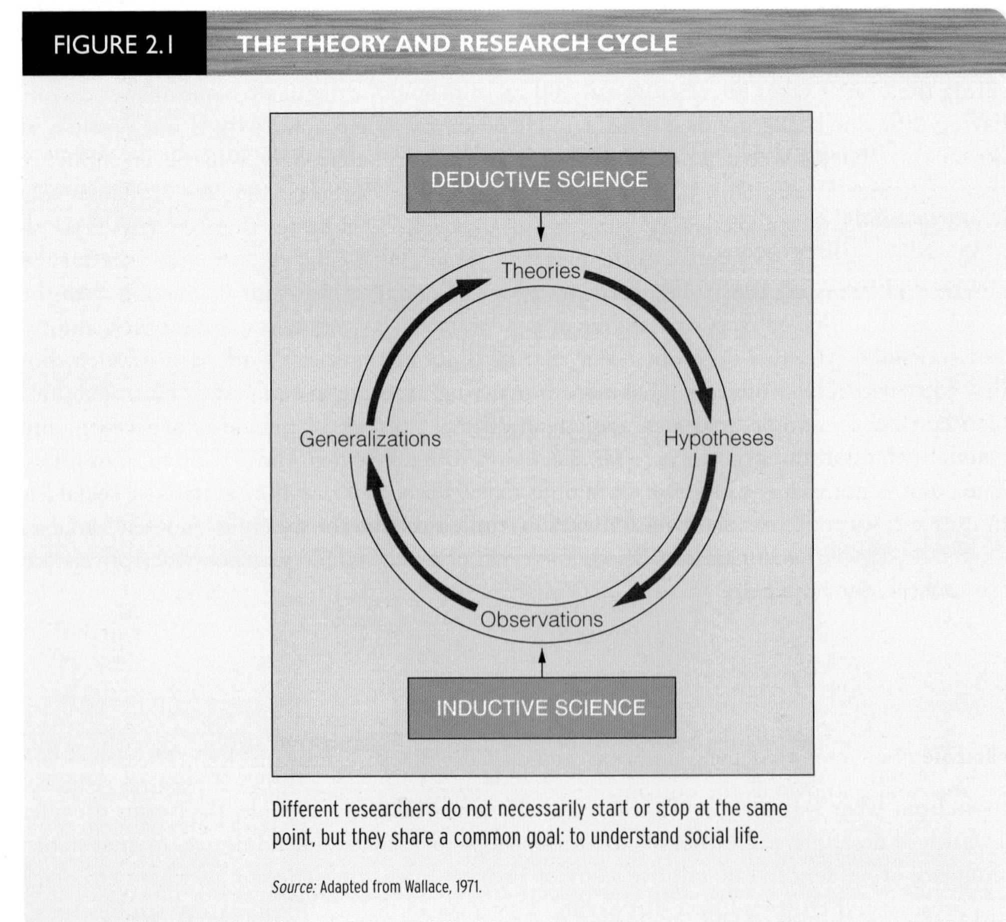

Different researchers do not necessarily start or stop at the same point, but they share a common goal: to understand social life.

Source: Adapted from Wallace, 1971.

Inductive theorists need at least rudimentary theories to guide their data collection, and deductive theorists, must refer constantly to the real world as they develop their theories. Researchers may break into the cycle at different points depending on what they want to know and what information is available. Theory gives meaning to research; research helps support theory.

THE SOCIOLOGICAL RESEARCH PROCESS LO-2

How would you go about conducting a sociological study? Not all sociologists conduct research in the same way. Some researchers engage primarily in *quantitative* research, whereas others engage in *qualitative* research. With quantitative research, the focus is on data that can be measured numerically. With qualitative research, interpretive description (words) rather than statistics (numbers) is used to analyze underlying meanings and patterns of social relationships. We will trace the steps in both of these research models.

The Quantitative Research Model

The steps in the quantitative model are outlined below:

SELECT AND DEFINE THE RESEARCH PROBLEM The first step is to select a research topic. A researcher's personal experience or social policy concerns can trigger interest in a topic. Other researchers select topics to fill gaps or challenge misconceptions in existing research or to test a specific theory.

Once you have selected a topic, ask, "What do I want to know about this topic?" Consider the issue of Good Samaritan laws discussed in Box 2.2. As a researcher, how would you approach the questions raised in the box?

REVIEW PREVIOUS RESEARCH Once you have defined your research problem, you need to review the literature (relevant books and scholarly articles) to see what others have learned about the topic. Knowledge of the literature helps refine the research problem, provides possible theoretical approaches, and indicates which aspects of the research topic have already been studied and where the gaps are.

FORMULATE THE HYPOTHESIS (IF APPLICABLE) After reviewing previous research, you may formulate a hypothesis—a statement of the relationship between two or more concepts. Concepts are the abstract elements representing some aspect of the world in simplified form (social integration and altruism are examples). As you formulate your hypothesis, you will need to convert concepts to variables. A **variable** is any concept with measurable traits or characteristics that can change or vary from one person, time, situation, or society to another. Variables are the observable and/or measurable counterparts of concepts. For example, when altruism is the concept, the percentage of the population who donate blood may be a variable.

Now you are ready to look at the relations between your variables. The most fundamental relationship is between a dependent variable and one or more independent variables. The **independent variable** is presumed to cause or determine a dependent variable. Sociologists often use characteristics such as age, sex, race, and ethnicity as independent variables. The **dependent variable** is assumed to depend on or be caused by the independent variable(s). The dependent variable is also known as the outcome or effect. Several researchers have tested the hypothesis that women are more altruistic than men. In this research, gender is the independent variable and the degree of altruism is the dependent variable. Whether a variable is dependent or independent depends on the context in which it is used, and a variable that is independent in one study may be dependent in another. For example, in a study of the relationship between

variable In sociological research, any concept with measurable traits or characteristics that can change or vary from one person, time, situation, or society to another.

independent variable A variable that is presumed to cause or determine a dependent variable.

dependent variable A variable that is assumed to depend on or be caused by one or more other (independent) variables.

BOX 2.2 **POINT/COUNTERPOINT**

Does the Law Require Us to Help?

Following Princess Diana's death in a Paris automobile crash in 1997, many Canadians were surprised to learn that France has a law requiring people to help others in distress. Such laws are referred to as Good Samaritan laws after the biblical story of altruistic behaviour. Because of their failure to help the princess, nine photographers and a press motorcyclist were placed under formal investigation—one step short of being charged—for failing to come to the aid of a person in danger.

What about Canada? Does the law require that we intervene in situations where others are in danger? Will we be compensated if we are injured when trying to help others?

In most cases, the answer to these questions is no—Canadian law does little to encourage or to protect Good Samaritans. Most provinces have Good Samaritan laws that protect healthcare professionals from liability if they provide assistance outside a hospital or office setting. Some provinces extend this protection to all citizens who provide emergency medical services or aid. However, only Quebec *requires* people to assist others. The Quebec Charter of Human Rights and Freedoms states:

> Every human being whose life is in peril has a right to assistance. Every person must come to the aid of anyone whose life is in peril, either personally or calling for aid, by giving him the necessary and immediate physical assistance, unless it involves danger to himself or a third person, or he has another valid reason.

What do you think? Should we be compelled to help each other, or should we rely on people's altruism? Can the law help to encourage altruism, or is it more a function of our backgrounds and social relationships?

Could sociological research help society's understanding of this issue? How could you assess the need for Good Samaritan laws and the impact of such laws on altruistic behaviour? Do you think most people are aware that such laws are—or are not—on the books? What does the public think about the need for such laws?

Sources: Nairne, 1998; Quinton, 1989.

a family's income and the likelihood of their child graduating from university, the dependent variable is university education. In another study looking at the relationship between university education and voting behaviour, university education is the independent variable.

Some variables are difficult to measure. How do we distinguish between criminals and noncriminals when virtually all of us have broken the law? We might define criminals as those who have been convicted of a crime. However, what do we do about people who have committed crimes but who have been found not guilty at a trial because the evidence against them was obtained illegally? What about corporate offenders whose behaviour may have injured people but who have violated government regulations rather than the criminal law?

The operational definition of altruism has also been debated. Earlier, we defined altruism as action intended to help others and done without any expectation of personal benefit. Warrant Officer Macauley and the other SARtechs, however, were paid to rescue people and their heroism was publicly recognized. Blood donors may someday receive the benefits of a transfusion. Mother Teresa received personal satisfaction from working with the poor and may become a saint. Thus we must consider altruism a matter of degree rather than an attribute that some people have and others do not.

DEVELOP THE RESEARCH DESIGN Sociologists use several different research methods, including experiments, survey research, field research, and secondary analysis of data, which are described in this chapter. In developing the research design, it is important to consider the advantages and disadvantages of each of these methods.

COLLECT AND ANALYZE THE DATA Next sociologists collect and analyze their data. No matter which method they choose, researchers must consider the reliability and validity of their data when designing a research project.

Adisa/Shutterstock

What if one of these people suddenly had a heart attack or got stabbed by another person? Under what conditions would others intervene to help? Social research has helped us answer this question.

reliability In sociological research, the extent to which a study or research instrument yields consistent results.

validity In sociological research, the extent to which a study or research instrument accurately measures what it is supposed to measure.

analysis The process through which data are organized so that comparisons can be made and conclusions drawn.

replication In sociological research, the repetition of the investigation in substantially the same way that it originally was conducted.

Reliability is the extent to which a study or research instrument yields consistent results when applied to different individuals at one time or to the same individual over time. A ruler is a reliable measure of length because it consistently gives the same results. In the social realm, an IQ test would be considered reliable if a person receives the same score when he or she takes the test more than once. **Validity** is the extent to which a study or research instrument accurately measures what it is supposed to measure. While IQ tests are quite reliable, their validity as a measure of intelligence is more controversial. Proponents believe they are good measures of people's natural abilities. However, some social scientists feel the tests measure only some components of intelligence, while others criticize their use among people whose language and cultural backgrounds are different from those of the researchers who designed the tests.

Once you have collected your data, they must be analyzed. **Analysis** is the process through which data are organized so that comparisons can be made and conclusions drawn.

DRAW CONCLUSIONS AND REPORT THE FINDINGS After analyzing the data, your first step in drawing conclusions is to relate the data to your hypotheses. Reporting the findings is the final stage. The report generally includes a review of each step taken in the research process to make the study available for **replication**—the repetition of the investigation in substantially the same way that it was originally conducted. This means that other researchers will see if they get the same results when they repeat your study. If your findings are replicated, the research community will have more faith in your conclusions.

© Kayte Deioma/PhotoEdit

Surveys and polls are common in many countries. This investigator is conducting her research in Taiwan.

The Qualitative Research Model

Although the same underlying logic is involved in both quantitative and qualitative sociological research, the *styles* of these two models are very different. Qualitative

© AP Photo/Eranga Jayawardena

Natural disasters, such as the tsunami in Sri Lanka, may be "living laboratories" for sociologists.

research is more likely to be used where the research question does not easily lend itself to numbers and statistical methods. Compared to a quantitative model, a qualitative approach often involves a different type of research question and a smaller number of cases. Qualitative studies are typically a detailed picture of some particular social phenomenon or social problem (King, Keohane, and Verba, 1994).

Qualitative researchers typically do not initially define their research problem in as much detail as quantitative researchers. The first step in qualitative research often consists of *problem formulation* to clarify the research question and formulate questions of interest to the research participants (Reinharz, 1992). Qualitative researchers typically gather data in natural settings, such as places where people live or work, rather than in a laboratory or over the phone. As a result, the qualitative approach can generate new theories and innovative findings that incorporate the perspectives of the research subjects.

The qualitative approach follows the conventional research approach in presenting a problem, asking a question, collecting and analyzing data, and seeking to answer the research question, but it also has several unique features (Creswell, 1998; Kvale, 1996):

1. The researcher begins with a general approach rather than a highly detailed plan. Flexibility is necessary because of the nature of the research question.
2. The researcher has to decide when the literature review and theory application should take place. Initial work may involve redefining existing concepts or reconceptualizing how existing studies have been conducted. The literature review may take place at an early stage, before the research design is fully developed, or it may occur after development of the research design and after collection of the data.
3. The study presents a detailed view of the topic. Qualitative research usually involves a smaller number of cases and many variables, whereas quantitative researchers typically work with a few variables and many cases (Creswell, 1998).

TIME TO REVIEW

- What are the different ways people use to understand their social and physical worlds? How does the scientific method differ from the other ways of knowing?
- Explain the cycle of theory and research. How do qualitative and quantitative researchers approach this cycle?

LO-3 RESEARCH METHODS

research methods
Specific strategies or techniques for conducting research.

How do sociologists decide which research method to use? Are some approaches better than others for particular research problems? **Research methods** are specific strategies or techniques for conducting research. *Qualitative* researchers frequently use field observation studies to help them understand the social world from the point of view of the people they are studying. *Quantitative* researchers generally use experimental designs, surveys, and secondary analysis of existing data. We will now look at these research methods.

Experiments

An **experiment** is a test conducted under controlled conditions in which an investigator tests a hypothesis by manipulating an independent variable and examining its impact on a dependent variable.

experiment A research method involving a carefully designed test in which the researcher studies the impact of certain variables on subjects' attitudes or behaviour.

TYPES OF EXPERIMENTS Experiments require that subjects be divided into an experimental group and a control group. **Experimental group** subjects are exposed to an independent variable to study its effect on them. The **control group** contains subjects who are not exposed to the independent variable. In an experiment, the independent variable is manipulated by the researcher and the dependent variable is hypothesized to change, based on the manipulation of the independent variable. Subjects are randomly assigned to each group or matched so that comparisons may be made between the groups. The researcher thereby ensures that the two groups are equivalent at the beginning of the study. In the simplest experimental design, (1) all subjects are pretested (measured in terms of the dependent variable); (2) subjects in the experimental group are then exposed to a stimulus (the independent variable); and (3) all subjects are post-tested (remeasured) in terms of the dependent variable. The experimental and control groups are then compared to see if they differ in relation to the dependent variable, and the hypothesis about the relationship of the two variables is confirmed or rejected.

experimental group Subjects in an experiment who are exposed to the independent variable.

control group Subjects in an experiment who are not exposed to the independent variable, but later are compared to subjects in the experimental group.

In a *laboratory experiment,* subjects are studied in a closed setting so researchers can maintain as much control as possible over the research. But not all experiments occur in laboratory settings. Researchers can stage events in natural settings by conducting *field experiments. Natural experiments* are real-life occurrences such as floods or earthquakes that provide researchers with "living laboratories." Can you think of how you might design a field experiment to help determine the value of microcredit programs, such as the one described in Box 2.3?

Experimental Research: Would You Help Another Person?

At 3 a.m. on March 13, 1964, Kitty Genovese was stabbed to death in the street near her home in New York City. Winston Moseley, her attacker, assaulted her three times over a period of half an hour. At one point, he left her and returned a few minutes later. During the assault, Ms. Genovese screamed, "Oh, my God, he stabbed me! Please help me!" However, she received no help from at least 38 neighbours who saw the attack and heard her cries for help. These neighbours did not turn away or ignore the attack; they continued to watch the murder from their apartment windows without coming to her assistance or calling the police. At Moseley's trial, several of these witnesses said they simply didn't want to get involved. Moseley himself said, "I knew they wouldn't do anything—they never do."

This case received worldwide attention. The killing also raised several questions for researchers: Why did Ms. Genovese's neighbours fail to act altruistically? Under what conditions will people be more or less likely to help others?

Among those who addressed these issues were social psychologists Bibb Latané and John Darley (1970). Their initial field studies found that in routine situations people were very willing to help. The vast majority willingly gave directions, told inquirers the time of day, and provided change for a quarter. However, their willingness to help could be changed by manipulating simple conditions, such as the wording of the request for assistance and the number of people asking for help.

BOX 2.3 SOCIOLOGY IN GLOBAL PERSPECTIVE

Altruism and Finance: The Grameen Bank

Much of the aid provided to poor countries is spent on large projects, such as dams and power plants. Critics have claimed that these infrastructure projects have done little to benefit the poor. However, in recent years the problem of development has been approached in a new way.

Muhammad Yunus has invented a new form of aid that directly benefits the poorest of the world's people. In the early 1970s, Yunus was the head of the economics department at Chittagong University in Bangladesh. In 1974, a terrible famine killed 1.5 million Bangladeshis and changed Yunus's life. Disturbed by the contrast between the economic theories he was teaching in his classes and the terrible poverty that surrounded him, he took his students to the affected towns and villages. On one of these visits, a woman told him that her profit from making bamboo stools was the equivalent of only two cents per day. Because she had no money, she could not buy the bamboo herself, even though it cost only 20 cents for a day's worth of the raw material. Instead, she had to get it from a trader who required that she sell the stools to him for a very low price. Yunus found 42 self-employed people in similar circumstances in the same village—together, they needed a total of $27 to become self-sufficient. Yunus lent them the money and then also tried to convince local banks to lend money to the poor. The banks refused, saying that people would not repay the money and that such small sums were not worth the trouble. So Yunus borrowed money himself and lent it to people in several villages.

Yunus eventually convinced the government to allow him to set up the Grameen Bank ("rural bank" in Bengali). The bank was funded by government loans and grants from international donors. While most banks lend money only to people who have money or property to use as collateral, the Grameen Bank deals solely with the destitute. Yunus lends mainly to women, as he has found that they are more likely to give the benefits to their families and to repay the money.

The bank charges interest and has several interesting requirements. For example, the bank will lend money only to groups of five borrowers. The five do not necessarily have to be in business together but are responsible for one another's loans. The group provides both peer support and peer pressure to ensure that the loans are repaid. Grameen also requires borrowers to make personal commitments to things like improving sanitation practices and sending their children to school.

The Grameen Bank has been phenomenally successful. About 98 percent of its loans are repaid, a much higher rate than other banks. The bank has expanded dramatically since it began operating in 1979. There are nearly eight million borrowers in Bangladesh, almost all of whom are women, and the bank is lending over a billion dollars each year. The bank is now self-sustaining and the idea of microcredit has spread to over 100 countries. Grameen has expanded into "social businesses" such as distributing fortified yogurt to poor children and building water treatment plants (Yunus, 2009).

Yunus, who is no longer involved with the Grameen bank, is an unusual banker. He was paid only $500 per month for this job, did not own a car, and has never charged anything on a credit card. However, he has won countless awards and honours and in 2006 he was awarded the Nobel Peace Prize for his revolutionary ideas and for the altruism he has shown in devoting his life to reducing poverty.

How would you study the impact of microcredit programs? You could conduct an observational study involving interviews with those who have received loans. You might also set up a field experiment that introduced microcredit programs into some communities that could then be compared with communities that did not have the programs.

Sources: Grameen Bank, 2005; Jolis, 1996; Mitchell, 1997; Stackhouse, 1998; and Yunus, 1997.

People are so willing to help in non-emergency situations that the question of why they may fail to respond to emergencies is difficult to understand. Latané and Darley rejected the view that this failure is due to apathy or indifference. Instead, they developed a *theoretical model* of the intervention process. Before a bystander will intervene in an emergency, they must notice that something is happening, interpret this event as an emergency, and decide that they are going to help. Latané and Darley proposed the hypothesis that the presence of other people will make people less likely to take each of these steps. They predicted the presence of others would inhibit the impulse to help because each of the potential helpers may look to others for guidance rather than acting quickly, potential helpers might be afraid of failing in front of other bystanders, and potential helpers may feel they are not obliged to help because someone else could take care of the problem.

Latané and Darley tested this hypothesis with a series of experiments, each scripted and designed like a short play. One of their studies simulated an emergency. Fifty-two university students were randomly assigned to groups of three different sizes: a two-person group (the subject and the victim), a three-person group, and a six-person group. Each of the students was seated at a table in a room, given a pair of headphones with a microphone, and told to listen for instructions.

Over the intercom, the subjects were told that the study concerned the personal problems facing students in a high-pressure urban environment. They were also told that, to maintain their anonymity when discussing personal matters, they had been placed in individual rooms and would talk and listen to others only through an intercom. The discussion would be controlled by a mechanical device that would turn each student's microphone on for two minutes at a time and then turn it off while the other students were talking. Thus only one student could be heard at a time and students could not talk with each other. To ensure spontaneity, the experimenter said he would not listen to the students' discussion but would get their reactions later.

These instructions were part of an elaborate script designed to see how the participants would respond to an emergency; in this case, an epileptic seizure in one of the subjects. After receiving the instructions, subjects heard a taped simulation that began with the future seizure victim discussing his difficulties adjusting to university and to big-city life. He also mentioned that he was prone to seizures during studying and exams. Each of the other people in the group, including the subject, then took their turns talking about their own adjustment problems.

The emergency occurred when it was again the victim's turn to talk. After beginning normally, he began to show obvious distress, then asked repeatedly for help, then made choking sounds and said he was going to die. After that, the intercom went quiet.

You will recall that Latané and Darley hypothesized that the presence of others would inhibit a helping response when people were faced with an emergency. The dependent variable was the time that elapsed from the start of the victim's seizure until the participant left the experiment room to get help. The independent variable was the number of other people each participant believed had also heard the victim's distress.

Did the experiment support the hypothesis? Figure 2.2 shows the results. Clearly, the number of bystanders had a significant effect on the likelihood of the student reporting the emergency. All the participants in the two-person groups reported the emergency, compared with 85 percent of the subjects in the three-person groups and only 62 percent of the subjects in the six-person groups. The participants in the two-person groups also responded more quickly than those in the larger groups.

What about those who failed to respond? They were not apathetic or unconcerned about the victim but were clearly upset by the episode. When the researcher entered the experiment room to end the study, the students who had not reported the seizure were often nervous and emotionally aroused. Many asked if the victim was "all right." While the students in the two-person groups clearly felt they had to intervene because nobody else knew of the victim's distress, those in the larger groups did worry about the victim but were also concerned about making fools of themselves by overreacting and ruining the experiment. Knowledge that others also knew of the emergency made it less likely that they would resolve this conflict by helping the victim.

STRENGTHS AND WEAKNESSES OF EXPERIMENTS The major advantage of the experiment is the researcher's control over the environment and the ability to isolate the experimental variable. This makes experiments the best way of testing cause-and-effect relationships. A second advantage is that since many experiments can be conducted with limited numbers of participants, it is often possible for researchers to replicate an experiment several times and thus increase confidence in the findings.

FIGURE 2.2 A STUDY OF ALTRUISTIC BEHAVIOUR

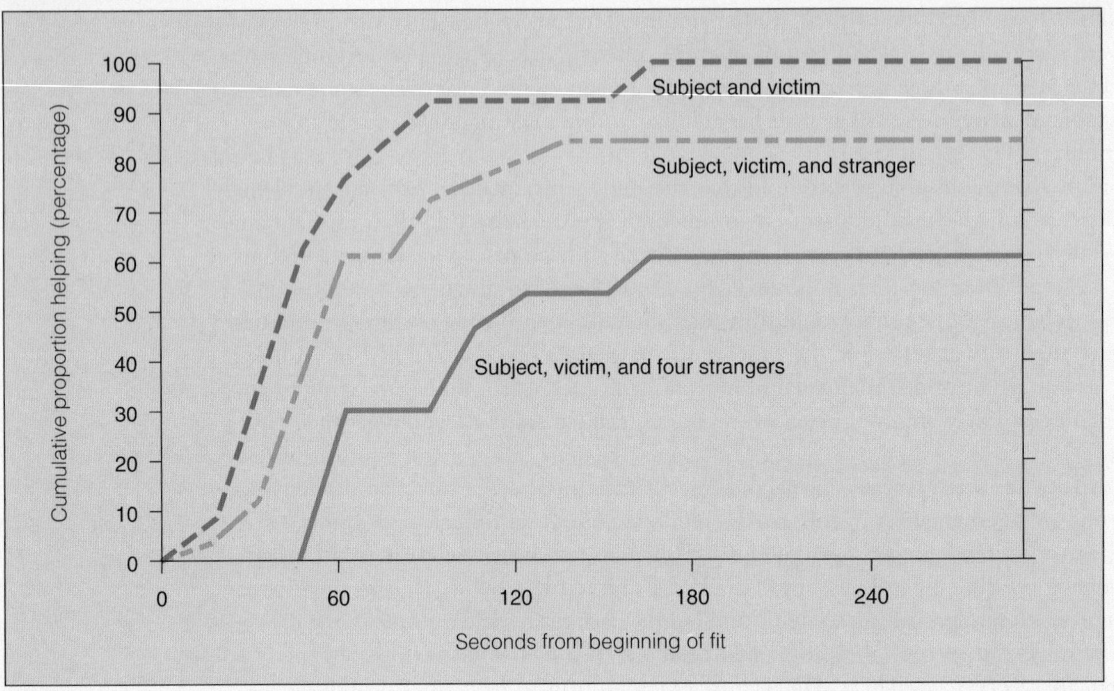

Cumulative proportion of subjects reporting seizure who think that they alone hear the victim or that one to four others also are present.

Source: Bibb Latané and John M. Darley, *The Unresponsive Bystander: Why Doesn't He Help?* New York: Appleton Century Crofts, 1970. Reprinted by permission of Prentice Hall.

reactivity The tendency of experiment participants to change their behaviour in response to the presence of the researcher or to the fact that they know they are being studied.

survey A research method in which a number of respondents are asked identical questions through a systematic questionnaire or interview.

respondent A person who provides data for analysis through an interview or questionnaire.

Artificiality is a major weakness of laboratory experiments. Participants in a laboratory obviously know they are participating in an experiment and may react to what they think the experiment is about or may not react realistically because they do not believe the scenario is real. **Reactivity** is the tendency of participants to change their behaviour in response to the presence of the researcher or to the fact that they know they are being studied. Latané and Darley tried to determine if some respondents chose not to intervene because they did not think the seizure was real. They concluded this was not a problem because the respondents were nervous when reporting the seizure, were surprised when they learned the true nature of the study, and made comments such as "My God, he's having a fit" during the simulated seizure.

A second limitation of experiments is that social scientists frequently rely on volunteers or captive audiences, such as students. As a result, the subjects of most experiments may not be representative of a larger population.

Third, experiments are limited in scope, as only a small number of variables can be manipulated.

Surveys

Survey research is the method perhaps most often associated with sociology. In a **survey**, a number of respondents are asked identical questions through a systematic questionnaire or interview. Researchers may select a representative sample from a larger population to answer questions about their attitudes, opinions, or behaviour. **Respondents** are persons who provide data for analysis through interviews or questionnaires. The Gallup and Ipsos Reid polls are among the most widely known large-scale surveys. Statistics Canada also conducts a variety of surveys, including the census, which attempts to gain information from all Canadians. Surveys are an important research method because they make it possible to study things that are not directly observable—such as people's attitudes and beliefs—and to describe a population too large to observe directly (Babbie, 2004).

TYPES OF SURVEYS Survey data are collected by using self-administered questionnaires, personal interviews, telephone surveys, or Internet surveys. A **questionnaire** is a research instrument containing a series of questions to which subjects respond.

Self-administered questionnaires have certain strengths. They are inexpensive to administer, they allow for rapid data collection and analysis, and they permit respondents to remain anonymous (an important consideration when the questions are personal). A major disadvantage is the low response rate. Mailed surveys sometimes have a response rate as low as 10 percent and those who respond may not be representative of the larger group. The response rate is usually higher if the survey is handed out to a group, such as a school class, that is asked to fill it out on the spot.

Survey data may also be collected by an **interview** in which an interviewer asks the respondent questions and records the answers. Survey research typically uses structured interviews, in which the interviewer asks questions from a standardized questionnaire.

Interviews are usually more effective in dealing with complicated issues and provide an opportunity for face-to-face communication between the interviewer and respondent. When open-ended questions are used, the researcher may gain new perspectives. The major disadvantage of interviews is the cost and time involved in conducting them.

Questionnaires may also be administered by *telephone surveys,* which save time and money compared to face-to-face interviews. Some respondents may be more honest over the phone than when they are facing an interviewer. Telephone surveys usually have much higher response rates than mailed questionnaires. However, caller identification systems, cellphones, and do-not-call lists have made telephone surveys more difficult, since many people are now less accessible to researchers. Survey researchers are now turning to questionnaires delivered on the Internet. Some problems with this technique involve difficulties in drawing a sample, particularly when the researcher is targeting the general population rather than specific groups, such as organizations where everyone's email address is known to the researcher.

SAMPLING CONSIDERATIONS Survey research usually involves some form of sampling. Researchers begin by identifying the population they want to study. They then draw a sample of that population.

The **population** is the group about which we wish to draw conclusions. A **sample** is the people who are selected from that population. A **representative sample** is a selection where the sample has the essential characteristics of the total population. For example, if you have to interview five students selected haphazardly from your sociology class, they would not be representative of your school's total student body. By contrast, if 500 students were selected from the total student body using a random sampling method, they would likely be representative of your school's students. A **simple random sample** is chosen by chance: Every member of an entire population being studied has the same chance of being selected. For example, you might draw a sample of the total student body by placing all the students' names in a rotating drum and drawing names from it.

questionnaire A research instrument containing a series of items to which subjects respond.

interview A research method using a data collection encounter in which an interviewer asks the respondent questions and records the answers.

population In a research study, those persons about whom we want to be able to draw conclusions.

sample The people who are selected from the population to be studied.

representative sample A selection where the sample has the essential characteristics of the total population.

simple random sample A selection in which everyone in the target population has an equal chance of being chosen.

Survey Research: Who Gives in Canada?

Many organizations depend upon charitable giving. Many buildings on your campus are likely named after people who have donated large sums of money to your institution; much of the research into the causes of cancer and other diseases is funded by donations; food banks depend on donations; and many Canadians contribute to fundraising drives during famines or natural

© Monkey Business Images/Shutterstock

Computer-assisted telephone interviewing is an easy and cost-efficient method of conducting research. The widespread use of voice mail, cellphones, and caller ID have made this form of research more difficult in the 21st century.

disasters. Because of the importance of charitable giving, we need to know more about the characteristics of those who give their money to help others.

Statistics Canada, in partnership with other government departments and several nonprofit and voluntary organizations, conducts a regular survey of Canadians—the Canada Survey of Giving, Volunteering and Participating—to learn more about charitable giving and volunteer work. In 2004, Statistics Canada drew a sample of 20,832 people 15 years of age and over for this study (Hall et al., 2006) (see Box 2.4). The survey used randomly generated phone numbers to contact respondents. The response rate for the survey was 57 percent, which meant that an interview was conducted with people at 57 percent of the numbers called. About 20 percent of those contacted refused to participate in the survey, and others could not be contacted.

This research examined some interesting questions. Which Canadians are most likely to donate their time or money? Are women more likely to donate money than men? Are young people more likely to volunteer their time than seniors?

You may be surprised to learn that the vast majority of Canadians—85 percent—had donated money to a charitable or nonprofit organization in the 12 months preceding the survey. The average person donated $400 and the total amount was $8.9 billion. The main recipients of these donations were religious organizations (45 percent of the total), health-related organizations (14 percent), and organizations delivering social services (10 percent) (Hall et al., 2006:9). The researchers were able to check the accuracy of their findings on the total amount donated by comparing it with information from income tax records and from a Statistics Canada survey on household spending. They found that $8.9 billion was reasonably close to the figures reported in the other two studies.

Who was most likely to donate? Women were slightly more likely to donate than men. Higher-income earners were more likely to donate than those with lower incomes and donated larger amounts of money. However, 69 percent of those in the lowest income bracket (less than $20,000 a year) donated. This compares with 92 percent of those who earned $100,000 or more. Older Canadians were more likely to donate than younger people.

Fewer people volunteered their time than gave their money—45 percent compared with 85 percent who donated funds. The patterns were similar to those for charitable giving, with the exception that young people (15 to 24) were the most likely to volunteer their time: 55 percent of this group had volunteered in the previous year, compared with 51 percent of the next highest group (35 to 44) and 32 percent of those 65 and over. While young people were not able to donate money (a scarce commodity for students and those new to the labour market), they were generous with their time.

One of the most interesting findings from the survey was that while there was a broad range of participation in the altruistic activities of charitable giving and volunteering, a core group did much more than others. About 13 percent of respondents were responsible for 57 percent of financial donations and 39 percent of volunteer hours. In the words of the researchers, "a lot do a little, but a little do a lot" (Hall et al., 2006:61).

STRENGTHS AND WEAKNESSES OF SURVEYS Survey research has several strengths. First, it is useful in describing the characteristics of a large population. Second, it enables the researcher to assess the relative importance of a number of variables. In the table in Box 2.4, we can compare the donation rates of people from different income levels.

BOX 2.4 PRESENTING SOCIOLOGICAL DATA

You have learned that sociologists have several ways of gathering data. These data are often presented numerically, and in this text you will find many tables showing the results of sociological studies. You should learn how to understand these tables and to develop the skill of presenting your own data.

In the study of charitable giving, Statistics Canada researchers wanted to determine if higher-income people were more or less likely to donate than those with lower incomes. Their data are presented below.

TABLE 2.1 DONOR RATE BY HOUSEHOLD INCOME (IN PERCENT)

HOUSEHOLD INCOME	LESS THAN $20,000	$20,000 TO $39,999	$40,000 TO $59,999	$60,000 TO $79,999	$80,000 TO $99,999	$100,000 OR MORE
Donated to Charity						
YES	69	82	86	88	91	92
NO	31	18	14	12	9	8
	100%	100%	100%	100%	100%	100%

Source: Hall et al., 2006.

The basic elements of a table are:

1. *Title or heading:* A brief description of the *content* of the table. The title "Donor Rate by Household Income" tells us that the table shows relationships between two variables: donor rate and household income.
2. *Categories of the variables:* The variable "Household Income" is divided into six categories based on reported income, and the variable "Donor Rate" is divided into the categories of Yes or No.
3. *Percentages:* The information in the table is stated in percentages. Using the raw numbers would make comparisons difficult for the reader. By comparing the percentages, we can see that as income increases, so does the likelihood of donating to charities.

Survey research also has weaknesses. One is that the use of standardized questions tends to force responses into categories that may not fit well. Moreover, people may be less than truthful, especially on emotionally charged issues or on issues, such as altruism, that have a strong element of social desirability. They may also be unwilling to provide information on sensitive issues, such as sexual activity, income, and criminal behaviour, and may also simply forget relevant information. This can make reliance on self-reported attitudes and behaviour problematic in some surveys. Finally, response rates have become so low for many surveys that their generalizability may be questionable.

field research The study of social life in its natural setting: observing and interviewing people where they live, work, and play.

Field Research

Field research is the study of social life in its natural setting: observing and interviewing people where they live, work, and play. Some kinds of behaviour are best studied by "being there"; a fuller understanding can be developed through observations, face-to-face discussions, and participation in events. Researchers use these methods to generate *qualitative* data: observations that are best described verbally rather than numerically. Although field research is less structured and more flexible than the other methods we have discussed, it also places many demands on the researcher. For example, field researchers must decide how to approach the target group, how to identify themselves as researchers, and whether to participate in the events they are observing.

complete observation Research in which the investigator systematically observes a social process, but does not take part in it.

participant observation A research method in which researchers collect systematic observations while being part of the activities of the group they are studying.

OBSERVATION Sociologists interested in observing social interaction may use either complete or participant observation. In **complete observation**, the researcher systematically observes a social process but does not take part in it. Observational research can take place just about anywhere. For example, sociologists David Karp and William Yoels (1976) became interested in why many students do not participate in classroom discussions. Observers sat in on various classes and took notes that included the average number of students who participated, the number of times they talked in class, and the sex of the instructor and of the students who talked in class. From these observations, Karp and Yoels found that, on average, a small number of students are responsible for most of the discussion that occurs in any class.

Subjects in observation studies may not realize that they are being studied, especially if the researcher remains unobtrusive. This type of observation helps us view behaviour as it is taking place. However, it provides limited opportunities to learn why people do certain things. One way for researchers to remain unobtrusive is through **participant observation**—collecting systematic observations while being part of the activities of the group they are studying. Participant observation generates more "inside" information than simply asking questions or observing from the outside. As Whyte noted in his classic participant observation study of a Boston low-income neighbourhood, "As I sat and listened, I learned the answers to questions I would not have had the sense to ask" (1957:303).

Canadians have always shown a strong willingness to help in natural disasters, such as the 2011 Manitoba flood.

FIELD RESEARCH: RESPONDING TO DISASTER During 2011, the provinces of Manitoba and Saskatchewan and the state of North Dakota suffered heavy flooding. In this and many other natural disasters, thousands of people pitch in to help by giving their time or their money to help out the victims. Natural disasters have brought people together in many parts of the world and have often shown human behaviour at its altruistic best. What motivates people to help after natural disasters? How effective is the aid that is provided to help others? What is the best way to help restore communities after a disaster?

Kamal Kapadia tried to answer these questions when she studied the impact of one of the world's greatest natural disasters. In December 2004, a devastating tsunami struck several countries surrounding the Indian Ocean. Nearly 250,000 people were killed and millions were left homeless. The global response to the disaster was massive as people around the world donated billions of dollars and their governments sent ships, aircraft, and disaster response teams to help with the recovery.

Because of the unprecedented global response, those involved in the reconstruction believed they could "build back better"—meaning that infrastructure such as housing and environmental protection to protect coasts could be improved and the poor could be helped to rebuild better lives.

Kapadia, who had lived and conducted research in Sri Lanka, moved back to that country to study the relief effort. As part of her field research, she worked as a volunteer for a Sri Lankan aid agency and so was directly involved with the aid effort. Her research was very thorough: She conducted a document review, analyzing the documents of 49 of the largest organizations involved with the aid effort; conducted 76 interviews with staff from these organizations; participated in dozens of meetings and workshops dealing with reconstruction; kept a database of newspaper clippings; used her volunteer work as an opportunity to learn about the aid effort; and moved to the small Sri Lankan village of Muhudupitiya for a month to observe the reconstruction activities, to spend time with people, and to conduct interviews with local residents. She also returned to this village several times after moving back to the city of Colombo (Kapadia, 2008).

Kapadia found her ethnographic field research with the villagers gave her an invaluable perspective on what was really happening at the community level during the relief effort. For example, when she visited the village as a representative of the aid group for which she volunteered, she was accompanied by village leaders and accepted their story that new housing was being allocated with the full participation of community members. However, when she was living in the village as a field researcher, she found that many of the villagers were not happy with the way housing was being allocated and felt the leaders were acting unfairly. Housing was not being distributed through participatory decision making but was being allocated through the village's normal political power structure. One of the villagers complained that:

> None of the projects are well managed or based according to actual needs. Those who run these projects show favoritism. If you know somebody powerful then you can get something. Some people are getting four houses even though only one house was damaged. (Kapadia, 2008:268)

Kapadia could not have discovered this information without having developed good relationships with the villagers.

Her fieldwork in the village also helped her to understand why the relief effort did not lead to an increase in Sri Lankans' standard of living. The relief strategy set out a plan for rehabilitating peoples' livelihoods by helping them build upon entrepreneurial activities such as farming and small business in the form of cottage industries. Her extensive contact with workers in the community showed her that activities that were categorized by aid agencies as "entrepreneurial" were actually just a form of casual labour. Muhudupitiya was considered a good site for entrepreneurial activities and relief money was used to support businesses manufacturing bricks, to purchase machines to allow local women to reestablish their businesses processing coconut husks into a fibre called coir, and processing coral to make lime that is used in construction. However, Kapadia found that many of the villagers participated in these businesses on a very short-term basis on contracts as short as one day. While the coir business involved workers on a more long-term basis, the women's income was very low, in part because the market for their product was limited. The women also typically only complete

© Imagestate Media Partners Limited-Impact Photos/Alamy

Case studies of homeless persons have added to our insights on the causes and consequences of this major social concern. Women are often the "invisible homeless."

one stage in the process, so they are doing piecework for middlemen rather than working as self-employed entrepreneurs. The global market for coir is limited, so the business has little potential to help move villagers out of their lives of poverty.

The aid agencies assumed that "if microfinance, training and assets were made available, people would quickly embrace these opportunities and escape poverty" (Kapadia, 2008:197). However, Kapadia found that relations of production and trade meant that these relief efforts made very little difference in the lives of most individuals. One specific example is the ongoing relationship that many poor villagers have with moneylenders. In many cases, these moneylenders are also employers, so villagers are bound to the people who hire them for casual labour by ties of history, tradition, and debt. The assistance that aid does provide helps those who have already escaped poverty through their business and moneylending activities. But even young people in the village were not attracted to entrepreneurship—most would much rather be employed in a government job.

Kapadia's field research is important because it shows that altruism—in this case, the donation of money, time, and materials to a country ravaged by a natural disaster—is not enough to guarantee that people can move out of poverty or even that their lives will soon return to normal. Without an understanding of the realities of life in the affected country, even the best-funded efforts will have little impact.

unstructured interview A research method involving an extended, open-ended interaction between an interviewer and an interviewee.

UNSTRUCTURED INTERVIEWS An **unstructured interview** is an extended, open-ended interaction between an interviewer and an interviewee. The interviewer has a general plan of inquiry but not a specific set of questions that must be asked, as is often the case with surveys. Unstructured interviews are essentially conversations in which interviewers establish the general direction by asking open-ended questions. Interviewers have the ability to "shift gears" and pursue specific topics raised by interviewees because answers to one question are used to suggest the next question or new areas of inquiry. This technique enables the interviewer to learn more about the interviewees' lives and thoughts.

GROUNDED THEORY Qualitative methods are frequently used to develop theories. The term *grounded theory* was developed by Glaser and Strauss (1967) to describe an inductive method of theory construction. Researchers who use grounded theory collect and analyze data simultaneously. For example, in her study in Sri Lanka, Kapadia did not begin with a theory but developed one as a result of her research:

> It was only when I became more deeply engaged with village life in Muhudupitiya, and started to acknowledge, as opposed to shut out, events and experiences that simply did not fit my conceptual categories, that I was able to see how the managerial and impact models were falling short. I am therefore, in effect, making the argument that one's theories are fundamentally shaped by one's methods, approaches, and experiences, and a self-reflective and engaged ethnographic research approach provides an excellent way to understand the workings of power, [and] the failings of reconstruction (and development) programs. (2008:338–39)

STRENGTHS AND WEAKNESSES OF FIELD RESEARCH Field research provides opportunities for researchers to view from the inside what may not be obvious to an outside observer. Field methods are useful when attitudes and behaviours can be understood best within their natural setting or when the researcher wants to study social processes and change over time. They provide detailed information about the reactions of people and let us generate theories from the data collected (Whyte, 1989).

Participant observation can also be difficult. Jack Haas describes his first day in the field in his study of high steel ironworkers:

> My traumatic introduction to the workday realities of high steel ironworking came the day the construction superintendent passed me through the construction gate, gave me a hard hat, and wished me good luck. Directly ahead were five incomplete levels of an emerging 21-storey office building. From my vantage point I observed a variety of workers engaged in the construction process. The most visible and immediately impressive group of workers were those on the upper level who were putting steel beams into place. These were the ironworkers I had come to participate with and observe. This chilling reality filled me with an almost overwhelming anxiety. I began to experience a trepidation that far exceeded any usual observer anxiety encountered in the first days of field research . . . the risks of firsthand observation were profoundly obvious. It was with fearful anticipation that I moved toward the job site. (1977:148)

Haas's understandable fear over the prospect of walking on 10-cm wide steel beams hundreds of metres above city streets helped to focus his research. He eventually learned that while the ironworkers did not talk publicly about their fears, they did share his concerns. However, they were careful not to let their colleagues know they were afraid and often took risks in order to prove themselves to the other workers.

Like other people in dangerous occupations, the ironworkers had developed a culture that helped them to deal with the risks of their work. They tried to control their work environment in such ways as making their own decisions about whether it was too dangerous to work rather than going along with the demands of their supervisors and by following a strict informal code of what types of behaviour were appropriate for their co-workers.

Most field research does not involve this degree of danger, but it can involve spending large blocks of time with very different types of people, long periods of time away from home, and complicated work schedules. Despite these difficulties, there is really no other way of experiencing the world of your research subjects. It is far different having someone describe what it is like to stand on a steel girder with nothing below than standing on such a piece of steel yourself.

Social scientists who believe that quantitative research methods such as survey research provide the most accurate means of measuring attitudes, beliefs, and behaviour are often critical of data obtained through field research. They argue that what is learned from a specific group or community cannot be generalized to a larger population. They also suggest that the data collected in natural settings are descriptive and do not lend themselves to precise measurement. However, field research provides a richness of data that cannot be obtained in any other way.

SECONDARY ANALYSIS OF EXISTING DATA LO-4

In **secondary analysis**, researchers use existing material and analyze data originally collected by others. Existing data sources include public records, official reports of organizations or government agencies, and surveys conducted by researchers in universities and private corporations. Research data gathered from studies are available in data banks. Other sources of secondary data are books, magazines, newspapers, radio and television programs, personal documents and Internet sites. Secondary analysis is *unobtrusive research* because it includes a variety of nonreactive research techniques—that is, techniques that have no impact on the people being studied. In most cases, they are not even aware they are being studied.

secondary analysis
A research method in which researchers use existing material and analyze data that originally was collected by others.

The case study in the next section shows how data collected for other purposes can be used to shed light on the phenomenon of altruism.

Secondary Analysis: Helping after Hurricane Katrina

In September 2005, Hurricane Katrina devastated the city of New Orleans and many other communities in Louisiana and Mississippi. More than a thousand people were killed and many more lost their homes and businesses as a result of the hurricane and the resulting flooding. African Americans and the elderly were disproportionately harmed by the storm, and governments at all levels were justifiably blamed for their inadequate planning and response.

While governments failed during Katrina, what about average citizens? Media images of the catastrophe showed New Orleans as a city in chaos, with disorganized rescue attempts, inadequate evacuation plans, and extensive looting and murder. Did members of the community really turn against one another rather than working together and behaving altruistically? Havidan Rodriguez and his colleagues at the University of Delaware's Disaster Research Center (Rodriguez and Dynes, 2006; Rodriguez, Trainor, and Quarantelli, 2006) studied how the media portrayed Hurricane Katrina and its aftermath.

Rodriguez and his colleagues used several sources of data:

1. A database of news sources in paper format and/or their website equivalent that were collected over the first month of the response . . . more than 2000 articles have been collected and catalogued by [Disaster Research Center] staff.
2. Reports disseminated by other formal organizations either in printed form or on their websites.
3. Stories from other informal sources such as bloggers on the Internet. (Rodriquez, Trainor, and Quarantelli, 2006:86)

They concluded that the media exaggerated many of the negative things that occurred during the catastrophe. This was particularly true of reports of mobs looting and killing people during the flooding. One example of the unfounded stories was:

> When the Louisiana National Guard at the Superdome [an evacuation site where there had been reports of major violence and disorder] turned over the dead to federal authorities, that representative arrived with an 18-wheel refrigerated truck since there were reports of 200 bodies there. The actual total was six; of these, four died of natural causes, one from a drug overdose and another had apparently committed suicide. While four other bodies were found in the streets near the Dome, presumably no one had been killed inside as had been previously reported. There were more reports that 30 to 40 bodies were stored in the Convention Center freezers in its basement. Four bodies were recovered: one appeared to have been slain. Prior to this discovery, there had been reports of corpses piled inside the building. (2006a:6)

In contrast to these exaggerated reports of civil disorder, Rodriguez, Trainor, and Quarentelli document the way in which community members and outsiders helped the hurricane's survivors. In several neighbourhoods, people organized themselves to help others. One group of friends that called itself "the Robin Hood Looters" evacuated their own families, then went back into the community with commandeered boats and spent two weeks rescuing people from their flooded homes. Their name came from the practice of taking food and water from abandoned homes to provide it to people who had none. Working with the police and National Guard, they became what sociologists call an "emergent group." They developed a structure and norms during the crisis that helped them operate effectively.

Many existing groups also rose to the occasion. For example, religious organizations that already had a role in helping the poor and homeless massively expanded their activities to take on many more volunteers to help cope with the demands of Katrina. Even the researchers from the Disaster Research Center benefited from altruistic behaviour, as they were housed and fed by local people. Thus the behaviour of people following the hurricane was not nearly as violent and chaotic as portrayed by the media, and many people worked hard to help restore their communities.

STRENGTHS AND WEAKNESSES OF SECONDARY ANALYSIS One strength of secondary analysis is that data are readily available and often are inexpensive to obtain. Another is that, because the researcher usually does not collect the data personally, the chances of bias may be reduced. Finally, if records have been kept over time, a researcher can analyze longitudinal data to identify trends or provide a historical context.

However, secondary analysis has inherent problems. For one thing, the data may be incomplete or inaccurate. If data on certain variables have not been collected, the information will not be available for later research. Since secondary data are often collected for administrative purposes, the categories may not reflect variables of interest to the researcher. Religion was important to Durkheim's research on suicide, but death records did not contain information on religion—he had to infer that each person who committed suicide belonged to the religious group most common in that community.

MULTIPLE METHODS: TRIANGULATION What is the best method for studying a particular topic? The Concept Snapshot compares the various social research methods. There is no one best research method; each method has its own strengths and weaknesses, so many sociologists believe that it is best to combine multiple methods in a given study. *Triangulation* is the term used to describe this approach (Denzin, 1989). **Triangulation** refers not only to research methods but also to multiple data sources, investigators, and theoretical perspectives in a study. Multiple data sources include persons, situations, contexts, and times.

triangulation Using several different research methods, data sources, investigators, and/or theoretical perspectives in the same study.

For example, in a study of homeless people, Snow and Anderson used as their primary data sources "the homeless themselves and the array of settings, agency personnel, business proprietors, city officials, and neighbourhood activities relevant to the routines of the homeless" (1991:158). They gained a detailed portrait of the homeless and their experiences and institutional contacts by tracking more than 700 homeless individuals through a network of seven institutions with which they had varying degrees of contact. The study also tracked a number of individuals over time and used a variety of methods, including "participant observation and informal, conversational interviewing with the homeless; participant and nonparticipation observation, coupled with formal and informal interviewing in street agencies and settings; and a systematic survey of agency records" (1991:158–169). This study is discussed in depth in Chapter 5.

Multiple methods and approaches provide a wider scope of information and enhance our understanding of critical issues. For a closer look at social research methods and new media, see Box 2.5 at **www.nelson.com/sociologyinourtimes6e.**

Feminist Research Methods

Feminist social scientists have been critical of traditional sociological research methodologies. Margrit Eichler (1988b) has identified several limitations in research that relate to gender, including *androcentricity* (which means approaching an issue from a male perspective or viewing women only in terms of how they relate to men); sexist language or concepts; research methods that are biased in favour of men (for example, in sampling techniques or questionnaire design); and research in which results that focus on members of one sex are used to support conclusions about both sexes.

CONCEPT SNAPSHOT

STRENGTHS AND WEAKNESSES OF SOCIAL RESEARCH

RESEARCH METHOD	STRENGTHS	WEAKNESSES
Experiments		
Laboratory	Control over research	Artificial by nature
Field	Ability to isolate experimental factors	Frequent reliance on volunteers or captive audiences
Natural	Relatively little time and money required; replication possible, except for natural experiments	Ethical questions of deception; problem of reactivity
Survey Research		
Self-administered questionnaire	Useful in describing features of a large population without interviewing everyone	Potentially forced answers
Interview	Relatively large samples possible	Respondent untruthfulness on emotional issues
Telephone survey	Multivariate analysis possible	Data that are not always "hard facts" presented as such in statistical analyses
Secondary Analysis of Existing Data		
Existing statistics	Data often readily available; inexpensive to collect	Difficulty in determining accuracy of some of the data
Content analysis	Longitudinal and comparative studies possible; replication possible	Failure of data gathered by others to meet goals of current research; questions of privacy when using diaries or other personal documents
Field Research		
Observation	Opportunity to gain insider's view	Problems in generalizing results to a larger population
Participant observation	Useful for studying attitudes and behaviour in natural settings	Data measurements not precise
Case study	Longitudinal/comparative studies possible; documentation of important social problems of excluded groups possible	Inability to demonstrate cause-effect relationships or test theories
Unstructured interviews	Access to people's ideas in their words; forum for previously excluded groups	Difficult to make comparisons because of lack of structure; not representative sample

No one method can be termed *the* feminist methodology. However, qualitative methods, and in particular in-depth interviews, tend to be associated with feminist research. Although feminist research may involve the same basic methods for collecting data as other research, the way in which feminists use these methods is different. First, women's experiences are important and women's lives need to be addressed in their own terms (Edwards, 1993). Feminist research is woman-centred; that is, "It puts women at the center of research that is nonalienating, nonexploitive, and potentially emancipating" (Scully, 1990:2–3). Second, the goal of feminist research is to provide explanations of women's lives that will help them improve their situations. It is important, therefore, to ensure that women's experiences are not objectified or treated as merely "research data." Indeed, feminist sociologist Dorothy Smith (1987) suggests that "giving voice" to disadvantaged and marginalized groups in society should be a primary goal of sociology. Finally, feminist research methods challenge the traditional role of the researcher as a detached, "value-free," objective observer. Rather, the researcher is seen as central to the research process, and her feelings and experiences should be analyzed as an integral part of the process (Edwards, 1993; Kirby and McKenna, 1989).

Raquel Bergen's research on marital rape has shown the need for the researcher's personal involvement in the research process. Bergen ensured that the women she interviewed knew that she was supportive and interested in helping them and that she was not simply exploiting their experiences for her own purposes. She shared her own views and experiences with her research subjects and carefully dealt with any emotional distress that was caused by her interviews:

> During the most emotionally difficult interview, I spent a long time offering support to a woman who became extremely upset when she described her husband . . . raping her in front of her child. This experience emphasized the need for researchers . . . to interview with conscious partiality. If I had been a detached and objective researcher merely collecting data, I might have either terminated the interview and discarded the data or possibly suggested that the woman receive outside counseling. As a feminist researcher, however, I was interacting with this woman on a personal level and her distress was deeply affecting. (1993:208)

Critical Research Strategies

Feminist research practice shows that some sociologists choose not to follow the traditional scientific approach presented earlier in this chapter. The scientific approach involves neutrality—researchers try not to let their values bias their research. However, some researchers feel that this neutral stance implicates the researchers in the dominant power structure that creates and maintains injustice: "To put the matter starkly, in a socially unjust world, knowledge of the social that does not challenge injustice is likely to play a role in reproducing it" (Carroll, 2004:3). By contrast, critical research strategies are rooted in a concern for social justice. William Carroll (2004) sets out three ways in which social inquiry can be considered "critical." First, inquiry can be *oppositional.* Researchers place themselves on the side of those who are victims of injustice and criticize structures that oppress people on the basis of distinctions, such as class, race, and gender. Second, inquiry can be *radical.* In other words, the researcher tries to get at the roots of dominance issues and to explore the interconnections between problems such as capitalism, the environment, and individual suffering. Third, inquiry can be *subversive.* Researchers try to question conventional assumptions in order to open the door for alternative understandings of the social world.

Critical scholars use a variety of research *techniques.* These include the traditional methods you have already learned about, field research, secondary analysis, and surveys among them. As examples, Karl Marx developed a workers' questionnaire in 1880 to investigate working conditions, and Friedrich Engels used ethnographic methods to document the plight of the working class in England in 1844 (Carroll, 2004).

The focus of critical scholars, however, is not so much on techniques but rather on strategies for social inquiry that can lead to a more just society. Among these are dialectical social analysis, institutional ethnography, critical discourse analysis, and participatory action research (Carroll, 2004). The critical approach can be illustrated by looking at institutional ethnography.

At the core of *institutional ethnography* is the view presented in the section on feminist methodology, that the lived experience of marginalized people should be at the centre of the research process. This focus sets the researcher apart from the institutionalized power structure and puts the researcher on the side of the oppressed. However, the strategy does not just consider the individual but rather looks at the social organization of the institutions that surround individual actors. These institutions are both local—the settings that people experience in their daily lives—and extra-local—"outside the boundaries of one's everyday experience" (Campbell and Gregory, 2006:170). Feminist scholar Dorothy Smith has done much of the work developing this research strategy. She set out three tasks that define how to conduct an institutional ethnography:

> The first task centers on ideology and involves addressing the ideological practices which are used to make an institution's processes accountable. The second task centers on work in a broad sense (not just paid employment), and involves studying the work activities through which people are themselves involved in producing the world they experience in daily life. The third task centers on social relations, and involves discovering the ways in which a localized work organization operates as part of a broader set of social relations which link multiple sites of human activity. (Grahame, 2004:185)

The results of this research will be very different from those of more conventional sociology in the manner in which it shows how the everyday experiences of marginalized people are shaped by larger social and economic factors.

TIME TO REVIEW

- How do researchers design experiments? What are the strengths and weaknesses of experimental design?
- What are the different ways in which researchers can conduct survey research? What are the strengths and weaknesses of survey research?
- Describe how a researcher would carry out an observational study. What are the strengths and weaknesses of observational research?
- Why would a researcher choose to use secondary analysis to help understand society? What are the strengths and weaknesses of secondary analysis?
- Discuss how feminist and critical methods differ from more mainstream research techniques.

LO-5 ETHICAL ISSUES IN SOCIOLOGICAL RESEARCH

The study of people ("human subjects") raises questions of ethics in sociological research. Researchers are required by a professional code of ethics to weigh the societal benefits of research against the potential physical and emotional costs to participants.

Sociologists must follow a number of basic ethical standards. Participation in research must be voluntary. No one should be enticed or forced to participate, and everyone must be told about the study and any possible risks so they can give their informed consent. Deception must not be used to obtain consent. Researchers must ensure that subjects are not harmed. For example, the researcher must be careful not to reveal information that would embarrass the participants or damage their personal relationships. Researchers must respect the rights of research subjects to anonymity and confidentiality. A respondent is *anonymous* when the researcher cannot link a given response to a given respondent. Anonymity is often extremely important in terms of obtaining information on "deviant" or illegal activities. Maintaining *confidentiality* means that the researcher is able to identify a given person's responses with that person but promises not to do so.

Sociologists are committed to adhering to ethical considerations and to protecting research participants; however, many ethical issues cannot be resolved easily. Research ethics is a difficult and often ambiguous topic, and there are disagreements among researchers concerning ethical issues. For example, is it ethical to give students extra marks in a course if they take part in an experiment? Is it ethical to persuade institutionalized young offenders to be interviewed about their crimes by offering payment? Different researchers might have different answers for each of these questions.

How honest do researchers have to be with potential participants? Let's look at a specific case to consider where the right to know ends and the right to privacy begins.

The Humphreys Research

Laud Humphreys (1970) decided to study homosexual behaviour for his doctoral dissertation. His research focused on homosexual acts between strangers meeting in "tearooms," or public restrooms in parks. He did not ask permission of his subjects, nor did he inform them that they were being studied. Instead, he took advantage of the typical tearoom encounter, which involved three men: two who engaged in homosexual acts and a third who kept a lookout for police and other unwelcome strangers. To conduct his study, Humphreys showed up at public restrooms that were known to be tearooms and offered to be the lookout. Then he systematically recorded details of the sexual encounters.

Humphreys decided to learn about the everyday lives of these tearoom participants. He recorded their car licence numbers and tracked down their names and addresses. Later, he arranged for these men to be included in a medical survey so that he could go out and interview them personally. He wore disguises and drove a different car so that they would not recognize him. From these interviews, he collected personal information and determined that most of the men were married and lived conventional lives.

Humphreys probably would not have gained access to these subjects if he had identified himself as a researcher. The fact that he did not do so produced widespread criticism. The police became very interested in his notes, but he refused to turn any information over to the authorities. His award-winning study, *Tearoom Trade* (1970), dispelled many myths about homosexual behaviour; however, his study remains controversial.

His research raises questions. Do you think Humphreys did his research ethically? Would these men willingly have agreed to participate in his research if he had identified himself as a researcher? What psychological harm might have come to these married men if people, outside of those involved in the encounters, knew about their homosexual behaviour? Today's university ethics committees would never permit this type of research to be conducted.

Ethical issues continue to arise in sociological research. The later Ogden case, outlined below, involved a different sort of question than the Humphreys research.

The Ogden Case

What should social scientists do when the ethical principles of confidentiality and not harming subjects conflict with the law? In 1992, Simon Fraser University student Russel Ogden began work on his master's thesis, a study of euthanasia (mercy killing) and assisted suicide involving AIDS patients (Ogden, 1994). Both euthanasia and assisted suicide are crimes in Canada. The university's ethics committee approved his research proposal, which included a promise to maintain the "absolute confidentiality" of any information provided to him by those he interviewed (Palys, 1997).

Shortly after Ogden defended his M.A. thesis in 1994, he was subpoenaed to give evidence at a coroner's inquest that was investigating the possible assisted suicide of an AIDS victim. Ogden refused to testify, citing the guarantee of confidentiality he had given to his respondents. The coroner charged Ogden with contempt of court. After a lengthy legal battle, the coroner agreed that Ogden's guarantee of confidentiality was in the public good and dropped the charges.

Despite this precedent in Ogden's favour, researchers do not know if other courts will support their right to maintain confidentiality. Academics do not have any legal exemption similar to that which exists between a lawyer and client, so without this exemption, decisions are made on a case-by-case basis. In the United States, researchers have gone to prison for refusing to testify about their research. In 2012, this issue arose again in the case of Luka Rocco Magnotta, who was accused of murdering and dismembering Lin Jun. Two University of Ottawa criminology professors, Christine Bruckert and Colette Parent, went to court to try to ensure that an interview they conducted with a research subject named "Jimmy"— a name sometimes used by Magnotta when he had worked as a male escort—was kept confidential and was not allowed as evidence in Magnotta's trial (Solyom, 2012). The outcome of the case was not known in 2012 when this chapter was written, but it could establish an important precedent concerning the rights of Canadian researchers to keep their research material private.

In this chapter, we have looked at the research process and the methods used to pursue sociological knowledge. The important thing to realize is that research is the lifeblood of sociology. Without research, sociologists would be unable to test existing theories and develop new ones. Research takes us beyond common sense and provides opportunities for us to use our sociological imagination to generate new knowledge.

TIME TO REVIEW

- Why is a code of research ethics needed?
- What are the key ethical principles that guide social research?

2

VISUAL SUMMARY

KEY TERMS

altruism Behaviour intended to help others and done without any expectation of personal benefit (p. 32).

analysis The process through which data are organized so that comparisons can be made and conclusions drawn (p. 37).

complete observation Research in which the investigator systematically observes a social process, but does not take part in it (p. 46).

control group Subjects in an experiment who are not exposed to the independent variable, but later are compared to subjects in the experimental group (p. 39).

deductive approach Research in which the investigator begins with a theory and then collects information and data to test the theory (p. 34).

dependent variable A variable that is assumed to depend on or be caused by one or more other (independent) variables (p. 35).

descriptive study Research that attempts to describe social reality or provide facts about some group, practice, or event (p. 33).

experiment A research method involving a carefully designed test in which the researcher studies the impact of certain variables on subjects' attitudes or behaviour (p. 39).

experimental group Subjects in an experiment who are exposed to the independent variable (p. 39).

LO-1 Understand the relationship between theory and research.

Image IS2012-1018-11, http://www.combatcamera.forces.gc.ca. Department of National Defence, 2012. Reproduced with permission of the Minister of Public Works and Government Services Canada, 2012.

Sociologists typically move back and forth from theory to research throughout the course of their inquiry. In fact, investigators rarely, if ever, begin with either just a theory or with research data. Inductive theorists need at least rudimentary theories to guide their data collection, and deductive theorists must refer constantly to the real world as they develop their theories. Researchers may break into the cycle at different points depending on what they want to know and what information is available. Theory gives meaning to research; research helps support theory.

LO-2 Identify the main steps in the sociological research process.

Adisa/Shutterstock

The four stages are: 1) Theories generate hypotheses; 2) these hypotheses lead to observations; 3) observations lead to generalizations; and (4) generalizations are used to support, refute, or modify the theory. Researchers following a deductive model will begin with theory, while inductive researchers will begin with their observations of the social world.

LO-3 Explain why it is important to have different methods of conducting social research and know something about each of these methods

© Monkey Business Images/Shutterstock

Through experiments, researchers study the impact of certain variables on their subjects. Surveys are polls used to gather facts about people's attitudes, opinions, or behaviours; a sample of respondents provides data through questionnaires or interviews. In secondary analysis, researchers analyze existing data, such as a government census, or cultural artifacts, such as a diary. In field research, sociologists study social life in its natural setting through participant and complete observation, case studies, unstructured interviews, and ethnography. Feminist and critical research methods bring a different perspective to sociological research by focusing on social justice for marginalized people.

LO-4 Discuss how research has contributed to our understanding of altruism.

© AP Photo/Eranga Jayawardena

Despite the media emphasis on bad-news stories, research on altruism has shown us that a high proportion of people are helpful to others. The vast majority of Canadians donate time and money to help others, and in disasters or emergencies many people will pitch in to help others. Experimental research has also found high rates of helping, though this could be suppressed if other people were also present.

LO-5 Explain why a code of ethics for sociological research is necessary.

© Imagestate Media Partners Limited-Impact Photos/Alamy

Researchers are required by a professional code of ethics to weigh the societal benefits of research against the potential physical and emotional costs to participants. Ethical principles include ensuring that research subjects provide informed consent; ensuring that subjects are not harmed; maintaining confidentiality unless the respondent waives this right; and ensuring that participation in research is voluntary.

explanatory study Research that attempts to explain relationships and to provide information on why certain events do or do not occur (p. 33).

field research The study of social life in its natural setting: observing and interviewing people where they live, work, and play (p. 46).

hypotheses Tentative statements of the relationship between two or more concepts or variables (p. 33).

independent variable A variable that is presumed to cause or determine a dependent variable (p. 35).

inductive approach Research in which the investigator collects information or data (facts or evidence) and then generates theories from the analysis of that data (p. 34).

interview A research method using a data collection encounter in which an interviewer asks the respondent questions and records the answers (p. 43).

objective Free from distorted subjective (personal or emotional) bias (p. 33).

participant observation A research method in which researchers collect systematic observations while being part of the activities of the group they are studying (p. 46).

population In a research study, those persons about whom we want to be able to draw conclusions (p. 43).

questionnaire A research instrument containing a series of items to which subjects respond (p. 43).

reactivity The tendency of experiment participants to change their behaviour in response to the presence of the researcher or to the fact that they know they are being studied (p. 42).

reliability In sociological research, the extent to which a study or research instrument yields consistent results (p. 37).

replication In sociological research, the repetition of the investigation in substantially the same way that it originally was conducted (p. 37).

representative sample A selection where the sample has the essential characteristics of the total population (p. 43).

research methods Specific strategies or techniques for conducting research (p. 38).

respondent A person who provides data for analysis through an interview or questionnaire (p. 42).

APPLICATION QUESTIONS

1. A local college has implemented a program limiting first-year classes to 30 students and wishes to evaluate the impact of this policy on students' subsequent performance. You have been asked to plan this evaluation. How would you proceed? What different research methods would you use?
2. Working with a group of your fellow students, conduct a content analysis of the way in which photographs in several of your textbooks portray people of different races and genders. Try to follow the steps in the sociological research process.
3. Feminist and critical researchers believe that researchers should not be value free in their research but should be advocates for social justice. Do you agree with this position, or do you feel that sociologists should maintain their objectivity and remain neutral about the way in which their findings are used?
4. For a class project, you want to study the relationship between students' grades and their willingness to cheat on examinations. What are some of the ethical issues to consider before you administer a survey to the other students in your class?
5. Have you ever participated in a behavioural experiment? If you have, do you think your responses were affected by the fact that you knew you were participating in a study?

sample The people who are selected from the population to be studied (p. 43).

secondary analysis A research method in which researchers use existing material and analyze data that originally was collected by others (p. 49).

simple random sample A selection in which everyone in the target population has an equal chance of being chosen; in other words, choice occurs by chance (p. 43).

survey A research method in which a number of respondents are asked identical questions through a systematic questionnaire or interview (p. 42).

triangulation Using several different research methods, data sources, investigators, and/or theoretical perspectives in the same study (p. 51).

unstructured interview A research method involving an extended, open-ended interaction between an interviewer and an interviewee (p. 48).

validity In sociological research, the extent to which a study or research instrument accurately measures what it is supposed to measure (p. 37).

variable In sociological research, any concept with measurable traits or characteristics that can change or vary from one person, time, situation, or society to another (p. 35).

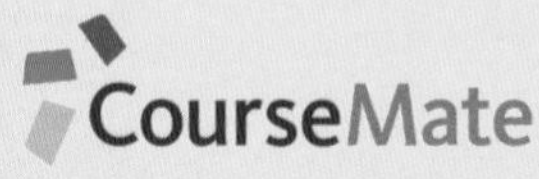

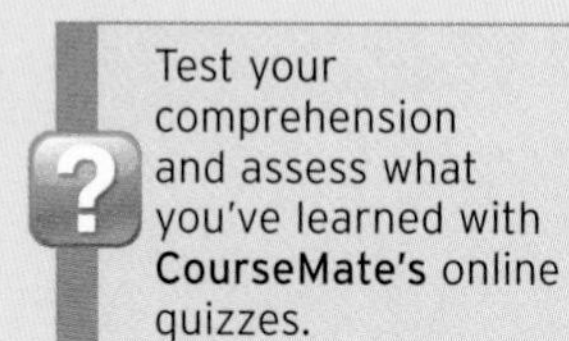
Test your comprehension and assess what you've learned with **CourseMate's** online quizzes.

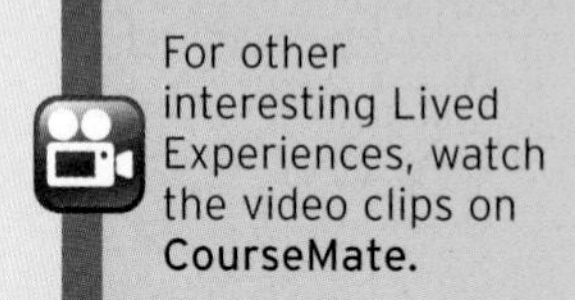
For other interesting Lived Experiences, watch the video clips on **CourseMate.**

Practise what you've learned with flashcards containing key terms and definitions on **CourseMate.**

CHAPTER 3 Culture

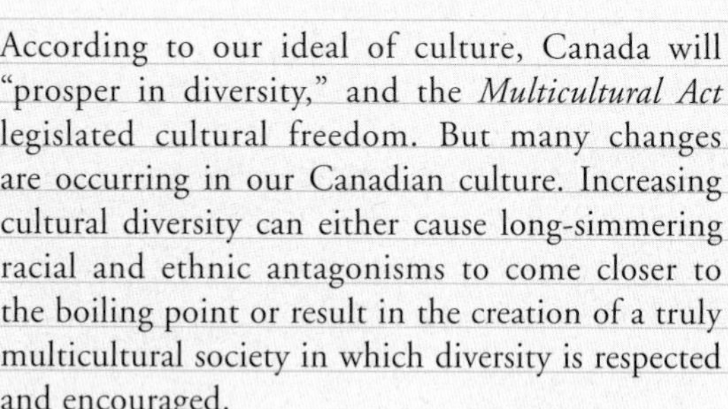

© CP PHOTO/Kevin Frayer

According to our ideal of culture, Canada will "prosper in diversity," and the *Multicultural Act* legislated cultural freedom. But many changes are occurring in our Canadian culture. Increasing cultural diversity can either cause long-simmering racial and ethnic antagonisms to come closer to the boiling point or result in the creation of a truly multicultural society in which diversity is respected and encouraged.

Since Canada's multiculturalism policy was first introduced more than 40 years ago, supporters and critics have debated the effects on the social, economic, and political integration of immigrants. Multiculturalism presents challenges for both new Canadians (who must fit in and succeed) and the native population (to accept and become comfortable with increasing diversity) (Environics, 2010:31). Multiculturalism remains a positive reality for the majority of Canadians. It has become a significant symbol of our Canadian identity and a source of national pride. However, it is not without its challenges. The following comments of student Kai James reflect some of these challenges:

> *My name is Kai, and I'm Canadian. However, I am unlike many other Black youth in Canada whose parents emigrated from the Caribbean in that I identify as a Canadian. Yes, I was born here and I'm one hundred percent Canadian. Whether they like it or not, even the majority of those youth born in the Caribbean but raised in Canada are Canadians. They are as Canadian as our first prime minister, Sir John A. Macdonald, who was not born in Canada but in Scotland.*
>
> *What makes Sir John A. Macdonald and millions of other citizens who have immigrated to this country Canadian is very simple. All have contributed to Canadian society to some extent, big or small, culturally, economically, and politically. And they continue to constantly reshape and redefine what we know as "Canadian," a notion that changes every day. So why do some Black youth constantly deny their Canadian identity even when they were born in Canada? . . .*
>
> *Only one thing is for certain. The current generation of Canadian Black youth is clearly Canadian. We are educated in the Canadian school system. We've been immersed in Canadian institutions, the Canadian political climate, and the Canadian geographic environment . . . At the same time, aspects of Caribbean culture are present in our style, slang, and values. Black youth in Canada have created a cultural blend that is truly unique and truly Canadian.* (James and Shadd, 2001:17–19)

As our world appears to grow increasingly smaller because of rapid transportation, global communications, and international business transactions and political alliances—and sometimes because of hostility, terrorism, and warfare—learning about cultural diversity, within our own nation and globally, is extremely important for our individual and collective well-being. Although the world's population shares a common humanity—and perhaps some components of culture—cultural differences pose crucial barriers to our understanding of others. Sociology provides us with a framework for examining and developing a greater awareness of culture and cultural diversity, as well as how cultures change over time and place.

What is culture? Why is it so significant to our personal identities? What happens when others are intolerant of our culture? **Culture** is the knowledge, language, values, customs, and material objects that are passed from person to person and from one generation to the next in a human group or society. As previously defined, a society is a large social grouping that occupies the same geographic territory and is subject to the same political authority and dominant cultural expectations. While a society is made up of people, a culture is made up of ideas, behaviour, and material possessions. Society and culture are interdependent; neither could exist without the other. If we look across the cultures of various nations, we may see opportunities for future cooperation based on our shared beliefs, values, and attitudes, or we may see potential for lack of understanding, discord, and conflict based on divergent ideas and worldviews. Before reading on, test your knowledge of multiculturalism in Canada by answering the questions in Box 3.1 and referring to Table 3.1, both on page 63.

In this chapter, we will examine society and culture, with special attention to the components of culture and the relationship between cultural change and diversity. We will also analyze culture from functionalist, conflict, feminist, interactionist, and postmodern perspectives.

Critical Thinking Questions

1. To what extent does our own culture keep us from understanding, accepting, or learning from other cultures?
2. Is intolerance toward "outsiders"—people who are viewed as being different from one's own group or way of life—accepted by some people in Canada? Why?
3. It has been suggested that the cultural freedom legislated by the *Multicultural Act* is more "symbolic" than real. Do you agree?

CHAPTER FOCUS QUESTION What part does culture play in shaping people and the social relations in which they participate?

LEARNING OBJECTIVES

AFTER READING THIS CHAPTER, YOU SHOULD BE ABLE TO

- **LO-1** Understand the importance of culture in our lives and those of others in society.
- **LO-2** Identify the essential components of culture.
- **LO-3** Describe what causes cultural change in societies.
- **LO-4** Compare and contrast ethnocentrism and cultural relativism as approaches to examining cultural differences.
- **LO-5** Explain how the various sociological perspectives view culture.

CULTURE AND SOCIETY IN A CHANGING WORLD

culture The knowledge, language, values, customs, and material objects that are passed from person to person and from one generation to the next in a human group or society.

Understanding how culture affects our lives helps us develop a sociological imagination. When we meet someone from a culture vastly different from our own, or when we travel in another country, it may be easier to perceive the enormous influence of culture on people's lives. However, as our society has become more diverse and communication among members of international cultures more frequent, the need to appreciate diversity and to understand how people in other cultures view their world has also increased (Samovar and Porter, 1991b). For example, many international travellers and businesspeople have learned the importance of knowing what gestures mean in various nations (see Figure 3.1). As a comparison, in Argentina, rotating an index finger around the front of the ear means someone has a telephone call, but in North American culture, it usually suggests that a person is "crazy" (Axtell, 1991).

LO-1 CULTURE AND SOCIETY

FIGURE 3.1 HAND GESTURES WITH DIFFERENT MEANINGS IN OTHER SOCIETIES

"Hook'em Horns"
or
"Your spouse is unfaithful"?

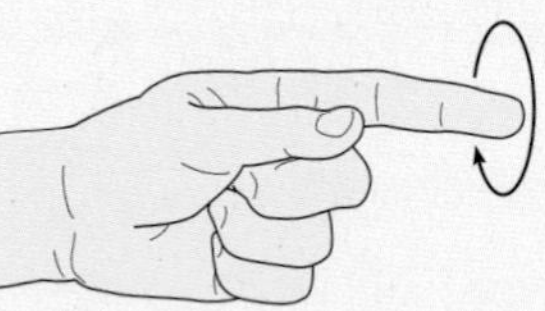

"He's crazy"
or
"You have a telephone call"?

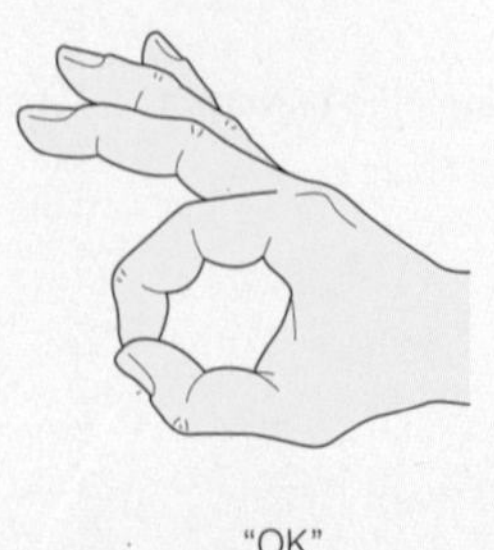

"OK"
or
"I'll kill you"?

As international travellers and businesspeople have learned, hand gestures may have very different meanings in different cultures.

The Importance of Culture

How important is culture in determining how people think and act daily? Simply stated, culture is essential for our individual survival and for our communication with other people. We rely on culture because we are not born with the information we need to survive. We do not know how to take care of ourselves, how to behave, how to dress, what to eat, which gods to worship, or how to make or spend money. We must learn about culture through interaction, observation, and imitation in order to participate as members of the group. Sharing a common culture with others simplifies day-to-day interactions. We must, however, also understand other cultures and the worldviews therein.

Just as culture is essential for individuals, it is also fundamental for the survival of societies. Culture has been described as "the common denominator that makes the actions of individuals intelligible to the group" (Haviland, 1993:30). Some system of making and enforcing rules necessarily exists in all societies. What would happen, for example, if *all* rules and laws in Canada suddenly disappeared? At a basic level, we need rules in order to navigate our bicycles and cars through traffic. At a more abstract level, we need laws to establish and protect our rights.

To survive, societies need rules about civility and tolerance toward others. We are not born knowing how to express kindness or hatred toward others, although some people may say, "Well, that's just human nature," when explaining someone's behaviour. Such a statement is built on the assumption that what we do as human beings is determined by *nature* (our biological and genetic makeup) rather than *nurture* (our social environment)—in other words, that our behaviour is

BOX 3.1 **SOCIOLOGY AND EVERYDAY LIFE**

How Much Do You Know About Multiculturalism in Canada?

True	False	
T	F	1. Canada is one of the most multicultural countries in the world.
T	F	2. A 2010 public opinion poll asked Canadians to describe what made them most proud of their country. Multiculturalism ranked fourth on the list.
T	F	3. Recent high levels of illegal immigration have led an increasing number of Canadians to reject multiculturalism.
T	F	4. The majority of Canadians regard multiculturalism as good for Canada.
T	F	5. Multiculturalism and social integration are mutually exclusive goals.

For answers to the quiz about multiculturalism in Canada, go to **www.nelson.com/sociologyinourtimes6e.**

TABLE 3.1 BASIS OF PRIDE IN BEING CANADIAN: TOP MENTIONS, 1994–2010

	1994	2003	2006	2010
Free country/freedom/democracy	31	28	27	27
Quality of life	5	6	3	10
Humanitarian/caring people	9	13	9	9
Multiculturalism	3	6	11	6
Healthcare system	3	2	6	—
Peaceful country	7	5	6	4
Beauty of the land	7	4	4	4
Born here/my country	5	4	2	3
Social programs	2	1	—	3

Source: Environics Institute, "Focus Canada 2010." Found at http://www.environicsinstitute.org/institute-projects/current-projects/focus-canada.

instinctive. An *instinct* is an unlearned, biologically determined behaviour pattern common to all members of a species that predictably occurs whenever certain environmental conditions exist. For example, spiders do not learn to build webs; they build webs because of instincts that are triggered by basic biological needs, such as protection and reproduction.

Humans do not have instincts. What we most often think of as instinctive behaviour can be attributed to reflexes and drives. A *reflex* is an unlearned, biologically determined involuntary response to a physical stimulus (such as a sneeze after breathing some pepper in through the nose or the blinking of an eye when a speck of dust gets in it). *Drives* are unlearned, biologically determined impulses common to all members of a species that satisfy needs, such as for sleep, food, water, and sexual gratification. Reflexes and drives do not determine how people will behave in human societies; even the expression of these biological characteristics is channelled by culture. For example, we may be taught that the "appropriate" way to sneeze (an involuntary response) is to use a tissue or turn our head away from others (a learned response). Most contemporary sociologists agree that culture and social learning—not nature—account for virtually all of our behaviour patterns.

Since humans cannot rely on instincts to survive, culture is a "tool kit" for survival. According to the sociologist Ann Swidler, culture is a "tool kit of symbols, stories, rituals, and world

material culture A component of culture that consists of the physical or tangible creations—such as clothing, shelter, and art—that members of a society make, use, and share.

technology The knowledge, techniques, and tools that make it possible for people to transform resources into usable forms, as well as the knowledge and skills required to use them after they are developed.

views, which people may use in varying configurations to solve different kinds of problems" (1986:273). The tools we choose will vary according to our own personality and the situations we face. We are not puppets on a string; we make choices from among the items in our own "toolbox."

Material and Nonmaterial Culture

Our cultural toolbox is divided into two major parts: *material* and *nonmaterial* culture (Ogburn, 1966/1922).

Material culture consists of the physical or tangible creations that members of a society make, use, and share. Initially, items of material culture begin as raw materials or resources, such as ore, trees, and oil. Through technology, these raw materials are transformed into usable items (ranging from books and computers to guns and bombs). Sociologists define **technology** as the knowledge, techniques, and tools that make it possible for people to transform resources into usable forms, as well as the knowledge and skills required to use them after they are developed. From this standpoint, technology is both concrete and abstract. For example, technology includes a pair of scissors and the knowledge and skill necessary to make

© Celia Peterson/Getty Images

© Frans Lemmens/Getty Images

© Eddie Gerald/Alamy

Food is a universal type of material culture, but what people eat and how they eat it vary widely, as shown in these cross-cultural examples from the United Arab Emirates (upper left), Holland (upper right), and China (bottom). What might be some of the reasons for the similarities and differences you see in these photos?

them from iron, carbon, and chromium (Westrum, 1991). At the most basic level, material culture is important because it is our buffer against the environment. For example, we create shelter to protect ourselves from the weather and provide ourselves with privacy. Beyond the survival level, we make, use, and share objects that are interesting and important to us. Why are you wearing the particular clothes you have on today? Perhaps you're communicating something about yourself, such as where you attend school, what kind of music you like, or where you went on vacation.

Nonmaterial culture consists of the abstract or intangible human creations of society that influence people's behaviour. Language, beliefs, values, rules of behaviour, family patterns, and political systems are examples of nonmaterial culture. A central component of nonmaterial culture is *beliefs*—the mental acceptance or conviction that certain things are true or real. Beliefs may be based on tradition, faith, experience, scientific research, or some combination of these. Faith in a supreme being, conviction that education is the key to success, and the opinion that smoking causes cancer are examples of beliefs. We also have beliefs in items of material culture. For example, most students believe that computers are the key to technological advancement and progress.

nonmaterial culture
A component of culture that consists of the abstract or intangible human creations of society—such as attitudes, beliefs, and values—that influence people's behaviour.

© Spencer Grant/PhotoEdit

© Mark Richards/PhotoEdit

© David Nunuk/All Canada Photos

The customs and rituals associated with weddings are one example of nonmaterial culture. What can you infer about beliefs and attitudes about marriage in the societies represented by these photographs?

© Stephen Finn/Shutterstock

The symbols shown here are international comparisons of road signs for elderly and disabled persons.

Cultural Universals

Because all humans face the same basic needs (such as food, clothing, and shelter), we engage in similar activities that contribute to our survival. Anthropologist George Murdock (1945:124) compiled a list of more than 70 **cultural universals**—customs and practices that occur across all societies. His categories included appearance (such as bodily adornment and hairstyles), activities (such as sports, dancing, games, joking, and visiting), social institutions (such as family, law, and religion), and customary practices (such as cooking, folklore, gift giving, and hospitality). These general customs and practices may be present in all cultures, but their specific forms vary from one group to another and from one time to another within the same group. For example, while telling jokes may be a universal practice, what is considered a joke in one society may be an insult in another.

How do sociologists view cultural universals? In terms of their functions, cultural universals are useful because they ensure the smooth and continual operation of society (Radcliffe-Brown, 1952). A society must meet basic human needs by providing food, shelter, and some degree of safety for its members so that they will survive. Children and other new members (such as immigrants) must be taught the ways of the group. A society also must settle disputes and deal with people's emotions. All the while, the self-interest of individuals must be balanced with the needs of society as a whole. Cultural universals help to fulfill these important functions of society.

cultural universals Customs and practices that occur across all societies.

From another perspective, however, cultural universals are not the result of functional necessity; these practices may have been *imposed* by members of one society on members of another. Similar customs and practices do not necessarily constitute cultural universals. They may be an indication that a conquering nation used its power to enforce certain types of behaviour on those who were defeated (Sargent, 1987). Sociologists might ask, Who determines the dominant cultural patterns? For example, although religion is a cultural universal, traditional religious practices of indigenous peoples (those who first live in an area) have often been repressed and even stamped out by subsequent settlers or conquerors who hold political and economic power over them.

TIME TO REVIEW

- What are cultural universals?
- Explain how functionalists and conflict theorists view cultural universals.

LO-2 COMPONENTS OF CULTURE

Even though the specifics of individual cultures vary widely, all cultures have four common nonmaterial cultural components: symbols, language, values, and norms. These components contribute to both harmony and conflict in a society.

Symbols

A symbol is anything that meaningfully represents something else. Culture could not exist without symbols because there would be no shared meanings among people. Symbols can simultaneously produce loyalty and animosity, love and hate. They help us communicate ideas, such as love or patriotism, because they express abstract concepts with visible objects. To complicate matters, however, the interpretation of symbols varies in different cultural contexts. For some Indo-Canadians, for example, the colour green rather than white symbolizes purity or virginity Similarly, although a swastika represents hate to most Canadians, to a member of the Church of Jesus Christ Christian/Aryan Nations, a swastika represents love.

Flags can stand for patriotism, nationalism, school spirit, or religious beliefs held by members of a group or society. In our technology-oriented society, *emoticons* are a new system of symbols used to express emotions when people are communicating on their computers via chat lines or email (see Figure 3.2.)

Symbols can stand for love (a heart or a valentine), peace (a dove), or hate (a Nazi swastika), just as words can be used to convey meanings. Symbols also can transmit other types of ideas. A siren is a symbol that denotes an emergency situation and sends the message to clear the way immediately. Gestures are also a symbolic form of communication—a movement of the head, body, or hands can express ideas or feelings to others. For example, in Canada, pointing toward your chest with your thumb or finger is a symbol for *me.* We are also all aware of how useful our middle finger can be in communicating messages to inconsiderate drivers.

Symbols affect our thoughts about class. For example, how a person is dressed or the kind of car he or she drives is often at least subconsciously used as a measure of that individual's economic standing or position. With regard to clothing, although many people wear casual clothes on a daily basis, where the clothing was purchased is sometimes used as a symbol of social status. Were the items purchased at Walmart, Old Navy, Club Monaco, or Holt Renfrew? What indicators on the clothing—such as the Nike swoosh, some other logo, or a brand name—say something about the product's status? Automobiles and their logos are also symbols that have cultural meaning beyond the shopping environment in which they originate.

FIGURE 3.2 EMOTICONS

:) = SMILE

:D = SMILE/LAUGHING/BIG GRIN

;) = WINK

:X = MY LIPS ARE SEALED

:P = STICKING OUT TONGUE

{ } = HUG

:(= FROWN

:'(= CRYING

0:) = ANGEL

}:> = DEVIL

The symbols shown here are examples of emoticons, or "smileys," a symbolic way to express moods in email or text messages. Turn the page sideways and the meaning of each emoticon will be clear.

Language

Language is a system of symbols that expresses ideas and enables people to think and communicate with one another. Verbal (spoken) and nonverbal (written or gestured) language help us describe reality. One of our most important human attributes is the ability to use language to share our experiences, feelings, and knowledge with others. Language can create visual images in our head, such as "the kittens look like little cotton balls" (Samovar and Porter, 1991a). Language also allows people to distinguish themselves from outsiders and maintain group boundaries and solidarity (Farb, 1973).

language A system of symbols that expresses ideas and enables people to think and communicate with one another.

Language is not solely a human characteristic. Other animals use sounds, gestures, touch, and smell to communicate with one another, but they use signals with fixed meanings that are limited to the immediate situation (the present) and cannot encompass past or future situations. For example, chimpanzees can use elements of Standard American Sign Language and manipulate physical objects to make "sentences," but they are not physically endowed with the vocal apparatus needed to form the consonants required for verbal language. As a result, nonhuman animals cannot transmit the more complex aspects of culture to their offspring. Humans have a unique ability to manipulate symbols to express abstract concepts and rules, and thus to create and transmit culture from one generation to the next.

LANGUAGE AND SOCIAL REALITY One key issue in sociology is whether language *creates* or simply *communicates* reality. Consider, for example, the terms used by organizations

© Norman Chan/Shutterstock

Notice that the sign conveys information about both wheelchair access and gender.

involved in the abortion debate: pro-life and pro-choice. Do such terms create or simply express a reality?

Anthropological linguists Edward Sapir and Benjamin Whorf have suggested that language not only expresses our thoughts and perceptions but also influences our perception of reality. According to the **Sapir–Whorf hypothesis**, language shapes its speakers' view of reality (Sapir, 1961; Whorf, 1956). If people are able to think only through language, language must precede thought. If language shapes the reality we perceive and experience, some aspects of the world are viewed as important and others are virtually neglected because people know the world only in terms of the vocabulary and grammar of their own language. For example, most Aboriginal languages focus on describing relationships between things rather than using language to judge or evaluate. One Aboriginal author explains, "No, we don't have any gender. It's a relationship . . . The woman who cares for your heart—that's your wife. Your daughters are the ones who enrich your heart. Your sons are the ones that test your heart!" (Ross, 1996:116). Consequently, many Aboriginal languages do not have any personal pronouns based on gender (such as words for *she* or *he*). As writer Rupert Ross explains:

> Because they don't exist there, searching for the correct ones often seems an artificial and unreasonable exercise. As a result, Aboriginal people are often as careless about getting them right as I am when speaking French and trying to remember whether a noun has "le" or "la" in front of it . . . On the more humorous side, my Aboriginal friends appear heartily amused by the frenzied Western debate over whether God is a "He" or a "She." (1996:117)

Sapir-Whorf hypothesis The proposition that language shapes its speakers' view of reality.

According to Ross, language does have a dramatic impact on our perception of the world. He describes two very different worlds experienced by English-speaking Canadians and Aboriginal peoples:

> I've struggled for some time to find a way to express how I perceive the difference between my English-speaking world and the world my Aboriginal friends tell me is given to them by their languages. I have this sense that if you decide that the first reality is constant change, if you discard your belief in the usefulness of judgmental absolutes like "good" and "bad" and choose to speak in terms of relative movement like "towards harmony" instead, then a lot of other things change as well. You start to sit in a room differently, in a car differently, everywhere differently. (1996:125)

If language does create reality, are we trapped by our language? Many social scientists agree that the Sapir–Whorf hypothesis overstates the relationship between language and our thoughts and behaviour patterns. While acknowledging that language has many subtle meanings and that the words used by people reflect their central concerns, most sociologists contend that language may *influence* our behaviour and interpretation of social reality, but it does not *determine* it.

LANGUAGE AND GENDER What is the relationship between language and gender? What cultural assumptions about women and men does language reflect? Scholars have suggested several ways in which language and gender are intertwined:

- The English language ignores women by using the masculine form to refer to human beings in general (Basow, 1992). For example, the word *man* is used generically in words like *chairman* and *mankind,* which allegedly include both men and women. However, *man* can mean either all human beings or a male human being (Miller and Swift, 1993:71).
- Use of the pronouns *he* and *she* affects our thinking about gender. Pronouns show the gender of the person we *expect* to be in a particular occupation. For instance, nurses, secretaries, and schoolteachers are usually referred to as *she,* while doctors, engineers, electricians, and presidents are referred to as *he* (Baron, 1986).
- Words have positive connotations when relating to male power, prestige, and leadership; when related to women, they carry negative overtones of weakness, inferiority, and immaturity (Epstein, 1988:224).
- A language-based predisposition to think about women in sexual terms reinforces the notion that women are sexual objects. Women are often described by terms such as *fox, broad, bitch, babe,* or *doll,* which ascribe childlike or even petlike characteristics to them. By contrast, performance pressures are placed on men. Words such as *dude, stud,* and *hunk* define them in terms of their sexual prowess (Baker, 1993).

Gender in language has been debated and studied extensively in recent years, and greater awareness and some changes have been the result. Many organizations and publications have established guidelines for the use of nonsexist language and have changed titles such as *chairman* to *chair* or *chairperson.* "Men Working" signs in many areas have been replaced with ones that say "People Working" (Epstein, 1988). Some occupations have been given genderless titles, such as *firefighter* and *flight attendant* (Maggio, 1988). Yet many people resist change, arguing that the English language is being ruined (Epstein, 1988). Still, many scholars suggest that a more inclusive language is needed to develop a more inclusive and equitable society (see Basow, 1992).

LANGUAGE, RACE, AND ETHNICITY Language may create and reinforce our perceptions about race and ethnicity by transmitting preconceived ideas about the superiority of one category of people over another. Let's look at a few images conveyed by words in the English language in regard to race and ethnicity.

- Words may have more than one meaning and create and reinforce negative images. Terms such as *blackhearted* (malevolent) and expressions such as *a black mark* (a detrimental fact) and *a Chinaman's chance of success* (unlikely to succeed) give the words *black* and *Chinaman* negative associations and derogatory imagery. By contrast, expressions such as "That's white of you" and "The good guys wear white hats" reinforce positive associations with the colour white.
- Overtly derogatory terms, such as *nigger, kike, gook, honkey, chink, squaw,* and *savage,* as well as other racial–ethnic slurs, have been "popularized" in movies, music, comic routines, and so on. Such derogatory terms are often used in conjunction with physical threats against persons.

Does language influence our perception of reality?

- Words are frequently used to create or reinforce perceptions about a group. For example, Aboriginal peoples have been referred to as *savages* and described as *primitive*, while blacks have been described as *uncivilized, cannibalistic,* and *pagan*.
- The "voice" of verbs may minimize or incorrectly identify the activities or achievements of members of various minority groups. For example, use of the passive voice in the statement "Chinese Canadians *were given* the right to vote" ignores how Chinese Canadians *fought* for that right. Active-voice verbs also may inaccurately attribute achievements to people or groups. Some historians argue that cultural bias is shown by the very notion that "Cabot discovered Canada." Canada was already inhabited by people who later became known as Aboriginal Canadians (see Stannard, 1992; Takaki, 1993).

In addition to these concerns about the English language, problems also arise when more than one language is involved.

LANGUAGE DIVERSITY IN CANADA Canada is a linguistically diverse society. The existence of Aboriginal languages, the presence of French- and English-speaking populations, and the increasing number of other languages commonly spoken are all evidence.

Language is the chief vehicle for understanding and experiencing one's culture. In 1969, the federal government passed the *Official Languages Act,* making both French and English the country's official languages. In doing so, Canada officially became a bilingual society. However, this action by no means resolved the complex issues regarding language in our society. According to the most recent census, 68 percent of Canadians speak English only, another 13 percent speak French only, and 17 percent are bilingual. Less than 2 percent, or 520,380 Canadians, indicated that they lacked the skills to converse in either French or English (Statistics Canada, 2006b). Although French versus English language issues have been a significant source of conflict over the years, bilingualism remains a distinct component of Canadian culture.

Canada's Aboriginal languages are many and diverse. The languages reflect distinctive histories, cultures, and identities linked to family, community, the land, and traditional knowledge. Aboriginal peoples' cultures are *oral cultures,* or cultures that are transmitted through speech rather than the written word. Many Aboriginal stories can be passed on only in the Aboriginal language in which they originated. Language is not only a means of communication, but also a link that connects people with their past and grounds their social, emotional, and spiritual vitality. For Aboriginal peoples, huge losses have already occurred as a result of the assimilationist strategies of missionaries and Jesuit priests running residential schools. At these schools, Aboriginal children were forbidden to speak their language. An Ojibwa woman from northwestern Ontario describes her experience:

> Boarding school was supposed to be a place where you forgot everything about being Anishinabe. And our language too. But I said, "I'm going to talk to myself"—and that's what I did, under my covers—talked to myself in Anishinabe. If we were caught, the nuns would make us stand in a corner and repeat over and over, "I won't speak my language." (Ross, 1996:122)

CENSUS PROFILE

Language Diversity in Canada

Among the categories of information gathered in the 2006 Census are data on the languages spoken in Canadian households. As shown below, two-thirds of Canadians speak English most often at home and just over one-fifth of the population speak French most often at home.

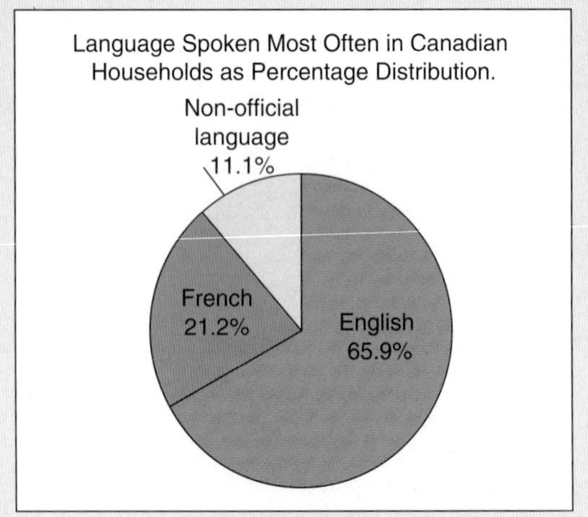

Source: Adapted from Statistics Canada Census 2006, "Language Highlight Tables," last modified March 2009. Found at http://www12.statcan.ca/census-recensement/2006/as-sa/97-555/p1-eng.cfm

Despite the efforts of Canadian Aboriginal peoples to maintain their languages, these languages are among the most endangered in the world. Only three of the more than 50 Aboriginal languages in Canada are in a healthy state; many have already disappeared or are near extinction. In the 2006 Canadian Census, only 18 percent of Aboriginal persons reported an Aboriginal language as their first language and even fewer spoke it at home (Bougie, 2010). Loss of their languages will have a profound effect on the cultural survival of Aboriginal peoples. According to Eli Taylor, a Dakota Sioux from Manitoba:

> Our native language embodies a value system about how we ought to live and relate to each other . . . Now if you destroy our language, you not only break down these relationships, but you also destroy other aspects of our Indian way of life and culture, especially those that describe man's connection with nature, the Great Spirit, the order of things. Without our language, we will cease to exist as a separate people. (Fleras and Elliott, 1992:151)

Steps to preserve indigenous languages include the introduction of Aboriginal language courses in schools and universities, Aboriginal media programming, and the recording of elders' stories, songs, and accounts of history in Aboriginal language (Bougie, 2010).

How does the presence of all these different languages affect Canadian culture? From the functionalist perspective, a shared language is essential to a common culture; language is a stabilizing force in society and an important means of cultural transmission. Through language, children learn about their cultural heritage and develop a sense of personal identity in relation to their group.

Conflict theorists view language as a source of power and social control; it perpetuates inequalities between people and between groups because words are used (intentionally or not) to "keep people in their place." As linguist Deborah Tannen has suggested, "The devastating group hatreds that result in so much suffering in our own country and around the world are related in origin to the small intolerances in our everyday conversations—our readiness to attribute good intentions to ourselves and bad intentions to others" (1993:B5). Furthermore, different languages are associated with inequalities. Consider this Aboriginal language instructor's comments on the lure of the English language: "It's to do with the perception of power. People associate English with prestige and power. We don't have movies in [Aboriginal language], we don't have hardcover books . . . or neon signs in our language" (Martin, 1996:A8). Language, then, is a reflection of our feelings and our values.

Values

Values are collective ideas about what is right or wrong, good or bad, and desirable or undesirable in a particular culture (Williams, 1970). Values do not dictate which behaviours are appropriate and which are not, but they provide us with the criteria by which we evaluate people, objects, and events. Values typically come in positive and negative pairs, such as being brave or cowardly, hardworking or lazy. Since we use values to justify our behaviour, we tend to defend them staunchly (Kluckhohn, 1961).

values Collective ideas about what is right or wrong, good or bad, and desirable or undesirable in a particular culture.

VALUE CONTRADICTIONS All societies have value contradictions. **Value contradictions** are values that conflict with one another or are mutually exclusive (achieving one makes it difficult, if not impossible, to achieve another). For example, core values of morality and humanitarianism may conflict with values of individual achievement and success. Similarly, although the majority of Canadians feel that people who are poor have a right to social assistance, they have also shown strong support for governments that have dramatically cut budgets to reduce financial deficits. Can you identify any value contradictions in the list of Canadian core values outlined previously?

value contradiction Values that conflict with one another or are mutually exclusive.

IDEAL VERSUS REAL CULTURE What is the relationship between values and human behaviour? Sociologists stress that a gap always exists between ideal culture and real culture in a society.

ideal culture The values and standards of behaviour that people in a society profess to hold.

real culture The values and standards of behaviour that people actually follow (as contrasted with *ideal culture*).

Ideal culture refers to the values and standards of behaviour that people in a society profess to hold. **Real culture** refers to the values and standards of behaviour that people actually follow. For example, we may claim to be law-abiding (ideal cultural value) but smoke marijuana (real cultural behaviour), or we may regularly drive over the speed limit but think of ourselves as "good citizens."

The degree of discrepancy between ideal and real culture is relevant to sociologists investigating social change. Large discrepancies provide a foothold for demonstrating hypocrisy (pretending to be what one is not or to feel what one does not feel). These discrepancies are often a source of social problems; if the discrepancy is perceived, leaders of social movements may use them to point out people's contradictory behaviour. For example, preserving our natural environment may be a core value, but our behaviour (such as driving energy-guzzling vehicles and polluting lakes) contributes to its degradation, as is further discussed in Chapter 22.

Norms

norms Established rules of behaviour or standards of conduct.

Values provide ideals or beliefs about behaviour but do not state explicitly how we should behave. Norms, on the other hand, have specific behavioural expectations. **Norms** are established rules of behaviour or standards of conduct. *Prescriptive norms* state what behaviour is appropriate or acceptable. For example, persons making a certain amount of money are expected to file a tax return and pay any taxes they owe. Norms based on custom direct us to open a door for a person carrying a heavy load. By contrast, *proscriptive norms* state what behaviour is inappropriate or unacceptable. Laws that prohibit us from driving over the speed limit and "good manners" that preclude texting or reading a newspaper during class are examples. Prescriptive and proscriptive norms operate at all levels of society, from our everyday actions to the formulation of laws.

FORMAL AND INFORMAL NORMS Not all norms are of equal importance; those that are most crucial are formalized. *Formal norms* are written down and involve specific punishments for violators. Laws are the most common type of formal norms; they have been codified and may be enforced by sanctions. **Sanctions** are rewards for appropriate behaviour or penalties for inappropriate behaviour. Examples of *positive sanctions* include praise, honours, or medals for conformity to specific norms. *Negative sanctions* range from mild disapproval to life imprisonment. In the case of law, formal sanctions are clearly defined and can be administered only by persons in certain official positions (such as police officers and judges). These people have the authority to impose the sanctions.

sanctions Rewards for appropriate behaviour or penalties for inappropriate behaviour.

Less important norms are referred to as *informal norms*—unwritten standards of behaviour understood by people who share a common identity. When individuals violate informal norms, other people may apply informal sanctions. *Informal sanctions* are not clearly defined and can be applied by any member of a group. Examples are frowning at someone or making a negative comment or gesture.

folkways Informal norms or everyday customs that may be violated without serious consequences within a particular culture.

FOLKWAYS Norms are also classified according to their relative social importance. **Folkways** are informal norms or everyday customs that may be violated without serious consequences within a particular culture (Sumner, 1959/1906). They provide rules for conduct but are not considered essential to society's survival. In Canada, folkways include using underarm deodorant, brushing one's teeth, and wearing appropriate clothing for a specific occasion. Folkways are not often enforced, and when they are, the resulting sanctions tend to be informal and relatively mild.

Folkways are culture-specific; they are learned patterns of behaviour that can vary markedly from one society to another. In Japan, for example, where the walls of restroom stalls reach to the floor, folkways dictate that a person should knock on the door before entering a stall (you cannot tell if anyone is inside without knocking). People in Canada find it disconcerting, however, when someone knocks on the door of a stall (Collins, 1991).

MORES Other norms are considered highly essential to the stability of society. **Mores** (pronounced MOR-ays) are strongly held norms with moral and ethical connotations that may not be violated without serious consequences in a particular culture. Since mores are based on cultural values and are considered crucial for the well-being of the group, violators are subject to more severe negative sanctions (such as ridicule, loss of employment, or imprisonment) than are those who fail to adhere to folkways. The strongest mores are referred to as taboos. **Taboos** are mores so strong that their violation is considered extremely offensive and even unmentionable. Violation of taboos is punishable by the group or even, according to certain belief systems, by a supernatural force. The incest taboo, which prohibits sexual or marital relations between certain categories of kin, is an example of a nearly universal taboo.

mores Strongly held norms with moral and ethical connotations that may not be violated without serious consequences in a particular culture.

taboos Mores so strong that their violation is considered extremely offensive and even unmentionable.

Folkways and mores provide structure and security in a society. They make everyday life more predictable and provide people with some guidelines for appearance and behaviour. As individuals travel in countries other than their own, they become aware of cross-cultural differences in folkways and mores. For example, women from Canada travelling in Muslim nations quickly become aware of mores, based on the *sharia* (the edicts of the Koran), that prescribe the dominance of men over women. In Saudi Arabia, for instance, women are not allowed to mix with men in public. Banks have branches with only women tellers—and only women customers. In hospitals, female doctors are supposed to tend only to children and other women (Alireza, 1990; Ibrahim, 1990).

LAWS **Laws** are formal, standardized norms that have been enacted by legislatures and are enforced by formal sanctions. Laws may be either civil or criminal. *Civil law* deals with disputes among persons or groups. Persons who lose civil suits may encounter negative sanctions, such as having to pay compensation to the other party or being ordered to stop certain conduct. *Criminal law,* on the other hand, deals with public safety and well-being. When criminal laws are violated, fines and prison sentences are the most likely negative sanctions.

laws Formal, standardized norms that have been enacted by legislatures and are enforced by formal sanctions.

As with material objects, all of the nonmaterial components of culture—symbols, language, values, and norms—are reflected in the popular culture of contemporary society.

TIME TO REVIEW

- What are the main types of norms?

TECHNOLOGY, CULTURAL CHANGE, AND DIVERSITY LO-3

Cultures do not generally remain static. There are many forces working toward change and diversity. Some societies and individuals adapt to this change, whereas others suffer culture shock and succumb to ethnocentrism.

Cultural Change

Societies continually experience cultural change at both material and nonmaterial levels. Changes in technology continue to shape the material culture of society. Although most technological changes are primarily modifications of existing technology, *new technologies* are changes that make a significant difference in many people's lives. Examples of new technologies include the introduction of the printing press more than 500 years ago and the advent of computers and electronic communications in the 20th century. The pace of technological change has increased rapidly in the past 150 years, as contrasted with the 4000 years before that, during which humans advanced from digging sticks and hoes to the plow.

All parts of a culture do not change at the same pace. When a change occurs in the material culture of a society, nonmaterial culture must adapt to that change. Frequently, this rate of change is uneven, resulting in a gap between the two. Sociologist William F. Ogburn (1966/1922) referred to this disparity as **cultural lag**—a gap between the technical development of a society and its moral and legal institutions. In other words, cultural lag occurs when material culture changes faster than nonmaterial culture, thus creating a lag between the two cultural components. For example, at the material cultural level, the personal computer and electronic coding have made it possible to create a unique health identifier for each person in Canada. Based on available technology (material culture), it would be possible to create a national data bank that includes everyone's individual medical records from birth to death. Using this identifier, health providers and insurance companies could rapidly transfer medical records around the globe and researchers could access unlimited data on people's diseases, test results, and treatments. The availability of this technology, however, does not mean that it will be used because, from a nonmaterial culture perspective, people may believe that such a national data bank would constitute an invasion of privacy and could easily be abused by others. Social conflict may arise between nonmaterial culture and the capabilities of material culture, often set in motion by discovery, invention, and diffusion.

cultural lag William Ogburn's term for a gap between the technical development of a society (material culture) and its moral and legal institutions (nonmaterial culture).

Discovery is the process of learning about something previously unknown or unrecognized. Historically, discovery involved unearthing natural elements or existing realities, such as "discovering" fire or the true shape of the earth. Today, discovery most often results from scientific research. For example, the discovery of a polio vaccine virtually eliminated one of the major childhood diseases. A future discovery of a cure for cancer or the common cold could result in longer and more productive lives for many people.

discovery The process of learning about something previously unknown or unrecognized.

As more discoveries have occurred, people have been able to reconfigure existing material and nonmaterial cultural items through invention. **Invention** is the process of reshaping existing cultural items into a new form. Guns, video games, airplanes, and the *Charter of Rights and Freedoms* are examples of inventions that positively or negatively affect our lives today.

invention The process of reshaping existing cultural items into a new form.

When diverse groups of people come into contact, they begin to adapt one another's discoveries, inventions, and ideas for their own use. **Diffusion** is the transmission of cultural items or social practices from one group or society to another through such means as exploration, military endeavours, the media, tourism, and immigration. To illustrate, piñatas can be traced back to the 12th century, when Marco Polo brought them back from China, where they were used to celebrate the springtime harvest, to Italy, where they were filled with costly gifts in a game played by the nobility. When the piñata travelled to Spain, it became part of Lenten traditions. In Mexico, it was used to celebrate the birth of the Aztec god Huitzilopochtli (Burciaga, 1993). Today, children in many countries squeal with excitement at parties as they swing a stick at a piñata. In our "shrinking globe," cultural diffusion moves at a rapid pace as countries continually seek new markets for their products (see Box 3.2 on page 77).

diffusion The transmission of cultural items or social practices from one group or society to another.

Cultural Diversity

Cultural diversity refers to the wide range of cultural differences found between and within nations. Cultural diversity between countries may be the result of natural circumstances (such as climate and geography) or social circumstances (such as level of technology and composition of the population). Some countries—such as Sweden—are referred to as *homogeneous societies,* meaning they include people who share a common culture and are typically from similar social, religious, political, and economic backgrounds. By contrast, other countries—including Canada—are referred to as *heterogeneous societies,* meaning they include people who are dissimilar in regard to social characteristics, such as nationality, race, ethnicity, class, occupation, or education (see Figure 3.3).

Canada has always been characterized by at least three main cultures. Although cultural diversity in our country is not only the result of immigration, immigration has certainly had a significant impact on the development of our culturally diverse society. Over the past 150 years, more than 13 million "documented," or legal, immigrants have arrived here; innumerable people have also entered the country as undocumented immigrants. Immigration can cause feelings of frustration and hostility, especially in people who feel threatened by the changes that large numbers of immigrants may produce. Often, people are intolerant of those who are different from themselves. When societal tensions rise, people may look for others they can blame—or single out persons because they are the "other," the "outsider," the one who does not belong. Sociologist Adrienne Shadd described her experience of being singled out as an "other":

With the widespread accessibility of television and the Internet, popular culture is increasingly accessible for both children and adults in their own homes. Studies show that many children spend more time watching television than they spend attending school.

> Routinely I am asked, "Where are you from?" or "What nationality are you?" as if to be Black, you have to come from somewhere else. I respond that I'm "Canadian" . . . I play along. The scenario usually unfolds as follows:
>
> "But where are you *originally* from?"
>
> "Canada."
>
> "Oh, *you* were born here. But where are your parents from?"
>
> "Canada."
>
> "But what about your grandparents?"
>
> As individuals delve further into my genealogy to find out where I'm "really" from, their frustration levels rise.
>
> "No, uh, I mean . . . your *people.* Where do your *people* come from?"
>
> At this point, questioners are totally annoyed and/or frustrated. After all, Black people in Canada are supposed to come from "the islands," aren't they? For those of us living in large urban centres, there are constant reminders that we are not regarded as truly "Canadian." (1994:11)

Have you ever been made to feel like an "outsider"? Each of us receives cultural messages that may make us feel good or bad about ourselves or may give us the perception that we belong or do not belong. However, in heterogeneous societies such as Canada, cultural diversity is inevitable. In Canada, this diversity has created some unique problems in terms of defining and maintaining our distinct Canadian culture. In fact, what is unique to Canada is the number of distinct subcultures that together make up our Canadian culture.

It has been suggested that complex societies are more likely to produce subcultures. This is certainly the case in Canada, where regional, ethnic, class, language, and religious subcultures combine to produce a highly diverse society.

subculture A group of people who share a distinctive set of cultural beliefs and behaviours that differ in some significant way from those of the larger society.

SUBCULTURES A **subculture** is a group of people who share a distinctive set of cultural beliefs and behaviours that differ in some significant way from those of the larger society. Emerging from the functionalist tradition, this concept has been applied to categories ranging from ethnic, religious, regional, and age-based categories to those categories presumed to be "deviant" or marginalized from the larger society. In the broadest use of the concept, thousands of categories of people residing in Canada might be classified as belonging to one or more subcultures, including Muslims, Italian Canadians, Orthodox Jews, Generation Xers, and bikers. However, many sociological studies of subcultures have limited the scope of inquiry to more visible distinct subcultures, such as the Hutterites, to see how subcultural participants interact with the dominant culture.

The Hutterites As a subculture, the Hutterities have fought for many years to maintain their distinct identity. The Hutterites are the largest family-type communal grouping in the Western world, with close to 30,000 members living in approximately 300 settlements. They live in colonies of about 15 families, but each family usually has its own home or apartment. Colonies range in size from about 60 to 150 people (CBC, 2006b).

The Hutterites are considered a subculture because their values, norms, and appearance differ significantly from those of members of the dominant culture. They have a strong faith in God and reject worldly concerns. Their core values include the joy of work, the

FIGURE 3.3 HETEROGENEITY OF CANADIAN SOCIETY

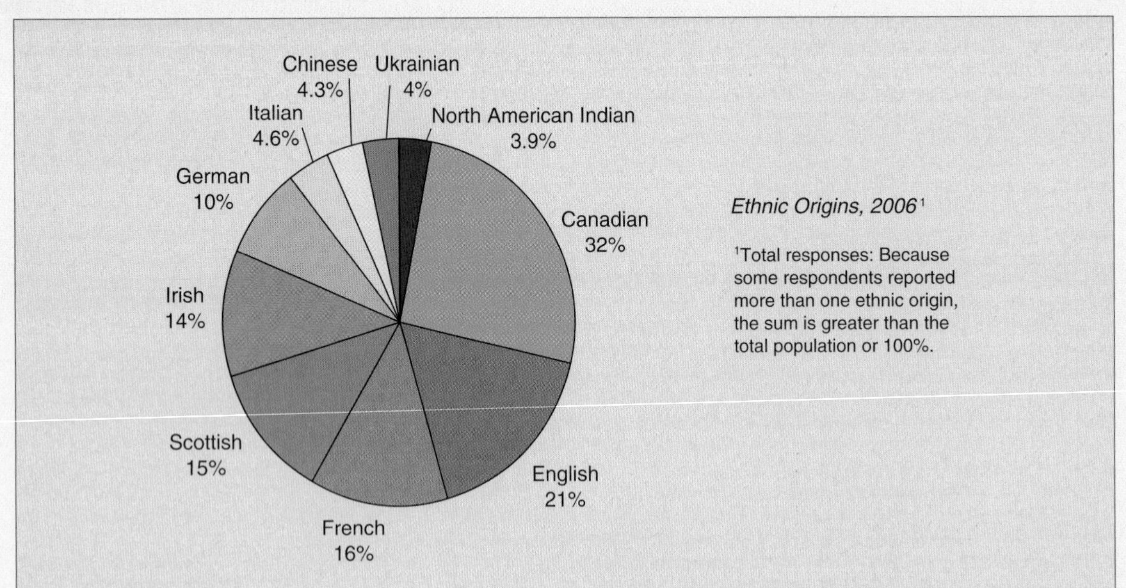

Throughout history, Canada has been heterogeneous. Today, Canada is represented by a wide variety of social categories, including our religious affiliations and ethnic origins.

Source: Statistics Canada, "2006 Census: Ethnic Origin, Visible Minorities, Place of Work and Mode of Transportation," The Daily, April 2, 2008.

BOX 3.2 **POINT/COUNTERPOINT**

Cultural Diffusion or Cultural Confusion: Advertising—The Global Market

Selling a product in a foreign culture requires that attention be paid to cultural differences. The world's smartest advertising minds have sometimes forgotten to do so and, as the examples below demonstrate, they have consequently come off as village idiots. Costly–often amusing–mistakes have been made by advertisers who have misread cultural attitudes, sensitivities, or superstitions, or something has simply been lost in the translation to the global marketplace. Here are a few examples:

- When the makers of Coca-Cola were launching their drink in China, they found a phrase that sounded perfect: "Ko-kou-ke-la." After printing thousands of signs, the Coke masterminds discovered that they had christened their drink "Bite the wax tadpole."
- When Colgate introduced a toothpaste called Cue in France, it turned out to be the same name as a well-known pornographic magazine.
- Most North Americans know the slogan for Kentucky Fried Chicken as "Finger-lickin' good." In China, after translation, the slogan became "Eat your fingers off."
- The American Dairy Council ran a "Got milk?" campaign that featured celebrities sporting milk moustaches. In converting the message to Spanish for its Mexican consumers, the council ended up asking, "Are you lactating?"
- "Come alive with the Pepsi Generation" was a perfectly good slogan–until it got translated into Taiwanese as "Pepsi will bring your ancestors back from the dead."
- The makers of Coors Light beer hired an agency to develop promotional materials aimed at Hispanics in the United States. In trying to translate the ad's catchphrase "Turn it loose" into Spanish, a copywriter ended up inviting customers to "Drink Coors and get diarrhea."

The lack of cultural awareness of corporate North America is obvious in the following blunders:

- When Coca-Cola introduced its two-litre bottles in Japan, it was unaware of the fact that few Japanese refrigerators are roomy enough to store such a large bottle.
- When trying to market its cake mixes in Japan in the 1960s, Betty Crocker discovered that most Japanese homes were missing a necessary ingredient: an oven.
- When McDonald's ventured into China, corporate mascot Ronald McDonald was there to clown around at the launch. Talk about a bozo move: To the Chinese, the clown is a symbol of death.
- A toothpaste company ran a commercial in Southeast Asia proclaiming that its product helped whiten teeth. The problem was that the people in the local target market were in the habit of chewing betel nut to achieve darkly stained teeth–a social sign of prestige.

Source: Reprinted by permission from Trish Snyder and Terri Foxman, authors of "The Global Marketing Hall of Shame" published in *Canadian Inflight Magazine* (July, 1998), 42-50.

primacy of the home, faithfulness, thriftiness, tradition, and humility. Hutterites hold conservative views of the family, believing that women are subordinate to men, birth control is unacceptable, and wives should remain at home. Children are cherished and seen as an economic asset: They help with the farming and other work.

Hutterite life is centred on the community rather than on the individual. All aspects of day-to-day life are based on sharing, right down to eating every meal in a community hall. Members of this group also have communal rather than private property; nobody is permitted to own as much as a pair of shoes (Curtis and Lambert, 1994). They have a "community of goods."

A predominant tenet of Hutterite faith is *nonassimilation*; that is, the Hutterites wish to maintain their separate status and not be absorbed into the dominant

Technology and tradition meet at the Fairholme Hutterite Colony as these young women try out a new digital camera at school.

culture. The fact that their colonies are usually located far from towns, cities, and highways emphasizes this. However, the Hutterites do not seek complete social isolation from the wider society. Although they strictly adhere to centuries-old traditions, the Hutterites do not hesitate to take advantage of 21st-century advancements (Lyons, 1998). They are successful farmers who trade with people in the surrounding communities, and they buy modern farm machinery. They also read newspapers, use home computers and telephones, and utilize the services of non-Hutterite professionals.

Applying the concept of subculture to our study of social life helps us understand how cultural differences may influence people; however, subcultural theory and research have been criticized for overstating the within-category similarities and making the assumption that most people primarily identify with others who are similar to themselves in ethnicity, religion, age, or other categories. Until recently, most studies of subcultures did not acknowledge that the experiences of women might be quite different from those of men in the same subcultural setting. Finally, some contemporary theorists argue that information technologies and the plurality and fragmentation of life in the 21st century have contributed to the creation of new subcultures in cyberspace and in the larger global community; subcultures need not be geographically specific or limited by time and space.

counterculture A group that strongly rejects dominant societal values and norms and seeks alternative lifestyles.

COUNTERCULTURES Some subcultures actively oppose the larger society. A **counterculture** is a group that strongly rejects dominant societal values and norms and seeks alternative lifestyles (Yinger, 1960, 1982). Young people are most likely to join countercultural groups, perhaps because younger persons generally have less invested in the existing culture. Examples of countercultures include the beatniks of the 1950s, the flower children of the 1960s, the drug enthusiasts of the 1970s, and members of non-mainstream religious sects, or cults.

TIME TO REVIEW

- How is cultural diversity reflected in society?

Culture Shock

culture shock The disorientation that people feel when they encounter cultures radically different from their own.

Culture shock is the disorientation that people feel when they encounter cultures radically different from their own and believe they cannot depend on their own taken-for-granted assumptions about life. When people travel to another society, they may not know how to respond to that setting. For example, Napoleon Chagnon (1992) was initially shocked at the sight of the Yanomamö (pronounced yah-noh-MAH-mah) tribe of South America in 1964.

The Yanomamö (also referred as the Yanomami) are a tribe of about 20,000 South American Indians who live in the rain forest. Although Chagnon travelled in a small aluminum motorboat for three days to reach these people, he was not prepared for the sight that met his eyes when he arrived:

> I looked up and gasped to see a dozen burly, naked, sweaty, hideous men staring at us down the shafts of their drawn arrows. Immense wads of green

> tobacco were stuck between their lower teeth and lips, making them look even more hideous, and strands of dark-green slime dripped from their nostrils—strands so long that they reached down to their pectoral muscles or drizzled down their chins and stuck to their chests and bellies. We arrived as the men were blowing *ebene,* a hallucinogenic drug, up their noses. As I soon learned, one side effect of the drug is a runny nose. The mucus becomes saturated with the drug's green powder, and the Yanomamö usually just let it dangle freely from their nostrils to plop off when the strands become too heavy.
>
> Then the stench of decaying vegetation and filth hit me, and I was almost sick to my stomach. I was horrified. What kind of welcome was this for someone who had come to live with these people and learn their way of life? (1992:12–14)

The Yanomamö have no written language, system of numbers, or calendar. They lead a nomadic lifestyle, carrying everything they own on their backs. They wear no clothes and paint their bodies; the women insert slender sticks through holes in the lower lip and the pierced nasal septum. In other words, the Yanomamö—like the members of thousands of other cultures around the world—live in a culture very different from that of Canada.

Even as global travel and the media make us more aware of people around the world, the distinctiveness of the Yanomamö in South America remains apparent.

LO-4 ETHNOCENTRISM AND CULTURAL RELATIVISM

ethnocentrism The tendency to regard one's own culture and group as the standard–and thus superior–whereas all other groups are seen as inferior.

cultural relativism The belief that the behaviours and customs of any culture must be viewed and analyzed by the culture's own standards.

When observing people from other cultures, many of us use our own culture as the yardstick by which we judge the behaviour of others. Sociologists refer to this approach as **ethnocentrism**—the tendency to regard one's own culture and group as the standard, and thus superior, whereas all other groups are seen as inferior. Ethnocentrism is based on the assumption that one's own way of life is superior to all others. For example, most schoolchildren are taught that their own school and country are the best. The school song and the national anthem are forms of *positive ethnocentrism*. However, *negative ethnocentrism* can also result from constant emphasis on the superiority of one's own group or nation. Negative ethnocentrism is manifested in derogatory stereotypes that ridicule recent immigrants whose customs, dress, eating habits, or religious beliefs are markedly different from those of dominant group members. Long-term Canadian residents who are members of racial and ethnic minority groups, such as First Nations and Indo-Canadians, have also been the target of ethnocentric practices by other groups.

An alternative to ethnocentrism is **cultural relativism**—the belief that the behaviours and customs of any culture must be viewed and analyzed by the culture's own standards. For example, the anthropologist Marvin Harris (1974, 1985) uses cultural relativism to explain why cattle, which are viewed as sacred, are not killed and eaten in India, where widespread hunger and malnutrition exist. From an ethnocentric viewpoint, we might conclude that cow worship is the cause of the hunger and poverty in India. However, according to Harris, the Hindu taboo against killing cattle is very important to their economic system. Live cows are more valuable than dead ones because they have more important uses than as a direct source of food. As part of the ecological system, cows consume grasses of little value to humans. Then they produce two valuable resources—oxen (the neutered offspring of cows), to power the plows, and manure, for fuel and fertilizer—as well as milk, floor covering, and leather. As Harris's study reveals, culture must be viewed from the standpoint of those who live in a particular society.

Cultural relativism also has a downside. It may be used to excuse customs and behaviour (such as cannibalism) that may violate basic human rights. Cultural relativism is a part of the sociological imagination; researchers must be aware of the customs and norms of the society they are studying and then spell out their background assumptions so that others can spot possible biases in their studies. According to some social scientists, however, issues surrounding ethnocentrism and cultural relativism may become less distinct in the future as people around the globe increasingly share a common popular culture.

HIGH CULTURE AND POPULAR CULTURE

What is the difference between high culture and popular culture? *High culture* consists of classical music, opera, ballet, live theatre, and other activities usually patronized by elite audiences, composed primarily of members of the upper-middle and upper classes, who have the time, money, and knowledge assumed to be necessary for its appreciation. *Popular culture* consists of activities, products, and services that are assumed to appeal primarily to members of the middle and working classes. These include rock concerts, spectator sports, movies, television soap operas, situation comedies, and, more recently, the Internet. Although we will distinguish between "high" and "popular" culture, some social analysts believe that high culture and popular culture have melded together with the rise of a consumer society in which luxury items have become more widely accessible to the masses. In a consumer society, the huge divide between the activities and possessions of wealthy elites may be indistinguishable from those of the middle and working classes.

Overall, most sociologists believe that culture and social class are intricately related. French sociologist Pierre Bourdieu's (1984) *cultural capital theory* views high culture as a device used by the dominant class to exclude the subordinate classes. According to Bourdieu, people must be trained to appreciate and understand high culture. Individuals learn about high culture in upper-middle and upper-class families and in elite education systems, especially higher education (university). Once they acquire this trained capacity, they possess a form of symbolic currency, or "cultural capital," that can be exchanged for employment and promotional opportunities in the workplace. The knowledge and skills acquired while earning a university degree (e.g., reading, writing, communication skills, logical reasoning) are valued resources on the job market, and people who possess this form of cultural capital are more likely to secure employment than people who do not. Persons from poor and working-class backgrounds typically do not acquire this cultural capital. Since knowledge and appreciation of high culture is considered a prerequisite for access to the dominant class, its members can use their cultural capital to deny access to subordinate group members and thus preserve and reproduce the existing class structure. Unlike high culture, popular culture is presumed to be available to everyone.

Activity fads, such as moshing, are particularly popular with young people. Why are such fads often short-lived?

Forms of Popular Culture

Three prevalent forms of popular culture are fads, fashions, and leisure activities.

A *fad* is a temporary but widely copied activity followed enthusiastically by large numbers of people. Most fads are short-lived novelties (Garreau, 1993). According to the sociologist John Lofland (1993), fads can be divided into four major categories. First, *object fads* are items that people purchase even though they have little use or intrinsic value. Past and present examples include Webkinz, Harry Potter wands, SpongeBob SquarePants items, and Silly Bandz. Second, *activity fads* include everyone you know playing games of Angry Birds on their cellphones, posting Facebook pictures of celebrity look-alikes (a "doppelganger") in place of their own photo, and 24/7 texting or Tweeting friends. Third are *idea fads*, such as New Age ideologies, the "Go Green" movement, and various eat local food movements and the resurgence of farmers' markets. Fourth are *personality fads*—for example, Lady Gaga, Beyoncé, Justin Bieber, and Matthew Morrison or other characters on *Glee*, a hit Fox television series about an unusual high school glee club. A *fashion* is a currently valued style of behaviour, thinking, or appearance that is longer lasting and more widespread than a fad. Examples of fashion are found in many areas, including child rearing, education, arts, clothing, music, and sports. Soccer is an example of a fashion in sports. Until recently, only schoolchildren played soccer in Canada, but now soccer has become a really popular sport, perhaps in part because of immigration from European countries and other areas of the world where soccer is widely played.

Like soccer, other forms of popular culture move across nations. In Canada, we often assess the quality of popular culture on the basis of whether it is a Canadian or American product. Canadian artists, musicians, and entertainers often believe they have "made it" only when they become part of American popular culture. Music, television shows, novels, and street fashions from the United States have become a part of our Canadian culture. People in this country continue to be strongly influenced by popular culture from nations other than the United States, too. For example, Canada's contemporary music and clothing reflect African, Caribbean, and Asian cultural influences, among others.

Will the spread of popular culture produce a homogeneous global culture? Critics argue that the world is not developing a global culture; rather, other cultures are becoming Westernized. Political and religious leaders in some nations oppose this process, which they view as **cultural imperialism**—the extensive infusion of one nation's culture into other nations. As discussed in Chapter 17, powerful countries often use the media to spread values and ideas that dominate and even destroy other cultures. For example, some view the widespread infusion of the English

cultural imperialism
The extensive infusion of one nation's culture into other nations.

© REUTERS/China Daily China Daily Information Corp - CDIC

Is the proliferation of massive shopping malls in China—containing stores from the United States and Western Europe as well as local entities—an example of cultural diffusion? Or is the malling of China an example of cultural imperialism? Can "culture" be sold?

language into countries that speak other languages as a form of cultural imperialism. On the other hand, the concept of cultural imperialism may fail to take into account various cross-cultural influences. For example, cultural diffusion of literature, music, clothing, and food has occurred on a global scale. A global culture, if it comes into existence, will most likely include components from many societies and cultures.

TIME TO REVIEW

- To what degree are we shaped by popular culture?

LO-5 SOCIOLOGICAL ANALYSIS OF CULTURE

Sociologists regard culture as a central ingredient in human behaviour. Although all sociologists share a similar purpose, they typically see culture through somewhat different lenses because they are guided by different theoretical perspectives in their research. What do these perspectives tell us about culture?

Functionalist Perspectives

As previously discussed, functionalist perspectives are based on the assumption that society is a stable, orderly system with interrelated parts that serve specific functions. Anthropologist Bronislaw Malinowski (1922) suggested that culture helps people meet their *biological needs* (including food and procreation), *instrumental needs* (including law and education), and *integrative needs* (including religion and art). Societies in which people share a common language and core values are more likely to have consensus and harmony.

How might functionalist analysts view popular culture? According to many functionalist theorists, popular culture serves a significant function in society in that it may be the "glue" that holds society together. Regardless of race, class, sex, age, or other characteristics, many people are brought together (at least in spirit) to cheer teams competing in major sporting events, such as the Grey Cup or the Olympic Games. Television and the Internet help integrate recent immigrants into the mainstream culture, whereas longer-term residents may become more homogenized as a result of seeing the same images and being exposed to the same beliefs and values (Gerbner et al., 1987).

Functionalists acknowledge, however, that all societies have dysfunctions that produce a variety of societal problems. When many subcultures are present within a society, discord results from a lack of consensus about core values. In fact, popular culture may undermine core cultural values rather than reinforce them (Christians, Rotzoll, and Fackler, 1987). For example, movies may glorify crime rather than hard work as the quickest way to get ahead. According to some analysts, excessive violence in music videos, movies, and television programs may be harmful to children and young people (Medved, 1992). From this perspective, popular culture may be a factor in antisocial behaviour as seemingly diverse as hate crimes and fatal shootings in public schools.

The functionalist perspective on culture has both strength and shortcomings. On the one hand, it focuses on the needs of society and the fact that stability is essential for society's continued survival. On the other hand, it overemphasizes harmony and cooperation. This approach also fails to fully account for factors embedded in the structure of society—such as class-based inequalities, racism, and sexism—that may contribute to conflict strife.

Conflict Perspectives

Conflict perspectives are based on the assumption that social life is a continuous struggle in which members of powerful groups seek to control scarce resources. According to this approach, values and norms help to create and sustain the privileged position of the powerful in society while excluding others. As early conflict theorist Karl Marx stressed, ideas are *cultural creations* of a society's most powerful members. Thus, it is possible for political, economic, and social leaders to use *ideology*—an integrated system of ideas that is external to, and coercive of, people—to maintain their positions of dominance in a society. As Marx stated:

> The ideas of the ruling class are in every epoch the ruling ideas, i.e., the class which is the ruling material force in society, is at the same time, its ruling intellectual force. The class, which has the means of material production at its disposal, has control at the same time over the means of mental production . . . The ruling ideas are nothing more than the ideal expression of the dominant material relationships, the dominant material relationships grasped as ideas. (Marx and Engels, 1970/1845–1846:64)

Many contemporary conflict theorists agree with Marx's assertion that ideas, a nonmaterial component of culture, are used by agents of the ruling class to affect the thoughts and actions of members of other classes.

How might conflict theorists view popular culture? Some conflict theorists believe that popular culture, which originated with everyday people, has been largely removed from their domain and has become nothing more than a part of the North American capitalist economy (Cantor, 1980, 1987; Gans, 1974). From this approach, U.S. media conglomerates, such as Time Warner, Disney, and Viacom, create popular culture, such as films, television shows, and amusement parks, in the same way that they would produce any other product or service. Creating new popular culture also promotes consumption of *commodities*—objects outside ourselves that we purchase to satisfy our human needs or wants (Fjellman, 1992). Recent studies have shown that moviegoers spend more money on popcorn, drinks, candy, and other concession stand food than they do on tickets to get into the theatre. Similarly, parkgoers at Disneyland and Walt Disney World spend as much money on merchandise—such as Magic Kingdom pencils, Mickey Mouse

© Scott Larson/Splash News/Newscom

Is this Japanese amusement park a sign of a homogeneous global culture or of cultural imperialism? Discuss.

hats, kitchen accessories, and clothing—as they do on admission tickets and rides (Fjellman, 1992).

From this perspective, people come to believe that they *need* things they ordinarily would not purchase. Their desire is intensified by marketing techniques that promote public trust in products and services provided by a corporation, such as the Walt Disney Company. Sociologist Pierre Bourdieu refers to this public trust as *symbolic capital:* "the acquisition of a reputation for competence and an image of respectability and honourability" (1984:291). Symbolic capital consists of culturally approved intangibles—such as honour, integrity, esteem, trust, and goodwill—that may be accumulated and used for tangible (economic) gain. Thus, people buy products at Walt Disney World (and Disney stores throughout the world) because they believe in the value of the items ("These children's pajamas are bound to be flame retardant—they came from the Disney store") and the integrity of the company ("I can trust Disney; it's been around for a long time").

Other conflict theorists examine the intertwining relationship among race, gender, and popular culture. According to sociologist K. Sue Jewell (1993), popular cultural images are often linked to negative stereotypes of people of colour, particularly black women. Jewell believes that cultural images depicting black women as mammies or domestics—such as those previously used in Aunt Jemima Pancake ads and recent resurrections of films like *Gone with the Wind*—affect contemporary black women's economic prospects in profound ways.

Conflict perspectives have two main strengths. The first is that they stress how cultural values and norms may perpetuate social inequalities. The second is that they highlight the inevitability of change and the constant tension between those who want to maintain the status quo and those who desire change.

A limitation is their focus on societal discord and the divisiveness of culture.

Symbolic Interactionist Perspectives

Unlike functionalists and conflict theorists, who focus primarily on macrolevel concerns, symbolic interactionists engage in a microlevel analysis that views society as the sum of all people's interactions. From this perspective, symbols make communication with others possible because they provide people with shared meanings and people create, maintain, and modify culture as they go about their everyday activities.

According to some symbolic interactionists, people continually negotiate their social realities. Values and norms are not independent realities that automatically determine our behaviour; instead, we reinterpret them in each social situation we encounter. However, the classical sociologist Georg Simmel warned that the larger cultural world—including both material and nonmaterial culture—eventually takes on a life of its own apart from the actors who daily recreate social life. As a result, individuals may be more controlled by culture than they realize.

Simmel (1990/1907) suggested that money is an example of how people may be controlled by their culture. According to Simmel, people initially create money as a means of exchange, but then money acquires a social meaning that extends beyond its purely economic function. Money becomes an end in itself, rather than a means to an end. Today, we are aware of the relative "worth" not only of objects but also of individuals. Many people revere wealthy entrepreneurs and highly paid celebrities, entertainers, and sports figures for how much money they make, not for their intrinsic qualities. According to Simmel, money makes it possible for us to *relativize* everything, including our relationships with other people. When social life can be reduced to money, people become cynical, believing that anything—including people, objects, beauty, and truth—can be bought if we can pay the price.

Although Simmel acknowledged the positive functions of money, he believed that the social interpretations people give to money often produce individual feelings of cynicism and isolation.

A symbolic interactionist approach highlights how people maintain and change culture through their interactions with others. However, interactionism does not provide a systematic framework for analyzing how we shape culture and how it, in turn, shapes us. It also does not provide insight into how shared meanings are developed among people, and it does not take into account the many situations in which there is disagreement on meanings. Whereas the functional and conflict approaches tend to overemphasize the macrolevel workings of society, the interactionist viewpoint often fails to take these larger social structures into account.

Postmodern Perspectives

Postmodern theorists believe that much of what has been written about culture in the Western world is Eurocentric—that it is based on the uncritical assumption that European culture (including its dispersed versions in countries such as Canada, the United States, Australia, and South Africa) is the true, universal culture in which all the world's people ought to believe (Lemert, 1997). By contrast, postmodernists believe that we should speak of *cultures* rather than *culture.*

However, Jean Baudrillard, one of the best-known French social theorists, believes that the world of culture today is based on *simulation,* not reality. According to Baudrillard, social life is much more a spectacle that simulates reality than reality itself. Many people gain "reality" from the media or cyberspace. For example, consider the many North American children who, upon entering school for the first time, have already watched more hours of television than the total number of classroom instruction hours they will encounter in their entire school careers (Lemert, 1997). Add to this the number of hours that some will have spent playing computer games or surfing the Internet. Baudrillard refers to this social creation as *hyperreality*—a situation in which the *simulation* of reality is more real than the thing itself. For Baudrillard, everyday life has been captured by the signs and symbols generated to represent it, and we ultimately relate to simulations and models as if they were reality.

Baudrillard (1983) uses Disneyland as an example of a simulation that conceals the reality that exists outside rather than inside the boundaries of the artificial perimeter. According to Baudrillard, Disney-like theme parks constitute a form of seduction that substitutes symbolic (seductive) power for real power, particularly the ability to bring about social change. From this perspective, amusement park "guests" may feel like "survivors" after enduring the rapid speed and gravity-defying movements of the roller coaster rides, or see themselves as "winners" after surviving fights with hideous cartoon villains on the "dark rides," when they have actually experienced the substitution of an *appearance* of power over their lives for the *absence* of real power.

In their examination of culture, postmodern social theorists make us aware of the fact that no single perspective can grasp the complexity and diversity of the social world. They also make us aware that reality may not be what it seems. According to the postmodern view, no one authority can claim to know social reality and we should *deconstruct*—take apart and subject to intense critical scrutiny—existing beliefs and theories about culture in hopes of gaining new insights (Ritzer, 1997).

Although postmodern theories of culture have been criticized on a number of grounds, we will mention only three. One criticism is postmodernism's lack of a clear conceptualization of ideas. Another is the tendency to critique other perspectives as being "grand narratives," whereas postmodernists offer their own varieties of such narratives. Finally, some analysts believe that postmodern analyses of culture lead to profound pessimism about the future.

© John Rowley/Thinkstock

New technologies have made educational opportunities available to a wider diversity of students, including persons with disabilities.

CONCEPT SNAPSHOT

COMPONENTS OF CULTURE

Symbol: Anything that meaningfully represents anything else.
Language: A set of symbols that express ideas and enable people to think and communicate with one another.
Values: Collective ideas about what is right or wrong, good or bad, and desirable or undesirable in a particular culture.
Norms: Established rules of behaviour or standards of conduct.

FUNCTIONALIST PERSPECTIVES

A functionalist analysis of culture assumes that a common language and shared values help produce consensus and harmony. Conversely, in a society that contains numerous subcultures, discord results from a lack of consensus and shared core values.

CONFLICT PERSPECTIVES

Conflict theorists suggest that values and norms help create and sustain a position of privilege for those in power in a society. Ideas are a cultural creation of society's most powerful members and can be used by the ruling class to affect the thoughts and actions of members of other classes.

SYMBOLIC INTERACTIONIST PERSPECTIVES

According to symbolic interactionists, people create, maintain, and modify culture during their everyday activities. Symbols assist in our communication with others by providing shared meanings.

POSTMODERN PERSPECTIVES

Postmodern theorists believe that culture today is based on a simulation of reality (e.g., what we see on television) rather than reality itself. According to the postmodern perspective, we should deconstruct existing beliefs and theories about culture in order to gain new insights.

VISUAL SUMMARY

3

LO-1 Understand the importance of culture in our lives and those of others in society.

© CP PHOTO/Kevin Frayer

Culture encompasses the knowledge, language, values, and customs passed from one generation to the next in a human group or society. Culture is essential for our individual survival because, unlike nonhuman animals, we are not born with instinctive information about how to behave and how to care for ourselves and others.

Culture can be a stabilizing force for society, providing a sense of continuity; however, culture also can be a force that generates discord, conflict, and violence.

There are both material and nonmaterial expressions of culture. Material culture consists of the physical creations of society. Nonmaterial culture is more abstract and reflects the ideas, values, and beliefs of a society.

© Stephen Finn/Shutterstock

LO-2 Identify the essential components of culture.

These components are symbols, language, values, and norms. Symbols express shared meanings; through them, groups communicate cultural ideas and abstract concepts. Language is a set of symbols through which groups communicate. Values are a culture's collective ideas about what is or is not acceptable. Norms are the specific behavioural expectations within a culture.

LO-3 Describe what causes cultural change in societies.

Cultural change takes place in all societies. Change occurs through discovery and invention and through diffusion, which is the transmission of culture from one society or group to another.

© Winnipeg Free Press, June 7, 1998. Reproduced with permission.

KEY TERMS

counterculture A group that strongly rejects dominant societal values and norms and seeks alternative lifestyles (p. 78).

cultural imperialism The extensive infusion of one nation's culture into other nations (p. 81).

cultural lag William Ogburn's term for a gap between the technical development of a society (material culture) and its moral and legal institutions (nonmaterial culture) (p. 74).

cultural relativism The belief that the behaviours and customs of any culture must be viewed and analyzed by the culture's own standards (p. 80).

cultural universals Customs and practices that occur across all societies (p. 66).

culture The knowledge, language, values, customs, and material objects that are passed from person to person and from one generation to the next in a human group or society (p. 62).

culture shock The disorientation that people feel when they encounter cultures radically different from their own (p. 78).

diffusion The transmission of cultural items or social practices from one group or society to another (p. 74).

discovery The process of learning about something previously unknown or unrecognized (p. 74).

ethnocentrism The tendency to regard one's own culture and group as the standard—and thus superior—whereas all other groups are seen as inferior (p. 80).

folkways Informal norms or everyday customs that may be violated without serious consequences within a particular culture (p. 72).

ideal culture The values and standards of behaviour that people in a society profess to hold (p. 72).

invention The process of reshaping existing cultural items into a new form (p. 74).

language A system of symbols that expresses ideas and enables people to think and communicate with one another (p. 67).

laws Formal, standardized norms that have been enacted by legislatures and are enforced by formal sanctions (p. 73).

material culture A component of culture that consists of the physical or tangible creations—such as clothing, shelter, and art—that members of a society make, use, and share (p. 64).

mores Strongly held norms with moral and ethical connotations that may not be violated without serious consequences in a particular culture (p. 73).

nonmaterial culture A component of culture that consists of the abstract or intangible human creations of society—such as attitudes, beliefs, and values—that influence people's behaviour (p. 65).

norms Established rules of behaviour or standards of conduct (p. 72).

real culture The values and standards of behaviour that people actually follow (as contrasted with *ideal culture*) (p. 72).

sanctions Rewards for appropriate behaviour or penalties for inappropriate behaviour (p. 72).

LO-4 Compare and contrast ethnocentrism and cultural relativism as approaches to examining cultural differences.

Ethnocentrism is the assumption that one's own culture is superior to other cultures. Cultural relativism counters culture shock and ethnocentrism by viewing and analyzing another culture in terms of its own values and standards.

© Corbis Sygma

© Scott Larson/Splash News/Newscom

LO-5 Explain how the various sociological perspectives view culture.

A functional analysis of culture assumes that a common language and shared values help produce consensus and harmony. According to some conflict theorists, culture may be used by certain groups to maintain their privilege and exclude others from society's benefits. Symbolic interactionists suggest that people create, maintain, and modify culture as they go about their everyday activities. Postmodern thinkers believe that there are many cultures in Canada alone. To gain a better understanding of how popular culture may simulate reality rather than being reality, postmodernists believe that we need a new way of conceptualizing culture and society.

APPLICATION QUESTIONS

1. Would it be possible today to live in a totally separate culture in Canada? In what ways could you avoid all influences from the mainstream popular culture or from the values and norms of other cultures? How would you avoid any change in your culture?
2. Do fads and fashions in popular culture reflect and reinforce or challenge and change the values and norms of a society? Consider a wide variety of fads and fashions: musical styles; computer and video games and other technologies; literature; and political, social, and religious ideas.
3. Make a list of three or four uniquely Canadian symbols. Then identify examples of symbols that represent other countries.
4. In what ways do we see cultural differences in our everyday life situations and experiences? Which different cultural groups are you a part of, and how do they intersect or interact?

KEY FIGURES

© Steve Pyke/Getty Images

Jean Baudrillard (1929-2007) One of the best-known French social theorists, Baudrillard views social life as more like a spectacle that simulates reality than a reality itself.

Sapir-Whorf hypothesis The proposition that language shapes its speakers' view of reality (p. 68).

subculture A group of people who share a distinctive set of cultural beliefs and behaviours that differ in some significant way from those of the larger society (p. 76).

taboos Mores so strong that their violation is considered extremely offensive and even unmentionable (p. 73).

technology The knowledge, techniques, and tools that make it possible for people to transform resources into usable forms, as well as the knowledge and skills required to use them after they are developed (p. 64).

value contradiction Values that conflict with one another or are mutually exclusive (p. 71).

values Collective ideas about what is right or wrong, good or bad, and desirable or undesirable in a particular culture (p. 71).

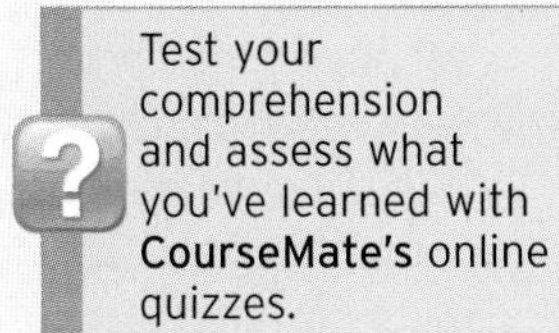
Test your comprehension and assess what you've learned with **CourseMate's** online quizzes.

For other interesting Lived Experiences, watch the video clips on **CourseMate.**

Practise what you've learned with flashcards containing key terms and definitions on **CourseMate.**

CHAPTER

4 Socialization

SCOTT DOBSON-MITCHELL STUDIES AT THE UNIVERSITY OF WATERLOO.

Consider his reflections on his first year of university and the suggestions he offers to new students who are adjusting to this new learning experience.

Assuming I couldn't accidentally cause some sort of butterfly effect that would prevent me being born, I wish I could travel back in time and tell my Freshman Self a few things about university. Considering I've already forgotten the answers to every exam, this is what I'd tell the younger me.

1. Plan ahead. WAY ahead.
It happens to me every semester. Searching through the course calendar, I find the perfect class. It sounds interesting, it fits perfectly into my schedule and it fulfills my upper-year science requirement. The prof checks out on RateMyProfessors and the course has a high score on Bird Courses. But I don't have one of the prerequisites! If I'd been smart enough to plan, I would have that first year zoology credit that's mandatory for nearly everything. Instead, I'm stuck with phytochemical biosystems.

2. You're richer than you think.
Or at least, you're less broke than you think. There are plenty of ways to get money beyond student loans—scholarships, bursaries, and work study programs that not only get you some cash but also valuable work experience. The Ontario Work Study Program is one example. If you're receiving student loans, then you're probably eligible. Also be sure to check out the Maclean's scholarship finder.

For students attending university for the first time, the socialization process is complex and immediate. What socialization issues did you face during your first term in higher education?

3. It's going to get easier.
The first year is the worst year. It's sort of like the first 20 minutes of the movie Inception, *when you have no idea what the hell is going on. But if you hang in there, things will start making sense. You'll realize that university isn't impossibly more difficult than high school. In fact, once you've acclimatized, it's easier in some ways. And it only gets better. Once some of those nasty prerequisites are out of the way, you can take courses that truly interest you. My interests happen to coincide with those listed on Bird Courses.*

4. It's easier to keep up than to catch up.
As a seasoned procrastinator, I can say with experience and authority that procrastination is not a good idea. Especially when you leave multiple things to the last minute. Here's

what I finally realized: There comes a point where writing an essay is less difficult than NOT writing an essay. After you've checked your email, looked at your Facebook notifications, watched a bunch of mindless videos on YouTube and then read some random Wikipedia articles, procrastinating actually becomes more difficult than finishing your work. A better option? Keep those pages closed. (Maclean's Campus Online, 2012)

(*Source:* Scott Dobson-Mitchell, "The Many Regrets of a Fourth-Year Student, from http://oncampus.macleans.ca/education/2012/01/27/the-many-regrets-of-a-fourth-year-student.)

Socialization is a lifelong process that includes socialization in early childhood, in adolescence, and in early and late adulthood. Each of these phases, or stages, of life presents its own special challenges as we are socialized or "resocialized" to new experiences, environments, and expectations. In fact, many of you are being socialized to university or college life with new practices of learning and new social dynamics both inside and outside the classroom.

Many of us experience stress when we take on new and seemingly unfamiliar roles and find that we must learn the appropriate norms regarding how persons in a specific role should think, act, and communicate with others.

Look around in your classes at the beginning of each semester, and you will probably see other students who are trying to find out what is going to be expected of them as a student in a particular course. What is the course going to cover? What are the instructor's requirements? How should students communicate with the instructor and other students in the class? Some information of this type is learned through formal instruction, such as in a classroom, but much of what we know about school is learned informally through our observations of other people, by listening to what they say when we are in their physical presence, or through interacting with them by cellphone, email, or text messaging when we are apart. Sociologists use the term *socialization* to refer to both the formal and informal processes by which people learn a new role and find out how to be a part of a group or organization. As we shall see in this chapter, this process takes place throughout our life.

In this chapter, we will examine the process of socialization and identify reasons why socialization is crucial to the well-being of individuals, groups, and societies. We will discuss both sociological and social psychological theories of human development. We will look at the dynamics of socialization—how it occurs and what shapes it. Throughout the chapter, we will focus on positive and negative aspects of the socialization process, including the daily stresses that may be involved in this process. Before reading on, test your knowledge about socialization and the university experience by taking the quiz in Box 4.1 on page 93.

Critical Thinking Questions

1. What socialization issues did you face during your first term in higher education?
2. What strategies did you use in acquiring information about your new role as a university student?
3. What suggestions would you offer to students struggling to learn new behaviours, attitudes, and norms for a university student, both inside and outside the classroom?

CHAPTER FOCUS QUESTION

How does socialization occur throughout our lives, including our university years?

LEARNING OBJECTIVES

AFTER READING THIS CHAPTER, YOU SHOULD BE ABLE TO:

- **LO-1** Discuss the purpose of socialization.
- **LO-2** Discuss the degree to which our unique physical and human characteristics are based on heredity and to what degree they are based on our social environment.
- **LO-3** Identify the key agents of socialization.
- **LO-4** Describe how sociologists explain our development of a self-concept.
- **LO-5** Review the main social psychological theories on human development.
- **LO-6** Describe socialization throughout various stages in the life course.

© Mandy Godbehear/Shutterstock

© iofoto/Shutterstock

© Monkey Business Images/Shutterstock

What are the consequences to children of isolation, as contrasted with social interaction and parental affection? Sociologists emphasize that social environment is a crucial part of an individual's socialization.

WHY IS SOCIALIZATION IMPORTANT? LO-1

Socialization—the lifelong process of social interaction through which individuals acquire a self-identity and the physical, mental, and social skills needed for survival in society—is the essential link between the individual and society. It enables each of us to develop our human potential and learn the ways of thinking, talking, and acting that are essential for social living.

socialization The lifelong process of social interaction through which individuals acquire a self-identity and the physical, mental, and social skills needed for survival in society.

Socialization is essential for the individual's survival and for human development. The many people who meet our early material and social needs are central to our establishing our own identity. During the first three years of life, we begin to develop a unique identity, as well as the abilities to manipulate things and to walk. We acquire sophisticated cognitive tools for thinking and analyzing a wide variety of situations, and we learn effective communication skills. As we do so, we begin a relatively long socialization process that culminates in our integration into a complex social and cultural system (Garcia Coll, 1990).

Socialization is also essential for the survival and stability of society. Members of a society must be socialized to support and maintain the existing social structure. From a functionalist perspective, individual conformity to existing norms is not taken for granted; rather, basic individual needs and desires must be balanced against the needs of the social structure. The socialization process is most effective when people conform to the norms of society because they believe that doing so is the best course of action. Socialization enables a society to "reproduce" itself by passing on this cultural content from one generation to the next.

While ways in which people learn beliefs, values, and rules of behaviour are somewhat similar in many countries, the content of socialization differs greatly from society to society. How people walk, talk, eat, make love, and wage war are all functions of the culture in which they are raised. At the same time, we are also influenced by our exposure to subcultures of class, ethnicity, religion, and gender. In addition, each of us has unique experiences in our families and friendship groupings. The kind of human being that we become depends greatly on the particular society and social groups that surround us at birth and during early childhood. What we believe about ourselves, our society, and the world is largely a product of our interactions with others.

BOX 4.1 SOCIOLOGY AND EVERYDAY LIFE

How Much Do You Know About Socialization and the University Experience?

True	False	
T	F	1. Professors are the primary agents of socialization for university students.
T	F	2. In recent studies, few students report that they spend time studying with other students.
T	F	3. Many students find that taking university courses is stressful because it is an abrupt change from high school.
T	F	4. University students typically find the socialization process in higher education less stressful than the one they experience when they enter an occupation or profession.
T	F	5. Getting good grades and completing schoolwork are the top sources of stress reported by University students.

For answers to the quiz about socialization and the university experience, go to **www.nelson.com/sociologyinourtimes6e.**

LO-2 Human Development: Biology and Society

What does it mean to be "human"? To be human includes being conscious of ourselves as individuals with unique identities, personalities, and relationships with others. As humans, we have ideas, emotions, and values. We have the capacity to think and to make rational decisions. But what is the source of "humanness"? Are we born with these human characteristics, or do we develop them through our interactions with others?

When we are born, we are totally dependent on others for our survival. We cannot turn ourselves over, speak, reason, plan, or do many of the things associated with being human. Although we can nurse, wet, and cry, most small mammals can also do those things. As discussed in Chapter 3, we humans differ from nonhuman animals because we lack instincts and must rely on learning for our survival. Human infants have the potential for developing human characteristics if they are exposed to an adequate socialization process.

Every human being is a product of biology, society, and personal experiences—that is, of heredity and environment, or, in even more basic terms, "nature" and "nurture." How much of our development can be explained by socialization? How much by our genetic heritage? Sociologists focus on how humans design their own culture and transmit it from generation to generation through socialization. By contrast, sociobiologists assert that nature, in the form of our genetic makeup, is a major factor in shaping human behaviour. **Sociobiology** is the systematic study of how biology affects social behaviour. According to zoologist Edward O. Wilson (1975), who pioneered sociobiology, genetic inheritance underlies many forms of social behaviour, such as war and peace, envy and concern for others, and competition and cooperation. Most sociologists disagree with the notion that biological principles can be used to explain all human behaviour. Obviously, however, some aspects of our physical makeup—such as eye colour, hair colour, height, and weight—are determined largely by our heredity.

sociobiology The systematic study of how biology affects social behaviour.

How important is social influence ("nurture") in human development? There is hardly a behaviour that is not influenced socially. Except for simple reflexes, most human actions are social, either in their causes or in their consequences. Even solitary actions, such as crying or brushing our teeth, are ultimately social. We cry because someone has hurt us. We brush our teeth because our parents (or dentist) told us it was important. Social environment probably has a greater effect than heredity on the way we develop and the way we act. However, heredity does provide the basic material from which other people help to mould an individual's human characteristics.

Our biological and emotional needs are related in a complex equation. Children whose needs are met in settings characterized by affection, warmth, and closeness see the world as a safe and comfortable place and other people as trustworthy and helpful. By contrast, infants and children who receive less than adequate care or who are emotionally rejected or abused often view the world as hostile and have feelings of suspicion and fear.

Social Isolation and Maltreatment

Social environment, then, is a crucial part of an individual's socialization. Even nonhuman primates, such as monkeys and chimpanzees, need social contact with others of their species to develop properly. As we will see, appropriate social contact is even more important for humans.

ISOLATION AND NONHUMAN PRIMATES Researchers have attempted to show the effects of social isolation on nonhuman primates raised without contact with others of their own species. In a series of laboratory experiments, psychologists Harry and Margaret Harlow (1962, 1977) took infant rhesus monkeys from their mothers and isolated them in separate cages. Each cage contained two nonliving "mother substitutes" made of wire, one with a feeding bottle attached and the other covered with soft terry cloth but without a bottle. The infant monkeys instinctively clung to the cloth "mother" and would not abandon it until hunger drove them to the bottle attached to the wire "mother." As soon as they were full, they went back to the cloth "mother," seeking warmth, affection, and physical comfort.

The Harlows' experiments show the detrimental effects of isolation on nonhuman primates. When the young monkeys were later introduced to other members of their species, they cringed in the corner. Having been deprived of social contact with other monkeys during their first six months of life, they never learned how to relate to other monkeys or to become well-adjusted adult monkeys—they were fearful of or hostile toward other monkeys (Harlow and Harlow, 1962, 1977). Because humans rely more heavily on social learning than do monkeys, the process of socialization is even more important for us.

ISOLATED CHILDREN Of course, sociologists would never place children in isolated circumstances so that they could observe what the effects were. However, there are cases in which parents or other caregivers failed to fulfill their responsibilities, leaving children alone or placing them in isolated circumstances. From analysis of these situations, social scientists have documented cases in which children were deliberately raised in isolation. A look at the lives of two children who suffered such emotional abuse provides insights into the importance of a positive socialization process and the negative effects of social isolation.

Anna Born in 1932 to an unmarried, mentally impaired woman, Anna was an unwanted child. She was kept in an attic-like room in her grandfather's house. Her mother, who worked on the farm all day and often went out at night, gave Anna just enough care to keep her alive; she received no other care. Sociologist Kingsley Davis described her condition when she was found in 1938:

> [Anna] had no glimmering of speech, absolutely no ability to walk, no sense of gesture, not the least capacity to feed herself even when the food was put in front of her, and no comprehension of cleanliness. She was so apathetic that it was hard to tell whether or not she could hear. And all of this at the age of nearly six years. (1940)

When she was placed in a special school and given the necessary care, Anna slowly learned to walk, talk, and care for herself. Just before her death at the age of 10, Anna reportedly could follow directions, talk in phrases, wash her hands, brush her teeth, and try to help other children (Davis, 1940).

Genie Almost four decades after Anna was discovered, Genie was found in 1970 at the age of 13. She had been locked in a bedroom alone, alternately strapped down to a child's potty chair or straitjacketed into a sleeping bag, since she was 20 months old. She had been fed baby food and beaten with a wooden paddle when she whimpered. She had not heard the sounds of human speech because no one talked to her, and there was no television or radio in her home (Curtiss, 1977; Pines, 1981). Genie was placed in a pediatric hospital, where one of the psychologists described her condition:

> At the time of her admission she was virtually unsocialized. She could not stand erect, salivated continuously, had never been toilet-trained and had no control over her urinary or bowel functions. She was unable to chew solid food and had the weight, height and appearance of a child half her age. (Rigler, 1993:35)

In addition to her physical condition, Genie showed psychological traits associated with neglect, as described by one of her psychiatrists:

> If you gave [Genie] a toy, she would reach out and touch it, hold it, caress it with her fingertips, as though she didn't trust her eyes. She would rub it against her cheek to feel it. So when I met her and she began to notice me standing beside her bed, I held my hand out and she reached out and took my hand and carefully felt my thumb and fingers individually, and then put my hand against her cheek. She was exactly like a blind child. (Rymer, 1993:45)

Extensive therapy was used in an attempt to socialize Genie and develop her language abilities (Curtiss, 1977; Pines, 1981). These efforts met with limited success: In the early 1990s, Genie was living in a board-and-care home for mentally challenged adults (see Angier, 1993; Rigler, 1993; Rymer, 1993).

CHILD MALTREATMENT What do the terms *child maltreatment* and *child abuse* mean to you? When asked what constitutes child maltreatment, many people first think of cases that involve severe injuries or sexual abuse. In fact, these terms refer to the violence, mistreatment, or neglect that a child may experience while in the care of someone he or she trusts or depends on, such as a parent, relative, caregiver, or guardian. There are many different forms of abuse, including physical abuse, sexual abuse or exploitation, neglect, and emotional abuse. A child who is abused often experiences more than one form of abuse.

Recent studies indicate that neglect is the most frequent form of child abuse. Child neglect occurs when a child's basic needs—including emotional warmth and security, adequate shelter, food, healthcare, education, clothing, and protection—are not met, regardless of the cause (Trocmé et al., 2001). The neglect usually involves repeated incidents over a lengthy time.

Any child—regardless of age, gender, race, ethnicity, socioeconomic status, sexual orientation, physical or mental abilities, and personality—may be at risk of being abused. Sociologists argue that child abuse is linked to inequalities in our society and the power imbalance that exists between adults and children. A child is usually dependent on his or her abuser and has little power to control the abusive circumstances. There is increasing understanding that a child's risk of being abused may be increased by other identifiable social factors, such as racism, sexism, homophobia, poverty, and social isolation. For example, historically, many children who were sent to institutions were abused. The majority of these children were from marginalized groups: Aboriginal children, children from racial and ethnic minorities, children with physical or mental disabilities, and children living in poverty (Department of Justice, 2002c).

Throughout history and across cultures, perceptions of what constitutes abuse or neglect have differed. What might have been considered appropriate disciplinary action by parents in the past (such as following the adage "Spare the rod, spoil the child") is today viewed by many as child abuse.

TIME TO REVIEW

- Why is healthy socialization so important?
- Explain what problems can develop when children receive inadequate socialization.

LO-3 AGENTS OF SOCIALIZATION

agents of socialization The persons, groups, or institutions that teach us what we need to know to participate in society.

Agents of socialization are the persons, groups, or institutions that teach us what we need to know to participate in society. We are exposed to many agents of socialization throughout our lifetime; in turn, we have an influence on those socializing agents and organizations. Here, we will look at those that are most pervasive in childhood—the family, the school, peer groups, and the mass media.

The Family

The family is the most important agent of socialization in all societies. As the discussion of child maltreatment has demonstrated, the initial love and nurturance we receive from our families are central to our cognitive, emotional, and physical development. As soon as we are born, our families begin to transmit cultural and social values to us. As we will discuss in Chapter 13, families in Canada vary in size and structure. Some families consist of two parents and their biological children, while others consist of a single parent and one or more children. Still other families reflect changing patterns of divorce and remarriage, and an increasing number are made up of same-sex partners and their children.

Theorists using a functionalist perspective emphasize that families serve important functions in society because they are the primary focus for the procreation and socialization of children. Most of us form an emerging sense of self and acquire most of our beliefs and values within the family context. We also learn about the larger dominant culture (including language, attitudes, beliefs, values, and norms) and the primary subcultures to which our parents and other relatives belong.

Families are also the primary source of emotional support. Ideally, people receive love, understanding, security, acceptance, intimacy, and companionship within families. The role of the family is especially significant because young children have little social experience beyond its boundaries; they have no basis for comparison or for evaluating how their family treats them.

To a large extent, the family is where we acquire our specific social position in society. From birth, we are a part of the specific ethnic, economic, religious, and regional subcultural grouping of our family. Studies show that families socialize their children somewhat differently based on ethnicity and class (Harrison et al., 1990; Kohn, 1977; Kohn et al., 1990; Kurian, 1991). For example, sociologist Melvin Kohn (1977; Kohn et al., 1990) has suggested that social class (as measured by parental occupation) is one of the strongest influences on what and how parents teach their children. On the one hand, working-class parents, who are closely supervised and expected to follow orders at work, typically emphasize to their children the importance of obedience and conformity. On the other hand, parents from the middle and professional classes, who have more freedom and flexibility at work, tend to give their children more freedom to make their own decisions and to be creative. Kohn concluded that differences in the parents' occupations were a better predictor of child-rearing practices than was social class itself.

Conflict theorists stress that socialization contributes to *false consciousness*—a lack of awareness and a distorted perception of class reality as it affects all aspects of social life. As a result, socialization reaffirms and reproduces the class structure in the next generation rather than challenging the conditions that currently exist. For example, children in poor and low-income families may be unintentionally socialized to believe that acquiring an education and aspiring to lofty ambitions are pointless because of existing economic conditions in the family (Ballantine, 2001). By contrast, middle- and upper-income families typically instill ideas of monetary and social success in children, as well as emphasizing the necessity of thinking and behaving in "socially acceptable" ways.

© Gaetano/Corbis

Daycare centres have become important agents of socialization for increasing numbers of children. Today, approximately 54 percent of all Canadian preschool children are in daycare of one kind or another (Bushnik, 2006).

The School

As the amount of specialized technical and scientific knowledge has expanded rapidly and the amount of time children spend in educational settings has increased, schools continue to play an enormous role in the socialization of young people. For many people, the formal education process is an undertaking that lasts up to 20 years.

As the numbers of one-parent families and families in which both parents work outside the home has increased dramatically, the number of children in daycare and preschool programs has grown rapidly as well (Bushnik, 2006). Generally, studies have found that daycare and preschool programs may have a positive effect on the overall socialization of children. These programs provide children with the opportunity to have frequent interactions with teachers and to learn how to build their language and literacy skills. High-quality programs also have a positive effect on the academic performance of children, particularly those from low-income families. Many researchers have found that children from all social classes and family backgrounds may benefit from learning experiences in early childhood education programs outside their homes (see UNICEF, 2008c). Today, however, the cost of child-care programs has become a major concern for many families.

Although schools teach specific knowledge and skills, they also have a profound effect on children's self-image, beliefs, and values. As children enter school for the first time, they are evaluated and systematically compared with one another by the teacher. Staff keep a permanent, official record of each child's personal behaviour and academic activities. From a functionalist perspective, schools are responsible for (1) socialization, or teaching students to be productive members of society; (2) transmission of culture; (3) social control and personal development; and (4) the selection, training, and placement of individuals on different rungs in the society (Ballantine and Hammack, 2009).

In contrast, conflict theorists assert that students have different experiences in the school system depending on their social class, their ethnic background, the neighbourhood in which they live, their gender, and other factors. According to sociologist Stephen Richer (1988), much of what happens in school amounts to teaching a *hidden curriculum* in which children learn to value competition, materialism, work over play, obedience to authority, and attentiveness. Richer's study of Ottawa classrooms indicated that success in school may be based more on students' ability to conform to the hidden curriculum than on their mastery of the formal curriculum. Therefore, students who are destined for leadership or elite positions acquire different skills and knowledge than those who will enter working-class and middle-class occupations

Peer Groups

peer group A group of people who are linked by common interests, equal social position, and (usually) similar age.

As soon as we are old enough to have acquaintances outside the home, most of us begin to rely heavily on peer groups as a source of information and approval about social behaviour. A **peer group** is a group of people who are linked by common interests, equal social position, and (usually) similar age. In early childhood, peer groups are composed of classmates in daycare, preschool, and elementary school. Studies have found that pre-adolescence—the latter part of the elementary school years—is a time in which the children's peer culture has an important effect on how they perceive themselves and on how they internalize society's expectations (Adler and Adler, 1998). In adolescence, peer groups are typically composed of people with similar interests and social activities. As adults, we continue to participate in peer groups of people with whom we share common interests and comparable occupations, income, and/or social position.

Peer groups function as agents of socialization by contributing to our sense of belonging and our feelings of self-worth. Unlike families and schools, peer groups provide children and adolescents with some degree of freedom from parents and other authority figures (Corsaro, 1992). Peer groups also teach and reinforce cultural norms while providing important information about "acceptable" behaviour. As a result, the peer group is both a product of culture and one of its major transmitters (Elkin and Handel, 1989).

BOX 4.2 POINT/COUNTERPOINT

"Good Job!" Mead's Generalized Other and the Issue of Excessive Praise

Hang out at a playground, visit a school, or show up at a child's birthday party, and there's one phrase you can count on hearing repeatedly: "Good job!" Even tiny infants are praised for smacking their hands together ("Good clapping!"). Many of us blurt out these judgments of our children to the point that it has become almost a verbal tic (Kohn, 2001).

Educational analyst Alfie Kohn describes the common practice of praising children for practically everything they say or do. According to Kohn, excessive praise or unearned compliments may be problematic for children because, instead of bolstering their self-esteem, such praise may increase a child's dependence on adults. As children increasingly rely on constant praise and on significant others to identify what is good or bad about their performance, they may not develop the ability to make meaningful judgments about what they have done. As Kohn suggests, "Sadly, some of these kids will grow into adults who continue to need someone to pat them on the head and tell them whether what they did was OK" (2001).

Kohn's ideas remind us of the earlier sociological insights of George Herbert Mead, who described how children learn to take into account the expectations of the larger society and to balance the "I" (the subjective element of the self: the spontaneous and unique traits of each person) with the "me" (the objective element of the self: the internalized attitudes and demands of other members of society and the individual's awareness of those demands). As Mead stated, "What goes on in the game goes on in the life of the child at all times. He is continually taking the attitudes of those about him, especially the roles of those who in some sense control him and on whom he depends" (1934:160). According to Mead, role-taking is vital to the formation of a mature sense of self as each individual learns to visualize the intentions and expectations of other people and groups. Excessively praising children may make it more difficult for them to develop a positive self-concept and visualize an accurate picture of what is expected of them as they grow into young adulthood.

Does this mean that children should not be praised? Definitely not! It means that we should think about when and how to praise children. What children may need sometimes is not praise but encouragement. As child development specialist Docia Zavitkovsky has stated:

> I sometimes say that praise is fine "when praise is due." We get into the habit of praising when it isn't praise that is appropriate but encouragement. For example, we're always saying to young children, "Oh, what a beautiful picture," even when their pictures aren't necessarily beautiful. So why not really look at each picture? Maybe a child has painted a picture with many wonderful colors. Why don't we comment on that—on the reality of the picture? (quoted in *Scholastic Parent & Child*, 2007).

From this perspective, Mead's concept of the generalized other makes us aware of the importance of other people's actions in how self-concept develops. Positive feedback can have a very important influence on a child's self-esteem because he or she can learn how to do a "good job" when engaging in a specific activity or accomplishing a task rather than simply being praised for any effort expended. What effect does receiving praise when we are young have on us when we are university students? Also, when we are dealing with our peers, how might we thoughtfully use the phrase "Good job!" without making it an overworked expression?

Is there such a thing as "peer pressure"? Individuals must earn their acceptance with their peers by conforming to a given group's norms, attitudes, speech patterns, and dress codes. When we conform to our peer group's expectations, we are rewarded; if we do not conform, we may be ridiculed or even expelled from the group. Conforming to the demands of peers frequently places children and adolescents at cross purposes with their parents. For example, children are frequently under pressure to obtain certain valued material possessions (such as toys, DVDs, clothing, or athletic shoes); they then pass this pressure on to

© Roy Morsch/Corbis

The pleasure of participating in activities with friends is one of the many attractions of adolescent peer groups. What groups have contributed the most to your own sense of belonging and self-worth?

their parents through emotional pleas to purchase the desired items. For more information on one such possession, see Box 4.3 (to read Box 4.3 on cellphones, go to **www.nelson.com/sociologyinourtimes6e**).

Mass Media

An agent of socialization that has a profound impact on both children and adults is the mass media, composed of organizations that use print and electronic means to communicate with large numbers of people, often at the same time. Books, magazines, radio, and newspapers are common types of mass media, as are the Internet, television, and movies.

The media function as socializing agents in several ways: (1) They inform us about events; (2) they introduce us to a wide variety of people; (3) they provide an array of viewpoints on current issues; (4) they make us aware of products and services that, if we purchase them, supposedly will help us to be accepted by others; and (5) they entertain us by providing the opportunity to live vicariously through other people's experiences. Although most of us take for granted that the media play an important part in contemporary socialization, we frequently underestimate the enormous influence this agent of socialization may have on children's attitudes and behaviour.

The use of social media such as Facebook and Twitter has grown exponentially in recent years. Today, over 95 percent of teens report that they use the Internet, and most indicate that they use it to interact with friends. Although boys are more likely to play video games, girls lead the charge in the use of blogs. Social networking has added another layer on existing media forms, particularly among young people. Recent studies have shown that North American children are spending more time in front of TV sets, computers, and video games than they did in the past. According to media educator Arlene Moscovitch, there is no doubt that media encounters are an inescapable part of everyday life:

> One thing is certain: we are living through a technological revolution which infuses every level of our lives and there is no going back. It's not clear where we're going but the young are leading the charge . . . Unlike most of their parents, the media embrace feels entirely natural to them. In fact, when detached in some ways from their iPods, cell phones or their laptops, they are likely to feel less than complete. (2007:23)

It is estimated that Canadian children spend just over two hours per day watching television and two hours more with computers, video games, or a DVD player. A recent survey about the Internet use of 5000 Canadians found that on an average weekday, Canadian students spend

- 54 minutes instant messaging
- 50 minutes downloading and listening to music
- 44 minutes playing online games (Moscovitch, 2007:8).

All of this adds up to thousands of hours per year where children are interacting with these media influences; by contrast, Canadian children spend about 1200 hours per year in school. This means that the average 16-year-old will have spent more time in front of a television or computer than attending school.

Parents, educators, social scientists, and public officials have widely debated the consequences of young people watching that much television. Television has been praised for offering numerous positive experiences to children. Some scholars suggest that television, when used wisely, can enhance children's development by improving their language abilities, concept-formation skills, and reading skills and by encouraging prosocial development (Winn, 1985). However, other studies have shown that children and adolescents who spend a lot of time watching television and playing video games often have lower grades in school, read fewer books, exercise less, and are overweight (Moscovitch, 2007; Sharif and Sargent, 2006).

Undoubtedly, all mass media socialize us in many ways we may or may not realize. Cultural studies scholars and some postmodern theorists believe that "media culture" has in recent years dramatically changed the socialization process for very young children.

TIME TO REVIEW

- Which of the primary socialization agents have the most significant influence on youth between the ages of 13 and 18? Why?

SOCIOLOGICAL THEORIES OF HUMAN DEVELOPMENT LO-4

Although social scientists acknowledge the contributions of psychoanalytic and psychologically based explanations of human development, sociologists focus on sociological perspectives in understanding how people develop an awareness of self and learn about the culture they live in. From a sociological perspective, we cannot form a sense of self or personal identity without intense social contact with others. The self represents the sum total of perceptions and feelings that an individual has of being a distinct, unique person—a sense of who and what one is. When we speak of the "self," we typically use words such as *I, me, my, mine,* and *myself* (Cooley, 1922/1902). This sense of self (also referred to as self-concept) is not present at birth; it arises in the process of social experience. **Self-concept** is the totality of our beliefs and feelings about ourselves (Gecas, 1982). Four components comprise our self-concept: (1) the physical self ("I am tall"), (2) the active self ("I am good at soccer"), (3) the social self ("I am nice to others"), and (4) the psychological self ("I believe in world peace"). Between early and late childhood, a child's focus tends to shift from the physical and active dimensions of self toward the social and psychological aspects (Lippa, 1994). Self-concept is the foundation for communication with others; it continues to develop and change throughout our lives (Zurcher, 1983).

self-concept The totality of our beliefs and feelings about ourselves.

Our *self-identity* is our perception about what kind of person we are. As we have seen, socially isolated children do not have typical self-identities because they have had no experience of "humanness." According to symbolic interactionists, we do not know who we are until we see ourselves as we believe others see us. We gain information about the self largely through language, symbols, and interaction with others. Our interpretation and evaluation of these messages are central to the social construction of our identity. However, we are not just passive reactors to situations, programmed by society to respond in fixed ways. Instead, we are active agents who develop plans out of the pieces supplied by culture and strive to execute these plans in social encounters (McCall and Simmons, 1978).

Cooley, Mead, and Symbolic Interactionist Perspectives

Social constructionism is a term that is applied to theories that emphasize the socially created nature of social life. This perspective is linked to symbolic interactionist theory, and its roots can be traced to the Chicago school and early theorists such as Charles Horton Cooley and George Herbert Mead.

© Monkey Business Images/Shutterstock

Our self-concept continues to be influenced by our interactions with others throughout our lives.

looking-glass self Charles Horton Cooley's term for the way in which a person's sense of self is derived from the perceptions of others.

COOLEY AND THE LOOKING-GLASS SELF According to sociologist Charles Horton Cooley (1864–1929), the **looking-glass self** refers to the way in which a person's sense of self is derived from the perceptions of others. Our looking-glass self is not who we are or what people think about us; it is based on our perception of how other people think of us (Cooley, 1922/1902). Cooley asserted that we base our perception of who we are on how we think other people see us and on whether this seems good or bad to us.

As Figure 4.1 shows, the looking-glass self is a self-concept derived from a three-step process:

1. We imagine how our personality and appearance will look to other people. We may imagine that we are attractive or unattractive, heavy or slim, friendly or unfriendly, and so on.
2. We imagine how other people judge the appearance and personality that we think we present. This step involves our *perception* of how we think they are judging us. We may be correct or incorrect!
3. We develop a self-concept. If we think the evaluation of others is favourable, our self-concept is enhanced. If we think the evaluation is unfavourable, our self-concept is diminished (Cooley, 1998/1902).

According to Cooley, we use our interactions with others as a mirror for our own thoughts and actions; our sense of self depends on how we interpret what they do and say. Consequently, our sense of self is not permanently fixed; it is always developing as we interact with others.

FIGURE 4.1 HOW THE LOOKING-GLASS SELF WORKS

MEAD AND ROLE-TAKING George Herbert Mead (1863–1931) extended Cooley's insights by linking the idea of self-concept to **role-taking**—the process by which a person mentally assumes the role of another person in order to understand the world from that person's point of view. Role-taking often occurs through play and games, as children try out different roles (such as being mommy, daddy, doctor, or teacher) and gain an appreciation of them. By taking the roles of others, the individual hopes to ascertain the intention or direction of the acts of others. Then the person begins to construct his or her own roles (role-making) and to anticipate other individuals' responses. Finally, the person plays at her or his particular role (role-playing) (Marshall, 1998).

role-taking The process by which a person mentally assumes the role of another person in order to understand the world from that person's point of view.

According to Mead (1962/1934), in the early months of life, children do not realize that they are separate from others. However, they do begin early on to see a mirrored image of themselves in others. Shortly after birth, infants start to notice the faces of those around them, especially the significant others, whose faces begin to have meaning because they are associated with experiences, such as feeding and cuddling. **Significant others** are those persons whose care, affection, and approval are especially desired and who are most important in the development of the self. Gradually, we distinguish ourselves from our caregivers and begin to perceive ourselves in contrast to them. As we develop language skills and learn to understand symbols, we begin to develop a self-concept. When we can represent ourselves in our own minds as objects distinct from everything else, our self has been formed.

significant others Those persons whose care, affection, and approval are especially desired and who are most important in the development of the self.

Mead divided the self into the "I" and the "me." The "I" is the subjective element of the self that represents the spontaneous and unique traits of each person. The "me" is the objective element of the self, which is composed of the internalized attitudes and demands of other members of society and the individual's awareness of those demands. Both the "I" and the "me" are needed to form the social self. The unity of the two constitutes the full development of the individual. According to Mead, the "I" develops first and the "me" takes form during the three stages of self development:

1. During the *preparatory stage,* up to about age three, interactions lack meaning and children largely imitate the people around them. At this stage, children are preparing for role-taking.
2. In the *play stage,* from about age three to five, children learn to use language and other symbols, which enable them to pretend to take the roles of specific people. At this stage, children begin to see themselves in relation to others but do not see role-taking as something that they have to do.
3. During the *game stage,* which begins in the early school years, children understand not only their own social position but also the positions of others around them. In contrast to play, games are structured by rules, are often competitive, and involve a number of other "players." At this time, children become concerned about the demands and expectations of others and of the larger society. Mead used the example of a baseball game to describe this stage because children, like baseball players, must take into account the roles of all the other players at the same time. Mead's concept of the **generalized other** refers to the child's awareness of the demands and expectations of the society as a whole or of the child's subculture.

generalized other George Herbert Mead's term for the child's awareness of the demands and expectations of the society as a whole or of the child's subculture.

How useful are symbolic interactionist perspectives in enhancing our understanding of the socialization process? Certainly, this approach contributes to our understanding of how the self develops (see Box 4.2 pg. 99). Sociologist Anne Kaspar (1986), for example, suggests that Mead's ideas about the social self may be more applicable to men than to women because women are more likely to experience inherent conflicts between the meanings they derive from their personal experiences and those they take from culture, particularly in regard to balancing the responsibilities of family life and paid employment.

Recent Symbolic Interactionist Perspectives

The symbolic interactionist approach emphasizes that socialization is a collective process in which children are active and creative agents, not passive recipients of the socialization process. From this view, childhood is a *socially constructed* category (Adler and Adler, 1998). Children are capable of actively constructing their own shared meanings as they acquire language skills and accumulate interactive experiences (Qvortrup, 1990). According to the "orb web model" of sociologist William A. Corsaro (1985, 1992, 1997), children's cultural knowledge reflects not only the beliefs of the adult world but also the unique interpretations and aspects of the children's own *peer culture*. Corsaro states that peer culture is "a stable set of activities or routines, artifacts, values, and concerns that children produce and share" (1992:162). This peer culture emerges through interactions as children "borrow" from the adult culture but transform it so that it fits their own situation. For example, when playing together, children often permit some children to gain access to their group and play area while preventing others from becoming a part of their group. Corsaro (1992) believes that the peer group is the most significant arena in which children and young people acquire cultural knowledge.

© Walter Hodges/Corbis

© muzsy/Shutterstock

© Rubberball Productions/Index Stock Imagery

According to sociologist George Herbert Mead, the self develops through three stages. In the preparatory stage, children imitate others; in the play stage, children pretend to take the roles of specific people; and in the game stage, children become aware of the "rules of the game" and the expectations of others.

SOCIAL PSYCHOLOGICAL THEORIES OF HUMAN DEVELOPMENT

LO-5

Up to this point, we have discussed sociologically oriented theories; we now turn to psychological theories that have influenced our understanding of how the individual personality develops.

Freud and the Psychoanalytic Perspective

The basic assumption in Sigmund Freud's (1924) psychoanalytic approach is that human behaviour and personality originate from unconscious forces within individuals. Sigmund Freud (1856–1939), known as the founder of psychoanalytic theory, lived in the Victorian era, when biological explanations of human behaviour were prevalent. It was also an era of extreme sexual repression and male dominance when compared to contemporary North American standards. Freud's theory was greatly influenced by these cultural factors, as reflected in the importance he assigned to sexual motives in explaining behaviour.

For example, Freud based his ideas on the belief that people have two basic tendencies: the urge to survive and the urge to procreate. According to Freud (1924), human development occurs in three stages that reflect different levels of the personality, which he referred to as the *id, ego,* and *superego.*

The **id** is the component of personality that includes all of the individual's basic biological drives and needs that demand immediate gratification. For Freud, the newborn child's personality is all id, and from birth the child finds that urges for self-gratification—such as wanting to be held, fed, or changed—are not going to be satisfied immediately. However, the id remains with people throughout their lives in the form of *psychic energy,* the urges and desires that account for behaviour.

id Sigmund Freud's term for the component of personality that includes all of the individual's basic biological drives and needs that demand immediate gratification.

By contrast, the second level of the personality, the ego, develops as infants discover their most basic desires are not always going to be met by others. The **ego** is the rational, reality-oriented component of personality that imposes restrictions on the innate pleasure-seeking drives of the id. The ego channels the desire of the id for immediate gratification into the most advantageous direction for the individual. The third level of the personality, the superego, is in opposition to both the id and the ego.

ego According to Sigmund Freud, the rational, reality-oriented component of personality that imposes restrictions on the innate pleasure-seeking drives of the id.

The **superego**, or conscience, consists of the moral and ethical aspects of personality. It is first expressed as the recognition of parental control and eventually matures as the child learns that parental control is a reflection of the values and moral demands of the larger society. When a person is well adjusted, the ego successfully manages the opposing forces of the id and the superego. Figure 4.2 illustrates Freud's theory of personality.

Although subject to harsh criticism, Freud's theories made people aware of the significance of early childhood experiences, including abuse and neglect. His theories have also had a profound influence on contemporary mental health practitioners and on other human development theories.

superego Sigmund Freud's term for the human conscience, consisting of the moral and ethical aspects of personality.

Piaget and Cognitive Development

Unlike psychoanalytic approaches, which focus primarily on personality development, cognitive approaches emphasize the intellectual (cognitive) development of children. The Swiss psychologist Jean Piaget (1896–1980) was a pioneer in the field of cognitive development. Cognitive theorists are interested in how people obtain, process, and use information—that is, in how we think. Cognitive development relates to changes over time in how we think.

According to Piaget (1954), in each stage of development (from birth through adolescence), children's activities are governed by their perception of the world around them. His four stages of cognitive development are organized around specific tasks that, when mastered, lead to the acquisition of new mental capacities, which then serve as the basis for the next level of development.

Piaget emphasized that all children must go through each stage in sequence before moving on to the next one, although some children move through them faster than others.

1. *Sensorimotor stage* (birth to age two). Children understand the world only through sensory contact and immediate action; they cannot engage in symbolic thought or use language. Children gradually comprehend *object permanence*—the realization that objects continue to exist even when the items are placed out of their sight.
2. *Preoperational stage* (ages two to seven). Children begin to use words as mental symbols and to form mental images. However, they are still limited in their ability to use logic to solve problems or to realize that physical objects may change in shape or appearance but still retain their physical properties.
3. *Concrete operational stage* (ages seven to 11). Children think in terms of tangible objects and actual events. They can draw conclusions about the likely physical consequences of an action without always having to try the action out. Children begin to take the role of others and start to empathize with the viewpoints of others.
4. *Formal operational stage* (age 12 through adolescence). Adolescents have the potential to engage in highly abstract thought and understand places, things, and events they have never seen. They can think about the future and evaluate different options or courses of action.

FIGURE 4.2 FREUD'S THEORY OF PERSONALITY

This illustration shows how Freud might picture a person's internal conflict over whether to commit an antisocial act, such as stealing a candy bar. In addition to dividing personality into three components, Freud theorized that our personalities are largely unconscious–hidden away outside our normal awareness. To dramatize his point, Freud compared conscious awareness (portions of the ego and superego) to the visible tip of an iceberg. Most of personality–including all of the id, with its raw desires and impulses–lies in the subconscious.

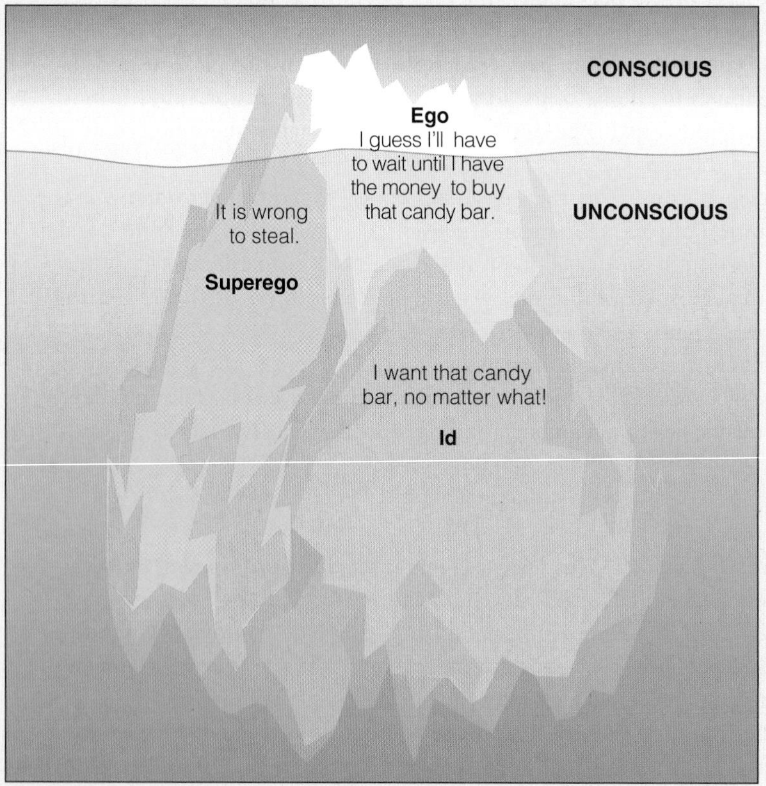

Using this cognitive model, Piaget also investigated moral development. In one study (1932), he told children stories and asked them to judge how "good" or "bad" the consequences were. One story involved a child who *accidentally* broke 15 cups, while another *deliberately* broke one cup. Piaget asked the children if they thought one child's behaviour was worse than the other's. He concluded that younger children (up to the age of eight or 10) believe that it is more evil to break a large number of cups (or steal large sums of money) than to break one cup (or steal small sums of money) for whatever reason. In contrast, older children (beginning at about age 11) are more likely to consider principles, including the intentions and motives behind other people's behaviour.

Piaget's stages of cognitive development provide us with useful insights into children's logical thinking and how they invent or construct the rules that govern their understanding of the world. Piaget asserted that children move from being totally influenced by external factors, such as parental and other forms of moral authority, to being more autonomous, thinking and acting based on their own moral judgments about behaviour. However, critics have pointed out that Piaget's theory fails to address individual differences, including how gender or culture may influence children's beliefs and actions.

Kohlberg and the Stages of Moral Development

Lawrence Kohlberg (1927–1987) elaborated on Piaget's theories of cognitive reasoning by conducting a series of studies in which respondents were presented with moral dilemmas that took the form of stories. Based on their responses, Kohlberg (1969, 1981) classified moral reasoning into three levels:

1. *Preconventional level* (ages seven to 10). Children's perceptions are based on punishment and obedience. Evil behaviour is that which is likely to be punished; good conduct is based on obedience and avoidance of unwanted consequences.
2. *Conventional level* (age 10 through adulthood). People are most concerned with how they are perceived by their peers and with how to conform to rules.
3. *Postconventional level* (few adults reach this stage). People view morality in terms of individual rights; "moral conduct" is judged by principles based on human rights that transcend government and laws.

Although Kohlberg presents interesting ideas about the moral judgments of children, some critics have challenged the universality of his stages of moral development. They have also suggested that the elaborate "moral dilemmas" he used are too abstract for children. In one story, for example, a husband contemplates stealing medicine for his critically ill wife. When questions are made simpler, or when children and adolescents are observed in natural settings, they often demonstrate sophisticated levels of moral reasoning (Darley and Schultz, 1990; Lapsley, 1990).

Gilligan's View on Gender and Moral Development

Psychologist Carol Gilligan (b. 1936) is one of the major critics of Kohlberg's theory of moral development. According to Gilligan (1982), Kohlberg's model was developed solely on the basis of research with male respondents. She suggested that women and men often have diverging views on morality based on differences in socialization and life experiences. Gilligan believes that men become more concerned with law and order, while women analyze social relationships and the social consequences of behaviour. For example, in Kohlberg's story about a man who is thinking about stealing medicine for his wife, Gilligan argues that male respondents are more likely to use *abstract standards of right and wrong,* whereas female respondents are more likely to be concerned about what *consequences* his stealing the drug might have for the man and his family. Does this constitute a "moral deficiency" on the part of either gender? Not according to Gilligan.

Subsequent research that directly compared women's and men's reasoning about moral dilemmas has supported some of Gilligan's assertions but not others. For example, some other researchers have not found that women are more compassionate than men (Tavris, 1993). Overall, however, Gilligan's argument that people make moral decisions according to both abstract principles of justice and principles of care is an important contribution to our knowledge about moral reasoning.

Although the sociological and psychological perspectives we have examined have often been based on different assumptions and reached somewhat different conclusions, an important theme emerges from these models of cognitive and moral development—through the process of socialization, people learn how to take into account other people's perspectives.

GENDER SOCIALIZATION

gender socialization The aspect of socialization that contains specific messages and practices concerning the nature of being female or male in a specific group or society.

Gender socialization is the aspect of socialization that contains specific messages and practices concerning the nature of being female or male in a specific group or society. Gender socialization is important in determining what we *think* the "preferred" sex of a child should be and in influencing our beliefs about acceptable behaviours for males and females.

In some families, gender socialization starts before birth. Parents who learn the sex of the fetus through ultrasound or amniocentesis often purchase colour-coded and gender-typed clothes, toys, and nursery decorations in anticipation of their daughter's or son's arrival. After birth, parents may respond differently toward male and female infants; they often play more roughly with boys and talk more lovingly to girls. Throughout childhood and adolescence, boys and girls are typically assigned different household chores and given different privileges (such as how late they may stay out at night).

When we look at the relationship between gender socialization and social class, the picture becomes more complex. Although some studies have found less rigid gender stereotyping in higher-income families (Brooks-Gunn, 1986; Seegmiller, Suter, and Duviant, 1980), others have found more (Bardwell, Cochran, and Walker, 1986). One study found that higher-income families are more likely than low-income families to give "male-oriented" toys (which develop visual–spatial and problem-solving skills) to children of both sexes (Serbin et al., 1990). And working-class families tend to adhere to more rigid gender expectations than middle-class families (Brooks-Gunn, 1986; Canter and Ageton, 1984).

Schools, peer groups, and the media also contribute to our gender socialization. From kindergarten through university, teachers and peers reward gender-appropriate attitudes and behaviour. Sports reinforce traditional gender roles through a rigid division of events into male and female categories. The media are also a powerful source of gender socialization; from an early age, children's books, television programs, movies, and music provide subtle and not-so-subtle messages about "masculine" and "feminine" behaviour.

Gender socialization is discussed in more depth in Chapter 11.

LO-6 SOCIALIZATION THROUGH THE LIFE COURSE

anticipatory socialization The process by which knowledge and skills are learned for future roles.

Why is socialization a lifelong process? Throughout our lives, we continue to learn. Each time we experience a change in status (such as becoming a university student or getting married), we learn a new set of rules, roles, and relationships. Even before we achieve a new status, we often participate in **anticipatory socialization**—the process by which knowledge and skills are learned for future roles. Many societies organize social experience according to age. Some have distinct *rites of passage,* based on age or other factors that publicly dramatize and validate changes in a person's status. In Canada and other industrialized societies, the most common categories of age are infancy, childhood, adolescence, and adulthood (often subdivided into young adulthood, middle adulthood, and older adulthood). See the Census Profile, which shows three categories as revised by Statistics Canada for the 2006 Census.

Childhood

Some social scientists believe that a child's sense of self is formed at a very early age and that it is difficult to change this sense later in life. Interactionists emphasize that during infancy and early childhood, family support and guidance are crucial to a child's developing self-concept. In some families, children are provided with emotional warmth, feelings of mutual trust, and a sense of security. These families come closer to our ideal cultural belief that childhood should be a time of carefree play, safety, and freedom from economic, political, and sexual responsibilities. However, other families reflect the discrepancy between cultural ideals and reality—children grow up in a setting characterized by fear, danger, and risks that are created by parental neglect, emotional abuse, or premature economic and sexual demands (Knudsen, 1992). Abused children often experience low self-esteem, an inability to trust others, feelings of isolation and powerlessness, and denial of their feelings.

Adolescence

In industrialized societies, the adolescent (or teenage) years represent a buffer between childhood and adulthood. In Canada, no specific rites of passage exist to mark children's move into adulthood; therefore, young people have to pursue their own routes to self-identity and adulthood. Anticipatory socialization is often associated with adolescence, when many young people spend much of their time planning or being educated for future roles they hope to occupy. However, other adolescents (such as 11- and 12-year-old mothers) may have to plunge into adult responsibilities. Adolescence is often characterized by emotional and social unrest. In the process of developing their own identities, some young people come into conflict with parents, teachers, and other authority figures who attempt to restrict their freedom. Adolescents may also find themselves caught between the demands of adulthood and their own lack of financial independence and experience in the job market. The experiences of individuals during adolescence vary according to their ethnicity, class, and gender Based on their family's economic situation and their own personal choices, some young people leave high school and move directly into the world of work, while others pursue a university education and may continue to receive advice and financial support from their parents. Others are involved in both the world of work and the world of higher education as they seek to support themselves and acquire more years of formal education or vocational/career training.

Adulthood

One of the major differences between child and adult socialization is the degree of freedom of choice. If young adults are able to support themselves financially, they gain the ability to make more choices about their own lives. In early adulthood (usually until about age 40), people work toward their own goals of creating meaningful relationships with others, finding employment, and seeking personal fulfillment. Of course, young adults continue to be socialized by their parents, teachers, peers, and the media, but they also learn new attitudes and behaviours. For example, when we marry or have children, we learn new roles as partners or parents. Adults often learn about fads and fashions in clothing, music, and

CENSUS PROFILE

Age of the Canadian Population

Just as age is a crucial variable in the socialization process, Statistics Canada gathers data about people's age so that the government and other interested parties will know how many individuals residing in this country are in different age categories. This chapter examines how a person's age is related to socialization and life experiences. The table below shows a depiction of the nation's population in the year 2006, separated into three broad age categories (which changed between the 2001 and 2006 censuses).

Age 0–14
17.6%

Age 15–64
68.6%

Age 65 and above
13.7%

Can age be a source of social cohesion among people? Why might age differences produce conflict among individuals in difference age groups? What do you think?

An important rite of passage for many Jewish Canadians is the bar mitzvah or bat mitzvah—a celebration of the adolescent's passage into manhood or womanhood. Can you see how this might be a form of anticipatory socialization?

language from their children. Parents in one study indicated that they had learned new attitudes and behaviours about drug use, sexuality, sports, leisure, and ethnic issues from their university-aged children (Peters, 1985).

Workplace (or occupational) socialization is one of the most important types of adult socialization. Sociologist Wilbert Moore (1968) divided occupational socialization into four phases: (1) career choice, (2) anticipatory socialization (learning different aspects of the occupation before entering it), (3) conditioning and commitment (learning the ups and downs of the occupation and remaining committed to it), and (4) continuous commitment (remaining committed to the work even when problems or other alternatives may arise). This type of socialization tends to be most intense immediately after a person makes the transition from school to the workplace; however, this process continues throughout our years of employment. Nowadays, many people experience continuous workplace socialization as a result of individuals having more than one career (Lefrançois, 1999).

Between the ages of 40 and 60, people enter middle adulthood, and many begin to compare their accomplishments with their earlier expectations. At this point, people either decide that they have reached their goals or recognize that they have attained as much as they are likely to achieve.

In older adulthood, some people are quite happy and content; others are not. Erik Erikson noted that difficult changes in adult attitudes and behaviour occur in the last years of life, when people experience decreased physical ability, lower prestige, and the prospect of death. Older adults in industrialized societies have experienced **social devaluation**, wherein a person or group is considered to have less social value than other individuals or groups. Social devaluation is especially acute when people are leaving roles that have defined their sense of social identity and provided them with meaningful activity (Achenbaum, 1978).

social devaluation A situation in which a person or group is considered to have less social value than other individuals or groups.

It is important to note that not everyone goes through passages or stages of a life course at the same age. Sociologist Alice Rossi (1980) suggests that human experience is much more diverse than life-course models suggest. She also points out that young people growing up today live in a different world, with a different set of opportunities and problems, than did the young people of previous generations (Epstein, 1988). Rossi further suggests that women's and men's experiences are not identical throughout the life course and that the life course of women today is remarkably different from that of their mothers and grandmothers because of changing societal roles and expectations. Life-course patterns are strongly influenced by ethnicity and social class as well.

RESOCIALIZATION

resocialization The process of learning a new and different set of attitudes, values, and behaviours from those in one's previous background and experience.

Resocialization is the process of learning a new and different set of attitudes, values, and behaviours from those in one's previous background and experience. It may be voluntary or involuntary. In either case, people undergo changes that are much more rapid and pervasive than the gradual adaptations that socialization usually involves. For many new parents, the process of resocialization involved in parenting is the most dramatic they will experience in their lifetimes.

Voluntary Resocialization

Resocialization is voluntary when we assume a new status (such as becoming a student, an employee, or a retiree) of our own free will. Sometimes, voluntary resocialization involves medical or psychological treatment or religious conversion, in which case the person's existing attitudes, beliefs, and behaviours must undergo strenuous modification to a new regime and a new way of life. For example, resocialization for adult survivors of emotional or physical child abuse includes extensive therapy to form new patterns of thinking and action, somewhat like Alcoholics Anonymous and its 12-step program that has become the basis for many other programs dealing with addictive behaviour (Parrish, 1990).

Involuntary Resocialization

Involuntary resocialization occurs against a person's wishes and generally takes place within a **total institution**—a place where people are isolated from the rest of society for a set period of time and come under the control of the officials who run the institution (Goffman, 1961a). Military boot camps, jails and prisons, concentration camps, and some mental hospitals are total institutions. In these settings, people are totally stripped of their former selves—or depersonalized—through a *degradation ceremony* (Goffman, 1961a). Inmates entering prison, for example, are required to strip, shower, and wear assigned institutional clothing. In the process, they are searched, weighed, fingerprinted, photographed, and given no privacy even in showers and restrooms. Their official identification becomes not a name but a number. In this abrupt break from their former existence, they must leave behind their personal possessions and their family and friends. The depersonalization process continues as they are required to obey rigid rules and to conform to their new environment.

total institution
Erving Goffman's term for a place where people are isolated from the rest of society for a set period of time and come under the control of the officials who run the institution.

After stripping people of their former identities, the institution attempts to build a more compliant person. A system of rewards and punishments (such as providing or withholding cigarettes and television or exercise privileges) encourages conformity to institutional norms. Some individuals may be rehabilitated; others become angry and hostile toward the system that has taken away their freedom. Although the assumed purpose of involuntary resocialization is to reform persons so that they will conform to societal standards of conduct after their release, the ability of total institutions to modify offenders' behaviour in a meaningful way has been widely questioned. In many prisons, for example, inmates may conform to the norms of the prison or of other inmates, but little relationship exists between those norms and the laws of society.

CONCEPT SNAPSHOT

SYMBOLIC INTERACTIONIST PERSPECTIVES **Key thinkers:** Charles Horton Cooley, George Herbert Mead, William A. Corsaro	According to Cooley, our sense of self is based on how others perceive and treat us. Mead extended Cooley's insights by linking the idea of self concept to role-playing. According to Mead, our self-concept is developed through role-playing and learning the rules of social interaction through others. More recently, Corsaro developed the "orb web model," arguing that children's socialization reflects not only knowledge from the adult world but also the unique interpretations of children's peer culture.
SOCIAL PSYCHOLOGICAL PERSPECTIVES **Key thinkers:** Sigmund Freud	According to Freud, the founder of psychoanalytic theory, the self is comprised of three interrelated components: id, ego, and superego. When a person is well adjusted, the three forces are in balance.
COGNITIVE MORAL PERSPECTIVES **Key thinkers:** Jean Piaget, Lawrence Kohlberg, Carol Gilligan	According to Swiss psychologist Jean Piaget, from birth through adolescence, children move through four states of cognitive development, which are organized around acquisition and mastery of specific tasks. Kohlberg classified moral development into six stages. Certain levels of cognitive development must occur before moral reasoning can develop. Gilligan critiqued Kohlberg's research as male-centred and suggested that men and women have different views on morality based on differences in socialization.

4 VISUAL SUMMARY

LO-1 Discuss the purpose of socialization.

© Walter Hodges/Corbis

Socialization is the lifelong process through which individuals acquire their self-identity and learn the physical, mental, and social skills needed for survival in society. The kind of person each of us becomes depends greatly on what we learn during our formative years from our surrounding social groups and social environment.

© Rubberball Productions/Index Stock Imagery

LO-3 Discuss the degree to which our unique physical and human characteristics are based on heredity and to what degree they are based on our social environment.

As individual human beings, we have unique identities, personalities, and relationships with others. Individuals are born with some of their unique physical and human characteristics; other characteristics and traits are gained during the socialization process. Each of us is a product of two forces: (1) heredity, referred to as "nature," and (2) the social environment, referred to as "nurture." While biology dictates our physical makeup, the social environment largely determines how we develop and behave.

LO-3 Identify the key agents of socialization.

© Gaetano/Corbis

The people, groups, and institutions that teach us what we need to know to participate in society are called agents of socialization. The agents include the family, schools, peer groups, the media, and the workplace. Families, which transmit cultural and social values to us, are the most important agents of socialization in all societies and have these roles: (1) procreating and socializing children, (2) providing emotional support, and (3) assigning social position. Schools are another key agent of socialization; they not only teach knowledge and skills but also deeply influence the self-image, beliefs, and values of children. Peer groups contribute to our sense of belonging and self-worth; they teach and reinforce cultural norms and are a key source of information about acceptable behaviour. The media function as socializing agents by (1) informing us about world events, (2) introducing us to a wide variety of people, and (3) providing an opportunity to live vicariously through other people's experiences.

KEY TERMS

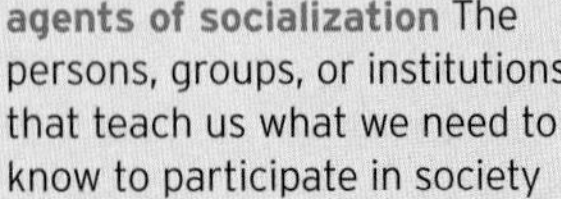

agents of socialization The persons, groups, or institutions that teach us what we need to know to participate in society (p. 96).

anticipatory socialization The process by which knowledge and skills are learned for future roles (p. 108).

ego According to Sigmund Freud, the rational, reality-oriented component of personality that imposes restrictions on the innate pleasure-seeking drives of the id (p. 105).

gender socialization The aspect of socialization that contains specific messages and practices concerning the nature of being female or male in a specific group or society (p. 108).

generalized other George Herbert Mead's term for the child's awareness of the demands and expectations of the society as a whole or of the child's subculture (p. 103).

id Sigmund Freud's term for the component of personality that includes all of the individual's basic biological drives and needs that demand immediate gratification (p. 105).

looking-glass self Charles Horton Cooley's term for the way in which a person's sense of self is derived from the perceptions of others (p. 102).

peer group A group of people who are linked by common interests, equal social position, and (usually) similar age (p. 98).

LO-4 Describe how sociologists explain our development of a self-concept.

© muzsy/Shutterstock

Charles Horton Cooley developed the image of the looking-glass self to explain how people see themselves through the perceptions of others. Our initial sense of self is typically based on how families perceive and treat us. George Herbert Mead linked the idea of self-concept to role-playing and to learning the rules of social interaction. According to Mead, the self is divided into the "I" and the "me." The "I" represents the spontaneous and unique traits of each person. The "me" represents the internalized attitudes and demands of other members of society.

LO-5 Review the main social psychological theories on human development.

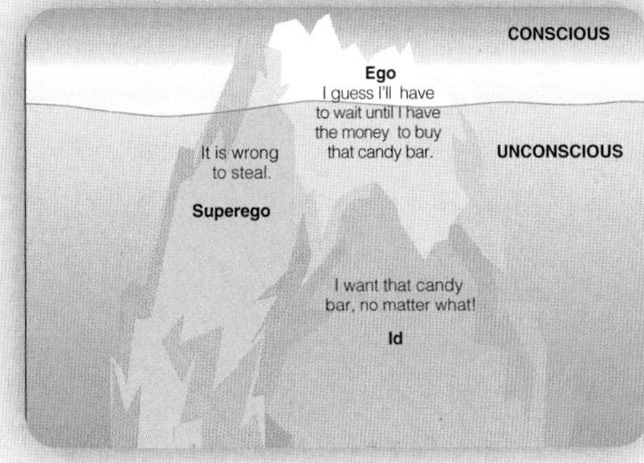

According to Sigmund Freud, the self emerges from three interrelated forces: id, ego, and superego. When a person is well adjusted, the three forces act in balance. Jean Piaget identified four cognitive stages of development; at each stage, children's activities are governed by how they understand the world around them. Lawrence Kohlberg classified moral development into six stages; certain levels of cognitive development are essential before corresponding levels of moral reasoning may occur. Carol Gilligan suggested that there are male–female differences regarding morality and identified three stages in female moral development.

© PhotoStock-Israel/Alamy

LO-6 Describe socialization throughout various stages in the life course.

Socialization is ongoing throughout the life course. We learn knowledge and skills for future roles through anticipatory socialization. Parents are socialized by their own children, and adults learn through workplace socialization. Resocialization is the process of learning new attitudes, values, and behaviours, either voluntarily or involuntarily.

resocialization The process of learning a new and different set of attitudes, values, and behaviours from those in one's previous background and experience (p. 110).

role-taking The process by which a person mentally assumes the role of another person in order to understand the world from that person's point of view (p. 103).

self-concept The totality of our beliefs and feelings about ourselves (p. 101).

significant others Those persons whose care, affection, and approval are especially desired and who are most important in the development of the self (p. 103).

social devaluation A situation in which a person or group is considered to have less social value than other individuals or groups (p. 110).

socialization The lifelong process of social interaction through which individuals acquire a self-identity and the physical, mental, and social skills needed for survival in society (p. 93).

sociobiology The systematic study of how biology affects social behaviour (p. 94).

superego Sigmund Freud's term for the human conscience, consisting of the moral and ethical aspects of personality (p. 105).

total institution Erving Goffman's term for a place where people are isolated from the rest of society for a set period of time and come under the control of the officials who run the institution (p. 111).

APPLICATION QUESTIONS

1. Consider the concept of the looking-glass self. How do you think others perceive you? Do you think most people perceive you correctly? Why or why not?
2. What are your "I" traits? What are your "me" traits? Which ones are stronger?
3. Is the attempted rehabilitation of a criminal offender—through boot camp programs, for example—a form of socialization or resocialization? Explain.
4. How might functionalist, conflict, symbolic interactionist, and postmodernist analysts view the role of television and computers in childhood socialization? What influence do you think television and computers have on your own socialization?

KEY FIGURES

Sigmund Freud (1856–1939) As the founder of psychoanalytic theory, Freud posited that the personality is comprised of the id, ego, and superego. Although subject to harsh criticism, Freud's analysis drew attention to the importance of early childhood experiences in healthy socialization.

© Pictorial Press Ltd/Alamy

George Herbert Mead (1863–1931) Mead divided the self into the "I" (the subjective component of the self) and the "me" (the objective element of the self). According to Mead, the "I" develops first and the "me" develops during three stages.

© DENNIS BRACK/Landov

Charles Horton Cooley (1864–1929) According to Cooley, how we see ourselves is based on how we think others see us. He referred to this as our looking-glass self.

© American Sociological Association

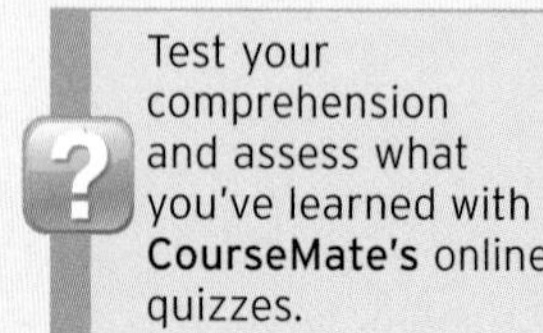

Test your comprehension and assess what you've learned with **CourseMate's** online quizzes.

For other interesting Lived Experiences, watch the video clips on **CourseMate.**

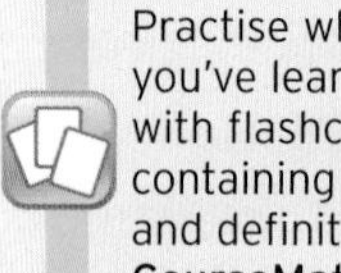

Practise what you've learned with flashcards containing key terms and definitions on **CourseMate.**

CHAPTER

5 Society, Social Structure, and Interaction

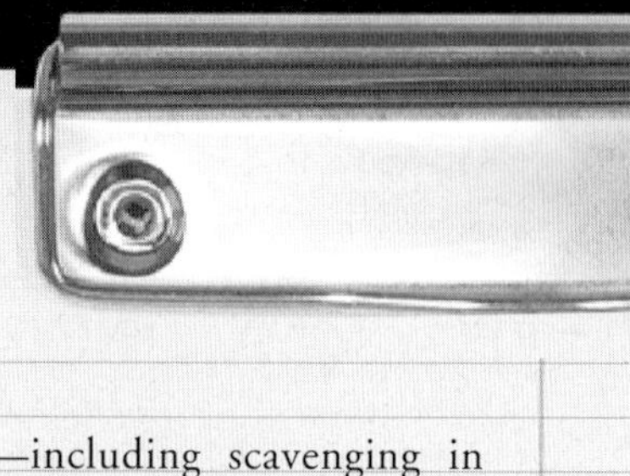

All activities in life—including scavenging in garbage bins and living "on the streets"—are social in nature. Here, Lars Eighner recalls his experiences as a Dumpster diver while he was living under a shower curtain in a stand of bamboo in a public park. Eighner became homeless when he was evicted from his "shack" after being unemployed for about a year.

> *I began Dumpster diving [scavenging in a large garbage bin] about a year before I became homeless . . . The area I frequent is inhabited by many affluent college students. I am not here by chance; the Dumpsters in this area are very rich. Students throw out many good things, including food. In particular they tend to throw everything out when they move at the end of a semester, before and after breaks, and around midterm, when many of them despair of college. So I find it advantageous to keep an eye on the academic calendar. I learned to scavenge gradually, on my own. Since then I have initiated several companions into the trade. I have learned that there is a predictable series of stages a person goes through in learning to scavenge. At first the new scavenger is filled with disgust and self-loathing. He is ashamed of being seen and may lurk around, trying to duck behind things, or he may dive at night . . . That stage passes with experience. The scavenger finds a pair of running shoes that fit and look and smell brand-new . . . He begins to understand: People throw away perfectly good stuff, a lot of perfectly good stuff. At this stage, Dumpster shyness begins to dissipate. The diver, after all, has the last laugh. He is finding all manner of good things that are his for the taking. Those who disparage his profession are the fools, not he.* (1993: 111–119)

© Bob Collins/The Image Works

All activities in life—including panhandling and living on the streets—are social. What types of interaction are normalized or made unusual and why?

Eighner's "diving" activities reflect a specific pattern of social behaviour. Homeless persons and domiciled persons (those with homes) live in social worlds that have predictable patterns of social interaction. **Social interaction** is the process by which people act toward or respond to other people and is the foundation for all relationships and groups in society. In this chapter, we will look at the relationship between social structure and social interaction. Homelessness is used as an example of how social problems occur and may be perpetuated within social structures and patterns of interaction.

Social structure is the stable pattern of social relationships that exist within a particular group or society. This structure is essential for the survival of society and for the well-being of individuals because it provides a social web of familial support and social relationships that connects each of us to the larger society. Many homeless people have lost this vital linkage. As a result, they often experience a loss of personal dignity and sense of moral worth because of their "homeless" condition (Neal, 2004). Although there have always been homeless people, there has been a significant increase in the number of Canadians without homes. The homeless category now includes people who have never before had to depend on social assistance for food, clothing, and a roof over their head. Before reading on, take the quiz on homelessness in Box 5.1 on page 119.

Critical Thinking Questions

1. Sociologists suggest that all activities are social in nature. Do you agree?
2. Identify predictable patterns of social interaction with a homeless person. How do you interact with a homeless person you may encounter in your day-to-day life?
3. It was suggested above that homeless persons may not have stable familial and social relationships that are vital to well-being. What are the stable familial and social relationships in your life?

CHAPTER FOCUS QUESTION How is homelessness related to the social structure of a society?

LEARNING OBJECTIVES

AFTER READING THIS CHAPTER, YOU SHOULD BE ABLE TO

- **LO-1** Identify the key components of social structure.
- **LO-2** Compare and contrast functionalist and conflict perspectives on social institutions.
- **LO-3** Explain how societies maintain stability in times of social change.
- **LO-4** Define and distinguish between *Gemeinschaft* and *Gesellschaft* societies.
- **LO-5** Understand Erving Goffman's dramaturgical perspective and the concepts of impression management, and front stage/back stage behaviours.

SOCIAL STRUCTURE: THE MACROLEVEL PERSPECTIVE

social interaction The process by which people act toward or respond to other people.

social structure The stable pattern of social relationships that exist within a particular group or society.

social marginality The state of being part insider and part outsider in the social structure.

Why do we need to know about social structure? Social structure provides the framework within which we interact with others. This framework is an orderly, fixed arrangement of parts that together comprise the whole group or society (see Figure 5.1). As defined in Chapter 1, a *society* is a large social grouping that shares the same geographical territory and is subject to the same political authority and dominant cultural expectations. At the macrolevel, the social structure of a society has several essential elements: social institutions, groups, statuses, roles, and norms.

Do social scientists agree about how social structure operates? No. Diverse theoretical approaches have different interpretations of how structure operates. For example, functional theorists emphasize that social structure creates order and predictability in a society (Parsons, 1951). Social structure is also important for human development: You and I develop a self-concept as each of us learns the attitudes, values, and behaviours of the people around us. When these attitudes and values are part of a predictable structure, it is easier for us to develop a positive self-concept.

By contrast, conflict theorists maintain that social structure helps determine social relations in a society and may be the source of inequality and injustice. For example, Karl Marx suggested that how economic production is organized is the most important structural aspect of society. In capitalistic societies, few people control the labour of many and the social structure helps create a system of domination and subordination that affects certain categories of people, including owners and workers, landlords and tenants, and rich celebrities and poor "nobodies."

Whether we look at social structure through the lens of functionalist or conflict theories, this structure creates boundaries that define persons and groups as "insiders," "outsiders," or "marginals." **Social marginality** is the state of being part insider and part outsider in the social

FIGURE 5.1 SOCIAL STRUCTURE FRAMEWORK

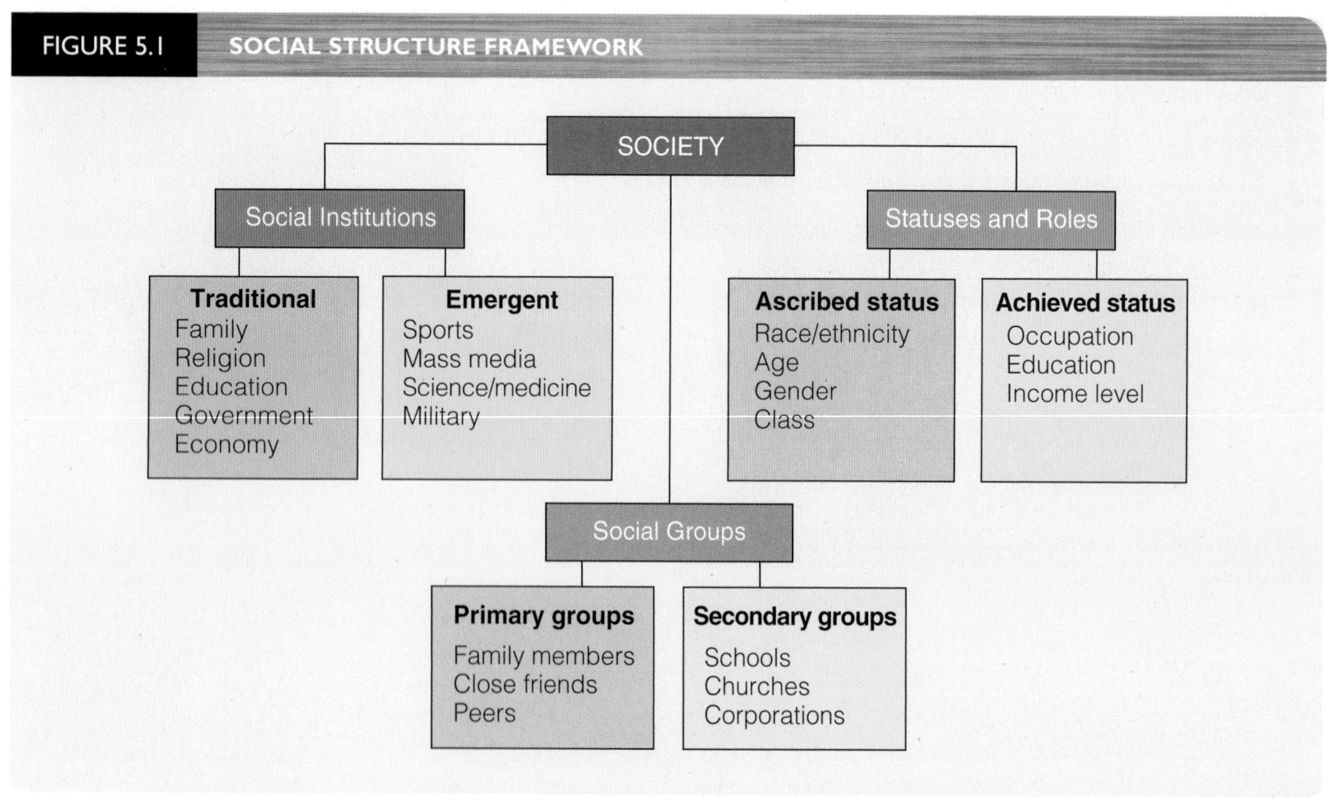

BOX 5.1 SOCIOLOGY AND EVERYDAY LIFE

How Much Do You Know About Homelessness?

True	False	
T	F	1. Most homeless people choose to be homeless.
T	F	2. The number of homeless persons in Canada has gradually declined over the past 30 years.
T	F	3. Most homeless people are mentally ill.
T	F	4. The number of homeless adolescents has increased in the past decade.
T	F	5. One out of every four homeless people is a child.

For answers to the quiz about homelessness, go to **www.nelson.com/sociologyinourtimes6e.**

structure. Sociologist Robert Park (1928) coined this term to refer to persons (such as immigrants) who simultaneously share the life and traditions of two distinct groups. Social marginality is an important concern for people because it often results in stigmatization. A **stigma** is any physical or social attribute or sign that so devalues a person's social identity that it disqualifies that person from full social acceptance (Goffman, 1963b). A convicted criminal wearing a prison uniform is an example of a person who has been stigmatized; the uniform says that the person has done something wrong and should not be allowed unsupervised outside the prison walls. The stigmatization of homelessness is discussed later in this chapter.

stigma According to Erving Goffman, any physical or social attribute or sign that so devalues a person's social identity that it disqualifies that person from full social acceptance.

Why is social structure important to you? Social structure gives us the ability to interpret the social situations we encounter. For example, we expect our families to care for us, our schools to educate us, and our police to protect us. When our circumstances change dramatically, most of us feel an acute sense of anxiety because we do not know what to expect or what is expected of us. Consider, for instance, why newly homeless individuals may feel disoriented when they do not know how to function in their new situation. These persons are likely to ask questions such as "How will I survive on the streets?" "Where do I go to get help?" "Should I stay at a shelter?" and "Where can I get a job?" Social structure helps people make sense out of their social setting even when they find themselves on the streets.

COMPONENTS OF SOCIAL STRUCTURE LO-1

What is included in the social structure of a society? The social structure of a society includes its social positions, the relationships among those positions, and the kinds of resources attached to each of the positions. Social structure also includes all of the groups that make up society and the relationships among those groups (Smelser, 1988). Let's start our study of the components of social structure by examining the social positions that are closest to us—the individual.

Status

status A socially defined position in a group or society characterized by certain expectations, rights, and duties.

No doubt you have heard the word *status* for many years. Sometimes we describe a person as "high status" or "low status," but sociologically speaking, what does the term really mean? A **status** is a socially defined position in a group or society characterized by certain expectations, rights, and duties. Statuses exist independently of the specific people occupying them (Linton, 1936); the statuses of professional athlete, rock musician, professor, university student, and homeless person all exist exclusive of the specific individuals who occupy these social positions. For example, although thousands of new students arrive on university campuses each year to occupy the status of first-year student, the status of university student and the expectations attached to that position have remained relatively unchanged.

As we previously mentioned, the term *status* does *not* refer to high-level positions only. Sociologists use it to refer to all socially defined positions—high rank and low rank. For example, both the position of director of Health Canada in Ottawa and that of a homeless person who is paid about five dollars a week (plus bed and board) to clean up the dining room at a homeless shelter are social statuses.

status set A term used to describe all the statuses that a person occupies at a given time.

Take a moment to answer this question: Who am I? To determine who you are, you must think about your social identity, which is derived from the statuses you occupy and is based on your status set. A **status set** is made up of all the statuses that a person occupies at a given time. For example, Marie may be a psychologist, a professor, a wife, a mother, a Roman Catholic, a school volunteer, an Alberta resident, and a French Canadian. All of these socially defined positions constitute her status set.

ascribed status A social position conferred on a person at birth or received involuntarily later in life.

achieved status A social position a person assumes voluntarily as a result of personal choice, merit, or direct effort.

ASCRIBED AND ACHIEVED STATUS Statuses are distinguished by the manner in which we acquire them. An **ascribed status** is a social position conferred on a person at birth or received involuntarily later in life, based on attributes over which the individual has little or no control, such as ethnicity, age, and gender. Marie, for example, is a female born to French Canadian parents; she was assigned these statuses at birth. An **achieved status** is a social position a person assumes voluntarily as a result of personal choice, merit, or direct effort. Achieved statuses (such as occupation, education, and income) are thought to be gained as a result of personal ability or successful competition. Most occupational positions in modern societies are achieved statuses. For instance, Marie voluntarily assumed the statuses of psychologist, professor, wife, mother, and school volunteer. However, not all achieved statuses are positions most people would want to attain: Being a criminal, a drug addict, or a homeless person, for example, is a negative achieved status.

Ascribed statuses have a significant influence on the achieved statuses we occupy. Ethnicity, gender, and age affect each person's opportunity to acquire certain achieved statuses. Those who are privileged by their positive ascribed statuses are more likely to achieve the more prestigious positions in a society. Those who are disadvantaged by their ascribed statuses may more easily acquire negative achieved statuses.

master status A term used to describe the most important status a person occupies.

MASTER STATUS If we occupy many different statuses, how can we determine which is the most important? Sociologist Everett Hughes has stated that societies resolve this ambiguity by determining master statuses. A **master status** is the most important status a person occupies; it dominates all the individual's other statuses and is the overriding ingredient in determining a person's general social position (Hughes, 1945). Being poor or rich is a master status that influences many other areas of life, including health, education, and life opportunities. Historically, the most common master statuses for women have related to positions in the family, such as daughter, wife, and mother. For men, occupation has usually been the most important status, although occupation is increasingly a master status for many women as well. "What do you do?" is one of the first questions many people ask when first meeting someone. Occupation provides important clues to a person's educational level, income, and family background. An individual's ethnicity may also constitute a master status in a society in which dominant group members single out members of other groups as "inferior" on the basis of real or alleged physical, cultural, or nationality characteristics (see Feagin and Feagin, 2003).

Master statuses confer high or low levels of personal worth and dignity on people. These are not characteristics that we inherently possess; they are derived from the statuses we occupy. For someone who has no residence, being a homeless person readily becomes a master status regardless of the person's other attributes. Homelessness is a stigmatized master status; it confers disrepute on its occupant because domiciled people often believe a homeless person has a "character flaw." The circumstances under which someone becomes homeless determine the extent to which that person is stigmatized.

© JOHN PAUL FILO/CBS/Landov

In the past, a person's status was primarily linked to his or her family background, education, occupation, and other sociological attributes. Today, some sociologists suggest that celebrity status has overtaken the more traditional status indicators.

STATUS SYMBOLS When people are proud of a particular social status they occupy, they often choose to use visible means to let others know about their position. A **status symbol** is a material sign that informs others of a person's specific status. For example, just as wearing a wedding ring proclaims that a person is married, owning a Rolls-Royce announces that one has "made it." In North American society, people who have "made it" frequently want symbols to inform others of their accomplishments.

Status symbols for the domiciled and the homeless may have different meanings. Among affluent persons, a full shopping cart in the grocery store and bags of merchandise from expensive department stores indicate a lofty financial position. By contrast, among the homeless, bulging shopping bags and overloaded grocery carts suggest a completely different status.

status symbol A material sign that informs others of a person's specific status.

TIME TO REVIEW

- Define ascribed status, achieved status, and master status.
- Is being unemployed an ascribed or achieved status?
- When does unemployment become a master status?

Roles

A role is the dynamic aspect of a status. Whereas we *occupy* a status, we *play* a role (Linton, 1936). A **role** is a set of behavioural expectations associated with a given status. For example, a carpenter (employee) hired to remodel a kitchen is not expected to sit down uninvited and join the family (employer) for dinner.

role A set of behavioural expectations associated with a given status.

Role expectation is a group's or society's definition of the way a specific role ought to be played. By contrast, **role performance** is how a person plays the role. Role performance does not always match role expectation. Some statuses have role expectations that are highly specific, such as that of surgeon or university professor. Other statuses, such as friend or significant other, have less structured expectations. The role expectations tied to the status of student are

role expectation A group's or society's definition of the way a specific role ought to be played.

role performance How a person plays a role.

role conflict A situation in which incompatible role demands are placed on a person by two or more statuses held at the same time.

role strain The strain experienced by a person when incompatible demands are built into a single status that the person occupies.

more specific than those for being a friend. Role expectations are typically based on a range of acceptable behaviour rather than on strictly defined standards.

Our roles are relational (or complementary); that is, they are defined in the context of roles performed by others. We can play the role of student because someone else fulfills the role of professor. Conversely, to perform the role of professor, the teacher must have one or more students.

Role ambiguity occurs when the expectations associated with a role are unclear. For example, it is not always clear when the provider–dependant aspect of the parent–child relationship ends. Should it end at age 18 or 21? When a person is no longer in school? Different people will answer these questions differently depending on their experiences and socialization, as well as on the parents' financial capability and willingness to continue contributing to the welfare of their adult children.

ROLE CONFLICT AND ROLE STRAIN Most people occupy a number of statuses, each of which has numerous role expectations attached. For example, Charles is a student who attends morning classes at the university and he is an employee at a fast-food restaurant where he works from 3 p.m. to 10 p.m. He is also Stephanie's boyfriend, and she would like to see him more often. On December 7, Charles has a final exam at 7 p.m., when he is supposed to be working. Meanwhile, Stephanie is pressuring him to take her to a movie. To top it off, his mother calls, asking him to fly home because his father is going to have emergency surgery. How can Charles be in all of these places at once? Such experiences of role conflict can be overwhelming.

© Jiang Jin/SuperStock

Parents often experience role conflict when they are trying to balance making a living and having a successful career with fulfilling their role as a good parent.

Role conflict occurs when incompatible role demands are placed on a person by two or more statuses held at the same time. When role conflict occurs, we may feel pulled in different directions. To deal with this problem, we may prioritize our roles and first complete the one we consider to be most important. Or we may compartmentalize our lives and "insulate" our various roles (Merton, 1968); that is, we may perform the activities linked to one role for part of the day and then engage in the activities associated with another role in some other time period or elsewhere. For example, under routine circumstances, Charles would fulfill his student role for part of the day and his employee role for another part of the day. In his current situation, however, he is unable to compartmentalize his roles.

What are the competing demands of working parents in contemporary societies? What sociological term best describes this situation?

Whereas role conflict occurs between two or more statuses (such as being homeless and being a temporary employee of a social services agency), role strain takes place within one status. **Role strain** occurs when incompatible demands are built into a single status that a person occupies (Goode, 1960). For example, parents may experience role strain because of the demands of managing their time, unclear expectations, unequal division of unpaid work in the home, and lack of emotional support from the other parent. The concepts of role expectation, role performance, role conflict, and role strain are illustrated in Figure 5.2.

FIGURE 5.2 ROLE EXPECTATION, PERFORMANCE, CONFLICT, AND STRAIN

The Role of "Student"

Oh, yes, Professor Bright. I know the answer, which is...

SUPER U

Role Expectation: a group's or society's definition of the way a specific role *ought* to be played.

Do I need to know that concept in order to pass this course?

NORMAL U

Role Performance: how a person does play a role.

I appreciate you letting me have Thursday off from work so I can study for my sociology exam!

SAM'S FAST FOOD

Role Conflict: what occurs when incompatible demands are put on a person by two or more statuses held at the same time.

Being a student is a lot more stressful than I thought it would be!

GRUMBLING U

Role Strain: what occurs when incompatible demands are built into a single status that the person holds.

When playing the role of "student," do you sometimes personally encounter these concepts?

Individuals frequently distance themselves from a role they find extremely stressful or otherwise problematic. *Role distancing* occurs when people consciously foster the impression of a lack of commitment or attachment to a particular role and merely go through the motions of role performance (Goffman, 1961b). People use distancing techniques when they do not want others to take them as the "self" implied in a particular role, especially if they think the role is "beneath them." While Charles is working in the fast-food restaurant, for example, he does not want people to think of him as a "loser in a dead-end job." He wants them to view him as a university student who is working there just to "pick up a few bucks" until he graduates. When customers from the university come in, Charles talks to them about what courses they are taking, what they are majoring in, and what professors they have. He does not discuss whether the bacon cheeseburger is better than the chili burger. When Charles is really involved in role distancing, he tells his friends that he "works there but wouldn't eat there." Role distancing is most likely to occur when people find themselves in roles in which the social identities implied are inconsistent with how they think of themselves or how they want to be viewed by others.

role exit A situation in which people disengage from social roles that have been central to their self-identity.

ROLE EXIT **Role exit** occurs when people disengage from social roles that have been central to their self-identity (Ebaugh, 1988). Sociologist Helen Rose Fuchs Ebaugh studied this

© REUTERS/Mario Anzuoni

Los Angeles Times columnist Steve Lopez met a homeless man, Nathaniel Ayers (above), and learned that he had been a promising musician studying at the Juilliard School who had dropped out because of his struggle with mental illness. In his 2008 book, *The Soloist*, Lopez chronicles the relationship that he developed with Ayers and how he eventually helped get Ayers off the street and treated for his schizophrenia. This story is an example of role exit, and you can see it in the movie version of *The Soloist*, released in 2009.

process by interviewing ex-convicts, ex-nuns, retirees, divorced men and women, and others who had exited voluntarily from significant social roles. According to Ebaugh, role exit occurs in four stages. The first stage is doubt, in which people experience frustration or burnout when they reflect on their existing roles. The second stage involves a search for alternatives; here, people may take a leave of absence from their work or temporarily separate from their marriage partner. The third stage is the turning point at which people realize that they must take some final action, such as quitting their job or getting a divorce. The fourth and final stage involves the creation of a new identity.

Exiting the "homeless" role is often very difficult. The longer a person remains on the streets, the more difficult it becomes to exit this role. Personal resources diminish over time. Personal possessions are often stolen, lost, sold, or pawned. Work experience and skills become outdated, and physical disabilities that prevent individuals from working are likely to develop on the streets. As 21-year-old Chris describes, breaking the ties with their street families and communities was often the most challenging aspect to their role exit:

> I found my biggest one [obstacle] was leaving the crowd that I was with, like my friends, the situation with my friends, 'cause they are all like, "No, don't go, stay down here and hang with us, go do that," and that was probably my biggest crutch, was getting away from my friends because I'd been friends with them my whole life and for me to just push them away and say, "No, I'm getting away from this, I'm getting out of this." It was a big step for me (Karabanow, 2008:783).

social group A group that consists of two or more people who interact frequently and share a common identity and a feeling of interdependence.

primary group A small, less specialized group in which members engage in face-to-face, emotion-based interactions over an extended time.

secondary group A larger, more specialized group in which the members engage in more impersonal, goal-oriented relationships for a limited time.

Groups

Groups are another important component of social structure. To sociologists, a **social group** consists of two or more people who interact frequently and share a common identity and a feeling of interdependence. Throughout our lives, most of us participate in groups, from our families and childhood friends, to our university classes, to our work and community organizations, and even to society.

Primary and secondary groups are the two basic types of social groups. A **primary group** is a small, less specialized group in which members engage in face-to-face, emotion-based interactions over an extended time. Typically, primary groups include our family, close friends, and school- or work-related peer groups. By contrast, a **secondary group** is a larger, more specialized group in which members engage in more impersonal, goal-oriented relationships for a limited time. Schools, churches, and corporations are examples of secondary groups. In secondary groups, people have few, if any, emotional ties to one another. Instead, they come together for some specific, practical purpose, such as getting a degree or a paycheque. Secondary groups are more specialized than primary ones; individuals relate to one another in terms of specific roles (such as professor and student) and more limited activities (such as course-related endeavours).

As discussed in Chapter 1, *social solidarity,* or cohesion, relates to a group's ability to maintain itself in the face of obstacles. Social solidarity exists when social bonds, attractions, or other forces hold members of a group in interaction over a period of time (Jary and Jary, 1991). For example, if a local church is destroyed by fire and congregation members still worship together in a makeshift setting, then they have a high degree of social solidarity.

© Bob Daemmrich/PhotoEdit

For many years, capitalism has been dominated by powerful "old-boy" social networks.

Many of us build social networks from our personal friends in primary groups and our acquaintances in secondary groups. A **social network** is a series of social relationships that link an individual to others. Social networks work differently for men and women, for different ethnic groups, and for members of different social classes. Research on homeless youth in Toronto and Vancouver revealed that informal social networks that the youth described as "street families" tended to form around issues of survival and support (Hagan and McCarthy, 1998). Individuals within these groups often assumed specialized roles that were defined in family terms, including references to street brothers and sisters, and even fathers and mothers.

social network A series of social relationships that link an individual to others.

A **formal organization** is a highly structured group formed for the purpose of completing certain tasks or achieving specific goals. Many of us spend most of our time in formal organizations, such as universities, corporations, or the government. Chapter 6 ("Groups and Organizations") analyzes the characteristics of bureaucratic organizations; however, at this point, we should note that these organizations are an important component of social structure in all industrialized societies. We expect such organizations to educate us, solve our social problems (such as crime and homelessness), and provide work opportunities.

formal organization A highly structured group formed for the purpose of completing certain tasks or achieving specific goals.

LO-2 Social Institutions

At the macrolevel of all societies, certain basic activities routinely occur—children are born and socialized, goods and services are produced and distributed, order is preserved, and a sense of purpose is maintained (Aberle et al., 1950; Mack and Bradford, 1979). Social institutions are the means by which these basic needs are met. A **social institution** is a set of organized beliefs and rules that establish how a society will strive to meet its basic social needs. In the past, these needs have centred around five basic social institutions: the family, religion, education, the economy, and the government or politics. Today, mass media, sports, science and medicine, and the military are also considered social institutions.

social institution A set of organized beliefs and rules that establish how a society will attempt to meet its basic social needs.

What is the difference between a group and a social institution? A group is composed of specific, identifiable people; an institution is a standardized way of doing something. The concept of family helps distinguish between the two. When we talk about your family or my family, we are referring to a specific family. When we refer to the family as a social institution, we are talking about ideologies and standardized patterns of behaviour that organize family life. For example, the family as a social institution contains certain statuses organized into well-defined relationships, such as husband–wife, parent–child, brother–sister, and so forth. Specific families do not always conform to these ideologies and behaviour patterns.

Functional theorists emphasize that social institutions exist because they perform five essential tasks:

1. *Replacing members.* Societies and groups must have socially approved ways of replacing members who move away or die.
2. *Teaching new members.* People who are born into a society or move into it must learn the group's values and customs.
3. *Producing, distributing, and consuming goods and services.* All societies must provide and distribute goods and services for their members
4. *Preserving order.* Every group or society must preserve order within its boundaries and protect itself from attack by outsiders.
5. *Providing and maintaining a sense of purpose.* To motivate people to cooperate with one another, a sense of purpose is needed.

Although this list of functional prerequisites is shared by all societies, the institutions in each society perform these tasks in somewhat different ways depending on their specific cultural values and norms.

Conflict theorists agree with functionalists that social institutions are originally organized to meet basic social needs; however, they do not agree that social institutions work for the common good of everyone in society. For example, the homeless lack the power and resources to promote their own interests when they are opposed by dominant social groups. This problem for homeless people, especially children and youth, exists not only in Canada, but throughout the world (see Box 5.2 on page 128). From the conflict perspective, social institutions, such as the government, maintain the privileges of the wealthy and powerful while contributing to the powerlessness of others (see Domhoff, 2002).

LO-3 STABILITY AND CHANGE IN SOCIETIES

Changes in social structure have a dramatic impact on individuals, groups, and societies. Social arrangements in contemporary societies have grown more complex with the introduction of new technology, changes in values and norms, and the rapidly shrinking "global village." How do societies maintain some degree of social solidarity in the face of such changes? Sociologists Émile Durkheim and Ferdinand Tönnies developed typologies to explain the processes of stability and change in the social structure of societies. A *typology* is a classification scheme containing two or more mutually exclusive categories that are used to compare different kinds of behaviour or types of societies.

Durkheim: Mechanical and Organic Solidarity

Émile Durkheim (1933/1893) was concerned with this question: How do societies manage to hold together? Durkheim asserted that preindustrial societies were held together by strong traditions and by the members' shared moral beliefs and values. As societies industrialized and developed more specialized economic activities, social solidarity came to be rooted in the members' shared dependence on one another. From Durkheim's perspective, social solidarity derives from a society's social structure, which, in turn, is based on the society's division of labour. *Division of labour* refers to how the various tasks of a society are divided up and performed.

People in diverse societies (or in the same society at different points in time) divide their tasks somewhat differently, however, based on their own history, physical environment, and level of technological development.

To explain social change, Durkheim developed a typology that categorized societies as having either mechanical or organic solidarity. **Mechanical solidarity** refers to the social cohesion in preindustrial societies, in which there is minimal division of labour and people feel united by shared values and common social bonds. Durkheim used the term *mechanical solidarity* because he believed that people in such preindustrial societies feel a more or less automatic sense of belonging. Social interaction is characterized by face-to-face, intimate, primary-group relationships. Everyone is engaged in similar work, and little specialization is found in the division of labour.

mechanical solidarity Émile Durkheim's term for the social cohesion that exists in preindustrial societies, in which there is a minimal division of labour and people feel united by shared values and common social bonds.

Organic solidarity refers to the social cohesion found in industrial (and perhaps postindustrial) societies, in which people perform specialized tasks and feel united by their mutual dependence. Durkheim chose the term *organic solidarity* because he believed that individuals in industrial societies come to rely on one another in much the same way that the organs of the human body function interdependently. Social interaction is less personal, more status-oriented, and more focused on specific goals and objectives. People no longer rely on morality or shared values for social solidarity; instead, they are bound together by practical considerations.

organic solidarity Émile Durkheim's term for the social cohesion that exists in industrial (and perhaps postindustrial) societies, in which people perform specialized tasks and feel united by their mutual dependence.

LO-4 Tönnies: *Gemeinschaft* and *Gesellschaft*

Sociologist Ferdinand Tönnies (1855–1936) used the terms *Gemeinschaft* and *Gesellschaft* to characterize the degree of social solidarity and social control found in societies. He was especially concerned about what happens to social solidarity in a society when a "loss of community" occurs.

The ***Gemeinschaft* (guh-MINE-shoft)** is a traditional society in which social relationships are based on personal bonds of friendship and kinship and on intergenerational stability. These relationships are based on ascribed rather than achieved status. In such societies, people have a commitment to the entire group and feel a sense of togetherness. Tönnies used the German term *Gemeinschaft* because it means commune or community; social solidarity and social control are maintained by the community. Members have a strong sense of belonging, but they also have limited privacy.

***Gemeinschaft* (guh-MINE-shoft)** A traditional society in which social relationships are based on personal bonds of friendship and kinship and on intergenerational stability.

By contrast, the ***Gesellschaft* (guh-ZELL-shoft)** is a large, urban society in which social bonds are based on impersonal and specialized relationships, with little long-term commitment to the group or consensus on values. In such societies, most people are "strangers" who perceive that they have little in common with most other people. Consequently, self-interest dominates and little consensus exists regarding values. Tönnies selected the German term *Gesellschaft* because it means association; relationships are based on achieved statuses, and interactions among people are both rational and calculated.

***Gesellschaft* (guh-ZELL-shoft)** A large, urban society in which social bonds are based on impersonal and specialized relationships, with little long-term commitment to the group or consensus on values.

Social Structure and Homelessness

In *Gesellschaft* societies, such as Canada, a prevailing core value is that people should be able to take care of themselves. Thus, many people view the homeless as "throwaways"—as beyond help or as having already had enough done for them by society. Some argue that the homeless made their own bad decisions, which led them into alcoholism or drug addiction, and should be held responsible for the consequences of their actions. In this

BOX 5.2 POINT/COUNTERPOINT

Homeless Rights versus Public Space

> I had a bit of a disturbing experience yesterday as I was running errands downtown. First, I was glad to see the south Queen sidewalk east of University open. (Months of construction on the new opera house had blocked it off.) As I continued walking eastward past the acclaimed new structure (where I have enjoyed a performance or two), I wondered why the sidewalk was so narrow. It seems this stretch of Queen should feel a bit grander. When I reached the corner of Queen and Bay, I saw some police officers and city workers "taking action on sidewalk clearance." They were clearing a homeless person's worldly belongings off the sidewalk. Using shovels. And a pickup truck . . .
>
> I think what I saw yesterday is unacceptable. Sure, the situation is complicated. Yes, there are a lot of stakeholders and stories to appreciate. But it's unfairness I want to see shovelled out of public space. Not people. Not blankets. Not kindness. And I hope I'm not alone. (Sandals, 2007)

"Protection of public space" has become an issue in many cities. Record numbers of homeless individuals and families seek refuge on the streets and in public parks because they have nowhere else to go. However, this seemingly individualistic problem is actually linked to larger social concerns, including long-term unemployment, lack of education and affordable housing, and cutbacks in government and social service budgets. The problem of homelessness also raises significant social policy issues, including the extent to which cities can make it illegal for people to remain for extended periods of time in public spaces.

Should homeless persons be allowed to sleep on sidewalks, in parks, and in other public areas? This issue has been the source of controversy. As cities have sought to improve their downtown areas and public spaces, they have taken measures to enforce city ordinances controlling loitering (standing around or sleeping in public spaces), "aggressive panhandling," and disorderly conduct. Advocates for the homeless and civil liberties groups have filed lawsuits claiming that the rights of the homeless are being violated by the enforcement of these laws. The lawsuits assert that the homeless have a right to sleep in parks because no affordable housing is available for them. Advocates also argue that panhandling is a legitimate livelihood for some of the homeless and is protected speech under the *Charter of Rights and Freedoms*. In addition, they accuse public and law enforcement officials of seeking to punish the homeless on the basis of their "status." According to ethics professor Arthur Schafer, punishing panhandlers is the wrong way to go about the issue:

> Do we, as a society, really want to rely upon still more laws to deal with the serious social problems of poverty, homelessness, and panhandling? Are we convinced that legal coercion, with its use of physical force backed by weapons, lawyers, courts and jails, will be effective in addressing what is essentially a social problem? Are we prepared to violate fundamental rights to freedom of expression and add further burdens to the least advantaged members of our society? (1998:1)

The "homeless problem" is not a new one for city governments. Of the limited public funding that is designated for the homeless, most has been spent on shelters that are frequently overcrowded and otherwise inadequate. Officials in some cities have given homeless people a one-way ticket to another city. Still others have routinely run them out of public spaces.

What responsibility does society have to the homeless? Are laws restricting the hours that public areas or parks are open to the public unfair to homeless persons? Some critics have argued that if the homeless and their advocates win these lawsuits, what they have won (at best) is the right for the homeless to live on the street under extremely adverse conditions. Others have disputed this assertion and note that if society does not make affordable housing and job opportunities available, the least it can do is stop harassing homeless people who are getting by as best they can.

Contrary to a popular myth that most homeless people are single drifters, an increasing number of families are now homeless.

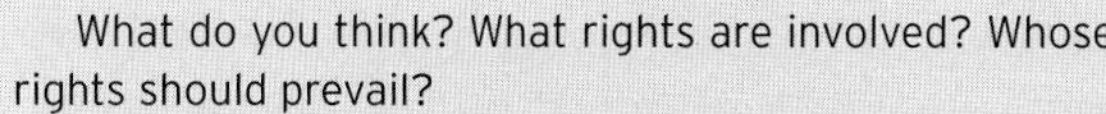

What do you think? What rights are involved? Whose rights should prevail?

© Bruce Ayres/Stone/Getty Images

Sources: Based on Kaufman, 1996; Sandals, 2007; Wood, 2002.

sense, homeless people serve as a visible example to others to "follow the rules" lest they experience a similar fate.

Alternative explanations for homelessness in *Gesellschaft* societies have been suggested. Elliot Liebow (1993) notes that homelessness is rooted in poverty; homeless people overwhelmingly are poor people who come from poor families. Homelessness is a "social class phenomenon, the direct result of a steady, across-the-board lowering of the standard of living of the working class and lower class" (1993:224). The problem is exacerbated by a lack of jobs and adequate housing. Clearly, there is no simple answer to the question about what should be done to help the homeless. Nor, as discussed in Box 5.2, is there any consensus on what legal rights the homeless have in public areas. The answers we derive as a society and as individuals are often based on our social construction of this reality of life.

SOCIAL INTERACTION: THE MICROLEVEL PERSPECTIVE

So far in this chapter, we have focused on society and social structure from a macrolevel perspective. We have seen how the structure of society affects the statuses we occupy, the roles we play, and the groups and organizations to which we belong. Functionalist and conflict perspectives provide a macrosociological overview because they concentrate on large-scale events and broad social features. By contrast, the symbolic interactionist perspective takes a microsociological approach, asking how social institutions affect our daily lives. We will now look at society from the microlevel perspective, which focuses on social interaction among individuals, especially face-to-face encounters.

Social Interaction and Meaning

When you are with other people, do you often wonder what they think of you? If so, you are not alone! Because most of us are concerned about the meanings others ascribe to our behaviour, we try to interpret their words and actions so that we can plan how we will react (Blumer, 1969).

© David Young-Wolff/PhotoEdit

These people are displaying what Goffman referred to as "civil inattention."

We know that others have expectations of us. We also have certain expectations about them. For example, if we enter an elevator that has only one other person in it, we do not expect that individual to confront us and stare into our eyes. As a matter of fact, we would be quite upset if the person did so.

Social interaction within a given society has certain shared meanings across situations. For instance, our reaction would be the same regardless of *which* elevator we rode in *which* building. Sociologist Erving Goffman (1963b) described these shared meanings in his observations about two pedestrians approaching each other on a public sidewalk. He noted that each will tend to look at the other just long enough to acknowledge the other's presence. By the time they are about two and a half metres away from each other, both individuals will tend to look downward. Goffman referred to this behaviour as *civil inattention*—the ways in which an individual shows awareness that others are present without making them the object of particular attention. The fact that people engage in civil inattention demonstrates that interaction does have a pattern, or *interaction order,* that regulates the form and processes (but not the content) of social interaction.

Does everyone interpret social interaction rituals in the same way? No. Ethnicity, gender, and social class play a part in the meanings we give to our interactions with others, including chance encounters on elevators or the street. Our perceptions about the meaning of a situation vary widely based on the statuses we occupy and our unique personal experiences.

Social encounters have different meanings for men and women, and for individuals from different social classes and ethnic groups. For example, sociologist Carol Brooks Gardner (1989) found that women frequently do not perceive street encounters to be "routine" rituals. They fear for their personal safety and try to avoid comments and propositions that are sexual in nature when they walk down the street. In another example, members of the dominant classes regard the poor, unemployed, and working class as less worthy of attention, frequently subjecting them to subtle yet systematic "attention deprivation" (Derber, 1983).

social construction of reality The process by which our perception of reality is shaped largely by the subjective meaning that we give to an experience.

The Social Construction of Reality

If we interpret other people's actions so subjectively, can we have a shared social reality? Some interaction theorists believe that there is little shared reality beyond that which is socially created. Interactionists refer to this as the **social construction of reality**—the process by which our perception of reality is shaped largely by the subjective meaning that we give to an experience (Berger and Luckmann, 1967). This meaning strongly influences what we "see" and how we respond to situations.

self-fulfilling prophecy A situation in which a false belief or prediction produces behaviour that makes the originally false belief come true.

Our perceptions and behaviour are influenced by how we initially define situations: We act on reality as we see it. Sociologists describe this process as the *definition of the situation,* meaning that we analyze a social context in which we find ourselves, determine what is in our best interest, and adjust our attitudes and actions accordingly. This can result in a **self-fulfilling prophecy**—a false belief or prediction that produces behaviour that makes the originally false belief come true (Thomas and Thomas, 1928:72). An example would be a person who has been told repeatedly that she or he is not a good student; eventually, this person might come to believe it to be true, stop studying, and receive failing grades.

People may define a given situation in very different ways. Consider sociologist Lesley Harman's initial reaction to her field research site, a facility for homeless women in an Ontario city: "The initial shock of facing the world of the homeless told me much about what I took for granted . . . The first day I lasted two very long hours. I went home and woke up severely depressed, weeping uncontrollably" (1989:42). In contrast, a resident typical of many of the women who lived there defined living in a hostel in this way: "This is home to me because I feel so comfortable. I can do what I really want, the staff are very nice to me, everybody is good to me, it's home, you know?" (1989:91). As these two examples show, we define situations from our own frame of reference, based on the statuses we occupy and the roles we play.

© Mike Theiler/Getty Images

Dominant group members with prestigious statuses may have the ability to establish how other people define "reality" (Berger and Luckmann, 1967:109). Some sociologists have suggested that dominant groups, particularly high-income white males in powerful economic and political statuses, perpetuate a dominant worldview that is frequently seen as "social reality."

Ethnomethodology

How do we know how to interact in a given situation? What rules do we follow? Ethnomethodologists are interested in the answers to these questions. **Ethnomethodology** is the study of the commonsense knowledge that people use to understand the situations in which they find themselves (Heritage, 1984:4). Sociologist Harold Garfinkel (1967) initiated this approach and coined the term: *ethno* for "people" or "folk" and *methodology* for "a system of methods." Garfinkel was critical of mainstream sociology for not recognizing the ongoing ways in which people create reality and produce their own world. Consequently, ethnomethodologists examine existing patterns of conventional behaviour in order to uncover people's *background expectancies*; that is, their shared interpretation of objects and events, as well as their resulting actions. According to ethnomethodologists, interaction is based on assumptions of shared expectancies. For example, when you are talking with someone, what are your expectations about taking turns? Based on your background expectancies, would you be surprised if the other person talked for an hour and never gave you a chance to speak?

© AP Images/Chris Gardner

Sharply contrasting perceptions of the same reality are evident in these people's views on the war in Iraq.

To uncover people's background expectancies, ethnomethodologists frequently break "rules" or act as though they do not understand some basic rule of social life so that they can observe other people's responses. In a series of *breaching experiments,* Garfinkel (1967) assigned different activities to his students to see how breaking the unspoken rules of behaviour created confusion.

ethnomethodology
The study of the commonsense knowledge that people use to understand the situations in which they find themselves.

In one experiment, when students were asked, "How are you?" they threw their questioners off balance by responding with detailed accounts rather than polite nothings.

The ethnomethodological approach contributes to our knowledge of social interaction by making us aware of subconscious social realities in our daily lives.

LO-5 Dramaturgical Analysis

dramaturgical analysis The study of social interaction that compares everyday life to a theatrical presentation.

impression management (or presentation of self) A term for people's efforts to present themselves to others in ways that are most favourable to their own interests or image.

Erving Goffman suggested that day-to-day interactions have much in common with being on stage or in a dramatic production. **Dramaturgical analysis** is the study of social interaction that compares everyday life to a theatrical presentation. Members of our "audience" judge our performance and are aware that we may slip and reveal our true character (Goffman, 1959, 1963a). Consequently, most of us attempt to play our role as well as possible and to control the impressions we give to others. **Impression management, or presentation of self**, refers to people's efforts to present themselves to others in ways that are most favourable to their own interests or image.

For example, suppose that a professor has returned graded exams to your class. Will you discuss the exam and your grade with others in the class? If you are like most people, you probably play your student role differently depending on whom you are talking to and what grade you received on the exam. In a study, researchers analyzed how students "presented themselves" or "managed impressions" when exam grades were returned. Students who all received high grades ("Ace–Ace encounters") willingly talked with one another about their grades and sometimes engaged in a little bragging about how they had "aced" the test. However, encounters between students who had received high grades and those who had received low or failing grades ("Ace–Bomber encounters")

© keith morris/Alamy

According to Erving Goffman, our day-to-day interactions have much in common with a dramatic production.

were uncomfortable. The Aces felt as if they had to minimize their own grades. Consequently, they tended to attribute their success to "luck" and were quick to offer the Bombers words of encouragement. On the other hand, the Bombers believed that they had to praise the Aces and hide their own feelings of frustration and disappointment. Students who received low or failing grades ("Bomber–Bomber encounters") were more comfortable when they talked with one another because they could share their negative emotions. They often indulged in self-pity and relied on face-saving excuses (such as an illness or an unfair exam) for their poor performances (Albas and Albas, 1988).

In Goffman's terminology, *face-saving behaviour* refers to the strategies we use to rescue our performance when we experience a potential or actual loss of face. When the Bombers made excuses for their low scores, they were engaged in face-saving; the Aces attempted to help them save face by asserting that the test was unfair or that it was only a small part of the final grade. Why would the Aces and Bombers both participate in face-saving behaviour? In most social interactions, all role players have an interest in keeping the "play" going so that they can maintain their overall definition of the situation in which they perform their roles.

Goffman noted that people consciously participate in *studied nonobservance,* a face-saving technique in which one role player ignores the flaws in another's performance to avoid embarrassment for everyone involved. Most of us remember times when we have failed in our role and know that it is likely to happen again; thus, we may be more forgiving of the role failures of others.

Social interaction, like a theatre, has a front stage and a back stage. The *front stage* is the area where a player performs a specific role before an audience. The *back stage* is the area where a player is not required to perform a specific role because it is out of view of a given audience. For example, when the Aces and Bombers were talking with each other at school, they were on the "front stage." When they were in the privacy of their own residences, they were in "back stage" settings—they no longer had to perform the Ace and Bomber roles and could be themselves.

The need for impression management is most intense when role players have widely divergent or devalued statuses. As we have seen with the Aces and Bombers, the participants often play different roles under different circumstances and keep their various audiences separated from one another. If one audience becomes aware of other roles that a person plays, the impression being given at that time may be ruined. For example, homeless people may lose jobs or the opportunity to get them when their homelessness becomes known. One woman, Kim, had worked as a receptionist in a doctor's office for several weeks but was fired when the doctor learned that she was living in a shelter. According to Kim, the doctor told her, "If I had known you lived in a shelter, I would never have hired you. Shelters are places of disease" (Liebow, 1993:53–54). The homeless do not passively accept the roles into which they are cast. For the most part, they attempt—as we all do—to engage in impression management in their everyday lives.

The dramaturgical approach helps us think about the roles we play and the audiences who judge our presentation of self; however, this perspective has also been criticized for focusing on appearances and not the underlying substance. This approach may not place enough emphasis on the ways in which our everyday interactions with other people are influenced by occurrences within the larger society. For example, if some political leaders or social elites in a community deride homeless people by saying they are "lazy" or "unwilling to work," it may become easier for everyday people walking down a street to treat homeless individuals poorly. Overall, however, Goffman's dramaturgical analysis has been highly influential in the development of the sociology of emotions, an important area of contemporary theory and research.

TIME TO REVIEW

- Provide three examples of self-fulfilling prophecies you have experienced in your interactions with others.
- Describe how daily interactions are similar to being onstage.

The Sociology of Emotions

Why do we laugh, cry, or become angry? Are these emotional expressions biological or social? To some extent, emotions are a biologically given sense (like hearing, smell, and touch), but they also are social in origin. We are socialized to feel certain emotions, and we learn how and when to express (or not express) those emotions (Hochschild, 1983).

How do we know which emotions are appropriate for a given role? Sociologist Arlie Hochschild (1983) suggests that we acquire a set of *feeling rules,* which shape the appropriate emotions for a given role or specific situation. These rules include how, where, when, and with whom an emotion should be expressed. For example, for the role of a mourner at a funeral, feeling rules tell us which emotions are required (sadness and grief, for example), which are acceptable (a sense of relief that the deceased no longer has to suffer), and which are unacceptable (enjoyment of the occasion expressed by laughing out loud) (see Hochschild, 1983:63–68).

Feeling rules also apply to our occupational roles. For example, the truck driver who handles explosive cargos must be able to suppress fear. Although all jobs place some burden on our feelings, *emotional labour* occurs only in jobs that require personal contact with the public or the production of a state of mind (such as hope, desire, or fear) in others (Hochschild, 1983). With emotional labour, employees must display only certain carefully selected emotions. For example, flight attendants are required to act friendly toward passengers, to be helpful and open to requests, and to maintain an "omnipresent smile" to enhance the customers' status. By contrast, bill collectors are encouraged to show anger and make threats to customers, thereby supposedly deflating the customers' status and wearing down their presumed resistance to paying past-due bills. In both jobs, the employees are expected to show feelings that are often not their true ones (Hochschild, 1983).

Social class and race are determinants in managed expression and emotion management. Emotional labour is emphasized in middle- and upper-class families. Because middle- and upper-class parents often work with people, they are more likely to teach their children the importance of emotional labour in their own careers than are working-class parents, many of whom work with things, not people (Hochschild, 1983). Race is also an important factor in emotional labour. Members of visible minorities spend much of their life engaged in emotional labour because racist attitudes and discrimination make it continually necessary to manage one's feelings.

Emotional labour may produce feelings of estrangement from one's "true" self. C. Wright Mills (1956) suggested that when we "sell our personality" in the course of selling goods or services, we engage in a seriously self-alienating process. In other words, the "commercialization" of our feelings may dehumanize our work role performance and create alienation and contempt that spill over into other aspects of our life (Hochschild, 1983; Smith and Kleinman, 1989).

Clearly, the sociology of emotions helps us understand the social context of our feelings and the relationship between the roles we play and the emotions we experience. However, it may overemphasize the cost of emotional labour and the emotional controls that exist outside the individual (Wouters, 1989).

Nonverbal Communication

In a typical stage drama, the players not only speak their lines but also convey information by nonverbal communication. In Chapter 3, we discussed the importance of language; now we will look at the messages we communicate without speaking. **Nonverbal communication** is the transfer of information between persons without the use of speech. It includes not only visual cues (gestures, appearances) but also vocal features (inflection, volume, pitch) and environmental factors (use of space, position) that affect meanings (Wood, 1999). Facial expressions, head movements, body positions, and other gestures carry as much of the total meaning of our communication with others as our spoken words do (Wood, 1999).

nonverbal communication The transfer of information between persons without the use of speech.

FUNCTIONS OF NONVERBAL COMMUNICATION Why is nonverbal communication important to you? We obtain first impressions of others from various kinds of nonverbal communication, such as the clothing they wear and their body positions. Head and facial movements may provide us with information about other people's emotional states, and others receive similar information from us (Samovar and Porter, 1991a). Through our body posture and eye contact, we signal that we do or do not wish to speak to someone. For example, we may look down at the sidewalk or off into the distance when we pass homeless persons who look as if they are going to ask for money.

Nonverbal communication establishes the relationship among people in terms of their responsiveness to and power over one another (Wood, 1999). For example, we show that we are responsive toward or like another person by maintaining eye contact and attentive body posture, and perhaps by touching and standing close. We can even express power or control over others through nonverbal communication. Goffman (1956) suggested that *demeanour* (how we behave or conduct ourselves) is relative to social power. People in positions of dominance are allowed a wider range of permissible actions than are their subordinates, who are expected to show deference. *Deference* is the symbolic means by which subordinates give a required permissive response to those in power; it confirms the existence of inequality and reaffirms each person's relationship to the other (Rollins, 1985).

TIME TO REVIEW

- Evaluate your nonverbal communication in an encounter with a police officer. What role would demeanour and deference play in this interaction having a positive or negative outcome?

FACIAL EXPRESSION, EYE CONTACT, AND TOUCHING Nonverbal communication is symbolic of our relationships with others. Who smiles? Who stares? Who makes and sustains eye contact? Who touches whom? All of these questions relate to demeanour and deference; the key issue is the status of the person who is *doing* the smiling, staring, or touching relative to the status of the recipient (Goffman, 1967).

Facial expressions, especially smiles, also reflect gender-based patterns of dominance and subordination in society. Women typically have been socialized to smile and frequently do so even when they are not happy (Halberstadt and Saitta, 1987). Jobs held predominantly by women (including flight attendant, secretary, elementary school teacher, and nurse) are more closely associated with being pleasant and smiling than are "men's jobs." In addition to smiling more frequently, many women tend to tilt their heads in deferential positions when they are talking or listening to others. By contrast, men tend to display less emotion through smiles or other facial expressions and instead seek to show that they are reserved and in control (Wood, 1999).

Women and men use eye contact differently during conversations. Women are more likely to sustain eye contact during conversations (but not otherwise) as a way of showing their interest in and involvement with others. By contrast, men are less likely to maintain prolonged eye contact during conversations but are more likely to stare at other people (especially other men) to challenge them and assert their own status (Pearson, 1985).

Eye contact can be a sign of domination or deference. For example, in a participant observation study of domestic (household) workers and their employers, sociologist Judith Rollins (1985) found that the domestics were supposed to show deference by averting their eyes when they talked to their employers. Deference also required that they present an "exaggeratedly subservient demeanour" by standing less erect and walking tentatively.

Touching is another form of nonverbal behaviour that has many different shades of meaning. Gender and power differences are evident in tactile communication from birth. Studies have shown that touching has variable meanings to parents: Boys are touched more roughly and playfully, while girls are handled more gently and protectively (Condry, Condry, and Pogatshnik, 1983). This pattern continues into adulthood, with women touched more frequently than men. Sociologist Nancy Henley (1977) attributed this pattern to power differentials between men and women and to the nature of women's roles as mothers, nurses, teachers, and secretaries. Clearly, touching has a different meaning to women than to men (Stier and Hall, 1984). Women may hug and touch others to indicate affection and emotional support, while men are more likely to touch others to give directions, assert power, and express sexual interest (Wood, 1999).

personal space The immediate area surrounding a person that the person claims as private.

PERSONAL SPACE How much space do you like between yourself and other people? Anthropologist Edward Hall (1966) analyzed the physical distance between people speaking to one another and found that the amount of personal space people prefer varies from one culture to another. **Personal space** is the immediate area surrounding a person that the person claims as private. Our personal space is contained within an invisible boundary surrounding our body, much like a snail's shell. When others invade our space, we may retreat, stand our ground, or even lash out, depending on our cultural background (Samovar and Porter, 1991a).

Age, gender, kind of relationship, and social class also have an impact on the allocation of personal space. Power differentials are reflected in personal space and privacy issues. With regard to age, adults generally do not hesitate to enter the personal space of a child (Thorne, Kramarae, and Henley, 1983). Similarly, young children who invade the personal space of an adult tend to elicit a more favourable response than do older uninvited visitors (Dean, Willis, and la Rocco, 1976). The need for personal space appears to increase with age (Aiello and Jones, 1971; Baxter, 1970), although it may begin to decrease at about age 40 (Heshka and Nelson, 1972).

For some people, the idea of privacy or personal space is an unheard of luxury afforded only to those in the middle and upper classes. As we have seen in this chapter, the homeless may

© Steve Vidler/SuperStock

© Roderick Chen/SuperStock

© Kwame Zikomo/SuperStock

Nonverbal communication can be thought of as an international language. What message do you receive from the facial expression and gestures of each of these people? Is it possible to misinterpret their messages?

have no space to call their own. Some may try to "stake a claim" on a heat grate or on the same bed in a shelter for more than one night, but such claims have dubious authenticity in a society in which the homeless are assumed to own nothing and have no right to lay claim to anything in the public domain.

In sum, all forms of nonverbal communication are influenced by gender, ethnicity, social class, and the personal contexts in which they occur. While it is difficult to generalize about people's nonverbal behaviour, we still need to think about our own nonverbal communication patterns. Recognizing that differences in social interaction exist is important. We should be wary of making value judgments—the differences are simply differences. Learning to understand and respect alternative styles of social interaction enhances our personal effectiveness by increasing the range of options we have for communicating with different people in diverse contexts and for varied reasons (Wood, 1999).

5 VISUAL SUMMARY

KEY TERMS

achieved status A social position a person assumes voluntarily as a result of personal choice, merit, or direct effort (p. 120).

ascribed status A social position conferred on a person at birth or received involuntarily later in life (p. 120).

dramaturgical analysis The study of social interaction that compares everyday life to a theatrical presentation (p. 132).

ethnomethodology The study of the commonsense knowledge that people use to understand the situations in which they find themselves (p. 131).

formal organization A highly structured group formed for the purpose of completing certain tasks or achieving specific goals (p. 125).

***Gemeinschaft* (guh-MINE-shoft)** A traditional society in which social relationships are based on personal bonds of friendship and kinship and on intergenerational stability (p. 127).

***Gesellschaft* (guh-ZELL-shoft)** A large, urban society in which social bonds are based on impersonal and specialized relationships, with little long-term commitment to the group or consensus on values (p. 127).

impression management (or presentation of self) A term for people's efforts to present themselves to others in ways that are most favourable to their own interests or image (p. 132).

master status A term used to describe the most important status a person occupies (p. 120).

LO-1 Identify the key components of social structure.

© JOHN PAUL FILO/CBS/Landov

Social structure comprises statuses, roles, groups, and social institutions. A status is a specific position in a group or society and is characterized by certain expectations, rights, and duties. Ascribed statuses, such as gender, class, and ethnicity, are acquired at birth or involuntarily later in life. Achieved statuses, such as education and occupation, are assumed voluntarily as a result of personal choice, merit, or direct effort. We occupy a status, but a role is a set of behavioural expectations associated with a given status. A social group consists of two or more people who interact frequently and share a common identity and sense of interdependence. A formal organization is a highly structured group formed to complete certain tasks or achieve specific goals. A social institution is a set of organized beliefs and rules that establish how a society attempts to meet its basic needs.

LO-2 Compare and contrast functionalist and conflict perspectives on social institutions.

© Bob Daemmrich/PhotoEdit

According to functionalist theorists, social institutions perform several prerequisites of all societies: to replace members; teach new members; produce, distribute, and consume goods and services; preserve order; and provide and maintain a sense of purpose. Conflict theorists, however, note that social institutions do not work for the common good of all individuals. Institutions may enhance and uphold the power of some groups but exclude others, such as the homeless.

LO-3 Explain how societies maintain stability in times of social change.

According to Durkheim, although changes in social structure may dramatically affect individuals and groups, societies manage to maintain some degree of stability. Mechanical solidarity refers to social cohesion in preindustrial societies, in which people are united by shared values and common social bonds. Organic solidarity refers to the cohesion in industrial societies, in which people perform specialized tasks and are united by mutual dependence.

© Jiang Jin/SuperStock

LO-4 Define and distinguish between *Gemeinschaft* and *Gesellschaft* societies.

According to Ferdinand Tönnies, the *Gemeinschaft* is a traditional society in which relationships are based on personal bonds of friendship and kinship and on intergenerational stability. The *Gesellschaft* is an urban society in which social bonds are based on impersonal and specialized relationships, with little group commitment or consensus on values.

© David Young-Wolff/PhotoEdit

© keith morris/Alamy

LO-5 Understand Erving Goffman's dramaturgical perspective and the concepts of impression management, and front stage/back stage behaviours.

According to Erving Goffman's dramaturgical analysis, our daily interactions are similar to dramatic productions. *Impression management* refers to efforts to present our self to others in ways that are most favourable to our own interests or self-image. The *front stage* is the area where a player performs a specific role before an audience. The *back stage* is the area where a player is not required to perform a specific role because it is out of view of a given audience.

APPLICATION QUESTIONS

1. Think of a person you know well who often irritates you or whose behaviour grates on your nerves (it could be a parent, friend, relative, or teacher). First, list that person's statuses and roles. Then analyze his or her possible role expectations, role performance, role conflicts, and role strains. Does anything you find in your analysis help to explain the irritating behaviour? (If not, change your method of analysis!) How helpful are the concepts of social structure in analyzing individual behaviour?
2. How does the structure of Canadian society influence the way in which we understand and respond to homelessness, both individually and collectively?
3. You are conducting field research on gender differences in nonverbal communication styles. How are you going to account for variations in age, ethnicity, and social class?
4. When communicating with other genders, ethnic groups, and ages, is it better to express and acknowledge different styles or to develop a common, uniform style? Why?

mechanical solidarity Émile Durkheim's term for the social cohesion that exists in preindustrial societies, in which there is a minimal division of labour and people feel united by shared values and common social bonds (p. 127).

nonverbal communication The transfer of information between persons without the use of speech (p. 134).

organic solidarity Émile Durkheim's term for the social cohesion that exists in industrial (and perhaps post-industrial) societies, in which people perform specialized tasks and feel united by their mutual dependence (p. 127).

personal space The immediate area surrounding a person that the person claims as private (p. 136).

primary group A small, less specialized group in which members engage in face-to-face, emotion-based interactions over an extended time (p. 124).

role A set of behavioural expectations associated with a given status (p. 121).

role conflict A situation in which incompatible role demands are placed on a person by two or more statuses held at the same time (p. 122).

role exit A situation in which people disengage from social roles that have been central to their self-identity (p. 123).

role expectation A group's or society's definition of the way a specific role ought to be played (p. 121).

role performance How a person plays a role (p. 121).

role strain The strain experienced by a person when incompatible demands are built into a single status that the person occupies (p. 122).

secondary group A larger, more specialized group in which the members engage in more impersonal, goal-oriented relationships for a limited time (p. 124).

self-fulfilling prophecy A situation in which a false belief or prediction produces behaviour that makes the originally false belief come true (p. 130).

social construction of reality The process by which our perception of reality is shaped largely by the subjective meaning that we give to an experience (p. 130).

social group A group that consists of two or more people who interact frequently and share a common identity and a feeling of interdependence (p. 124).

social institution A set of organized beliefs and rules that establish how a society will attempt to meet its basic social needs (p. 125).

social interaction The process by which people act toward or respond to other people (p. 118).

social marginality The state of being part insider and part outsider in the social structure (p. 118).

social network A series of social relationships that link an individual to others (p. 125).

social structure The stable pattern of social relationships that exist within a particular group or society (p. 118).

status A socially defined position in a group or society characterized by certain expectations, rights, and duties (p. 119).

status set A term used to describe all the statuses that a person occupies at a given time (p. 120).

status symbol A material sign that informs others of a person's specific status (p. 121).

stigma According to Erving Goffman, any physical or social attribute or sign that so devalues a person's social identity that it disqualifies that person from full social acceptance (p. 119).

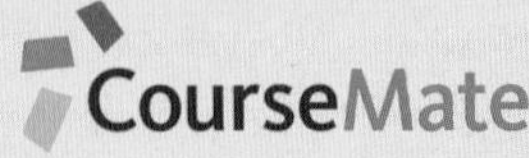

KEY FIGURES

Ferdinand Tönnies (1855–1936) German sociologist Ferdinand Tonnies used the terms *Gemeinschaft* (traditional societies) and *Gesellschaft* (large urban societies) to describe the degree of social solidarity and social control in different societies.

© American Sociological Association

Erving Goffman (1922–1982) Canadian-born sociologist Erving Goffman, author of *The Presentation of Self in Everyday Life*, used a theatre metaphor in his study of social interaction. According to Goffman day-to-day interactions are similar to a theatre production—we have a front stage and a back stage and we use "impression management" to ensure that our audience judges our performance favourably.

Test your comprehension and assess what you've learned with **CourseMate's** online quizzes.

For other interesting Lived Experiences, watch the video clips on **CourseMate.**

Practise what you've learned with flashcards containing key terms and definitions on **CourseMate.**

CHAPTER

6 Groups and Organizations

© JUPITERIMAGES/Creatas/Alamy

KENNETH PAYNE DESCRIBES HIS JOURNEY THROUGH A BUREAUCRATIC MAZE:

> *Since November, I have spent six to eight hours a day trying to persuade the authorities to accommodate me, but it just goes around in a circle . . . It's George Orwell's* Big Brother *. . . The bureaucracy is making me prove a negative and it turns "innocent until proven guilty" on its head . . . There's no common sense here. It's an inflexible bureaucracy where nobody takes any responsibility.* (Reed, 1998:A11)

What is Mr. Payne's problem? The former carpenter wants to be a schoolteacher. He has a degree in education and teaching experience. However, he is unable to get a permanent job teaching because he has a skin disease that causes the skin on his hands to blister and peel.

Why should this disqualify Mr. Payne from teaching? California legislators passed a law requiring that all teachers be fingerprinted so that they could be checked for criminal records. Because of Mr. Payne's disease, he has never had proper fingerprints, so there is no file to check against. Mr. Payne has appealed to the state and offered to prove in other ways that he has no criminal record, but he has been unable to get an exemption from the rule.

Why do people in organizations behave so inflexibly? Some rules are necessary. Even in small groups, such as families or friendship groups, informal rules help to ensure that people interact smoothly. In a large bureaucracy, an explicit system of rules and regulations means that employees and clients know what is expected of them. These rules help to ensure that everyone receives equal treatment from the organization. Unfortunately, adherence to the rules can stifle individual judgment, and some bureaucrats become so inflexible that they hurt the organization and its clients. In Mr. Payne's case, it made sense for the school system to do its best to protect children by establishing background checks for prospective teachers. However, in this case, the bureaucrats focused on fingerprinting, which is just one way of ensuring that people with criminal records are not hired as teachers. An official who was concerned with the *goal* of the policy (protecting children) rather than with one of the *means* of achieving that goal (fingerprinting) would have accepted the other ways in which Mr. Payne could have proven that he was not an offender.

While Mr. Payne suffered personal hardship, the consequences of bureaucratic inflexibility can be much more severe. In August 2005, Hurricane Katrina devastated the city of New Orleans. Tens of thousands of evacuees were not properly cared for and law and order broke down. There were massive failures in planning for the disaster and in coordinating the response after the city was flooded. While the most serious flaw was probably a lack of coordination among the local, state, and federal agencies responsible for the emergency, bureaucratic inflexibility was also pervasive.

Several incidents show that even in the face of the largest natural disaster ever to hit North America, some bureaucrats were focused more on rules and regulations than on saving lives. Despite the desperate need for water for hurricane survivors, there were occasions where truckloads of water were turned back because the drivers didn't have the proper paperwork (Lipton et al., 2005). A group of doctors were evacuated from their hospital and taken to the New Orleans airport. They offered to help tend the many sick people who had also been taken to the airport, but federal authorities were worried about liability issues and told them they could best help by mopping floors (CNN, 2005). While the doctors cleaned floors, patients died because of the lack of medical care. Another example of goal displacement occurred when hundreds of firefighters from around the United States were forced by the U.S. Federal Emergency Management Agency to delay their deployment into the emergency zone to take several days of community relations and sexual harassment training.

Much of our time is spent dealing with bureaucratic organizations. Most of us are born in hospitals, educated in schools, fed by restaurants and supermarket chains, entertained by communications companies, employed by corporations, and buried by funeral companies. Some people think of bureaucracies in a negative way because of their red tape and impersonality. While they can be inflexible and inhumane, bureaucracies are essential to modern life. Bureaucracies have been the best way of managing large numbers of people who must accomplish a common task. They are an essential part of our industrialized society.

In this chapter, you will learn about different types of groups and organizations, including bureaucracies. We live our lives in groups and they constantly affect our behaviour. Before reading on, test your knowledge about bureaucracies by taking the quiz in Box 6.1 on page 145.

Critical Thinking Questions

1. What bureaucracies have you recently encountered? What do you think are the benefits and shortcomings of this form of social organization?
2. Have you ever run into the kind of bureaucratic inflexibility we have described above? If you have, how did that make you feel about the organization that behaved unreasonably?
3. How do you think bureaucracies could be changed so they treat people more like individuals than is now the case?

CHAPTER FOCUS QUESTION

How can we explain the behaviour of people who work in bureaucracies?

LEARNING OBJECTIVES

AFTER READING THIS CHAPTER, YOU SHOULD BE ABLE TO

LO-1 Identify the differences among social groups, aggregates, and categories.

LO-2 Understand the effect that size has on the functioning of groups.

LO-3 Explain the impact of groups on people's behaviour.

LO-4 Identify the characteristics that define a bureaucracy and the "other face" of bureaucracies.

LO-5 Discuss the form large organizations may take in the future.

© Lebrecht Music and Arts Photo Library/Alamy

Napoleon's defeat at Waterloo in 1815 showed that massive armies could not be led in the traditional way, by a single commander responsible for everything. Subsequently, armies developed more effective organizational structures.

LO-1 SOCIAL GROUPS

We spend most of our lives in groups, including families, friends, and school and work groups, so it is important to understand the characteristics and dynamics of groups ranging from small, informal groups to large bureaucracies.

Consider these situations. Three strangers are standing at a street corner waiting for a traffic light to change. Do they constitute a group? Five hundred people are first-year students at a university. Do they constitute a group? In everyday usage, we use the word *group* to mean any collection of people. According to sociologists, however, the answer to these questions is no; individuals who happen to share a common feature or to be in the same place at the same time do not constitute social groups.

Groups, Aggregates, and Categories

aggregate A collection of people who happen to be in the same place at the same time but have little else in common.

category A number of people who may never have met one another but who share a similar characteristic.

A *social group* is a collection of two or more people who interact frequently with one another, share a sense of belonging, and have a feeling of interdependence. Several people waiting for a traffic light to change constitute an **aggregate**—a collection of people who happen to be in the same place at the same time but have little else in common. Shoppers in a department store and passengers on an airplane are also examples of aggregates. People in aggregates share a common purpose (such as purchasing items or arriving at their destination) but generally do not interact with one another. The first-year students, at least initially, constitute a **category**—a number of people who may never have met one another but who share a similar characteristic (such as education level, age, ethnicity, and gender). Men and women make up categories, as do First Nations peoples and victims of sexual harassment. Categories are not social groups because the people in them usually do not create a social structure or have anything in common other than a particular trait.

Occasionally, people in aggregates and in categories form social groups. People within the category of "students" become an aggregate when they meet for an orientation. Some of them may form social groups as they interact with one another in classes, find that they have mutual interests and concerns, and develop a sense of belonging to the group.

Social groups can change over time. For example, an aggregate or category of people may become a formal organization with a specific structure and clear-cut goals. A *formal organization* is a structured group formed to achieve specific goals in the most efficient manner. Universities, factories, corporations, and the military are examples of formal organizations. Before we examine formal organizations, we need to know more about groups in general and about how they function.

Types of Groups

Groups have varying degrees of social solidarity and structure. This structure is flexible in some groups and more rigid in others. Some groups are small and personal; others are large and impersonal. We more closely identify with the members of some groups than we do others.

PRIMARY AND SECONDARY GROUPS Sociologist Charles H. Cooley (1962/1909) used the term *primary group* to describe a small, less specialized group in which members engage in face-to-face, emotion-based interactions over an extended time. We have primary relationships with other individuals in our primary groups—that is, with our *significant others*.

In contrast, a *secondary group* is a larger, more specialized group in which members engage in more impersonal, goal-oriented relationships for a limited time. The size of a secondary group may vary. Twelve students in a university seminar may start out as a secondary group but eventually become a primary group as they get to know one another and communicate on a more personal basis. Formal organizations are secondary groups, but they also contain many primary groups within them. There are many thousands of primary groups within the secondary group setting of your university.

BOX 6.1 SOCIOLOGY AND EVERYDAY LIFE

How Much Do You Know About Bureaucracy?

True	False	
T	F	1. Large bureaucracies have existed for about a thousand years.
T	F	2. Because of the efficiency and profitability of the new factory bureaucracies, people were eager to leave farms to work in the factories.
T	F	3. Bureaucracies are deliberately impersonal.
T	F	4. The organizational principles used by McDonald's restaurants are being adopted by other sectors of the global economy.
T	F	5. The rise of Protestantism helped create the social conditions favourable to the rise of modern bureaucracies.

For answers to the quiz about bureaucracy, go to **www.nelson.com/sociologyinourtimes6e**.

© Gari Wyn Williams/Alamy

Visiting spectators to the game form an outgroup in relation to the home team fans.

INGROUPS AND OUTGROUPS Groups set boundaries by distinguishing between insiders, who are members, and outsiders, who are not. William Graham Sumner (1959/1906) coined the terms *ingroup* and *outgroup* to describe people's feelings toward members of their own and other groups. An **ingroup** is a group to which a person belongs and with which the person feels a sense of identity. An **outgroup** is a group to which a person does not belong and toward which the person may feel a sense of competitiveness or hostility. Distinguishing between our ingroups and our outgroups helps us establish our individual identity.

Group boundaries may be formal, with clearly defined criteria for membership. For example, a country club that requires applicants for membership to be recommended by four current members and pay a $25,000 initiation fee and $1000 per month membership dues has set requirements for its members. The club may even post an entrance sign that states "Members Only" and use security personnel to ensure that nonmembers do not encroach on its grounds. Boundary distinctions are often reflected in symbols, such as emblems or clothing. Country club members are given membership cards to gain access to the club's facilities.. They may wear shirts with the country club's logo on them. These symbols denote that the individual is a member of the ingroup.

> **ingroup** A group to which a person belongs and with which the person feels a sense of identity.

> **outgroup** A group to which a person does not belong and toward which the person may feel a sense of competitiveness or hostility.

Group boundaries are not always as formal as they are in a private club. Friendship groups, for example, usually do not have clear guidelines for membership. Rather, the boundaries tend to be informal and vaguely defined.

Ingroup and outgroup distinctions may encourage social cohesion among members, but they also may promote classism, racism, sexism, and ageism. Ingroup members typically view themselves positively and may view members of outgroups negatively. These feelings of group superiority, or *ethnocentrism,* can be detrimental to groups and individuals not part of the ingroup. Sexual harassment and racial discrimination are two negative consequences of ethnocentrism.

> **reference group** A group that strongly influences a person's behaviour and social attitudes, regardless of whether that individual is an actual member.

REFERENCE GROUPS Ingroups provide us not only with a source of identity but also with a point of reference. A **reference group** is a group that strongly influences a person's behaviour and social attitudes, regardless of whether that individual is an actual member. When we evaluate our appearance, ideas, or goals, we automatically refer to the standards of a group. Sometimes, we will refer to our membership groups, such as family or friends. Other times, we will rely on groups to which we do not belong but that we might wish to join in the future, such as a social club or a profession.

> **network** A web of social relationships that link one person with other people and, through them, with more people that those people know.

NETWORKS A **network** is a web of social relationships that link one person with other people and, through them, with more people that those people know. Frequently, networks connect people who share common interests but who otherwise might not interact with one another. For example, if A is tied to B and B is tied to C, then a network may be formed among individuals A, B, and C. Think of the experiences that you and your friends have had looking for summer jobs. If your friend works at a company that needs more people, he or she may recommend you to the potential employer. This recommendation helps you get a job and gives the employer the assurance that you are likely to be a good employee. Research shows that networks play a very important role for graduating students in finding employment (Granovetter, 1994).

It's a Small World: Networks of Acquaintances On September 11, 2001, nearly 3000 people died when terrorists crashed two planes into New York City's World Trade Center and a third into the Pentagon. Many people around the world were surprised to learn that they, or some of their acquaintances, knew someone who had been personally touched by the tragedy. Social scientists were not surprised by this because of a fascinating research project done more than 40 years ago by psychologist Stanley Milgram (1967).

Milgram sent packages of letters to people in the Midwestern United States. The objective was to get the letters to one of two target recipients in Boston using personal contacts. Those originating the chain were given the name of the target recipient and told that the person was either a Boston stockbroker or the wife of a Harvard divinity student. They were asked to mail the letter to an acquaintance who they felt would be able to pass it on to another acquaintance even closer to the intended target. Milgram found that it took an average of five contacts to get the letters to the intended recipient.

The research was popularized through the play and movie *Six Degrees of Separation,* and the popular trivia game *Six Degrees of Kevin Bacon,* in which the objective is to link actors to other actors who have appeared in films with Kevin Bacon. Thus, Nicole Kidman has a Kevin Bacon number of 2, as she appeared in *Eyes Wide Shut* with Tom Cruise, who worked with Kevin Bacon in the film *A Few Good Men.* Since virtually no American actor has a Bacon number larger than 4, the challenge for movie trivia experts is to figure out the linkages. (See the Oracle of Bacon website at oracleofbacon.org.)

The "small world" research has important implications. Strogatz and Watts (1998) have studied the mathematics behind the phenomenon and have documented the importance of "bridges"—people who bridge very different social worlds. For example, in Milgram's study, the Boston stockbroker received 64 letters, 16 of which were delivered by the owner of a clothing store in Boston. Perhaps you can think of friends or acquaintances who come from other countries or who have unusual interests, hobbies, or jobs that would enable them to bridge vast distances or widely different social groups. The study of networks and of the role of bridges has important implications for researchers in many fields, including *epidemiology,* which is the study of the spread of disease. For example, the spread of HIV/AIDS was hastened by a Canadian flight attendant (Patient X) whose travels meant that he bridged several different networks of gay males (Saulnier, 1998).

While Milgram's research was influential, Kleinfeld (2002) found that most of Milgram's letters never reached their intended destination. We do not know if the connections failed because the participants could not think of anyone who could act as the next link in the chain, or simply because they did not bother moving the letter along toward the intended recipient. However, a study using email contacts had lower failure rates and had similar results to Milgram's. Dodds and his colleagues (2003) found that those who continued the chain needed an average of five to seven contacts to reach their targets, even when in another country. A recent study found that there was an average of just under four degrees of separation among Facebook users around the world, so social media may be bringing people closer together (Backstrom et al., 2011).

Research points out an interesting aspect of social networks. Korte and Milgram (1970) found a significantly higher number of completed chains when both the sender and the recipient were the same race, and Dodds et al. (2003) found that people most frequently contacted persons of the same gender. They found that workplace and educational contacts were most likely to be used in completing chains. These findings imply that members of groups that are less powerful and less educated may be disadvantaged in a world that is increasingly dependent upon geographically dispersed social networks.

Why is this important? We live in a world where many things get done through networks. Granovetter (1995) showed that social networks are important for employers and for people looking for work. Most people get their jobs through personal contacts rather than through formal job-search mechanisms. Those with good networks will have the advantage in their search for work, while those without extensive networks or those whose networks are not oriented to the labour market will be at a great disadvantage. If most of your friends are unemployed, they cannot help you find a job. This can perpetuate unemployment among groups, including some visible minorities and women, who may not have had the opportunity to build up strong networks.

Network analysis is becoming more important in sociology. For example, email patterns may tell us a great deal about the way in which organizations work. How do ideas spread within an organization? Do email messages frequently pass between different levels of an organization, or are communications restricted to one level? Do women and visible minorities have the same interaction patterns as white males, and are they able to bridge different parts of their organizations? On a broader level, can genuine communities flourish in cyberspace, or does the Internet reduce community by reducing the personal contact between people?

LO-2 GROUP CHARACTERISTICS AND DYNAMICS

© Roy Morsch/zefa/Corbis

Our most intense relationships occur in dyads—groups composed of two members. How might the interaction of these two people differ if they were with several other people?

What purpose do groups serve? Why do individuals give up some of their freedom to participate in groups? According to functionalists, groups meet peoples' instrumental and expressive needs. *Instrumental,* or task-oriented, needs cannot always be met by one person, so the group works cooperatively to fulfill a specific goal. For example, you could not function as a one-person football team or single-handedly build a skyscraper. Groups help members do jobs that are difficult or impossible to do alone. They also help people meet their *expressive,* or emotional, needs, especially for self-expression and support from family, friends, and peers.

Conflict theorists and symbolic interactionists, of course, have a different understanding of groups. While not disputing that groups ideally perform positive functions, conflict theorists suggest that groups also involve power relationships whereby the needs of individual members may not be equally served. Symbolic interactionists focus on how the size of a group influences the kind of interaction that takes place among members.

To many postmodernists, groups and organizations—like other aspects of postmodern societies—are generally characterized by superficiality and by shallow social relationships. One postmodern thinker who focuses on this issue is the literary theorist Fredric Jameson, whose works have had a significant influence on contemporary sociology. According to Jameson (1984), postmodern organizations (and societies as a whole) are characterized not only by superficial relations and lack of depth but also by people experiencing a waning of emotion because the world and the people in it have become more fragmented (Ritzer, 1997). For example, Ritzer (1997) examined fast-food restaurants and concluded that both restaurant employees and customers interact in extremely superficial ways that are largely scripted by large-scale organizations: The employees learn to follow scripts in taking and filling customers' orders ("Would you like fries with that?"), while customers respond with their own "recipied" action.

Group Size

The size of a group is important. Interactions are more personal and intense in a **small group**, in which all members are acquainted with one another and interact simultaneously.

small group A collectivity small enough for all members to be acquainted with one another and to interact simultaneously.

Simmel (1950/1902–1917) suggested that small groups have distinctive interaction patterns. According to Simmel, in a **dyad**—a group composed of two members—the active participation of both members is crucial for the group's survival. If one member withdraws from interaction, or "quits," the group ceases to exist. Examples of dyads include two people who are best friends, and married couples. Dyads provide an intense bond and a sense of unity not found in most larger groups.

dyad A group consisting of two members.

Adding a third person forms a **triad**. The nature of the relationship and interaction patterns change with the addition of the third person. In a triad, even if one member ignores another or declines to participate, the group can still function. In addition, two members may unite to create a coalition that can subject the third member to group pressure to conform. A *coalition* is an alliance created in an attempt to reach a shared objective or goal. If two members form a coalition, the other member may be seen as an outsider or intruder.

triad A group composed of three members.

As group size increases beyond three, members tend to specialize in different tasks and communication patterns change. In groups of more than six or seven people, it becomes increasingly difficult for everyone to participate in the same conversation, so several conversations will likely take place simultaneously. In groups of more than 10 or 12 people, it becomes virtually impossible for all members to participate in a single conversation unless one person serves as moderator and facilitates the discussion. Figure 6.1 shows that when the size of the group increases, the number of possible social interactions increases dramatically.

FIGURE 6.1 GROWTH OF POSSIBLE SOCIAL INTERACTIONS BASED ON GROUP SIZE

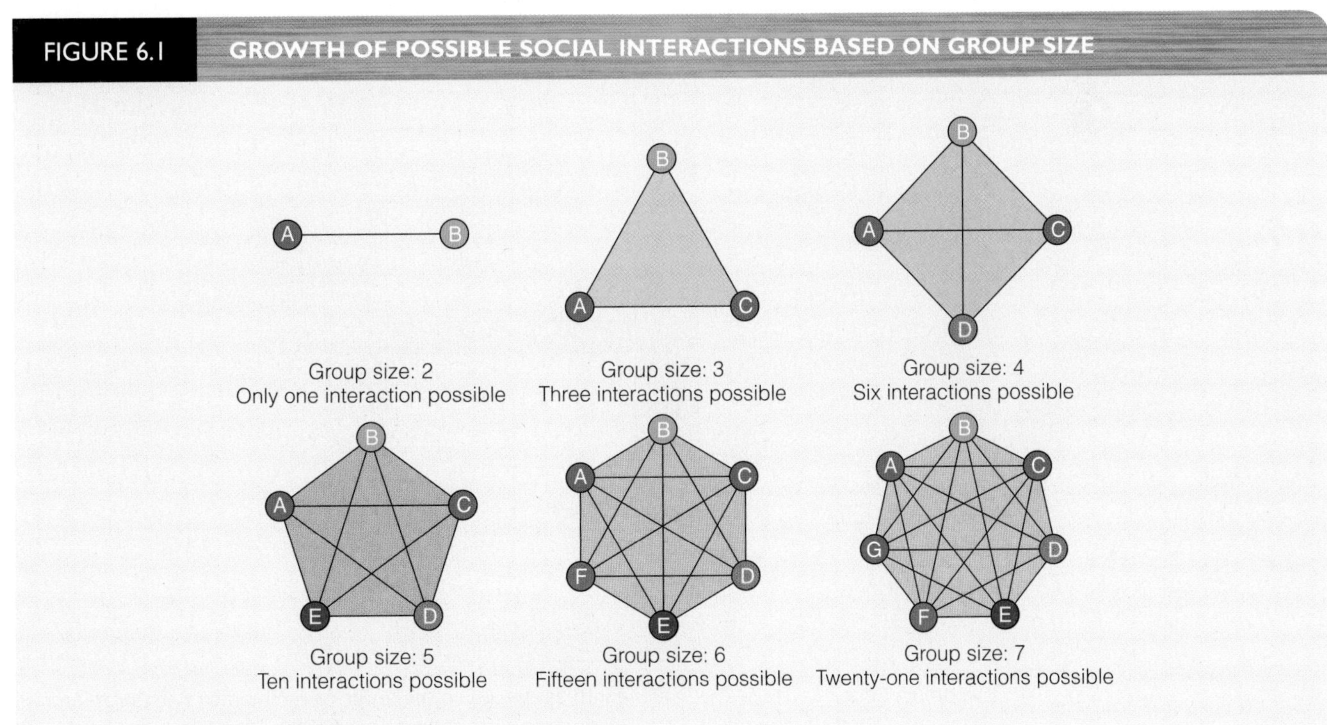

LO-3 Group Conformity

conformity The process of maintaining or changing behaviour to comply with the norms established by a society, subculture, or other group.

Groups exert a powerful influence in our lives. To gain and then retain our membership in groups, most of us are willing to exhibit a high level of conformity to the wishes of other group members. **Conformity** is the process of maintaining or changing behaviour to comply with the norms established by a society, subculture, or other group. We often experience powerful pressure from other group members to conform. In some situations, this pressure may be almost overwhelming.

Several researchers have found that the pressure to conform can cause group members to say they see something they don't see or to do something they otherwise would be unwilling to do. As we look at two of these studies, ask yourself what you might have done if you had been involved in this research.

ASCH'S RESEARCH Pressure to conform is especially strong in small groups. In a series of experiments conducted by Solomon Asch (1955, 1956), the pressure toward group conformity was so great that participants were willing to contradict their own best judgment rather than disagree with other group members.

One of Asch's experiments involved groups of undergraduate men (seven in each group) who supposedly were recruited for a study of visual perception. All the men were seated in chairs. However, the person in the sixth chair did not know that he was the only actual subject; all of the others were assisting the researcher. The participants were first shown a large card with a vertical line on it and then a second card with three vertical lines (see Figure 6.2). Each of the seven participants was asked to indicate which of the three lines on the second card was identical in length to the "standard line" on the first card.

FIGURE 6.2 ASCH'S CARDS

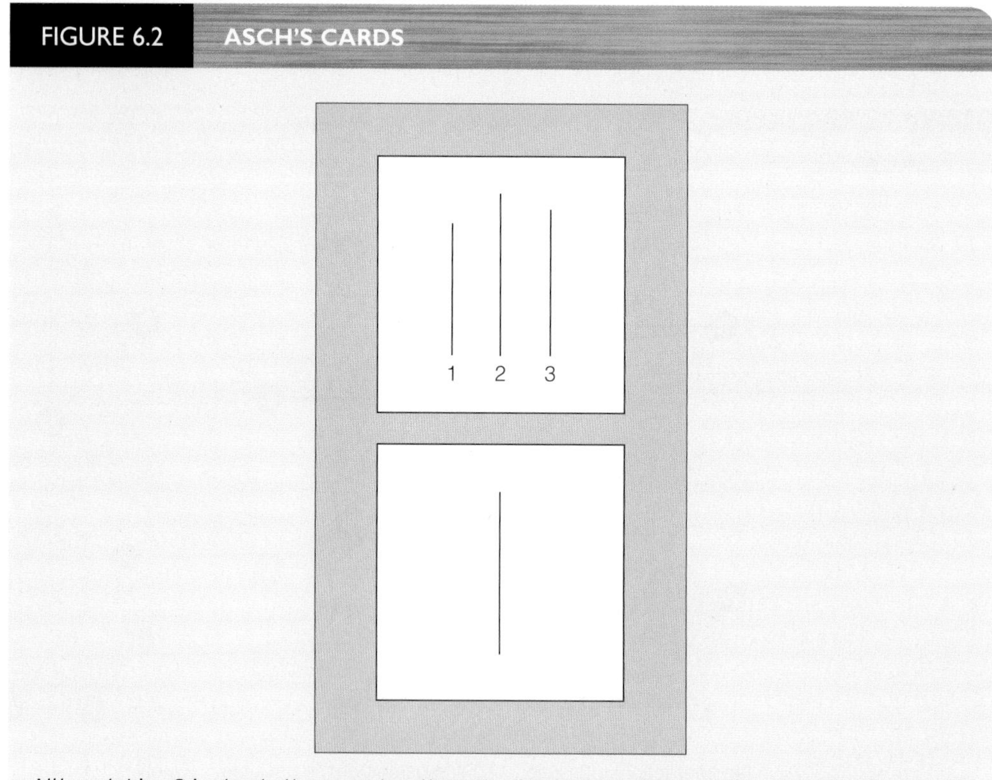

Although Line 2 is clearly the same length as the line in the lower card, Solomon Asch's research assistants tried to influence "actual" participants by deliberately picking Line 1 or Line 3 as the correct match. Many of the participants went along rather than risk the opposition of the "group."

In the first test with each group, all seven men selected the correct matching line. In the second trial, all seven still answered correctly. In the third trial, however, the subject became very uncomfortable when all of the others selected the incorrect line. The subject could not understand what was happening and became even more confused as the others continued to give incorrect responses on 11 out of the next 15 trials.

If you had been in the position of the subject, how would you have responded? Would you have continued to give the correct answer, or would you have been swayed by the others? When Asch (1955) averaged the responses of the 50 actual subjects who participated in the study, he found that about 33 percent routinely chose to conform to the group by giving the same (incorrect) responses as Asch's assistants. Another 40 percent gave incorrect responses in about half of the trials. Although 25 percent always gave correct responses, even they felt very uneasy and "knew that something was wrong." In discussing the experiment afterward, most of the subjects who gave incorrect responses indicated that they had known the answers were wrong but decided to go along with the group to avoid ridicule or ostracism.

In later studies, Asch found that if even a single assistant did not agree with the others, the subject was reassured by hearing someone else question the accuracy of incorrect responses and was much less likely to give a wrong answer. Figure 6.3 shows how group size was related to conformity. This shows the power that groups have to produce conformity among members.

MILGRAM'S RESEARCH ON OBEDIENCE How willing are we to do something because someone in a position of authority has told us to do it? How far are we willing to go in following that individual's demands? Stanley Milgram (1963, 1974) conducted a series of controversial experiments to answer these questions about people's obedience to authority. Milgram wanted to understand atrocities, such as the Holocaust, where ordinary citizens behaved brutally when they were ordered to do so.

FIGURE 6.3 EFFECT OF GROUP SIZE IN THE ASCH CONFORMITY STUDIES

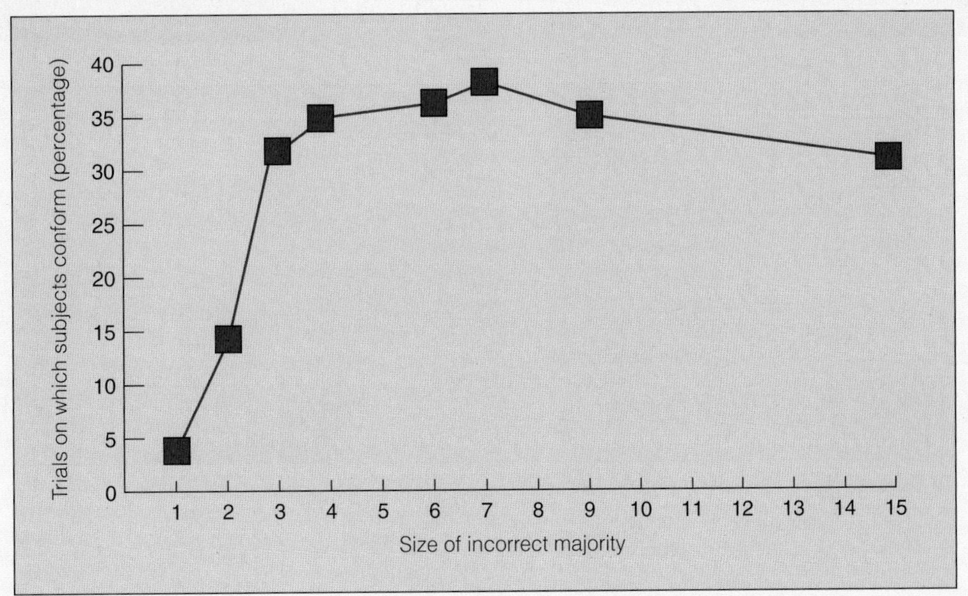

As more people are added to the "incorrect" majority, subjects' tendency to conform by giving wrong answers increases—but only up to a point. Adding more than seven people to the incorrect majority does not further increase subjects' tendency to conform—perhaps because subjects are suspicious about why so many people agree with one another.

Source: Asch, 1955.

Milgram's subjects were men who had responded to an advertisement for participants in an experiment. When the first (actual) subject arrived, he was told that the study concerned the effects of punishment on learning. After the second subject (an assistant of Milgram's) arrived, the two men were directed to draw slips of paper from a hat to get their assignments as either the "teacher" or the "learner." Because the drawing was rigged, the actual subject always became the teacher and the assistant the learner. Next, the learner was strapped into a chair with protruding electrodes that looked something like an electric chair. The teacher was placed in an adjoining room and given a realistic-looking but nonoperative shock generator. The "generator's" control panel showed levels that went from "Slight Shock" (15 volts) on the left, to "Intense Shock" (255 volts) in the middle, to "DANGER: SEVERE SHOCK" (375 volts), and finally "XXX" (450 volts) on the right.

The teacher was instructed to read aloud a pair of words and then repeat the first of the two words. At that time, the learner was supposed to respond with the second of the two words. If the learner could not provide the second word, the teacher was instructed to press the lever on the shock generator so that the learner would be punished for forgetting the word. Each time the learner gave an incorrect response, the teacher was supposed to increase the shock level by 15 volts. The alleged purpose of the shock was to determine whether punishment improves a person's memory.

What was the maximum level of shock that a "teacher" was willing to inflict on a "learner"? The learner had been instructed (in advance) to beat on the wall between himself and the teacher as the experiment continued, pretending that he was in intense pain. The teacher was told that the shocks might be "extremely painful" but would cause no permanent damage. At about 300 volts, when the learner quit responding to questions, the teacher often turned to the experimenter to see what he should do next. When the experimenter indicated that the teacher should give increasingly painful shocks, 65 percent of the teachers administered shocks all the way up to the "XXX" (450 volt) level (see Figure 6.4). By this point in the process, the teachers were frequently sweating, stuttering, or biting on their lip.

FIGURE 6.4 RESULTS OF MILGRAM'S OBEDIENCE EXPERIMENT

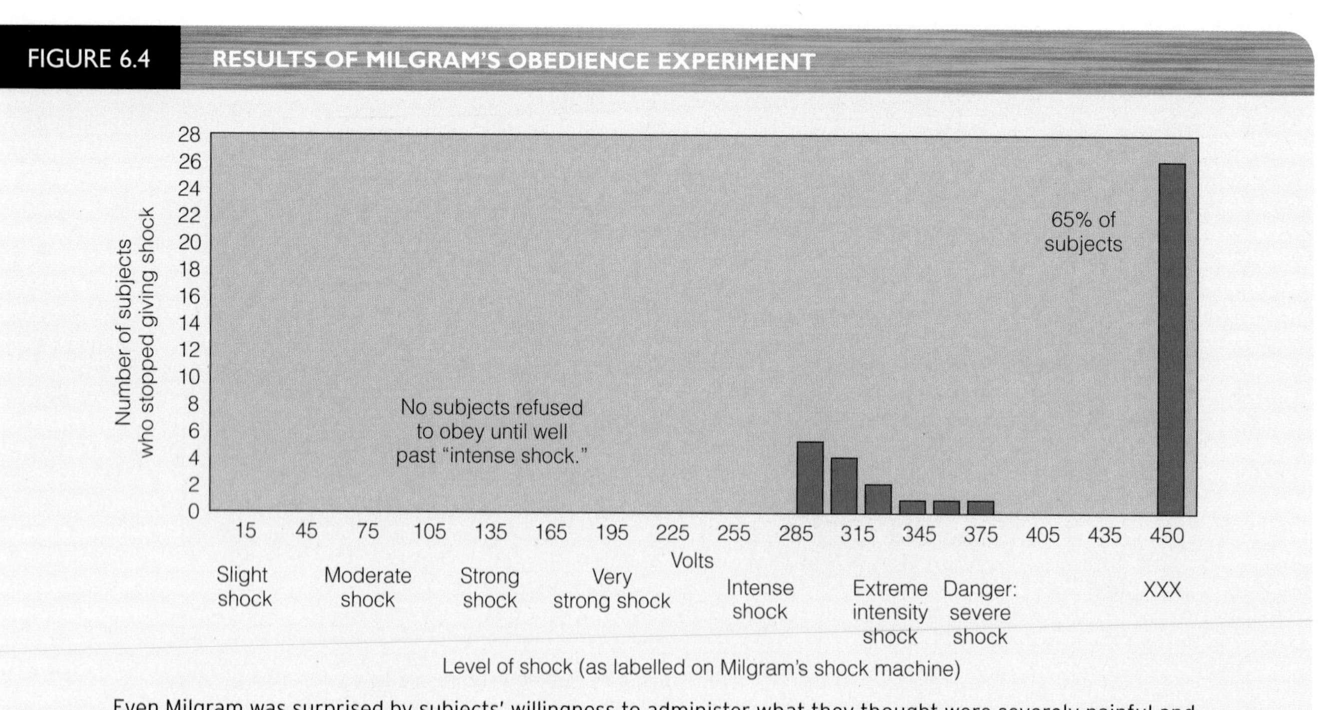

Even Milgram was surprised by subjects' willingness to administer what they thought were severely painful and even dangerous shocks to a helpless "learner."

Source: Graph is based on Table 2 in Milgram, 1963: 376.

According to Milgram, the teachers—who were free to leave whenever they wanted to—continued in the experiment because they were being given directions by a person in a position of authority (a scientist wearing a white coat).

What can we learn from Milgram's study? The study suggests that obedience to authority may be more common than most of us would like to believe. None of the "teachers" challenged the process before they had applied 300 volts. Almost two-thirds went all the way to what could have been a painful jolt of electricity if the shock generator had been real. Burger (2009) has recently conducted a partial replication of Milgram's work and found that rates of obedience were similar to those of the earlier study. Most people went to the end of the experiment, and women were as likely to obey as men.

This research raises ethical questions. Milgram's subjects were deceived about the nature of the study. Many found the experiment extremely stressful, and some suffered anxiety so severe that the experimental sessions had to be ended (Milgram, 1963). It would be impossible today to obtain permission to replicate this experiment in a university setting, though such studies were common in the 1960s. Burger's partial replication of the study made a number of changes, including stopping the experiment at the 150-volt level, to obtain ethics approval. Burger felt this was justified because in Milgram's work, most people who went past this level continued all the way to the end.

In addition to ethical problems, some critics feel that Milgram's study was also methodologically flawed. Brannigan (2004) has raised the issue of whether the subjects actually believed that they were hurting people. The more realistic Milgram made the experiment, the more likely the subjects were to refuse to proceed. One critic explains why he does not take the results of Milgram's study seriously:

> Every experiment was basically preposterous . . . the entire experimental procedure from beginning to end could make no sense at all, even to the laymen. A person is strapped to a chair and immobilized and is explicitly told he is going to be exposed to extremely painful electric shocks . . . The task the student is to learn is evidently impossible. He can't learn it in a short time . . . No one could learn it . . . This experiment becomes more incredulous and senseless the further it is carried. (Mantell, 1971:110–111)

Because of the artificiality of the laboratory situation, Brannigan is very doubtful that this experiment tells us anything about why German citizens were willing to participate in the atrocities of the Holocaust. The issue of artificiality means that we should always be cautious when we consider the findings of laboratory experiments involving human behaviour.

GROUPTHINK As we have seen, individuals often respond differently in a group context than if they were alone. Janis (1972, 1989) examined group decision making and found that major blunders may be attributed to pressure toward group conformity. To describe this phenomenon, he coined the term **groupthink**—the process by which members of a cohesive group arrive at a decision that many individual members privately believe is unwise. Why not speak up at the time? Members usually want to be "team players." They may not want to be the ones who undermine the group's consensus or who challenge the leadership. Consequently, members often withhold their opinions and focus on consensus rather than on exploring all the options and making the best decision. Figure 6.5 summarizes the dynamics and results of groupthink.

groupthink The process by which members of a cohesive group arrive at a decision that many individual members privately believe is unwise.

Similarly, in 1986, the launch of the space shuttle Challenger, which exploded 73 seconds into its flight, killing all seven crew members, provides an example of groupthink. On the day preceding the launch, engineers at the company that designed and manufactured the shuttle's rocket boosters became concerned that freezing temperatures at the launch site would interfere with the proper functioning of the O-ring seals in the boosters. When they expressed their misgivings, they were overruled by higher officials at the company and with NASA (the government agency that administers the U.S. space program), where executives were impatient because of earlier delays. A presidential commission that investigated the tragedy concluded that neither the manufacturer nor NASA responded adequately to warnings about the seals (Lippa, 1994).

FIGURE 6.5 JANIS'S DESCRIPTION OF GROUPTHINK

Process of Groupthink	Example: *Columbia* Explosion
PRIOR CONDITIONS Isolated, cohesive, homogeneous decision-making group Lack of impartial leadership High stress	NASA had previously orchestrated many successful shuttle missions and was under pressure to complete additional space missions that would fulfill agency goals and keep its budget intact.
SYMPTOMS OF GROUPTHINK Closed-mindedness Rationalization Squelching of dissent "Mindguards" Feelings of righteousness and invulnerability	Although *Columbia*'s left wing had been damaged on takeoff when a chunk of insulated foam from the external fuel tank struck it, NASA did not regard this as a serious problem because it had occurred on previous launches. Some NASA engineers stated that they did not feel free to raise questions about problems.
DEFECTIVE DECISION MAKING Incomplete examination of alternatives Failure to examine risks and contingencies Incomplete search for information	The debate among engineers regarding whether the shuttle had been damaged to the extent that the wing might burn off on re-entry was not passed on to the shuttle crew or to NASA's top officials in a timely manner because either the engineers harboured doubts about their concerns or were unwilling to believe that the mission was truly imperilled.
CONSEQUENCES Poor decisions	The shuttle *Columbia* was destroyed during re-entry into the Earth's atmosphere, killing all seven crew members and strewing debris across large portions of the United States.

© AP Photo/Chris O'Meara

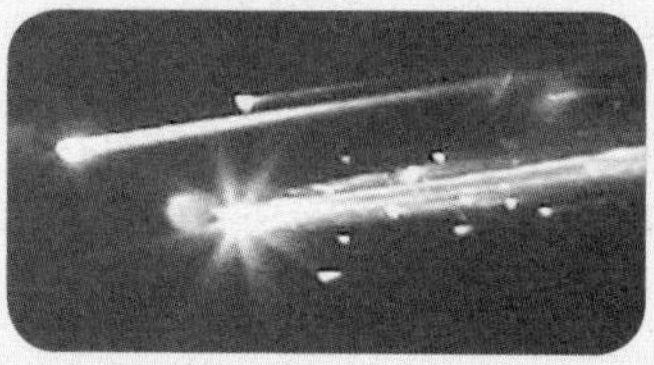

© AP Images/Dr. Scott Lieberman

In Janis's model, prior conditions, such as a highly homogeneous group with committed leadership, can lead to potentially disastrous "groupthink," which short-circuits careful and impartial deliberation. Events leading up to the tragic 2003 launch of the space shuttle *Columbia* provide an example of this process.

Why did people agree to the launch despite these safety concerns? It is one thing to doubt your judgment about the length of a line, as in the Asch experiments, and quite another to send seven people to their deaths. The engineers closest to the situation almost unanimously opposed the launch. The decision, however, was ultimately made by managers more focused on the schedule than on safety concerns. NASA managers were under great pressure to keep the shuttle flights on schedule because they feared budget cuts. When the contractor suggested delaying the launch until air temperatures were above 53°F (11.7°C), NASA managers responded angrily. One said, "My God . . . when do you want me to launch, next April?" (President's Commission, 1986:96). Another said, "I'm appalled by your recommendation" (President's Commission, 1986:94). Faced with this pressure, the contractor, who was about to begin negotiating a new billion-dollar agreement with NASA, had second thoughts. Senior managers overruled the recommendations of their engineers and recommended launch. NASA managers and the contractor managers risked other people's lives to accomplish their own bureaucratic goals.

Groupthink can be hard to eliminate. Despite the clear analysis of NASA's errors in the *Challenger* case, groupthink may also have contributed to the 2003 crash of the space shuttle *Columbia*, as administrators did not listen to engineers' concerns about foam that had broken from a fuel tank on seven previous flights. Damage caused by this foam led to the destruction of the shuttle. One of the investigation board members concluded that dissent was still not welcome at NASA, even when safety was involved.

© Franz Pedrick/The Image Works

Although telephone- and computer-based procedures have streamlined registration at many schools, for many students registration exemplifies the worst aspects of academic bureaucracy. Yet students and other members of the academic community depend upon the bureaucracy to establish and administer procedures that enable the complex university system to operate smoothly.

TIME TO REVIEW

- Discuss the differences between groups, aggregates, and categories.
- Explain the importance of the difference between primary and secondary groups.
- Discuss how people interact though networks.
- Explain how groups can lead people to make bad decisions. How does "groupthink" affect peoples' behaviour?
- Discuss the impact of group size on interaction patterns within groups.

FORMAL ORGANIZATIONS LO-4

In earlier times, life was centred in small, informal groups, such as the family and the village. With the advent of industrialization and urbanization (as discussed in Chapter 1), people's lives became increasingly dominated by large, formal organizations. A formal organization is a highly structured group formed for the purpose of completing certain tasks or achieving specific goals. Formal organizations (such as corporations, schools, and government agencies) usually keep their basic structure for many years.

Bureaucracies

The bureaucratic model of organization is the most universal organizational form in government, business, education, and religion. A **bureaucracy** is an organizational model characterized by a hierarchy of authority, a clear division of labour, explicit rules and procedures, and impersonality in personnel matters.

bureaucracy An organizational model characterized by a hierarchy of authority, a clear division of labour, explicit rules and procedures, and impersonality in personnel matters.

When we think of a bureaucracy, we may think of "buck-passing," such as occurs when we are directed from one office to the next without receiving an answer to our question or a solution to our problem. We also may view a bureaucracy in terms of red tape because of the situations in which there is so much paperwork and so many incomprehensible rules that no one really understands what to do. However, bureaucracy originally was not intended to be this way; it was seen as a way to make organizations *more* productive and efficient. Weber (1968/1922) was interested in the historical trend toward bureaucratization that accelerated during the Industrial Revolution. To Weber, the bureaucracy was the most efficient means of attaining organizational goals because of its coordination and control.

WHY BUREAUCRACY? While much of the rest of this chapter focuses on how bureaucracies work, it is also important to understand why they exist. The simple answer is that they exist because organizations grew too large to be managed in any other way. However, large organizations existed for thousands of years before the birth of bureaucracy, so we must also consider social conditions to explain why the modern bureaucratic form of social organization arose in the 19th century in Europe and North America. Weber suggested that this growth required both cultural and structural changes that did not occur until then.

The cultural change was the rejection of *traditional authority* and the acceptance of *rational-legal authority* as the basis of conduct. This means that people were less willing to accept rules based on tradition and more willing to grant legitimacy to a set of rules intended to achieve certain ends (Weber, 1947). Weber's influential work on the relationship between the rise of Protestantism and the development of capitalism (Weber, 1976) analyzes the factors that led to this change.

The social conditions for factory bureaucracies were established during the Industrial Revolution, when peasants were forced off the farms. These former peasants became the first large labour pool for the factories, as they had no alternative but to work for whatever wages the owners would pay them. The system of wage employment gave the profits from the workers' labour to the factory owner, while the workers were paid only a subsistence wage. This cheap labour provided a tremendous incentive for the factory owners to expand their enterprises. Owners used the capital their factories generated to mechanize the factories; they also developed the systems of specialization and standardization that most efficiently achieved productivity and profitability. Of course, breaking down production into specialized tasks required managers to coordinate activities, so the factories quickly became hierarchical organizations.

The success of the factory bureaucracy was important because it encouraged other organizations to adopt the same principles. The bureaucratic form quickly spread to governments, schools, and churches. Even today, we find pressure for other organizations to follow the lead of industry. Governments are continually urged to become more "businesslike," and universities face pressure to become more efficient and to meet the specialized needs of industry rather than providing students with a broader education.

FORMAL CHARACTERISTICS OF BUREAUCRACY Weber set forth several characteristics of bureaucratic organizations. Although real bureaucracies may not feature all of these ideal characteristics, Weber's model highlights the organizational efficiency and productivity that bureaucracies strive for.

Division of Labour Bureaucracies are characterized by specialization, and each member has a specific status with certain assigned tasks to fulfill. This division of labour requires the employment of specialized experts. In a university, for example, a distinct division of labour exists between the faculty and the administration.

Hierarchy of Authority Hierarchy of authority, or chain of command, includes each lower office being under the control of a higher one. Hierarchical authority takes the form of a pyramid. Those few individuals at the top have more power and exercise more control than do the many at the lower levels. Hierarchy inevitably influences social interaction. People lower in the hierarchy report to (and often take orders from) those above them. Persons at the upper levels are responsible not only for their own actions but also for those of the individuals they supervise.

Rules and Regulations Weber asserted that rules and regulations establish authority within an organization. These rules are typically standardized and provided to members in a written format. In theory, written rules and regulations offer clear-cut standards for determining satisfactory performance. They also provide continuity so that each new member does not have to reinvent the rules and regulations.

Qualification-Based Employment Bureaucracies hire staff members and professional employees based on specific qualifications. Favouritism, family connections, and other subjective factors not relevant to organizational efficiency are not acceptable criteria for employment. Individual performance is evaluated against specific standards, and promotions are based on merit as spelled out in personnel policies.

Impersonality A detached approach should prevail toward clients so that personal feelings do not interfere with organizational decisions. Officials must interact with subordinates based on their status in the organization, not on the officials' personal feelings.

INFORMAL STRUCTURE IN BUREAUCRACIES An organizational chart makes the official, formal structure of a bureaucracy readily apparent. In practice, however, bureaucracies have patterns of activities and interactions that cannot be accounted for by organizational charts and formal rules. In addition to its formal structure, every bureaucracy has an informal structure, which has been called "bureaucracy's other face" (Page, 1946).

An organization's **informal structure** comprises those aspects of participants' day-to-day activities and interactions that ignore, bypass, or do not correspond with the official rules and procedures of the bureaucracy. An example is an informal "grapevine" that spreads information (with varying degrees of accuracy) much faster than do official channels of communication, which tend to be slow and unresponsive. The informal structure also includes the ideology and practices of workers on the job. Workers create a work culture to help deal with the constraints of their jobs and to guide their interactions with co-workers.

informal structure
Those aspects of participants' day-to-day activities and interactions that ignore, bypass, or do not correspond with the official rules and procedures of the bureaucracy.

HAWTHORNE STUDIES AND INFORMAL NETWORKS The Hawthorne studies first made social scientists aware of the effect of informal networks on workers' productivity.

Researchers observed 14 men in the "bank wiring room" who were responsible for making parts of switches for telephone equipment. Although management had offered financial incentives to encourage the men to work harder, the men persisted in working according to their own informal rules. They tended to work rapidly in the morning and to ease off in the afternoon. They frequently stopped their own work to help another person who had fallen behind. When they got bored, they swapped tasks so their work was more varied. They played games and bet on horse races and baseball.

Why did these men insist on lagging behind even when they had been offered financial incentives to work harder? Perhaps they feared that the required productivity levels would increase if they showed that they could do more. Some of them also may have feared that they would lose their jobs if the work was finished more rapidly. One finding stood out: The men's productivity level was clearly related to the pressure they received from other members of their informal networks. Those who worked too hard were called "speed kings" and "rate busters"; individuals who worked too slowly were referred to as "chiselers." Those who broke the informal norm against telling a supervisor about someone else's shortcomings were called "squealers." Negative sanctions such as striking a person on the shoulder made the workers adhere to the informal norms of their work group. Ultimately, the level of productivity was determined by the workers' informal networks, not by the levels set by management (Blau and Meyer, 1987; Roethlisberger and Dickson, 1939).

© THE CANADIAN PRESS/Richard Lam

Corporal Catherine Galliford is one of a number of members and former members who have launched sexual harassment suits against the RCMP. Sociologists have found that women in male-dominated fields are less likely than men to be included in informal networks and more likely to be harassed on the job. Are these two factors related? What steps could be taken to reduce the problems of harassment and lack of networks?

POSITIVE AND NEGATIVE ASPECTS OF INFORMAL STRUCTURE Is informal structure good or bad? Should it be controlled or encouraged? Two schools of thought have emerged with regard to these questions. One approach emphasizes control of informal groups; the other suggests that they should be nurtured.

Traditional management theories are based on the assumption that people are basically lazy and motivated by greed. Consequently, informal groups must be controlled (or eliminated) to ensure greater worker productivity. Proponents of this view cite the bank wiring room study to demonstrate the importance of controlling informal networks.

The other school of thought asserts that people are capable of cooperation. Thus, organizations should foster informal groups that permit people to work more efficiently toward organizational goals. Barnard (1938) discussed the functional aspects of informal groups. He suggested that informal groups help organizations by providing understanding and motivation for participants. Research on soldiers in combat has shown that bonds with other soldiers in each small squad or platoon have much more impact on performance than abstract notions of patriotism and love for one's country (Marshall, 1947). Even in huge organizations, close interpersonal relationships provide meaning and a sense of belonging to individual workers.

Informal groups can have a negative impact on employees who are excluded from them. While some scholars have argued that women and visible minorities receive fairer treatment in larger bureaucracies than they do in smaller organizations, others feel that they may be excluded from networks that are important for survival and advancement in the organization (Benokraitis and Feagin, 1986; Kanter, 1977; South et al., 1982). Women and visible minorities who are employed in positions traditionally held by white men (such as firefighters, police officers, and construction workers) are often excluded from the informal structure. Not only do they lack an informal network to "grease the wheels," they also may be harassed and endangered by their co-workers. For example, in 2012, many female RCMP members and ex-members sued the RCMP, claiming they had suffered sexual harassment, gender discrimination, and exposure to pornography throughout their careers. In sum, the informal structure is critical for employees—whether they are allowed to participate in it or not.

Shortcomings of Bureaucracies

Weber's description of bureaucracy was intentionally an idealized model of a rationally organized institution. However, the characteristics that make up this "rational" model have a dark side that has frequently given bureaucracies a bad name (see Figure 6.6). Three of the major problems of bureaucracies are inefficiency and rigidity; resistance to change; and perpetuation of gender, race, and class inequalities.

INEFFICIENCY AND RIGIDITY Bureaucracies experience inefficiency and rigidity throughout the organization. The self-protective behaviour of officials at the top may render

FIGURE 6.6 CHARACTERISTICS AND EFFECTS OF BUREAUCRACY

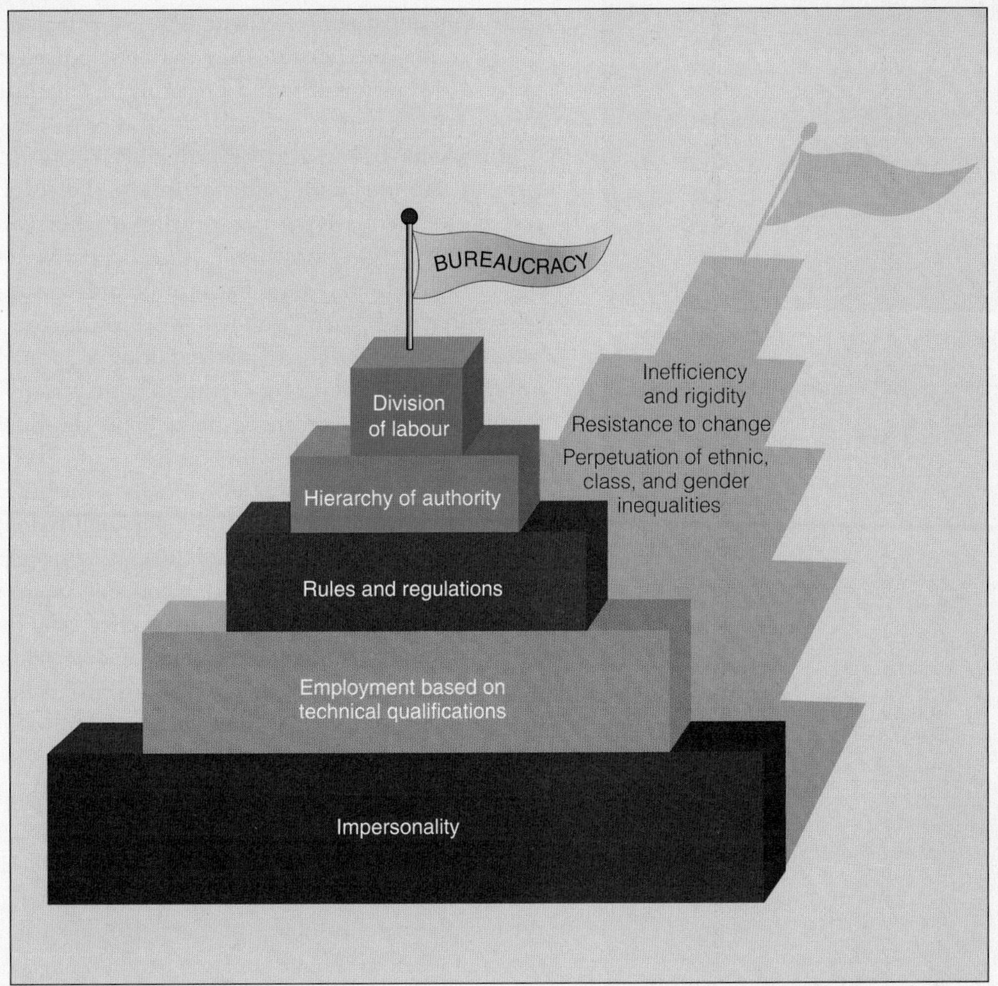

The very characteristics that define Weber's idealized bureaucracy can create or worsen the problems that many people associate with this type of organization.

the organization inefficient. One type of self-protective behaviour is the monopolization of information. Information is crucial for decision making at all levels of an organization. However, those in positions of authority may guard information because it is a source of power for them—others cannot second-guess their decisions without access to relevant (and often confidential) information (Blau and Meyer, 1987).

This information blockage is intensified by the hierarchical arrangement of officials and workers. While those at the top may use their power and authority to monopolize information, they may also fail to communicate with workers at the lower levels. As a result, they are often unaware of potential problems facing the organization. Meanwhile, those at the bottom of the structure hide their mistakes from supervisors, a practice that ultimately may result in problems for the organization.

goal displacement A process that occurs in organizations when the rules become an end in themselves rather than a means to an end.

Policies and procedures also contribute to inefficiency and rigidity. Bureaucratic regulations are often written out in great detail to ensure that almost all conceivable situations are covered (Blau and Meyer, 1987). **Goal displacement** occurs when the rules

© CP/AP Photo/Barry Sweet

© CLARO CORTES IV/Reuters/Landov

The "organization man" of the computer age varies widely in manner and appearance, as shown in the contrast between the top photo of a casually clad employee at Apple Computer and the one of Bill Gates, the formally dressed chairman of Microsoft.

become an end in themselves rather than a means to an end (Merton, 1968). Administrators tend to overconform to the rules because their expertise is knowledge of the regulations and they are paid to enforce them. They also fear that if they bend the rules for one person, they may be accused of violating the norm of impersonality and engaging in favouritism (Blau and Meyer, 1987).

Bureaucrats may also be inflexible because they fear criticism or liability if they do not follow the rules closely. In the case of Kenneth Payne, the aspiring teacher you read about at the beginning of this chapter, bureaucrats were afraid to waive the need for fingerprints because of public concern about the possibility of sexual offenders working in the schools. These bureaucrats were able to avoid taking responsibility for their unreasonable decision by saying that they were "just following the rules." Mistakes can be blamed on the bureaucracy rather than on the individuals who run it.

Rigidity can also occur at lower levels of the bureaucracy. Merton (1968) used the term **bureaucratic personality** to describe workers who are more concerned with following correct procedures than they are with getting the job done correctly. Such workers are usually able to handle routine situations effectively but may be incapable of handling a unique problem or an emergency. Box 6.2 shows how bureaucratic inefficiency contributed to serious terrorist attacks in Canada and the United States.

RESISTANCE TO CHANGE Resistance to change occurs in all bureaucratic organizations. This resistance can make it difficult for organizations to adapt to new circumstances. Many workers are reluctant to change because they have adapted their professional and personal lives to the old way of doing their jobs. Some workers have also seen previous change efforts fail and do not want to commit to the latest effort at transforming their organization. Those trying to implement change can have a difficult task breaking through this resistance.

The hierarchical structure of bureaucracies can make this situation worse. Management is separated from labour, clerical workers from professional workers, and people doing one function from those doing another. This creates structural barriers to communication and to joint problem solving. Information is restricted and problems are dealt with in a segmented way. People are rewarded for not taking risks and punished when they try to make changes. Often, people have no structural way of getting innovative ideas from the bottom to the top, so they give up trying. Kanter provides an example of this kind of blockage in a textile company that had been dealing with frequent and costly yarn breakages for decades:

bureaucratic personality A psychological construct that describes those workers who are more concerned with following correct procedures than they are with doing the job correctly.

> A new plant manager interested in improving employee communication and involvement discovered a foreign-born worker with an ultimately successful idea for modifying the machine to reduce breakage—and was shocked to learn that the man had wondered about the machine modification for thirty-two years. "Why didn't you say something before?" the manager asked. The reply: "My supervisor wasn't interested and I had no one else to tell it to." (Kanter, 1983:70)

BOX 6.2 POINT/COUNTERPOINT

How Bureaucratic Inefficiency Contributed to Terrorist Attacks

Bureaucratic inefficiency can impede information flow within and between large-scale organizations. Failures of governmental organizations to properly utilize information have contributed to the success of major terrorist strikes in Canada and the United States.

In 1985, an explosion destroyed Air India Flight 182, killing 329 people. The flight had originated in Vancouver and most of the victims were Canadians. After nearly two decades of investigation, two Sikh militants were tried for the crime, but they were acquitted in 2005.

Following the trial, an inquiry into the bombing was critical of the work of the RCMP and the Canadian Security and Intelligence Service (CSIS). The investigation into the bombing was seriously flawed and there was little cooperation between the RCMP and CSIS. Both the RCMP and CSIS had information that could have prevented the attack but took no action. Bureaucratic inefficiencies facilitated the attack and hindered the subsequent investigation.

One specific problem is that CSIS and the RCMP have different roles. CSIS is responsible for collecting intelligence on possible terrorist activity, while the RCMP is responsible for investigating criminal matters and assisting in the prosecution of accused persons. There has been a history of poor relationships between these agencies, and information collected by one agency has not always been made available to the other. CSIS did not process information on the prime suspect, prematurely erased wiretap evidence, and did not share evidence with the RCMP. The RCMP did not provide CSIS with intelligence information that would have allowed them to correctly assess the threat: "Unforgivably, the RCMP did not forward to CSIS the June 1st Telex that set out Air India's own intelligence, forecasting a June terrorist attempt to bomb an Air India flight by means of explosives hidden in checked baggage" (Commission of Inquiry into the Investigation of the Bombing of Air India Flight 182, 2010:23). The failure of these agencies to properly assess and share evidence contributed to the murder of hundreds of people.

These problems are not unique. Following the 2001 terrorist attacks on the United States, the Federal Bureau of Investigation (FBI), the Central Intelligence Agency (CIA), and other U.S. governmental organizations faced similar criticism about how they used and shared information before these attacks. The U.S. Senate Judiciary Committee conducted hearings in an effort to learn what information about terrorist activities and possible U.S. targets had been available to federal agencies before September 11 and why the government had not acted on this information to prevent the attacks. The judiciary committee interviewed FBI agent Coleen Rowley, who testified that she believed the culture of the FBI had prevented the organization from acting on what it knew before the attacks (*New York Times*, 2002b):

> Agent Rowley: We have a culture in the FBI that there's a certain pecking order, and it's pretty strong. And it's very rare that someone picks up the phone and calls a rank or two above themselves. It would have to be only on the strongest reasons. Typically, you would have to . . . pick up the phone and talk to somebody who is at your rank. So when you have an item that requires review by a higher level, it's incumbent for you to go to a higher-level person in your office and then for that person to make a call . . .
>
> Senator Grassley: In your letter [to the FBI director], you mention a culture of fear, especially a fear of taking action, and the problem of careerism. Could you talk about how this hurts investigations in the field, what the causes are, and what you think might fix these problems?
>
> Agent Rowley: [W]hen I looked up the definition [of careerism], I really said [it's] unbelievable how appropriate that is. I think the FBI does have a problem with that. And if I remember right, it means, "promoting one's career over integrity." So, when people make decisions, and it's basically so that [they] can get to the next level and not rock—either it's not rock the boat or do what a boss says without question. And either way that works, if you're making a decision to try to get to the next level, but you're not making that decision for the real right reason, that's a problem . . .

Organizations that resist change, rather than adapt to it, may not survive and certainly will not flourish. Thus leaders of many different organizations face the task of developing new organizational models that are better suited to today's environment. Consider the challenges faced by leaders of corporations such as those discussed in Box 6.3, "Organizations and New Media" (see Box 6.3 at **www.nelson.com/sociologyinourtimes6e**).

PERPETUATION OF GENDER, RACE, AND CLASS INEQUALITIES Bureaucracies can perpetuate inequalities of gender, race, and class. Power at the top of most North American bureaucracies still remains in the hands of affluent white men. These divisions can be perpetuated by the "dual labour market" in which bureaucracies provide different career paths for different categories of workers. Middle- and upper-class employees are more likely to have careers characterized by higher wages, job security, and opportunities for advancement. By contrast, poor and working-class employees (who are more likely to be women and members of racial minorities) work in occupations characterized by low wages, lack of job security, and few opportunities for promotion. This dual labour market not only reflects class, race, and gender inequities but also perpetuates them. See Box 6.4 on page 164.

While the situation has improved over the past several decades, women and members of racial minorities may also find themselves excluded from informal networks. Kanter (1977) conducted an important study of the difficulties faced by workers who did not fit the white male stereotype. There are enormous pressures on "tokens"—group members who were different from the dominant group members. Tokens were singled out and were often viewed as representatives of their group rather than as individual workers. These pressures led to higher turnover rates and to reduced performance by those in the token groups.

To counteract these pressures, organizations must establish policies that ensure supportive environments for members of disadvantaged groups. Pryor and McKinney (1991) showed how people respond to environments that condone sexist behaviour. Their experiments examined the dynamics of sexual harassment on university campuses. In one experiment, a graduate student (a member of the research team) led research subjects to believe that they would be training undergraduate women to use a computer. The actual purpose of the experiment was to observe whether the trainers (subjects) would harass the women if given the opportunity and encouraged to do so. By design, the graduate student purposely harassed the women (who were also part of the research team), setting an example for the subjects to follow.

Pryor and McKinney found that when the "trainers" were led to believe that sexual harassment was condoned and were then left alone with the women, they took full advantage of the situation in 90 percent of the experiments. One of the women on the research team felt vulnerable because of the permissive environment created by the men in charge:

> So it kind of made me feel a little bit powerless as far as that goes because there was nothing I could do about it. But I also realized that in a business setting, if this person really was my boss, that it would be harder for me to send out the negative signals or whatever to try to fend off that type of thing. (1995)

TIME TO REVIEW

- Why have bureaucracies become the most universal organizational form in modern society?
- Describe the five characteristics that Weber believed characterized bureaucracies.
- How can the informal structure affect the way bureaucracies operate?
- Why do bureaucracies sometimes become rigid, inefficient and resistant to change?
- How do bureaucracies perpetuate inequalities of gender, race, and class?

McDonaldization

Weber's work on bureaucracy was based on his view that rationalization was an inevitable part of the social world. George Ritzer has updated Weber's work by looking at what he calls *McDonaldization*—"the process by which the principles of the fast-food restaurant are coming to dominate more and more sectors of American society, as well as of the rest of the world" (2004:1). Ritzer believes that McDonald's restaurants embody the principles of rationalization and establish a model that is emulated by many other types of organizations. To Ritzer, fast-food restaurants go beyond Weber's model of bureaucracy. The basic elements of McDonaldization are as follows:

- *Efficiency.* Fast-food restaurants operate like an assembly line. Food is cooked, assembled, and served according to a standardized procedure. Customers line up or move quickly past a drive-through window. Despite the McDonald's slogan "We do it all for you," it is the customer who picks up the food, takes it to the table, and cleans up the garbage at the end of the meal.
- *Calculability.* The emphasis is on speed and quantity rather than quality. Cooking and serving operations are precisely timed, and the emphasis on speed often results in poor employee morale and high turnover rates. Restaurants are designed to encourage customers to leave quickly.
- *Predictability.* Standard menus and scripted encounters with staff make the experience predictable for customers. The food is supposed to taste the same wherever it is served.
- *Control.* Fast-food restaurants have never allowed individual employees much discretion; instead, employees must follow detailed procedures. The degree of control has been enhanced through technology. For example, automatic french fry cookers and other devices ensure a standardized product. Nobody claims to be a chef in a fast-food restaurant.
- *Irrationalities of rationality.* Fast-food restaurants are dehumanizing for both customers and employees. The examples of bureaucratic inflexibility used at the beginning of this chapter demonstrate this dehumanization, or **rationality**—the process by which traditional methods of social organization, characterized by informality and spontaneity, are gradually replaced by efficiently administered formal rules and procedures (bureaucracy). Kenneth Payne was denied a teaching career because of an inflexible interpretation of the rules, and the real human concerns of the victims of the New Orleans hurricane were subordinated to organizational rules.

rationality The process by which traditional methods of social organization, characterized by informality and spontaneity, are gradually replaced by efficiently administered formal rules and procedures (bureaucracy).

Ritzer feels that McDonaldization is expanding to other parts of our lives and to other parts of the world. Many universities process huge numbers of students by giving them classes in large lecture theatres and testing them using machine-graded, multiple-choice exams. The questions on these examinations are often taken from test banks provided by the textbook publishers, who also provide instructors with many of their teaching aids. Students who are more interested in efficiency than in learning can purchase their term papers online so they don't have to spend time writing them.

Recent increases in the number of babies born via surgery, using cesarean sections rather than waiting for a natural birth, show that even the birth process is being rationalized. Families and doctors may welcome the predictability associated with scheduling birth on a specific day during normal working hours rather than waiting for nature to take its course.

ORGANIZATIONS OF THE FUTURE: THE NETWORK ORGANIZATION LO-5

The form of organizations has changed over time. While we can never be certain about the future, broad social trends, such as globalization, technological innovation, and the increased prevalence of an economy based on services, make it likely that *networks* will become the dominant organization of the future. Social theorist Manuel Castells argues that "the old order, governed by discrete individual units in the pursuit of money, efficiency, happiness, or power,

BOX 6.4 POINT/COUNTERPOINT

Dilbert and the Bureaucracy

Our experiences with red tape and other bureaucratic inefficiencies have been satirized by cartoonist (and disillusioned bureaucrat) Scott Adams. In the late 1980s, Adams began passing his cartoons around the office at Pacific Bell. Since then, *Dilbert* has become a phenomenal success and is read in more than 2000 papers in 70 countries. *Dilbert* ridicules many of the worst features of bureaucracy, including stupid bosses, cubicles, management consultants, pointless meetings, and inflexibility. (For examples of the cartoon, go to www.unitedmedia.com/comics/dilbert).

Workers enjoy *Dilbert*. The cartoons are posted on office doors, walls, and desks, and many of Adams's ideas come from readers' suggestions. The British magazine *The Economist* attributes *Dilbert's* popularity to the fact that the comic strip taps into three trends that are troubling workers:

1. Employees are forced to labour harder to compensate for the effects of downsizing.
2. Workers are afraid of being laid off and see their wage increases falling far behind those of their managers.
3. New management fads have led to constant reorganization but have had little impact on efficiency or on job satisfaction.

Ironically, while many workers feel *Dilbert* says what they are thinking about ineffective and uncaring managers, the leaders of many of North America's largest corporations have used the cartoons for training and corporate communications.

Sources: The Economist, 1997; Merton, 1968; Whitaker, 1997.

is being replaced by a novel one in which motives, decisions, and actions flow from ever more fluid, yet ever-present networks. It is networks, not the firm, bureaucracy, or the family, that gets things done" (Esping Anderson, 2000:68).

You can learn how global networks operate by reading about the structure of terrorist organizations in Box 6.5, or by thinking about the ways in which illicit drugs get from the coca fields of Colombia and the poppy fields of Afghanistan to users on the streets of Halifax, Toronto, and Victoria. Large bureaucracies are not involved in either of these complex global enterprises, as terrorists and drug dealers operate very effectively through decentralized global networks. One reason that drug suppression strategies have not succeeded is because there is no company called Global Drugs Inc. that can be easily located and destroyed by law enforcement agencies. Instead, there are shifting, fluid networks of people who are difficult to identify and who are easily replaced when the legal system takes them out of the network. Similar problems face those who are trying to deal with the threat of terrorism.

Another example of the operation of a flexible global network is the production of open source software, such as the Linux operating system and the Firefox Internet browser. This software was not produced by a large profit-making corporation, but by networks of people working together with no expectation of profit. The product is available freely to anyone who wishes to download it, and programmers all over the world can make improvements in the software. While some coordination is necessary to develop a product that can be used by the public, no large bureaucracy is required and individual users are free to modify programs to suit their own needs.

Networks have always had an advantage over other organizational forms because they are agile and can quickly adapt to new circumstances. However, the ability to coordinate network activities has been weak compared to hierarchical bureaucratic organizations that

BOX 6.5 SOCIOLOGY IN GLOBAL PERSPECTIVE

The Structure of Terrorist Networks

The growth of large armies, such as the Prussian army, contributed to the development of the bureaucratic form of organization. These large armies represented the governments of established countries; however, many of today's wars are not between two countries.

Terrorist attacks around the globe and the difficulties in fighting the insurgency in Afghanistan have drawn attention to what military planners refer to as *asymmetrical warfare.* This term refers to attacks by small groups of people, who usually do not represent states or governments, upon much larger and stronger opponents. Terrorists do not directly confront their opponents, since they would be quickly defeated in such a confrontation. Rather, they use covert tactics, such as car bombs and suicide bombings, which are difficult to prevent.

To fight successfully against larger and more powerful opponents, terrorist groups must develop organizational structures that are difficult to identify and to fight against. Rather than forming large hierarchical armies, terrorist groups such as al-Qaeda have evolved sophisticated network structures. These networks are made up of loosely coupled cells, each of which has only a few members. This structure allows for a high level of secrecy, flexibility, and innovation. Participants in the network operate in a coordinated way because they have relationships with other members of the network, with whom they share a common vision of the future, not because of bureaucratic control. Al-Qaeda network members are linked by a common religious background and philosophy and through the leadership of now-deceased Osama bin Laden and his associates. Figure 6.7 is a simplified diagram of the al-Qaeda network. This structure is very different from the hierarchical organization charts of the military and security organizations that are trying to defeat al-Qaeda. This loose and flexible network structure makes it difficult to defeat terrorist organizations. For example, the network has roots in many different countries, and information and funds can flow relatively freely from one jurisdiction to another. On the other hand, security and intelligence agencies are based in individual countries and for a variety of reasons find it difficult to work cooperatively (Arquilla and Ronfeldt, 2001). The fluid network of al-Qaeda shown in the figure contrasts with the hierarchical, vertical structure of the armies and governments opposing it. Using modern communications technology, including the Internet, information can flow to all parts of the network much more easily than can information that must be filtered through national governments and their internal bureaucracies (see Box 6.2).

Krebs (2002) analyzed the relationships between the hijackers responsible for the September 11 attacks on the United States. Mohamed Atta, who was the leader of the attacks, had contacts with each of the teams of hijackers. However, most of the others had no contact with teams other than their own. The strategy of minimizing ties among members of the network is deliberate—if security personnel identify or apprehend one or two members of the network, they can provide only limited information about other members so the entire network would not be jeopardized. In a videotape that was found at an al-Qaeda training camp in Afghanistan, Osama bin Laden said, "Those who were trained to fly didn't know the others. One group of people did not know the other group" (Department of Defense, 2001, cited in Krebs, 2002:46). It is very difficult for those opposing such networks to be able to target more than a limited part of the terrorist organization.

Sources: Arquilla and Ronfeldt, 2001; Krebs, 2002.

(*continued*)

FIGURE 6.7 SIMPLIFIED REPRESENTATION OF THE AL-QAEDA NETWORK

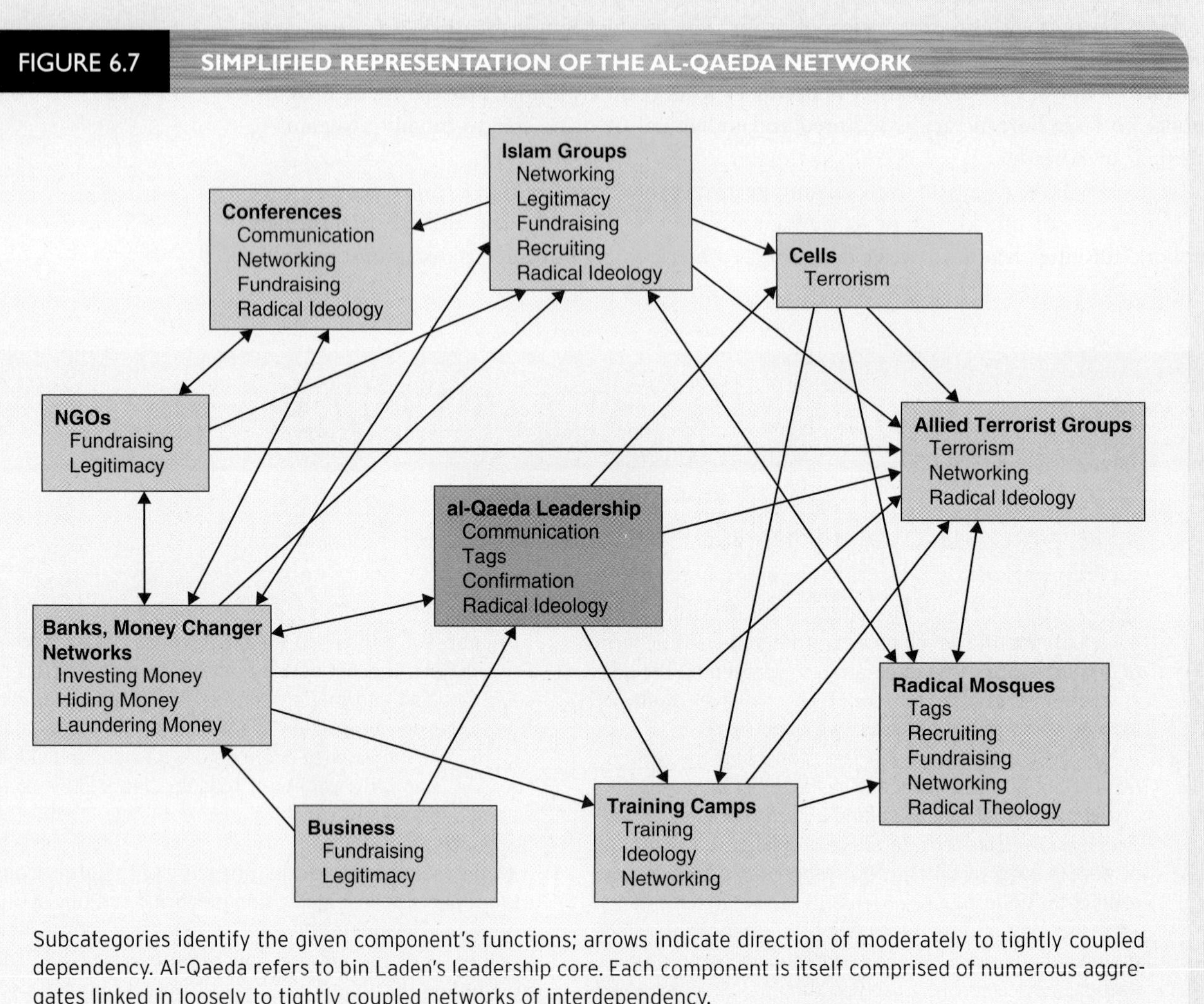

Subcategories identify the given component's functions; arrows indicate direction of moderately to tightly coupled dependency. Al-Qaeda refers to bin Laden's leadership core. Each component is itself comprised of numerous aggregates linked in loosely to tightly coupled networks of interdependency.

Source: Russ Marion and Mary Uhl-Bien, "A Complexity Theory and Al-Qaeda: Examining Complex Leadership," *Emergence* 5 (1), 2003, pp. 54–76.

have well-specified lines of communication and means of coordination. This has meant that bureaucracies have had a competitive advantage in handling complex tasks (Castells, 2000b). Modern information and communication technology has now provided networks with a competitive advantage. Each part of a network can communicate instantly with other parts, and those responsible for the network can constantly monitor performance even if the network is globally distributed. With this technology, the network can quickly shift and change, as pieces can be eliminated if they are no longer useful or can be temporarily set aside if they are not needed for a particular project (Castells, 2000b).

It is more difficult to centrally control a network than a traditional hierarchical organization because, once the network has been programmed and set in motion, it may be difficult for anyone, even those who started the network, to shut it down. With no central communication and control system, parts of the network can continue to operate even if the central core is eliminated. Thus, opponents of al-Qaeda could not shut down the network by simply closing down some of its pieces. Even Osama bin Laden would have had difficulty closing down the network or changing its goals if other members of al-Qaeda and its affiliated groups around the world wanted to continue with their activities.

Castells (2000a, 2000b) speaks of a new type of economic organization called the **network enterprise**, in which separate businesses, which may be companies or parts of companies, join together for specific projects that become the focus of the network. This structure gives those responsible for the network a great deal of flexibility, as they can select and change network partners based upon factors such as cost, efficiency, and technological innovation. The Dell laptop computer that you may be working on is the product of a network enterprise (Friedman, 2005). Dell sells its products over the Internet and by telephone rather than in stores, so your order may be taken by a person in Bangalore, India, rather than a clerk in your own city. The hardware that makes up the computer was manufactured by companies in Israel, the Philippines, Malaysia, Costa Rica, China, Taiwan, South Korea, Germany, Japan, Mexico, Singapore, Indonesia, India, and Thailand. The computers are assembled in Dell factories located in Ireland, China, Brazil, Malaysia, and the United States. Thomas Friedman describes how the company fills its orders:

network enterprise Separate businesses, which may be companies or parts of companies, join together for specific projects that become the focus of the network.

> "In an average day, we sell 140,000 to 150,000 computers," explained Dick Hunter, one of Dell's three global production managers. "Those orders come over Dell.com or over the telephone. As soon as these orders come in, our suppliers know about it. They get a signal based on every component in the machine you ordered, so the supplier knows just what he has to deliver. If you are supplying power cords for desktops, you can see minute by minute how many power cords you are going to have to deliver." Every two hours, the Dell factory in Penang [Malaysia] sends an email to the various SLCs [supplier logistics centres] nearby, telling each one what parts and what quantities of those parts it wants delivered within the next 90 minutes—and not one minute later. Within 90 minutes, trucks from the various SLCs around Penang pull up to the Dell manufacturing plant and unload the parts needed for all those notebooks ordered in the last two hours. This goes on all day, every two hours," said Hunter. (2005:415)

This system is a major reason why Dell helped to dramatically reduce computer prices during the 1990s and early 2000s. A critical factor in the development of widely dispersed network organizations has been the development of modern communications technology. Networks are held together by the rapid flow of information rather than by bricks and mortar and a rigid organizational chart like that of the industrial organization. The globalized production processes used by Dell and many other large companies would not be possible without instant global communication. The Internet itself is a decentralized and loosely coupled structure. The Internet was originally designed as way of ensuring that communications systems would survive an attack targeted at the central hubs of information systems. Instead of flowing from a central hub, information on the Internet is transmitted in small packets that can follow a wide range of electronic routes and are put together at the destination computer (Castells, 2000a). Nobody owns the Internet, so it is universally accessible to anyone who has a computer and a connection. While the Internet is vulnerable to a variety of threats, including computer hacking, it would be almost impossible to completely shut it down. Flexibility and resilience are what make the Internet such a valuable tool for networks.

Castells (2004) points out that it is not simply the technology that is critical, but also the cultural and organizational means of using the technology. This means that just having computers is not enough to guarantee access to the networked global economy. Countries with ineffective systems of government, few trained workers, and no entrepreneurial culture that supports innovation will be excluded from these networks. India has been successful in getting involved in network enterprises because of an entrepreneurial culture, a democratic government, and the presence of a well-educated workforce with English language skills, while many parts of Africa and Latin America have less involvement in the new economy.

Sociologists are also concerned with assessing the impact of network enterprises on people. While this network structure can help corporations to become more profitable, the impact on workers has not always been as positive. For example, unions lose much of their bargaining power when production at one plant can be quickly moved to another part of the network in a different country. Thus a strike may result in the permanent closure of a factory and the movement of jobs offshore. It is likely that the future work lives of today's university students will be affected in many ways—some positive but others negative—by the shift to networked organizations. Because network enterprises are fluid and can quickly transform themselves, you should anticipate that your working lives may also change rapidly after you enter the labour market.

Finally, there are inherent dangers in networked organizations. These dangers were illustrated in August 2003 when the power went off for several days in much of Ontario because of a power outage in Ohio that cascaded through the transmission networks covering the northeastern U.S. and Ontario. A similar network failure led to the global financial crisis in 2008 in which lax U.S. mortgage practices affected the global economy and billions of people who had not even invested in these mortgages (Watts, 2009). Our reliance on complex physical and social networks places us at risk, and these risks are not always predictable. Global transportation networks facilitate the spread of disease; email viruses threaten our computers; a moment of indiscretion can be spread around the globe through YouTube; and any disruption of traffic between Detroit and Windsor would have a serious impact on North American automobile production and food distribution because of the system of parts manufacture and supply. Governments will be challenged in the future to determine ways of minimizing this risk.

TIME TO REVIEW

- Explain Ritzer's theory that the principles that guide McDonald's operations are expanding to other parts of our lives and to other parts of the world.
- How does the network structure increase the effectiveness of terrorist groups?
- According to Castells, what are the advantages of network enterprises over traditional businesses?
- How is the Internet changing the way businesses operate?

VISUAL SUMMARY

6

LO-1 Identify the differences among social groups, aggregates, and categories.

A social group is a collection of two or more people who interact frequently, share a sense of belonging, and depend on one another. People who happen to be in the same place at the same time are considered an aggregate. Those who share a similar characteristic are considered a category. Neither aggregates nor categories are considered social groups.

© Gari Wyn Williams/Alamy

© Roy Morsch/zefa/Corbis

LO-2 Understand the effect that size has on the functioning of groups.

In small groups, all members know one another and interact simultaneously. In groups with more than three members, the dynamics of communication change and members tend to assume specialized tasks. As groups grow larger, keeping them operating effectively becomes increasingly challenging.

LO-3 Explain the impact of groups on people's behaviour.

Groups have a significant influence on our values, attitudes and behaviour. Most of us our willing to exhibit a high level of conformity to the wishes of other group members. This sometimes leads to groupthink—the process by which members of a cohesive group arrive at a decision that many individual members privately believe is unwise.

© AP Photo/Chris O'Meara

KEY TERMS

aggregate A collection of people who happen to be in the same place at the same time but have little else in common (p. 144).

bureaucracy An organizational model characterized by a hierarchy of authority, a clear division of labour, explicit rules and procedures, and impersonality in personnel matters (p. 155).

bureaucratic personality A psychological construct that describes those workers who are more concerned with following correct procedures than they are with doing the job correctly (p. 160).

category A number of people who may never have met one another but who share a similar characteristic (p. 144).

conformity The process of maintaining or changing behaviour to comply with the norms established by a society, subculture, or other group (p. 150).

dyad A group consisting of two members (p. 149).

goal displacement A process that occurs in organizations when the rules become an end in themselves rather than a means to an end (p. 159).

groupthink The process by which members of a cohesive group arrive at a decision that many individual members privately believe is unwise (p. 153).

informal structure Those aspects of participants' day-to-day activities and interactions that ignore, bypass, or do not correspond with the official rules and procedures of the bureaucracy (p. 157).

ingroup A group to which a person belongs and with which the person feels a sense of identity (p. 146).

network A web of social relationships that link one person with other people and, through them, with more people that those people know (p. 146).

network enterprise Separate businesses, which may be companies or parts of companies, join together for specific projects that become the focus of the network (p. 167).

outgroup A group to which a person does not belong and toward which the person may feel a sense of competitiveness or hostility (p. 146).

rationality The process by which traditional methods of social organization, characterized by informality and spontaneity, are gradually replaced by efficiently administered formal rules and procedures (bureaucracy) (p. 163).

reference group A group that strongly influences a person's behaviour and social attitudes, regardless of whether that individual is a member (p. 146).

small group A collectivity small enough for all members to be acquainted with one another and to interact simultaneously (p. 149).

triad A group composed of three members (p. 149).

LO-4 Identify the characteristics that define a bureaucracy and the "other face" of bureaucracies.

© Lebrecht Music and Arts Photo Library/Alamy

A bureaucracy is a formal organization characterized by hierarchical authority, division of labour, explicit procedures, and impersonality. Bureaucracy's "other face" is the informal structure of daily activities and interactions that bypass the official rules and procedures. Informal networks may enhance productivity or may be counterproductive to the organization. They also may be detrimental to those who are excluded from them.

LO-5 Discuss the form large organizations may take in the future.

© CLARO CORTES IV/Reuters/Landov

While we can never be certain about the future, broad social trends, such as globalization, technological innovation, and the increased prevalence of a service economy, make it likely that networks will be the dominant organization of the future. Networked organizations, which are made possible by modern communications technology, are flexible and can respond quickly to social change.

APPLICATION QUESTIONS

1. Do you think the insights gained from Milgram's research on obedience outweigh the elements of deception and stress that were forced on his subjects?
2. Many students have worked at a McDonald's or at some other fast-food restaurant. Relate your experience (or that of your friends) to George Ritzer's analysis of "McDonaldization."
3. Technology is changing the way organizations have to operate. Consider the entertainment industry. Downloading music and movies from the Internet has become very popular, and the film and music industries are trying hard to convince the Canadian government to pass new legislation to combat this downloading. What are the arguments of those who think that this material should be widely available on the Internet? What are the counterarguments of those who wish to see downloading regulated? Which side do you support in this debate?
4. What happens to people when they violate bureaucratic regulations? What range of sanctions do bureaucracies have to enforce these regulations?
5. Networks are important organizational forms. How have social networking sites changed the way in which people stay connected with their personal and professional networks?

KEY FIGURES

Used courtesy of George Ritzer

George Ritzer (b. 1940) Ritzer is a prolific social theorist who is perhaps best known for his work on the concept of "McDonaldization." This work is a contemporary extension of Weber's study of rationalization.

Used courtesy of Manuel Castells

Manuel Castells (b. 1942) One of the foremost theorists of network theory, Castells is a Spanish sociologist who has taught for many years in the U.S. His other work has focused on the influence of the media, globalization, and the processes of urban life.

Photo by Eric Kroll

Stanley Milgram (1933-1984) Milgram was a social psychologist whose work contributed to the study of social organization. His best-known research involves his study of the "small world" and his controversial obedience studies.

Rosabeth Moss Kanter (b. 1943) A professor at Harvard Business School, much of Kanter's work has focused on change management. One of her best-known books, *Men and Women of the Corporation* (1977), examined the difficulties faced by members of token groups, including women, in formal organizations.

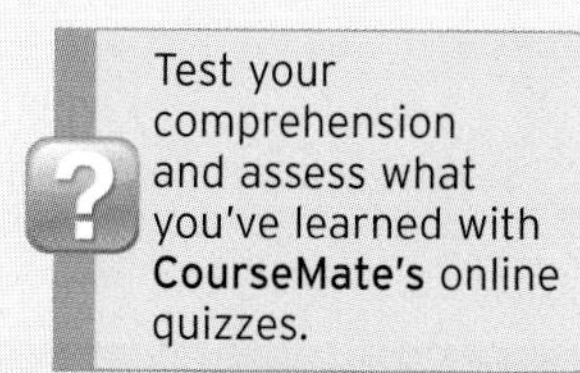
Test your comprehension and assess what you've learned with **CourseMate's** online quizzes.

For other interesting Lived Experiences, watch the video clips on **CourseMate.**

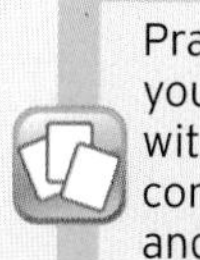
Practise what you've learned with flashcards containing key terms and definitions on **CourseMate.**

CHAPTER 7 Crime and Deviance

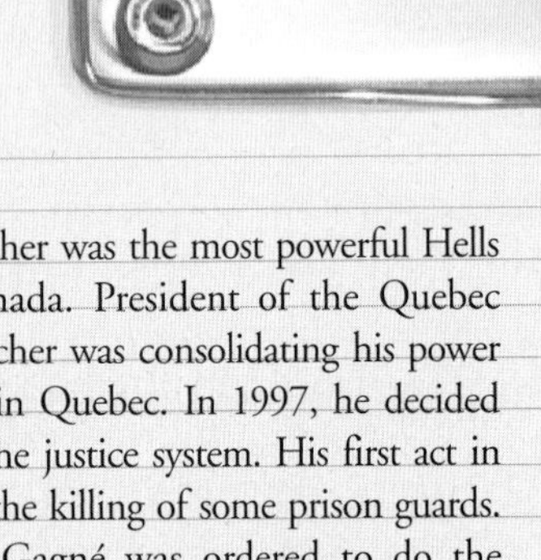

© CP/Ryan Remiorz

Maurice "Mom" Boucher was the most powerful Hells Angels leader in Canada. President of the Quebec Nomads chapter, Boucher was consolidating his power over organized crime in Quebec. In 1997, he decided to go to war against the justice system. His first act in this war was to order the killing of some prison guards. Stéphane "Godasse" Gagné was ordered to do the killings. Gagné was a member of the Rockers, a Hells Angels' puppet gang that did much of the Angels' dirty work. For several years, he enforced drug debts, served as a bodyguard, and did other jobs for the Hells Angels.

On two separate operations, Gagné and another gang member killed guards Diane Lavigne and Pierre Rondeau. Gagné was eventually arrested and confessed to the murders. In exchange for some minor concessions, he also agreed to testify against Mom Boucher for ordering the murders.

In 1998, Boucher was acquitted, but the Crown successfully appealed and Boucher was convicted at a second trial in 2002 and is currently serving a life sentence. At Boucher's first trial, Gagné testified about Boucher's role in the murders. In his cross-examination, Boucher's lawyer, Jacques Larochelle, tried to discredit Gagné's testimony by highlighting his criminal past. Gagné's responses illustrate the brutality of organized crime:

> *"During this entire time, you evidently had no respect for authority?"*
> *"No."*
> *"No respect for other people's property."*
> *"No."*
> *"No respect for the truth?"*
> *"No."*

Larochelle then tried to show Gagné's readiness to do anything he thought would please the Hells Angels. He recalled a hunger strike at Sorel prison that Mom ordered because he was sick of eating shepherd's pie. One inmate broke ranks and ate the meal.

> *"And without anyone asking you to do it," Larochelle asked, "you went over and beat him up?"*
> *"Yes."*
> *"In fact you courageously waited until he was asleep and you went to attack him in his bed, is that correct?"*
> *"Yes."*
> *"You hit him so hard with your fist that the bone came out his nose—all so that you would be noticed, is that correct?"*
> *"Yes."*

Larochelle also elicited the sordid details of Gagné's attempted murder of the drug dealer Christian Bellemare. He showed how Gagné acted

Source: Excerpted from *The Road to Hell: How the Biker Gangs are Conquering Canada* by Julian Sher and William Marsden.

alone, deciding to kill him because he owed him money.

> *"The first two bullets hit Bellemare in the throat or in that area. But the other bullets didn't fire, and Bellemare was still alive?" Larochelle said, taking the jurors back to the scene of the crime.*
>
> *"Yes," Gagné agreed.*
>
> *"You went running up to Bellemare and you put your fingers around his neck, your two hands around his neck, and squeezed?"*
>
> *"Yes."*
>
> *"He tries to talk, is that correct?" Larochelle pushed. "You have a good idea of what he is trying to tell you, I imagine?"*
>
> *"Yes."*
>
> *"Don't kill me, or something like that?" the lawyer suggested.*
>
> *"Something like that, yes," said Gagné.*
>
> *"That didn't impress you?"*
>
> *"I had a job to do," he admitted.* (Sher and Marsden, 2003:147-148)

Despite the attempts of the Hells Angels to convince the public that they are just a social club, supporting the community through events such as toy runs, they are one of Canada's most powerful criminal organizations. The violence of Godasse Gagné is typical of the methods used by organized criminals and explains why nearly one in every five Canadian homicides—94 killings in 2010—is gang-related (Mahony, 2011).

Organized crime is one of a wide range of behaviours that society has defined as deviant and/or criminal. For many years, crime and deviance have been of special interest to sociologists. Many of the issues they have examined remain important today: What is deviant behaviour, and how does it differ from criminal behaviour? Why are some people considered to be "deviants" or "criminals" while others are not? How should society deal with those who break the rules? Before reading on, take the quiz on crime and organized crime in Box 7.1 on page 175.

Critical Thinking Questions

1. The violence perpetrated by the Hells Angels and other organized crime groups is fed by the huge amounts of money made by selling illegal drugs. Many of the people who buy these drugs are otherwise respectable lawyers, electricians, and even students. How do you think these people justify sustaining organized crime?
2. In the *Safe Streets and Communities Act*, passed in 2012, the federal government imposed mandatory minimum penalties for some relatively minor drug offences, including growing six marijuana plants and selling or sharing the crop. Do you think these mandatory penalties will help reduce drug crime in Canada?
3. Should so-called victimless crimes such as recreational drug use and prostitution be decriminalized? What do you think would be the positive and negative effects of decriminalization?

CHAPTER FOCUS QUESTION What are the causes and consequences of crime in Canada?

LEARNING OBJECTIVES

AFTER READING THIS CHAPTER, YOU SHOULD BE ABLE TO

LO-1 Explain the meanings of the terms *crime* and *deviance*.

LO-2 Understand the way in which crime and deviance are explained by functionalist, conflict, interactionist, feminist, and postmodern theories.

LO-3 Describe how sociologists count and classify crimes.

LO-4 Understand how age, gender, class, and race are related to deviance and crime.

LO-5 Describe how the criminal justice system deals with crime.

© CP/Paul Chiasson

Outlaw motorcycle gangs such as the Hells Angels are highly profitable criminal organizations.

LO-1 WHAT IS DEVIANCE?

How do societies determine what behaviour is acceptable and what is unacceptable? All societies have norms that govern acceptable behaviour. If we are to live and to work with others, these rules are necessary. We must also have a reasonable expectation that other people will obey the rules. Think of the chaos that would result if each driver decided which side of the road she would drive on each day or which stop sign he would decide to obey. Most of us usually conform to the norms our group prescribes. Of course, not all members of the group obey all the time. All of us have broken many rules, sometimes even important ones. These violations are dealt with through various mechanisms of **social control**—systematic practices developed by social groups to encourage conformity and discourage deviance. One form of social control takes place through the process of socialization, whereby individuals *internalize* societal norms and values. A second form of social control is the use of *negative sanctions* to punish rule-breakers and nonconforming acts. Later in this chapter, you will read about the legal system, which is a *formal* means of social control

Although the purpose of social control is to ensure some level of conformity, all societies have some degree of **deviance**—any behaviour, belief, or condition that violates cultural norms in the society or group in which it occurs (Adler and Adler, 1994).

social control Systematic practices developed by social groups to encourage conformity and discourage deviance.

deviance Any behaviour, belief, or condition that violates cultural norms in the society or group in which it occurs.

Defining Deviance

According to sociologists, deviance is *relative*—that is, an act becomes deviant when it is socially defined as such. Definitions of deviance vary widely from place to place, from time to time, and from group to group. For example, you may have played the Pick 3 lottery. To win, you must pick a three-digit number matching the one drawn by the government lottery agency. Television commercials encourage us to risk our money on this game from which the government profits. Several years ago, the same game was called the numbers racket and was the most popular form of gambling in many low-income neighbourhoods. The two main differences between now and then are that the game used to be run by organized criminals, and those criminals paid the winners a higher share of the take than the government now does. While the profits now go to social services rather than into the pockets of criminals, the example illustrates the point that the way societies define behaviour can be more important than the harm caused by that behaviour, as legalized gambling involves far more people suffering losses than was the case when gambling was illegal.

Definitions of deviance are continually changing. Several hundred thousand "witches" were executed in Europe during the Middle Ages; now the crime of witchcraft doesn't exist. Racist comments used to be socially acceptable; now they are not. Tattoos and piercings are now common among students, but 30 years ago they were almost unknown.

Deviance can be difficult to define. Good and evil are not two distinct categories. The two overlap, and the line between deviant and nondeviant can be *ambiguous.* For example, how do we decide if someone is mentally ill? What if your brother begins to behave in a strange fashion? He occasionally yells at people for no apparent reason and keeps changing topics when you talk to him. He begins to wear clothes that don't match and phones you in the middle of the night to talk about people who are threatening him. How would you respond to this change in

BOX 7.1 SOCIOLOGY AND EVERYDAY LIFE

How Much Do You Know About Crime and Organized Crime?

True	False	
T	F	1. Official statistics accurately reflect the amount of crime in Canada.
T	F	2. Most organized criminals are affiliated with the Italian Mafia.
T	F	3. Organized crime exists largely to provide goods and services demanded by "respectable" members of the community.
T	F	4. Rates of murder and other violent crimes have been steadily rising for the past 20 years.
T	F	5. Gang-related killings have been declining at about the same rate as other types of homicides in Canada.

For answers to the quiz about crime and organized crime, go to **www.nelson.com/sociologyinourtimes6e.**

behaviour? Would it make any difference if you knew that your brother was drinking heavily at the time or was under a lot of stress at work? Would it make a difference if he behaved this way once a year or twice a week? When would you decide that he had a problem and should seek help? What is the difference between someone who is eccentric and someone who is mentally ill? These questions reflect the difficulty we have in defining deviance.

Deviant behaviour also varies in seriousness, ranging from mild transgressions to quite serious violations of the law. Have you kept a library book past its due date or cut classes? If so, you have broken the rules. Others probably view your infraction as relatively minor; at most, you might have to pay a fine. Violations of other university regulations—such as cheating on an examination—are viewed as more serious infractions and are punishable by stronger sanctions, such as academic probation or expulsion. Some forms of deviant behaviour are defined as crimes. A **crime** is an act that violates criminal law and is punishable with fines, jail terms, and other sanctions. Crimes range from minor—running an illegal bingo game or disorderly conduct—to major offences such as sexual assault and murder.

crime An act that violates criminal law and is punishable with fines, jail terms, and other sanctions.

Sociologists study the behaviours that are defined as deviant, who does the defining, how and why people become deviants, and how society deals with deviants (Schur, 1983). In this chapter, we present several sociological explanations of deviance. These theories are quite different from one another, but each contributes in its own way to our understanding of deviance. No one perspective provides a comprehensive explanation of all deviance. In many respects, the theories presented in this chapter can be considered complementary.

SOCIOLOGICAL PERSPECTIVES ON CRIME AND DEVIANCE LO-2

Functionalist Perspectives on Crime and Deviance

STRAIN THEORY: GOALS AND THE MEANS TO ACHIEVE THEM According to Robert Merton (1938, 1968), in a smoothly functioning society, deviance will be limited because most people share common cultural goals and agree upon the appropriate means for reaching them.

However, societies that do not provide sufficient avenues to reach these goals may also lack agreement about how people may achieve their aspirations. Deviance may be common in such societies because people may be willing to use whatever means they can to achieve their goals. According to **strain theory**, people feel strain when they are exposed to cultural goals that they are unable to obtain because they do not have access to culturally approved means of achieving these goals. The goals may be material possessions and money; the approved means may include an education and jobs. When denied legitimate access to these goals, some people seek access through deviant means.

strain theory The proposition that people feel strain when they are exposed to cultural goals that they are unable to obtain because they do not have access to culturally approved means of achieving these goals.

Typically, strain theory has been used to explain the deviance of the lower classes. Denied legitimate access to the material goods that are such an important part of North American culture, some individuals may turn to illegal activities to achieve their goals. However, not only the poor turn to illegal ways of achieving their goals. Some sociologists feel that strain theory can help explain upper-class deviance as well. In 2007, Conrad Black, one of Canada's wealthiest and most influential businessmen (and as Lord Black of Crossharbour, also a member of the British House of Lords), was convicted of fraud and obstruction of justice and sentenced to three and a half years in prison. Despite his wealth, Black took money from the Hollinger company that rightfully belonged to shareholders. A committee established to investigate Black's activities concluded that "Black and [his partner] Radler were motivated by a ravenous appetite for cash . . . and Hollinger International, under their reign 'lost any sense of corporate purpose, competitive drive or internal ethical concerns' as the two executives looked for ways to 'suck cash' out of the company" (McNish and Stewart, 2004:288).

OPPORTUNITY THEORY: ACCESS TO ILLEGITIMATE OPPORTUNITIES Expanding on Merton's strain theory, Richard Cloward and Lloyd Ohlin (1960) suggested that for deviance to occur, people must have access to **illegitimate opportunity structures**—circumstances that provide an opportunity for people to acquire through illegitimate activities what they cannot achieve through legitimate channels. For example, members of some communities may have insufficient legitimate means to achieve conventional goals of status and wealth but have much greater access to illegitimate opportunity structures—such as theft, drug dealing, or robbery—through which they can achieve these goals.

illegitimate opportunity structures Circumstances that provide an opportunity for people to acquire through illegitimate activities what they cannot achieve through legitimate channels.

According to Cloward and Ohlin (1960), three different forms of delinquent subcultures—criminal, conflict, and retreatist—emerge based on the type of illegitimate opportunities available in a specific area. The criminal subculture focuses on economic gain and includes acts such as theft, extortion, and drug dealing. Elijah Anderson (1990) suggested that the "drug economy [is an] employment agency superimposed on the existing gang network" for many young men who lack other opportunities. For young men who grow up in a gang subculture, running drug houses and selling drugs on street corners provides illegitimate opportunities. Using the money from these "jobs," they can support themselves and their families, as well as purchase material possessions to impress others. When illegitimate economic opportunities are not available, gangs may become conflict subcultures that fight over turf (territory) and adopt a value system of toughness, courage, and similar status-enhancing qualities. Those who lack the opportunity or ability to join one of these gangs may turn to retreatist forms of deviance, such as drinking and drug use.

Opportunity theory expands strain theory by pointing out the relationship between deviance and the availability of illegitimate opportunity structures. Some studies of gangs have supported this premise by pointing out that gang membership provides some women and men in low-income central-city areas with an illegitimate means to acquire money, entertainment, refuge, and physical protection (Esbensen and Huizinga, 1993; Jankowski, 1991).

CONTROL THEORY: SOCIAL BONDING Early social control theories explained how some types of social structures led to high rates of deviance. Communities characterized by poverty, physical deterioration, and internal conflict were too disorganized to exert effective control over residents' behaviour. These communities often had high rates of suicide, mental illness, substance abuse, and crime.

Although most of the research documenting the correlation between community disorganization and crime has been done in large, urban areas, Linda Deutschmann (2002) has applied the theory to frontier areas as well. Many small Canadian communities were created solely to develop an economic resource. Such towns have grown up around mines, railroads, pulp mills, and hydro dams. These towns may be lasting or short-lived depending on the nature of the project or the life of the resource. Deutschmann notes that in these towns' early stages, the absence of controls, such as families and churches, means that deviant behaviour, such as fighting and alcohol abuse, may be common. In later stages of development, the strains of a booming town may also facilitate deviance.

While work in this tradition continues, most of the recent work on control theory has focused on the individual rather than on the community. In doing so, it has posed the fundamental question about causes of deviance in a new way. Most theories of deviance ask this question: Why do they do it? Control theorists reverse this question. They ask: Why don't we *all* do it? Or, put another way, they wonder: Why do some people *not* engage in deviant behaviour? In answer to this question, Travis Hirschi (1969) suggested that deviant behaviour is minimized when people have strong bonds that bind them to families, school, peers, churches, and other social institutions.

Social bond theory holds that the likelihood of deviant behaviour increases when a person's ties to society are weakened or broken. According to Hirschi, social bonding consists of (1) *attachment* to other people; (2) *commitment* to conventional lines of behaviour, such as schooling and job success; (3) *involvement* in conventional activities; and (4) *belief* in the legitimacy of conventional values and norms. The variables of attachment and commitment are much more strongly related to delinquency than involvement and belief. Although Hirschi did not include females in his study, others who have replicated it with both females and males have found that the theory explains the delinquency of both (Linden and Fillmore, 1981).

social bond theory
The proposition that the likelihood of deviant behaviour increases when a person's ties to society are weakened or broken.

While Hirschi's theory did not differentiate between bonds to conventional and to deviant others, several researchers have modified the theory and suggested that the probability of crime or delinquency increases when a person's social bonds are weak and when peers promote antisocial values and deviant behaviour (Linden and Fillmore, 1981). Gang members may bond with one another rather than with persons who subscribe to dominant cultural values. As one gang member explains:

> Before I joined the gang, I could see that you could count on your boys to help in times of need and that meant a lot to me. And when I needed money, sure enough they gave it to me. Nobody else would have given it to me; my parents didn't have it, and there was no other place to go. The gang was just like they said they would be, and they'll continue to be there when I need them. (Jankowski, 1991:42)

Symbolic Interactionist Perspectives on Crime and Deviance

According to symbolic interactionists, deviance is learned in the same way as conformity—through interaction with others. Differential association and labelling theory are two interactionist theories of deviance.

differential association theory
The proposition that individuals have a greater tendency to deviate from societal norms when they frequently associate with persons who favour deviance over conformity.

DIFFERENTIAL ASSOCIATION THEORY Edwin Sutherland (1939) developed a theory to explain how people learn deviance through social interaction. **Differential association theory** states that individuals have a greater tendency to deviate from societal norms when they frequently associate with persons who favour deviance over conformity. According to Sutherland, people learn the necessary techniques and the motives, drives, rationalizations, and attitudes of deviant behaviour from people with whom they associate.

Misha Glenny described the transition of a "whitehat" computer hacker named Max Vision into a criminal "blackhat" hacker named Iceman. Vision had been working for the U.S. government searching for vulnerabilities in their website security. For reasons that were unclear, Vision left a U.S. Air Force website vulnerable to later attack and was sentenced to prison. After his release, Vision decided to change his life:

> Abandoned by his wife for another man, forsaken by his erstwhile friends in the FBI, Max Vision tumbled down the abyss, at the bottom of which lay a deep depression. Here he landed next to a fellow inmate, one Jeffrey Normington, who extended a hand of friendship when nobody else would.
>
> On his release from prison, Vision was unable to find regular work that paid more than the minimum wage. He . . . was offered senior positions in security companies abroad, but as he was on parole, he was not eligible for a passport. In Silicon Valley, nobody wanted to employ someone whose CV included an indelible conviction for computer crime.
>
> His debts mounted as his despair deepened. Then one day friend Normington reappeared, promising a path out of the abyss and back into California's sunshine . . . Normington promised him a top-of-the-line Alienware laptop, a must-have but expensive accessory for hackers. That was just for starters. He said he'd find Vision an apartment and pay for it. Normington would arrange everything.
>
> In exchange for a few favors.
>
> Crime was not Vision's sole option. There were other avenues to explore. He could have gone to friends and family. But he was tired, he felt abandoned and Normington was convincing . . .
>
> Max Vision, all-round good guy, was discarded back into an abyss. In his place, Iceman emerged—all-round bad guy. . . . (2011:102)

Vision is now in prison, serving a 13-year sentence for credit card hacking that cost consumers over $85 million.

Differential association is most likely to result in deviant activity when a person has extensive interaction with rule-breakers. Ties to other deviants can be particularly important in organized crime, where the willingness of peers to stand up for one another is a response to violent competitors. Daniel Wolf, an anthropologist who rode with an Edmonton biker gang, describes this solidarity:

> For an outlaw biker, the greatest fear is not of the police; rather, it is of a slight variation of his own mirror image: the patch holder [full-fledged member] of another club. Under slightly different circumstances those men would call each other "brother." But when turf is at stake, inter-club rivalry and warfare completely override any considerations of the common bonds of being a biker—and brother kills brother. None of the outlaws that I rode with enjoyed the prospect of having to break the bones of another biker. Nor did they look forward to having to live with the hate–fear syndrome that dominates a conflict in which there are no rules . . .
>
> When a patch holder defends his colours, he defends his personal identity, his community, his lifestyle. When a war is on, loyalty to the club and one another arises out of the midst of danger, out of apprehension of possible injury, mutilation, or worse. Whether one considers this process as desperate, heroic, or just outlandishly foolish and banal does not really matter. What matters is that, for patch holders, the brotherhood emerges as a necessary feature of their continued existence as individuals and as a group. (1996:11)

Group ties are not only important in organized crime groups such as motorcycle gangs. Think of the different subcultural groups that are involved in deviant activities in many Canadian high schools. Whether the focus of the group is graffiti, using drugs, or fighting, the encouragement and support of peers is vital to recruiting and teaching new members and to sustaining the group.

Differential association theory contributes to our knowledge of how deviant behaviour reflects the individual's learned techniques, values, attitudes, motives, and rationalizations. However, critics question why many individuals who have had extensive contact with people who violate the law still conform most of the time. They also assert that the theory does not adequately assess possible linkages between social inequality and criminal behaviour.

LABELLING THEORY Two complementary processes are involved in the definition of deviance. First, some people act (or are believed to act) in a manner contrary to the expectations of others. Second, others disapprove of and try to control this contrary behaviour. Part of this social control process involves labelling people as deviants. A very important contribution to the study of deviance was made by sociologists who asked this question: Why are some people labelled as deviants while others are not? **Labelling theory** suggests that deviants are those people who have been successfully labelled as such by others. The process of labelling is directly related to the power and status of those persons who do the labelling and those who are being labelled. To the labelling theorist, behaviour is not deviant in and of itself; it is defined as such by a social audience (Erikson, 1962). Labels are applied most easily to those who lack the power to resist them.

labelling theory The proposition that deviants are those people who have been successfully labelled as such by others.

William Chambliss (1973) witnessed the labelling process when he observed members of two groups of high school boys: the Saints and the Roughnecks. Both groups were "constantly occupied with truancy, drinking, wild parties, petty theft, and vandalism." The Saints committed more offences than the Roughnecks, but the Roughnecks were labelled as troublemakers by school and law enforcement officials, while the Saints were seen as being likely to succeed. Unlike the Roughnecks, none of the Saints was ever arrested.

Chambliss attributed this contradictory response by authorities to the fact that the Saints came from "good families," did well in school, and thus were forgiven for their "boys will be boys"–type behaviour. By contrast, the Roughnecks came from lower-income families, did poorly in school, and generally were viewed negatively. Although both groups engaged in similar behaviour, only the Roughnecks were stigmatized by a deviant label.

The concept of secondary deviance is important to labelling theory because it suggests that when people accept a negative label or stigma that has been applied to them, the label may contribute to the type of behaviour it was initially meant to control (see Figure 7.1). According to Lemert (1951), **primary deviance** is the initial act of rule breaking. **Secondary deviance** occurs when a person who has been labelled deviant accepts that new identity and continues the deviant behaviour. For example, a person may shoplift, not be labelled deviant, and subsequently decide to forgo such acts in the future. Secondary deviance occurs if the person steals from a store, is labelled a "shoplifter," accepts that label, and then continues to steal.

primary deviance A term used to describe the initial act of rule breaking.

secondary deviance A term used to describe the process whereby a person who has been labelled deviant accepts that new identity and continues the deviant behaviour.

Labelling theorists have made an important contribution to our understanding of the process by which society defines behaviours and individuals as deviant and of the consequences of that definition. Let us first look at the impact of labelling on a person who is defined as deviant.

Robert Scott (1969) conducted a fascinating study that examined the effects of two different ways of treating blind people. One agency defined the blind as helpless, dependent people and developed programs to accommodate them. Their clients were driven to the agency's offices, where they worked in sheltered workshops and ate food that had been cut before being served.

FIGURE 7.1 LABELLING THEORY

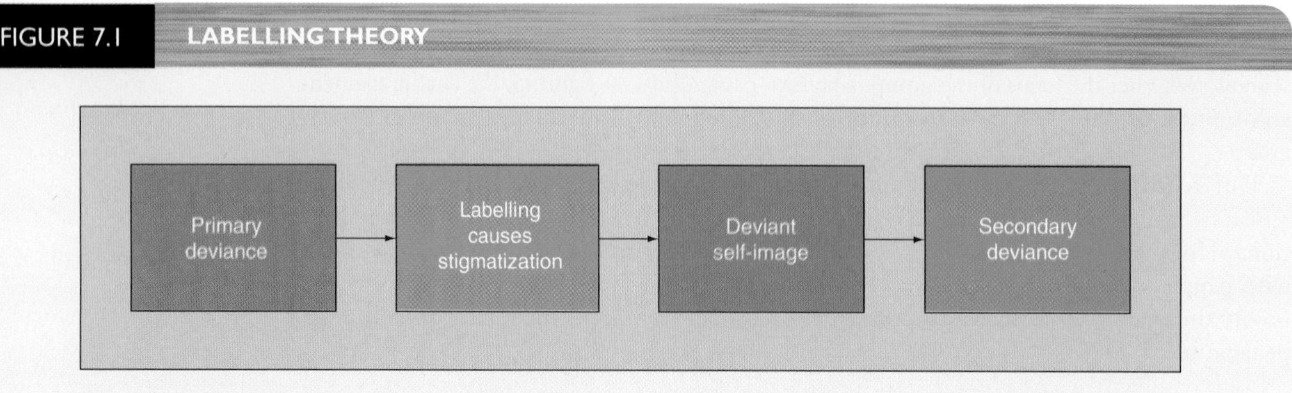

When an act is labelled as deviant, the label may cause the behaviour it was intended to control. The individual may find that others now respond differently to him or her because of the stigmatization of being labelled as deviant. While some individuals may successfully resist the label, others may develop a deviant self-image and subsequently get involved in secondary deviance.

Not surprisingly, the clients had trouble adapting to life outside the agency. Another agency, which dealt mainly with Vietnam War veterans, used a different approach. Their goal was to reintegrate clients into the community. Instead of being driven places, they were trained to take public transit. They were given confidence training and encouraged to live on their own and work in normal job settings. Scott concluded that these different approaches, with different labels for the visually impaired clients, had a significant impact on the self-image and social adjustment of the blind clients.

Think of the impact that labels can have on a person's self-concept and life chances. Being labelled a drug addict can lead to serious difficulties in getting a job even after successful treatment. If the label prevents the former addict from reintegrating into the conventional community, that person may accept this deviant status and return to his or her friends in the drug world. Similar problems come with other deviant labels. The impact of the label "mentally ill" is described by Tom, an ex-patient:

> Having been diagnosed as a psychiatric patient with psychotic tendencies is the worst thing that has ever happened to me. It's shitty to be mentally ill; it's not something to be proud of. It makes you realize just how different you are from everybody else—they're normal and you're not. Things are easy for them; things are hard for you. Life's a ball for them; life's a bitch for you. I'm like a mental cripple! I'm a failure for life! (Herman, 1996:310)

Not everyone passively submits to the labelling process—some people successfully resist the imposition of a label. This can be done individually or by working with others. The leader of one Ontario group of former psychiatric patients described the aims of his group:

> Simply put, we're tired of being pushed around. We reject everything society says about us, because it's just not accurate . . . We don't like the meaning of the words [people] use to describe us—"mentals" and "nuts." We see ourselves differently, just as good and worthy as everybody out there. In our newsletter, we're trying to get across the idea that we're not the stereotypical mental patient you see in movies. We're real people who want to be treated equally under the Charter of Rights. We're not sitting back, we're fighting back! (Herman, 1996:323)

The view that deviance is socially defined draws our attention to the question of why particular behaviours are defined as deviant and others are not. One of the answers highlights the role of **moral entrepreneurs**—people or groups who take an active role in trying to have particular behaviours defined as deviant (Becker, 1963). Think of the role that groups such as Mothers Against Drunk Driving (MADD) have played in getting governments to increase the penalties for drunk driving and in educating the public about the dangers of this behaviour. Similarly, in recent years, health advocates have stigmatized cigarette smoking and many of our communities have passed legislation banning smoking in most public places. A few decades ago, there was little opposition to smoking; people smoked on buses, in airplanes, in classrooms, in offices, and in virtually all other public places. Because of the health risks of smoking, the antismoking movement was able to overcome tobacco company lobbying and convince governments to impose restrictions on smoking. Not only is smoking banned in public places, but many people now define smokers as deviants who threaten public health (Tuggle and Holmes, 2000). Thus, smoking has moved from a normative behaviour to a stigmatized behaviour over a period of about 30 years.

moral entrepreneurs People or groups who take an active role in trying to have particular behaviours defined as deviant.

Moral entrepreneurs often create **moral crusades**—public and media awareness campaigns that help generate public and political support for their causes. In recent years, we have seen moral crusades against abortion providers, wife abusers, squeegee kids, panhandlers, prostitutes, and a wide variety of other real or perceived threats to society. Some crusades have been more successful than others. The campaign by women's groups for zero-tolerance policies mandating arrest in domestic violence cases has been successful. However, anti-abortion groups have drawn attention to their cause but have been unable to bring about changes in the law.

moral crusades Public and media awareness campaigns that help generate public and political support for moral entrepreneurs' causes.

Some groups succeed in changing perceptions and laws and others do not. A major reason for the difference is the distribution of power and resources in society. Those who control the levers of power are much more likely to be able to impose their definitions of what is right and wrong on the rest of society.

Labelling theory has had an important impact on the justice system. It has led to an increased use of diversion for minor offences so a formal label would not be applied. Critics argue that this theory neither explains what causes the original acts that make up primary deviance nor provides insight into why some people accept deviant labels and others do not (Cavender, 1995).

Conflict Perspectives on Crime and Deviance

Who determines what behaviours are deviant or criminal? Conflict theorists feel that people in positions of power maintain their advantage by using the law to protect their own interests. Conflict theorists suggest that lifestyles considered deviant by political and economic elites are often defined as illegal. The activities of poor and lower-income individuals are more likely to be defined as criminal than those of persons from middle- and upper-income backgrounds. For example, those who commit welfare fraud are more likely to face criminal charges than are professionals whose misconduct is generally dealt with by disciplinary committees of their peers rather than by the criminal courts. The relative social harm caused by either of these groups seems to have little relevance in the determination of who is defined as criminal; what matters more is the power of some groups to resist sanctions.

THE CONFLICT APPROACH Although Karl Marx wrote very little about deviance and crime, many of his ideas influenced a critical approach that is based on the assumption that the criminal justice system protects the power and privilege of the capitalist class.

As you learned in Chapter 1, Marx based his critique of capitalism on the inherent conflict that he believed existed between the capitalists and the working class. According to Marx, social institutions (such as law, politics, and education) make up a superstructure that legitimizes the class structure and maintains the capitalists' dominant position in it. Crime is an expression of the individual's struggle against the unjust social conditions and inequality produced by capitalism.

According to Quinney (1980), people with economic and political power define as criminal any behaviour that threatens their own interests. For example, drug laws enacted early in the 20th century were passed and enforced in an effort to control immigrant workers, particularly Chinese workers, who were more inclined than most other residents of Canada to smoke opium. The laws were motivated by racism more than by a real concern with drug use (Cook, 1969). By contrast, while the Canadian government passed anti-combines legislation in 1889 in response to concerns expressed by labour and small-business people about the growing power of monopoly capitalists, the law had no impact. Large companies still engaged in price fixing and other means of limiting competition. Having symbolic anti-combines laws on the books merely made the government appear responsive to public concerns about big business (Smandych, 1985).

Why do people commit crimes? Some conflict theorists believe that the affluent commit crimes because they are greedy and want more than they have. Corporate and white-collar crimes, such as stock market manipulation, land speculation, and price fixing, often involve huge sums of money and harm many people. By contrast, street crimes, such as robbery and aggravated assault, generally involve small sums of money and cause harm to limited numbers of victims (Bonger, 1969). According to conflict theorists, the poor commit street crimes to survive; they cannot afford the necessary essentials, such as food, clothing, and shelter. Thus, some crime represents a rational response by the poor to the unequal distribution of resources in society (Gordon, 1973). Further, living in poverty may lead to violent crime and victimization *of the poor by the poor.* For example, violent gang activity may be a collective response of young people to seemingly hopeless poverty (Quinney, 1979).

In sum, the conflict approach argues that the law protects the interests of the affluent and powerful. The way laws are written and enforced benefits the capitalist class by ensuring that individuals at the bottom of the class structure do not take the property or threaten the safety of those at the top (Reiman, 1984). However, this theory explains some types of laws but not others. People of all classes share a consensus about the criminality of certain acts. For example, laws that prohibit murder, rape, and armed robbery protect not only middle- and upper-income people but also low-income people, who are frequently the victims of such violent crimes (Klockars, 1979). While some laws do protect the rich and powerful, others reflect the interests of all citizens.

This British Columbia accident killed 3 farm workers and injured 14 when their employer transported 17 people in a 10-passenger van with wooden benches and no seat belts. While the RCMP recommended 33 criminal charges, none were laid and the driver was only fined $2000.

Feminist Perspectives on Crime and Deviance

The few early studies that were conducted on "women's crimes" focused almost exclusively on prostitution and attributed the cause of this crime to women's biological or psychological "inferiority." As late as the 1980s, researchers were still looking for unique predisposing factors that led women to commit crime, which was often seen as individual psychopathology rather than as a response to their social environment. These theories, which reinforce existing female stereotypes, have had a negative impact on our understanding and treatment of female offenders.

A new interest in women and deviance developed in 1975 when two books—Freda Adler's *Sisters in Crime* and Rita James Simons's *Women and Crime*—declared that women's crime rates were going to increase significantly as a result of the women's liberation movement. Although this so-called emancipation theory of female crime has been strongly criticized by subsequent analysts (Comack, 2012), Adler's and Simons's works encouraged feminist scholars to examine the relationship between gender, deviance, and crime more closely.

Feminist scholars have concluded that the roots of female criminality lie in a social structure that is "characterized by inequalities of class, race, and gender" (Comack, 2012:173). Women's deviance and crime is seen as a rational response to gender discrimination experienced in work, marriage, and interpersonal relationships. Some female crimes are attributed to women's lack of job opportunities and to stereotypical expectations about appropriate roles for women. Other theorists feel that women are exploited by capitalism and patriarchy. Because most females have had relatively low-wage jobs and few economic resources, minor crimes, such as prostitution, shoplifting, and passing bad cheques, were means to earn money or acquire consumer products. Increases in women's criminality during the 1970s and 1980s reflect the fact that the number of single female parents living in poverty grew significantly during this period.

Some of the most interesting work on female criminality has focused on the simultaneous effects of race, class, and gender on deviant behaviour. Arnold (1990) attributes many of the women's offences to living in families in which sexual abuse, incest, and other violence left them few choices except deviance. Economic marginality and racism also contributed to their victimization.

These conclusions are reinforced by the work of Elizabeth Comack, who examined the relationship between women's victimization and their subsequent involvement in Manitoba's criminal justice system. The incidence of prior victimization was pervasive among the 24 women she interviewed while they were incarcerated in a provincial jail. The abuse suffered by the women was connected to their criminal behaviour in several ways. Some women turned to crime as a means of coping with their abuse. "Meredith" had been sexually abused by her father since the age of four or five. She was in jail for fraud and had been involved in drug use and prostitution:

> Some people are violent, some people take it out in other ways, but that was my only way to release it. It was like, it's almost orgasmic, you know, you'd write the cheques, and you'd get home and you'd go through all these things and it's like, "There's so much there. I have all these new things to keep my mind off. I don't have to deal with the old issues." And so you do it. And it becomes an escape. (1996b:86)

Others broke the law while resisting abuse. "Janice" had been raped as a teenager and turned to alcohol as a way to cope. Serving time for manslaughter, she recounts the offence:

> Well I was at a party, and this guy, older, older guy, came, came on to me. He tried telling me, "Why don't you go to bed with me. I'm getting some money, you know." And I said, "No." And then he started hitting me and then he raped me and then [pause] I lost it. Like I just, I went, I got very angry and I snapped. And I started hitting him. I threw a coffee table on top of his head and then I stabbed him, and then I left. (1996b:96)

While abuse was strongly related to the women's law violations, Comack also found that race and class were factors contributing to their criminal behaviour—most were Aboriginal and poor.

Feminist theorists feel that women who violate the law are not "criminal women" but "criminalized women" (Laberge, 1991). This means that they commit crimes and acts of deviance because they have been forced into difficult situations that are not of their own making. The women interviewed by Comack faced many social pressures caused by race, class, and gender, and had few options for escaping their situations and improving their lives.

Feminist scholars have also focused attention on violence against women. Much of this violence was hidden, as sexual assault and domestic violence were rarely reported and were not taken seriously by the justice system. Several studies focusing on how rapes were dealt with by the justice system, including an important work by Clark and Lewis (1977), led to new sexual assault legislation in 1983 that changed some of the worst parts of the old law, including a section that gave husbands the right to rape their wives (Comack, 2012).

Feminist research has also helped to change the way domestic violence is dealt with by the justice system. Until the 1970s, little was known about this crime. In 1980, the Canadian Council on the Status of Women released a report showing that wife abuse was a major problem (MacLeod, 1980). Attitudes toward domestic violence at that time were illustrated by the fact that when these findings were released in the male-dominated House of Commons, parliamentarians responded with laughter. Despite this response, some legislators did take the issue seriously and recognized that the police response to domestic violence was inadequate. As a result, many provinces implemented mandatory charging policies for domestic violence complaints. This dramatically increased the number of charges laid for this offence (Ursel, 1996).

Postmodern Perspectives on Crime and Deviance

How do postmodernists view deviance and social control? In his book *Discipline and Punish* (1979), Michel Foucault analyzed the intertwining nature of power, knowledge, and social control. In his study of prisons from the mid-1800s to the early 1900s, Foucault found that many penal institutions stopped torturing prisoners who disobeyed the rules and began using new surveillance techniques to maintain social control. Although the prisons appeared to be more humane in the post-torture era, Foucault contends that the new means of surveillance impinged more on prisoners and brought greater power to prison officials. Foucault described the *Panopticon*—a structure that gives prison officials the possibility of complete observation of inmates at all times. The Panopticon might be a tower in the centre of a circular prison from which guards can see all the cells. The prisoners know they can be observed at any time but do not know precisely when their behaviour is being scrutinized. As a result, prison officials are able to use their knowledge as a form of power over inmates. Eventually, the guards would not even have to be present all the time because prisoners would believe that they were under constant scrutiny by officials in the observation post.

How does Foucault's perspective explain social control in the larger society? Technologies such as the Panopticon make widespread surveillance and disciplinary power possible in many settings, including the police network, factories, schools, and hospitals. And current technology has the potential to expand surveillance far more broadly than Foucault could have imagined. The computer can act as a modern Panopticon that gives workplace supervisors virtually unlimited capabilities for surveillance. Technological developments have broadened the capacity of governments and corporations to control our behaviour. The Japanese have designed a toilet that companies can use to determine whether employees have recently used illegal drugs (Newham, 2004). Many people who were responsible for the 2010 Stanley Cup riots in Vancouver were identified and arrested because of facial recognition software that was used to analyze digital photos of the riots, and the police in many cities have licence plate recognition cameras that can identify wanted drivers and track stolen vehicles.

These technologies can be valuable tools in improving public safety. Closed-circuit television cameras in the subway were used to identify the people who carried out the July 2005 bombings that took more than 50 lives in London. Licence number recognition cameras have helped the police to get many auto thieves and suspended drivers off the road. DNA technology has freed many people who had been unjustly convicted of serious crimes and has enabled the justice system to imprison others who have committed crimes, such as sexual assault and murder. A system that would allow us to log on to our computers by scanning the iris of our eyes or our fingerprints would eliminate the confusing number of security passwords that each of us must remember.

However, these technologies raise important issues of privacy and individual rights, and society will have to decide whether greater protection is worth our loss of personal privacy. What are your views on this issue? Where should the balance lie between collective security and individual rights?

We have examined functionalist, interactionist, conflict, feminist, and postmodern perspectives on deviance and crime (see the Concept Snapshot). These explanations help us understand the causes and consequences of certain kinds of behaviour and provide us with guidance about how we might reduce crime and deviance. However, they also make us aware of how limited our knowledge of deviance and crime really is.

CONCEPT SNAPSHOT

FUNCTIONALIST PERSPECTIVES **Key thinkers:** Robert Merton, Richard Cloward, Lloyd Ohlin	In a smoothly functioning society, deviance will be limited because most people will share common culture goals and agree upon the appropriate means for reaching them. However, societies that do not provide sufficient avenues to reach these goals may also lack agreement about how people may achieve their aspirations. Deviance may be common in such societies because people may feel free to use whatever means they can to achieve their goals.
INTERACTIONIST PERSPECTIVES **Key thinkers:** Edwin Sutherland, Howard Becker, Edwin Lemert	Deviance is learned in the same way as conformity—through interaction with others. A person becomes deviant when exposure to law-breaking attitudes is more meaningful to them than exposure to law-abiding attitudes. Societal reaction to someone who has been labelled as deviant may also cause people to develop a deviant self-concept.
CONFLICT PERSPECTIVES **Key thinkers:** Karl Marx, Richard Quinney	The powerful use law and the criminal justice system to protect their own class interests. The way laws are written and enforced benefits the capitalist class by ensuring that individuals at the bottom of the class structure do not take the property or threaten the safety of those at the top. The poor may also be forced to commit crimes to survive.
FEMINIST PERSPECTIVES **Key thinker:** Elizabeth Comack	The structured inequalities of race, class, and gender lead to the criminalization of women. Women's deviance and crime is seen as a rational response to gender discrimination experienced in work, marriage, and interpersonal relationships. Some female crimes are attributed to women's lack of job opportunities and to stereotypical expectations about appropriate roles for women. Other theorists feel that women are exploited by capitalism and patriarchy.
POSTMODERN PERSPECTIVES **Key thinker:** Michel Foucault	Power, knowledge and social control are intertwined. In prisons, for example, new means of surveillance make prisoners think they are being watched all the time. This gives prison officials power over the inmates. Modern technologies make widespread surveillance and disciplinary power possible in many settings, including the police network, factories, schools, and hospitals.

TIME TO REVIEW

- Discuss how crime differs from deviance.
- Describe how functionalist theorists explain the causes of crime and deviance. How do strain theories differ from control theories of deviance?
- Explain the two interactionist theories described in the text—differential association theory and labelling theory.
- Describe how conflict theorists critically assess the justice system and blame capitalism for causing crime.
- How do feminist theorists link women's criminality with inequalities of class, race, and gender?
- Explain how postmodern theorists such as Foucault view deviance and social control.

LO-3 CRIME CLASSIFICATION AND STATISTICS

There are many different types of crimes. To study them, sociologists have put them into broader categories.

How Sociologists Classify Crime

Sociologists categorize crimes based on how they are committed and how society views the offences. We will examine four types: (1) street crime; (2) occupational, or white-collar, and corporate crime; (3) organized crime; and (4) political crime. There is also a box on the relatively new category of **cybercrime**—offences where a computer is the object of a crime or the tool used to commit a crime (see Box 7.2 at **www.nelson.com/sociologyinourtimes6e**). As you read about these types of crime, ask yourself how you feel about them. Should each be a crime? How severe should the sanctions be against each type?

cybercrime Offences where a computer is the object of a crime or the tool used to commit a crime.

STREET CRIME When people think of crime, they most commonly think of **street crime**, which includes all violent crime, certain property crimes, and certain morals crimes. Examples are robbery,

street crime All violent crime, certain property crimes, and certain morals crimes.

© Blazej Lyjak/Shutterstock

Computers are increasingly being used as a means of committing a wide variety of crimes ranging from the distribution of child pornography to industrial espionage and identity theft.

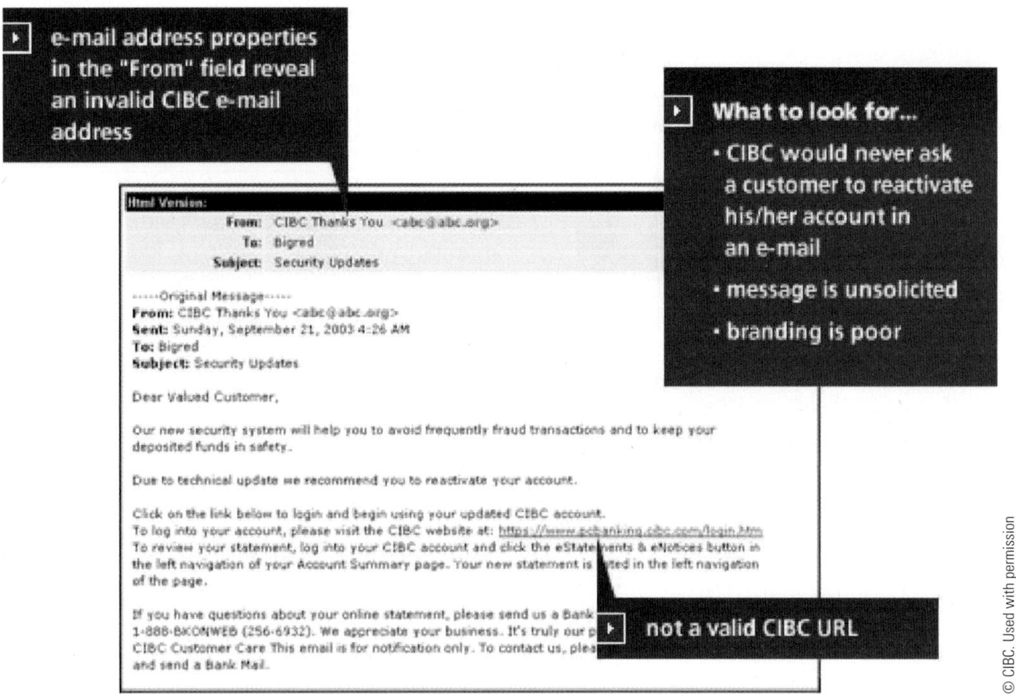

For some people, the "information superhighway" is a new avenue of illegitimate opportunity. Computer mischief and crime demonstrate how new opportunity structures can elicit new forms of deviance. This is an attempt by CIBC to educate its banking customers to avoid Internet fraud.

assault, and break and enter. These crimes occupy most of the criminal justice system's time. All street crime does not occur on the street; it frequently occurs in the home, workplace, and other locations.

Violent crime involves force or the threat of force against others, including murder, sexual assault, robbery, and aggravated assault. Violent crimes are probably the most anxiety-provoking of all criminal behaviour. Victims are often physically injured or even lose their lives, and the psychological trauma may last for years (Parker, 1995). Violent crime receives the most sustained attention from law enforcement officials and the media. While much attention may be given to the violent stranger, the vast majority of violent crime victims are injured by someone they know: family members, friends, neighbours, or co-workers (Silverman and Kennedy, 1993).

Property crimes include break and enter, theft, motor vehicle theft, and arson. While violent crime receives the most publicity, property crime is much more common. In most property crimes, the primary motive is to obtain money or some other valuable.

Morals crimes involve an illegal action voluntarily engaged in by the participants, such as prostitution, illegal gambling, the use of illegal drugs, and illegal pornography. Many people assert that such conduct should not be labelled as a crime. These offences are often referred to as "victimless crimes" because they involve exchanges of illegal goods or services among willing adults (Schur, 1965).

occupational or white-collar, crime A term used to describe illegal activities committed by people in the course of their employment or in dealing with their financial affairs.

OCCUPATIONAL AND CORPORATE CRIME **Occupational, or white-collar, crime** consists of illegal activities committed by people in the course of their employment or in dealing with their financial affairs. Much of white-collar crime involves the violation of positions of trust. These activities include employee theft of company property or profits, soliciting bribes or kickbacks, and embezzling. Some white-collar criminals set up businesses for the sole purpose of victimizing the general public, engaging in activities such as land swindles, securities thefts, and consumer fraud.

corporate crime An illegal act committed by corporate employees on behalf of the corporation and with its support.

In addition to acting for their own profit, some white-collar offenders become involved in criminal conspiracies designed to improve the profitability of their companies. This is known as **corporate crime**—illegal acts committed by corporate employees on behalf of the corporation and with its support. Examples include antitrust violations; false advertising; infringements on patents, copyrights, and trademarks; price fixing; and financial fraud. These crimes involve deliberate decisions made by corporate personnel to enhance profits at the expense of competitors, consumers, and the general public.

© Dick Loek/GetStock.com

Conrad Black, one of Canada's most influential businessmen, has now completed a three-and-a half-year sentence in a Florida prison for misappropriating millions of dollars from shareholders of his newspaper chain.

The cost of white-collar and corporate crimes far exceeds that of street crime. Tax evasion costs Canadians billions of dollars a year. In one of the world's biggest white-collar crimes, investors in Calgary's Bre-X gold-mining company lost about $5 billion when it was learned that geologist Michael de Guzman had salted core samples with gold to make a worthless mining property look like the world's biggest gold find. In 2011, investors discovered that Sino-Forest, a Canadian-listed company that claimed to control vast amounts of Chinese forests, may have issued fraudulent reports. If these accusations are true, the losses may exceed those of Bre-X.

At the individual level, while few bank robbers get away with more than a few thousand dollars, Earl Jones, a Montreal investment adviser, defrauded clients of more than $50 million to support his lavish lifestyle. Many investors trusted Jones with their life savings and were financially devastated by his actions (Sutherland, 2009).

Corporate crimes can also be costly in terms of lives lost and injury. Laureen Snider (1988) found that occupational accidents and illnesses were the third leading cause of death in Canada. She attributes at least half of these deaths to unsafe and illegal working conditions. Working conditions in the mining industry, for example, have been especially dangerous. Decades ago, large numbers of Canadian miners died because their employers failed to protect them from mine hazards. Coal miners died of black lung, a condition caused by inhaling coal dust, and fluorspar miners died from the effects of inhaling silica dust in unventilated mineshafts. Not only did the mine owners fail to provide safe working conditions, but company doctors were also told not to advise the miners of the seriousness of their illnesses (Leyton, 1997).

One reason why many employers have been reluctant to implement required safety measures is because the penalties for violating workplace health and safety laws are so light. Typically, companies have been fined only a few thousand dollars even when employees died because of their employers' negligence.

Although people who commit occupational and corporate crimes can be arrested, fined, and sent to prison, many people do not regard such behaviour as "criminal." In Canada, punishment for such offences is usually a fine or a relatively brief prison sentence at a minimum-security facility; in the United States, however, penalties have become much more severe.

The concept of white-collar crime also fits some people who wear blue collars. Thus, *occupational crime* may be a more accurate term. Many tradespeople defraud the government by doing work "off the books" in order to avoid sales taxes, and some blue-collar businesses, such as auto repair, have bad records of consumer fraud.

organized crime A business operation that supplies illegal goods and/or services for profit.

ORGANIZED CRIME **Organized crime** is a business operation that supplies illegal goods and/or services for profit. Organized crime includes drug trafficking, prostitution, liquor and cigarette smuggling, loan sharking, money laundering, and large-scale theft, such as truck hijacking (Simon and Eitzen, 1993). No single organization controls all organized crime, but many groups operate at all levels of society. Organized crime thrives because there is great demand for illegal goods and services. This public demand has produced illicit supply systems with global connections. These activities are highly profitable, since groups that have a monopoly over goods and services the public strongly desires can set their own price. Legitimate competitors are excluded because of the illegality; illegitimate competitors are controlled by force.

Gang-related killings have been increasing in Canada. The deadly nature of organized crime has been shown in Metro Vancouver. In early 2009, there were 16 gang-related shootings, seven of them fatal, in less than a month. Many of the shootings took place in public places, including streets and mall parking lots. In one incident, a woman was fatally shot one morning while driving her car with a four-year-old child in the back seat. Arrests in such incidents are rare.

Along with their illegal enterprises, organized crime groups have infiltrated the world of legitimate business. Linkages with organized crime exist in many businesses, including immigration consulting, real estate, garbage collection, vending machines, construction, and trucking.

POLITICAL CRIMES **Political crime** involves illegal or unethical acts involving the misuse of power by government officials, or illegal or unethical acts perpetrated against a government by outsiders seeking to make a political statement or to undermine or overthrow the government. Government officials may use their authority unethically or illegally for material gain or political power. They may engage in graft (taking advantage of political position to gain money or property) through bribery, kickbacks, or "insider" deals that financially benefit them. While Canadian governments have a better record than those of most other countries, there have been a number of scandals. In the late 1990s, several members of former premier Grant Devine's Saskatchewan government were charged with fraud and many—including the former deputy premier—received prison sentences for misusing government funds. The 2005 Gomery Inquiry exposed serious wrongdoing by some members of Prime Minister Jean Chrétien's Liberal government who illegally funnelled millions of dollars to Quebec advertising agencies in exchange for their political support.

political crime Illegal or unethical acts involving the usurpation of power by government officials, or illegal or unethical acts perpetrated against a government by outsiders seeking to make a political statement or to undermine or overthrow the government.

Crime Statistics

It is difficult to measure crime. While citizens, police, and policymakers all wish to know how much crime there is and what forms this crime takes, those who commit crimes normally try to conceal their actions. Thus our information about crime will always be incomplete and we can never be certain of its accuracy. Our main sources of information about crime are police statistics and victimization surveys.

OFFICIAL STATISTICS Our most important source of crime data is the Canadian Uniform Crime Reports (CUCR) system, which summarizes crimes reported to all Canadian police departments. Most of our public information about crime comes from the CUCR. When we read that the homicide rate in British Columbia is higher than the national average, or that in 2010 more than 2.2 million offences were reported to the police, the information is usually based on CUCR data. Figure 7.2 shows trends in violent and property crimes, and Figure 7.3 shows Canada's homicide rates. These figures show that crime has declined significantly over the past two decades. The decline is particularly significant in the case of homicide, where rates are now the lowest they have been in more than 30 years.

Crime figures should be interpreted cautiously. While one can have confidence in homicide and auto theft statistics, the accuracy of other crime statistics is less certain. Since many policy decisions by governments, as well as decisions by individuals about their personal safety, are based on CUCR statistics, it is important to recognize their limitations.

The major weakness of the CUCR is that police statistics always underreport the actual amount of crime. The vast majority of offences reported in the CUCR come to the attention of the police from the reports of victims of crime, and victims do not report all crimes. Official crime rates are the result of a criminal act, a complaint by a victim or witness, and a response by the criminal justice system. A change in any of these will lead to an increase or decrease in crime rates. As a result, it can be difficult to analyze crime patterns and trends.

For example, Figure 7.2 shows that rates of reported violent crimes increased significantly in Canada during the late 1980s and early 1990s, almost doubling between 1980 and 1990. We know that at least part of the increase in reported crime was because violence against women was more likely to be reported rather than because violence actually increased (Linden, 1994). In the mid-1980s, many provincial governments directed police to lay charges in all suspected cases of domestic violence. These zero-tolerance policies have been made progressively more effective since they were first implemented. This visible support of the justice system may have encouraged more victims to report spousal assaults. The impact of these changes was seen in

FIGURE 7.2 CANADIAN CRIME RATES, 1962–2011

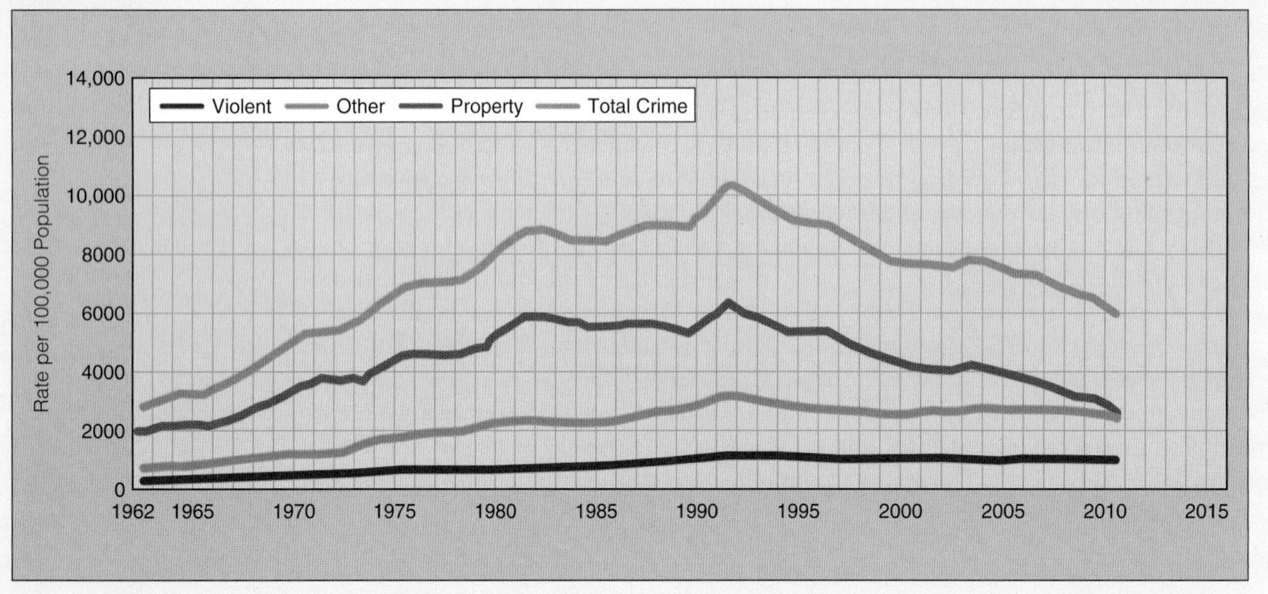

Sources: Adapted from Statistics Canada, *Crime Statistics in Canada 2007*, Cat. no. 85-002-X, Vol. 28 no. 7, 2008; Brennan, Shannon, *Police-reported Crime Statistics in Canada, 2011*, Statistics Canada, Cat. no 85-002-X, 2012.

FIGURE 7.3 CANADIAN HOMICIDE RATES, 1961–2011

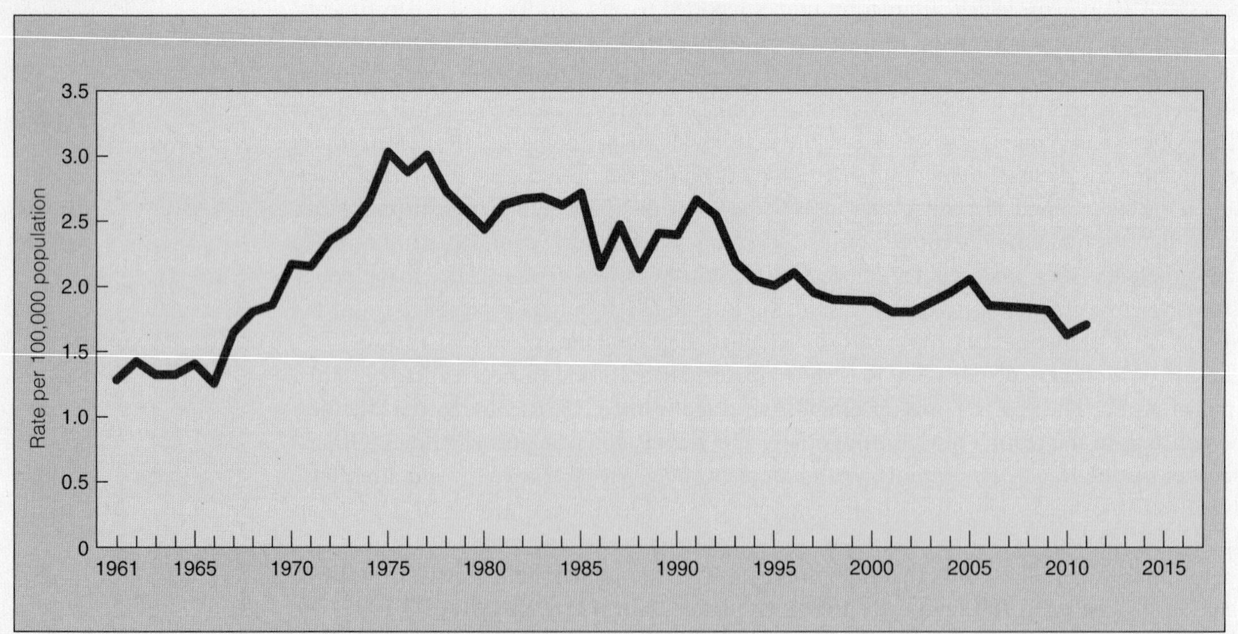

As of 1971, population estimates were adjusted to reflect new methods of calculation.

Sources: Statistics Canada, *Crime Statistics in Canada 2007*, Cat. no. 85-002-X, Vol. 28 no. 7, 2008; Brennan, Shannon, *Police-reported Crime Statistics in Canada, 2011*, Statistics Canada, Cat. no 85-002-X, 2012.

Winnipeg, where the police instituted a mandatory charging policy and where the province set up a special family violence court for spouse abuse cases. The number of domestic violence cases dealt with by this court rose from 1444 in 1990, the first year of the court's operation, to 3387 three years later (Ursel, 1996). This increase was likely due to changes in the reporting and recording of domestic assaults rather than to any increase in family violence.

Another weakness of official statistics is that many crimes committed by persons of higher socioeconomic status are routinely handled by administrative bodies or by civil courts. To avoid negative publicity, many companies prefer to deal privately with offences like embezzlement committed by their employees, and these cases may not be reported to the police. As a result, many elite crimes are never classified as "crimes," nor are the businesspeople who commit them labelled as "criminals."

VICTIMIZATION SURVEYS The weaknesses of the CUCR have led to the development of the *victimization survey.* Because many people do not report their victimization to police, governments conduct surveys in which members of the public are directly asked if they have been victims of crime. In the latest Canadian survey, only 31 percent of the victimizations reported by respondents had been reported to the police (Perreault and Brennan, 2010). Thus, reported crimes are only the tip of the iceberg. People reported that they did not report a crime because they considered the incident too minor, because they felt it was a personal matter, because they preferred to deal with the problem in another way, or because they did not feel the police could do anything about the crime.

Victimization surveys provide us with information about crimes that have not been officially reported. The additional information that they provide has helped to confirm that the rise in violent crime during the 1980s and early 1990s was due to an increase in the reporting and recording of domestic assaults. Assaults did not likely increase during this period—we just did a better job of counting them.

These surveys, however, also have weaknesses: People may not remember minor types of victimization; they may not report honestly to the interviewer; and they do not provide any information about "victimless crimes," such as drug use and illegal gambling. Despite these flaws, victimization surveys have shed new light on the extent of criminal behaviour. They are a valuable complement to other ways of counting crimes.

WHO COMMITS CRIMES: CHARACTERISTICS OF OFFENDERS LO-4

Given the limitations of official statistics, is it possible to determine who commits crimes? Age, gender, class, and race are important *correlates of crime.* That is, they are factors associated with criminal activity. One method of testing theories of crime is to see how well they explain these correlates.

Age and Crime

The offender's age is one of the most significant factors associated with crime and most other kinds of deviance. Arrests increase from early adolescence, peak in young adulthood, and steadily decline with age. There is some variation in this pattern—for example, violent crimes peak at a later age than property crimes—but the general pattern is almost always the same. Crime is a young person's game, with rates peaking between the ages of 15 and 18.

The relationship between age and criminality exists in every society for which we have data (Hirschi and Gottfredson, 1983). This is also true for most other types of high-risk behaviours, some of which are considered to be deviant. Adolescence and early adulthood are the peak times for both offending and victimization. Possible explanations for the decline in crime and deviance rates after early adulthood are the physical effects of aging, which make some criminal activity more difficult, and the realization by older chronic offenders that further arrests will result in very long jail sentences. Perhaps the best explanation for maturational reform, though, is related to the different social positions of youth and adults. Adolescents are between childhood and adult life. They have few responsibilities and no clear social role. Adolescence is also a time when young people are breaking away from the controls of their parents and others and preparing to live on their own. As we age, we begin to acquire commitments and obligations that limit our freedom to choose a lifestyle that includes crime and other forms of deviance.

Gender and Crime

Another consistent correlate of crime is gender. Most crimes are committed by males. Females are more likely to be victims than offenders. As with age and crime, this relationship has existed in almost all times and cultures. However, while the age distribution is remarkably stable, there is considerably more variation in male/female crime ratios in different places, at different times, and for different types of crime.

Men make up more than 80 percent of those charged with crimes in Canada. As Figure 7.4 shows, the degree of involvement of males and females varies substantially for different crimes. The most important gender differences in arrest rates are reflected in the proportionately greater involvement of men in violent crimes and major property offences.

The difference between male and female involvement in crime has narrowed over the past three decades. Hartnagel (2004) found that the percentage of *Criminal Code* offences committed by females nearly doubled, from 9 percent to 17 percent, between 1968 and 2000. While there was virtually no change in the percentage of homicides committed by women (11 percent versus 10 percent), women's involvement in serious theft (9 percent versus 23 percent), fraud (11 percent versus 30 percent), and minor theft (22 percent versus 28 percent) increased substantially.

FIGURE 7.4 PERCENTAGE OF CHARGES IN ADULT CRIMINAL COURTS, BY GENDER, 2010–11 (SELECTED CRIMINAL OFFENCES)

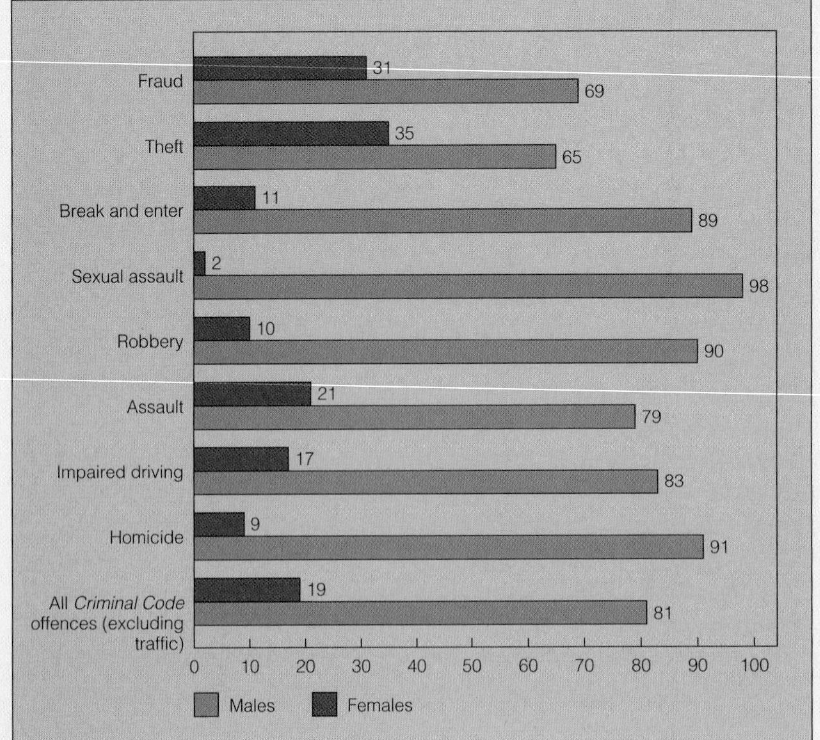

Source: Statistics Canada, CANSIM Table 252-0053. Integrated Criminal Court Survey.

What has caused this change in the sex distribution of crime? One clue comes from cross-cultural data showing very large differences in sex ratios of criminal involvement in different parts of the world. We know from comparisons of different countries that women's rates of crime are lowest in countries having the greatest differences between the roles of men and women. Where women follow traditional roles in which their lives are centred exclusively on the home, their crime rates are low. On the other hand, where women's lives are more similar to men's, their crime rates will be higher. This finding is consistent with the change in women's crime rates over the past several decades in Canada, where the role of women has come to resemble that of men.

While role convergence may explain some of the reduction in the gap between male and female crime rates, the convergence in crime rates had almost stopped over two decades ago, and it does not seem likely that women will ever become as involved in crime as men or that they will adopt male patterns of crime, particularly for violent crime. The increase in female crime has been greatest for property crimes, such as theft and fraud. These two categories include offences such as shoplifting, credit card fraud, and passing bad cheques, which are among the least serious property offences. Comack (2009) has concluded that this reflects the feminization of poverty rather than any convergence of gender roles. Thus, much of the increase in female crime may reflect the increased economic marginalization of poor women.

While female crime rates have increased more rapidly than male crime rates, it is important to remember that the numbers seem more dramatic than they are because the percentage changes are based on very low numbers of female crimes in earlier decades. Women have a long way to go to reach equality in crime with men, and the increases in female crime have now levelled off.

Social Class and Crime

Many theories assume that crime is economically motivated and that poverty will lead to criminal behaviour. However, the evidence concerning the impact of economic factors on crime is mixed. We know that persons from lower socioeconomic backgrounds are more likely to be arrested for violent and property crimes. However, we also know that these crimes are more likely to come to the attention of the police than are the white-collar crimes that are more likely to be committed by members of the upper class. Because the vast majority of white-collar crimes are never reported, we lack the data to fully assess the relationship between class and crime.

Before looking at some of the data on social class and crime, let us consider several other economic variables. Does crime increase during times of high unemployment? Do poor cities, provinces, and countries have higher crime rates than richer communities? The answer to both these questions is no. Historically, crime rates are at least as likely to rise during periods of prosperity as during recessionary times. We are also as likely to find high crime rates in rich countries as in poor ones. Within Canada, the poorer provinces of Quebec and New Brunswick have crime rates far lower than the wealthier provinces of British Columbia and Alberta (see Map 7.1 on page 197). Hartnagel (2012) has concluded that the *degree of inequality*—poverty amid affluence—is a better predictor of crime than is the amount of poverty.

We know that lower-class people are overrepresented in arrest and prison admission statistics; however, we do not know if lower-class people commit more crimes or if the justice system treats them more harshly. To get closer to actual behaviour, researchers developed self-report surveys in which respondents were asked to report the number of deviant acts they had committed during a specified time. There is some disagreement about the conclusions that should be drawn from this research, most of which has used adolescent subjects. However, the most likely conclusion is that for the vast majority of people, class and crime or delinquency are not related. However, the most frequent and serious offenders are most likely to come from the bottom of the class ladder—from an underclass that is severely disadvantaged economically, educationally, and socially. There is also some evidence that other forms of deviance, such as suicide, alcoholism, mental illness, and drug addiction, are also more common among the underclass.

A unique victimization survey reinforces this conclusion. More than 12,000 Canadian women were interviewed for the national Violence Against Women Survey (Johnson, 1996). Several findings supported the view that violence is greatest at the very bottom of the class ladder. First, men with high school educations assaulted their wives at twice the rate of men with university degrees. Second, men who were out of work committed assaults at twice the rate of men who were employed. Third, men in the lowest income category (less than $15,000 a year) assaulted their wives at twice the rate of men with higher incomes. Above this $15,000 level, however, there was no relationship between income and crime. This again suggests that the highest crime rates can be found at the bottom of the economic ladder, but that above this level there is no relationship.

Race and Ethnicity and Crime

In societies with culturally heterogeneous populations, some ethnic and racial groups will have higher crime rates than others. For example, in the United States, African Americans and Hispanics are overrepresented in arrest data. However, because Statistics Canada does not routinely collect data about racial and ethnic correlates of crime, we know relatively little about the situation in Canada.

In addition to data about Aboriginal Canadians, which will be discussed later, there have been several Canadian studies dealing with minorities and crime. The first of these examined race and ethnicity in the federal prison system. Offenders from non-Aboriginal visible ethnic minorities were *underrepresented* in the federal correctional system's population (Thomas, 1992). Specifically, the study found that in 1989, 5.2 percent of the federal corrections population were members of ethnic minority groups, while these groups made up more than 6.3 percent of the general population. The second study, which examined provincial youth and adult correctional centres in British Columbia, arrived at similar findings. Only 8.2 percent of the prison population were members of non-Aboriginal visible ethnic minorities, yet these groups made up 13.5 percent of the province's population. Contrary to the common view that immigrants have high crime rates, only 11 percent of B.C. inmates were not born in Canada, compared with 22 percent of the population of the province. The Commission on Systemic Racism in the Ontario Criminal Justice System (1995) reported that the rate of imprisonment for black adults in Ontario was five times higher than the rate for white adults. Black adults were also more likely to be imprisoned while awaiting trial, particularly for discretionary charges, such as drug possession and drug trafficking. Most recently, the *Toronto Star* used Canada's criminal records database to show that 16.7 percent of people with a criminal record in Canada were "non-white" (Rankin and Powell, 2008). This is below the percentage of visible minorities and Aboriginal people in the Canadian population, which is about 20 percent.

While statistics on other minorities are limited, there are extensive data on Aboriginal peoples because of special inquiries held to find out whether the justice system has discriminated against Aboriginal people. Many studies have demonstrated the overinvolvement of Aboriginal people (Hartnagel, 2009). For example, while Aboriginal people made up about 4 percent of the population in 2006, they made up about 24 percent of admissions to provincial prisons and 18 percent of admissions to federal prisons (Landry and Sinha, 2008). They also made up 23 percent of those accused of homicide between 1997 and 2004 (Brzozowski, Taylor-Butts, and Johnson, 2006). It is important to note that there is much variation in Aboriginal crime rates among different communities and different parts of the country (Wood and Griffiths, 1996).

What is the reason for these racial and ethnic differences in crime rates? One answer is that there has often been discrimination against minority groups. The treatment of blacks in South Africa and in the Southern United States are obvious examples. Discrimination against

BOX 7.3 POINT/COUNTERPOINT

"If It Bleeds, It Leads": Fear of Crime and the Media

Most Canadians learn about crime through the media, which shape our views about crime and criminals. However, the media do not simply "report" the news. Editors and reporters select the crime news and construct the way this news is presented to us (McKnight, 2012).

Unfortunately, the picture of crime we receive from the media is distorted. For example, while most crime is property crime, most media stories deal with violent crime. Gabor (1994) reviewed all the crime-related stories reported over two months in an Ottawa newspaper. More than half the stories focused on violent crimes, particularly murders. However, violent crimes made up only 7 percent of reported crimes in Ottawa, and the city averaged just six murders per year. While violent crimes were overreported, property crimes rarely received much attention.

The portrayal of crime in the fictional media is even more distorted. Video games, television programs, and movies are often extremely violent. Consider the partial list of the 221 violent acts depicted in *South Park: Bigger, Longer & Uncut*, the R-rated movie based on the animated series *South Park*, and ask whether the list reflects the reality of life in your community:

> 130 weapons fired (with multiple killings), 18 electric shocks, 10 blows to the body, 8 blood spatterings, 3 burnings, 3 hanging-body scenes, 1 breaking of body in half, 1 assault with a chainsaw, 1 attempted electrocution, and 1 dog attack. (Media Index, 1999)

Why do the media misrepresent crime? The primary goal of the media is to make profits by selling advertising. Stories about violent crime will boost ratings and circulation, even if these stories give people a false picture of crime. The informal media rule "If it bleeds, it leads" reflects the public fascination with sensationalized, bloody stories, such as those of mass murders. Commenting on his experience with the media, the executive director of a provincial legal society said, "If there's no blood and gore, or there's no sex, it's not newsworthy. And if it falls into the category of being newsworthy, then they have to show the dead body. They've got to show the corpse" (McCormick, 1995:182). Some parts of the media also have an ideological agenda, as they favour "tough on crime" policies that are more likely to be supported by members of the public who fear being victimized by violent crime.

The media's crime coverage is selective in other ways. Some have blamed the media for failing to cover the story of large numbers of missing women in Vancouver until Robert Pickton was charged with 26 murders. While a missing child from a middle-class home will generate an avalanche of publicity, the stories of dozens of missing lower-class women—many of whom were sex trade workers—were not seen as important. Robert Pickton's trial generated international coverage, but the media focused on the gruesome crimes and did not consider larger social issues such as legal policies that endanger sex trade workers, the structural reasons why so many of the victims were Aboriginal, and the role of the state in producing socially impoverished neighbourhoods such as Vancouver's Downtown Eastside, where Pickton found most of his victims (Hugill, 2010). What is the impact of the media's misrepresentation of crime? First, Canadians greatly overestimate the amount of violent crime and have a fear of crime that is higher than the risk of victimization justifies (McKnight, 2012). Meanwhile, global coverage of violence means that violent crimes, such as school shootings in Europe or Australia, are reported as immediately and as thoroughly as if they had happened in our own communities.

The media also provide a distorted stereotype of offenders. Violent crimes are most often committed by relatives, friends, and acquaintances, not by the anonymous stranger so many of us fear. Corporate and white-collar criminals are responsible for a great deal of social harm, but except for the most dramatic cases—such as Conrad Black in Canada and Bernie Madoff in the United States—their activities rarely receive much attention in the media. Reporting of these cases is typically limited to the business section rather than the headlines.

Members of the media pursue a vehicle containing convicted murderer Karla Homolka following a court hearing.

Aboriginal people in Canada, Australia, and New Zealand has also been well documented by commissions of inquiry. Members of minority groups, who tend to be poor, may go to prison for minor offences if they are unable to pay fines. While this type of discrimination may be unintentional, it is nonetheless real. The justice system also tends to focus its efforts on the types of crimes that are committed by low-income people rather than on white-collar crimes, so members of poor minority groups may be overrepresented in crime statistics. Discrimination accounts for some, but not all, of the high rates of criminality of some minority groups.

To provide a further explanation, consider the case of Canada's Aboriginal people. Their situation is unique, but the same kinds of factors may apply in other racial contexts. While a number of theories have been advanced to explain Aboriginal overinvolvement (Hartnagel, 2004; Wood and Griffiths, 2000), consider the following explanation, which has been drawn from conflict and social control theories. Canada's Aboriginal people have far less power and fewer resources than other Canadians. They must cope with systems of education and religion that have been imposed on them from outside their cultural communities and that are incompatible with their customs and traditions. In the past, forced attendance at residential schools and forced adoption outside the community weakened family ties. Crippling rates of unemployment in many areas mean no job ties, and school curricula that are irrelevant to the lives of Aboriginal students mean that children do not become attached to their schools. Under these conditions, strong social bonds are difficult to develop and high rates of crime can be predicted. Manitoba's Aboriginal Justice Inquiry concluded: "We believe that the relatively high rates of crime among Aboriginal people are a result of the despair, dependency, anger, frustration and sense of injustice prevalent in Aboriginal communities, stemming from the cultural and community breakdown that has occurred over the past century" (Hamilton and Sinclair, 1991:91).

TIME TO REVIEW

- Compare the different categories used by sociologists to classify different types of crime.
- Discuss some of the different types of cybercrime.
- What are the strengths and weaknesses of official crime statistics, self-reported crime statistics, and victimization surveys?
- Explain how and why age, gender, class, and race are correlated with crime.

LO-5 THE CRIMINAL JUSTICE SYSTEM

The criminal justice system includes the police, the courts, and prisons. However, the term criminal justice *system* is misleading because these institutions do not work together and each has considerable autonomy.

The Police

Most people think that the main function of the police is to enforce the law. That is indeed one of their functions, but there are several others, including order maintenance and the provision of social services. *Order maintenance* refers to keeping the peace and includes things like stopping arguments, controlling the areas where skid-row alcoholics drink, and making a group of

MAP 7.1 2011 CRIME RATES PER 100,000 POPULATION (*CRIMINAL CODE* EXCLUDING TRAFFIC OFFENCES)

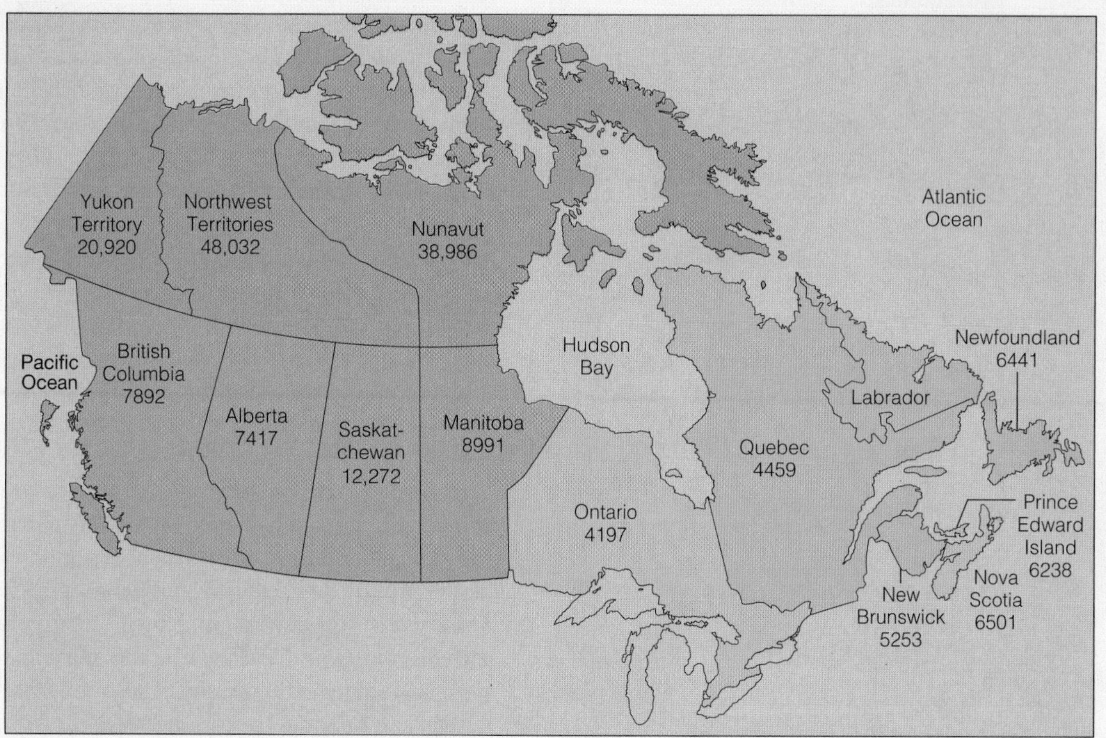

There are major regional differences in crime rates within Canada. Crime rates are highest in the West and the North, and lowest in Central Canada.

Source: Statistics Canada, "Police-Reported Crime Statistics in Canada, 2011," Catalogue no. 85-002-X, p. 27.

boisterous teenagers move away from the parking lot of a convenience store. While the main concern in law enforcement is arresting a suspect, the main concern in order maintenance is restoring peace in the community. The service role, also important, consists of many different activities, including finding lost children, counselling crime victims, and notifying next of kin in fatal accidents.

Two questions you might ask are these: Why do the police have such a broad range of responsibilities? What ties these diverse activities together? In answer to the first question, there are several reasons why the police have the broad responsibilities they do:

1. The police are one of the few public agencies open 24 hours a day.
2. In many cases, the police are serving clients that other agencies may not be interested in. The poor, the homeless, and the mentally ill may become police clients almost by default. If no other agency will look after intoxicated people who pass out on downtown streets, the police must do it.
3. The police may not know about, or have access to, other agencies that could handle some of their cases.

The second question—What ties these diverse activities together?—is best answered by looking at two dimensions of the police role. First, the police have the *authority* (and often the duty) to intervene in situations where something must be done immediately. This authority is the same whether the incident is an armed robbery in progress, a naked man standing on a busy street

© CP PHOTO/Halifax Chronicle Herald - Darren Pittman

A Nova Scotia Board of Inquiry found that a member of the Halifax Police Service discriminated against boxer Kirk Johnson when Mr. Johnson was stopped, ticketed, and had his car impounded despite having committed no offenses.

screaming at people, or a complaint that someone's pet boa constrictor has just appeared in someone else's apartment. Second, the authority is backed up by *non-negotiable force.* If someone refuses to obey a police officer, the officer can use force (usually arrest) to back up his or her demands. Even professional caregivers may resort to calling the police when clients refuse to cooperate with them. Egon Bittner has summed up the patrol officer's role: "What policemen do appears to consist of rushing to the scene of any crisis whatever, judging its needs in accordance with canons of common sense reasoning, and imposing solutions upon it without regard to resistance or opposition" (1980:137).

The police have a high degree of discretion in that they often have to decide which rules to apply and how to apply them. For example, if a police officer stops a driver for speeding and the driver has alcohol on his or her breath, several outcomes are possible. The police officer may warn the person and tell her or him to go straight home, write a speeding ticket, or administer a Breathalyzer and lay charges of impaired driving.

The use of discretion by the police is unavoidable. If discretion is dispensed equitably and in a manner consistent with community standards and the rule of law, this is not a problem. However, if it is based on extra-legal factors, such as race or class, or if it is used to favour certain individuals over others, it can be considered *discriminatory.* Issues of racial discrimination have generated the most discussion in Canada in recent years, as inquiries have been held in many provinces following police shootings of minority group members.

Earlier in this chapter, we discussed some of the ways in which the justice system discriminates against Aboriginal people. Similar conclusions may also apply to other groups. Many blacks, particularly young people, feel that they are harassed by the police and that they are stopped and questioned because of their race. Carl James interviewed a number of black youth in several Ontario cities about their experiences with the police. Their comments show that they do not feel they have been treated equitably by the police:

> You can't win. As long as you're Black you are a target.
>
> They drive by. They don't glimpse your clothes, they glimpse your colour. That's the first thing they look at. If they judge the clothes so much why don't they go and stop those white boys that are wearing those same things like us?
>
> No matter what the situation that you're in, what your dress is like . . . they will find a negative way of thinking about you, because you're Black, and secondly because you're Somali, and thirdly because you're an immigrant and you speak a different language. (1998:165–168)

A survey conducted for the Commission on Systemic Racism in the Ontario Criminal Justice System (1995) also found that black respondents were much more likely than white and Chinese respondents to report that they had been stopped by the police and were more likely to report feeling that the police had treated them unfairly. These perceptions of racial profiling have been supported by research done in Toronto (Wortley and Tanner, 2003) and Kingston (CTV, 2005) showing that black drivers are more likely to be stopped by the police than drivers of other races. While not all researchers agree that these studies demonstrate racial profiling (see Melchers, 2003), there is little doubt that being more frequently stopped does contribute to the perception of police harassment felt by many black people.

Most recently, Peter Carrington and Robin Fitzgerald also reported that minority youth were more likely than white youth to be questioned by the police. This difference could not be explained by the extent of differential involvement in crime by minority youth. They conclude that the evidence suggests that the "disproportionate minority youth contact with the police in Canada is at least partly a result of racially discriminatory policing practices" (2012:195).

The Courts

Criminal courts decide the guilt or innocence of those accused of committing a crime. In theory, justice is determined in an adversarial process in which the prosecutor (a lawyer representing the state) argues that the accused is guilty and the defence lawyer asserts that the accused is innocent. Proponents of the adversarial system feel this system best provides a just decision about guilt or innocence.

The essence of the adversarial system can be seen in the defence lawyer's role, which is to defend the accused. This role was described by Lord Brougham, the defence lawyer in an 1821 case that could have had disastrous consequences for the British government had his defence been successful:

> An advocate, in the discharge of his duty, knows but one person in all the world, and that person is his client. To save that client by all means and expedients, and at all hazards and costs to their persons, and amongst them, to himself, is his first and only duty; and in performing this duty he must not regard the alarm, the torments, the destruction which he may bring upon others. Separating the duty of a patriot from that of an advocate, he must go on reckless of the consequences, though it should be his unhappy fate to involve his country in confusion. (cited in Greenspan, 1982:201)

We can add that in an adversarial system, the defence lawyer is obliged to fulfill this duty to the client without concern for the client's guilt or innocence.

Most of those working in the courts view the adversarial system as one of the cornerstones of a free and democratic society. Many of the procedures that seem to restrict the ability of the court to get at the "truth," such as the rule that accused persons cannot be forced to testify against themselves, were adopted to prevent the arbitrary use of state power against the accused. However, some critics feel that our system does not deal adequately with crime because it places more emphasis on winning than on doing what is best for the accused, for the victim, and for society.

Not all Western countries use the adversarial court system. Several European countries use systems in which the judge takes a much more active role in ensuring that justice is done. At the trial, the judge leads the questioning and there is much more concern with getting at the truth and less on legal constraints of the kind that exist in our system. The holistic, restorative approach to justice advocated by many Aboriginal people is another alternative to our current system. This approach tries to take into account the needs of the victim, the accused, and the community, rather than simply applying formal legal rules and procedures.

Restorative Justice

For many years, we have relied on the formal justice system to deal with crime. Community members have been discouraged from participating in their own protection and have had little say in the services they received. After the victim called the police, the police would arrive to take care of the problem, and if an arrest was made, processing the case was left in the hands of the formal justice system. Some of those found guilty by the court were removed from the community and sent away to jail. Professionals controlled each step in the system, and victims and other community members had little involvement.

While most people have come to accept this as the proper way of dealing with crime, some feel the system has failed them. Victims feel left out, as their injury is forgotten and they are relegated to the role of witnesses. Offenders are also dealt with impersonally and are rarely reminded of the personal harm they have done. The public is often dissatisfied with a justice system that does not respond to their concerns.

Many critics have proposed an alternative system that is intended to restore social relationships rather than simply to punish (Church Council on Justice and Corrections, 1996). Advocates of *restorative justice* seek a system that will repair the harm that has been done to the victim and to the community. A key element is the involvement of the victim and other members of the community as active participants in the process in order to reconcile offenders with those they have harmed and to help communities reintegrate victims and offenders.

Restorative justice has its roots in traditional societies where the restoration of order was crucial to society's survival. In Canada, Aboriginal communities are leading the way in the return to restorative justice practices. They have used a variety of different methods, including *sentencing circles,* which bring an offender together with the victims and other community members, to resolve disputes. Two of the most widespread contemporary restorative justice methods are *victim–offender reconciliation* and *family group conferencing.*

Victim–offender reconciliation was devised in Elmira, Ontario, as an initiative to persuade a judge to deal in a positive fashion with two youths who had vandalized property belonging to 22 different victims. Mediators worked with the victims and the offenders to reach an acceptable resolution. As a result, the youths had to deal personally with each of their victims and to make restitution for the damage they had caused. The restorative process gave victims a say in what happened and gave offenders the chance to make amends.

Family group conferencing is similar to sentencing circles. It typically applies to young offenders and normally involves the victim, the offender, and as many of their family and friends as possible. All parties speak and then discuss how to repair the harm done to the victim. Negotiation continues until a plan is agreed on and written down. The coordinator then establishes mechanisms for enforcing the plan. The family and friends of both the victim and the offender are encouraged to offer continuing help to ensure that the resolution arrived at during the conference is carried out in the community.

While there have been concerns about issues such as the potential for net-widening through including offenders who might otherwise be screened out and dealt with in less formal ways, restorative justice programs provide us with a valuable alternative to the formal justice system.

Prisons

The incarceration rate in Canada in 2008 was 116 per 100,000 people. This rate is lower than the rates in the United States (756) and England and Wales (153), but higher than the rates in many other countries, including Italy (92), Germany (89), and Denmark (63) (Public Safety Canada, 2010). And prisons are very expensive—it costs $110,000 a year to keep an inmate in a federal penitentiary.

Why do we send people to jail? We deprive people of their liberty for several reasons:

1. *Retribution.* We send people to jail to punish them for their crimes.
2. *Incapacitation.* We imprison offenders so they cannot commit further crimes.
3. *Rehabilitation.* We seek to return offenders to the community as law-abiding citizens.
4. *Deterrence.* We try to reduce criminal activity by instilling a fear of punishment.

You can see that these goals may conflict. Those who focus on retribution and deterrence may want to make the prison experience as punitive and harsh as possible. This conflicts with rehabilitation, however, because this goal is best accomplished by providing inmates with the skills to get jobs following release, by helping them deal with the issues that led them into crime, and by carefully reintegrating them into their communities.

While prisons are very costly, we do not know as much as we should about their effectiveness. The research you learn about in Box 7.4 shows that longer prison sentences are not effective

BOX 7.4 POINT/COUNTERPOINT

Do Tougher Prison Sentences Reduce Crime?

The law clearly deters. Most people do not deliberately park where they know their car will be towed away and do not speed if they see a police car behind them. However, the more important question concerns the limits of deterrence. How can we change the system to make it more effective?

The Canadian government has decided to "crack down" on crime, and since 2006, Parliament has passed several pieces of legislation designed to put more people in jail for longer periods of time. Prisons are expensive—the cost of keeping someone in a federal penitentiary is $110,000 per year (Public Safety Canada, 2010)—so it is important to know whether this policy of sending more people to jail for longer periods reduces crime rates or whether other crime reduction strategies would keep Canadians safer.

The research tells us that longer sentences do *not* reduce crime rates. Steven Durlauf and Daniel Nagin reviewed the evidence on the deterrent effect of imprisonment and conclude that long prison sentences "are difficult to justify on a deterrence-based, crime prevention basis" (2011:38). Some of the research they reviewed suggests that imprisonment may actually *increase* an individual's likelihood of future criminal behaviour.

The most conclusive studies reviewed by Durlauf and Nagin are the evaluations of laws requiring mandatory minimum prison sentences for particular offences or for offenders with significant prior records. Mandatory minimum sentences have become widely used—they are part of many of Canada's new laws—and there has been much debate about their effectiveness.

The harshest mandatory sentencing law in any Western country is California's three-strikes law. This law provides a mandatory sentence of 25 years in prison for a third felony conviction following two earlier convictions for serious felonies (a category that includes residential burglary). This has resulted in some bizarre sentences, including cases where two men will spend 25 years in prison, one for stealing a slice of pizza and the other for shoplifting a small package of meat.

The three-strikes law has been costly. The California State Auditor (2010) calculated that the cost of three-strikes sentences was $20 billion more than if the inmates had been sentenced for the crimes they committed rather than for the "strikes" against them. California can no longer afford its prison system and in 2012 the U.S. Supreme Court ordered the state to release 32,000 inmates because of severe overcrowding. Mandatory minimum sentences also significantly increase court costs because individuals facing long mandatory penalties are more likely to insist on a trial rather than pleading guilty. The law is also very hard on the offenders and their families.

The high social and financial costs of mandatory minimum sentences might be worthwhile if they reduced crime rates. However, they do not. Michael Tonry concluded: "Mandatory penalties are a bad idea. They often result in injustice to individual offenders . . . And the clear weight of the evidence is, and for nearly 40 years has been, that there is insufficient credible evidence to conclude that mandatory penalties have significant deterrent effects" (2009:100).

Tonry bases this conclusion in part on a series of evaluations of California's three-strikes laws. While California's crime rate has declined since the passage of three strikes in 1994, this decline was not a result of the three-strikes laws. Only one of 15 studies reviewed by Tonry concluded that the legislation reduced crime rates. Several studies, including those by Marvell and Moody (2001) and Chen (2008), showed that crime rates in California did not decline faster than in other states even though the penalties in California were far more severe than in any other state. Zimring (2012) found that crime rates in New York City dropped far more than in Los Angeles and San Diego between 1990 and 2009 despite the fact that incarceration actually declined substantially in New York as it climbed in California.

Why don't severe penalties such as mandatory sentences deter crime? One reason is because offenders may not feel they are at risk of receiving those penalties. And potential offenders are actually correct in believing that their next crime is unlikely to lead to punishment. Most crimes are not reported, most reported offences do not result in arrests, most arrests do not lead to convictions, and most convictions do not result in imprisonment. Nearly 2.2 million crimes were reported to Canadian police in 2009 (Dauvergne and Turner, 2010). Vicitmization surveys have shown that less than one-third of all crimes are reported to the police, so there are likely over seven million crimes each year in Canada. Despite this huge number of offences, only about 5000 people were sentenced to federal penitentiaries (all sentences of two years or more) and 80,000 to provincial custody each year (Public Safety Canada, 2011). Thus, the likelihood of being arrested, convicted, and punished for any offence is so low that tinkering with the level of punishment makes no difference. Governments promise

(*continued*)

to "crack down" on crime, but this promise is kept so rarely that it is ignored by potential offenders, who know from their own experience (and from that of their peers) that the odds of getting away with a crime are in their favour. This means that a harsh system like California's is really one of randomized severity in which some offenders receive very harsh sentences while many others with similar patterns of offending remain on the streets.

Evaluations show that techniques such as improving the lives of high-risk youth and policing targeted toward high-crime locations and high-rate offenders can be very effective at reducing crime (Linden, 2012) . Why do you think the Canadian government has chosen to pursue a prison-based strategy they know will not work?

Canada's latest mandatory minimum sentences require a mandatory sentence of at least six months in prison for growing as few as six marijuana plants if the grower is involved in marijuana trafficking. Do you think this will have any impact on marijuana use in your community?

Source: Rick Linden, *Criminology: A Canadian Perspective* (7th ed.), Toronto: Nelson, 2012.

deterrents. Research on rehabilitation has shown that prison programs can reduce recidivism (getting in trouble again) if three principles are followed (Smith, Gendreau, and Swartz, 2009):

1. *The risk principle.* Rehabilitation programs should be based on the offender's risk of reoffending.
2. *The needs principle.* Interventions should address the offender's individual needs.
3. *The responsivity principle.* This means that programs should be "based on cognitive, behavioral, and social learning theories" (2009:154) and offenders should be matched with treatments and with particular treatment staff.

While these principles are well established, prison managers seldom explicitly utilize them in dealing with inmates. While virtually all inmates are released back into the community, governments have not made effective rehabilitation a priority.

Community Corrections

Our relatively high incarceration rate has led some to suggest that Canada should rely more heavily on community corrections. These dispositions include programs such as community probation, community service orders, intensive probation supervision, and bail supervision.

The movement toward community-based sanctions has been driven by three major concerns. First, these programs are much cheaper. It costs $30,000 for community supervision, which is about one-quarter the cost of imprisonment (Public Safety Canada, 2010). The second concern is humanitarian. Prison life is unpleasant and it can be unfair to send people to jail for relatively minor offences. Finally, an offender may benefit from maintaining ties with family and community, which may make subsequent involvement in crime less likely.

TIME TO REVIEW

- Explain why the police have such a broad range of responsibilities.
- Discuss the use of discretion in the criminal justice system.
- How does the adversarial system affect the way our court system operates?
- Explain how the restorative approach to justice differs from the normal operation of our criminal justice system.
- Explain why our society sends some convicted criminals to jail. What are some of the alternatives to this practice?

LO-1 Explain the meanings of the terms *crime* and *deviance*.

Deviant behaviour is any act that violates established norms. Deviance varies from culture to culture and in degree of seriousness. Crime is seriously deviant behaviour that violates written laws and that is punishable by fines, incarceration, or other sanctions.

© Blazej Lyjak/Shutterstock

© CP/Ryan Remiorz

LO-2 Understand the way in which crime and deviance are explained by functionalist, conflict, interactionist, feminist, and postmodern theories.

There are many different ways of explaining crime and deviance. Strain theory says that if people are denied legitimate access to cultural goals, some will engage in illegal behaviour to achieve these goals. Social control theory says that our social bonds help to keep us from crime and deviance, while differential association theory focuses on ties to deviant peers. The emphasis of labelling theory is on those who apply a deviant label to people who break the rules, because that label may lead to subsequent deviance. Conflict theories examine the impact of social inequality. Those with power exploit the lower classes and the legal order protects people at the top. Feminist theorists conclude that women's deviance and crime is a response to gender discrimination experienced in work, marriage, and interpersonal relationships. Postmodern theorists have focused on social control and discipline based on the use of knowledge, power, and technology.

LO-3 Describe how sociologists count and classify crimes.

Official crime statistics are taken from the Canadian Uniform Crime Reports survey, which lists crimes reported to the police. We also use victimization surveys that interview households to determine the incidence of crimes, including those not reported to police.

© JEAN-PHILIPPE KSIAZEK/AFP/Getty Images

KEY TERMS

corporate crime An illegal act committed by corporate employees on behalf of the corporation and with its support (p. 187).

crime An act that violates criminal law and is punishable by fines, jail terms, and other sanctions (p. 175).

cybercrime Offences where a computer is the object of a crime or the tool used to commit a crime (p. 186).

deviance Any behaviour, belief, or condition that violates cultural norms in the society or group in which it occurs (p. 174).

differential association theory The proposition that individuals have a greater tendency to deviate from societal norms when they frequently associate with persons who favour deviance over conformity (p. 177).

illegitimate opportunity structures Circumstances that provide an opportunity for people to acquire through illegitimate activities what they cannot achieve through legitimate channels (p. 176).

labelling theory The proposition that deviants are those people who have been successfully labelled as such by others (p. 179).

moral crusades Public and media awareness campaigns that help generate public and political support for moral entrepreneurs' causes (p. 181).

moral entrepreneurs People or groups who take an active role in trying to have particular behaviours defined as deviant (p. 181).

occupational 'or white collar' crime A term used to describe illegal activities committed by people in the course of their employment or in dealing with their financial affairs (p. 187).

organized crime A business operation that supplies illegal goods and/or services for profit (p. 188).

political crime Illegal or unethical acts involving the usurpation of power by government officials, or illegal or unethical acts perpetrated against a government by outsiders seeking to make a political statement or to undermine or overthrow the government (p. 189).

primary deviance A term used to describe the initial act of rule breaking (p. 179).

secondary deviance A term used to describe the process whereby a person who has been labelled deviant accepts that new identity and continues the deviant behaviour (p. 179).

social bond theory The proposition that the likelihood of deviant behaviour increases when a person's ties to society are weakened or broken (p. 177).

social control Systematic practices developed by social groups to encourage conformity and discourage deviance. (p. 174).

strain theory The proposition that people feel strain when they are exposed to cultural goals that they are unable to obtain because they do not have access to culturally approved means of achieving these goals (p. 176).

street crime All violent crime, certain property crimes, and certain morals crimes (p. 186).

LO-4 Understand how age, gender, class, and race are related to deviance and crime.

© Dick Loek/GetStock.com

Persons under the age of 25 have the highest rates of crime. Persons arrested for assault and homicide and white-collar criminals are generally older. Women have much lower rates of crime than men. Persons from lower socioeconomic backgrounds are more likely to be arrested for violent and property crimes, while corporate crime is more likely to occur among upper socioeconomic classes.

© CP/Paul Chiasson

LO-5 Describe how the criminal justice system deals with crime.

The criminal justice system includes the police, the courts, and prisons. These agencies often have considerable discretion in dealing with offenders. The police often use discretion in deciding whether to act on a situation. Prosecutors and judges use discretion in deciding which cases to pursue and how to handle them.

KEY FIGURES

© Pictorial Parade/Staff/Getty Images

Robert Merton (1910–2003) Merton was one of the most important figures in the development of sociology in the United States. His work in criminology was important because it placed the sources of crime in the social structure rather than in individual psychopathology.

© American Sociological Association

Edwin Sutherland (1883–1950) Sutherland was also a key figure in criminological theory. He is best known for his differential association theory and identification of white-collar crime as a serious problem.

KEY FIGURES

Michel Foucault (1926–1984) Foucault's work spanned a wide variety of areas in the field of social theory. He was also one of the first to recognize the potential of new surveillance technologies on all members of society.

© Jean Pierre FOUCHET/RAPHO/Gamma-Rapho/Getty

Elizabeth Comack (b. 1952) Comack's work has focused on the intersections of gender, race, and crime and on the sociology of law. Her most recent research has been on inner-city crime and on racialized policing.

Courtesy of Elizabeth Comack

APPLICATION QUESTIONS

1. As a sociologist armed with a sociological imagination, how would you propose to deal with the problem of crime in Canada? What programs would you suggest enhancing? What programs would you reduce?
2. Do you ever feel afraid of being a crime victim? How do you think that people like you can best reduce their likelihood of being victimized?
3. Legalized gambling provides Canadian governments with billions of dollars in revenue each year. Some provinces now even allow online gambling. What are the positive and negative consequences of this gambling? Do you think that gambling laws should be liberalized, or should gambling be restricted? Why?
4. Look at today's paper or an online media site. What sorts of crimes are in the headlines? How well do these media reports reflect the reality of crime in your community?
5. Legislation passed by the federal government in 2012 provided mandatory penalties for some marijuana offences that were as long or longer than sentences for sexually abusing children. Do you think these mandatory minimum sentences reflect society's attitudes toward these offences? Why do you think the government passed such harsh laws against growing marijuana?

Test your comprehension and assess what you've learned with **CourseMate's** online quizzes.

For other interesting Lived Experiences, watch the video clips on **CourseMate.**

Practise what you've learned with flashcards containing key terms and definitions on **CourseMate.**

CHAPTER

8 Social Class and Stratification in Canada

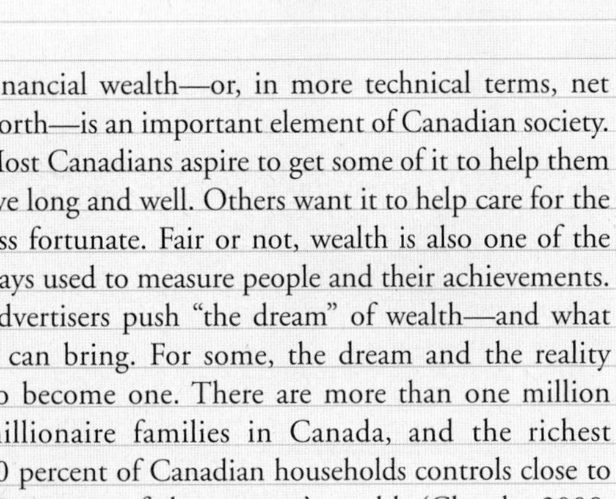

Financial wealth—or, in more technical terms, net worth—is an important element of Canadian society. Most Canadians aspire to get some of it to help them live long and well. Others want it to help care for the less fortunate. Fair or not, wealth is also one of the ways used to measure people and their achievements. Advertisers push "the dream" of wealth—and what it can bring. For some, the dream and the reality do become one. There are more than one million millionaire families in Canada, and the richest 10 percent of Canadian households controls close to 60 percent of the country's wealth (Chawla, 2008; Yalnizyan, 2010).

© Shepard Sherbell/Corbis Saba

For many, however, the dream never does become the reality. Their reality regarding wealth may consist of having enough to live just above the poverty line. The poorest 10 percent of Canadian households have more debts than assets—a negative net wealth. The bottom half of all households controls less than 10 percent of the wealth (Sauvé, 2012).

Grades 4 and 5 students in North Bay, Ontario, were asked to respond to this question: What does poverty mean? Here are their responses:

Poverty is . . .
Not being able to go to McDonald's.
Getting a basket from the Santa Fund.
Feeling ashamed when my dad can't get a job.
Not buying books at the book fair.
Not getting to go to birthday parties.
Hearing my mom and dad fight over money.
Not ever getting a pet because it costs too much.
Wishing you had a nice house.
Not being able to go camping.
Not getting a hot dog on hot dog day.
Not getting pizza on pizza day.
Not being able to have your friends sleep over.
Pretending you forgot your lunch.
Being afraid to tell your mom that you need gym shoes.
Not having breakfast sometimes.
Not being able to play hockey.
Sometimes really hard because my mom gets scared and she cries.
Not being able to go to Cubs or play soccer.
Not being able to take swimming lessons.
Not being able to afford a holiday.
Not having pretty barrettes for your hair.
Not having your own private backyard.
Being teased for the way you are dressed.
Not getting to go on school trips.

Source: The Interfaith Social Assistance Reform Coalition, *Our Neighbours' Voices: Will We Listen?* James Lorimer & Company Ltd., p. 107.

A recent opinion survey found that two-thirds of Canadians believe that it is possible to go from "rags to riches" (Canadian Centre for Policy Alternatives, 2006). In Canadian society, we are socialized to believe that hard work is the key to personal success. In other words, anyone can go from poverty to wealth if she or he works hard enough and plays by the rules. Conversely, we are taught that individuals who fail—who do not achieve success—do so as a result of personal inadequacies. Poverty is attributable to personal defect; it is up to the individual to find a way to break the cycle of poverty. Do you agree? Or do you think that structural factors in Canadian society affect the degree of success that individuals achieve?

In this chapter, we will examine systems of social stratification and how the Canadian class system may make it easier for some individuals to attain (or maintain) top positions in society while others face significant obstacles in moving out of poverty or low-income origins. Before we explore class and stratification, test your knowledge of wealth and poverty in Canada by taking the quiz in Box 8.1 on page 209.

Critical Thinking Questions

1. What factors–individual, social, or structural–do you think contribute to a person living in poverty?
2. If a child is raised in poverty, what chance does he or she have of changing his or her economic position later in life? What would be the best way to accomplish this?
3. Is it true that "the rich are getting richer and the poor are getting poorer" in Canadian society?

CHAPTER FOCUS QUESTION

How are the lives of Canadians affected by social inequality?

LEARNING OBJECTIVES

AFTER READING THIS CHAPTER, YOU SHOULD BE ABLE TO

LO-1 Identify three types of stratification systems.

LO-2 Discuss the extent of social inequality in Canada based on measures of income and wealth.

LO-3 Understand the classical analysis of social class by Karl Marx and Max Weber.

LO-4 Provide an overview of poverty and its effects in Canada.

LO-5 Compare and contrast a functionalist view and a conflict perspective on social inequality.

WHAT IS SOCIAL STRATIFICATION?

social stratification The hierarchical arrangement of large social groups based on their control over basic resources.

life chances Max Weber's term for the extent to which individuals have access to important societal resources, such as food, clothing, shelter, education, and healthcare.

Social stratification is the hierarchical arrangement of large social groups based on their control over basic resources. Stratification involves patterns of structural inequality that are associated with membership in each of these groups, as well as the ideologies that support inequality. Sociologists examine the social groups that make up the hierarchy in a society and seek to determine how inequalities are structured and persist over time.

Max Weber's term **life chances** refers to the extent to which individuals have access to important societal resources, such as food, clothing, shelter, education, and healthcare. According to sociologists, more affluent people typically have better life chances than the less affluent because they have greater access to quality education, safe neighbourhoods, high-quality nutrition and healthcare, police and private security protection, and an extensive array of other goods and services. In contrast, persons with low- and poverty-level incomes tend to have limited access to these resources. *Resources* are anything valued in a society. They range from money and property to medical care and education; they are considered scarce because of their unequal distribution among social categories. If we think about the valued resources available in Canada, for example, the differences in life chances are readily apparent. Our life chances are intertwined with our class, race, gender, and age.

All societies distinguish among people by age. Young children typically have less authority and responsibility than older persons. Older persons, especially those without wealth or power, may find themselves at the bottom of the social hierarchy. Similarly, all societies differentiate between females and males: Women are often treated as subordinate to men. From society to society, people are treated differently as a result of their religion, race and ethnicity, appearance, physical strength, disabilities, or other distinguishing characteristics. All of these differentiations result in inequality. However, systems of stratification are also linked to the specific economic and social structure of a society and to a nation's position in the system of global stratification, which is so significant for understanding social inequality that we will devote Chapter 9 to this topic.

LO-1 SYSTEMS OF STRATIFICATION

social mobility The movement of individuals or groups from one level in a stratification system to another.

intergenerational mobility The social movement (upward or downward) experienced by family members from one generation to the next.

intragenerational mobility The social movement (upward or downward) experienced by individuals within their own lifetime.

Around the globe, one of the most important characteristics of systems of stratification is their degree of flexibility. Sociologists distinguish among such systems based on the extent to which they are open or closed. In an *open system,* the boundaries between levels in the hierarchies are more flexible and may be influenced (positively or negatively) by people's achieved statuses. Open systems are assumed to have some degree of social mobility. **Social mobility** is the movement of individuals or groups from one level in a stratification system to another (Rothman, 2001). This movement can be either upward or downward. **Intergenerational mobility** is the social movement experienced by family members from one generation to the next. By contrast, **intragenerational mobility** is the social movement of individuals within their own lifetime. Both intragenerational mobility and intergenerational mobility may be downward as well as upward. In a *closed system,* the boundaries between levels in the hierarchies of social stratification are rigid and people's positions are set by ascribed status.

Open and closed systems are ideal-type constructs; no stratification system is completely open or closed. The systems of stratification that we will examine—slavery, caste, and class—are characterized by different hierarchical structures and varying degrees of mobility.

BOX 8.1 SOCIOLOGY AND EVERYDAY LIFE

How Much Do You Know About Wealth and Poverty in Canada?

True	False	
T	F	1. There is less child poverty in Canada today than there was 20 years ago.
T	F	2. Individuals over the age of 65 have the highest rate of poverty.
T	F	3. Men account for two out of every three impoverished adults in Canada.
T	F	4. Most poor children live in female-headed, single-parent households.
T	F	5. Age plays a key role in wealth accumulation in Canada.
T	F	6. The richest 10 percent of Canadian households account for approximately one-third of all wealth.
T	F	7. Fewer than 1 percent of Canadian households have a net worth of at least a million dollars.
T	F	8. The income gap between poor families and rich families has widened in the past 10 years.

For more questions and the answers to the quiz about wealth and poverty in Canada, go to **www.nelson.com/sociologyinourtimes6e**.

Slavery

Slavery is an extreme form of stratification in which some people are owned by others. It is a closed system in which people designated as "slaves" are treated as property and have little or no control over their lives. According to some social analysts, throughout recorded history only five societies have been slave societies or a society in which the social and economic impact of slavery was extensive: ancient Greece, the Roman Empire, the United States, the Caribbean, and Brazil (Finley, 1980). Others suggest that slavery existed in the Americas before European settlement and throughout Africa and Asia (Engerman, 1995).

slavery An extreme form of stratification in which some people are owned by others.

Many Canadians are not aware of the legacy of slavery in our own country. Beginning in the 1600s, people were forcibly imported to what are now Canada and the United States to serve as slaves and cheap labour. Slavery existed in what are now the provinces of Quebec, New Brunswick, Nova Scotia, and Ontario until the early 19th century (Satzewich, 1998).

As practised in North America, slavery had four primary characteristics: (1) It was for life and was inherited (children of slaves were considered slaves); (2) slaves were considered property, not human beings; (3) slaves were denied rights; and (4) coercion was used to keep slaves "in their place" (Noel, 1972).

The Caste System

Like slavery, caste is a closed system of social stratification. A **caste system** is a system of social inequality in which people's status is permanently determined at birth based on their parents' ascribed characteristics. Vestiges of caste systems exist in contemporary India and South Africa.

caste system A system of social inequality in which people's status is permanently determined at birth based on their parents' ascribed characteristics.

In India, caste is based in part on occupation, while in South Africa it was based on race and a sense of moral superiority. In India, families have typically performed the same type of work from generation to generation. By contrast, the caste system of South Africa was based on racial classifications and the belief of white South Africans (Afrikaners) that they were morally superior to the black majority. Until the 1990s, the Afrikaners controlled the government, the police, and the military by enforcing *apartheid*—the separation of the races. Blacks were denied full citizenship and restricted to segregated hospitals, schools, residential neighbourhoods, and other facilities. Whites held almost all the desirable jobs; blacks worked as manual labourers and servants.

In a caste system, marriage is *endogamous,* meaning that people are allowed to marry only within their own group. In India, parents have traditionally selected marriage partners for their children. In South Africa, interracial marriage was illegal until 1985.

Cultural beliefs and values sustain caste systems. Hinduism, the primary religion of India, reinforced the caste system by teaching that people should accept their fate in life and work hard as a moral duty. However, caste systems grow weaker as societies industrialize: The values reinforcing the system break down, and people begin to focus on the types of skills needed for industrialization.

As we have seen, in closed systems of stratification, group membership is hereditary and it is almost impossible to move up within the structure. Custom and law frequently perpetuate privilege and ensure that higher-level positions are reserved for the children of the advantaged (Rothman, 2001).

The Class System

class system A type of stratification based on the ownership and control of resources and on the type of work people do.

The **class system** is a type of stratification based on the ownership and control of resources and on the type of work people do (Rothman, 2001). At least theoretically, a class system is more open than a caste system because the boundaries between classes are less distinct than the boundaries between castes. In a class system, status comes at least partly through achievement rather than entirely by ascription.

In class systems, people may become members of a class other than that of their parents through both intergenerational and intragenerational mobility, either upward or downward. *Horizontal mobility* occurs when people experience a gain or loss in position and/or income that does not produce a change in their place in the class structure. For example, a person may get a pay increase and a more prestigious title but still not move from one class to another. By contrast, movement up or down the class structure is *vertical mobility.* Martin, a commercial artist who owns his own firm, is an example of vertical intergenerational mobility:

> My family came out of a lot of poverty and were eager to escape it . . . My [mother's parents] worked in a sweatshop. My grandfather to the day he died never earned more than $14 a week. My grandmother worked in knitting mills while she had five children . . . My father quit school when he was in eighth grade and supported his mother and his two sisters when he was twelve years old. My grandfather died when my father was four and he basically raised his sisters. He got a man's job when he was twelve and took care of the three of them. (quoted in Newman, 1993:65)

Martin's situation reflects upward mobility; however, people may also experience downward mobility, caused by any number of reasons, including a lack of jobs, low wages and employment instability, marriage to someone with fewer resources and less power than oneself, and changing social conditions (Ehrenreich, 1989; Newman, 1988, 1993). Ascribed statuses, such as race and ethnicity, gender, and religion, also affect people's social mobility. Sometimes, the media portray upward social mobility as something that is easily achieved by a few lucky people regardless of their ascribed or achieved statuses. We will return to the ideals versus the realities of social mobility when we examine the Canadian class structure later in the chapter.

TIME TO REVIEW

- How does social mobility differ in the three systems of stratification?
- Is it possible to have vertical or horizontal mobility in a caste system? Why or why not?

Systems of stratification include slavery, caste, and class. As shown in these photos, the life chances of people living in each of these systems differ widely.

LO-2 INEQUALITY IN CANADA

Throughout human history, people have argued about the distribution of scarce resources in society. Disagreements often concentrate on whether the share people get is a fair reward for their effort and hard work. Social analysts have recently pointed out that the old maxim "the rich get richer" continues to be valid in Canada. To understand how this happens, let us take a closer look at income and wealth inequality in our country.

Money is essential for acquiring goods and services. People without money cannot acquire food, shelter, clothing, legal services, education, and the other things they need or desire. Money—in the form of both income and wealth—is unevenly distributed in Canada (see Figure 8.1). Among the approximately 20 industrialized nations of North America and Europe, Canada has a poor record pertaining to income inequality, following only the United States and the United Kingdom (Picot and Myles, 2004).

income The economic gain derived from wages, salaries, income transfers (governmental aid), and ownership of property.

Income Inequality

Income is the economic gain derived from wages, salaries, income transfers (governmental aid), and ownership of property. One common method of analyzing the distribution of

FIGURE 8.1 MEDIAN AFTER-TAX INCOME, FAMILIES OF TWO PERSONS OR MORE, PROVINCES AND TARGETED CENSUS METROPOLITAN AREAS, 2010

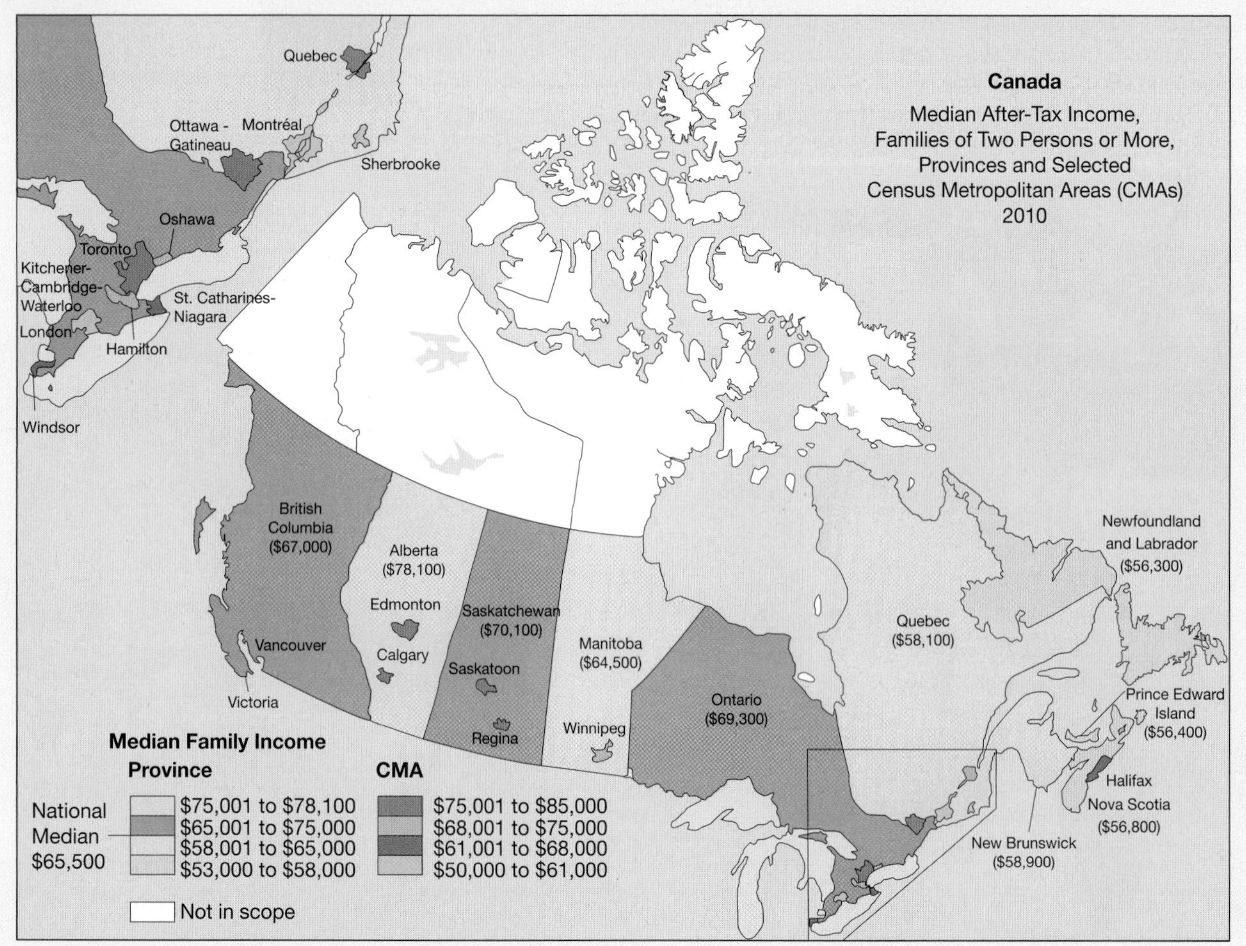

Source: Statistics Canada (2011), "Income in Canada," Catalogue no. 13-F0022XIE. Retrieved from http://www.statcan.gc.ca/pub/75-202-x/75-202-x2009000-eng.htm.

income is the concept of income *quintiles* comprised of five income groups ranging from the lowest-income group to the highest-income group. As shown in Table 8.1, the top quintile represents the 20 percent of families with the lowest incomes and the bottom quintile represents the 20 percent of families with the highest incomes. Sociologist Dennis Gilbert (2003) compares the distribution of income to a national pie that has been cut into portions ranging from stingy to generous, for distribution among segments of the population. Today, the wealthiest 20 percent of households receive close to 70 percent of the total income "pie," while the poorest receive only 4 percent of all income (Statistics Canada, 2011). Analysts further report that incomes have remained remarkably stable over time. In 1990, average family income was just under $60,000, and by 2009, it had increased to only $65,500 (Statistics Canada, 2011). However, a closer examination of the data reveals that focusing on the overall average family income tends to conceal wide variations between different segments of the population and hides increasing inequities in the distribution of income in Canada. Overall, the average family income of the three lowest income groups has increased slightly during the past decade, while that of the two highest income groups has continued to increase much more rapidly (Sauvé, 2012).

© Photodisc/Getty Images

People's life chances are enhanced by access to important societal resources, such as education. How will the life chances of students who have the opportunity to pursue a university degree differ from those of young people who do not have the chance to go to university?

There is considerable variation on other fronts, too. Consider regional variation in income across the country. As shown in Figure 8.1, family income is highest in Saskatchewan, Ontario, and Alberta and lowest in the Atlantic provinces and Quebec (Statistics Canada, 2011). There is also significant income variation among particular racial–ethnic groups. For example, recent statistics indicate almost 40 percent of visible minorities are in the low-income group, as compared to 20 percent of the general population. Beyond that, the data clearly demonstrate the inequities in income distribution experienced by Aboriginal peoples in Canada; their average income is less than two-thirds the average income of the general population (Quebec Population Health Research Network 2008).

wealth The value of all of a person's or family's economic assets, including income and property, such as buildings, land, farms, houses, factories, and cars, as well as other assets, such as money in bank accounts, corporate stocks, bonds, and insurance policies.

Wealth Inequality

Income is only one aspect of wealth. **Wealth** includes property, such as buildings, land, farms, houses, factories, and cars, as well as other assets, such as money in bank accounts, corporate stocks, bonds, and insurance policies. Wealth is computed by subtracting all debt obligations and converting the remaining assets into cash. The terms *wealth* and *net worth,* therefore, are used interchangeably. For most people in Canada, wealth is invested primarily in property that generates no income, such as a house or a car. In contrast, the wealth of an elite minority is often in the form of income-producing property.

Research on the distribution of wealth in Canada reveals that wealth is more unevenly distributed among the Canadian population than is income. Although the term *wealthy,* like the term *poor,* is relative, analysts generally define the wealthy as those whose total assets after debt

TABLE 8.1 AVERAGE ADJUSTED AFTER-TAX INCOME BY AFTER-TAX INCOME QUINTILES IN CANADA, 2010

2010	
Lowest quintile	16,000
Second quintile	28,000
Third quintile	38,500
Fourth quintile	50,600
Highest quintile	85,500

Source: Statistics Canada, "Survey of Labour and Income Dynamics," Cat. no. 75-202-X2010000 (CANSIM Table 202-0707).

TABLE 8.2 WEALTHIEST CANADIANS, 2011

NAME	WEALTH ($ BILLION)
David Thomson	21.0
Galen Weston	8.0
Irving Family	7.8
Ted Rogers Jr.	6.0
James (Jimmy) Pattison	5.7
Lino Saputo and family	4.3
Paul Demarais	4.3
Jeff Skoll	3.7
Fred and Ron Mannix	3.4
Bernard (Barry) Sherman	3.3
Clay Riddell	3.2

Source: "The Rich 100." *Canadian Business,* 2011. Retrieved August 2, 2012, from http://list.canadianbusiness.com/rankings/rich100/2011/Default.aspx?sp2=1&dl=a&scl=0. x

payments are more than $250,000. Now, 1.1 million Canadian households can claim millionaire status because their net worth is at least $1 million. Recent estimates indicate that, on average, millionaire families hold 10 times as much wealth as non-millionaire families do (Chawla, 2008).

Most of the wealthiest people in Canada are inheritors, with some at least three or four generations removed from the original fortune. As shown in Table 8.2, the combined wealth of Canada's richest families totals approximately $66 billion, $21 billion of which is accounted for by Canada's richest person, former newspaper publisher Kenneth Thomson (*Canadian Business*, 2011). It is clear that a limited number of people own or control a huge portion of the wealth in Canada. Indeed, one survey of wealth concluded that there is "gross and persistent inequality in the distribution of wealth in Canada. A surprisingly small number of Canadians have huge slices of the wealth pie, and a surprisingly large number of Canadians have no more than a few crumbs" (Kerstetter, 2002:6).

Whether we consider distribution of income or wealth, though, it is relatively clear that social inequality is a real, consistent, and enduring feature of life in Canadian society.

LO-3 CLASSICAL PERSPECTIVES ON SOCIAL CLASS

Early sociologists grappled with the definition of class and the criteria for determining people's location within the class structure. Both Karl Marx and Max Weber viewed class as an important determinant of social inequality and social change, and their works have had a profound influence on contemporary class theory.

Karl Marx: Relation to Means of Production

capitalist class (bourgeoisie) Karl Marx's term for those who own the means of production.

working class (proletariat) Karl Marx's term for those who must sell their labour in order to earn enough money to survive.

According to Karl Marx, class position is determined by people's work situation, or relationship to the means of production. As we have previously seen, Marx stated that capitalistic societies are made up of two classes—the capitalists and the workers. The **capitalist class (bourgeoisie)** consists of those who own the means of production—the land and capital necessary for factories and mines, for example. **The working class (proletariat)** consists of those who must sell their labour to the owners in order to earn enough money to survive (see Figure 8.2).

According to Marx, class relationships involve inequality and exploitation. The workers are exploited as capitalists maximize their profits by paying workers less than the resale value of what they produce but do not own. Marx believed that a deep level of antagonism exists between capitalists and workers because of extreme differences in the *material interests* of the people in these two classes. According to the sociologist Erik O. Wright, material interests are "the interests people have in their material standard of living, understood

FIGURE 8.2 MARX'S VIEW OF SOCIAL CLASS

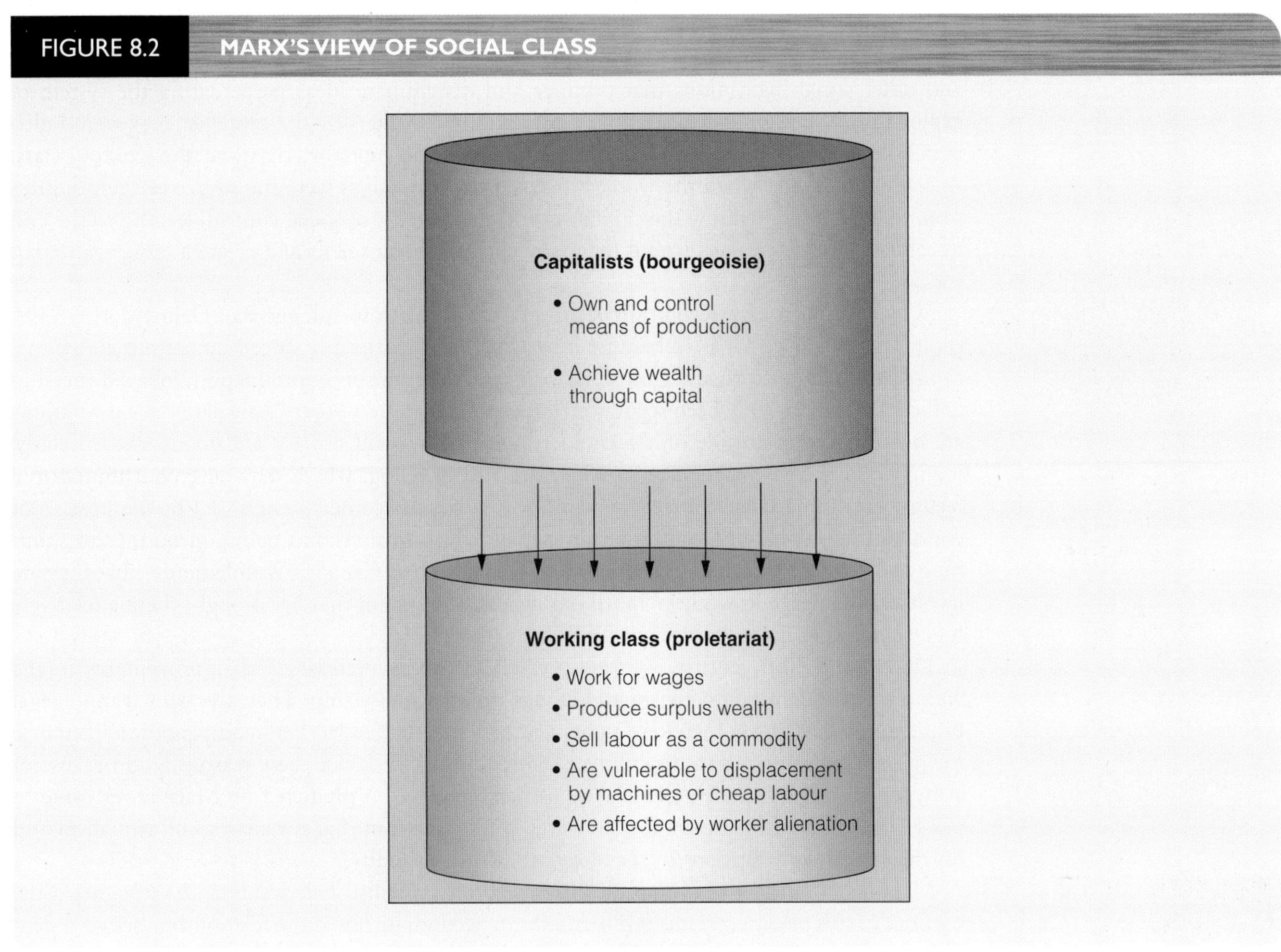

as the package of toil, consumption, and leisure. Material interests are thus not interests of maximizing consumption *per se,* but rather interests in the trade-off between toil, leisure, and consumption" (1997:5). Wright suggests that *exploitation* is the key concept for understanding Marx's assertion that *interests* are generated by class relations: "In an exploitative relation, the exploiter needs the exploited since the exploiter depends upon the effort of the exploited." In other words, the capitalists *need* the workers to derive profits; therefore, capitalists benefit when workers do not have adequate resources to provide for themselves and hence must sell their labour power to the capitalist class. As Marx suggests, exploitation involves ongoing interactions between the two antagonistic classes, which are structured by a set of social relations that binds together the exploiter and the exploited (Wright, 1997).

Continual exploitation results in worker alienation—a feeling of powerlessness and estrangement from other people and from oneself. In Marx's view, alienation develops as workers manufacture goods that embody their creative talents, but the goods do not belong to them. Workers are also alienated from the work because they are forced to perform it to live. Because the workers' activities are not their own, they feel self-estrangement. Moreover, the workers are separated from others in the factory because they individually sell their labour power to the capitalists as a commodity.

In Marx's view, the capitalist class maintains its position at the top of the class structure by control of the society's *superstructure,* which is composed of the government, schools, churches, and other social institutions that produce and disseminate ideas perpetuating the system of exploitation. Marx predicted that the exploitation of workers by the capitalist class would ultimately lead to class conflict—the struggle between the capitalist class and the working class. According to Marx, when the workers realized that capitalists were the source of their oppression, they would overthrow the capitalists and their agents of social control, leading to the end of capitalism. The workers would then take over the government and create a more egalitarian society.

Why has no workers' revolution occurred? According to sociologist Ralf Dahrendorf (1959), capitalism may have persisted because it has changed significantly since Marx's time. Individual capitalists no longer own and control factories and other means of production; today, ownership and control have largely been separated. For example, contemporary transnational corporations are owned by a multitude of shareholders but run by paid officers and managers. Similarly, many workers have experienced a rising standard of living, which may have contributed to a feeling of complacency. Moreover, many people have become so engrossed in the process of consumption—including acquiring more material possessions and going on outings to shopping malls, movie theatres, and amusement parks, such as Canada's Wonderland—that they are less likely to engage in workers' rebellions against the system that has brought them a relatively high standard of living (Gottdiener, 1997).

During the 20th century, workers pressed for salary increases and improvements in the workplace through their activism and labour union membership. They also gained more legal protection in the form of workers' rights and benefits, such as workers' compensation insurance for job-related injuries and disabilities (Dahrendorf, 1959). For these reasons, and because of a myriad of other complex factors, the workers' revolution predicted by Marx never came to pass. The failure of his prediction, however, does not mean that his analysis of capitalism and his theoretical contributions to sociology are without validity.

Marx had a number of important insights about capitalist societies. First, he recognized the economic basis of class systems (Gilbert, 2003). Second, he noted the relationship between people's location in the class structure and their values, beliefs, and behaviour. Finally, he acknowledged that classes may have opposing (rather than complementary) interests. For example, capitalists' best interests are served by a decrease in labour costs and other expenses and a corresponding increase in profits; workers' best interests are served by well-paid jobs, safe working conditions, and job security.

Max Weber: Wealth, Prestige, and Power

Max Weber's analysis of class builds upon earlier theories of capitalism (particularly those by Marx). Living in the late 19th and early 20th centuries, Weber was in a unique position to see the transformation that occurred as individual, competitive, entrepreneurial capitalism went through the process of shifting to bureaucratic, industrial, corporate capitalism. As a result, Weber had more opportunity than Marx did to see how capitalism changed over time.

Weber agreed with Marx's assertion that economic factors are important in understanding individual and group behaviour. However, he emphasized that no one factor (such as economic divisions between capitalists and workers) was sufficient to define people's location within the class structure. For Weber, the access that people have to important societal resources (such as economic, social, and political power) is crucial in determining their life chances. To highlight the importance of life chances for categories of people,

Weber developed a multidimensional approach to *social stratification* that reflects the interplay among wealth, prestige, and power. In his analysis of these dimensions of class structure, Weber viewed the concept of class as an *ideal type* (which can be used to compare and contrast various societies), rather than as a specific category of "real" people (Bourdieu, 1984).

Weber placed categories of people who have a similar level of wealth and income in the same class. For example, he identified a privileged commercial class of *entrepreneurs*—wealthy bankers, ship owners, professionals, and merchants who possess similar financial resources. He also described a class of *rentiers*—wealthy individuals who live off their investments and do not have to work. According to Weber, entrepreneurs and rentiers have much in common. Both are able to purchase expensive consumer goods, control other people's opportunities to acquire wealth and property, and monopolize costly status privileges (such as education) that provide contacts and skills for their children.

Weber divided those who work for wages into two classes: the middle class and the working class. The middle class consists of white-collar workers, public officials, managers, and professionals. The working class consists of skilled, semiskilled, and unskilled workers.

The second dimension of Weber's system of social stratification is **prestige**—the respect with which a person or status position is regarded by others. Fame, respect, honour, and esteem are the most common forms of prestige. A person who has a high level of prestige is assumed to receive deferential and respectful treatment from others. Weber suggested that individuals who share a common level of social prestige belong to the same status group regardless of their level of wealth. They tend to socialize with one another, marry within their own group of social equals, spend their leisure time together, and safeguard their status by restricting outsiders' opportunities to join their ranks (Beeghley, 2000).

prestige The respect or regard with which a person or status position is regarded by others.

The other dimension of Weber's system is **power**—the ability of people or groups to achieve their goals despite opposition from others. The powerful shape society in accordance with their own interests and direct the actions of others (Tumin, 1953). According to Weber, social power in modern societies is held by bureaucracies; individual power depends on a person's position within the bureaucracy. Weber suggested that the power of modern bureaucracies was so strong that even a workers' revolution, as predicted by Marx, would not lessen social inequality (Hurst, 2007).

power According to Max Weber, the ability of people or groups to achieve their goals despite opposition from others.

Weber stated that wealth, prestige, and power are separate continuums on which people can be ranked from high to low. As shown in Figure 8.3, individuals may be high in one dimension while being low in another. For example, people may be very wealthy but have little political power (for example, a recluse who has inherited a large sum of money). They also may have prestige but not wealth (for instance, a university professor who receives teaching excellence awards but lives on a relatively low income). In Weber's multidimensional approach, people are ranked in all three dimensions. Sociologists often use the term **socioeconomic status (SES)** to refer to a combined measure that attempts to classify individuals, families, or households in terms of indicators, such as income, occupation, and education, to determine class location.

socioeconomic status (SES) A combined measure that attempts to classify individuals, families, or households in terms of indicators, such as income, occupation, and education, to determine class location.

What important insights does Weber provide in regard to social stratification and class? Weber's analysis of social stratification contributes to our understanding by emphasizing that people behave according to both their economic interests and their values. He also added to Marx's insights by developing a multidimensional explanation of the class structure and identifying additional classes. Both Marx and Weber emphasized that capitalists and workers are the primary players in a class society, and both noted the importance of class to people's life chances. However, they saw different futures for capitalism and the social system. Marx saw these structures being overthrown; Weber saw increasing bureaucratization of life even without capitalism.

FIGURE 8.3 WEBER'S MULTIDIMENSIONAL APPROACH TO SOCIAL STRATIFICATION

According to Max Weber, wealth, power, and prestige are separate continuums. Individuals may rank high in one dimension and low in another, or they may rank high or low in more than one dimension. They may also use their high rank in one dimension to achieve a comparable rank in another.

TIME TO REVIEW

- Explain the statement "The rich get richer and the poor get poorer." Does this apply to both income and wealth?
- Explain how prestige, power, and wealth determine social class.

CONTEMPORARY SOCIOLOGICAL MODELS OF THE CLASS STRUCTURE IN CANADA

How many social classes exist in Canada today? What criteria are used for determining class membership? No broad consensus exists about how to characterize the class structure of this country. Canadians do not like to talk about social class, and many deny that class distinctions even exist. Most people like to think of themselves as middle class; it puts them in a comfortable middle position—neither rich nor poor.

Sociologists have developed a few models of the class structure. One is based on a Weberian approach, the other on a Marxian approach. We will examine each of these models briefly.

A Weberian Model of Class Structure

Expanding on Weber's analysis of the class structure, sociologists Dennis Gilbert (2003) and Joseph A. Kahl (1998) developed a widely used model of social classes based on three elements: (1) education, (2) occupation of the family head, and (3) family income. This model can be used to describe the social class structure in Canadian society.

THE UPPER CLASS The upper class is the wealthiest and most powerful class in Canada. Members of the upper class own substantial income-producing assets (such as real estate, stocks, and bonds) and operate at both the national and international levels. It is difficult to determine the exact size and composition of this group because information about the very rich is difficult to obtain. However, it has been estimated that approximately 3 percent of the population is in this class, which owns and controls the major economic assets in Canada (Naiman, 2000).

Some models further divide the upper class into *upper-upper class* ("old money") and *lower-upper class* ("new money"). Because such a small number (about 1 percent) are members of the upper-upper class, many analysts have referred to it as the *elite* class (Clement, 1975; Clement and Myles, 1994). Members of this class come from prominent families that possess tremendous wealth that they have held for several generations. For example, the net worth of the Thomson family was recently estimated at close to $21 billion (*Canadian Business*, 2011).

Numerous scholars have examined the distribution of wealth and power in Canada and found one consistent result: A small number of individuals—in the upper-upper class—yield an enormous amount of power. For example, John Porter's classic study identified just over 900 individuals who controlled all of the major corporations in Canada (1965:579). Author Peter Newman identified slightly less than 1000 individuals as members of what he described as "the Canadian establishment." As Newman points out, members of the upper-upper class share more than wealth and power; they tend to have strong feelings of ingroup solidarity. They belong to the same exclusive clubs, share social activities, and support high culture (such as the symphony, opera, ballet, and art museums). Their children are educated at prestigious private schools and universities. In general, children of the upper class are socialized to view themselves as different from others; they may also learn that they are expected to marry within their own class (Johnson, 1974; Mills, 1959a; Warner and Lunt, 1941).

Members of the lower-upper class may be extremely wealthy but have not attained as much prestige as the members of the upper-upper class. The "new rich" have earned most of their money as entrepreneurs, presidents of major corporations, sports or entertainment celebrities, or top-level professionals.

UPPER-MIDDLE CLASS Persons in the upper-middle class are often highly educated professionals who have established careers as physicians, lawyers, stockbrokers, or corporate managers. Others have derived their income from family-owned businesses. A combination of three factors qualifies people for the upper-middle class: a university education, authority and independence on the job, and high income. Of all the class categories, the upper-middle class is the one that is most influenced by education.

Across racial–ethnic and class lines, children are encouraged to acquire the higher education necessary for upper-middle-class positions that typically have high prestige in the community. However, many social analysts point out that racism still diminishes the life chances of people of colour even when they achieve a high income and a prestigious career (see Henry and Tator, 2006).

THE MIDDLE CLASS In past decades, a high school diploma was required to qualify for most middle-class jobs. Today, undergraduate university degrees or college programs have replaced the high school diploma as an entry-level requirement for employment in many middle-class occupations, including medical technicians, nurses, legal and medical secretaries, lower-level managers, semiprofessionals, and nonretail salespersons. Traditionally, most middle-class positions have been relatively secure and provided more opportunities for advancement (especially with increasing levels of education and experience) than working-class positions. Recently, however, four factors have diminished the chances for material success for members of this class: (1) escalating housing prices, (2) occupational insecurity, (3) blocked upward mobility on the job, and (4) the cost-of-living squeeze that has penalized younger workers, even when they have more education and better jobs than their parents (Newman, 1993).

THE WORKING CLASS An estimated 30 percent of the Canadian population is in the working class. The core of this class is made up of semiskilled machine operators who work in factories and elsewhere. Members of the working class also include some workers in the service sector and salespeople whose job responsibilities involve routine, mechanized tasks requiring little skill beyond basic literacy and a brief period of on-the-job training (Gilbert, 2003). Within the working class are also **pink-collar occupations**—relatively low-paying, nonmanual, semiskilled positions primarily held by women, such as daycare workers, checkout clerks, cashiers, and waitresses.

pink-collar occupation Relatively low-paying, nonmanual, semiskilled positions primarily held by women.

How does life in the working-class family compare with that of individuals in middle-class families? According to sociologists, working-class families not only earn less than middle-class families, but they also have less financial security, particularly with high rates of layoffs and corporate downsizing in some parts of the country. Few people in the working class have more than a high school diploma, which makes job opportunities increasingly scarce in our "high-tech" society (Gilbert, 2003).

THE WORKING POOR The working poor account for about 20 percent of the Canadian population. Members of the working-poor class live from just above to just below the poverty line. They typically hold unskilled jobs, seasonal jobs, lower-paid factory jobs, and service jobs (such as counter help at restaurants). Employed single mothers often belong to this class; consequently, children are overrepresented in this category. Members of some visible minority groups, Aboriginal peoples, and recent immigrants are also overrepresented among the working poor (Canadian Council on Social Development, 2009). For the working poor, living from paycheque to paycheque makes it impossible to save money for emergencies, such as periodic or seasonal unemployment, which is a constant threat to any economic stability they may have.

Social critic and journalist Barbara Ehrenreich (2001) left her upper-middle-class lifestyle for a time to see whether the working poor could live on the wages they were being paid as restaurant servers, salesclerks at discount department stores, aides in nursing homes, house cleaners for franchise maid services, and other similar jobs. She conducted her research by holding those jobs for periods of time and seeing if she could live on the wages she received. Through her research, Ehrenreich persuasively demonstrated that people who work full time, year-round for poverty-level wages must develop survival strategies that include getting help from relatives or constantly moving from one residence to another to have a place to live. Like many other researchers, Ehrenreich found that minimum-wage jobs cannot cover the full cost of living, such as rent, food, and the rest of an adult's monthly needs, even without considering the needs of children or other family members.

THE UNDERCLASS According to Gilbert (2003), people in the underclass are poor, seldom employed, and caught in long-term deprivation that results from low levels of education and income and high rates of unemployment. Some are unable to work because of age or disability; others experience discrimination based on race or ethnicity. Single mothers are overrepresented in this class because of lack of jobs, affordable child care, and many other impediments to their future and that of their children. People without a "living wage" must often rely on public or private assistance programs for their survival. Studies by various social scientists have found that satisfactory employment opportunities are the critical missing link for people on the lowest rungs of the social class ladder. According to these analysts, job creation is essential for people to have the opportunity to earn a decent wage; have medical coverage; live meaningful, productive lives; and raise their children in a safe environment (see Fine and Weis, 1998; Nelson and Smith, 1999; Newman, 1999; Wilson, 1996).

A Conflict Model of Class Structure

The earliest Marxian model of class structure identified ownership or nonownership of the means of production as the distinguishing feature of classes. From this perspective, classes are social groups organized around property ownership, and social stratification is created and maintained by one group to protect and enhance its own economic interests. Moreover,

Erik Olin Wright's conflict model of the class system emphasizes the differing interests of the capitalist class, exemplified by the small-business class (top left); the managerial class (top right); the capitalist class—Phil Knight, the founder of Nike (bottom left); and the working class (bottom right).

societies are organized around classes in conflict over scarce resources. Inequality results when the more powerful exploit the less powerful.

Contemporary Marxian (or conflict) models examine class in terms of people's relationships with others in the production process. For example, conflict theorists attempt to determine what degree of control workers have over the decision-making process and the extent to which they are able to plan and implement their own work. They also analyze the type of supervisory authority, if any, that a worker has over other workers. According to this approach, most employees are a part of the working class because they do not control either their own labour or that of others.

Erik Olin Wright (1978, 1979, 1985, 1997), one of the leading stratification theorists to examine social class from a Marxian perspective, has concluded that Marx's definition of "workers" does not fit the occupations found in advanced capitalist societies. For example, many top executives, managers, and supervisors who do not own the means of production (and thus would be "workers" in Marx's model) act like capitalists in their zeal to control workers and maximize profits. Likewise, some experts hold positions in which they have control over money and the use of their own time even though they are not owners. Wright views Marx's category of "capitalist" as being too broad as well. For instance, small-business owners might be viewed as capitalists because they own their own tools and have a few people working for them, but they have little in common with large-scale capitalists and do not share the interests of factory workers. Figure 8.4 compares Marx's model and Wright's model.

Wright (1979) argues that classes in modern capitalism cannot be defined simply in terms of different levels of wealth, power, and prestige, as in the Weberian model. Consequently, he outlines four criteria for placement in the class structure: (1) ownership of the means of production, (2) purchase of the labour of others (employing others), (3) control of the labour of others (supervising others on the job), and (4) sale of one's own labour (being employed by someone else). Wright (1978) assumes that these criteria can be used to determine the class placement of all workers, regardless of race and ethnicity, in a capitalist society.

Let's take a brief look at Wright's (1979, 1985) four classes—(1) the capitalist class, (2) the managerial class, (3) the small-business class, and (4) the working class—so that you can compare them to those found in the Weberian model.

THE CAPITALIST CLASS According to Wright, this class holds most of the wealth and power in society through ownership of capital—for example, banks, corporations, factories, mines, news and entertainment industries, and agribusiness firms. The "ruling elites," or "ruling class," within the capitalist class hold political power and are often elected or appointed to influential political and regulatory positions (Parenti, 1994).

This class is composed of individuals who have inherited fortunes, own major corporations, or have extensive stock holdings or control of company investments because they are top corporate executives. Even though many top executives have only limited *legal ownership* of their corporations, they have substantial economic ownership and exert extensive control over investments, distribution of profits, and management of resources. The major sources of income for the capitalist class are profits, interest, and very high salaries. Members of this class make important decisions about the workplace, including which products and services to make available to consumers and how many workers to hire or fire.

According to *Forbes* magazine's 2011 list of the richest people in the world, Carlos Slim Helú of Telecom was the wealthiest capitalist with a net worth of $69 billion. Bill Gates (co-founder of Microsoft Corp., the world's largest microcomputer software company) was a close second with a net worth of $61 billion. Investor Warren E. Buffett came in third with $44 billion. Although some of the men who made the *Forbes* list of wealthiest people have gained their fortunes through entrepreneurship or as chief executive officers (CEOs) of large corporations, women who made the list typically acquired their wealth through inheritance, marriage, or both. In 2012, only 20 women were heads of Fortune 500 companies (Catalyst Canada, 2012).

FIGURE 8.4 COMPARISON OF MARX'S AND WRIGHT'S MODELS OF CLASS STRUCTURE

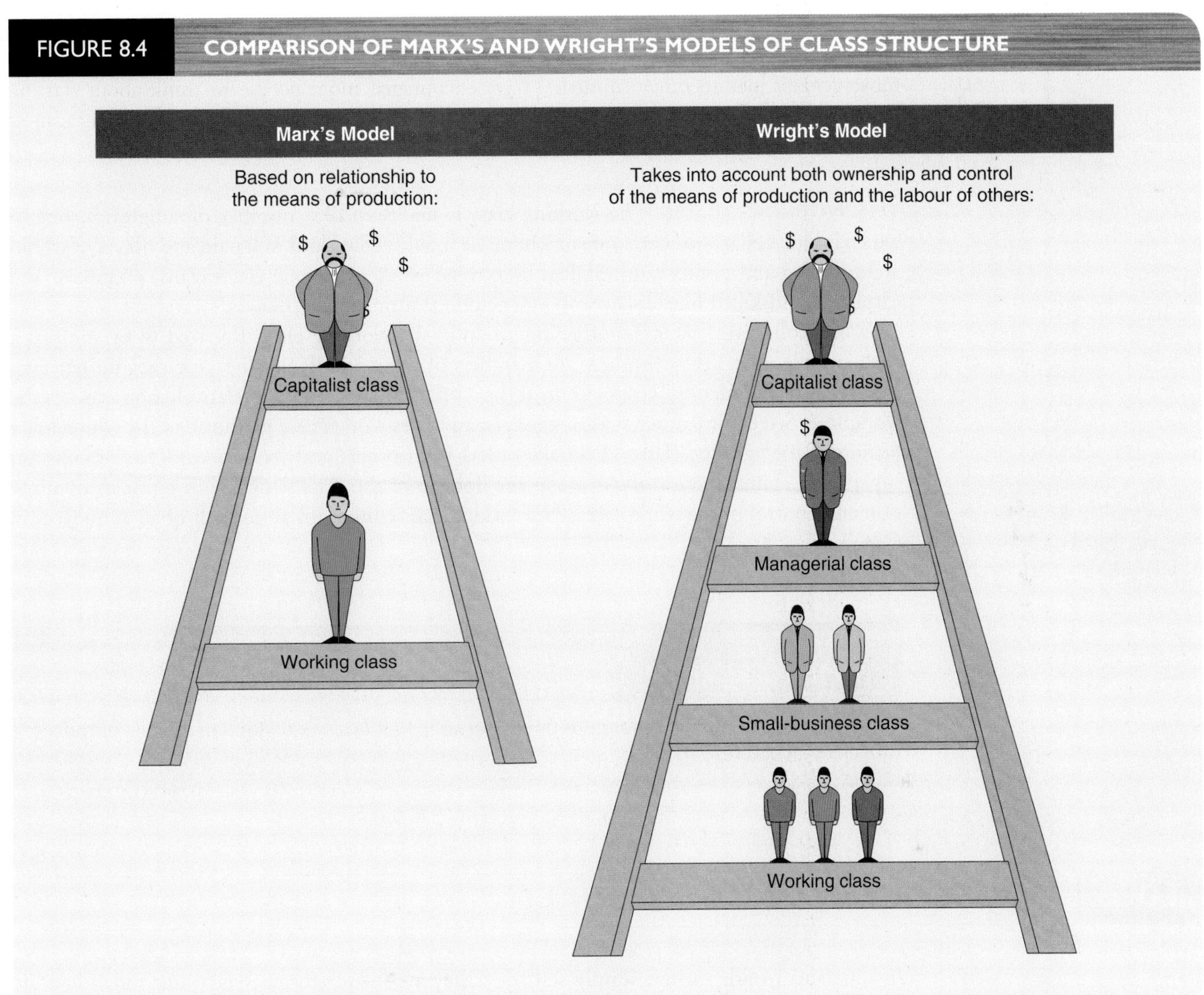

THE MANAGERIAL CLASS People in the managerial class have substantial control over the means of production and over workers; however, these upper-level managers, supervisors, and professionals typically do not participate in key corporate decisions, such as how to invest profits. Lower-level managers may have some control over employment practices, including the hiring and firing of some workers

Top professionals, such as physicians, lawyers, accountants, and engineers, may control the structure of their own work; however, they typically do not own the means of production and may not have supervisory authority over more than a few people. Even so, they may influence the organization of work and the treatment of other workers. Members of the capitalist class often depend on these professionals for their specialized knowledge.

THE SMALL-BUSINESS CLASS This class consists of small-business owners and craftspeople who may hire a few employees but largely do their own work. Some members own businesses, such as "mom and pop" grocery stores, retail clothing stores, and jewellery stores. Others are doctors and lawyers who receive relatively high incomes from selling their services. Some of these professionals now share attributes with members of the capitalist class because they have formed corporations that hire and control the employees who produce profits for the professionals.

It is in the small-business class that we find many people's hopes of achieving upward mobility. Recent economic trends, including corporate downsizing, telecommuting, and the movement of jobs to other countries, have encouraged more people to think about starting their own business. As a result, more people today are self-employed or own a small business than at any time in the past.

THE WORKING CLASS The working class is made up of a number of subgroups, one of which is blue-collar workers, some of whom are highly skilled and well paid and others of whom are unskilled and poorly paid. Skilled blue-collar workers include electricians, plumbers, and carpenters; unskilled blue-collar workers include janitors and gardeners.

White-collar workers are another subgroup of the working class. Referred to by some as a "new middle class," these workers are members of the working class because they do not own the means of production, do not control the work of others, and are relatively powerless in the workplace. Secretaries, other clerical workers, and sales workers are members of the white-collar faction of the working class. They take orders from others and tend to work under constant supervision. Thus, these workers are at the bottom of the class structure in terms of domination and control in the workplace. The working class consists of about half of all employees in Canada.

TIME TO REVIEW

- What are the fundamental differences between Weberian and Marxian models of the class structure?

LO-4 CONSEQUENCES OF INEQUALITY

Income and wealth are not simply statistics; they are intricately related to our individual life chances. Persons with a high income or substantial wealth have more control over their lives. They have greater access to goods and services, and they can afford better housing, more education, and a wider range of medical services. Similarly, those with greater access to economic resources fare better when dealing with the criminal justice system (Linden, 2009; Reiman, 1979). Persons with less income, especially those living in poverty, must spend their limited resources on the basic necessities of life.

Physical and Mental Health and Nutrition

People who are wealthy and well educated and who have high-paying jobs are much more likely to be healthy than are poor people. As people's economic status increases, so does their health status. People who are poor have shorter life expectancies and are at greater risk for chronic illnesses, such as diabetes, heart disease, and cancer, as well as for infectious diseases, such as tuberculosis (see Chapter 16).

For example, a report by Prof. Dennis Raphael at York University (2001) concluded that the economic and social conditions under which Canadians live their lives are greater determinants of whether they develop heart disease than medical and lifestyle factors (such as poor diet, lack of activity, and smoking). If all Canadians had the cardiovascular health of the wealthiest Canadians, there would be approximately 6000 fewer deaths a year from heart disease. According to Raphael's report, the economic and social conditions that most contribute to heart disease are poverty and low income. Specifically, poverty and low income lead to heart disease in three ways:

1. People on low incomes live under conditions of material deprivation that produce a cardiovascular heart burden that accumulates over the life span.
2. Living on low incomes creates excessive stress that damages the cardiovascular system.
3. The stressful conditions associated with low incomes lead to unhealthy behaviours, such as smoking (Raphael, 2001).

There is also increasing evidence that societies with large income gaps between the wealthy and the poor are the most likely to produce the conditions that lead to heart disease.

Children born into poor families are at much greater risk of dying during their first year of life. Some die from disease, accidents, or violence. Others are unable to survive because they are born with low birth weight, a condition linked to birth defects and increased probability of infant mortality. Low birth weight in infants is attributed, at least in part, to the inadequate nutrition received by many low-income pregnant women. Most of the poor do not receive preventive medical and dental checkups; many do not receive adequate medical care after they experience illness or injury. Furthermore, many high-poverty areas lack an adequate supply of doctors and medical facilities (Campaign 2000, 2010). The higher death rates among Aboriginal peoples in Canada are partly attributable to unequal access to medical care and nutrition (Quebec Population Health Research Network, 2008).

Although the precise relationship between class and health is not known, analysts suggest that people with higher incomes and greater wealth tend to smoke less, exercise more, maintain a healthy body weight, and eat nutritious meals. As a category, affluent people tend to be less depressed and face less psychological stress, conditions that tend to be directly proportional to income, education, and job status (Ross and Roberts, 1997).

Good health is basic to good life chances, and adequate amounts of nutritious food are essential for good health. Hunger is related to class position and income inequality. After spending 60 percent of their income on housing, low-income families are often unable to provide enough food for their children. Consider the following comments by a mother on her attempts to manage her food budget:

> I remember opening up the fridge just to see what was in there. There was a green pepper, an onion in the drawer and a bag of frozen rhubarb in the freezer, and that was all the food we had in the entire house. We used to eat peanut butter by the spoonful, if we had any peanut butter. We used to make rhubarb soup. And we'd throw in whatever we could find. (Canadian Council on Social Development, 1996:21)

The highest rate of food bank use since 1997 was reported in 2010, when close to 900,000 Canadians had to rely on food banks each month to help make ends meet. This increase clearly indicates that many Canadians are unable meet their nutritional needs (Campaign 2000, 2010).

Education

Educational opportunities and life chances are directly linked. Some functionalist theorists view education as the "elevator" to social mobility. Improvements in the educational achievement levels (measured in number of years of schooling completed) of the poor, visible minorities, and women have been cited as evidence that students' abilities are now more important than their class, race, or gender. From this perspective, inequality in education is declining and students have an opportunity to achieve upward mobility through achievements at school. Functionalists generally see the education system as flexible, allowing most students the opportunity to attend university if they apply themselves (Ballantine, 2001).

In contrast, most conflict theorists stress that schools are agencies for reproducing the capitalist class system and perpetuating inequality in society. From this perspective, education perpetuates poverty. Parents with a limited income are not able to provide the same educational opportunities for their children as are families with greater financial resources. Today, great disparities exist in the distribution of educational resources. Because funding for education comes primarily from local property taxes, school districts in wealthy suburban areas generally pay higher teachers' salaries, have newer buildings, and provide state-of-the-art equipment. By contrast, schools in poorer areas have a limited funding base. Students in core area schools and poverty-stricken rural areas often attend schools that lack essential equipment and teaching resources.

Poverty exacts such a toll that many young people will not have the opportunity to finish high school, much less enter university, which subsequently affects job prospects, employment patterns, and potential earnings.

Crime and Lack of Safety

Along with diminished access to quality healthcare, nutrition, and housing and unequal educational opportunities, crime and lack of safety are other consequences of inequality. As discussed in Chapter 7, although people from all classes commit crimes, they commit different kinds of crimes. Capitalism and the rise of the consumer society may be factors in the criminal behaviour of some upper-middle-class and upper-class people, who may be motivated by greed or the competitive desire to stay ahead of others in their reference group. By contrast, crimes committed by people in the lower classes may be motivated by feelings of anger, frustration, and hopelessness.

According to Marxist criminologists, capitalism produces social inequalities that contribute to criminality among people, particularly those who are outside the economic mainstream. Poverty and violence are also linked. In his ethnographic study of inner-city life, sociologist Elijah Anderson suggests that what some people refer to as "random, senseless street violence" (1999:33) is often not random at all, but instead a response to profound social inequalities in the inner city.

Consequences of inequality include both crime and lack of safety on the streets, particularly for people who feel a profound sense of alienation from mainstream society and its institutions. Those who are able to take care of themselves and protect their loved ones against aggression are accorded deference and regard by others. However, Anderson believes that it is wrong to place blame solely on individuals for the problems that exist in urban ghettos; instead, he asserts that the focus should be on the socioeconomic structure and public policy that have threatened the well-being of people who live in poverty.

POVERTY IN CANADA

When many people think about poverty, they think of people who are unemployed or on welfare; however, many hardworking people with full-time jobs live in poverty. In the United States, the government established an *official poverty line,* which is based on what is considered the minimum amount of money required for living at a subsistence level. The poverty level is computed by determining the cost of a minimally nutritious diet and multiplying this figure by three to allow for nonfood costs. Canada, however, has no official definition of poverty, no official method for measuring poverty, and no official set of poverty lines (Zhang, 2010). As a result, in Canada, there is ongoing and contentious debate with respect to how prevalent and how serious the problem of poverty is.

low-income cutoff
The income level at which a family may be in "straitened circumstances" because it spends considerably more on the basic necessities of life (food, shelter, and clothing) than the average family.

The most accepted and commonly used definition of poverty is Statistics Canada's before-tax **low-income cutoff**—the income level at which a family may be in "straitened circumstances" because it spends considerably more on the basic necessities of life (food, shelter, and clothing) than the average family. The low-income cutoff depends on family and community size. According to this measure, any individual or family that spends more than 70 percent of their income on the three essentials of life—food, clothing, and shelter—is considered to be living in poverty. There is no single cutoff line for all of Canada because living costs vary by family size and place of residence. When sociologists define poverty, they distinguish between absolute and relative poverty.

absolute poverty A level of economic deprivation in which people do not have the means to secure the basic necessities of life.

relative poverty A level of economic deprivation in which people may be able to afford basic necessities but still are unable to maintain an average standard of living.

Absolute poverty exists when people do not have the means to secure the most basic necessities of life. This definition comes closest to that used by the corporate think tanks, such as the Fraser Institute. Absolute poverty often has life-threatening consequences, such as when a homeless person freezes to death on a park bench. By comparison, **relative poverty** exists when people may be able to afford basic necessities but still are unable to maintain an average standard of living (Lee, 2000). The relative approach is based on equity—that is, on some acknowledgment of the extent to which society should tolerate or accept inequality in the distribution of income and wealth. This definition recognizes that people who have so little that they stand out in relation to their community will feel deprived (Canadian Council on Social Development, 1996:3). In short, regardless of how it is defined, poverty is primarily about deprivation, as this woman's comments reveal:

> There are times when I am so scared that I'm not going to find a job, I think, "What the hell is wrong with me?" . . . I can get scared to death . . . I have periods of insomnia. I'll get very short tempered with my husband and with the children. (Burman, 1998:195)

With the exception of a small percentage of the Canadian population that is living at a bare subsistence level or below, most of the poor people in our society suffer the effects of a relentless feeling of being boxed in, a feeling that life is dictated by the requirements of simply surviving each day. If something unexpected happens, such as sickness, an accident, a family death, fire, theft, or a rent increase, there is no buffer to deal with the emergency. Life is just today because tomorrow offers no hope (Ross, Scott, and Smith, 2000). As analyst Roger Sauvé sums up after an evaluation of what low-income families do without:

> Money may not buy happiness . . . but the lack of money clearly reduces the probability of accessing many of the goods and services that are enjoyed by others. The poorest fifth of households are short of cash, skip on food, are much less likely to achieve home ownership, less likely to own a car, and give up spending on recreation, camps, investing, dental insurance and many other items. (2008:5)

Who Are the Poor?

As might be expected, those who are society's most vulnerable, most disadvantaged, and least equipped to compete in a highly competitive, fast-polarizing labour market are most likely to be living in poverty (Pohl, 2002). Poverty in Canada is not randomly distributed, but rather is highly concentrated among certain groups of people—specifically, women, children, persons with disabilities, and Aboriginal peoples. When people belong to more than one of these categories—for example, Aboriginal children—their risk of poverty is even greater.

AGE Today, children are at much greater risk of living in poverty than are people over age 65. A generation ago, older persons were at greatest risk of being poor; however, increased government transfer payments and an increase in the number of elderly individuals retiring with private pension plans have led to a decline in poverty among the elderly. Recent statistics indicate that the poverty rate for children under age 18 is approximately 9.5 percent. More than 600,000 Canadian children are living in poverty, and a large number of children hover just above the official poverty line (Campaign 2000, 2011).

As shown in Table 8.3 on page 230, child poverty rates are even higher among vulnerable groups. These include children living in female lone-parent families, children with disabilities,

BOX 8.2 SOCIOLOGY IN GLOBAL PERSPECTIVE

How Does Child Poverty in Canada Compare with Child Poverty in Other Nations?

The UNICEF report *Child Poverty in Rich Nations* ranks Canada a lowly 24 out of the 35 industrialized countries belonging to the Organisation for Economic Co-operation and Development (OECD) (see the figure below).

The international rankings show that a nation's level of wealth does not predetermine its ability to prevent children from falling into poverty. Countries with higher economic growth do not necessarily have a lower poverty ranking. Many of the countries with the lowest poverty rates have relatively lower wealth rankings. The wealthiest nation, the United States, has the highest poverty ranking. The contention that child poverty can be addressed only through increased economic growth is contradicted by the available evidence.

UNICEF states that the reason why countries are able to address child poverty with such varying degrees of success relates to how each chooses to set priorities according to its wealth. Most of the nations that have been more successful than Canada at keeping low levels of child poverty are willing to counterbalance the effects of unemployment and low-paid work with substantial investments in family policies. The comprehensive approach to the well-being of children adopted by many European countries includes generous income security and unemployment benefits and national affordable housing programs, as well as widely accessible early childhood education and care.

The contrast of early childhood education and care services in Canada and in Europe is instructive. A recent OECD review of 12 nations found that early childhood education and care had experienced a "surge of policy attention" in Europe during the past decade. The same has not been true in Canada. While the nations of Western Europe now provide universal full-day early childhood education and care for all three- to five-year-olds, Canada has not even begun to consider this. Yet there is widespread agreement, including among Canadian researchers, that early childhood education and care is a critical component of comprehensive family policy and of an effective antipoverty strategy.

Source: Unicef Innocenti Research Centre, 2000.

POVERTY RATES FOR CHILDREN AND THE TOTAL POPULATION, 2008

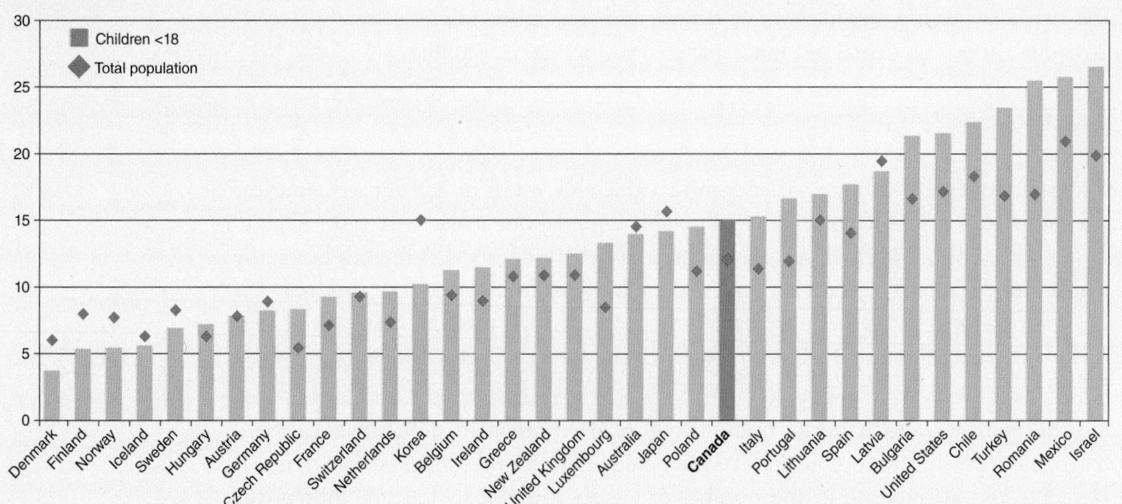

This bar graph shows the percentage of children (0-17 years) in households with an income equivalent to less than 50 percent of the median.

Source: Adapted from Chart CO2.2.A, "Poverty rates for children and the total population, 2008" from "OECD Family Database www.oecd.org/social/familiesandchildren/41929552.df.

immigrant families, and Aboriginal families. Approximately 30 percent of children in all of these groups are living in poverty (Campaign 2000, 2011).

Despite the 1989 promise made by the House of Commons to alleviate child poverty by the year 2000, little progress has been made (see Table 8.3). It makes little difference whether they live in one- or two-parent families: Children as a group are poorer now than they were at the beginning of the 1980s. More than half of all poor children live in two-parent families, while the number of poor children living in single-parent households is increasing. These children are poor because their parents are poor, and one of the main reasons for poverty among adults is a lack of good jobs. Government cuts to employment insurance benefits, employment programs, income supports, and social services for families and children will affect not only those who need these services but also the children of these individuals. (See Box 8.2 for a look at child poverty in Canada and other wealthy nations.)

© David Bacon/The Image Works

The "feminization of poverty" refers to the fact that two out of three impoverished adults in North America are women. Should we assume that poverty is primarily a women's issue? Why or why not?

GENDER About two-thirds of all adults living in poverty in Canada are women. Women in all categories are at greater risk for poverty than men, but the risk is particularly significant in single-parent families headed by women (Naiman, 2008). As Figure 8.5 shows,

FIGURE 8.5 POVERTY RATE BY FAMILY TYPE

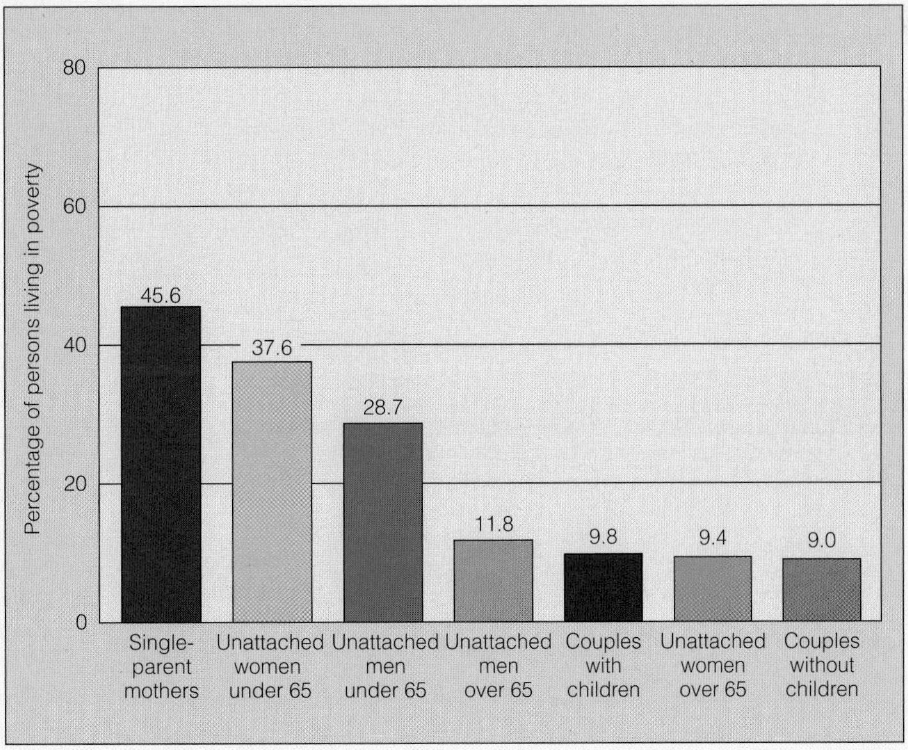

Family type	Percentage of persons living in poverty
Single-parent mothers	45.6
Unattached women under 65	37.6
Unattached men under 65	28.7
Unattached men over 65	11.8
Couples with children	9.8
Unattached women over 65	9.4
Couples without children	9.0

Source: Canadian Council on Social Development, 2009.

FIGURE 8.6 POVERTY RATE FOR CHILDREN IN LOW-INCOME FAMILIES, 1989–2009

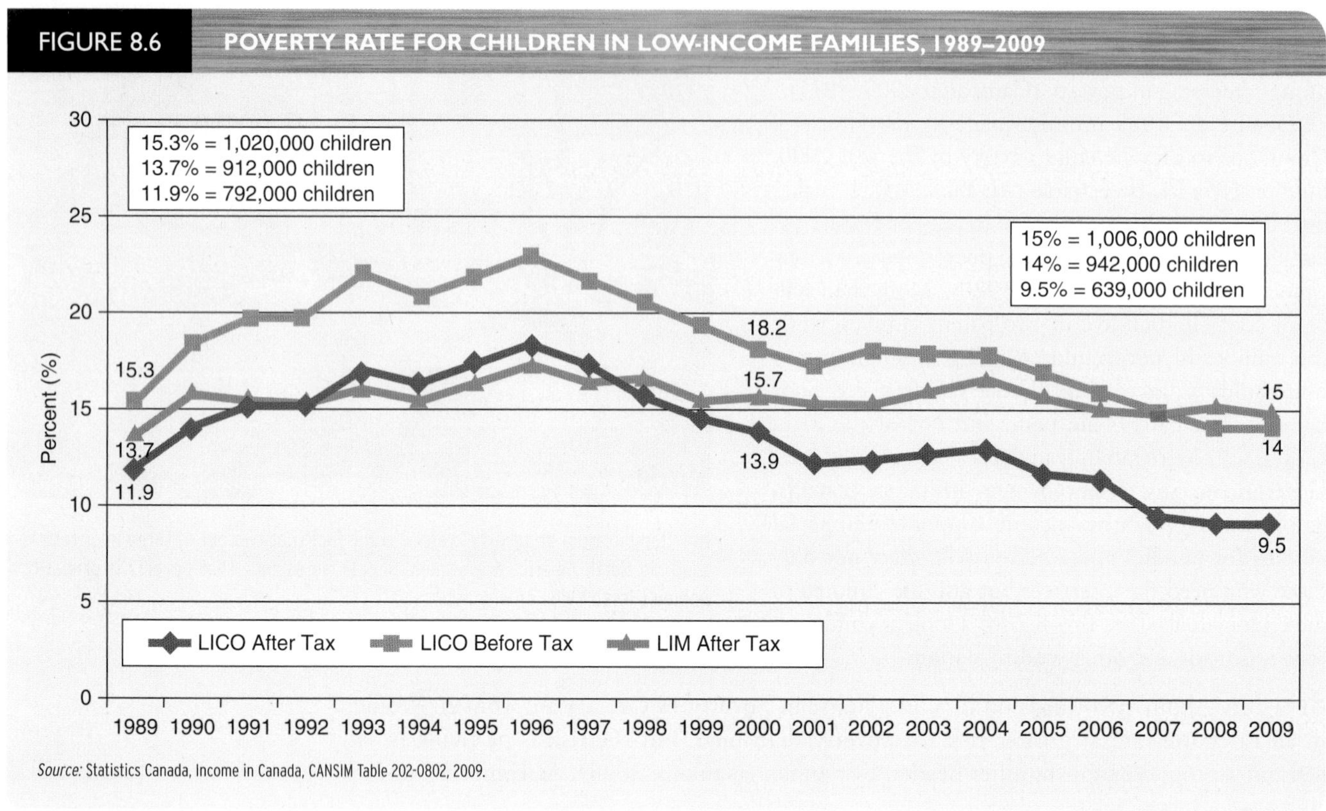

Source: Statistics Canada, Income in Canada, CANSIM Table 202-0802, 2009.

single-parent families headed by women have a poverty rate of 45 percent, compared with a rate of 10 percent for two-parent families (see Figure 8.6 above). Furthermore, women are among the poorest of the poor. Poor single mothers with children under 18 are the worst off, struggling on incomes more than $9000 below the low-income cutoff (Campaign 2000, 2011). Sociologist Diana Pearce (1978) coined a term to describe this problem. The **feminization of poverty** refers to the trend in which women are disproportionately represented among individuals living in poverty. According to Pearce, women have a higher risk of being poor because they bear the major economic burden of raising children as single heads of households but earn only 70 cents for every dollar a male worker earns—a figure that has changed little over four decades. More women than men are unable to obtain regular, full-time, year-round employment, and the lack of adequate affordable daycare exacerbates this problem. As we will see in Chapter 9, the feminization of poverty is a global phenomenon.

feminization of poverty The trend in which women are disproportionately represented among individuals living in poverty.

Does the feminization of poverty explain poverty in Canada today? Is poverty primarily a women's issue? On one hand, this thesis highlights a genuine problem—the link between gender and poverty. On the other hand, several major problems exist with this argument. First, women's poverty is not a new phenomenon. Women have

TABLE 8.3 PREVALENCE OF LOW INCOME AMONG CHILDREN IN CANADA, BY SOCIAL GROUP

Group	Prevalence of Low Income (Percent)
All children	9.5%
Children (under 15 years) in recent immigrant families	39.3%
First Nations children (under 15 years)	33.7%
Children in racialized families	34.0%
Children with disabilities	28.0%

Sources: Statistics Canada Catalogue no. 97-564-X2006002, 6 December 2008; Statistics Canada, CANSIM table 202-0802; Statistics Canada, Canada Census 2001, Statistics Canada Catalogue no. 97-564-XCB2006008, 17 December 2008.

always been more susceptible to poverty (see Katz, 1989). Second, all women are not equally susceptible to poverty. Many in the upper and upper-middle classes have the financial resources, education, and skills to support themselves regardless of the presence of a man in the household. Some women, however, experience what has been described as *event-driven poverty* as a result of marital separation, divorce, or widowhood (Bane, 1986). Third, event-driven poverty does not explain the realities of poverty for many visible minority women, who instead may experience *reshuffled poverty*—a condition of deprivation that follows them regardless of their marital status or the type of family in which they live. Some women experience *multiple jeopardies,* a term that refers to the even greater risk of poverty experienced by women who are immigrants, members of visible minorities, or Aboriginal or who have disabilities (Gerber, 1990).

Finally, poverty is everyone's problem, not just women's. When women are impoverished, so are their children. Moreover, many of the poor people in our society are men, especially the chronically unemployed—older persons, the homeless, persons with disabilities, and members of a visible minority. These men have spent their adult lives without hope of finding work.

RACE/ETHNICITY According to some stereotypes, most of the poor and virtually all welfare recipients are visible minorities. Such stereotypes are perpetuated because a disproportionate percentage of the impoverished in Canada are Aboriginal persons and recent immigrants. Members of both of these groups have significantly higher rates of poverty and unemployment and much lower incomes. These families often live in crowded housing, and parents often worry about being able to afford food for their children (Campaign 2000, 2011).

Aboriginal people in Canada are among the most severely disadvantaged. About one-third live in poverty, and some live in conditions of extreme poverty. The median income for Aboriginal persons is just over $15,000—$11,000 below the national average income of $26,000 (Gionet, 2009). A study by the Department of Indian Affairs found that the quality of life for Aboriginal persons living on reserves ranks worse than in countries such as Mexico and Thailand. Similarly, the United Nations Human Development Index put their living conditions in line with those in Russia (Tjepkema, 2002). For Aboriginal persons living off reserves, the quality of life is slightly better. The unemployment rate for Aboriginal persons in Canada ranges from 15 to 25 percent, while the national average is about 5 percent.

In short, the erosion of Canada's social safety net has had a particularly negative impact on those who have historically experienced exclusion and disadvantage in Canadian society (Campaign 2000, 2011).

PERSONS WITH DISABILITIES Awareness that persons with disabilities are discriminated against in the job market has increased in recent years. As a result, they now constitute one of the recognized "target groups" in efforts to eliminate discrimination in the workplace. People with disabilities have more opportunities to work today than they had a decade ago. Today, although more than 50 percent of people with disabilities are in the labour force, many continue to be excluded from the workplace not because of the disability itself but because of environmental barriers in the workplace (Galarneau and Radulescu, 2009). The effects of this systemic discrimination continue to be felt by disabled persons, as they are still, as a group, vulnerable to poverty. As discussed in Chapter 16, adults with disabilities have significantly lower incomes than Canadians without disabilities. Recent estimates indicate that close to half of employed persons with disabilities had incomes below $10,000. Once again, when gender and disability are combined, we find that women with disabilities are doubly disadvantaged (Galarneau and Radulescu, 2009).

Economic and Structural Sources of Poverty

Poverty has both economic and structural sources. The low wages paid for many jobs is the major cause: About one in three low-income children has at least one parent who is working full-time but is still in poverty. These parents are not finding jobs with sufficient pay, reasonable amounts of hours of work, and decent benefits that would allow them to move above the poverty line. In 1972, minimum-wage legislation meant that someone who worked 40 hours a week, 52 weeks a year could earn a yearly income 20 percent over the poverty line. By today's standards, the same worker would have to earn more than $11 per hour simply to reach the poverty line. Minimum wages across Canada range from just over $10 to a high of about $11 per hour. In other words, a person with full-time employment in a minimum-wage job cannot keep a family of four above the official poverty line.

Structural problems contribute to both unemployment and underemployment. The rapid worldwide transformation that is taking place today is changing our societies from industrial-based ones to information-based ones. Automation in the industrial heartland of Quebec and Ontario has made the skills and training of thousands of workers obsolete. Many of these workers have become unemployable and poor. Corporations have been deinvesting in Canada, displacing millions of people from their jobs. Economists refer to this displacement as the *deindustrialization of North America* (Bluestone and Harrison, 1982). Even as they have closed their Canadian factories and plants, many corporations have opened new facilities in other countries where "cheap labour" exists because people of necessity will work for lower wages. **Job deskilling**—a reduction in the proficiency needed to perform a specific job, which leads to a corresponding reduction in the wages for that job—has resulted from the introduction of computers and other technology (Hodson and Parker, 1988). The shift from manufacturing to service occupations has resulted in the loss of higher-paying positions and their replacement with lower-paying and less secure positions that do not offer the wages, job stability, or advancement potential of the disappearing manufacturing jobs. Consequently, there are not enough good jobs available in Canada to enable families to lift themselves out of poverty. In addition, the lack of affordable, high-quality daycare for women who need to earn an income means that many jobs are inaccessible, especially to women who are single parents. The problems of unemployment, underemployment, and poverty-level wages are even greater for members of visible minorities and young people (Canadian Council on Social Development, 2009).

job deskilling A reduction in the proficiency needed to perform a specific job, which leads to a corresponding reduction in the wages paid for that job.

LO-5 SOCIOLOGICAL EXPLANATIONS OF SOCIAL INEQUALITY

Obviously, some people are disadvantaged as a result of social inequality. Is inequality therefore always harmful to a society? Why are all societies stratified?

Functionalist Perspectives

According to sociologists Kingsley Davis and Wilbert Moore (1945), social inequality is not only inevitable but necessary for the smooth functioning of society. The *Davis–Moore thesis,* which has become the definitive functionalist explanation for social inequality, can be summarized as follows:

1. All societies have important tasks that must be accomplished and certain positions that must be filled.
2. Some positions are more important for the survival of society than others.

3. The most important positions must be filled by the most qualified people.
4. The positions that are the most important for society, and that require talent that is scarce and extensive training or both, must be the most highly rewarded.
5. The most highly rewarded positions should be those on which people in other positions rely for expertise, direction, or financing and that are functionally unique (no one outside the position can perform the same function).

Davis and Moore use the physician as an example of a functionally unique position. Doctors are very important to society and require extensive training, but individuals would not be motivated to go through years of costly and stressful medical training without incentives to do so. The Davis–Moore thesis assumes that social stratification results in **meritocracy**—a hierarchy in which all positions are rewarded based on people's ability and credentials.

meritocracy A hierarchy in which all positions are rewarded based on people's ability and credentials.

Critics have suggested that the Davis–Moore thesis ignores inequalities based on inherited wealth and intergenerational family status (Rossides, 1986). The thesis assumes that economic rewards and prestige are the only effective motivators for people, and fails to take into account other intrinsic aspects of work, such as self-fulfillment (Tumin, 1953). It also does not adequately explain how such a reward system guarantees that the most qualified people will gain access to the most highly rewarded positions.

Conflict Perspectives

From a conflict perspective, people with economic and political power are able to shape and distribute the rewards, resources, privileges, and opportunities in society for their own benefit. Conflict theorists do not believe that inequality serves as a motivating force for people; they argue that powerful individuals and groups use ideology to maintain their favoured positions at the expense of others. A stratified social system is accepted because of the dominant ideology of the society, the set of beliefs that explain and justify the existing social order (Marchak, 1975). Core values in Canada emphasize the importance of material possessions, hard work, and individual initiative to get ahead, as well as behaviour that supports the existing social structure. These same values support the prevailing resource distribution system and contribute to social inequality.

Are wealthy people smarter than others? According to conflict theorists, certain stereotypes suggest that this is the case; however, the wealthy may be "smarter" than others only in the sense of having "chosen" to be born to wealthy parents from whom they could inherit assets. Conflict theorists also note that laws and informal social norms support inequality in Canada. For the first half of the 20th century, both legalized and institutionalized segregation and discrimination reinforced employment discrimination and produced higher levels of economic inequality. Although laws have been passed to make these overt acts of discrimination illegal, many forms of discrimination still exist in educational and employment opportunities.

Feminist Perspectives

According to feminist scholars, the quality of an individual's life experiences is a reflection of both class position and gender. These scholars examine the secondary forms of inequality and oppression occurring *within* each class that have been overlooked by the classical theorists. Feminist theorists focus on the combined effect that gender has on class inequality. Some feminist scholars view class and gender as reinforcing one another and creating groups that are "doubly oppressed." This combined effect of one's class and gender may manifest itself in the workplace or the home or both. Subsequently, feminist authors have identified such terms as the *double ghetto* (Armstrong and Armstrong, 1994) and *second shift* (Hochschild, 1989) to describe women's experiences in the segregated workforce or the home (see Chapters 11 and 13). Rather than male and female spouses maintaining similar class positions within a family unit, women hold a subordinate position. A feminist perspective emphasizes that within any class, women are less advantaged than men in their access to material goods, power, status, and possibilities for self-actualization. The causes of the inequality lie in the organization of capitalism itself (Ritzer, 1996:321). For example, upper-class women are wealthy but often remain secondary to their husbands in terms of power. Middle-class women may be financially well off but often lack property or labour force experience and are vulnerable to financial instability in cases of divorce or separation. The position of working-class women varies based on their participation in the paid labour force. Typically, the working-class woman has little income, primary responsibility for the household work, and an inferior position in terms of power and independence to her husband. As a result, the female spouse may become "the slave of a slave" (Mackinnon, 1982:8), allowing the working-class male to compensate for his lower class position in society. The family is viewed as an institution that supports capitalism and encourages or exacerbates the exploitation of women.

Symbolic Interactionist Perspectives

Symbolic interactionists focus on microlevel concerns and usually do not analyze larger structural factors that contribute to inequality and poverty. However, many significant insights on the effects of wealth and poverty on people's lives and social interactions can be derived from applying a symbolic interactionist approach. Using qualitative research methods and influenced by a symbolic interactionist approach, researchers have collected the personal narratives of people across all social classes, ranging from the wealthiest to the poorest people.

A few studies provide rare insights into the social interactions between people from vastly divergent class locations. Sociologist Judith Rollins's (1985) study of the relationship between household workers and their employers is one example. Based on in-depth interviews and participant observation, Rollins examined rituals of deference that were often demanded by elite white women of their domestic workers, who were frequently women of colour. According to Erving Goffman (1967), *deference* is a type of ceremonial activity that functions as a symbolic means whereby appreciation is regularly conveyed to a recipient. In fact, deferential behaviour between non-equals (such as employers and employees) confirms the inequality of the relationship and each party's position in the relationship relative to that of the other. Rollins identified three types of linguistic deference between domestic workers and their employers: use of the first names of the workers, contrasted with titles and last names (Mrs. Adams) of the employers; use of the term *girls* to refer to female household workers regardless of their age; and deferential references to employers, such as, "Yes, ma'am." Spatial demeanour, including touching and how close one person stands to another, is an additional factor in deference rituals across class lines. Rollins concludes:

> The employer, in her more powerful position, sets the essential tone of the relationship; and that tone . . . is one that functions to reinforce the inequality of the relationship, to strengthen the employer's belief in the rightness of her advantaged class and racial position, and to provide her with justification for the inegalitarian social system. (1985:232)

Many concepts introduced by the sociologist Erving Goffman (1959, 1967) could be used as springboards for examining microlevel relationships between inequality and people's everyday interactions. What could you learn about class-based inequality in Canada by using a symbolic interactionist approach to examine a setting with which you are familiar?

CONCEPT SNAPSHOT

FUNCTIONALIST PERSPECTIVES **Key thinkers:** Kingsley Davis and Wilbert Moore	Inequality is necessary for the smooth functioning of society. Social stratification leads to *meritocracy:* a hierarchy in which all positions are rewarded based on ability and credentials.
CONFLICT PERSPECTIVES	Dominant groups maintain and control the distribution of rewards, resources, privileges, and opportunities at the expense of others. Marxist conflict theorists explain that growing inequality is a result of the *surplus value*, profit that is generated when the cost of labour is less than the cost of the goods and services being produced.
FEMINIST PERSPECTIVES	Class and gender reinforce one another and create inequalities and oppressions for women "within" different social classes.
SYMBOLIC INTERACTIONIST PERSPECTIVES	Focus is on the microlevel effects of wealth and poverty on people's social interactions. For example, in its various forms, *deference* confirms inequality between individuals in differing social class positions.

8

VISUAL SUMMARY

KEY TERMS

absolute poverty A level of economic deprivation in which people do not have the means to secure the basic necessities of life (p. 227).

capitalist class (bourgeoisie) Karl Marx's term for those who own the means of production (p. 214).

caste system A system of social inequality in which people's status is permanently determined at birth based on their parents' ascribed characteristics (p. 209).

class system A type of stratification based on the ownership and control of resources and on the type of work people do (p. 210).

feminization of poverty The trend in which women are disproportionately represented among individuals living in poverty (p. 230).

income The economic gain derived from wages, salaries, income transfers (governmental aid), and ownership of property (p. 212).

intergenerational mobility The social movement (upward or downward) experienced by family members from one generation to the next (p. 208).

intragenerational mobility The social movement (upward or downward) experienced by individuals within their own lifetime (p. 208).

job deskilling A reduction in the proficiency needed to perform a specific job, which leads to a corresponding reduction in the wages paid for that job (p. 232).

LO-1 Identify three types of stratification systems.

© Jake Norton/Alamy

Slavery is an extreme form of stratification in which some people are owned by others. It is a closed system in which people designated as "slaves" are treated as property and have little or no control over their lives. Like slavery, caste is a closed system of social stratification. A *caste system* is a system of social inequality in which people's status is permanently determined at birth based on their parents' ascribed characteristics. Vestiges of caste systems exist in contemporary India and South Africa. The *class system* is a type of stratification based on the ownership and control of resources and on the type of work people do. At least theoretically, a class system is more open than a caste system because the boundaries between classes are less distinct than the boundaries between castes. In a class system, status comes at least partly through achievement rather than entirely by ascription.

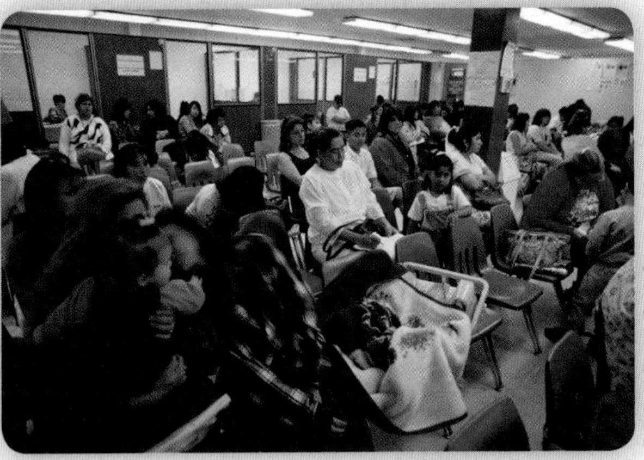

© Shepard Sherbell/Corbis Saba

LO-2 Discuss the extent of social inequality in Canada based on measures of income and wealth.

Based on measures of income and wealth, there is significant social inequality in Canada. The richest 20 percent of households receive close to 70 percent of the total income "pie," while the poorest receive only 4 percent of all income. Wealth is more unevenly distributed among the Canadian population than is income—the richest 10 percent of Canadian households control close to 60 percent of the country's wealth. The stratification of society into different social groups results in wide discrepancies in income and wealth and in variable access to available goods and services. People with high incomes or wealth have a greater opportunity to control their own lives. People with lower incomes have fewer life chances and must spend their limited resources to acquire basic necessities.

LO-3 Understand the classical analysis of social class by Karl Marx and Max Weber.

Karl Marx and Max Weber acknowledged social class as a key determinant of social inequality and social change. For Marx, people's relationship to the means of production determines their class position. Weber developed a multidimensional concept of stratification that focuses on the interplay of wealth, prestige, and power.

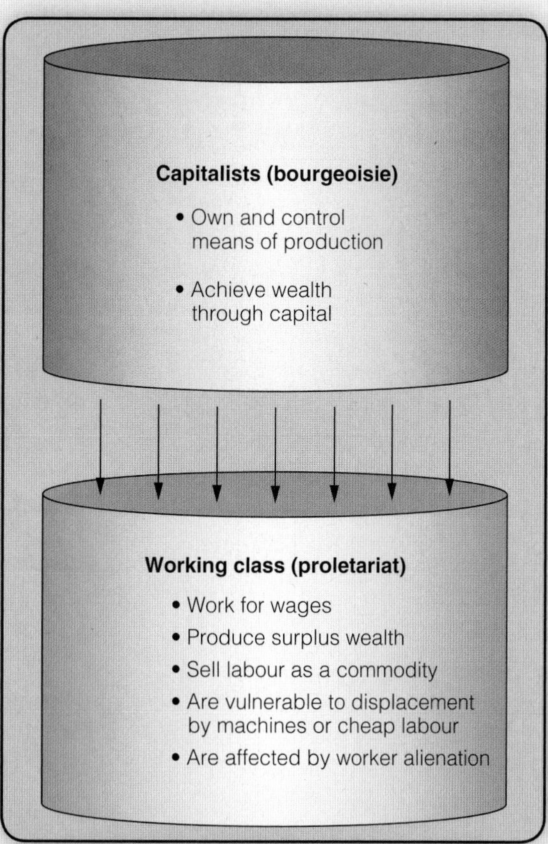

© David Bacon/The Image Works

LO-4 Provide an overview of poverty and its effects in Canada.

Sociologists distinguish between absolute and relative poverty. Absolute poverty exists when people do not have the means to secure the basic necessities of life. Relative poverty exists when people may be able to afford basic necessities but still are unable to maintain an average standard of living. Age, gender, race and ethnicity, and disability tend to be factors in poverty. Children have a greater risk of being poor than do the elderly, while women have a higher rate of poverty than do men. Although white persons account for approximately two-thirds of those below the poverty line, Aboriginal peoples and members of visible minorities account for a disproportionate share of the impoverished in Canada. As the gap between rich and poor and between employed and unemployed widens, social inequality will clearly increase in the future.

life chances Max Weber's term for the extent to which individuals have access to important societal resources, such as food, clothing, shelter, education, and healthcare (p. 208).

low-income cutoff The income level at which a family may be in "straitened circumstances" because it spends considerably more on the basic necessities of life (food, shelter, and clothing) than the average family (p. 226).

meritocracy A hierarchy in which all positions are rewarded based on people's ability and credentials (p. 233).

pink-collar occupation Relatively low-paying, nonmanual, semiskilled positions primarily held by women (p. 220).

power According to Max Weber, the ability of people or groups to achieve their goals despite opposition from others (p. 217).

prestige The respect or regard with which a person or status position is regarded by others (p. 217).

relative poverty A level of economic deprivation in which people may be able to afford basic necessities but still are unable to maintain an average standard of living (p. 227).

slavery An extreme form of stratification in which some people are owned by others (p. 209).

social mobility The movement of individuals or groups from one level in a stratification system to another (p. 208).

social stratification The hierarchical arrangement of large social groups based on their control over basic resources (p. 208).

socioeconomic status (SES) A combined measure that attempts to classify individuals, families, or households in terms of indicators, such as income, occupation, and education, to determine class location (p. 217).

wealth The value of all of a person's or family's economic assets, including income and property, such as buildings, land, farms, houses, factories, and cars, as well as other assets, such as money in bank accounts, corporate stocks, bonds, and insurance policies (p. 213).

working class (proletariat) Karl Marx's term for those who must sell their labour in order to earn enough money to survive (p. 214).

LO-5 Compare and contrast a functionalist view and a conflict perspective on social inequality.

© Katie Deits/Index Stock Imagery

According to the Davis–Moore thesis, stratification exists in all societies and some inequality is not only inevitable but also necessary for the ongoing functioning of society. The positions that are most important within society and that require the most talent and training must be highly rewarded. Conflict perspectives on inequality are based on the assumption that social stratification is created and maintained by one group to enhance and protect its own economic interests. Conflict theorists measure inequality according to people's relationships with others in the production process.

APPLICATION QUESTIONS

1. Based on the functionalist model of class structure, what is the class location of each of your 10 closest friends or acquaintances? What is their location in relation to yours? To one another? What does their location tell you about friendship and social class?
2. Should employment be based on merit, need, or affirmative action policies? Discuss.
3. If the gap between rich and poor people continues to widen, what might happen in Canada in the future?

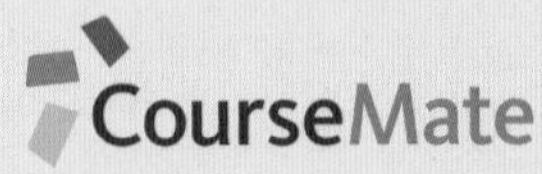

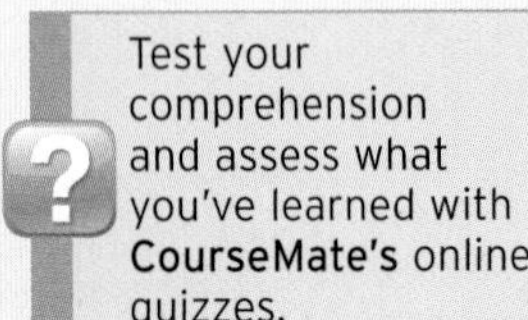
Test your comprehension and assess what you've learned with **CourseMate's** online quizzes.

For other interesting Lived Experiences, watch the video clips on **CourseMate.**

Practise what you've learned with flashcards containing key terms and definitions on **CourseMate.**

CHAPTER

9 Global Stratification

© AFP/Getty Images

The following is an excerpt from a letter that a mother in the Philippines wrote to her daughters explaining her commitment to political activism:

> *Today, both of you are in University. In less than five years, you will join the ranks of the 40 to 50 percent unemployed and underemployed Filipinos. If you are lucky and do find jobs, you will painfully experience the discrepancy between the daily cost of living at 354 pesos and the minimum wage pegged by the government at 150 pesos. I won't be surprised if you find yourselves in the 70 percent of the population considered below the poverty line and the 40 percent below the food threshold. Even now, that is what we see happening.*
>
> *I fear that very soon, even the environment will no longer be a dependable support system. What with biologically dead rivers, contaminated drinking water, and depleted marine resources because of the mine tailings spewed by mining companies, the likes of Marcopper and its Canadian partner, Placer Dome, what with dry rice fields that have to be abandoned due to the lack of water for irrigation brought about by open pit mining operations of giant establishments . . . What with two-thirds of the whole Cordillera region apportioned to Australian, American, and Canadian mining companies . . .*
>
> *The road is long that leads to progress—too long in fact, that hope could easily be snuffed out. But this one thing I can say, Mitzi May and Lily Joyce: I HAVE NOT LOST HOPE. This is why I have opted to leave you for a while—to join the many hopeful Filipinos who have put their lives on the line. And I will continue to put my life on the line for as long as this insensitive government rides roughshod on our people's God-given rights.* (Ruiz-Duremdes, n.d.)

(*Source:* Ruiz-Duremdex, Sharon Rose Joy, "An Open Letter to My Children," *Transformation: An International Journal of Holistic Mission Studies*, Volume 15 (3): 6. July 1, 1998 Reprinted by Permission of SAGE.)

You might be surprised to learn that of all the narratives we have used to open the chapters in this book, this was the most difficult to find. The world's poorest people have no voice. Even researchers who study global stratification rarely let them tell their own stories. Books are full of statistics that tell the stories of nations that cannot feed their citizens and researchers' descriptions of the lives of people living at the margins of survival. However, the poor remain faceless. If not for the haunting images of famine or civil war that we see in the media, most of us would know nothing about the more than one billion people who live out their lives in abject poverty. They are equally invisible to those managing the global corporations and the international organizations whose decisions have life-and-death consequences for those at the bottom of the global stratification system.

The quotation we did select is not really representative of the world's poor. The mother writing to her children is educated, articulate, and a political activist. While her country, the Philippines, is poor, it is far wealthier than many other nations. However, her letter does articulate many of the problems of people in developing countries—unemployment, foreign control of resources, environmental degradation, economic restructuring, and political discontent.

In this chapter, we will examine global stratification and discuss the perspectives that have been developed to explain this inequality. It can be difficult to connect the lives of people living in poverty in distant countries to our own lives in one of the world's wealthiest countries. When television shows us thousands of people starving in Somalia or babies being treated for dehydration at aid stations in Darfur, it is sometimes hard to realize that the people we see are individual human beings just as we and our friends are. The global stratification system determines who will live long, prosperous lives, like those of most Canadians, and who will live short, miserable lives, eking out a marginal existence in subsistence agriculture and subject to the vagaries of rain, floods, and political instability.

Why do these inequities persist? In this chapter, you will learn why the life prospects of billions of people remain so dismal. When you read the explanations of global stratification, you should remember that these are not just academic theories. Rather, these are the ideas shaping the way governments and international organizations, such as the United Nations, deal with the problem of global poverty. As you will see, decisions based on the wrong theories can be disastrous for the poor.

Before reading on, test your knowledge of global wealth and poverty by taking the quiz in Box 9.1 on page 243.

Critical Thinking Questions

1. What role do you think higher-income countries play in the continuing poverty of people in lower-income countries?
2. When global corporations such as Apple move their production from North America and Europe to countries where wages are low and government regulation is limited, do you think they make life better or worse for workers living in those countries?
3. You will learn in this chapter that educating women is such an important strategy for improving the lives of people living in poor countries that the UN recognized it as a Millennium Development Goal. Why do you think women's education is so important?

CHAPTER FOCUS QUESTION

What is global stratification, and how does it contribute to economic inequality?

LEARNING OBJECTIVES

AFTER READING THIS CHAPTER, YOU SHOULD BE ABLE TO

LO-1 Understand the concept of global stratification and its impact on the lives of billions of people.

LO-2 Understand the relationship between global poverty and human development.

LO-3 Discuss Rostow's modernization theory and explain the stages that modernization theorists believe all societies must go through.

LO-4 Describe how dependency theory differs from modernization theory.

LO-5 Understand how world-systems analysis views the global economy.

LO-6 Understand the international division of labour theory.

© vietnam/Alamy

Many of the things we buy are produced in low-income countries. Many workers in these countries are poorly paid and work in harsh conditions.

LO-1 WEALTH AND POVERTY IN GLOBAL PERSPECTIVE

Global stratification refers to the unequal distribution of wealth, power, and prestige on a global basis, resulting in people having vastly different lifestyles and life chances. Just as Canada can be divided into classes, the world can be divided into unequal segments characterized by extreme differences in wealth and poverty. *High-income countries* have highly industrialized economies; technologically advanced industrial, administrative, and service occupations; and relatively high levels of income. In contrast, *low-income countries* are undergoing the transformation from agrarian to industrial economies and have lower levels of income.

Where you are born has a huge influence on your life chances. A World Bank report (2006) contrasts the prospects of two children: Nthabiseng, born in a rural area of South Africa, and Sven, born in Sweden. The chance of Sven dying in his first year of life is only 0.3 percent, compared with the 7.2 percent risk faced by Nthabiseng. Sven will likely complete 11.4 years of schooling, while Nthabiseng will have less than one year of formal education. Sven will have access to clean water, good housing, proper food, and excellent medical care, while Nthabiseng may have none of these advantages. As a result, Sven will likely live to the age of 80, while Nthabiseng will likely die before she is 50.

Consumption and Poverty

Progress in reducing world poverty has been slow, despite a great deal of talk and billions of dollars in foreign aid flowing from high-income to low-income nations. The notion of "development" has become the primary means of attempting to alleviate global poverty. Often, the nations that have been unable to reduce poverty are blamed for not establishing the necessary social and economic reforms to make change possible. However, some analysts have suggested that the problem of inequality lies not in poverty but in excess:

> "The problem of the world's poor," defined more accurately, turns out to be "the problem of the world's rich." This means that the solution to the problem is not a massive change in the culture of poverty so as to place it on the path of development, but a massive change in the culture of superfluity in order to place it on the path of counter-development. It does not call for a new value system forcing the world's majority to feel shame at their traditionally moderate consumption habits, but for a new value system forcing the world's rich to see the shame and vulgarity of their over-consumption habits, and the double vulgarity of standing on other people's shoulders to achieve those consumption habits. (Lummis, 1992:50)

The United Nations *Human Development Report* (1998) showed how excessive consumption in rich countries threatens the environment, depletes natural resources, and wastes money that might otherwise provide for the needs of the desperately poor in low-income countries. The wealthiest 20 percent of the world's people account for 86 percent of private consumption, while the poorest 20 percent account for only 1.3 percent. See Figure 9.1.

What is overconsumption? Canadians spend $21 billion a year on clothing (Lin, 2003). Much of this is spent keeping up with changes in style. The young Winnipeg woman interviewed for the *Winnipeg Free Press* style section who said her fashion essential was "Shoes, mostly heels. I buy, like, two pairs a week" (2009:F9) was not just trying to protect her feet from the elements. She was motivated by other concerns. Spending even a small portion of our money on disease prevention or education in low-income countries rather than on the latest style of shoes could keep hundreds of thousands of people alive in low-income countries.

But aren't the world's needs so great that channelling some of the money we spend on excessive consumption would make little difference in the lives of the world's poor? Surprisingly, the

BOX 9.1 **SOCIOLOGY AND EVERYDAY LIFE**

How Much Do You Know About Global Wealth and Poverty?

True	False	
T	F	1. Because of foreign aid and the globalization of trade, the gap between the incomes of people in the poorest countries and the richest countries has narrowed over the past several decades.
T	F	2. The percentage of people living in extreme poverty in the world has declined since 1990 (See Figure 9.1).
T	F	3. The richest one-fifth of the world's population receives about 75 percent of the world's total income.
T	F	4. The political role of governments in policing the activities of transnational corporations has expanded as companies' operations have become more globalized.
T	F	5. In low-income countries, poverty affects women more than men.

For answers to the quiz about global wealth and poverty, go to **www.nelson.com/sociologyinourtimes6e**.

FIGURE 9.1 THE NUMBER OF PEOPLE LIVING IN EXTREME POVERTY HAS BEEN FALLING SINCE 1990

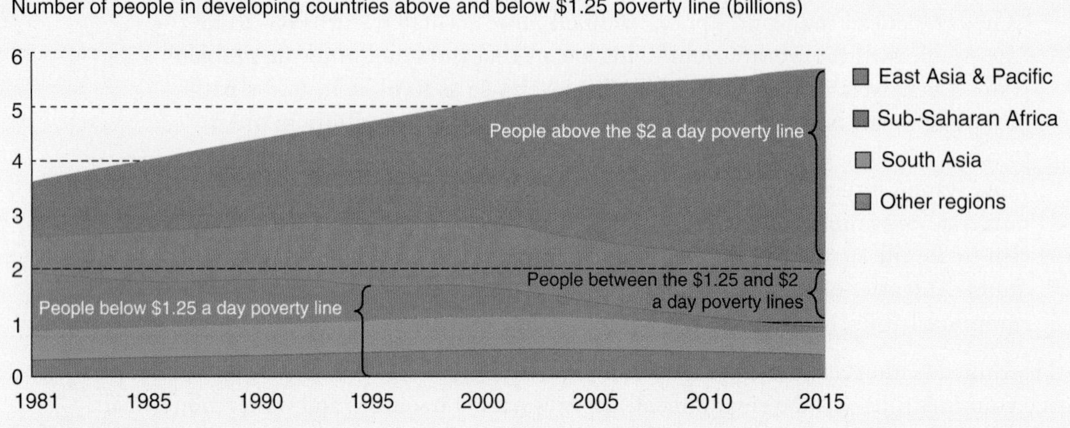

Efforts to alleviate global poverty have been succeeding and the number of people living in extreme poverty has declined significantly. However, progress has been uneven, as some countries lag behind and the disparity between rich and poor has been increasing.

Source: World Bank, *World Development Report 2010*, p. 5.

Vast inequalities in income and lifestyle are evident in this photo of slums and nearby higher-priced housing in Mumbai, India. Similar patterns of economic inequality exist in many other cities.

amount of money required to meet some basic human needs is not that great. *The Hindu,* an Indian newspaper, put these needs in perspective:

> Consumers in Europe and the U.S. spend $17 billion every year on pet foods. Yet the world cannot find the additional $13 billion that is needed every year to provide basic health services to all people in developing countries. Consumers in Europe and the U.S. annually spend $12 billion on perfumes. This is the additional amount needed to meet the basic reproductive health needs of the women in developing countries. Consumers in Europe spend $11 billion every year buying ice cream, which is more than the extra $9 billion required to provide universal access to drinking water and sanitation in the developing countries. (*The Hindu,* 1998:25)

DEFINING GLOBAL INEQUALITY

There has been a debate over the best way to define global inequality, since these definitions imply judgments about countries, particularly those with low incomes.

The Levels of Development Approach

There are several ways of describing global inequality. Terminology based on levels of development includes concepts such as developed nations, developing nations, less developed nations, and underdevelopment. Let's look first at the contemporary origins of the ideas of underdevelopment and underdeveloped nations.

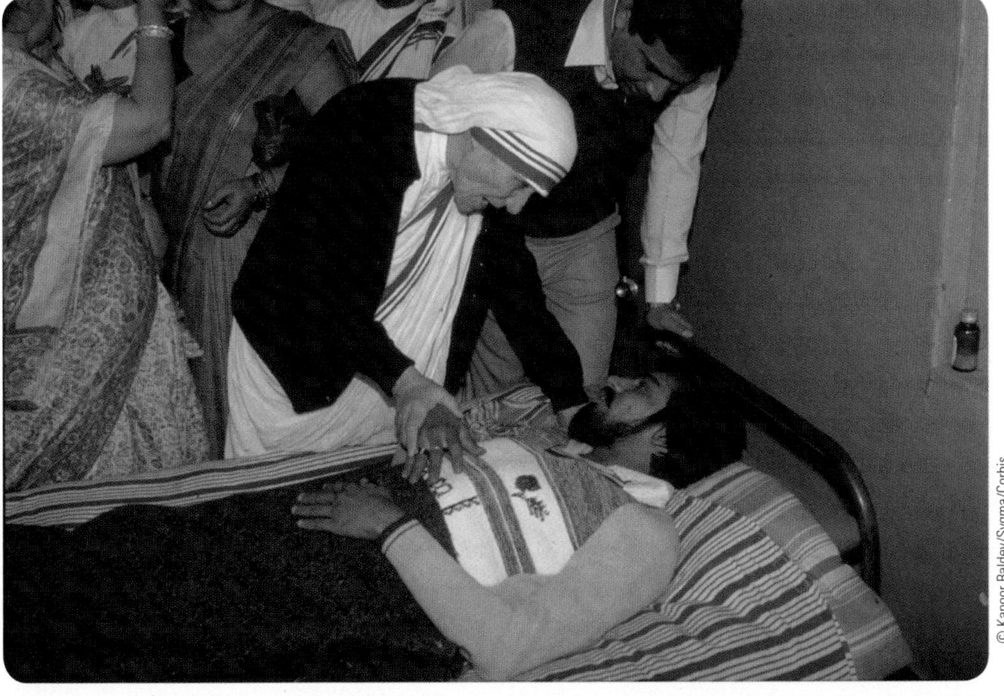

© Kapoor Baldev/Sygma/Corbis

In 1997, people around the world were saddened by the death of Mother Teresa, who had dedicated her life to ministering to the poor and unfortunate in low-income nations, especially India. According to Mother Teresa, people who are not poor have much to learn from the poor.

gross national income (GNI) All the goods and services produced in a country in a given year, plus the income earned outside the country by individuals or corporations.

low-income economies Countries with an annual per capita gross national income of $US1005 or less.

lower-middle-income economies Countries with an annual per capita gross national income between $US1005 and $US3975.

upper-middle-income economies Countries with an annual per capita gross national income between $US4,036 and $US12,476.

high-income economies Countries with an annual per capita gross national income of $US12,476 or more.

Following World War II, the terms *underdevelopment* and *underdeveloped nations* emerged out of the Marshall Plan, which provided massive sums of money to rebuild the European economic base destroyed during World War II. Given the Marshall Plan's success, U.S. political leaders decided that Southern Hemisphere nations that had recently been released from European colonialism could also benefit from a massive financial infusion and rapid economic development. Leaders of developed nations argued that problems, such as poverty, disease, and famine, could be reduced through the transfer of finance, technology, and experience from the developed nations to less developed countries. From this perspective, economic development is the primary way to solve the poverty problem. Hadn't economic growth brought the developed nations to their own high standard of living? Moreover, "self-sustained development" in a nation would require that people in the less developed nations accept the beliefs and values of people in the developed nations, so the development movement had an explicitly political component.

In his 1949 inaugural address, U.S. President Harry S. Truman stated his view that the nations in the Southern Hemisphere were "underdeveloped areas" because of their low **gross national income (GNI)**—a term that refers to all the goods and services produced in a country in a given year, plus the income earned outside the country by individuals or corporations. If nations could increase their GNI, then social and economic inequality within the country could also be reduced. Accordingly, Truman believed that it was necessary to help the people of economically underdeveloped areas raise their *standard of living*. An increase in the standard of living meant that a nation was moving toward economic development, which typically includes greater exploitation of natural resources by industrial development.

After several decades of economic development fostered by organizations such as the United Nations and the World Bank, it became apparent by the 1970s that improving a country's GNI did *not* tend to reduce the poverty of the poorest people in that country. In fact, global poverty and inequality were increasing, and the initial optimism of a speedy end to underdevelopment faded. Even in developing countries that had achieved economic growth, the gains were not shared by everyone. For example, the poorest 20 percent of the Brazilian population receives less than 3 percent of the total national income, whereas the richest 20 percent of the population receives more than 63 percent (World Bank, 2003).

Why did inequality increase even with greater economic development? Many attribute this to the impact of actions taken by the industrialized countries. These actions include foreign aid programs and debt-control policies, both of which will be discussed later in this chapter. Some analysts have also linked the growing global inequality to relatively high rates of population growth in the poorest nations.

© Alison Wright/The Image Works

Based on the assumption that economic development is the primary way to reduce poverty in low-income nations, the United Nations has funded projects such as this paper company in Nepal.

Classification of Economies by Income

An alternative way of describing the global stratification system is simply to measure a country's per capita income. The World Bank (2010) classifies nations into four economic categories: **low-income economies** (a GNI per capita of $US1005 or less), **lower-middle-income economies** (a GNI per capita between $US1005 and $US3975), **upper-middle-income economies** (a GNI per capita between $US4,036 and $US12,475), and **high-income economies** (a GNI per capita of $US12,476 or more).

LOW-INCOME ECONOMIES About half of the world's population lives in the 49 low-income economies, where most people engage in agricultural pursuits, reside in nonurban areas, and are impoverished (World Bank, 2008). As shown on Map 9.1, low-income economies are found primarily in countries in Asia and Africa. Included are such nations as Rwanda, Ethiopia, Nigeria, Cambodia, Afghanistan, and Bangladesh. Caribbean and Latin American nations with low-income economies include Haiti and Nicaragua.

Women and children are particularly affected by poverty in low-income economies. Many women worldwide are unable to increase their economic power because they do not have the time to invest in additional work that could bring in more income. Also, many poor women worldwide do not have access to commercial credit and have been trained only in traditionally female skills that are unpaid or produce low wages. These factors have contributed to the *global feminization of poverty,* whereby women tend to be more impoverished than men (Durning, 1993). Despite some gains, the income gap between men and women continues to grow wider in many low-income developing nations.

MIDDLE-INCOME ECONOMIES About one-third of the world's population resides in the 95 nations with middle-income economies (World Bank, 2008c). The World Bank divides middle-income economies into lower-middle-income and upper-middle-income. Countries classified as lower-middle-income include the Latin American nations of Bolivia, Colombia, El Salvador, and Honduras. Even though these countries are referred to as "middle-income," more than half of the people residing in many of them live in poverty, defined as $US1.25 per day in purchasing power (World Bank, 2008c).

Other lower-middle-income economies include Russia, Ukraine, and Romania. These countries had centrally planned—that is, socialist—economies until dramatic political and economic changes occurred in the late 1980s and early 1990s. Since then, these nations have been going through a transition to a market economy. Some nations have been more successful than others in making the change and achieving a higher standard of living. High rates of inflation, the growing gap between the rich and the poor, low life-expectancy rates, and homeless children

MAP 9.1 HIGH-, MIDDLE-, AND LOW-INCOME ECONOMIES IN GLOBAL PERSPECTIVE

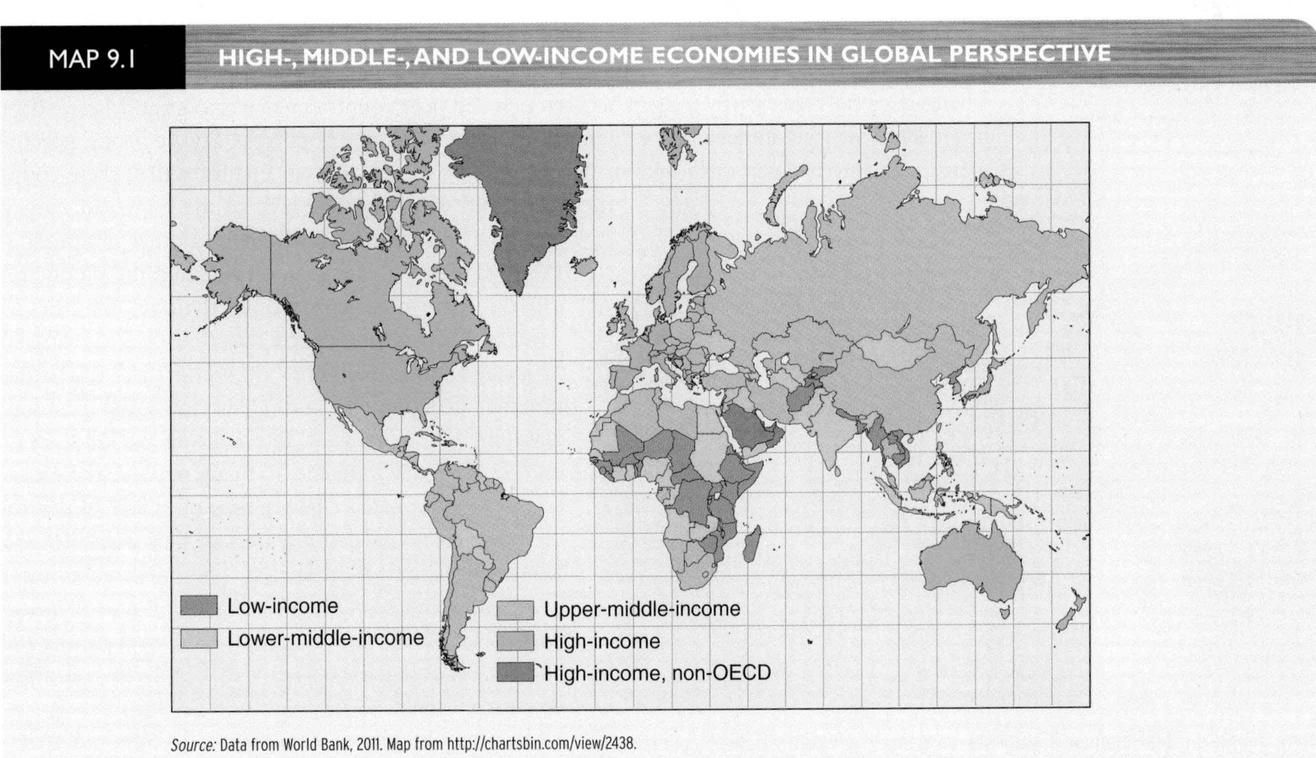

Source: Data from World Bank, 2011. Map from http://chartsbin.com/view/2438.

© Jochen Tack/Glow Images

In developing nations, such as Turkey, many families support themselves by creating handmade products, such as rugs. The loom in this home is a common sight throughout Turkey.

are visible signs of problems in the transition toward a free-market economy in countries such as Russia.

Compared with lower-middle-income economies, nations with upper-middle-income economies have a somewhat higher standard of living and export diverse goods and services, ranging from manufactured goods to raw materials and fuels. Upper-middle-income economies include Saudi Arabia, Chile, Hungary, and Mexico.

HIGH-INCOME ECONOMIES High-income economies are found in 65 nations, including Canada, the United States, Japan, and Germany (World Bank, 2008c). High-income economies dominate the world economy.

The only significant group of middle- and lower-middle-income economies to close the gap with the high-income industrialized economies over the past few decades has been the nations of East Asia. South Korea has been reclassified from a middle-income to a high-income economy, and other countries, including China, have grown dramatically over the past two decades. Despite its recent economic growth, the East Asian region remains home to more than 300 million people living on less than $1.25 a day (World Bank, 2010).

THE IMPACT OF DEBT AND FOREIGN AID

Why do low-income countries remain poor despite all the efforts that have been made to improve their economic conditions? Some of this is due to the policies of high-income countries.

Debt and Global Stratification

There are several reasons why the gap between rich and poor countries remains so great. Massive debt has made it virtually impossible for some countries to move out of poverty. Private banks, governments, and international organizations have lent more money to poor countries than these countries can afford to pay back. Much of the borrowed money was spent on military hardware and other nonproductive investments rather than on building the productive capacity that would have allowed the poor countries to develop. Many countries were forced by the International Monetary Fund (IMF) and the World Bank to restructure their economies by cutting back on social spending, devaluing their currencies, and reducing the funds spent on economic development. In many respects, these governments lost whatever power they once had to control their own economic destinies because they were forced to follow the dictates of the lenders. This happened to most Latin American economies during the 1980s, to many East Asian and Eastern European economies during the late 1990s, and more recently to European countries, including Greece.

© AP Photo/Ahn Young-joon/CP Images

Many people protest economic summits involving the world's richest countries because they feel these countries promote the interests of capitalism at the expense of the world's poor.

In many countries, this externally imposed structural adjustment had disastrous consequences. Debt repayment takes money that could otherwise be used to provide social services and expand the country's economic base. In addition, debt repayment and economic restructuring have caused massive unemployment, reduced incomes, and soaring prices that have led to drastically reduced living standards, declines in investment, and political instability. The problem has been summarized by Michel Chossudovsky:

> The movement of the global economy is "regulated" by "a worldwide process of debt collection" which constricts the institutions of the national state and contributes to destroying employment and economic activity . . . Internal purchasing power has collapsed, famines have erupted, health clinics and schools have been closed down, hundreds of millions of children have been denied the right to a primary education. In several regions of the developing world, the reforms have been conducive to resurgence of infectious diseases including tuberculosis, malaria, and cholera. (1997:33)

Many countries, particularly those in sub-Saharan Africa, have no chance of progressing economically unless the burden of debt repayment is eased by the richer debtholder countries.

In 2005, the wealthy countries agreed to cancel $40 billion in debt—money that would otherwise have gone to interest payments—to allow some of the poor countries to spend on education, agriculture, healthcare, and infrastructure. While this was a significant step, hundreds of billions of dollars in debt remain to be repaid, and between 2005 and 2007 overall foreign aid declined from $107 billion to $104 billion, largely because of a reduction in debt relief (United Nations, 2008). Also, some of the most indebted nations, including Nigeria, Sudan, and Congo, were not included in the deal because their governments were considered too corrupt and the donor countries were concerned that the benefits of debt cancellation would go to a few powerful rulers rather than the poorest citizens.

Foreign Aid and Global Stratification

We have all been moved by the plight of starving people in developing countries where droughts or floods have destroyed the annual harvest. Most of us support the emergency exports of food to these countries to prevent famine. However, some analysts have questioned whether this type of aid hurts more than it helps. Consider, for example, Somalia, now one of the world's poorest and most politically unstable countries. While Somalia's troubles are commonly blamed on drought and clan rivalries, some analysts feel that economic restructuring and food aid are the real causes (Chossudovsky, 1997). Because of droughts and other internal problems, food aid to Somalia increased dramatically from the mid-1970s to the mid-1980s. This donated food was sold into local markets very cheaply and undercut the price of locally grown food. At the same time, a currency devaluation demanded by the IMF as a condition for restructuring Somalia's foreign debt made the cost of farm equipment and fuel more expensive. The combined result of the financial restructuring and the lower food prices was the virtual destruction of Somalia's agricultural system. While we normally think that a shortage of food is the cause of starvation, the global oversupply of grain may have contributed to famine by destroying the agricultural base of developing countries, making them vulnerable to future food shortages (Chossudovsky, 1997).

Foreign aid can damage low-income countries in other ways. First, aid can be tied to specific projects or objectives that may meet the interests of the donor country more than the interests of the recipients. For example, military aid will do little to help the lives of those who are poor and may do them great harm. Similarly, aid devoted to large infrastructure projects, such as dams, may cause more problems than it solves.

Second, aid may be given to achieve political objectives. The United States provides aid to many countries of strategic interest, including several Latin American countries. Such aid is dependent on the low-income country's continuing political support for the donor country's activities, something that can severely constrain the government's power to make decisions based on its own interests.

Third, even when aid is targeted to individuals, it may not filter down to people who are poor. For example, donor countries may intend food aid to be distributed to those who need it without payment, but elites may simply take the food, sell it, and keep the money.

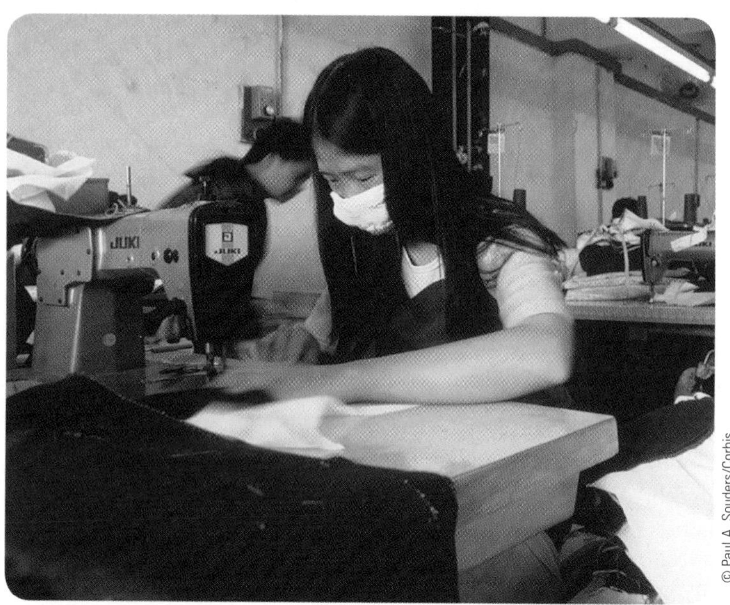

© Paul A. Souders/Corbis

A young Hong Kong woman wearing a dust mask sews in a garment sweatshop under poor conditions.

Finally, there is not enough aid to help low-income countries solve their problems. Overall foreign aid has been declining over the past decade. During the 1990s, Canada's foreign aid budget declined by about 20 percent, although it has increased since then. Yet despite Canada's target of donating 0.7 percent of its gross domestic product (GDP) to foreign aid, the amount donated in 2010 was only 0.3 percent of GDP and cuts to that amount were announced in 2012. And not only is there not enough aid, but the aid that is provided is often not spent effectively.

There are signs of change, however. Many aid agencies have changed their focus away from large infrastructure programs, such as dams and railroads, to programs that focus directly on the poor. New ideas include using labour-intensive technologies and other strategies to create employment; providing basic social services, such as healthcare, nutrition, and education; and giving assistance directly to the poorest people in low-income countries (Martinussen, 1997). Above all, aid recipients themselves must have a say in aid programs and should be empowered to make decisions about how the money is spent. Otherwise, foreign aid can be a double-edged sword that creates more problems than it solves.

In addition, high-income countries need to change trade policies that are often devastating to the economies of poor countries and can negate the benefits of the aid provided. For example, in the mid-1990s, Canada gave an average of $44 million per year in aid to Bangladesh. However, Canadian quotas (now removed) that restricted the export of textiles from Bangladesh cost the Bangladeshi people $36 for every dollar in aid provided (Oxfam, 2001). These quotas were designed to protect Canadian manufacturers from foreign competition, but they also prevented developing nations from building a viable economic base.

Developed countries often force poor countries to liberalize their own trade laws, then sell heavily subsidized products into the poor countries' internal markets. The United States devastated Haiti's rice farmers by forcing Haiti to reduce its tariffs on imported rice and selling Haiti large quantities of subsidized American-grown rice. This action depressed local prices and resulted in a 40 percent reduction in Haitian rice production (Oxfam, 2001). By 2002, the United States and the countries making up the European Union were spending more than $450 billion to subsidize their farmers, making it impossible for farmers in poor countries to compete, particularly in the export market. At the same time, the aid given by wealthy countries to poor countries was only $75 billion. Such practices need to be changed to achieve the goal of alleviating global poverty. However, it has been difficult to convince wealthy countries to lower their agricultural subsidies. Figure 9.2 illustrates the size of agricultural subsidies in the European Union, Japan, and the United States compared to the average income in sub-Saharan Africa and the aid given these countries.

TIME TO REVIEW

- Why does the country you're born in play such an important role in determining your life chances?
- How does excessive consumption in high-income countries affect people living in poverty in low-income countries?
- How have experts conceptualized world poverty and global stratification?
- Discuss the role of debt in determining the economic future of low-income nations.
- Why does foreign aid not always work to the benefit of people in low-income countries?

FIGURE 9.2 COWS AND COTTON RECEIVE MORE AID THAN PEOPLE, 2000

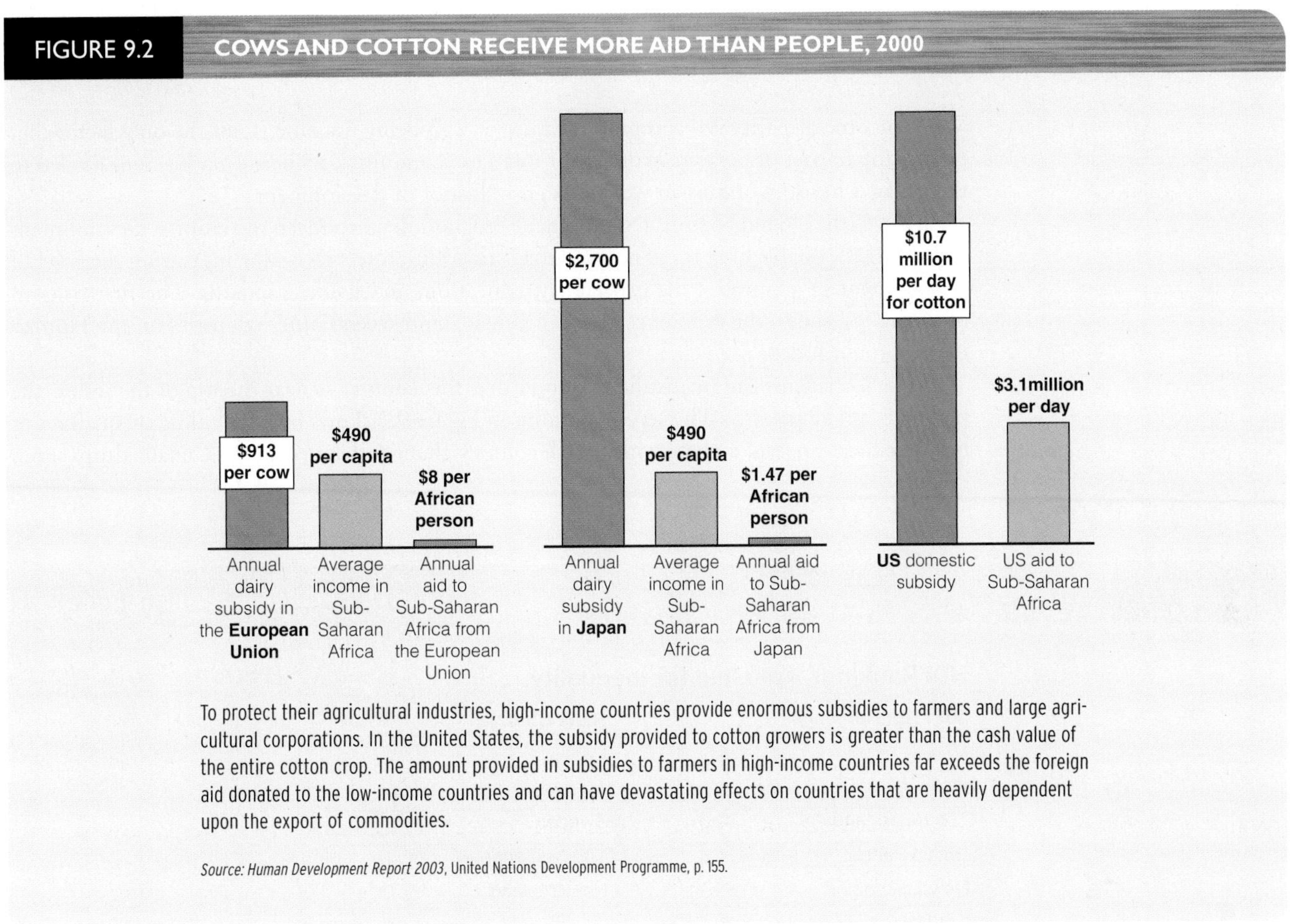

To protect their agricultural industries, high-income countries provide enormous subsidies to farmers and large agricultural corporations. In the United States, the subsidy provided to cotton growers is greater than the cash value of the entire cotton crop. The amount provided in subsidies to farmers in high-income countries far exceeds the foreign aid donated to the low-income countries and can have devastating effects on countries that are heavily dependent upon the export of commodities.

Source: Human Development Report 2003, United Nations Development Programme, p. 155.

MEASURING GLOBAL WEALTH AND POVERTY

How is poverty defined on a global basis? Researchers and policy analysts have developed several ways of measuring global wealth and poverty.

Absolute, Relative, and Subjective Poverty

Defining poverty involves more than comparisons of personal or household income; it also involves social judgments made by researchers. From this point of view, *absolute poverty*—a condition in which people do not have the means to secure the most basic necessities of life—would be measured by comparing personal or household income or expenses with the cost of buying a given quantity of goods and services. The World Bank (2008c) has defined absolute poverty as living on less than $1.25 a day, and this definition is commonly used by other international organizations. *Relative poverty*—when people may be able to afford basic necessities but are still unable to maintain an average standard of living—would be measured by comparing one person's income with the income of others. Finally, *subjective poverty* would be measured by comparing the actual income against the income earner's expectations and perceptions. However, for low-income nations in economic transition, data on income and levels of consumption are typically difficult to obtain and often ambiguous when they are available. Defining levels of poverty involves several dimensions: (1) how many people are poor, (2) how far below the poverty line people's incomes fall, and (3) how long they have been poor (is the poverty temporary or long term?) (World Bank, 2003).

LO-2 GLOBAL POVERTY AND HUMAN DEVELOPMENT ISSUES

While income disparity is a common measure of well-being, income is not the only factor that defines the impact of poverty. Work by prominent economists, such as Amartya Sen, has led to the use of a measure of human welfare as an indicator of development.

In 1990, the United Nations Development Programme introduced the Human Development Index (HDI), establishing three new criteria—in addition to GNI—for measuring the level of development in a country: life expectancy, education, and living standards. The first column of Figure 9.3 shows the difference between Canada and several other countries on the Human Development Index.

While Canadians can be justifiably proud that this country is near the top of the index, the picture is not all positive. The second column in Figure 9.3 shows how including inequalities of health, education, and income within each country changes these rankings. Canada drops seven

FIGURE 9.3 HUMAN DEVELOPMENT INDEX AND HDI RANKINGS, ADJUSTED FOR INEQUALITY

HDI Rankings Adjusted for Inequality

2011 HDI Rankings		Rank Change*	
Norway	1	Norway	0
Australia	2	Australia	0
The Netherlands	3	Sweden	+5
United States	4	The Netherlands	-1
New Zealand	5*	New Zealand	*
Canada	6	Iceland	+5
Ireland	7	Ireland	0
Liechtenstein	8*	Liechtenstein	*
Germany	9	Germany	0
Sweden	10	Denmark	+4
Switzerland	11	Switzerland	0
Japan	12*	Japan	*
Hong Kong	13*	Hong Kong	*
Iceland	14	Slovenia	+7
Republic of Korea	15	Finland	+7
Denmark	16	Canada	-7
Israel	17	Czech Republic	+9
Belgium	18	Austria	+1
Austria	19	Belgium	-1
France	20	France	0
Slovenia	21	Israel	-8
Finland	22	United States	-19
Czech Republic	27	Republic of Korea	-17

*IHDI data not available; rank change is based on countries for which IHDI is calculated.

Source: *Human Development Report 2011*, United Nations Development Programme.

places on this index largely because of our relatively high degree of income inequality. One factor in this is the position of Canada's Aboriginal people, who rank far below other Canadians on the Human Development Index.

Life Expectancy

Although some advances have been made in increasing life expectancy in middle- and low-income countries, major problems still exist. On the positive side, average life expectancy has increased by about one-third in the past four decades and is now more than 70 years in 87 countries (United Nations Development Programme, 2003). However, the average life expectancy at birth in the 20 countries ranked highest on human development is about 80 years, compared with 49 years in the bottom 20 countries (United Nations Development Programme, 2008). Especially striking are the declines in life expectancies in sub-Saharan Africa, where estimated life expectancy has dropped significantly in many countries, largely because of HIV/AIDS. While the Safe Motherhood Initiative has had some success, more than 50,000 women still die each year in pregnancy and childbirth (UNICEF, 2009).

One major cause of shorter life expectancy in low-income nations is the high rate of infant mortality. Comparison of Map 9.1 on page 247 with Map 9.2 on page 253 shows that low-income countries are also those with high rates of infant mortality. The infant mortality rate is more than eight times higher in low-income countries than in high-income countries (World Bank, 2003). Low-income countries typically have higher rates of illness and disease, and they lack adequate healthcare facilities. Malnutrition is a common problem among children, many of whom are underweight, stunted, and have anemia—a nutritional deficiency with

MAP 9.2 INFANT MORTALITY RATES, 2012

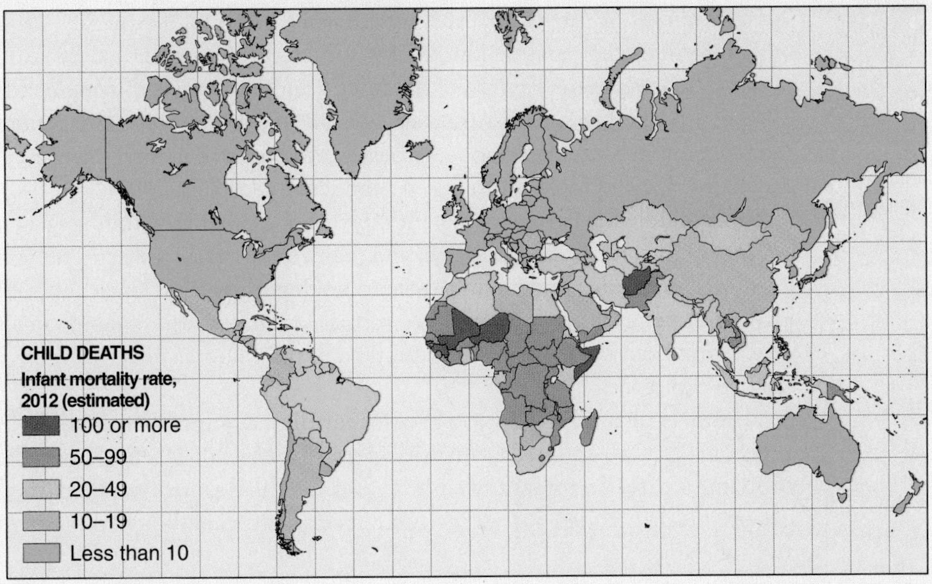

Mortality rates for children under one year of age in developing countries have dropped substantially since 1990. Yet many children die every day, most from preventable causes and almost half of them in sub-Saharan Africa.

Source: Based on data from *CIA World Factbook*. Retrieved from https://www.cia.gov/library/publications/the-world-factbook/rankorder/2091rank.html.

serious consequences for child mortality. Consider this journalist's description of a child she saw in Haiti:

> Like any baby, Wisly Dorvil is easy to love. Unlike others, this 13-month-old is hard to hold.
>
> That's because his 10-pound frame is so fragile that even the most minimal of movements can dislocate his shoulders.
>
> As lifeless as a rag doll, Dorvil is starving. He has large, brown eyes and a feeble smile, but a stomach so tender that he suffers from ongoing bouts of vomiting and diarrhea. Fortunately, though, Dorvil recently came to the attention of U.S. aid workers. With round-the-clock feeding, he is expected to survive.
>
> Others are not so lucky. (Emling, 1997:A17)

Nearly one billion people suffer from chronic malnutrition and more than nine million people die each year from hunger-related causes (World Food Program, 2009). To put this figure in perspective, the number of people worldwide dying from hunger-related causes is the equivalent of more than 60 jumbo-jet crashes a day with no survivors, and half the passengers are children. However, some progress has been made. Since 1955, life expectancy has increased from 46 to 67 years and infant mortality has been cut in half in low-income countries through simple measures such as basic immunization and malaria nets (World Health Organization, 2003, 2009).

Health

Health is defined by the World Health Organization as "a state of complete physical, mental and social well-being and not merely the absence of disease or infirmity" (Smyke, 1991:2).

Many people in low-income nations do not have physical, mental, and social well-being—2.5 billion people do not have proper sanitation and one billion do not have safe water. Many do not have adequate housing or access to modern health services (World Bank, 2010). Millions of people die each year from HIV/AIDS, diarrhea, malaria, tuberculosis, and other infectious and parasitic illnesses (World Health Organization, 2012a). Infectious diseases persist in many nations because of unsanitary and overcrowded living conditions and a lack of basic healthcare. Disease, in turn, can have an impact on economic conditions. For example, the economy in Swaziland stopped growing and began to contract because the AIDS epidemic decimated the workforce and reduced productivity (Nolen, 2007).

Some middle-income countries are experiencing rapid growth in degenerative diseases, such as cancer and coronary heart disease, and many more deaths are expected from smoking-related diseases. Despite the decrease in tobacco smoking in high-income countries, there has been an increase in per capita consumption of tobacco in low- and middle-income countries, many of which have been targeted for free samples and promotional advertising by U.S. and European tobacco companies.

Health is also affected by war and conflict. Countries including Afghanistan, Iraq, and Somalia have suffered from widespread conflict in recent years. These crises not only contribute directly to serious injury and death, but also weaken the effectiveness of a nation's health-related infrastructure. As a result, people are more vulnerable to disease and mortality.

Education and Literacy

Education is fundamental to reducing both individual and national poverty. Thus, school enrollment is used as a measure of human development. Literacy is an important result of education, and the adult literacy rate in low-income countries is much lower than that of the high-income

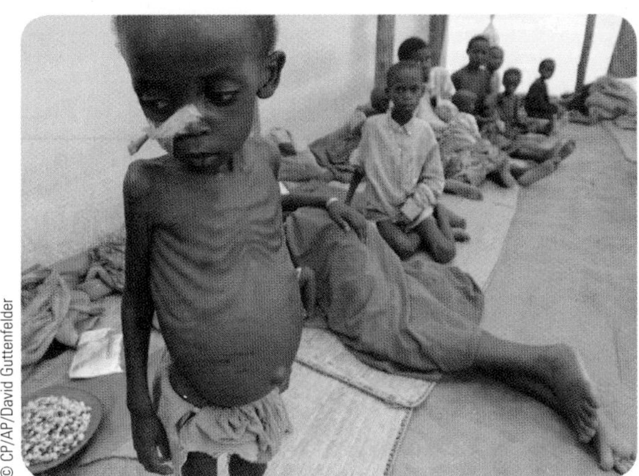

© CP/AP/David Guttenfelder

© Mark Snelling/British Red Cross

Malnutrition is a widespread health problem in many low-income nations. On the left, a Rwandan refugee child waits for help in a field hospital in Zaire; on the right, people in the Sahel region line up to receive food aid.

countries. For women in these countries, the rate is even lower. However, educational achievements have improved dramatically around the globe. Since 1990, rates of literacy have risen from 73 percent to 84 percent and the average number of years of schooling has gone up by two years. While progress in human development is usually quite uneven, since 1970 no countries have had declines in literacy rates or years of schooling (United Nations Human Development Report, 2010).

Gender and Equality

According to the World Bank, women suffer more than men from global inequality:

> Women have an enormous impact on the well-being of their families and societies—yet their potential is not realized because of discriminatory social norms, incentives, and legal institutions. And while their status has improved . . . gender inequalities remain pervasive.
>
> Gender inequality starts early and keeps women at a disadvantage throughout their lives. In some countries, infant girls are less likely to survive than infant boys because of parental discrimination and neglect. Girls are more likely to drop out of school and to receive less education than boys because of discrimination, education expenses, and household duties. (2004:1)

Although more women have paid employment than in the past, women are still living in poverty because of increases in single-person and single-parent households headed by women, and because low-wage work is often the only source of livelihood available to them. According to an analyst for the Inter-American Development Bank, women experience sexual discrimination in employment and also in wages:

> In Honduras, for example, coffee and tobacco farmers prefer to hire girls and women as laborers because they are willing to accept low wages and are more reliable workers. Especially in poor countries, female labor is primarily sought for low-paid positions in services, agriculture, small-scale commerce, and in the growing, unregulated manufacturing and agribusiness industries, which pay their workers individual rather than family wages, offer seasonal or part-time employment, and carry few or no benefits. Hence, this explains the seemingly contradictory trends of women's increased economic participation alongside their growing impoverishment. (Buvinić, 1997:47)

FIGURE 9.4 EDUCATED WOMEN LEAD DIFFERENT LIVES

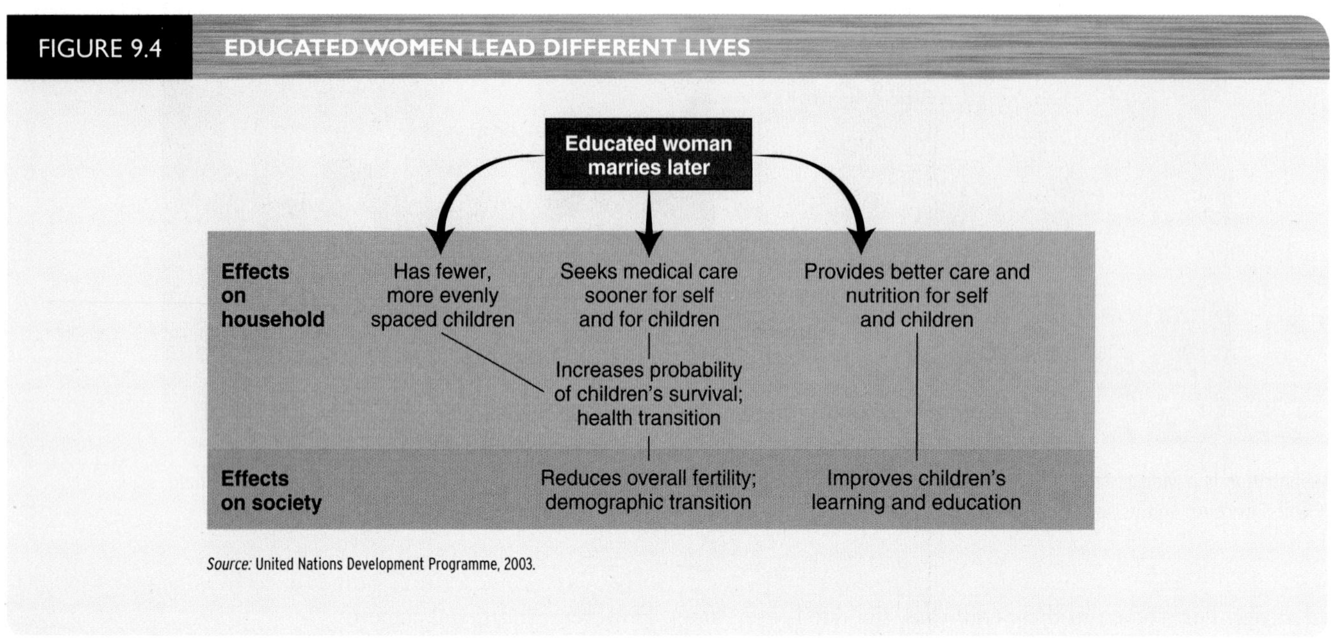

Source: United Nations Development Programme, 2003.

Researchers have found that women play a critical role in development. Women's education is particularly important because it has an impact on many other factors that contribute to human development (United Nations Development Programme, 2003). Figure 9.4 above illustrates how educated females marry later and have smaller families. They do a better job feeding their families and getting medical care, so more of their children survive. The children of illiterate mothers have an under-five mortality rate that is twice as high as the mortality rate for the children of mothers who have a middle school education (United Nations Development Programme, 2005:31). Higher child survival rates lead to a reduction in birth rates, which allows better child care and less strain on the educational system. In societies where educated women are allowed to work outside the home, they make a significant contribution to family income.

© Scott Wallace/World Bank

Researchers have found that the education of girls is one of the most important factors in furthering development in low-income countries.

Women's education is improving. According to the World Bank (2010) 64 developing countries now have gender parity in primary education and 73 in secondary education, while 20 more will likely achieve parity in primary education and 14 in secondary education by 2015. However, 22 countries, most in sub-Saharan Africa, lag seriously behind in primary education and 29 in secondary education.

TIME TO REVIEW

- In what ways has the Human Development Index helped change people's understanding of global poverty?
- Discuss some of the trends in health and education in low-income nations over the past few decades.
- Why does global inequality affect women more than men?

THEORIES OF GLOBAL INEQUALITY

Social scientists have developed several theories of global stratification that view the causes and consequences of global inequality somewhat differently. We will examine the development approach and modernization theory, dependency theory, world-systems analysis, and the new international division of labour theory. Modernization theory is part of the functionalist tradition, while the other perspectives are rooted in conflict theory. These approaches are depicted in Figure 9.5.

LO-3 Development and Modernization Theories

According to some social scientists, global wealth and poverty are linked to a society's level of industrialization and economic development. These theorists maintain that low-income nations have progressed less than the wealthier industrial countries. They feel that industrialization and economic development are essential steps that nations must go through to reduce poverty and improve the living conditions of their citizens.

The most widely known development theory is **modernization theory**—a perspective that links global inequality to different levels of economic development and suggests that low-income economies can move to middle- and high-income economies by achieving self-sustained economic growth. According to Langdon, modernization theory holds that undeveloped countries must follow the road travelled by successful Western capitalist, democratic societies, such as Britain and the United States:

> The usually implicit assumption was that economic development and growth involved a process of becoming like those societies and would be achieved essentially as those societies had achieved it: through economic change focused around industrialization, through social changes that would introduce Western institutions based on universalism and merit/achievement, and through political changes marked by secularization and the bureaucratic efficiency of the state. (1999:41)

modernization theory
A perspective that links global inequality to different levels of economic development and that suggests that low-income economies can move to middle- and high-income economies by achieving self-sustained economic growth.

Just as Weber had concluded that the adoption of a "spirit of capitalism" facilitated economic development, modernization theorists felt that development would be accompanied by changes in people's beliefs, values, and attitudes toward work. With modernization, the values of people in developing countries should become more similar to those of people in high-income nations.

The most widely known modernization theory is that of Walt Rostow (1971, 1978). To Rostow, one of the largest barriers to development in low-income nations was the traditional cultural values people held, particularly fatalistic beliefs such as viewing extreme hardship and economic deprivation as inevitable and unavoidable facts of life. Fatalistic people do not see

FIGURE 9.5 APPROACHES TO STUDYING GLOBAL INEQUALITY

Modernization Theory: Low-income, less-developed countries can move to middle- and high-income economies by achieving self-sustained economic growth.

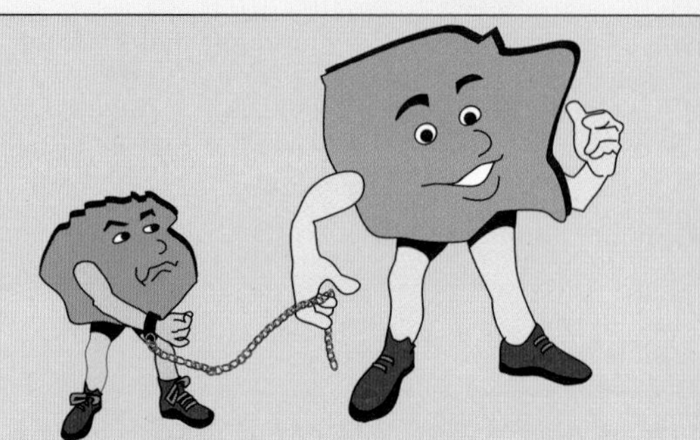

Dependency Theory: Global poverty can at least partially be attributed to the fact that low-income countries have been exploited by high-income economies; the poor nations are trapped in a cycle of dependency on richer nations.

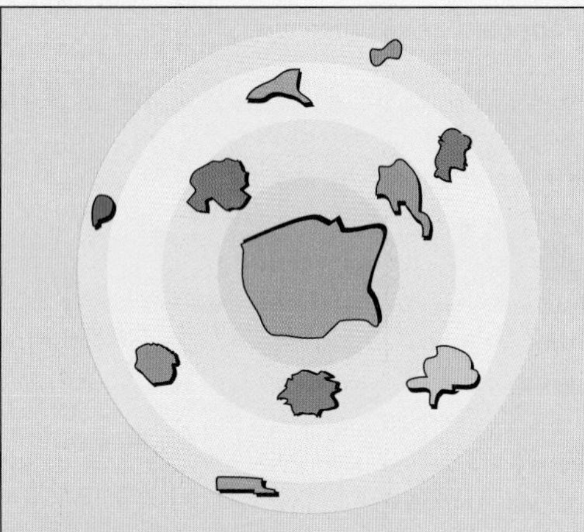

World Systems Analysis: How a country is incorporated into the global capitalist economy (e.g., a core, semiperipheral, or peripheral nation) is the key feature in determining how economic development takes place in that nation.

The New International Division of Labour Theory: Commodity production is split into fragments, each of which can be moved (e.g., by a transnational corporation) to whichever part of the world can provide the best combination of capital and labour.

What causes global inequality? Social scientists have developed a variety of explanations, including the four theories shown here.

Source: United Nations Development Programme, 2003.

any need to work to improve their lot in life: Their future is predetermined for them, so why bother? According to modernization theory, poverty can be attributed to people's cultural failings, which are reinforced by governmental policies interfering with the smooth operation of the economy.

Rostow suggested that all countries go through four stages of economic development with identical content, regardless of when these nations began to industrialize. He compares the stages of economic development to an airplane flight. The first stage is the *traditional stage,* in which people do not think much about changing their circumstances and in which people hold a fatalistic value system, do not subscribe to the work ethic, and save little money. The second stage is the *take-off stage*—a period of economic growth accompanied by a growing belief in individualism, competition, and achievement. People start to look toward the future, to save and invest money, and to discard traditional values. For Rostow, the development of capitalism is essential for the transformation from a traditional, simple society to a modern, complex one. With the financial help and advice of the high-income countries, low-income countries will be able to "fly" and enter the third stage of economic development, moving toward *technological maturity.* The country improves its technology, invests in new industries, and embraces the beliefs, values, and social institutions of the developed nations. In the fourth and final stage, the country reaches the phase of *high mass consumption* and a high standard of living.

According to proponents of this approach, studies have supported the assertion that economic development occurs more rapidly in a capitalist economy. The countries that have moved from low- to middle-income status have typically been those most centrally involved in the global capitalist economy. For example, many East Asian countries have successfully made the transition from low-income to higher-income economies through factors such as a high rate of savings, an aggressive work ethic among employers and employees, and the fostering of a market economy.

Critics of modernization theory point out that it is Eurocentric in its analysis of low-income countries, which it implicitly labels as backward (see Evans and Stephens, 1988). In many respects, modernization was equated with Westernization, as modernization theorists assumed that the problems of low-income countries would be alleviated only once they adopted Western values, culture, and economic models. Modernization theory does not take into account the possibility that all nations do not industrialize in the same manner. Allahar (1989) points out that leading industrial nations, such as the United States, Britain, and Japan, followed dissimilar paths to industrialization. Thus, we might also assume that the modernization of low-income nations in the early 21st century will require novel policies, sequences, and ideologies that are not accounted for in Rostow's approach (see Gerschenkron, 1962). The theory also does not tell us what causes the move from one stage to another, but simply assumes they are natural stages that must be followed as societies advance economically and socially.

One of the most influential critics of modernization theory was Andre Gunder Frank (1969). Frank's research in Latin America convinced him that modernization theory was badly flawed. While Rostow felt that all societies had to move in a linear fashion from underdevelopment to industrialization, Frank pointed out that underdevelopment was not an original stage but a condition created by the imperial powers that had created dependency through actions, such as the deindustrialization of India, the damage done to African societies during the years of the slave trade, and the destruction of Native civilizations in Central and Latin America (Hettne, 1995). All societies were *un*developed at one time, but not all became *under*developed. While some countries moved from being undeveloped to developed, others moved from being undeveloped to a condition of underdevelopment in which they were dependent on other nations. These dependent countries had structures and institutions that effectively blocked any further development (Allahar, 1989).

Frank's critique of modernization theory was also a critique of the social policies that grew out of the theory. Frank felt that the Western powers, particularly the United States, were imposing their views of development through both political and military means. Modernization theory was linked to the fight against communism during the Cold War. Because communism was an obstacle on the road to modernization, it was necessary to persuade or force countries to adopt alternative forms of government. Many critics felt that modernization theory contributed to underdevelopment by encouraging policies that perpetuated global inequality (Langdon, 1999). The inadequacies of modernization theory and the political injustices that resulted from policies based on it, such as the Vietnam War, moved the next generation of development theorists to *dependency theory,* an approach based on the conflict perspective.

LO-4 DEPENDENCY THEORY

According to dependency theorists, rich countries have an interest in maintaining the dependent status of poor countries, as this ensures them a source of raw materials and a captive market for manufactured goods exported to the dependent nations. Business and political leaders in the poor nations find it in their interests to accept dependence and willingly work with the advanced nations to impose policies that maintain the dependent relationship. Any surpluses created in the dependent country will be taken by the affluent capitalist country rather than being used to build up production infrastructure or raise the standard of living in the dependent nation. Unless this situation changes, poor countries will never match the sustained economic growth patterns of the more advanced capitalist economies.

dependency theory The perspective that global poverty can at least partially be attributed to the fact that low-income countries have been exploited by high-income countries.

Dependency theory states that global poverty can be at least partially attributed to the fact that the low-income countries have been exploited by the high-income countries. Dependency theorists see the greed of the rich countries as a source of increasing impoverishment of the poorer nations and their people. Due to their need for infusions of foreign capital and external markets for their raw materials, poorer nations are trapped in a cycle of structural dependency on the richer nations. This makes it impossible for the poorer nations to pursue their own economic and human development agendas. Frank and other scholars believed that the best way for low-income countries to move ahead was to break their links with the industrialized countries and establish independent socialist governments.

Dependency theory has been most often applied to the newly industrializing countries (NICs) of Latin America, but scholars examining the NICs of East Asia have found that dependency theory has little or no relevance to that part of the world. Therefore, dependency theory has been expanded to encompass transnational economic linkages that affect developing countries, including foreign aid, foreign trade, foreign direct investment, and foreign loans. On the one hand, in Latin America and sub-Saharan Africa, transnational linkages, such as foreign aid, investments by transnational corporations, foreign debt, and export trade, have been significant impediments to development within countries. On the other hand, East Asian countries, such as Hong Kong, Taiwan, South Korea, and Singapore, have also had high rates of dependency on foreign aid, foreign trade, and interdependence with transnational corporations but have still experienced high rates of economic growth.

© NCG/Shutterstock

Residential and commercial buildings in Singapore: A variety of factors, including foreign investment and the presence of transnational corporations, has contributed to the economic growth of nations such as Singapore.

Dependency theory has contributed to our understanding of global poverty by pointing out that "underdevelopment" is not necessarily the cause of inequality. Rather, this theory points out that exploitation of one country by another, and also of countries by transnational corporations, may limit or slow a country's economic growth and human development.

What remains unexplained is how some East Asian countries have had successful "dependency management" whereas many Latin American countries have not (Gereffi, 1994). In fact, between 1998 and 2005, the annual economic growth in emerging East Asian countries averaged 9 percent, which was much higher than growth in the West (Gill and Kharas, 2007).

Although dependency theory has contributed to our understanding of global stratification, even its proponents feel it is no longer adequate. In addition to the problem of explaining the success of the East Asian economies that were closely linked with global capitalist structures, the dependency theorists have had their faith in development through socialist revolution shaken by the failure of many socialist economies, including that of the former Soviet Union (Frank, 1981). Most have concluded that the global economy is so pervasive that it is impossible for low-income countries to disconnect themselves from the industrialized world and proceed with their own development (Martinussen, 1997).

LO-5 World-Systems Analysis

Drawing on Karl Marx's ideas, world-systems analysis suggests that what exists under capitalism is a truly global system held together by economic ties. From this perspective, global inequality does not emerge solely as a result of the exploitation of one country by another. Instead, economic domination involves a complex world system in which the industrialized, high-income nations benefit from other nations and exploit the citizens of those nations. Wallerstein (1979, 1984) believed that a country's mode of incorporation into the capitalist work economy is the key feature in determining how economic development takes place in that nation. According to **world-systems analysis**, the capitalist world economy is a global system divided into a hierarchy of three major types of nations—core, semiperipheral, and peripheral—in which upward or downward mobility is conditioned by the resources and obstacles that characterize the international system.

world-systems analysis The perspective that the capitalist world economy is a global system divided into a hierarchy of three major types of nations–core, semiperipheral, and peripheral–in which upward or downward mobility is conditioned by the resources and obstacles that characterize the international system.

Core nations are dominant capitalist centres characterized by high levels of industrialization and urbanization. Core nations, such as the United States, Japan, and Germany, possess most of the world's capital and technology. They can thereby exert massive control over world trade and economic agreements across national boundaries.

core nations According to world-systems analysis, dominant capitalist centres characterized by high levels of industrialization and urbanization, as well as a high degree of control over the world economy.

Most low-income countries in Africa, South America, and the Caribbean are **peripheral nations**—nations that are dependent on core nations for capital, have little or no industrialization, and have uneven patterns of urbanization. According to Wallerstein, the wealthy in peripheral nations benefit from the labour of poor workers and from their economic relations with core nation capitalists, whom they uphold to maintain their own wealth and position. At a global level, uneven economic growth results from capital investment by core nations. Disparity between the rich and the poor within the major cities in these nations is increased in the process. The United States–Mexico border is an example of disparity and urban growth: Transnational corporations have built *maquiladora* plants just over the border in Mexico so that goods can be assembled by low-wage workers to keep production costs down. Because of the demand for low-wage workers, thousands of people have moved from the rural regions of Mexico to urban areas along the border in hope of earning a higher wage.

peripheral nations According to world-systems analysis, nations that are dependent on core nations for capital, have little or no industrialization, and have uneven patterns of urbanization.

This influx has pushed already overcrowded cities far beyond their capacity. Many people live on the edge of the city in shantytowns made from discarded materials or in low-cost rental housing in central-city slums because their wages are low and affordable housing is nonexistent (Flanagan, 1999). In fact, housing shortages are among the most pressing problems in many peripheral nations. According to most world-systems analysts, it will be very difficult for peripheral countries to change their structural position in the capitalist world economy (Wallerstein, 1979).

Semiperipheral nations are more developed than peripheral nations but less developed than core nations. Nations in this category—South Korea, Mexico, Brazil, India, South Africa, and Nigeria are examples—typically provide labour and raw materials to core nations within the world system. These nations constitute a midpoint between the core and peripheral nations that promotes the stability and legitimacy of the three-tiered world economy. According to Wallerstein, semiperipheral nations exploit peripheral nations, just as the core nations exploit both the semiperipheral and the peripheral nations.

semiperipheral nations According to world-systems analysis, nations that are more developed than peripheral nations but less developed than core nations.

Wallerstein (1991) acknowledges that world-systems analysis is an "incomplete, unfinished critique" for long-term, large-scale social change that affects global inequality. However, most scholars acknowledge that nations throughout the world are influenced by a relatively small number of countries and transnational corporations that have prompted a shift from an international to a more global economy (see Knox and Taylor, 1995; Wilson, 1997).

LO-6 The New International Division of Labour Theory

new international division of labour theory The perspective that commodity production is being split into fragments that can be assigned to whichever part of the world can provide the most profitable combination of capital and labour.

According to the **new international division of labour theory**, commodity production is being split into fragments that can be assigned to whichever part of the world can provide the most profitable combination of capital and labour. Consequently, the new international division of labour has changed the pattern of geographic specialization between countries and high-income countries have become dependent on low-income countries for labour. Low-income countries provide transnational corporations with the ability to pay lower wages and taxes and face fewer regulations regarding workplace conditions and environmental protection (Waters, 1995).

This new division of labour is part of a global economy based on free trade among countries. Multilateral trade agreements, such as the General Agreement on Tariffs and Trade (GATT) and the North American Free Trade Agreement (NAFTA), have allowed the freer transfer of goods and services among countries, and global corporations now view all the countries of the world both as potential markets and as potential locations for production.

© Ross Kinnaird/Getty Images

Tiger Woods makes more money by endorsing Nike products than the combined salaries of thousands of the workers who manufacture the products. According to Nike's chief executive officer, marketing is more important to the company's success than is the manufacturing of their products (Klein, 2000).

These trade liberalization agreements would appear to be beneficial for poor countries, but often they are not. The movement of production into developing countries brings jobs to countries with chronically high unemployment; however, few of the profits stay in these countries. For example, a study of garment manufacturing in Bangladesh found that less than 2 percent of the final value of the product went to production workers and that 1 percent went to the local producer. The rest of the money went to profit those who owned the company and to pay expenses, such as shipping and storage costs, and customs duties and sales taxes in high-income countries (Chossudovsky, 1997). There is little hope of higher wages for workers because the jobs are unskilled and can quickly be moved to another poor country if workers begin to put pressure on the companies (Klein, 2000).

Many large corporations have global operations. Typically, labour-intensive manufacturing operations, ranging from textiles to computers, are established in low-wage countries. Even service industries—such as completing income tax forms, booking airline flights, and processing insurance claims forms—have now become exportable through electronic transmission and the Internet. These activities make up *global commodity chains,* a complex pattern of international labour and production processes that result in a finished commodity ready for sale in the marketplace.

Commodity chains are most common in labour-intensive consumer goods industries, such as toys, garments, and footwear (Gereffi, 1994). Athletic footwear companies, such as Nike and Reebok, and clothing companies, such as The Gap and Liz Claiborne, are examples of this model. Since manufacturing these products is labour-intensive, the factory system is typically very competitive and globally decentralized. Workers in commodity chains are often exploited by low wages, long hours, and poor working conditions. Most cannot afford the products they make. Tini Heyun Alwi, on the assembly line of the shoe factory in Indonesia that makes Reebok sneakers, is an example: "I think maybe I could work for a month and still not be able to buy one pair" (quoted in Goodman, 1996:F1). Since Tini earned only 2,600 Indonesian rupiah ($1.28) per day working a 10-hour shift six days a week, her monthly income would fall short of the retail price of the athletic shoes (Goodman, 1996).

> We live in a world where (1) the political unit is *national,* (2) industrial production is *regional,* and (3) capital movements are *international.* The rise of Japan and the East Asian [newly industrializing countries] in the 1960s and 1970s is the flip side of the "deindustrialization" that occurred in the United States and much of Europe. Declining industries in North America have been the growth industries in East Asia. (Gereffi, 1994:225)

These changes have had a mixed impact on people living in these countries (see Box 9.2). For example, Indonesia has been able to attract foreign business into the country, but workers remain poor despite working full time in factories making such consumer goods as Nike shoes (Gargan, 1996). As employers feel pressure from workers to raise wages, clashes erupt between the workers and managers or owners. Governments in these countries fear that rising wages and labour strife will drive away the businesses, leaving behind workers who have no other hopes for employment and become more impoverished than they previously were.

THE "FLYING GEESE" MODEL OF DEVELOPMENT The flying geese model was developed by Japanese economist Akamatsu Kaname and is an extension of international division of labour theory. The model has been used to explain the rapid development of East Asian economies following World War II (Korhonen, 1994). This process involves one country—in this case, Japan—leading other less developed countries into more prosperous times. The countries go through the sequential steps of importing goods, manufacturing to serve domestic markets, and, finally, exporting goods. Factors such as labour costs cause production to shift from advanced to less advanced economies. This boosts the standard of living of the less advanced economies, raises wages, and, in turn, leads to a shift in production to countries that are even less developed. In the 1960s, Japan was the only developed economy in Asia but was then followed by the "Asian tigers"—Singapore, Hong Kong, Taiwan, and South Korea. Development in these countries was followed by industrialization in Malaysia, Indonesia, the Philippines, and Thailand, and most recently by China and India.

One example of this process has been in textiles, where Japan had a thriving export business for a number of years. When wages in Japan became globally uncompetitive, production shifted to the next tier of countries while Japan moved into the production of higher-technology goods such as automobiles and electronics. Production of these goods has also moved to lower-tier countries that have upgraded their technological skills. Companies such as South Korea's Hyundai and Samsung are now producing very high-quality high-technology products that are displacing some Japanese products in global markets.

This perspective provides a dynamic picture of the global division of labour that gives us some reason for optimism as we see technology being transferred from more to less industrialized countries. It is not clear that the flying geese model will apply outside East Asia or whether unique circumstances led to the pattern of development in those countries. However, the fact that a Taiwanese company employs 10,000 people in the African country of Lesotho manufacturing Levi's jeans for sale in North America provides some hope that this process will continue (Kristof, 2012b).

TIME TO REVIEW

- What are the stages that modernization theorists feel all societies must go through before they can become high-income economies?
- According to dependency theorists, in what ways do rich countries exploit the economies of poor countries?
- In world-systems analysis, how do core, semiperipheral, and peripheral countries interact with each other?
- Discuss the ways in which the new international division of labour theory explains current trends in globalization. How does the flying geese hypothesis extend this theory?

BOX 9.2 **POINT/COUNTERPOINT**

The Foxconn Suicides

In May 2010, the Apple corporation became the world's most valuable technology company when its value jumped over that of Microsoft. The same month, a worker at a Foxconn factory in Shenzhen, China, became the ninth worker to jump to his death from one of the company's buildings that year. The connection between these two events is that the Foxconn factory is one of the largest producers of Apple products, including iPods, iPhones, and iPads. It also produces items for other companies, including Dell, Microsoft, and Sony.

Like many of its competitors, Apple manufactures most of its products outside North America because of lower wages. Apple employs 43,000 people in the United States, but most of its production is done by 700,000 workers employed by offshore contractors (Duhigg and Bradsher, 2012). Foxconn is a Taiwan-based company that has large factories in mainland China. The Shenzhen plant, which employs more than 400,000 people, is modern and working conditions are much better than in the sweatshops that exist in many poor countries. However, the pay averages only $130 per month and workers are pressured to work long hours of overtime. Many of the workers are rural young people who migrated to Shenzhen to get jobs and who live in company dormitories where they have little contact with their families and friends. The workers who have killed themselves may have seen little in their futures except endless hours on an assembly line. Black has provided two examples of what it is like to work at Foxconn:

> Some workers' legs swelled so much they waddled. "It's hard to stand all day," said Zhao Sheng, a plant worker.
>
> Banners on the walls warned the 120,000 employees: "Work hard on the job today or work hard to find a job tomorrow." (2012)

While Apple's former leader, Steve Jobs, was extremely demanding about the design and functioning of Apple products, he was obviously less demanding in ensuring that the people assembling his products were treated well.

In response to the suicides, Foxconn significantly increased salaries and placed netting around its buildings to prevent workers from jumping. At the same time, unprecedented strikes in China, including at several Honda factories, have resulted in large wage hikes for workers and dissatisfaction seems to be growing across the country over low wages and poor working conditions. It is too soon to know if this unrest will spread to other companies.

The Foxconn situation illustrates the flying geese model. Work sent offshore from North America might at one time have been done in Foxconn's home country of Taiwan but is now done in the lower-wage environment of China. If Chinese workers succeed in getting higher wages, some low-skill work will likely move from China to poorer countries where workers are still desperate for jobs.

The suicides raise another issue. Labour costs make up very little of the final cost of most high-technology products. About $4 of the cost of a $299 iPod can be attributed to the labour costs of final assembly in China (Linden, Kraemer, and Dedrick, 2007). Doubling or tripling these wages would mean that you would have to pay a few dollars more for these products or that Apple would make slightly less profit.

In response to the negative publicity over the suicides, Apple has opened its offshore production facilities for inspection by the Fair Labor Association and reached an agreement with Foxconn to reduce overtime and improve working conditions. However, as late as 2012, suicides continued to occur at Foxconn factories.

What are your views about this issue? Would you pay a few dollars more for the technology you use to ensure that the people who manufactured it were being paid a fair wage? Are purchasers who continue to buy these devices contributing to a system that exploits foreign workers, or is sending work offshore an important step in improving the living conditions of people in low-income countries?

GLOBAL INEQUALITY IN THE FUTURE

What are the future prospects for greater equality across and within nations? Social scientists disagree on the answer to this question. Depending on their theoretical framework, they may see either an optimistic or a pessimistic future scenario.

In some regions, economic development has stalled and persistent and growing poverty continues to undermine human development and future possibilities for socioeconomic change. Most of the countries where human development has worsened are in sub-Saharan Africa and Eastern Europe. Many of these countries have been affected by the HIV/AIDS epidemic or are adjusting to the collapse of the former Soviet Union and then the global recession of 2009. Others have suffered from low prices for the agricultural products that are their main source of income.

The situation of coffee farmers illustrates how low-income producers may fail to benefit from rising prices in high-income countries. Canadians have become used to paying two or three dollars for a cup of coffee at chains like Tim Hortons and Starbucks. Many of us assume that the people who grow the coffee receive a fair share of this price. However, according to the United Nations, between 1990 and 2005, the retail value of coffee sold in high-income countries increased from $30 billion to $80 billion (United Nations Development Programme, 2005). Over the same period, the income received by coffee exporters dropped from $12 billion to $5.5 billion even though the amount of coffee exported increased. The farmer receives only 1 cent of each dollar you pay for your cup of coffee. The reduction in income has had devastating effects on human development in countries such as Ethiopia, Uganda, and Nicaragua, which rely heavily on coffee exports. At the same time, chains that serve coffee have been enormously profitable because they can charge high prices while paying almost nothing for their raw materials. While consumers in North America and Europe are content to pay high prices for their double-espresso low-fat lattes, coffee retailers have taken advantage of an oversupply of coffee beans to reduce their costs.

© Lou Linwei/Alamy

According to a United Nations study, the number of people living in absolute poverty in China was reduced by nearly half during the 1990s. The photo above, taken in 2006, shows shoppers outside an IKEA store in Beijing—a sure sign that China's growing middle class is taking on the consumer habits of their counterparts in Western nations.

In the future, continued population growth, urbanization, and environmental degradation will threaten even the meagre living conditions of people in low-income nations. Environmental problems will be catastrophic if billions of people in countries such as China and India begin to live like middle-class North Americans, as we are setting an example that is wasteful and resource-intensive.

From this perspective, the future looks dim not only for people in low- and middle-income countries but also for those in high-income countries, who will see their quality of life diminish as natural resources are depleted, the environment is polluted, and high rates of immigration and global political unrest threaten the standard of living.

Others see a more optimistic scenario. Globally, health is improving, a higher proportion of people are educated, incomes have increased, far more females are enrolled in schools, and more countries are holding democratic elections. According to the United Nations, only three countries (the Democratic Republic of the Congo, Zambia, and Zimbabwe) have lower human development scores than they did in 1970 (United Nations Human Development Programme, 2010). Most of this improvement has been in East Asia—particularly in China—where the number of people living in absolute poverty was reduced by nearly half during the 1990s (United Nations Development Programme, 2003). It will be challenging to maintain these improvements and to make similar progress in areas, such as sub-Saharan Africa, that have largely been left behind.

These improvements show that it will be possible to alleviate global poverty, but if this positive change is to continue, the practices of global corporations, foreign aid donors, and international lending organizations must begin to focus on the needs of low-income countries rather than solely on the perceived demands of the marketplace. These needs were formally recognized in 2000, when most of the world's heads of state adopted the UN Millennium Declaration that committed countries to make dramatic improvements in the lives of the poor. The declaration contains a series of specific goals and targets that are being monitored to track the progress being made (see Figure 9.6).

As shown in Figure 9.7 on page 268, substantial progress has been made toward achieving these goals, but much more remains to be done. The most progress has been made in meeting the educational goals, improving maternal health (attended births), and providing access to safe water. There has been much less success in reducing infant mortality and providing people with proper sanitation. Figure 9.7 also shows that while progress is being made at the global level, many countries lag seriously behind.

The United Nations has suggested six policy changes that will help low-income countries to improve their situations (United Nations Development Programme, 2003:4):

1. Invest in basic education and health and encouraging the equality of women will help to encourage economic growth.
2. Help to improve the productivity of small farmers.
3. Improve roads, ports, communications systems, and the other infrastructure necessary for production and trade.

FIGURE 9.6 MILLENNIUM DEVELOPMENT GOALS AND TARGETS

Goal 1: Eradicate extreme poverty and hunger.
- Target 1: Halve, between 1990 and 2015, the proportion of people whose income is less than $1 a day.
- Target 2: Halve, between 1990 and 2015, the proportion of people who suffer from hunger.

Goal 2: Achieve universal primary education.

Goal 3: Promote gender equality and empower women.

Goal 4: Reduce child mortality.
- Target 1: Reduce by two-thirds, between 1990 and 2015, the under-five mortality rate.

Goal 5: Improve maternal health.
- Target 1: Reduce by two-thirds, between 1990 and 2015, the maternal mortality rate.

Goal 6: Combat HIV/AIDS, malaria, and other diseases.

Goal 7: Ensure environmental sustainability.
- Target 1: Integrate the principles of sustainable development into country policies and programs and reverse the loss of environmental resources.
- Target 2: Halve, by 2015, the proportion of people without sustainable access to safe drinking water and basic sanitation.
- Target 3: Have achieved, by 2020, a significant improvement in the lives of at least 100 million slum dwellers.

Goal 8: Develop a global partnership for development.

Source: © United Nations Development Programme, *Human Development Report, 2003.*

4. Promote the development of small- and medium-sized businesses to help countries move away from dependence on exporting commodities.
5. Promote democratic governance and human rights, to help ensure that economic growth benefits the poorest people within low-income countries rather than just the elite.
6. Ensure environmental sustainability and urban planning.

Making these changes is beyond the capability of the poorest countries, so progress will depend on the willingness of the rest of the world to work with them to meet the Millennium Development Goals, as achieving these goals is very important to the world's poorest people.

We will continue to focus on issues pertaining to global inequality in subsequent chapters as we discuss such topics as race, gender, education, health and medicine, population, urbanization, social change, and the environment.

© CARE/A. John Watson

CARE water trucks, like this one, help provide clean drinking water to more than a quarter-million residents of Kabul, Afghanistan.

FIGURE 9.7 PROGRESS TOWARD THE MILLENNIUM DEVELOPMENT GOALS, BY COUNTRY

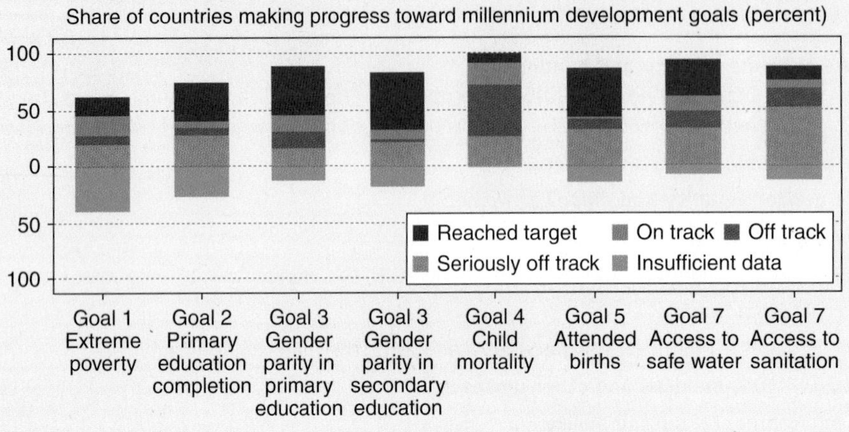

Source: World Bank, 2010, p. 2.

VISUAL SUMMARY

9

LO-1 Understand the concept of global stratification and its impact on the lives of billions of people.

© vietnam/Alamy

Global stratification refers to the unequal distribution of wealth, power, and prestige on a global basis, which results in people having vastly different lifestyles and life chances both within and among the nations of the world. The income gap between the richest and the poorest people in the world continues to widen and hundreds of millions of people are living in abject poverty.

© Mark Snelling/British Red Cross

LO-2 Understand the relationship between global poverty and human development.

Income disparities are not the only factor that defines poverty and its effect on people. The United Nations Human Development Index measures the level of development in a country through indicators such as life expectancy, infant mortality rate, proportion of underweight children under age five, and adult literacy rate for low-income, middle-income, and high-income countries.

LO-3 Discuss Rostow's modernization theory and explain the stages that modernization theorists believe all societies must go through.

© Lou Linwei/Alamy

Modernization theory links global inequality to different levels of economic development and suggests that low-income economies can move to middle- and high-income economies by achieving self-sustained economic growth. According to Rostow, all countries go through four stages of economic development: (1) the traditional stage; (2) the take-off stage; (3) the technological maturity stage; and (4) the high mass consumption stage.

KEY TERMS

core nations According to world-systems analysis, dominant capitalist centres characterized by high levels of industrialization and urbanization, as well as a high degree of control over the world economy (p. 261).

dependency theory The perspective that global poverty can at least partially be attributed to the fact that low-income countries have been exploited by high-income countries (p. 260).

gross national income (GNI) All the goods and services produced in a country in a given year, plus the income earned outside the country by individuals or corporations (p. 246).

high-income economies Countries with an annual per capita gross national income of $US12,275 or more (p. 246).

lower-middle-income economies Countries with an annual per capita gross national income between $US1005 and $US3975 (p. 246).

low-income economies Countries with an annual per capita gross national income of $US1005 or less (p. 246).

modernization theory A perspective that links global inequality to different levels of economic development and that suggests that low-income economies can move to middle- and high-income economies by achieving self-sustained economic growth (p. 257).

new international division of labour theory The perspective that commodity production is being split into fragments that can be assigned to whichever part of the world can provide the most profitable combination of capital and labour (p. 262).

peripheral nations According to world-systems analysis, nations that are dependent on core nations for capital, have little or no industrialization, and have uneven patterns of urbanization (p. 261).

semiperipheral nations According to world-systems analysis, nations that are more developed than peripheral nations but less developed than core nations (p. 261).

upper-middle-income economies Countries with an annual per capita gross national income between $US3976 and $US12,274 (p. 246).

world-systems analysis The perspective that the capitalist world economy is a global system divided into a hierarchy of three major types of nations—core, semiperipheral, and peripheral—in which upward or downward mobility is conditioned by the resources and obstacles that characterize the international system (p. 261).

LO-4 Describe how dependency theory differs from modernization theory.

© NCG/Shutterstock

Dependency theory states that global poverty can be at least partially attributed to the fact that low-income countries have been exploited by high-income countries. Whereas modernization theory focuses on how societies can reduce inequality through industrialization and economic development, dependency theorists see the greed of the rich countries as a source of increasing impoverishment of the people in poorer nations.

© CARE/A. John Watson

LO-5 Understand how world-systems analysis views the global economy.

According to world-systems analysis, the capitalist world economy is a global system divided into a hierarchy of three major types of nations: core, peripheral, and semiperipheral. Core nations benefit from their relationships with peripheral and semiperipheral nations.

LO-6 Understand the international division of labour theory.

© Ross Kinnaird/Getty Images

The international division of labour theory is based on the assumption that commodity production is split into fragments that can be assigned to whichever part of the world can provide the most profitable combination of capital and labour. This division of labour has changed the pattern of geographic specialization among countries and high-income countries have become dependent on low-income countries for labour. The low-income countries provide transnational corporations with a situation in which they can pay lower wages and taxes and face fewer regulations regarding workplace conditions and environmental protection. A variation of this theory—the flying geese theory—helps explain how manufacturing technology is successively transferred to lower-income countries.

KEY FIGURES

Walt Whitman Rostow (1916–2003) Rostow was an economist who taught at several universities and worked at high levels of the U.S. government. As a national security advisor to U.S. presidents John F. Kennedy and Lyndon Johnson, he has been criticized for his role in planning Vietnam War strategy. His best-known academic work involved his theory of modernization.

© Stan Wayman//Time Life Pictures/Getty Images

Amartya Sen (b. 1933) Sen was born in what is now Bangladesh. Raised in India, much of his later work was influenced by sectarian violence in that country in the 1940s and by the Bengal famine that killed two million to three million people in 1943. He became an economist and philosopher and received the Nobel Prize for Economics in 1998. Along with his colleague Mahbub ul Haq, Sen developed the Human Development Index for the United Nations Development Programme.

© Rick Maiman/Sygma/Corbis

Immanuel Wallerstein (b. 1930) Wallerstein is a sociologist who taught at McGill University during the 1970s before returning to the United States. His major work involved the development of world-systems analysis. This work has inspired many of those involved in the anti-globalization movement.

Used with permission of Immanuel Wallerstein

APPLICATION QUESTIONS

1. You have decided to study global wealth and poverty. How would you approach your project? Which research methods would provide the best data for analysis? What do you think you might find if you compared your research data with popular presentations—such as films and advertising—of everyday life in low- and middle-income countries?
2. What are some of the positive aspects of globalization? How might the globalization of manufacturing and service industries benefit the world's poorest people?
3. In what ways are people and cultures negatively affected by the practices of global corporations?
4. Using the theories discussed in this chapter, devise a plan to alleviate poverty in low-income countries. Assume that you have the necessary resources, including wealth and political power. Share your plan with others in your class and create a consolidated plan that represents the best ideas and suggestions presented.

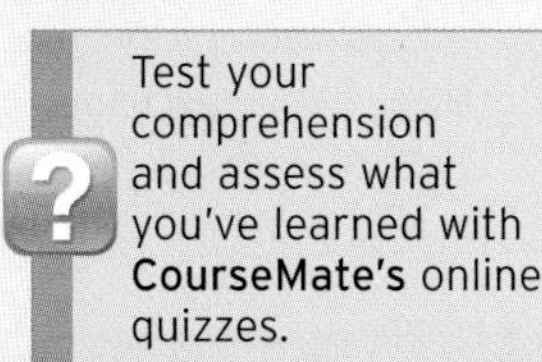

Test your comprehension and assess what you've learned with **CourseMate's** online quizzes.

For other interesting Lived Experiences, watch the video clips on **CourseMate.**

Practise what you've learned with flashcards containing key terms and definitions on **CourseMate.**

CHAPTER

10 Ethnic Relations and Race

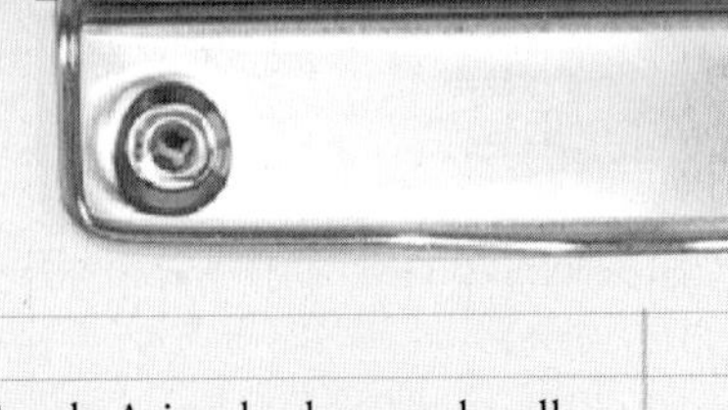

Keisha, a student of South Asian background, tells the story of the racism she experienced when she first went to university in southern Ontario. She describes her first "big shock":

> *I came to university with a big mind and an open mind and I was here to learn and it was an environment where my fellow peers, I had hoped, would have the same stand or the same understanding of a lot of things. So walking into lecture one day, I was a little bit late, so I just turned around to one of the girls and asked what was happening, and she turned to me and said something that was very awful and I will quote. She said: "Don't talk to me, filthy Paki." She was pretty loud, and the girls in front of me and behind me kind of heard and there were a couple of guys who heard and they turned around . . . I was so shocked that I couldn't respond because I couldn't fathom that someone my age, someone in the same society that I grew up in or at least at the level of education system that we were in, would not have an open mind and would say some thing like that . . . I couldn't respond because I'm a person who is very naïve . . . I didn't say anything. But I was hoping, I guess, that the people who were sitting in front of me or behind me would've said something.* (James, 2010:235)

Canada is a diverse and complex society composed of racially and ethnically different groups. Our country has a reputation as a tolerant and compassionate country whose success in race and ethnic relations has received worldwide admiration (Fleras and Elliott, 2003). Canada is widely renowned for its "cultural democracy" and "harmonious" ethnic diversity (James, 2005). Without question, significant gains have been made in the past 50 years for "visible" and "non-visible" minority groups in Canada (Hier and Singh Bolaria, 2007).

From a distance, Canada maintains its enviable status. However, upon closer examination, we see evidence of a more complex picture in terms of race and ethnic relations. Despite our claims that Canadians are "colour-blind," racist ideas and practices affect individuals and groups in very real ways. Racism is something that is not only part of Canada's history, but also an important aspect of current circumstances (Satzewich and Liodakis, 2007).

In this chapter, racism will be central to the discussion of race and ethnicity. One of the most important and reliable sources of information on racism is the individuals who have experienced it directly. Therefore, we will explore the subjective impact of race and ethnicity on people's lives—and examine whether those effects are changing. Before reading on, test your knowledge about race and ethnic relations in Canada by taking the quiz in Box 10.1 on page 275.

(*Source:* James, Carl E. *Seeing Ourselves: Exploring Race, Ethnicity and Culture*, 4th edition (2010). Thompson Books.)

Critical Thinking Questions

1. How do you think you would have responded if you had witnessed the racist incident outlined earlier?
2. How might you have responded if you, like Keisha, were the target of such racial hatred?
3. To what extent do you think race plays a part in Canadian society? In global societies?

CHAPTER FOCUS QUESTION

What is the significance of race in Canadian society?

LEARNING OBJECTIVES

AFTER READING THIS CHAPTER, YOU SHOULD BE ABLE TO

LO-1 Distinguish between race and ethnicity.

LO-2 Define and explain prejudice, discrimination, and racism.

LO-3 Explain the major sociological perspectives on race and ethnic relations.

LO-4 Discuss the unique historical experiences of the racial and ethnic groups in Canada.

LO-5 Describe how Canada's immigration policies have affected the composition of Canada's racial and ethnic population today.

LO-1 RACE AND ETHNICITY

March 21 is recognized annually as the International Day for the Elimination of Racial Discrimination because on that day, in 1960, police opened fire and killed 69 people at a peaceful demonstration against apartheid in South Africa.

What is "race"? Some people think it refers to skin colour (the Caucasian "race"); others use it to refer to a religion (the Jewish "race"), nationality (the British "race"), or the entire human species (the human "race") (Marger, 2009). Popular usages of *race* have been based on the assumption that a race is a grouping or classification based on *genetic* variations in physical appearance, particularly skin colour. However, social scientists and biologists dispute the idea that biological race is a meaningful concept (Johnson, 1995). In fact, the idea of race has little meaning in a biological sense because of the enormous amount of interbreeding that has taken place within the human population. For these reasons, sociologists sometimes place "race" in quotation marks to show that categorizing individuals and population groups on biological characteristics is neither accurate nor based on valid distinctions between the genetic makeup of differently identified "races" (Marshall, 1998).

Race is a *socially constructed reality,* not a biological one. Understanding what we mean when we say that race is a social construct is important to our understanding of how race affects all aspects of social life and society. Race as a *social construct* means that races as such do not actually exist, but some groups are still racially defined because the *idea* persists in many people's minds that races are distinct biological categories with physically distinguishable characteristics and a shared common cultural heritage. However, research on the human genome has been unable to identify any racially based genetic differences in human beings, and fossil and DNA evidence also point to humans all being of one race. Race continues to be an important concern in the 21st century, however, not because it is a biological reality but because it takes on a life of its own when it is socially defined and shapes how we see others and ourselves. Race also has significant social consequences, such as which individuals experience prejudice and discrimination and which have the best life chances and opportunities. When we look at race in this way, the *social significance* that people accord to race is more important than any biological differences that might exist among people who are placed in arbitrary racial categories (Frankenberg, 1993).

A **race** is a category of people who have been singled out as inferior or superior, often on the basis of real or alleged physical characteristics, such as skin colour, hair texture, eye shape, or other subjectively selected attributes (Feagin and Feagin, 2011). Categories of people frequently thought of as racial groups include Asian Canadians, African Canadians, and Native or Aboriginal peoples.

race A term used by many people to specify groups of people distinguished by physical characteristics, such as skin colour; also, a category of people who have been singled out as inferior or superior, often on the basis of real or alleged physical characteristics, such as skin colour, hair texture, eye shape, or other subjectively selected attributes.

How do you classify yourself with regard to race? For an increasing number of people, this is a difficult question to answer. What if you were asked about your ethnic origin or your ethnicity? The Canadian census, unlike that of the United States, collects information on ethnic origin rather than race. Whereas race refers only to *physical* characteristics, the concept of ethnicity refers to *cultural* features. An **ethnic group** is a collection of people distinguished, by others or by themselves, primarily on the basis of cultural or nationality characteristics (Feagin and Feagin, 2011). Ethnic groups share five main characteristics:

ethnic group A collection of people distinguished, by others or by themselves, primarily on the basis of cultural or nationality characteristics.

1. Unique cultural traits, such as language, clothing, holidays, or religious practices.
2. A sense of community.
3. A feeling of ethnocentrism.
4. Ascribed membership from birth.
5. Territoriality, or the tendency to occupy a distinct geographic area.

BOX 10.1 **SOCIOLOGY AND EVERYDAY LIFE**

How Much Do You Know About Racial and Ethnic Relations in Canada?

True	False	
T	F	1. Canadians are significantly less racist than Americans.
T	F	2. Racism occurs only in times of economic decline and recession.
T	F	3. Canada continues to employ racial criteria in the selection of new immigrants.
T	F	4. No civil rights movement has ever existed in Canada.
T	F	5. Slavery has never existed in Canada.

For answers to the quiz about racial and ethnic relations in Canada, go to **www.nelson.com/sociologyinourtimes6e**.

Although some people do not identify with any ethnic group, others participate in social interaction with the individuals in their group and feel a sense of common identity based on cultural characteristics, such as language, religion, or politics. Ethnicity provides individuals with a sense of identity and belonging based not only on their perception of being different but also on others' recognition of their uniqueness. Consider the comments from this university student:

> My ethnic identity is Polish. My parents were born in Poland and came to Canada in 1967 . . . I saw my ethnicity as an advantage and disadvantage during my lifetime. When I was younger, I didn't want to admit that I was Polish. Even though I was born here, I felt that admitting my ethnicity would be a barrier to joining the "in crowd" or the "cool group" at school . . . As I became older, I realized I couldn't change my ethnicity. I was who I was. I became more proud of my Polish background. It felt good to be a part of a Polish community where I was able to participate in ceremonies and activities based on my Polish background. It gave me a sense of belonging to a group, a sense of identity, a sense of security. (James, 2010:62)*

The Social Significance of Race and Ethnicity

Race and ethnicity take on great social significance because how people act in regard to these terms drastically affects other people's lives, including what opportunities they have, how they are treated, and even how long they live. It matters because it provides privilege and power for some. Fleras and Elliott discuss the significance of being white and enjoying what has sometimes been referred to as *white privilege:*

> Think for a moment about the privileges associated with whiteness, many of which are taken for granted and unearned by accident of birth. Being white means you can purchase a home in any part of town and expect cordial treatment rather than community grumblings about a plummeting in real estate values. Being white saves you the embarrassment of going into a shopping mall with fears of being followed, frisked, monitored, or finger printed. Being white means you can comment on a variety of topics without having someone question your objectivity or second-guess your motives. Being white provides a peace of mind in that your actions are judged not as a betrayal of or a credit to your race, but in terms of individual idiosyncracies . . . Finally, being white ensures one the satisfaction of socializing at night, without being pulled over by the police or patted down. (2003:35)

**Source:* James, Carl E. *Seeing Ourselves: Exploring Race, Ethnicity and Culture*, 4th edition (2010). Thompson Books.

Ethnicity, like race, is a basis of hierarchical ranking in society. John Porter (1965) described Canada as a "vertical mosaic," made up of different ethnic groups wielding varying degrees of social and economic power, status, and prestige. Porter's analysis of ethnic groups in Canada revealed a significant degree of ethnic stratification, with some ethnic groups heavily represented in the upper strata, or elite, and other groups heavily represented in the lower strata. The dominant group holds power over other (subordinate) ethnic groups. To what extent does a "vertical mosaic" still exist in Canada? A 2009 study by Philip Oreopoulos found that, despite the fact that immigrants to Canada are selected on the basis of their optimal skills, education, and professional qualifications, immigrants and ethnic minority Canadians still have significantly lower incomes and higher rates of unemployment. Oreopoulis constructed "mock" resumés representative of recent immigrants from the three largest countries of origin (China, India, and Pakistan) and Britain, as well as nonimmigrants with and without ethnic-sounding names. Six thousand resumés were sent out to apply to online job postings in the Toronto area. The findings indicated that applicants with English-sounding names with Canadian education and experience received callbacks 40 percent more often than did applicants with Chinese, Indian, or Pakistani names who had similar Canadian education and experience (Oreopoulos, 2009). This study provides evidence of continued ethnic stratification based on what Oreopoulos described as "substantial discrimination" by employers. Ethnic stratification is one dimension of a larger system of structured social inequality, as examined in Chapter 8.

Majority and Minority Groups

majority (dominant) group A group that is advantaged and has superior resources and rights in a society.

minority (subordinate) group A group whose members, because of physical or cultural characteristics, are disadvantaged and subjected to unequal treatment by the dominant group and who regard themselves as objects of collective discrimination.

visible minority An official government category of nonwhite, non-Caucasian individuals.

The terms *majority group* and *minority group* are widely used, but what do they actually mean? To sociologists, a **majority** (or **dominant) group** is one that is advantaged and has superior resources and rights in a society (Feagin and Feagin, 2011). In Canada, whites with northern European ancestry (often referred to as Euro-Canadians or white Anglo-Saxon Protestants, or WASPs) are considered the majority group. A **minority** (or **subordinate) group** is one whose members, because of physical or cultural characteristics, are disadvantaged and subjected to unequal treatment by the dominant group and who regard themselves as objects of collective discrimination. All visible minorities and white women are considered minority group members in Canada. The term **visible minority** refers to an official government category of nonwhite, non-Caucasian individuals. Included in this category are Chinese, Japanese, Koreans, Filipinos, Asians, South Asians, Arabs, Southeast Asians, blacks, Latin Americans, and Pacific Islanders (Statistics Canada, 2008). Aboriginal people form a separate category of individuals with minority group status.

Today, more than five million Canadians—close to one in six—identified themselves as members of a visible minority, and, it is estimated that 20 years from now, Canada could be home to more than 14 million people belonging to a visible minority group. South Asians and Chinese will still comprise the largest visible minority groups (Statistics Canada, 2011).

Although the terms *majority group* and *minority group* are widely used, their actual meanings are not clear. In the sociological sense, *group* is misleading because people who merely share ascribed racial or ethnic characteristics do not constitute a group. Further, *majority* and *minority* have meanings associated with both numbers and domination. Numerically speaking, *minority* means that a group is smaller in number than a dominant group. In countries such as South Africa and India, however, this has not historically been true.

TIME TO REVIEW

- Explain the statement "Race is a social construct."
- How significant do you think this social construct is in the lives of visible minority group members?
- What is the significance of race in the lives of majority group members?

PREJUDICE LO-2

Prejudice is a negative attitude based on preconceived notions about members of selected groups. The term *prejudice* comes from the Latin words *prae* ("before") and *judicium* ("judgment"), which means that people may be biased either for or against members of other groups before they have had any contact with them. Although prejudice can be either *positive* (bias in favour of a group—often our own) or *negative* (bias against a group—one we deem less worthy than our own), it most often refers to the negative attitudes people may have about members of other racial or ethnic groups. **Racial prejudice** involves beliefs that certain racial groups are innately inferior to others or have a disproportionate number of negative traits.

prejudice A negative attitude based on preconceived notions about members of selected groups.

racial prejudice Beliefs that certain racial groups are innately inferior to others or have a disproportionate number of negative traits.

Stereotypes

Prejudice is rooted in stereotypes and ethnocentrism. When used in the context of racial and ethnic relations, ethnocentrism refers to the tendency to regard one's own culture and group as the standard—and thus superior—whereas all other groups are seen as inferior. Ethnocentrism is maintained and perpetuated by **stereotypes**—overgeneralizations about the appearance, behaviour, or other characteristics of members of particular groups. The term *stereotype* comes from the Greek word *stereos* ("solid") and refers to a fixed mental impression. Although all stereotypes are hurtful, negative stereotypes are particularly harmful to members of minority groups. Consider for example, Naomi's experience:

stereotype An overgeneralization about the appearance, behaviour, or other characteristics of members of particular groups.

> People whom I meet frequently ask, "What are you?" as a way of determining my racial background. I then proceed to tell them that I am Canadian. Then they ask me, "Where are your parents from?" I tell them Poland and they then look confused . . . And then when they learn that I am Jewish, their responses always amaze me. People express surprise and say, "You are Jewish!" as if I had a disease or something. And some people think they are paying me a compliment by saying, "We do not think of you as Jewish; you are different than most Jewish people we know." This is an outright insult to my ethnicity, of which I am proud. Another typical comment is that I "do not look Jewish." I do not understand what it means to "look Jewish" considering that there are Jewish people from all over the world. (James, 2010:216)*

How do people develop these stereotypes? The media are a major source of racial and ethnic stereotypes. Another source is ethnic jokes that portray minorities in a derogatory manner. Take a moment and think of an ethnic joke you have heard recently. Do you think this joke is harmful? Would you tell the joke to the member of the ethnic group that the joke is about? Paul, a student in a race and ethnic relations course at a Canadian university, discusses this issue:

> I laugh at a joke that uses a Black . . . because I associate a stereotype with what has been said, I am a bigot. For example, what do you call a Black guy in a new car? A thief. Funny, eh? No, the joke itself is not funny, but it makes reference to a stereotype about Blacks that they're all thieves, which I do not find funny . . . That kind of joke is not funny. It does not point out a funny stereotype of a certain race . . . it is pure malice and cruelty against a specific group. (James, 2001:107)†

*†*Source:* James, Carl E. *Seeing Ourselves: Exploring Race, Ethnicity and Culture,* 4th edition (2010). Thompson Books.

Theories of Prejudice

Are some people more prejudiced than others? To answer this question, some theories focus on how individuals may transfer their internal psychological problems onto an external object or person. Others look at factors such as social learning and personality types.

The frustration-aggression hypothesis states that people who are frustrated in their efforts to achieve a highly desired goal will respond with a pattern of aggression toward others (Dollard et al., 1939). The object of their aggression becomes the **scapegoat**—a person or group that is incapable of offering resistance to the hostility or aggression of others (Marger, 2009). Scapegoats are often used as substitutes for the actual source of the frustration. For example, members of subordinate racial and ethnic groups are often blamed for societal problems (such as unemployment or an economic recession) over which they have no control.

scapegoat A person or group that is incapable of offering resistance to the hostility or aggression of others.

According to some symbolic interactionists, prejudice results from social learning; in other words, it is learned from observing and imitating significant others, such as parents and peers. Initially, children do not have a frame of reference from which to question the prejudices of their relatives and friends. When they are rewarded with smiles or laughs for telling derogatory jokes or making negative comments about outgroup members, children's prejudiced attitudes may be reinforced.

Psychologist Theodor W. Adorno and his colleagues concluded that highly prejudiced individuals tend to have an **authoritarian personality**, which is characterized by excessive conformity, submissiveness to authority, intolerance, insecurity, a high level of superstition, and rigid, stereotypic thinking (Adorno et al., 1950). It is most likely to develop in a family environment in which dominating parents who are anxious about status use physical discipline but show very little love in raising their children (Adorno et al., 1950). Other scholars have linked prejudiced attitudes to traits such as submissiveness to authority, extreme anger toward outgroups, and conservative religious and political beliefs (Altemeyer, 1981, 1988; Weigel and Howes, 1985).

authoritarian personality A personality type characterized by excessive conformity, submissiveness to authority, intolerance, insecurity, a high level of superstition, and rigid, stereotypic thinking.

DISCRIMINATION

discrimination Actions or practices of dominant group members (or their representatives) that have a harmful impact on members of a subordinate group.

Whereas prejudice is an attitude, **discrimination** involves actions or practices of dominant group members (or their representatives) that have a harmful impact on members of a subordinate group (Feagin and Feagin, 2011). For example, people who are prejudiced toward South Asian, Jewish, or Aboriginal people may refuse to hire them, rent an apartment to them, or allow their children to play with them. In these instances, discrimination involves the differential treatment of minority group members not because of their ability or merit but because of irrelevant characteristics, such as skin colour or language preference. Discriminatory actions vary in severity from the use of derogatory labels to violence against individuals and groups.

Discrimination takes two basic forms: *de jure,* or legal discrimination, which is encoded in laws; and *de facto,* or informal discrimination, which is entrenched in social customs and institutions. *De jure* discrimination has been supported with explicitly discriminatory laws, such as the *Chinese Exclusionary Act*, which restricted immigration to Canada on the basis of race, or the Nuremberg laws passed in Nazi Germany, which imposed restrictions on Jews. The *Indian Act* provides other examples of *de jure* discrimination. According to the act, a Native woman who married a non-Native man automatically lost her Indian status rights and was no longer allowed to live on a reserve. Native men had no such problem. The *Indian Act* also specified that Native people who graduated from university, or who became doctors, lawyers, or ministers before 1920, were forced to give up their status rights. An amendment to the *Indian Act* in 1985 ended this legalized discrimination. The *Charter of Rights and Freedoms* prohibits discrimination on the basis of race, ethnicity, or religion. As a result, many cases of *de jure* discrimination have been eliminated. *De facto* discrimination is more subtle and less visible to public scrutiny and therefore much more difficult to eradicate.

Prejudiced attitudes do not always lead to discriminatory behaviour. Sociologist Robert Merton (1949) identified four combinations of attitudes and responses. *Unprejudiced nondiscriminators* are not personally prejudiced and do not discriminate against others. These are individuals who believe in equality for all. *Unprejudiced discriminators* may have no personal prejudices but still engage in discriminatory behaviour because of peer group pressure or economic, political, or social interests—for example, an employee who has no personal hostility toward members of certain groups but is encouraged by senior management not to hire them. *Prejudiced nondiscriminators* hold personal prejudices but do not discriminate due to peer pressure, legal demands, or a desire for profits. Such individuals are often referred to as "timid bigots" because they are reluctant to translate their attitudes into action (especially when prejudice is considered to be "politically incorrect"). Finally, *prejudiced discriminators* hold personal prejudices and actively discriminate against others—for example, the landlord who refuses to rent an apartment to an Aboriginal couple and then readily justifies his actions on the basis of racist stereotypes.

Merton's typology shows that some people may be prejudiced but not discriminate against others. Do you think it is possible for a person to discriminate against some people without holding a prejudiced attitude toward them? Why or why not?

RACISM

Racism is a set of ideas that implies the superiority of one social group over another on the basis of biological or cultural characteristics, together with the power to put these beliefs into practice in a way that denies or excludes minority women and men.

racism A set of ideas that implies the superiority of one social group over another on the basis of biological or cultural characteristics, together with the power to put these beliefs into practice in a way that denies or excludes minority women and men.

Racism involves elements of prejudice, ethnocentrism, stereotyping, and discrimination. For example, racism is present in the belief that some racial or ethnic groups are superior while others are inferior—this belief is a prejudice. Racism may be the basis for unfair treatment toward members of a racial or ethnic group. In this case, the racism involves discrimination.

Fleras and Elliott (2003) make distinctions among a number of diverse types of racism (see Table 10.1). **Overt racism (or redneck or hate racism)** may take the form of deliberate and highly personal attacks, including derogatory slurs and name-calling toward members of a racial or ethnic group who are perceived to be "inferior" (James, 2010). Examples of overt racism, although rare, are available in Canada. In 2009, a Winnipeg case made national headlines when family service agencies removed two children from their parents' home and sought permanent custody because their parents were teaching the children racist views. Social workers became involved when the young girl attended school with white supremist symbols and slogans drawn all over her skin. The girl told social workers that she watched violent racist videos in her home and her parents regularly discussed killing minorities. Overt racism is also demonstrated in the racist violence perpetuated by members of white supremacist groups, including the Heritage Front, White Aryan Nation, and Western Guard, that are active in Canada. These groups are committed to an ideology of racial supremacy in which the white "race" is seen as superior to other races. This type of overt racism is becoming increasingly unacceptable in Canadian society, and few people today will tolerate the open expression of racism. In fact, overt acts of discrimination are now illegal. *The Criminal Code*, the *Charter of Rights and Freedoms,* and human rights legislation have served to limit the expression of overt racist ideology.

overt racism (or redneck or hate racism) Racism that may take the form of deliberate and highly personal attacks, including derogatory slurs and name-calling toward members of a racial or ethnic group who are perceived to be "inferior."

While blatant forms of racism have dissipated to some extent, less obvious expressions of bigotry and stereotyping that allow people to discuss their dislike of certain groups in "coded language" remain in our society. **Polite racism** is an attempt to disguise a dislike of others through behaviour that is outwardly nonprejudicial. This type of racism may be operating when members of visible minority groups are ignored or turned down for jobs or promotions on a regular basis. Polite racism may consist of subtle remarks or looks that result in members of visible minority groups feeling inferior or out of place (Fleras and Elliott, 2003). A number of studies have examined the extent to which this type of racism manifests itself in the workplace (Henry, 2006; Kunz, Milan, and Schetagne, 2000; Oreopoulis, 2009). Researchers have found that members of particular visible minority groups are often ignored; assigned unpleasant tasks at work; turned down for interviews, jobs, and promotions; or excluded from the inner circle of their workplace.

polite racism A term used to describe an attempt to disguise a dislike of others through behaviour that is outwardly nonprejudicial.

TABLE 10.1 THE FACTS OF RACISM

	WHAT: CORE SLOGAN	WHY: DEGREE OF INTENT	HOW: STYLE OF EXPRESSION	WHERE: MAGNITUDE AND SCOPE
Overt racism	"X, get out."	Conscious	Personal and explicit	Interpersonal
Polite racism	"Sorry, the job is taken."	Moderate	Discreet and subtle	Personal
Subliminal racism	"I'm not racist, but . . ."	Ambivalent	Oblique	Cultural
Institutionalized racism	"We treat everyone the same here."	Unintentional or intentional	Impersonal	Institutional and societal

Sources: Fleras and Elliott, 1996, 2003.

subliminal racism A term used to describe an unconscious racism that occurs when there is a conflict of values.

Polite racism may be largely hidden in our "politically correct" society, but the effects on victims are similar to the more obvious forms of the past—control, exclusion, and exploitation (Fleras and Elliott, 2003:70).

Subliminal racism is a form of subconscious racism that occurs when there is a conflict of values. Subliminal racism is not directly expressed but is demonstrated in opposition to progressive minority policies (such as Canada's immigration policy) or programs (such as employment equity or affirmative action). For example, after the 9/11 terrorist attacks, there were insinuations that Canada's "weak" immigration policies allowed the terrorists to enter the United States. Subliminal racism allows us to understand how mainstream whites can simultaneously demonstrate nearly universal support for principles of equality and at the same time undermine progressive policies and strategies directed at achieving that equality. As Fleras and Elliott highlight:

> Refugee claimants are not condemned in blunt racist terminology; rather their landed entry into Canada is criticized on procedural grounds ("jumping the queue"). Or they are belittled for taking unfair advantage of Canada's generosity or ability to shoulder the processing costs . . . Minority peoples have rights, but minority demands that fall outside conventional channels are criticized as a threat to national identity or social harmony . . . Employment equity initiatives are endorsed in principle but rejected in practice as unfair to the majority. (2003:73)

© AFP/Getty Images

Recent anti-Semitic attacks on Jewish synagogues are an unfortunate indicator that some forms of overt racism still exist.

Subliminal racism, more than any other type, demonstrates the ambiguity concerning racism. Values that support racial equality are publicly supported while, at the same time, resentment at the prospect of moving over and making space for newcomers is also present. Subliminal racism enables individuals to maintain two apparently conflicting values—one rooted in the egalitarian virtues of justice and fairness, the other in beliefs that result in resentment and selfishness (Fleras and Elliott, 2003).

Institutionalized racism occurs where the established rules, policies, and practices within an institution or organization produce differential treatment of various groups based on race. Although institutions can no longer openly discriminate against minorities without attracting legal sanctions, negative publicity, or consumer resistance, this type of racism nevertheless continues to exist (Fleras and Kunz, 2001). The practice of word-of-mouth recruitment is an example of an institutional practice that has the result of excluding racial minorities from the hiring selection process.

institutionalized racism A situation where the established rules, policies, and practices within an institution or organization produce differential treatment of various groups based on race.

Institutional racism may also be reflected in organizational practices, rules, and procedures that have the unintended consequence of excluding minority group members. For example, occupations such as police officer and firefighter historically had minimum weight, height, and educational requirements for job applicants. These criteria resulted in discrimination because they favoured white applicants over members of many minority groups, as well as males over females. Other examples of this type of institutional racism include the requirement of a college or university degree for nonspecialized jobs, employment regulations that require people to work on their Sabbath, and the lack of recognition of foreign credentials. Institutional racism is normally reflected in statistical underrepresentation of certain groups within an institution or organization. For example, a given group may represent 15 percent of the general population but only 2 percent of those promoted to upper-management positions in a large company.

Efforts to eliminate this kind of disproportionate representation are the focus of employment equity legislation. The target groups for employment equity in Canada are visible minorities, women, persons with disabilities, and Aboriginal peoples. Strategies include modified admissions tests and requirements, enhanced recruitment of certain target groups, establishment of hiring quotas for particular minority groups, or specialized training or employment programs for specific target groups. Consideration of affirmative action strategies inevitably leads to claims of reverse discrimination by some individuals who enjoy majority group status. (For a more detailed discussion of reverse discrimination, see Box 10.2.) Consider the comments from this white male student:

> I am a white male and I am discriminated against all the time. Faced with trying to get jobs that have been reserved for minorities and not the best candidate. There is racism in Canada and as a white male I feel lots of it is aimed at myself. There was an article not long ago that Toronto Police want to hire more minority police. I think that comment in itself is racist. We don't want the best person for the job anymore? (James, 2010:243)*

The most recent analysis of employment equity programs indicates that these programs have had the most significant effect on women and Aboriginal peoples, while people with disabilities have made the fewest gains. As for members of visible minorities, although they have higher levels of education, on average, than other Canadians and very high labour-force participation rates, they continue to be concentrated in low-status, low-paying occupations (Henry and Tator, 2006, Oreopoulos, 2009).

TIME TO REVIEW

- Identify all the types of racism that exist in our society.
- In considering all of these, which type do you think is the most difficult to control? Which type does the most damage?

**Source:* James, Carl E. *Seeing Ourselves: Exploring Race, Ethnicity and Culture*, 4th edition (2010). Thompson Books.

BOX 10.2 POINT/COUNTERPOINT

The Myth of Reverse Racism

Is reverse racism possible? According to race relations scholars Augie Fleras and Jean Leonard Elliott, the answer is no. In the following excerpt from *Unequal Relations* (2003), they explain why:

> Are affirmative actions policies that favour visible minority group members and Aboriginal persons racist? Can minority women and men express racism ("reverse racism") against the majority sector? Can ethnic minorities be racist toward other ethnic minorities? Is it racist for Aboriginal peoples to accuse all whites of complicity in the destruction of Indigenous societies? Answers to these questions may never be settled to everyone's satisfaction, given the politics or intellectual dishonesty at play, but their very asking provides a sharper understanding of racism.
>
> Responses depend on how one defines racism—as biology or power. A reading of racism as biology suggests that anyone who approaches, defines, or treats someone else on the basis of race is a racist. Thus, minorities can be racist if they criticize or deny whites because of their whiteness ("reverse racism").
>
> But reference to racism as power points to a different conclusion. Accusations of minority ("reverse") racism must go beyond superficial appearances. There is a world of difference in using race to create equality (employment equity) versus its use to limit opportunity (discrimination), even if the rhetoric sounds the same. Emphasis must be placed instead on the context of the actions and their social consequences. Racism is not about treating others differently because they are different. Rather, it involves different treatment in colour-conscious contexts of power that limit opportunity or privileges (Blauner 1972).
>
> In short, racism is about the politics of difference within the context of power. Statements made by a minority group, however distasteful or bigoted, may not qualify as racist in the conventional sense of outcomes. They are largely preferences or prejudices without the capacity for harm, since minorities lack the institutional power to put bigotry into practice in a way that "stings."
>
> To be sure, minorities are not entirely powerless; after all, there is recourse to alternative sources of power-brokering, such as boycotts, civil disobedience, lobby groups, and moral suasion. And even though they may not have institutional power, minorities may have other ways to put bigotry into practice (e.g., stealing from a store owned by a member of another minority or threatening others on the basis of appearance).
>
> Still, the power that minority individuals wield in certain contexts rarely has the potential to deny or exclude. Those without access to institutionalized power or resources cannot racialize the other in ways that demean, control, or exploit. Minorities do not have the power to dominate and enforce prejudices, oppression, or subdomination. They have neither the resources to topple the dominant sector nor the critical mass to harass, exclude, exploit, persecute, dominate, or undermine the empowered. Conditions of relative powerlessness reduce minority hostility to the level of rhetoric or a protective shell in defence of minority interests. In other words, reverse racism may be a contradiction in terms. Racism is not a two-way street; more accurately, it resembles an expressway with controlled access points for those privileged enough to control the switches.

Source: Fleras & Elliot 2003.

LO-3 SOCIOLOGICAL PERSPECTIVES ON RACE AND ETHNIC RELATIONS

Symbolic interactionist, functionalist, conflict, and feminist perspectives examine race and ethnic relations in different ways. Symbolic interactionists examine how microlevel contacts between people may produce either greater racial tolerance or increased levels of hostility. Functionalists focus on the macrolevel intergroup processes that occur among members of majority and minority groups in society. Conflict theorists analyze power and economic differentials between the dominant group and subordinate groups. Feminists highlight the interactive effects of racism and sexism on the exploitation of women, who are members of a visible minority.

Symbolic Interactionist Perspectives

What happens when people from different racial and ethnic groups come into contact with one another? In the *contact hypothesis,* symbolic interactionists point out that contact between people from divergent groups should lead to favourable attitudes and behaviour when certain factors are present. Members of each group must (1) have equal status, (2) pursue the same goals, (3) cooperate with one another to achieve their goals, and (4) receive positive feedback when they interact with one another in positive, nondiscriminatory ways (Allport, 1958; Coakley, 2004).

What happens when individuals meet someone who does not conform to their existing stereotype? Frequently, they will ignore anything that contradicts the stereotype or will interpret the situation to support their prejudices (Coakley, 2004). For example, a person who does not fit the stereotype may be seen as an exception—"You're not like other [persons of a particular race]."

When a person is seen as conforming to a stereotype, he or she may be treated simply as one of "you people." Former Los Angeles Lakers basketball star Earvin "Magic" Johnson described how he was categorized along with all other African Americans when he was bused to a predominantly white school:

> On the first day of [basketball] practice, my teammates froze me out. Time after time I was wide open, but nobody threw me the ball. At first I thought they just didn't see me. But I woke up after a kid named Danny Parks looked right at me and then took a long jumper. Which he missed.
>
> I was furious, but I didn't say a word. Shortly after that, I grabbed a defensive rebound and took the ball all the way down for a basket. I did it again and a third time, too.
>
> Finally Parks got angry and said, "Hey, pass the [bleeping] ball."
>
> That did it. I slammed down the ball and glared at him. Then I exploded. "I *knew* this would happen!" I said. "That's why I didn't want to come to this [bleeping] school in the first place!"
>
> "Oh, yeah? Well, you people are all the same," he said. "You think you're gonna come in here and do whatever you want? Look, hotshot, your job is to get the rebound. Let us do the shooting." (1992:31–32)

The interaction between Johnson and Parks demonstrates that when people from different racial and ethnic groups come into contact with one another, they may treat one another as stereotypes, not as individuals. Symbolic interactionist perspectives make us aware of the importance of intergroup contact and the fact that it may either intensify or reduce racial and ethnic stereotyping and prejudice.

Functionalist Perspectives

How do members of subordinate racial and ethnic groups become part of the dominant group? To answer this question, early functionalists studied immigration and patterns of majority and minority group interaction.

ASSIMILATION **Assimilation** is a process by which members of subordinate racial and ethnic groups become absorbed into the dominant culture. To some analysts, assimilation is functional because it contributes to the stability of society by minimizing group differences that otherwise might result in hostility and violence.

assimilation A process by which members of subordinate racial and ethnic groups become absorbed into the dominant culture.

Assimilation occurs at several distinct levels, including the cultural, structural, biological, and psychological stages. *Cultural assimilation,* or *acculturation,* occurs when members of an ethnic group adopt dominant group traits, such as language, dress, values, religion, and food preferences. Cultural assimilation in this country initially followed an "Anglo-conformity" model; members of subordinate ethnic groups were expected to conform to the culture of the dominant white Anglo-Saxon population (Gordon, 1964). However, members of some groups, such as Aboriginal peoples and Québécois, refused to be assimilated and sought to maintain their unique cultural identity.

Structural assimilation, or *integration,* occurs when members of subordinate racial or ethnic groups gain acceptance in everyday social interaction with members of the dominant group. This type of assimilation typically starts in large, impersonal settings, such as schools and workplaces, and only later (if at all) results in close friendships and intermarriage.

Biological assimilation, or *amalgamation,* occurs when members of one group marry those of other social or ethnic groups. Biological assimilation has been more complete in some other countries, such as Mexico and Brazil, than in Canada.

Psychological assimilation involves a change in racial or ethnic self-identification on the part of an individual. Rejection by the dominant group may prevent psychological assimilation by members of some subordinate racial and ethnic groups, especially those with visible characteristics, such as skin colour or facial features that differ from those of the dominant group.

ETHNIC PLURALISM Instead of complete assimilation, many groups share elements of the mainstream culture while remaining culturally distinct from both the dominant group and other social and ethnic groups. **Ethnic pluralism** is the coexistence of a variety of distinct racial and ethnic groups within one society.

ethnic pluralism
The coexistence of a variety of distinct racial and ethnic groups within one society.

Equalitarian pluralism, or *accommodation,* is a situation in which ethnic groups coexist in equality with one another. Switzerland has been described as a model of equalitarian pluralism; more than six million people with French, German, and Italian cultural heritages peacefully coexist there.

Has Canada achieved equalitarian pluralism? The *Canadian Multiculturalism Act* of 1988 stated that "All Canadians are full and equal partners in Canadian society." The Department of Multiculturalism and Citizenship was established in 1991 with the goal of encouraging ethnic minorities to participate fully in all aspects of Canadian life while at the same time maintaining their distinct ethnic identities and cultural practices. The objective of multiculturalism is to "promote unity through diversity." Under multiculturalism, citizens are accepted as racially or ethnically different yet no less Canadian, with a corresponding package of citizen rights and entitlement, regardless of origin, creed, or colour (Fleras and Elliott, 2003:280). Multiculturalism programs provide funding for education, consultative support, and a range of activities, including heritage language training, race relations training, ethnic policing and justice, and ethnic celebrations. In implementing this pluralistic strategy, Canada gained international respect and admiration as a society

© A. Gottfried/The Image Works

The members of this adult education class are learning English as their second language. What type of assimilation does this represent?

that is both united and distinct, where citizens are valued as "different" yet recognized as "equal."

In recent years, multiculturalism policies have been under increasing attack. For example, multiculturalism has been described as a policy that creates and maintains an "illusion" of respect for racial and ethnic differences when in reality the pressures toward conformity and the experiences with exclusion and discrimination are very similar for Canadian "multicultural minorities" and racial and ethnic minorities living in the American "melting pot" (Reitz and Breton, 1994). Neil Bissoondath, author of *Selling Illusions: The Cult of Multiculturalism in Canada* (1994), suggests that multiculturalism does not promote equalitarian pluralism. Rather, he argues, multiculturalism serves to discourage immigrants from thinking of themselves as Canadian; it exaggerates differences, which fosters racial animosity; and it alienates people from the mainstream society, which detracts from national unity. Bissoondath argues:

> Whatever policy follows multiculturalism it should support a new vision of Canadianness. A Canada where no-one is alienated with hyphenation. A nation of cultural hybrids, where every individual is unique and every individual is a Canadian, undiluted and undivided. A nation where the following conversation, so familiar— and so enervating—to many of us will no longer take place: "What nationality are you?" "Canadian." "No, I mean, what nationality are you *really*?" (1998:1)

The challenge for a pluralistic society such as Canada lies in attaining some degree of balance between the equally important values of racial and ethnic equality and national unity. To date, any consensus on multiculturalism in terms of definition, policy, or practice remains illusive.

segregation A term used to describe the spatial and social separation of categories of people by race/ethnicity, class, gender, and/or religion.

INEQUALITARIAN PLURALISM, OR SEGREGATION *Inequalitarian pluralism,* or *segregation,* exists when specific ethnic groups are set apart from the dominant group and have unequal access to power and privilege (Marger, 2000). **Segregation** is the spatial and social separation of categories of people by race, ethnicity, class, gender, and/or religion. Segregation may be enforced by law (*de jure*) or by custom (*de facto*).

An example of *de jure* segregation was the Jim Crow laws, which legalized the separation of the races in all public accommodations (including hotels, restaurants, transportation, hospitals, jails, schools, churches, and cemeteries) in the Southern United States after the Civil War (Feagin and Feagin, 2011).

De jure segregation of blacks is also part of the history of Canada. Blacks in Canada lived in largely segregated communities in Nova Scotia, New Brunswick, and Ontario, where racial segregation was evident in the schools, government, the workplace, residential housing, and elsewhere. Segregated schools continued in Nova Scotia until the 1960s. Residential segregation was legally enforced through the use of

© Clark Brennan/Alamy

Segregation laws existed and were enforced with signs such as these in both Canada and the United States until the 1960s.

racially restrictive covenants attached to deeds and leases. Separation and refusal of service were common in restaurants, theatres, and recreational facilities (Henry and Tator, 2006). Sociologist Adrienne Shadd describes her experiences growing up in North Buxton, Ontario, in the 1950s and 1960s:

> When we would go into the local ice cream parlour, the man behind the counter would serve us last, after all the Whites had been served, even if they came into the shop after us. Southwestern Ontario may as well have been below the Mason-Dixon line in those days. Dresden, home of the historic Uncle Tom's cabin, made national headlines in 1954 when Blacks tested the local restaurants after the passage of the *Fair Accommodation Practices Act* and found that two openly refused to serve them. This came as no surprise, given that for years certain eateries, hotels, and recreational clubs were restricted to us, and at one time Blacks could only sit in designated sections of movie theatres (usually the balcony) if admitted at all. (1991:11)

One of the most blatant examples of segregation in Canada is the federal government's reserve system for status Indians, which resulted in segregation of Aboriginal peoples on reserves in remote areas across the country.

With that exception, legally sanctioned forms of racial segregation have been all but eliminated, but *de facto* segregation, which is enforced by custom, still exists. Although functionalist explanations provide a description of how some early white ethnic immigrants assimilated into the cultural mainstream, they do not adequately account for the persistent racial segregation and economic inequality experienced by some minority group members.

TIME TO REVIEW

- Compare and contrast assimilation, ethnic pluralism, and segregation.

Conflict Perspectives

Why do some ethnic groups continue to experience subjugation after many years? Conflict theorists focus on economic stratification and access to power in their analysis of race and ethnic relations.

internal colonialism According to conflict theorists, a situation in which members of a racial or ethnic group are conquered or colonized and forcibly placed under the economic and political control of the dominant group.

INTERNAL COLONIALISM Conflict theorists use the term **internal colonialism** to refer to a situation in which members of a racial or ethnic group are conquered or colonized and forcibly placed under the economic and political control of the dominant group. Groups that have been subjected to internal colonialism often remain in subordinate positions longer than groups that voluntarily migrated to North America.

Aboriginal peoples in Canada were colonized by Europeans and others who invaded their lands and conquered them. In the process, Aboriginal peoples lost property, political rights, aspects of their culture, and often their lives (Frideres and Gadacz, 2005). The capitalist class acquired cheap labour and land through this government-sanctioned racial exploitation. The effects of past internal colonialism are reflected today in the number of Aboriginal people who live in extreme poverty on government reserves (Frideres and Gadacz, 2005).

The experiences of internally colonized groups are unique in three ways: (1) They have been forced to exist in a society other than their own; (2) they have been kept out of the economic and political mainstream, so it is difficult for them to compete with dominant group members; and (3) they have been subjected to severe attacks on their own culture, which may lead to its extinction (Blauner, 1972).

The internal colonialism model is rooted in historical foundations of racial and ethnic inequality in North America. However, it tends to view all voluntary immigrants as having many more opportunities than do members of colonized groups. Thus, this model does not explain the continued exploitation of some immigrant groups, such as Chinese, Filipinos, and Vietnamese, and the greater acceptance of others, primarily those from Northern Europe (Cashmore, 1996).

split labour market A term used to describe the division of the economy into two areas of employment: a primary sector, or upper tier, composed of higher-paid (usually dominant group) workers in more secure jobs; and a secondary sector, or lower tier, composed of lower-paid (often subordinate group) workers in jobs with little security and hazardous working conditions.

THE SPLIT LABOUR MARKET THEORY Who benefits from the exploitation of visible minorities? The split labour market theory states that both white workers and members of the capitalist class benefit from the exploitation of visible minorities. **Split labour market** refers to the division of the economy into two areas of employment: a primary sector, or upper tier, composed of higher-paid (usually dominant group) workers in more secure jobs, and a secondary sector, or lower tier, made up of lower-paid (often subordinate group) workers in jobs with little security and hazardous working conditions (Bonacich, 1972, 1976). According to this perspective, white workers in the upper tier may use racial discrimination against nonwhites to protect their positions. These actions most often occur when upper-tier workers feel threatened by lower-tier workers hired by capitalists to reduce labour costs and maximize corporate profits. In the past, immigrants were a source of cheap labour that employers could use to break strikes and keep wages down. Agnes Calliste (1987) applied the split labour market theory in her study of sleeping-car porters in Canada. Calliste found a doubly submerged split labour market with three levels of stratification in this area of employment. While "white" trade unions were unable to

The effects of past colonialism are reflected in the poor housing conditions of many Aboriginal persons living on reserves today.

restrict access to porter positions on the basis of race, they were able to impose differential pay scales. Consequently, black porters received less pay than white porters, even though they were doing the same work. Furthermore, the labour market was doubly submerged because black immigrant workers from the United States received even less pay than both black and white Canadian porters. Throughout history, higher-paid workers have responded with racial hostility and joined movements to curtail immigration and thus do away with the source of cheap labour (Marger, 2009).

Proponents of the split labour market theory suggest that white workers benefit from racial and ethnic antagonisms. However, these analysts typically do not examine the interactive effects of race, class, and gender in the workplace.

Feminist Perspectives

Minority women (women of colour, immigrant women, and Aboriginal women) are doubly disadvantaged as a result of their gender. The term *gendered racism* refers to the interactive effect of racism and sexism in the exploitation of women of colour. According to social psychologist Philomena Essed (1991), women's particular position must be explored within each racial or ethnic group, because their experiences will not have been the same as the men's in each grouping. For example, university-educated immigrant women have a more difficult time finding a job than university-educated male immigrants.

Capitalists do not equally exploit all workers. Gender and race or ethnicity are important in this exploitation. Historically, the high-paying primary labour market has been monopolized by white men. People of colour and most white women more often hold lower-tier jobs (Arat-Koc, 1999). Below that tier is the underground sector of the economy, characterized by illegal or quasi-legal activities, such as drug trafficking, prostitution, and working in sweatshops that do not meet minimum wage and safety standards. Many undocumented workers and some white women and people of colour attempt to earn a living in this sector (Amott and Matthaei, 1991).

Postmodern Perspectives

Conventional theories of race and ethnicity tend to see racial or ethnic identities as organized around social structures that are fixed and closed, such as nations, tribes, bands, and communities. As such, there is little movement in or out of these groups. Postmodern perspectives, in contrast, view ethnic and racial identities as largely a consequence of personal choice and subjective definition. Ethnic and racial identities are socially constructed and given meaning by our fragmented society. These identities are constantly evolving and subject to the continuous interplay of history, power, and culture.

A postmodernist framework may ask how social actors come to understand who they are in "race" terms. Central to a postmodern perspective on race is the concept of *discourse.* Based on the work of Michael Foucault, *discourse* is used to refer to "different ways of structuring knowledge and social practice" (Fiske, 1994, cited in Henry and Tator, 2006). Postmodernists view reality as constructed through a broad range of discourses, which includes all that is written, spoken, or otherwise represented through language and communication systems (Anderson, 2006:394). Analysts using this perspective focus on *deconstructing,* which means analyzing the assumptions and meanings embedded in scientific works (Anderson, 2006).

Postmodernist scholars use this perspective to shift the frame of analysis away from race relations to an examination (deconstruction) of racist discourse. *Racist discourse,* or *racialized discourse,* is defined as a collection of words, images, and practices through which racial power is directed against ethnic and racial minority groups. An analysis of racist discourse is central to understanding the ways in which a particular society gives a voice to racism and advances the interests of whites.

Frances Henry and Carol Tator (2006) have identified examples of racist discourse that serve to sustain or perpetuate racism in our society. For example, the *discourse of denial* suggests that racism does not exist in our Canadian democratic society. When racism is shown to exist, the discourse of denial will explain it away as an isolated incident rather than an indication of systemic racism. There are numerous examples of the discourse of denial in policing agencies across the country. Despite numerous complaints of racism directed at visible minority groups and Aboriginal persons, police agencies continue to respond to allegations with, "We don't have a problem with racism within our organization," or "I have never witnessed a racist incident."

A second, related, discourse identified by Henry and Tator is "the discourse of colour-blindness," in which white people insist that they do not notice the skin colour of a racial minority. In doing so, white people also fail to "recognize that race is a part of the 'baggage' that people of colour carry with them, and the refusal to recognize racism as part of everyday values, policies, programs, and practices is part of the psychological power of racial constructions" (2006:25). By claiming to be colour-blind, members of the dominant white majority are allowed to ignore the power differentials they experience as a result of their "whiteness," as well as negating the racialized experiences of visible minority persons.

A postmodern perspective not only examines how identities of racial and ethnic minorities are formed, but also asks the same question about white identities. For example:

> [W]hite people are "raced" just as men are "gendered." And in a social context where white people have too often viewed themselves as nonracial or racially neutral, it is crucial to look at the "racialness" of the white experience . . . Whiteness is first a location of structural advantage of race privilege. Second, a "standpoint," a place from which white people look at ourselves, at others, at society. Third, "whiteness" refers to a set of cultural practices that are usually unmarked and unnamed. (Frankenberg, 1993, cited in Gann, 2000)

An Alternative Perspective: Critical Race Theory

Emerging out of scholarly law studies on racial and ethnic inequality, critical race theory derives its foundation from the U.S. civil rights tradition and the writing of people like Martin Luther King, Jr., W.E.B. Du Bois, Malcolm X, and Cesar Chavez. The growth of critical race theory began in Canada during the 1980s, and it is based on the same theoretical foundation as its American counterpart; that is, a growing dissatisfaction with the failure to acknowledge and recognize the critical roles that race and racism have played in the political and legal structures of Canadian society (Aylward, 1999).

Critical race theory has several major premises, including the belief that racism is such an ingrained feature of North American society that it appears to be ordinary and natural to many people (Delgado, 1995). As a result, civil rights legislation and affirmative action laws (formal equality) may remedy some of the more overt, blatant forms of racial injustice but have little effect on subtle, business-as-usual forms of racism that people of colour experience as they go about their everyday lives. According to this approach, the best way to document racism and ongoing inequality in society is to listen to the lived experiences of people who have experienced such discrimination. In this way, we can learn what actually happens in regard to racial oppression and the many effects it has on people, including alienation, depression, and certain physical illnesses (Razack, 1998).

Central to this argument is the belief that *interest convergence* is a crucial factor in bringing about social change. According to the legal scholar Derrick Bell, white elites tolerate or encourage racial advances for people of colour *only* if the dominant-group members believe that their own self-interest will be served in so doing (cited in Delgado, 1995). From this approach, civil rights laws have typically benefited white North Americans as much as (or more than) people of colour because these laws have been used as mechanisms to ensure that "racial progress occurs at just the right pace: change that is too rapid would be unsettling to society at large; change that is too slow could prove destabilizing" (Delgado, 1995:xiv).

Critical race theory is similar to postmodernist approaches in that it calls our attention to the fact that things are not always as they seem. Formal equality under the law does not necessarily equate to actual equality in society.

LO-4 ETHNIC GROUPS IN CANADA

How do racial and ethnic groups come into contact with one another? How do they adjust to one another and to the dominant group over time? Sociologists have explored these questions extensively; however, a detailed historical account of each group is beyond the scope of this chapter. Given the diversity of our population, imposing any kind of conceptual order on a discussion of ethnic groups in Canada is difficult. We will look briefly at some of the predominant ethnic groups in Canada. In the process, we will examine a brief history of racism with respect to each group.

CONCEPT SNAPSHOT

SYMBOLIC INTERACTIONIST PERSPECTIVES	Symbolic interactionists examine how microlevel contacts between individuals may produce greater racial tolerance or increase levels of hostility. According to the contact hypothesis, when members of divergent groups have equal status, shared goals, cooperation, and positive feedback, favourable attitudes and behaviour between groups can result.
FUNCTIONALIST PERSPECTIVES	Early functionalists examined immigration and patterns of majority and minority group interaction Intergroup processes include cultural, biological, structural, and psychological assimilation and ethnic pluralism—equalitarian and inequalitarian pluralism (segregation).
CONFLICT PERSPECTIVES	Conflict theorists focus on power and economic differentials between dominant and subordinate groups. Internal colonialism occurs when members of racial or ethnic groups are conquered or colonized and forcibly controlled by the dominant group. Split labour market theory examines the division of the economy into two unequal areas of employment.
FEMINIST PERSPECTIVES	Feminist perspectives highlight the fact that minority women are doubly disadvantaged as a result of their gender. *Gendered racism* describes the interactive effect of racism and sexism in the exploitation of visible minority women.
POSTMODERN PERSPECTIVES	Postmodern perspectives view racial and ethnic identities as socially constructed through a range of discourses. Postmodern perspectives focus is deconstructing racialized and racist discourse that serves to sustain and reinforce patterns of discrimination against racial and ethnic minorities.
CRITICAL RACE THEORY	Critical race theorists believe that racism is such an ingrained feature of society that it appears to be ordinary and natural to many. According to critical race theorists, human rights legislation and employment equity strategies may remedy overt discrimination but have little effect on subtle racism. Interest convergence is required to effect positive change for visible minority group members.

Aboriginal Peoples

Canada's Aboriginal peoples are believed to have migrated to North America from Asia about 14,000 years ago. The term *Aboriginal* itself refers to the "first," or indigenous, occupants of this country (Fleras and Elliott, 2003). Aboriginal peoples are an extremely diverse group with varying access to resources, development levels, and social health. Today, the terms *Native, First Nations,* or *Aboriginal* refer to over 600 bands across the country with approximately 50 Aboriginal languages, including Inuktitut, Cree, Ojibway, Wakashan, and Haida. Other categories of Aboriginal peoples are status Indians (those Indians with legal rights under the *Indian Act),* nonstatus Indians (those without legal rights), Métis, and Inuit. Those who settled in the southern part of Canada, Yukon, and the Mackenzie Valley can be termed *North American Indians.* Those located in the eastern Arctic and northern islands, who were formerly referred to as Eskimos, are now referred to as *Inuit.* A third category, *Métis,* who live mostly on the Prairies, are descendants of Indian and non-Indian unions (primarily French settlers and Indian women) (Dyck, 2008).

When European settlers arrived on this continent, the Aboriginal inhabitants' way of life was changed forever. Experts estimate that approximately two million Aboriginal people lived in North America at the time of contact; by 1900, however, their numbers had been reduced to under 240,000. What factors led to this drastic depopulation?

GENOCIDE, FORCED MIGRATION, AND FORCED ASSIMILATION Aboriginal people have been the victims of genocide and forced migration. Many Native Americans were either massacred or died from European diseases (such as typhoid, smallpox, and measles) and starvation (Cook, 1973; Wagner and Stearn, 1945). In battle, Aboriginal people often were no match for the Europeans, who had the latest weaponry (Amott and Matthaei, 1991). Europeans justified their aggression by stereotyping Aboriginals as "savages" and "heathens" (Frideres and Gadacz, 2004).

Aboriginal nations were forced to move in order to accommodate the white settlers. The "Trail of Tears" was one of the most disastrous of the forced migrations to occur in North America. In the coldest part of the winter of 1832, more than half of the Cherokee Nation died during or as a result of their forced relocation from the southeastern United States to the Indian Territory in Oklahoma (Thornton, 1984).

First Nations rights were clearly defined in the *Royal Proclamation* of 1763, which divided up the territory acquired by Britain. In the large area called the Indian Territory, the purchase or settlement of land was forbidden without a treaty (Dyck, 1996:154). The government broke treaty after treaty as it engaged in a policy of wholesale removal of Indigenous nations to clear the land for settlement by Anglo-Saxon "pioneers" (Green, 1977). The Canadian government then passed the *Indian Act* of 1876, which provided for federal government control of almost every aspect of Indian life. The regulations under the act included prohibitions against owning land, voting, purchasing and consuming alcohol, and leaving reserves without permission and a ticket from the government's agent (Frideres and Gadacz, 2005).

Aboriginal children were placed in residential boarding schools to facilitate their assimilation into the dominant culture. The Jesuits and other missionaries who ran these schools believed that Aboriginal peoples should not be left in their "inferior" natural state and considered it their mission to replace Aboriginal culture with Christian beliefs, values, rituals, and practices (Bolaria and Li, 1988). Many Aboriginal children who attended these schools were sexually, physically, and emotionally abused. They were not allowed to speak their language or engage in any of their traditional cultural practices. The coercive and oppressive nature of this educational experience is one of the most blatant examples of institutionalized racism (Henry et al., 1996:62). It was not until 2008 that Prime Minister Stephen Harper offered a formal apology acknowledging that the policy of forced assimilation "was wrong, has caused great harm, and has no place in our country" and that the treatment of children in residential schools "is a sad chapter in our history" (CBC News, 2008).

ABORIGINAL PEOPLES TODAY According to the 2006 Census, more than one million people reported they were Aboriginal, including 698,025 First Nations (North American Indian), 389,785 Métis, and 50,485 Inuit. These numbers represent approximately 4 percent of Canada's total population (Statistics Canada, 2008b). Figure 10.1 displays the composition of the Aboriginal population. Although the majority of registered Indians live on reserves, the majority of all Aboriginal people live off reserves. The Aboriginal population is unevenly distributed across Canada, with the heaviest concentrations in western and northern Canada.

The results of government assimilationist policies, forced segregation, and discrimination continue to be experienced by First Nations children, youth and families across the country. In terms of income, employment, housing, nutrition, and health, Aboriginal peoples are the most disadvantaged racial or ethnic group in Canada (Frideres, 2007). The life chances of Aboriginal peoples who live on reserves are especially limited. According to a United Nations report, First Nations children in Western countries live in Third World conditions, with an estimated 80 percent of urban Aboriginal children under the age of six living in poverty. Aboriginal people living in urban areas were more than twice as likely as non-Aboriginal people to live in poverty. And the number of Aboriginal children involved with the child welfare system across Canada continues to grow. In some provinces, over 95 percent of children involved with family services are Aboriginal. Aboriginal peoples have the highest rates of infant mortality and death by exposure and malnutrition, as well as high rates of tuberculosis, alcoholism, and suicide (Frideres, 2007). The overall life expectancy of Aboriginal people in Canada is five years less than that of non-Aboriginals, largely due to poor health services and inadequate housing on reserves. Aboriginal peoples also have had limited educational opportunities (the functional illiteracy rate for Aboriginal peoples is 45 percent, compared with the overall Canadian rate of 17 percent).

Economic disadvantage is reflected in both employment and income inequality among First Nations populations. Their rate of unemployment is twice that for non-Aboriginal Canadians. On reserves, the unemployment rate is about 29 percent, nearly three times the Canadian rate (Frideres, 2007). Finally, incomes for Aboriginal persons are about two-thirds the level of non-Aboriginals. For First Nations people on reserves, average incomes are less than half the rest of the population's incomes (National Aboriginal Economic Development Board, 2012).

Despite the state's efforts to assimilate Aboriginal peoples into Canadian culture and society, many Aboriginal people have been successful in resisting oppression. National organizations like the Assembly of First Nations, Inuit Tapiriit Kanatami, the Native Council of Canada, and the Métis National Council have been instrumental in bringing the demands of those they represent into the political and

FIGURE 10.1 ABORIGINAL IDENTITY POPULATION, 2006

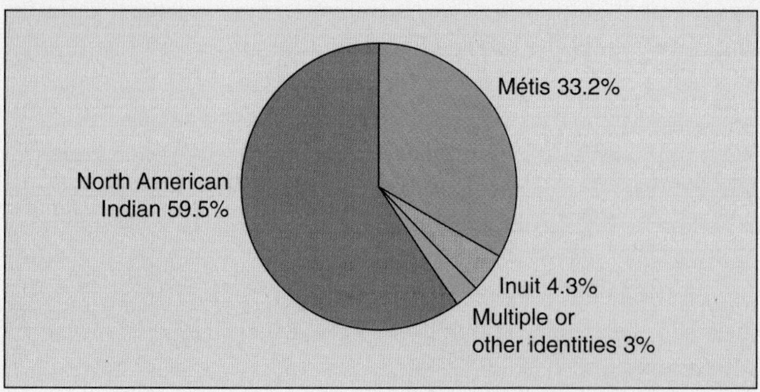

Note: Some respondents indicated they consider themselves members of more than one Aboriginal group.

Source: Statistics Canada, Census of Population, 2006, found at: http://www12.statcan.ca/english/census06/data/highlights/Aboriginal/index.cfm?Lang=E

constitutional arenas. Of these demands, the major ones have been—and still are—self-government, Aboriginal rights, and the resolution of land claims (see Frideres and Gadacz, 2005).

Aboriginal peoples today are in a period of transition from a long history marked by racism, exploitation, and domination to a contemporary life in which they are regaining control of programs directed at protecting their children, delivering education, and promoting and restoring health and commerce in Aboriginal communities. Many see the challenge for Aboriginal peoples today as being to erase negative stereotypes while maintaining their heritage and obtaining recognition for their contribution to this country's development and growth. A report released in 2012 indicated that Aboriginal Canadians are making some measurable progress toward improving their economic outcomes. However, as Chief Clarence Louie comments:

> Significant gaps remain between Aboriginal and non-Aboriginal Canadians. Clearly, much of our economic potential remains unrealized, and there is still much work to be done before Aboriginal Canadians are in the same position as other Canadians to contribute to and benefit from one of the world's wealthiest economies. (National Aboriginal Economic Development Board, 2012:5)

The North American Indigenous Games, held on Vancouver Island in 2008, are a reflection of Aboriginal peoples' sustained efforts to maintain their unique cultures. For thousands of years before European contact, Aboriginal peoples held games throughout North America.

The Québécois

The French were the first Europeans to immigrate to Canada in large numbers, establishing settlements in what was then known as Acadia and along the St. Lawrence River. In 1608, the first permanent settlement in New France was established at Quebec City. At this time, France's North American empire extended from Hudson Bay to Louisiana.

Following the British conquest of the French in Canada in the Seven Years' War (1756–1763), Canada became a British dominion and the French found themselves in an inferior position (Weinfeld, 1995). However, given the numerical dominance of the French, their links to the fur trade, and the fact that the French colony shared a border with the United States, the British felt it advantageous to accommodate the French. What emerged was a plural, or segmented, society in which the French were able to maintain French civil law, language, and religion; however, the overall economic, social, and political power passed to English Canada (Breton, 1988).

The British North America Act (1867) formally acknowledged the rights and privileges of the French and British as the founding, or charter, groups of Canadian society. French was recognized as an official language in Quebec and the provincial government in Quebec was able to maintain significant authority over culture and education. The Catholic Church was also able to retain control over educational and religious matters and many other aspects of Quebec society. During this time, it was assumed that in the future, French- and English-speaking groups would coexist and complement one another. However, during the period between Confederation and World War II, the French struggled for cultural survival because English-speaking Canadians controlled the major economic institutions in both English Canada and Quebec. During the early 1960s, the Catholic Church's control began to erode and the old elite consensus began to break down, laying the foundation for what was described as the Quiet Revolution (Satzewich and Liodakis, 2007).

During the Quiet Revolution (1960–1966), Quebec nationalism grew sharply. Under the leadership of Premier Jean Lesage, Quebec began undergoing a rapid process of modernization. During this time, the authority of the Catholic Church over the educational system was reduced as the Quebec government established a department of education. More French Canadians began pursuing higher education, particularly in business and science. The Church also lost some of its influence over moral issues, which was reflected in a declining birth rate and an increase in common-law marriages. Finally, nonfrancophone immigrants were challenging French culture by choosing to learn English and having their children learn English rather than French. Francophones came to view their language and culture as endangered, and as a result, many rejected their Canadian identity and adopted a distinctly Québécois identity.

In the 1970s, the separatist Parti Québécois was elected under the leadership of Premier René Lévesque. During this time, the controversial Bill 101 was introduced and established French as the sole official language in Quebec. In 1980, the Parti Québécois held a referendum on the question of pursuing a more independent relationship with Canada called *sovereignty association.* The proposal was narrowly rejected, but the matter was once again addressed in a second referendum in 1995 (Dyck, 2000). Although Quebeckers once again rejected sovereignty (this time by a narrow margin of 1 percent) the issue remains controversial (see Chapter 20).

FRENCH CANADIANS TODAY Today, almost 23 percent of the Canadian population is francophone, of which 85 percent is located in Quebec; 81 percent of Quebeckers are French-speaking and over 90 percent of French-speaking Canadians live in Quebec (Dyck, 2008). Many Quebec nationalists now see independence or separation as the ultimate protection against cultural and linguistic assimilation, as well as the route to economic power. As political scientist Rand Dyck comments:

> Given their historic constitutional rights, given their geographic concentration in Quebec and majority control of such a large province, and given their modern-day self-consciousness and self-confidence, the French fact in Canada cannot be ignored. If English Canada wants Quebec to remain a part of the country, it cannot go back to the easy days of pre-1960 unilingualism and federal government centralization. (2008:116)

French Canadians have at least forced Canada to take its second language and culture seriously, which is an important step toward attaining cultural pluralism.

Canada's Multicultural Minorities

Home to approximately six million foreign-born immigrants, Canada is well described as a land of immigrants. Approximately 75 percent of immigrants arriving in Canada today are members of a visible minority group (Statistics Canada, 2008). But Canada's policies toward some of these groups have been far from exemplary. In fact, initial Canadian immigration policies have been described as essentially racist in orientation, assimilationist in intent, and exclusionary in outcome. For example, the *Immigration Act* of 1869 excluded certain types of undesirables, such as criminals and the diseased, and imposed strict limitations on the Japanese, Chinese, and East Asians. A "racial pecking order" was established to select potential immigrants on the basis of race and perceived ability for assimilation (Lupul, 1988; Walker, 1997, cited in Fleras and Elliott, 2003). As much energy was expended in keeping out certain "types" as was put into encouraging others to settle.

A preferred category was that of *white ethnics*—a term coined to identify immigrants who came from European countries other than England, such as Scotland, Ireland, Poland, Italy, Greece, Germany, Yugoslavia, and Russia and other former Soviet republics. Immigration from "white" countries was encouraged to ensure the British character of Canada. With the exception of visa formalities, this category of "preferred" immigrants was virtually exempt from entry restrictions (Fleras and Elliott, 2003:253). On the other hand, Jews and other Mediterranean populations required special permits for entry, and Asian populations were admitted only because they could serve as cheap labour for Canadian capitalist expansion. The restrictions regarding the Chinese, Japanese, and Jews highlighted the racist dimension of Canada's early immigration policies (Satzewich, 1998).

© Al Harvey

As more Chinese Canadians have made gains in education and employment, many have also made a conscious effort to increase awareness of Chinese culture and develop a sense of unity and cooperation. This Chinese dragon parade exemplifies the desire to maintain traditional celebrations.

CHINESE CANADIANS The initial wave of Chinese migrants came to Canada in the 1850s, when Chinese men were attracted to emigrate by the British Columbia gold rush and by employment opportunities created by the expansion of a national railroad. Nearly 17,000 Chinese were brought to Canada at this time to lay track for the Canadian Pacific Railway. The work was brutally hard and dangerous, living conditions were appalling, food and shelter were insufficient, and due to scurvy and smallpox the fatality rate was high. These immigrants were "welcomed" only as long as there was a shortage of white workers. However, they were not permitted to bring their wives and children with them or to have sexual relations with white women, because of the fear they would spread the "yellow menace" (Henry and Tator, 2006).

The Chinese were subjected to extreme prejudice and were referred to by derogatory terms, such as *coolies, heathens,* and *Chinks.* Some were attacked by working-class whites who feared they would lose their jobs to Chinese immigrants. In 1885, the federal government passed its first anti-Chinese bill, the purpose of which was to limit Chinese immigration, and a $50 head tax was imposed on all Chinese males arriving in Canada. In 1903, the tax was raised to $500 in a further attempt to restrict entry to Canada (Satzewich and Loidakis, 2007). Other hostile legislation included a range of racist exclusionary policies, such as prohibiting the Chinese from voting, serving in public office, serving on juries, participating in white labour unions, and working in the professions of law and pharmacy. Not until after World War II were these discriminatory policies removed from the *Immigration Act.* After immigration laws were further relaxed in the 1960s, the second and largest wave of Chinese immigration occurred, with immigrants coming primarily from Hong Kong and Taiwan (Henry and Tator, 2006).

JAPANESE CANADIANS When Japanese Canadians first arrived in British Columbia in the 1870s, they experienced similar discriminatory policies and practices. Like Chinese immigrants two decades earlier, the Japanese were viewed as a threat by white workers and became victims of racism and discrimination. They were paid lower wages than white labourers, had restrictions placed on their fishing licences, and were segregated in schools and public places.

In 1907, an organization known as the Asiatic Exclusion League was formed with the goal of restricting admission of Asians to Canada. Following the arrival of a ship carrying more than a thousand Japanese and a few hundred Sikhs, the league carried out a demonstration that precipitated a race riot. After the riot, the Canadian government negotiated a "gentlemen's agreement" that permitted entry only of certain categories of Japanese persons. In this agreement, the government further allowed only 400 Japanese to immigrate to Canada in a given year (Henry and Tator, 2006).

Japanese Canadians also experienced one of the most vicious forms of discrimination ever sanctioned by Canadian law. During World War II, when Canada was at war with Japan, nearly 23,000 people of Japanese ancestry—13,300 of whom were Canadian-born—were placed in jails and internment camps, forced to work, and had their property confiscated. Those interned in camp were not released until two years after the war was over (Miki and Kobayashi, 1991). German immigrants avoided this fate even though Canada was at war with both Japan and Germany. Four decades after these events, the Canadian government issued an apology for its actions and agreed to pay $20,000 to each person who had been placed in an internment camp (Henry and Tator, 2006).

SOUTH ASIANS Immigrants from India were also subjected to widespread anti-immigration sentiments in the early 20th century. One of the first discriminatory immigration laws was the "continuous passage" rule of 1908, which specified that South Asians could immigrate only if they came directly from India and did not stop at any ports on the way. This law made it almost impossible for them to enter the country, since no ships made direct journeys from India. For example, in 1914, a Sikh businessman chartered a ship in Hong Kong to transport more than 300 Indian passengers to Canada. On arrival in Vancouver, the passengers were refused entry. After a two-month standoff, the ship was forced to return to India (Satzewich and Liodakis, 2007).

South Asians who did manage to immigrate to Canada were subject to ongoing exclusion and hostility. Their property and businesses were frequently attacked, and they were denied citizenship and the right to vote in British Columbia until 1947 (Henry and Tator, 2006). Because they were denied their political rights, they were also precluded from entering the more prestigious professions of law, medicine, education, and pharmacy.

JEWISH CANADIANS Between 1933 and 1945, many Jews sought refuge from the persecution of the Nazis. During this time, Canada admitted fewer Jewish refugees as a percentage of its population than any other Western country. In 1942, a ship carrying Jewish refugees from Europe attempted to land in Halifax and was denied entrance. Jews who did immigrate experienced widespread discrimination in employment, business, and education. Other indicators of anti-Semitism included restrictions on where Jews could live, buy property, and attend university. Signs posted along Toronto's beaches warned, "No dogs or Jews allowed." Many hotels and resorts had policies prohibiting Jews as guests (Abella and Troper, 1982, quoted in Henry and Tator, 2000:80).

IMMIGRATION TRENDS POST WORLD WAR II TO THE PRESENT LO-5

Although the more blatantly racist aspects of immigration policy were moderated after World War II, the underlying philosophy behind immigration to Canada retained its discriminatory agenda—immigration needed to be carefully controlled, the encouragement of nonwhite immigration was not in the best interests of the country, and any economic benefits of immigration needed to be measured against the potential "social costs" of unrestrained immigration of visible minority immigrants. This philosophy was clearly articulated by Prime Minister William Lyon Mackenzie King in a 1947 speech to the House of Commons:

> The people of Canada do not wish, as a result of mass immigration, to make a fundamental alteration in the character of our population. Large scale immigration from the Orient would change the fundamental composition of the Canadian population. Any considerable oriental immigration would, moreover, be certain to give rise to social and economic problems. (Canada, 1947: Debates of the House of Commons, cited in Satzewich and Liodakis, 2007)

After the war, some of the more overtly racist immigration legislation, such as the *Chinese Immigration Act* and the continuous journey stipulations, were repealed and immigration from India was permitted on a fixed quota basis of 300 persons per year. However, the focus of postwar immigration continued to be on the "preferred" white immigrants from Europe and the United States (Satzewich and Liodakis, 2007:54).

Changes to the *Immigration Act* in 1962 opened the door to immigration on a nonracial basis. Canada became one of the first countries in the world to announce that "any suitable qualified person from anywhere in the world" would be considered for immigration, based solely on the criteria of personal merit. Education, occupation, and language skills replaced ethnicity and nationality as criteria for admission (Fleras and Elliott, 2003). The criteria for immigration underwent further reform in 1967 when a *points system* was introduced. All applicants, regardless of origin or colour, were rated according to the total of points given for the following: job training, experience, skills, level of education, knowledge of English or French, degree of demand for the applicant's occupation, and job offers (Henry and Tator, 2006). Although, as shown in Figure 10.2, this act opened the doors to those from previously excluded countries, critics have suggested that it maintained some of the same racist policies. In 2002, in response to the numerous concerns of continued exclusionary and racist immigration practices, the *Immigration and Refugee Protection Act* was implemented. This act recognizes three classes of immigrants—economic, family class, and refugee—and reflects a more open policy with selection criteria based on language skills, education, age, employment experience, and a category called "adaptability" (Henry and Tator, 2006:78).

Growing Racial and Ethnic Diversity in Canada

Racial and ethnic diversity is increasing in Canada. This changing demographic pattern is largely the result of the elimination of overtly racist immigration policies and the opening up of immigration to low-income countries. Canada has evolved from a country largely inhabited

FIGURE 10.2 REGION OF BIRTH OF RECENT IMMIGRANTS TO CANADA, 1971 TO 2006

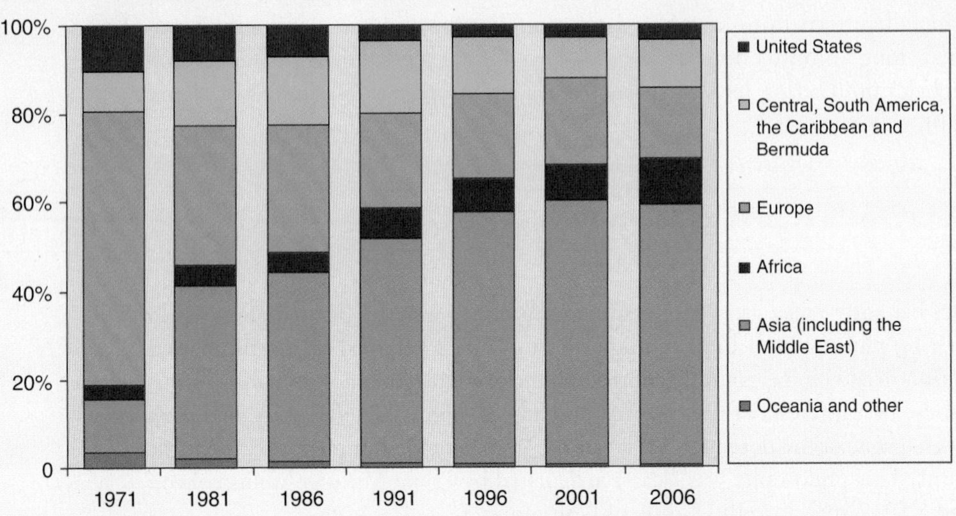

Notes:
1. "Recent immigrants" refers to landed immigrants who arrived in Canada within five years before a given census.
2. "Other" includes Greenland, St. Pierre and Miquelon, and the category "other country," as well as a small number of immigrants born in Canada.

Source: Chui, Tran, and Maheux, 2007.

by whites and Aboriginal peoples to a country made up of people from more than 70 countries. Today, people born outside of Canada make up more than 20 percent of the total population of Canada (see Figure 10.3). Newcomers from Asia make up the largest proportion of immigrants, followed by newcomers from Europe (Chui, Tran, and Maheux, 2007).

Almost all immigrants to Canada live in cities. Recent immigrants are especially attracted to Canada's three largest cities. The majority of recent immigrants have chosen to live in Toronto, Montreal, or Vancouver. Today, nearly half of the population of Toronto and nearly two-fifths of the population of Vancouver is composed of immigrants. As author Neil Bissoondath explains:

> In the new millennium Toronto, Canada's largest city, will mark an unusual milestone. In a city of three million, the words "minorities" and "majority" will be turned on their heads and the former will become the latter. Reputed to be the most ethnically diverse city in the world, Toronto has been utterly remade by immigration, just as Canada has been remade by a quarter of a century of multiculturalism. (1998:1)

What effect will these changes have on racial and ethnic relations? Several possibilities exist. On the one hand, conflict between whites and racial and ethnic minorities may become more overt and confrontational. Certainly, the concentration of visible minorities will mean that these groups will become more visible than ever in some Canadian cities. Increasing contact may lead to increased intergroup cohesion and understanding, or it may bring on racism or prejudice. Rapid political changes and the global economy have made people fearful about their future and may cause some to blame "foreigners" for their problems People may continue to use *discourses of denial*—personal beliefs that reflect larger societal mythologies, such as "I am not racist" or "I have never discriminated against anyone"—even when these are inaccurate perceptions (Henry and Tator, 2006).

FIGURE 10.3 NUMBER AND SHARE OF THE FOREIGN-BORN POPULATION IN CANADA, 1901 TO 2006

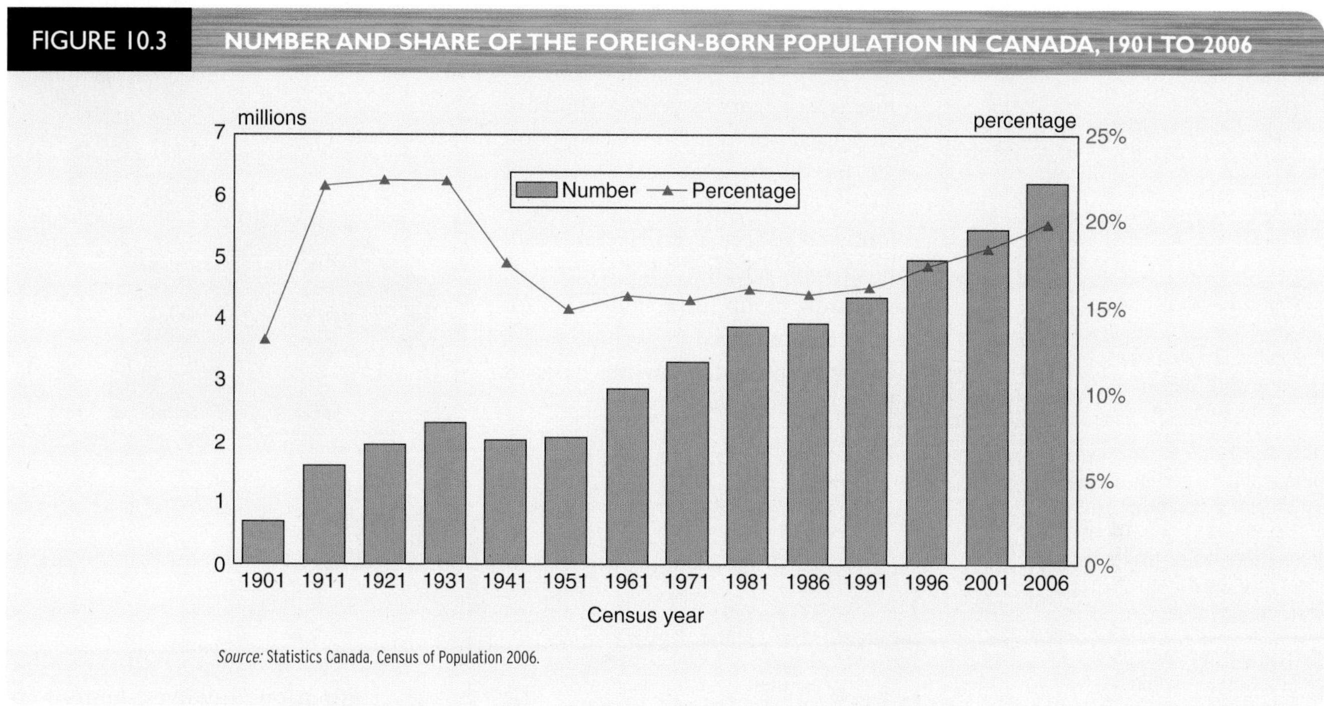

Source: Statistics Canada, Census of Population 2006.

On the other hand, there is reason for cautious optimism. Throughout Canadian history, subordinate racial and ethnic groups have struggled to gain the freedom and rights that were previously withheld from them. Today, employment equity programs are alleviating some of the effects of past discrimination against minority groups, as well as addressing systemic and institutional forms of racism that exist in employment. Movements made up of both whites and visible minorities continue to oppose racism in everyday life, to seek to heal divisions among racial groups, and to teach children about racial tolerance (Rutstein, 1993). Many groups hope not only to affect their own countries but also to contribute to worldwide efforts to end racism (Ford, 1994).

10

VISUAL SUMMARY

LO-1 Distinguish between race and ethnicity.

A race is a category of people who have been singled out as inferior or superior, often on the basis of real or alleged physical characteristics, such as skin colour, hair texture, eye shape, or other subjectively selected characteristics. An ethnic group is a collection of people distinguished by others or by themselves, primarily on the basis of culture or nationality.

© CP/Kevin Frayer

© Clark Brennan/Alamy

LO-2 Define and explain prejudice, discrimination, and racism.

Prejudice involves attitudes, but discrimination involves actions or practices of dominant group members that have a harmful impact on members of a subordinate group. Discriminatory actions range from name-calling to violent actions and can be either *de jure* (encoded in law) or *de facto* (informal). *Racism* refers to an organized set of beliefs about the innate inferiority of some racial groups, combined with the power to discriminate on the basis of race. There are many different ways in which racism may manifest itself, including overt racism, polite racism, subliminal racism, and institutionalized racism.

LO-3 Explain the major sociological perspectives on race and ethnic relations.

© A. Gottfried/The Image Works

Interactionists suggest that increased contact between people from divergent groups should lead to favourable attitudes and behaviour when members of each group (1) have equal status, (2) pursue the same goals, (3) cooperate with one another to achieve goals, and (4) receive positive feedback when they interact with one another. Functionalists stress that members of subordinate groups become absorbed into the dominant culture. Conflict theorists focus on economic stratification and access to power in race and ethnic relations. Feminist analysts highlight the fact that women who are members of racial and ethnic minorities are doubly disadvantaged as a result of their gender. There is an interactive effect of racism and sexism on the exploitation of women of colour. Postmodern theorists view racial and ethnic identities as fluid and examine how these concepts are socially constructed. Critical race theorists emphasize the significant role that race and racism have played in legal and political structures in society.

KEY TERMS

assimilation A process by which members of subordinate racial and ethnic groups become absorbed into the dominant culture (p. 283).

authoritarian personality A personality type characterized by excessive conformity, submissiveness to authority, intolerance, insecurity, a high level of superstition, and rigid, stereotypic thinking (p. 278).

discrimination Actions or practices of dominant group members (or their representatives) that have a harmful impact on members of a subordinate group (p. 278).

ethnic group A collection of people distinguished, by others or by themselves, primarily on the basis of cultural or nationality characteristics (p. 274).

ethnic pluralism The coexistence of a variety of distinct racial and ethnic groups within one society (p. 284).

institutionalized racism A situation where the established rules, policies, and practices within an institution or organization produce differential treatment of various groups based on race (p. 281).

internal colonialism According to conflict theorists, a situation in which members of a racial or ethnic group are conquered or colonized and forcibly placed under the economic and political control of the dominant group (p. 286).

majority (dominant) group An advantaged group that is advantaged and has superior resources and rights in a society (p. 276).

© CP PHOTO/Winnipeg Free Press - Jeff de Booy

LO-4 Discuss the unique historical experiences of the racial and ethnic groups in Canada.

When European settlers arrived on this continent, the Aboriginal inhabitants' were the victims of genocide and forced migration. Aboriginal children were placed in residential boarding schools to facilitate their assimilation into the dominant culture. Although the French were the first Europeans to immigrant to Canada in large numbers when they were defeated by the English following the seven years war they found themselves in an inferior position. Although the French were able to maintain French civil law, language, and religion; however, the overall economic, social, and political power passed to English Canada. Non-white immigrants (including Chinese, Japanese, and South Asians) were only welcomed into Canada as a source of cheap labour and were subject to racist laws and immigration policies.

LO-5 Describe how Canada's immigration policies have affected the composition of Canada's racial and ethnic population today.

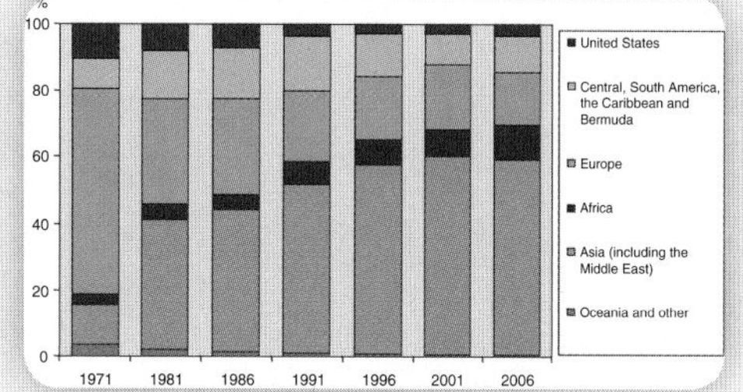

Canada's early immigration policies were described as racist and included exclusionary policies directed at Asian populations, including Chinese, Japanese, and South Asians, as well as Jews. "White ethnics" who came from European countries comprised the preferred category of immigrants. Changes to the *Immigration Act* in 1962 involving the implementation of a points system opened the door to immigration on a nonracial basis. In 2002, the *Immigration and Refugee Protection Act* was implemented, with selection criteria based on attributes of human capital and the skills of potential immigrants.

minority (subordinate) group A group whose members, because of physical or cultural characteristics, are disadvantaged and subjected to unequal treatment by the dominant group and who regard themselves as objects of collective discrimination (p. 276).

overt racism (or redneck or hate racism) Racism that may take the form of deliberate and highly personal attacks, including derogatory slurs and name-calling toward members of a racial or ethnic group who are perceived to be "inferior" (p. 279).

polite racism A term used to describe an attempt to disguise a dislike of others through behaviour that is outwardly nonprejudicial (p. 279).

prejudice A negative attitude based on preconceived notions about members of selected groups (p. 277).

race A term used by many people to specify groups of people distinguished by physical characteristics, such as skin colour; also, a category of people who have been singled out as inferior or superior, often on the basis of real or alleged physical characteristics, such as skin colour, hair texture, eye shape, or other subjectively selected attributes (p. 274).

racial prejudice Beliefs that certain racial groups are innately inferior to others or have a disproportionate number of negative traits (p. 277).

racism A set of ideas that implies the superiority of one social group over another on the basis of biological or cultural characteristics, together with the power to put these beliefs into practice in a way that denies or excludes minority women and men (p. 279).

scapegoat A person or group that is incapable of offering resistance to the hostility or aggression of others (p. 278).

segregation A term used to describe the spatial and social separation of categories of people by race/ethnicity, class, gender, and/or religion (p. 285).

split labour market A term used to describe the division of the economy into two areas of employment: a primary sector, or upper tier, composed of higher-paid (usually dominant group) workers in more secure jobs; and a secondary sector, or lower tier, composed of lower-paid (often subordinate group) workers in jobs with little security and hazardous working conditions (p. 287).

stereotype An overgeneralization about the appearance, behaviour, or other characteristics of members of particular groups (p. 277).

subliminal racism A term used to describe an unconscious racism that occurs when there is a conflict of values (p. 280).

visible minority An official government category of nonwhite, non-Caucasian individuals (p. 276).

KEY FIGURES

© World History Archive/Alamy

W.E.B. Du Bois (1868–1963) Born in Massachusetts, Du Bois was both a race relations scholar and a civil rights activist. Du Bois was the first African American to earn a PhD at Harvard University. Over the years, he became frustrated with the lack of progress in race relations and became a co-founder of the National Association for the Advancement of Colored People (NAACP).

Courtesy of Frances Henry

Frances Henry Now retired as a professor emerita from York University, Henry is one of Canada's leading experts in the study of racism and antiracism. Since the mid-1970s, when she published the first study of attitudes toward people of colour, she has consistently pioneered research in this field. She is co-author with Carol Tator of The Colour of Democracy: Racism in Canadian Society and more recently Racism in the Canadian University.

Courtesy of Carol Tator

Carol Tator Tator is the author of numerous books on racism in Canada, including *Racism in the Canadian University* and *Racial Profiling in Canada: Challenging the Myth of "A Few Bad Apples."* For more than three decades, she has worked on the front lines of the antiracism and equity movement in the areas of the development and implementation of antiracism policies and programs, strategic planning, training, and research.

APPLICATION QUESTIONS

1. Do you consider yourself defined more by your race, your ethnicity, or neither of these concepts? Explain.
2. Given that minority groups have some common experiences, why is there such deep conflict between certain minority groups?
3. What would need to happen in Canada, both individually and institutionally, for a positive form of ethnic pluralism to flourish in the 21st century?
4. Is it possible for members of racial minorities to be racist? Discuss.

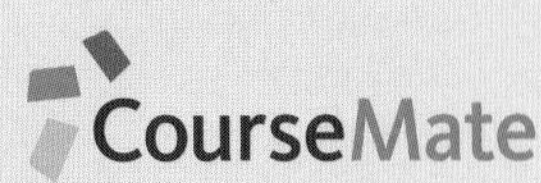

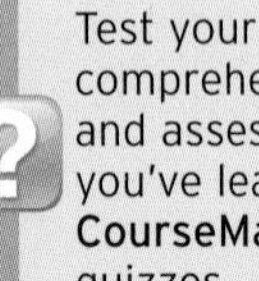

Test your comprehension and assess what you've learned with **CourseMate's** online quizzes.

For other interesting Lived Experiences, watch the video clips on **CourseMate.**

Practise what you've learned with flashcards containing key terms and definitions on **CourseMate.**

CHAPTER 11

Gender

Andrew Paterson/Alamy

Professor Ted Cohen describes an exercise he uses in his gender studies class to demonstrate the significance of gender in the lives of men and women:

> *Close your eyes and think carefully about what you believe life must be like for the "opposite sex." Then complete the following statements:*
>
> *"The best thing(s) about being a (male/female) in this society must surely be . . ."*
>
> *"The worst thing(s) about being a (male/female) in this society must surely be . . ."*

Professor Cohen has the male students answer the questions about being female and the female students respond to the statements about being male. Following is a summary of the most common responses by his students.

Women's Views of the Best Things About Being Male

- Higher pay, access to higher-status positions
- Respect
- Freedom of movement, less fear about safety and the possibility of rape
- No monthly periods, no PMS
- Not having to worry about pregnancy, childbirth, and child care
- Less concern about one's appearance

Women's Views of the Worst Things About Being Male

- Need to be stoic and emotionally strong, and tendency to be inexpressive
- Pressure to be the breadwinner or devote oneself to work
- Depleted emotional or physical health: earlier death
- Restricted intimacy

Men's Views of the Best Things About Being Female

- Freedom to show feelings, especially vulnerability or affection
- Ability to choose—though within limits—whether to work outside the home or raise children
- Depth of connection felt in relationships
- Giving birth
- Longer life span

Men's Views of the Worst Things About Being Female

- Being sexually harassed, assaulted, or objectified
- Being judged and related to so much in terms of one's appearance
- Being underpaid, occupationally segregated, and discriminated against
- Having so much responsibility for children, families, and households

- Having to think so much about one's safety and potential vulnerability
- Being trivialized in conversation and patronized in relationships*

This exercise highlights the significant impact that gender has on our lives. As Professor Cohen explains, gender both constrains and enables us. To further emphasize the impact of "gender," he asks his students one last question:

> *Imagine and describe how your life would differ if you had been born and were living as the opposite sex.* (2001:2-3)

Although significant gains have been made in recent years, the responses of Professor Cohen's students clearly demonstrate that gender inequality still exists. As this exercise further demonstrates, this inequality has negative consequences for both men and women. Young men and women continue to live "gendered lives" with societal "scripts" that impose accepted parameters of being male or female. Specific ideas of femininity and masculinity are inescapable products of the society in which we are socialized. Although significant changes have occurred in the last half of the 20th century in terms of work activities, notions of gender remain firmly embedded in social institutions and relationships. Gender is so much a part of who we are that it often goes unexamined. As sociologist Judith Lorber explains, we often take gender and the profound effect it has on our lives for granted:

*From Cohen, *Men and Masculinity*, 1E. © 2001 Cengage Learning.

> *Gender is so much the routine ground of everyday activities that questioning its taken-for-granted assumptions and presuppositions is like thinking about whether the sun will come up. Gender is so pervasive that in our society we assume it is bred into our genes. Most people find it hard to believe that gender is constantly created and re-created out of human interaction, out of social life, and is the texture and order of that social life. Gender, like culture, is a human production that depends on everyone constantly "doing gender."* (2001:19)

In this chapter, we will examine the issue of gender: what it is and how it affects us. Before reading on, test your knowledge about gender inequality by taking the quiz in Box 11.1 on page 306.

Critical Thinking Questions

1. How would you respond to Professor Cohen's questions? What would you identify as the best and worst aspects of being female or male in today's society?
2. How would you answer Professor Cohen's follow-up question? Describe how your life would differ if you had been born and were living as the opposite sex.
3. What do your answers reveal about gender equality?

CHAPTER FOCUS QUESTION

What effect does gender inequality have on men and women?

LEARNING OBJECTIVES

AFTER READING THIS CHAPTER, YOU SHOULD BE ABLE TO

LO-1 Understand how gender is defined and how it differs from "sex."

LO-2 Explain the significance of gender in our everyday lives.

LO-3 Discuss how the nature of work affects gender equality in societies

LO-4 Identify and discuss the primary agents of gender socialization.

LO-5 Explain the causes of gender inequality in Canada.

LO-6 Understand how functionalist, conflict, feminist, and interactionist perspectives on gender stratification differ.

BOX 11.1 **SOCIOLOGY AND EVERYDAY LIFE**

How Much Do You Know About Gender Inequality?

True	False	
T	F	1. The average earnings of employed women are still substantially lower than those of men, even when they are employed full time.
T	F	2. Men continue to outnumber women in Canadian universities.
T	F	3. Most Canadians living in poverty are female.
T	F	4. Men in Canada have a shorter life expectancy than women.
T	F	5. Married couples today who both work full time tend to share the "unpaid labour" fairly equally.

For answers to the quiz about gender inequality, go to **www.nelson.com/sociologyinourtimes6e.**

LO-1 UNDERSTANDING GENDER

gender The culturally and socially constructed differences between females and males found in the meanings, beliefs, and practices associated with "femininity" and "masculinity."

Gender refers to the culturally and socially constructed differences between females and males found in the meanings, beliefs, and practices associated with "femininity" and "masculinity." In contrast, as we will see in Chapter 12, *sex* refers to the biological and anatomical differences between females and males. Although biological differences between women and men are important, most "sex differences" are socially constructed "gender differences." According to sociologists, social and cultural processes—not biological "givens"—are most important in defining what females and males are, what they should do, and what sorts of relations do or should exist between them. Sociologist Judith Lorber summarizes the importance of gender:

> Gender is a human invention, like language, kinship, religion, and technology; like them, gender organizes human social life in culturally patterned ways. Gender organizes social relations in everyday life as well as in the major social structures, such as social class and the hierarchies of bureaucratic organizations. (1994:6)

Virtually everything social in our lives is *gendered:* People continually distinguish between males and females and evaluate them differentially. Gender is an integral part of the daily experiences of both women and men (Mandell, 2001).

gender role Attitudes, behaviour, and activities that are socially defined as appropriate for each sex and are learned through the socialization process.

gender identity A person's perception of the self as female or male.

A microlevel analysis of gender focuses on how individuals learn gender roles and acquire a gender identity. **Gender role** refers to the attitudes, behaviour, and activities that are socially defined as appropriate for each sex and are learned through the socialization process (Lips, 2007). For example, in Canadian society, males traditionally are expected to demonstrate aggressiveness and toughness, while females are expected to be passive and nurturing. **Gender identity** is a person's perception of the self as female or male. Typically established between 18 months and three years of age, gender identity is a powerful aspect of our self-concept (Lips, 2007). Although this identity is an individual perception, it is developed through interaction with others. As a result, most people form a gender identity that matches their biological sex: Most biological females think of themselves as female and most biological males think of themselves as male.

A macrolevel analysis of gender examines structural features, external to the individual, that perpetuate gender inequality. These structures have been referred to as *gendered institutions,* meaning that gender is one of the major ways by which social life is organized in all sectors of society. Gender is embedded in the images, ideas, and language of a society and is used as a means to divide up work, allocate resources, and distribute power. For example, every society uses gender to assign certain tasks—ranging from child rearing to warfare—to females and males, and differentially rewards those who perform these duties.

These institutions are reinforced by a *gender belief system* that includes all of the ideas regarding masculine and feminine attributes that are held to be valid in a society. This belief system is legitimated by religion, science, law, and other societal values (Lorber, 2005). For example, gendered belief systems may change over time as gender roles change. Many fathers take care of young children today, and there is a much greater acceptance of this change in roles. However, popular stereotypes about men and women, as well as cultural norms about gender-appropriate appearance and behaviour, serve to reinforce gendered institutions in society.

LO-2 The Social Significance of Gender

Gender is a social construction with important consequences in everyday life. Just as stereotypes regarding race and ethnicity have built-in notions of superiority and inferiority, gender stereotypes hold that men and women are inherently different in attributes, behaviour, and aspirations. Stereotypes define men as strong, rational, dominant, independent, and less concerned with their appearance. Women are stereotyped as weak, emotional, nurturing, dependent, and anxious about their appearance.

The social significance of gender stereotypes is illustrated by eating problems. The three most common eating problems are anorexia, bulimia, and obesity. With *anorexia,* a person must have lost at least 25 percent of body weight due to a compulsive fear of becoming fat (Ressler, 1998). With *bulimia,* a person binges by consuming large quantities of food and then purges the food by induced vomiting, laxatives, or fasting (Renzetti and Curran, 1992). A relatively new eating disorder—activity bulimia—may become more dangerous than both anorexia and bulimia. *Activity bulimia* is characterized by excessive exercising, usually attached to feelings of guilt about eating. The danger with this eating disorder is that it is virtually impossible to detect until serious health problems arise (Sharell, 1996). With *obesity,* individuals are 20 percent or more above their ideal weight, as established by the medical profession. For a woman 1.7 m (5 ft., 4 in.) tall, that is about 11 kg (25 lbs); for a man 1.8 m (5 ft., 10 in.) tall, that is about 13.5 kg (30 lbs) (Burros, 1994:1).

Sociologist Becky W. Thompson argues that, based on stereotypes, the primary victims of eating problems are presumed to be white, middle-class, heterosexual women. However, such problems also exist among women of colour, working-class women, lesbians, and some men. According to Thompson, explanations for the relationship between gender and eating problems must take into account a complex array of social factors, including gender socialization and women's responses to problems such as racism and emotional, physical, and sexual abuse (Thompson, 1994; see also Heywood, 1998).

Bodybuilding is another gendered experience. *Bodybuilding* is the process of deliberately cultivating an increase in mass

© Fabio Cardoso/zefa/Corbis

For males, objectification and gender stereotyping may result in excessive bodybuilding.

and strength of the skeletal muscles by means of lifting and pushing weights (Mansfield and McGinn, 1993). In the past, bodybuilding was predominantly a male activity; musculature connoted power, domination, and virility (Klein, 1993). Today, an increasing number of women engage in this activity.

As gendered experiences, eating problems and bodybuilding have more in common than we might think. Women's studies scholar Susan Bordo (2004) has noted that the anorexic body and the muscled body are not opposites but instead are both united against the common enemy of soft, flabby flesh. In other words, the body may be objectified in both compulsive dieting and in compulsive bodybuilding.

Sexism

sexism The subordination of one sex, usually female, based on the assumed superiority of the other sex.

patriarchy A hierarchical system of social organization in which cultural, political, and economic structures are controlled by men.

matriarchy A hierarchical system of social organization in which cultural, political, and economic structures are controlled by women.

Sexism is the subordination of one sex, usually female, based on the assumed superiority of the other sex. Sexism directed at women has three components: (1) negative attitudes toward women; (2) stereotypical beliefs that reinforce, complement, or justify the prejudice; and (3) discrimination—acts that exclude, distance, or keep women separate (Lott, 1994).

Can men be victims of sexism? Although women are more often the target of sexist remarks and practices, men can be victims of sexist assumptions. According to the social psychologist Hilary M. Lips (2007), an example of sexism directed against men is the mistaken idea that it is more harmful for female soldiers to be killed in battle than male soldiers.

Like racism, sexism is used to justify discriminatory treatment. When women participate in what is considered gender-inappropriate endeavours in the workplace, at home, or in leisure activities, they often find that they are the targets of prejudice and discrimination. Obvious manifestations of sexism are found in the undervaluing of women's work, in hiring and promotion practices that effectively exclude women from an organization or confine them to the bottom of the organizational hierarchy. Even today, some women who enter nontraditional occupations (such as firefighting and welding) or professions (such as dentistry and architecture) encounter hurdles that men do not face.

Sexism is interwoven with **patriarchy**—a hierarchical system of social organization in which cultural, political, and economic structures are controlled by men. By contrast, **matriarchy** is a hierarchical system of social organization in which cultural, political, and economic structures are controlled by women; however, few societies have been organized in this manner. Patriarchy is reflected in the way men may think of their position as men as a given, while women may deliberate on what their position in society should be (see Box 11.2 for an example).

LO-3 WORK AND GENDER INEQUALITY

How do tasks in a society come to be defined as "men's work" or "women's work"? Three factors are important in determining the gendered division of labour in a society: (1) the type of subsistence base, (2) the supply of and demand for labour, and (3) the extent to which women's child-rearing activities are compatible with certain types of work. *Subsistence* refers to the means by which a society gains the basic necessities of life, including food, shelter, and clothing. Based on subsistence, societies are classified as hunting and gathering, horticultural and pastoral, agrarian, industrial, or post-industrial. The first three of these categories are *preindustrial* societies.

Preindustrial Societies

The earliest known division of labour between women and men is in hunting and gathering societies. While the men hunt for wild game, women gather roots, nuts, seeds and berries. A relatively equitable relationship exists because neither sex has the ability to provide all the food

BOX 11.2 **SOCIOLOGY IN GLOBAL PERSPECTIVE**

The Rise of Islamic Feminism in the Middle East?

> I would like for all of the young Muslim girls to be able to relate to Iman, whether they wear the hijab [head scarf] or not. Boys will also enjoy Iman's adventures because she is one tough, smart girl! Iman gets her super powers from having very strong faith in Allah, or God. She solves many of the problems by explaining certain parts of the Koran that relate to the story.
>
> —Rima Khoreibi, an author from Dubai (United Arab Emirates), explaining that she has written a book about a female Islamic superhero because she would like to dispel a widely held belief that sexism in her culture is deeply rooted in Islam (see theadventuresofiman.com, 2007; Kristof, 2006)

Although Rima Khoreibi and many others who have written fictional and nonfictional accounts of girls and women living in the Middle East typically do not deny that sexism exists in their region or that sexism is deeply interwoven with patriarchy around the world, they dispute the perception that Islam is inherently misogynistic (possessing hatred or strong prejudice toward women). As defined in this chapter, patriarchy is a hierarchical system of social organization in which cultural, political, and economic structures are controlled by men. The influence of religion on patriarchy is a topic of great interest to contemporary scholars, particularly those applying a feminist approach to their explanations of why persistent social inequalities exist between women and men and how these inequalities are greater in some regions of the world than in others.

According to some gender studies specialists, a newer form of feminist thinking is emerging among Muslim women. Often referred to as "feminist Islam" or "Islamic feminism," this approach is based on the belief that greater gender equality may be possible in the Muslim world if the teachings of Islam, as set forth in the Qur'an, the Islamic holy book, are followed more closely. Islamic feminism is based on the principle that Muslim women should retain their allegiance to Islam as an essential part of their self-determination and identity, but that they should also work to change patriarchal control over the basic Islamic worldview (Wadud, 2002). According to journalist Nicholas D. Kristof, both Islam and evangelical Christianity have been on the rise in recent years because both religions provide "a firm moral code, spiritual reassurance and orderliness to people vexed by chaos and immorality around them, and they offer dignity to the poor" (2006:A22).

Islamic feminists believe that the rise of Islam might contribute to greater, rather than less, equality for women. From this perspective, stories about characters such as Iman may help girls and young women realize that they can maintain their deep religious convictions and their head scarf (hijab) while working for greater equality for women and more opportunities for themselves. In *The Adventures of Iman*, the female hero always wears a pink scarf around her neck and she uses the scarf to cover her hair when she is praying to Allah. Iman quotes the Qur'an when she is explaining to others that Muslims are expected to be tolerant, kind, and righteous. For Iman, religion is a form of empowerment, not an extension of patriarchy.

The focus of Islamic feminism is quite different from what most people view as Western feminism. For example, Islamic feminism puts less emphasis than might be expected on issues such as the wearing of the hijab or the fact that in Saudi Arabia, a woman may own a motor vehicle but cannot legally drive it. As rapid economic development and urbanization affect the lives of many people, however, change is clearly under way in many regions of the Middle East and in other areas of the world.

In light of such differences, consider the following. Why is women's inequality a complex issue to study across nations? What part does culture play in defining the roles of women and men in various societies? How do religious beliefs influence what we think of as "appropriate" or "inappropriate" behaviours for men, women, and children? What do you think?

Sources: Kristof, 2006; theadventuresofiman.com, 2007; Wadud, 2002.

necessary for survival. When wild game is nearby, both men and women may hunt. When it is far away, hunting becomes incompatible with child rearing (which women tend to do because they breastfeed their young) and women are placed at a disadvantage in terms of contributing to the food supply (Lorber, 1994). In most hunting and gathering societies, women are full economic partners with men; relations between them tend to be cooperative and relatively egalitarian (Bonvillain, 2001; Chafetz, 1984). Little social stratification of any kind is found because people do not acquire a food surplus.

In horticultural societies, which first developed 10,000 to 12,000 years ago, a steady source of food becomes available. People are able to grow their own food because of hand tools, such as the digging stick and the hoe. Women make an important contribution to food production because cultivation with hoes is compatible with child care. A fairly high degree of gender equality exists because neither sex controls the food supply.

When inadequate moisture in an area makes planting crops impossible, *pastoralism*—the domestication of large animals to provide food—develops. Herding is primarily done by men, and women contribute relatively little to subsistence production in such societies. In some herding societies, women have relatively low status; their primary value is their ability to produce male offspring so that the family lineage can be preserved and enough males will exist to protect the group against attack (Nielsen, 1990). Even so, the relationship between men and women is more equitable than it is in agrarian societies, which first developed about 8000 to 10,000 years ago.

In agrarian societies, gender inequality and male dominance become institutionalized. Agrarian societies rely on agriculture—farming done by animal-drawn or mechanically powered plows and equipment. Because agrarian tasks require more labour and greater physical strength than horticultural ones, men become more involved in food production. It has been suggested that women are excluded from these tasks because they are viewed as too weak for the work and because child-care responsibilities are considered incompatible with the full-time labour that the tasks require (Nielsen, 1990). Most of the world's population currently lives in agrarian societies in various stages of industrialization.

Why does gender inequality increase in agrarian societies? Scholars cannot agree on an answer; however, some suggest that it results from private ownership of property. When people no longer have to move continually in search of food, they can acquire a surplus. Men gain control over the disposition of the surplus and the kinship system, and this control serves men's interests (Lorber, 1994). The importance of producing "legitimate" heirs to inherit the surplus increases significantly, and women's lives become more secluded and restricted as men attempt to ensure the legitimacy of their children. Premarital virginity and marital fidelity are required; indiscretions are punished (Nielsen, 1990). However, some scholars argue that male dominance existed before the private ownership of property (Firestone, 1970; Lerner, 1986).

Industrial Societies

An *industrial society* is one in which factory or mechanized production has replaced agriculture as the major form of economic activity. As societies industrialize, the status of women tends to decline further. Industrialization in North America created a gap between the nonpaid work performed by women at home and the paid work that was increasingly performed by men and unmarried young women (Krahn and Lowe, 2007).

In Canada, the division of labour between men and women in the middle and upper classes became much more distinct with industrialization. The men were viewed as "breadwinners"; the women were seen as "homemakers." In this new "cult of domesticity" (also referred to as the "cult of true womanhood"), the home became a private, personal sphere in which women created a haven for the family. Those who supported the cult of domesticity argued that women were the natural keepers of the domestic sphere and that children were the mother's responsibility. Meanwhile, the "breadwinner" role placed enormous pressures on men to support their families—providing for them well was considered a sign of manhood. This gendered division of labour increased the economic and political subordination of women.

The cult of true womanhood not only increased white women's dependence on men but also became a source of discrimination against women of colour, based on both their race and the fact that many of them had to work to survive. Employed, working-class white women were similarly stereotyped; they became more economically dependent on their husbands because their wages were so much lower.

Post-Industrial Societies

Chapter 5 defines *post-industrial societies* as societies in which technology supports a service- and information-based economy. In such societies, the division of labour in paid employment is increasingly based on whether people provide or apply information or are employed in service jobs, such as fast-food restaurant counter help or healthcare workers. For both women and men in the labour force, formal education is increasingly crucial for economic and social success. However, even as some women have moved into entrepreneurial, managerial, and professional occupations, many others have remained in the low-paying service sector, which affords few opportunities for upward advancement.

Will technology change the gendered division of labour in post-industrial societies? Scholars do not agree on the effects of computers, the Internet, cellphones, tablets, and many other newer forms of communications technology on the role of women in society. For example, some feminist writers had a pessimistic view of the impact of computers and monitors on women's health and safety, predicting that women in secretarial and administrative roles would experience an increase in eyestrain, headaches, and problems such as carpal tunnel syndrome. However, some medical experts now believe that such problems extend to both men and women, as computers have become omnipresent in more people's lives. The term *24/7* has come to mean that a person is available 24 hours a day, seven days a week, via cellphone, email, and other means of communication, whether the individual is at the office or a continent away on "vacation."

Although some analysts presumed that technological developments would reduce the boundaries between women's and men's work, researchers have found that the gender stereotyping associated with specific jobs has remained remarkably stable even when the nature of work and the skills required to perform it have been radically transformed. Today, men and women continue to be segregated into different occupations, and this segregation is particularly visible within individual workplaces (as discussed later in the chapter).

How does the division of labour change in families in post-industrial societies? For a variety of reasons, more households are headed by women with no adult male present. This means that women in these households truly have a double burden, both from family responsibilities and from the necessity of holding gainful employment in the labour force. Even in single-person or two-parent households, programming "labour-saving" devices (if they can be afforded) often means that a person must have some leisure time to learn how to do the programming. According to analysts, leisure is deeply divided along gender lines and women have less time to "play in the house" than do men and boys. Some websites seek to appeal to women who have economic resources but are short on time, making it possible for them to shop, gather information, "telebank," and communicate with others at all hours of the day and night.

In post-industrial societies such as Canada, close to 80 percent of adult women are in the labour force. This reality means that despite living in an information- and service-oriented economy, women will continue to bear the heavy burden of finding time to care for children, help aging parents, and meet the demands of the workplace (Marshall, 2011).

How people accept new technologies and the effect these technologies have on gender stratification are related to how people are socialized into gender roles. However, gender-based stratification remains rooted in the larger social structures of society, which individuals have little ability to control.

TIME TO REVIEW

- How do new technologies influence gender relations in the workplace and the division of labour in the home?
- Is it likely that technology will increase or decrease the divisions between men and women at work and home?

LO-4 GENDER AND SOCIALIZATION

We learn gender-appropriate behaviour through the socialization process. Our parents, teachers, friends, and the media all serve as gendered institutions that communicate to us our earliest, and often most lasting, beliefs about the social meanings of being male or female and thinking and behaving in masculine or feminine ways. Some gender roles have changed dramatically in recent years; others remain largely unchanged over time.

Many parents prefer boys to girls because of stereotypical ideas about the relative importance of males and females to the future of the family and society. Although some parents prefer boys to girls because they believe old myths about the biological inferiority of females, research suggests that social expectations also play a major role in this preference. We are socialized to believe that it is important to have a son, especially as a first or only child. For many years, it was assumed that a male child could support his parents in their later years and carry on the family name.

Across cultures, boys are preferred to girls, especially when the number of children that parents can have is limited by law or economic conditions. For example, in China, which strictly regulates the allowable number of children to one per family, a disproportionate number of female fetuses are aborted. In India, the practice of aborting female fetuses is widespread and female infanticide occurs frequently. As a result, both India and China have a growing surplus of young men who will face a shortage of women their own age. In Canada, sex selection through the use of assisted reproductive technologies has been officially banned since 2004.

Parents and Gender Socialization

© BananaStock/Thinkstock

Are children's toys a reflection of their own preferences and choices? How do toys reflect gender socialization by parents and other adults?

From birth, parents treat children differently on the basis of the child's sex. Baby boys are perceived to be less fragile than girls and tend to be treated more roughly by their parents. Girl babies are thought to be "cute, sweet, and cuddly" and receive more gentle treatment. Parents strongly influence the gender-role development of children by passing on—both overtly and covertly—their own beliefs about gender. When girl babies cry, parents respond to them more quickly, and parents are more prone to talk and sing to girl babies (Wharton, 2004).

The toys that parents select for their children are a significant source of gender socialization. Children's toys reflect their parents' gender expectations. In a study of preschoolers, for example, little boys selected the tool sets over dish sets, indicating that their fathers thought playing with dishes is "bad" (Raag, 1999). Gender-appropriate toys for boys include computer games, trucks and other vehicles, sports equipment, and war toys, such as guns and soldiers. Girls' toys include Barbie dolls, play makeup, and homemaking items.

When children are old enough to help with household chores, boys and girls are often assigned different tasks. Maintenance chores (such as mowing the lawn) are assigned to boys, while domestic chores (such as shopping, cooking, and cleaning the table) are assigned to girls. Chores may also become linked with future occupational choices and personal characteristics. Girls who are responsible for domestic chores, such as caring for younger brothers and sisters, may learn nurturing behaviours that later translate into employment as a nurse or schoolteacher. Boys may learn about computers and other types of technology that lead to different career options.

In the past, most studies of gender socialization focused on white middle-class families and paid little attention to ethnic differences (Raffaelli and Ontai, 2004). According to earlier studies in the United

States, children from middle- and upper-income families are less likely to be assigned gender-linked chores than children from lower-income backgrounds. In addition, gender-linked chore assignments occur less frequently in African American families, where both sons and daughters tend to be socialized toward independence, employment, and child care (Bardwell, Cochran, and Walker, 1986; Hale-Benson, 1986). Sociologist Patricia Hill Collins (1991) suggests that African American mothers are less likely to socialize their daughters into roles as subordinates; instead, they are likely to teach them a critical posture that allows them to cope with contradictions.

In contrast, a recent study of gender socialization in U.S. Latino/Latina families suggests that adolescent females of Mexican, Puerto Rican, Cuban, or other Central or South American descent receive different gender socialization by their parents than do their male siblings (Raffaelli and Ontai, 2004). Latinas are given more stringent curfews and are allowed less interaction with members of the opposite sex than are the adolescent males in their families. Rules for dating, school activities, and part-time jobs are more stringent for the girls because many parents want to protect their daughters and keep them closer to home.

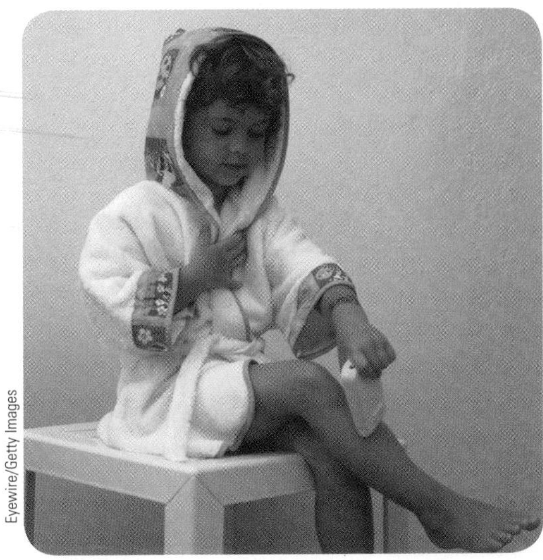
Eyewire/Getty Images

From an early age, we are encouraged by a number of societal influences to learn gender-appropriate behaviour.

Many parents are aware of the effect that gender socialization has on their children and make a conscientious effort to provide nonsexist experiences for them. Mothers' education and employment have a significant effect on the gender attitudes of their sons and daughters. Many fathers also take an active role in socializing their sons to be thoughtful and caring individuals who do not live by traditional gender stereotypes. However, children's peers often make nontraditional gender socialization much more difficult for parents and their children.

Peers and Gender Socialization

Peers help children learn prevailing gender role stereotypes, as well as gender-appropriate—and inappropriate—behaviour. During the school years, same-sex peers have a powerful effect on how children see their gender roles; during adolescence, they are often more influential agents of gender socialization than adults (Maccoby and Jacklin, 1987).

Children, especially boys, are more socially acceptable to their peers when they conform to implicit societal norms governing the "appropriate" ways that girls and boys should act in social situations. Male peer groups place more pressure on boys to do "masculine" things than female peer groups place on girls to do "feminine" things. For example, girls wear jeans and other "boy" clothes, play soccer and softball, and engage in other activities traditionally associated with males. But if a boy wears a dress, plays hopscotch with girls, and engages in other activities associated with being female, he will be ridiculed by his peers. This distinction between the relative value of boys' and girls' behaviours strengthens the cultural message that masculine activities and behaviour are more important and more acceptable.

The male bonding that occurs during adolescence is believed to reinforce masculine identity (Gaylin, 1992) and to encourage gender-stereotypical attitudes and behaviour (Huston, 1985; Martin, 1989). For example, male peers have a tendency to ridicule and bully others about their appearance, size, and weight. One woman painfully recalled walking down the halls at school when boys would flatten themselves against the lockers and cry, "Wide load!" At lunchtime, the boys made a production of watching her eat lunch and frequently made sounds like pig grunts or moos (Kolata, 1993). Because peer acceptance is so important for both males and females during their first two decades, such actions can have very harmful consequences for the victims.

As young adults, men and women still receive many gender-related messages from peers. Among university students, for example, peers are organized largely around gender relations and play an important role in career choices and the establishment of long-term, intimate relationships (Holland and Eisenhart, 1990).

Peer pressure is often at its strongest in relation to norms of appearance. As other researchers have shown, peer pressure can strongly influence a person's body consciousness. Women in university often feel pressure to be very thin, as Karen explains:

> "Do you diet?" asked a friend [in my first year of university], as I was stuffing a third homemade chocolate chip cookie in my mouth. "Do you know how many calories there are in that one cookie?"
>
> Stopping to think for a moment as she and two other friends stared at me, probably wanting to ask me the same question, I realized that I really didn't even know what a calorie was . . .
>
> From that moment, I'd taken on a new enemy, one more powerful and destructive than any human can be. One that nearly fought me to the death—my death . . .
>
> I just couldn't eat food anymore. I was so obsessed with it that I thought about it every second . . . In two months, I'd lost thirty pounds . . . Everyone kept telling me I looked great . . .
>
> I really didn't realize that anything was wrong with me . . . There were physical things occurring in my body other than not having my period anymore. My hair was falling out and was getting thinner . . . I would constantly get head rushes every time I stood up . . . When my friends would all go out to dinner or to a party I stayed home quite often, afraid that I might have to eat something, and afraid that my friends would find out that I didn't eat. (Twenhofel, 1993:198)

Feminist scholars have concluded that eating problems are not always psychological "disorders" (as they are referred to by members of the medical profession). Instead, eating (or not eating) may be a strategy for coping with problems, such as unrealistic social pressures about slenderness (see Hesse-Biber, 2006) or social injustices caused by racism, sexism, and classism in society (Thompson, 1994).

Teachers, Schools, and Gender Socialization

From kindergarten through university, schools operate as gendered institutions. Teachers provide important messages about gender through both the formal content of classroom assignments and informal interaction with students. Sometimes, gender-related messages from teachers and other students reinforce gender roles that have been taught at home; however, teachers may also contradict parental socialization. During the early years of a child's schooling, the teacher's influence is very powerful; many children spend more hours per day with their teachers than they do with their parents.

gender bias Behaviour that shows favouritism toward one gender over the other.

According to some researchers, the quantity and quality of teacher–student interactions often vary between the education of girls and that of boys (Wellhousen and Yin, 1997). **Gender bias** consists of showing favouritism toward one gender over the other. Gender bias is displayed in a number of different ways in academic settings: through teacher–student interactions, biased or stereotyped resources, and responses to male and female interactions. Although girls are more academically successful than boys, close examination of what goes on in our classrooms shows that girls and boys continue to be socialized in ways that work against gender equality (Chapman, 2003). For example, research indicates that males receive more praise for their contributions and are called on more frequently in class, even when they do not volunteer. Teachers also influence how students treat one another during school hours. Many teachers use sex segregation as a way to organize students, resulting in unnecessary competition between females and males. Competition based on gender often reinforces existing misconceptions about the skills and attributes of boys and girls, and may contribute to overt and subtle discrimination in the classroom and beyond.

The effect of gender bias is particularly problematic if teachers take a boys-will-be-boys attitude when boys and young men make derogatory remarks or demonstrate aggressive behaviour against girls and young women. When girls complain of **sexual harassment**—unwanted sexual advances, requests for sexual favours, or other verbal or physical conduct of a sexual nature—their concerns are sometimes overlooked or downplayed by teachers and school administrators. Sexual harassment is prohibited by law, and teachers and administrators are obligated to investigate such incidents.

© Mary Kate Denny/ PhotoEdit

Teachers often use competition between boys and girls because they hope to make a learning activity more interesting. Here, a middle school girl leads other girls against boys in a Spanish translation contest. What are the advantages and disadvantages of gender-based competition in classroom settings?

Girls, however, are not alone in experiencing sexual harassment at school. A national U.S survey of more than 2000 public school students in Grades 8 through 11 found that 83 percent of girls and 79 percent of boys reported having experienced sexual harassment at least once, and that one in four of the students surveyed had experienced such harassment often. The same survey found that girls experienced more forms and a higher frequency of harassment than boys (AAUW, 2001). Similar results were reported in Canadian surveys of sexual harassment. For example, a 1994 survey of secondary students in Ontario found over 80 percent of female students reported they had been sexually harassed in a school setting. The pervasiveness of sexual harassment in the lives of girls and young women was reconfirmed in a 2002 Canada-wide study of elementary and high school students (Berman, 2002; Mancini, 2012).

sexual harassment
Unwanted sexual advances, requests for sexual favours, or other verbal or physical conduct of a sexual nature.

Women now constitute a larger proportion of all college and university students. In some academic fields of study, however, women remain a distinct minority and may be more marginalized in classrooms and interpersonal interactions with professors and other students. Men still constitute the majority of majors in architecture, engineering, computer technology, and the physical sciences. Despite such obstacles, women are more likely than men to earn an undergraduate degree, but at the graduate level, the number of women to earn a degree declines dramatically. See Figure 11.1.

Mass Media and Gender Socialization

The media, including newspapers, magazines, television, movies, and Internet sources, are powerful sources of gender stereotyping. Although some critics argue that the media simply reflect existing gender roles in society, others point out that the media have a unique ability to shape ideas (see Box 11.3 on page 317). Think of the impact that television might have on children if they spend one-third of their waking time watching it, as has been estimated.

From children's cartoons to adult shows, television programs offer more male than female characters. Furthermore, the male characters act in a strikingly different manner from female ones. Male characters in both children's and adult programs are typically aggressive, constructive, and direct, while some female characters defer to others or manipulate them by acting helpless, seductive, or deceitful.

In prime-time television, several significant changes in the past several decades have reduced gender stereotyping; however, men still outnumber women as leading characters, and they are often "in charge" in any setting where both men and women are portrayed. In the popular ABC series *Grey's Anatomy,* for example, the number of women's and men's roles is evenly balanced, but the male characters typically are the top surgeons at the hospital,

FIGURE 11.1 UNIVERSITY DEGREES AWARDED, BY SEX, 2011

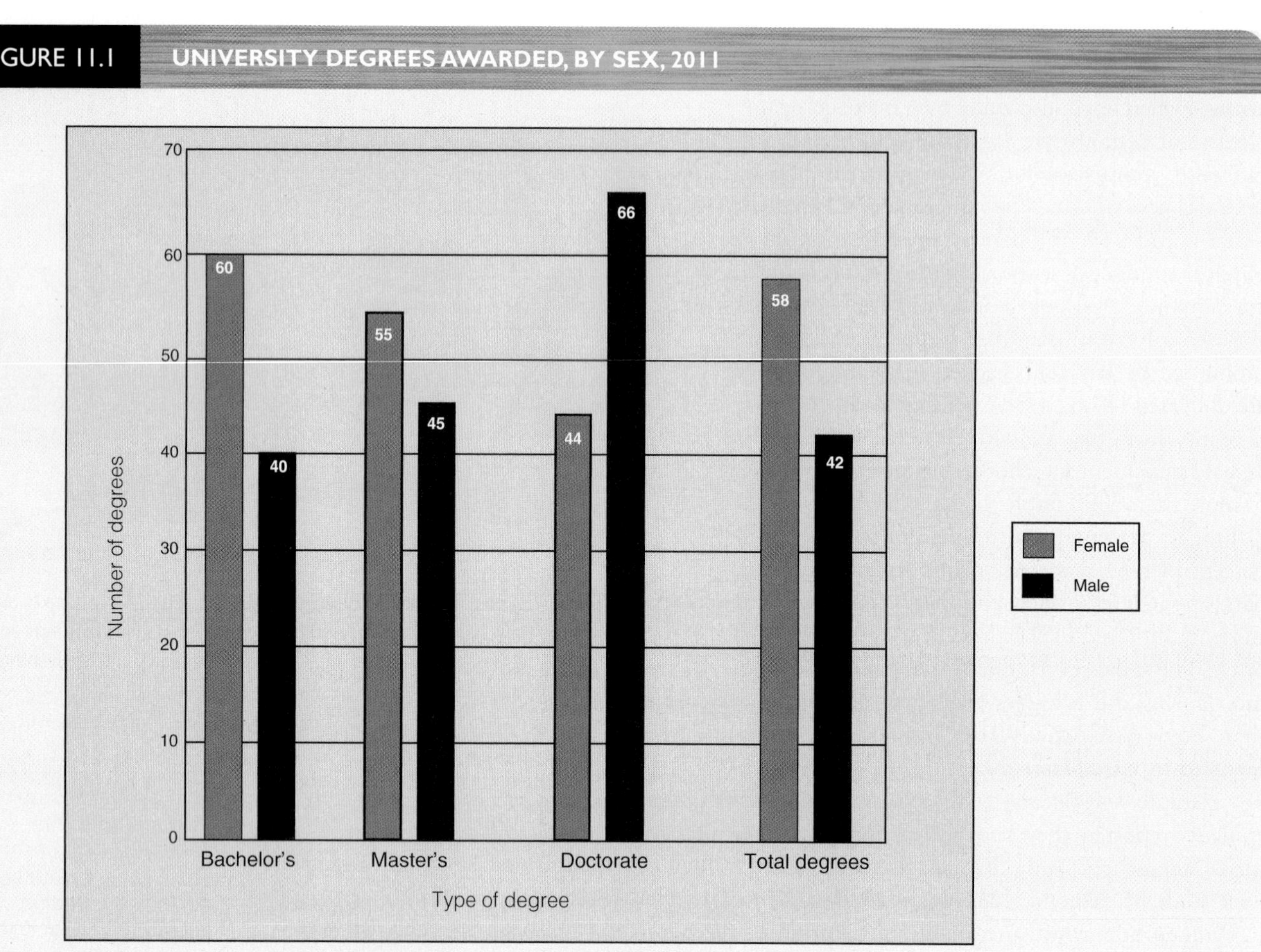

Source: Cara Williams, "Women in Canada: A Gender-Based Statistical Report," 6th ed., Statistics Canada Cat. No 89-503-XIE 2101110, 2011.

whereas the female characters are residents, interns, or nurses. In shows with predominantly female characters, such as *Desperate Housewives or Cougar Town,* the women are typically attractive, thin, and ultimately either hysterical or compliant when dealing with male characters (Stanley, 2004).

Whether on television and billboards or in magazines and newspapers, advertising can send out persuasive messages about gender roles. The intended message is clear to many people: If they embrace traditional notions of masculinity and femininity, their personal and social success is assured; if they purchase the right products and services, they can enhance their appearance and gain power over other people. In commercials, men's roles are typically portrayed differently from women's roles: Men are more likely to be shown working or playing outside the house rather than inside, whereas women are more likely to be doing domestic tasks, such as cooking, cleaning, shopping, or taking care of the children. As such, television commercials may act as agents of socialization, showing children and others what women's and men's designated activities are (Kaufman, 1999).

A study by the sociologist Anthony J. Cortese (2004) found that women—regardless of what they were doing in a particular ad—were frequently shown in advertising as being young, beautiful, and seductive. Although such depictions may sell products, they may also have the effect of influencing how we perceive ourselves and others with regard to issues of power and subordination.

BOX 11.3 POINT/COUNTERPOINT

"You Can Never Be Too Beautiful" and Teen Plastic Surgery

News Item: **Cosmetic Surgery Is Teenagers' Reward for Passing Exams**

Chinese teenagers are being given cosmetic surgery by their parents as a reward for their hard work in school. Three hospitals in Guangzhou reported that 90 percent of their plastic surgery patients were middle school graduates . . . [whose] parents were paying for the surgery to reward children for passing university entrance exams.

—Ananova News Service, 2005

News Item: **Teenagers Opt for Cosmetic Surgery**

I'm only a 32B so having a bigger bust would make me feel happier in my clothes . . . I could wear better tops and not have to resort to wearing padded bras to create the illusion of a larger bust.

—Kimberley Brooke, a college student in the United Kingdom, describing why she is interested in having cosmetic surgery (quoted in Atkins, 2005)

News Item: **For More Teenage Girls, Adult Plastic Surgery**

My family was upset that I was so young. But I explained to them that it was about being confident.

—Nicole Castro of the United States, explaining why she had breast implant surgery (quoted in Boodman, 2004:A1)

Although both men and women seek plastic surgery, the majority of elective cosmetic surgery procedures are performed on women. In the United States and other nations, the number of young women seeking procedures such as rhinoplasty (nose reshaping), breast implants, and liposuction appears to be increasing (Boodman, 2004).

Why do young women want to undergo surgical procedures to make their bodies more "beautiful" or "perfect"? According to some analysts, the pressure to improve one's appearance comes primarily from acquaintances; however, other researchers assert that how the media frame stories about personal appearance influences the way we think about ourselves and the improvements that we may believe our bodies require. If this assertion is correct, media framing plays an important role in the growing phenomenon of young women opting for cosmetic enhancement or change.

For example, television reality shows such as *Extreme Makeover* may encourage people to believe that cosmetic surgery could be the answer to all their problems. These programs are framed in such a manner that the negative attributes of a person's "before" appearance are emphasized and often exaggerated, while the positive aspects of the "after" appearance are carefully highlighted and enhanced for media audiences. This type of framing gives audiences a perception that things were originally worse than they were, that everything afterward is much better than it is, and that surgery is a simple matter. Such stories often have a profound influence on how viewers see themselves and others. And in some cases, media framing even suggests that we should want to look like a celebrity. Consider MTV's *I Want a Famous Face*, where contestants in the second season stated their desire to look like celebrities such as Carmen Electra, Tiffani-Amber Thiessen, Arnold Schwarzenegger, Jennifer Aniston, Britney Spears, Ricky Martin, and Janet Jackson (MTV, 2005).

Before performing cosmetic surgery, physicians are encouraged to carefully evaluate teenagers on factors such as their level of physical and emotional maturity (Canadian Society of Plastic Surgeons, 2009); however, this kind of scrutiny may be overwhelmed by intense media framing of stories that suggests young people are inadequate; by advertising that uses models to sell all kinds of products; and by the advertisements for physical improvements and plastic surgery that are omnipresent in newspapers, magazines, and cable television shows. Magazines for teenage girls, including *Teen Vogue* and *Seventeen*, regularly carry ads for products such as herbal breast enhancement tablets and often have articles about "problems" associated with having small breasts. Music videos make teenagers cognizant of their breast size as they are constantly bombarded with images of scantily clad, generously endowed women (Quart, 2003). Some researchers have found that popular magazines typically describe very tall, very thin women as beautiful and those who are shorter or thicker as plain. As a result of constantly seeing images of tall, thin bodies in the media, many females begin to compare themselves to a body type that is unattainable for 99 percent of all women (Kilbourne, 2000).

Clearly, the media industry is a big business that makes billions of dollars by selling magazines, producing television shows, and reaching audiences through various other avenues; however, it is important for all of us, as media consumers, to ask ourselves if we are being sold ideal images of beauty that are not only unattainable but

(continued)

also subject us to procedures, such as cosmetic surgery, that may have adverse consequences. Harvard Medical School psychologist Nancy Etcoff notes that plastic surgery isn't just "someone waving a magic wand and you look better. You're subjecting yourself to potential dangers" (quoted in Kornblum, 2004). Should we be concerned about girls and young women who become so obsessed with their looks that they are willing to pursue risky procedures that may not have the result they so hope to achieve? What do you think?

Sources: Ananova News Service, 2005; Atkins, 2005; Boodman, 2004; Canadian Society of Plastic Surgeons, 2009; Kilbourne, 2000; Kornblum, 2004; MTV, 2005; Quart, 2003.

TIME TO REVIEW

- Consider all of the primary socialization agents considered in this section. Which of these socialization agents have had the greatest impact on your gender identity?

LO-5 CONTEMPORARY GENDER INEQUALITY

According to feminist scholars, women experience gender inequality as a result of economic, political, and educational discrimination. Women's position in the Canadian workforce reflects their overall subordination in society.

Gendered Division of Paid Work

The workplace is another example of a gendered institution, and where people are located in the occupational structure of the labour market has a major effect on their earnings. In industrialized countries, most jobs are segregated by gender and by race and ethnicity. Lorber notes that in most workplaces, employees are either gender-segregated or all of the same gender. *Gender-segregated work* refers to the concentration of women and men in different occupations, jobs, and places of work (Reskin and Padavic, 2002). Despite some progress, the majority of employed women continued to work in occupations in which they have been traditionally concentrated. In 2009, 67 percent of all employed women were working in teaching, nursing and related health occupations, clerical or other administrative positions, or sales and service occupations (Ferrao, 2010).

To eliminate gender-segregated jobs in North America, more than half of all men or all women workers would have to change occupations. Moreover, women are severely underrepresented at the top Canadian corporations, at only about 17 percent of the corporate officers in the *Financial Post 500* list (comprising the 500 largest companies in Canada). Of these, only about 6 percent hold the highest corporate officer titles, and only 23 women serve as chief executive officer (Catalyst Canada, 2012). Based on current rates of change, the number of women reaching the top ranks of corporate Canada will not reach an acceptable level of 25 percent until the year 2025. See Table 11.1 for more on gender segregation in occupations.

Although the degree of gender segregation in parts of the professional labour market has declined since the 1970s, racial–ethnic segregation has remained deeply embedded in the social structure. The relationship between visible minority status and occupational status is complex and varies by gender, however. Visible minority males are overrepresented in both lower- and

TABLE 11.1 GENDER SEGREGATION BY OCCUPATION

PERCENTAGE OF WOMEN IN THE 10 HIGHEST-PAYING OCCUPATIONS	
Judges	25%
Specialist physicians	34%
General practitioners and family physicians	38%
Dentists	31%
Senior managers (goods production, utilities, transportation, construction)	12%
Senior managers (financial, communications, other business)	21%
Lawyers	39%
Senior managers (trade, broadcasting, other services)	19%
Engineering managers	10%
Banking, credit, and investment managers	55%
PERCENTAGE OF WOMEN IN THE 10 LOWEST-PAYING OCCUPATIONS	
Sewing machine operators	91%
Cashiers	84%
Ironing, pressing, and finishing occupations	70%
Artisans and craftspersons	52%
Bartenders	55%
Harvesting labourers	54%
Service station attendants	20%
Food service attendants and food preparers	75%
Food and beverage servers	76%
Babysitters, nannies, and parents' helpers	98%

Source: UN Platform for Action Committee, 2005.

higher-status occupations; nonwhite women are heavily overrepresented in lower-paying, low-skilled jobs (Krahn, Lowe, and Hughes, 2007).

Labour market segmentation—the division of jobs into categories with distinct working conditions—results in women having separate and unequal jobs (Amott and Matthaei, 1996; Lorber, 2005). The pay gap between men and women is the best documented consequence of gender-segregated work (Reskin and Padavic, 2002). Most women work in lower-paying, less prestigious jobs with little opportunity for advancement. Because many employers assume that men are the breadwinners, men are expected to make more money than women to support their families. For many years, women have been viewed as supplemental wage earners in a male-headed household, regardless of the women's marital status. Consequently, women have not been seen as legitimate workers but mainly as wives and mothers (Lorber, 2005).

Gender-segregated work affects both men and women. Men are often kept out of certain types of jobs. Those who enter female-dominated occupations often have to justify themselves and prove that they are "real men." They have to fight stereotypes (gay, "wimpy," and passive) about why they are interested in such work (Williams, 2004). Even if these assumptions do not push men out of female-dominated occupations, they affect how the men manage their gender identity at work. For example, men in occupations such as nursing emphasize their masculinity, attempt to distance themselves from female colleagues, and try to move quickly into management and supervisory positions (Williams, 2004).

Occupational gender segregation contributes to stratification in society. Job segregation is structural; it does not occur simply because individual workers have different abilities, motivations, and material needs. As a result of gender and racial segregation, employers are able to pay many men of colour and all women less money, promote them less often, and provide fewer benefits. If they demand better working conditions or wages, workers are often reminded of the number of individuals (members of Marx's "reserve army") who would like to have their jobs.

The Gender Wage Gap

wage gap A term used to describe the disparity between women's and men's earnings.

Occupational segregation contributes to a second form of discrimination—the **wage gap**, a term used to describe the disparity between women's and men's earnings. It is calculated by dividing women's earnings by men's to yield a percentage, also known as the *earnings ratio* (Reskin and Padavic, 2002). Today, women who work full time for the whole year still earn just over 70 cents for each dollar earned by their male counterparts (Williams, 2010). One study found that the majority of this wage gap can be explained by fields of study chosen by men and women, the continued overrepresentation of women in low-paying sectors of the economy, and gender differences in the division of time between caregiving and paid employment (Cool, 2010; Drolet, 2011). Marital status has a dramatic impact on the wage gap. The wage gap is smallest between single, never-married men and women (86 percent) and biggest between married men and women (65 percent). As shown in Figure 11.2, the gender wage gap exists for all levels of education. In 2008, women with a bachelor's degree who worked full time for the full year earned 85 cents for every dollar earned by their male counterparts. Once again, this gap is partially attributable to occupational segregation. The majority of female university students enroll in degree programs in education, health professions, fine arts, and the humanities, while males continue to dominate in the fields of science and engineering. Even within occupations that require specialized educational credentials, the wage gap does not disappear—for every dollar earned by men, women earned 65 cents as dentists, 68 cents as lawyers, and 77 cents as university professors (Statistics Canada, 2008k).

Pay Equity and Employment Equity

A number of strategies have been implemented in an attempt to achieve greater gender equality in the labour market. *Pay equity* attempts to raise the value of the work traditionally performed

FIGURE 11.2 EVOLUTION OF THE GENDER WAGE GAP, 1993–2008

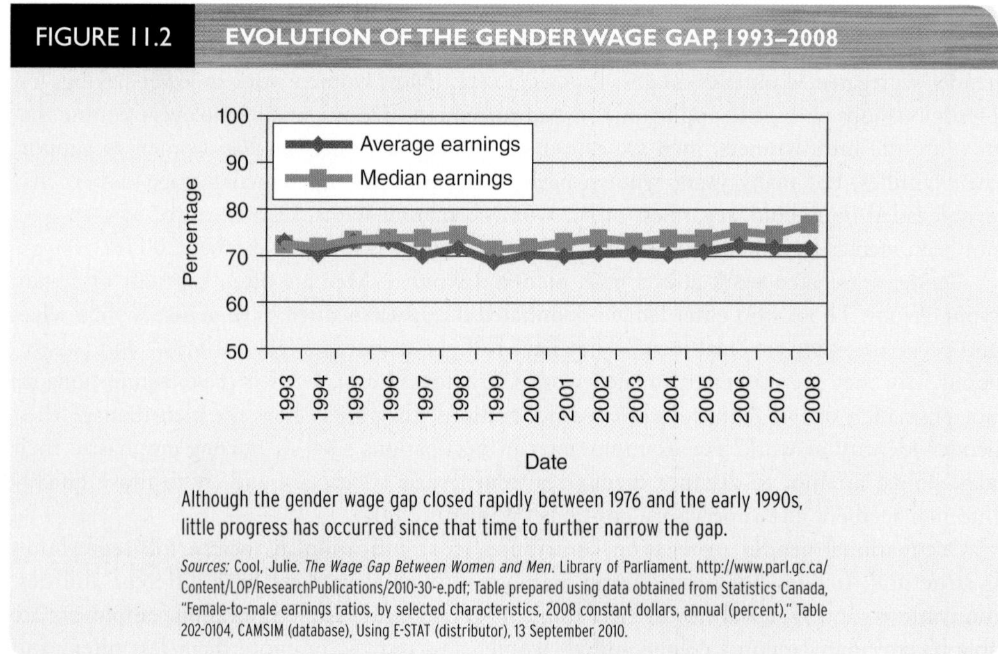

Although the gender wage gap closed rapidly between 1976 and the early 1990s, little progress has occurred since that time to further narrow the gap.

Sources: Cool, Julie. *The Wage Gap Between Women and Men.* Library of Parliament. http://www.parl.gc.ca/Content/LOP/ResearchPublications/2010-30-e.pdf; Table prepared using data obtained from Statistics Canada, "Female-to-male earnings ratios, by selected characteristics, 2008 constant dollars, annual (percent)," Table 202-0104, CAMSIM (database), Using E-STAT (distributor), 13 September 2010.

by women. *Employment equity* strategies focus on ways to move women into higher paying jobs traditionally held by men. Since the 1980s, the federal government, some provincial governments, and several private companies have implemented pay equity and employment equity policies (Nelson, 2006).

Pay equity (or, as it is sometimes called, **comparable worth**) reflects the belief that wages ought to reflect the worth of a job, not the gender or race of the worker (Kemp, 1994). How can the comparable worth of different kinds of jobs be determined? One way is to compare the work involved in women's and men's jobs and see if there is a disparity in the salaries paid for each. To do this, analysts break a job into components—such as the education, training, and skills required, the extent of responsibility for others' work, and the working conditions—and then allocate points for each (Lorber, 2005). For pay equity to exist, men and women in occupations that receive the same number of points should be paid the same. In short, pay equity promotes the principle of equal pay for work of equal value.

pay equity (comparable worth) The belief that wages ought to reflect the worth of a job, not the gender or race of the worker.

A second strategy for addressing inequality in the workplace is **employment equity**—a strategy to eliminate the effects of discrimination and to make employment opportunities available to groups who have been excluded (Krahn, Lowe, and Hughes, 2007). The target groups for employment equity are visible minorities, persons with disabilities, Aboriginal peoples, and women. In comparison with pay equity, which addresses wage issues only, employment equity covers a range of employment issues, such as recruitment, selection, training, development, and promotion. Employment equity also addresses issues pertaining to conditions of employment, such as compensation, layoffs, and disciplinary action. Critics of employment equity policies have pointed out that the *Employment Equity Act* of 1996 has jurisdiction over a tiny percentage of the population; it covers only federal government employers or companies that have contracts with the federal government. As shown in Figure 11.2 these policies represent a start in the right direction, male resistance and poor regulation and enforcement have resulted in minimal progress toward gendered employment equity (Nelson, 2006). See Figure 11.3.

employment equity A strategy to eliminate the effects of discrimination and to make employment opportunities available to groups who have been excluded.

Paid Work and Family Work

As previously discussed, the first big change in the relationship between family and work occurred with the Industrial Revolution and the rise of capitalism. The cult of domesticity kept many middle- and upper-class women out of the workforce during this period. Primarily working-class and poor women had to deal with the work/family conflict. Today, however, the issue spans the entire economic spectrum. The typical married woman in Canada combines paid work in the labour force and family work as a homemaker. Although this change has occurred at the societal level, individual women bear the brunt of the problem.

Today, women who work full time for the whole year still earn just over 70 cents for each dollar earned by their male counterparts.

FIGURE 11.3 THE WAGE GAP

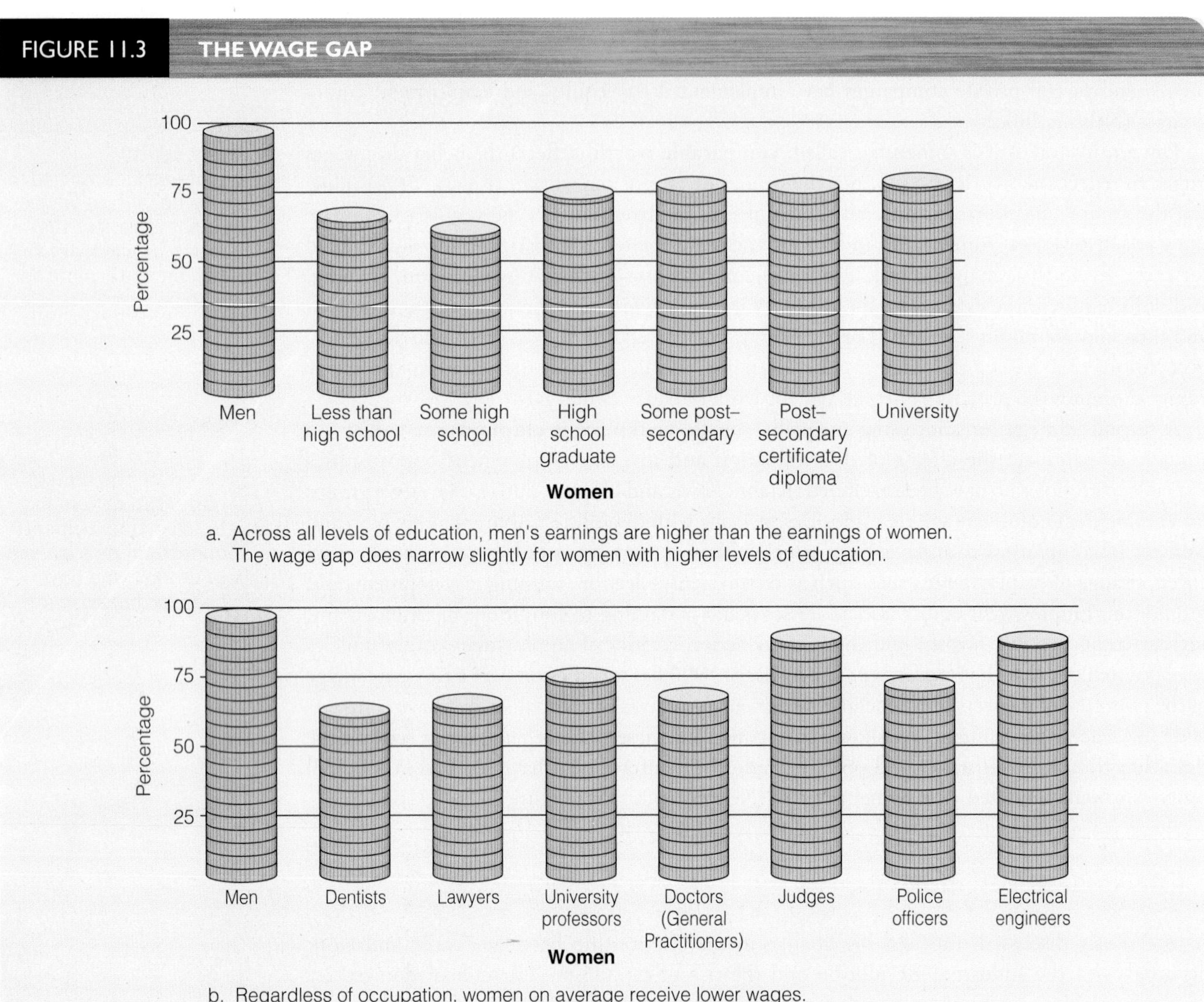

a. Across all levels of education, men's earnings are higher than the earnings of women. The wage gap does narrow slightly for women with higher levels of education.

b. Regardless of occupation, women on average receive lower wages.

Sources: Statistics Canada, 2001f; UN Platform for Action Committee, 2005.

While dramatic changes have occurred in women's participation in the workforce, men's entry into housework has been gradual, prompting some to refer to the latter as a "stalled revolution" (Cooke, 2004, cited in Marshall, 2006:16). Recent time-use surveys have confirmed that the burden of unpaid work continues to rest disproportionately on women. Even when women work full time, most maintain primary responsibility for child care, elder care, housework, shopping, and meal preparation. Among couples, the woman does close to two hours per day more housework than her male partner. Consequently, many women have a "double day" or "second shift" because of their dual responsibilities for paid and unpaid work (Hochschild, 1989, 2003; see also Chapter 13). Working women have less time to spend on housework; if husbands do not help do routine domestic chores, some chores do not get done or get done less often. Although the income that many women earn is essential for the economic survival of their families, they must spend part of their earnings on family maintenance, such as daycare, fast food, and laundry and housecleaning, in an attempt to keep up with their obligations.

© Tony Freeman/PhotoEdit

© Spencer Grant/PhotoEdit

What stereotypes are associated with men in female-oriented occupations? With women in male-oriented occupations? Do you think such stereotypes will change in the near future?

Especially in families with young children, domestic responsibilities consume much time and energy. Although some kinds of housework can be put off, the needs of children often cannot be ignored or delayed. When children are ill or school events cannot be scheduled around work, parents (especially mothers) may experience stressful role conflicts. ("Shall I be a good employee or a good mother?")

Many working women care not only for themselves, their husbands, and their children but also for elderly parents or in-laws. Some analysts refer to these women as "the sandwich generation"—caught between the needs of their young children and elderly relatives. Many women try to solve their time crunch by forgoing leisure time and sleep. When Arlie Hochschild first interviewed working mothers, she found that they talked about sleep "the way a hungry person talks about food" (1989:9). In more recent research, Hochschild (1997) learned that some married women with children found more fulfillment at work and worked longer hours because they liked work better than facing the pressures of home (see Chapter 13).

Although the transition into housework has been slow for men, there is room for optimism as the household–work gender gap slowly narrows. As shown in Figure 13.2 (see page 388), gender differences in the division of labour remain, but they are slowly diminishing. Since 1986, as women have increased their participation in paid work, men have increased their time spent on housework. In particular, men have made significant changes in their participation in core housework, such as meal preparation and cleanup, cleaning, and laundry. For couples with children, there have also been noticeable changes in men's participation in meeting child-care responsibilities and duties (Marshall, 2011). See Figure 11.4.

FIGURE 11.4 GENERATIONAL CHANGE IN PAID AND UNPAID WORK

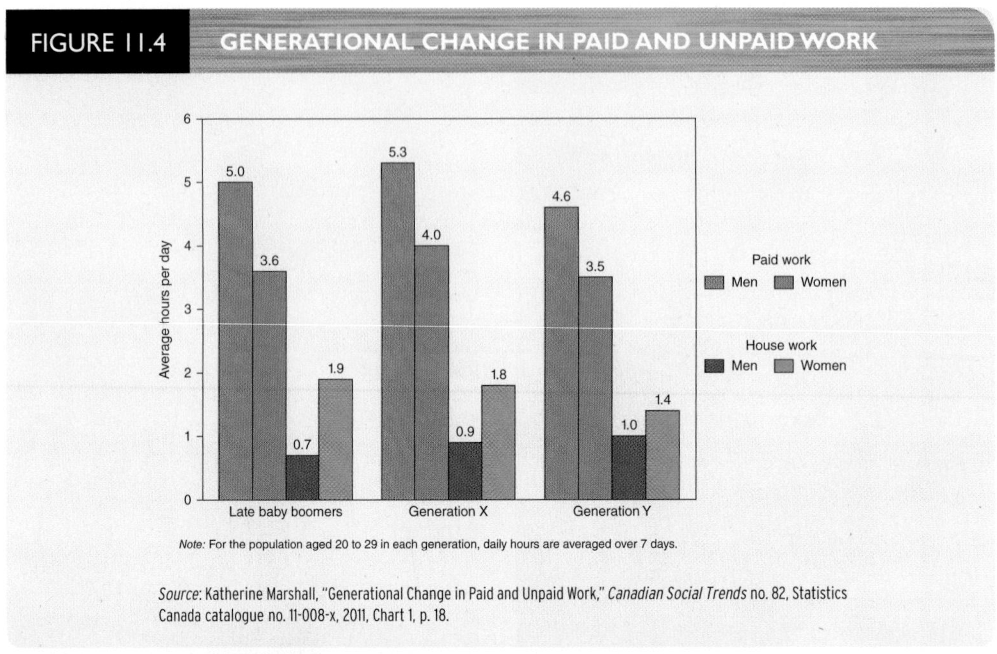

Note: For the population aged 20 to 29 in each generation, daily hours are averaged over 7 days.

Source: Katherine Marshall, "Generational Change in Paid and Unpaid Work," *Canadian Social Trends* no. 82, Statistics Canada catalogue no. 11-008-x, 2011, Chart 1, p. 18.

TIME TO REVIEW

- Based on your understanding of the gender wage gap, do you think the gap will get larger, smaller, or disappear completely as younger men and women enter the paid workforce? Why or why not?
- Analysts believe that the burden of the "double day" or "second shift" will likely preserve women's inequality at home and in the workplace for another generation. If this is the case, what needs to be done to address the gendered division of unpaid work?

LO-6 PERSPECTIVES ON GENDER STRATIFICATION

Sociological perspectives on gender stratification vary in their approach to examining gender roles and power relationships in society. Some focus on the roles of women and men in the domestic sphere; others note the inequalities arising from a gendered division of labour in the workplace. Still others attempt to integrate both the public and private spheres into their analyses. The Concept Snapshot on page 330 outlines the key aspects of each sociological perspective on gender stratification.

Functionalist and Neoclassical Economic Perspectives

As seen earlier, functionalist theory views men and women as having distinct roles that are important for the survival of the family and society. The most basic division of labour is biological: Men are physically stronger, while women are the only ones able to bear and nurse children. Gendered belief systems foster assumptions about appropriate behaviour for men and women and may have an impact on the types of work women and men perform.

THE IMPORTANCE OF TRADITIONAL GENDER ROLES According to functional analysts such as Talcott Parsons (1955), women's roles as nurturers and caregivers are even more pronounced in contemporary industrialized societies. While the husband performs the *instrumental* tasks of providing economic support and making decisions, the wife assumes the *expressive* tasks of providing affection and emotional support for the family. This division of family labour ensures that important societal tasks will be fulfilled; it also provides stability for family members.

This view has been adopted by a number of conservative analysts who assert that relationships between men and women are damaged when changes in gender roles occur and that family life suffers as a consequence. From this perspective, the traditional division of labour between men and women is the natural order of the universe.

THE HUMAN CAPITAL MODEL Functionalist explanations of occupational gender segregation are similar to neoclassical economic perspectives, such as the human capital model (Horan, 1978; Kemp, 1994). According to this model, individuals vary widely in the amount of human capital they bring to the labour market. *Human capital* is acquired by education and job training; it is the source of a person's productivity and can be measured in terms of the return on the investment (wages) and the cost (schooling or training) (Kemp, 1994; Stevenson, 1988).

From this perspective, what individuals earn is the result of their own choices (the kinds of training, education, and experience they accumulate, for example) and of the labour market need (demand) for and availability (supply) of certain kinds of workers at specific times. For example, human capital analysts argue that women diminish their human capital when they leave the labour force to engage in childbearing and child-care activities. While women are out of the labour force, their human capital deteriorates from non-use. When they return to work, women earn lower wages than men because they have fewer years of work experience and because their education and training may have become obsolete. They have "atrophied human capital" (Kemp, 1994:70).

Other neoclassical economic models attribute the wage gap to such factors as (1) the different amounts of energy men and women expend on their work (women who spend much energy on their family and household have less to put into their work), (2) the occupational choices women make (choosing female-dominated occupations so that they can spend more time with their families), and (3) the crowding of too many women into some occupations (which suppresses wages because the supply of workers exceeds demand) (Kemp, 1994).

EVALUATION OF FUNCTIONALIST AND NEOCLASSICAL ECONOMIC PERSPECTIVES Although Parsons and other functionalists did not specifically endorse the gendered division of labour, their analysis views it as natural and perhaps inevitable. Critics argue that problems inherent in traditional gender roles, including the strains placed by these roles on both men and women, and the social costs to society, are minimized by this approach. For example, men are assumed to be "money machines" for their families when they might prefer to spend more time in child-rearing activities. Also, the woman's place is assumed to be in the home, an idea that ignores the fact that many women hold jobs out of economic necessity.

Couples & Families CD 79

According to the human capital model, women earn less in the labour market because of their child-rearing responsibilities. What other explanations are offered for the lower wages that women receive?

Another limitation of the functionalist approach is that it does not take a critical look at the structure of society—especially the economic inequalities—that make educational and occupational opportunities more available to some than to others. Furthermore, it fails to examine the underlying power relations between men and women or to consider that the tasks assigned to women and men are unequally valued by society (Kemp, 1994). Similarly, the human capital model is rooted in the premise that individuals are evaluated based on their human capital in an open, competitive market where education, training, and other job-enhancing characteristics are taken into account. From this perspective, those who make less money (often men from visible minority groups and all women) have no one to blame but themselves.

Conflict Perspectives

According to many conflict analysts, the gendered division of labour within families and in the workplace results from male control of and dominance over women and resources. Differentials between men and women may exist in terms of economic, political, physical, and/or interpersonal power. The importance of a male monopoly in any of these arenas depends on the significance of that type of power in a society (Richardson, 1993). In hunting and gathering and horticultural societies, male dominance over women is limited because all members of the society must work to survive (Collins, 1971; Nielsen, 1990). In agrarian societies, however, male sexual dominance is at its peak. Male heads of household gain a monopoly not only on physical power but also on economic power, and women become sexual property.

Although men's ability to use physical power to control women diminishes in industrial societies, men still remain the household heads and control the property. Men also gain more power through their predominance in the most highly paid and prestigious occupations and the highest elected offices. In contrast, women have the ability to trade their sexual resources, companionship, and emotional support in the marriage market for men's financial support and social status; as a result, however, women as a group remain subordinate to men (Collins, 1971; Nielsen, 1990).

All men are not equally privileged, though. Some analysts argue that women and men in the upper classes are more privileged, because of their economic power, than men in lower-class positions and members of some minority groups (Lorber, 1994). In industrialized societies, persons who occupy elite positions in corporations, universities, the mass media, and government or who have great wealth have the most power (Richardson, 1993). Most, however, are men.

Conflict theorists in the Marxist tradition assert that gender stratification results from private ownership of the means of production; some men not only gain control over property and the distribution of goods but also gain power over women. According to Friedrich Engels and Karl Marx, marriage serves to enforce male dominance. Men of the capitalist class instituted monogamous marriage (a gendered institution) so that they could be certain of the paternity of their offspring, especially sons, whom they wanted to inherit their wealth. Feminist analysts have examined this theory, among others, as they have sought to explain male domination and gender stratification.

Feminist Perspectives

feminism The belief that women and men are equal and that they should be valued equally and have equal rights.

Feminism—the belief that women and men are equal and that they should be valued equally and have equal rights—is embraced by many men as well as women. Gender is viewed as a socially constructed concept that has important consequences in the lives of all people (Craig, 1992). According to sociologist Ben Agger (1993), men can be feminists and propose feminist theories; both women and men have much in common as they seek to gain a better understanding of the causes and consequences of gender inequality.

Although all feminist perspectives begin with the assumption that the majority of women occupy a subordinate position to men, they often diverge in terms of their explanations of how and why women are subordinated and the best strategies for achieving true equality for women (Chunn, 2000). Feminist perspectives vary in their analyses of the ways in which norms, roles, institutions, and internalized expectations limit women's behaviour. Taken together, they all seek to demonstrate how women's personal control operates even within the constraints of a relative lack of power (Stewart, 1994).

LIBERAL FEMINISM In liberal feminism, gender equality is equated with equality of opportunity. Liberal feminists assume that women's inequality stems from the denial to them of equal rights (Mandell, 2001). Liberal feminism strives for sex equality through the elimination of laws that differentiate people by gender. Only when these constraints on women's participation are removed will women have the same chance of success as men. This approach notes the importance of gender-role socialization and suggests that changes need to be made in what children learn from their families, teachers, and the media about appropriate masculine and feminine attitudes and behaviour. Liberal feminists fight for better child-care options, a woman's right to choose an abortion, and elimination of sex discrimination in the workplace.

RADICAL FEMINISM According to radical feminists, male domination causes all forms of human oppression, including racism and classism (Tong, 1989). Radical feminists often trace the roots of patriarchy to women's childbearing and child-rearing responsibilities, which make them dependent on men (Chafetz, 1984; Firestone, 1970). In the radical feminist view, men's oppression of women is deliberate, and ideological justification for this subordination is provided by other institutions, such as the media and religion. For women's condition to improve, radical feminists claim, patriarchy must be abolished. If institutions currently are gendered, alternative institutions—such as women's organizations seeking better health care, daycare, and shelters for victims of domestic violence and sexual assault—should be developed to meet women's needs.

SOCIALIST FEMINISM Socialist feminists suggest that the oppression of women results from their dual roles as paid *and* unpaid workers in a capitalist economy. In the workplace, women are exploited by capitalism; at home, they are exploited by patriarchy (Kemp, 1994). Women are easily exploited in both sectors; they are paid low wages and have few economic resources. Gendered job segregation is "the primary mechanism in capitalist society that maintains the superiority of men over women, because it enforces lower wages for women in the labour market" (Hartmann, 1976:139). As a result, women must do domestic labour either to gain a better-paid man's economic support or to stretch their own wages (Lorber, 1994). According to socialist feminists, the only way to achieve gender equality is to eliminate capitalism and develop a socialist economy that would bring equal pay and rights to women.

MULTICULTURAL FEMINISM During the "second wave" of feminism (1970–1990), the mainstream feminist movement was criticized for ignoring the experiences of poor women, women of colour, and women with disabilities. Feminism in its various forms described middle-class white women's experiences as the norm, and other women's experiences were treated as "different" (Cassidy, Lord, and Mandell, 2001). Recently, academics and activists have been attempting to address these criticisms and working to include the experiences of women of colour and Aboriginal women. Antiracist feminist perspectives are based on the belief that women of colour experience a different world than do middle-class white women because of multilayered oppression based on race and ethnicity, gender, and class (Khayatt, 1994). Building on the civil rights and feminist movements of the late 1960s and early 1970s, contemporary feminists have focused on the cultural experiences of marginalized women, such as women of colour, immigrant women, and Aboriginal women. A central assumption of this analysis is that race, class, and gender are forces that simultaneously oppress some women (Hull, Bell-Scott, and Smith, 1982). The effects of these statuses cannot be adequately explained as "double" or "triple" jeopardy (class plus race plus gender) because these ascribed characteristics are not simply added to one another. Instead, they are multiplicative (race times class times gender); different characteristics may be more significant in one situation than another. For example, a wealthy white woman (class) may be in a position of privilege as compared with people of colour (race) and men from lower socioeconomic positions (class), yet be in a subordinate position as compared to a white man (gender) from the capitalist class (Andersen and Collins, 1998). To analyze the complex relationship among these characteristics, the lived experiences of women of colour and other previously "silenced" people must be heard and examined within the context of particular historical and social conditions.

Feminists who analyze race, class, and gender suggest that equality will occur only when all women, regardless of race and ethnicity, class, age, religion, sexual orientation, or ability (or disability), are treated more equitably (Cassidy, Lord, and Mandell, 2001).

POSTMODERNIST FEMINISM One of the more recent feminist perspectives to emerge is *postmodernist feminism*. Postmodernist feminists argue that the various feminist theories—liberal, Marxist, radical, and socialist among them—that advocate a single or limited number of causes for women's inequality and oppression are flawed, inadequate, and typically based on suppression of female experiences. In keeping with the assumptions of postmodernist theory, postmodernist feminists resist making generalizations about "all women." Rather, they attempt to acknowledge the individual experiences and perspectives of women of all classes, races, ethnicities, abilities, sexualities, and ages. To postmodernist feminists, a singular feminist theory is impossible because there is no essential "woman." The category *woman* is seen as a social construct that is "a fiction, a non-determinable identity" (Cain, 1993, cited in Nelson, 2006:94).

Given that the category *woman* is regarded as socially constructed, the challenge of postmodernist feminism is to "deconstruct" these notions of the natural or essential woman. For example, the traditional sciences, in particular medicine, have viewed reproduction as a central construct of "woman." As Phoenix and Woolett have argued, "Women continue to be defined in terms of their biological functions" such that "motherhood and particularly childbearing continues to be defined as the supreme route to physical and emotional fulfillment and as essential for all women" (1991:7). Postmodernist feminists challenge the concept of the reproductive woman as essential and highlight the oppressive nature of such so-called scientific knowledge.

Postmodernist feminists strive to deconstruct our traditional understanding of what constitutes being female or male in society today. They argue that nothing is essentially male or female. In fact, they go so far as to challenge the idea of any real biological categories of male or female—suggesting, rather, that our understanding of biological differences between the sexes is of socially constructed categories that have emerged from specific cultural and historical contexts. Some scholars view the distinction between sex and gender as false because it is based on the assumption of biological differences as real. In sum, the categories of male and female, and man and woman, are viewed by postmodernist feminists as fluid, artificial, and malleable (Anderson, 2006:395).

Critics have suggested that this understanding of gender contradicts the fundamental principle of other feminist perspectives—that is, a central focus on women. As one critic asks, "How can it ascribe to be feminist, since feminism is a theory that focuses on the unitary category 'woman'?" (Cain, 1993:76).

EVALUATION OF CONFLICT AND FEMINIST PERSPECTIVES Conflict and feminist perspectives provide insights into the structural aspects of gender inequality in society. These approaches emphasize factors external to individuals that contribute to the oppression of women; however, they have been criticized for emphasizing the differences between men and women without taking into account their commonalities. Feminist approaches have also been criticized for their emphasis on male dominance without a corresponding analysis of the ways in which some men also may be oppressed by patriarchy and capitalism.

Symbolic Interactionist Perspectives

In contrast to functionalist, conflict, and feminist theorists, who focus primarily on macrolevel analysis of structural and systemic sources of gender differences and inequities, symbolic interactionists focus on a microlevel analysis that views a person's identity as a product of social interactions. From this perspective, people create, maintain, and modify gender as they go about their everyday lives. Candace West and Don Zimmerman utilized a symbolic interactionist perspective to explain what they refer to as "doing gender." An individual is "doing gender" whenever he or she interacts with another in a way that displays characteristics of a particular gender. This perspective views gender not as fixed in biology or social roles, but rather as something that is "accomplished" through interactions with others. They explain:

> Gender is not a set of traits, nor a variable, nor a role, but the product of social doings of some sort. What then is the social doing of gender? It is more than the continuous creation of the meaning of gender through human actions. We claim that gender itself is constituted through interaction. (1991:16)

In illustrating the concept of "doing gender," West and Zimmerman refer to a case study of Agnes, a transgender raised as a boy until she adopted a female identity at age 17. Although Agnes underwent a sex reassignment operation several years later, she had the challenging task of displaying herself as female even though she had never experienced the everyday interactions that women use to attach meaning to the concept of being female. Agnes had to display herself as a woman while simultaneously learning what it was to be a woman. To make matters more difficult, she was attempting to do so when most people at that age "do gender" virtually without thinking. As West and Zimmerman explain, this does not make Agnes's gender artificial:

> She was not faking what real women do naturally. She was obliged to analyze and figure out how to act within socially constructed circumstances and conceptions of femininity that women born with the appropriate biological credentials take for granted early on . . . As with others who must "pass" . . . Agnes's case makes visible what culture has made invisible—the accomplishment of gender. (1991:18)

Can you think of ways in which you "do gender" in your daily interactions? Using a symbolic interactionist perspective helps us to understand how we create, sustain, or change the gender categories that constitute being a man or a woman in our society. Analysts emphasize that socialization into gender roles is not simply a passive process whereby people internalize others' expectations, but rather people can choose to "do gender" (Messner, 2000, cited in Anderson, 2006). The interactionist perspective has been criticized for failing to address the power differences between men and women, as well as the significant economic and political advantages that exist in the larger social structure (Anderson, 2006).

TIME TO REVIEW

- Do any of these socialization agents discussed previously provide you with conflicting messages about how you "do gender"?

CONCEPT SNAPSHOT

FUNCTIONALIST PERSPECTIVES **Key thinker:** Talcott Parsons	According to functionalists, the division of labour into instrumental tasks for men and expressive tasks for women ensures stability in society.
NEOCLASSICAL ECONOMIC PERSPECTIVE	Human capital analysts argue that women create "atrophied human capital" when they leave the labour force to engage in childbearing and child-care activities. While women are out of the labour force, their human capital deteriorates from nonuse. When they return to work, women earn lower wages than men because they have fewer years of work experience and because their education and training may have become obsolete.
CONFLICT PERSPECTIVES **Key thinkers:** Friedrich Engels, Karl Marx	According to conflict theorists Engels and Marx, marriage serves to enforce male dominance. Men of the capitalist class instituted monogamous marriage (a gendered institution) so that they could be certain of the paternity of their offspring, especially sons, whom they wanted to inherit their wealth.
FEMINIST PERSPECTIVES	Feminist perspectives vary in their analyses of the ways in which norms, roles, institutions, and internalized expectations limit women's behaviour. Taken together, they all seek to demonstrate how women's personal control operates even within the constraints of a relative lack of power.
SYMBOLIC INTERACTIONIST PERSPECTIVES **Key thinkers:** Candace West, Don Zimmerman	From this perspective, people create, maintain, and modify gender as they go about their everyday lives. Candace West and Don Zimmerman utilized a symbolic interactionist perspective to explain what they refer to as "doing gender" whenever he or she interacts with another in a way that displays characteristics of a particular gender.

LO-1 Understand how gender is defined and how it differs from "sex."

Sex refers to the biological categories and manifestations of femaleness and maleness; *gender* refers to the socially constructed differences between females and males. In short, sex is what we (generally) are born with; gender is what we acquire through socialization.

Andrew Paterson/Alamy

© Fabio Cardoso/zefa/Corbis

LO-2 Explain the significance of gender in our everyday lives.

Gender role encompasses the attitudes, behaviours, and activities that are socially assigned to each sex and that are learned through socialization. Gender identity is an individual's perception of self as either female or male. Gendered institutions are those structural features that perpetuate gender inequality.

LO-3 Discuss how the nature of work affects gender equality in societies.

© Spencer Grant/PhotoEdit

In most hunting and gathering societies, fairly equitable relationships exist because neither sex has the ability to provide all of the food necessary for survival. In horticultural societies, cultivation with hoes is compatible with child care and a fair degree of gender equality exists because neither sex controls the food supply. In agrarian societies, male dominance is apparent; agrarian tasks require more labour and physical strength, and women often are excluded from these tasks because they are viewed as too weak or too tied to child-rearing activities. In industrialized societies, a gap exists between nonpaid work performed by women at home and paid work performed by men and women. A wage gap also exists between men and women in the marketplace. In post-industrial societies, the division of labour in paid employment is increasingly based on whether people provide or apply information or are employed in service jobs.

KEY TERMS

employment equity A strategy to eliminate the effects of discrimination and to make employment opportunities available to groups who have been excluded. (p. 321).

feminism The belief that women and men are equal and that they should be valued equally and have equal rights (p. 326).

gender The culturally and socially constructed differences between females and males found in the meanings, beliefs, and practices associated with "femininity" and "masculinity." (p. 306).

gender bias Behaviour that shows favouritism toward one gender over the other (p. 314).

gender identity A person's perception of the self as female or male (p. 306).

gender role Attitudes, behaviour, and activities that are socially defined as appropriate for each sex and are learned through the socialization process (p. 306).

matriarchy A hierarchical system of social organization in which cultural, political, and economic structures are controlled by women (p. 308).

patriarchy A hierarchical system of social organization in which cultural, political, and economic structures are controlled by men (p. 308).

pay equity (comparable worth) The belief that wages ought to reflect the worth of a job, not the gender or race of the worker (p. 321).

sexism The subordination of one sex, usually female, based on the assumed superiority of the other sex (p. 308).

sexual harassment Unwanted sexual advances, requests for sexual favours, or other verbal or physical conduct of a sexual nature (p. 315).

wage gap A term used to describe the disparity between women's and men's earnings (p. 320).

LO-4 Identify and discuss the primary agents of gender socialization.

Parents, peers, teachers and schools, sports, and the media are agents of socialization that tend to reinforce stereotypes of gender-appropriate behaviour.

© Mary Kate Denny/ PhotoEdit

© Tony Freeman/PhotoEdit

LO-5 Explain the causes of gender inequality in Canada.

Gender inequality results from economic, political, and educational discrimination against women. In most workplaces, jobs are either gender-segregated or the majority of employees are of the same gender. Although the degree of gender segregation in the professional workplace has declined since the 1970s, racial and ethnic segregation remains deeply embedded.

LO-6 Understand how functionalist, conflict, feminist, and interactionist perspectives on gender stratification differ.

According to functional analysts, women's roles as caregivers in contemporary industrialized societies are crucial in ensuring that key societal tasks are fulfilled. Whereas the husband performs the instrumental tasks of economic support and decision making, the wife assumes the expressive tasks of providing affection and emotional support to the family. According to conflict analysis, the gendered division of labour within families and the workplace—particularly in agrarian and industrial societies—results from male control and dominance over women and resources.

Couples & Families CD 79

Although feminist perspectives vary in their analyses of women's subordination, they all advocate social change to eradicate gender inequality. In liberal feminism, gender equality is connected to equality of opportunity. In radical feminism, male dominance is seen as the cause of oppression. According to socialist feminists, women's oppression results from their dual roles as paid and unpaid workers. Antiracist feminists focus on including knowledge and awareness of the lives of marginalized women in the struggle for equality. Postmodernist feminists focus on deconstructing what they see as fluid, artificial notions of the category *woman*. Symbolic interactionists view gender not as fixed in biology or social roles, but rather as something that is "accomplished" through interactions with others. An individual is viewed as "doing gender." whenever he or she interacts with another in a way that displays characteristics of a particular gender.

APPLICATION QUESTIONS

1. As discussed throughout this chapter, gender may be viewed as a social construction. "Doing gender," whether you are male or female, is something you have learned through a process of socialization. What changes would you have to make in your "gender performance" if you were to wake up one morning as the opposite gender?

2. Do the media reflect societal attitudes on gender, or do the media determine and teach gender behaviour? (As a related activity, watch television for several hours and list the roles women and men play in the shows and the advertisements.)

3. Examine the various academic departments at your university. What is the gender breakdown of the faculty in selected departments? What is the gender breakdown of undergraduates and graduate students in those departments? Are there major differences among various academic areas of teaching and study? What hypotheses can you come up with to explain your observations?

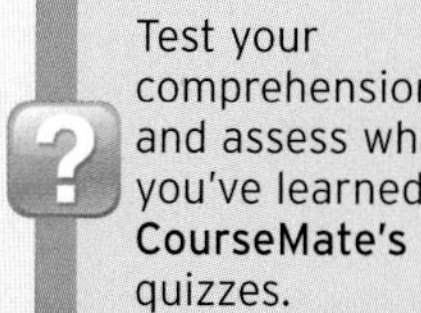

Test your comprehension and assess what you've learned with **CourseMate's** online quizzes.

For other interesting Lived Experiences, watch the video clips on **CourseMate.**

Practise what you've learned with flashcards containing key terms and definitions on **CourseMate.**

CHAPTER

12 Sex, Sexualities, and Intimate Relationships

With contributions by Caitlin Forsey

Peter Bernik/Shutterstock

Hookups, friends with benefits, $%!$ buddies, booty call,* and a variety of other terms are used to describe casual sexual relationships or sexual encounters outside of committed relationships. Although it is unlikely that these phenomena are new, it appears that less committed relationships may be more common among today's youth and young adult population than in previous generations (Weaver, MacKeigan, and MacDonald, 2011).

Generally speaking, hooking up includes a range of behaviours, from kissing to intercourse. Most research on the hookup culture to date has focused primarily on heterosexual college and university students to the exclusion of other sexual orientations. Despite a significant amount of inconsistency in how the term *hooking up* is used, it has become a significant way to initiate sexual and romantic relationships among heterosexual young adults.

In their classic sociological analysis, Gagnon and Simon (1973) argue that sexuality, like other forms of human behaviour, is socially learned and that we internalize "sexual scripts" in order to learn how to interact with those we desire. Sociologist Kathleen Bogle's (2008) qualitative study of college students and young alumni from two universities indicated that hooking up has its own sexual script, with its own norms on how to meet, get together, become sexually intimate, and manage the potential formation of relationships. Students from universities and colleges across North America shared what they had learned about the "hookup script." Many of these students explained that hookups allowed them to be sexual without the demands of a relationship. For example, Emily, a second-year university student, explains:

> *More often than not it happens once and it doesn't happen again. I think that's the accepted way that it is and I think that people drink and then they hook up and maybe there's attraction there and then it's not there anymore or maybe it's awkward or maybe you hook up with someone you don't really know and then you don't really take the time to get their number. Like sometimes when I hook up with people like I might not have any interest in them but it just happens to happen and you don't expect any more from it.* (Bogle, 2008:40)

As the following comments from a female student demonstrate, hooking up helped them clarify their values, embrace their own sexuality, and learn how to enforce their boundaries:

> *Every experience that I have had with these guys has taught me more about who I am and what type of role sex has in my life. I am no longer afraid to give into my desires, but I am also aware of what I feel is right and wrong.* (Wade, 2011)

Because hookup scripts are less defined and more varied than other sexual scripts (e.g., dating scripts), the "rules" of hookup culture are often difficult to decode and navigate. As third-year university student, Tony explains, even the definition of hookup is difficult to articulate:

> *If you take someone home and hook up, then that's hooking up . . . it depends on who the person is, like I can read my friends really, really easily. Like if one of my roommates says he "hooked up," that means he brought a girl home and this, that and the other thing . . . But, like if other kids tell me they hooked up, you got to ask, not to pry into their life, but it could mean a lot of things.* (Bogle, 2008:24)*

It becomes apparent in listening to these students that sexuality can often be confusing, ambiguous, and full of contradictions. Unquestionably, sexual scripts are changing, as are sexual values and practices.

In 2011, a Manitoba judge determined that a convicted rapist would not go to jail because the victim sent signals that "sex was in the air" through her suggestive attire and flirtatious conduct (McIntyre, 2011). This judgment, which created public outrage and debate, highlights the ambiguity that continues to revolve around issues of sex and sexuality. What is "normal"? What is "natural"? What is acceptable and what is morally reprehensible? The simple answer is, "It depends." According to sociologist Tracey Steele:

> *Sex—including our sexual activities and desires, our understanding of what sex is, and what sex means to us as individuals, depends—it depends on such things as when and where you where born, your sex, age, ethnicity, social class, and marital status, who your friends and family are, what kind of a job you have (or plan to have), the status of the economy, and even the god, gods or goddesses that you worship.* (Steele, 2005:2)

In this chapter, we will examine sex and sexuality, what it is and how it affects us. We will also consider issues pertaining to sex and sexuality such as sexual orientation, intimate relationships, and sexual health. It is also important to examine some of the more controversial issues related to sexuality, such as intimate partner violence and the sexual double standard. The voices of individuals will be utilized whenever possible to assist in understanding the complexities and challenges faced by young adults in developing and managing their sexuality. Before reading on, test your knowledge of sexuality by taking the quiz in Box 12.1 on page 336.

(*Source:* Bogle, Kathleen. *Hooking Up: Sex, Dating, and Relationships on Campus.* © 2008 New York University Press, p. 40.)

Critical Thinking Questions

1. How do you think sexual scripts, sexual values, and sexual practices have changed since your parents were your age? Do you agree that we live in more permissive times?
2. What effects will changes in sexual scripts have on young Canadians as they are struggling to establish their sexuality?

CHAPTER FOCUS QUESTION What are some of the current attitudes toward sexuality, and how have these changed in recent decades?

LEARNING OBJECTIVES

AFTER READING THIS CHAPTER, YOU SHOULD BE ABLE TO

LO-1 Explain how the terms *sex*, *gender*, and *sexuality* relate to one another and how they are different.

LO-2 Understand how various social scientists have classified sexual orientation.

LO-3 Compare and contrast monogamous and polyamorous intimate relationships.

LO-4 Explain a functionalist, conflict, symbolic interactionist, and postmodern analysis of sexuality.

LO-5 Evaluate the sexual health of Canadian youth and young adults.

LO-6 Identify the significant issues and controversies regarding sexuality in Canadian society.

BOX 12.1 **SOCIOLOGY AND EVERYDAY LIFE**

How Much Do You Know About Sexuality?

True	False	
T	F	1. The age of first intercourse has remained relatively stable among Canadian youth since the 1970s.
T	F	2. Youth today are more inclined than previous generations to have multiple sexual partners.
T	F	3. Today's youth are experiencing better sexual health and are more proactive about protecting their sexual health than were previous generations.
T	F	4. "Hooking up" has largely replaced committed relationships among university and college students.
T	F	5. Young people are having more sex at an earlier age and in a more casual context than their baby boomer parents did.

For answers to the quiz about sexuality, go to **www.nelson.com/sociologyinourtimes6e.**

LO-1 UNDERSTANDING SEXUALITY

Sexuality includes our sexual identity, sexual orientation, sexual acts, and intimate relationships. Specific ideas of sex, sexuality, and intimate relationships are the products of the society in which we live. As such, sexuality is a social construction that has significant consequences in our everyday lives.

Sex and Gender

sex A term used to describe the biological and anatomical differences between females and males.

primary sex characteristics The genitalia used in the reproductive process.

secondary sex characteristics The physical traits (other than reproductive organs) that identify an individual's sex.

Sex refers to the biological and anatomical differences between females and males. *Gender,* as discussed in Chapter 11, refers to the distinctive culturally and socially created qualities associated with being a man or a woman (masculinity and femininity). These two concepts are often used interchangeably. This is because *sex*—the biological and physiological aspects of the body—interacts with *gender*— the roles and responsibilities associated with the socially constructed concepts of "masculinity" and "femininity." Given the interdependence of these two concepts, it is virtually impossible to think about sex without thinking about gender at the same time.

At the core of sex differences is the chromosomal information transmitted at the moment a child is conceived. The mother contributes an X chromosome and the father either an X chromosome (which produces a female embryo) or a Y chromosome (which produces a male embryo). At birth, male and female infants are distinguished by **primary sex characteristics**—the genitalia used in the reproductive process. At puberty, an increased production of hormones results in the development of **secondary sex characteristics**—the physical traits (other than reproductive organs) that identify an individual's sex. For women, these include larger breasts, wider hips, and narrower shoulders, a layer of fatty tissue covering the body, and menstruation. For men, they include development of enlarged genitals, a deeper voice, greater height, a more muscular build, and more body and facial hair.

Sex and Sexuality

Once again, the terms *sex* and *sexuality* are often used interchangeably in our everyday speech. For example, although *sex* may refer to the biological determination of being male or female, it may also be used to describe a range of behaviours or feelings associated with human sexuality (e.g., "sex was in the air," he had "sex" with his girlfriend, she is "sexy"). The fact that the terms *sex* and *sexuality* are used interchangeably may contribute to many common misconceptions about the biological determination of human sexuality, such as uncontrollable sexual urges. For our purposes, **sexuality** and **sexual** will refer to the range of human activities designed to produce erotic response and pleasure. Sexuality, like other forms of human behaviour is shaped by the society and culture we live in. **Sexual scripts** are culturally created guidelines that define how, where, with whom, and under what conditions a person is to behave as a sexual being (Nelson, 2006).

© NHAT V. MEYER/MCT/Landov

Three years after Olympic athlete Caster Semenya had to undergo genital exams in 2009 to verify that she was female—an experience she described as "unwarranted and invasive"—she successfully competed in the 2012 Olympics.

Intersexed Individuals and Transsexuals

In our society, sex is usually viewed as either one of only two categories—male or female. But sex is not always clear-cut. That is, not all individuals are distinctly male or female. The complexities of sex and gender recently came to light in the controversial case of Olympic runner Caster Semenya. After her gold-metal performance at the 2009 World Athletics Championship, Semenya was asked to undergo medical testing to verify that she was in fact "female." Fortunately, the South African sports ministry refused to make the results public and Semenya was able to keep her gold medal. In 2012, Semenya proudly walked into the opening ceremonies in London carrying her country's flag. The case of Caster Semenya is not unique. At the 1996 Olympics Games in Atlanta, eight female athletes were determined to have XY chromosomes and were not allowed to compete. Later studies showed that they were physiologically female even though their genes said they were male, and they were reinstated (Greenemeier, 2009).

Intersexed individuals are persons whose sexual differentiation is ambiguous or incomplete. In one case, for example, a chromosomally normal (XY) male was born with a penis just 1 cm long and a urinary opening similar to that of a female (Money and Ehrhardt, 1972). In another case, a newborn male had his penis irreversibly damaged during a circumcision and had his gender "reassigned" to female (see Box 12.2). Occasionally, a hormone imbalance before birth produces a hermaphrodite. This term has been used incorrectly to describe intersexed individuals. A **hermaphrodite** has male testes and female ovaries. In the past, persons born with ambiguous genitalia were thought to have an abnormal and problematic condition that called for immediate surgical intervention. If ambiguous genitalia are rarely detrimental to a person's physical health, why the need for surgical intervention as quickly as possible after the child's birth? According to social psychologist Suzanne Kessler, the "treatment" that intersexed infants are subjected to is based not on the well-being of the child but rather on cultural beliefs about a dichotomous conception of sex as either male or female. As she explains:

> Lest there be any doubt about whom the genitals are for, one team of researchers justified doing surgery by saying that it "relieves parental anxiety" about the child with relatives and friends. Another surgical group is even more explicit in concluding that "for a small infant, the initial objective is an operation to feminize the appearance of the baby to make it acceptable to the parents and family." (1998:55)

sexuality (sexual)
The range of human activities designed to produce erotic response and pleasure.

sexual scripts
Culturally created guidelines that define how, where, with whom, and under what conditions a person is to behave as a sexual being.

intersexed individuals
Persons whose sexual differentiation is ambiguous or incomplete.

hermaphrodite
An individual born with male testes and a female ovary.

Guided largely by the pioneering work of Money and Ehrhardt (1972), physicians have attempted to relieve the distress of parents of intersexed infants by assuring them that early surgical "correction" would allow intersexed children to perceive themselves as clearly one sex or another—allowing them to grow up as "whole men" or "whole women." More recently, feminist critiques have challenged these medical practices, in particular many of the incorrect assumptions made about sex, gender, and gender identity. For example, gender reassignment surgeries are based on the assumption that unaltered intersexed persons have no clear identities. There is no research evidence to support this assumption. Furthermore, medical practitioners assume that "typical" women and men feel completely at home in their bodies and gender identities and do not experience crises in relating their identity and appearance (Holmes, 2002:162). Finally, the voices of intersexed individuals tell a story of feeling deeply ashamed and abused by their medical treatments.

transsexual A person who believes that he or she was born with the body of the wrong sex.

transvestite A male who lives as a woman or a female who lives as a man but does not alter the genitalia.

Some people may be genetically of one sex but have the gender identity of the other. That is true for a **transsexual**, a person who believes that he or she was born with the body of the wrong sex. Some transsexuals take hormone treatments or have a sex change operation to alter their genitalia to achieve a body congruent with their own sense of sexual identity (Basow, 1992). Many transsexuals who receive hormone treatments or undergo surgical procedures go on to lead lives that they view as being compatible with their true sexual identity. Transsexuality may occur in conjunction with homosexuality, but this is frequently not the case. Some researchers believe that both transsexuality and homosexuality have a common prenatal cause, such as a critically timed hormonal release due to stress in the mother or the presence of certain hormone-mimicking chemicals during critical steps of fetal development. Researchers continue to examine this issue and to debate the origins of transsexuality and homosexuality.

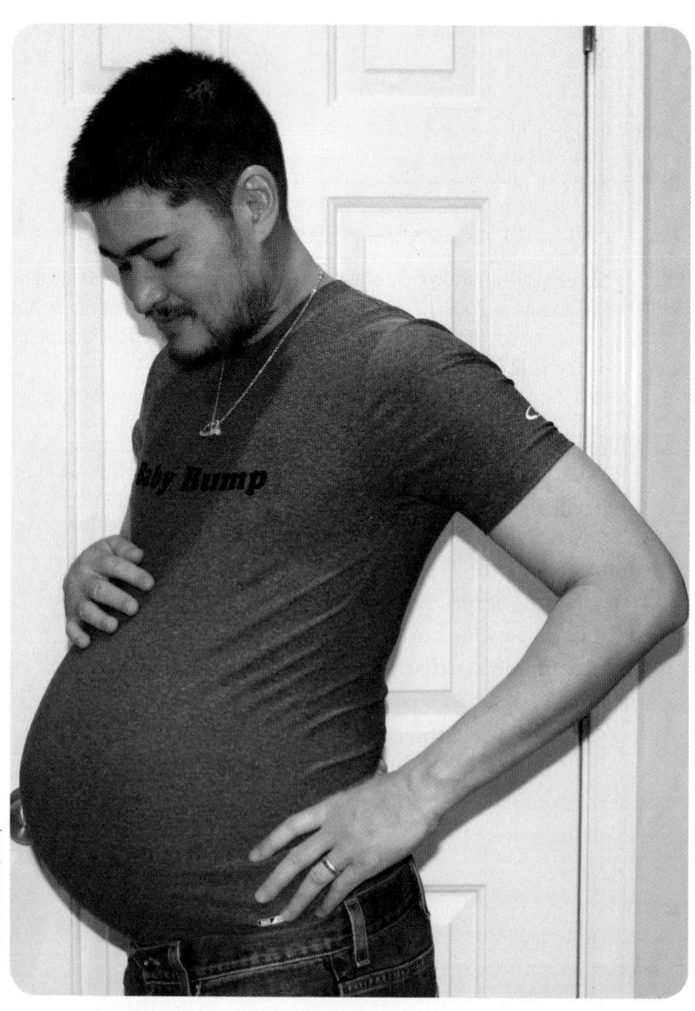

© Barcroft Media/Getty

Thomas Beatie, born a woman, underwent a sex-change operation but kept his reproductive organs. He made headlines in 2007 after pictures of his pregnant belly became public.

Western societies acknowledge the existence of only two sexes; some other societies recognize three—men, women, and *berdaches* (or *hijras* or *xaniths*), biological males who behave, dress, and work and are treated in most respects as women. Although outside observers viewed the berdache as shameful or deviant, multiple sex and/or gender roles were common in many Native American societies. In many Indigenous cultures, stories of creation involved themes of sex/gender ambiguity and absence of sexual differentiation and transformation from one sex to another (Nanda, 2000:20). More recently, the term *berdache* has been rejected as insulting and inaccurate in its presentation of diversity in Aboriginal cultures. A more widely accepted term is *two-spirited,* which emphasizes that in Indigenous societies, gender variance is respected and valued and seen as a source of spiritual power (Brotman et al., 2002).

The closest approximation to a third sex in Western societies is a **transvestite**, a male who lives as a woman or a female who lives as a man but does not alter the genitalia. Although transvestites are not treated as a third sex, they often "pass" for members of that sex because their appearance and mannerisms fall within the range of what is expected from members of the other sex.

BOX 12.2 POINT/COUNTERPOINT

Gender Reassignment: "As Nature Made Him"

On April 27, 1966, in Winnipeg, Manitoba, an infant boy's routine circumcision went terribly wrong. Through a medical error, eight-month-old Bruce Reimer was left without a penis. The circumcision of his twin brother, Brian, had gone smoothly and his male genitalia remained intact. In desperation, the twins' parents consulted Dr. John Money, medical director of the Gender Identity Clinic at the world-renowned Johns Hopkins University.

Based on his research, Dr. Money asserted that a person's gender identity and sexual orientation were not biologically determined but rather the result of socialization. Tragically, Bruce Reimer became the "test case" used to prove this theory.

Dr. Money convinced Bruce's parents to have their son surgically transformed into a girl (he was renamed Brenda), based on his assurance that, with appropriate parenting, she would grow up to be a feminine, heterosexual woman (LeVay, 2000:1). Dr. Money monitored Brenda and her identical twin, Brian, during their childhood, and he reported extensively in books, journals, and lectures that this "experiment" had been a complete success. According to Dr. Money, Brenda had grown up happily feminine, displaying many of the stereotypical traits associated with being female: She was shy, neat, and pretty, and she enjoyed playing with dolls and cooking. Most important, Brenda's own gender identity was that of a female, supporting Dr. Money's theory that gender was malleable.

This "test case" gave Dr. Money enormous professional acclaim and success as it became one of the most famous cases in modern medicine and the social sciences. The case was cited repeatedly for 30 years as proof that our sense of being female or male is not inborn but primarily the result of how we are raised. The case also established a medical precedent for the gender reassignment of thousands of other newborns who were similarly injured during circumcision or who were born with ambiguous genitals.

This "experiment" was, in fact, a failure from the start and had disastrous results for the Reimer family. "Brenda" did not see herself as female, nor did her peers. She preferred to play with her twin brother's toys. She was tormented at school, nicknamed "Cavewoman," and teased for her masculine qualities. Brenda failed at school and was frequently in fights. When she was a teenager, after years of depression and a suicide attempt, her parents told her the truth about her gender reassignment. In response, Brenda assumed a male gender identity and underwent surgery to create a cosmetic penis. He changed his name to David (in reference to David and Goliath) and eventually married a woman who had three children.

Dr. Money failed to report this final outcome, but in 1996, it was exposed. Sexologist Milton Diamond, from the University of Hawaii, found David and revealed the truth to the medical community. Dr. Money claimed that he had lost track of the Reimer family, despite the fact that they had never moved (Nussbaum, 2003:1). His professional reputation was destroyed.

The true facts of this case have been particularly helpful in dealing with the treatment of hermaphroditic infants, who in the past were "normalized" to female. Evidence now shows that many, like David, had rejected their medically created gender and been traumatized by the medical intervention. Tragically, on May 4, 2004, David Reimer committed suicide at the age of 38.

What conclusions do you draw about sex and gender identity from David Reimer's case? Consider the formation of your own gender identity. What factors have contributed to your being a female or a male? What role does society play in the formulation of gender identity, both in general and in your own life in particular?

Sources: Colapinto, 2001; LeVay, 2000; Nussbaum, 2003.

LO-2 Sexual Orientation

Sexual orientation refers to an individual's preference for emotional–sexual relationships with members of the opposite sex (heterosexuality), the same sex (homosexuality), or both (bisexuality) (Lips, 2001). Some scholars believe that sexual orientation is rooted in biological factors that are present at birth; others believe that sexuality has both biological and social components and is not preordained at birth.

sexual orientation A person's preference for emotional-sexual relationships with members of the opposite sex (heterosexuality), the same sex (homosexuality), or both (bisexuality).

The terms *homosexual* and *gay* are most often used in association with males who prefer same-sex relationships; the term *lesbian* is used in association with females who prefer same-sex relationships. Heterosexual individuals, who prefer opposite-sex relationships, are sometimes referred to as *straight*. However, it is important to note that heterosexual people are much less likely to be labelled by their sexual orientation than are people who are gay, lesbian, or bisexual.

What criteria do social scientists use to classify individuals as heterosexual, gay, lesbian, bisexual, or homosexual? For more than 40 years, the work of biologist Alfred C. Kinsey was considered the definitive research on human sexuality. It was Kinsey's research that first challenged the idea that human beings could be categorized simply as either "heterosexual" or "homosexual." As he explained in his first book, *Sexual Behaviour in the Human Male:*

> Males do not represent two discrete populations, heterosexual and homosexual. The world is not divided into sheep and goats . . . Only the human mind invents categories and tries to force fit individuals into separated pigeon holes. The living world is a continuum in each and every one of its aspects. The sooner we learn this concerning human sexual behaviour the sooner we will reach a sound understanding of the realities of sex. (Kinsey et al., 1948:639, cited in Nelson, 2006)

Instead of three categories (heterosexual, homosexual, bisexual), Kinsey constructed a seven-point scale of sexual behaviour (see Figure 12.1). This scale was constructed to measure the fluidity of human sexual experience. An eighth category, for asexuals, was later added by Kinsey's associates. The term **asexual** refers to an absence of sexual desire toward either sex.

asexual An absence of sexual desire toward either sex.

Findings from Kinsey's research indicated that while 60 percent of his nonrandom sample of white males reported engaging in some same-sex experiences before adulthood (37 percent of which led to orgasm), only 4 percent developed exclusively homosexual patterns of sexuality as adults. He further found that although 13 percent of his sample of women reported experiencing at least one same-sex experience leading to orgasm, only 3 percent reported being "mostly" or "exclusively" lesbian as adult women. As a result of Kinsey's research, it became widely known that bisexuality was much more common than exclusive homosexuality and human sexuality was much less definitive and much more fluid than previously believed (Kinsey, 1948, 1953).

FIGURE 12.1 KINSEY'S HETEROSEXUAL–HOMOSEXUAL RATING SCALE

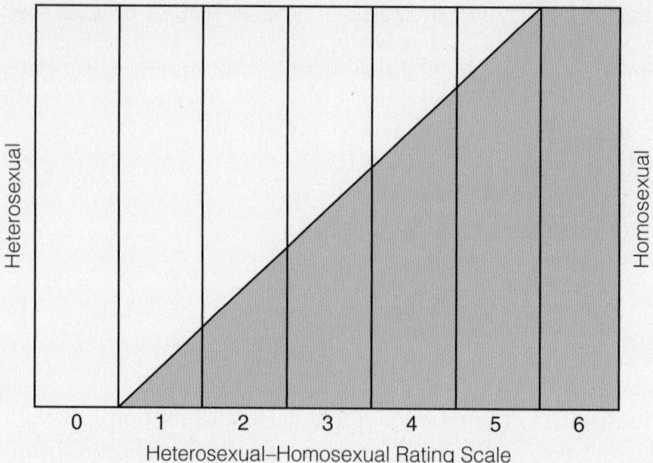

Source: The Kinsey Institute, 2012. "Kinsey's Homosexual-Heterosexual Rating Scale" retrieved August 1, 2012 http://www.iub.edu/~kinsey/research/akhhscale.html. Reprinted by permission of The Kinsey Institute for Research in Sex, Gender, and Reproduction, Inc.

Recently, the work of Kinsey and his associates has been superseded by the National Health and Social Life Survey conducted by the National Opinion Research Center at the University of Chicago. Based on interviews with more than 3400 men and women age 18 to 59, this random survey tended to reaffirm the significance of the dominant sexual ideologies. The researchers established three criteria for identifying people as homosexual or bisexual: (1) *sexual attraction* to persons of one's own gender, (2) *sexual involvement* with one or more persons of one's own gender, and (3) *self-identification* as gay, lesbian, or bisexual (Michael et al., 1994). According to these criteria, then, having engaged in a homosexual act does not necessarily classify a person as homosexual. Many respondents in the University of Chicago study reinforced this idea by indicating that, although they may have had at least one homosexual encounter when they were younger, they were no longer engaged in homosexual conduct and had never identified themselves as gay, lesbian, or bisexual. Most respondents reported that they engaged in heterosexual relationships, although 9 percent of the men said they had had at least one homosexual encounter resulting in orgasm. While 6.2 percent of men and 4.4 percent of women said that they were at least somewhat attracted to others of the same gender, only 2.8 percent of men and 1.4 percent of women identified themselves as gay or lesbian.

Gender can be "ambiguous," and individuals whose appearance, behaviour, or self-identification does not conform to common social rules of gender expression are often referred to as being *transgendered*.

More recent studies have examined how sexual orientation is linked to identity. Sociologist Kristin G. Esterberg (1997) interviewed lesbian and bisexual women to determine how they "perform" lesbian or bisexual identity through daily activities, such as choice of clothing and hairstyles, as well as how they use body language and talk. According to Esterberg, some of the women viewed themselves as being "lesbian from birth," whereas others had experienced shifts in their identities depending on social surroundings, age, and political conditions at specific periods in their lives.

Another study looked at gay and bisexual men. Human development scholar Ritch C. Savin-Williams found that gay/bisexual youths often believe from an early age that they are different from other boys:

> The pattern that most characterized the youths' awareness, interpretation, and affective responses to childhood attractions consisted of an overwhelming desire to be in the company of men. They wanted to touch, smell, see, and hear masculinity. This awareness originated from earliest childhood memories; in this sense, they "always felt gay." (2004:131)

However, most of the boys and young men realized that these feelings were not typical of other males. They were uncomfortable when others attempted to make them conform to the established cultural definitions of masculinity, such as showing a great interest in team sports, competition, and aggressive pursuits.

The term *transgender* was created to describe individuals whose appearance, behaviour, or self-identification does not conform to common social rules of gender expression. "Transgenderism" is sometimes used to refer to those who cross-dress, to transsexuals, and to others outside mainstream categories. Although some gay and lesbian advocacy groups oppose the concept of transgender as being somewhat meaningless, others applaud the term as one that might help unify diverse categories of people based on sexual identity. Various organizations of gays, lesbians, and transgender persons have been unified in their desire to reduce hate crimes and other forms of **homophobia**—extreme prejudice directed at gays, lesbians, bisexuals, and others who are perceived as not being heterosexual.

homophobia Extreme prejudice directed at gays, lesbians, bisexuals, and others who are perceived as not being heterosexual.

TIME TO REVIEW

- How has research on intersexed and transsexual individuals changed our perception of gender and gender identity?
- Discuss how the research on homosexuality has changed our understanding of sexuality since Kinsey's pioneering work.

LO-3 LOVE AND INTIMACY

It has been said that North Americans are "in love with love." Why is this so? Perhaps the answer lies in the fact that our ideal culture emphasizes *romantic love,* which refers to a deep emotion, the satisfaction of significant needs, a caring for and acceptance of the person we love, and involvement in an intimate relationship (Lamanna and Riedmann, 2011). Although the methods we employ to pursue romance may have changed, we are certainly no less enthralled with the idea.

How have Canadians viewed love and intimacy in the past? During the Industrial Revolution in the late 19th century, people came to view work and home as separate spheres in which different feelings and emotions were appropriate (Coontz, 1992). The public sphere of work—men's sphere—emphasized self-reliance and independence. In contrast, the private sphere of the home—women's sphere—emphasized the giving of services, the exchange of gifts, and love. Accordingly, love and emotions became the domain of women, and work and rationality the domain of men (Lamanna and Riedmann, 2011).

Although the roles of women and men have changed dramatically over the past century, men and women still do not always share the same perspectives about romantic love. According to sociologist Francesca Cancian (1990), women tend to express their feelings verbally, whereas men tend to express their love through nonverbal actions, such as running an errand for someone or repairing a child's broken toy.

Love, intimacy, and sexuality are closely intertwined. Intimacy may be psychic ("the sharing of minds") or sexual or both. Although sexuality is an integral part of many intimate relationships, perceptions about sexual activities vary from one culture to the next and from one era to another. For example, depending on the time and place, a kiss may (or may not) be regarded as a sexual act, a health threat, a ceremonial celebration, or a disgusting behaviour. Psychologist Leonore Tiefer explains that while sexual kissing is customary in Western cultures, many African and Asian cultures view kissing negatively. When the Thonga of Africa first saw Europeans kissing, they laughed, remarking, "Look at them—they eat each other's saliva and dirt" (2005:24).

marriage A legally recognized and/or socially approved arrangement between two or more individuals that carries certain rights and obligations and usually involves sexual activity.

Intimate Relationships

Across cultures, intimate relationships are characterized by different forms. All sexual or intimate relationships, whether they are monogamous or nonmonogamous, are a social product.

MONOGAMY In Canada, marriage continues to be the most common form of committed intimate relationship among adults. **Marriage** is a legally recognized and/or socially approved arrangement between two or more individuals that carries certain rights and obligations and usually involves sexual activity. In Canada, the only legally sanctioned form of marriage is **monogamy**—an intimate relationship with only one person at a time. For some people, this takes the form of marriage as a lifelong commitment that ends only with the death of a partner.

monogamy
An intimate relationship with one person at a time.

Members of some religious groups believe that marriage is "forever"; if one spouse dies, the surviving spouse is precluded from marrying anyone else. For others, marriage is a commitment of indefinite duration. Through a pattern of marriage, divorce, and remarriage, some people practise *serial monogamy*—a succession of relationships in which a person has several partners over a lifetime but is legally married to only one person at a time.

Extramarital or, more generally, sexual infidelity in monogamous relationships is common. Infidelity can involve a wide range of behaviours occurring outside of a committed relationship. Most research on heterosexual relationships focuses on vaginal sex occurring outside of a marital relationship. However, behaviours can range from intense emotional relationships or close friendships to kissing, oral sex, or other sexual behaviours, and the primary dyad need not be married (Mark, Janssen, and Milhausen, 2011). And the Internet has created a new forum for infidelity that provides individuals with an opportunity to engage in secretive, anonymous, often sexually charged interactions with others online. Consider, for example, the website AshleyMadison.com, which has more than 12 million users looking for extramarital intimacy.

Research on infidelity in heterosexual relationships suggests that approximately one-third of men and one-quarter of women may engage in sexual relationships outside of their committed relationship at least once in their lives (Kinsey, Pomeroy, and Martin, 1948; Kinsey et al., 1953; Mark, Janssen, and Milhausen, 2011). According to a University of Chicago study, persons who engaged in extramarital sex found their activities to be more thrilling than those with their marital partner, but they also felt guilty. Persons in sustained relationships, such as marriage or cohabitation, found sexual activity to be the most satisfying emotionally and physically (Milhausen and Mark, 2009).

Research on infidelity in same-sex relationships is less prevalent and fraught with the same measurement issues faced by researchers studying infidelity in heterosexual unions. However, one study on infidelity in same-sex relationships found that 45.2 percent of gay men who indicated they were in committed, monogamous relationships reported that they or their partner had had sex with a third party since the beginning of their relationship (Milhausen and Mark, 2009).

According to sociologist Eric Anderson, author of *The Monogamy Gap: Men, Love and the Reality of Cheating* (2012), monogamy does not necessarily provide a lifetime of sexual contentment. Anderson interviewed 40 heterosexual male undergraduate university students in England about their experience with monogamy and cheating. The participants very clearly described competing social scripts of emotional desire for monogamy and sexual desire for cheating. For example, Tony says, "I struggle all the time. I get mad at her. I want sex with other women, and I know she'd never let me, so sometimes I just feel like cheating because I'm not supposed to." Similarly, another participant, James, indicates he desperately wants other women: "I can't stop thinking about other women, I'm sure I'll cheat. I mean, I don't want to but I will. It sucks, really it sucks. I don't want to cheat, but I really want sex [with someone other than his girlfriend]" (Anderson, 2010:859).

Anderson concludes that monogamy is a cultural illusion imposed on young men and women that falsely promises that once they find true love, they will no longer experience sexual boredom and the desire to cheat. Although society cherishes monogamy for most couples, the expectation of exclusive sexual activity may be unsustainable. The solution, according to Anderson, is to explore alternatives to monogamy. He suggests:

> We may need to investigate other relationship models: open arrangements or . . . "monogamish" relationships in which couples have flings, affairs or threesomes. These ways of loving, along with polyamorous relationships and even singlehood, should be as equally culturally valued as monogamy. Only when men and women are able to make sexual choices free of stigma will people be honest with their partners about their desires (2012b).

One alternative to monogamy is a form of intimate relationship that is increasingly presenting itself as an option in North American society—polyamory.

polyamory
Intimate relationships that involve mutually acknowledged emotional, sexual, or romantic relationships with multiple partners.

NONMONOGAMY **Polyamory** involves mutually acknowledged emotional, sexual, or romantic relationships with multiple partners. The Latin part of *polyamory* means "love" and the Greek part means "many," so the word translates into "many loves" or "more than one love" (Kress, 2006). In the following narrative, Angi talks about her polyamorous family and some of the challenges she faces:

> It is continually surprising to me that people, in general, seem far more able to accept the possibility of sharing a partner sexually than they are able to accept the possibility of having multiple loves. It says a great deal about our society's rigid definition of romantic love that people are able to somewhat easily accept the concept of sexually open relationships—and even dishonest infidelity—while insisting that it cannot be possible to actually love multiple partners simultaneously. Frustratingly, I have been told on more than one occasion that what I share with my partners cannot, by definition, be love, as if anyone can define for others what love is and what it is not. These attitudes strike me as incredibly reminiscent of a society that—30 years ago—viewed same-sex relationships only as a deviant sexual behaviour. (Stevens, 2012)

Polyamory includes a wide range of relationship and sexual practices, including open or closed group marriages, triads (three partners), and quads (four partners). Polyamorous partners may be primary, secondary, or tertiary, depending on the level of commitment and amount of time they spend with the partner(s). Unlike other sexual relationships involving multiple partners, such as swinging or casual sex, love is central to polyamorous relationships. Christian Klesse conducted interviews with 44 men and women from the United Kingdom who were in polyamorous relationships. His subjects emphasized the importance of love, friendship, and commitment in these relationships and de-emphasized the importance of sexuality. As Marianne explained:

> I mean sometimes when I try to explain polyamory to my friends, they don't get it, because they say . . . I mean especially, if it's relationships that aren't sexual, they say, "Oh but they're just close friendships." And I'm trying to explain that "No, they're not just close friendships—they're closer than a close friendship—they're people that I love." And you know, some of my friends that probably are truly monogamous, they just don't get it. Erm, it's funny really. (Klesse, 2006:568)

© Catchlight Visual Services/Alamy

Unlike other sexual relationships involving multiple partners, love is central to poyamorous relationships.

The blurring of the boundaries between friend, partner, and lover is an important aspect of polyamory. Consequently, having sex with friends is not unusual and may work in a number of different directions: Sometimes, long-standing friendships can turn into more sexual relationships; sometimes, sexual attraction marks the beginning of a later nonsexual relationship. Pal describes his approach to polyamory as a fluid process of moving from friendship to partnership:

> I am very much coming from becoming very, very close friends and then having those friends being very intimate, much more intimate and

> sort of sharing a life with them, but I really don't like the idea of having a mould for a relationship in the way of doing it. (Klesse, 2006:570)

Individuals in polyamorous unions describe their intimate relationships as "responsible non-monogamy" because all partners are aware of and share a consensus on the nonmonogamous aspect of their relationship. As such, honesty is central to the success of these relationships (Jamieson, 2004).

Despite media portrayals of patriarchal and nonegalitarian forms of polyamory in *Sister Wives* and *Big Love,* the voices of individuals in committed polyamorous relationships tell a different story. For example, Angi says:

> I don't know that there's any way to offer a universal definition of romantic love. I certainly don't claim to be up to the task. What I do know is that my partners, while vastly different from one another, share several important qualities. They are my two best friends in the world. They are both men I can sit up all night talking with. They are both men who support and embrace my feminism. They are both men who I laugh with almost every single day. They both make me feel loved, respected, and desired. And I can say with as much certainly as it is ever possible to have about such things that I am madly in love them both, and want to live the rest of my life with them both by my side. (Stevens, 2012:3)

polygamy The concurrent marriage of a person of one sex with two or more members of the opposite sex.

polygyny The concurrent marriage of one man with two or more women.

polyandry The concurrent marriage of one woman with two or more men.

CROSS-CULTURAL VARIATIONS IN INTIMATE RELATIONSHIPS **Polygamy** is the concurrent marriage of a person of one sex with two or more members of the opposite sex (Ward and Belanger, 2001). The most prevalent form of polygamy is **polygyny**—the concurrent marriage of one man with two or more women. Polygyny has been practised, for example, in a number of Islamic societies, including in some regions of contemporary Africa and southern Russia. The reality television show *Sister Wives*, which documents the life of a polygamist family that includes a husband with four wives and 17 children, certainly challenges traditional notions of family.

The second type of polygamy is **polyandry**—the concurrent marriage of one woman with two or more men. Polyandry is rare; when it does occur, it is typically found in societies where men greatly outnumber women because of high rates of female infanticide or where marriages are arranged between two brothers and one woman (fraternal polyandry). According to recent research, polyandry is never the only form of marriage in a society: Whenever polyandry occurs, polygyny co-occurs (Trevithick, 1997). Although Tibetans are the most frequently studied population where polyandry exists, anthropologists have also identified the Sherpas, Paharis, Sinhalese, and various African groups as sometimes practising polyandry (Trevithick, 1997). An anthropological study of Nyinba, an ethnically Tibetan population living in northwestern Nepal, found that fraternal polyandry (two brothers sharing the same wife) is the normative form of marriage and that the practice continues to be highly valued culturally (Levine and Silk, 1997).

In Canada, the notion of romantic love is deeply intertwined with our beliefs about how and why people develop intimate relationships and establish families. Not all societies share this concern with romantic love.

TIME TO REVIEW

- Discuss the alternatives to monogamy.
- How pervasive is infidelity? What are some of the reasons why people may have relationships outside of their committed relationships?
- What are some of the different types of polyamorous relationships?

LO-4 THEORETICAL PERSPECTIVES ON SEX, SEXUALITY, AND INTIMATE RELATIONS

Sociological perspectives on sex, sexuality, and intimate relations vary in their emphasis on the function of sexuality, the relationship between sexuality and social inequality, the commodification of sex, the role of gender in the social ordering of sexuality, the meaning people attach to sexual scripts, the historical emergence of sexuality as a mechanism of social control, and the degree to which sexual identity is understood as either a fixed state or an ongoing process.

Functionalist Perspectives

Functionalists use the terms *functional* and *dysfunctional* to describe how certain practices and norms contribute to the stability of social institutions and society more generally. On a biological level, sexual reproduction is functional because it ensures the continuation of the human species. For this reason, regulating norms and values surrounding sexual reproduction is an important aspect of maintaining social stability. Most members of society share a common set of values, beliefs, and behavioural expectations regarding legitimate and illegitimate sexual reproduction. The incest taboo is one of the oldest and most universally recognized norms that forbids marriage and sexual relations between certain relatives. In Canada, Europe, Mexico, and some U.S. states, first cousin marriage is permitted; however, both law and cultural norms prohibit marriage and sexual relations between brothers and sisters, as well as between parents and their children. Part of the reason is biological, since reproduction between close relatives increases the odds of genetic abnormalities. However, functionalists also recognize that regulating sexual contact between close relatives integrates people into society, limits sexual competition within the family, protects children, and reinforces the legal rights and obligations that are defined through kinship ties.

Although sexual relations between close relatives are considered dysfunctional because they threaten the stability of the family, functionalists argue that a certain amount of deviance is necessary for the overall stability of society because deviance clarifies social norms and helps maintain social control. The societal consensus regarding when and with whom people should engage in sexual activity has shifted considerably over time. A 2009 public opinion poll conducted by Angus Reid shows that 87 percent of Canadians consider premarital sex between men and women to be "morally acceptable," compared with 81 percent of Canadians in 2007. In a 1990 national survey, Bibby and Posterki (1992) found that 80 percent of Canadians "agreed" or "strongly agreed" that premarital sex was acceptable, compared with 68 percent in 1975. While these statistics point to a growing trend toward viewing sex as a legitimate form of intimacy and recreation outside of marriage, they exist alongside very strict attitudes concerning extramarital affairs. In Canada, extramarital sex is widely condemned with more than 85 percent of adults reporting that adultery is "almost always wrong" or "always wrong" (Bibby, 1995a). Through negative reactions to sexual infidelity within marriage, Canadian society reaffirms its commitment to norms surrounding appropriate sexual conduct and ensures the stability of the family.

From a functionalist perspective, some sexual practices are both functional *and* dysfunctional for society. Although prostitution is often considered harmful to society because it exploits women and spreads disease, Kingsley Davis (1937) argues that prostitution will always serve an important function in societies where restrictive norms govern sexual conduct. From a functionalist perspective, prostitution offers quick, impersonal sexual gratification for people who are not looking for emotional attachment or long-term relationships. It also provides a sexual outlet for people who may not have ready access to sex because they are single, socially inept, unattractive, or too busy to maintain ongoing sexual relationships. Prostitution also provides people with the opportunity to engage in sexual practices that regular sex partners may consider distasteful or immoral (e.g., multiple sex partners, anal intercourse, sadomasochism). For people with no formal education and limited job skills, prostitution provides a means for establishing social contacts and generating income.

In viewing society as a set of interrelated parts, functionalists recognize that solutions to a social problem such as prostitution can also lead to undesirable social consequences. According to Becki Ross (2010), the expulsion of prostitutes from Vancouver's lively West End neighbourhood to the uninhabited industrial tracts of the city's Downtown Eastside had lethal consequences for outdoor sex workers in the city. Some of the abolitionist strategies used by community members and other stakeholders intent on transforming Vancouver into a "world class city" included "throwing eggs, tomatoes and beer bottles at community meetings and during public altercations" (Ross, 2010:200). Community residents also joined forces with business owners, politicians, lobbyists, journalists, urban planners, and police to strengthen prostitution laws and implement traffic controls that hindered occupational and geographic mobility for outdoor sex workers. As a result, many sex workers were displaced to an isolated, poorly lit industrial zone where they began to go "missing" (Jiwani and Young, 2006). In 2007, Robert William "Willie" Pickton stood trial for murdering 27 women, many of them Aboriginal sex workers from the Downtown Eastside.

Conflict Perspectives

Whereas the functionalist perspective views society as comprised of different parts that work together, the conflict perspective explores issues of power, inequality, and competition over scarce resources. In a Marxist sense, the relationship between the economic system and sexuality is largely a question of exploitation. Scholars working in this tradition are primarily interested in the workers, consumers, and unequal relations of power that affect who benefits and who loses when sex is bought and sold. The commodification of sex and sexuality raises important questions about social and economic power, especially given the relative power of those who control the marketplace—men over other men, men over women, adults over children, and wealthy over poor.

Although Giddens (1992) uses the phrase *intimacy as democracy* to suggest that erotic inequality has improved in recent years, others are not so convinced (e.g., Jamieson, 1999). In terms of prostitution laws, enforcement is largely unequal and women tend to face more serious consequences than men. While two (or more) people may be involved in the purchase of sexual services, research shows that police are far more likely to arrest and convict less powerful female prostitutes than more powerful male clients. In Canada, men convicted of "communicating for the purposes of prostitution" are more likely to receive fines, whereas women convicted of the same offence are more likely to receive probation and jail sentences (Duschesne, 1995).

Similarly, of all women engaged in sex work, street prostitutes—women with the least income and most likely to be visible minorities—face the highest risk of arrest (Ross, 2010). Street prostitutes also occupy the lowest stratum and receive the strongest dose of stigma from the general public and other sex workers in the industry (Weitzer, 2005). Control over working conditions is lowest among street prostitutes, many of whom do not have access to resources for protection, do not have the freedom to refuse abusive clients or particular sex acts, and are dependent on pimps or other third parties (Chapkis, 2000). Disparities in social and economic status place street prostitutes at risk for victimization, especially when compared to indoor prostitutes who work in brothels, massage parlours, and escort agencies. In Canada, for instance, Lowman and Fraser (1995) found that female street prostitutes were more likely than escorts to be robbed, kidnapped, sexually assaulted, beaten, and killed. Although the literature on male and transgendered prostitutes is somewhat limited, findings indicate that males tend to be less dependent on prostitution as a source of income, have more control over their working conditions due to greater physical strength, and are less likely to experience violence from customers (Aggleton, 1999; Prestage, 1994; West, 1993).

Prostitution and pornography are multi-billion dollar industries geared primarily toward adults, though often at the expense of children. The sexual exploitation of children has become an increasing concern, especially in economically poor countries such as Thailand and India where sex tourism flourishes. The commercialized use of children for sex is also a problem in North America, where the Internet plays an important role in facilitating direct, anonymous contact between adults and children. Adult predators will use the Internet to persuade children to perform sexual acts via webcam, to meet in person for sex, or to recruit young girls into prostitution (Jaffer and Brazeau, 2011). In these situations, the relationship between the victim and the exploiter is often economic in nature, since the "customer" is an adult who purchases sexual services from the child in exchange for something of value, such as money, food, clothing, shelter, drugs, video games, and even affection. Given the social, economic, and maturational disparities between adults and children, these "exchanges" can never be equal and therefore compromise the dignity and well-being of the child.

Feminist Perspectives

The Western feminist movement of the 1960s and 1970s politicized the personal and was instrumental in bringing the issue of sexuality out of the private realm and into the public arena. During this time, feminists challenged the sexual double standard, raised questions about what counted as sex, and demanded protection from sexual violence and coercion. Feminists have made important contributions to theorizing sexuality, especially in terms of its relationship to gender.

During the late 19th and early 20th centuries, the connection between gender and sexuality was often described in biological, medical, and psychological terms. Central to these early accounts was the assumption that the relationship between gender and sexuality expressed a natural order, one that relied on universal and fixed dualisms that were presumed to complement each other (male/female, heterosexual/homosexual, masculine/feminine). From this perspective, sex/gender/sexuality relate in a hierarchical, coherent manner for which "a disruption in expectations to one element presumably carries consequences for all the other elements" (Ponse, 1978:170).

Feminists put forward new ideas about the relationship between gender and sexuality that challenged earlier perspectives that viewed sex as a product of biological forces and sexual identities as fixed and stable. Feminist analysis paved the way for thinking about the *social* relationship between the sex and gender. Most of the early work in this area was dominated by structural analysis that prioritized gender over sexuality. In these debates, the relationship between gender and sexuality is viewed as one of the key mechanisms by which gender inequalities are maintained. Marxist feminists, and others not clearly aligned with this perspective, view gender as the outcome of a hierarchy in which one class of people (usually men) have systematic power and privilege over another class of people (usually women).

According to some feminist writers, sexuality is central to the maintenance of patriarchal domination where institutionalized heterosexuality is enforced through sexual coercion and violence. According to Kathleen Gough (1971), some of these methods include denying women their own sexuality (e.g., clitoridectomy, chastity belts, capital punishment for female adultery), forcing male sexuality upon women (e.g., rape, arranged marriage, idealization of heterosexual romance), exploiting the reproductive labour of women (e.g., male control of abortion, contraception, sterilization, and childbirth), limiting visibility and movement (e.g., sexual harassment, purdah, high heels, and other "feminine" modes of dress), and using women as objects of exchange (e.g., geisha girls, pimping, bride price).

Adrienne Rich (1980) uses the concept of "compulsory heterosexuality" to draw links between the social ordering of gender and the regulation of sexuality. Specifically, Rich questions the assumption that women are naturally heterosexual and argues that heterosexuality is imposed upon women and reinforced by a variety of social constraints. Cannon's (1998) analysis of the *Indian Act* builds on the concept of compulsory heterosexuality to explore how sexual relations between Aboriginal men and women are regulated in Canada. While the literature suggests that a broad range of erotic relationships existed prior to European settlement, compulsory heterosexuality was instituted in Aboriginal communities through the *Indian Act* of 1876, in which heterosexual marriage became the only possible avenue through which to convey Indian status and rights. Elements of sexism also appear in the status and citizenship sections of the *Indian Act* that denied Indian status to Aboriginal women—along with their children—who marry non-Aboriginal men. Although this section of the *Indian Act* may have protected reserve lands from white male encroachment (Sanders, 1972), it did not apply equally to men (Aboriginal men and their children retained Indian status regardless of whom they married) and constituted an attempt to assimilate Aboriginal communities into Canadian society "through a system of patrilineal descent and heterosexual marriage" (Cannon 1998: 10). Some of these inequalities in law were addressed in 1985 when the *Indian Act* was amended. For recent developments in sexuality and the law, see Box 12.3 at **www.nelson.com/sociologyinourtimes6e.**

Symbolic Interactionist Perspectives

Symbolic interactionists are interested in shared meaning and ongoing social interaction between members of society. Symbolic interactionist perspectives on sexuality emerged in the 1960s alongside theories of deviance that stress the importance of social definition, or "labelling," rather than the features of particular acts and actors. One of the earliest studies that draws on this view is Marcy McIntosh's (1968) analysis of the "homosexual role." Rather than viewing homosexuality as an innate or acquired condition, McIntosh draws on labelling theory to argue that expectations regarding homosexuality vary according to culture and history. Thus, while in Western societies there is an expectation that homosexual men are effeminate and exclusively homosexual, other societies in Australia, Greece, and Northern Africa accept homosexual liaisons between men as part of a varied heterosexual pattern.

William Simon and John Gagnon (1986) also played an important role in the development of interactionist perspectives on sexuality. Simon and Gagnon argue that feelings, practices, and body parts are not inherently sexual. Instead, they derive their sexual significance through the application of *sexual scripts*—cultural guidelines that prescribe "with whom one should have sexual activity, when and where sexual activity should occur, what types of activities are appropriate, and acceptable reasons for participating (or not) in sexual activity" (Baber and Murray, 2001:25).

There are normative sexual scripts that guide how men and women think about themselves as sexual beings and make choices about partners and sexual practices (see Box 12.4, "Hooking Up In/To the Seduction Community," at **www.nelson.com/sociologyinourtimes6e**) (Brown, 2012). For instance, some of the messages women and girls receive about sex include: Say no to sex (or be swept away); pursue love, security, and romance; "get a man" (aim to be attractive but passive); and don't be too knowledgeable about sex or ask for what you want (Crane and Crane-Seeber, 2003). In contrast, men and boys receive messages about sex that include: Get as much sex as you can; love is a trap/responsibility; "be a man" (get a woman); don't give up, she'll give in; and act like you know all about sex (Crane and Crane-Seeber, 2003).

Sexual scripts may also vary in response to the social messages received by people with different cultural backgrounds. Shirpak, Maticka-Tyndale, and Chinichiani (2007) analyze the social meaning Iranian immigrants attribute to sexuality in Canada and draw attention to the tensions that exist between Canadian and Iranian sexual scripts. In Iran, for instance, women who publicly expose body parts other than their hands, feet, and face are considered immodest because they are believed to inspire enticing thoughts and feelings of sexual arousal among men other than their spouse. Although negative stereotypes are sometimes ascribed to women who wear revealing clothing, the sexual scripts regarding appropriate dress for women are more permissive in Canada. The cultural tension between these sexual scripts is evident among Iranian immigrants who ascribe the symbolism of sexual availability and seduction to the dress of Canadian women. As one study participant put it, "Here in Canada women dress in a revealing way and their body is visible. Some Iranian men's minds might become preoccupied with that. The way men dress [in Canada] is not different from Iran. Women are different" (2007:118).

Postmodern Perspectives

Postmodern approaches to sex and sexuality stress the importance of historical context, variations among people, and change over time. Postmodern thinkers reject claims that sexuality is presocial and biologically based. Within this broad tradition, *queer theory* has emerged as an approach to theorizing gender and sexuality that emphasizes the fluidity of identity and the normalizing tendencies of the heterosexual order. Broadly speaking, the term *queer* describes any mismatch between sex, gender, and sexual desire that disrupts *heteronormativity*—a cultural bias toward heterosexuality that privileges sexual relations between men and women. This area of scholarship is heavily influenced by the work of Judith Butler and Michel Foucault, both of whom use the term *discourse* to describe ways of speaking and writing about the social world that limit what can be written and said.

In *The History of Sexuality, Volume 1* (1978), Foucault challenges the idea that sexuality was silenced and repressed during the 18th century and traces the historical emergence of discourse on sexuality. Foucault (1978:11) is not investigating sexuality as a pregiven object of analysis; instead, he is exploring how sex is "put into discourse" and how this discourse produces power. Specifically, Foucault points to the Christian practice of confessing sinful desires and the 19th-century science of sex as evidence of how discourse surrounding sexuality proliferated during the Victorian era. The operation of power through these sexual discourses was not repressive; rather, it created new sexual subjects and new modes of being. From this perspective, homosexuality is not a preexisting form of sexuality but a product of the discourses that construct *the* homosexual as a "personage" that makes it possible to *be* a homosexual. The relationship between sex and gender is often made complicated by the body, especially when primary and secondary sex characteristics appear in combinations that deviate from norms established by the medical community. Intersexed bodies create problems for any sex/gender/sexuality system that insists bodies are limited by an absolute dimorphism. Because intersexuals unravel meaning by disrupting the presumed connection between sex, gender, and sexuality, they are not considered intelligible within the boundaries of what Judith Butler (1999) calls a "heterosexual matrix." The cultural anxiety about bodies that do not fit this scheme, and responses to that expression launched by the medical community, position intersexed persons as targets for neutralization of abnormalities (Fausto-Sterling 2002). This is achieved through hormonal therapy and surgical management, both of which render intersexed bodies "intelligible" or "recognizable" in a matrix that uses heterosexuality to define how sex, gender, and sexuality should correspond. In other words, an individual whose sex assignment is male is expected to have a masculine gender identity, act in a masculine way, and be sexually attracted (only) to women.

One of the principal tasks of queer theory is to interrogate and subvert the norms that constrain modes of being. Anne Fausto-Sterling (2002) points to the importance of thinking about sex as a malleable continuum and proposes three new sex categories to account for the huge variability among individuals who present aspects of male and female genitalia: Intersexed persons or hermaphrodites (herms) possess one testis and one ovary; male pseudohermaphrodites (merms) have testes, some female genitalia, but no ovaries; and female pseudohermaphrodites (ferms) have ovaries, some male genitalia, but no testes. Lebenkoff (2011) draws attention to the transgressive potential of gay weddings and reports a number of practices through which gay couples disrupt heteronormative wedding rituals, such as walking down the aisle together rather than having the father "give the bride away." Otnes and Pleck (2003) describe how one same-sex Jewish couple defined smashing the glass as the symbolic destruction of the second Jewish temple *and* the destruction of homophobia.

CURRENT ISSUES IN SEXUALITY

Given that sex and issues of sexuality permeate most aspects of our daily lives, it is no surprise that sex is often a contributing factor to significant social problems and issues. The sexual health of youth, including birth control, teen pregnancy, sexually transmitted infections, and sexual violence, are all issues of significant concern in today's society.

LO-5 The Sexual Health of Youth

Despite media claims of an unprecedented increase in sexual behaviour among youth today—including dramatic increases in the transmission of sexually transmitted infections, unplanned pregnancies, masturbatory displays via Facebook, YouTube, and smartphones, and oral sex games involving multiple partners—there is strong evidence that young people are experiencing better sexual health than ever before.

Sexual health is multidimensional and includes such factors as mutually rewarding intimate relationships, positive attitudes toward sexuality, and avoidance of negatives outcomes such as sexually transmitted infections and, in the case of heterosexual health, unplanned pregnancies. Promoting sexual health involves equipping young people with the knowledge, motivation, and behaviours to enhance their sexual health and avoid sexual health-related problems. Trends in teen pregnancy, sexually transmitted infections, age of first intercourse, and condom use are often used to evaluate the status of the sexual health of Canadian youth (McKay, 2009). Sociologist Eleanor Maticka-Tyndale (2009) compared the sexual health and behaviours of Canadian youth today to that of adolescents from previous generations and found that in terms of a number of criteria, today's youth are experiencing better sexual health.

TEEN PREGNANCY The overall teen pregnancy rate has declined in the past 30 years as a result of an increase in the availability of contraception, an increase in the awareness of the dangers of unprotected sex brought on by the HIV/AIDs epidemic, and legal access to abortion. More recently, youth also now have legal and medical access to emergency contraception, commonly referred to as the morning-after pill (Maticka-Tyndale, 2008). In 2009, an estimated 15,000 women age 15 to 19 gave birth and a slightly larger number in this age range (approximately 17,000) had an abortion. Over the past decades, the teen pregnancy rate in Canada has dropped significantly, with an almost 40 percent drop between 1996 and 2006 (see Figure 12.2). According to Alexander McKay, author of a recent report for the Sex and Education Council of Canada:

> This is a good news story. It's important to look at teen pregnancy rates because they're a basic fundamental indicator of young women's sexual and reproductive health. While not all teen pregnancies are a bad thing, when we see [rates] dropping, it's a fairly clear indicator that young women are doing increasingly well in terms of controlling and protecting their reproductive health." (Bielski, 2010)

FIGURE 12.2 TEEN BIRTH AND ABORTION RATES PER 1,000 15- TO 19-YEAR-OLDS, CANADA, 1974–2003

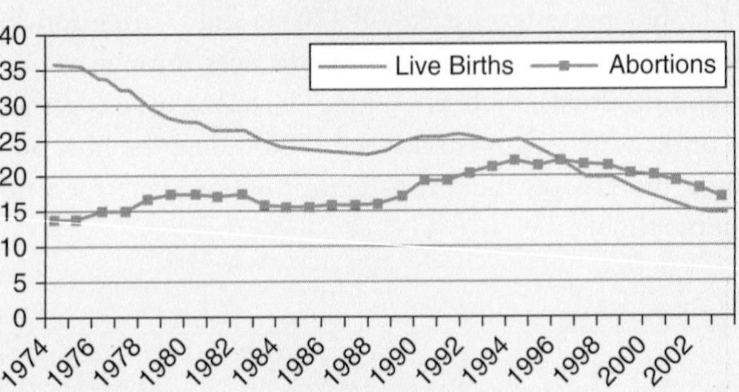

Source: McKay, A. (2006). "Trends in Teen Pregnancy in Canada with Comparisons to U.S.A. and England/Wales," *The Canadian Journal of Human Sexuality*, Vol. 15, (3-4), 157-161. Used with permission of Sex Information and Education Council of Canada.

This decline is not unique to Canada; the United States, England, Wales, and Sweden have witnessed decreases in teenage pregnancies in recent years (McKay, 2010). However, Canada's teenage pregnancy birth rate is less than half that of the United States. This is largely attributable to cultural differences in approaches to teenage sexuality, with Canadians taking a more open and accepting approach to sexuality while certain regions in the U.S. continue to advocate an abstinence approach to sexuality, which contributes to lower rates of contraceptive use and higher rates of unplanned pregnancies (McKay, 2009).

SEXUALLY TRANSMITTED INFECTIONS In comparison to the successes displayed by Canadian youth in pregnancy prevention, the picture in terms of sexually transmitted infections is not as positive. Sexually transmitted diseases (STIs) can be transmitted from one person to another during unprotected oral, anal, or vaginal sex. STIs pose a significant threat to the health and well-being of Canadian youth, and the prevalence of common STIs, such as chlamydia and human papillomavirus (HPV), is highest among youth and young adults. Chlamydia is of particular concern because, if left untreated, it can have serious long-term consequences for the reproductive health of women. Following a steady decline in reported rates of chlamydia (the number of positive test reports made to public health agencies) in the 1990s, rates have been increasing steadily (Maticka-Tyndale, 2008). It is important to recognize, however, that reported rates are not a measure of prevalence (the percentage of the population that is infected) and that much of the increase in the reported rate of chlamydia is likely due to the increasing use of more sensitive testing technologies and the greater number of young people being tested (McKay and Barrett, 2008). Rates of chlamydia infection range from approximately 3 percent among young women tested at family physicians' offices to almost 11 percent among female street youth.

By Public Health Agency of Canada's standards, the prevalence of chlamydia infection among youth and young adult Canadians is unacceptably high. In fact, a range of STIs—including HPV and herpes simplex virus (HSV)—are common in youth and require that both general health campaigns and school-based sex education programs continue to educate youth around using effective methods to protect themselves from STIs (Maticka-Tyndale, 2008). It has been suggested that today's youth are less sensitive to the potential risks of sexual activity than those who grew up in the fear-filled era of the HIV/AIDS epidemic of the 1980s and early 1990s. People who became sexually active in the 1980s did so with a clear understanding that sexual choices were life and death choices. In contrast, today's youth may believe, incorrectly, that sexual risk is easily managed through condom use during intercourse. Sex education programs have reinforced this idea by focusing safe sex practices on vaginal-penile intercourse. Many youth are not aware that oral sex carries a significant risk of infection—incorrectly equating safe sex with oral sex. Researchers suggest that this misconception may contribute to their willingness to engage in the sexually risky behaviour of engaging in unprotected oral sex with multiple partners (Heldman and Wade, 2010:329).

AGE OF FIRST INTERCOURSE, MULITIPLE PARTNERS, AND CONDOM USE For a majority of Canadians, their first sexual intercourse occurs during the teenage years (Maticka-Tyndale, 2008, Rotermann, 2008). Overall, the percentage of Canadian youth who report ever having had sexual intercourse has declined since the mid-1990s. The data from the Canadian Community Health Survey indicate that the percentage of 18- to 19-year-olds who had ever had intercourse declined between 1996–1997 and 2005 (Rotermann, 2008). Research from both Canada and the United States indicates that oral sex is about as common as intercourse and typically occurs at about the same time as intercourse, although up to a quarter of teens may begin having oral sex before starting to have intercourse. As Eleanor Maticka-Tyndale explains, "With respect to oral sex, it is important to remember that over the last 30 to 40 years oral sex has become a normative aspect of the adult sexual script and this trend has been followed by youth" (2008:86). As shown in Figure 12.3, the percentage of youth who became sexually active before 15 also declined in the period between 1996–1997 and 2005. The average age of first intercourse among Canadian youth age 15 to 24 is 16.5 years for both male and females (Rotermann, 2008).

Multiple sexual partners is an important indicator of sexual risk behaviour, especially in terms of the risk of contracting an STI. As shown in Figure 12.4, approximately one-third of youth reported having sex in the previous year with more than one partner. Also indicated in Figure 12.4 is the fact that males are slightly more likely to have multiple sexual partners than females—a reflection, perhaps, that a sexual double standard still exists.

FIGURE 12.3 PERCENTAGE OF 15- TO 19-YEAR-OLDS WHO HAD SEXUAL INTERCOURSE BEFORE AGE 15 OR AT AGE 15 AND 16, BY GENDER AND AGE GROUP, CANADA

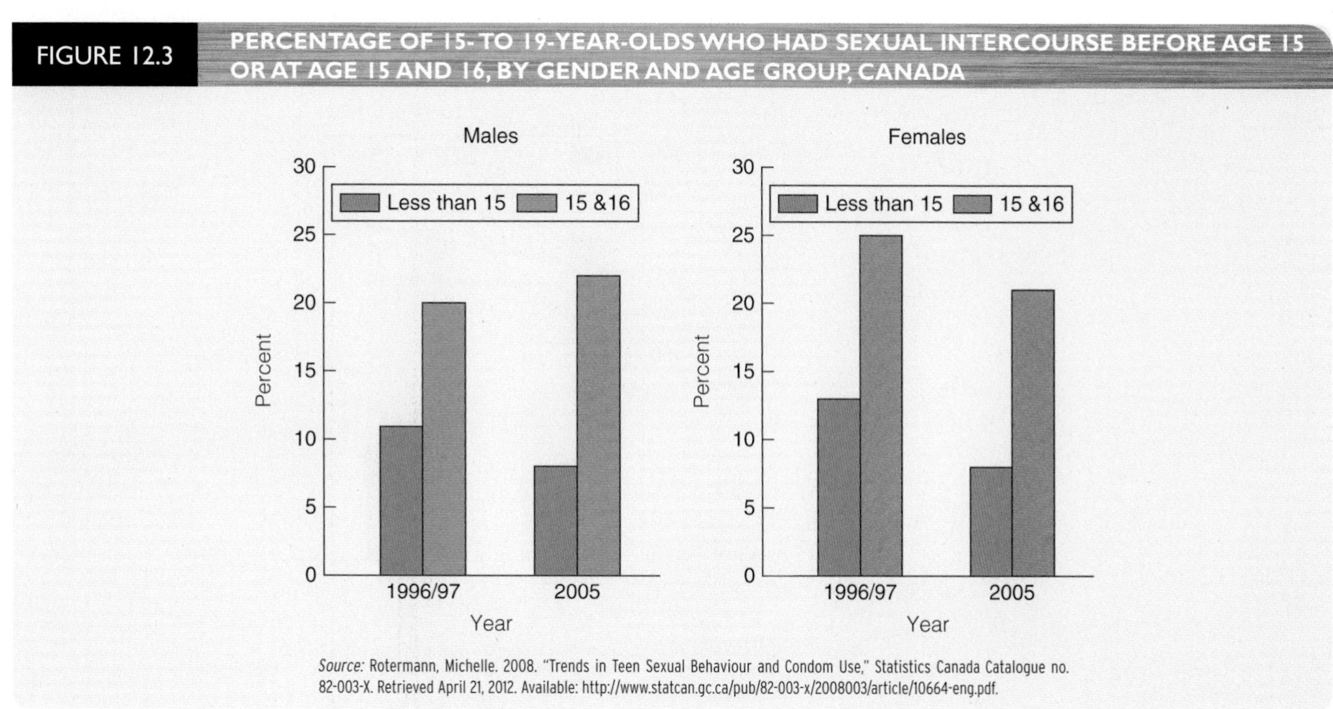

Source: Rotermann, Michelle. 2008. "Trends in Teen Sexual Behaviour and Condom Use," Statistics Canada Catalogue no. 82-003-X. Retrieved April 21, 2012. Available: http://www.statcan.gc.ca/pub/82-003-x/2008003/article/10664-eng.pdf.

Condom use is an effective means of both preventing unplanned pregnancy and providing protection against sexually transmitted infections. As shown in Figure 12.5, the majority of sexually active youth are effectively protecting their sexual health by using condoms. However, a large proportion of young people move from one sexually active dating relationship to another over the course of their teen and young adult years. A common behavioural pattern is for dating couples to use condoms the first time they have sex but discontinue condom use as the relationship progresses and contraceptive pill use increases. A study in Toronto in 2009 involved interviews with young women in dating relationships, age 18 to 24, about their use

FIGURE 12.4 PERCENTAGE OF SEXUALLY ACTIVE 15- TO 19-YEAR-OLDS WHO REPORTED HAVING MULTIPLE PARTNERS IN THE PAST YEAR, BY GENDER AND AGE GROUP, CANADA

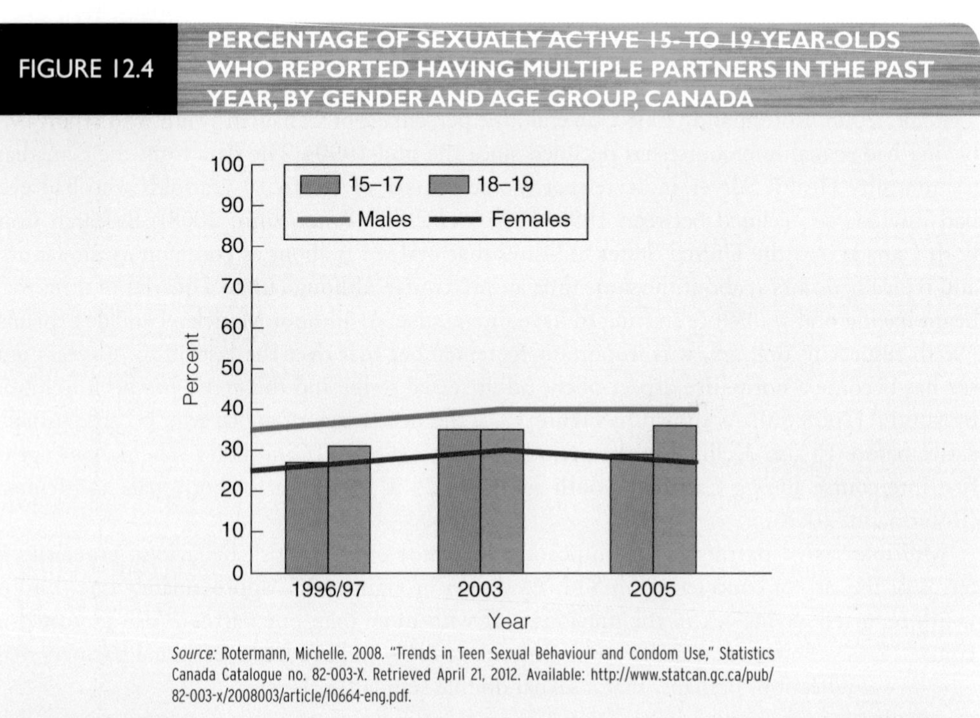

Source: Rotermann, Michelle. 2008. "Trends in Teen Sexual Behaviour and Condom Use," Statistics Canada Catalogue no. 82-003-X. Retrieved April 21, 2012. Available: http://www.statcan.gc.ca/pub/82-003-x/2008003/article/10664-eng.pdf.

FIGURE 12.5 PERCENTAGE OF SEXUALLY ACTIVE YOUTH WHO USED A CONDOM THE LAST TIME THEY HAD INTERCOURSE, BY GENDER AND AGE GROUP, CANADA

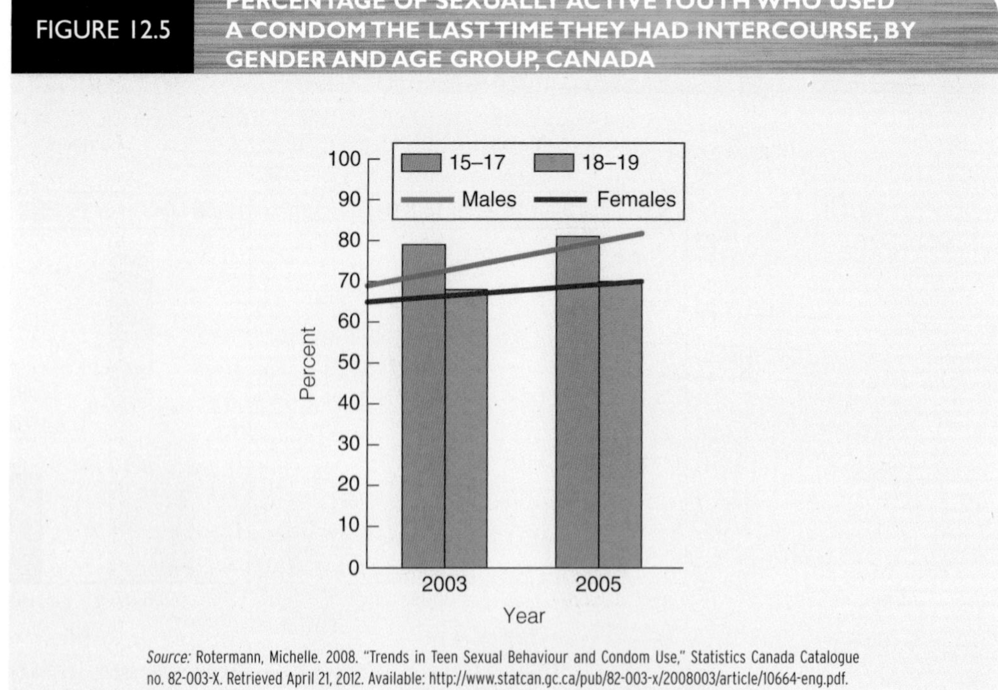

Source: Rotermann, Michelle. 2008. "Trends in Teen Sexual Behaviour and Condom Use," Statistics Canada Catalogue no. 82-003-X. Retrieved April 21, 2012. Available: http://www.statcan.gc.ca/pub/82-003-x/2008003/article/10664-eng.pdf.

and discontinuation of condom use. Most of the participants simply assumed that they were in a monogamous relationship without explicitly discussing sexual exclusivity with their partners. As one participant explained:

> I did ask him before we had sex. I said "Look, do I need to be worried about things like sexually transmitted diseases cause if so, put that back in your pants." And he was like, "No, no, no." So I was like, "Okay, you don't need to worry about that with me either." So this is okay. So we have had that discussion without going into detail. (Bolton, McKay, and Schneider, 2010:97)

A repeated pattern of discontinuing condom use in a series of dating relationships over time places individuals at an increased risk of an STI. Sexual health educators need to caution young adults that assumed monogamy is, for a number of reasons, a poor indicator of low STI risk (Bolton, McKay, and Schneider, 2010).

VULNERABLE GROUPS The improvements in sexual health experienced by the majority of Canadian youth are not evenly distributed. In particular, youth living in low-income families, in isolated rural areas, or in regions with greater concentrations of rural and Aboriginal populations are more likely to be sexually active in their early teens, more susceptible to STIs, and more likely to experience unplanned pregnancies and sexual abuse (Yee, 2010). Aboriginal populations are particularly vulnerable to poor sexual health. For example, in First Nations, 20 percent of births involve a teenage mother and reported cases of chlamydia are seven times higher than the general population (Health Canada, 2009).

Another group of youth who are particularly at risk for poor sexual health are gay, lesbian, bisexual, transgendered, or questioning (GLBTQ) teens. The First National Climate Survey on Homophobia in Canadian High Schools found that GLBTQ youth face frequent discrimination in their school lives. One of the nearly 4000 students surveyed across Canada made the following comment:

> Most of the gay community in my school are bullied, we all stick together, but that doesn't always help. Many gays are depressed because of this, and teachers and adults need to help and stand up for our community. We are not aliens, we're people, and we have rights. (Taylor and Peter, 2011:307)

Respondents also indicated that they received insufficient sexual health information relevant to their needs. GLBTQ youth also experience higher levels of distrust of health and social services providers that leads them to feel they must hide their sexual identities (Maticka-Tyndale, 2008).

SEX EDUCATION School-based programs are one of the primary avenues for educating young people about sexual health. The primary objective of sexual health education is to provide young people with the necessary knowledge, motivation, and strategies to make informed choices that promote their sexual health and overall well-being (McKay, 2009). Most sex education programs use a biomedical approach focusing on anatomy and biology rather than more complex issues related to human sexuality and intimacy, such as developing a positive sexual identity or equality in sexual relationships. Sociologists emphasize that sex education programs could be improved by incorporating these social issues related to sexual health rather than focusing almost exclusively on the biological and medical measures of sexual health. When schools avoid presenting alternative perspectives, including those that incorporate a discussion of eroticism and pleasure, they may perpetuate existing class, race, gender, and sexuality hierarchies (Schneider and Jenness, 2005:396).

One GLBTQ student in the First National Climate Survey on Homophobia in Canadian High Schools wrote:

> Teachers must be educated. They discuss other teachers' sexuality, other students' sexuality, they tell homophobic jokes and do not realize. They also must implement resources into the curriculum, or LGBT individuals will always be viewed as one-dimensional abstractions. I am not satisfied with my rights in the school curriculum. (Taylor and Peter, 2011:207)

An effective sexual health education curriculum needs to "recognize that responsible individuals may choose a variety of paths to achieve sexual health" (Public Health Agency, 2008:25). This would include information on a variety of options for youth, including the necessary information for youth who choose not to engage in sexual activity, as well as information on sexual diversity issues. To ensure the sexual health and overall well-being of our youth, Canadian families, schools, healthcare providers, public health agencies, and communities must share in the responsibility of providing effective and inclusive sexual health education and services (McKay, 2009).

LO-6 Violence in Intimate Relationships

intimate partner violence The physical and nonphysical violence experienced by women and men at the hands of current or former partners.

It has been suggested that "intimacy can be hazardous to one's health." Unfortunately this statement reflects the sad reality that we often suffer the most damage within our intimate relationships. The term **intimate partner violence** refers to the physical and nonphysical violence experienced by women and men at the hands of current or former partners. Across cultures and over time, women have been particularly vulnerable to frequent, severe, and sometimes lethal intimate partner violence. According to the World Health Organization, although women can be violent in relationships with men, and violence is sometimes found in same-sex partnerships, the overwhelming burden of partner violence is borne by women at the hands of men (Krug et al., 2002, cited in Johnson, 2011:64). Physical assault, emotional abuse, sexual assault, sexual harassment, and stalking occur at disturbingly high rates within intimate relationships in various forms—dating partners, common-law partners, married partners.

The extent of violence in relationships was first discovered in the 1980s largely as a result of the efforts of the feminist movement. What had been considered a "private" matter became a "public" issue, precipitating a dramatic increase in services and organizations to serve victims of domestic violence, as well as significant reforms in social policy, law, and police practices. Although significant gains have been made over the past 30 years in reducing various forms of intimate partner violence against women, the numbers remain shocking. According to the Canadian Violence Against Women Survey in 1993, three in 10 women who have ever been married or lived in a common-law relationship have experienced violence at the hands of their partner, and almost four in 10 women have been sexually assaulted. The same survey found that 16 percent of women aged 15 or over had been assaulted by a date or boyfriend. In 2004, approximately 200,000 women in Canada were physically assaulted and another 100,000 were sexually assaulted by their intimate partners. According to police data, in 2006 almost 40,000 incidents of spousal violence were reported and women comprised almost 85 percent of the victims (Johnson and Dawson, 2011). In 2010, 70 women were murdered by their intimate partners (Hotton and Mahony, 2011). In a survey of over 3000 students in colleges and universities across the country, 22 percent of female students reported that they had been physically abused and 29 percent reported being sexually abused by a boyfriend or male acquaintance in the previous year. It is evident from these statistics that violence within intimate relationships continues to be a reality for far too many women today. Given that sexual assault and domestic violence are discussed elsewhere in the text (see Chapters 7 and 13), we will focus here on the most recent form of intimate violence—dating violence.

DATING VIOLENCE Consider this story told to sociologist Kathleen Bogle when she was interviewing university students about their experiences with hooking up:

> I'll tell you this story . . . It was final week my junior year and I was done finals . . . so I went out for some drinks . . . There were these two girls there and the bartender started feeding her shots and next thing you know I started talking to her. The bar wasn't crowded at all. Next thing you know we are back at my frat house, she's like, she can't even walk, she is really messed up. So we start hooking up, nothing major. She's coherent, she knows what is going on, but she is really drunk. So we are hooking up and we are sleeping together and she gets sick on me. She's on top of me and throws up on me . . . There were two guys out there watching TV, I'm like, "One of you guys has to help me". . . We put her in the shower and she is like all out of it. My friend that was helping me out tried to help me clean her up a bit, I put her up on his bed . . . I go back in and she's totally fine, she is totally coherent. So we start "going at it" again [laughs] and then she starts calling me by the wrong name . . . I can't believe I am telling you this. (2008:91)*

How do you respond to this story? How would you define the actions of the young man telling the story? Is this a story of a "bad date," or is it a story of sexual assault? Scenarios like this one inevitably come up in discussions about dating violence. These debates emphasize once again that definitions of intimate violence remain unclear for many.

dating violence A term used for various forms of sexually and nonsexually assaultive behaviours that occur within dating relationships.

date rape Acts in which a date or boyfriend forced or attempted to force any type of sexual activity through threats or use of violence.

The term **dating violence** refers to various forms of sexually and nonsexually assaultive behaviours that occur within dating relationships. According to the Canadian Violence Against Women Survey, an estimated 1.7 million Canadian women have experienced at least one incident of physical or sexual assault by a date or boyfriend since the age of 16. Included in the category of "dates or boyfriends" were "one-night stands," first dates, long-term boyfriends, and committed relationships (Johnson, 1996). Overall, women reported higher rates of sexual assaults than physical assaults. Consequently, most discussions of dating violence have focused on the subject of date rape or acquaintance rape. **Date rape** is defined as acts in which a date or boyfriend forced or attempted to force any type of sexual activity through threats or use of violence. Date rape is especially common on college and university campuses, where it is estimated that approximately one in four, or 25 percent, of female university students will be date-raped (Brownridge, 2006a; Schwartz, 2001).

Numerous explanations have been offered as to why women continue to be viewed by some men as legitimate targets of sexual violence. Sociologist Diana Russell (1974) describes sexual assault as an *overconforming act,* or an exaggerated form of "normal" relations that exist between the sexes. Sexual aggression, even violent assault, represents qualities regarded by some men as "supermasculine"—strength, power, forcefulness, domination, toughness. As Russell explains, "to conquer, to win, to induce respect through force" are all attributes commonly associated with masculinity in our culture. Especially for men who feel powerless or inadequate, the conquest or domination of a woman may become a means through which they maintain their sense of masculinity and self-esteem.

The fact that men can sexually assault women in their dating or intimate relationships is facilitated by a set of highly stereotyped beliefs and values about women. Studies have shown that holding stereotypical beliefs about women is strongly related with abusive sexual relationships, acceptance of rape myths, and tolerance of violence against women (Anderson, 2011). For example, DeKeseredy and Kelly measured the existence of patriarchal beliefs among male university students with the following four statements:

1. A man has the right to decide whether or not his wife/partner should work outside the home.
2. A man has the right to decide whether or not his wife/partner should go out in the evening with her friends.

**Source:* Bogle, Kathleen. *Hooking Up: Sex, Dating, and Relationships on Campus.* © 2008 New York University Press, p. 91.

3. Sometimes it is important for a man to show his wife/partner that he is the head of the house.
4. A man has the right to have sex with his wife/partner when he wants, even though she might not want to. (1993:33)

Although the research clearly demonstrated that the majority of male students did not hold attitudes or beliefs supportive of male dominance in intimate relationships, the male students who did hold these attitudes and beliefs were most likely to commit date rape.

DeKeseredy and Kelly's research also determined a strong link between sexually aggressive behaviour and male peer support. Specifically, they found that some men formed attachments with male peers who were abusive to their partners and who validated the belief that abuse of girlfriends is acceptable. These peers provided abusive men with a *rapist vocabulary* comprised of shared motives and rationalizations that consistently blame the victim. Common messages in rapist vocabulary are "Some women need to be raped," "Some women deserve to be raped," and "Some women want to be raped." Consider, for example, the comments of this young man:

> These dumb broads don't know what they want. They get you worked up and then they chicken out. You let' em get away with stuff like that and the next thing you know they'll be walking all over you. Women like a strong man who will knock them around once in a while—that way they know the man is in charge.

Now consider the explanation for date rape provided by the following second-year university student:

> I met a girl at a party and I considered her snobbish and phony. She latched onto me at the party, and we laughed and had a good time and went somewhere else. She was an attractive woman in her thirties, but she irritated me. When I took her home to her apartment she was telling me goodnight and I raped her. I didn't really feel the urge. As a matter of fact, I had a hell of a time getting an erection . . . I'd had quite a bit of booze. But I forced myself to do it to prove a point to her, to prove that she wasn't as big as she thought she was. (Johnson, 1995:218)

It is through interactions with like-minded male peers that these young men develop the justifications for their actions, which allow them to maintain a favourable self-image and define themselves as normal despite their abuse of their dating partners.

Not all women are equally at risk of intimate partner violence. Aboriginal women are four times more likely to experience intimate partner violence than non-Aboriginal women. In addition, Aboriginal women are not only more likely to experience violence at the hands of their current or former spouses, but the violence is more frequent, more serious, more likely to result in injury, and more likely to result in the women fearing for their lives (Brennan, 2011; Brownridge, 2008). It is also estimated that persons with disabilities are between 50 and 100 percent more likely than those without disabilities to have experienced spousal violence (Brownridge, 2006b; Perrault, 2009).

TIME TO REVIEW

- Describe the trends in Canada's teenage pregnancy rates over the past 30 years.
- Discuss the characteristics of youth who are at high risk of poor sexual health. Why are these groups particularly vulnerable? What might be done to reduce their risk of sexually transmitted infections and unwanted pregnancies?
- Discuss the issue of intimate partner violence among young people. Why do you think that some men believe women are legitimate targets for sexual violence?

SEXUALITY AND SOCIAL CHANGE

After the Sexual Revolution

The term **sexual revolution** refers to the dramatic changes that occurred regarding sexual attitudes, behaviours, and values during the 1960s. These rapid and dramatic social changes were precipitated by a number of factors, and not surprisingly, many of the changes associated with the sexual revolution were, in fact, changes in women's sexuality. The women's liberation movement, for example, challenged gender-role stereotyping, advocating that women should be free to be sexual both in and out of marriage and that not only "bad" girls like sex. Changes in reproductive technologies also played a role. The availability of the birth control pill, along with the liberalization of attitudes toward sexuality, led to significant changes in sexual norms and values and much greater sexual freedom. Sexual intercourse before marriage was no longer viewed as "taboo," particularly for women. Rather, it was viewed as a sign of intimacy and physical pleasure (Freedman and D'Emilio, 1988). Expressions such as "If it feels good, do it" and "Make love, not war" were mantras of the baby boomers, who were becoming young adults during this era. The gay and lesbian movement also played an important role during this time by bringing issues of sexual diversity and sexual oppression into the public realm and profoundly changing levels of tolerance and understanding of lesbian and gay sexuality (Anderson, 2011:295).

sexual revolution
A term used for the dramatic changes that occurred regarding sexual attitudes, behaviours, and values during the 1960s.

Women's sexual behaviour has changed more than men's since the 1960s, narrowing the differences and inequities between the sexual experiences of men and women. Today, if one considers several factors, such as age of first intercourse, number of sexual partners, and the variety of sexual behaviours, women and men are more similar than different. As sociologists Barbara Risman and Pepper Schwartz explained more than a decade ago:

sexual double standard
The belief that men and women are expected to conform to different standards of sexual conduct.

> The sexual revolution is a fait accompli; no counterrevolution has taken place. Instead, the revolution was such an overwhelming success that it has revised the entire framework of how [North] American society thinks about sex. Premarital, unmarried, and post-divorce sex are now seen as individual choices for both women and men. The revolutionary principle that divorced the right to sexual pleasure from marriage (at least for adults) is no longer controversial; it goes unchallenged by nearly everyone but the most conservative of religious fundamentalists. (2002:21)

If the sexual revolution is over, what about the gender revolution? According to Risman and Schwartz (2002), the gender revolution is unfinished and still progressing. There is evidence that this revolution is still in the making when we examine the sexual double standard.

© Spencer Grant/Getty Images

Gay pride and Lesbian pride parades originated in the 1970s as a celebration of sexual diversity. Today they reflect tolerance and respect for lesbian and gay and transgendered sexuality.

The Gender Revolution and the Sexual Double Standard

The **sexual double standard** refers to the belief that men and women are expected to conform to different standards of sexual conduct. In other words, there are different guidelines for men and women when it comes to what is acceptable sexual behaviour. For example, according to the sexual double standard, boys and men are expected to desire and pursue sexual opportunities regardless of context, while girls and women are stigmatized and viewed critically for similar behaviour (Bogle, 2008). The sexual double standard is believed to inhibit young women's sexual behaviour, particularly "promiscuous" behaviour, by making it socially costly in terms of negative labels, peer group relations, or disrespect (Lyons et al., 2011:437). There is considerable debate regarding the extent to which this sexual double standard still exists. For example, is it acceptable in today's society for both women and men to have multiple sexual partners? To engage in casual sex? Are there expectations in terms of who initiates sex? Although numerous studies have examined the sexual double standard in various contexts, the results remain inconclusive (Kreager and Staff, 2009).

The rules for men's sexual behaviour have remained relatively consistent throughout the 20th century and the first part of this century. Single men are expected to pursue sexual activity and have sex whenever they have the opportunity to do so. Historically, women were expected to "keep their virginity" and "remain chaste" until they were married. It was acceptable for married women to engage in sexual intercourse, however, primarily for procreation rather than sexual fulfillment or gratification. Single women who had sexual intercourse were seen as "sexually immoral," promiscuous, or "loose." The societal standard for female sexual behaviour meant that women were viewed as either "good" girls or "bad" girls—madonnas or whores (Bogle, 2008:203).

To what extent has the double standard changed since the sexual revolution? Is there a contemporary or modern sexual double standard? According to sociologists Mary Crawford and Danielle Popp:

> The heterosexual double standard has been a "now you see it, now you don't phenomenon . . . despite claims that double standards are progressively fading, they may exist in contemporary forms that influence the behaviour of both men and women. (2003:14)

What does the contemporary form of the sexual double standard look like? To what extent does it continue to constrain the sexual behaviour of young men and women today? The relevance of these questions for healthy sexual development and gender inequality has prompted substantial research over the past 50 years. A 2009 study by Kreager and his staff using the National Longitudinal Study of Adolescent Health found that greater numbers of sexual partners was viewed as a source of peer acceptance. For example, a study involving focus groups of late adolescent girls found that women were labelled "sluts" for the same sexual behaviour that earned boys the label "stud." Milhausen and Herold (2001) found evidence for the erosion of the sexual double standard, finding that although a small minority of men continued to endorse a sexual double standard, the majority of both men and women judged men and women's sexual behaviour from a single standard. More recently, principle researcher Heidi Lyons (Lyons et al., 2011) asked young women to evaluate the sexual activity of other female peers with multiple sexual partners. Interestingly, although the interviewees recognized the continued existence of a sexual double standard at a societal level, their associations with peers with similar sexual attitudes served as a buffer against negative labels.

Is the gender revolution over? Are women and men equals as sexual partners? Although women and men today are equally likely to be sexually active, a remnant of the sexual double standard appears to be alive and well. According to Reisman and Schwartz:

> Young women still report being worried about being labeled a slut. A new definition of the word *slut*, however, has surfaced—one that demonstrates that the sexual revolution is over, even while the gender revolution has hardly been won. Girls today may be able to have sex without stigma, but only with a steady boyfriend. For girls, love justifies desire. A young woman still cannot be respected if she admits an appetite-driven sexuality. If a young woman has sexual liaisons outside of publically

> acknowledged "coupledom," she is at risk of being defamed. If a girl changes boyfriends too often and too quickly, she risks being labeled a slut. This puts her one down as a power player in her relationship, because her boyfriend does not have to worry about moving on too quickly and being stigmatized for his sexual choices. (2002:20)

Similarly, sociologist Kathleen Bogle's qualitative research on the hookup culture on university and college campuses found similar evidence of a modern sexual double standard in the hookup scripts of university students. A senior at a large U.S. university explains how the label of "slut" is assigned:

> The perception is that if a girl sleeps with a lot of guys she's a slut. If a guy sleeps with a lot of girls he's a stud . . . I mean, I see it every day . . . you can ask anyone on campus randomly, and they would say that would be the perception. (2008:104)*

For a more detailed discussion of the sexual double standard in the hookup culture, see Box 12.5.

BOX 12.5 **POINT/COUNTERPOINT**

Is the Hookup Culture Bad for Girls?

Is the hookup culture reflective of increased sexual freedom for men and women and a demonstration of young women's sense of empowerment and control over their sexuality? Or is the hookup culture another variation on inequalities that continue to exist between men and women's sexuality?

In the following article, sociologists Elizabeth Armstrong, Laura Hamilton, and Paula England examine the divergent viewpoints and assumptions underlying this debate.

Is Hooking Up Bad for Young Women?

"Girls can't be guys in matters of the heart, even though they think they can," says Laura Sessions Stepp, author of *Unhooked: How Young Women Pursue Sex, Delay Love, and Lose at Both*, published in 2007. In her view, "hooking up"—casual sexual activity ranging from kissing to intercourse—places women at risk of "low self-esteem, depression, alcoholism, and eating disorders."

Stepp is only one of half a dozen journalists currently engaged in the business of detailing the dangers of casual sex. On the other side, pop culture feminists such as Jessica Valenti, author of *The Purity Myth: How America's Obsession with Virginity is Hurting Young Women* (2010), argue that the problem isn't casual sex but a "moral panic" over casual sex. And still a third set of writers, like Ariel Levy, author of *Female Chauvinist Pigs: Women and the Rise of Raunch Culture* (2005), question whether it's empowering for young women to show up at parties dressed to imitate porn stars or to strip in "Girls Gone Wild" fashion. Levy's concern isn't necessarily moral, but rather that these young women seem less focused on their own sexual pleasure and more worried about being seen as "hot" by men.

Following on the heels of the mass media obsession, sociologists and psychologists have begun to investigate adolescent and young adult hookups more systematically, drawing on systematic data and studies of youth sexual practices over time to counter claims that hooking up represents a sudden and alarming change in youth sexual culture. The research shows that there is some truth to popular claims that hookups are bad for women. However, it also demonstrates that women's hookup experiences are quite varied and far from uniformly negative and that monogamous, long-term relationships are not an ideal alternative. Scholarship suggests that pop culture feminists have correctly zeroed in on sexual double standards as a key source of gender inequality in sexuality.

Before examining the consequences of hooking up for girls and young women, we need to look more carefully at the facts. *Unhooked* author Stepp describes girls "stripping in the student center in front of dozens of boys they didn't know." She asserts that "young people have virtually abandoned dating" and that "relationships have been replaced by the casual sexual encounters known as

(continued)

**Source:* Bogle, Kathleen. *Hooking Up: Sex, Dating, and Relationships on Campus.* © 2008 New York University Press, p. 104.

hookups." Her sensationalist tone suggests that young people are having more sex at earlier ages in more casual contexts than their baby boomer parents did.

This characterization is simply not true. Young people today are not having more sex at younger ages than their parents did. The sexual practices of American youth changed in the 20th century, but the big change came with the baby boom cohort, who came of age more than 40 years ago. The pervasiveness of casual sexual activity among today's youth may be at the heart of boomers' concerns. England surveyed more than 14,000 students from 19 universities and colleges about their hookup, dating, and relationship experiences. Seventy-two percent of both men and women participating in the survey reported at least one hookup by their senior year in college. What the boomer panic may gloss over, however, is the fact that college students do not, on average, hook up that much. By senior year, roughly 40 percent of those who ever hooked up had engaged in three or fewer hookups, 40 percent between four and nine hookups, and only 20 percent in 10 or more hookups. About 80 percent of students hook up, on average, less than once per semester over the course of college.

In addition, the sexual activity in hookups is often relatively light. Only about one-third had engaged in intercourse in their most recent hookup. Another third had engaged in oral sex or manual stimulation of the genitals. The other third of hookups only involved kissing and nongenital touching. A full 20 percent of survey respondents in their fourth year of college had never had vaginal intercourse. In addition, hookups between total strangers are relatively uncommon, while hooking up with the same person multiple times is common. Ongoing sexual relationships without commitment are labelled as "repeat," "regular," or "continuing" hookups, and sometimes as "friends with benefits." Often there is friendship or socializing both before and after the hookup.

Hooking up hasn't replaced committed relationships. Students often participate in both at different times during college. By their senior year, 69 percent of heterosexual students had been in a college relationship of at least six months. Hookups sometimes became committed relationships and vice versa; generally the distinction revolved around the agreed upon level of exclusivity and the willingness to refer to each other as "girlfriend/boyfriend."

And, finally, hooking up isn't radically new. As suggested above, the big change in adolescent and young adult sexual behaviour occurred with the baby boomers. This makes sense, as the forces giving rise to casual sexual activity among the young—the availability of the birth control pill, the women's and sexual liberation movements, and the decline of *in loco parentis* on college campuses—took hold in the 1960s. But changes in youth sexual culture did not stop with the major behavioural changes wrought by the sexual revolution. Contemporary hookup culture among adolescents and young adults may rework aspects of the sexual revolution to get some of its pleasures while reducing its physical and emotional risks. Young people today are expected to delay the commitments of adulthood while they invest in careers. They get the message that sex is okay, as long as it doesn't jeopardize their futures; STDs and early pregnancies are to be avoided. This generates a sort of limited-liability hedonism. For instance, friendship is prioritized a bit more than romance, and oral sex appeals because of its relative safety. Hookups may be the most explicit example of a calculating approach to sexual exploration. They make it possible to be sexually active while avoiding behaviours with the highest physical and emotional risks (e.g., intercourse, intense relationships). Media panic over hooking up may be at least in part a result of adult confusion about youth sexual culture—that is, not understanding that oral sex and sexual experimentation with friends are actually some young people's ways of balancing fun and risk.

Even though hooking up in college isn't the rampant hedonistic free-for-all portrayed by the media, it does involve moving sexual activity outside of relationships.

Hookup Problems, Relationship Pleasures

Hookups are problematic for girls and young women for several related reasons. As many observers of North American youth sexual culture have found, a sexual double standard continues to be pervasive. As one woman Hamilton interviewed explained, "Guys can have sex with all the girls and it makes them more of a man, but if a girl does, then all of a sudden she's a 'ho' and she's not as quality of a person." Sexual labelling among adolescents and young adults may only loosely relate to actual sexual behaviour; for example, one woman complained in her interview that she was a virgin the first time she was called a "slut." The lack of clear rules about what is "slutty" and what is not contributes to women's fears of stigma.

The most commonly encountered disadvantage of hookups, though, is that sex in relationships is far better for women. England's survey revealed that women orgasm more often and report higher levels of sexual satisfaction in relationship sex than in hookup sex. This is in part because sex in relationships is more likely to include sexual activities conducive to women's orgasm. In hookups, men are much more likely to receive fellatio than women are to receive cunnilingus. In relationships, oral sex is more likely to be reciprocal. In interviews conducted by England's research team, men report more concern with the sexual pleasure of girlfriends than hookup partners, while women seem equally invested in pleasing hookup partners and boyfriends.

The continuing salience of the sexual double standard mars women's hookup experiences. In contrast, relationships provide a context in which sex is viewed as acceptable for women, protecting them from stigma and establishing sexual reciprocity as a basic expectation. In addition, relationships offer love and companionship.

Toward Gender Equality in Sex

Like others, Stepp, the author of *Unhooked*, suggests that restricting sex to relationships is the way to challenge gender inequality in youth sex. Certainly, sex in relationships is better for women than hookup sex. However, research suggests two reasons why Stepp's strategy won't work. First, relationships are also plagued by inequality. Second, valorizing relationships as the ideal context for women's sexual activity reinforces the notion that women shouldn't want sex outside of relationships and stigmatizes women who do. A better approach would challenge gender inequality in both relationships and hookups. It is critical to attack the tenacious sexual double standard that leads men to disrespect their hookup partners. Fostering relationships among young adults should go hand in hand with efforts to decrease intimate partner violence and to build egalitarian relationships that allow more space for other aspects of life—such as school, work, and friendship.

Source: Armstrong, Elizabeth, Laura Hamilton, and Paula England, *Contexts* (August 2010, Vol. 9, No. 3), pp. 22 -27, copyright © 2010 by SAGE Publications. Reprinted by permission of SAGE Publications.

TIME TO REVIEW

- Describe the factors that led to the sexual revolution. What changes occurred in the lives of men and women during this period?
- What is the sexual double standard? Why do you think this double standard still exists?

12

VISUAL SUMMARY

KEY TERMS

asexual An absence of sexual desire toward either sex (p. 340).

date rape Acts in which a date or boyfriend forced or attempted to force any type of sexual activity through threats or use of violence (p. 357).

dating violence A term used for various forms of sexually and nonsexually assaultive behaviours that occur within dating relationships (p. 357).

hermaphrodite An individual born with male testes and a female ovary (p. 337).

homophobia Extreme prejudice directed at gays, lesbians, bisexuals, and others who are perceived as not being heterosexual (p. 342).

intersexed individuals Persons whose sexual differentiation is ambiguous or incomplete (p. 337).

intimate partner violence The physical and nonphysical violence experienced by women and men at the hands of current or former partners (p. 356).

marriage A legally recognized and/or socially approved arrangement between two or more individuals that carries certain rights and obligations and usually involves sexual activity (p. 342).

monogamy An intimate relationship with one person at a time (p. 343).

polyamory Intimate relationships that involve mutually acknowledged emotional, sexual, or romantic relationships with multiple partners (p. 344).

LO-1 Explain how the terms *sex, gender,* and *sexuality* relate to one another and how they are different.

© NHAT V. MEYER/MCT/Landov

The terms *sex* and *gender* are often used interchangeably. *Sex* refers to the biological and anatomical differences between females and males. *Gender* refers to culturally and socially created qualities associated with being a man or a woman (masculinity and femininity). *Sex*—the biological and physiological aspects of the body—interacts with *gender*—the roles and responsibilities associated with the socially constructed concepts of "masculinity" and "femininity." Similarly, the terms *sex* and *sexuality* are used interchangeably. *Sexuality* refers to the range of human activities designed to produce erotic response and pleasure. Sexuality, like other forms of human behaviour, is shaped by the society and culture we live in.

LO-2 Understand how various social scientists have classified sexual orientation.

© Guy Moberly/Alamy

Sexual orientation refers to an individual's preference for emotional–sexual relationships with members of the opposite sex (heterosexuality), the same sex (homosexuality), or both (bisexuality). Alfred Kinsey constructed a seven-point scale of sexual behaviour to emphasize the fluidity of human sexual experience. Kinsey's scale did not measure sexual identity or unacted-upon sexual feelings. More recently, researchers at the University of Chicago established three criteria for identifying people as homosexual or bisexual: (1) *sexual attraction* to persons of one's own gender, (2) *sexual involvement* with one or more persons of one's own gender, and (3) *self-identification* as gay, lesbian, or bisexual.

LO-3 Compare and contrast monogamous and polyamorous intimate relationships.

Monogamy refers to the practice of having an intimate relationship with only one person at a time. Some people practise *serial monogamy*—a succession of relationships in which a person has several partners over a lifetime but is legally married to only one person at a time. Polyamory involves mutually acknowledged emotional, sexual, or romantic relationships with multiple partners.

© Catchlight Visual Services/Alamy

LO-4 Explain a functionalist, conflict, symbolic interactionist, and postmodern analysis of sexuality

© Dick Hemingway

According to functionalists, the regulation of norms and values surrounding sexual reproduction is functional because it maintains social stability. Some sexual practices, such as prostitution, can be both functional and dysfunctional. Conflict theorists draw attention to the exploitative aspects of sexuality focusing on workers and consumers and unequal power relations in the buying and selling of sex. Symbolic interactionists argue that sexual feelings, practices and body parts are giving meaning through the application of sexual scripts. Postmodern theorists view gender identities and sexual identities as fluid and malleable rather than presocial and biologically based.

LO-5 Evaluate the sexual health of Canadian youth and young adults.

In terms of using birth control, rates of teenage pregnancy, and condom use, today' youth are doing a good job of protecting their sexual health and well-being. The picture in terms of sexually transmitted infections (STIs) is not as positive. A range of STIs, including human papillomavirus (HPV) and herpes simplex virus (HSV), are common in youth and require that both general health campaigns and school-based sex education programs continue to educate youth around using effective methods to protect themselves from STIs.

LO-6 Identify the significant issues and controversies regarding sexuality in Canadian society.

Intimate partner violence—the physical and nonphysical violence experienced by women and men at the hands of their current or former intimate partners—remains a significant social problem. Women are particularly vulnerable to frequent, severe, and sometimes lethal intimate partner violence. Dating violence, which includes forms of sexually and nonsexually assaultive behaviours that occur within dating relationships, has been found to be far too common. The sexual double standard—the belief that men and women are expected to conform to different standards of sexual conduct—continues to constrain the sexual behaviour of young men and women today.

© Peter Bernik/Shutterstock

polyandry The concurrent marriage of one woman with two or more men (p. 345).

polygamy The concurrent marriage of a person of one sex with two or more members of the opposite sex (p. 345).

polygyny The concurrent marriage of one man with two or more women (p. 345).

primary sex characteristics The genitalia used in the reproductive process (p. 336).

secondary sex characteristics The physical traits (other than reproductive organs) that identify an individual's sex (p. 336).

sex A term used to describe the biological and anatomical differences between females and males (p. 336).

sexual double standard The belief that men and women are expected to conform to different standards of sexual conduct (p. 359).

sexual orientation A person's preference for emotional-sexual relationships with members of the opposite sex (heterosexuality), the same sex (homosexuality), or both (bisexuality) (p. 339).

sexual revolution A term used for the dramatic changes that occurred regarding sexual attitudes, behaviours, and values during the 1960s (p. 359).

sexual scripts Culturally created guidelines that define how, where, with whom, and under what conditions a person is to behave as a sexual being (p. 337).

sexuality (sexual) The range of human activities designed to produce erotic response and pleasure (p. 337).

transsexual A person who believes that he or she was born with the body of the wrong sex (p. 338).

transvestite A male who lives as a woman or a female who lives as a man but does not alter the genitalia (p. 338).

KEY FIGURES

© Arthur Siegel/Time & Life Pictures/Getty Images

Alfred Kinsey (1894-1956) Kinsey was a biologist and professor of zoology who in 1947 founded the Institute for Sex Research at Indiana University. Kinsey's research on human sexuality provoked controversy in the 1940s and 1950s and profoundly influenced social and cultural values regarding sexuality in North American society.

© Jean Pierre FOUCHET/RAPHO/Gamma-Rapho/Getty

Michel Foucault (1926-1984) Foucault was a French philosopher, social theorist, and historian. In one of his best-known works, the three-volume *History of Sexuality* (1976–1984), Foucault develops an "analytics of power"—the conceptual instruments that make it possible to analyze sex in terms of power. He emphasized that the power mechanisms of sexuality are socially constructed, unstable, and historically situated.

APPLICATION QUESTIONS

1. The media claim that young people engage in far more sexual behaviour than their predecessors did. Assess the validity of this claim.
2. Describe some of the possible consequences if a culture in which people are more likely to hook up than to engage in long-term committed relationships continues to evolve.
3. Discuss cases in which sex and gender do not correspond. What are the consequences for the individuals involved?
4. Our culture believes that marriage should be monogamous. Do you think this is a realistic expectation for marital partners to have for themselves and their partners? Why or why not?
5. The evidence suggests that sexual health among young people is improving. Why do you think this improvement has occurred?
6. Imagine that your parents have just informed you that you were born intersexed and had undergone gender reassignment surgery. How would this affect you? Who do you think should make decisions regarding surgical interventions with intersexed newborns? When do think these decisions should be made?

Test your comprehension and assess what you've learned with **CourseMate's** online quizzes.

For other interesting Lived Experiences, watch the video clips on **CourseMate.**

Practise what you've learned with flashcards containing key terms and definitions on **CourseMate.**

CHAPTER 13

Families

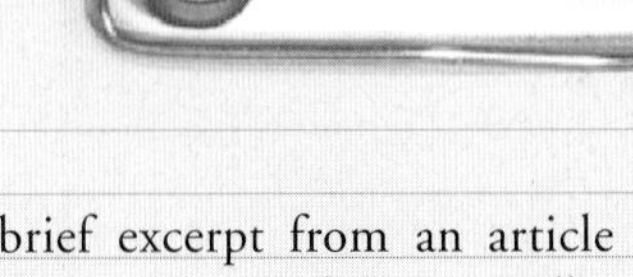

© LWA-Dann Tardif/Corbis

The following is a brief excerpt from an article entitled "Out Family Values" by Prof. James Miller from the University of Western Ontario:

The family I live in as a father is also the family I live out in as a gay man. I call it an "out family" for three reasons: its openness to homosexual membership; its opposition to heterosexist conformity (the prejudicial assumption of heterosexuality as normal and proper); and its overtness within the contemporary lesbian and gay movement.

Mine is a family that opens out, steps out, and stands out. It opens out to people traditionally excluded from the charmed circle of Home; it steps out beyond the polite and policed borders of the Normal; and it stands out as a clear new possibility on the horizon of what used to be called—in the heady days following Pierre Trudeau's decriminalization of homosexuality in Canada (1969)—the Just Society. Against the drone of current conservative rhetoric urging decent citizens to protect "family values" from homefront activists like me, I shall try to spell out here the distinctive qualities that my family has discovered in itself to meet the challenges of living in a pervasively homophobic culture that would rather we closed down, stepped in, and stood back . . .

When I first came out to my children in January of 1990, they immediately wanted to know whether they were gay, too. Not necessarily, I told them, trying to allay their time-honoured fears without compromising my newfound sense of pride. Yet was I not outing them by outing myself? For better or worse, I realized my uncloseted gayness was bound to be socially projected onto all who lived with me. Whatever my children's sexual orientations might be, their close association with me would effectively gay them in the eyes of straight society and queer their cultural outlook. So look out, I warned them, the World likes to see things straight.

They have taken my warning to heart by setting the record straight about me and them ("Our Dad's gay, but we're probably not") for any curious soul who comes into our domestic space . . . An out family must learn to speak about itself in unaccustomed ways, develop its own outlandish frontier lingo, for its members are always proudly, if at times also painfully, aware of their strategic positioning outside the normative vision of heterosexual monogamy. . . . My out family bravely resists the exclusionary pressures of heterosexist institutions and their defenders simply by existing as such, by brazenly occupying hallowed spaces like "family rooms" and "family cottages" and even "family restaurants" where we're not supposed to exist. (2003:104)

Fifty years ago, the majority of Canadian families consisted of two adults in a permanent union that produced three to five children. Other kinds of families were the exception. Today, when we think of families, we think of diversity and change, and exceptions are the rule. The experiences of the family in the above narrative certainly are not unique. Other variations on what has been described as a "traditional" family are also common. Separation and divorce, remarriage, and blended or reconstituted families are a reality for many Canadians. Regardless of the form it takes, family life continues to be a source of great personal satisfaction and happiness.

In this chapter, we will examine the diversity and complexity of families and intimate relationships. Pressing social issues, such as same-sex marriage, divorce, child care, and new reproductive technologies, will be used as examples of how families and intimate relationships continue to change. Before reading on, test your knowledge about the changing family by taking the quiz in Box 13.1 on page 371.

Critical Thinking Questions

1. It has been suggested that variations of the "traditional" family are common today. Identify some of these alternative family forms.
2. James Miller "came out" to his children in 1990. Do you think childen of gay parents would have a similar experience today? What changes have occurred in the past 20 years that might make this experience easier for both parent and child?
3. Which, if any, heterosexist institutions continue to place exclusionary pressures on families with gay parents today?

CHAPTER FOCUS QUESTION

How is social change affecting the Canadian family?

Learning Objectives

AFTER READING THIS CHAPTER, YOU SHOULD BE ABLE TO

LO-1 Explain why it is difficult to define family.

LO-2 Understand the key assumptions of functionalist, conflict, feminist, symbolic interactionist, and postmodernist perspectives on families.

LO-3 Understand the various options available to Canadian families in establishing families.

LO-4 Describe the challenges facing families today.

LO-5 Identify the primary problems facing Canadian families today.

© BuzzFoto/FilmMagic/Getty Images

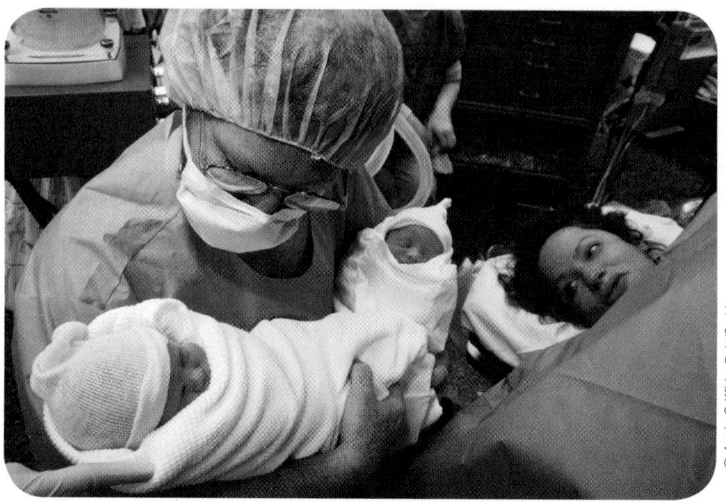

© Annie Griffiths Belt/Corbis

Despite the idealized image of "the family," North American families have undergone many changes in the past century, as exemplified by the increase in the number of families using assisted reproductive technologies to start a family.

LO-1 DEFINING FAMILY

What is a family? Although we all have a family of some form or another and we all understand the concept of family, it is not an easy word to define. More than ever, this term means different things to different people. As the nature of family life and work has changed in high-, middle-, and low-income nations, the issue of what constitutes a family has been widely debated. For example, Hutterite families in Canada live in communal situations in which children from about the age of three spend most of their days in school. The children also eat their meals in a communal dining hall, away from their parents. In this case, the community is the family, as opposed to a traditional nuclear family.

Some Aboriginal families in Canada also tend to have a much broader idea of family membership. Children are often cared for by relatives in the extended family. A social worker may define a family as consisting of parents and children only. Some Aboriginal parents may be perceived as neglecting their children when the parents feel they are safe and well cared for by "their family"—that is, by uncles, grandparents, siblings, or other relatives (Vanier Institute of the Family, 2009a).

Similarly, gay men and lesbians often form unique families. Many gay men and lesbians have **families we choose**—social arrangements that include intimate relationships between couples and close familial relationships with other couples, as well as with other adults and children (Ambert, 2005).

families we choose Social arrangements that include intimate relationships between couples and close familial relationships with other couples, as well as with other adults and children.

In a society as diverse as Canada, talking about "a family" as though a single type of family exists or ever did exist is inaccurate. In reality, different groups will define their family lives in unique ways, depending on a number of factors, such as their socioeconomic background, immigrant status, religious beliefs, or cultural practices and traditions (Baker, 2009).

For many years, a standard sociological definition of family has been a group of people who are related to one another by bonds of blood, marriage, or adoption and who live together, form an economic unit, and bear and raise children (Benokraitis, 2005). Many people believe that this definition should not be expanded—that social approval should not be extended to other relationships simply because the persons in those relationships wish to be considered a family. Others, however, challenge this definition because it simply does not match the reality of family life in contemporary society. Today's families include many types of living arrangements and relationships, including single-parent households, unmarried couples, lesbian and gay couples, and multiple generations (such as grandparents, parents, and children) living in the same household. To accurately reflect these changes in family life, we need an encompassing definition of what constitutes a family. Accordingly, we will define a **family** as a relationship in which people live together with commitment, form an economic unit and care for any young, and consider their identity to be significantly attached to the group. Sexual expression and parent–children relationships are a part of most, but not all, family relationships (based on Benokraitis, 2005; Lamanna and Riedmann, 2011).

family A relationship in which people live together with commitment, form an economic unit and care for any young, and consider their identity to be significantly attached to the group.

In our study of families, we will use our sociological imaginations to see how our personal experiences are related to the larger happenings in our society. At the microlevel, each of us has our own "biography," based on our experience within a family; at the macrolevel, our families are embedded in a specific social context that has a major impact on them (Aulette, 1994). We will examine the institution of the family at both of these levels, beginning with family structure and characteristics.

Family Structure and Characteristics

In preindustrial societies, the primary form of social organization is through kinship ties. **Kinship** refers to a social network of people based on common ancestry, marriage, or adoption. Through kinship networks, people cooperate so that they can acquire the basic necessities of life, including food and shelter. Kinship systems can also serve as a means by which property is transferred, goods are produced and distributed, and power is allocated.

kinship A social network of people based on common ancestry, marriage, or adoption.

In industrialized societies, other social institutions fulfill some of the functions previously taken care of by the kinship network. For example, political systems provide structures of social control and authority, and economic systems are responsible for the production and distribution of goods and services. Consequently, families in industrialized societies serve fewer and more specialized purposes than do families in preindustrial societies. Contemporary families are primarily responsible for regulating sexual activity, socializing children, and providing affection and companionship for family members.

BOX 13.1 **SOCIOLOGY AND EVERYDAY LIFE**

How Much Do You Know About the Changing Family in Canada?

True	False	
T	F	1. Today, people in Canada are more inclined to get married than at any time in history.
T	F	2. Men are as likely as women to be single parents.
T	F	3. One out of every two marriages ends in divorce.
T	F	4. Age of first marriage has increased significantly in the past 40 years for both men and women.
T	F	5. In recent years, the number of extended families where members live together in the same home has decreased.

For answers to the quiz about the changing family in Canada, go to **www.nelson.com/sociologyinourtimes6e.**

family of orientation The family into which a person is born and in which early socialization usually takes place.

family of procreation The family that a person forms by having or adopting children.

extended family A family unit composed of relatives in addition to parents and children who live in the same household.

FAMILIES OF ORIENTATION AND PROCREATION During our lifetime, many of us will be members of two different types of families—a family of orientation and a family of procreation. The **family of orientation** is the family into which a person is born and in which early socialization usually takes place. Although most people are related to members of their family of orientation by blood ties, those who are adopted have a legal tie that is patterned after a blood relationship. The **family of procreation** is the family that a person forms by having or adopting children (Benokraitis, 2005). Both legal and blood ties are found in most families of procreation. The relationship between a husband and wife is based on legal ties; however, the relationship between a parent and child may be based on either blood ties or legal ties, depending on whether the child has been adopted or is by marriage (Aulette, 1994).

Although many young people leave their families of orientation as they reach adulthood, finish school, and/or get married, recent studies have found that many people maintain family ties across generations, particularly as older persons have remained actively involved in relationships with their adult children.

EXTENDED AND NUCLEAR FAMILIES Sociologists distinguish between extended and nuclear families based on the number of generations that live within a household. An **extended family** is a family unit composed of relatives in addition to parents and children who live in the same household. These families often include grandparents, uncles, aunts, or other relatives who live in close proximity to the parents and children, making it possible for family members to share resources (see Box 13.2). In horticultural and agricultural societies, extended families are extremely important; having a large number of family members participate in food production may be essential for survival. Today, extended families are becoming more common across North America and Britain. This trend is related to an increase in the number of families caring for aging seniors in their homes, an increase in the number of grandparents with children and grandchildren living with them for economic reasons, and an increase in immigration from countries where extended family living is the norm (Milan, Keown, and Robles Urquijo, 2011).

BOX 13.2 SOCIOLOGY IN GLOBAL PERSPECTIVE

Buffering Financial Hardship: Extended Families in the Global Economy

- Day after day, Nang Pajik sews collars on workshirts at a factory in Vientiane, Laos, so that she can send money home to her six brothers and sisters and her extended family in her home village (Bradsher, 2006).
- Odilon Hernandez bought a television and several appliances from La Curacao, a Los Angeles store, for his parents in Puebla, Mexico. La Curacao delivers items directly to the extended families of U.S. immigrant workers from the store's warehouse in Mexico, which was set up for that purpose (Associated Press, 2006).
- A United Kingdom building society estimates that the number of homes containing three generations of a family will triple in England during the next 20 years. The causes are rising levels of debt and the high cost of property. According to a Skipton Building Society spokesperson, "These issues are likely to get worse and so combining incomes and sharing mortgage repayments may well be the only alternative for some families." (BBC News, 2004)

Although many people think of the extended family as primarily a thing of the past, current evidence suggests that the extended family is far from becoming obsolete. What unique benefits do extended families offer? The answer is quite simple: Extended families offer a financial safety net that is unavailable in the typical nuclear family. For many families in the United Kingdom, purchasing a house is a possibility only if multiple generations combine their incomes and share their living expenses and mortgage payments. However, as the cost of child care rises in the United Kingdom, extended family residential patterns are important not only for house purchases but also for child care because expenditures are greatly reduced when grandparents serve as live-in childminders (BBC News, 2004).

In low-income and immigrant families, the extended family is particularly important: Pooling resources often means economic survival for the family. In the poorest of nations, such as Laos, some family members remain in the home village to tend the family's rice plot while other members migrate to the city to earn money that can be shared with relatives at home.

To people in high-income nations, the thought of earning wages of $50 a month for factory work is unheard of. For individuals with few educational opportunities or little experience using machines, however, moving from a village to the city to work in a factory constitutes a major economic improvement (even if it is only temporary) in the standard of living for their entire family.

The stories above could be repeated in many nations. In Africa, for example, extended family systems help buffer inequality through the exchanges of resources and fostering of children across nuclear family units. At this time, it does not appear that globalization or greater exposure to other cultural norms of family life will change this pattern significantly. The African HIV/AIDS epidemic has left many children dependent on relatives for their survival. Like children, many older adults benefit from extended family patterns. In a study of elderly Asians living in Britain, researchers found that the grandmothers in their study had better mental health—were "better adjusted"—when they resided in an extended family rather than in a nuclear family (Guglani, Coleman, and Sonuga-Barke, 2000).

What conclusions might we draw from this brief look at extended families in the global economy? Apparently, extended families meet specific needs that are not easily met by nuclear families, and current evidence suggests that extended family patterns are not likely to disappear in the near future. Do you or does someone you know live in an extended family? What are the strengths and limitations of this arrangement?

In the global economy, many immigrant workers regularly send portions of their paycheques to relatives living in their country of origin. What other important functions do extended family patterns serve in the 21st century?

A **nuclear family** is a family composed of one or two parents and their dependent children, all of whom live apart from other relatives. A traditional definition specifies that a nuclear family is made up of a "couple" and their dependent children; however, this definition became outdated as a significant shift occurred in the family structure. For the first time ever, there are more families without children than families with children. As shown in the Census Profile, in 2006 about 41 percent of all households were composed of couples with children under the age of 18, while 43 percent of couples did not have children living at home. This latter group consisted of childless couples and empty nesters, or couples whose children no longer lived at home (Statistics Canada, 2007c).

nuclear family A family made up of one or two parents and their dependent children, all of whom live apart from other relatives.

Nuclear families are smaller than they were 20 years ago; whereas the average family size in 1971 was 3.7 persons, in 2006 it was 2.5 persons. This decrease has been largely attributed to decisions to postpone or forgo childbearing and to increases in separation and divorce rates (Milan, Keown, and Robles Urquijo, 2011).

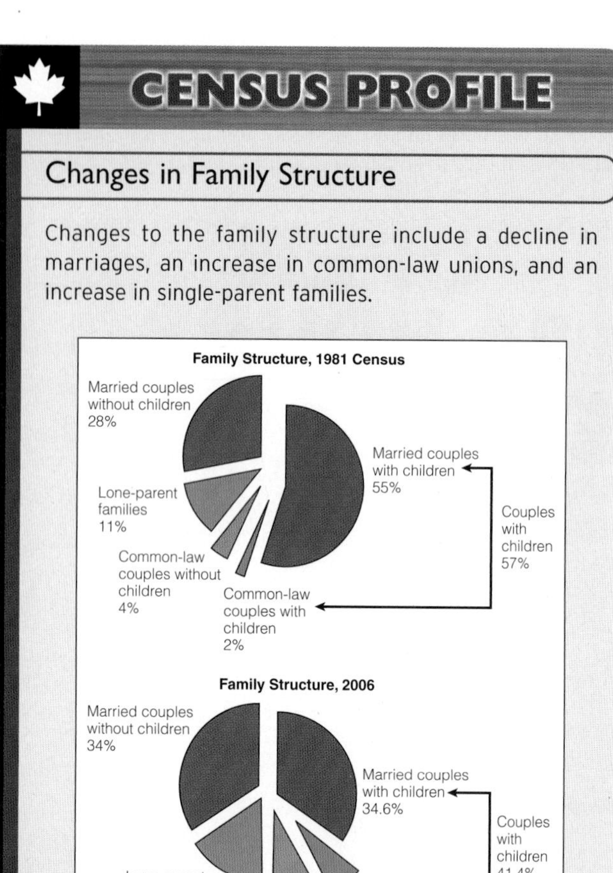

Marriage Patterns

Across cultures, families are characterized by different forms of marriage. **Marriage** is a legally recognized and/or socially approved arrangement between two or more individuals that carries certain rights and obligations and usually involves sexual activity. In Canada, the only legally sanctioned form of marriage is **monogamy**—marriage to one person at a time. For some people, marriage is a lifelong commitment that ends only with the death of a partner.

Members of some religious groups believe that marriage is "forever"; if one spouse dies, the surviving spouse is precluded from marrying anyone else. For others, marriage is a commitment of indefinite duration. Through a pattern of marriage, divorce, and remarriage, some people practise *serial monogamy*—a succession of marriages in which a person has several spouses over a lifetime but is legally married to only one person at a time.

Polygamy refers to the concurrent marriage of a person of one sex with two or more members of the opposite sex. The most prevalent form of polygamy is **polygyny**—the concurrent marriage of one man with two or more women. Polygyny has been practised in a number of Islamic societies, including in some regions of contemporary Africa and southern Russia. The reality television show *Sister Wives*, which documents the life of polygamist family which includes a husband with four wives and 17 children certainly challenges traditional notions of family. How many wives and children might a polygynist have at one time? Some analysts believe that the practice of polygamy contributes to the likelihood that families will live in poverty (Chipungu, 1999).

The second type of polygamy is **polyandry**—the concurrent marriage of one woman with two or more men. Polyandry is rare; when it does occur, it is typically found in societies where men greatly outnumber women because of high rates of female infanticide or where marriages are arranged between two brothers and one woman (fraternal polyandry). According to recent research, polyandry is never the only form of marriage in a society: Whenever polyandry occurs, polygyny co-occurs (Trevithick, 1997). Although Tibetans are the most frequently studied population where polyandry exists, anthropologists have also identified the Sherpas, Paharis, Sinhalese, and various African groups as sometimes practising polyandry (Trevithick, 1997). An anthropological study of Nyinba, an ethnically Tibetan population living in northwestern Nepal, found that fraternal polyandry (two brothers sharing the same wife) is the normative form of marriage and that the practice continues to be highly valued culturally (Levine and Silk, 1997).

marriage A legally recognized and/or socially approved arrangement between two or more individuals that carries certain rights and obligations and usually involves sexual activity.

monogamy marriage to one person at a time.

polygamy The practice of having more than one spouse at a time.

polygyny The concurrent marriage of one man with two or more women.

polyandry The concurrent marriage of one woman with two or more men.

Patterns of Descent and Inheritance

Even though a variety of marital patterns exist across cultures, virtually all forms of marriage establish a system of descent so that kinship can be determined and inheritance rights established. In preindustrial societies, kinship is usually traced through one parent (unilineally). The most common pattern of unilineal descent is **patrilineal descent**—a system of tracing descent through the father's side of the family. Patrilineal systems are set up in such a manner that a legitimate son inherits his father's property and sometimes his position upon the father's death. In nations such as India, where boys are seen as permanent patrilineal family members and girls are seen only as temporary family members, girls tend to be considered more expendable than boys (O'Connell, 1994).

Even with the less common pattern of **matrilineal descent**—a system of tracing descent through the mother's side of the family—women may not control property. However, inheritance of property and position is usually traced from the maternal uncle (mother's brother) to his nephew (mother's son). In some cases, mothers may pass on their property to daughters.

By contrast, in industrial societies, kinship is usually traced through both parents (bilineally). The most common form is **bilateral descent**—a system of tracing descent through both the mother's and father's sides of the family. This pattern is used in Canada for the purpose of determining kinship and inheritance rights; however, children typically take the father's last name.

patrilineal descent A system of tracing descent through the father's side of the family.

matrilineal descent A system of tracing descent through the mother's side of the family.

bilateral descent A system of tracing descent through both the mother's and father's sides of the family.

Power and Authority in Families

Descent and inheritance rights are intricately linked with patterns of power and authority in families. A **patriarchal family** is a family structure in which authority is held by the eldest male (usually the father). The male authority figure acts as head of the household and holds power and authority over the women and children as well as over other males. A **matriarchal family** is a family structure in which authority is held by the eldest female (usually the mother). In this case, the female authority figure acts as head of the household. Although there has been a great deal of discussion about matriarchal societies, scholars have found no historical evidence to indicate that true matriarchies ever existed.

The most prevalent pattern of power and authority in families is patriarchy—a hierarchical system of social organization in which cultural, political, and economic structures are controlled by men. Across cultures, men are the primary (and often sole) decision makers regarding domestic, economic, and social concerns facing the family. The existence of patriarchy may give men a sense of power over their own lives, but it also can create an atmosphere in which some men feel greater freedom to abuse women and children (O'Connell, 1994). According to some feminist scholars and journalists, hostility and violence perpetrated by men against women and children are the results of patriarchal attitudes, economic hardship, rigid gender roles, and societal acceptance of aggression (Johnson and Dawson, 2011). Moreover, some economists believe that the patriarchal family structure (along with prevailing market conditions and public policy) limits people's choices in employment. According to this view, the patriarchal family structure has remained largely unchanged in this country, even as familial responsibilities in the paid labour market have undergone dramatic transformation. In the post-industrial age, for example, gender-specific roles may have been reduced; however, women's choices remain limited by the patriarchal tradition in which women do most of the unpaid labour, particularly in the family. Despite dramatic increases in the number of women in the paid workforce, there has been little movement toward gender equity, which would equalize women's opportunities (Lindsay, 2008).

patriarchal family A family structure in which authority is held by the eldest male (usually the father).

matriarchal family A family structure in which authority is held by the eldest female (usually the mother).

egalitarian family A family structure in which both partners share power and authority equally.

An **egalitarian family** is a family structure in which both partners share power and authority equally. In egalitarian families, issues of power and authority may be frequently negotiated as the roles and responsibilities within the relationship change over time. Recently, a trend toward more egalitarian relationships has been evident in a number of countries as women have sought changes in their legal status and greater educational and employment opportunities. Some degree of economic independence makes it possible for women to delay marriage or to terminate a problematic marriage (Ward, 2005). However, one study of the effects of egalitarian values on the allocation and performance of domestic tasks in the family found that changes were relatively slow in coming. According to the study, fathers were more likely to share domestic tasks in nonconventional families where members held more egalitarian values. Similarly, children's gender-role stereotyping was more closely linked to their parents' egalitarian values and nonconventional lifestyles than to the domestic tasks they were assigned (Marshall, 2011).

While the relationship between husband and wife is based on legal ties, relationships between parents and children may be established either by blood ties or by legal ties.

TIME TO REVIEW

- Describe how Canadian families have changed in recent years in their structure and characteristics. In particular, comment on changes in nuclear and extended families, patterns of descent and inheritance, and power and authority in families.
- What social factors have driven these changes?

LO-2 THEORETICAL PERSPECTIVES ON FAMILIES

sociology of family The subdiscipline of sociology that attempts to describe and explain patterns of family life and variations in family structure.

The **sociology of family** is the subdiscipline of sociology that attempts to describe and explain patterns of family life and variations in family structure. Functionalist perspectives emphasize the functions that families perform at the macrolevel of society, while conflict and feminist perspectives focus on families as a primary source of social inequality. By contrast, symbolic interactionists examine microlevel interactions that are integral to the roles of different family members. Finally, postmodern theorists emphasize the fact that families today are diverse and variable.

Functionalist Perspectives

Functionalists emphasize the importance of the family in maintaining the stability of society and the well-being of individuals. According to Émile Durkheim, marriage is a microcosmic replica of the larger society; both marriage and society involve a mental and moral fusion of physically distinct individuals (Lehmann, 1994). Durkheim also believed that a division of labour contributed to greater efficiency in all areas of life—including marriages and families—even though he acknowledged that this division imposed significant limitations on some people.

Talcott Parsons was a key figure in developing a functionalist model of the family. According to Parsons (1955), the husband/father fulfills the *instrumental role* (meeting the family's economic needs, making important decisions, and providing leadership), while the wife/mother fulfills the *expressive role* (running the household, caring for children, and meeting the emotional needs of family members).

Contemporary functionalist perspectives on families derive their foundation from Durkheim and Parsons. Division of labour makes it possible for families to fulfill a number of functions that no other institution can perform as effectively. In advanced industrial societies, families serve four key functions:

1. *Sexual regulation.* Families are expected to regulate the sexual activity of their members and thus control reproduction so that it occurs within specific boundaries. At the macrolevel, incest taboos prohibit sexual contact or marriage between certain relatives. For example, virtually all societies prohibit sexual relations between parents and their children and between brothers and sisters.
2. *Socialization.* Parents and other relatives are responsible for teaching children the necessary knowledge and skills to survive. The smallness and intimacy of families makes them best suited for providing children with the initial learning experiences they need.
3. *Economic and psychological support.* Families are responsible for providing economic and psychological support for members. In preindustrial societies, families are economic production units; in industrial societies, the economic security of families is tied to the workplace and to macrolevel economic systems. In recent years, psychological support and emotional security have been increasingly important functions of the family.
4. *Provision of social status.* Families confer social status and reputation on their members. These statuses include the ascribed statuses with which individuals are born, such as race and ethnicity, nationality, social class, and sometimes religious affiliation. One of the most significant and compelling forms of social placement is the family's class position and the opportunities (or lack thereof) resulting from that position. Examples of class-related opportunities include access to quality health care, higher education, and a safe place to live.

Conflict Perspectives

Both conflict and feminist analysts view functionalist perspectives on the role of the family in society as idealized and inadequate. Rather than operating harmoniously and for the benefit of all members, families are sources of social inequality and conflict over values, goals, and access to resources and power (Benokraitis, 2005).

In his classic work *The Origin of the Family, Private Property and the State* (1972/1884), Friedrich Engels argued that the family in a capitalist society is an exploitive social institution that oppresses women. According to some conflict theorists, families in capitalist economies are similar to workers in a factory. Women are dominated by men in the home in the same manner that workers are dominated by capitalists and managers in factories (Engels, 1970/1884). Although childbearing and care for family members in the home contribute to capitalism, these activities also reinforce the subordination of women through unpaid (and often devalued) labour. Engels predicted that the oppression of women would end when women moved out of the private sphere of the home and into the paid workforce. As discussed in Chapter 11, women's oppression has not disappeared as a result of the dramatic increases in the number of women in the paid workforce.

Other conflict analysts are concerned with the effect that class conflict has on the family. The exploitation of the lower classes by the upper classes contributes to family problems, such as high rates of divorce and overall family instability.

Feminist Perspectives

The contributions of feminist theorists have resulted in radical changes in the sociological study of families. Feminist theorists have been primarily responsible for redefining the concept of the family by focusing on the diversity of family arrangements. Some feminist scholars reject the "monolithic model of the family" (Eichler, 1981:368), which idealizes one family form—the family with a male breadwinner and stay-at-home wife and children—as the normal household arrangement. Feminist theorists argue that limiting our concept of family to this traditional

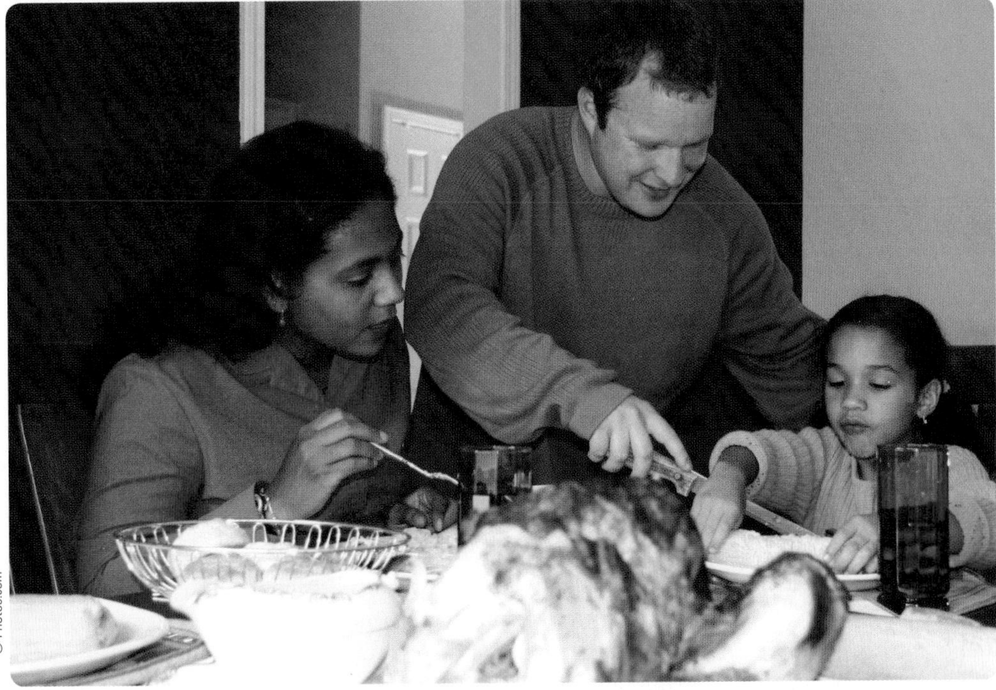

Functionalist theorists believe that families serve a variety of important functions that no other social institution can adequately fulfill. In contrast, conflict and feminist analysts believe that the functionalist perspective is idealistic and inadequate for explaining problems in contemporary families.

form means ignoring or undervaluing diverse family forms, such as single-parent families, childless families, gay or lesbian families, and stepfamilies. Roles within the family are viewed by feminist theorists as primarily socially constructed rather than biologically determined (Smith, 1974). Feminist scholars have challenged a number of common assumptions about family life and the roles women fulfill within families. For example, they question whether all "real" women want to be mothers and whether the inequality between traditional husbands and wives is "natural" (Mandell and Duffy, 2005).

Feminist perspectives on inequality focus on patriarchy. From this viewpoint, men's domination over women existed long before private ownership of property and capitalism (Mann, 1994). Women's subordination is rooted in patriarchy and men's control over women's labour power (Hartmann, 1981). The division of labour by gender, both within the larger society and within households, is a fundamental focus of feminist analysis (Luxton and Corman, 2001, cited in Ambert, 2006a:21). Although the division of labour may appear to be an equal pooling of contributions within the family unit, feminist scholars view women as giving much but receiving less in return. According to sociologist Patricia Mann, "Male power in our society is expressed in economic terms even if it does not originate in property relations; women's activities in the home have been undervalued at the same time as their labor has been controlled by men" (1994:42).

Many women resist male domination. Women can control their reproductive capabilities through contraception and other means, and they can take control of their labour power from their husbands by working for wages outside the home (Mann, 1994). However, men may be reluctant to relinquish their status as family breadwinner. Why? Although only 15 percent of families in Canada are supported solely by a male breadwinner, many men continue to construct their ideal of masculinity around this cultural value.

Feminist perspectives on families also draw attention to the problems of dominance and subordination inherent in relationships. Specifically, feminist theorists have acknowledged what has been described as the "dark side of the family," focusing research efforts on issues such as child abuse, wife abuse, and violence against the elderly (Ambert, 2001; Johnson and Dawson, 2011; Smith, 1985). The idea that family relations, including wife abuse and child abuse, are private, personal matters has been challenged by feminists and successfully brought into the public domain of social policy and legislative changes. As a result, feminist analysis of families is viewed not only as a theoretical perspective, but also as a broad movement for social change (Johnson and Dawson, 2011).

Symbolic Interactionist Perspectives

Early symbolic interactionists, such as Charles Horton Cooley and George Herbert Mead, provided key insights on the roles we play as family members and how we modify or adapt our roles to the expectations of others—especially significant others, such as parents, grandparents, siblings, and other relatives. How does the family influence the individual's self-concept and identity? Contemporary symbolic interactionist perspectives examine the roles of husbands, wives, and children as they act out their own parts and react to the actions of others. From such a perspective, what people think, as well as what they say and do, is very important in understanding family dynamics.

According to sociologists Peter Berger and Hansfried Kellner (1964), interaction between marital partners contributes to a shared reality. Although newlyweds bring separate identities to a marriage, over time they construct a shared reality as a couple. In the process, the partners redefine their past identities to be consistent with new realities. Development of a shared reality is a continuous process, taking place not only in the family but also in any group in which the couple participates together. Divorce is the reverse of this process; couples may start with a shared reality and, in the process of uncoupling, gradually develop separate realities (Vaughan, 1985).

Symbolic interactionists explain family relationships in terms of the subjective meanings and everyday interpretations people give to their lives. Sociologist Jessie Bernard (1982/1973) pointed out that women and men experience marriage differently and that a marriage contains two marriages: "his marriage" and "her marriage." While a husband may see his marriage positively, his wife may feel less positive about her marriage, and vice versa. Researchers have found that husbands and wives may give very different accounts of the same event and their two "realities" frequently do not coincide (Safilios-Rothschild, 1969).

Other symbolic interactionists have examined ways in which individuals communicate with one another and interpret these interactions. According to Lenore Walker (1979), females are socialized to be passive and males are socialized to be aggressive long before they take on the adult roles of battered and batterer. However, even women who have not been socialized by their parents to be helpless and passive may be socialized into this behaviour by abusive husbands. Three factors contribute to the acceptance of the roles of batterer and battered: (1) low self-esteem on the part of both people involved, (2) a limited range of behaviours (he only knows how to be jealous and possessive; she only knows how to be dependent and eager to make everyone happy), and (3) a belief by both in stereotypic gender roles (she should be feminine and pampered; he should be aggressive and dominant). Other analysts suggest that this pattern is changing as more women are gaining paid employment and becoming less dependent on their husbands or male companions for economic support.

Postmodern Perspectives

Although postmodern theorists disparage the idea that a universal theory can be developed to explain social life, a postmodern perspective might provide insights on questions such as this: How is family life different in the Information Age? Social scientist David Elkind (1995) describes the postmodern family as *permeable*—capable of being diffused or invaded in such a manner that an entity's original purpose is modified or changed. According to Elkind, if the nuclear family is a reflection of the age of modernity, the permeable family reflects the postmodern assumptions of difference, particularity, and irregularity.

Difference is evident in the fact that the nuclear family is now only one of many family forms. Similarly, under modernity, the idea of romantic love has given way to the idea of consensual love: Individuals agree to have sexual relations with others they have no intention of marrying or, if they marry, do not necessarily see the marriage as having permanence. Maternal love has also been transformed into shared parenting, which includes not only mothers and fathers but also caregivers, who may be either relatives or nonrelatives (Elkind, 1995).

Urbanity is another characteristic of the postmodern family. The boundaries between the public sphere (the workplace) and the private sphere (the home) are becoming more open and flexible. As a result, family life may be negatively affected by the decreasing distinction between what is work time and what is family time. As more people are becoming connected "24/7" (24 hours a day, seven days a week), the boss who before would not have called at 11:30 p.m. or when an employee was on vacation may send an email or text asking for an immediate response to some question that has arisen while the person is away with family members.

Social theorist Jean Baudrillard's idea that the simulation of reality may come to be viewed as "reality" by some people can be applied to family interactions in the Information Age. Does the ability to contact someone anywhere and any time of the day or night provide greater happiness and stability in families? Or is "reach out and touch someone" merely an ideology promulgated by the consumer society? Journalists have written about the experience of watching a family gathering at an amusement park, restaurant, mall, or other location, only to see family members pick up their cellphones to receive or make calls to individuals not present, rather than spending "face time" with those family members who are present.

The Concept Snapshot on the next page summarizes these sociological perspectives on the family. Taken together, these perspectives on the social institution of families help us understand both the good and bad sides of familial relationships. Now we shift our focus to love, marriage, intimate relationships, and family issues in Canada.

CONCEPT SNAPSHOT

FUNCTIONALIST PERSPECTIVES **Key thinker:** Talcott Parsons	In modern societies, families serve the functions of sexual regulation, socialization, economic and psychological support, and provision of social status.
CONFLICT PERSPECTIVES **Key thinker:** Friedrich Engels	Families both mirror and help perpetuate social inequalities based on class and gender.
FEMINIST PERSPECTIVES **Key thinkers:** Nancy Mandell, Ann Duffy	Women's subordination is rooted in patriarchy and men's control over women's labour power.
SYMBOLIC INTERACTIONIST PERSPECTIVES **Key thinker:** Jessie Bernard	Family dynamics, including communication patterns and the subjective meanings that people assign to events, mean that interactions within families create a shared reality.
POSTMODERN PERSPECTIVES **Key thinker:** David Elkind	In postmodern societies, families are diverse and fragmented. Boundaries between the workplace and home are also blurred.

LO-3 ESTABLISHING FAMILIES

Cohabitation

cohabitation The sharing of a household by a couple who live together without being legally married.

Cohabitation refers to the sharing of a household by a couple who live together without being legally married. Attitudes about cohabitation have changed in the last few decades, something that is reflected in Figure 13.1. In Canada, cohabitation (most commonly referred to as a common-law union) has become an increasingly popular alternative to marriage. The growth of common-law families is the strongest of all family structures. Since the early 1980s, the number of persons living common-law has doubled, going from 700,000 in 1981 to 1.4 million in 2006 (Statistics Canada, 2007c). Almost half of these common-law-couple families included children, whether born to the current union or brought to the family from previous unions. The proportion of people in common-law unions varies considerably by province. In Quebec, one in three couples lives common-law, making it the province with the highest rate of common-law families.

Those most likely to cohabit are young adults between the ages of 25 and 29. Based on the Statistics Canada census data, approximately one in four Canadians in this age group lives in a common-law union. However, the largest growth in common-law unions has occurred among couples in their early 60s, reflecting a growing acceptance among older generations of what was previously a living arrangement of young adults. While "living together" is often a prelude to marriage for young adults, common-law unions are also becoming a popular alternative both to marriage and to remarriage following divorce or separation (Milan, Keown, and Robles Urquijo, 2011).

Today, some people view cohabitation as a form of "trial marriage," but for others, cohabitation is not a first step toward marriage. Some people who have cohabited do eventually marry the person with whom they have been living, whereas others do not. And studies over the past decade

FIGURE 13.1 PROPORTION OF COMMON-LAW FAMILIES GROWS WHILE IT DECLINES FOR MARRIED FAMILIES, CANADA

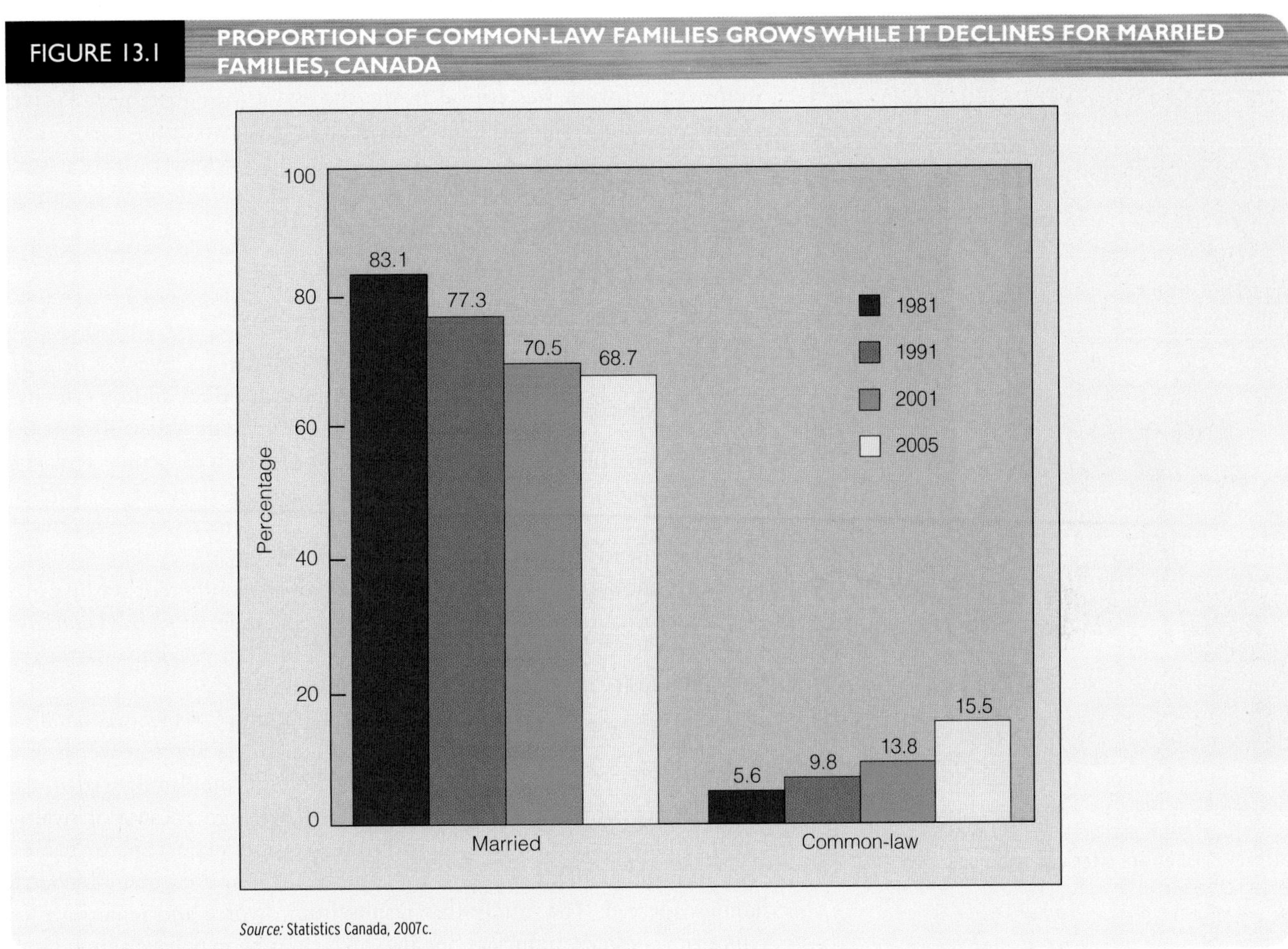

Source: Statistics Canada, 2007c.

have supported the proposition that couples who cohabit before marriage do not necessarily have a stable relationship once they are married (Clark and Crompton, 2006).

Marriage

Despite the prevalence of divorce in our society, marriage continues to be an extremely popular institution. The majority of Canadians will marry at some point in their lives. Furthermore, although marriages today experience many problems, for better or worse the majority of marriages in Canada do last a lifetime (Ward and Belanger, 2011).

Why do people get married? Couples get married for a variety of reasons. Some do so because they are "in love," desire companionship and sex, want to have children, feel social pressure, are attempting to escape from a bad situation in their parents' home, or believe that they will have more money or other resources if married. These factors notwithstanding, the selection of a marital partner is fairly predictable. Most people in Canada tend to choose marriage partners who are similar to themselves. **Homogamy** refers to the pattern of individuals marrying those who have similar characteristics, such as race/ethnicity, religious background, age, education, or social class. However, homogamy provides only the general framework within which people select their partners; people are also influenced by other factors. For example, some researchers claim that people want partners whose personalities match their own in significant ways. As a result, people who are outgoing and friendly may be attracted to people with those same traits. Other researchers, however, claim that people look for partners whose personality traits differ from but complement their own.

homogamy The pattern of individuals marrying those who have similar characteristics, such as race/ethnicity, religious background, age, education, or social class.

Regardless of the individual traits of marriage partners, research indicates that communication and emotional support are crucial to the success of marriages. Common marital problems include

Geostock/Getty Images

Dual-earner marriages are a challenge for many children as well as their parents. While parents are at work, latchkey children are often at home alone.

lack of emotional intimacy, poor communication, and lack of companionship. One study concluded that for many middle- and upper-income couples, women's paid work was critical to the success of their marriages. People who have a strong commitment to their work have two distinct sources of pleasure—work and family. For members of the working class, however, work may not be a source of pleasure. For all women and men, balancing work and family life is a challenge (Marshall, 2011).

Remarriage

Most people who divorce get remarried. In recent years, over 30 percent of all marriages were between previously married brides and/or grooms. Among individuals who divorce before age 35, about half will remarry within three years of their first divorce. Most divorced people remarry others who have been divorced. However, remarriage rates vary by gender and age. A greater proportion of men than women remarry, often relatively soon after the divorce, regardless of age (Ambert, 2009).

As a result of divorce and remarriage, complex family relationships are often created. Some people become part of stepfamilies or *blended families,* which consist of a husband and wife, children from previous marriages, and children (if any) from the new marriage.

There has been a dramatic increase in the number of blended families in North America over the last 30 years. Today there are just over half a million stepfamilies in Canada (Vanier Institute for the Family, 2010). At least initially, levels of family stress may be fairly high because of rivalry among the children and hostilities directed toward stepparents or babies born into the family. In spite of these problems, however, many blended families succeed. The family that results from divorce and remarriage is typically a complex, binuclear one in which children may have a biological parent and a stepparent, biological siblings and stepsiblings, and an array of other relatives, including aunts, uncles, and cousins.

According to sociologist Andrew Cherlin (1992), the norms governing divorce and remarriage are ambiguous. Because there are no clear-cut guidelines, people must make decisions about family life (such as decisions about Christmas, birthdays, and weddings) based on their own beliefs and feelings about the people involved. Consider the following example of a couple who both brought children to their new marriage:

> The first couple of years after we got married, we had two Christmas trees, one in the living room, and one in the rec room. Once they [Angie's biological children and stepchildren] got older, I could say to them, "It's a really big hassle," but the first couple of years, there was so much decoration and everybody wanted everything: my kids wanted this because we had always had it on our tree, and the other kids wanted that because they had it on their tree. (Church, 2003:66)

Because there are few norms governing these family relationships, it may take years for them to come together, clarify roles and responsibilities, and establish a solid identity as a family unit (Preese, 2004).

TIME TO REVIEW

- Compare and contrast marriage versus cohabitation. Based on what you have learned about these forms of establishing committed relationships, which do you predict will be most common in your generation?

CHILD-RELATED FAMILY ISSUES AND PARENTING LO-4

Not all couples become parents. Those who decide not to have children often consider themselves "child free," whereas those who do not produce children through no choice of their own may consider themselves "childless."

Deciding to Have Children

Cultural attitudes about having children and the ideal family size began to change in North America in the late 1950s. On average, women are now having 1.5 children. However, rates of fertility differ across racial and ethnic categories. For example, Aboriginal women have a total fertility rate of 2.6 (Statistics Canada, 2007c).

Over the past five decades, advances in birth control techniques—including the birth control pill and contraceptive patches and shots—have made it possible for people to decide whether they want to have children and how many they wish to have, and to determine (at least somewhat) the spacing of their births. Sociologists suggest, however, that fertility is linked not only to reproductive technologies but also to women's beliefs that they do or do not have other opportunities in society that are viable alternatives to childbearing (Lamanna and Riedmann, 2011).

The concept of reproductive freedom includes both the desire *to have* or *not to have* one or more children. Women, more often than men, are the first to choose a child-free lifestyle By age 40, more than 10 percent of Canadian women intend to remain child free (Edmonston, Lee, and Wu, 2008). However, the desire not to have children often comes in conflict with our society's *pronatalist bias,* which assumes that having children is the norm and can be taken for granted, while those who choose not to have children believe they must justify their decision to others (Lamanna and Riedmann, 2011). Many diverse reasons account for why individuals decide not to have children, including never having wanted any, not finding themselves in the right circumstances, and having religious or environmental concerns (Stobert and Kemeny, 2003).

Some couples experience involuntary infertility, whereby they want to have a child but they are physically unable to do so. **Infertility** is defined as an inability to conceive after one year of unprotected sexual relations. Research suggests that fertility problems originate in females in approximately 30 to 40 percent of cases and with males in about 40 percent of cases; in the other approximately 20 percent of cases, the cause is impossible to determine. It is estimated that about half of infertile couples who seek treatments, such as fertility drugs, artificial insemination, and surgery to unblock fallopian tubes, can be helped; however, some are unable to conceive despite expensive treatments such as in vitro fertilization, which costs as much as $15,000 per attempt (IVF.ca, 2012).

infertility An inability to conceive after one year of unprotected sexual relations.

People who are involuntarily childless may choose to become parents by adopting a child.

Adoption

Adoption is a legal process through which the rights and duties of parenting are transferred from a child's biological and/or legal parents to new legal parents. This procedure gives the adopted child all the rights of a biological child. In most adoptions, a new birth certificate is issued and the child has no future contact with the biological parents. In Canada, adoption is regulated provincially. Therefore, adopted persons' access to information regarding their "biological parents" varies, as does their desire to access this information.

Matching children who are available for adoption with prospective adoptive parents can be difficult. The available children have specific needs, and the prospective parents often set specifications on the type of child they want to adopt. There are fewer infants available for adoption today than in the past because better means of contraception exist, abortion is more readily available, and more single parents decide to keep their babies. As a result, many prospective parents pursue international adoptions from countries including China, Haiti, South Korea, and India (Vanier Institute of the Family, 2008).

Assisted Reproductive Technologies

In recent years, there has been an explosion of research, clinical practice, and experimentation in the area of reproductive technology. For example, in 2007, a Quebec woman froze some of her embryos so that her seven-year-old daughter, who is infertile, could use them. In 2009, a 60-year-old woman gave birth to twin boys in Calgary (she had undergone in vitro fertilization in India) (CBC, 2009). Also in 2009, a woman in California gave birth to eight babies with the use of assisted reproductive technologies. These procedures, in particular, have raised some controversial ethical issues in terms of what role medical science should play in the creation of human life (Marquardt, 2006).

Procedures used in the creation of new life, such as artificial insemination and in vitro fertilization, are referred to as "methods of assisted reproduction" (Achilles, 1996). Artificial insemination is the oldest, simplest, and most common type of assisted reproduction. The most common form of artificial insemination is *intrauterine insemination,* which involves a physician inserting sperm directly into the uterus near the time of ovulation. Inseminations may be performed with donor sperm.

Intrauterine insemination with donor sperm raises several complex issues concerning its moral, legal, and social implications. In most cases, the woman is given no information about the donor and the donor is not told if a pregnancy has occurred. The result of this anonymity is that neither the mother nor the individuals conceived through donor insemination will have access to information regarding the biological father (Achilles, 1996). The term *test-tube baby* is often used incorrectly to describe babies conceived through in vitro fertilization. A real test-tube baby would require conception, gestation, and birth to occur outside of a woman's body. To date, this technology has not been developed (Achilles, 1996). *In vitro* (Latin for "in glass") *fertilization* involves inducing ovulation, removing the egg(s) from a woman, fertilizing the egg(s) with the sperm in a petri dish, and then implanting the fertilized egg(s) (embryos) into the woman.

Another alternative available to couples with fertility problems is the use of a surrogate, or substitute, mother to carry a child for them. There are two types of surrogacy. In *traditional surrogacy,* the surrogate is artificially inseminated with the father's sperm. In this case, the egg is the surrogate's and the child is biologically related to the surrogate and the father. This type of surrogacy is typically used in cases where the woman is infertile or when there is a risk of passing on a serious genetic disorder from mother to child. In the second type of surrogacy, *gestational surrogacy,* the sperm and the eggs from the infertile couple are transferred to the surrogate using an assisted reproductive technology (such as in vitro fertilization). With gestational surrogacy, the surrogate carries the child but is not biologically or genetically related to it. The genetic parents are the man and woman whose eggs and sperm were donated to the surrogate.

The availability of a variety of reproductive technologies is having a dramatic impact on traditional concepts of the family and parenthood. In light of all the assisted reproductive technologies available, what does the term *parent* mean? How many "parents" does the child have? Is *mother* an accurate term for the gestational surrogate mother? Consider the comments of sociologist Christine Overall:

> Thanks to reproductive technology, a baby could, potentially, have five different parents: its genetic mother and genetic father, who supply the ovum and the sperm; its carrying mother, who gestates the embryo produced by the union of the ovum and sperm; and finally, its social mother and father, the individuals who rear the child produced by the carrying mother. (1991:473)

How do the children conceived with assisted reproductive technologies define their families? There are now approximately one million donor-conceived children in the world. Now that they are able to speak for themselves, these children have raised some difficult questions about the rights of the child, biology, identity, and families. Some of these issues are highlighted in the following narrative:

> Is it right to deprive people of knowing who their natural parents are? What happens to your sense of identity when one of your biological parents is missing? Is there a difference when you're raised by "social" rather than biological parents? What if those parents are two women, or two men, or perhaps three people? Are children's understandings of parenthood as flexible as we would like to think? How do kids feel about all this? And do their feelings matter? (Wente, 2006:A21)

In 2004, the federal government enacted legislation to monitor and regulate assisted reproductive technologies. This legislation specifies what practices are forbidden: These include human cloning, sex selection, and buying or selling human embryos and sperm. It also outlines allowed practices, including surrogate mothers, donation of human sperm and embryos, and the use of human embryos and stem cells for scientific research (Department of Justice, 2009a). In 2006, a regulatory agency was established to ensure that these standards are followed.

The issues raised by legislation in this area are complex and emotional, not just scientific and technical (see Box 13.3 for a more detailed discussion). They also have legal, social, moral, and ethical implications. For example, fertility clinics across the country can send cells from embryos conceived through in vitro fertilization to labs in the United States to test them for disorders the new parents want to avoid. As a result of these new technologies, it is possible to screen for a number of life-threatening conditions. However, it is also possible to screen for other conditions that are less severe and may never present themselves until late adulthood if ever. Most disturbing, however, is the suggestion that these new technologies may lead to the creation of what has been described as "unnatural selection," allowing parents to select for traits such as height, weight, hair and eye colour, and athletic ability (Abraham, 2012).

Despite these concerns and unintended consequences, these new reproductive technologies have enabled some infertile couples to become parents. For them, the benefits far outweigh the costs.

BOX 13.3 **POINT/COUNTERPOINT**

Baby by Stealth: Reproduction Law Forcing "Dangerous Alternatives"

At the same time as reproductive technologies stretch the notion of the family beyond the nuclear, and just as Canada bends to accommodate that evolution, a prevailing piece of federal legislation is being accused of inadvertently forcing a slew of prospective parents underground.

At the root of this underworld, some argue, is the 2004 *Assisted Human Reproduction Act*—the Canadian government's most comprehensive attempt to regulate reproductive technologies. Some onlookers fear that the legislation has created a secretive black market, where couples seek sperm and egg donors on Craigslist or in university libraries.

Where those couples quietly compensate donors for their gametes, despite the legislation that criminalizes doing so. Where lesbian couples lie to doctors about their sexual orientation to avoid paying to quarantine a friend's sperm for six months. And where doctors and counsellors sometimes adopt the credo of "Don't ask, don't tell."

The act—which is a result of the Royal Commission on New Reproductive Technologies in 1993—has triggered condemnation from the right and left, and was the focal point of an International Women's Day conference in Toronto last week. There, at the Law Society of Upper Canada, panellists argued that some of the legislation

(continued)

does more to imperil and confuse prospective parents and their offspring than it does to protect them.

The act's aftermath has some significant real-world, legal implications, said lawyer Kelly Jordan, who specializes in family law and assisted reproductive technologies at Toronto firm Jordan Battista.

"Right now, we don't have any guidance about the rights of donors, carriers and surrogates, and there has been virtually no case law in Canada to deal with those questions," Ms. Jordan said.

"For example, if an egg donor in Ontario dies without a will, do her genetic children inherit her estate? Can a sperm donor be ordered to pay child support? Those are some of the questions that have yet to be answered."

Ms. Jordan said there is also the lingering issue of jurisdiction: The act is federal, but health falls under provincial purview. In 2008, the Quebec Court of Appeal ruled that large parts of the legislation, including those related to regulating the treatment of infertility, fall under provincial jurisdiction and are therefore unconstitutional. The case made it to the Supreme Court in April 2009 but, nearly a year later, the court has yet to release a decision.

Looking back, Canada has a history of amending its laws to accommodate the evolution of what constitutes a family, and citizens have long fought for the right to create a family no matter their sexual orientation, race, religion, ability or class.

For some, the right to family has gone too far, sacrificing the sanctity of family in the unfounded quest for equity. For others, the concept of the "family" is still too constrained.

What do you think? Where should the government draw the line in terms of a parent's right to use reproductive technologies to establish a family?

Source: Kathryn Blaze Carlson, "Baby By Stealth: Reproduction Law Forcing Dangerous Alternatives," *National Post*, March 12 2010. Material reprinted with the express permission of National Post, a division of Postmedia Network Inc.

TIME TO REVIEW

- What are the some of the legal, social, moral, and ethical implications of assisted reproductive technologies?

Single-Parent Households

Single parenting is not a new phenomenon in Canada. However, one of the most significant changes in Canadian families is the dramatic increase in single-parent families. Today, there are more than one million single parents in Canada, and more than 80 percent of them are women (Ward and Belanger, 2011). In the past, most single-parent families were created when one parent died. Today, the major causes of single parenthood for women are divorce and separation. Even for a person with a stable income and a network of friends and family to help with child care, raising a child alone can be an emotional and financial burden. Children in mother-only families are more likely than children in two-parent families to have poor academic achievement, higher school absentee and dropout rates, higher early marriage and parenthood, higher divorce rates, and more drug and alcohol abuse (Ambert, 2006b). Does living in a one-parent family cause all of this? Certainly not! Many other factors—including poverty, discrimination, unsafe neighbourhoods, and high crime rates—contribute to these problems.

Currently, men head close to one-fifth of lone-parent families; among many of the men, a pattern of "involved fatherhood" has emerged (Ward and Belanger, 2011). While some single fathers remain actively involved in their children's lives, others may become less involved, spending time with their children around recreational activities and on special occasions. Sometimes this limited role is by choice, but more often it is caused by workplace demands on time and energy, the location of the ex-wife's residence, and the limitations placed on the visitation arrangements. Although the courts continue to award mothers custody in divorces, an increasing number of fathers are attempting to gain sole or joint custody of their children.

As a result, we can expect to see an increase in the number of single fathers in the future (Ward and Belanger, 2011).

Housework and Child-Care Responsibilities

Thirty years ago, most Canadian families relied on one wage earner. Today, approximately 70 percent of all families in Canada are **dual-earner families**—families in which both partners are in the labour force. More than half of all employed women hold full-time, year-round jobs. Even when their children are very young, most working mothers work full time. Moreover, as discussed in Chapter 11, many married women leave their paid employment at the end of the day and go home to perform hours of housework and child care. Difficulty in balancing work and family is the defining feature of family life today. Parents must make difficult decisions—decisions often driven by economic necessity—between the amount of time they spend at work and the amount of time they can be at home with their children (Barrette, 2009; Marshall, 2011). Sociologist Arlie Hochschild (1989, 2003) refers to this as the **second shift**—the domestic work that employed women perform at home after they complete their workday on the job. Thus, many women today contribute to the economic well-being of their families and also meet many of the domestic needs of family members by cooking, cleaning, shopping, taking care of children, and managing household routines. In households with small children or many children, the amount of housework increases. Hochschild points to the second shift in many families as a sign that the gender revolution has stalled:

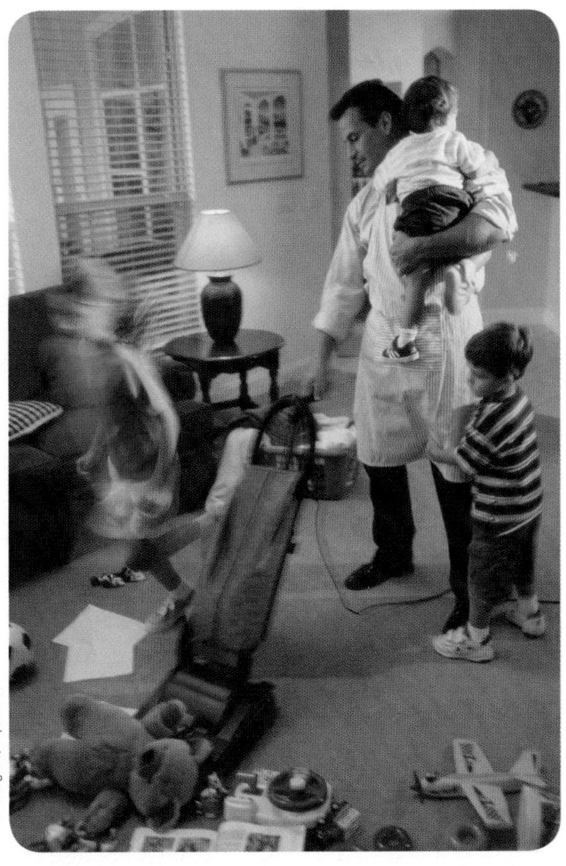

In recent years, many more fathers and mothers alike have been confronting the unique challenges of single parenting.

> The move of masses of women into the paid workforce has constituted a revolution. But the slower shift in ideas of "manhood," the resistance of sharing work at home, and the rigid schedules at work make for a "stall" in this gender revolution. It is a stall in the change of institutional arrangement of which men are the principal keepers. (2003:28)

dual-earner families Families in which both partners are in the labour force.

second shift Arlie Hochschild's term for the domestic work that employed women perform at home after they complete their workday on the job.

As Hochschild points out, the second shift remains a problem for many women in dual-earner marriages. However, recent time-use surveys of Canadian households indicate that the "stalled" revolution may be picking up the pace. Although a division of labour still exists within families, the hours of paid work, average earnings, and time spent on domestic labour and child care are becoming more similar between spouses in Canada (Marshall, 2011:13). As women's participation in the paid labour market has increased, men's involvement in housework and child care has also risen. In the mid-1980s, only half of men, with or without children, participated in daily housework. Today, approximately seven out of 10 men do so. In recent years, more husbands are sharing more of the household and child-care responsibilities, especially in families in which the wife's earnings are essential to family finances.

Despite the narrowing of the differences, men continue to have an overall greater involvement in paid work and a lesser involvement in housework An examination of men and women aged 20 to 29 in dual-earner couples confirms the trend that spouses are increasingly sharing economic and domestic responsibilities. For example, in 2010, dual-earner women aged 20 to 29 did 47 percent of couples' total paid work and 53 percent of couples' housework. Also similar to past trends, however, dependent children at home tend to increase the gap between

© Morgan Lane Photography/Shutterstock

Juggling housework, child care, and a job in the paid workforce are all part of the average day for many women. Why does sociologist Arlie Hochschild believe that many women work a second shift?

paid and unpaid work within young dual-earner couples (Marshall, 2011). Couples with more egalitarian ideas about the roles of women and men tend to share more equally in food preparation, housework, and child care.

Women who are employed full time and who are single parents have the greatest burden of all: complete responsibility for the children and the household, often with little or no help from ex-husbands or relatives. Recent statistics indicate that female single parents with full-time employment work, on average, 11 hours per day when paid and unpaid work are combined (Vanier Institute of the Family, 2009b). See Figure 13.2.

In Canada, millions of parents rely on child care so they can work and their young children can benefit from early educational experiences that will help in their future school endeavours. For millions more parents, after-school care for their school-aged children is an urgent concern because the children need productive and safe activities to engage in while their parents are working. (Children who are in daycare for extended hours often come to think of child-care workers and other caregivers as members of their extended families because they may spend nearly as many hours with them as they do with their own parents.) Obtaining child care for children of divorced parents and other young people living in single-parent households is often an especially pressing concern because of the limited number of available adults and a lack of financial resources (Friendly and Prentice, 2009).

FIGURE 13.2 TIME SPENT ON PAID AND UNPAID WORK, MEN AND WOMEN

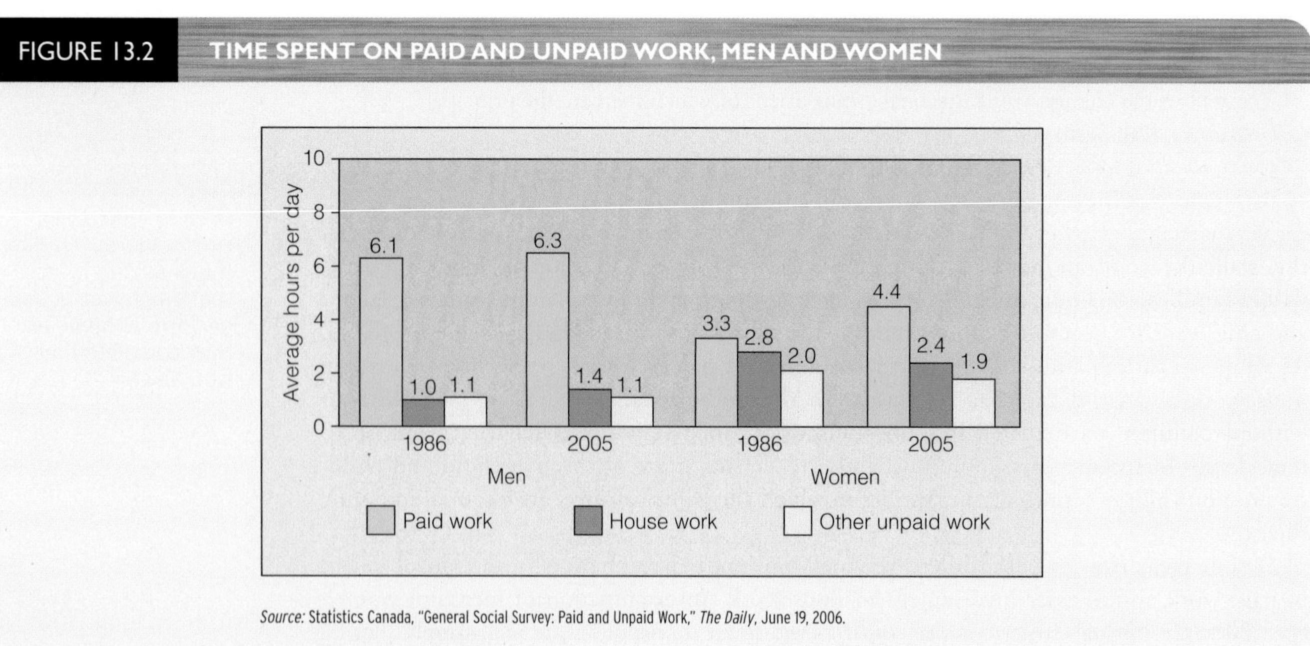

Source: Statistics Canada, "General Social Survey: Paid and Unpaid Work," *The Daily*, June 19, 2006.

TRANSITIONS AND PROBLEMS IN FAMILIES LO-5

Families go through many transitions and experience a wide variety of problems ranging from separation and divorce to unplanned pregnancy to family violence. These all-too-common experiences highlight two important facts about families: (1) For good or ill, families are central to our existence, and (2) the reality of family life is far more complicated than the idealized image found in the media and in many political discussions. Whereas some families provide their members with love, warmth, and satisfying emotional experiences, other families may be hazardous to the individual's physical and mental well-being. Because of this dichotomy in family life, sociologists have described families as both a "haven in a heartless world" (Lasch, 1977) and a "cradle of violence" (Gelles and Straus, 1988).

Family Violence

Violence between men and women in the home is often referred to as spouse abuse or domestic violence. *Spouse abuse* refers to the violence or mistreatment that a woman or man may experience at the hands of a marital, common-law, or same-sex partner. Forms of spousal abuse include physical abuse, emotional abuse, sexual abuse, and economic/financial abuse. These various forms of violence often occur in combination with one another. As discussed in Chapter 4, *child abuse* refers to physical or sexual abuse and/or neglect by a parent or caregiver.

How much do we know about violence in families? Women, as compared with men, are more likely to be victims of violence perpetrated by intimate partners. Recent statistics indicate that women are five times more likely than men to experience such violence and that many of these women live in households with children witnessing the violence (Ogrodnik, 2008). However, we cannot know the true extent of family violence because much of it is not reported to police. For example, results from the 2009 General Social Survey indicated that just under one-quarter (22 percent) of victims of spousal violence reported the incident to police (Department of Justice, 2011).

Although everyone in a household where family violence occurs is harmed psychologically, children are especially affected by household violence. Children who are raised in an environment of violence suffer profoundly, even if they are not the direct targets. Their own physical and emotional needs are often neglected, and they may learn by example to deal with conflict through violence (Johnson and Dawson, 2011). Not surprisingly, the research indicates that domestic violence and child maltreatment often take place in the same household.

It is estimated that approximately one million Canadian children witness some form of domestic violence in their homes each year (Beattie, 2005b). Long-term effects associated with witnessing violence include aggressive behaviour, emotional problems, and effects on social and academic development (Ross, Scott, and Kelly, 1996). In some situations, family violence can be reduced or eliminated through counselling, the removal of one parent from the household, or other steps that are taken either by the family or by social service agencies or law enforcement officials. However, as noted above, children who witness violence in the home may display certain emotional and behavioural problems that adversely affect their school life and communication with other people. In short, there are no easy solutions to a problem as complex as family violence.

Although differences in power and privilege between women and men do not inevitably result in violence, gender-based inequalities can still produce sustained marital conflicts. In any case, a common consequence of marital strife and unhappiness is divorce.

Although public awareness of domestic violence has increased in recent years, society is far from finding an effective solution for this pressing social problem.

Divorce

Divorce is the legal process of dissolving a marriage that allows former spouses to remarry if they so choose. Prior to 1968, it was difficult to obtain a divorce in Canada. A divorce was granted only on the grounds of adultery. In 1968, the grounds for divorce were expanded to include marital breakdown—that is, desertion, imprisonment, or separation of three or more years—and marital offences (physical or mental cruelty). As shown in Figure 13.3, the divorce rate increased dramatically as a result of the wider grounds for divorce. In 1985, the *Divorce Act* introduced "no fault" provisions that made marital breakdown the sole ground for divorce. Under no-fault divorce laws, proof of "blameworthiness" is no longer necessary. When children are involved, however, the issue of blame may assume greater importance in the determination of parental custody.

Have you heard statements such as "One out of every two marriages ends in divorce"? Statistics might initially appear to bear out this statement. In 2008, for example, 147,000 Canadian couples married and 70,229 divorces were granted (Vanier Institute for the Family, 2011). However, comparing the number of marriages with the number of divorces from year to year can be misleading. The couples who are divorced in any given year are unlikely to come from the group that married that year. Some people also may go through several marriages and divorces, thus skewing the divorce rate. The likelihood of divorce goes up with each subsequent marriage in the serial monogamy pattern (Ambert, 2009).

To accurately assess the probability of a marriage ending in divorce, it is necessary to use what is referred to as a *cohort approach*. This approach establishes probabilities based on assumptions about how the various age groups (cohorts) in society might behave, given their marriage rate, their age at first marriage, and their responses to various social, cultural, and economic changes. Canadian estimates based on a cohort approach are that 35 to 40 percent of marriages will end in divorce (Ambert, 2009).

CAUSES OF DIVORCE Why do divorces occur? As you will recall from Chapter 2, sociologists look for correlations (relationships between two variables) in attempting to answer questions such as this. Existing research has identified a number of factors at both the macro- and microlevels that make some couples more or less likely to divorce. At the macrolevel, societal factors contributing to higher rates of divorce include changes in social institutions such as religion, the family, and the legal system. Some religions have taken a more lenient attitude toward divorce, and the social stigma associated with divorce has lessened. Further, as we have seen in this chapter, the family has undergone a major change that has resulted in less economic and emotional dependency among family members—and thus reduced a barrier to divorce. And, as Figure 13.3 demonstrates, the liberalization of divorce laws in Canada has had a dramatic impact on the divorce rate.

At the microlevel, a number of factors contribute to a couple's "statistical" likelihood of becoming divorced. Anne-Marie Ambert (2009) has identified some of the primary risk factors for divorce:

- youthful marriage
- low incomes and poverty, as well as rapid upward social mobility
- cohabitation prior to marriage
- remarriage

- parents who are divorced or have unhappy marriages
- low religiosity
- the presence of children (depending on their gender and age at the beginning of the marriage)

The interrelationship of these and other factors is complicated. For example, the effect of age is intertwined with economic resources: Persons from families at the low end of the income scale tend to marry earlier than those at more affluent income levels. Thus, the question becomes whether age is a factor or whether economic resources are more closely associated with divorce.

CONSEQUENCES OF DIVORCE Divorce may have a dramatic economic and emotional impact on family members. Few children want their parents to divorce, no matter how unhappy the marriage is. For children, divorce results in the most significant changes they have experienced in their lifetimes—new relationships with each parent, often new residences, changes in schedules to accommodate visitation privileges, and, in some cases, a new parental figure.

The exact number of children affected by divorce in Canada is difficult to determine because no official information is available on out-of-court custody decisions, but approximately 40,000 Canadian children per year are involved in custody disputes. In the majority of these cases, the children reside primarily with their mother, meaning that the mother has *physical* custody of the children. Only about 10 percent of children live with their father despite the fact that joint *legal* custody now represents almost 50 percent of custody orders awarded. Parental joint custody is also an option for some divorcing couples. When joint custody is a voluntary arrangement, and when there is motivation to make it work, it has benefits for both children and parents (Ambert, 2009). However, this arrangement may also create unique problems for children, who must adjust to living in two homes and to the fact that their parents no longer live together. The worst thing that can happen to children after a divorce is that their parents remain in conflict (Buchanan, Maccoby, and Dornbusch, 1996).

The consequences of divorce are not entirely negative. There is no doubt that some children are better off after their parents divorce. For some people, divorce may be an opportunity to

FIGURE 13.3

DIVORCES IN CANADA, 1950–2010

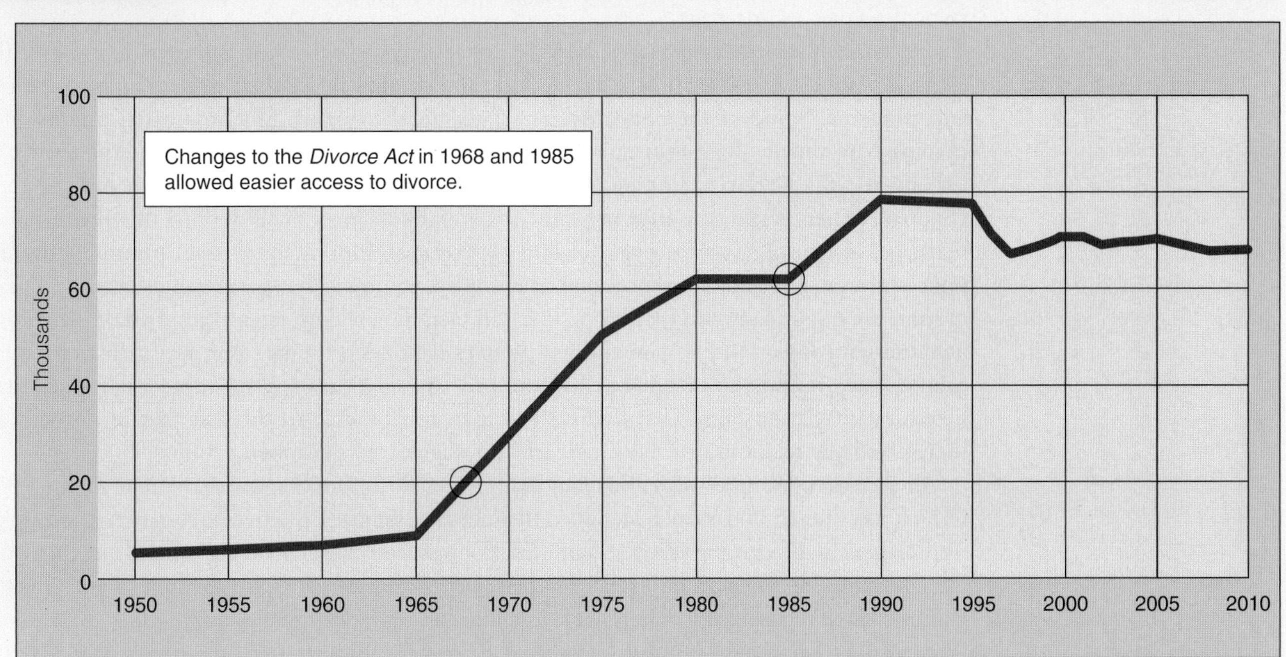

Sources: Statistics Canada, 2005d, 2012c.

terminate destructive relationships. For others, it may represent a way to achieve personal growth by enabling them to manage their lives and social relationships and establish their own identity.

DIVERSITY IN FAMILIES

Gay and Lesbian Families

Lesbians and gay men grow up in families, establish long-lasting, committed, emotional relationships, and sometimes become parents. Nevertheless, until recently, discussions of gay and lesbian relationships and families have been excluded from discussions of the family. These relationships were considered by many as threatening to notions of the traditional family. Lesbians and gay men were viewed as existing entirely outside families, and many people felt that recognition of gay and lesbian relationships would result in the demise of "the family." Notions of the family that are limited to unions between members of the opposite sex are examples of **heterosexism**—an attitude in which heterosexuality is considered the only valid form of sexual behaviour, and gay men, lesbians, and bisexuals are considered inferior to heterosexual people.

heterosexism An attitude in which heterosexuality is considered the only valid form of sexual behaviour, and gay men, lesbians, and bisexuals are considered inferior to heterosexual people.

In Canada, the law grants particular rights, benefits, and privileges only to heterosexual relationships, especially legally married partners. Until recently, gays and lesbians have been prohibited from sponsoring the immigration of their partners to Canada, from obtaining custody of their children, from jointly adopting children, or from receiving spousal benefits and survivors' pensions. Until very recently, same-sex couples were prohibited from legally marrying. In 2003, the Ontario Court of Appeal ruled that Canada's legal definition of marriage is unconstitutional and redefined it as "the voluntary union for life of two persons to the exclusion of all others." In her ruling, the judge further explained that "the existing common law rule is inconsistent with the constitutional values in modern Canadian society and offends the equality rights of gays and lesbians" (Kome, 2002:1). In response to this ruling, Prime Minister Jean Chrétien announced that the federal government would rewrite the legal definition of marriage to recognize same-sex marriages. In 2005, Canada became the third country in the world to recognize same-sex marriage.

The issue of same-sex marriages, however, remains a hotly debated and divisive issue for the Canadian public. Even for those who support same-sex marriages there remain many questions and concerns. Some of the concerns are related to the quality of homosexual unions—for example, are they as long-lasting and committed? Many are concerned about the ability of lesbians and gay men to parent and the effect that living in same-sex families may have on their children. Others argue that allowing same-sex couples to marry will devalue the institution of marriage. In contrast to stereotypes of same-sex relationships as short-term, promiscuous, and noncommittal, research on homosexual relationships indicates that partnerships lasting 20 years or more are not uncommon (Ambert, 2009). In fact, the breakup rates of married or cohabiting heterosexual couples and lesbian and gay couples have been found to be approximately equal. Studies have found, however, that lesbian and gay relationships are more egalitarian than heterosexual relationships. This finding is in part attributable to the fact that in virtually all lesbian and gay relationships, both partners are wage earners (Ambert, 2005a).

An increasing number of lesbians and gay males form families with children. In the 2006 Census, just over 45,000 couples identified themselves as same-sex married or common-law couples. Approximately 10 percent of these same-sex couples had children living with them (Statistics Canada, 2008). In many cases, lesbian mothers and gay fathers may have children from a previous marriage or relationship. However, not all children in same-sex families are products of previous heterosexual relationships. Lesbians may become pregnant through *alternative insemination* (sexual relations as a means of getting pregnant or artificial insemination) (Epstein, 2003). Lesbian mothers and gay fathers may also form families through fostering or adoption. Unlike many heterosexual families in which both mother and father have genetic links to their children, gay and lesbian families always have a nonbiological parent. These nonbiological parents are often not regarded as parents either socially or legally. For example, nonbiological parents may not be granted admission to parent–teacher interviews or may be denied permission to make important medical decisions for their children if the biological parent is unavailable.

Many people believe that being parented by same-sex couples is emotionally unhealthy for children and can cause them confusion about their own sexuality. However, the research has shown that the children of lesbians and gay men are as well adjusted as children who grow up in heterosexual households. In addition, these children experience no psychological damage, and they are no more likely to be homosexual than are children raised by heterosexual parents (Ambert, 2005a). According to Rachel Epstein (2003), there can be positive effects of being raised by lesbian or gay parents, such as a greater appreciation of diversity and increased tolerance, since the children are taught to accept social differences in others.

© Ronnie Kaufman/Corbis

Adoption is a complex legal process for most parents; it can be even more complicated for gay and lesbian couples.

TIME TO REVIEW

- What are some of the most significant challenges facing lesbian and gay families today?
- What progress has been made in recent years?

Diversity Among Singles

While marriage at increasingly younger ages was the trend in Canada during the first half of the 20th century, by the 1960s the trend had reversed and many more adults were remaining single. In 1971, close to half of Canadians aged 20 to 24 were already married. Today, almost 90 percent of Canadians aged 20 to 24 are single (Statistics Canada, 2007c). Currently, approximately 25 percent of households in Canada are one person households. This estimate, however, includes people who are divorced, widowed, or have never married. Given the fact that nine out of 10 Canadians marry at some time in their lives, single status is often temporary. Some never-married singles remain single by choice. Reasons include more opportunity for a career (especially for women), the availability of sexual partners without marriage, the belief that the single lifestyle is full of excitement, and the desire for self-sufficiency and freedom to change and experiment (Stein, 1976, 1981). According to some marriage and family analysts, individuals who prefer to remain single hold more individualistic values and are less family-oriented than those who choose to marry. Friends and personal growth tend to be valued more highly than marriage and children (Alwin, Converse, and Martin, 1985; Crompton, 2005).

© David Clarke/The Province

Secondary school systems are being pressured to address issues of family diversity in the classroom. In Surrey, British Columbia, in 2002, a battle was fought over the censorship of books about same-sex families.

Other never-married singles remain single out of necessity. For some people, being single is an economic necessity: They cannot afford to marry and set up their own households. Structural changes in the economy have limited the options of many working-class young people. Even some university and college graduates have found that they cannot earn enough money to set up a household separate from that of their parents. Consequently, a growing proportion of young adults are living with one or both parents (Beaupré, Turcotte, and Milan, 2006; Turcotte, 2006).

Aboriginal Families

It is difficult to discuss Aboriginal families, given the fact that Aboriginal peoples in Canada are by no means a homogeneous group. Aboriginal peoples are composed of many distinct nations with different histories, cultures, economic bases, and languages (Ward and Belanger, 2011). In all Aboriginal families, however, the extended family was seen as central to both the individual and the community. The concept of family was defined very broadly. For example, to the Ojibwa, *family* referred to individuals who worked together and were bound together by responsibility and friendship as well as kinship ties. Family size averaged between 20 and 25 persons (Shkilnyk, 1985). A band member describes the economic cooperation and sharing that once existed within the Ojibwa family:

> Trapping kept the family together because everyone in the family had something to do; the man had to lay traps and check them; the woman skinned the animals, cooked, and looked after the kids. The grandparents helped with the kids; they taught them manners, how to behave, and told them stories about our people. The kids, if they were old enough, had work to do. (Shkilnyk, 1985:81)

Under this cooperative family system, Aboriginal families were extremely successful in ensuring the survival and well-being of their members.

Four hundred years after contact with the European settlers, the current state of family disruption is evident when you consider the following data. Aboriginal children represent 40 percent of children placed in home care in Canada; the rate of wife abuse among Aboriginal peoples is five times the national average; the rate of spousal homicide is eight times higher among Aboriginal women compared to non-Aboriginal women; and the suicide rate of Aboriginal peoples is double the rate of the general population (Assembly of First Nations, 2008; Ogrodnik, 2008). How did this happen? Aboriginal family life was profoundly changed in the 20th century as a result of the interventionist strategies employed by the Canadian church and state. Families were displaced from their traditional lands, moved to reserves, and denied access to the resources that were central to the economic survival of the extended family unit. An estimated 125,000 Aboriginal children were forcibly removed from their families and placed in residential schools (where they were often sexually and physically abused). This was part of a government "assimilation policy," directed at preventing Aboriginal children from learning their traditional language and culture. The result of this action is the trauma that many Aboriginal families continue to struggle with today. In the 1960s and 1970s, Aboriginal children were once again forcibly removed from their families and adopted by non-Aboriginal families. "In many cases, children were taken from parents whose only crime was poverty and being aboriginal" (Fournier and Crey, 1997:85, cited in Ambert, 2006a). Generations of Aboriginal children were separated from their families and their communities, and this separation also served to sever links with Aboriginal identity, culture, and languages (Frideres, 2007). Consider Chief Cinderina Williams's description of the impact of residential schools on the family:

> Later when these children returned home, they were aliens. They did not speak their own language, so they could not communicate with anyone other than their own counterparts. Some looked down on their families because of their lack of English, their lifestyle, and some were just plain hostile. They had formed no bonds with their families, and some couldn't survive without the

> regimentation they had become so accustomed to . . . Consequently, when these children became parents, and most did at an early age, they had no parenting skills. They did not have the capability to show affection. (Godin-Beers and Williams, 1994, cited in Castellano, 2002)

After generations of cultural and spiritual destruction, Aboriginal peoples are now reclaiming their culture. They have also united behind the goal of self-government, especially in the areas of social services, education, and child welfare (Castellano, 2002). Aboriginal peoples believe in maintaining the ties between children and their natural parents, as well as caring for children within their Aboriginal communities. This they see as essential to the rebuilding of Aboriginal families in Canada. Many Aboriginal communities are striving to return to the practices and values that traditionally nourished Aboriginal family life: respect for women and children, mutual responsibility, and, above all, the general creed of sharing and caring (Royal Commission of Aboriginal Peoples, 1995:81).

FAMILY ISSUES IN THE FUTURE

As we have seen, families and intimate relationships have changed dramatically over the last century. Some people believe the family as we know it is doomed. Others believe that a return to traditional values will save this important social institution and create greater stability in society.

Regardless of problems facing families today, the family remains the central institution in the lives of most Canadians. A national opinion poll found that more than three-quarters of Canadians regard the family as the most important thing in their lives—more important than their career or religion—and 92 percent of the respondents with young children at home indicated that the family is becoming *more* important to them. Finally, an overwhelming majority demonstrated their faith in the family by indicating that they want to marry and have children (although fewer than in the past) (Bibby, 2004). Individuals in families are now freer to establish the kinds of family arrangements that best suit them. As Clarence Lochhead, executive director of the Vanier Institute, explains:

> We just have to come to grips with the diversity that actually is within our experience. Then we need to find ways to address and take on the challenges that face families, but do it in an inclusive way that makes sense for the reality and not some ideal notion of what a family is or ought to be (CBC, 2010b).

13

VISUAL SUMMARY

KEY TERMS

bilateral descent A system of tracing descent through both the mother's and father's sides of the family (p. 375).

cohabitation The sharing of a household by a couple who live together without being legally married (p. 380).

dual-earner families Families in which both partners are in the labour force (p. 387).

egalitarian family A family structure in which both partners share power and authority equally (p. 375).

extended family A family unit composed of relatives in addition to parents and children who live in the same household (p. 372).

families we choose Social arrangements that include intimate relationships between couples and close familial relationships with other couples, as well as with other adults and children (p. 370).

family A relationship in which people live together with commitment, form an economic unit and care for any young, and consider their identity to be significantly attached to the group (p. 371).

family of orientation The family into which a person is born and in which early socialization usually takes place (p. 372).

family of procreation The family that a person forms by having or adopting children (p. 372).

heterosexism An attitude in which heterosexuality is considered the only valid form of sexual behaviour, and gay men, lesbians, and bisexuals are considered inferior to heterosexual people (p. 392).

homogamy The pattern of individuals marrying those who have similar characteristics, such as race/ethnicity, religious background, age, education, or social class (p. 381).

LO-1 Explain why it is difficult to define family.

© LWA-Dann Tardif/Corbis

© BuzzFoto/FilmMagic/Getty Images

Families may be defined as relationships in which people live together with commitment, form an economic unit and care for any young, and consider their identity to be significantly attached to the group.

CONCEPT SNAPSHOT

FUNCTIONALIST PERSPECTIVES **Key thinker:** Talcott Parsons	In modern societies, families serve the functions of sexual regulation, socialization, economic and psychological support, and provision of social status.
CONFLICT PERSPECTIVES **Key thinker:** Friedrich Engels	Families both mirror and help perpetuate social inequalities based on class and gender.
FEMINIST PERSPECTIVES **Key thinkers:** Nancy Mandell, Ann Duffy	Women's subordination is rooted in patriarchy and men's control over women's labour power.
SYMBOLIC INTERACTIONIST PERSPECTIVES **Key thinker:** Jessie Bernard	Family dynamics, including communication patterns and the subjective meanings that people assign to events, mean that interactions within families create a shared reality.
POSTMODERN PERSPECTIVES **Key thinkers:** David Elkind	In postmodern societies, families are diverse and fragmented. Boundaries between the workplace and home are also blurred.

LO-2 Understand the key assumptions of functionalist, conflict, feminist, symbolic interactionist, and postmodernist perspectives on families.

Functionalists emphasize the importance of the family in maintaining the stability of society and the well-being of the individuals. Functions of the family include sexual regulation, socialization, economic and psychological support, and provision of social status. Conflict and feminist perspectives view the family as a source of social inequality and an arena for conflict over values, goals, and access to resources and power. Symbolic interactionists explain family relationships in terms of the subjective meanings and everyday interpretations people give to their lives. Postmodern analysts view families as permeable, reflecting the individualism, particularity, and irregularity of social life in the Information Age.

LO-3 Understand the various options available to Canadian families in establishing families.

© Photos.com

Families are changing dramatically in Canada. Cohabitation has increased significantly in the past two decades. The number of single-parent families has also increased sharply in recent decades. Marriage continues to be an extremely popular institution with the majority of Canadians marrying at some point in their lives. As a result of divorce and remarriage, stepfamilies or *blended families* may be established, which consist of a husband and wife, children from previous marriages, and children (if any) from the new marriage.

LO-4 Describe the challenges facing families today.

© Morgan Lane Photography/Shutterstock

Canadian families are faced with many challenges as a result of the increasing diversity and choice available to individuals establishing intimate relationships. These include choosing among a wide range of reproductive choices and establishing ways to maintain balance between paid work and family responsibilities. With the increase in dual-earner marriages, women increasingly have been burdened by the "second shift"—the domestic work that employed women perform at home after they complete their workday on the job

© 1997-2012 Centre for Children and Families in the Justice System, London Family Court Clinic Inc., http://www.lfcc.on.ca

LO-5 Identify the primary problems facing Canadian families today.

Two of the most significant problems facing families are family violence and divorce. Both *spouse abuse* (violence or mistreatment that a woman or man may experience at the hands of a marital, common-law, or same-sex partner) and *child abuse* (physical or sexual abuse and/or neglect by a parent or caregiver) occur at alarming rates in Canadian families. Divorce is the legal process of dissolving a marriage. At the macrolevel, changes in social institutions may contribute to an increase in divorce rates; at the microlevel, factors contributing to divorce include age at marriage, economic resources, religiosity, and parental marital happiness. Divorce has contributed to greater diversity in family relationships, including stepfamilies or blended families and the complex binuclear family.

APPLICATION QUESTIONS

1. In your own thinking, what constitutes an ideal family?
2. Based on your understanding of the term *family*, should the following be considered families? Why or why not?
   - Man, woman, no children; married but living apart
   - Woman, woman, and child of one woman living together; women a same-sex couple
   - Man, his biological child, and woman (not his wife) with whom he has a sexual relationship living together
   - Four adults sharing household for many years; none a same-sex couple

infertility An inability to conceive after one year of unprotected sexual relations (p. 383).

kinship A social network of people based on common ancestry, marriage, or adoption (p. 371).

marriage A legally recognized and/or socially approved arrangement between two or more individuals that carries certain rights and obligations and usually involves sexual activity (p. 374).

matriarchal family A family structure in which authority is held by the eldest female (usually the mother) (p. 375).

matrilineal descent A system of tracing descent through the mother's side of the family (p. 374).

monogamy An intimate relationship with one person at a time (p. 374).

nuclear family A family made up of one or two parents and their dependent children, all of whom live apart from other relatives (p. 373).

patriarchal family A family structure in which authority is held by the eldest male (usually the father) (p. 375).

patrilineal descent A system of tracing descent through the father's side of the family (p. 374).

polyandry The concurrent marriage of one woman with two or more men (p. 374).

polygamy The practice of having more than one spouse at a time (p. 374).

polygyny The concurrent marriage of one man with two or more women (p. 374).

second shift Arlie Hochschild's term for the domestic work that employed women perform at home after they complete their workday on the job (p. 387).

sociology of family The subdiscipline of sociology that attempts to describe and explain patterns of family life and variations in family structure (p. 376).

Test your comprehension and assess what you've learned with **CourseMate's** online quizzes.

For other interesting Lived Experiences, watch the video clips on **CourseMate.**

Practise what you've learned with flashcards containing key terms and definitions on **CourseMate.**

CHAPTER

14 Education

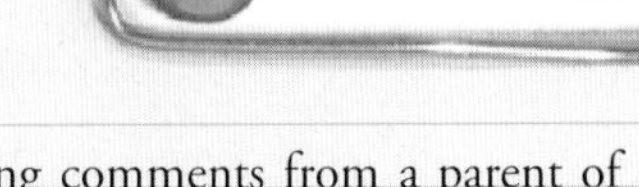

Courtesy of Jane Murray

Consider the following comments from a parent of three university students:

I picked up a university education on the weekend.

I did it with a rented U-Haul trailer, enough room, almost, for the yearly needs of two first-year students at a small university a few hours from Ottawa.

We took them down in September; it required two U-Hauls: one for their clothes, CDs, snowboards, skateboards, hockey equipment, birdfeeders, posters, computers, and—oh, yes—pen and paper in case they ever needed to take a few notes; and one trailer, of course, for the money to get them through a year of higher Canadian education.

It is really quite simple. You remortgage the house, cash in your RRSPs, take back the beer bottles, fill up the U-Haul with hard cash, add a couple of shovels and tell the kids to fill up the first black hole when they reach campus.

I do not begrudge this state of affairs. We are among the extremely fortunate in that we can help out and besides, who could ever put a price on seeing all those slim, healthy young men and women hugging and weeping openly as they say their goodbyes in the residence parking lot while their overweight, sweating, near-cardiac arrest parents do all the heavy lifting?

Still, one cannot help but think of the changes that have come about since we became the first generation in Canada who were given to take higher education as a basic rite of passage, thanks to the world of student loans and generous grants you never even had to consider paying back.

Going to school was a simple project. You worked in the summer, socked away your $1000; you got your student loan of $600, your student grant of $600, and that was it. Sometimes you ran unbelievably short—I will spare you my own horror stories—but you survived and, one day, you went out into the world owing a couple of thousand dollars in student loans which you soon paid off and never again thought about.

Never again, that is, until your own kids were suddenly headed off to similar schools.

At one point, no one would ever dare question the value of an education, and even today it makes one feel slightly queasy to do so, but there are just too many stories hanging around to ignore it. We have three at university this year, and one suspects even Bill Gates would blanch at the costs, even with the kids themselves contributing. (MacGregor, 2002)

More than ever before, education—in particular, higher education—is regarded as the key to success.

Most young Canadians today will attend university, correct? Although you may be one of the fortunate ones, the answer to this question is no. Increasingly, a university education is becoming a valuable life asset that only a few can afford to obtain. The most recent statistics indicate that only 25 percent (or one in four) of Canadians aged 25 to 64 have a university degree (Statistics Canada, 2010b). Given the costs associated with attaining this higher level of education, these numbers should come as no surprise. Students from families in the highest income group are twice as likely to attend university than students whose families come from the lowest income group (Drolet, 2005). It is not only in the system of higher education that we are witnessing unequal access to "intellectual capital." Parents can contribute directly to a young child's educational success by providing a supportive environment for learning or indirectly by paving the way for a higher level of educational attainment. Increasingly, we hear of parents opting out of the public school system, placing their children in private schools, charter schools, home-schooling, or "supplementing" their education with specialized extracurricular programming—computer camps, mini-universities, or private tutoring—in an effort to make sure their child "makes it." It is apparent that only parents with the financial resources (that is, middle- or upper-income families) can afford these programs.

Does this mean that education is stratified by social class? What effect will this have on students from low-income families? Education is one of the most significant social institutions in Canada and other high-income nations. Although most social scientists agree that schools are supposed to be places where people acquire knowledge and skills, not all of them agree on how a wide array of factors—including class, race, gender, age, religion, and family background—affect individuals' access to educational achievement or to the differential rewards that accrue at various levels of academic achievement. Canada has become a "schooled society," and the education system has become a forum for competition.

In this chapter, we will explore the issue of educational inequality in Canada, as well as look at other problems facing contemporary elementary, secondary, and higher education. Before reading on, test your knowledge about education in Canada by taking the quiz in Box 14.1 on page 401.

(*Source:* MacGregor, Roy, "Questioning the Value of an Education," *National Post*, April 25, 2002. Available: http://www.nationalpost.com. Material reprinted with the express permission of National Post, a division of Postmedia Network Inc.)

Critical Thinking Questions

1. All children in Canada have an equal opportunity to participate in elementary and secondary public schools. Does this mean that all students have an equal opportunity to succeed in school?
2. Is education in Canada stratified by social class?
3. What effects do you think this is likely to have on students from low-income families?

CHAPTER FOCUS QUESTION How do race, class, and gender affect people's access to and opportunities in education?

LEARNING OBJECTIVES

AFTER READING THIS CHAPTER, YOU SHOULD BE ABLE TO

LO-1 Explain how education differs in preliterate, preindustrial, and industrial nations.

LO-2 Identify the key assumptions of functionalist, conflict, feminist, symbolic interactionist, and postmodern perspectives on education.

LO-3 Describe the major problems in elementary and secondary schools in Canada today.

LO-4 Identify the major challenges facing students in higher education institutions.

LO-1 AN OVERVIEW OF EDUCATION

education The social institution responsible for the systematic transmission of knowledge, skills, and cultural values within a formally organized structure.

cultural transmission The process by which children and recent immigrants become acquainted with the dominant cultural beliefs, values, norms, and accumulated knowledge of a society.

informal education Learning that occurs in a spontaneous, unplanned way.

formal education Learning that takes place within an academic setting, such as a school, that has a planned instructional process and teachers who convey specific knowledge, skills, and thinking processes to students.

Education is the social institution responsible for the systematic transmission of knowledge, skills, and cultural values within a formally organized structure. As a social institution, education imparts values, beliefs, and knowledge considered essential to the social reproduction of individual personalities and entire cultures (Bourdieu and Passeron, 1990). Education grapples with issues of societal stability and social change, reflecting society even as it attempts to shape it. Education serves an important purpose in all societies. At the microlevel, people must acquire the basic knowledge and skills they need to survive in society. At the macrolevel, the social institution of education is an essential component in maintaining and perpetuating the culture of a society across generations. **Cultural transmission**—the process by which children and recent immigrants become acquainted with the dominant cultural beliefs, values, norms, and accumulated knowledge of a society—occurs through informal and formal education. However, the process of cultural transmission differs in preliterate, preindustrial, and industrial nations.

The earliest education in *preliterate societies*, which existed before the invention of reading and writing, was informal in nature. People acquired knowledge and skills through **informal education**—learning that occurs in a spontaneous, unplanned way—from parents and other group members who provided information on survival skills, such as how to gather food, find shelter, make weapons and tools, and get along with others. Formal education for elites first came into being in *preindustrial societies*, where few people knew how to read and write. **Formal education** is learning that takes place within an academic setting, such as a school, that has a planned instructional process and teachers who convey specific knowledge, skills, and thinking processes to students. Perhaps the earliest formal education occurred in ancient Greece and

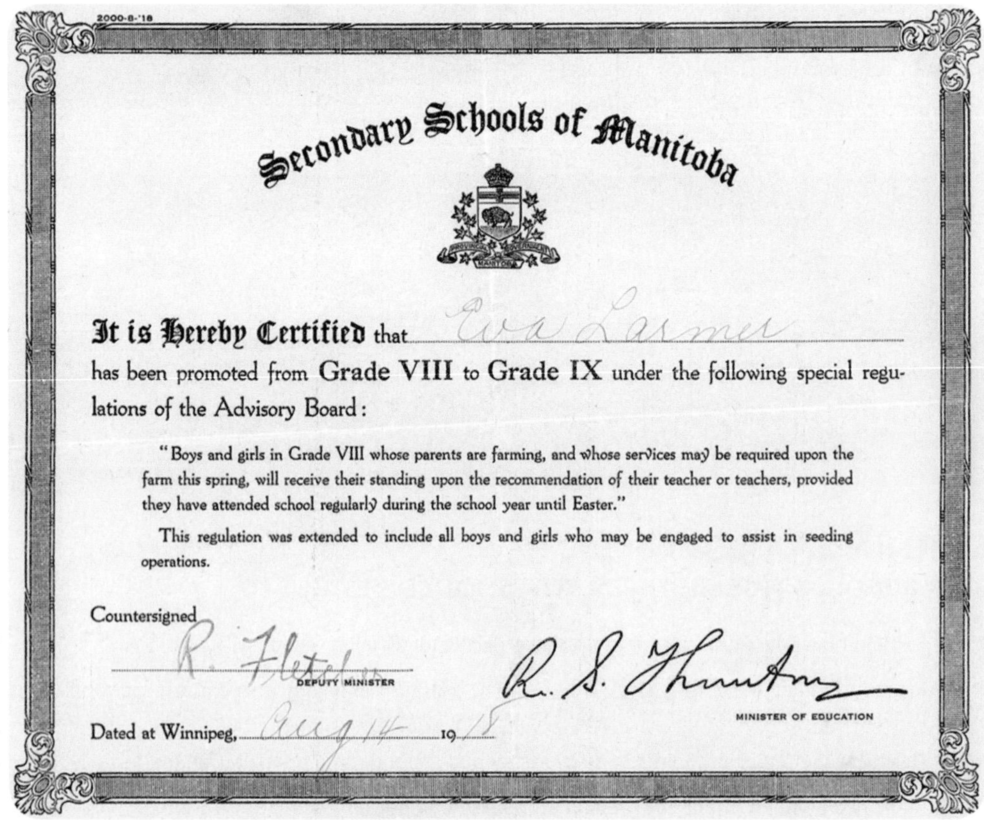

2000-8-'18

Secondary Schools of Manitoba

It is Hereby Certified that

has been promoted from **Grade VIII** to **Grade IX** under the following special regulations of the Advisory Board:

"Boys and girls in Grade VIII whose parents are farming, and whose services may be required upon the farm this spring, will receive their standing upon the recommendation of their teacher or teachers, provided they have attended school regularly during the school year until Easter."

This regulation was extended to include all boys and girls who may be engaged to assist in seeding operations.

Countersigned

DEPUTY MINISTER

MINISTER OF EDUCATION

Dated at Winnipeg, 19

Courtesy of Jane Murray

The first schools in Canada, typically one-room schoolhouses, combined children of all ages. Attendance was sparse, as other priorities, such as working on the farm, took precedence.

Rome, where philosophers such as Socrates, Plato, and Aristotle taught elite males the skills required to become thinkers and orators who could engage in the art of persuasion (Ballantine and Hammack, 2012). During the Middle Ages, the first colleges and universities were developed under the auspices of the Catholic Church. In the Renaissance era, the focus of education shifted to the importance of developing well-rounded and liberally educated people. With the rapid growth of industrial capitalism and factories during the Industrial Revolution, it became necessary for workers to have basic skills in reading, writing, and arithmetic, and pressure to provide formal education for the masses increased significantly.

In Canada, the school reformers of the late 1800s began to view education as essential to economic growth. Ontario school reformer Egerton Ryerson promoted free schooling for all children, arguing that sending rich and poor children to the same schools would promote social harmony (Tepperman, 1994). By the early 1900s, **mass education**—providing free, public schooling for wide segments of a nation's population—had taken hold in Canada as the provinces established free, tax-supported elementary schools available to all children. As industrialization and bureaucratization intensified, managers and business owners demanded that schools educate students beyond the third or fourth grade so that well-qualified workers would be available for rapidly emerging "white-collar" jobs in management and clerical work.

mass education Free, public schooling for wide segments of a nation's population.

Today, schools attempt to meet the needs of industrial and post-industrial society by teaching a wide diversity of students a myriad of topics, including history and science, computer skills, how to balance a chequebook, and how to avoid contracting sexually transmitted diseases (STIs). According to sociologists, many functions performed by other social institutions in the past are now under the auspices of the public schools.

BOX 14.1 **SOCIOLOGY AND EVERYDAY LIFE**

How Much Do You Know About Education in Canada?

True	False	
T	F	1. Canada has the largest population with a university education among developed countries.
T	F	2. Children of parents with high levels of education are more likely to pursue a university education.
T	F	3. Students from families of low socioeconomic status are more likely to have difficulty in school.
T	F	4. More young men than young women in Canada have university degrees.
T	F	5. Tuition fees for postsecondary education have doubled in the past 15 years.

For answers to the quiz about education in Canada, go to **www.nelson.com/sociologyinourtimes6e**.

SOCIOLOGICAL PERSPECTIVES ON EDUCATION LO-2

Sociologists have divergent perspectives on education in contemporary society. Here, we examine functionalist, conflict, feminist, symbolic interactionist, and postmodernist approaches to analyzing schooling.

Functionalist Perspectives

Functionalists view education as one of the most important components of society. According to Émile Durkheim, education is crucial for promoting social solidarity and stability in society:

© Dick Hemingway

What values are these children being taught? Is there a consensus about what today's schools should teach? Why or why not?

Education is the "influence exercised by adult generations on those that are not yet ready for social life" (1956:28) and helps young people travel the great distance that it has taken people many centuries to cover. In other words, we can learn from what others have already experienced. Durkheim also asserted the importance of *moral education* because it conveys moral values—the foundation of a cohesive social order. He believed that schools are responsible for teaching a commitment to the common morality.

From this perspective, students must be taught to put the group's needs ahead of their individual desires and aspirations. Contemporary functionalists suggest that education is responsible for teaching social values. The 1994 Royal Commission on Learning outlined three purposes of schooling: first, to ensure for all students high levels of literacy by building on basic reading, writing, and problem-solving skills; second, to develop an appreciation of learning, the wish to continue learning, and the ability and commitment to do so; and, finally, to prepare students for responsible citizenship, including developing "basic moral values, such as a sense of caring and compassion, respect for the human person and anti-racism, a commitment to peace and non-violence, honesty and justice" (Osborne, 1994:4).

Functionalists emphasize that "shared" values should be transmitted by schools from kindergarten through university. However, not all analysts agree on what those shared values should be or what functions education should serve in contemporary societies. In analyzing the values and functions of education, sociologists using a functionalist framework distinguish between manifest and latent functions. Manifest and latent functions are compared in Figure 14.1.

MANIFEST FUNCTIONS OF EDUCATION Some functions of education are *manifest functions*—previously defined as open, stated, and intended goals or consequences of activities within an organization or institution. Education serves six major manifest functions in society:

1. *Socialization.* From kindergarten through university, schools teach students the student role, specific academic subjects, and political socialization.

FIGURE 14.1 MANIFEST AND LATENT FUNCTIONS OF EDUCATION

Manifest functions—open, stated, and intended goals or consequences of activities within an organization or institution. In education, these are

- socialization
- transmission of culture
- social control
- social placement
- change and innovation

Latent functions—hidden, unstated, and sometimes unintended consequences of activities within an organization. In education, these include

- restricting some activities
- matchmaking and production of social networks
- creation of a generation gap

2. *Transmission of culture.* Schools transmit cultural norms and values to each new generation. However, questions remain as to *whose* culture is being transmitted. Because of the great diversity in Canada today, it is virtually impossible to define a single culture.
3. *Multiculturalism.* Schools promote awareness of and appreciation for cultural differences so that students can work and compete successfully in a diverse society and a global economy.
4. *Social control.* Schools are responsible for teaching values, such as discipline, respect, obedience, punctuality, and perseverance. Schools teach conformity by encouraging young people to be good students, conscientious future workers, and law-abiding citizens.
5. *Social placement.* Schools are responsible for identifying the most qualified people to fill the positions available in society. As a result, students are channelled into programs based on individual ability and academic achievement. Graduates receive the appropriate credentials to enter the paid labour force.
6. *Change and innovation.* Schools are a source of change and innovation to meet societal needs. Faculty members are responsible for engaging in research and passing on their findings to students, colleagues, and the general public.

LATENT FUNCTIONS OF EDUCATION Education serves at least three *latent functions*, which we have previously defined as hidden, unstated, and sometimes unintended consequences of activities within an organization or institution:

1. *Restricting some activities.* States have *mandatory education laws* that require children to attend school until they reach a specified age (usually 16) or complete a minimum level of

formal education (generally the eighth grade). Out of these laws grew one latent function of education: keeping students off the streets and out of the full-time job market until they are older.

2. *Matchmaking and production of social networks.* Because schools bring together people of similar ages, social class, and race and ethnicity, young people often meet future marriage partners and develop lasting social networks.
3. *Creation of a generation gap.* Students learn information and develop technological skills that may create a generation gap between them and their parents, particularly as the students come to embrace a newly acquired perspective.

Functionalists acknowledge that education has certain dysfunctions. Some analysts argue that education systems in Canada are not promoting the high-level skills in reading, writing, science, and mathematics that are needed in the workplace and the global economy. However, when it comes to reading, mathematics, and science, a new international report that assesses the skill levels of students nearing the end of their compulsory education ranked Canadian students among the best in the world. Among the students of 32 participating nations, 15-year-old Canadians ranked second in science and third in reading and mathematics (OECD, 2009).

TIME TO REVIEW

- To what extent do you think schools today are fulfilling the manifest and latent functions outlined by functionalists?

Conflict Perspectives

Conflict theorists emphasize that schools solidify the privileged position of some groups at the expense of others by perpetuating class, racial–ethnic, and gender inequalities (Ballantine and Hammack, 2012). Contemporary conflict theorists also focus on how politics and corporate interests dominate schools, particularly higher education.

CULTURAL CAPITAL AND CLASS REPRODUCTION Although many factors—including intelligence, family income, motivation, and previous achievement—are important in determining how much education a person will attain, conflict theorists argue that access to high-quality education is closely related to social class. From this approach, education is a vehicle for reproducing existing class relationships. According to French sociologist Pierre Bourdieu, the school legitimates and reinforces the social elites by engaging in specific practices that uphold the patterns of behaviour and the attitudes of the dominant class. Bourdieu asserts that students from diverse class backgrounds come to school with differing amounts of **cultural capital**—social assets that include values, beliefs, attitudes, and competencies in language and culture (Bourdieu and Passeron, 1990). Cultural capital involves "proper" attitudes toward education, socially approved dress and manners, and knowledge about books, art, music, and other forms of high and popular culture. Middle- and upper-income parents endow their children with more cultural capital than do working-class and poverty-level parents. And because cultural capital is essential for acquiring an education, children with less cultural capital have fewer opportunities to succeed in school. For example, standardized tests that are used to group students by ability and assign them to classes often measure students' cultural capital rather than their "natural" intelligence or aptitude. Thus, a circular effect occurs: Students with dominant cultural values are more highly rewarded by the educational system; in turn, the educational system teaches and reinforces those values that sustain the elite's position in society.

cultural capital Pierre Bourdieu's term for people's social assets, including their values, beliefs, attitudes, and competencies in language and culture.

TRACKING AND SOCIAL INEQUALITY Closely linked to the issue of cultural capital is how tracking in schools is related to social inequality. Conflict theorists who study ability grouping focus on how the process of tracking affects students' educational performance. Ability grouping, which is based on the assumption that it is easier to teach students with similar abilities, is often used in elementary schools. However, class-based factors also affect which children are most likely to be placed in "high," "middle," or "low" groups, often referred to by such innocuous terms as "Blue Birds," "Red Birds," and "Yellow Birds."

In middle school, junior high, and high school, most students experience **tracking**—the assignment of students to specific courses and educational programs based on their test scores, previous grades, or both. Ruben Navarrette, Jr. talks about his experience with tracking:

tracking The assignment of students to specific courses and educational programs based on their test scores, previous grades, or both.

> One fateful day, in the second grade, my teacher decided to teach her class more efficiently by dividing it into six groups of five students each. Each group was assigned a geometric symbol to differentiate it from the others. There were the Circles. There were the Squares. There were the Triangles and Rectangles.
>
> I remember something else, an odd coincidence. The Hexagons were the smartest kids in the class. These distinctions are not lost on a child of seven. Even in the second grade, my classmates and I knew who was smarter than whom. And on the day on which we were assigned our respective shapes, we knew that our teacher knew, too.
>
> As Hexagons, we would wait for her to call on us, then answer by hurrying to her with books and pencils in hand. We sat around a table in our "reading group," chattering excitedly to one another and basking in the intoxication of positive learning. We did not notice, did not care to notice, over our shoulders, the frustrated looks on the faces of Circles and Squares and Triangles who sat quietly at their desks, doodling on scratch paper or mumbling to one another.
>
> We knew also that, along with our geometric shapes, our books were different and that each group had different amounts of work to do. The Circles had the easiest books and were assigned to read only a few pages at a time. Not surprisingly, the Hexagons had the most difficult books of all, those with the biggest words and the fewest pictures, and we were expected to read the most pages.
>
> The result of all of this education by separation was exactly what the teacher had imagined that it would be: Students could, and did, learn at their own pace without being encumbered by one another. Some learned faster than others. Some, I realized only [later], did not learn at all. (1997:274–275)*

As Navarrette suggests, tracking does make it possible for students to work together based on their perceived abilities and at their own pace; however, it also extracts a serious toll from students who are labelled as "underachievers" or "slow learners." Race, class, language, gender, and many other social categories may determine the placement of children in elementary tracking systems, as much as or more than their actual academic abilities and interests.

The practice of tracking continues in middle school/junior high and high school. Although schools in some communities bring together students from diverse economic and racial and ethnic backgrounds, the students do not necessarily take the same courses or move on the same academic career paths (Gilbert, 2010). Today, however, extreme forms of tracking are relatively rare. Most tracking involves grouping students by ability within subjects so that they are assigned to advanced, regular, or basic courses depending on their past performance.

The detracking movement, stressing that students should be deliberately placed in classes of mixed ability, has influenced some schools and teachers. An important benefit of detracking is closing the achievement gap among students based on class or race; however, detracking is a major concern to parents of high-achieving students because they believe their children should have classes that maximize their potential, rather than holding them back with less able or less talented students. According to sociologist Maureen Hallinan (2005), rather than tracking students, schools should provide more engaging lessons for all students, alter teachers' assumptions about students, and raise students' performance requirements. Eventually, independent studies and technologies such as online learning may eliminate the "tracking" debate.

hidden curriculum The transmission of cultural values and attitudes, such as conformity and obedience to authority, through implied demands found in the rules, routines, and regulations of schools.

THE HIDDEN CURRICULUM According to conflict theorists, the **hidden curriculum** is the transmission of cultural values and attitudes, such as conformity and obedience to authority, through implied demands found in the rules, routines, and regulations of schools (Snyder, 1971). Although students from all social classes are subjected to the hidden curriculum, working-class and poverty-level students may be affected the most adversely (Ballantine, 2001, Davies and Guppy, 2006; Polakow, 1993). When teachers are from a higher-class background than their students, they tend to use more structure in the classroom and to have lower expectations for students' academic achievement. In a study of five elementary schools located in different communities, significant differences were found in the manner in which knowledge was transmitted to students even though the curriculum was organized similarly (Anyon, 1980, 1997). Schools for working-class students emphasize procedures and rote memorization without much decision making, choice, and explanation of why something is done a particular way. Schools for middle-class students stress the processes (such as calculating and decision making) involved in getting the right answer. Schools for affluent students focus on creative activities in which students express their own ideas and apply them to the subject under consideration. Schools for students from elite families work to develop students' analytical powers and critical thinking skills, applying abstract principles to problem solving.

Through the hidden curriculum, schools make working-class and poverty-level students aware that they will be expected to take orders from others, arrive at work on time, follow bureaucratic rules, and experience high levels of boredom without complaining (Ballantine,

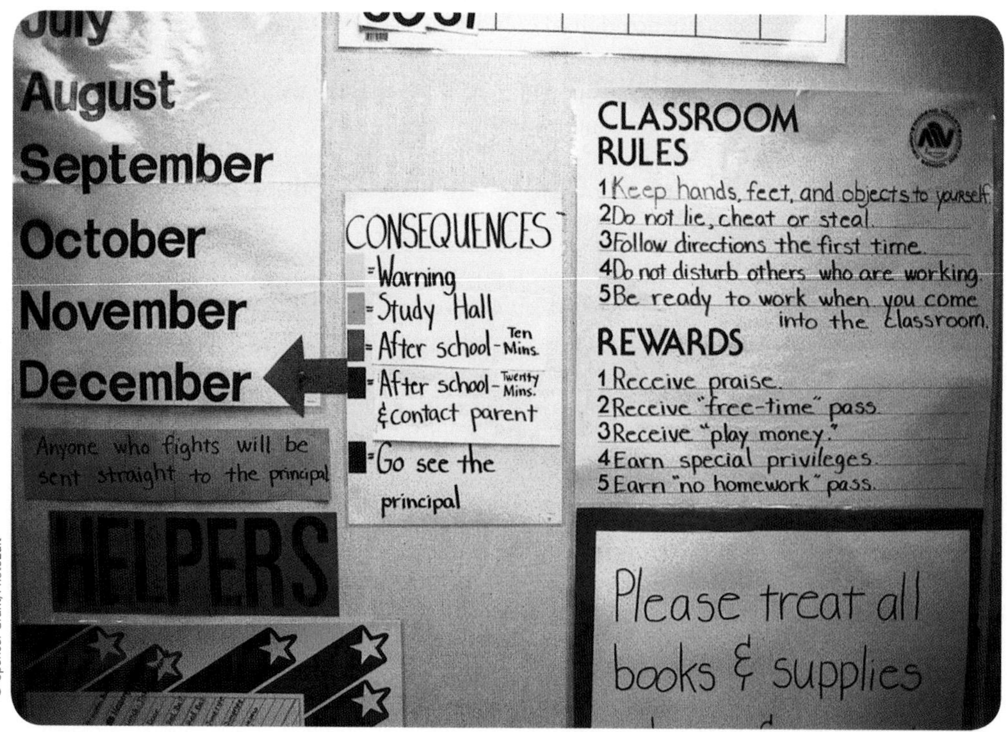

Signs in this elementary classroom list the rules, rewards, and consequences of different types of student behaviour. According to conflict theorists, schools impose rules on working-class and poverty-level students so that they will learn to follow orders and be good employees in the workplace. How would functionalists and symbolic interactionists interpret these same signs?

2001). Over time, these students may be disqualified from higher education and barred from obtaining the credentials necessary for well-paid occupations and professions (Bowles and Gintis, 1976). Educational credentials are extremely important in societies that emphasize **credentialism**—a process of social selection in which class advantage and social status are linked to the possession of academic qualifications (Collins, 1979; Marshall, 1998). Credentialism is closely related to meritocracy—previously defined as a social system in which status is assumed to be acquired through individual ability and effort (Young, 1994). Persons who acquire the appropriate credentials for a job are assumed to have gained the position through what they know, not who they are or whom they know. According to conflict theorists, the hidden curriculum determines in advance that the most valued credentials will primarily stay in the hands of the elites. Therefore, Canada is not as meritocratic as some might claim.

credentialism A process of social selection in which class advantage and social status are linked to the possession of academic qualifications.

Feminist Perspectives

As mentioned in previous chapters, feminism represents not only a theoretical perspective but also a broad movement for social change. One social institution on which feminism has had a significant impact is the educational system. As feminist scholar Jane Gaskell explains, "When feminists demanded equal opportunity for women, education was one of the first areas targeted for reform and rethinking" (2009:17).

GENDER BIAS AND GENDER STEREOTYPING Early feminist analysis of schooling focused on questions about sexism in the classroom and curricula, and unequal distributions of male and female educators in the system (Wotherspoon, 2009). In Canada, in the late 1960s, the Royal Commission on the Status of Women examined the relationship between education and patterns of gender inequality. It identified gender bias and gender stereotyping in the educational curriculum as a significant issue that had to be addressed. For example, girls were underrepresented in the school books, and when they were included, they appeared in rigid sex-typed roles. Boys and girls were also segregated in the playgrounds and in sporting activities. Furthermore, boys received more attention from teachers than girls, and teachers displayed stereotypical expectations of male and female students' aptitudes and interests.

In response to this report, ministries of education across the country appointed advisory groups on sexism and established guidelines to eliminate gender bias and stereotyping in school curriculum and classroom practices. According to Gaskell, "These changes had an effect . . . the critique of stereotyping had caught on. The idea that biology did not mean destiny, that equality meant open access and equal treatment, was increasingly accepted. The numbers of women in science and math, in universities, and in leadership positions in the teaching profession increased" (2009:21).

These strategies are characteristic of liberal feminism (see Chapter 11). Reforms focus on creating change within the existing social, educational, and economic systems—eliminating gender bias is an example (Wotherspoon, 2009).

More than 40 years later, women now surpass men on a number of educational indicators. This gap in favour of women is evident at a young age—girls get better marks than boys in elementary and high school, are less likely to drop out, and are more likely to graduate from high school in the requisite number of years. At a postsecondary level, the gender gap in educational attainment and enrollment has narrowed to the extent that university and college enrollments for women now surpass those of their male counterparts. Today, over 60 percent of university graduates are female and women outnumber men in the faculties of law and medicine (Statistics Canada, 2011). However, differences still remain. As shown in Table 14.1, females are highly overrepresented in nursing and teaching, while men are overrepresented in engineering, computer science, and applied mathematics.

Rather than focusing on the elimination of gender bias and stereotyping, some feminist scholars have directed our attention to the economic consequences of educational attainment, arguing that gender inequalities are not only built into the structure of schooling but also its links to the labour market. Radical feminism points out that patriarchy, or the systematic

TABLE 14.1 CANADIAN UNIVERSITY GRADUATES' TOP 10 FIELDS OF STUDY, BY SEX, 2006

MEN	
Business, management, marketing and related support services	801,605
Mechanic and repair technologies/technicians	542,370
Engineering	450,960
Engineering technologies/technicians	427,840
Construction trades	388,990
Precision production	290,625
Computer and information sciences and support services	257,385
Health professions and related clinical sciences	204,560
Education	196,165
Social sciences	194,795
WOMEN	
Business, management, marketing and related support services	1, 357,160
Health professions and related clinical sciences	1, 080,745
Education	583,560
Personal and culinary services	271,825
Visual and performing arts	182,880
Social sciences	182,625
Family and consumer sciences/human sciences	170,020
Computer and information sciences and support services	150,220
Legal professions and studies	130,190
Public administration and social service professions	126,575

Source: Adapted from Statistics Canada, Census of Population 2006, Analysis Series, Table 7, last modified July 2009.

oppression of women, is reflected in the relationship between education and work. Although one might assume that more education will lead to higher income and a better job, that assumption is not borne out for many women. As Gaskell explains:

> Instead of arguing that equality will be achieved when there are as many girls as boys in mathematics and physics classes, radical feminism critiques the wages and prestige associated with the jobs that women have traditionally done. Equal-pay legislation has forced employers to recognize that the work women have done is underpaid in relation to the skills, education, and responsibility it entails. Day care workers have been paid less than dog catchers; secretaries are paid less than male technicians with equal levels of education. (2009:24)

Feminist scholars have also challenged common assumptions about learning and traditional teaching methods. They argue that men and women learn in different ways and that formal educational institutions may not adequately attend to women's "ways of knowing" (Gaskell, 2009:23). Language, science, politics, and the economy, for example, are organized around ways of knowing and doing that take the male experience as the norm. In contrast, women are frequently absent as subjects and objects of study, and women's experiences are undermined and relegated to the margins of what is considered socially important (Wotherspoon, 2009:43). Rather than denying difference, some feminists emphasize the need to recognize and incorporate female strategies of learning as well as value the knowledge constructed by women.

TIME TO REVIEW

- What are the indicators of greater gender equity in elementary schools? In universities and colleges?

Symbolic Interactionist Perspectives

Unlike functionalist analysts, who focus on the functions and dysfunctions of education, and conflict theorists, who focus on the relationship between education and inequality, symbolic interactionists focus on classroom communication patterns and educational practices that affect students' self-concept and aspirations. Labelling is one such educational practice.

LABELLING AND THE SELF-FULFILLING PROPHECY According to symbolic interactionists, the process of labelling is directly related to the power and status of those persons who do the labelling and those who are being labelled. Chapter 7 explains that *labelling* is the process whereby others identify a person as possessing a specific characteristic or exhibiting a certain pattern of behavior, such as being deviant. In schools, teachers and administrators are empowered to label children in various ways, including grades, written comments on classroom behaviour, and placement in classes. For some students, labelling amounts to a *self-fulfilling prophecy*—an unsubstantiated belief or prediction resulting in behaviour that makes the originally false belief come true (Merton, 1968).

A classic form of labelling and the self-fulfilling prophecy has occurred for many years through the use of various IQ (intelligence quotient) tests, which claim to measure a person's inherent intelligence apart from any family or school influences on the individual. Schools have used IQ tests as one criterion in determining student placement in classes and ability groups (see Figure 14.2). The way in which IQ test scores may become a self-fulfilling prophecy was revealed in the 1960s when two social scientists conducted an experiment in an elementary school during which they intentionally misinformed teachers about the scores of students in their classes (Rosenthal and Jacobson, 1968). Although the students had no measurable differences in intelligence, the researchers informed the teachers that some of the students had extremely high IQ test scores whereas others had average to below-average scores. As the researchers observed, the teachers began to teach "exceptional" students in a different manner from other students. In turn, the "exceptional" students began to outperform their "average" peers and to excel in their classwork. This study called attention to the labelling effect of IQ scores.

Is IQ a good indicator of a person's potential? In their controversial book *The Bell Curve: Intelligence and Class Structure in American Life*, Richard J. Herrnstein and Charles Murray (1994) argue that intelligence is genetically inherited and that people cannot be "smarter" than they are born to be, regardless of their environment or education. According to Herrnstein and Murray, certain racial–ethnic groups differ in average IQ and are likely to differ in "intelligence

FIGURE 14.2 IQ TEST SAMPLE QUESTION

Question 2: Consider the following two statements: all farmers who are also ranchers cannot come near town; and most of the ranchers who are also farmers cannot surf. Which of the following statements MUST be true?

- Most of the farmers who cannot come near town can surf.
- Only some farmers who ranch can surf near town.
- A surfer who ranches and farms cannot surf near town.
- Some ranchers who farm can come to town to learn to surf.
- Any farmer who cannot surf also ranches.

IQ tests containing items such as this are often used to place students in ability groups. Such placement can set the course of a person's entire education.

genes" as well. Herrnstein and Murray claimed the people with lower intelligence are more likely to commit crimes, drop out of school, and live in poverty. In contrast, people with high intelligence are more likely to be successful. Many scholars disagree with Herrnstein and Murray's conclusions, pointing out that what these authors claim to be immutable intelligence is actually acquired skills (Weinstein, 1997).

In 2008, the British psychologist Richard Lynn's *The Global Bell Curve: Race, IQ, and Inequality Worldwide* expanded the ideas of Herrnstein and Murray to include the nations of the world. According to Lynn, in multiracial nations, people of Jewish and East Asian ancestry have the highest average IQ scores and socioeconomic positions, followed by whites, South Asians, Hispanics, and people of African descent. Lynn attributes people's positions in the socioeconomic hierarchy to differences in intelligence on the basis of race and ethnicity.

Today, so-called IQ fundamentalists continue to label students and others on the basis of IQ tests, claiming that these tests measure some identifiable trait that predicts the quality of people's thinking and their ability to perform. Critics of IQ tests continue to argue that these exams measure a number of factors—including motivation, home environment, type of socialization at home, and quality of schooling—not intelligence alone (Yong, 2011).

Postmodern Perspectives

Postmodern theories often highlight *difference* and *irregularity* in society. From this perspective, education—like the family—is a social institution characterized by its permeability. In contemporary schools, a wide diversity of family kinship systems is recognized and educators attempt to be substitute parents and promulgators of self-esteem in students. Urbanity is reflected in multicultural and anti-bias curriculums that are initially introduced in early childhood education. Similarly, autonomy is evidenced in policies, such as voucher systems, under which parents have a choice about which schools their children will attend. Since the values of individual achievement and competition have so permeated contemporary home and school life, social adjustment, or how to deal with others, has become of little importance to some people (Elkind, 1995).

How might a postmodern approach describe higher education? Postmodern views of higher education might incorporate the ideas of the sociologist George Ritzer, who believes that "McUniversity" can be thought of as a means of educational consumption that allows students to consume educational services and eventually obtain "goods," such as degrees and credentials:

> Students (and often, more importantly, their parents) are increasingly approaching the university as consumers; the university is fast becoming little more than another component of the consumer society . . . Parents are, if anything, likely to be even more adept as consumers than their children and because of the burgeoning cost of higher education more apt to bring a consumerist mentality to it. (1998:151–152)

Savvy college and university administrators are aware of the permeability of higher education and the students-as-consumers model:

> [Students] want education to be nearby and to operate during convenient hours—preferably around the clock. They want to avoid traffic jams, to have easy, accessible and low cost parking, short lines, and polite and efficient personnel and services. They also want high-quality products but are eager for low costs. They are willing to shop—placing a premium on time and money. (Levine, 1993:4)

To attract new students and enhance current students' opportunities for consumption, many campuses have student centres equipped with amenities such as food courts, ATMs (automatic teller machines), video games, Olympic-sized swimming pools, and massive rock-climbing walls. "High-tech," or "wired," campuses are also a major attraction for student consumers, and virtual classrooms make it possible for some students to earn postsecondary credits without having to look for a parking place at the traditional bricks-and-mortar campus.

The permeability of contemporary universities may be so great that eventually it will be impossible to distinguish higher education from other means of consumption. For example, Ritzer believes that officials of "McUniversity" will start to emphasize the same kinds of production values as CNN or MTV, resulting in a simulated world of education somewhat like postmodernist views of Disneyland. Based on Baudrillard's fractal stage, where everything interpenetrates, Ritzer predicts that we may enter a "trans-educational" era: "Since education will be everywhere, since everything will be educational, in a sense nothing will be educational" (1998:160). Based on a postmodern approach, what do you believe will be the predominant means by which future students will consume educational services and goods at your college or university? The Concept Snapshot summarizes the major theoretical perspectives on education, while Box 14.2 provides details on the technology revolution in the classroom (to read Box 14.2, go to **www.nelson.com/sociologyinourtimes6e**).

CURRENT ISSUES IN ELEMENTARY AND SECONDARY SCHOOLS LO-3

Public schools in Canada today are a microcosm of many of the issues and problems facing the country. Canada is the only advanced industrialized country without a federal educational system—a fact that has made it difficult to coordinate national educational and teaching standards. Each province enacts its own laws and regulations, with local school boards frequently making the final determinations on the curriculum. Accordingly, no general standards exist as to what is to be taught to students or how, although many provinces have now adopted standards for what (at a minimum) must be learned in order to graduate from high school.

Inequality in Public Schools versus Private Schools

Often, there is a perceived conflict between public and private schools for students and financial resources. However, far more students and their parents are dependent on public schools than on private ones for providing a high-quality education. Enrollment in Canadian elementary and secondary education (kindergarten through Grade 12) totals approximately five million students. More than 90 percent of elementary and secondary students are educated in public schools.

CONCEPT SNAPSHOT

FUNCTIONALIST PERSPECTIVES	Education is one of the most important components of society: Schools teach students not only content but also to put group needs ahead of the individual's.
CONFLICT PERSPECTIVES	Schools perpetuate class, racial-ethnic, and gender inequalities through what they teach to whom.
FEMINIST PERSPECTIVES	Schools perpetuate gender bias and stereotyping. Educational institutions also fail to recognize that men and women have different ways of learning and knowing.
SYMBOLIC INTERACTIONIST PERSPECTIVES	Labelling and the self-fulfilling prophecy are an example of how students and teachers affect one another as they interpret their interactions.
POSTMODERNIST PERSPECTIVES	In contemporary schools, educators attempt to become substitute parents and promulgators of self-esteem in students; students and their parents become the consumers of education

About 6 percent of all students are educated in private schools, and approximately 1 percent of all students attend private schools with tuition of more than $5000 a year (Statistics Canada, 2010b).

Private secondary boarding schools tend to be reserved for students from high-income families and for a few lower-income or minority students who are able to acquire academic or athletic scholarships that cover their tuition, room and board, and other expenses. The average cost for seven-day tuition and room and board at secondary boarding schools is nearly $20,000 a year, whereas day-school tuition can be as high as $8000.

An important factor for many parents whose children attend private secondary schools is the emphasis on academics that they believe exists in private as opposed to public schools. Another is the moral and ethical standards that they believe private secondary schools instill in students. Overall, many families believe that private schools are a better choice for their children because they are more academically demanding, more motivating, more focused on discipline, and without many of the inadequacies found in public schools. However, according to some social analysts, there is little to substantiate the claim that private schools—other than elite academies attended by the children of the wealthiest and most influential families—are inherently better than public schools (Zehr, 2006).

Dropping Out

Although the overall school dropout (or school leaver) rate has significantly decreased in recent decades, a little less than 10 percent of people under the age of 20 still leave school before earning a high school diploma. Ethnic and class differences are important factors in the data on dropout rates. For example, Aboriginal students have a dropout rate of slightly less than 24 percent (Statistics Canada, 2010b). According to the Toronto District School Board, in 2009, over 30 percent of black students had failed to complete high school.

In response to these disturbingly high dropout rates, alternative specialized Aboriginal and Afrocentric schools have been established across the country. As the Africentric Alternative School Support Committee explains:

> Students who have been failed by the current system will have the opportunity to learn the importance and value of their own histories and community. By learning from a perspective that cherishes the learner and his/ her own history, students will be motivated to succeed. (2009:7)

Despite claims by critics that these schools are exclusionary and promote segregation, students and teachers from alternative schools report successes in terms of higher grades, lower drop out rates, and greater student motivation.

The dropout rate also varies by region—Manitoba, Alberta, and Quebec had the highest proportion of school dropouts in 2005, while British Columbia had the lowest dropout rate of 7.5 percent (McMullen, 2005).

Why do students drop out of school? Some students believe that their classes are boring; others are skeptical about the value of schooling and think that completing high school will not increase their job opportunities. Upon leaving school, many dropouts have high hopes of making money and enjoying newfound freedom; however, many find that few jobs are available and that they do not have the minimum education required for any "good" jobs that exist.

Although critics of the public education system point to high dropout rates as proof of failure in the public education system, these rates have steadily declined in Canada since the 1950s, when more than 70 percent of students did not complete high school (Luciw, 2002).

Equalizing Opportunities for Students with Disabilities

Another relatively recent concern in education has been how to provide better educational opportunities for students with disabilities. See Figure 14.3.

FIGURE 14.3 PERSONS WITH AND WITHOUT DISABILITIES BY EDUCATIONAL ATTAINMENT

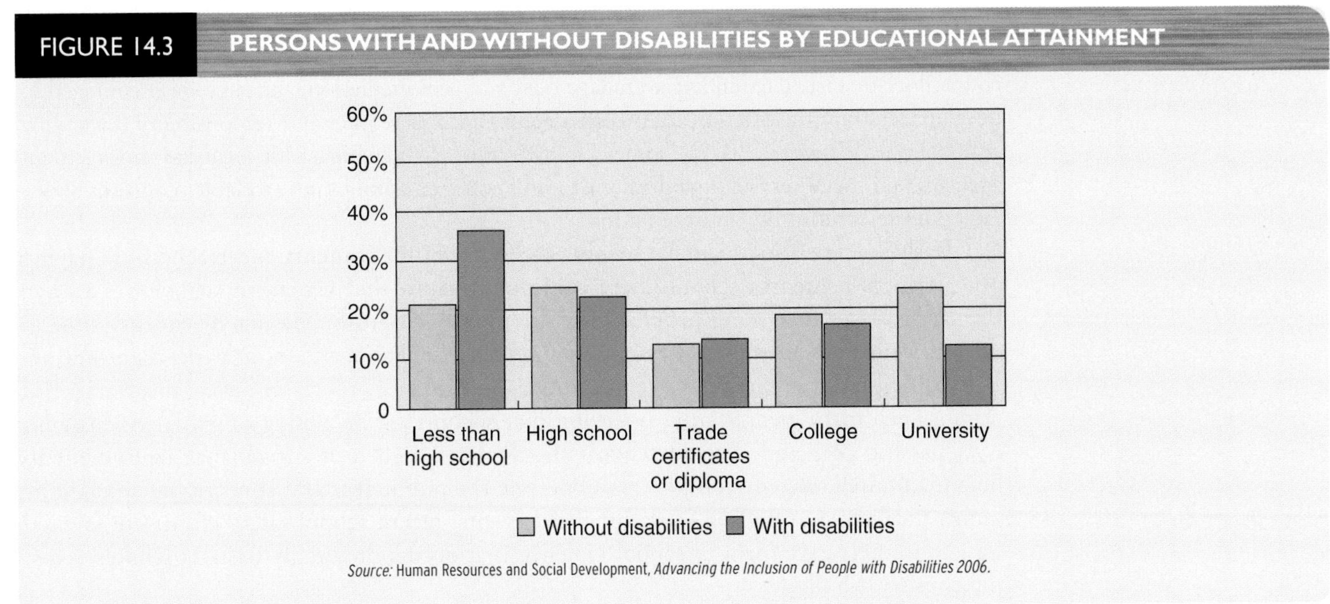

Source: Human Resources and Social Development, *Advancing the Inclusion of People with Disabilities 2006.*

As we will see in Chapter 16, the term *disability* has a wide range of definitions (see Shapiro, 1993). For the purposes of this chapter, disability is regarded as any physical and/or mental condition that limits students' access to, or full involvement in, school life.

The barriers facing students with disabilities are slowly being removed or surmounted by new legislation. Today, most people with disabilities are no longer prevented from experiencing the full range of academic opportunities. Under various provincial human rights guidelines and the *Charter of Rights and Freedoms,* all children with disabilities are guaranteed a free and appropriate public education. This guarantee means that local school boards must make the necessary efforts and expenditures to accommodate students with special needs (Uppal, Kohen, and Khan, 2007).

Many schools have attempted to *mainstream* children with disabilities by *inclusion programs,* under which the special education curriculum is integrated with the regular education program and each child receives an *individualized education plan* that provides annual education goals. (Inclusion means that children with disabilities work with a wide variety of people; over the course of a day, children may interact with their regular education teacher, the special education teacher, a speech therapist, an occupational therapist, a physical therapist, and a resource teacher, depending on the child's individual needs.) Today, more than 85 percent of children with disabilities are integrated into mainstream schools. Twenty years ago, more than 80 percent of these children were placed in segregated schools. This dramatic change reflects growing acceptance of the fact that children with a range of disabilities often thrive in an integrated learning environment.

School Safety and Violence

Violence and fear of violence continue to be pressing problems in schools This concern extends from kindergarten through Grade 12 because violent acts, although rare, have hit close to home in the past 10 to 20 years. In 1989, 14 women were shot and killed at Montreal's École Polytechnique. In 1999. a 14-year-old boy walked into his high school in Taber, Alberta, and began shooting, killing one student and wounding another. In September 2006, 18 students were shot and one student was killed at Dawson College in Montreal. The aftermath of each of these tragedies saw a massive outpouring of public sympathy and a call for greater campus security. Gun-control advocates called for greater control over the licensing and ownership of firearms and for heightened police security on college campuses.

Today, officials in schools from the elementary years to two-year colleges and four-year universities are focusing on how to reduce or eliminate violence. In many schools, teachers and counsellors are instructed in anger management and peer mediation, and they are encouraged to develop classroom instruction that teaches values such as respect and responsibility (Canadian Safe Schools Network, 2012). Some schools create partnerships with local law enforcement agencies and social service organizations to link issues of school safety to larger concerns about safety in the community and the nation.

Clearly, some efforts to make schools a safe haven for students and teachers are paying off. Statistics related to school safety continue to show that Canadian schools are among the safest places for young people. They are more likely to be victims of violent crime at or near their home, on the streets, at commercial establishments, or at parks than they are at school (National Center for Educational Statistics, 2010a). However, these statistics do not keep many people from believing that schools are becoming more dangerous with each passing year and that all schools should have high-tech surveillance equipment to help maintain a safe environment. And despite the public fear and concern precipitated by highly publicized and often sensationalized events, recent school safety efforts are focused on a more pervasive form of school violence that occurs on a daily basis in schools across the country—bullying.

Bullying affects up to 60 percent of students, depending on grade level and gender. Over 90 percent of students have witnessed bullying in their school environment (Pepler, Craig, and O'Connell, 2010). This type of school violence takes many forms and includes physical, psychological, and emotional abuse, threats, and intimidation. Victims are often targeted on the basis of race or ethnic origin, sexual orientation, or disability. A more recent form of bullying, cyberbullying, has become a common method of accessing both students and teachers with some degree of anonymity.

The effects of bullying can include learning problems, low self-esteem, mental health problems, such as anxiety and depression, substance abuse, and, in far too many cases, suicide. Tragic cases of Canadian children who have died or been seriously impaired by bullying has raised awareness of the seriousness of bullying problems for both children who bully and children who are victimized. As a result, antibullying and safe schools programs have been established at a local, provincial, and national level to create public awareness and reduce the incidence of this form of violence (PrevNet.ca, 2012).

TIME TO REVIEW

- What strategies are being used in Canadian schools to address the problem of school violence and bullying?

LO-4 The Cost of Postsecondary Education

Who attends college or university? What sort of college or university do they attend? Even for students who complete high school, access to colleges and universities is determined not only by prior academic record but also by the ability to pay.

Postsecondary education has been described as the dividing line of the modern labour market. Today more than ever before, employers want employees with a university degree, college diploma, or some other form of postsecondary educational certificate. As shown in Figure 14.4, for most Canadians, higher education will result in higher earnings. To obtain a university education, however, students must have the necessary financial resources. What does a university education cost?

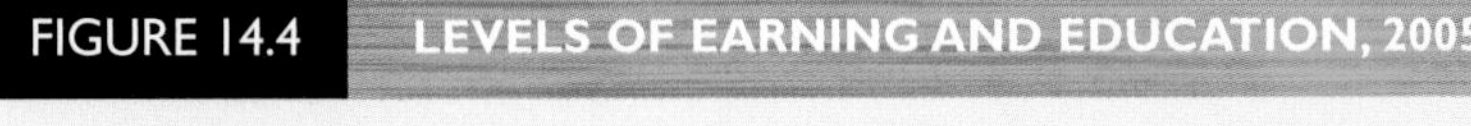

FIGURE 14.4 LEVELS OF EARNING AND EDUCATION, 2005

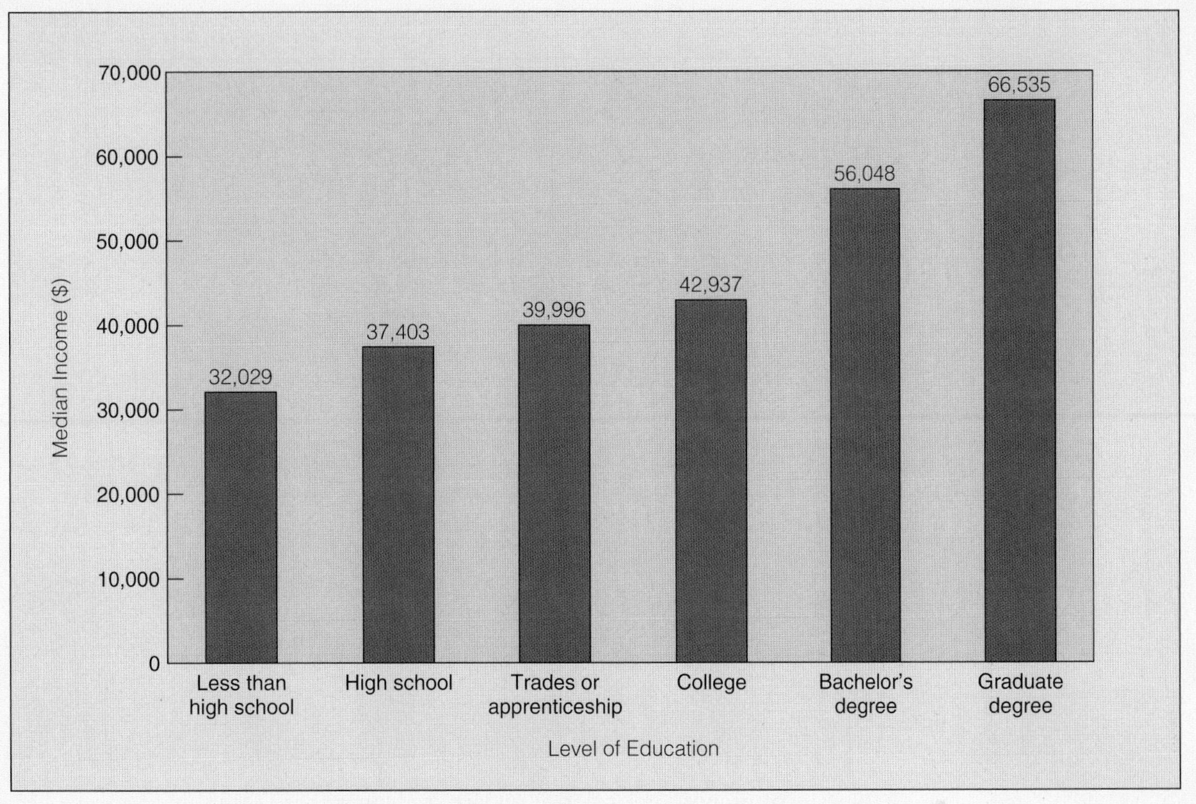

Source: Adapted from Statistics Canada, Census of Canada 2006, 2008 Income and Earnings Highlight Tables.

In Canada, postsecondary education is funded by the federal and provincial governments, and by parents and students through personal savings. As governments cut their funding to higher education, an increasing financial burden is falling on the shoulders of students and their parents. To make matters worse, the cost of attending university has increased dramatically over the past 20 years. Tuition fees have been rising faster than the rate of inflation (see Figure 14.5). For example, between 1991 and 2012, average tuition fees for an undergraduate degree went from approximately $1500 to more than $5500. College fees, although lower than the price of university, have also increased (Statistics Canada, 2012d). Despite the soaring cost of postsecondary education, the percentage of young people attending university continued to rise in the first years of the 1990s; however, undergraduate enrollments have started to level off in the past five years, an indication that for some students, the cost of a university education has become prohibitive (Statistics Canada, 2012d).

How do students afford this increasingly costly education? In a survey that explored this question, both college and university graduates identified employment earnings and student loan programs as their primary sources of funding. Parents ranked a close third for university graduates. Scholarships, fellowships, grants, and bursaries were rarely identified as a significant source of funding. Approximately one-third of college and university students indicated that they relied on student loans to finance their education. And close to 30 percent of students surveyed anticipated debt of more than $10,000 once their education was completed (EKOS Research Associates, 2003).

FIGURE 14.5 INCREASES IN TUITION FEES, 1990–2012

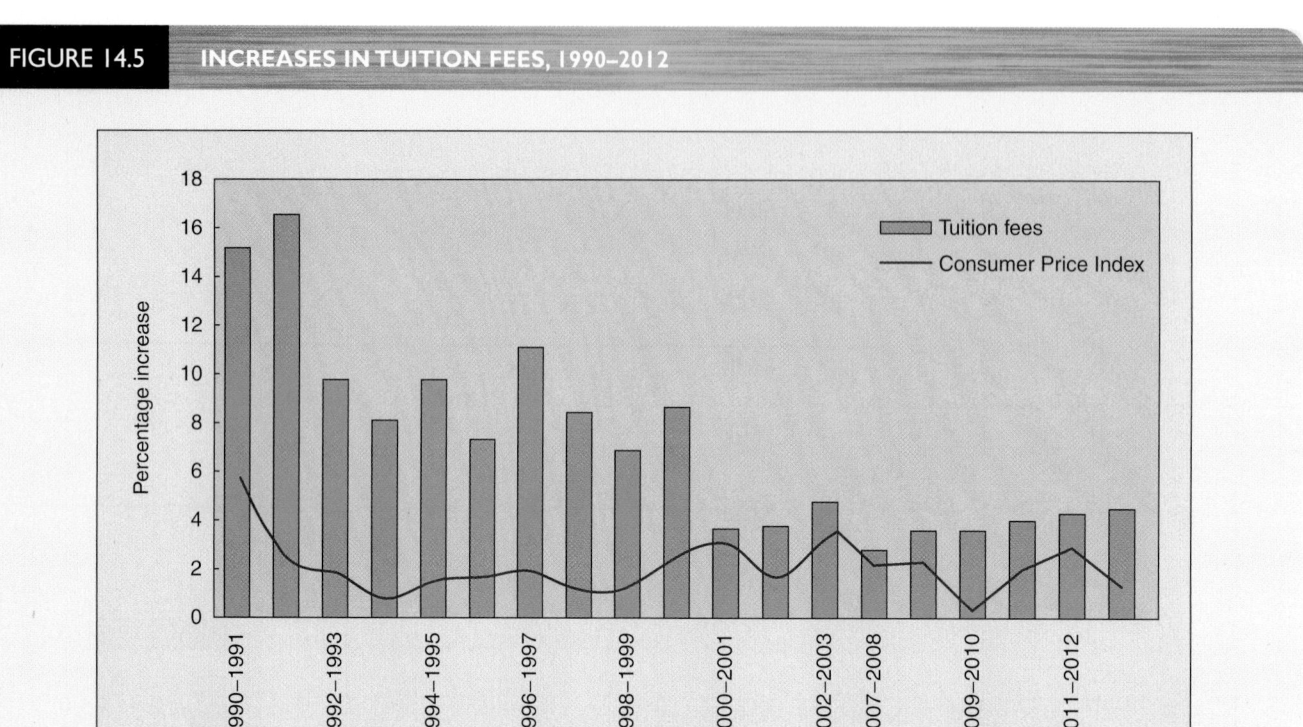

Sources: Statistics Canada, 2004; Statistics Canada, 2012d.

A substantial proportion of postsecondary students choose community college because of the lower costs. However, the overall enrollment of low-income students in community colleges has dropped as a result of increasing costs and also because many students must work full time or part time to pay for their education. Many Canadian colleges have implemented three- and four-year degree-granting programs that are an excellent option but may be cost and

Will distance learning courses change the face of the typical college or university classroom? What do you believe education will be like in the future?

time prohibitive for low-income students. In contrast, students from more affluent families are more likely to attend prestigious public universities or private colleges outside of Canada, where tuition fees alone may be more than $20,000 per year.

According to some social analysts, a university education is a bargain—even at about $90 a day for private schools or $35 for public schools—because for their money students receive instruction, room, board, and other amenities, such as athletic facilities and job placement services. However, other analysts believe that the high cost of a university education reproduces the existing class system: Students who lack money may be denied access to higher education, and those who are able to attend college or university tend to receive different types of education based on their ability to pay. For example, a community college student who receives an associate's degree or completes a certificate program may be prepared for a position in the middle of the occupational status range, such as a dental assistant, computer programmer, or auto mechanic. In contrast, university graduates with four-year degrees are more likely to find initial employment with firms where they stand a chance of being promoted to high-paying management and executive positions. Although higher education may be a source of upward mobility for talented young people from poor families, the Canadian system of higher education is sufficiently stratified that it may also reproduce the existing class structure (Barlow and Robertson, 1994; Davies and Guppy, 2006; Gilbert, 1998).

14

VISUAL SUMMARY

KEY TERMS

credentialism A process of social selection in which class advantage and social status are linked to the possession of academic qualifications (p. 407).

cultural capital Pierre Bourdieu's term for people's social assets, including their values, beliefs, attitudes, and competencies in language and culture (p. 404).

cultural transmission The process by which children and recent immigrants become acquainted with the dominant cultural beliefs, values, norms, and accumulated knowledge of a society (p. 400).

education The social institution responsible for the systematic transmission of knowledge, skills, and cultural values within a formally organized structure (p. 400).

formal education Learning that takes place within an academic setting, such as a school, that has a planned instructional process and teachers who convey specific knowledge, skills, and thinking processes to students (p. 400).

hidden curriculum The transmission of cultural values and attitudes, such as conformity and obedience to authority, through implied demands found in the rules, routines, and regulations of schools (p. 406).

informal education Learning that occurs in a spontaneous, unplanned way (p. 400).

mass education Free, public schooling for wide segments of a nation's population (p. 401).

tracking The assignment of students to specific courses and educational programs based on their test scores, previous grades, or both (p. 405).

LO-1 Explain how education differs in preliterate, preindustrial, and industrial nations.

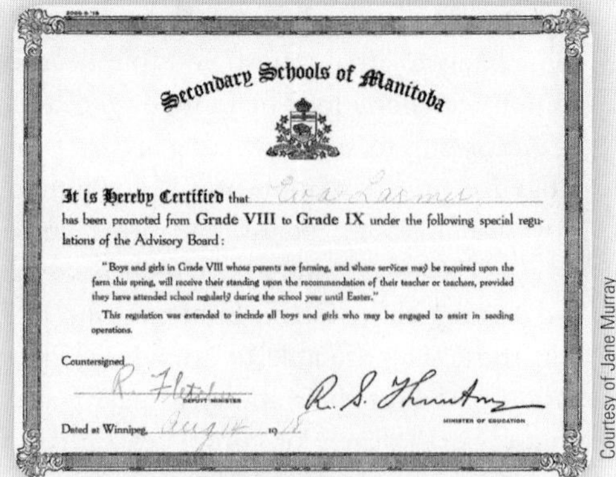

Secondary Schools of Manitoba

It is Hereby Certified that

has been promoted from Grade VIII to Grade IX under the following special regulations of the Advisory Board:

"Boys and girls in Grade VIII whose parents are farming, and whose services may be required upon the farm this spring, will receive their standing upon the recommendation of their teacher or teachers, provided they have attended school regularly during the school year until Easter."

This regulation was extended to include all boys and girls who may be engaged to assist in seeding operations.

Countersigned

DEPUTY MINISTER

MINISTER OF EDUCATION

Dated at Winnipeg, 19

Courtesy of Jane Murray

In preliterate societies, people acquired knowledge and skills through informal education from parents and other group members. Formal education—learning that takes place within an academic setting such as a school, that has a planned instructional process and teachers who convey specific knowledge—first became available to members of the elite class in preindustrial societies. In industrial and post-industrial societies, education is provided through mass education, where all members of society have access to publicly funded education.

© Dick Hemingway

LO-2 Identify the key assumptions of functionalist, feminist, conflict, symbolic interactionist, and postmodern perspectives on education.

According to functionalists, education has both manifest functions (socialization, transmission of culture, multiculturalism, social control, social placement, and change and innovation) and latent functions (keeping young people off the streets and out of the job market, matchmaking and producing social networks, and creating a generation gap). From a conflict perspective, education is used to perpetuate class, racial–ethnic, and gender inequalities through tracking, ability grouping, and a hidden curriculum that teaches subordinate groups conformity and obedience. Feminist scholars direct our attention to Gender bias and stereotyping, the economic consequences of educational attainment. They also argue that men and women learn in different ways and that formal educational institutions may not adequately attend to women's "ways of knowing". Interactionists examine classroom dynamics and study ways in which a practice, such as labelling, may become a self-fulfilling prophecy for some students, such that these students come to perform up—or down—to the expectations held for them by teachers. Some postmodernists suggest that in a consumer culture, education becomes a commodity that is bought by students and their parents. Colleges and universities function as "McUniversities" that allow students to consume educational services and obtain goods such as degrees and credentials.

LO-3 Describe the major problems in elementary schools and secondary schools in Canada today.

Dropping out, unequal educational opportunities for students with disabilities, and school violence, primarily in the form of bullying, are among the most pressing issues in elementary and secondary schools.

Courtesy of Jane Murray

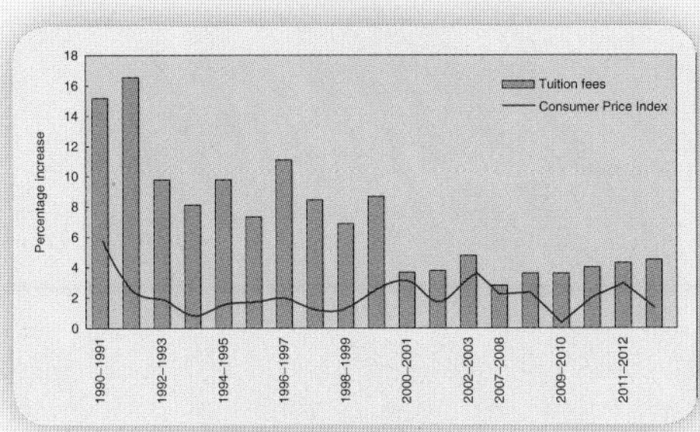

LO-4 Identify the major challenges facing students in higher education institutions.

The combined effects of funding cuts and the soaring cost of a college or university education are among the pressing issues in higher education in Canada today.

APPLICATION QUESTIONS

1. Why do some theorists believe that education is a vehicle for decreasing social inequality whereas others believe that education reproduces existing class relationships?
2. Why does so much controversy exist over what should be taught in Canadian public schools?
3. How has education shaped your life in both direct and indirect ways?

Test your comprehension and assess what you've learned with **CourseMate's** online quizzes.

For other interesting Lived Experiences, watch the video clips on **CourseMate.**

Practise what you've learned with flashcards containing key terms and definitions on **CourseMate.**

CHAPTER 15

Religion

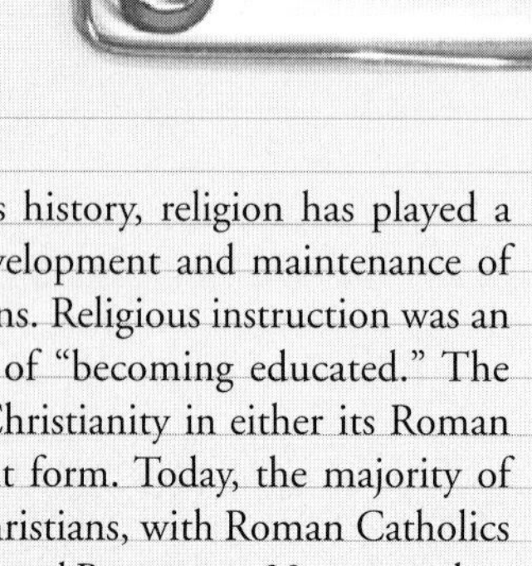

© Lindsay Hebberd/Corbis

For most of Canada's history, religion has played a major role in the development and maintenance of educational institutions. Religious instruction was an essential component of "becoming educated." The religion taught was Christianity in either its Roman Catholic or Protestant form. Today, the majority of Canadians are still Christians, with Roman Catholics making up 43 percent and Protestants 29 percent, but other religions, such as Hinduism, Islam, Buddhism, Confucianism, and Sikhism, are now part of our Canadian mosaic (Statistics Canada, 2003j).

There is no longer any consensus among Canadians regarding the role religion should play in education. Should students receive religious instruction in the classroom? If so, which religions should be included? Should prayer be offered in schools? In our multicultural society, these questions are becoming increasingly difficult to answer.

Some parents believe religious instruction is necessary and suggest that secularization in the public school system is contributing to a declining morality. Albertans Dick and Joanne Barendregt teach their children at home. Although home-schooling is common in Canada, the Barendregts are part of a growing network of parents who disobey the law by not registering their children or allowing provincial officials to monitor their children's education—they believe this would interfere with their religious freedom. The couple decided to educate their children at home after they found that one of their children's textbooks had a section on evolution that conflicted with their religious views.

Joanne Barendregt feels that "in two or three years, they're going to regulate what we feed our children . . . and after that it will be our reproductive systems . . . We feel the highest calling a girl can have is to be a wife and mother first. We teach that that is their purpose . . . We are not changing. You [society] have changed. You're trying to destroy our [religious] heritage." Her husband says they will not register with the government because "We will not have a partnership with a government that promotes and allows homosexuality to continue, and abortion" (Mitchell, 1999:A7).

In contrast to the Barendregts, many Canadians feel that the school curriculum should be secular and that, in our multicultural society, no religion should be endorsed.

How can schools teach religious values that might conflict with the values and customs of a significant number of students? How might students and teachers who come from diverse religious and cultural backgrounds feel about instruction or organized prayer in public schools? Rick Nelson, a teacher in the public school system, explains his concern about the potential impact of religion in his classroom:

> *I think it really trivializes religion when you try to take such a serious topic with so many different viewpoints and cover it in the public schools . . . I am not opposed to individual*

prayer by students. But when there is a group prayer, who's going to lead the group? (CNN, 1994)

This debate has a long history. Controversies have arisen over topics such as the teaching of creationism versus evolutionism, moral education, sex education, school prayers, and the content of textbooks and library books.

What role does religion play in Canada's school systems today? The simple answer is that religion plays almost no role in the public school system. Most of those who wish to combine education with religious instruction must do so through private schooling. Education falls within provincial jurisdiction, however, and some provinces provide public funding to Roman Catholic separate schools (Holmes, 1998). Saskatchewan and Ontario fully fund Roman Catholic schools, but Ontario does not support schools operated by members of other religious denominations, while Saskatchewan does provide funding for private schools, including religious schools. Manitoba and British Columbia provide funding to a wide variety of private schools (many of which are religious schools) based on academic criteria. In Ontario, the teaching of the Christian religion in the public school system, which was once mandatory, is now forbidden. At the same time, Roman Catholic schools are fully funded. This means that the Protestant majority cannot teach its understanding of Christianity in the public schools, while the Roman Catholic minority has its own funded system. All other minorities and Protestants who wish a religious-based education receive no provincial support (Holmes, 1998).

As the issue of religious education suggests, religion can be a highly controversial topic. One group's deeply held beliefs or cherished religious practices may be a source of irritation to another. Religion is a source of both stability and conflict throughout the world. In this chapter, we will examine how religion influences life in Canada and in other areas of the world. Before reading on, test your knowledge about how religion affects public education in this country by taking the quiz in Box 15.1 on page 423.

Critical Thinking Questions

1. In 2004, a Canadian university was criticized for not providing prayer space for Muslim students. Do you think that secular universities should be required to provide on-campus prayer space for all observant students?

2. How does religion appear in your life? Does it ever come up in everyday conversations? Is it discussed in any of your classes? Do you see any differences between your acquaintances who are religious and those who are not?

3. In 2012, a Nova Scotia high school student was suspended for a week for wearing a T-shirt saying "Life is wasted without Jesus" (Winnipeg Free Press, 2012). Do you think the school was justified in restricting this student's freedom of expression when other students are allowed to wear religious symbols to school? Would you have a different view if the student had been aggressively trying to get other students to support his Christian beliefs?

CHAPTER FOCUS QUESTION

What is the relationship between society and religion, and what role does religion play in people's everyday lives?

LEARNING OBJECTIVES

AFTER READING THIS CHAPTER, YOU SHOULD BE ABLE TO

LO-1 Describe what religion is and understand its purpose in society.

LO-2 Understand the differences between the functionalist, conflict, interactionist, feminist, and postmodern perspectives on religion.

LO-3 Understand the different types of religious organizations.

LO-4 Discuss the impact of religion on people's attitudes and behaviour.

LO-5 Consider the future role of religion in Canada.

LO-1 THE SOCIOLOGICAL STUDY OF RELIGION

religion A system of beliefs, symbols, and rituals, based on some sacred or supernatural realm, that guides human behaviour, gives meaning to life, and unites believers into a community.

faith Unquestioning belief that does not require proof or scientific evidence.

sacred A term used to describe those aspects of life that are extraordinary or supernatural.

profane A term used for the everyday, secular, or "worldly" aspects of life.

rituals Regularly repeated and carefully prescribed forms of behaviour that symbolize a cherished value or belief.

What is religion? **Religion** is a system of beliefs, symbols, and rituals, based on some sacred or supernatural realm, that guides human behaviour, gives meaning to life, and unites believers into a community (Durkheim, 1995/1912). Religion is one of our most significant social institutions and consists of a variety of elements, including beliefs about the sacred or supernatural, rituals, and a social organization of believers drawn together by their common religious tradition (Kurtz, 1995). Most religions attempt to answer fundamental questions about the meaning of life and death, and how the world was created. Most religions also provide comfort to persons facing emotional traumas, such as illness, suffering, grief, and death.

According to Kurtz, religious beliefs are typically woven into a series of narratives, including stories about how ancestors and other significant figures had meaningful experiences with supernatural powers (1995:9). Religious beliefs are linked to practices that bind people together and to rites of passage, such as birth, marriage, and death. People with similar religious beliefs and practices often come together in a moral community (based on a church, mosque, temple, or synagogue) where they can engage with similarly minded people.

Religious Belief and Ritual

Religions seek to answer important questions, such as why we exist and what happens after death. Peter Berger (1967) referred to religion as a *sacred canopy*—a sheltering fabric hanging over people that gives them security and provides answers to the questions of life. However, this sacred canopy requires that people have **faith**—unquestioning belief that does not require proof or scientific evidence. The answers provided by religion point to the **sacred**, those aspects of life that are extraordinary or supernatural—those things that are set apart as "holy" (Durkheim, 1995/1912). People feel a sense of awe, reverence, deep respect, or fear for what is considered sacred. Across cultures and at different times, many things have been considered sacred, including invisible gods, spirits, specific animals or trees, altars, crosses, and holy books (Collins, 1982). Those things that people do not set apart as sacred are referred to as the **profane**—the everyday, secular, or "worldly" aspects of life (Collins, 1982). Sacred beliefs are rooted in the holy or supernatural, whereas secular beliefs have their foundation in scientific knowledge or everyday explanations. For example, in the educational debate over creationism and evolutionism, creationists view their belief as founded in sacred teachings, but evolutionists argue that their beliefs are based on scientific data.

In addition to beliefs, religion also comprises symbols and rituals. People often perform religious **rituals**—regularly repeated and carefully prescribed forms of behaviour that symbolize a cherished value or belief (Kurtz, 1995). Rituals range from songs and prayers to offerings and sacrifices that worship or praise a supernatural being or a set of supernatural principles. For example, Muslims bow toward Mecca,

This Nova Scotia student was suspended from high school for wearing a t-shirt expressing his religious beliefs.

BOX 15.1 **SOCIOLOGY AND EVERYDAY LIFE**

How Much Do You Know About the Impact of Religion on Education in Canada?

True	False	
T	F	1. Parents who home-school their children for religious reasons are free to teach the children whatever curriculum they wish.
T	F	2. Enrollment in parochial (religious) schools has decreased in Canada as interest in religion has waned.
T	F	3. In Canada, the public school system recognizes only Christian religious holidays by giving students those days off.
T	F	4. The number of children from religious backgrounds other than Christian and Judaic has grown steadily in schools over the past several decades.
T	F	5. Debates over textbook content focus only on elementary education because of the vulnerability of young children.

For answers to the quiz about the impact of religion on education in Canada, go to **www.nelson.com/sociologyinourtimes6e.**

the holy city of Islam, five times a day at fixed times to pray to God, and Christians participate in Holy Communion to commemorate the life, death, and resurrection of Jesus Christ. The rituals involved in praying or in observing communion are carefully orchestrated and must be followed with precision. According to Collins, "In rituals, it is the forms that count. Saying prayers, singing a hymn, performing a primitive sacrifice or a dance, marching in a procession, kneeling before an idol or making the sign of the cross—in these, the action must be done the right way" (1982:34).

The importance of rituals and other religious regulations can be understood if you recall that the purpose of religion is to explain fundamental questions, such as death and the meaning of life. Rodney Stark has pointed out that religions do more for humans than "supply them with answers to questions of ultimate meaning. The assumption that the supernatural exists raises a new question: *What does the supernatural want or expect from us?"* (1998:386). Thus, religions also provide the faithful with rules about how they must act if they are to please the gods. These rules are justified in religious terms, and following the rules is a sign of faith.

Bob Daemmrich Photography Inc.

Throughout the world, people seek the meaning of life through traditional and nontraditional forms of religion. These Italian spiritual seekers are meeting together at a Mayan ruin, in quest of harmonic convergence.

Categories of Religion

simple supernaturalism The belief that supernatural forces affect people's lives either positively or negatively.

animism The belief that plants, animals, or other elements of the natural world are endowed with spirits or life forces that have an impact on events in society.

theism A belief in a god or gods.

monotheism A belief in a single, supreme being or god who is responsible for significant events, such as the creation of the world.

polytheism A belief in more than one god.

Anthropologists have concluded that all known groups over the past 100,000 years have had some form of religion (Haviland, 1993). Religions have been classified into four main categories based on their dominant belief: simple supernaturalism, animism, theism, and transcendent idealism (McGee, 1975). In simple preindustrial societies, religion often takes the form of **simple supernaturalism**—the belief that supernatural forces affect people's lives either positively or negatively. This type of religion does not acknowledge specific gods or supernatural spirits but focuses instead on impersonal forces that may exist in people or natural objects. For example, simple supernaturalism has been used to explain mystifying events of nature, such as sunrises and thunderstorms, and ways that some objects may bring a person good or bad luck. By contrast, **animism** is the belief that plants, animals, or other elements of the natural world are endowed with spirits or life forces that have an impact on events in society. Animism is associated with early hunting and gathering societies in which everyday life is not separated from the elements of the natural world (Albanese, 1992).

The third category of religion is **theism**—a belief in a god or gods. Horticultural societies were among the first to practise **monotheism**—a belief in a single, supreme being or god who is responsible for significant events, such as the creation of the world. Three of the major world religions—Christianity, Judaism, and Islam—are monotheistic. By contrast, Shinto and a number of the indigenous religions of Africa are forms of **polytheism**—a belief in more than one god. The fourth category of religion, transcendent idealism, is a **nontheistic religion**—a religion based on a belief in divine spiritual forces, such as sacred principles of thought and conduct, rather than a god or gods. Transcendent idealism focuses on principles, such as truth, justice, affirmation of life, and tolerance for others, and its adherents seek an elevated state of consciousness in which they can fulfill their true potential.

LO-2 SOCIOLOGICAL PERSPECTIVES ON RELIGION

nontheistic religion A religion based on a belief in divine spiritual forces, such as sacred principles of thought and conduct, rather than a god or gods.

The major sociological perspectives have very different views about the relationship between religion and society. Functionalists emphasize the ways in which religious beliefs and rituals can bind people together. Conflict explanations suggest that religion can be a source of false consciousness in society. Interactionists focus on the meanings that people give to religion in their everyday lives. Feminists look at the ways in which women's religious experiences differ from those of men. Postmodern theorists examine the changing nature and role of religion in the 21st century.

The Concept Snapshot later in this chapter outlines what the proponents of various perspectives say about religion.

Functionalist Perspectives on Religion

DURKHEIM ON RELIGION Durkheim emphasized that religion is essential to the maintenance of society. He suggested that religion was found in all societies because it met basic human needs and served important societal functions.

For Durkheim, the central feature of all religions is the presence of sacred beliefs and rituals that bind people together in a collectivity. In his studies of the religion of the Australian Aborigines, for example, Durkheim found that each clan had established its own sacred totem, which included kangaroos, trees, rivers, rock formations, and other animals or natural creations. To clan members, their totem was sacred; it symbolized some unique quality of their clan. People developed a feeling of unity by performing ritual dances around their totem, which caused them to abandon individual self-interest. Durkheim suggested that the correct performance of the ritual gives rise to religious conviction.

FUNCTIONS OF RELIGION Religion has three important functions in any society:

1. *Providing meaning and purpose to life.* Religion offers meaning for the human experience. Some events create a profound sense of loss for both individuals and groups. Individual losses might be the death of a loved one; group ones might be famine or an earthquake. Inequality may cause people to wonder why their personal situation is no better than it is. Most religions offer explanations for these concerns. Explanations differ among religions, but each tells the individual or group that life is part of a larger system (McGuire, 1997). Some (but not all) religions even offer the hope of an afterlife for persons who follow the religion's tenets of morality in this life. Such beliefs help make injustices in this life easier to endure.
2. *Promoting social cohesion and a sense of belonging.* By emphasizing shared symbolism, religious teachings and practices help promote social cohesion. The Christian ritual of Holy Communion not only commemorates a historical event but also allows followers to participate in their unity ("communion") with other believers (McGuire, 1997). Religion can also help members of subordinate or minority groups develop a sense of social cohesion and belonging. For example, in the late 1980s and early 1990s, Russian Jewish immigrants to Canada found a sense of belonging in their congregations. Even though they did not speak the language of their new country, they had religious rituals and a sense of history in common with others in the congregation. In Calgary, the Baptist minister at a church with a congregation made up of 1500 people of Korean background commented, "The church is more than a Christian institution, it is also a means of cultural fellowship. It is a place to feel comfortable. They are in a strange country and here there is friendship" (Nemeth, Underwood, and Howse, 1993:33).
3. *Providing social control and support for the government.* If individuals consider themselves part of a larger order that holds the ultimate meaning in life, they will feel bound to one another (and to past and future generations) in a way that otherwise might not be possible (McGuire, 1997). Religion also helps maintain social control by conferring supernatural legitimacy on the norms and laws in society. In some societies, social control occurs as a result of direct collusion between the dominant classes and the dominant religious organizations. Absolute monarchs have often claimed that God gave them the right to rule so their citizens could not question their legitimacy to govern.

Conflict Perspectives on Religion

KARL MARX ON RELIGION While most functionalists feel that religion serves a positive role, many conflict theorists view religion negatively. For Marx, *ideologies*—"systematic views of the way the world ought to be"—are embodied in religious doctrines and political values (Turner, Beeghley, and Powers, 1995:135). These ideologies also justify the status quo and block social change. The capitalist class uses religious ideology to mislead the workers about their true interests. For Marx, religion is the "opiate of the masses." People become complacent because they have been taught to believe in an afterlife in which they will be rewarded for their suffering and misery in this life. Although these religious teachings soothe the masses, any relief is illusory. Religion unites people under a "false consciousness" that leads them to believe they have common interests with members of the dominant class (Roberts, 1995b).

From a conflict perspective, religion also tends to promote strife between groups and societies. The conflict may be *between* religious groups (religious wars), *within* a religious group

© Bettmann/Corbis

The shared experiences and beliefs associated with religion have helped many groups maintain a sense of social cohesion and a feeling of belonging in the face of prejudice and discrimination.

(a splinter group leaving an existing denomination), or between a religious group and *the larger society* (conflict over religion in the classroom). Conflict theorists assert that, in attempting to provide meaning and purpose in life while at the same time promoting the status quo, religion is used by the dominant classes to impose their own control over society and its resources (McGuire, 1992).

WEBER'S RESPONSE TO MARX Whereas Marx believed that religion hindered social change, Weber argued just the opposite: that religion could help produce social change. In *The Protestant Ethic and the Spirit of Capitalism* (1976/1904–1905), Weber asserted that the religious teachings of John Calvin were directly related to the rise of capitalism. Calvin emphasized the doctrine of *predestination*—the belief that all people are divided into two groups, the saved and the damned. Only God knows who will go to heaven (the elect) and who will go to hell. Because people cannot know whether they will be saved, they look for earthly signs that they are among the elect. According to the Protestant ethic, those who have faith, perform good works, and achieve economic success are more likely to be among the chosen of God. As a result, people work hard, save their money, and do not spend it on worldly frivolity; instead, they reinvest it in their land, equipment, and labour (Chalfant, Beckley, and Palmer, 1994).

The spirit of capitalism grew under the Protestant ethic. As people worked harder to prove their religious piety, structural conditions in Europe led to the Industrial Revolution, free markets, and the commercialization of the economy—developments that worked hand in hand with Calvinist religious teachings. From this viewpoint, wealth was an unintended consequence of religious piety and hard work.

Like Marx, Weber was aware that religion could reinforce existing social arrangements, especially the stratification system. The wealthy can use religion to justify their power and privilege: It is a sign of God's approval of their hard work and morality. As for the poor, if they work hard and live a moral life, they will be richly rewarded in another life.

Is Weber's thesis about the relationship between religion and the economy supported by other researchers? Collins reexamined Weber's claim that the capitalist breakthrough occurred just in Christian Europe and concluded that it is only partially accurate. According to Collins, the foundations for capitalism in Asia, particularly Japan, were laid in the Buddhist monastic economy of late medieval Japan: "The temples were the first entrepreneurial organizations in Japan: the first to combine control of the factors of labor, capital, and land so as to allocate them for enhancing production" (1997:855). Due to an ethic of self-discipline and restraint on consumption, high levels of accumulation and investment took place in medieval Japanese Buddhism. Gradually, secular capitalism emerged from temple capitalism as new guilds, independent of the temples, arose, and the gap between the clergy and everyday people narrowed. The capitalist dynamic in the monasteries was eventually transferred to the secular economy, opening the way to the Industrial Revolution in Japan.

From the works of Weber and Collins, we can conclude that the emergence of capitalism through a religious economy happened in several parts of the world, not just one, and that it occurred in both Christian and Buddhist forms (Collins, 1997).

Symbolic Interactionist Perspectives on Religion

Thus far, we have looked at religion primarily from a macrolevel perspective. Symbolic interactionists focus on a microlevel analysis that examines the meanings that people give to religion in their everyday lives.

RELIGION AS A REFERENCE GROUP For many, religion serves as a reference group to help them define themselves. For example, religious symbols have meaning for many people. The Star of David holds special significance for Jews, just as the crescent moon and star do for Muslims and the cross does for Christians. It has been said that the symbolism of religion is so powerful because it "expresses the essential facts of our human existence" (Collins, 1982:37).

© Hemis/Alamy

According to Marx and Weber, religion serves to reinforce social stratification in a society. According to Hindu belief, for example, a person's social position in his or her current life is a result of behaviour in a former life.

RELIGIOUS CONVERSION John Lofland and Rodney Stark (1965) wanted to find out why people converted to nontraditional religious movements. What would attract people to a small movement outside the religious mainstream, and why were some movements successful at attracting people while most others failed? In the early 1960s, Lofland and Stark studied a small religious movement that had been brought to the San Francisco area from Korea. They called the movement the Divine Precepts but later revealed that the group was the Unification Church, better known as "the Moonies" after their founder, Sun Myung Moon.

Lofland and Stark spent a great deal of time observing the group's activities and conducting interviews. They proposed a seven-step theory of conversion and concluded that the most important personal characteristics that made conversion likely were as follows:

1. Individuals had an important tension or strain in their lives, such as financial problems, marital issues, or sexual identity problems.
2. They had a religious problem-solving perspective. While other people respond to strain in their lives by taking direct action (such as divorce or bankruptcy), going to a psychiatrist, or joining a political movement, these individuals try to solve their problems through spiritual means.
3. They defined themselves as religious seekers trying to resolve their problems through some system of religious meaning. Some had tried a wide variety of different religious alternatives before encountering the Moonies.

These background factors were present before the potential converts came to the Divine Precepts. Several situational factors then increased the likelihood of conversion:

4. Individuals had come to a turning point in their lives. Some of the future converts had just failed or dropped out of school, while others had moved, lost a job, or experienced some other major life change. This turning point not only increased the tension experienced but gave the people the opportunity to turn to something new.
5. Potential converts had close personal ties with a member of the Divine Precepts. While many religious seekers heard the message of the Divine Precepts, only those who also developed a personal bond with a member underwent conversion. One of the converts, who had recently recovered from a serious illness, described the process:

> I felt as if I had come to life from a numb state and there was spiritual liveliness and vitality within me by being among this group. As one feels when he comes from a closed stuffy room into the fresh air, or the goodness and warmth after freezing coldness was how my spirit witnessed its happiness. Although I could not agree with the message intellectually I found myself one with it spiritually. (1965:871)

6. There was a lack of ties with people outside the group. Few of those who converted had strong ties outside the group.
7. Those who converted had been exposed to intensive interaction with Divine Precepts members. The Divine Precepts recognized this and strongly encouraged those who had verbally converted to move into a shared residence with other group members. This tactic helped to secure converts' total commitment to the movement.

Feminist Perspectives on Religion

There is evidence that in early societies, female goddesses played a predominant role in religious beliefs. As societies became more stratified, however, male gods became more important. Religious leadership was restricted to men, and women were restricted to subordinate roles in church activities. In many religions, women were not even permitted to study religious texts; only men could.

Former U.S. president Jimmy Carter left the Baptist Church because he disagreed with their views on the role of women in that church. However, he believed that the problem was far broader than just among Baptists:

> This view that women are somehow inferior to men is not restricted to one religion or belief. It is widespread. Women are prevented from playing a full and equal role in many faiths. Nor, tragically, does its influence stop at the walls of the church, mosque, synagogue, or temple. This discrimination, unjustifiably attributed to a higher authority, has provided a reason or excuse for the deprivation of women's equal rights across the world for centuries. The male interpretations of religious texts and the way they interact with and reinforce traditional practices justify some of the most pervasive, persistent, flagrant, and damaging examples of human-rights abuses. (quoted in Prose, 2012)

As President Carter points out, religious discrimination against women is not just a religious matter, as it is used as justification for discrimination in other aspects of life, including education and marriage.

HIS RELIGION AND HER RELIGION Because men and women often play different roles in the church, they may belong to the same religious group but their experience of religion may not be the same. Some religious groups are inclusive, but in others, women's versions of particular religions may differ markedly from men's versions (McGuire, 1997). For example, while an Orthodox Jewish man may focus on his roles in public rituals and his discussion of sacred texts, Orthodox Jewish women have few ritual duties and are more likely to focus on their responsibilities in the home. Consequently, the meaning of being Jewish may be different for women than for men.

Consider one woman's reaction to the serving of Holy Communion in her Protestant church:

> Following the sermon, the worshippers are invited to participate in the celebration of the Lord's Supper. As the large group of male ushers marches down the aisle to receive the communion elements and distribute them to the congregation, I am suddenly struck with the irony of the situation. The chicken suppers, the ham suppers, the turkey suppers in the church are all prepared and served by the women. But not the Lord's Supper . . . the privilege of serving the Lord's Supper in worship is reserved for the men. This particular morning I find it very difficult to swallow the bread and drink the wine, knowing that within the Body of Christ, the Church, the sisters of Christ are not given the same respect and privileges as are his brothers. (Johnstone, 1997:237)

Religious symbolism and language create a social definition of the roles of men and women. Sometimes, females are depicted as negative or evil spiritual forces. Historically, language has been male-centred in the world's major religions. Phrases such as *for all men* in Roman Catholic and Anglican services have gradually been changed to *for all*, but some churches retain the traditional liturgy (Briggs, 1987). Many women resist the subordination they have experienced in organized religion and object to its patriarchal nature. Some advocate a break from traditional religions, while others seek to reform religious language, symbols, and rituals to eliminate the elements of patriarchy (Renzetti and Curran, 1992).

WOMEN IN THE MINISTRY

> I believe in God, the Father Almighty, Creator of Heaven and Earth, and in Jesus Christ, His only Son. (MacDonald, 1996:47)

> A woman can't represent Christ. Men and women are totally different—that's not my fault—and Jesus chose men for his disciples. (MacDonald, 1996:47)

These quotations highlight two issues that are important to women: the gender inclusiveness of religion and the absence of women in significant roles within many religious institutions. Women from many religious backgrounds are demanding an end to traditions that do not reflect their religious commitment. Some women are choosing alternative spiritual belief systems, while others are working inside their church to create change. The battles have been intense, and the issue of the role of women has polarized some churches. In 1992, the Church of England allowed the ordination of women priests. In response, a British vicar made a point of telling the media that he would "burn the bloody bitches" (MacDonald, 1996:47).

Despite opposition, there have been some advances. Women make up an increasing proportion of the clergy in some religious denominations. The United and Anglican churches have significant numbers of female clergy. Reform Judaism has ordained women as rabbis since the early 1970s, and Aboriginal Canadian religions have traditionally given status to women in spiritual leadership. The Roman Catholic Church, for one, however, will not allow women to serve as clergy, and women are still struggling to make their voices heard. In 2012, Pope Benedict was highly critical of the largest association of U.S. nuns, the Leadership Conference of Women Religious (LCWR). The nuns were accused of pursuing a radical feminist agenda of social justice and poverty reduction by disagreeing with official Catholic Church positions on the ordination of women, ministry to homosexuals, and several other issues. The pope appointed an archbishop (of course a male) to oversee the LCWR to ensure that they follow Catholic doctrine more faithfully.

While women are a distinct minority among religious leaders, they make up a substantial majority of the faithful. Rodney Stark has concluded that "in every sizable religious group in the Western world, women outnumber men, usually by a considerable margin" (2004:61). Thus, many churches discriminate against their most faithful members.

Postmodern Perspectives on Religion

THE SECULARIZATION DEBATE One of the most important debates within the sociology of religion deals with the question of whether the world is becoming more secular and less religious or whether we are seeing a renewal of religious belief. The view that modern societies are becoming more secular goes back to the work of Weber, Durkheim, and Marx. For example, Weber felt that as societies became modernized, the role of religion as the sole source of authority would inevitably diminish as other social institutions—particularly economic and political ones—became dominant. Hadden has summarized the *secularization* perspective:

> Once the world was filled with the sacred—in thought, practice, and institutional form. After the Reformation and the Renaissance, the forces of modernization swept across the globe and secularization . . . loosened the dominance of the sacred. In due course, the sacred shall disappear altogether except, possibly, in the private realm. (1987:598)

Proponents of this view link modernization with secularization. These theorists predict that as the world becomes more rational and bureaucratized, and as knowledge becomes more science-based, the influence of religion will decline. According to Fukuyama, Weber's prediction has proven accurate in many ways: "Rational science-based capitalism has spread across the globe, bringing material advancement to large parts of the world and welding it together into the iron cage we call globalization" (2005:2). Religion has become much less important in Canada and in almost all Western industrial countries other than the United States. Church membership in these countries has dramatically declined over the past 50 years.While many people still report an interest in spiritual matters, they do not pursue these interests through the organized church.

Most critics of secularization theory concede that in most Western industrialized countries, the separation between church and state has increased and church attendance has declined. At the same time, however, religion is becoming more important in other parts of the world. Religion remains strong in Islamic societies, even in countries that have begun to modernize, such as Turkey and Pakistan. In the former Soviet bloc, where religion had been banned, there has been a dramatic resurgence in religious participation since the end of the communist era. Pentecostal churches are growing very rapidly in South America. The United States, perhaps the world's most modernized society, is still a very religious country, showing that modernization does not inevitably cause a decline in religiosity.

The proportion of the world's population that holds religious beliefs is now growing because of high birth rates in religious countries (Norris and Inglehart, 2004). Even in more secular countries, religious people have higher birth rates than those who are not religious. Because of this, some sociologists, such as Rodney Stark, disagree with secularization theory: "After nearly three centuries of utterly failed prophecies and misrepresentations of both past and present, it seems time to carry the secularization doctrine to the graveyard of failed theories, and there to whisper ['rest in peace']" (1999:270).

Jeff Haynes (1997) has looked at this situation from the postmodern perspective and concludes that both sides in this debate are partially correct. While secularization continues in much of the industrialized West, the postmodern condition has led people in many low-income countries to turn to religion. The structural conditions of postmodernism, including the negative consequences of globalization and its perceived threats to the moral order, can destabilize local values and traditions. Instead of leading to secularization, these conditions can lead to a strengthening of faith as some people resist these threats by turning to religion. Proponents of secularization theory would not have predicted the role played by religion in global politics in the past four decades. Religion has been critical in major political events as diverse as the ongoing conflicts between India and Pakistan and between Israel and the Palestinians; the violent breakup of the former Yugoslavia; and the Republican political victories in the United States in 2000, 2004, and 2010. See Box 15.2.

Haynes explains the coexistence of secularization in some parts of the world and the spread of religion elsewhere by hypothesizing that secularization will continue, except in circumstances where religion "finds or retains work to do other than relating people to the supernatural . . . only when religion does something other than mediate between man and God does it retain a high place in people's attentions and in their politics" (1997:713). Thus, in countries where organized religion fills other functions for adherents, it will flourish, and in countries, such as Canada, where religion retains only its premodern spiritual role, it will continue to stagnate or decline.

Haynes predicts that religion will retain or increase its importance in societies where it helps defend culture against perceived threats from outside or from the threat of internal cultural change. Global capitalism has weakened national sovereignty and carries with it only the values of the marketplace. Many people view their own governments as part of the enemy (Juergensmeyer, 2003). The comments of Joanne Barendregt in the chapter introduction show how even some Canadians feel threatened by this social change. And Islamic militant Sayyid Qutb, who was tortured and executed by Egyptian police in 1966, stated his disgust with the Westernization of the Arab world, which he felt was destroying his basic Islamic values:

> Humanity today is living in a large brothel! One has only to glance at its press, films, fashion shows, beauty contests, ballrooms, wine bars, and broadcasting stations! Or observe its mad lust for naked flesh, provocative postures, and sick, suggestive statements in the literature, the arts and the mass media! (Ruthven, 2004:37)

One way for people to deal with these threats is to turn to fundamentalist beliefs. These beliefs do more than mediate between people and their God. To people who feel that their values and identities are under threat from globalization, poverty, immorality, religious pluralism, or corrupt government, religious fundamentalism provides certainty in an uncertain world. According to Haynes, "For many people, especially in the Third World, postmodernism is synonymous with poverty, leading the poor especially to be receptive to fundamentalist arguments which supply a mobilising ideology" (1997:719). In large part, these fundamentalist religious institutions are based on strong local community organizations. They not only fill people's spiritual needs and provide a moral code that protects them from the consequences of globalization, but they also provide adherents with the support of a strong moral community that can replace older structures that have been weakened by rapid social change.

BOX 15.2 SOCIOLOGY IN GLOBAL PERSPECTIVE

Religious Terrorism

Religious terrorism has become a serious threat in postmodern societies. While there is a long history of religious wars among states and many earlier instances of religious terrorism, this type of terrorism has intensified over the past three decades. Following the September 11, 2001, attacks on the United States and subsequent bombings in Madrid, Bali, London, Mumbai, and elsewhere, much of the world's attention is now focused on Islamic terrorists, including members of al-Qaeda. However, all of the world's major religious traditions—as well as many minor religious movements—have been linked with terrorism. Among the questions that interest sociologists are: What are the causes of religious terrorism? How does it differ from other types of terrorist activities?

Violent extremism is not limited to any one faith. In Northern Ireland, the Catholic Irish Republican Army (IRA) exploded hundreds of bombs and killed hundreds of civilians in an attempt to free Northern Ireland from British rule. In 1994, a Jewish right-wing settler, Dr. Baruch Goldstein, shot and killed more than 30 Palestinians who were praying at the Tomb of the Patriarchs in Hebron. On the other side of the Israeli-Palestinian conflict, hundreds of Israelis have been killed by Palestinian suicide bombers. In Canada and the United States, there have been numerous bombings of abortion clinics and several doctors who perform abortions have been killed or wounded—some of these attacks were carried out by Christian ministers, and others were supported by militant Christian groups.

continued

BOX 15.2 SOCIOLOGY IN GLOBAL PERSPECTIVE

Religious Terrorism (Continued)

The largest domestic terrorism incident in the United States was the bombing of the Oklahoma City federal building, which killed 168 people. The bomber, Timothy McVeigh, was inspired by the white supremacist book *The Turner Diaries*. This book condemns the dictatorial secularism that it alleges has been imposed on the United States by a Jewish and liberal conspiracy. McVeigh's religious group, Christian Identity, shared these values and beliefs (Juergensmeyer, 2003).

Militant Sikhs, fighting for an independent homeland, have committed many acts of terrorism. These include the assassination of Indian prime minister Indira Gandhi by her own bodyguards. Sikh extremists were also responsible for Canada's worst act of terrorism, the Air India bombing that killed 329 people (see Chapter 20).

In 1995, members of an apocalyptic Japanese Buddhist sect released sarin nerve gas into the Tokyo subway system—this was the first attempt by religious terrorists to use a weapon of mass destruction. While the attack killed 12 people, thousands more would have died if the terrorists had been able to find a more effective way of vaporizing the sarin gas.

There are differences in the motivation behind these different attacks. The IRA bombing campaign had a strong political component, while members of the Japanese sect had few identifiable political goals. In each of the instances, however, the religious ideology of the terrorists helps to define the enemy and provides a justification for killing innocents. According to Bruce Hoffman, there are important differences between religious and secular terrorism:

> For the religious terrorist, violence first and foremost is a sacramental act or divine duty executed in direct response to some theological demand or imperative. Terrorism assumes a transcendental dimension, and its perpetrators are thereby unconstrained by the political, moral, or practical constraints that seem to affect other terrorists . . . Thus, religion serves as a legitimizing force—conveyed by sacred text or imparted via clerical authorities claiming to speak for the divine. (1995:272)

The acts of secular terrorists may be restrained by their fear of alienating potential supporters. Religious terrorists must please only themselves and their God, and can justify attacks against all "nonbelievers." Finally, purely religious terrorists are not seeking modifications of an existing system, such as a change in the ruling government. Rather, they wish to transform the social order. Unlike groups, such as the IRA, that combined their religious ideology with specific and limited political goals, Islamic fundamentalist leaders have not been not trying to replace governments but to destroy the enemy and transform the world. According to Osama bin Laden:

> It is no secret that warding off the American enemy is the top duty after faith and that nothing should take priority over it . . . jihad has become [obligatory] upon each and every Muslim . . . The time has come when all the Muslims of the world, especially the youth, should unite and soar . . . and continue jihad till these forces are crushed to naught, all the anti-Islamic forces are wiped off the face of this earth and Islam takes over the whole world and all the other false religions. (quoted in Juergensmeyer, 2003:431)

Because negotiating with religious terrorists is almost impossible and because contemporary terrorist organizations have a loose networked form (see Box 6.4), they are very difficult to control. While religious terrorism is a serious threat, we should keep religion in perspective by remembering that the mass genocides of the 20th century, including the Holocaust, Stalin's purges, China's Cultural Revolution, Pol Pot's massacre in Cambodia, and the atrocities in Rwanda, were committed in the name of political ideology, not religion.

Haynes's theory is supported by data from the World Values Survey. Several indicators of religiosity are strongly correlated with a country's level of development (see Figure 15.1). Respondents in agrarian countries (including Nigeria, Tanzania, and Zimbabwe) are twice as likely as those in industrialized, high-income countries to attend religious services at least weekly and to pray daily, and three times as likely to say that religion is "very important" in their lives (Norris and Inglehart, 2004). The major exceptions to this pattern are the United States and Ireland, which are both wealthy and religious countries.

FIGURE 15.1 RELIGIOSITY BY TYPE OF SOCIETY

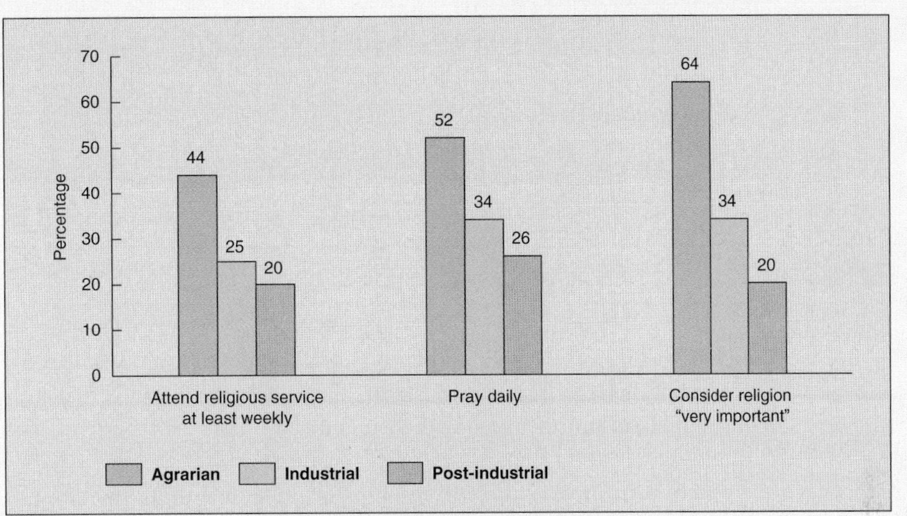

The level of a country's development is strongly related to the religiosity of its citizens.

Source: Pippa Norris and Ronald Inglehart, *Sacred and Secular: Religion and Politics Worldwide*, Cambridge: Cambridge University Press, 2004.

CONCEPT SNAPSHOT

FUNCTIONALIST PERSPECTIVES **Key thinkers:** Emile Durkheim, Max Weber	Durkheim considered religion to be essential to the maintenance of society. Religion performs three important functions: (1) providing meaning and purpose to life; (2) promoting social cohesion; (3) providing social control and support for government. Weber believed that religion could lead to positive change in society. His main example was the way in which he believed the religious teachings of Calvinist Protestantism were directly related to the rise of capitalism.
CONFLICT PERSPECTIVES **Key thinker:** Karl Marx	Conflict theorists believe that the capitalist class uses religious ideology as a tool of domination to mislead the working class about their true interests. According to Marx, religion is the "opiate of the masses" and unites people under a false consciousness that leads them to believe they have common interests with the capitalists.
INTERACTIONIST PERSPECTIVES **Key thinkers:** John Lofland, Rodney Stark	Interactionists look at the role of religion in people's everyday lives. Lofland and Stark studied conversion to a nontraditional religious movement. This conversion was more likely if individuals had certain predisposing background factors; had come to a turning point in their lives; had close personal ties to members of the group; had a lack of ties to people outside the group; and had intensive interaction with group members.
FEMINIST PERSPECTIVES **Key thinker:** Meredith McGuire	For many feminist scholars, even though they may belong to the same religious groups, men and women experience religion in different ways. Religious doctrine and language typically create a social definition of the roles of men and women. Typically, these definitions place women in subordinate roles in the church.
POSTMODERN PERSPECTIVES **Key thinker:** Jeff Haynes	The structural conditions of postmodernism, including the negative consequences of globalization and its perceived threats to the moral order, can destabilize local values and traditions. Instead of leading to secularization, these conditions can lead to a strengthening of faith as some people resist these threats by turning to religion.

TIME TO REVIEW

- Why is ritual important in the practice of religion?
- Describe the forms that religion can take in different societies.
- How do theorists from each of the functionalist, conflict, interactionist, feminist, and postmodern perspectives analyze religion?

LO-3 CHURCHES, SECTS, AND CULTS

Religious groups vary widely in their organizational structure. While some groups are large and bureaucratically organized, others are small, with a relatively informal authority structure. Some require total commitment from their members; others expect members to have only a partial commitment.

To help explain the different types of religious organizations, Ernst Troeltsch (1960/1931) and his teacher, Max Weber (1963/1922), developed a typology that distinguishes between the characteristics of churches and sects (see Table 15.1). A **church** is a large, bureaucratically organized religious body that tends to seek accommodation with the larger society in order to maintain some degree of control over it. Church membership is largely based on birth; children of church members typically are baptized as infants and become lifelong members of the church, though older people can also join if they go through a training process. Leadership is hierarchical, and clergy generally have many years of formal education. Religious services are highly ritualized; they are often led by clergy who wear robes, enter and exit in a formal processional, administer sacraments, and read services from a prayer book or other standardized liturgical format.

church A large, bureaucratically organized religious body that tends to seek accommodation with the larger society in order to maintain some degree of control over it.

By contrast, a **sect** is a relatively small religious group that has broken away from another religious organization to renew what it views as the original version of the faith. Sects offer members a more personal religion and an intimate relationship with a supreme being, who is depicted as taking an active interest in the individual's everyday life. Whereas churches use formalized prayers, often from a prayer book, sects often have informal prayers composed at the time they are given. Whereas churches typically appeal to members of the middle and upper classes, sects seek to meet the needs of people who are low in the stratification system (Stark, 1992).

sect A relatively small religious group that has broken away from another religious organization to renew what it views as the original version of the faith.

TABLE 15.1 CHARACTERISTICS OF CHURCHES AND SECTS

CHARACTERISTIC	CHURCH	SECT
Organization	Large, bureaucratic organization, led by a professional clergy	Small, faithful group, with high degree of lay participation
Membership	Open to all; members usually from middle and upper classes	Closely guarded membership, usually from lower classes
Type of worship	Formal, orderly	Informal, spontaneous
Salvation	Granted by God, as administered by the church	Achieved by moral purity
Attitude toward other institutions and religions	Tolerant	Intolerant

© Pecold/Shutterstock

Christians around the world have been drawn to cathedrals such as Notre-Dame de Paris (built between 1163 and 1257) to worship God and celebrate their religious faith.

© AP Photo/Ahn Young-joon

This mass wedding ceremony of thousands of brides and grooms brought widespread media attention to Rev. Sun Myung Moon and the Unification church, which many people view as a religious cult.

Cults/New Religious Movements

cult A religious group with practices and teachings outside the dominant cultural and religious traditions of a society.

While sects represent attempts to renew old religions, cults represent new religious practices. A **cult** is a religious group with practices and teachings outside the dominant cultural and religious traditions of a society. Even though many of the world's major religions began as cults, the term now has a negative connotation for many people outside the field of sociology, so some sociologists use the term *new religious movement* to refer to these groups (Barrett, 2001). Cult leadership is based on charismatic characteristics of the individual (Stark, 1992). An example is the religious movement started by Rev. Sun Myung Moon, a Korean electrical engineer who believed that God had revealed to him that Judgment Day was rapidly approaching. Out of this movement, the Unification church, or "Moonies," grew and flourished, recruiting new members through their personal attachments to present members (Stark, 1992). Some cult leaders have not fared well. These include Jim Jones, whose ill-fated cult members ended up committing mass suicide in Guyana, and David Koresh, of the also ill-fated Branch Davidians in Waco, Texas.

© Julie Thompson/Alamy

These protesters in Vancouver are drawing attention to the persecution of members of Falun Gong by the Chinese government.

Are all cults short-lived? Over time, most cults disappear. However, others undergo transformation into sects or denominations. Some researchers view cults as a means of reviving religious practice when existing churches do not provide satisfaction to those seeking a spiritual home.

In some countries, new religious movements are harshly repressed. This is because they may challenge state religions or, as in the case of the Falun Gong movement in China, are seen by the country's leadership as a potential political threat.

TRENDS IN RELIGION IN CANADA

Canada's Religious Mosaic

Until the end of the 19th century, Canada's population was made up almost entirely of Protestants and Roman Catholics. The Roman Catholic Church was the dominant religious force during the early settlement of Canada, a situation that continued well into the 19th century. With the arrival of the United Empire Loyalists from the American colonies in the 1780s, the Protestant population in Canada became larger than the French Catholic population. However, this changed as the combined share of the Protestant churches declined from 51 percent in 1951 to 36 percent in 1991 (McVey and Kalbach, 1995). Changes in the population of the major religious groups in Canada are illustrated in Figure 15.2. In 2001(the last year for which statistics are available), Roman Catholics, at 43 percent of the population, were the largest religious group in Canada.

FIGURE 15.2 RELIGIOUS AFFILIATION IN CANADA

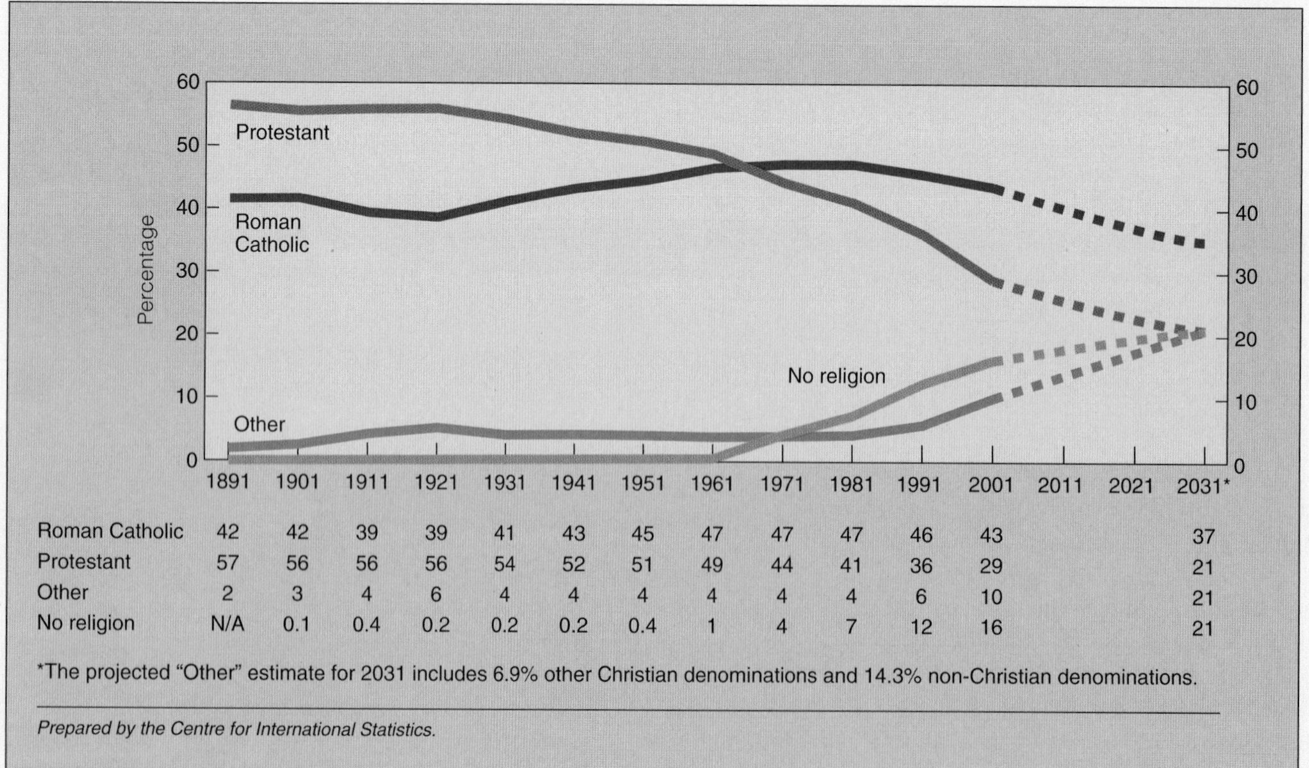

	1891	1901	1911	1921	1931	1941	1951	1961	1971	1981	1991	2001	2011	2021	2031*
Roman Catholic	42	42	39	39	41	43	45	47	47	47	46	43			37
Protestant	57	56	56	56	54	52	51	49	44	41	36	29			21
Other	2	3	4	6	4	4	4	4	4	4	6	10			21
No religion	N/A	0.1	0.4	0.2	0.2	0.2	0.4	1	4	7	12	16			21

*The projected "Other" estimate for 2031 includes 6.9% other Christian denominations and 14.3% non-Christian denominations.

Prepared by the Centre for International Statistics.

Source: Vanier Institute of the Family, 1994. Reprinted by permission. Statistics Canada, 2003j. Malenfant, Lebel, and Martel, 2010.

Other religions than Christianity were practised in Canada prior to European colonization. Aboriginal peoples were excluded from the earliest census collections. Even so, in 1891, almost 2 percent of Canadians reported practising religions other than Christianity. In 2001, more than 6 percent of Canadians were affiliated with "other" religions, including Judaism; Eastern non-Christian religions, such as Islam, Buddhism, Hinduism, and Sikhism; and para-religious groups (see Figure 15.3). As a result of changing immigration patterns, Eastern non-Christian religious populations have grown significantly since the 1960s. Statistics Canada projects that by 2031, the percentage of Muslims in Canada will have increased from 2 percent in 2001 to about 7 percent (Malenfant, Lebel, and Martel, 2010). The percentage of Hindus and Sikhs is much smaller, but is also forecast to double by 2031.

The numbers who fall under the category *no religion* have also increased, going from less than 1 percent in 1951 to 16 percent in 2001 and to a projected 21 percent in 2031. Does this mean that Canadians are rejecting religion? We can answer this question by examining other recent trends in religion in Canada.

Religiosity

Is Canada a religious society? The answer depends on how you look at things. Nationally, attendance at religious services, public confidence in religious leadership, and religious influence have all gradually declined since the late 1940s.

Over the past 60 years, attendance at religious services has declined precipitously (Clark, 1998). A 1946 Gallup poll reported that 67 percent of Canadian adults reported attending religious services during the previous week. By 2001, the General Social Survey (GSS) found that reported attendance at weekly religious services had declined to only 20 percent (Clark, 2003). A generation ago, most Canadians attended religious services; today only a small minority attend regularly.

Different denominations have seen different rates of decline (Clark, 1998). In 1996, 24 percent of Roman Catholics attended weekly services, down from 37 percent attendance in 1986. Nearly one in three Roman Catholics did not attend church at all in 1996, compared with one in

FIGURE 15.3 MAJOR RELIGIOUS DENOMINATIONS, CANADA, 2001

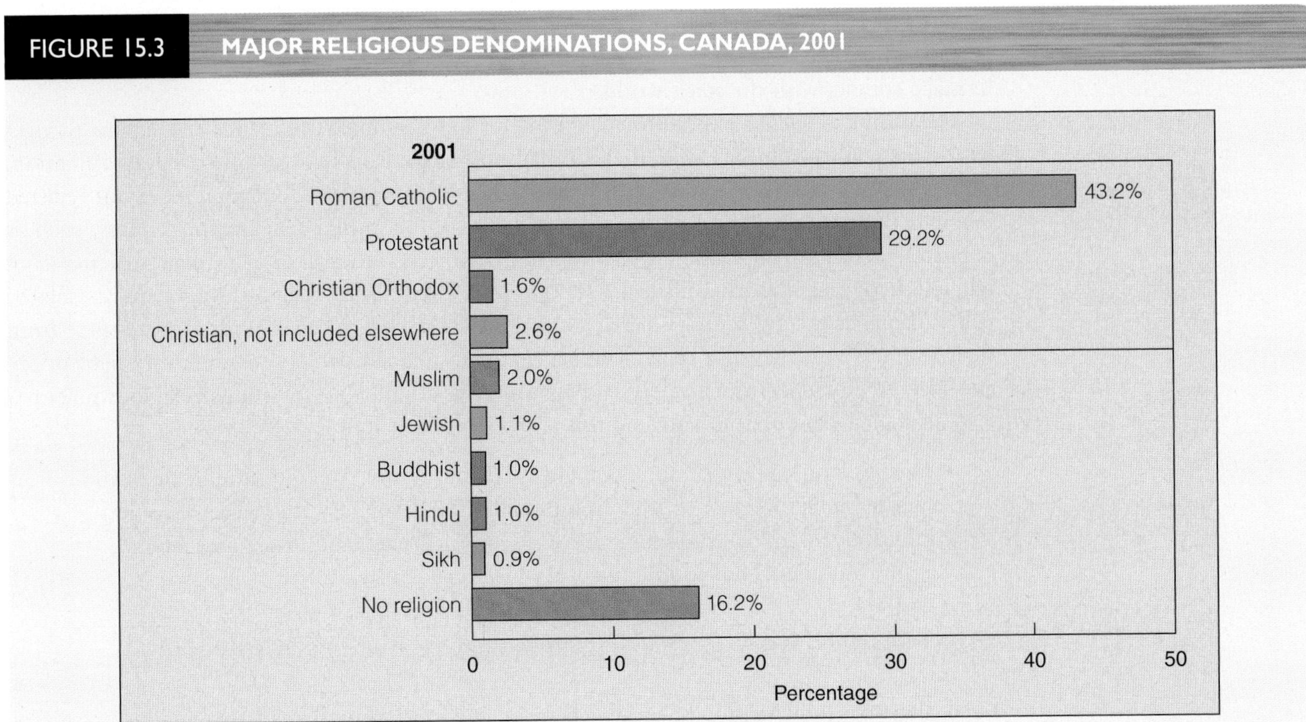

Source: Adapted from Statistics Canada, 2003j.

seven in 1986. While attendance in the mainline Protestant denominations (United, Anglican, Presbyterian, and Lutheran) was very low (14 percent), conservative Protestant denominations (Baptist and Pentecostal) have maintained 50 percent to 60 percent attendance rates. Other religions (including Judaism, Hinduism, Buddhism, and Sikhism) have also seen serious declines in the percentage of people attending services, though some have seen a stabilization or even an increase because of immigration.

The most recent research (Eagle, 2011) shows that the decline in attendance has continued to 2008 but that most of the recent decline is among Catholics. Attendance among Protestants appears to have stabilized.

While attendance rates have declined for all age groups, the drop has been greatest for younger people: 34 percent of those 65 years of age and over regularly attend religious services, compared with only 12 percent of people 15 to 24 years old. This loss of young members does not bode well for the future of Canadian religions, as the vast majority of adults who attend regularly also attended regularly in childhood. This means that as older members die, fewer and fewer people will likely take their places in the pews.

Despite the decline in church attendance, the vast majority of Canadians still report a religious affiliation and affirm that they believe in God. However, both of these measures have also declined in recent years. In 1961, only 1 percent of Canadians reported no religious affiliation; by 2001, this number had increased to 16 percent (Statistics Canada, 2003j). In 1975, 89 percent of Canadians reported that they believed in God, compared with 81 percent in 1995 (Bibby, 1995b). A 2012 survey found that 42 percent of Canadians reported that religion was an important aspect of their lives and that those over 65 were almost twice as likely as those 18 to 24 to report that religion was important (Association for Canadian Studies, 2012).

According to Clark and Schellenberg (2006), although only about one-third of Canadians attended services once or more a month, over half (53 percent) carried out some religious practice, such as praying, on their own. In 2000, Bibby (2001) found that 76 percent of Canadian young people identified with a religious group. Table 15.2 shows some of Bibby's other findings. In addition to their religious beliefs, Canadians show an interest in other aspects of spirituality. The table shows that most Canadians believe that some people have psychic powers; that supernatural and evil forces exist; that there is life after death; and that some people have extrasensory perception. A significant minority believe that astrology has some merit and that it is possible to make contact with the spirit world.

The results of these surveys provide an interesting paradox. Attendance at religious services has dramatically declined despite the fact that most Canadians report some religious affiliation, express a belief in God, and believe in other spiritual aspects of life. People have not rejected religious institutions completely, as most still rely on organized religion for services, such as baptisms, weddings, and funerals (Bibby, 2002). However, they are not regular participants in religious activities, choosing instead to adopt what Bibby calls "religious fragments"—isolated beliefs, isolated practices, and isolated services (1987). They receive spiritual sustenance from their religions, but they also draw from alternatives, such as astrology, extrasensory perception, and New Age practices, such as crystals, that serve as adjuncts to traditional religious practice.

Theologian Tom Harpur sums up this approach to religion:

> There is a huge spiritual quest going on. There's a lot of attempts at quick fixes and spiritual junk food as well. But even the silly fringe is part of it . . . People seem intuitively aware that something is missing in their lives, and there's a reaction against traditional religion. (quoted in MacDonald, 1996:42)

Why Have Canadians Turned Away from the Church?

According to Bibby, people have moved from religious commitment to religious consumption. Religious consumers look at the church as just one of many different options for solving their spiritual or worldly problems. Even those with a high religious commitment may not feel

TABLE 15.2 SPIRITUAL BELIEFS AND INVOLVEMENT OF CANADIANS, 2000

"I BELIEVE . . ."	ADULTS	TEENS
	Percentage Agreeing	
Conventional		
God exists	81%	73%
In life after death	68%	78%
Less Conventional		
In ESP	66%	59%
One can have contact with the spirit world	45%	43%
In astrology	35%	57%
"I . . ."		
Group Involvement		
Am committed to Christianity or another faith	55%	48%
Attend weekly	21%	22%
Am open to possibility of greater involvement	57%	43%
Spirituality		
Have spiritual needs	73%	48%
Find spirituality very important	34%	30%
Pray privately weekly or more often	47%	33%

Source: Bibby, 2001.

church attendance is the best way to express that commitment. As one of Bibby's respondents commented:

> I've been through a great deal in life and my faith is very strong. But I believe that one is closer to God in their own home and garden than a church. I see going to church these days as "keeping up with the Joneses." (1987:83)

A postmodernist would explain that as our culture has become more individualistic, people are less likely to accept the dictates of an organized church. Religion has now been internalized, and rather than depending on the dictates of organized religion, people can make up their own version of spirituality that meets their needs.

It is apparent that organized religion no longer seems relevant to the lives of many Canadians. One of Bibby's subjects illustrates this view: "The major issues of the day seem to me to have little to do with religion and morality; economic and political factors are far more important" (1993:59).

When it has tried to address contemporary issues, the church has often had problems. Several Protestant denominations have had major conflicts over the role of homosexuals in the church. Debates over issues ranging from the tolerance of homosexuality to the ordination of homosexual ministers have led to serious divisions. These moral issues have distracted the churches from other activities. Some churches, notably the United Church, have tried to become more socially relevant by focusing on social justice issues; however, this strategy has not attracted new members (Bibby, 1993) and may have driven older members away.

The alienation of women has contributed to the decline in attendance. As one journalist has written:

> Women—the traditional mainstays of organized religion—in huge numbers abruptly rejected the church's patriarchal exemplar of them as chaste, submissive "angels in the house" with all of the social and moral responsibility for community and family but none of the authority. (Valpy, 2007:A17)

© The United Church of Canada, WonderCafe.ca

What do you think of the use of this bobblehead Jesus to help advertise the United Church?

Many churches have not adapted to the changed role of women. Patriarchal practices can be difficult or impossible to change, as traditional gender roles are part of the core religious ideology of some churches. The quotation from Joanne Barendregt in the chapter opening illustrates the fundamentalist view that a woman's sacred duty is submission to her husband. Some women welcome this role, but this subordination is seen as unacceptable by many others. Failure to address women's concerns will have serious consequences, as women are more likely to participate in church activities than are men and are also instrumental in ensuring that their children go to church.

The image of the church has also suffered from thousands of charges of child sexual abuse by ministers and priests. The abuse was most pervasive in residential settings, such as the church-run schools that were established for Aboriginal children during the first half of the 20th century. More than 125,000 children attended these schools before the system was closed in the 1980s, and by 1999 more than a thousand abuse complaints had been laid against church officials who worked in the schools (Cheney, Matas, and Roberts, 1998). The problem was not limited to the abuse of Aboriginal youth, however; the first major residential school scandal in Canada grew out of offences committed by members of the Christian Brothers order at Newfoundland's Mount Cashel orphanage.

The image of the church was further damaged by the fact that, in many cases, senior church officials knew about the problem, did little or nothing to stop it, and tried to cover it up. These incidents make it more difficult for the churches to speak credibly on moral issues. Some critics have linked abuse within the Roman Catholic Church to its patriarchal structure and its celibate male priesthood and have called into question these fundamental principles of the church.

Finally, we can look at the special case of Quebec. The early development of French and English Canada was strongly influenced by religious principles. In Quebec, most social institutions came under the influence of the Roman Catholic Church. For example, much of the education system was church-run. The Roman Catholic Church was politically powerful and dominated the province's social and moral life.

However, following the Quiet Revolution in the mid-1960s, the church's influence in Quebec dwindled rapidly. Weekly church attendance dropped from a remarkable high of 90 percent in the 1940s (Bibby, 1993) to less than 30 percent by 1990 and it continues to decline (Clark, 2003). As Quebec became a secular society, the church lost its influence in fields such as education and social services. Church policies, such as the prohibitions on birth control, premarital sex, abortion, and divorce and the refusal to ordain women priests, also turned people away. The reduced influence of the church is shown by the fact that the province with the

TIME TO REVIEW

- What are the key differences between churches, sects, and cults?
- How has church attendance in Canada changed over the past 100 years?
- What are the demographic characteristics of those who are most likely to attend church in Canada?
- Describe the spiritual practices that appear to be replacing formal participation in church services.
- What factors account for the decline in church membership and attendance in Canada?

highest proportion of Roman Catholics (Quebec) also has Canada's highest rate of common-law marriages, a practice that is contrary to Roman Catholic teachings.

Bibby (2012) has recently described a polarization of religiosity. About one-quarter of Canadians have little or no interest in the church, about one-third are committed members, and about 40 percent are "marginals" who are not active in the church but could possibly be attracted back. The decisions made by the people in this category will determine the future of organized religion in Canada.

Fundamentalism

As many mainline denominations have been losing membership, some fundamentalist churches have steadily grown. The term *religious fundamentalism* refers to a religious doctrine that is conservative, is typically opposed to modernity, and rejects "worldly pleasures" in favour of otherworldly spirituality. Whereas "old" fundamentalism usually appealed to people from lower-income, rural backgrounds, the "new" fundamentalism appears to appeal to persons from all socioeconomic levels, geographical areas, and occupations.

As you read in the chapter introduction, many fundamentalists feel that, instead of offering children a proper Christian education, the public schools are teaching things that seem to the child to prove that their parents' lifestyle and religion are inferior and perhaps irrational (Carter, 1994:52). The new-right fundamentalists claim that banning the teaching of Christian beliefs in the classroom while teaching things that are contrary to their faith is an infringement on their freedom of religion (Jenkinson, 1979). The selection of textbooks and library materials is an especially controversial issue. Conservative religious groups have protested the use of books that they felt had morally objectionable subject matter or language. For example, a small group of parents in Ontario convinced the Durham District School Board to restrict the classroom reading of the Harry Potter books because they contain references to witchcraft and magic.

We began this chapter with a discussion of the place of religion in our educational system. Numerous recent incidents have raised the issue of what is and is not acceptable in schools. See Box 15.3. To promote a multicultural environment, some Toronto schools have excluded all references to Christian symbols or doctrine from their annual Christmas celebrations. One Toronto high school renamed its Christmas assembly a "holiday assembly" and eliminated all references to Christianity. Another school banned the singing of religious Christmas carols on the grounds that references to Christianity would upset the non-Christian children (more than 30 percent of Toronto's school population). A Toronto school recently became involved in a controversy when it allowed an imam from a nearby mosque to conduct school prayers in the school cafeteria. Girls were required to sit at the back of the room during these prayers, leading several critics to raise the issue of whether the school was allowing gender discrimination (Fatah, 2012).

The overall effect of such incidents has been the increased secularization of the public school system. For example, in 1990, the Ontario Court of Appeal ruled against religious instruction in public elementary schools because it violates an individual's rights to freedom of religion (Fleras and Elliott, 1992). In 1995, Newfoundlanders voted to eliminate church-run schools in favour of a public, nondenominational education system, and in 2006, the Quebec government said it would shut down unlicensed evangelical schools that did not follow the provincial curriculum by teaching evolution (Alphonso and Seguin, 2006).

The changing role of religion in education is but one example of the declining influence of organized religion in Canadian society. Many religious institutions in Canada face a bleak future as church attendance and membership continue to decline. The Roman Catholic Church faces the additional difficulty that the number of priests and nuns has declined dramatically as few young people are attracted to these occupations.

Some see hope for the future in our aging population. They feel that as the baby boomers age, they are likely to search for spiritual meaning and some may turn back to the religions of their youth. However, there is little evidence that the baby boomers are returning and church membership continues to stagnate. Even if the organized church continues to decline, however, spirituality will remain important to many Canadians:

BOX 15.3 POINT/COUNTERPOINT

A Legal Challenge to Religious Holidays in Schools

Like millions of other young Canadians, 14-year-old Aysha Bassuny returned to school in September 1994, but she did so two days later than some. The Ottawa Board of Education delayed the start of her school year for two days so that Jewish students could observe the Jewish New Year–Rosh Hashanah. Bassuny was one of many in Ottawa's Islamic community who were upset that the board refused to close schools for two Muslim holy days. "It's not fair," said Bassuny, a Grade 10 student at suburban Brookfield High School who wears the traditional Islamic head scarf, the hijab. "I have to miss school for my holy days and the Jewish kids don't. You cannot have it for one group and not the other."

In July 1995, the Islamic Schools Federation of Ontario launched a lawsuit against the Ottawa Board of Education, alleging that the rights of Muslims to freedom of conscience and religion under the *Charter of Rights and Freedoms* were undermined by the board's actions. The lawsuit argued that schools with significant numbers of Muslim students should be required to observe two important Islamic holidays. The Islamic Schools Federation sued the Ottawa Board of Education as a test case, hoping to set a precedent for the rest of the country.

The dispute began when the Ottawa board agreed to a request from Ottawa's Jewish community to delay the start of the school year so that Jewish students could observe Rosh Hashanah without missing the first two days of school. This did not mean a permanent change in the school year: Rosh Hashanah coincides with the opening of school only once every 40 years.

On the other side of the issue, the lawyer for the Islamic Schools Federation of Ontario said that the problem was "the recognition of two religions, Christian and Jewish, and the rejection of another, Muslim."

Those involved in the dispute recognized that, if taken to its logical extreme, the rapid growth of Canada's Muslim, Buddhist, Hindu, and Sikh communities could lead to a school year with as many as 15 religious holidays. At the time, one school board member conceded that it was "a tough problem," and one that an increasingly multicultural society would be unable to avoid. Ultimately, the lawsuit was rejected by the Ontario Divisional Court and in July 1997, the Court of Appeal for Ontario refused to hear an appeal. This means that Ontario schools are not required to recognize the holidays of minority religious groups.

Do you think it is fair that Christian holidays are recognized, while the holidays of other religions are not? Should any religious holidays be recognized by the public school system?

Source: Fisher, Luke, "A Holy War Over Holidays." *Maclean's*, August 12, 1994, p. 26.

> [People] know that religion, for all its institutional limitations, holds a vision of life's unity and meaningfulness, and for that reason it will continue to have a place in their narrative. In a very basic sense, religion itself was never the problem, only social forms of religion that stifle the human spirit. The sacred lives on and is real to those who can access it. (Roof, 1993:261)

LO-4 Does Religion Make a Difference?

Research looking at the impact of religion on attitudes and behaviour has shown mixed results. Bibby (1998) concluded that religiosity has little impact on personal characteristics, such as happiness and contentment. While religion may help some people to be happy and content, others find the same level of satisfaction through other means. He also found that people with strong religious beliefs were no different from other Canadians in terms of relationships with other people, compassion, and tolerance of others (Bibby, 1995a). However, a Statistics Canada study found that people who attended church weekly were much more likely to feel satisfied with their lives and much less likely to feel that their lives were stressful than people who did not attend (Clark, 1998).

Storefront missions such as this seek to win religious converts and offer solace to people in low-income, central-city areas.

Religiosity also influences other aspects of behaviour. All religions have ethical codes that govern personal and social behaviour. There is some evidence that religious commitment does influence people's moral conduct. For example, religiosity reduces involvement in delinquent and criminal behaviour (Linden, 2009). This relationship is complex, however. First, it is greatest where there is a strong religious community (Stark, Doyle, and Kent, 1982). Second, it has more impact on behaviour that is not universally condemned by other segments of society than on behaviour that most other social institutions also disapprove of. That means religiosity has more influence on matters such as illegal drug use than it does on theft and assault (Linden and Currie, 1977).

Religiosity is also associated with marital stability. Weekly church attenders place more importance on marriage and children than people who do not attend, although the differences are not large. Church attenders have longer and happier marriages than non-attenders do, and the marriages of church attenders are less than half as likely to break down as the marriages of couples who do not attend (Clark, 1998).

What about the impact of religion on health? In many small-scale societies, the same individual—the healer or *shaman*—was responsible for both physical and spiritual needs. Some people are once more trying to reintegrate medicine and religion. The increasing popularity of alternative medicine has led to an openness to nontraditional approaches, and polls show that many people (including some doctors) believe that religious faith can help cure disease and therefore use prayer as medical therapy (Sloan, Bagiella, and Powell, 1999).

Many researchers have examined the relationship between religion and medical outcomes. In a humorous attempt to test the hypothesis, the eminent British scientist Sir Francis Galton sought to determine whether prayer could increase longevity. He assumed that nobody in England received more prayers for longevity than the British royal family. People sang "God Save the Queen [or King]" and regularly expressed concerns for their rulers in their prayers. Recognizing that the upper-class lifestyle of royalty made them more likely to live longer, Galton knew he had to compare them with other wealthy people. He selected for his comparison group wealthy lawyers, arguing that nobody would pray that lawyers live longer lives. Contrary to his hypothesis, he found that the lawyers lived longer and concluded that prayer had little efficacy in this regard.

Other, more serious studies found that religious people live longer, but failed to account for risk factors. Studies show that priests, monks, and nuns have less illness and live longer than members of the general population. However, the studies have weak validity because they do not control for the lower exposure of those in religious orders to a variety of risk factors. Similarly, studies of Israelis living on secular and religious kibbutzim found that the religious Jews lived longer than those who were nonreligious, but did not control for risk factors, such as smoking, blood cholesterol, and marital status (Sloan, Bagiella, and Powell, 1999).

In their review of research in this area, Sloan and his colleagues (1999) concluded that the evidence of an association between religiosity and health is weak and inconsistent. If it does not affect physical health, however, there is evidence that religion can play a role in comforting the sick. For example, one study found that 40 percent of a group of hospitalized adults reported that their religious faith was the most important factor in their ability to cope with their illness (Johns Hopkins, 1998).

LO-5 RELIGION IN THE FUTURE

What significance will religion have in the future? Religion will continue to be important because it provides answers to basic questions that are important to many people. Moreover, the influence of religion is felt in global politics. In many nations, the rise of *religious nationalism* has led to the blending of strongly held religious and political beliefs. The rise of religious nationalism is especially strong in the Middle East, where Islamic nationalism has continued to spread after the revolutions Egypt, Tunisia, and Libya in 2011. In Canada, the influence of religion will be evident in ongoing political battles over social issues, such as school prayer, abortion, and family issues. On the one hand, religion may unify people; on the other, it may result in tensions and confrontations between individuals and groups. For an examination of religion and new media, see Box 15.4 at **www.nelson.com/sociologyinourtimes6e.**

TIME TO REVIEW

- Discuss the meaning of the term *religious fundamentalism.*
- What impact does religion have on individuals and on their behaviour?
- What is religious nationalism, and what impact is it having around the world?
- What factors have limited the impact of immigration on religious life in Canada?

VISUAL SUMMARY

15

LO-1 Describe what religion is and understand its purpose in society.

Religion, based on some sacred or supernatural realm, is a system of beliefs, symbols, and rituals that guides human behaviour, gives meaning to life, and unites believers into a community.

© Bettmann/Corbis

LO-2 Understand the differences between the functionalist, conflict, interactionist, feminist, and postmodern perspectives on religion.

© Julie Thompson/Alamy

According to functionalists, religion has three important functions: (1) providing meaning and purpose to life, (2) promoting social cohesion and a sense of belonging, and (3) providing social control and support for the government. From a conflict perspective, religion can have negative consequences. The capitalist class uses religion as a tool of domination to mislead workers about their true interests. However, Max Weber believed that religion could be a catalyst for social change. Symbolic interactionists focus on a microlevel analysis of religion, examining the meanings people give to religion and the meanings they attach to religious symbols in their everyday life. Feminist theorists have pointed out that even though they may belong to the same religious groups, men and women experience religion in different ways. Religious doctrine and language create a social definition of the roles of men and women that place women in subordinate roles in some religions. Some postmodern theorists have proposed that the structural conditions of postmodernism, including the negative consequences of globalization and its perceived threats to the moral order, can destabilize local values and traditions. Instead of leading to secularization, these conditions can lead to a strengthening of faith as some people resist these threats by turning to religion.

LO-3 Understand the different types of religious organizations.

Religious organizations can be categorized as churches, sects, and cults.

© Pecold/Shutterstock

KEY TERMS

animism The belief that plants, animals, or other elements of the natural world are endowed with spirits or life forces that have an impact on events in society (p. 424).

church A large, bureaucratically organized religious body that tends to seek accommodation with the larger society in order to maintain some degree of control over it (p. 435).

cult A religious group with practices and teachings outside the dominant cultural and religious traditions of a society (p. 435).

faith Unquestioning belief that does not require proof or scientific evidence (p. 422).

monotheism A belief in a single, supreme being or god who is responsible for significant events, such as the creation of the world (p. 424).

nontheistic religion A religion based on a belief in divine spiritual forces, such as sacred principles of thought and conduct, rather than on a god or gods (p. 424).

polytheism A belief in more than one god (p. 424).

profane A term used to describe the everyday, secular, or "worldly" aspects of life (p. 422).

religion A system of beliefs, symbols, and rituals, based on some sacred or supernatural realm, that guides human behaviour, gives meaning to life, and unites believers into a community (p. 422).

rituals Regularly repeated and carefully prescribed forms of behaviour that symbolize a cherished value or belief (p. 422).

sacred A term used to describe those aspects of life that are extraordinary or supernatural (p. 422).

sect A relatively small religious group that has broken away from another religious organization to renew what it views as the original version of the faith (p. 434).

simple supernaturalism The belief that supernatural forces affect people's lives either positively or negatively (p. 424).

theism A belief in a god or gods (p. 424).

LO-4 Discuss the impact of religion on people's attitudes and behaviour.

John Neubauer/PhotoEdit Inc

Research looking at the impact of religion on attitudes and behaviour has had mixed results. Religiosity reduces involvement in delinquent and criminal behaviour. Religious people have longer and happier marriages than nonreligious people. Religion and prayer appear to have little impact on health, though they play a strong role in comforting the sick.

© The United Church of Canada, WonderCafe.ca

LO-5 Consider the future role of religion in Canada.

Religion in Canada is clearly in decline and the prognosis for the future is not bright. However, Canadians still have a strong interest in spiritual matters and continue to identify with the church. If it is to take advantage of these factors, churches must find new ways to become relevant to the daily lives of Canadians.

APPLICATION QUESTIONS

1. Do you think religion will continue as a major social institution in Canada? What factors lead people to turn away from religion? What factors promote a renewed or continued interest in religion?
2. The church is a place where many people mark the milestones in their lives—births, baptisms, marriages, and deaths are all celebrated in church and recorded in church documents. Do you think that social media sites such as Facebook are now replacing churches as the preferred site for recording this information?
3. How does religion contribute to social stability? How is religion a force for social change?
4. How are Canada's religious institutions addressing important social issues such as rising social inequality and women's role in society?
5. What do you think religious leaders could do to attract more young people to their faiths?

KEY FIGURES

© Pictorial Press Ltd./Alamy

Émile Durkheim (1858–1917) Many of the early sociological theorists tried to understand the role of religion in social life. Durkheim's work focused on the role religion plays in contributing to social stability. His book *The Elementary Forms of the Religious Life* is one of the classic works in this field.

© Mondadori Portfolio/Getty Images

Max Weber (1864–1920) Weber was another of the early sociologists who studied religion. Weber is best known for his work on the role of Calvinist Protestantism in the development of capitalism. For Weber, the new way of thinking that was part of Protestantism set the stage for the development of the rational, bureaucratized, capitalist economic system.

Courtesy of Rodney Stark

Rodney Stark (b. 1934) Rodney Stark is one of the most prolific sociology of religion scholars. His work has looked at a wide range of religious issues, including examining how religions attract converts, studying the degree to which a rational choice model applies to religion, and debating whether societies have become more secular over time.

Courtesy of Reginald Bibby

Reginald Bibby (b. 1943) Sociologist Reginald Bibby holds the Board of Governors Research Chair at the University of Lethbridge. Much of his work has been based on a series of national surveys he has conducted looking at trends in religious attitudes and behaviour. He has been particularly active in the debate over whether the decline in participation in formal religious activity has ended.

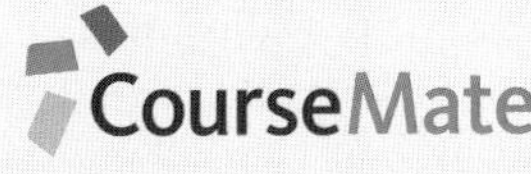

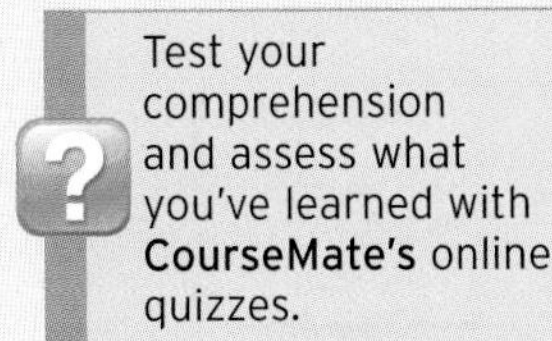
Test your comprehension and assess what you've learned with **CourseMate's** online quizzes.

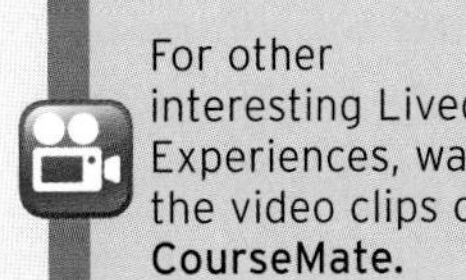
For other interesting Lived Experiences, watch the video clips on **CourseMate.**

Practise what you've learned with flashcards containing key terms and definitions on **CourseMate.**

CHAPTER

16 Health, Healthcare, and Disability

CP/AP/Eraldo Peres

RAE LEWIS-THORNTON DESCRIBES HER EXPERIENCE WITH HIV/AIDS IN THE FOLLOWING WAY:

> *The day I found out [I was HIV-positive] I was so calm . . . I walked out of the . . . Red Cross office and into the . . . sunshine, flagged a cab and went back to work. I worked late that night . . . I was 24. I'd just been given a death sentence . . . I'm young . . . Well educated. Professional. Attractive. Smart. I've been drug and alcohol-free all my life. I'm a Christian. I've never been promiscuous. Never had a one-night stand. And I am dying of AIDS.*
>
> *I've been living with the disease for nine years, and people still tell me that I am too pretty and intelligent to have AIDS. But I do. I discovered I was HIV-positive when I tried to give blood at the office. I have no idea who infected me or when it happened. Still, there is one thing I am absolutely certain of; I am dying now because I had one sexual partner too many. And I'm here to tell you one is all it takes.* (Lewis-Thornton, 1994:63)

AIDS has taken a huge toll on individuals, families, cities, and nations. The disease known as AIDS (acquired immune deficiency syndrome) is caused by HIV, the human immunodeficiency virus, which gradually destroys the immune system by attacking the white blood cells, making the person with HIV more vulnerable to other types of illnesses. The United Nations estimated that 34 million people were infected with HIV/AIDS and 1.8 million people died of AIDS in 2010 (UNAIDS, 2011). In Canada, 65,000 people were living with HIV in 2008 (Public Health Agency of Canada, 2010). Map 16.1 on page 450 outlines the global distribution of the virus.

Because of a massive global effort, progress has been made in the fight against AIDS. Because of antiretroviral therapy, the number of AIDS deaths has declined from 2.2 million in 2005 to 1.8 million in 2010—and the number of new infections declined from 3 million in 2001 to 2.7 million in 2010 (UNAIDS, 2008).

HIV/AIDS has nonetheless had a devastating impact in sub-Saharan Africa, which has 68 percent of all AIDS cases and half of AIDS deaths (UNAIDS, 2011). Many of the new infections in Africa are among people aged 15 to 24, and many newborns are infected by their mothers—the disease is thereby destroying much of Africa's future. The average life expectancy in some countries there has dropped by as much as 17 years, and the cost of providing even minimal treatment for the disease is taking away many of the hard-won economic gains of some countries.

The problem of AIDS illustrates how sociology can be applied to what, at first glance, appears to be a purely medical matter:

> *AIDS demonstrates that disease not only affects health, but one's definition of self, relations with others, and behaviours. As well, AIDS has had a significant impact on social institutions. The healthcare system has been most directly affected, requiring assessments of the adequacy of research, treatment modalities, and health care facilities. Legislators have wrestled with issues of privacy and human rights protections for people with AIDS. AIDS has resulted in social and sexual mores and lifestyles being reassessed.* (Grant, 1993:395)

This chapter will explore the dynamics of health and healthcare. In the process, we will periodically focus on HIV/AIDS and its impact on society. While we will use HIV/AIDS as an example throughout this chapter, you should be aware that, globally, several other causes of death are more common. The leading cause of death is heart disease (12.2 percent), followed by cerebrovascular disease (9.7 percent), lower respiratory infections (7.0 percent), chronic obstructive pulmonary disease (5.1 percent), diarrheal diseases (3.6 percent), and HIV/AIDS (3.5 percent) (World Health Organization, 2009). Before reading on, test your knowledge about HIV/AIDS by taking the quiz in Box 16.1 on page 450.

Critical Thinking Questions

1. What is the role of alternative therapies such as naturopathy and acupuncture in healthcare? Have you or your friends or relatives made use of alternative treatments?
2. Lifelong health is partly determined by habits in diet, exercise, smoking, and drug and alcohol use developed by young people. Are you aware of any efforts made by governments and medical practitioners to encourage you to develop healthy habits? How could this be done more effectively?
3. Look at the global distribution of HIV-positive people in Map 16.1. What does this map tell you about the social and cultural factors involved in this disease?

CHAPTER FOCUS QUESTION What effect has HIV/AIDS had on the health of the global population?

LEARNING OBJECTIVES

AFTER READING THIS CHAPTER, YOU SHOULD BE ABLE TO

LO-1 Understand the ways in which sociological factors influence health and disease.

LO-2 Compare how functionalist, symbolic interactionist, conflict, feminist, and postmodern theories differ in their analyses of health.

LO-3 Understand how social inequality affects health and healthcare.

LO-4 Identify the consequences of disability.

LO-5 Discuss the state of the healthcare system in Canada today and explain how it could be improved.

MAP 16.1 NUMBER OF HIV-POSITIVE PEOPLE AROUND THE WORLD IN 2010

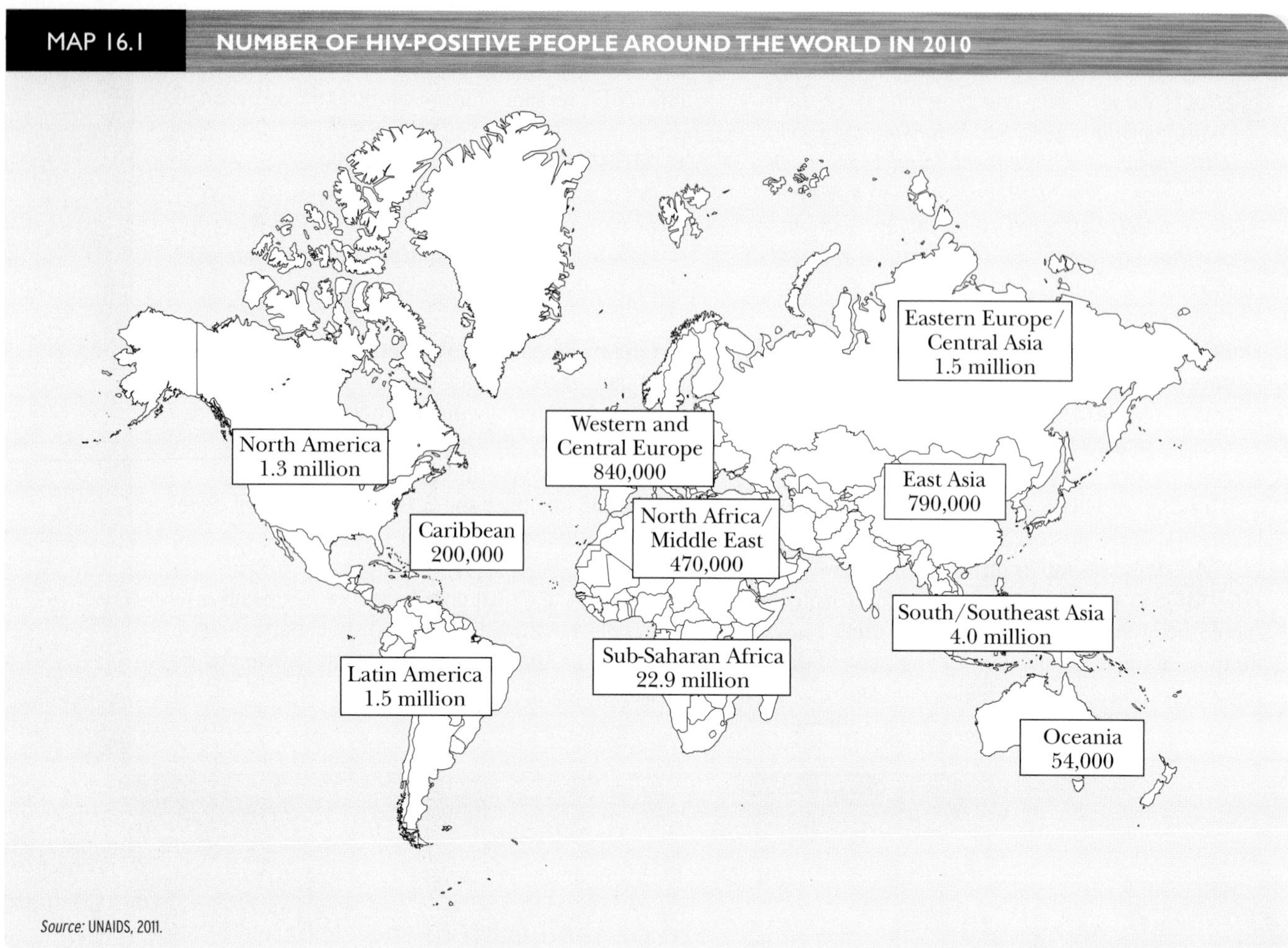

Source: UNAIDS, 2011.

BOX 16.1 SOCIOLOGY AND EVERYDAY LIFE

How Much Do You Know About HIV/AIDS?

True	False	
T	F	1. Worldwide, most people with AIDS are gay men.
T	F	2. In Canada, you can be sent to prison if you knowingly transmit HIV.
T	F	3. HIV is spreading rapidly among women in some nations.
T	F	4. Young people are particularly vulnerable to HIV.
T	F	5. One of the major concerns of AIDS activists is reducing the stigmatization of HIV/AIDS victims.

For answers to the quiz about HIV/AIDS, go to **www.nelson.com/sociologyinourtimes6e.**

HEALTH AND MEDICINE LO-1

What does the concept of health mean to you? If you were asked if you are healthy, how would you respond? Although the definition of health may appear obvious, consensus on it remains elusive. Health was once considered to be simply the absence of disease. The World Health Organization (WHO) provides a more inclusive definition of **health**, calling it the state of complete physical, mental, and social well-being. This definition of health has several dimensions; physical, social, and psychological factors are all important. Health does not depend solely on the absence of disease or sickness. Health is socially defined and therefore varies over time and between cultures (Farley, 1992). For example, in our society, obesity is viewed as unhealthy, while in other times and places it has signalled prosperity and good health.

Medicine is an institutionalized system for the scientific diagnosis, treatment, and prevention of illness. Medicine is a vital part of the broader concept of **healthcare**, which is any activity intended to improve health. In North America, medicine is typically used when there is a failure in health. When people get sick, they seek medical attention to make them healthy again. The field of **preventive medicine**—medicine that emphasizes a healthy lifestyle in order to prevent poor health before it occurs, is receiving increasing attention (Appelbaum and Chambliss, 1997).

health The state of complete physical, mental, and social well-being.

medicine An institutionalized system for the scientific diagnosis, treatment, and prevention of illness.

healthcare Any activity intended to improve health.

preventive medicine Medicine that emphasizes a healthy lifestyle in order to prevent poor health before it occurs.

SOCIOLOGICAL PERSPECTIVES ON HEALTH AND MEDICINE LO-2

Functionalist Perspectives on Health: The Sick Role

For functionalists, people are normally healthy and contribute to their society. Talcott Parsons (1951) viewed illness as dysfunctional both for the individual who is sick and for the larger society. Sick people may be unable to fulfill their social roles, such as parenting or working in the paid labour force. Thus illness can cause the social system to malfunction. Societies must therefore establish definitions of who is legitimately sick. They also expect that those who are sick will get well so that they can once again contribute to the healthy functioning of the social system. According to Parsons, all societies have a **sick role**—patterns of behaviour defined as appropriate for people who are sick. The characteristics of the sick role are:

1. The sick person is temporarily exempt from normal social responsibilities. When you are sick, you are not expected to go to work or school.
2. The sick person is not responsible for his or her condition, so individuals should not be blamed or punished.
3. The sick person must want to get well. The person who does not do everything possible to return to a healthy state is no longer a legitimately sick person and may be considered a hypochondriac or a malingerer.
4. The sick person should seek competent help and cooperate with healthcare practitioners to hasten his or her recovery.
5. Physicians are the "gatekeepers" who maintain society's control over people who enter the sick role.

sick role Patterns of behaviour defined as appropriate for people who are sick.

Italian School/Getty Images

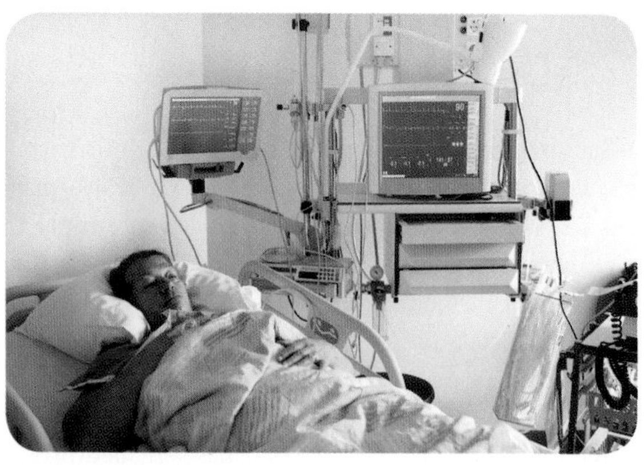
ariadna de raadt/Shutterstock

The treatment of the sick, and indeed the way in which we conceive of "the sick," depends upon time and place. Contrast the illustration of the medieval patient surrounded by family and various healers with the modern patient, who is constantly monitored by technology.

Critics of this view of health and illness argue that it places too much responsibility for illness upon the sick people, neglecting the fact that the actions of other people may be the cause of someone's illness. For example, a child may be born with fetal alcohol syndrome because the mother consumed alcohol while pregnant. Individuals living in poverty may become sick because of inadequate food and shelter. Also, contrary to the functionalist view, individuals may be blamed for their illness, as people who contract HIV or lung cancer often are.

Conflict Theories: Inequalities in Health and Healthcare

The conflict approach emphasizes the political, economic, and social forces that affect health and the healthcare system and the inequities that result from these forces. Among the issues of concern for conflict theorists are the ability of all citizens to obtain healthcare; the impact of race, class, and gender on health and healthcare; the relative power of doctors compared with other health workers; and the dominance of the medical model of healthcare.

We will consider several of these issues later in this chapter because they are important enough to consider in depth. For now, the role of conflict in the health field is sufficiently illustrated in the debate over the allocation of money for research and treatment for different diseases. Advocates for different diseases compete for funds, as money spent doing research on cancer cannot be spent on heart disease. There is also conflict among those who take different approaches to research and treatment of a particular disease. Should funds be spent on treatment or prevention? Should nontraditional treatment methods be studied, or is the medical model the only legitimate way of responding to disease?

Groups representing victims of particular diseases have lobbied governments to give their problem more funding. Thus the priority given to research, prevention, and medical care for particular types of diseases may reflect the power of lobby groups as well as the seriousness of the problem. AIDS activists have been particularly successful in having their concerns reflected in policy. Breast cancer advocates have also been highly successful, though some of their funding methods have been controversial (see Box 16.2).

BOX 16.2 **POINT/COUNTERPOINT**

Pink Ribbons, Inc.: The Corporatization of Medical Charities

Medical charities compete for the millions of dollars Canadians donate each year. One of the most successful campaigns has been run by the breast cancer movement. Most of us know someone who has walked, run, or paddled a dragon boat to raise funds for breast cancer, and we have all seen the pink ribbon used in campaigns run by the Canadian Breast Cancer Foundation (Kedrowski, 2010).

The breast cancer movement has been very successful in breaking down the negative stereotypes and shame that used to be attached to breast cancer. They have also provided a way for family and friends to show their support for cancer victims—most of the largest breast cancer charities were founded by relatives of women who died of the disease. Thousands of women have found friendship and support through the breast cancer movement and have also received enormous satisfaction from helping other breast cancer victims.

Despite this success, the movement has its critics. In 2012, Canada's National Film Board produced the documentary *Pink Ribbons, Inc.* based on a book by Samantha King from Queen's University. According to King, during the early years of the breast cancer movement in the 1990s, it was focused on broader women's health issues as well as on breast cancer. Now the emphasis has changed to "the individual breast cancer patient and her participation in uplifting and profit-generating activities to fund high-stakes medical research to the virtual exclusion of other considerations" (2006:113).

King is particularly critical of the way in which the breast cancer movement has partnered with corporations. Many of these corporations use this sponsorship as a marketing tool. Rather than using philanthropy as a way to give something back to society, some corporations use it to increase profits. Many corporations use cause-related marketing to attract customers. This means that corporations tie themselves to a specific cause in order to "build the reputation of a brand, increase profit, develop employee loyalty to the company, and add to their reputation as good corporate citizens" (King, 2006:9). Many of these sponsorships last for years, so the corporate brand becomes strongly linked with the charity. Some corporations choose to provide support by donating a portion of the money received for each product sold. However, in some cases the amount of money has been very small compared to the cost of the product ($1 for each $200 Eureka vacuum cleaner sold), and in others the product was inappropriate (pink Smith and Wesson handguns and pink shotgun ammunition in the U.S.).

Some women with life-threatening breast cancer have complained about the upbeat message that everyone can beat cancer if they have the proper attitude and the will to beat the disease. They argue that cancer is not feminine and normal, as many of the campaigns imply, but a terrible disease that kills 5100 Canadian women each year (Canadian Cancer Society, 2011), so not everyone does beat it. Other critics believe that the increase in breast cancer rates over the past few decades is caused by environmental factors such as pollution and the use of carcinogenic chemicals in products including cosmetics. If cosmetic companies such as Avon and Revlon are important sponsors, projects that ask questions about these environmental issues will not be funded.

The breast cancer movement has made some changes in response to these criticisms. Recently, the Susan G. Komen Foundation, the largest breast cancer organization in the U.S., has sponsored a major study on environmental factors and may be moving toward a more preventive approach.

This debate leaves many questions for you to consider. Should we rely on mainstream medical science to find a cure for cancer, or should we look more broadly at environmental and social factors? What role do you think corporations should play in funding health-related charities? Should corporations use health-funding campaigns to market their products? Do corporate donors restrict the questions that foundation-funded researchers are allowed to ask? Should people who wish to fight against disease focus on specific campaigns against problems such as heart disease or breast cancer or work more broadly for better healthcare policy?

Feminist Perspectives on Health and Illness

Feminist scholars have studied many different aspects of health and healthcare. One of the first problems they identified was that most medical research was centred on males and ignored diseases that primarily affected females. Other feminist researchers have studied the discrimination against women working in a healthcare system that has traditionally been dominated by male doctors. Women were relegated to subservient roles and have lacked access to leadership roles within the system. Some of the most important work done by feminist scholars has looked at the ways in which medicalization has affected women.

medicalization The process whereby an object or a condition becomes defined by society as a physical or psychological illness.

THE MEDICALIZATION OF WOMEN'S LIVES **Medicalization** refers to the process whereby an object or a condition becomes defined by society as a physical or psychological illness. Medicalization has been a focus of feminist researchers because women's health issues, including those pertaining to childbirth, menopause, PMS, and contraception, have been particularly susceptible to medicalization and this has not necessarily served the interests of women. Historically, women's health needs, including pregnancy and childbirth, were looked after by other women in their communities (Findlay and Miller, 2002). The era of women looking after women ended when the male profession of medicine successfully challenged midwives and other traditional health practitioners and claimed exclusive jurisdiction over conditions such as childbirth and menopause, which were redefined as medical problems. Medical doctors won this struggle despite the fact that traditional practices often had more favourable outcomes than those of the new profession of medicine. Healing became "men's work." While this development helped to raise the status of the medical profession, it reduced women's control over their own bodies. Medicalization had a profound effect on the practices of childbirth, child rearing, and mothering.

Feminist researchers have also questioned the role of medicine in shaping the ways in which women view their physical appearance: "Medical rhetoric itself acts to exacerbate the already powerful cultural demands on women to overemphasize their bodily appearance" (Findlay and Miller, 2002:197).

A paper by the American Society for Plastic and Reconstructive Surgery offers a rather extreme example of this medical rhetoric. This society, the major professional organization representing plastic surgeons, wanted the U.S. government to loosen its restrictions on the use of breast implants. The society based its case on the view that having small breasts constituted a disease. It alleged that this disease (called *micromastia*) resulted in "feelings of inadequacy, lack of self-confidence, distortion of body image, and a total lack of well-being due to a lack of self-perceived femininity" (cited in Weitz, 1996:123). Of course, this "disease" could be cured if the victims received expensive, potentially dangerous breast implants. It is not difficult to imagine the harm that the plastic surgeons' lobbying effort encouraging women to think of their biologically normal bodies as "diseased" might have on some women's self-images. For example, reports of a Penticton, B.C., contest in which 36 women competed for a chance to win breast implants said that many of the losers felt they had "lost a chance at gaining self-confidence" (Carmichael, 2005). The fact that breast size is still a measure of these young women's sense of self-worth, and that many other aspects of physical appearance have come under medical control, is a clear indication of the degree to which women's appearance has become medicalized.

Findlay and Miller feel that the medicalization of women's lives individualizes and depoliticizes their problems. Medicalization also forces women to conform to traditional social norms and "limits women's options—in behaviour, in appearance, and in relationships" (2002:201). There have been incremental changes that may reduce some of the negative effects of medicalization while retaining the benefits of the modern medical system. Women have made headway in reestablishing midwifery and natural childbirth methods that return some of the control over the birthing process to the mother. They have also forced the medical profession to share more information and to empower clients in other ways.

Symbolic Interactionist Theories: The Social Construction of Illness

Interactionists try to understand the meanings and causes that we attribute to particular events. They focus on how the meaning that social actors give their illness or disease affects their self-concept and their relationships with others. The interactionist approach is illustrated by society's response to AIDS.

We often try to explain disease by blaming it on those who are ill. This practice reduces the uncertainty of those of us who fear the disease. Nonsmokers who learn that a cancer victim had a two-pack-a-day smoking habit feel comforted that the guilty have been punished and that the same fate is unlikely to befall them. Because of the association of their disease with promiscuous homosexuality and intravenous drug use, victims of AIDS have particularly suffered from blame. How is a person's self-concept affected when he or she is diagnosed with AIDS? How does this diagnosis affect how the person relates with others in his or her social world?

In the case of AIDS, the social definition of the illness can have as profound an impact on the AIDS patient as the medical symptoms. AIDS is an example of illness as stigma (Giddens, 1996). A *stigma* is any physical or social attribute or sign that so devalues a person's social identity that it disqualifies that person from social acceptance. While other illnesses may provoke sympathy or compassion, an illness such as AIDS is perceived by some people as dishonourable or shameful, and sufferers are rejected by the healthy population. Children with AIDS have been driven from their schools, homes of people with AIDS have been burned, employees have been fired, and medical professionals have refused treatment to AIDS patients. These events have happened despite the fact that AIDS cannot be transmitted by casual everyday contact. However, the social definition of an illness is not always based on medical fact. The incidents of hostility and discrimination directed at individuals with AIDS have a profound impact on their self-concept, social relationships, and ability to cope with the illness.

THE SOCIAL DEFINITION OF HEALTH AND ILLNESS: THE PROCESS OF MEDICALIZATION Feminist scholars are not the only ones who have studied medicalization. Interactionists have also focused on the subjective component in the way illness is defined. This subjective component is important when we look at conditions that are more ambiguous than cancer or a broken bone. For example, a child who has difficulty learning may be diagnosed as having attention deficit hyperactivity disorder (ADHD), a man who occasionally behaves strangely may be called mentally ill, and a woman experiencing menopause may be defined as having a hormonal deficiency disease. Alternatively, we could view these conditions as part of the range of normal human behaviour. The child might be seen as a student who needs extra support, the man as a bit eccentric, and the woman as a person going through the normal aging process. The way we view these individuals will depend on our cultural perspectives, which can change over time.

CP PHOTO/Nathan Denette

This AIDS memorial in Toronto is a striking reminder that AIDS has taken a toll on individuals, families, cities, and nations. In some countries, AIDS is a significant cause of mortality.

Conrad and Schneider (1992) found that medicalization is typically the result of a lengthy promotional campaign conducted by interest groups, often culminating in legislative or other official changes that institutionalize a medical treatment for the new "disease." The interest groups may include scientists acting on the results of their research, those who have the disease and may be seeking either a cure or a socially acceptable excuse for their behaviour, and members of the medical industry interested in increasing their profits.

Conrad and Schneider (1980) also emphasize that many behaviours that were at one time defined as "badness" have been redefined as "sicknesses" or "illnesses." Until the medical condition "attention deficit hyperactivity disorder" (ADHD) was established, children who had difficulty sitting still and concentrating or were impulsive and full of energy were labelled "active" or "energetic"—or called "problem children" (Conrad, 1975). In the early 1970s, the medical profession began to treat such children as deviant. The "discovery" of ADHD coincided with the development of Ritalin, a drug that suppresses hyperactive behaviours, and medication became the accepted treatment for this condition. For schools, the social construction of this illness results in fewer disruptive students and more manageable classrooms—the illness also creates a huge new patient population for doctors and a profitable new market for the pharmaceutical industry. Ritalin can help children whose problem behaviour is organically based by enabling them to concentrate and function better in the classroom. However, for children whose disruptive behaviour is a reflection of their acting "like children" rather than symptomatic of ADHD, it results in unnecessary medication.

In 2012, a controversy emerged over the American Psychiatric Association's attempt to classify grief after the death of a loved one as a mental illness. The eminent British medical journal *The Lancet* opposed this medicalization:

> Medicalizing grief, so that treatment is legitimized routinely with antidepressants . . . is not only dangerously simplistic, but also flawed . . . Grief is not an illness; it is more usefully thought of as part of being human and a normal response to death of a loved one . . . For those who are grieving, doctors would do better to offer time, compassion, remembrance, and empathy, than pills. (2012:589)

Behaviours can also be *demedicalized.* For many years, homosexuality was defined as a mental illness and gays and lesbians were urged to seek psychiatric treatment. Gay activists fought for years to convince the American Psychiatric Association to remove homosexuality from the association's psychiatric diagnostic manual. Women's groups have been trying to demedicalize childbirth and menopause, and to redefine them as natural processes rather than as illnesses.

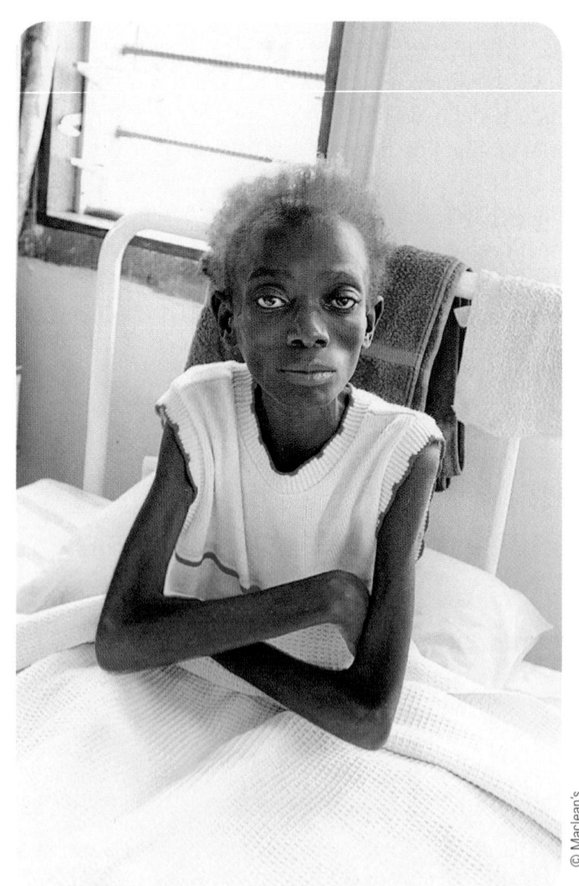

AIDS is a severe burden on the healthcare systems of poor countries. Sixteen-year-old Lucy Bwanali died in a hospice far from her home in northern Zambia because the palliative care system cannot meet the needs of the huge numbers of people who are dying of the disease.

Postmodern Perspectives on Health: The Crossroads of Biology and Culture

David Morris has proposed a postmodern perspective on health that understands disease and illness "whatever [their] particular causes, as created in the convergences between biology and culture" (1998:76). While most of us are aware of the biological dimensions of disease and illness, culture is a factor in health in many ways. Human activities, such as coal mining and the pollution caused by the burning of fossil fuels, have health implications for workers and for the general population. Culture also affects how we experience illness. The experience of having cancer—part of which involves the "sick role" described by

Parsons—is very different for someone in a poor village in Uganda than it is for someone in a Canadian city. While the biological factors may be identical, the understanding of the illness, the treatment available, the suffering experienced by the patient, and the likelihood of survival differ greatly between the two cultural contexts. According to Morris, another characteristic of illness, viewed through a postmodern lens, is an ambiguity about the nature of some disorders. Patients and doctors have contested the existence of ailments such as chronic fatigue syndrome, post-traumatic stress disorder, and even some types of addictions. Our understanding of, and experience with, health and illness is socially constructed—it is not simply a matter of biology.

Postmodern culture has a fixation on health. Health-related products are heavily advertised, new developments in health research are widely reported in the media, and healthcare is an important political issue. While 16th-century explorers sailed the world searching for the Fountain of Youth, people in postmodern societies search for immortality through medical research, plastic surgery, fitness programs, and miracle cures. In this search for perfection, "our culture has declared war on biology" (Morris, 1998:2). Alexander Segall and Christopher Fries (2011) have noted that the way people look after their bodies has become a measure of their self-worth.

One aspect of this war on biology is the belief in the perfectibility of the body. People now have "the option of transforming bodies into a facsimile of their own ideal vision" (Morris, 1998:138). The desire for bodily perfection is manifested in many ways, including cosmetic surgery, legal and illegal performance-enhancing drugs used by athletes, the very different body types attained by competitive bodybuilders and by anorexics, and the growing occupation of personal trainer. We can alter our bodies for aesthetic purposes through devices such as breast implants or make them function more effectively by replacing defective body parts with artificial hips, knees, and heart valves.

While these measures may change the look of the body, the search for perfection may also be harmful. The premature deaths caused by anorexia and steroid use, and the psychological consequences of realizing that no matter what one does, perfection is not attainable, show the futility of pursuing a vision of bodily perfection. Also, this utopian vision is ultimately contradicted by the biology of aging and the inevitability of death. When old age is seen as just another stage in an active life rather than as a time to prepare for the end, physical decline is viewed as an embarrassment and there is often a denial of death.

Even when death is imminent, postmodern patients are trapped between two conflicting realities. The first is the ability of biomedicine to keep failing bodies alive almost indefinitely; the second is the public pressure in many cultures to allow doctor-assisted suicide to alleviate suffering and provide a dignified death at a time of the patient's choosing. Doctors, patients, and policymakers find it difficult to resolve this impasse.

While Morris feels that modernist Western biomedicine is being challenged by the postmodern emphasis on culture, the future of our culture's understanding of health and illness is not yet clear:

> It is an untold, unnoticed story in which the cultural fantasy of living forever—or at least pushing back death through an unending series of medical purchases—creates sickly lives obsessed with heartburn, bowels, megavitamins, and miracle cures. This new postmodern narrative, in short, represents for us the confusing historical moment we are living through when the biomedical model has begun to reveal its inherent limitations but when a biocultural model . . . has not yet proven its power to constitute a satisfying and coherent replacement. (1998:278)

CP/Edmonton Journal/Bruce Edwards

Alzheimer's disease is a tragedy for the afflicted individuals and for their families. As our population ages, such debilitating conditions as Alzheimer's will also increasingly place a burden on our healthcare system and on the taxpayers who fund it.

TIME TO REVIEW

- How do functionalists define the sick role? What are some of the criticisms of this view of health and illness?
- What are some of the questions conflict theorists ask about health and healthcare?
- Describe how the process of medicalization has affected women's lives.
- What do interactionists mean when they say that illness is socially constructed? Is this a complete explanation of illness?
- How do people's ideas of the perfectibility of the body affect the way they think about health and healthcare?

CONCEPT SNAPSHOT

FUNCTIONALIST PERSPECTIVES **Key thinker:** Talcott Parsons	Illness is dysfunctional both for the individual who is sick and for the larger society. All societies have a sick role—patterns of behaviour defined as appropriate for people who are sick.
CONFLICT PERSPECTIVES	Among the issues for conflict theorists are the ability of all citizens to obtain healthcare; the impact of race, class, and gender on healthcare; the relative power of doctors and the medical model in the healthcare system; and the role of profit in the healthcare system.
INTERACTIONIST PERSPECTIVES **Key thinkers:** Peter Conrad and Joseph Schneider	Interactionists examine how the meaning that people give their illness or disease affects their self-concept and their relationships with others and at how the social definition of disease affects those who are ill. A related subjective component of illness is medicalization—the process whereby an object or a condition becomes defined by society as a physical or psychological illness.
FEMINIST PERSPECTIVES **Key thinkers:** Deborah Findlay and Leslie Miller	Feminist scholars have been critical of the male-centred focus of medical research and of discrimination against women working in the healthcare system. They have also studied the way that medicalization blames women for their physical condition and forces women to conform to traditional role expectations, limiting their freedom of behaviour, appearance, and relationships.
POSTMODERN PERSPECTIVES **Key thinker:** David Morris	Some postmodern theorists who study illness and disease focus on the interaction between biology and culture. Culture is a factor in health in many ways—human activities contribute to disease and culture affects how we experience illness. Our culture also emphasizes the perfectability of the body, and many people seek to alter their bodies through surgery, exercise and drugs.

LO-3 SOCIAL FACTORS IN HEALTH: AGE, SEX, AND SOCIAL CLASS

We often think of health in only physical terms. However, the health of any group is a product of the interaction of a wide range of physiological, psychological, spiritual, historical, sociological, cultural, economic, and environmental factors (Waldram, Herring, and Young, 1995). In this section, we will see how these factors affect the health of people of different ages, genders, and classes in Canada.

A basic premise of conflict theory is that groups compete with one another for access to scarce resources. Conflict theorists would predict that, because of this competition, the quality of health and healthcare will vary by age, sex, and class. Do these differences exist?

Age

Rates of illness and death are highest among the old and the very young. Mortality rates drop shortly after birth and begin to rise significantly during the middle years. After age 65, rates of chronic illness and mortality increase rapidly. This has obvious implications for individuals and their families but also has an impact on society.

Canada is an aging society. About 12 percent of the population is 65 or over; by 2036, this will double to 25 percent. Because healthcare costs are high for some older people, these costs will rise as the baby boomers age. Between 1998 and 2008, however, healthcare spending increased by an average of 7.4 percent each year and population aging only accounted for 0.8 percent of this increase (Canadian Institute for Health Information, 2011a), so we should not overestimate the impact of aging on these costs (see Chapter 18, "Aging").

BOX 16.3 **POINT/COUNTERPOINT**

AIDS and Public Health

In 2009, a Hamilton jury found Johnson Aziga guilty of two counts of first-degree murder and 10 counts of aggravated sexual assault. Aziga, a former research analyst for the Ontario government, was the first person convicted of murder in Canada for knowingly infecting others with HIV. Despite being diagnosed with HIV, Aziga had unprotected sex with 13 women. Seven of these women contracted HIV and two died.

Aziga learned he had HIV in 1996. He was counselled to tell potential sexual partners of his disease and to avoid unprotected sex. However, despite several warnings and a Health Protection and Promotion order, he continued to have unprotected sex with multiple partners and he did not tell his partners that he was HIV positive.

Canada has no specific law against knowingly infecting others with a sexually transmittable disease, although such laws exist in several other countries. Nonetheless, the Supreme Court of Canada determined that if someone does not disclose HIV, that person does not have his or her partner's consent and can be found guilty of assault. Almost a hundred men and women have been charged with criminal offences for exposing partners to HIV.

Controlling the spread of HIV has been controversial. The normal steps for dealing with infectious diseases include reporting the names of those who have positive tests and tracing contacts to inform them that they have been exposed to the disease. Quarantine has even been used. In Ontario, 12 diseases, including syphilis, gonorrhea, and tuberculosis, are defined as virulent and people with these diseases can be forced to stay in a hospital or jail for up to four months for treatment. However, HIV/AIDS is not included in this category. Because it is incurable, health authorities have reasoned, it does not make sense to force victims to have treatment. In the 1990s, when Dr. Richard Schabas, Ontario's medical officer of health, suggested classifying HIV/AIDS as a virulent disease in order to control rare, irresponsible victims who knowingly spread the disease, AIDS activists burned Dr. Schabas in effigy and he was given police protection when he received death threats. More recently, several people, including Dr. Mark Wainberg, the former head of the International AIDS Society, have been critical of the use of the criminal law in cases like Aziga's.

Why do some feel that the criminal law should not be used in HIV/AIDS transmission cases and oppose treating HIV/AIDS like other communicable diseases? Dr. Wainberg feels that these cases will discourage people from getting tested, thus increasing the chances of further transmission of the disease. He also feels that prosecutions will further stigmatize HIV/AIDS victims. There is no question that HIV/AIDS victims have been stigmatized, and to some AIDS activists, Dr. Schabas's suggestion that AIDS victims could be involuntarily detained raised the possibility of homophobic governments locking up large numbers of gay men simply because they were ill.

What are your views on this issue? Should all known partners of HIV victims be informed of their risk? Because medical advances can slow the progress of HIV, should more effort go into identifying those with HIV so that they can be treated? Can attitudes be changed so that the consequences of being labelled an HIV/AIDS victim are less severe? Should it be a crime to knowingly spread HIV, or should the problem be dealt with outside the criminal courts?

Sources: Burr, 1997; Weston and Jeffery, 1994.

Sex

Prior to the 20th century, women had shorter lives than men because of high mortality rates during pregnancy and childbirth. Childbirth is now much safer and women now live longer than men. Females born in Canada in 2008 could expect to live about 83 years, compared with 78.5 years for males (Statistics Canada, 2011d). Three factors contribute to this sex difference in life expectancy (Waldron, 1994). First, differences in gender roles mean that females are less likely than males to engage in risky behaviour, such as using alcohol and drugs, driving dangerously, and fighting. Males are also more likely to work in dangerous occupations, such as commercial fishing and mining. Second, females are more likely to seek medical care and so may have problems identified at an earlier, more treatable stage than men, who are more reluctant to consult doctors. Third, there may be biological differences, as females have higher survival rates than males at every stage from fetus to old age.

As the social roles played by females have changed, the mortality gap has narrowed. Women are moving into traditionally male-dominated occupations, such as farming and policing, where they face the same risks as males. As female rates of participation in risky behaviour, such as smoking and illicit drug use, approach those of males, females are paying the price in illness and early death.

While women live longer than men, they also have higher rates of disease and disability. While men at every age have higher rates of fatal diseases, women have higher rates of nonfatal chronic conditions (Waldron, 1994).

One important women's health issue is the lack of medical research on women. Many major studies of diseases such as heart disease have excluded women. These studies, however, are the basis for the diagnosis and treatment of both sexes, even though there appear to be sex differences in the diseases. Most funding agencies now require researchers to include both men and women subjects unless there are clear reasons for limiting the study to one sex. However, much of our existing medical knowledge is based on the earlier male-centred research.

Social Class

People who are poor have worse health and die earlier than the rich. This observation is also true of poor and rich countries, as illness and mortality rates are far higher in low-income countries than in high-income countries. In Canada, males living in the highest-income neighbourhoods have a life expectancy of almost five years greater than males in the lowest-income neighbourhoods. For women, the difference is about two years (Statistics Canada, 2002m). The infant mortality rate in Canada's poorest urban neighbourhoods was more than 50 percent higher than that in the richest neighbourhoods (Statistics Canada, 2002m). Low-income Canadians had higher rates of major chronic diseases, such as emphysema and high blood pressure, than those with middle and upper incomes and also had much higher mortality rates (Statistics Canada, 1998b). Children from low-income families were more than twice as likely as those from families in the highest income category to have functional health problems (see Figure 16.1). A recent study has shown that the level of inequality in a neighbourhood was related to mortality even after controlling for individual income levels (Auger et al., 2011).

Good healthcare policy can help reduce the health effects of poverty. Providing the poor with access to medical advice and treatment through universal medicare is one way of doing this. A study comparing cancer survival rates for the poorest one-third of Toronto residents, who all had government-funded healthcare, with their counterparts in Detroit, who typically had little or no health insurance, showed the benefits of providing adequate healthcare for the poor (Gorey et al., 1997). Survival rates were higher in Toronto for 12 of the 15 most common types of cancer. For many of these cancers, survival rates after five years were 50 percent higher among the poor in Toronto than in Detroit. The benefits of government-funded care go particularly to the poor, as this study found no differences among middle- or high-income patients in the two countries.

If access to medical care improves the health of the poor, why are Canada's poor less healthy than its middle and upper classes despite our universal healthcare? The answer is that medical

FIGURE 16.1 CHILDREN WITH LOWER FUNCTIONAL HEALTH, BY AVERAGE HOUSEHOLD INCOME[1]

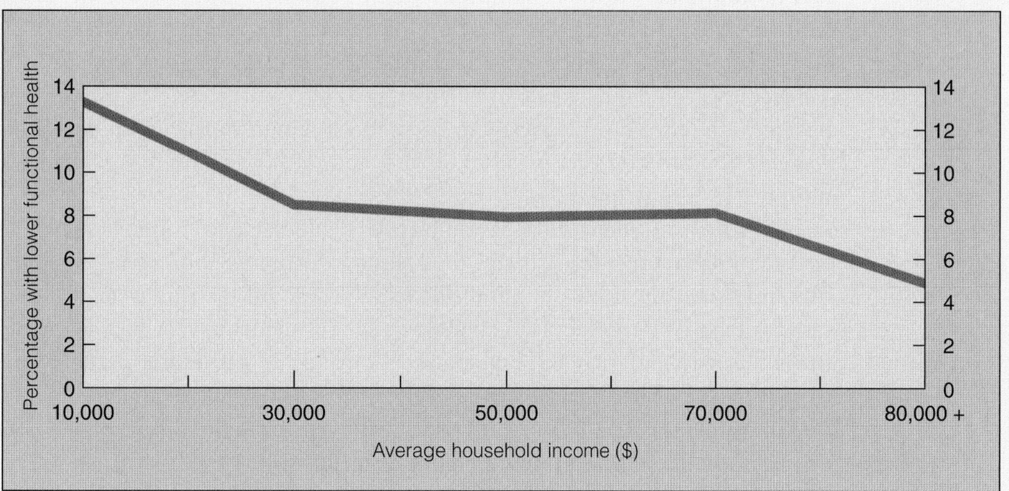

Children from low-income families are more likely to have health problems than children whose families have higher incomes.

[1]Statistics Canada has based functional health on eight attributes: vision, hearing, speech, mobility, dexterity, cognition, emotion, and pain and discomfort.
Note: Two-parent families with children age 4 to 11.

Source: Prepared by the Canadian Council on Social Development, using the National Longitudinal Survey of Children and Youth, 1994-1995. Reprinted by permission.

care cannot compensate for the other disadvantages of poverty, such as poor housing, hazardous employment, inadequate diet, greater exposure to disease, and the psychological stresses of poverty. People who are poor are more likely to engage in unhealthy behaviours, such as smoking and excessive drinking. One recent study found that class differences in smoking accounted for over half the difference in death rates between upper and lower classes (Jha et al., 2006).

Poor people may also lack knowledge of preventive strategies and services. For example, college-educated women are twice as likely as women who have not graduated from high school to have mammograms, which means that less educated women are at higher risk of dying of breast cancer. Their health is worse despite the availability of care once the medical problem has occurred or been identified. Finally, when they are ill, the poor are less likely to visit doctors than are wealthier people (Roos et al., 2004).

While differences remain between rich and poor, it is encouraging to note that the gap in life expectancy between people living in the highest- and lowest-income neighbourhoods has declined substantially (Statistics Canada, 2002m). One reason for this is that the difference in infant mortality rates between high- and low-income neighbourhoods declined from 9.8 deaths per 1000 births in 1971 to 2.4 deaths per 1000 births in 1996 and has remained low since then.

RACE, CLASS, AND HEALTH: CANADA'S ABORIGINAL PEOPLES

The experience of Canada's Aboriginal peoples illustrates how the disadvantages of race can interact with those of class to cause health problems.

Health Problems Among Aboriginal Peoples in Canada

epidemics Sudden, significant increases in the numbers of people contracting a disease.

Aboriginal people have a history of serious health problems that begins with their early contact with Europeans. **Epidemics**—sudden, significant increases in the numbers of people contracting a disease—of contagious diseases such as tuberculosis, measles, smallpox, and influenza broke out in the early years of this contact. These epidemics occurred partly because Aboriginal people had no immunity to these European diseases. Another factor was new patterns of trade that led to contact with more diverse groups of people after European settlement. Trade also led to higher population densities around trading posts, and this density helped to sustain epidemics. Tuberculosis epidemics were particularly devastating in the late 19th century, when Aboriginal people were moved to reserves. Crowded and lacking proper sanitation facilities, the reserves were ideal settings for the spread of disease, and mortality rates for tuberculosis remained high until the 1950s.

While their mortality rates have improved significantly, Aboriginal people still have shorter lives than other Canadians. Infant mortality rates among Aboriginal people have declined significantly since the 1970s but are still well above the Canadian average. The infant mortality rate for First Nations people is about twice the Canadian average and for the Inuit it is four times the national average (Smylie and Adomako, 2009). Life expectancy is seven years less than average for First Nations men and five years less for First Nations women (Health Canada, 2005). While most infectious diseases have been brought under control among Aboriginal people (though their rates remain higher than those of other Canadians), their health problems are now chronic diseases, such as heart disease and diabetes. HIV/AIDS is also having a serious impact on Aboriginal people, whose rates of new HIV infection are 3.6 times higher than those of other Canadians. The majority of Aboriginal people contracted HIV through intravenous drug use (Public Health Agency of Canada, 2010).

What are the reasons for the poorer health of Aboriginal people? The major factor is poverty. Aboriginal people are among the poorest in Canada and suffer from the poor nutrition and other social conditions that go with poverty. Because of the high costs of transporting food to remote reserves, it is difficult for some families to afford a well-balanced diet, so health problems due to nutritional deficiencies are common.

Many of the diseases that affect Aboriginal people can also be traced to the inadequate housing, crowding, and poor sanitary conditions common on reserves and in other communities where they live. In 2008, for example, 93 reserves were under orders to boil their water because it was not safe to drink (Eggertson, 2008). The isolation of many Aboriginal communities is also a factor; an illness that could be easily treated in a city hospital can be fatal in a community 800 km from the nearest doctor.

Aboriginal people also have high rates of violent death, with rates of death by murder and suicide higher than those of other Canadians. Rates of adolescent suicide are particularly high, especially in Nunavut. Accidental deaths, particularly by motor vehicle accidents and drowning, are also higher for Aboriginal people.

Finally, the legacy of colonialism still affects Aboriginal people's health. Anastasia Shkilnyk (1985), who studied the Ojibwa community of Grassy Narrows in northwestern Ontario, attributed the high rates of suicide and violent death, as well as health problems on the reserve, to colonial actions such as the destruction of Aboriginal language and religion, the family breakdown caused by enforced attendance at residential schools, and the forced relocation of the community by the Department of Indian Affairs. Environmental destruction by local industries that dumped methyl mercury into the lakes and rivers around the reserve was another contributor. This toxic substance had a direct impact on the health of Grassy Narrows residents, and also an indirect impact because it destroyed the fishery that was the foundation of the community's way of life.

Aboriginal Healing Methods

Aboriginal healing traditions are holistic and deal with the interactions between spirit, mind, emotions, and body. However, the Western model of medicine has been as dominant in Aboriginal communities as in the rest of Canada. Traditional healing practices fell into disuse for many years but are becoming popular again. Medical authorities have responded to Aboriginal demands that culturally appropriate healing methods should be available, though the acceptance of these methods has been mixed. Some hospitals and clinics now have Aboriginal healers, and combine traditional and Western treatment methods—a plaque in a Kenora, Ontario, hospital reads: "We believe traditional Native healing and culture have a place in our provision of health-care services to the Native people" (Waldram Herring, and Young, 1995). Aboriginal people are also gaining greater control over the delivery of medical services in their communities. These changes mean that in the future, Aboriginal people will be more involved in the healthcare system and traditional and Western medical traditions will be better integrated.

Evidence supports the idea that restoring Native control over their healthcare will lead to improved health among Aboriginal people (Canadian Institute for Health Information, 2004b). Moreover, researchers in many parts of the world have found that many traditional medicines are effective. Acting on this, pharmaceutical companies now market many products (including Aspirin) with the same chemical composition as traditional remedies. However, it will take much more than better healthcare for Aboriginal people to become as healthy as the rest of Canadian society.

social determinants of health The conditions in which people are born, grow, live, work and age, including the health system.

SOCIAL DETERMINANTS OF HEALTH

The strong correlations between health and social variables such as class, race, and sex have led researchers to consider the social determinants of health. According to the World Health Organization, "The **social determinants of health** are the conditions in which people are born, grow, live, work and age, including the health system. These circumstances are shaped by the distribution of money, power and resources at global, national and local levels, which are themselves influenced by policy choices. The social determinants of health are mostly responsible for health inequities—the unfair and avoidable differences in health status seen within and between countries" (2012).

Rather than placing responsibility for illness on individuals ("Don't smoke," "Eat a proper diet," "Stay fit") this perspective focuses on factors—race, class, social inequality—that cannot be controlled by individuals. Keep this perspective in mind when you read the next section, which provides a global view of social development and health.

Social Development and Health: A Global Perspective

Poverty and colonialism have affected the health of Canada's Aboriginal people. These factors also operate on a global scale. For example, Hunt (1989) attributes the rapid spread of diseases, such as HIV/AIDS in Africa (see Box 16.4), to the underdevelopment and dependency that are the legacy of colonialism. The underlying roots of this health problem lie in the economic and social marginalization of most African people.

The difference between rich and poor countries is dramatically reflected in infant mortality rates. While five of every 1000 infants in Canada die before their first birthday, infant mortality in the world's poorest countries is far higher. Afghanistan, Nigeria, and Rwanda, for instance, have infant mortality rates of 152, 94, and 82 per 1000 live births respectively (CIA, 2009). Life expectancy is correspondingly low. For persons born in Canada in 2008, life expectancy at birth was about 81 years (Statistics Canada, 2011d),

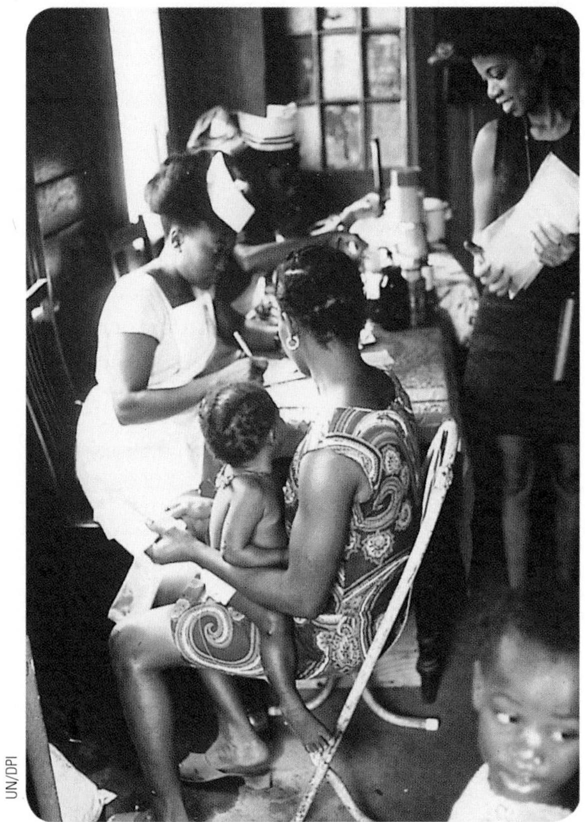
UN/DPI

A nurse interviews a mother at a rural health clinic in Sierra Leone. With the support of the World Health Organization, these clinics were established to reduce infant mortality and improve the health of mothers and their children.

© AP Photo/Tsvangirayi Mukwazhi

The availability of safe water has been a major reason why life expectancy has risen dramatically since the 1950s.

compared with less than 45 years in many poor African nations. Most deaths in less developed countries are caused by diseases now rare in the industrialized world.

A UNICEF (2009) report on the health of the world's children puts the situation in stark terms. More than nine million children under five years of age die each year. This figure is the equivalent of 60 Boeing 747 crashes each day of the year—and most of these deaths could be prevented easily. Most child deaths are caused by malnutrition and by preventable diseases, including measles, diarrhea, malaria, and pneumonia. As Sharma and Tulloch tell us, "Children in rich countries do not die from the common, preventable diseases of childhood. Children in poor countries do" (1997:1).

Tremendous progress has nevertheless been made in saving the lives of children. The number of child deaths is now less than half the 20 million who died in 1960 (UNICEF, 2010) and the decline is continuing. Measures such as immunization, rehydration therapy for diarrhea, and child mosquito nets save the lives of millions of children each year. Millions more deaths could be prevented through simple measures such as improved sanitation, clean water, better immunization programs, and the provision of better local health services.

Of course, not only children are dying in poor countries. Each year, more than 500,000 women die of complications arising from pregnancy and childbirth. Virtually all of these deaths take place in poor countries. In Niger, one in seven women will die in childbirth, compared with one in 8000 women in high-income countries (UNICEF, 2009). Many other diseases, such as malaria, take millions of lives, but drug companies are not interested in developing cures because the residents of poor countries where these diseases are epidemic cannot afford to pay high prices for such drugs.

Despite these problems, tremendous progress has been made in improving world health. Since 1955, the average life expectancy in the world has increased from 46 years to 67 years (World Health Organization, 2003, 2009). Life expectancy has risen to more than 70 years in 84 countries, up from only 55 countries in 1990. This increase has been attributed to a number of factors, one of the most important being the development of a safe water supply. The percentage of the world's population with access to safe water nearly doubled between 1990 and 2000 (United Nations Development Programme, 2003).

TIME TO REVIEW

- Life expectancy is far lower in poor countries than in wealthy ones. What could the global community do to increase the life expectancy of the poorest people?

LO-4 DISABILITY

What is a disability? There are many different definitions. In business and government, it is often defined in terms of work—for instance, "an inability to engage in gainful employment." Medical professionals tend to define it in terms of organically based impairments—the problem being entirely within the body (Albrecht, 1992). However, this definition is too narrow. Many of you have vision problems that would make it difficult for you to read this text. Do these people consider themselves disabled? The answer is no, because eyeglasses or contact lenses can make it possible for most people to function normally. Thus the definition of disability must have a social component. Thus we can define a **disability** as a physical or health condition that reduces a person's ability to perform tasks he or she would normally do at a given stage of life and that may result in stigmatization or discrimination against the person. This definition of disability is based not only on physical conditions but also on social attitudes and the social and physical environments in which people live.

disability A physical or health condition that reduces a person's ability to perform tasks he or she would normally do at a given stage of life and that may result in stigmatization or discrimination against the person.

Society has not provided the universal access that would allow people with disabilities to participate fully in all aspects of life (Blackford, 1996). For example, many buildings are

BOX 16.4 SOCIOLOGY IN GLOBAL PERSPECTIVE

The AIDS Epidemic in Africa

> Rakai, Uganda: From the shadows of his hut, the gaunt and weary young man stares outside at the pigs playing in the dust under the banana palms. His chest is covered with open sores; skin rashes have left his ebony arms looking as if they are covered in chalk; his army fatigues hang loosely around his waist.
>
> Outside, Charles Lawanga glances toward his ailing second son and lowers his voice. Last year, when the Ugandan army gave him his medical furlough, his son was sick, but at least he could walk, says Lawanga.
>
> Lawanga's brows are furrowed; he has the face of a man who is watching his son die. His eyes sharpen when he hears that an American journalist knows many of the Western doctors working on the disease. He knows that the United States is a country of immense wealth, and that the medicine that will save his country and his son will probably come from there. Tears gather in his brown eyes, and he asks, "When will it come? When will there be the cure?" (Shilts, 1988:621)

In the mid-1990s, Uganda had the highest number of recorded HIV cases in Africa—around 1.5 million—and AIDS has touched virtually all families in this country. Uganda was, however, the first African country to make major gains in the fight against HIV/AIDS. One key indicator was the infection rate of pregnant women: Between 1992 and 1998, this rate dropped from 31 percent to 14 percent in the capital city of Kampala and from 21 percent to 8 percent in the rest of the country. The rate among men attending clinics for sexually transmitted diseases dropped from 46 percent to 20 percent over the same period (Global Health Council, 2002).

The fight against HIV/AIDS was personally led by Uganda's President Museveni. The government worked with community partners to implement school sex education programs that encouraged abstinence but also promoted condom use for those who were sexually active; quick treatment of other sexually transmitted diseases; and same-day results for HIV tests and immediate counselling for those who were tested. Uganda developed the ABC approach to AIDS prevention: Abstinence, Be faithful to one partner, and use Condoms. This program was implemented through grassroots organizations throughout the country and received funding from the World Bank and from the United States (Avert, 2005). Successful programs in Thailand and Senegal have also been based on encouraging condom use and discouraging risky sexual behaviour, such as casual sex and sex with prostitutes (Global Health Council, 2002).

Unfortunately, few other countries have followed Uganda's lead. Many countries deny that they have a problem and others reject modern treatment methods. South Africa's former president, Thabo Mbeki, denied that AIDS was caused by HIV and his government refused to provide treatment to pregnant women to prevent the transmission of HIV to their children. His health minister promoted garlic and beets as remedies for AIDS. These policies resulted in hundreds of thousands of needless deaths.

In other countries, public discussion of sexual behaviour is so taboo that governments and other leaders refuse to address rising infection rates. Even in Uganda, progress was slowed because under former president George W. Bush, U.S.-based funding organizations discouraged the promotion of condoms and advocated "abstinence-only" programs. In response, President Museveni condemned condom use as immoral and the safe-sex advertising campaign and free distribution of condoms were drastically curtailed. As evidence clearly shows that condom use is a vital component of successful AIDS prevention programs and that abstinence-only programs do not work, the ideology of the faith-based organizations that helped deliver U.S. funding jeopardized the lives of millions of Ugandans (Avert, 2005; New York Times, 2005). These restrictions were modified under President Barack Obama.

© BH Generic Stock Images/Alamy

Does life expectancy take on a different meaning for persons with chronic disabilities? While he was still in college, British theoretical physicist Stephen Hawking learned he had Lou Gehrig's disease (amyotrophic lateral sclerosis). Hawking nevertheless went on to develop a quantum theory of gravity that forever changed our view of the universe. As a result, he is considered one of the leading figures in modern cosmology.

still not accessible to persons using a wheelchair. In this context, disability derives from a lack of accommodation, not simply from someone's physical condition. Oliver (1990) used the term *disability oppression* to describe the barriers that exist for disabled persons in Canadian society. These include economic hardship (from the additional costs of accessibility devices, transportation, and attendant care or from employment discrimination), inadequate government assistance programs, and negative social attitudes toward disabled persons. According to disability rights advocates, disability must be thought of in terms of how society causes or contributes to the problem—not in terms of what is "wrong" with the person with a disability.

Sociological Perspectives on Disability

How do sociologists view disability? Functionalists often apply Parsons's sick role model, which is referred to as the *medical model* of disability. According to the medical model, disability is deviance. The deviance framework is also apparent in some symbolic interactionist perspectives. According to symbolic interactionists, people with a disability experience *role ambiguity* because many people equate disability with deviance (Murphy et al., 1988). By labelling individuals with a disability as "deviant," other people can avoid them or treat them as outsiders. Society marginalizes people with a disability because they have lost old roles and statuses and are labelled as "disabled" persons.

According to Freidson (1965), people are labelled based on: (1) their degree of responsibility for their impairment, (2) the apparent seriousness of their condition, and (3) the perceived legitimacy of the condition. Freidson concluded that the definition of and expectations for people with a disability are socially constructed factors.

Like Freidson, Titchkosky feels that disability can be understood only by considering its social and cultural context. A main feature of this context is "the fact that disability is necessarily an experience of marginality" (2003:232). Titchkosky describes how the arrival of a guide dog affected her partner, a professor whose sight had been deteriorating for years but who was usually able to pass as a sighted person:

> I had not anticipated that acquiring a guide dog would also mean acquiring a new identity. Rod arrived home with a beautiful new dog and an expert guide. But there was more. With Smokie, Rod was seen as blind. Staring, grabbing, helping, offers of prayers or medical advice, groping for words or even a voice are some of the many ways in which sighted people show that they are seeing a blind person. Through these interactions, Rod was given the identity—blind person. (2003:82)

Finally, from a conflict perspective, persons with a disability are members of a subordinate group in conflict with persons in positions of power in the government, in the healthcare industry, and in the rehabilitation business, all of whom are trying to control their destinies (Albrecht, 1992). Those in positions of power have created policies and artificial barriers that keep people with disabilities in a subservient position (Asch, 1986; Hahn, 1987). In a capitalist economy, disabilities are big business. Persons with a disability have an economic value as consumers of goods and services that will allegedly make them "better" people. Many persons with a disability endure the same struggle for resources faced by people of colour, women, and older persons. Individuals who hold more than one of these ascribed statuses, combined with experiencing disability, are doubly or triply oppressed by capitalism.

Disability in Contemporary Society

An estimated 4.4 million people age 15 and over, representing 14 percent of the adult population in Canada, report having one or more physical or mental disabilities (Statistics Canada, 2007h). This number is increasing for several reasons. First, with advances in medical technology, many people who formerly would have died from an accident or illness now survive, although with an impairment. Second, as people live longer, they are more likely to experience disabling diseases such as arthritis that may have disabling consequences (Albrecht, 1992). Third, persons born with serious disabilities are more likely to survive infancy because of medical technology. Finally, there is some indication that people are now more willing to report disabilities (Statistics Canada, 2007h).

Some people are more likely to become disabled than others. Aboriginal people and persons with lower incomes have higher rates of disability (Bolaria and Bolaria, 1994). Environment, lifestyle, and working conditions all contribute to disability. Air pollution and smoking lead to a higher incidence of chronic respiratory disease and lung damage. In industrial societies, workers in many types of low-status jobs are at greatest risk for certain health hazards and disabilities. Employees in data processing and service-oriented jobs may also be affected by work-related disabilities, such as arthritis and carpal tunnel syndrome.

People with disabilities have been kept out of the mainstream. They have been denied equal opportunities in education by being consigned to special education classes or special schools. Snowdon (2012) has described the social isolation of children with disabilities. The majority of parents reported that their disabled child had "no close friends" or "only one close friend."

Many people with disabilities have been restricted from entry into schools and the workforce, not due to their own limitations, but by societal barriers. Why are disabled persons excluded? Susan Wendell offers an explanation:

> In a society that idealizes the body, the physically disabled are often marginalized. People learn to identify with their own strengths (by cultural standards) and to hate, fear, and neglect their own weaknesses. The disabled are not only de-valued for their de-valued bodies; they are constant reminders to the able-bodied of the negative body—of what the able-bodied are trying to avoid, forget, and ignore . . . In a culture which loves the idea that the body can be controlled, those who cannot control their bodies are seen (and may see themselves) as failures. (1995:458)

© CP/Tom Hanson

Steven Fletcher, appointed Minister of State for Transport by Prime Minister Stephen Harper, is the first quadriplegic to be elected to Canada's House of Commons. After he was injured in an automobile accident, Fletcher served two terms as president of the University of Manitoba's Students' Union while earning his M.B.A. That was the beginning of his political career.

The combination of a disability and society's reaction to the disability has an impact on the lives of many people. The disabled often suffer from stereotyping. Movies often depict villains as individuals with disabilities (think of the villains in the Batman movies, such as the *Dark Knight,* in which both the Joker and former District Attorney Harvey Dent were driven to crime by serious disfigurement). Charitable fundraising campaigns may contribute to the perception of the disabled as persons who are to be pitied. Prejudice against persons with disabilities may result in either subtle or overt discrimination. According to Asch, "Many commentators note that people with disabilities are expected to play no adult social role whatsoever; to be perceived as always, in every social interaction, a recipient of help and never a provider of assistance" (2004:11). This attitude is part of the reason why people with disabilities have difficulty finding employment.

While the role of persons with disabilities has expanded in the Canadian labour force in recent years, compared with nondisabled adults, a much smaller proportion of the disabled population is employed. Overall, the unemployment rate for adults aged 25 to 54 with activity limitations was over 50 percent higher than that of people without activity limitations, and many more were not in the labour force at all because of their conditions (Crompton, 2011). As a result, people with activity limitations were more likely to be poor (Crompton, 2011). Not surprisingly many persons with disabilities feel that they are disadvantaged in terms of employment and that they have been discriminated against in the workplace because of their condition (Statistics Canada, 2008i).

Ensuring equality for people with disabilities is not just a matter for governments. While legislation is important, social attitudes also must change. Adrienne Asch, who is a blind university professor, says that even her close friends do not treat her in the same way as they treat others. For example, they "do not feel comfortable accepting my offers to pick up food as part of a dinner we plan to have . . . or who would prefer that a high-school-age stranger take care of their six-year-old son for an evening than have me do it, even though I have known their son and their home ever since his birth" (2004:11). Thus equality isn't just a matter of ending discrimination against people with disabilities, but rather of ensuring full integration into mainstream society.

TIME TO REVIEW

- What is the relationship between health and the variables of age, sex, and social class? How do these relationships affect the healthcare system?
- Discuss why Canada's Aboriginal people are much less healthy than the rest of the population.
- What is the role of traditional practices in Aboriginal healthcare?
- Describe the state of health and healthcare in the world's poorest countries.
- Discuss the degree to which disabilities are a function of the social and physical environments in which people live.

Healthcare in Canada

Healthcare is an important social and political issue in Canada. Healthcare costs are increasing steadily, while governments have made cuts in other areas such as support for college and university students. However, attempts by governments to make changes in the way healthcare is provided often meet with great resistance from the public and from those who work in the healthcare system. See Figure 16.2.

Universal Healthcare

universal healthcare system System in which all citizens receive medical services paid for through taxation revenues.

Canadians have a **universal healthcare system**; that is, one in which all citizens receive medical services paid for through taxation revenues. Prior to the early 1960s, Canadians had a user-pay system, in which people paid for healthcare directly out of their pockets. Individuals who did not have health insurance and who required expensive medical procedures or long-term care or who developed a chronic illness often suffered severe financial losses. Under our universal system, if you are sick, you have the right to receive medical care regardless of your ability to pay. Individuals do not pay doctor or hospital costs directly, but they are responsible for at least part of the costs of other medical services, such as prescription drugs and ambulances.

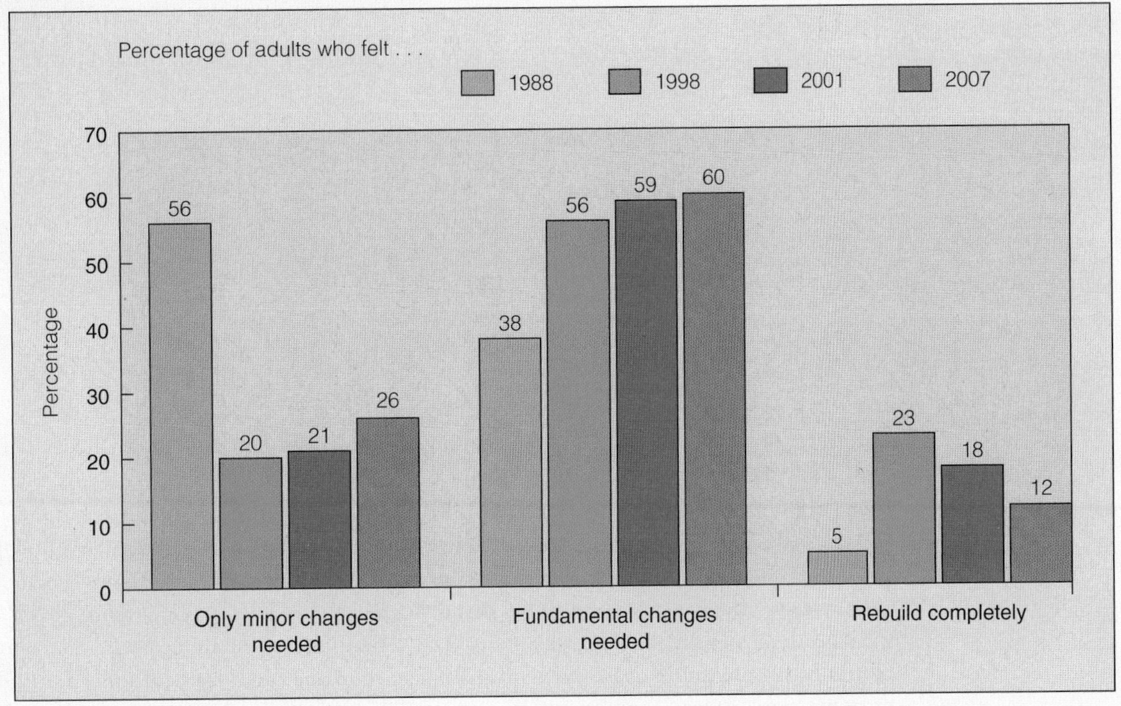

Sources: Commonwealth Fund, 2002, 2007.

Healthcare is a provincial and territorial responsibility, and each province and territory has its own healthcare system. However, the federal government contributes billions of dollars to the provinces for healthcare and enforces basic standards that each province must follow. Provincial plans must meet the following requirements:

1. *Universality.* All Canadians should be covered on uniform terms and conditions.
2. *Comprehensiveness.* All necessary medical services should be guaranteed, without dollar limit, and should be available solely on the basis of medical need.
3. *Accessibility.* Reasonable access should be guaranteed to all Canadians.
4. *Portability.* Benefits should be transferable from province to province.
5. *Public administration.* The system should be operated on a nonprofit basis by a public agency or commission (Grant, 1993:401).

Canada spends over 11 percent of its gross domestic product on healthcare. While this figure is low in comparison with the United States (see Table 16.1), it is higher than in most other industrialized countries and represents a huge expenditure. Canada's 2011 healthcare expenditures were $200 billion (Canadian Instititute for Health Information, 2011b). Of this amount, $140 billion came from government funding, while the remainder came from individuals and medical insurance companies for services not covered by medicare. Healthcare costs are rising faster than government revenues, and factors such as greater use of technology and the aging baby boomers will place further demands on the system.

One cause of increasing costs is overutilization of healthcare services. Some of this is a result, for example, of people using emergency rooms for routine care instead of visiting a doctor's office. However, while members of the public may not always make the most economical choices, many of the costs of our system are controlled by doctors, who prescribe drugs, admit patients to hospitals, determine patients' lengths of stay in hospital, order tests and examinations, determine

TABLE 16.1 LIFE SPAN AND HEALTHCARE EXPENDITURE, 2008

COUNTRIES IN ORDER OF LIFE EXPECTANCY	LIFE EXPECTANCY AT BIRTH, IN YEARS	TOTAL EXPENDITURE ON HEALTH, % OF GDP	EXPENDITURE ON HEALTH, PER CAPITA[1]
Japan	83	8.1%	$2878
Canada	81	11.4%	$4363
France	81	11.8%	$3978
United Kingdom	80	8.5%	$3487
Germany	80	10.8%	$4218
United States	78	17.4%	$7690

[1]In U.S. dollars adjusted for purchasing power parities.

Source: OECD, 2011.

the course of treatment that will be used, and recommend follow-up visits. Since patients will do almost anything to ensure their health and since they do not pay directly, they have no incentive to question doctors' recommendations. On the other hand, doctors have a financial interest in providing more treatment. Ensuring that doctors make decisions about treatment only on medical grounds is a major challenge faced by taxpayer-funded healthcare systems.

Another reason for the high costs of the healthcare system is the system's focus on hospitals and doctors. Our healthcare system has overemphasized acute care and underemphasized community care and disease prevention. Cheaper forms of noninstitutional healthcare, such as home-care services, are not subject to national standards, so these services vary widely from province to province and may not be available even when they are the most cost-effective type of care. Thus, people who need minimal care may be taking up expensive acute-care hospital beds because community alternatives are not available. Use of the Internet, however, may enable people to have greater control over their own healthcare (see Box 16.5 at **www.nelson.com/sociologyinourtimes6e**).

Healthcare in the United States

The United States is the only industrialized country that does not provide universal health coverage to all its citizens. While Canada and Western European countries treat healthcare as a basic human right, the United States sees it as a market commodity. Most Americans receive healthcare coverage through private insurance programs that are sometimes paid for or subsidized by their employers. However, many Americans cannot afford to buy insurance and others are denied coverage because of medical conditions. Some of the uninsured are covered by government-funded Medicare and Medicaid programs that are available for seniors, people with disabilities, and some people with low incomes. Approximately 15 percent of the U.S. population—47 million people—have no medical coverage (U.S. Census Bureau, 2008). Many others lack adequate coverage, and the expenses incurred in treating a serious medical condition can lead to financial ruin. Medical expenses are the leading cause of personal bankruptcy in the United States (Himmelstein et al., 2005). President Obama has implemented a healthcare plan that will broaden coverage in the future, but it will not provide the level of coverage found in Canada and other industrialized countries. However, this program has been very controversial, as many Americans feel the government's role in providing medical services should be limited.

Despite the lack of universal coverage, per capita healthcare costs in the United States are much higher than in Canada and are growing more rapidly. Table 16.1 shows that per capita healthcare costs in the United States of $7690 were much higher than Canada's cost of $4363. Much of the difference in costs between Canada and the United States reflects the efficiency of Canada's government insurance system compared with the fragmented U.S. system, with its large number of different healthcare insurers and providers, each eager to maximize profits and each adding its costs to the final bill. The salaries of healthcare workers, particularly doctors, are lower in Canada than in the United States. A comparison of the costs of heart bypass surgery in Canada and the United States (Eisenberg et al., 2005) found that the same operation cost twice as much in the United States ($20,673 as opposed to $10,373 in Canada), even though the success rate for the procedure was the same in both countries.

In the debates over healthcare reform, many U.S. politicians and lobbyists are critical of Canada's "socialized" healthcare. They claim that the Canadian system is beset with delays and that we get care that is inferior to that provided in the United States. Are these critics correct? Do Canadians have an inferior system that forces people to travel to the United States to get proper treatment?

The answer to these questions is no. Despite the higher costs of U.S. healthcare, Canadians are healthier than Americans and have better access to healthcare. Canada has lower infant mortality and longer life expectancy than the United States; these two indicators are often used as broad measures of the quality of healthcare. Many studies demonstrate the superiority of our system. A study cited earlier in this chapter showed that poor Canadians had much higher cancer survival rates than poor Americans. Another study comparing the outcomes of 10 different surgical procedures for elderly persons in Manitoba with those in the New England states found that long-term survival rates were higher in Canada than in the United States for nine of the 10 procedures studied (Roos et al., 1992). Other research confirms that the outcome differences are primarily because of worse health outcomes among lower-income Americans (Sanmartin and Ng, 2004). These differences between the countries are recognized by the public; 34 percent of Americans say that their healthcare system needs to be completely rebuilt, compared with 12 percent of Canadians (Commonwealth Fund, 2007). Figure 16.2 shows how Canadians' satisfaction with their health care system has improved since the late 1990s.

APPROACHES TO HEALTHCARE LO-5

The Medical Model of Illness

The medical model has been the predominant way of thinking about illness in industrialized societies for many years. This model has five basic assumptions: that illness is "(1) deviation from normal, (2) specific and universal, (3) caused by unique biological forces, (4) similar to the breakdown of a machine whose parts can be repaired, and (5) defined and treated through a neutral scientific process" (Weitz, 1996:129). Acceptance of this model has given great power to doctors, who are viewed as the experts in diagnosing and treating illness. Doctors have gone to great lengths to protect their role at the centre of the healthcare system. For example, they have actively resisted those with conflicting views, such as midwives, advocates of natural healing methods, and those more concerned with preventing disease than with treating it.

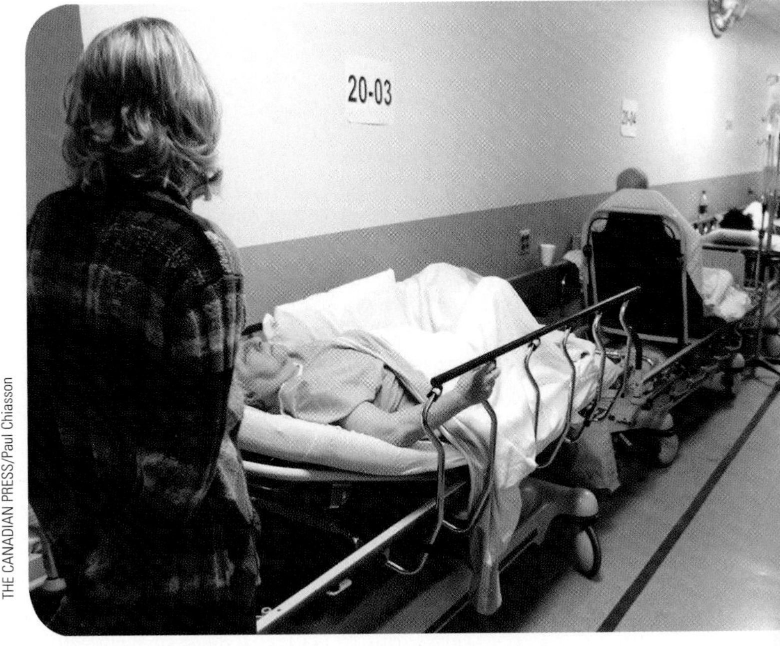

THE CANADIAN PRESS/Paul Chiasson

One of the consequences of the demands on Canada's healthcare system has been hospital overcrowding. In some hospitals, patients are forced to spend time in emergency room hallways because no rooms are available.

Alternative Approaches

Despite the successes of modern medicine, the medical model of illness is losing some of its dominance as

Canadians are recognizing that their health needs cannot be met by medical services alone and that more medical care does not necessarily lead to better health. Rising medical costs have led the federal government to implement programs emphasizing environmental and lifestyle factors in health promotion. For example, education about the hazards of smoking, combined with more effective legislation against the use and advertising of tobacco products, has improved public health and saved the money spent treating smoking-related diseases such as emphysema and lung cancer. Responsibility for healthcare is shifting away from the government and the healthcare system and toward the individual and the family.

Winnipeg Free Press/Jeff Debooy

Government home-care workers marched at the Manitoba legislature in April 1997, protesting the provincial government's plans to contract out their services to private companies. Public opposition to this privatization convinced the government to scale back its plans to a small trial project. Later in the year, the government found that privatization would not save any money and returned all responsibility for home care to government workers.

The popularity of holistic healthcare is a further indication of the move toward a new definition of health. Holism reflects the orientations of many ancient therapeutic systems, including those of Canadian Aboriginal peoples. Modern scientific medicine has been widely criticized for focusing on diseases and injuries rather than on preventing illness and promoting overall well-being. Critics say the medical model looks at problems in a mechanical fashion without considering their context, while the holistic approach emphasizes the interdependence of body, mind, and environment.

Holism is adaptable to traditional medical practice and is being adopted by some medical doctors and nurses as well as by practitioners of alternative healthcare, including chiropractors, osteopaths, acupuncturists, and naturopathic doctors. Supporters of the holistic health movement encourage people to take greater individual responsibility for their health and healthcare, especially with regard to lifestyle-related diseases and disabilities.

The holistic approach's emphasis on the role of social factors in illness is now receiving support in research done by traditional practitioners. For example, authors of a *Journal of the American Heart Association* article found that middle-aged men with high levels of despair had a 20 percent greater chance of developing atherosclerosis—narrowing of the arteries—than more optimistic men with similar physiological risk factors. This difference in the risks for heart disease was as great as that between a nonsmoker and a pack-a-day smoker (Cable News Network, 1997). Research on the health of older adults has also shown that nonmedical factors, such as isolation, the death of a family member or a friend, and the loss of status after retirement, have a major influence on health. Accordingly, programs for the elderly must deal with these issues as well as with physical problems (Crichton et al., 1997).

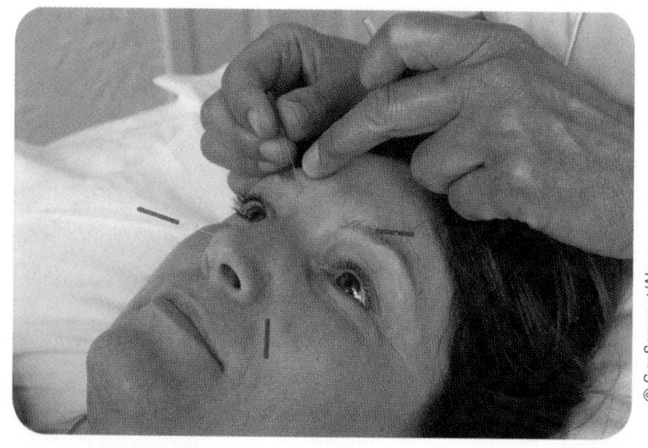

© Guy Somerset/Alamy

Canadians are increasingly using alternative healthcare methods, such as acupuncture.

The National Population Health Survey found that many Canadians were making use of alternative medicine. While about 20 percent of those surveyed had consulted an alternative practitioner within the previous year, few of them had relied exclusively on alternative medicine (Statistics Canada, 2005e). Thus it seems that alternative medicine is being used as a complement to traditional medicine rather than as a replacement. Christopher Fries (2008) has described some of the factors that have facilitated the integration of traditional medicine and alternative techniques. He reports that people no longer accept the dominance of traditional medicine and shop around for whatever combination of treatment they feel meets their physical and psychological needs. Their goal is not just to avoid sickness but to achieve a state of well-being. This individualized view of consuming healthcare is reinforced by the government's attempt to encourage people to take responsibility for their own health rather than relying on the healthcare system.

While its use is growing, some types of alternative medicine have been criticized. The main criticism is that some of the claims of alternative medical practice have not been empirically verified. Beyerstein blames the acceptance of such claims on the fact that most people know little about science:

> Even an elementary understanding of chemistry should raise strong doubts about the legitimacy of homeopathy; a passing familiarity with human anatomy would suggest that "subluxations" of the vertebrae cannot cause all the diseases that chiropractors believe they do; and a quite modest grasp of physiology should make it apparent that a coffee enema is unlikely to cure cancer. But when consumers have not the foggiest idea of how bacteria, viruses, carcinogens, oncogenes, and toxins wreak havoc on bodily tissues, then shark cartilage, healing crystals, and pulverized tiger penis seem no more magical than the latest breakthrough from the biochemistry laboratory. (1997:150)

Beyerstein does see some benefits in alternative medicine. It has, he says, added a comforting human component to a medical world that has become increasingly impersonal and technological. Many alternative healers offer sound advice about prevention and a healthy lifestyle, and some alternative practices do have strong scientific backing. However, he fears that some alternatives can divert sick people from more effective treatment. People will need to be sufficiently well informed about the variety and nature of the options available to make sound treatment choices in the future. These options will certainly grow in number as alternative therapies become more widely accepted and as more become integrated with conventional medicine.

TIME TO REVIEW

- What requirements must provinces meet in Canada's universal healthcare system?
- How has the Internet enabled people to take more control over their own health and healthcare?
- How does the U.S. healthcare system differ from that of Canada and most other industrialized countries? Discuss how these differences affect health outcomes.
- Discuss the strengths and weaknesses of alternative approaches to healthcare.

16 VISUAL SUMMARY

LO-1 Understand the ways in which sociological factors influence health and disease.

The health of any group is a product of the interaction of a wide range of factors. Sociological variables such as age, race, sex, and social class have a major impact on the health of every individual.

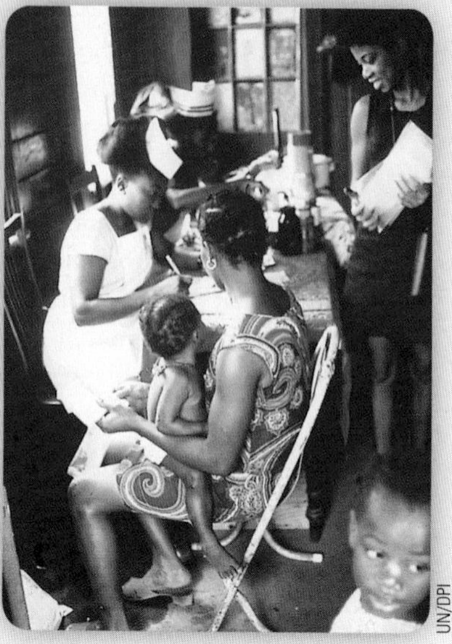

UN/DPI

ariadna de raadt/Shutterstock

LO-2 Compare how functionalist, symbolic interactionist, conflict, feminist, and postmodern theories differ in their analyses of health.

Functionalists see illness as dysfunctional for both the individual who is sick and for society. Sickness may result in an inability on the part of the sick person to fulfill his or her necessary social roles. The conflict approach to health and illness considers the political and social forces that affect health and the healthcare system, as well as the inequities that result from these forces. Feminist scholars have studied a variety of issues, including the manner in which medicalization has affected the lives of women, the male-centred focus of medical research, and discrimination against women working in the healthcare system. Symbolic interactionists attempt to understand the specific meanings and causes that we attribute to particular events. In studying health, interactionists focus on the fact that the meaning that people give their illness or disease will affect their self-concept and their relationships with others. Finally, postmodern theorists have examined the relationship between biology and culture.

LO-3 Understand how social inequality affects health and healthcare.

People with low incomes have worse health and die earlier than the rich. Illness and mortality rates are far higher for low-income than high-income countries. Within the industrialized world, citizens of those countries with the most equal distribution of income have the best health as measured by life expectancy.

© AP Photo/Tsvangirayi Mukwazhi

KEY TERMS

disability A physical or health condition that reduces a person's ability to perform tasks he or she would normally do at a given stage of life and that may result in stigmatization or discrimination against the person (p. 465).

epidemics Sudden, significant increases in the numbers of people contracting a disease (p. 461).

health The state of complete physical, mental, and social well-being (p. 451).

healthcare Any activity intended to improve health (p. 451).

medicalization The process whereby an object or a condition becomes defined by society as a physical or psychological illness (p. 454).

medicine An institutionalized system for the scientific diagnosis, treatment, and prevention of illness (p. 451).

preventive medicine Medicine that emphasizes a healthy lifestyle in order to prevent poor health before it occurs (p. 451).

sick role Patterns of behaviour defined as appropriate for people who are sick (p. 451).

social determinants of health The conditions in which people are born, grow, live, work and age, including the health system (p. 463).

universal healthcare system System in which all citizens receive medical services paid for through taxation revenues (p. 468).

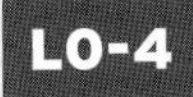

LO-4 Identify the consequences of disability.

Disability may result in stigmatization or discrimination. Persons with disabilities are more likely to be unemployed or underemployed and poor.

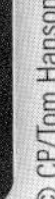

© CP/Tom Hanson

Winnipeg Free Press/Jeff Deboov

LO-5 Discuss the state of the healthcare system in Canada today and explain how it could be improved.

The costs of the healthcare system are increasing faster than those of almost any other social institution. Those responsible for the system need to reduce cost increases and provide better service to Canadians.

APPLICATION QUESTIONS

1. Some doctors are refusing to treat people who smoke, and increasing numbers of pediatricians have begun to remove families from their practices if the parents refuse to have their children vaccinated. Do you think that medical practitioners should have the right to "fire" patients who refuse to look after their own health, or should everyone have the right to be treated?
2. Find some sites on the Web that promise cures for cancer and other serious diseases—you can start with some of the treatments at www.cancure.org. How do these sites try to convince people with illnesses to buy their products? What are some of the negative consequences that could happen to people who follow these treatments?
3. In 2012, the Northern Ontario community of Attawapiskat received national media attention because of its desperately inadequate housing, which was overcrowded, physically deteriorated, mould-ridden, and lacked running water. Consider how these conditions explain the higher mortality rates and comparatively bad health of First Nations people.
4. Find examples of the ways the media encourage people to look for perfection in their bodies. What techniques do advertisers, such as those for plastic surgery or drugs that grow hair, use to try to encourage people to buy these products or services?

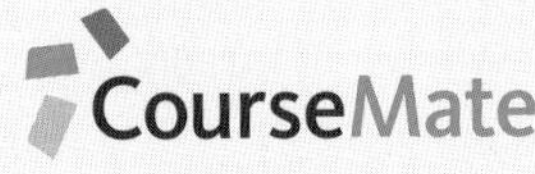

Test your comprehension and assess what you've learned with **CourseMate's** online quizzes.

For other interesting Lived Experiences, watch the video clips on **CourseMate.**

Practise what you've learned with flashcards containing key terms and definitions on **CourseMate.**

CHAPTER 17

Mass Media

SOCIAL MEDIA AND REVOLUTION

In 2011, people living in Tunisia, Egypt, and Libya overthrew their despotic and corrupt governments. These revolutions were unique in their use of social media as an organizing tool. Ayat Mneina, a Libyan-born University of Manitoba student, describes how she helped in the fight for political freedom in her home country:

The resentment toward the regime and the desire for change are sentiments I share with the youth in Libya. Upon seeing the uprisings take place in neighbouring Tunisia and Egypt in January, a friend (Omar Amer) and I made a conscious decision to get involved if the youth of Libya were ever to take action.

We decided to observe social media outlets used by Libyan youth, predominantly Facebook, to gauge the potential for action. We simultaneously monitored the use of social media, including Twitter, by Tunisian and Egyptian youth in case we had to mobilize.

Within weeks of the Jasmine Revolution in Tunisia, Facebook groups emerged calling for a Day of Rage in Libya, setting the date for February 17, 2011. Although we could not predict whether or not the youth would in fact take to the streets, as the day grew near we equipped ourselves with a Twitter account (called @ShababLibya), a small network of friends and relatives on the ground who we could contact for updates, a Skype account, a YouTube account, a Gmail account, and a Facebook account and page all complementing our effort—which we chose to call the Libyan Youth Movement (ShababLibya).

Ayat Mneina

Used with permission of Ayat Mneina

Because of premature protests occurring on February 15—due to the arrest of a young human rights lawyer named Fathi Terbil and reports of increased security in the resistance stronghold of Benghazi—we grew skeptical about the upcoming Day of Rage. On the evening of the 16th, we received confirmation from several sources that youth were in fact planning to take to the streets the next morning. Fully equipped with caffeine, laptops, and our complete toolbox of social media, we began the task of filling the void that existed because independent and international media were not allowed to operate in Libya.

Overnight, we found ourselves tweeting urgent messages to the world and international media calling for the coverage of what we soon understood was the brutal and indiscriminate murder of innocent, unarmed protesters across the country. The images, reports, and accounts we received were unlike anything we could have prepared for, and in the next week we became the number one source of information on the Libyan uprising. We tweeted and posted reports as we received them, confirmed from the ground based on accounts from at least three people. We also provided media outlets with interviews and contacts with protesters on the ground, and we were even able to deliver coordinates of Gaddafi forces to NATO. We rallied for international support, and effectively became the voice of the Libyan youth during the revolution. I have seen our humble efforts thrive and grow to include more than 49,000 followers on Twitter, nearly 23,000 subscribers to our Facebook page, a website that sees thousands of visitors every week (www.shabablibya.org), and a handful of dedicated volunteers located around the globe who have tirelessly given their time and effort to this cause.

At the same time, people in Libya were using their mobile phones to record the fighting and to post their videos on YouTube. Outside reporters were not allowed to work freely in the parts of Libya controlled by Gaddafi, so these videos were important in helping to convince other countries to provide support to the revolution.

Social media have played a prominent role in other political events. Repressive governments control their local media and constantly transmit government propaganda. Satellite TV helped to break this control—the Al Jazeera network gave many people in the Middle East their first real look at the outside world and showed the harm being done by their own repressive regimes. The Internet and the World Wide Web further opened up the world and for the first time enabled two-way communication inside and outside these countries. Cellphones enabled people who could not afford computers to access the Internet and to share information through social media. Revolutionaries no longer needed to seize state radio and television stations to get their message out. The transformation of media communication from "one-to-many" to "many-to-many" (Zakaria, 2011) made it possible for citizens to use the media to organize against the state.

People do not need social media to overturn oppressive governments—revolutions occurred long before the Internet. However, social media help people to get their message out and to mobilize others. Social media allow opponents to share information without the knowledge of the government and also to send news about their situation to the rest of the world.

Repressive governments do not just passively allow their opponents to use social media. More than 40 countries, including China, Iran, and Cuba, restrict Internet access (Canada Centre for Global Security Studies, 2011), and during times of crisis, governments may try to shut down the Internet and other social media entirely. During protests in 2009, the Iranian government shut down Tehran's cellphone network on days when demonstrations were planned and severely restricted Internet use. In 2011, the Egyptian government also tried shutting down social media in an unsuccessful attempt to save the regime of Hosni Mubarak.

While the Internet is a valuable tool, people cannot just dial up a revolution. The efforts in Egypt, Tunisia, and Libya would not have been successful without the courage of thousands of local residents who were willing to give their lives to change their government. Gaddafi would likely still be in power in Libya if the rebels had not also received military assistance from NATO. However, this support would probably not have happened without the work of people like Ayat Mneina, who collected information and put together a story that attracted the attention of individuals and governments around the world. The social media message is part of a media ecosystem that can help to amplify a message to enough audiences that a huge undertaking like a revolution becomes possible (Zuckerman, 2011).

Before reading on, test your knowledge of the media by taking the quiz in Box 17.1. on page 478.

(*Source:* Used with permission of Ayat Mneina)

Critical Thinking Questions

1. Think of a political issue that you and your friends are interested in (tuition fees, student loan policies, environmental issues,). How could you use social media to help promote your views on this issue?

2. In the 2008 U.S. presidential election, Barack Obama based much of his campaign strategy on organizing support through social media. Do you think young voters would be more receptive to political participation if more politicians follow President Obama's example?

3. Do any of your friends or classmates come from countries with repressive governments? If so, are any of them involved in using social media to help people who oppose these governments?

CHAPTER FOCUS QUESTION

What impact are the media having on our culture, our social institutions, and our communities?

LEARNING OBJECTIVES

AFTER READING THIS CHAPTER, YOU SHOULD BE ABLE TO

- **LO-1** Understand what is meant by the term *mass media.*
- **LO-2** Consider how the impact of the media is explained by functionalist, conflict, feminist, interactionist, and postmodern theories.
- **LO-3** Understand how new media both bring people together and keep them apart.
- **LO-4** Understand how social media sites profit from the information you provide them.
- **LO-5** Think about the role played by the media in globalization.

LO-1 WHAT ARE THE MASS MEDIA?

mass media Any technologically based means of communicating between large numbers of people distributed widely over space or time.

The media connect those who produce messages with those who receive them. The **mass media** can be defined as any technologically based means of communicating between large numbers of people distributed widely over space or time (Pavlik and McIntosh 2011:18).

Traditionally, the mass media have involved one-way communication in which a single source sent out a message to a large number of people who passively received that message. Think of the early days of television when there were only one or two channels and families gathered in their living rooms to watch their favourite programs. There was no opportunity for direct interaction between the media and members of the audience and little choice of programs.

BOX 17.1 **SOCIOLOGY AND EVERYDAY LIFE**

How Much Do You Know About the Media?

True	False	
T	F	1. You do not need to be concerned about your privacy when using social media sites such as Facebook.
T	F	2. Canadians spend more time watching television than using the Internet.
T	F	3. Canadian radio stations can broadcast any songs they wish.
T	F	4. When people design their online avatars in virtual worlds such as Second Life, they are not bound by our real-life cultural preferences about body size, hairstyles, and dress.
T	F	5. While Internet dating sites are becoming more common, most people still meet their partners through traditional means such as family, school, and church.

For answers to the quiz about the media, go to **www.nelson.com/sociologyinourtimes6e.**

The nature of the media has changed dramatically. Social media such as blogs, Facebook, and Twitter allow many individuals or groups to send out messages to many others, and the monopoly of those who control transmission has been broken. We have access to hundreds of television channels and millions of websites, there are countless YouTube videos to watch, and we can communicate directly with people anywhere in the world, thanks to the **Internet**—the network infrastructure that links together the world's millions of computers.

Internet The network infrastructure that links together the world's millions of computers.

Over the past decade, the development of smartphones, tablets, and other portable devices has meant that we can stay constantly connected with family and friends and with the vast range of information available on the **World Wide Web**—the computer language that allows us to access information on the Internet. There used to be a clear separation of the different media, but media convergence has blended them together. Now we can watch movies and television programs, read novels and online newspapers, listen to music, and send text and voice messages on the same digital media device. We now live in a world where anyone can become a publisher or broadcaster through blogs, YouTube videos, or publishing services such as Amazon's CreateSpace—and the traditional media will have to adapt to this new reality.

World Wide Web The computer language that allows us to access information on the Internet.

In this chapter, we will discuss some of the ways in which we are affected by the media and how new media technology is changing many aspects of our lives.

SOCIOLOGICAL PERSPECTIVES ON THE MASS MEDIA LO-2

The media play an important role in our lives. Media theorist Douglas Kellner has set out some of the ways the media affect us:

> Radio, television, film, and the other products of media culture provide materials out of which we forge our very identities; our sense of selfhood; our notion of what it means to be male or female; our sense of class, of ethnicity and race, of nationality, of sexuality; and of "us" and "them." Media images help shape our view of the world and our deepest values: what we consider good or bad, positive or negative, moral or evil. Media stories provide the symbols, myths, and resources through which we constitute a common culture and through the appropriation of which we insert ourselves into this culture. Media spectacles demonstrate who has power and who is powerless, who is allowed to exercise force and violence, and who is not. They dramatize and legitimate the power of the forces that be and show the powerless that they must stay in their places or be oppressed . . .
>
> The media . . . contribute to educating us how to behave and what to think, feel, believe, fear, and desire—and what not to do. The media . . . show us how to dress, look, and consume: how to react to members of different social groups; how to be popular and successful and how to avoid failure; and how to conform to the dominant system of norms, values, practices, and institutions. Consequently, the gaining of critical media literacy is an important resource for individuals and citizens in learning how to cope with a seductive cultural environment. (2011:7)

The Center for Media Literacy defines **media literacy** as the ability to access, analyze, evaluate, and create media in a variety of forms (2011). Sociology provides many of the tools we need to become media literate and to understand the role of the media in our society. Different sociological theories provide us with a variety of perspectives that help us to explain how the media operate in our society and to understand the impact the media have on our attitudes and behaviour.

media literacy The ability to access, analyze, evaluate, and create media in a variety of forms.

Functionalist Perspectives on the Media

FUNCTIONS OF THE MEDIA Charles Wright was one of the earliest sociologists to analyze the media from a functionalist perspective. Wright (1959) described four functions of the mass media:

- *Surveillance.* The media tell us what is happening in the world. By warning us about imminent storms, reporting the latest economic news, or telling us about the newest Hollywood movies, the media play an important role in informing the public.
- *Interpretation.* The media also interpret what is going on and tell us how we should respond to events. In editorials and in the selection of news stories, the media advance a particular agenda. Many parts of the mass media advocate particular political perspectives and try to influence how citizens vote.
- *Socialization.* The media transmit information, values, and norms from one generation to another and to newcomers. We can learn about society's rules, customs, and ways of behaving from the media.
- *Entertainment.* The media provide us with content that we find interesting and enjoyable. Many of us spend a significant part of our day being entertained by television, video games, radio programs, and recorded music.

Most would agree that the media do indeed fill these functions. The media sometimes do an excellent job of telling us what is going on—people around the world instantly learned of disasters like the 2011 earthquake and tsunami in Japan and the 2008 economic collapse. However, media coverage can be selective, so we learn more about some events than others. For example, while a terrorist bombing in a Western industrialized country will receive massive coverage in the media, atrocities elsewhere in the world may remain virtually uncovered—most Canadians are unaware of mass atrocities going on in countries such as the Democratic Republic of the Congo because the media do not want to spend money covering conflicts in little-known countries. Coverage of the Rwandan genocide took a back seat to the massive coverage of the O.J. Simpson murder trial in California and other events such as the war in the former Yugoslavia (Jackson, Nielsen, and Hsu, 2011).

One important form of socialization is that the media share images and experiences that allow us to imagine ourselves as part of a nation state. The invention of the printing press played an important role in developing a unified culture in France and other European countries (Straw, 2011). For centuries, France consisted of decentralized regional cultures with little sense of a national identity. Print media helped to standardize the French language, and the news and entertainment media contributed to a shared identity throughout the country. Straw also reports that the media, particularly television, drew the regions of Quebec together following

These early CBC logos highlight the organization's mandate of reflecting Canada and its regions.

the Quiet Revolution of the 1960s. The media play the same role everywhere in the world through broadcasting events such as the Olympics, legislative sessions, and national elections.

In many countries, the media have a legislated nation-building mandate. Canada's *Broadcasting Act* specifically gives the Canadian Broadcasting Corporation (CBC) the mandate to be "predominantly and distinctively Canadian, reflect Canada and its regions to national and regional audiences, while serving the special needs of those regions," to "actively contribute to the flow and exchange of cultural expression," to "contribute to shared national consciousness and identity," and to "reflect the multicultural and multiracial nature of Canada." (See Box 17.2.)

BOX 17.2 **POINT/COUNTERPOINT**

Should We Regulate the Media?

Many countries strictly regulate their media. China has imprisoned hundreds of journalists over the past decade, and "The Great Firewall of China" (formally named the Golden Shield Project) is one of many ways the Chinese government restricts free access to the Internet. Iran, Cuba, and several other countries are also known for their harsh treatment of journalists who are critical of the government.

Many other governments have also passed laws regulating the media. While Canadian media regulations may not censor free political expression, they do restrict who can own media companies, they regulate the use of the airwaves, and they put restrictions on media content. Children cannot view certain types of movies, and tobacco advertising is prohibited. One of the most interesting laws regulates the music played by Canadian radio stations.

In 1971, the Canadian government passed legislation specifying the amount of Canadian music that must be played on Canadian radio. York has explained why this legislation was passed:

> The average Top Forty station was programmed by an American broadcasting consultant, who told the station what to play, how to play it, and who to hire and fire. The station played either English or American records or both; it employed primarily American deejays; and it modeled itself after the best (or worst, whichever way you personally hear it) U.S. stations in Boston, Chicago and New York. The yardstick of success was just how close you could come to sounding exactly like these American stations. (Ranson, 2008)

In the 1950s and 1960s, few Canadian musicians were as popular as those from the United States and England. This situation changed when the Canadian Radio-television and Telecommunications Commission (CRTC) required radio and television stations to promote Canadian culture by broadcasting a regulated amount of content written and performed by Canadians. Television stations must broadcast material with 60 percent Canadian content (50 percent during evening hours), and radio stations must play music with 35 percent Canadian content. These regulations have had a positive impact. Canadian popular musicians flourished, and many have become international stars (Ranson, 2008). For example, Arcade Fire won the Grammy Award for best album of 2010, and in December 2011, four of the seven best-selling albums in North America were recorded by Canadian artists—Michael Bublé (#1), Justin Bieber (#3), Nickelback (#6), and Drake (#7).

While this effort to promote Canadian artists was successful, in 1999 the CRTC decided not to regulate the Internet. The CRTC felt that regulation would stifle creativity and innovation and that most of the content of the Internet at that time was mainly text-based and did not involve broadcasting content (CRTC, 2011). The CRTC also felt that enough Internet content was being produced in Canada, so no regulation was necessary at that time.

The CRTC revisited this issue in 2009, and several groups, including those representing actors, urged the CRTC to regulate online content in the same way as it regulates television and radio because they felt the new media are just providing alternate platforms for viewing and listening to cultural products. While it is easy to control the content produced by radio and television stations operating in Canada, however, Internet content can be transmitted from anywhere in the world. Transmitting radio over the Internet requires few resources other than a computer, a microphone, and some MP3 files—all of which are very portable, so regulation would likely be futile (Ranson, 2008). Thus, Internet content is still not regulated.

What are your views on this issue? Now that we are able to access radio and video broadcasts from anywhere in the world, should the federal government try to regulate content on the Internet to protect Canadian artists?

Building a national consciousness is not always positive. The 1994 genocide in Rwanda was spread by radio stations and newspapers that promoted hatred against the Tutsi minority, and the media were heavily used by the Nazis to promote their vision of German racial superiority prior to World War II (Jackson, Nielsen, and Hsu, 2011).

Bookman (2011) has pointed out that today's interactive media also allow us to become members of very different types of imagined communities. These include online communities such as Second Life and FarmVille, as well as communities organized around interests such as cooking, sports, and environmental issues that can include members from around the globe.

OTHER FUNCTIONS OF THE MEDIA Wright's four categories do not exhaust the functions of the media. For example, new forms of social media give the public a forum to express their views and perspectives. Traditional mass media tightly control what is transmitted, but we are now living in an era when anyone can set up a website, write a blog, or comment on a news story. As you read in Ayat Mneina's story in the chapter introduction, people can be mobilized through these sites. The July 2011 edition of the Vancouver-based anti-consumer magazine *Adbusters* included the message "What is our one demand? . . . #OCCUPYWALLSTREET, September 17" (Mickleburgh, 2011), which precipitated the Occupy movement in 2011. This movement spread quickly to many other cities throughout North America and Europe and at least temporarily drew attention to the increasing degree of inequality in Western countries. And some politicians follow public sites and even analyze Twitter feeds to help them develop policies that might appeal to voters.

The media can also link people through means such as Facebook, dating sites, and sales sites such as eBay. The importance of being able to stay close to people who are important to us is shown by the fact that in 2011, Skype reported 300 million minutes of video calls each day, an increase of 900 percent since 2007 (Caukin, 2011).

status conferral The process of giving prominence to particular individuals by focusing media attention on them.

The media also have a **status conferral** function—attention by the media can give people high status. This status can apply to people who have made real contributions to society and deserve recognition, but today's mass media also confer "star" status on people who have no particular talent but are simply "famous for being famous."

The Occupy movement spread to many Canadian cities, including to this site in Toronto. Did this movement make you more aware of income inequality in Canada?

The celebrity socialite is not a new phenomenon, but reality television and the new social media have magnified the popularity of people such as the Kardashians (Gerds, 2011). Reality television shows enhance celebrity by showing us the details of their homes, cars, parties, holidays, and other personal details that make fans feel they have a close relationship with the celebrity, many of whom have blogs they use to reinforce these intimate ties with fans. Fans can respond to the blog postings, which helps them believe that they have a mutual relationship with the celebrity. Frequent tweets by the stars also give fans the sense that they are part of the celebrity's life. People grieved the deaths of celebrities such as Princess Diana and Michael Jackson as if they were close friends rather than people who were known only through media images (Hodkinson, 2011). The fact that people feel they are friends with people they will never meet blurs the distinction between reality and fiction—an issue that will be discussed later in this chapter when we discuss postmodern theories of media.

DYSFUNCTIONS OF THE MEDIA The media can also be *dysfunctional*. More than 60 years ago, long before the development of the Internet and the 24-hour global news cycle, Paul Lazarsfeld and Robert Merton (1948) coined the term *narcotization* to describe a situation in which people become so overwhelmed by the amount of information they receive that they become numb and do not act on the information. Nonstop broadcasts of scenes from a natural disaster such as the earthquake in Japan in 2011 can mobilize people to contribute to relief efforts, but as the bad news continues, people become desensitized and their attention moves on to other things.

Another dysfunction is that the free flow of news can threaten the status quo. News of what is happening elsewhere can be contagious. For example, the overthrow of the Tunisian government in 2011 quickly led to the successful revolutions in Egypt and Libya and to unsuccessful movements in several other countries, including Bahrain and Syria.

The media can also deliberately distort the news to sway public opinion. For example, Anderson and Robertson have documented the way in which the media have perpetuated stereotypes that have reinforced notions that "degrade, denigrate, and marginalize" Aboriginal people (2011:6). For nearly 150 years, the media have contributed to the marginalization of Aboriginal people by portraying them as inferior and by failing to present the Aboriginal case in discussions of issues such as land claims. Thus Aboriginal people have been largely excluded from the nation-building narrative presented by mainstream newspapers.

Other distortions, which are mainly being spread through the Web rather than through traditional media, include claims that the U.S. government was behind the 9/11 attacks on the World Trade Center and that President Obama is not legally the president because he was born outside the United States. These stories survive because the new media provide so many possible sources of information that almost every bias and interest can find support online.

The impact of these false stories may also be greater because of the new media. A person who watches network news or reads a mainstream newsmagazine will be exposed to a variety of issues and perspectives. However, if news comes through a customized daily news feed—what MIT Media Lab founder Nicholas Negroponte (1995) has called "The Daily Me"—the recipient may be exposed only to points of view he or she already supports. This new information will reinforce these beliefs rather than encouraging the recipient to consider alternative views. However, there has not yet been sufficient research to know whether the Internet will lead to selective exposure to a narrow range of opinions or whether people will use its power to find sources that challenge their views.

Conflict Perspectives on the Media

Conflict theorists argue that the media help the dominant class control society by reinforcing its capitalist ideology and by encouraging a mass consumer culture that allows those who own the means of production to sell us unnecessary products and services.

MASS MEDIA AND MASS DECEPTION Max Horkheimer and Theodor Adorno (1972) were two of the earliest critics of the mass media. During the 1940s, they asserted that the *culture*

Image courtesy of The Advertising Archives

Conflict theorists believe that capitalism uses the media to create false needs for consumer products. One example of this is advertising for makeup products that try to sell people on the ideal of everlasting youth and beauty.

industry has turned artistic expression into just another marketable commodity—a commodity that keeps people passively entertained and politically apathetic. Consumption of this mass media culture destroys individual creativity and prevents consumers from taking a critical approach to their life situation. While "true" artistic activities may lead to independent thought and criticism of existing social arrangements, monopoly capitalism has used popular culture to promote its own values and to help preserve the status quo. According to these critics, the culture industry has been responsible for the mass deception and control of the public.

Through advertising and the images created by the popular media, capitalism also creates false needs for consumer products while people's true needs—including freedom and creativity—are ignored. And of course these products are manufactured and sold by the capitalist system that created the need for them. These false needs keep workers motivated to work even harder for their capitalist employers.

The mass culture industry also provides workers with a way of escaping the boredom and routine that define their lives. The cultural products the workers consume are standardized and follow a consistent formula so that the consumer does not have to think much about them or engage with them intellectually. People can just come home after work and absorb media products such as television programs without engaging with others, without thinking about their problems, and without thinking critically about their lives under capitalism.

MEDIA CONCENTRATION Conflict theorists are critical of the fact that members of the dominant class control the media. They feel the media exploit the working class by promoting the cultural values and beliefs of the rich and powerful and by creating a false consciousness among workers. The media in most democratic countries claim to be objective, but conflict theorists reject this claim. For example, Herman and Chomsky (1998) describe the reasons why concentrated capitalist control means that stories critical of capitalism will not appear in the popular media. These include the following: Massive media companies profit from capitalism; their advertisers would not allow them to be critical of corporations; and governments and other organizations, such as pressure groups and corporations, influence media organizations. These factors mean that the public does not receive any information that would seriously threaten the interests of the dominant class.

The Senate has concluded that the ownership of media is more highly concentrated in Canada than in most other countries and has recommended that the government take steps to ensure that media concentration is limited (Parliament of Canada, 2006). However, since the Senate report, there has been even more concentration: Shaw recently purchased the broadcasting assets of Canwest, and Bell bought the portion of CTV network it did not already control. Both of these transactions are examples of media convergence as telecommunications companies (Shaw and Bell) have merged with media companies (Canwest and CTV). All the largest media companies show this convergence. For example, Rogers Communications provides cellular and home phone service, Internet, and cable television. Along with these telecommunications services, Rogers owns 54 radio stations and two television networks; 70 magazines, including *Maclean's* and *Chatelaine*; and several television channels, including The Shopping Channel and Rogers Sportsnet. Rogers also owns the Toronto Blue Jays baseball team. In 2011, Rogers and Bell each purchased 37.5 percent of the Toronto Maple Leafs, the Toronto Raptors, and the Toronto FC soccer club.

Thus, Rogers (and its major competitors Bell, Telus, and Shaw) owns some of the content as well as the means of distributing that content. Content can easily be shifted from one platform to another, and advertising can be targeted to very specific audiences. This gives these corporations a very powerful place in the digital world. They have always been hugely profitable, as they spent many years as monopolies—for decades, in many areas, people had only one choice of a cable television provider, so the companies that received these licences were guaranteed large profits. While some of their business has now been deregulated, the massive cost of entering the market helps to limit competition.

Why is media concentration an issue? Those who control the media control the message, and if ownership is concentrated, there will be less likelihood of diverse messages. Conflict theorists such as Hall (1982) believe that the media support the values and interests of the dominant class. For example, while the Fox News Network describes itself as "fair and balanced," it actually has a very deliberate right-wing bias (Martin, 2008) and vigorously supports America's economic elites. While television networks such as Fox (and Sun News, its Canadian counterpart) do not hide their ideological bias, conflict theorists believe that other media that claim to be objective are also biased. For example, Parenti argues that

> [Media bias] moves in more or less consistent directions, favoring management over labor, corporations over corporate critics, affluent whites over low income minorities, officialdom over protestors . . . privatization and free market 'reforms' over public sector development, U.S. dominance of the Third World over revolutionary or populist social change, and conservative commentators and columnists over progressive or radical ones. (2001)

How is media reporting biased? The media report some stories, ignore others that might challenge the dominant view of the world, and discredit stories that do not support the message of the established elites. They may also use loaded words: "freedom fighter" is a positive label, while "terrorist" is a negative label used to describe the same behaviour. Referring to "Third World" countries implicitly adopts the perspective that these countries are inferior to industrialized Western countries. The media also often deal with issues and events at a superficial level, which has the effect of supporting the status quo. Election campaigns focus on things like the latest poll results or a candidate's bus breaking down rather than on fundamental issues like inequality or the environment. Crime stories provide us with all the gruesome details, and the discussion is often racialized so that particular racial groups are blamed, deflecting attention from the social causes of crime.

While media concentration has been an important concern, the new social media have begun to change the situation. The chapter introduction showed how social media were able to break the media monopoly of repressive governments, and anyone can set up a blog to get out information that might not be published or broadcast by media conglomerates. The music industry has much less control over its products since downloading became possible, and individual artists are now able to sell their work online without going through a record company.

Interactionist Perspectives on the Media

Symbolic interactionists tell us that individuals continually negotiate their social realities. In his looking-glass-self theory, Charles Horton Cooley (1922/1902) proposed that a person's sense of self is derived from the perceptions of others. According to Cooley, we use our interactions with others as a mirror for our own thoughts and actions; our sense of self depends on how we interpret what they do and say. Consequently, our sense of self is always developing as we interact with others.

Cooley developed his theory more than a century ago, so it is interesting to see how it applies to our new social media. Do these social media affect our sense of self? Does interacting with others online have positive or negative effects on our self-concepts? Do our online representations affect our sense of self and our behaviour?

SOCIAL MEDIA AND GENDER IDENTITY Shapiro has studied the impact of the Internet on transgendered people. The Internet has made it easier for everyone to learn more about transgenderism, which makes it easier for the transgendered to work out new identities. It has also helped them to "shape their own gender identity and self-esteem and manage feelings of fear, isolation, and anger" (Shapiro, 2010:107).

Differently gendered people can feel isolated because they are afraid of public stigmatization (Schrock et al., 2004). However, the Internet can help them construct their identities by providing them with information through blogs and information sites. Perhaps more importantly, online discussion forums provide a way of discussing their lives with others who share the same experience. The importance of this contact is apparent in the expression of joy posted by a cross-dresser who had just discovered an online news group:

> just couldn't resist sharing my *elation* at having found you! I stumbled across the group by accident during lunch today and my heart skipped, then skipped again, and again. i've been a t-something as long as i can recall, but never had much hope of meeting anyone else. it's so *good* to see you all out there. (Schrock et al., 2004:66)

This contact can help people construct their gender identities. Hill asked members of Toronto's trans community (including cross-dressers, transsexuals, and transgendered persons) how they came to their sense of identity as trans persons. Many of his respondents reported that communications technologies had played an important role in this process. For example, Miqqi said:

> The biggest impact on the transgender world has been the Internet . . . I cannot overestimate its importance. It is . . . more than anything else how contact has been made for hundreds and hundreds of people who are isolated and otherwise out of contact. (Hill, 2005:39)

Another respondent, Melisa, who had been very isolated in a small northern community, described how she began to develop her trans identity based on her online contacts:

> I got on the Internet and the first thing I did, you know, was talk to anybody I could talk to about it . . . I wanted to talk to anybody or anything I could just to get some kind of rationale behind it, the vocabulary, do something with it . . . To build a story, to build a way to talk about it . . . It was something I could never do before. (Hill, 2005:41)

This research suggests that new social media can affect how people develop their identity, particularly for people who are isolated from other role models.

VIRTUAL IDENTITIES AND REALITY Many people blur the difference between reality and simulation by using the virtual world to experiment with their identity. Audrey, a subject interviewed by Sherry Turkle, told her that creating avatars and Facebook profiles is a "performance of you":

> Making an avatar and texting. Pretty much the same. You're creating your own person; you don't have to think of things on the spot really, which a lot of people can't really do. You're creating your own little ideal person and sending it out. Also on the Internet, with sites like MySpace and Facebook, you put up the things you like about yourself, and you're not going to advertise the bad aspects of you . . . You can write anything about yourself; these people don't know. You can create who you want to be . . . maybe in real life it won't work for you, you can't pull it off. But you can pull it off on the Internet. (2011:191)

Audrey uses her online virtual life to help construct her real identity. She uses Facebook and Second Life to try different styles—flirting one day and being witty on another—and notes how others respond. If the new style gets a poor response, she changes it, and if her online friends respond positively, she incorporates that into her real-life identity. One of Turkle's respondents came out as gay online to help him deal with this process in real life. Another, who needed a prosthetic leg following a car accident, practised sexual intimacy through her online avatar (which also had a prosthetic leg) before considering a sexual relationship in real life. The Internet's anonymity means that these identity experiments are much less risky than if they were done in real life. Just as a pilot can safely learn to fly and to handle aircraft emergencies in a flight simulator, some people can learn to handle real-life problems by practising online.

We know that people create idealized images of themselves when they create avatars on sites such as Second Life (LeBlanc, 2011). Yee and Bailenson (2007) have addressed the interesting question of whether the process works the other way as well—do our avatars also affect our real-life behaviour?

Yee and Bailenson assigned volunteers to either attractive or unattractive avatars and asked the volunteers to interact online with other avatars. They wanted to see whether their subjects conformed to the stereotypes of their avatars. They found that those with attractive avatars were more confident and friendlier toward others than were subjects with unattractive avatars. They chatted more often with the other avatars and positioned themselves much more closely to their companions than did the unattractive avatars. In a second experiment, taller avatars did better in a negotiation than shorter avatars. The finding that the nature of our avatars affects the way we behave may help to explain why virtual communities are friendlier and more intimate than real life because people tend to create attractive avatars.

This effect also spills over into our real lives. Yee, Bailenson, and Duchenault (2009) found that the effects of the height of avatars continued when the volunteers later engaged in face-to-face real-life negotiations. Yee and his colleagues conclude that, "Together these studies suggest that neither the virtual nor the physical self can ever be truly liberated from the other. What we learn in one body is shared with other bodies we inhabit, whether virtual or physical" (2009:309). As more people spend more time online with their digital avatars, it will be interesting to see what impact this will have on behaviour and on our interactions with others.

The new media raise some interesting questions concerning the meaning of the "self" in a digital world. Nancy Baym asks where our true selves reside: "[W]hat if the selves enacted through digital media don't line up with those we present face to face, or if they contradict one another? If someone is nurturing face to face, aggressive in one online forum, and needy in another online forum, which is real? Is there such a thing as a true self anymore? Was there ever?" (2010:3). Of course, sociologists such as Goffman (1959) long ago showed us that all of us present ourselves in different ways depending on the circumstances, so perhaps this is not just limited to our digital worlds.

Feminist Perspectives on the Media

Gender scripts are our "blueprints for behavior, belief, and identity" (Shapiro, 2010:9). These scripts guide how we perform gender roles, and one of the ways we learn about these scripts is through the media. Many feminists are critical of the media's stereotyping of women, and research supports their view that television shows, newspaper stories, advertisements, movies, songs, and video games use sexist imagery to define women. If the media help us define our gender identities, the distorted mirror they hold up to women will have a negative impact.

Some of this bias can be attributed to the fact that the majority of people working in the media are male, and this male overrepresentation is particularly great at the senior management level (Straw, 2011). Advertising has been particularly criticized for being sexist, and most of the people employed in advertising agencies, particularly those who create the ads, are white males (Leiss et al., 2006).

WOMEN IN THE NEWS Since 1995, the Global Media Monitoring Project (2010) has reported on the representation of women in the media. Its first study, which looked at 71 countries (now expanded to 108 countries), found that women were greatly underrepresented in newspaper, television, and radio stories in every country. Between 1995 and 2010, the percentage of stories that mentioned women increased from 17 percent to 24 percent. However, this meant that women were still neglected in media reports. The study also found that media reports stereotyped women's social roles. Women were more likely to appear in stories dealing with science and health than in stories dealing with politics or the economy. Women were underrepresented in all occupational categories except homemakers and students, so their role in other occupations and professions was minimized. Stories about women were more likely to mention their age and their family status than were stories about men. Thus, the media play an important role in reinforcing unequal gender stereotypes around the globe (Global Media Monitoring Project, 2010).

WOMEN IN ADVERTISING Gender roles are an important part of media advertising. While most products are designed to have some practical use, marketers also try to give their products a symbolic value that will encourage consumers to buy (Hodkinson, 2011). Consumers are invited to associate themselves with the image presented in advertising.

The image that many advertisers wish to hold up to women was illustrated by American feminist leader Gloria Steinem. Steinem, the founding editor of *Ms.* magazine, described a conversation she had with Leonard Lauder, president of the Estée Lauder cosmetics company:

> *Ms.* isn't appropriate for his ads anyway, he explains. Why? Because Estée Lauder is selling a "kept-woman mentality."
>
> I can't quite believe this. Sixty percent of the users of his products are salaried, and generally resemble *Ms.* readers. Besides, his company has the appeal of having been started by a creative and hardworking woman, his mother, Estée Lauder.
>
> That doesn't matter, he says. He knows his customers, and they would *like* to be kept women. That's why he will never advertise in *Ms.* (2011:241)

The lack of advertising from Estée Lauder and other companies led to the eventual sale of the magazine.

One of the few companies that did use a feminist message was a tobacco company. During the 1960s and 1970s, advertising for Virginia Slims cigarettes used the slogan "You've Come a Long Way, Baby" to co-opt the progressive image of the feminist movement as a way of attracting women to their product.

Despite decades of criticism, advertisers continue to show women in the role of caregivers or sex objects (Leiss et al., 2006). Current ads for GoDaddy.com—a company that registers Internet domain names—portray several female athletes, including Danica Patrick, in a sexualized manner. When not doing these commercials, Patrick has been breaking down stereotypes in the very dangerous, male-dominated sport of high-performance auto racing, but in the ads she is depicted only as an attractive, scantily clad woman. Other advertisements have depicted women as needing a man's help—sink stains required the help of the Ajax White Knight, and dirty floors and doors led to a call for Mr. Clean to rescue the woman of the house (O'Reilly, 2011). While women prefer advertising that shows them in more egalitarian roles (Leiss et al., 2006), advertisers still persist in showing women in these traditional ways.

Erving Goffman (1979) went beyond the content of the ads to look at other ways in which advertisers engage in gender stereotyping. He looked at the details of print advertisements and found several ways in which women and men were portrayed differently. Women were more often sitting down or even lying on the floor or a bed, while men were more often standing. Men were authorities, while women were more often in subordinate positions—men were shown instructing women or as doctors who had authority over female nurses. The exception to this was ads showing a kitchen, where women were in charge and were typically shown cooking for or serving men. If men were shown doing household chores, they were typically doing an incompetent job, often under the scrutiny of a woman.

The media perpetuate traditional gender roles, despite the dramatic changes in the role of women over the past 40 years. Why should we be concerned about this depiction of women? Media stereotypes may make it harder for women to move into nontraditional roles and to break through the glass ceiling that still exists in many occupations. The way the media portray ideals of personal appearance also influences how people think about themselves and the improvements that they believe their bodies require. Researchers have found, for example, that the media ideal of thin female bodies can lead to body dissatisfaction and depression among those who are most exposed to these idealized images (Mastro and Stern, 2006). If this view is correct, media framing plays an important role in the growing phenomenon of young women opting for cosmetic surgery.

© Badgley Mischka/Splash News/Newscom

This shoe advertisement, featuring actor Teri Hatcher, shows how advertisers use gender stereotypes to market their products.

Postmodern Perspectives on the Media

The new social media are postmodern developments, so it should not be surprising that we can use the tools of postmodern theory to analyze some of the latest media trends. We can consider several examples of the way postmodern scholars have analyzed new media.

CREATING AVATARS IN SECOND LIFE Cathie LeBlanc (2011) used a postmodern framework to help us understand how participants design their avatars in Second Life. Postmodern theorist Michel Foucault showed that we live in a society where technologies make widespread surveillance possible in many different social settings. Because people feel they are always being watched, they govern their own behaviour through self-surveillance. While some have predicted that virtual environments such as Second Life will enable people to freely choose the bodies of their avatars without concern for physical limitations or cultural constraints, LeBlanc believes that self-surveillance will enforce social constraints on the appearance of avatars.

When people first move into the Second Life environment, they can select a default body, but the default body of a newcomer reduces their status in the virtual world, so most quickly customize their avatar as it becomes clear that the avatar's external appearance matters. The expectation is that Second Life residents will design an avatar to match their idealized view of who they really are and that this avatar will also meet conventional standards of attractiveness.

Avatars are designed by Second Life residents who are sitting outside the online environment looking at their on-screen representations. Like a cosmetic surgeon, residents can change those aspects of their avatar that do not match their view of who they are or would like to be. As residents of Second Life move through their online world, they see both the landscape and the back of their avatar. This creates a feeling that the body is "both a subject and an object" (LeBlanc, 2011:116). This sense of detachment reinforces a self-surveillance that enforces the norms of the virtual community.

Used with permission of Marissa Ashkenaz

These rather normal-looking avatars are the "plus-sized" bodies that generated hostile comments on Second Life. Why do you think people responded so negatively to the appearance of these avatars?

What are these norms? Despite the hope that virtual space would enable people to free themselves from real-life bodily constraints, what actually happens is that external appearance becomes as important online as it is in the real world. Just as people use cosmetic surgery, makeup, tattoos, piercings, and clothing to try to communicate who they are in real life, online residents are bound by cultural constraints. In effect, self-surveillance is even more explicit online than it is in the real world. This explains one researcher's finding that in Second Life, "Almost everyone was thin, beautiful, well dressed, and had chosen features typical of North American societies' Anglo-European ideals including skin tone, facial and body structure" (Shapiro, 2010:89).

Thus, people who could be whatever they wanted chose to follow the familiar cultural norms they had learned in the real-life world. It seems likely that this was largely the result of self-surveillance, but there was also pressure from others online to use attractive avatars. For example, one researcher found that many fellow Second Lifers were hostile toward the plus-sized avatars that she and several friends used (Ashkenaz, 2008). Typical of the comments were the following:

> Kess also experienced some biting comments from her friends about her new weight gain:
>
> Grow: Hi fatass :P
>
> *Then later on:*
>
> Grow: Kess you put on weight over xmas, hun.
>
> Jad: Eat too much for xmas, kess?

FANTASY FOOTBALL

> For the fantasy football fanatic, the seventh day is hardly an occasion for rest. From the moment he wakes, the clock begins ticking toward kickoff. There are statistical match-ups to analyze; weather and injury reports to consult; imaginary rosters to juggle. He is still a fan, but a very different kind of fan, and while he may not be alone in managing and cheering on his particular fantasy squad, he is not at all alone in his quest for fantasy success. (Serazio, 2008:229)

Fantasy sports have become a significant part of North American culture. Fantasy sports leagues enable people to draft real players onto their fantasy teams. The fantasy "owners" decide who is going to play and can trade players to other teams. The results are based on the performance of each of their chosen players in actual games.

Websites, magazines, talk shows, apps, and statistical services are dedicated to fantasy sports (Harper and Ploeg, 2011). The Internet has had a huge impact on fantasy sports because it enables the real-time tracking of statistics so that participants do not have to spend time making these calculations.

The blending of real performance with the fantasy ownership of a team has changed the way people watch and relate to the game (Serazio, 2008). While sports fans normally cheer for a favourite team and often identify strongly with that team, fantasy team owners are concerned about the performance of the individual players who make up their virtual teams. And of course these teams are not really "teams" in the sense of being a group of people who work together to attain the common goal of winning but exist only in the simulated realm of fantasy. To the participants, however, the results of their fantasy teams do feel very real and can have real consequences if there are financial prizes for the best teams.

Jean Baudrillard (1995) developed the notion of **hyperreality**—a situation in which the distinction between reality and simulation has become blurred. We are saturated in media that have become a central part of our lives and that help to define our experiences and our understanding of the world. Manufactured images and representations are part of our reality and in turn affect the way we interpret subsequent images.

hyperreality A situation in which the distinction between reality and simulation has become blurred.

Harper and Ploeg argue that fantasy sports illustrate the world of hyperreality: "Reality is no longer diametrically opposed to fantasy; it is indistinguishable from it. Ironically, in *fantasy* sports, fans abandon the dichotomized framework of fantasy/reality and, instead, embrace the paradigm of the hyperreal" (2011:156).

FARMVILLE The Internet game FarmVille provides another example of hyperreality in which players can sometimes lose track of the difference between their real and virtual lives. Emily Hall (2011) describes how the designers have built into the game many ways of rewarding players through awards and prizes. This recognition can lead some players to feel that they get more appreciation from their simulated work in FarmVille than from their real jobs. Life online can be simpler than real life, and players can become very absorbed in the game as they build up their farms, add decorations that show their prosperity, and receive gifts from their online neighbours.

The creators of FarmVille have developed ways of keeping players involved and expanding the numbers playing the game. Crops grow in real time, so individual participants must keep checking online in order to harvest them at the proper time. Players have incentives for bringing new people into the game, and players are encouraged to create communities where people are farming with their real-life friends as their online neighbours. Players can also join co-ops whose members are rewarded for accomplishing collective goals. This places pressure on each member to stay involved with the game because all co-op members will suffer if one fails to do his or her part.

These techniques have helped FarmVille become the most popular online game. According to Patrick Liskiewicz, a game that he feels is actually boring and difficult to play has become a huge success because game developers have built in social pressures to play:

> My mother began playing *Farmville* last fall, because her friend asked her to join and become her in-game neighbor. In *Farmville*, neighbors send you gifts, help you tend your farm, post bonuses to their Facebook pages, and allow you to earn larger plots of land. Without at least eight in-game neighbors, in fact, it is almost impossible to advance in *Farmville* without spending real money. This frustrating reality led my mother—who was now obligated to play because of her friend—to convince my father, two of her sisters, my fiancée and (much to my dismay) myself to join *Farmville*. Soon, we were all scheduling our days around harvesting, sending each other gifts of trees and elephants, and posting ribbons on our Facebook walls. And we were convincing our own friends to join *Farmville*, too. Good times.
>
> The secret to *Farmville*'s popularity is neither gameplay nor aesthetics. *Farmville* is popular because it entangles users in a web of social obligations. When users log into Facebook, they are reminded that their neighbors have sent them gifts, posted bonuses on their walls, and helped with each others' farms. In turn, they are obligated to return the courtesies . . . We play *Farmville*, then, because we are trying to be good to one another. We play *Farmville* because we are polite, cultivated people. (2010)

Zynga, the corporation that owns FarmVille, makes hundreds of millions of dollars each year, most of which comes from participants who use real money to buy land, animals, and other in-game products, so these strategies are used to increase their profits. Here again, the difference between the real and the simulated is blurred as real-life social relations are manipulated by the creators of a simulated world in order to make real-life profits (Hall, 2011).

Finally, consider a recent tragic consequence of the hyperreality created by FarmVille. A man in England robbed a blind man to obtain money so he could buy animals for his virtual farm and then killed a family friend so he could pay back the money before his victim reported him to the police (Osuh, 2011).

TIME TO REVIEW

- Describe the role played by social media in the 2011/12 revolutions in the Middle East and North Africa.
- What are the functions and dysfunctions of the media?
- Discuss how conflict theorists feel the media support capitalist societies. What role does media concentration play in this support?
- How do interactionists help us to understand the way the new media helps people develop their identities?
- Discuss how stereotyped gender roles are used in advertising to promote products.
- How do online games fit Baudrillard's notion of hyperreality?

CONCEPT SNAPSHOT

FUNCTIONALIST PERSPECTIVES **Key thinker:** Charles Wright	Functionalists have shown that the media help us to learn what is happening in the world; suggest how we should interpret and respond to these events; teach us about our society's rules, customs, and ways of behaving; and keep us entertained. The media also provide us with community forums, link people together, and confer status on certain individuals. The media also have dysfunctions, including misinforming us and "narcotizing" us to the extent that we do not respond to social issues.
CONFLICT PERSPECTIVES **Key thinkers:** Max Horkheimer, Theodor Adorno	Conflict theorists argue that the media help the dominant class control society by reinforcing capitalist ideology and by encouraging a mass consumer culture that allows those who own the means of production to sell us unnecessary products and services. Conflict theorists are highly critical of the fact that the conventional media are dominated by a few very large corporations that control the message that goes out to media consumers.
INTERACTIONIST PERSPECTIVES **Key thinkers:** Sherry Turkle, Jeremy Bailenson	Interactionists tell us that individuals continually negotiate their social realities. The media, particularly the new social media, play an important role in creating our sense of self. Many people are now experimenting with identities online through the persona they put on their Facebook pages and through avatars in online games and virtual reality communities.
FEMINIST PERSPECTIVES **Key thinkers:** Gloria Steinem, Erving Goffman	Feminist sociologists have been critical of the stereotyped manner in which women are portrayed in the media. Most stories in the media focus on males and women are depicted in typical gender-linked roles. This is especially true in advertisements, where women tend to be depicted as traditional homemakers and caregivers or as sex objects. These media stereotypes may make it more difficult for women to move into non-traditional social roles.
POSTMODERN PERSPECTIVES **Key thinkers:** Michel Foucault, Cathie LeBlanc, Jean Baudrillard	Postmodern theorists have approached the media in several different ways. One of the most interesting of these is Baudrillard, whose theory of hyperreality points out how the distinction between reality and simulation has become blurred. Manufactured images and representations are part of our reality and in turn affect the way we interpret subsequent images.

THE IMPACT OF SOCIAL MEDIA LO-3

In this section, we will look at some of the ways in which new media technologies are reshaping the ways we interact with each other. Texting is replacing face-to-face contact, and we are increasingly likely to meet our romantic partners online rather than through family or school. It is important to think about the impact of these changes on our culture and our social relationships.

Alone Together: Do Social Media Bring Us Together or Keep Us Apart?

Sherry Turkle was one of the first to study computer culture. When she began her work in the 1980s, phones were mounted on kitchen walls, people were playing simple video games that plugged into their television sets, and a few hobbyists were building and programming their own home computers. Turkle was interested in learning how these tools were shaping individuals and their cultures.

The relationship between people and their communication devices changed dramatically in the 1990s and continues to rapidly evolve. Many of us are connected all the time and communicating electronically is becoming the way we live rather than just something we do. The Internet has dramatically increased the scope of possible relationships, as it is now just as easy to communicate with people halfway around the world as with the people next door. Your parents' old wall-mounted telephones were just a means of communication, but our portable devices have become a "portal that enable[s] people to live parallel lives in online worlds" (Turkle, 2011:xi).

What impact has this had on our lives? Do social media hold us together or keep us apart? Two facets of social media are having a dramatic impact on our social relationships: Mobile devices mean that we can always be contacted, and we can develop online identities in addition to living our "real" lives.

WE ARE ALWAYS AVAILABLE Mobile connections such as smartphones mean that people are no longer tethered to their computers but can carry their online lives with them everywhere. This means that we can always be available to others and have difficulty escaping this contact even if we wish to do so.

Some people have become dependent on this constant connection. In 2011, when a problem affected many subscribers' use of their BlackBerry smartphones for several days, many called it a "disaster" and filed lawsuits against the manufacturer. Some of Turkle's respondents describe the loss of a cellphone as feeling "like a death" (2011:16).

Communications professor Danna Walker required her students to avoid all electronic media for 24 hours. Many of the students found this painful. One wrote, "I was in shock . . . I honestly did not think I could accomplish this task. The 24 hours I spent in what seemed like complete isolation became known as one of the toughest days I have had to endure" (2007). Walker commented that another "apparently did not see the irony in this statement: 'I felt like I would be wasting my time doing the project. I did not want to give up my daily schedule, which mainly includes lying on my couch, watching television and playing The Sims 2 . . . computer game" (2007). Another said, "There was a moment in my day when I felt homeless . . . I couldn't go home because I knew that would be too tempting . . . I was walking down the street literally with nowhere to go, and I just didn't know what I was going to do" (2007).

The fact that we can be constantly available to friends and family might help us to strengthen our relationships with these significant others. However, Turkle concluded that the new media may actually be keeping us apart: "We are increasingly connected to each other but oddly more alone: in intimacy, new solitudes" (2011:19).

Think of how some people pay more attention to their mobile phones than to the people they are with. Face-to-face conversations are routinely interrupted by the beep or buzz of the mobile device

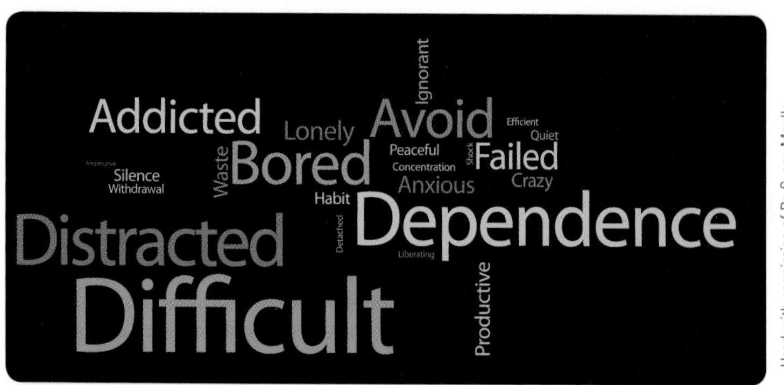

The first of these word clouds shows the feelings of students who had spent 24 hours without media. The second shows their responses to a question about the advantages of unplugging. What lesson can you draw from these two word clouds?

as a text message is given priority over face-to-face communication because our new cultural norms demand an instant response. The average teenager sends more than 3300 text messages each month, and teenage girls send an average of 4050 (Nielsen, 2010). While each text message may not take long, sending more than a hundred texts a day takes an enormous amount of time. The time spent using social media—whether responding to hundreds of texts each day, spending hours in virtual reality, or playing an online game—is time that is not spent interacting with other people. Face-to-face relationships are being replaced by networked relationships. This point was highlighted by another of Danna Walker's students who had to give up electronic media for a day: "My mother is thrilled that I'm doing this . . . to her it means I get to spend the day with her. I bite, and we walk into town for some brunch. I draw out the brunch as long as possible" (2007).

The ability to chat online certainly broadens our range of contacts. People can keep in touch with hundreds of Facebook friends. However, we can ask whether having many brief contacts with a broad range of "friends" is as meaningful as more intimate personal relationships with fewer people.

Technology can be used to keep people at a distance: "Texting puts people not too close, not too far, but at just the right distance" (Turkle, 2011:15). Turkle also discusses an extreme form of distancing one's self from others when she describes an interview with a reporter from *Scientific American* who accused her of intolerance because she did not think it was appropriate that people might someday have sexual relationships with robots and even marry them. Turkle subsequently interviewed several people who would have welcomed such relationships because they came without the risks inherent in relationships with other humans. Real-life marital partners can cheat, become alcoholics, and be judgmental about their partner's behaviour. Robotic spouses would be completely predictable and could be programmed to do whatever their partners/owners wished. Many young people have been raised with robotic pets, and some seniors now have robot companions to keep them from getting lonely.

WE CAN LIVE ALTERNATIVE LIVES Social media can provide us with online lives that may be more satisfying to some people than their real lives. Consider the promises made by Second Life (secondlife.com): "Who will you meet in Second Life? Where will you explore? What will you discover? Who will you be? Anything is possible in Second Life. A whole new world is waiting."

To someone who is lonely and unhappy, the promise of virtual reality can be compelling. A new identity, a glamorous appearance, and the chance to live an adventurous lifestyle lie ahead.

Your Second Life avatar can help you live your dreams, and you are in control in a way that would never be possible in the real world.

Consider Pete, one of Turkle's interview subjects. Pete was a 46-year-old man who was devoted to Second Life. His online avatar is a handsome young man who had married a young and beautiful avatar, Jade, at a wedding attended by their virtual best friends. While Pete has never met the anonymous woman (or man) who is behind Jade, he shares with Jade a relationship that is both socially and physically intimate. Pete prefers his Second Life to his "real life": "Second Life gives me a better relationship than I have in real life. This is where I feel most myself. Jade accepts who I am. My relationship with Jade makes it possible for me to stay in my marriage, with my family" (2011:159). To Turkle, "The ironies are apparent: an avatar who has never seen or spoken to him in person and to whom he appears in a body nothing like his own seems, to him, most accepting of his truest self" (2011:159).

While Pete used his online life to help cope with an unhappy family situation, others who are dissatisfied with their real lives may completely withdraw into their online worlds. Adam was another of Turkle's respondents. He got little satisfaction from his life and turned to online games such as Quake and Civilization:

> These games take so long, you can literally play it for days. One time when I played it, I had just got the game and I got so addicted, I stayed home the next day and I played . . . I think it was like noon the next day, or like nine o'clock the next day, I played all night long. And I ended up winning. You get so advanced. You get super-advanced technology. (2011:222)

Adam felt good only when he was playing games, and he was emotionally attached to the bots he played with. He was letting the rest of his life slip away, and his difficulties dealing with reality turned him even more toward the virtual world.

How Social Media Affect Our Lives

Even those who are not hooked on virtual worlds or online games can be affected by the demands and distractions of the new media. Many of our activities require concentration, but it can be difficult to focus on a task when texts and emails keep arriving and any fleeting thought can lead us to waste minutes or hours tracking something down on the Internet. Many of our students have told us how difficult it can be to study when their friends expect an immediate response to text messages. The Internet has been an invaluable resource that has helped us write this text—we no longer need to walk to the library to find the most recent crime rates or to read an article in an academic journal—but it is also a source of distraction that makes it more difficult to meet deadlines. Sometimes watching cat videos or checking the latest hockey scores is more interesting than writing about how to conduct survey research or why social class affects educational success.

There are other, more serious consequences of distractions. An iPhone app named Type n Walk uses the iPhone camera to show the ground ahead of you so you do not walk into a tree or a lamppost while you are texting on your phone. Hundreds of people are killed each year in North America because drivers continue to text and talk on cellphones while they are driving despite a vast amount of evidence showing that this practice is at least as dangerous as drunk driving. For some people, the need to be in constant contact with others outweighs the need to walk or drive safely.

Some researchers have studied problematic Internet use (Tokunaga and Rains, 2010), which consists of behaviours such as not being able to control the amount of time spent using the Internet, a preference for online interaction over in-person interaction, and withdrawal when the Internet is not available. Some consider the Internet addictive—South Korea has set up Internet addiction recovery programs for young people, and 12-step recovery programs for Internet addiction are even available online (Blascovich and Bailenson, 2011).

Elias Aboujaoude (2010) suggests that virtual technology may have a much more profound impact than earlier forms of mass media—in the 18th century, the new popularity of novels led to fears of "reading mania" (Korkeila, 2010)—because the new media have immersive and interactive qualities that the earlier media did not have. Blascovich and Bailenson (2011) speculate that 3-D immersive virtual reality experiences are potentially much more addictive than current online games and activities because the experiences are closer to those of real life. Online avatars will look like humans and will be controlled as easily as we control our own bodies, so the line between real and simulation will continue to fade.

While there may be negative effects, the popularity of social media show that most people who use it consider it a valuable part of their lives. Families share news and photos on social media, and friends can stay in touch with each other, even if they live in different cities. The earlier discussion of the impact of the Internet on the transgendered and transsexual community shows how important it can be for people to be able to meet like-minded others online. The ability to have friends and role models from anywhere in the world can be liberating to people whose physical condition, sexual preferences, or other characteristics make them different. The GimpGirl Community, established online by women with disabilities, is another example of how the Internet enables people to set up networks of friendship and support from hundreds of communities to interact with one another.

WILL YOU MEET YOUR PARTNER ON THE INTERNET? THE RISE OF ONLINE DATING The Internet has dramatically changed the way many people meet their partners. In the 1940s and 1950s, most heterosexual couples met through family, friends, and school (Rosenfeld and Thomas, 2012). The family and school have steadily declined as sources of connection since then, but friends are still very important in making introductions, and the proportion of people who meet their future partners in bars and restaurants has doubled since the 1940s. The most significant change has been that in just over a decade, the percentage of people who met their partners on the Internet jumped from zero to 22 percent and it is now the third most common way of meeting (see Figure 17.1). These people meet through dating sites, online personal ads, online gaming sites, and sites focused on interests such as religion or hobbies.

Same-sex couples were much more likely to meet over the Internet: 61 percent of same-sex couples met online (see Figure 17.2 on page 498). Rosenfeld and Thomas believe this is because the Internet may be particularly useful to people facing thin dating markets—those who are seeking partners who are harder to find and where relationships may meet with social disapproval from some people. Parents will not be helpful in introducing a gay or lesbian child to a future partner if they disapprove of same-sex marriage or if their child has not come out to them. However, the Internet allows for a very efficient search process far beyond local neighbourhoods and friendship groups. Older heterosexuals also have a limited range of potential partners because most people in their age group already have partners and also have much higher than average rates of finding partners online. Rosenfeld and Thomas found that couples who met online were just as satisfied with their relationships as people who met in other ways and were no more likely to break up their relationships.

WILL ONLINE DATING BROADEN OUR SOCIAL TIES? How will digital media transform our social relationships? A Super Bowl ad for telecommunications company MCI told us, "There is no race, there are no genders, there is no age, there are no infirmities, there are only minds. Utopia? No, the Internet" (Baym, 2010:34). However, others feel social media will just reinforce our existing social networks. Those who favour this view cite research on the impact of the telephone, which increased people's ability to communicate but did not change people's social networks because they used the phone to communicate with their existing network of friends and relatives. Rosenfeld and Thomas examined the impact of the Internet on dating and marriage.

FIGURE 17.1 THE CHANGING WAYS AMERICANS MEET THEIR PARTNERS: HETEROSEXUAL COUPLES

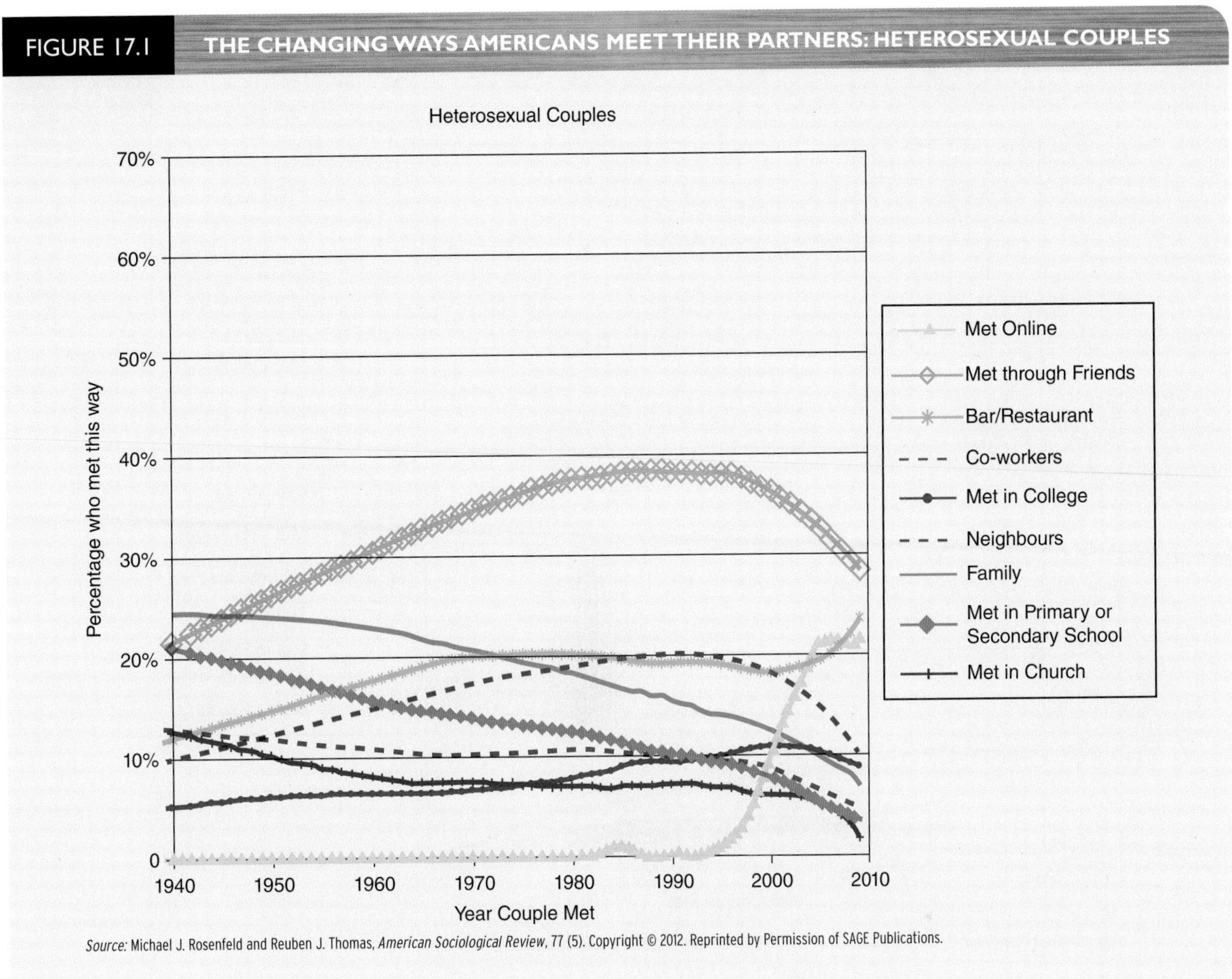

Source: Michael J. Rosenfeld and Reuben J. Thomas, *American Sociological Review*, 77 (5). Copyright © 2012. Reprinted by Permission of SAGE Publications.

Before World War II, most people chose their mates from their local neighbourhoods, schools, and churches. Because these institutions were homogeneous, people married partners with very similar class and race backgrounds. Does the broader reach of the Internet mean that people will meet potential partners who come from more diverse economic, racial, and religious backgrounds?

The Internet has had a limited effect on broadening social contacts. While couples from different religions were more likely than those from the same religion to have met online, the opposite was true for couples from different racial backgrounds, although the latter difference was not strong. There were only very small class differences between those who met online and those who met in other ways (Rosenfeld and Thomas, 2012).

DO PEOPLE TELL THE TRUTH ABOUT THEMSELVES ONLINE? While people are able to hide their identities in much of the online universe, this does not work in online dating, where the ultimate goal is a real-life romantic relationship. Those seeking a romantic attachment online face a dilemma. To attract potential partners, a person wants to create a positive impression. For online dating, physical attractiveness is particularly important in self-presentation, so people may use their most flattering photographs, photographs taken several years ago, or photographs that have been digitally altered (Toma and Hancock, 2010). However, the person must take care in constructing an online image. If reality is distorted too much, the potential partner may be very disappointed at the first face-to-face meeting—it is immediately obvious if

FIGURE 17.2 THE CHANGING WAYS AMERICANS MEET THEIR PARTNERS: SAME-SEX COUPLES

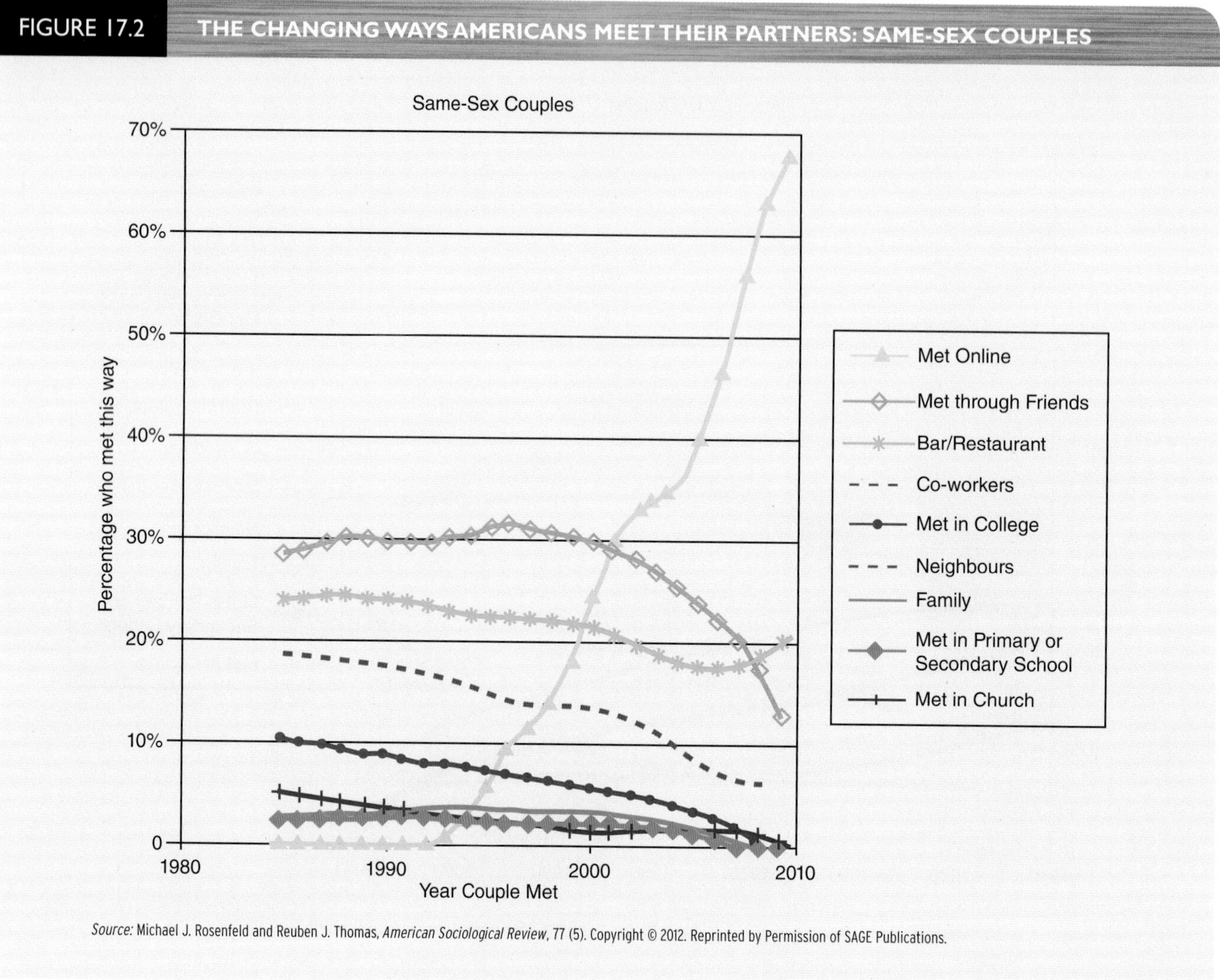

Source: Michael J. Rosenfeld and Reuben J. Thomas, *American Sociological Review*, 77 (5). Copyright © 2012. Reprinted by Permission of SAGE Publications.

a man is 20 cm shorter or 40 kg heavier than his dating profile had claimed, or if he really does not own a Ferrari and live in a mansion.

Toma and Hancock (2010) assessed the accuracy of daters' online reports of physical attractiveness. Those who were the least attractive were the most likely to enhance their online photographs and to lie about height, weight, and age. They were slightly more likely than more attractive online daters to lie about factors such as income and occupation. On the other hand, attractive daters posted more photographs of themselves, presumably to showcase their desirability.

Given the possibility of distortion, how do those seeking a partner reduce the chance of being disappointed when they actually meet their online contact? In relationships that begin through social contacts, some information about a potential partner can often be obtained from family, friends, and co-workers. Also, when we meet people in person, we know how they look, and we can use nonverbal cues to give us some clues about their personality.

These information sources are not available in online dating, but there are other ways of checking out another person (Gibbs, Ellison, and Lai, 2011). Networking sites such as Facebook and LinkedIn, public records (such as property tax assessments), and Google searches provide information about potential partners. Some online daters also ask direct questions and disclose more of their own personal information in online conversations in the hope of getting their potential partner to disclose more of their information.

Toma and Hancock used computerized linguistic analysis to find clues to the truthfulness of potential partners. These clues can be found in the language people used to describe themselves. The less truthful used fewer first-person pronouns (words such as *I*), used more negatives, and had shorter self-descriptions than those who were being honest (Rosenbloom, 2011).

PROFITING FROM SOCIAL MEDIA LO-4

The early Internet was not about money because it was originally designed to allow scientists to communicate with one another. Businesses soon began to seek ways of profiting from Web activities, however, and the ideologies of "free" versus "profit" have battled throughout the history of the Internet. For example, early in the development of the Web, Microsoft forced computer manufacturers to include Internet Explorer in their computers. Eventually, Explorer captured 97 percent of the browser market and put most of its competitors out of business. This monopoly was broken by the courts, and other browsers, such as Firefox and Chrome, have become popular.

Another economic battle was fought after the invention of Napster, which was the first widely available means of downloading music. This had a huge impact on the music industry as millions of people began to share music online rather than purchasing it from music stores. This permanently changed the music business, although legal music sources such as iTunes have helped the music companies and the artists regain some of their profits.

The new social media are also trying to become profitable. Most users do not understand the role of Facebook (Rushkoff, 2010). They think they are *clients* of Facebook, but they are actually its *products*—because Facebook makes money by selling access to personal information. Because of the information people provide to the site, Facebook can charge a premium for ads that are tailored to the interests of a particular audience. At the end of 2011, the estimated value of Facebook was $100 billion; Zynga, the producer of FarmVille, was valued at almost $10 billion. However, both declined in value in 2012 as questions arose about their ability to make profits (see Box 17.3).

There are many ways of profiting from the new media . Many corporations, including Nike, Nissan, and Sears, have become part of Second Life with stores, showrooms, and virtual products. They hope to use the site to get potential customers interested in their real-life products. Movies have had virtual premieres complete with red carpets and glamorous virtual stars. Religious institutions are also becoming part of Second Life, so we now see virtual missionaries who try to spread the faith online. According to one religious spokesperson, "This virtual Second Life is becoming populated with churches, mosques, temples, cathedrals, synagogues, places of prayer of all kinds. And behind an avatar, there is a man or woman, perhaps searching for God and faith, perhaps with very strong spiritual needs" (quoted in Rhoten and Lutters, 2009).

IBM has more than 50 "islands" in Second Life where it conducts meetings and other events (Rhoten and Lutters, 2009). This saves the company travel costs and is considered more personal than conference calls or video conferencing. The boundaries between real and virtual worlds were narrowed in 2007 when nearly 2000 avatars invaded one of IBM's islands to protest against the company's threats to cut employees' pay in Italy. The protest was successful in the real world, and is now commemorated in a museum on Union Island in Second Life (Rhoten and Lutters, 2009). Many other political and social issues have also been addressed in Second Life, including Palestinian statehood and the animal rights movement.

We are barely touching the surface of the commercial exploitation of the new media. Advertisers have developed a strategy of *self-endorsing,* which means that an avatar or other representation of the consumer is used in an advertisement. Ahn and Bailenson (2011) found that this was a highly effective technique. If the avatar is shown using the product, favourable brand attitude and purchase intentions increased. For example, if the avatar was shown wearing a particular brand of clothing, the research subjects were more likely to prefer that brand to others representing similar products. The closer avatars were in appearance to the consumer, the more positive the brand attitude.

BOX 17.3 **POINT/COUNTERPOINT**

New Media and Privacy

You have just tweeted a friend that you're going for coffee. As you pass a coffee shop, a coupon arrives on your phone offering 50 cents off a large cup of coffee. A friend who is travelling to Paris uses an online site to book a hotel room. Because she is using a Mac computer, the hotels that come up on the booking list are more expensive than if she had used a PC. A new college graduate has submitted a resumé for a job. The potential employer looks at the applicant's Facebook site, finds photos of the applicant using soft drugs at parties, and decides not to hire the person. In each of these cases, information that a person might expect to be private has been used by a third party. In the first two cases, the information was sold to an advertiser.

Online sites such as Facebook, Google, and Twitter provide a useful service for hundreds of millions of users. However, from the perspective of those who own these sites, the service is actually provided to advertisers rather than to users. The commodity they provide to these advertisers is personal information about users that allows advertisers to carefully target their ad campaigns. Advertisers are interested in knowing your location, relationship status, travel plans, musical tastes, occupation, and other interests.

Search engines such as Google make billions of dollars from tracking the key words you use. If you search for terms such as *headache* or *upset stomach*, you may receive ads or coupons for remedies for these maladies. Google also tracks your information across its different products, such as Gmail and YouTube, to develop more complete profiles of users in order to personalize the service.

Facebook and other networking sites frequently change their privacy policies with little notice. In 2009, Facebook suddenly made lists of friends publicly available. This change had serious consequences for many people. For example, the Iranian government detained people who were Facebook friends with people who were critics of the government (Andrews, 2012). The people who bought shares of Facebook when they were first offered to the public in 2012 valued each of its one billion users at $100. At that time, the company was earning only an average of $1 per user, so its shareholders will be putting pressure on Facebook executives to find new ways of selling people's information that will put increasing pressure on privacy. Meanwhile, Google has paid large fines after admitting to using its Street View camera cars to collect people's wireless data and to violating rules by bypassing privacy settings on the Safari browsers used on iPhones and computers.

While people may feel that receiving targeted advertising is an acceptable price to pay for using the services of a search engine or networking site, many of us are not aware of the other organizations that use these data. Insurance companies may search for evidence of risky activities or chronic illnesses that individuals may not report on their application forms. Law enforcement agencies and tax officials use social media sites to find information about potential wrongdoing and do not need search warrants that would be required if they were accessing the information in another fashion. Law enforcement agencies can also track people by using their cellphone records and obtain a great deal of personal information through this tracking:

> The United States Court of Appeals for the District of Columbia Circuit, ruling about the use of tracking devices by the police, noted that GPS data can reveal whether a person "is a weekly church goer, a heavy drinker, a regular at the gym, an unfaithful husband, an outpatient receiving medical treatment, an associate of particular individuals or political groups—and not just one such fact about a person, but all such facts." (Maass and Rajagopalan, 2012)

Information may last forever on the Internet. Do most people know that personal information they and their friends post online can come back to haunt them in the future when they apply for a job, run for political office, or try to convince their teenage children that they behaved perfectly when they were attending university or college? What about sites such as Banjo that allow people to track you and receive a message if you are near their location? Does it concern you that if you search for information on HIV/AIDS for a term paper, a data aggregator may infer that you have AIDS? Should people have the right to know what data are being collected about them and to prohibit companies from tracking their information without their consent?Would you prefer to pay a fee for Facebook rather than letting them sell your personal information to advertisers? These and other issues need to be worked out as new media technologies become more pervasive in our lives.

Sources: Andrews, 2012; Maass and Rajagopalan, 2012.

GLOBALIZATION AND THE MEDIA LO-5

Media Technology and Globalization

With its dots and dashes transmitted through a wire, the telegraph seems a very primitive means of communication compared with today's media technologies. After its introduction in the 1840s, however, people predicted it would have a revolutionary impact because, for the first time, people could instantly communicate over a distance:

> Universal peace and harmony seem at this time more possible than ever before, as the telegraph binds together by a vital cord all the nations of the earth. It is impossible that old prejudices and hostilities should any longer exist, while such an instrument has been created for an exchange of thought between all nations of the earth. (Czitrom, 1982:10)

Canadian media scholar Marshall McLuhan was one of the first to recognize the potential impact of modern media technologies. McLuhan believed these technologies would create a **global village** in which people around the world share information through interactive media: "'Time' has ceased, 'space' has vanished. We now live in a global village . . . a simultaneous happening" (McLuhan, Fiore, and Fairey, 1967:63). McLuhan optimistically believed that the global village would empower people and foster the growth of democracy and equality.

global village
A world in which distances have been shrunk by modern communications technology so that everyone is socially and economically interdependent.

Today's media make it possible to form communities of shared interest even though people have no direct contact with each other. For McLuhan, it was important that this communication was not one way and linear but decentralized and multidirectional:

> In the electric age, when our central nervous system is technologically extended to involve us in the whole of mankind and to incorporate the whole of mankind in us, we necessarily participate, in depth, in the consequences of our every action. It is no longer possible to adopt the aloof and disassociated role of the literate Westerner . . . As electronically contracted, the globe is no more than a village. (McLuhan, 1964:4–5)

McLuhan believed that media technology would change society and shape our social lives. While McLuhan's work predated the Internet by three decades, the impact of today's media has at least partly supported his views. Examples such as the global response to natural disasters such as the 2010 Haitian earthquake and the 2011 Japanese earthquake and tsunami are fostered by the fact that people around the globe could follow the disaster in real time through the mass media. Other examples of positive change are technologies that enable people in isolated rural areas anywhere on the globe to educate themselves, care for their health, and conduct business—a farmer with an Internet connection can easily find the most lucrative place to market her products rather than accepting the price offered by local buyers.

Not everyone is as positive about the impact of the media on globalization as McLuhan. Schiller (1992) argued that media technologies would lead to **cultural imperialism**—a process whereby, powerful countries use the media to spread values and ideas that dominate and even destroy other cultures, and local cultural values are replaced by the cultural values of the dominant country. The dominant media culture is that of the United States, and the media enable large transnational corporations to profit from their global domination at the expense of cultural diversity. The globalization of culture means that local cultural values are replaced by Western values such as consumerism.

cultural imperialism
A process whereby powerful countries use the media to spread values and ideas that dominate and even destroy other cultures, and local cultural values are replaced by the cultural values of the dominant country.

Cultural imperialism has occurred—many people around the world are familiar with Lady Gaga, the Disney characters, and many other products of American culture. However, the flows are becoming multidirectional as there is now a reverse flow of cultural products, such as India's Bollywood movies, which have become popular in many parts of the world, including North America. Countries including China and Brazil have very significant cultural industries that dominate their own local media and are now being exported.

The Qatar-based television news network Al Jazeera has become a significant cultural force since its establishment in 1996. Al Jazeera has transformed news reporting in many Middle

THE CANADIAN PRESS IMAGES/Dominic Chan

Indian actor Anil Kapoor is shown in Toronto at the opening ceremonies of the 2011 "Bollywood Oscars." This was the first time the event had been held in North America.

Eastern countries, where coverage was often limited because of restrictions imposed by dictatorial governments. It has provided a global alternative to Western media, and its English language services have provided people in Europe and North America with a very different perspective on Middle Eastern issues than they have been given by traditional news sources.

The Digital Third World

Information and communications technologies are changing the world, but are these technologies helping people who are poor or just increasing the gap between rich and poor?

Some feel that the ability to share information from around the globe will help low-income countries develop by providing them with the opportunity to become knowledge societies that can compete with industrialized nations. New technologies will help them streamline industry and government, and their competitive advantage in wages will allow them to attract business. Technology can speed up educational reform and help build a more participatory civil society through the sharing of information and ideas. India has generated hundreds of thousands of jobs based on new information and communication technologies (Friedman, 2005). See Figure 17.3.

However, there is a danger that the move to a world linked by new information and communications technology will lead to a greater polarization between the rich, who can exploit the new technologies, and the poor, who do not have access to them. The poor may be excluded from the global information society—and this includes the poor in industrialized countries, as the "digital Third World" does not follow international borders. See Figure 17.4.

The major barrier to the spread of information and communications technology is cost. To become part of the "digital world," low-income countries must build expensive communications infrastructures. Because of these costs, high-income residents of high-income countries are most likely to have access to the Internet. In 2011, 78 percent of North Americans and 58 percent of Europeans had access to the Internet compared with 24 percent of Asians and only 11 percent of residents of Africa. However, there has been significant growth in Internet use in low-income countries. For example, even though it is still low, Internet use in Africa increased by 2500 percent between 2000 and 2011 (Internet World Stats, 2012). Similarly, mobile phone use is much lower in low-income countries but is also growing very rapidly. Between 2000 and 2008, mobile phone ownership in Africa increased from 2 percent to 28 percent of the population (Tryhorn, 2009). Despite this growth, it will take many years before access to modern communications approaches that of people in wealthier parts of the world.

Language issues also act as a barrier to Internet access in many parts of the world. Most of the content on the Internet is in English. Without multilingual sites, the name "World Wide Web" will never be accurate. A Web that is dominated linguistically by English and technologically and culturally by the United States will never reflect the point of view of people in low-income countries. The magnitude of this problem was demonstrated by Charles Kenny (2003), who searched for Web pages in Igbo, a language spoken by 17 million Nigerians. Kenny found only five sites that used the Igbo language.

Much remains to be done if low-income countries are to build on-ramps to the information superhighway. Rather than following the North American model, involving individual access to communications technology, it is likely that solutions in low-income countries will involve shared infrastructure and public access facilities, such as Internet phones accessed through individuals who make their living by sharing their phones with neighbours for a small fee. These intermediaries help to share the financial burden and are also important in helping teach unskilled people to utilize complex technology (Jensen, 2002).

FIGURE 17.3 **WORLD CONNECTIONS**

This graphic shows the relative density of Internet connectivity across the globe. You can see how North America, Europe, and Japan are far more connected than other parts of the world.

Source: http://www.chrisharrison.net/index.php/Visualizations/InternetMap. Used with permission of Chris Harrison.

FIGURE 17.4 **CITY-TO-CITY CONNECTIONS**

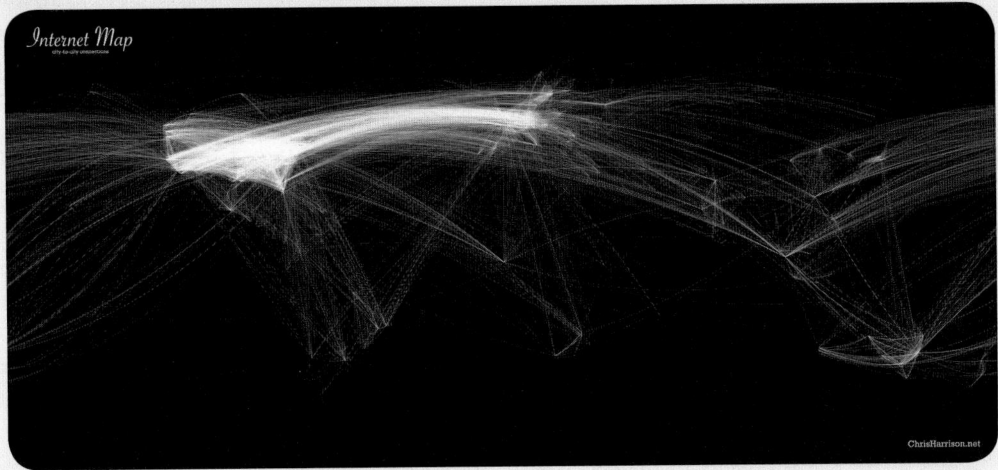

This graphic shows the network ties around the globe. North America and Europe are clearly at the core of the digital world, while other countries are on its periphery.

Source: http://www.chrisharrison.net/index.php/Visualizations/InternetMap. Used with permission of Chris Harrison.

TIME TO REVIEW

- What impact does the constant connectivity of smartphones have on our lives?
- Discuss the implications of living a life online through networks such as Second Life along with your life in the 'real' world.
- What are some of the positive and negative consequences of the way people use new social media.
- How has the Internet changed the process of selecting a potential spouse?
- Describe how the pressure to make a profit can affect people's privacy rights.
- Do you think that new media will help or harm the world's poor?

17 VISUAL SUMMARY

KEY TERMS

cultural imperialism A process whereby powerful countries use the media to spread values and ideas that dominate and even destroy other cultures, and local cultural values are replaced by the cultural values of the dominant country (p. 501).

global village A world in which distances have been shrunk by modern communications technology so that everyone is socially and economically interdependent (p. 501).

hyperreality A situation in which the distinction between reality and simulation has become blurred (p. 491).

Internet The network infrastructure that links together the world's millions of computers (p. 479).

mass media Any technologically based means of communicating between large numbers of people distributed widely over space or time (p. 478).

media literacy The ability to access, analyze, evaluate, and create media in a variety of forms (p. 479).

status conferral The process of giving prominence to particular individuals by focusing media attention on them (p. 482).

World Wide Web The computer language that allows us to access information on the Internet (p. 479).

LO-1 Understand what is meant by the term *mass media*.

The media connect those who produce messages with those who receive them. The mass media are "any technologically based means of communicating between large numbers of people distributed widely over space or time" (Pavlik and McIntosh 2011:18).

© CBC

© Jen Grantham/iStockphoto

LO-2 Consider how the impact of the media is explained by functionalist, conflict, feminist, interactionist, and postmodern theories.

Functionalist theorists believe the media exist because of the functions they play for society. For example, the media keep us informed, help societies socialize their members, and entertain us. Conflict theorists argue that the media help the dominant class control society by reinforcing capitalist ideology. Interactionist theorists show us how people use the media to help develop their individual identities. Feminist theorists have been critical of the way the media perpetuate gender stereotyping. Postmodern theorists have showed us how the media blur the distinction between reality and simulation, creating a new condition that Baudrillard called "hyperreality."

LO-3 Understand how new media both bring people together and keep them apart.

Social media can enable us to stay connected with friends and family even though we may be living in different parts of the world. However, many people spend so much time interacting with media that they may neglect their personal relationships.

© Philip Street. Used with permission

LO-4 Understand how social media sites profit from the information you provide them.

© Badgley Mischka/Splash News/Newscom

Companies like Facebook and Zynga (the makers of FarmVille) are worth many billions of dollars. They make money by selling information about their subscribers to advertisers or by selling things that people use in their online lives. We need to be aware of how these organizations make their money in order to ensure that we are not exploited through such factors as violations of our privacy.

THE CANADIAN PRESS IMAGES/Dominic Chan

LO-5 Think about the role played by the media in globalization.

McLuhan believed that media technologies would create a global village in which people around the world shared information through interactive media. This would empower people and foster the growth of democracy and equality. Not everyone agrees with this view. There is a huge digital divide between people living in rich countries and those living in poor countries. Without action to reduce this technological gap, the disparity between rich and poor will get worse, not better.

APPLICATION QUESTIONS

1. The chapter opener described how social media helped to overthrow Libya's repressive government. Progressive movements are not the only ones to use social media, however, as groups such as al-Qaeda and the Taliban also have a strong online presence. Using information you find on the Internet, examine how these groups make use of social media and consider how successful they have been.
2. In what ways do the media make you feel more Canadian? In what ways do the media make you feel like a citizen of the world (part of the global village) rather than like a Canadian?
3. Some people use virtual reality scenarios, such as those in Second Life, to try out new identities. Which personality trait(s) would you like to "test drive" in virtual reality?
4. People can have strong emotional attachments through their avatars in Second Life and other online worlds. If a married person's avatar has an intimate relationship with another avatar, should that be grounds for divorce in that person's real-life marriage? Why or why not?
5. Why do you think so many people are meeting their partners online? Do you think that this way of meeting is better than relying on traditional ways, such as meeting people through your family, at church, or in school? Why or why not?

KEY FIGURES

© INTERFOTO/Alamy

Theodor Adorno (1903–1969) Philosopher Theodor Adorno was one of the earliest critics of the media. He was a member of the Frankfurt School of critical theory, which looked at the role of social factors in the oppression of the lower classes. His work with Max Horkheimer focused on the way in which the culture industry had turned into just another marketable commodity.

© INTERFOTO/Alamy

Jean Baudrillard (1929–2007) Postmodern scholar Jean Baudrillard is best known for his work on the way in which postmodern societies are organized around simulation, which can be more involving than reality. He developed the notion of hyperreality, which refers to a situation in which the distinction between reality and simulation has been blurred.

© Bettmann/Corbis

Marshall McLuhan (1911–1980) McLuhan was Canada's foremost media theorist. One of his best-known assertions was that because of the power of the media, we live in a global village in which people around the world share information through interactive media.

Peter Urban

Sherry Turkle (b. 1948) Psychologist Sherry Turkle was one of the first scholars to study how our lives are affected by the new technology of computers and social media. Her most recent work looks at how social media may cause a flight from conversation to mere connection, thereby reducing the richness of human communication.

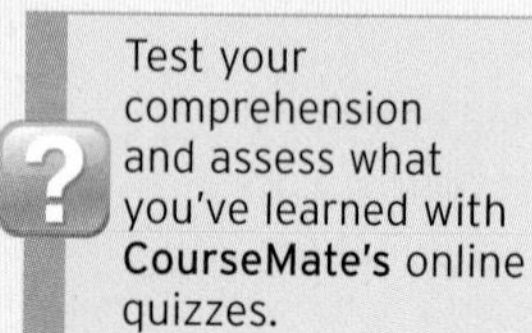

Test your comprehension and assess what you've learned with **CourseMate's** online quizzes.

For other interesting Lived Experiences, watch the video clips on **CourseMate.**

Practise what you've learned with flashcards containing key terms and definitions on **CourseMate.**

CHAPTER 18 Aging

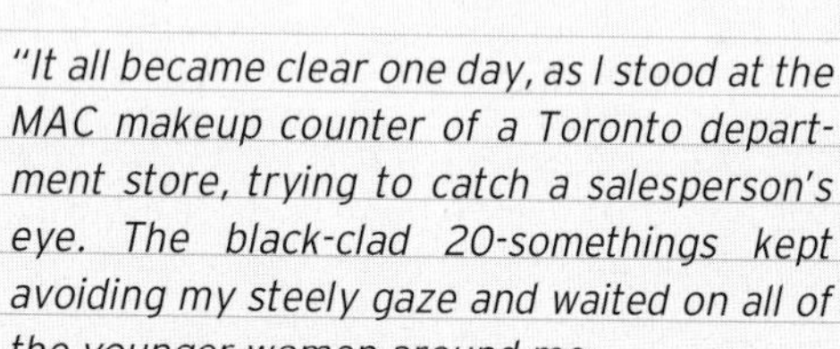

AP Photo/Jim McKnight

"It all became clear one day, as I stood at the MAC makeup counter of a Toronto department store, trying to catch a salesperson's eye. The black-clad 20-somethings kept avoiding my steely gaze and waited on all of the younger women around me.

"I worried that perhaps I was in the middle of a dream, or possibly even invisible. When I finally grabbed a young man at the counter with a couple of piercings to his lower lip, he apologized. 'I thought you were with your daughter,' he said, pointing to one of the Goths beside me. God forbid a woman in her 40s should buy lipstick on her own.

"I realized then that part of me was starting to disappear. Unlike Alice, in Woody Allen's movie of the same name, who was given potions to make her invisible, all I had to do was continue to sit around and age and I, too, would start to fade away.

"I did what many women do when they first realize they're disappearing—I fought back. We can be perked up or puffed out. I coloured my hair, increased my daily dosage of makeup . . . And started wearing my daughter's clothes . . .

"What I didn't realize initially is that invisibility runs deeper than just our skin." (Binks, 2003)

"When Morley Callaghan turned 80, his sons gave him a birthday party in a fine restaurant. During a graceful thank-you speech, the novelist said, `Being 80 is like walking through a jungle: you never know what is going to pounce on you next.'

"I've been 80 for a few months now and I don't see it as a very big deal. My packaging is wearing out: my skin is too big for me and falls in folds, I have less hair, I am shorter and stooped, and my knees hurt on stairs. Plus a bit of cancer. But I'm still me; exactly me, irreducibly, for better and also for worse, me.

"When I was young, I expected that age would make me sage and I would become so serene that strangers would stop to take my pulse. I now realize that all age does is make you old.

"Almost all the invincible women of the 1950s are now widows. I am almost the only one of our gang with a living husband. After 60 years, our marriage is a mellow one. We seem to be bobbing on a sea of affection, and disagreements are rare. Perhaps we are maturing. Just in time." (Callwood, 2005:56)

(*Source:* Excerpt from article "On Turning 80" by June Callwood is used with permission of Rogers Publishing Ltd.

Michael Kinsley describes an early morning swim in an apartment pool. He describes a fellow swimmer: "It was a tiny old man in a tiny black bathing suit. He was slowly, slowly completing a lap in the next lane . . . He saw me, beamed, and said, 'I'm ninety years old.' It was clearly a boast, not a lament, so I followed his script and said, 'Well, isn't that marvelous' and 'You certainly don't look it' . . . He beamed some more, I beamed, and briefly we were both happy . . .

"Perhaps sensing some condescension in my praise, he then stuck out his chest and declared, 'I used to be a judge.' And I started to resent this intruder on my morning and my pool. Did I now have to tell him it was marvelous that he used to be a judge? . . . What was his point? But even as he said this, a panicky realization of its absurd irrelevance seemed to pass across his face, and then a realization of its pathos. When he was a judge . . . he had not felt the need to accost strangers and tell them he was a judge. And then he seemed to realize that he had overplayed his hand. He has left this stranger in the pool thinking the very thought he had wanted to dispel: the old fool is past it." (2008)

We will all be affected by aging. **Aging** is the physical, psychological, and social processes associated with growing older (Atchley, 1997). As the experiences you have just read suggest, the way in which societies and individals respond to aging can be at least as important as the physical processes in determining how we will spend our older years.

In some societies, including Canada, older people may be the targets of prejudice and discrimination based on myths about aging. For example, older people may be viewed as incompetent solely because of their age. Although some older people may need assistance, many others are physically, socially, and financially independent. In this chapter, we will examine the sociological aspects of aging. We will examine how older people live in a society that often devalues people who do not fit the ideal norms of youth, beauty, physical fitness, and self-sufficiency. Before reading on, test your knowledge about aging and age-based discrimination by taking the quiz in Box 18.1 on page 511.

Critical Thinking Questions

1. Why do you think older people are devalued in our society?
2. Is it necessary to have a mandatory retirement age? As Canada becomes more flexible about retirement, who is most likely to benefit and who is most likely to be hurt by this policy change?
3. Older people are often the victims of social stereotypes. What are some of these stereotypes? How do you think these affect the lives of older people?

CHAPTER FOCUS QUESTION

Given the fact that aging is an inevitable consequence of living (unless an individual dies young), why do many people in Canada devalue older persons?

Learning Objectives

AFTER READING THIS CHAPTER, YOU SHOULD BE ABLE TO

LO-1 Explain how functional age differs from chronological age.

LO-2 Discuss how views of aging differ in preindustrial and industrialized societies.

LO-3 Explain ageism and elder abuse.

LO-4 Understand the differences between the functionalist, symbolic interactionist, conflict, feminist, and postmodern explanations of aging.

LO-5 Identify the most common living arrangements for older people.

LO-1 THE SOCIAL SIGNIFICANCE OF AGE

aging The physical, psychological, and social processes associated with growing older.

chronological age A person's age based on date of birth.

functional age A term used to describe observable individual attributes–such as physical appearance, mobility, strength, coordination, and mental capacity–that are used to assign people to age categories.

life expectancy The average length of time a group of individuals of the same age will live.

cohort A category of people born within a specified period of time or who share some specified characteristic.

"How old are you?" is one of the most frequently asked questions in our society. Age is socially significant because it defines what is appropriate for or expected of people at various stages. Age is one of the few ascribed statuses that changes over time. Thus behaviour that is considered appropriate at one stage of a person's life may be considered unusual at another stage. Nobody thinks it is unusual if a person in her 20s goes bungee jumping . If her 85-year-old grandfather does the same thing, however, he may receive some odd looks and even media coverage because he is defying norms regarding age-appropriate behaviour.

We all have a **chronological age**—a person's age based on date of birth. However, we often assess people on the basis of their **functional age**—observable individual attributes, such as physical appearance, mobility, strength, coordination, and mental capacity, that are used to assign people to age categories (Atchley and Barusch, 2004). Characteristics such as youthful appearance or grey hair and wrinkled skin are common criteria for determining whether someone is "young" or "old." Feminist scholars have noted that functional age works differently for women and men—as they age, men may be viewed as distinguished or powerful, whereas when women grow older, they are thought to be "over the hill" or grandmotherly (Banner, 1993).

Trends in Aging

Just as people get older, so can societies age. Today, older Canadians make up about 14 percent of the population, and the number of people over 65 will continue to increase as the baby boomers get older (see Figure 18.1). In 1981, the median age (the age at which half the people are younger and half are older) was 30. By 2001, it was 38. This substantial increase—eight years in two decades—is partly the result of the baby boomers (people born between 1946 and 1964) moving into middle age and partly the result of more people living longer. Figure 18.2 shows that the number of older people (65 and above) began to increase dramatically in the 1970s.

© Corbis Premium RF/Alamy

Many older persons seek dignity, autonomy, and empowerment in a society that values youth, beauty, physical fitness, and self-sufficiency.

This *greying of Canada* resulted from an increase in life expectancy combined with a decrease in birth rates following the baby boom. **Life expectancy** is the average length of time a group of individuals of the same age will live. Life expectancy shows the average length of life of a **cohort**—a category of people born within a specified period of time or who share some specified characteristic. For the cohort born in 2008, for example, life expectancy at birth was 83 for females and 79 for males (Statistics Canada, 2011). Figure 18.3 on page 512 shows the sex differences in life expectancy.

In 1900, about 5 percent of the Canadian population was over age 65; by 1981, that number had risen to approximately 10 percent. By 2011, this had increased to 14 percent and then it will increase to 22 percent in 2031 (Figure 18.2).

Since the beginning of the 20th century, life expectancy has steadily increased as industrialized nations developed better water and sewage systems, improved nutrition, and made tremendous advances in medical science. The economic development that contributed to the lower death rate also helped lower the birth rate. In industrialized nations, children came to be viewed as an economic liability: They could not contribute to the family's financial well-being and had to be supported.

BOX 18.1 SOCIOLOGY AND EVERYDAY LIFE

How Much Do You Know About Aging?

True	False	
T	F	1. Most older persons have serious physical disabilities.
T	F	2. Women in Canada have a longer life expectancy than men.
T	F	3. Scientific studies have documented the fact that women age faster than men.
T	F	4. The majority of older people have incomes below the poverty line.
T	F	5. Studies show that advertising no longer stereotypes older persons.

For answers to the quiz about aging, go to **www.nelson.com/sociologyinourtimes6e.**

FIGURE 18.1 PROJECTED POPULATION BY AGE GROUP, CANADA, 1992–2036

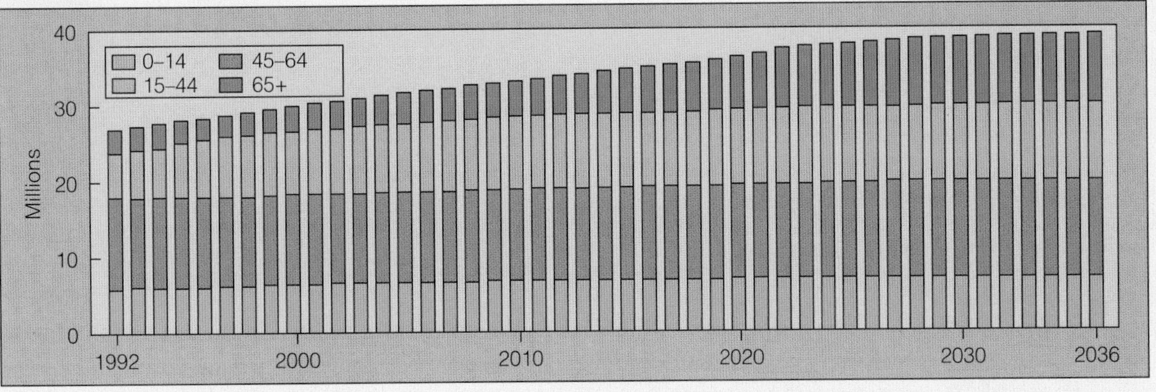

Source: Adapted from the Statistics Canada publication "Population projections for Canada, provinces and territories," Catalogue 91-520, 2005-2031, released December 15, 2005.

FIGURE 18.2 POPULATION AGED 65 AND OVER, CANADA, 1901–2031

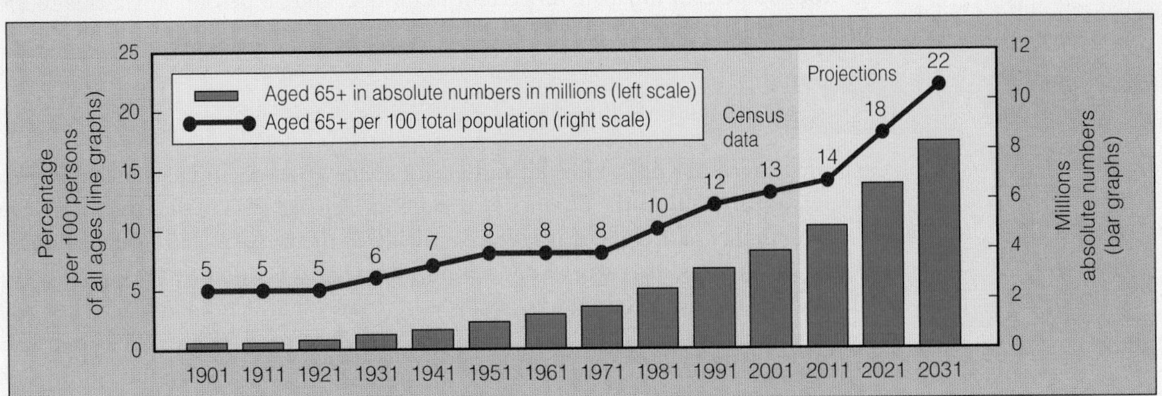

Source: Adapted from the Statistics Canada publication "Population projections for Canada, provinces and territories," Catalogue 91-520, 2005 to 2031. Released December 15, 2005.

FIGURE 18.3 EVOLUTION OF LIFE EXPECTANCY AT BIRTH BY AGE AND SEX, CANADA, 1921–2008

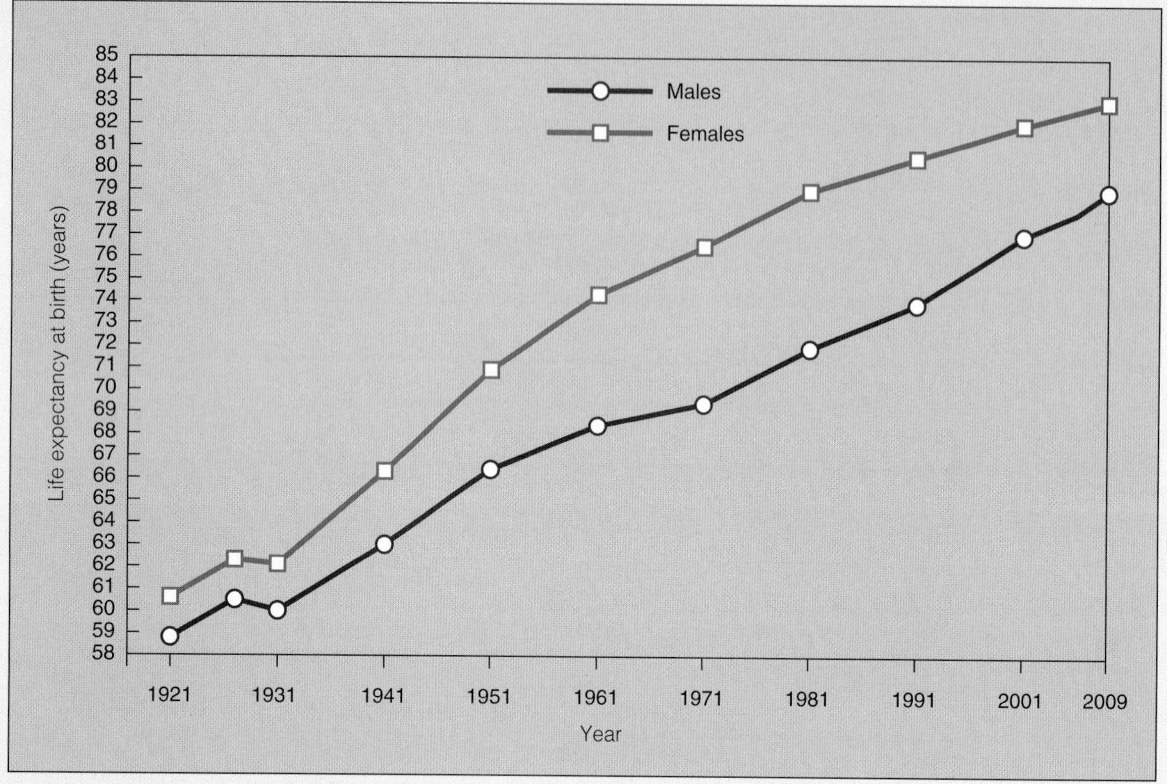

Source: Statistics Canada, CANSIM database table 102-0511 (1990 to 2006), 2011.

The distribution of the Canadian population is depicted in the age pyramid in Figure 18.4. If, every year, the same number of people are born as in the previous year and a certain number die in each age group, the plot of the population distribution should be pyramid-shaped because fewer people survive to reach the next age level. Figure 18.4 is not a perfect pyramid; rather, it reflects declining birth rates since the baby boom. This decline has resulted in fewer young people at the bottom of the pyramid and a higher average age.

Populations in all parts of the world are aging. Novak and Campbell (2006) looked at forecasts of populations who will be over the age of 60 in 2050. They found that percentages will range from 42 percent in Japan, 37 percent in Europe, and 30 percent in Canada to 23 percent in Asia and only 10 percent in Africa.

LO-2 Age in Historical Perspective

People are assigned to different roles and positions based on a particular society's age and role structures. *Age structure* is the number of persons at each age level within the society; *role structure* is the number and types of positions available to them (Riley and Riley, 1994). Over the years, the age continuum has been divided into finer and finer points. Two hundred years ago, people divided the age spectrum into "babyhood," a *very* short childhood, and then adulthood. What we would consider "childhood" today was very different 200 years ago, when agricultural societies needed many people to work on the land. When most of the population was involved in food production, categories such as toddlers, preschoolers, preteens, teenagers, young adults, the middle-aged, or older persons did not exist.

FIGURE 18.4 DIFFERENT COHORTS AMONG THE AGE PYRAMID OF CANADA, 2006

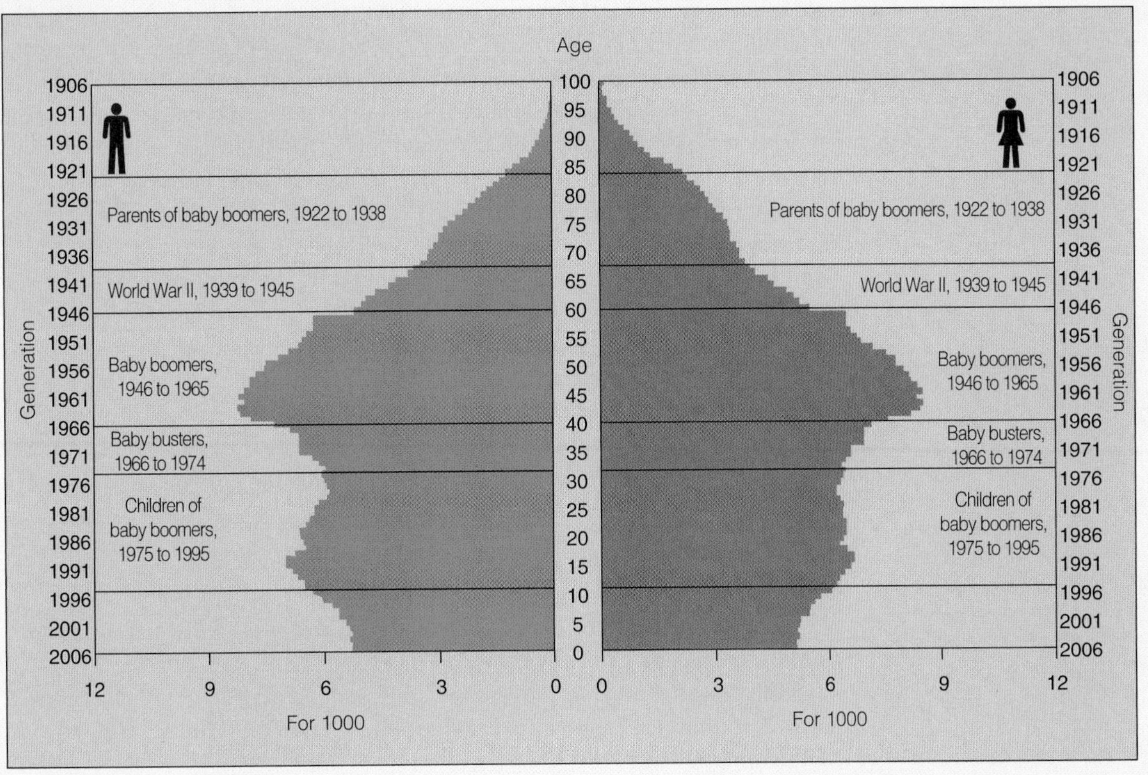

Source: Statistics Canada, 2006 Census of the Population.

If the physical labour of young persons is necessary for society's survival, then young persons are considered "little adults" and are expected to act like adults and do adult work. Older persons are also expected to continue to be productive for as long as they are physically able. During the 17th and 18th centuries in North America, for example, older individuals helped with the work and were respected because they were needed—and because few people lived that long (Gratton, 1986). The presence of older people in large numbers is a modern phenomenon and their place in society is still evolving.

Today, many retired persons have good health and the resources to enjoy an active life.

Late Adulthood

Late adulthood is generally considered to begin at age 65—the "normal" retirement age. Some gerontologists—researchers who study aging (**gerontology**)—subdivide late adulthood into three categories: (1) the "young-old" (ages 65 to 74), (2) the "old-old" (ages 75 to 85), and (3) the "oldest-old" (over age 85) (see Moody, 1998). Although these are somewhat arbitrary divisions, the "young-old" are less likely to suffer from disabling illnesses than the "old-old" (Belsky, 1990).

gerontology The study of aging and older people.

Still, older persons have increased chances of serious illness. Some diseases affect virtually only persons in late adulthood. Alzheimer's disease (a progressive and irreversible deterioration of brain tissue) is an example; about 55 percent of all organic mental disorders in the older population are caused by Alzheimer's (Atchley and Barusch, 2004). Persons with this disease have an impaired ability to function in everyday social roles. Eventually, they can no longer recognize people they have always known and lose all sense of their own identity. They become totally dependent upon help from others. We do not know the cause of this disease and there is no cure. About half a million Canadians suffer from Alzheimer's disease and related dementias. By the year 2034, this number will likely grow to well over a million (Alzheimer Society of Canada, 2009).

Fortunately, most older people do not suffer from Alzheimer's and are not incapacitated by their physical condition. Only about 5 percent of older people live in nursing homes, about 10 percent have visual impairment, and about 50 percent have some hearing loss (Naeyaert, 1990; Novak, 1993). Although older people experience some decline in strength, flexibility, stamina, and other physical capabilities, much of that decline does not result simply from the aging process—it is avoidable. With proper exercise, some of it is even reversible (Lefrançois, 1999).

Along with physical changes come changes in roles. One that most people enjoy is being a grandparent. An extended family is a great source of pleasure for many older Canadians. Grandparenting is an interesting role because it "has no clearly defined responsibilities, expectations, or rights" (McPherson, 1998:209). This gives members of younger and older generations the opportunity to build relationships that are to their mutual benefit. Some of the benefits of having grandparents are described in the following comments by Grade 3 students about the role of a grandmother:

> When they read to us they don't skip words and they don't mind if it is the same story.
>
> They don't have to be smart, only answer questions like why dogs hate cats, and how come God isn't married.
>
> Grandmas are the only grownups who have got time—so everybody should have a grandmother, especially if you don't have television. (Huyck, cited in McPherson, 1998:213)

Some of the physical and psychological changes that come with increasing age can cause stress. According to Erik Erikson (1963), older people must accept that the life cycle is inevitable and that their lives are nearing an end. Mark Novak interviewed several older people about what he termed "successful aging." One respondent, Joanne, commented:

> For me getting older was very painful at first because I resisted change. Now I'm changed, and it's okay. I would say I have a new freedom . . . I thought I had no limits, but for me a great learning [experience] was recognizing my limits. It was a complete turnover, almost like a rebirth. I guess I've learned we're all weak really. At least we should accept that—being weak—and realize, "Hey, I'm only a fragile human being." (1995:125)

Despite its negative aspects, aging has many positive dimensions and most older people are quite content with their lives. Many are financially secure, with home mortgages paid off and no children remaining at home. They thereby have a great deal of personal freedom. Most report that they are in good or excellent health (Norland, 1994). Northcott found that older Edmonton residents were happier with their lives than younger respondents (1982). A national study (Health and Welfare Canada, 1998) found that older people were much less likely than younger people to report that their lives were stressful, and the vast majority (92 percent) reported that they were quite or even very happy. And Connidis (1989) reports that married people over 65 have a higher level of satisfaction with their romantic relationships than married people of any other age.

Retirement

Retirement means the end of a status that has been a source of income and personal identity. Perhaps the loss of a valued status explains why many retired persons introduce themselves by saying, "I'm retired now, but I was a [banker, lawyer, plumber, supervisor, and so on] for 40 years."

Retirement is a recent phenomenon. The first national pension system was established in Germany in 1889. In Canada, the *Old Age Pension Act* was introduced in 1927 to provide a basic income to needy retired people. This started a shift in the burden of retirement from the individual to the state. However, people were still expected to look after themselves or to receive help from their families. Initially, pensions were given only to needy people over the age of 70 and payments were minimal. Retirement was not common until the amount paid to retirees by public pension plans increased. Pension coverage became universal in 1951, and benefits were improved between 1951 and 1975 (Northcott, 1982).

All working people in Canada are covered by the Canada or Quebec pension plans, and all those over age 65 receive the Old Age Security pension, though this is taxed back from higher-income recipients. About 1.6 million lower-income Canadians also receive the benefits of the Guaranteed Income Supplement program. These programs are responsible for the reduction in poverty among older people (see Figure 18.5, which shows how the overall situation for people with low incomes has improved over time). Many people have company pension plans and others have invested in registered retirement savings plans (RRSPs).

Retirees in some other countries are not as fortunate as Canadians. Many Western industrial countries, including the United States, have underfunded their government pension plans and will be forced to raise taxes or reduce benefits. In other parts of the world, there are no pension plans because families have always been expected to care for their own members. Pensions are very limited in China, and the one child per family policy means that many workers will be responsible for supporting both of their parents during their retirement years.

Retirement plays an increasingly important part in the lives of Canadians. When the first retirement laws were passed, the retirement age (usually 70) was much higher than the average life expectancy. As a result, most people never retired, and for those who did, retirement was typically short. Today, about 10 percent of seniors are still working—15 percent of men and 6 percent of women (Uppal, 2010). Since the retirement age has been declining and life expectancy has been increasing, the retirement years will likely make up an increasing proportion of people's lives. On the other hand, many people—prefer to work past the normal retirement age of 65. Most provinces no longer allow mandatory retirement.

Retirement can be a major transition, as retirees lose a source of income, identity, lifestyle, and friends that they may have had for most of their adult lives. This is especially true of workers who achieve a great deal of satisfaction from their jobs. Jack Culberg explains the difficulties of his transition:

FIGURE 18.5 LOW-INCOME RATE, PEOPLE 65 AND OLDER, 1980–2006

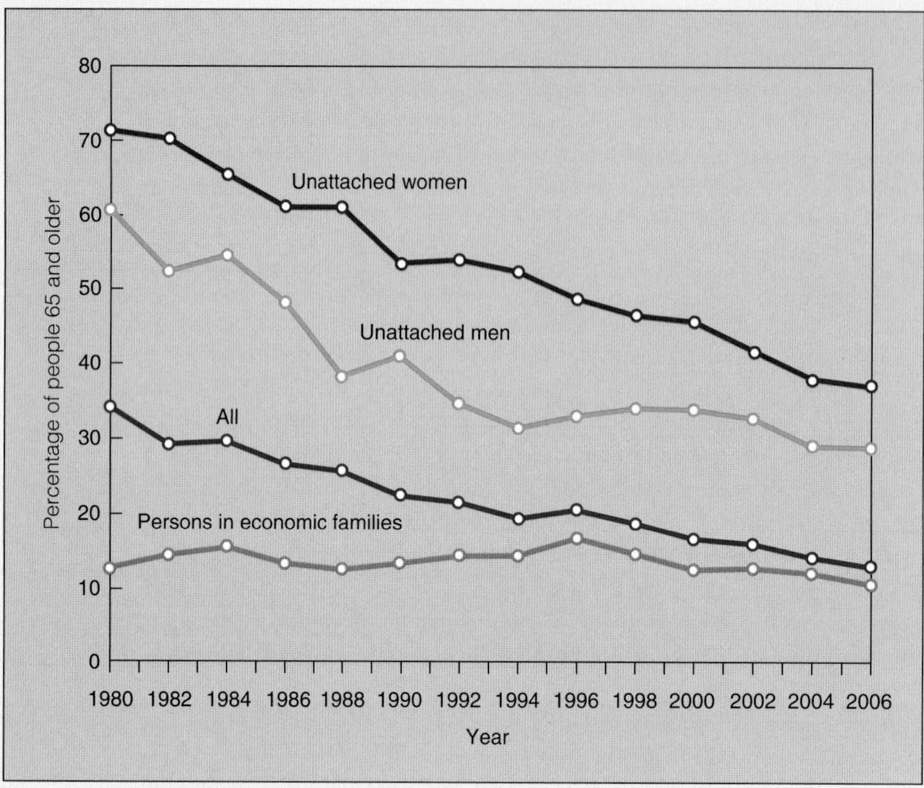

Poverty rates have steadily declined for all categories of older people, though there are still large differences between couples and unattached people, particularly females.

Source: Statistics Canada, E-Stat CANSIM table 2002-0802; Lindsay, 2002: 108-110.

> When you suddenly leave [the corporate jungle], life is pretty empty. I was sixty-five, the age people are supposed to retire. I started to miss it quite a bit. The phone stops ringing. The king is dead. You start wanting to have lunch with old friends. At the beginning, they're nice to you, but then you realize that they're busy, they're working. They've got a job to do and just don't have the time to talk to anybody where it doesn't involve their business . . . You hesitate to call them. (quoted in Terkel, 1996:9–10)

As Culberg's statement indicates, reaching "retirement age" moves people out of the mainstream. To ease this transition, researchers suggest that people plan ways of remaining occupied and engaged in society. Those who are involved with activities, such as volunteer work and hobbies that continue after retirement, are happier and healthier than those who have few retirement interests and withdraw from social life. Many organizations are encouraging older workers to make gradual transitions to retirement by working part time. This allows the organization to retain the skills of senior employees and enables the individual to make a comfortable transition to retirement.

A Statistics Canada survey found that more than half of retirees would have liked to continue working, particularly if they were allowed more flexible working hours and more time off (Schellenberg and Silver, 2004). While the vast majority of seniors do retire by 65, between 1996 and 2001 the number of seniors who were working increased at nearly twice the rate of the growth in the senior population.

Recent research has found that people have very different reasons for retirement (Park, 2011). Many retired because they had adequate pensions and wanted to stop working, but a significant proportion retired under less favourable circumstances: 24 percent retired for medical reasons, and others left work because they were restructured out of a job or because they had to help others with caregiving. Some of these involuntary retirees have low incomes and are not well prepared for retirement. And many workers return to the labour force after retirement, mainly because the workers' pensions are not sufficient for a comfortable retirement and to help ease the transition between work and retirement for those nearing the end of their working lives (Hébert and Luong, 2008).

The costs of pensions and health care have led to concerns about whether Canada can afford the increasing numbers of retired people. Consider the arguments presented in Box 18.2.

BOX 18.2 POINT/COUNTERPOINT

Will There Be a Generational War Between the Old and the Young?

> Canadians enjoy retirement, and why not? Most retirees are having the time of their lives: long, lazy summers at the cottage, gambling jaunts to Vegas in the winter, golf all year round . . .
>
> Retirement as we know it–ten or twenty years of fun, partly at public expense, as a reward for showing up at work during our adult lives–is doomed. The happy coincidence of generous governments and the postwar economic and population boom that made it possible has come undone. The web of government-sponsored seniors' programmes that pays retirees largely from the taxes of those still working has become unsustainable . . .
>
> Funding leisure in later life must become a personal responsibility, not a social obligation. Retirees must stop insisting that they have a right to siphon money from their kids to help make their golden years enjoyable. (Taylor, 1995:18)

Is Taylor correct? Will our social welfare system go bankrupt as the baby boomers reach retirement age? Will young people be impoverished by their parents and grandparents? Are the fears of Canadians that the aging baby boomers will reduce the quality of the healthcare system realistic? Let us look at the likely future.

Much of Canada's social welfare system supports the young and the old. An informal social contract between generations obliges the working-age population to support dependent children and older adults. In exchange, these workers received support during their own childhoods and could expect to receive support in their old age.

After World War II, governments in most industrial countries began providing old-age pensions for seniors, and initially this effort was successful. However, in the mid-1970s, people began to worry that increasing numbers of elderly and increasing entitlements would cause the collapse of the Old Age Security program (Myles, 1999).

These worries led people, such as Taylor, to suggest that the social contract between generations has been broken and that young people will have to pay far more to support older people than they will ever receive in return. The huge numbers of aging baby boomers, who themselves supported a relatively small number of older people, will have to be supported in their old age by a much smaller number of workers.

This debate flourished during the 1980s and 1990s, when unemployment rates were high, particularly for young people, and when massive social service cuts were pitting one group against the other. This conflict was symbolized by seniors activist Solange Denis, who in 1985 confronted Prime Minister Brian Mulroney on Parliament Hill and helped force him to back down on pension cuts. Because of their numbers, baby boomers have a great deal of political power, so it will be difficult for politicians to change the current pension system.

The tension between the generations is increased by public images, as expressed in the quotation at the beginning of this box, that suggest older people are living the good life while younger people struggle economically. Some critics have suggested that benefits be cut, that the age for payment of government pensions be raised, or that healthcare to older people be rationed.

However, you should not be too concerned about the gloomy future predicted by Taylor. Ellen Gee (2000) has described the alarmist view of the costs of aging as "voodoo demography." And several factors should help to alleviate the problem before it turns

Continued

into a crisis. First, because of declining fertility rates, fewer resources will be required to look after children and it will be easier to direct resources to older people (Desjardins, 1993). Second, the government has taken action to reduce the future burden on our pension system. The 1999 increase in Canada Pension Plan contributions guarantees that government pensions will be available for all Canadians in the future. In 2012, the age at which people collect Old Age Security was changed from 65 to 67 for those born after 1963 to ensure that this program remains affordable. Finally, many older persons will be well off and paying high levels of tax on their retirement income. Many seniors give money and other support to younger family members and contribute significant amounts of volunteer labour. Older people do not just take from their children and grandchildren.

It is also unlikely that the aging baby boomers will cause a crisis in healthcare—the "silver tsunami" predicted by the Canadian Medical Association (2010). A British Columbia study found that aging added only about 1 percent per year to the cost of healthcare—less than other cost drivers such as the increasing prices of pharmaceutical drugs (Morgan and Cunningham, 2011). Community support programs (discussed later in this chapter) can reduce costs. Older people have responded to health promotion efforts focused on diet, exercise, and lifestyle, so their use of the healthcare system should lessen. Finally, we can develop policies that address the fact that a large proportion of healthcare costs occur in the final six months of life. These costs include keeping the dying patient in an acute-care facility, ordering tests, and using life support to prolong life even when it is clear that the patient is dying. Many dying patients could be cared for in hospices or in chronic-care hospitals, rather than in more expensive acute-care hospitals.

What do you think about this issue? Are you prepared to pay to support your parents and grandparents? Do you think older people should be viewed as mentors who have valuable experience to pass along or as consumers living the good life on the backs of younger people? How can people be persuaded to act in ways that will reduce their need for healthcare when they are older; for example, by exercising and not smoking? The changes to Old Age Security mean that most of you will not be able to collect this pension at the same age as your parents—do you think this is fair?

LO-3 INEQUALITIES RELATED TO AGING

In previous chapters, we have seen how prejudice and discrimination may be directed toward individuals based on ascribed characteristics—such as ethnicity or gender—over which they have no control. The same holds true for age.

In some respects, older people are treated very well in Canada. Most have adequate incomes—though some do not—and all have access to publicly funded medical care. Many older people feel their biggest problem is that other people have negative views of aging and of the capabilities of older people.

Ageism

ageism Prejudice and discrimination against people on the basis of age, particularly when they are older.

Stereotypes of older persons reinforce **ageism**—prejudice and discrimination against people on the basis of age, particularly when they are older (Butler, 1975). Ageism is rooted in the assumption that older people become unattractive, unintelligent, asexual, unemployable, and mentally incompetent as they grow older (Comfort, 1976).

One-sided and exaggerated images of older people are used repeatedly in everyday life. Older persons are often stereotyped as thinking and moving slowly and as living in the past and therefore unable to change and grow (Belsky, 1990). They are viewed as cranky, sickly, and lacking in social value (Atchley and Barusch, 2004); as egocentric and demanding; as shallow and enfeebled; and as absent-minded (Belsky, 1990).

The media also contribute to negative images of older persons. Advertising often portrays older people as unattractive and incompetent (Pomice, 1990). Stereotypes contribute to the view that women are "old" 10 or 15 years sooner than men. The multibillion-dollar cosmetics industry helps perpetuate the myth that age reduces the "sexual value" of women but increases

© Tony Freeman/PhotoEdit

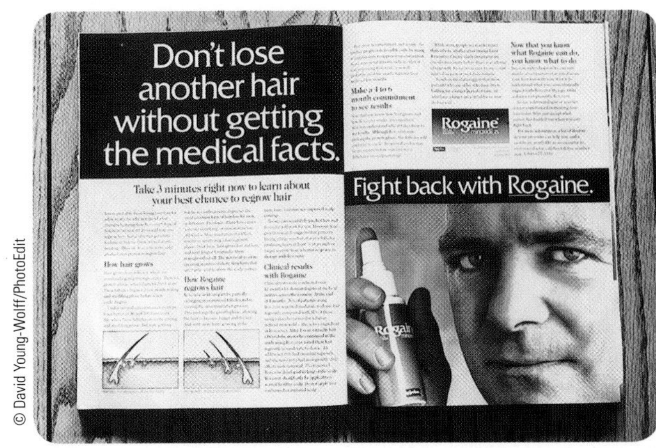

© David Young-Wolff/PhotoEdit

For many years, advertisers have bombarded women with messages about the importance of a youthful appearance. Increasingly, men, too, are being targeted by advertising campaigns that play on fears about the "ravages" of aging.

it for men. Men's sexual value is defined more in terms of personality, intelligence, and earning power than physical appearance. For women, however, sexual attractiveness is based on youthful appearance. By idealizing this "youthful" image of women and playing up the fear of growing older, sponsors sell thousands of products that claim to prevent the "ravages" of aging. Many recent movies provide examples of how older male film stars represent wealth and virility, while their female co-stars are often half their age.

In recent years, there has been a change in the media coverage of older persons. Analysis of books, magazines, advertisements, and television shows has shown that media images of older people have begun to become more positive (Kaufert and Lock, 1997; Novak, 1997). Features such as a segment on the CBC show *The Mercer Report* showing Mississauga mayor Hazel McCallion, then 88, rushing through her day and bowling, playing hockey, and exercising with host Rick Mercer draw attention to the contributions, talents, and stamina of older persons rather than offering stereotypical and negative portrayals. Because of the increasing consumer power of older persons, this trend will likely continue. Older people will not want to buy from companies that demean them in their advertising.

Stereotyping does continue, however. In 2009, TD Canada Trust promoted its Mobile Mortgage program through television commercials featuring two "Grumpy Old Men" who complain about modern conveniences such as bank employees who come to the home or another location to arrange mortgage financing (Laird, 2009). These characters continued to be used by the bank in 2012.

Research has also documented the negative stereotypes of "the elderly" held by some people. Levin (1988) showed photographs of the same man (disguised to appear as ages 25, 52, and 73 in various photos) to a group of college students and asked them to evaluate these apparently different men for employment purposes. Based purely on the photographs, the "73-year-old" was viewed by many of the students as being less competent, less intelligent, and less reliable than the "25-year-old" and the "52-year-old."

Reprinted with permission, from the Summer 2010 issue of Zoomer magazine. Photography by Bryan Adams.

CBC/Rick Mercer Report

Many older people are challenging traditional views of aging. CBC's Rick Mercer did a show featuring Hazel McCallion, mayor of Mississauga, Ontario, since 1978, who won the 2010 election with 76 percent of the vote. In addition to exercising with Mercer, Mayor McCallion—a former professional women's hockey player—also demonstrated her puck-handling skills on one of the city's rinks, beat Mercer at bowling, and performed in a music video in her hockey uniform.

Although not all people act on appearances alone, Patricia Moore, an industrial designer, found that many do. At age 27, Moore disguised herself as an 85-year-old woman by donning age-appropriate clothing and placing baby oil in her eyes to create the appearance of cataracts. She supplemented the "aging process" with latex wrinkles, stained teeth, and a grey wig. For three years, "Old Pat Moore" went to various locations to see how people responded to her:

> When I did my grocery shopping while in character, I learned quickly that the Old Pat Moore behaved—and was treated—differently from the Young Pat Moore. When I was 85, people were more likely to jockey ahead of me in the checkout line. And even more interesting, I found that when it happened, I didn't say anything to the offender, as I certainly would at age 27. It seemed somehow, even to me, that it was okay for them to do this to the Old Pat Moore, since they were undoubtedly busier than I was anyway. And further, they apparently thought it was okay, too! After all, little old ladies have plenty of time, don't they? What it all added up to was that people feared I would be trouble, so they tried to have as little to do with me as possible. And the amazing thing is that I began almost to believe it myself . . . I think perhaps the worst thing about aging may be the overwhelming sense that everything around you is letting you know that you are not terribly important anymore. (Moore with Conn, 1985:75–76)

If we apply our sociological imagination, we find that "Old Pat Moore's" experiences reflect what many older persons already know—it is not their age, but other people's *reactions* to their age that place them at a disadvantage.

These attitudes can have serious consequences. Many older people, particularly women, have negative views about the way others see them and distinguish their outward selves from whom they "really" are. A woman of 71 interviewed by Laura Hurd Clarke reported:

> I don't really think about my body much. I know it's there, but I'm still me inside. The outside is sort of a shell. I know some people would look at me and think, "Oh, well, that's an old lady walking her dog." . . . But that isn't me really. I always have that idea that I'm still inside. I'm me inside. And I've always been me . . . Doesn't matter what the outside looks like or crazy actions I might have on the outside. That isn't really me—that's me inside. (2001:448)

Researchers have discovered that physical abilities deteriorated among older people who were exposed to negative images of aging. In the longer term, older persons who held negative images of aging had greater memory loss, worse health, and earlier deaths than comparable people who had more positive views about aging (Kolata, 2006).

Stereotypes of aging can also have an impact on older people who find themselves unemployed due to layoffs or plant closures. Because of their age, they often find it difficult to find new jobs. Both employers and employment counsellors say that there is age-related bias against older workers (Lipovenko, 1997; Underhill, Marshall, and Deliencourt, 1997).

Wealth, Poverty, and Aging

Aging is easier for those with financial resources. However, many older people have meagre incomes and few savings. For these people, aging is not so much a matter of seeking to defy one's age as it is a matter of simply surviving in a society where they do not have sufficient financial resources and where they are devalued because of their age. The consequences of a weak social safety network are shown in Box 18.3.

How have older Canadians as a group fared economically in recent decades? The elderly comprise an extremely diverse group. Some of Canada's wealthiest individuals are old. At the same time, a significant number of this country's older citizens are poor.

To assess the economic situation of older people, it is necessary to address two questions. First, has the economic situation of older Canadians improved? The answer is yes—rather dramatically. The income of people over the age of 65 has improved much more than the income of younger people in the past three decades. According to Lindsay and Almey (2006), the incomes of males over 65 increased by 24 percent and the income of females over 65 increased by 32 percent between 1981 and 2003. This compares with an increase of 2 percent in the incomes of males under 65 years of age.

The second question is whether older Canadians are able to maintain a satisfactory standard of living. The answer to this question is more complex. It is important to remember that although the economic situation of seniors has improved, many still have low incomes. While income has risen in the past few years for older people in general, certain groups still have incomes below the poverty line in old age. Older people from lower-income backgrounds, people who cannot speak English or French, people with limited education, and people in small towns tend to have low incomes. Very old people and unattached individuals—especially women (see Figure 18.5 on page 516)—often live at or below the poverty line. Older Aboriginal people are more likely than other older Canadians to be poor. Many older Aboriginal people also suffer from chronic diseases such as diabetes and live in substandard housing in communities that lack healthcare services.

Elder Abuse

Abuse and neglect of older persons has received increasing attention due to the rising number of older people and the establishment of more vocal groups to represent their concerns. **Elder abuse** refers to physical abuse, psychological abuse, financial exploitation, and medical abuse or neglect of people age 65 or older (Patterson and Podnieks, 1995).

elder abuse A term used to describe physical abuse, psychological abuse, financial exploitation, and medical abuse or neglect of people age 65 or older.

It is difficult to determine the extent of elder abuse. Many victims are understandably reluctant to talk about it. The 1999 General Social Survey interviewed more than 4000 seniors who were living in private households and asked if they had experienced emotional, financial, physical, or sexual abuse in the previous five years (Dauvergne, 2003). Seven percent of seniors reported having experienced one of these forms of abuse from an adult child, caregiver, or spouse. Emotional abuse was the most common form reported, followed by financial abuse and physical and sexual abuse. Police records showed that those over 65 were more likely to be victimized by a family member than were younger victims. The perpetrators were most likely to be adult children, followed by spouses (Ogrodnik, 2007).

BOX 18.3 SOCIOLOGY IN GLOBAL PERSPECTIVE

Aging in Russia

After the breakup of the Soviet Union in 1991, Russia struggled in its transition from communism to capitalism. Faced with a crumbling economy and an ineffective government, as well as being plagued by corruption and organized crime, the Russian economy had difficulty providing for the needs of its citizens. Under the communist regime, older persons were provided for by the state. While they were not well off by Canadian standards, they had basic medical care and a state pension. Today, the healthcare system has problems and pensions are inadequate.

Political change had a dramatic impact on the structure of the Russian population (see the figure below). As the economic and political structure changed, birth rates dropped and death rates rose (the figure in this box means that for every 110 children born in 2008, there were 160 deaths). Death rates are particularly high for working-age males, many of whom die prematurely because of accidents, alcohol consumption, and coronary problems. This means that males have a very low life expectancy—about 63 years in 2009.

The difference between birth rates and death rates means that the population of Russia is declining. The decline was about 750,000 per year, but in recent years, that has improved somewhat because of higher birth rates. The population distribution means that fewer working-age people are supporting larger numbers of older persons.

As you read in Box 18.2, the increasing ratio of old to young persons is an issue in Canada, but is the cause of far greater difficulties for Russia. With a weak economy, it will be difficult to maintain services for older people.

The cause of Russia's difficulties was summed up by Natalia Rimachevskaya, a Russian delegate to a United Nations conference, who said: "[T]he old principles and social structures had been destroyed but nothing new

FIGURE 18.6 BIRTH AND DEATH RATES IN RUSSIA, 1979–2008

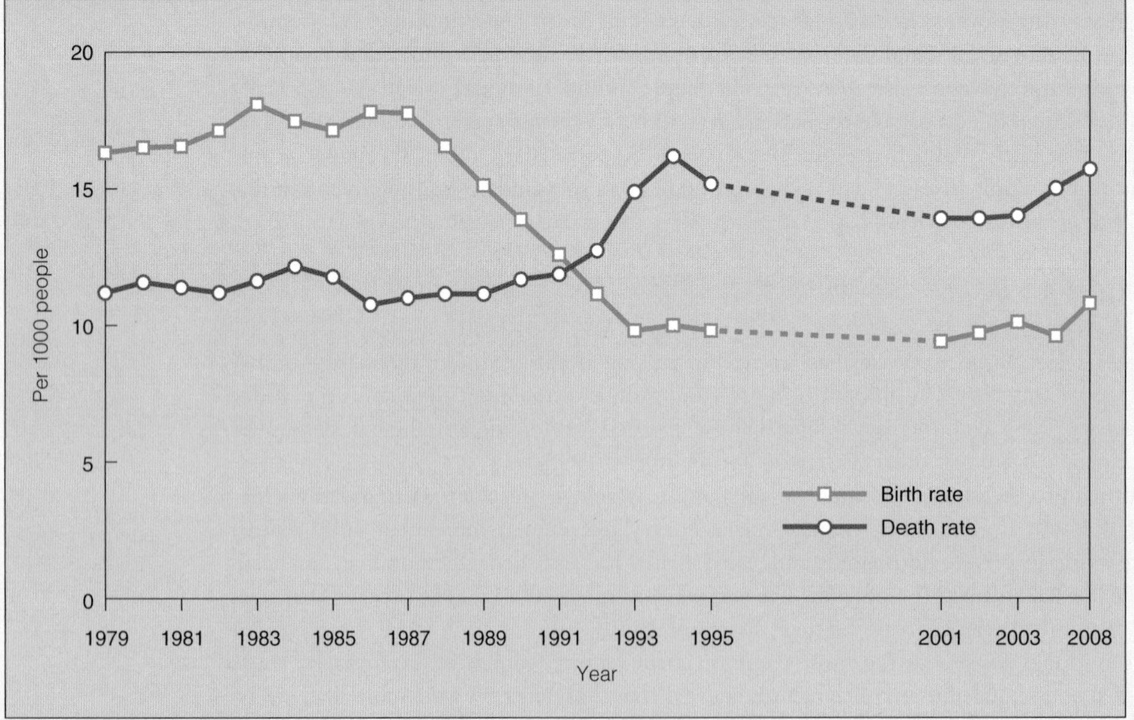

Source: Sourbojina, 2001; CIA, 2001, 2004, 2008.

had really been created" (United Nations, 1997b). As usual, the burden of these difficulties falls heavily on the most vulnerable, including children and older people. Because of oil revenues, rates of poverty had begun to decline until the 2009 recession, but for many Russians, the situation remains desperate.

While older people in Russia are having a difficult time, the situation is also bad in other parts of the world. Many developing countries will see a rapid increase in the percentage of people over age 60. By 2050, 30 percent of China's population and 24 percent of Mexico's population will be over 60 (United Nations, 2002). Most developing countries do not have the formal support systems needed, such as pensions, housing, and healthcare, to properly care for older people. Africa may be particularly hard hit, as HIV/AIDS has decimated the working-age population: Many older people will not have the family caregivers who have traditionally looked after their elders. The burden on older people will be compounded by the fact that, in many cases, they have been left to care for their orphaned grandchildren.

As in Russia, another consequence of low birth rates and an aging population will be depopulation. Japan, Spain, and Italy will lose over 20 percent of their population within the next 50 years. And China's one child per family policy will mean that the average age of the population will increase very rapidly and caring for older people will be difficult.

While rates of crime victimization of seniors are lower than for the rest of the population (Ogrodnik, 2007), the consequences of victimization may be more serious. For example, seniors may be dependent upon their caregivers and cannot readily escape a dangerous or threatening situation. Also, a young person who is knocked down by a stranger may get up unharmed, while in a similar incident an older person may be seriously hurt.

TIME TO REVIEW

- Why is age such a socially significant characteristic?
- What will the age structure of Canada look like in 2031?
- Describe some of the changes that happen to people as they age.
- How has retirement changed over the past hundred years?
- What are some of the inequities associated with aging?

SOCIOLOGICAL PERSPECTIVES ON AGING LO-4

Sociologists have developed a number of explanations of the social effects of aging. Some of the early theories were based on a microlevel analysis of how individuals adapt to changing social roles. More recent theories have used a macrolevel approach to examine the inequalities produced by **age stratification**—the inequalities, differences, segregation, or conflict between age groups—at the societal level.

age stratification The inequalities, differences, segregation, or conflict between age groups.

Functionalist Perspectives on Aging

Functionalist explanations examine how older persons adjust to their changing roles. According to Talcott Parsons (1960), the roles of older persons need to be redefined by society. Parsons suggested that devaluing the contributions of older persons is dysfunctional for society; older persons often have knowledge and wisdom to share with younger people.

How does society cope with the disruptions resulting from its members growing older and dying? According to **disengagement theory**, older persons make a normal and healthy adjustment to aging when they detach themselves from their social roles and prepare for

disengagement theory The proposition that older persons make a normal and healthy adjustment to aging when they detach themselves from their social roles and prepare for their eventual death.

their eventual death (Cumming and Henry, 1961). Cumming and Henry (1961) concluded that disengagement can be functional for both the individual and society. Disengagement facilitates a gradual and orderly transfer of statuses and roles from one generation to the next, and the withdrawal of older persons from the workforce provides employment opportunities for younger people. Retirement, then, can be thought of as recognition for years of service and acknowledgment that the person no longer fits into the world of paid work (Williamson, Duffy Rinehart, and Blank, 1992). The younger workers who move into the vacated positions will bring current training and new ideas to their jobs, which should be functional for their organizations.

Critics of this perspective object to the assumption that all older persons want to disengage while they are still productive and gain satisfaction from their work. Disengagement may be functional for organizations but not for individuals. A corporation that has compulsory retirement may be able to replace higher-paid older workers with lower-paid younger workers, but retirement may hurt some older workers. Contrary to disengagement theory, a number of studies have found that social activity is *more* important as people get older.

Symbolic Interactionist Perspectives on Aging

What does growing old mean to you? Do all people experience aging in the same way? Are there cultural differences in the aging experience? Symbolic interactionists look at how people deal with aging and at how this experience can vary. For example, a person's culture provides broad ideas of what constitutes aging. Symbolic interactionists show us that the experience of older people in a culture that respects them as sources of wisdom and stability is dramatically different from the experience in a culture in which they are seen as a drain on the resources of younger people. Contrast the earlier discussion of Patricia Moore, who felt diminished and irrelevant when she posed as "Old Pat Moore" with those of older people in Korea whose 60th birthday is celebrated for several days or a Tibetan group whose elders have such status that people exaggerate their ages to "age" more quickly (Tirriton, 2003). Tirriton reports that attitudes toward older people became more negative as societies moved from agrarian to industrial. One reason for this is that people on farms could adjust their workload to match their physical abilities, while owners of factories and large businesses were less likely to make accommodations for older workers (Synge, 1980).

Within their broader cultural context, individuals find different ways of dealing with aging. **Activity theory** states that people tend to shift gears in late middle age and find substitutes for previous statuses, roles, and activities (Havighurst, Neugarten, and Tobin, 1968).

activity theory The proposition that people tend to shift gears in late middle age and find substitutes for previous statuses, roles, and activities.

Whether they invest their energies in grandchildren, travelling, hobbies, or new work roles, social activity among retired persons is directly related to longevity, happiness, and health (Palmore, 1981). Consider these differences in the perceptions of people who do and do not remain active:

> The Richardsons came for lunch: friends we hadn't seen for twenty years . . . Helen and Martin had owned and worked together in a very fine women's clothing shop . . . Having some mistaken notion they were getting too old and should retire and "enjoy themselves," they sold the business ten years ago.
>
> During lunch, Larry and I realized we were dealing with two seriously depressed people, in excellent health but with no place to go. When Larry asked Helen what she'd been doing, she replied bitterly, "Who has anything to do?" Martin said sadly he was sorry he gave up tennis ten years ago; if he'd kept it up he could still play . . .
>
> We were embarrassed to indicate we were still so busy that we couldn't see straight. They seemed genuinely shocked that we had no plans to retire at seventy-one and seventy-four. (LeShan, 1994:221–222)

Studies have confirmed that healthy people who remain active have a higher level of life satisfaction than do those who are inactive or in ill health (Havighurst, Neugarten, and Tobin, 1968). Among those whose mental capacities decline later in life, deterioration is most rapid in people who withdraw from social relationships and activities.

Other symbolic interactionist perspectives focus on role and exchange theories. Role theory poses this question: What roles are available for older people? Some theorists have noted that industrialized, urbanized societies typically do not have roles for older people (Cowgill, 1986). Analysts examining the relationship between ethnicity and aging have found that many older persons are able to find active roles within their own ethnic group. While their experiences may not be valued in the larger society, they are esteemed within their ethnic subculture because they provide a rich source of knowledge of ethnic lore and history. For example, Mildred Cleghorn, an 80-year-old Aboriginal woman, passes on information to younger people by the use of dolls:

> I decided . . . to show that we were all not the same, by making dolls that said we were just as different as our clothes are different. I made four dolls . . . representing the four tribes there—then seven more . . . for the tribes living here. Now, over the years, I have a collection of forty-one fabric dolls, all different tribes. The trouble is there are thirty-two more to go! (quoted in Mucciolo, 1992:23)

Cleghorn's unique knowledge about the various First Nations has been a valuable source of information for young Aboriginal people who otherwise might be unaware of the great diversity found among First Nations peoples. According to Donald E. Gelfand (1994), older people can "exchange" their knowledge for deference and respect from younger people.

Conflict Perspectives on Aging

Conflict theorists view aging as especially problematic in capitalist societies. As people grow older, their power tends to diminish unless they are able to maintain wealth. Consequently, those who have been disadvantaged in their younger years become even more so in late adulthood. Women's incomes decline significantly following the deaths of their husbands (Statistics Canada, 2006d) and women 75 and over are among the most disadvantaged because, after outliving their spouses, they must often rely solely on government support payments.

Members of racial and ethnic minority groups may also suffer disadvantages. Some do not speak English, and because of racism and geographic isolation, many have been excluded from the broader society. Many come from cultures in which older people are viewed with respect and have an important role to play; they may feel distressed at the way they are treated in Canada.

Aboriginal people who live on reserves often face poverty, poor housing, and second-class medical care. These living conditions lead to higher rates of disability and more health problems among older Aboriginal people than among the rest of the population (Frideres, 1994). One positive trend in Aboriginal communities is an enhanced role for elders, who are serving more and more as resources for mentoring and teaching and filling other leadership roles. Taking on these important roles can help ease some of the stresses of aging (Novak and Campbell, 2001).

Conflict analysis highlights the diversity in the older population. Differences in social class, gender, and ethnicity divide older people just as they do everyone else. Wealth cannot forestall aging indefinitely, but it can minimize economic hardships. The conflict perspective adds to our understanding of aging by focusing on how capitalism devalues older people, especially women. Critics assert, however, that this approach ignores the fact that industrialization and capitalism have greatly enhanced the longevity and quality of life for many older persons.

© Strauss/Curtis/Corbis

© Mark Richards/PhotoEdit

What happens as we grow older? Activity theory assumes that we will find substitutes for our previous roles and activities. Disengagement theory assumes that we will detach ourselves from social roles and prepare for death. Which scenario do you prefer for your future?

Feminist Perspectives on Aging

Feminist scholars analyze the gender-based inequalities that affect older women:

> One conclusion stands out . . . Poverty in old age is largely a woman's problem, and is becoming more so every year. (National Council of Welfare, cited in Novak, 1993:239)

The poverty rate for elderly women is double that for elderly men. *Unattached* elderly women are at the greatest risk of poverty, with a rate that is double that of married elderly women (see Figure 18.5). Why do women have such low incomes in old age? According to the National Council of Welfare, "after a lifetime spent taking care of their spouses and children, these women who had no opportunity to become financially self-sufficient are now abandoned by the generation that benefited most from their work" (quoted in Novak, 1993:239).

Hardy and Hazelrigg (1993) found that gender was more directly related to poverty in older persons than was ethnicity, educational background, or occupational status. Many women who are now 65 or older spent their early adult lives as financial dependants of husbands or as working women trying to support themselves in a culture that did not see women as the heads of households or as sole providers of family income. Because they were not viewed as being responsible for the family's financial security, women were paid less and did not receive the same promotions and pay raises as their male counterparts. Many took years off work or worked part time to raise families, so their pensions are lower. Therefore, older women may rely on inadequate income replacement programs originally designed to treat them as dependants. Furthermore, women tend to marry men who are older than they are, and women live longer than men. Consequently, nearly half of all women over age 65 are widowed and living alone on fixed incomes.

Young women today will be much better equipped to deal with the financial pressures of old age as a result of a number of structural changes in Canadian society. The majority of women are working in the paid labour force, they have begun to enter male-dominated professions, and more of them have private pension plans. At retirement, they will be in much better financial shape than their mothers and grandmothers.

Postmodern Perspectives on Aging

A central theme of postmodern theory is the notion that identity is a social construct. This implies that we can alter the way our culture thinks about aging—what theorists

CONCEPT SNAPSHOT

FUNCTIONALIST PERSPECTIVES **Key thinkers:** Talcott Parsons, Elaine Cumming, William Henry	Functionalists look at how people adjust to their changing roles as they grow older. Disengagement theory argues that it is good for society if people detach themselves from their social roles in order to transfer statuses and roles to the next generation. Other functionalists feel that societies also need to provide the opportunity for older persons to share their knowledge and wisdom with younger people.
SYMBOLIC INTERACTIONIST PERSPECTIVES **Key thinkers:** Robert Havighurst, Donald Cowgill	Symbolic interactionists look at how people deal with aging and at how this experience can vary under different circumstances. Older people who live in a culture that values and respects them have a different experience than those who live in a culture in which they are seen as a drain on society's resources.
CONFLICT PERSPECTIVES	As people grow older, their power tends to diminish unless they are able to maintain their health. Those who have been disadvantaged in their younger years become even more disadvantaged in late adulthood. Many conflict theorists feel that aging is particularly problematic in capitalist societies where the people's status and power depends on their wealth.
FEMINIST PERSPECTIVES **Key thinkers:** Melissa Hardy, Lawrence Hazelrigg	Feminists argue that for older people, poverty has become feminized. Because many older women grew up in an era in which women were not treated as men's financial equals, they are much more likely than men to be poor in old age. These women stayed home to raise families or were restricted to low-wage jobs and so they do not have adequate pensions or savings. Because of changes in the role of women, the current generation of women will be much better-prepared for retirement than their predecessors.
POSTMODERN PERSPECTIVES **Key thinkers:** Stephen Katz, Larry Polivka	A central theme of postmodern theory is the notion that identity is a social construct. Postmodern society has eroded the rigid states of the life course, and older people are now able to experiment with new identities with the assistance of anti-aging technologies including surgery, hormone replacement therapy, Botox, and fitness programs.

call our *cultural narratives.* Steven Katz has characterized the postmodern approach to aging as one in which the rigid stages of "childhood, middle age and old age are eroding under pressure from cultural directions that have accompanied profound changes in labor, retirement and the welfare state, and the globalization of Western consumer economies and lifestyles" (1999:3). Katz's analysis emphasizes the role played by marketers of consumer products in portraying an ageless image of older people. Consumers do not want to buy products that are targeted to "old" people, so marketers have developed strategies that mask the dimension of age. At a time when the number of older persons is increasing dramatically, the physical aspects of aging are being concealed (Woodward, 1991). In the postmodern world, nobody should look or act as if they are old.

Technology allows us to change our appearance. No longer must we allow our bodies to visibly change if we choose to surgically mask the aging process. A Toronto plastic surgeon commented on the emerging trend for men to get cosmetic surgery:

> This is a very youth-oriented culture . . . so a lot of men feel they have to look fresh, young and vigorous to get the next promotion at work. And many of these same men are divorced or separated and back in the dating game, often competing for much younger women with guys who are frequently 10, 15 or 20 years younger. (Collison, 2006)

Meredith Jones (2004) has compared cosmetic surgery to postmodern architecture. In a world in which anti-aging technologies, such as Botox injections, breast implants, and hormone replacement therapy, have been normalized and in which tattoos and piercings are common, the postmodern notion that we can simply choose from a variety of ages and alter that choice at will does not seem out of place. Jones illustrates this by quoting Kathryn Morgan's idea of celebrating old age:

> Bleaching one's hair white and applying wrinkle-inducing "wrinkle-creams," having one's face and breasts surgically pulled down (rather than lifted), and having wrinkles sewn and carved into one's skin. (Morgan, 1991:46, cited in Jones, 2004:99)

Unlike traditional societies in which well-defined roles and statuses are attached to older persons, contemporary society has less certainty. We are not surprised to hear of a 72-year-old person being in a nursing home, nor are we surprised to hear of another 72-year-old running a large company and spending vacations downhill skiing. Retirement at age 65 is no longer mandatory in most provinces, so we no longer have clear signals about when someone should move into a new role as a retired person. This blurring of identity can make it difficult for older people to define themselves.

Negotiating an identity as an older person can be particularly hard for lower-income people who cannot afford to define themselves by what they buy and where they travel and who cannot afford cosmetic surgery and other anti-aging technologies (Polivka, 2000). As the media increasingly portray older people as active and youthful, those who cannot live up to this standard may feel they are to blame for their condition (Hodgetts, Chamberlain, and Bassett, 2003) and feel marginalized.

On a more positive note, postmodern culture provides older people with the freedom to experiment. Older people no longer have to fit into stereotyped roles, so they can shape their own identities. For example, through the technology of in vitro fertilization, a Calgary woman of 60 gave birth to twins to fulfill her lifelong dream of motherhood. Affluent seniors can resist traditional aging through pharmaceuticals, cosmetic surgery, technology, and participation in the consumer culture. Older people can keep working but with flexible work times and new paid or volunteer occupations. Some older people now take up activities such as surfing at age 80 or playing tennis at 90. Adopting attitudes such as these may allow seniors to extend active living for many years before biology finally takes its toll—older people can remain creative and engaged with life.

© Chuck Savage/Corbis

What does the concept of nursing homes imply about the ability of residents to live out their lives with dignity and respect?

This perspective is very different than the functionalist view of old age as a time for gradual disengagement and preparation for death.

TIME TO REVIEW

- Discuss how disengagement theory explains the aging process.
- According to interactionist theorists, how do different individuals deal with aging?
- How do conflict theorists analyze the aging process?
- According to feminist theorists, what types of discrimination face women as they age?
- According to postmodern theorists, how do people construct their identities as they get older?

LIVING ARRANGEMENTS FOR OLDER ADULTS LO-5

Many older people live alone or in a family setting where care is provided informally by family or friends. Relatives, usually women, provide most of the care. Many women caregivers are employed outside the home; some are still raising a family. The responsibilities of informal caregivers have become more complex. For frail, older persons, for example, family members are often involved in nursing regimes—such as chemotherapy and tube feeding—that were previously performed in hospitals (Glazer, 1990).

Only a small percentage of older persons live in nursing homes or other special-care facilities. About 10 percent of older women and 5 percent of older men live in these facilities (Cranswick, 2003). As one would expect, the older the people are, the more likely it is they will live in institutions. Few people under age 75 are in nursing homes, compared with about one-third of those age 85 and over (Cranswick, 2003). Increased social supports and community care have led to a significant decline in rates of institutionalization over the past three decades.

Despite this, having those seniors in the community, where they are cared for by relatives or friends, poses a few problems. While most caregivers find this task rewarding, it does have a significant negative impact on many of them (Cranswick, 2003). If seniors are to be cared for in the community, mechanisms must be found to support the caregivers, many of whom are themselves seniors—often spouses of those needing care (Stobert and Cranswick, 2004).

Japan provides an interesting case study on the impact of an aging population on caregiving. Because of lower birth rates, Japan has an older population than Canada. By 2030, about one-third of the population will be 65 or over. In the past, it was widely assumed that older people in Japan were respected and revered. However, recent studies suggest that sociocultural changes and population shifts are producing a gradual change in the social importance of the elderly. For example, in 1980, 70 percent of older people were living with a child. By 2010, this had declined to 42 percent (International Longevity Centre Japan, 2012). At least part of this decline may be related to younger and middle-aged couples working long hours and feeling they do not have time to look after their parents.

Support Services

Declining family sizes mean that the baby boomers will likely require higher levels of formal care than the preceding generation of seniors because there will be fewer children to do this work for their parents. Support services help older individuals cope with the problems in their day-to-day care. For older persons, homemaker services perform basic chores such as light housecleaning and laundry; other services (such as Meals on Wheels) deliver meals to homes.

Support services and daycare for older persons can be costly, but they are far less expensive than institutional care. Even intensive services that provide the support to allow older persons with serious physical problems to live in their homes may cost only 25 percent of the costs of a nursing home. More important, these services allow older persons to live in a familiar environment and retain much of their independence.

A British Columbia program illustrates how careful planning can save money and enhance the quality of life of older persons (Novak, 1997). The Quick Response Team (QRT) was designed to deal with patients who have been admitted to hospital because of medical emergencies, such as broken bones and strokes. After the emergency has been dealt with, the acute-care hospital can do little more for the patient. However, many patients are unable to return home because they cannot care for themselves. The QRT arranges for community support for these patients. These supports depends on the patient's needs and can include live-in homemaker services, transportation, home nursing, Meals on Wheels, physiotherapy, and household equipment, such as walkers and bath seats. Because it costs over $1500 per day to keep a patient in an acute-care hospital, programs such as the QRT can be a cost-effective way of providing high-quality services to older persons.

CP Photo/Fred Chartrand

Older persons seek to be fully accepted as participants in everyday life, as this seniors' protest demonstrates.

Nursing Homes

A nursing home is defined as any institution that offers medical care for chronically ill older people but is not a hospital (Novak, 1997:148). It is the most restrictive environment for older persons.

Why do people live in nursing homes? Many residents have major physical and/or cognitive problems that prevent them from living elsewhere or do not have available caregivers in their family. Women are more likely to enter nursing homes because of their greater life expectancy, higher rates of chronic illness, and higher rates of widowhood. Lower-income seniors are also more likely to stay in institutions because they do not have the financial resources to live on their own (Trottier et al., 2000). Some of the facilities available to the poor do not offer high-quality care.

Some people adjust well to life in a nursing home. For many others, however, the transition to an institutional setting can be stressful. Mortality rates are higher after admission to nursing homes. In part, this is due to the fact that the sickest older people enter these institutions. However, researchers have concluded that institutionalization itself can lower levels of well-being and accelerate mortality (Novak, 1997). Cases of neglect, excessive use of physical restraints, overmedication of patients, and other complaints have been rampant in many of the homes. Friedan (1993:516) believes that even the best-run nursing homes "deny the personhood of age [because they] reify the image of age as inevitable decline and deterioration."

One solution to this problem is to provide higher levels of support so people can remain in the community. However, there will always be people whose physical or mental condition makes institutional care necessary. Gerontologists have found that nursing homes can do many things to reduce the negative effects of institutionalization. They can make life in the institution as much like life outside as possible (MacLean and Bonar, 1983). They can allow patients as much freedom of choice as possible. They should have programs that allow patients to remain active and maintain their daily, monthly, and yearly rhythms of life (Novak, 1997). It is also important for patients to have a normal social life and to keep enough of their own possessions that the institution becomes their home and not just a place where they are forced to stay. The idea of ethnic-focused nursing homes has been very successful, as many older people prefer to live in a facility that serves familiar food and allows them to share lifelong cultural practices with other seniors. People wait as long as a decade to get into facilities such as Mississauga's Yee Hong Centre for Geriatric Care (Bascaramurty, 2012).

Contrasting views of nursing home life that illustrate some of these points are expressed by two nursing home residents:

> My eyesight and ability to walk are very bad. I have a hard time getting around. But I am feeling alright because I have enough money, thanks to my pension, and I am in a home where people look after me. I don't have any family but like being here because everybody is a friend.
>
> They take care of me here but they don't do it the same as I would myself. I can't take care of myself because I'm all crippled up. Sometimes I think this place is run more for the convenience of the staff than for the residents. I resent having to go to bed early just to suit them . . . I have only $90 a month to get by on. That is not very much. It is very hard for me to take a car or a bus to go anywhere. (National Advisory Council on Aging, 1992)

DEATH AND DYING

Historically, death has been a common occurrence at all stages of the life course. Until the 20th century, the chances that a newborn child would live to adulthood were slight. Poor nutrition, infectious diseases, accidents, and natural disasters took their toll on men and women of all ages. In contemporary industrial societies, however, death is seen as unnatural because it has largely been removed from everyday life. Most deaths now occur among older persons and in institutional settings. In the past, explanations for death and dying were rooted in custom or religious beliefs; today, they have been replaced by medical and legal explanations and definitions, and ongoing medical and legal battles.

The Canadian courts have not yet resolved several controversial issues that relate to the right to die with dignity. Should guardians of incompetent persons in permanent vegetative states have the legal right to refuse medical treatment? Should individuals suffering from an incurable terminal illness have the right to decide when their life should end? In 1993, the Supreme Court of Canada considered this question in the case of Sue Rodriguez, a British Columbia woman suffering from Lou Gehrig's disease. The Court decided that the right to life, liberty, and security of the person (as outlined in the *Charter of Rights and Freedoms*) does not include the right to take action to end one's life. Furthermore, the Court decided that prohibition of physician-assisted suicide did not constitute cruel and unusual treatment. However, the lack of consensus over this complex issue was reflected in a strong dissenting vote expressed by four of the nine justices. Justice Beverley McLachlin wrote:

> The denial to Sue Rodriguez of a choice available to others cannot be justified. Such a denial deprived Sue Rodriguez of her security of the person (the right to make decisions concerning her own body which affect only her own body) in a way that offended the principles of fundamental justice. (quoted in Bolton, 1995:391)

After the Supreme Court declined her challenge for a legal physician-assisted suicide, Rodriguez took her own life with the help of an anonymous doctor. Currently, the *Criminal Code* specifies that anyone who counsels or "aids and abets" a suicide is guilty of an indictable offence and subject to 14 years in prison (McGovern, 1995). The patient's consent cannot be used as a defence.

In 2012, the British Columbia Supreme Court found this law unconstitutional on the grounds that it discriminated against people with a physical disability. While the judge in the case suspended her ruling for one year to allow the government time to change the law, one of the plaintiffs was given an exception to the law if she chooses to end her life. The ruling has been appealed by the federal government.

A related issue concerns the legality of a doctor's hastening the death of a terminally ill patient. Ethical guidelines allow doctors to remove life support with the consent of the patient or the patient's family if the patient is incapable of responding. After life support is removed, doctors may administer painkilling drugs to make the patient comfortable even if these drugs may hasten death. However, Halifax doctor Nancy Morrison was charged with murder over her role in the 1996 death of a patient who was near death and in terrible pain. Dr. Morrison administered two drugs that were not painkillers but that would stop the patient's heart. After a colleague reported the occurrence to police, the hospital was raided by 60 police officers and Dr. Morrison was arrested on a charge of first-degree murder. The charges were subsequently dismissed by a judge who did not think that the Crown could prove its charges. However, the case led to a major debate about proper medical practice. In 2012, the Supreme Court will likely hear the case of Hassan Rasouli, whose family is challenging the right of doctors to remove his life support.

Many people have chosen to have a say in how their own lives might end by signing a *living will*—a document stating their wishes about the medical circumstances under which their life should be terminated. Most provinces recognize living wills.

Many issues pertaining to the quality of life and to death with dignity may remain unresolved, but the debate about the right to die will continue. The number of deaths in Canada will increase from about 252,000 per year in 2011 to 500,000 per year in 2039 as the lives of the baby boomers end (Kettle, 1998; Statistics Canada, 2011d).

The way a person dies is shaped by many social and cultural factors. According to Hooyman and Kiyak, "The dying process is shaped by an individual's own personality and philosophy of life, by the specific illness, and by the social context (e.g., whether at home surrounded by family who encourage the expression of feelings, or isolated in a hospital)" (1996:417).

In recent years, the process of dying has become an increasingly acceptable topic for public discussion. Such discussions helped further the hospice movement in the 1970s (Weitz, 1995). A **hospice** is a homelike facility that provides supportive care for patients with terminal illnesses. The hospice philosophy asserts that people should participate in their own care and have control over as many decisions pertaining to their life as possible. Pain and suffering should be minimized, but artificial measures should not be used to sustain life. This approach is family-based and provides support for family members and friends, as well as for the person who is dying (see Corr, Nabe, and Corr, 2003). Many hospitals have established palliative care units designed to make the process of dying more compassionate and humane.

hospice A homelike facility that provides supportive care for patients with terminal illnesses.

AGING IN THE FUTURE

The size of the older population in Canada will soon increase dramatically. By 2031, there will be an estimated 8 million persons age 65 and older, compared with 3.2 million in 1991. More people will survive to age 85, and more will reach the 95 and over cohort. In almost all societies, institutions including government, the family, industry, education, and healthcare will have to change to accommodate the increasing age of the population. The baby boomers have had a huge impact on social and political matters because of the size of this cohort. The fact that nearly one-quarter of the population will be over 65 means that they will continue to have a significant impact because of their votes. Thus we can anticipate many changes in government policies related to seniors.

Retirement will be redefined in the future. Mandatory retirement has been abolished for most people, and as people stay healthy and active into their later years, many will choose to work. Margaret Wente expressed the views of many seniors in her comments on the life of television personality Andy Rooney, who was still on U.S. network television into his 90s:

> I used to think retirement might be kind of fun. But the older I get, the worse the whole idea seems. After you go Elderhostelling around the world, take some art lessons and clean the cupboards, then what? I hate golf, and I'm no good at bridge. To tell the truth, I'm not that eager for my husband to retire, either. I'm afraid he'd just be underfoot.
>
> The retirement fantasies we're peddled are a crock. Typically, they feature attractive older people who seem to spend their days in endless rounds of play, and their nights sipping champagne in their adult-lifestyle condos. Retirement living is depicted as a sort of resort vacation that goes on until you die. No wonder Andy Rooney hated it. His idea of the good life was to get up, read the newspapers, go to work, come home, read some more, watch a bit of TV, and do it all again the next day. That seems like a decent formula for happiness to me. (2011)

It is important to note that delaying retirement will be much easier for writers like Ms. Wente than it will be for people working doing hard physical labour in meat packing plants or outdoor construction sites. Thus, people who are poor may be negatively affected by changing views of retirement.

One of the most positive consequences of population aging is that there will be considerably less age segregation. When the elderly comprise one-quarter of the population, there will be much more interaction between individuals of all age groups. This development should lead to decreases in both ageism and negative stereotypes of old age (Dooley and Frankel, 1990).

As biomedical research on aging and disabilities continues, new discoveries in genetics may eliminate life-threatening diseases and make early identification of others possible. Any major

extension of life expectancy will also lead to changes in the way our society defines realities like retirement and old age.

Advances in technology and design will alleviate some of the difficulties that come with aging. Just as eyeglasses, heart pacemakers, and accessible buses have improved life for older persons in the past, computers, robots, and household elevators will make things easier in the future. Even simple changes, such as buttons that can be done up with arthritic fingers, can improve the ability of older people to care for themselves. To see how new media may affect seniors, see Box 18.4 at **www.nelson.com/sociologyinourtimes6e.**

Will these advances help everyone or just some segments of the population? This question is very important for the future. Many of the benefits and opportunities of living in a highly technological, affluent society are not available to all people. Classism, racism, sexism, and ageism all serve to restrict individuals' access to education, medical care, housing, employment, and other valued goods and services in society.

For older persons, the issues discussed in this chapter are not merely sociological abstractions; they are part of their everyday lives. Older people have resisted ageism by organizing politically, and with their increased numbers, older people will have far more political power in the future than they have had in the past.

Finally, your own actions will help to determine how aging affects Canadian society in the future. Results of the National Population Health Survey have confirmed the fact that personal choices play a major role in determining the health and happiness of people over 65 (Martel et al., 2005). As someone pursuing postsecondary education, you have already made a positive contribution to your future, as education and income are important factors in successful aging. The study also showed that people were at greater risk of losing their health in later life if they smoked, if they were overweight, or if they were inactive. While individuals will benefit if they continue their education and live healthy, active lifestyles, society will also benefit through a reduction in the costs of healthcare and the need for institutional or home care for elderly persons.

TIME TO REVIEW

- Discuss the living arrangements of most older people.
- Why are community support services so important for older people?
- What are some of the ways in which nursing homes can improve the quality of life for their residents?
- How is the process of dying changing? What are some of the legal issues involved in the dying process?
- How will aging change in the future?

18 VISUAL SUMMARY

KEY TERMS

activity theory The proposition that people tend to shift gears in late middle age and find substitutes for previous statuses, roles, and activities (p. 524).

age stratification The inequalities, differences, segregation, or conflict between age groups (p. 523)

ageism Prejudice and discrimination against people on the basis of age, particularly when they are older (p. 518).

aging The physical, psychological, and social processes associated with growing older (p. 510).

chronological age A person's age based on date of birth (p. 510).

cohort A category of people born within a specified period in time or who share some specified characteristic (p. 510).

disengagement theory The proposition that older persons make a normal and healthy adjustment to aging when they detach themselves from their social roles and prepare for their eventual death (p. 523).

elder abuse A term used to describe physical abuse, psychological abuse, financial exploitation, and medical abuse or neglect of people age 65 or older (p. 521).

functional age A term used to describe observable individual attributes—such as physical appearance, mobility, strength, coordination, and mental capacity—that are used to assign people to age categories (p. 510).

gerontology The study of aging and older people (p. 513).

LO-1 Explain how functional age differs from chronological age.

Chronological age is a person's age based on their date of birth. Functional age is the age a person appears to be based on observable individual attributes, such as physical appearance, mobility, strength, coordination, and mental capacity, that are used to assign people to age categories.

© Corbis Premium RF/Alamy

CBC/Rick Mercer Report

Discuss how views of aging differ in preindustrial and industrialized societies.

In preindustrial societies, people of all ages are expected to share the work and the contributions of older people are valued. In industrialized societies, however, older people are often expected to retire so that younger people can take their place.

LO-3 Explain ageism and elder abuse.

Ageism is prejudice and discrimination against people on the basis of age, particularly against older persons. Elder abuse includes physical abuse, psychological abuse, financial exploitation, and medical abuse or neglect of people aged 65 or older. Passive neglect is the most common form of abuse.

© Tony Freeman /PhotoEdit

© Strauss/Curtis/Corbis

LO-4 Understand the differences between the functionalist, symbolic interactionist, conflict, feminist, and postmodern explanations of aging.

Functionalist explanations focus on how older persons adjust to their changing roles in society; gradual transfer of statuses and roles from one generation to the next is necessary for the functioning of society. Interactionist theorists show us that the experience of older people in a culture that respects them as sources of wisdom and stability is dramatically different from the experience in a culture in which they are seen as a drain on the resources of younger people. Conflict theorists link the loss of status and power experienced by many older persons to their lack of ability to produce and maintain wealth in a capitalist economy. Feminist scholars have analyzed the gender-based inequalities that affect older women, who are much more likely than men to be poor in old age and who also face other forms of discrimination based on their physical appearance. Postmodern theorists have shown that because identity is a social construct, people are actively trying to avoid being categorized as "old" through means such as plastic surgery, exercise, and staying active in the labour market.

hospice A homelike facility that provides supportive care for patients with terminal illnesses (p. 532).

life expectancy The average length of time a group of individuals of the same age will live (p. 510).

LO-5 Identify the most common living arrangements for older people.

© Chuck Savage/Corbis

Many older persons live alone or in an informal family setting. Support services and daycare help older individuals who are frail or disabled cope with their day-to-day needs, although many older people do not have the financial means to pay for these services. Nursing homes are the most restrictive environment for older persons. Many nursing home residents have major physical and/or cognitive problems that prevent them from living in any other setting, or they do not have caregivers available in their family.

APPLICATION QUESTIONS

1. Analyze your grandparents (or other older persons you know well, or even yourself if you are older) in terms of disengagement theory and activity theory. Which theory seems to provide the most insight? Why?
2. Pay close attention to the commercials the next time you spend an evening watching television. How do these commercials portray older persons? What type of products target their advertisements toward older people?
3. In the past 150 years, life expectancy has doubled, from 40 to 80 years. How would our society change if life expectancy doubled again, to 160 years of age?

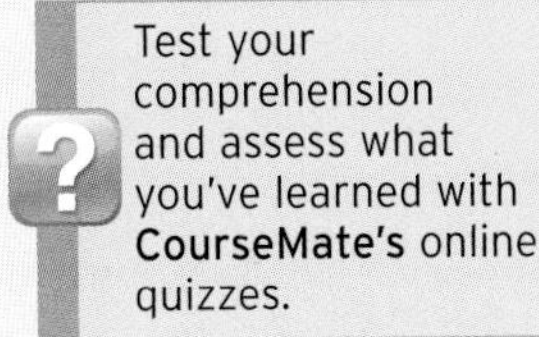
Test your comprehension and assess what you've learned with **CourseMate's** online quizzes.

For other interesting Lived Experiences, watch the video clips on **CourseMate.**

Practise what you've learned with flashcards containing key terms and definitions on **CourseMate.**

CHAPTER

19 The Economy and Work

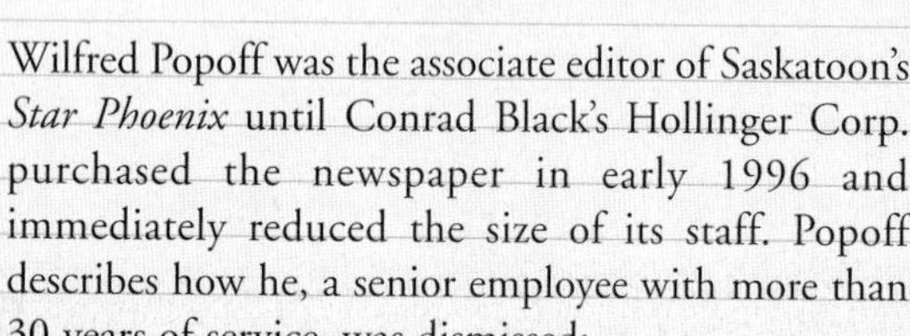

Wilfred Popoff was the associate editor of Saskatoon's *Star Phoenix* until Conrad Black's Hollinger Corp. purchased the newspaper in early 1996 and immediately reduced the size of its staff. Popoff describes how he, a senior employee with more than 30 years of service, was dismissed:

I can only attribute my sudden firing, within several months of possible retirement, a dignified retirement I had seen so many others receive, to total abandonment of common civility, a phenomenon more and more prevalent today. You see, I was fired not because of anything I did or didn't do, but because of the need to cut costs in the quest for fantastic profits. And how the affair was stage-managed tells more than one wishes to know about the uncivil environment surrounding contemporary capitalism.

On a Friday afternoon all employees, about 300 in all, received a terse letter from the boss commanding attendance at a meeting in a hotel the following morning. The arrangement was reminiscent of military occupations portrayed in countless movies. The vanquished are summoned to the market square where officers of the occupying army register all people and direct them to various camps. In our case the officers were employees of a consulting firm, also strangers, who directed employees to various rooms, separating survivors from those marked for elimination. Of course, I was in the second group, although none of us knew what fate awaited us. Eventually the boss entered, gripped the lectern and read a brief statement: We were all finished, the decision was final.

© Stephen Coburn/Shutterstock

Not only were we finished, our place of work a few blocks away had been locked up, incapacitating our entry cards, and was under guard. We could never go back except to retrieve our personal belongings, and this under the watchful eye of a senior supervisor and one of the newly retained guards. I felt like a criminal. In my time I had managed large portions of this company, had represented it the world over and, until the previous day, had authority to spend its money. Now I couldn't be trusted not to snitch a pencil or note pad . . . The current phenomenon known as downsizing is threatening to hurt capitalism by depriving it of the very thing it needs most: a market. This, however, speaks to the stupidity of capitalism today, not its abandonment of civility. But perhaps there is a connection. (1996:A22)

Many Canadians face unemployment when their employers restructure or shut down because of business problems. However, Popoff and his colleagues at the *Star Phoenix* lost their jobs because the new owner wanted to cut costs to increase profits. Although the paper had been quite profitable under its previous owners, new owner Conrad Black wanted higher profits so that he and other shareholders would receive a greater return on their investment. Firing staff is often the quickest route to short-term profits, so the termination consultants were called. In an interesting postscript to this story, Conrad Black recently completed a three-and-a-half-year sentence in a Florida prison for misappropriating some of the profits of his publicly owned newspaper chain.

Unemployment shows the linkage between the economy and work. Changes in the economy affect us all, but those who lose their jobs will feel an acute sense of financial and personal loss. For many people, work helps define who they are. When someone is introduced to another, the first question often asked is, Where do you work? or What do you do for a living? Job loss may cause people financial problems that could range from the loss of their cars and homes to bankruptcy, as well as bringing on personal problems, such as depression and divorce.

In this chapter, we will discuss the economy and the world of work—how people feel about their work, how work is changing, what impact these changes may have on students and other current and future workers, and the connections between work and the larger economic structure in Canada and in the global economy. We will also look at how workers have sought better wages and working conditions through unions. Before reading on, test your knowledge about the economy, work, and workers by taking the quiz in Box 19.1 on page 538.

(*Source:* Popoff, 1996. Reprinted by permission of the author.)

Critical Thinking Questions

1. In the years since Wilfred Popoff was fired, the gap between the pay of those running corporations and their workers has become wider. What factors do you think have led to this increased disparity between those at the top and those at the bottom?
2. In 2011 and 2012, the Occupy movement began to draw public attention to the growing power of the "1 percent" who were doing well while the rest of society suffered. Do you think social movements like Occupy can help to redress the imbalance between rich and poor in Western societies?
3. Why do you think that the job a person does is so central to that person's identity?

CHAPTER FOCUS QUESTION

How is work in Canada affected by changes in the economy?

LEARNING OBJECTIVES

AFTER READING THIS CHAPTER, YOU SHOULD BE ABLE TO

LO-1 Understand the primary function of the economy.

LO-2 Describe the differences between the primary, secondary, and tertiary sectors of economic production.

LO-3 Discuss the differences between the three major contemporary economic systems—capitalism, socialism, and mixed economies.

LO-4 Understand the functionalist, conflict, symbolic interactionist, and feminist perspectives on the economy and work.

LO-5 Understand the role of labour unions and identify the challenges currently faced by the union movement.

LO-6 Consider how globalization has affected Canadian workers.

LO-1 THE ECONOMY

economy The social institution that ensures the maintenance of society through the production, distribution, and consumption of goods and services.

The **economy** is the social institution that ensures the maintenance of society through the production, distribution, and consumption of goods and services. *Goods* are tangible objects that are necessary or desired. Necessary objects include food, clothing, and shelter; desired objects may include smartphones and stylish clothing. *Services* are activities for which people are willing to pay (such as a haircut, a movie, legal advice, or medical care). *Labour* consists of the physical and intellectual services, including training, education, and individual abilities, which people contribute to the production process (Boyes and Melvin, 1994). *Capital* is wealth (money or property) owned or used in business by a person or corporation. Money, or financial capital, is needed to invest in the physical capital (such as machinery, equipment, buildings, warehouses, and factories) used in production.

The Sociology of Economic Life

Sociologists focus on interconnections among the economy and other social institutions, and the social organization of work. At the macrolevel, sociologists may study the impact of multinational corporations on industrialized and developing nations. At the microlevel, sociologists might study people's job satisfaction. To better understand the Canadian economy, we will examine the evolution of economic systems and how they have changed over time.

LO-2 Historical Changes in Economic Systems

primary sector production The sector of the economy that extracts raw materials and natural resources from the environment.

The nature of work in Canada has changed dramatically since preindustrial times. This section will illustrate how economic systems have evolved.

PREINDUSTRIAL ECONOMIES Hunting and gathering, horticultural and pastoral, and agrarian societies are all preindustrial economies. Most workers engage in **primary sector production**—the extraction of raw materials and natural resources from the environment. These materials and resources are typically consumed or used without much processing.

BOX 19.1 **SOCIOLOGY AND EVERYDAY LIFE**

How Much Do You Know About the Economy and the World of Work?

True	False	
T	F	1. Women are dramatically increasing their representation in the professions of law and medicine.
T	F	2. Sociologists have developed special criteria to distinguish professions from other occupations.
T	F	3. Workers' skills are usually upgraded when new technology is introduced in the workplace.
T	F	4. Many of the new jobs being created in the service sector pay poorly and offer little job security.
T	F	5. Women are more likely than men to hold part-time jobs.

For answers to the quiz about the economy and the world of work, go to **www.nelson.com/sociologyinourtimes6e**.

© Bettman/Corbis

In the wake of the Industrial Revolution, many observers were dismayed by the mechanization of work and its effects on the dignity of workers. Filmmaker Charlie Chaplin bitingly satirized the new relationship between workers and machines in the classic *Modern Times*.

Preindustrial societies show a progression from work by family members to the use of other people to fulfill specialized tasks. In hunting and gathering societies, most goods are produced by family members and the division of labour is by age and gender. The ability to produce surplus goods increases as people learn to domesticate animals and grow their own food. In horticultural and pastoral societies, the economy becomes distinct from family life. The distribution process becomes more complex with the accumulation of a *surplus* because some people can engage in activities other than food production. In agrarian societies, production is related primarily to producing food. Workers, however, have a greater variety of specialized tasks. For example, warriors are necessary to protect surplus goods from theft by outsiders. Commercial enterprises operate on a small scale, and the vast majority of the population still lives in small rural communities.

Most manufactured goods were produced by artisans with the help of family members and apprentices. Under this system, the individual artisans had control over the work process and kept the profits from their labour. Sjoberg described the flexibility of work schedules:

> Merchants and handicraft workers generally do not adhere to any fixed schedule. Shopkeepers open and close their shops as they see fit. They may open one morning at nine, the next at ten, and so on. The lunch hour is likely to be longer on some days than on others. (1960:209)

The Granger Collection, New York

© Tomasz Wieja/Shutterstock

In the days before assembly lines, goods were manufactured by individual artisans such as the 15th-century French cabinetmaker shown on the left. These artisans were supported and regulated by guilds made up of their fellow craftsmen. On the right, the elaborate guildhalls in Brussels' town square show the wealth of some of the guilds.

Craft work was controlled through guilds, made up of artisans such as weavers and stonemasons (Volti, 2008). The guilds set and enforced standards, provided social activities, and gave assistance to members who were having difficulties. Guilds also controlled entrance to the trades, ensuring that the number of tradespeople did not exceed the demand for the product because this would have led to competition and decreased wages.

INDUSTRIAL ECONOMIES The nature of work and life changed dramatically with industrialization. At the beginning of the 20th century, the majority of workers in Canada were farmers (Drucker, 1994). By the end of the century, however, only 3 percent were agriculture workers and other primary sector workers were equally rare. Industrialization dramatically changed the system of production and the distribution of goods and services. Drawing on new forms of energy (steam, gasoline, and electricity) and technology, factories became the primary means of producing goods and wage labour became the dominant form of employment. Workers sold their labour to others rather than working independently or with family members. In a capitalist system, this means that the product belongs to the factory owner and not to the workers who create it.

secondary sector production The sector of the economy that processes raw materials (from the primary sector) into finished goods.

Most workers engage in **secondary sector production**—the processing of raw materials into finished goods. For example, steel workers process metal ore and auto workers then convert the steel into automobiles. In industrial economies, work becomes specialized and repetitive, activities become bureaucratically organized, and workers primarily work with machines instead of with one another.

This differs greatly from craftwork, where individual artisans perform all the steps in the production process. Think of the difference between a skilled artisan, who creates an elegant piece of furniture from pieces of wood, and a relatively unskilled assembly line worker who staples a cabinet together as it passes by on an assembly line. The jobs of the craftworkers were taken over by machines and by unskilled labourers. The work was broken into simple tasks that labourers repeated hour after hour. This approach was much less costly than using craftspeople because more goods are produced in a shorter time on an assembly line and because labourers received a lower wage than more skilled workers. However, workers lost control over their work, and some began to see themselves as part of the machinery, not as human beings.

Industrialization also had a major impact on women's lives. In preindustrial times, much production took place within the household and men and women often worked together. Factories separated production from the household, causing a gendered division of labour. Men became responsible for the family's income and women for domestic tasks (Cohen, 1993).

In the early days of industrialization, work hours were long, wages were low, and workers had no pensions, vacation, or overtime pay. A parliamentary committee in the 1880s documented the exploitation of child labour:

National Archives of Canada/CP

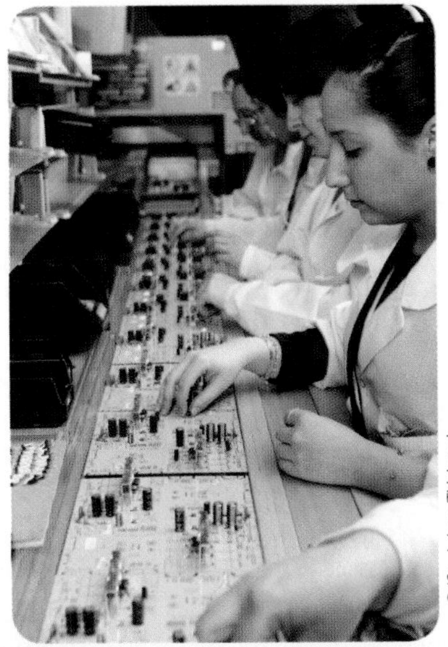

© iStockphoto/Thinkstock

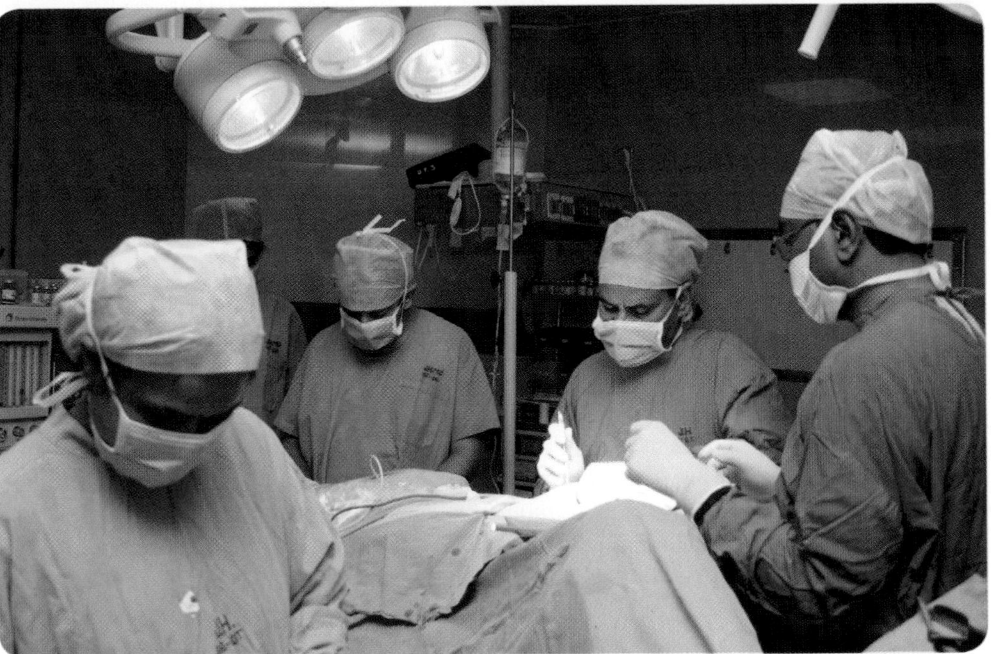

© Girish Menon/Shutterstock.com

The nature of work is very different in the three main types of economies. In preindustrial economies, most workers are directly involved in extracting raw materials. In industrial economies, production and distribution of goods are much more complex and much work is specialized and repetitive. In post-industrial economies, workers increasingly provide services, such as healthcare, rather than manufacturing goods.

© SimplyCreativePhotography/iStockphoto

The Blackberry, manufactured by Waterloo's Research in Motion company, was one of the first products that made it possible to stay in contact with work day and night and from almost anywhere in the world.

> Many children of tender age, some of them not more than nine years old, were employed in cotton, glass, tobacco and cigar factories . . . Some of them worked from six o'clock in the morning till six in the evening, with less than an hour for dinner, others worked from seven in the evening till six in the morning. (quoted in Rinehart, 1996:xx)

By the 1950s, unionized industrial workers had gained better working conditions and better wages, but many of these gains were lost by the end of the 20th century as manufacturing jobs disappeared in the *post-industrial economy.*

POST-INDUSTRIAL ECONOMIES During the first half of the 20th century, Canada shifted from a primary sector economy to one focused on manufacturing and service industries. By 1951, 47 percent of Canadian workers were employed in the service sector, 31 percent were employed in manufacturing, and the remaining 22 percent worked in primary industries. Manufacturing has steadily declined in importance as technology (such as robots) has replaced workers and as production has shifted offshore to low-wage countries; we have moved to a service-based economy. By 2008, only 4 percent of workers remained in primary industries, while 20 percent were employed in manufacturing and construction. Fully 77 percent worked in service industries (Krahn, Lowe, and Hughes, 2011). We now have a **post-industrial economy** that is based on the provision of services rather than goods. The service sector includes activities such as food services, transportation, communication, healthcare, education, legal services, sports, and entertainment.

post-industrial economy An economy that is based on the provision of services rather than goods.

In a post-industrial economy:

1. *Information displaces property as the central focus of the economy.* Post-industrial economies are characterized by ideas, and computer and communications technology is becoming the infrastructure of the future. In 1971, knowledge workers comprised 14 percent of the workforce. By 2001, they comprised 25 percent (Statistics Canada, 2003t).
2. *Workplace culture shifts away from factories and toward a diversity of work settings.* Many people continue to be employed in traditional workplaces with set workdays, but these jobs are increasingly being affected by layoffs and outsourcing.
3. *The traditional boundaries between work and home are being set aside.* Communications technology allows many workers to work away from the office, and globalization means that some businesses operate 24 hours a day.

Challenging, well-paid jobs in the service sector have grown dramatically, and highly skilled "knowledge workers" have benefited from the post-industrial economy. However, these benefits are not shared by those who do routine production work, such as data entry, and workers who provide personal services, including restaurant workers and salesclerks. The positions filled by these workers form a poorly paid second tier. Many jobs in the service sector emphasize productivity, often at the expense of job satisfaction. Fast-food restaurants are an example, as the manager of a McDonald's explains:

> As a manager I am judged by the statistical reports which come off the computer. Which basically means my crew's labour productivity. What else can I really distinguish myself by? . . . O.K., it's true, you can overspend your [maintenance and repair] budget; you can have a low fry yield; you can run a dirty store, every Coke spigot is monitored. Every ketchup squirt is measured. My costs for every item are set. So

> my crew labour productivity is my main flexibility . . . Look, you can't squeeze a McDonald's hamburger any flatter. If you want to improve your productivity there is nothing for a manager to squeeze but the crew. (quoted in Garson, 1989:33–35)

"McDonaldization" is built on many of the ideas and systems of industrial society, including bureaucracy and the assembly line (Ritzer, 1993) (see Box 19.2 and Chapter 6).

Machines and offshore production have eliminated many of the well-paying manufacturing jobs that were formerly available to young people with low levels of education and training. These people now work in lower-paying service sector jobs. This change was particularly hard on young men between the ages of 18 and 24 with full-time jobs, whose earnings (in constant dollars) declined by 20 percent between 1977 and 1997 (Gadd, 1998). Over the same period, earnings for young women declined by 9 percent, but their incomes levelled off during the 1990s. Many young men have been stuck in entry-level jobs with few prospects for advancement or for additional training. Some economists believe that the wage restructuring was permanent and that many of these young men may never move into a more favourable job situation.

BOX 19.2 POINT/COUNTERPOINT

McJobs: Assembling Burgers in the Global Economy

> Yesterday I was meant to go home at midnight, after working 8 hours. But they were short-staffed and asked me to clean up until 2:30 a.m. I didn't want to but there was nothing I could do. Same thing happened night before. Lots of us are working 12 hours sometimes without proper breaks . . . John hasn't had a day off for months—they keep ringing him up on his rest day—and a bloke who refused to come in one Saturday was reported to head office.
>
> —Julie, a worker at a McDonald's in London, England (quoted in McSpotlight 1999)

"McJobs" at McDonald's and other fast-food restaurants worldwide have received both praise and criticism from employees and social analysts in recent years. When the first McDonald's restaurant opened in 1955, nobody could have predicted the company would grow to more than 33,000 restaurants, serving tens of millions of customers a day in 119 countries and employing 1.7 million people (McDonald's, 2012).

Some argue that McDonald's provides a service by giving job opportunities to people who might otherwise be out of work. Many young people have had their first jobs at McDonald's and were happy to receive some training and a paycheque. However, critics complain that McDonald's and other fast-food restaurants intentionally hire young workers and members of minority groups because they can be more easily exploited for corporate profits. From this perspective, McDonald's vast profits are derived at the expense of workers who are paid low wages, given few breaks, and often required to work shifts that meet the fluctuating demands of customers. According to critics, companies like McDonalds are net destroyers of jobs. They use low wages and the huge size of their businesses to undercut local food outlets and force them out of business (McSpotlight, 1999). McSpotlight (www.mcspotlight.org), a website critical of McDonald's, states that the restaurant chain "feeds" on foreign visitors, women, students, and ethnic minorities who, with few other opportunities, are forced to accept the poor wages and conditions (McSpotlight, 1999). McDonald's spokespersons adamantly disagree. For example, the manager of a McDonald's restaurant in England stated, "We don't look at people's colour or nationality but their availability" (quoted in McSpotlight, 1999).

Could McDonald's workers organize to achieve better working conditions? Labour union activists state that McDonald's blocks workers' attempts at unionization. For example, Natalya Gracheva, an employee of McDonald's Russia, wanted to form a trade union in the company's factory outside Moscow. However, she quickly learned that the company would block all her efforts for pay raises and more rest periods (Charlton, 1999). By contrast, McDonald's spokespersons state that the franchise restaurants provide equitable compensation for their workers and that their employees are happy. McDonald's Russia responded to the complaints of Natalya Gracheva and others by forming a company-supervised "workers' council," and, in return, hundreds of employees agreed to sign a document stating that they did not want a union (Charlton, 1999).

As such disputes have arisen on a global basis, the question remains: Are corporations such as McDonald's good employers and good corporate citizens in the global community? What do you think?

LO-3 CONTEMPORARY ECONOMIC SYSTEMS

Capitalism and socialism have been the principal economic models in industrialized countries. Sociologists often use two criteria—property ownership and market control—to distinguish between types of economies. Keep in mind, however, that no society has a purely capitalist or socialist economy.

Capitalism

capitalism An economic system characterized by private ownership of the means of production, from which personal profits can be derived through market competition and without government intervention.

Capitalism is an economic system characterized by private ownership of the means of production, from which personal profits can be derived through market competition and without government intervention. Most of us think of ourselves as "owners" of private property because we own a car, an iPhone, or other possessions. However, most of us are not capitalists; we are consumers who *spend money* on the things we own rather than *making money* from them. Relatively few people control the means of production, and the rest are paid to work for these capitalists. "Ideal" capitalism has four distinctive features: (1) private ownership of the means of production, (2) pursuit of profit, (3) competition, and (4) lack of government intervention.

PRIVATE OWNERSHIP OF THE MEANS OF PRODUCTION Capitalist economies are based on the right of individuals to own income-producing property, such as land and factories, and to "buy" people's labour.

The early Canadian economy was based on the sale of *staples*—goods associated with primary industries, including lumber, wheat, and minerals. Harold Innis (1984/1930) showed how the early Canadian economy was driven by the demand for raw materials by the colonial powers of France and Britain. In 1670, a British royal charter gave the privately held Hudson's Bay Company exclusive control over much of what is now Western Canada, which was the source of the lucrative fur trade. This was *commercial capitalism,* in which fortunes were made by merchants who controlled the trade in raw materials.

Inventions such as the steam engine led to factory production and the dramatic transformation to *industrial capitalism.* Industrial capitalism did not just alter the means of production; it changed the very nature of European and North American societies. Urbanization, the growth of the modern nation-state, and the struggle for democracy can all be traced to the growth of industrial capitalism (Krahn, Lowe, and Hughes, 2011). In the early stages of industrial capitalism (1850–1890), virtually all investment capital was individually owned and a few individuals and families controlled all the major trade and financial organizations in Canada.

corporations Large-scale organizations that have legal powers, such as the ability to enter into contracts and buy and sell property, separate from their individual owners.

Under early monopoly capitalism (1890–1940), most ownership shifted from individuals to huge **corporations**—large-scale organizations that have legal powers, such as the ability to enter into contracts and buy and sell property, separate from their individual owners. Major industries came under the control of a few corporations owned by shareholders. For example, the automobile industry in North America was dominated by the "Big Three"—General Motors, Ford, and Chrysler.

Industrial development in Canada lagged behind that of many other countries as business focused on exporting raw materials that others could use in manufacturing. Many of the industries that did establish themselves in Canada were branch plants of large American and British corporations whose profits flowed back to their home countries. By 1983, Canada received more direct foreign investment than any other country (Laxer, 1989). Economist Kari Levitt (1970) was among the first to show how this foreign private investment posed a threat to Canadian sovereignty, as fundamental economic decisions were made outside the country and did not necessarily take Canadian interests into account. While foreign investment has declined (see Figure 19.1), many of our industries are still controlled by foreign parent corporations, such as General Motors, Toyota, and Walmart, and large corporations, including most of our largest mining companies, continue to be bought by foreign owners.

multinational corporations Large companies that are headquartered in one country and have subsidiaries or branches in other countries.

Today, **multinational corporations**—large companies that are headquartered in one country and have subsidiaries or branches in other countries—play a major role in the economies and governments of many nations. Some of these corporations are very large and powerful. The 200

FIGURE 19.1 PERCENTAGE OF CANADIAN NONFINANCIAL INDUSTRIES UNDER FOREIGN CONTROL

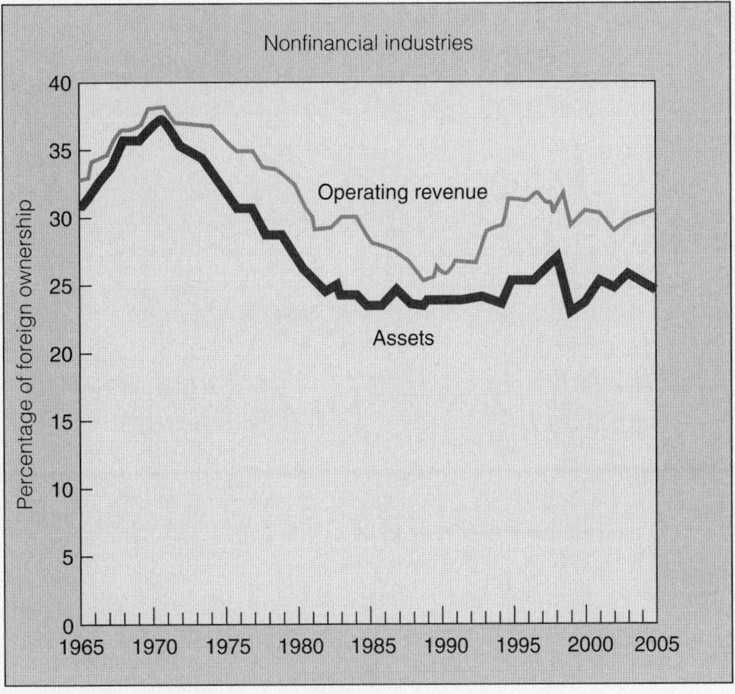

Foreign control was at its peak in the early 1970s.

Source: Statistics Canada, *The Daily*, November 2, 2004.

largest global corporations have sales that are greater than the economies of many countries. For example, Walmart's sales are greater than the economies of all but 18 countries. Over 50 percent of the global market in several industries, including the automotive, aerospace, and electronics industries, is controlled by no more than five corporations (Brownlee, 2005). Such corporations are not dependent on the labour, capital, or technology of any one country and may move their operations to countries where wages and taxes are lower and potential profits are higher. Many formerly Canadian jobs have been moved to developing nations. There, workers are paid significantly less money than Canadians would accept, so labour costs are lower.

PURSUIT OF PROFIT Capitalist doctrine holds that people are free to maximize their individual gain through personal profit and the entire society will benefit from their activities (Smith, 1976/1776). Economic development is assumed to benefit both capitalists and workers, and the general public also benefits from public expenditures (such as for roads, schools, and parks) made possible through business tax revenues.

© AP Photo/The Canadian Press, Dave Chidley

Caterpillar closed this plant in London, Ontario, when workers refused to agree to a wage cut from $35 to $18 an hour. The jobs were moved to a plant in the United States, where high unemployment rates have forced workers to accept lower wages. At the time the plant was closed, Caterpillar was reporting record revenues and profits.

During the period of industrial capitalism, however, specific individuals and families, not the general public, were the primary recipients of profits. For many generations, descendants of some of the early industrial capitalists have benefited from the economic deeds (and misdeeds) of their ancestors. For example, much of the Seagram distillery fortune was based on profits made from smuggling liquor from Canada to the U.S. during Prohibition. While families are now much less involved in business, corporations are still focused on profits. Nobel Prize–winning economist Milton Friedman famously stated his belief that the only responsibility of business is to engage in activities designed to increase its profits. According to this view, corporations should not be concerned about their social responsibilities but only about maximizing the money they make for shareholders. Thus, investing in communities, training workers, protecting the environment, and producing safe products should not be of concern unless doing these things will make the corporation more profitable. Businesses that maximize their profits will provide the jobs and investment that are essential to strong communities. To Friedman, the corporate downsizing that cost Wilfred Popoff his job (see the chapter introduction) was positive because of the social benefits Friedman believed would flow from higher profits.

COMPETITION In theory, competition acts as a balance to excessive profits. When producers compete for customers, they must be able to offer innovative goods and services at competitive prices. However, the trend has been toward less, rather than more, competition among companies because profits are higher when there is less competition.

One way of decreasing competition is by increasing concentration *within* a particular industry. For example, Microsoft so dominates certain segments of the computer software industry that it has virtually no competitors. Large companies may also try to restrict competition by temporarily setting prices so low that weaker competitors are forced out of business. Ultramar, a chain of gasoline stations in Quebec and Atlantic Canada, was accused of starting a gasoline price war that saw gas prices in Quebec fall by almost two-thirds. One Nova Scotia independent station owner complained that Ultramar was charging him more for wholesale gasoline than its retail price at its own nearby Ultramar station. While cutting prices provides a temporary benefit to consumers, it reduces competition by forcing small retailers out of the market. The large companies recoup their losses when the competition has disappeared.

oligopoly The situation that exists when several companies overwhelmingly control an entire industry.

What appears to be competition among producers *within* an industry really may be "competition" among products, all of which are produced and distributed by relatively few corporations. Much of the beer in Canada is produced by Molson Coors and Labatt (both now foreign-owned companies), which use a wide variety of different brand names for their products.

An **oligopoly** exists when several companies control an entire industry. An example is the music industry, in which four giant companies have controlled most of the labels and artists. This number will soon shrink further, as Sony has purchased EMI's music catalogue and Universal Music has applied for approval to purchase its recorded music division.

© Matthew Staver/Bloomberg/Getty Images

Many of the brands of beer sold in Canada are actually owned by a small number of companies such as Molson Coors.

LACK OF GOVERNMENT INTERVENTION Proponents believe that capitalism works best without government intervention. This policy of *laissez-faire* was advocated by economist Adam Smith in 1776. Smith argued that when people pursue their own selfish interests, they are guided "as if by an invisible hand" to promote the best interests of society (see Smith, 1976/1776). Today, terms such as *market* *economy* and *free enterprise* are often used, but the underlying assumption is the same: that free market competition, not the government, should regulate prices and wages.

However, the "ideal" of unregulated markets benefiting all citizens has seldom been realized. Individuals and companies in pursuit of higher profits have run roughshod over weaker competitors, and small businesses have grown into large, monopolistic corporations. Accordingly, governments implemented regulations in an effort to curb the excesses of the marketplace. While its effectiveness can be debated, Canada has a Competition Bureau to ensure that corporations compete fairly.

Ironically, much of government intervention has been in the form of *aid* to business. Canadian governments have always provided financial support to business. To encourage settlement of the West, the government gave subsidies and huge tracts of land to the Canadian Pacific Railway for the construction of a national railway. Many corporations receive government assistance in the form of public subsidies and protection from competition by way of tariffs, patents, and trademarks. Governments provide billions of dollars in tax credits for corporations, large subsidies or loan guarantees to manufacturers, and subsidies and tariff protection for farmers. While most corporations have gained much more than they have lost through government involvement in the economy, the free enterprise mythology still persists.

Socialism

socialism An economic system characterized by public ownership of the means of production, the pursuit of collective goals, and centralized decision making.

Socialism is an economic system characterized by public ownership of the means of production, the pursuit of collective goals, and centralized decision making. Marx described socialism as a temporary stage en route to a communist society, but like "pure" capitalism, "pure" socialism does not exist.

Although the terms *socialism* and *communism* are associated with Marx and are often used interchangeably, they are not identical. Marx defined communism as an economic system characterized by common ownership of all economic resources (Marshall, 1998). In *The Communist Manifesto* and *Das Kapital,* he predicted that the working class would become increasingly impoverished and alienated under capitalism. As a result, the workers would become aware of their own class interests, revolt against the capitalists, and overthrow the entire system. After the revolution, private property would be abolished and capital would be controlled by collectives of workers who would own the means of production. The government would no longer be necessary. People would contribute according to their abilities and receive according to their needs (Marx, 1967/1867; Marx and Engels, 1967/1848). Over the years, state control was added as an organizing principle for communist societies. "Ideal" socialism has three distinct features: (1) public ownership of the means of production, (2) pursuit of collective goals, and (3) centralized decision making.

PUBLIC OWNERSHIP OF THE MEANS OF PRODUCTION In a socialist economy, the means of production are owned and controlled by the state, not by private individuals or corporations. Prior to the early 1990s, the state owned all the natural resources and almost all the capital in the Soviet Union. At least in theory, goods were produced to meet the needs of people. Access to housing and medical care was considered a right. In the 1990s, leaders of the former Soviet Union and other Eastern European nations abandoned government ownership and control of the means of production because the system was so inefficient. Shortages and widespread unrest led to the reform movement headed by Soviet president Mikhail Gorbachev in the late 1980s.

China—previously the world's other major communist economy—has privatized many state industries. In *privatization,* resources are converted from state to private ownership and the state protects private property rights. China now has an economy made up of both capitalism and an autocratic form of Communist Party governance. Rapid economic growth has led to significant improvements in the lives of many Chinese, so it is likely that this combination of communism and a modified form of capitalism will remain for the foreseeable future.

PURSUIT OF COLLECTIVE GOALS Ideal socialism is based on the pursuit of collective goals, rather than on personal profits. Equality in decision making replaces hierarchical relationships, such as between owners and workers or political leaders and citizens. Everyone shares the goods and services of society—especially necessities, such as food, clothing, shelter, and medical care—based on need, not on ability to pay. In reality, however, few societies pursue purely collective goals.

CENTRALIZED DECISION MAKING Another tenet of socialism is centralized decision making. In theory, economic decisions are based on the needs of society, and the government is responsible for ensuring the production and distribution of goods and services. Central planners set wages and prices. When problems, such as shortages and unemployment, arise, they can be dealt with quickly and effectively by the central government (Boyes and Melvin, 1994).

In the former Soviet Union, broad economic policy decisions were made by the highest authorities of the Communist Party. The production units (the factories and farms) at the bottom of the structure had little voice in the decision-making process. Wages and prices were based on political priorities and eventually came to be completely unrelated to supply and demand. Thus, while some factories kept producing goods that nobody wanted, there were chronic shortages of other goods. The collapse of state socialism in the former Soviet Union was due partly to the declining ability of the Communist Party to govern and partly to the growing incompatibility of central planning with the requirements of a modern economy (see Misztal, 1993).

mixed economy An economic system that combines elements of a market economy (capitalism) with elements of a command economy (socialism).

While the socialist system as practised in the Soviet Union was not sustainable, privatization has proven difficult. More than two decades after centralized decision making was abolished in Russia, people are still faced with high unemployment and crime rates, and the prices of goods and services have risen greatly. Organized criminal groups have muscled their way into business and trade, and many workers feel their future is dim. While the situation has begun to improve because of Russia's oil resources, the transition to a capitalist economy will take decades.

democractic socialism An economic and political system that combines private ownership of some of the means of production, governmental distribution of some essential goods and services, and free elections.

Mixed Economies

No economy is truly capitalist or socialist; most economies have elements of both. A **mixed economy** combines elements of a market economy (capitalism) with elements of a command economy (socialism). Sweden is an example of a mixed economy, sometimes referred to as **democratic socialism**—an economic and political system that combines private ownership of some of the means of production, governmental distribution of some essential goods and services, and free elections. Government ownership in Sweden is limited primarily to railroads, mineral resources, a public bank, and liquor and tobacco operations (Feagin and Feagin, 1994). Compared with capitalist economies, however, the government in a mixed economy plays a larger role in setting rules, policies, and objectives.

© Stuart Nimmo/GetStock.com

Gasoline price wars benefit consumers. However, they may also be part of a strategy in which major companies put smaller competitors out of business.

The government is also heavily involved in providing services, such as medical care, child care, and transportation. In Sweden, all residents have health insurance, housing subsidies, child allowances, paid parental leave, and daycare subsidies. Public funds help subsidize cultural institutions, such as theatres and orchestras ("General

Facts on Sweden," 2005; Kelman, 1991). While Sweden has a very high degree of government involvement, all industrial countries provide support and services to their citizens. There are, however, significant differences in the degree to which these services are provided. For example, Canada provides medical care to all its citizens, while about 47 million Americans have no health insurance at all, a figure that may be reduced because of legislation passed by President Obama (U.S. Census Bureau, 2008).While Canada is much closer to a mixed economy than the United States, our government provides fewer benefits than do most Western European countries.

© CP/AP

One of the 20th century's most important leaders was Mikhail Gorbachev, who began reforms that led to the end of the socialist economy in the former Soviet Union.

TIME TO REVIEW

- What is the economy and what is its role in society?
- How did most people earn their living in preindustrial societies?
- How did the new technology of the industrial era change the nature of work?
- What is the most common form of labour in post-industrial society?
- What are the differences between capitalist, socialist, and mixed economies?

PERSPECTIVES ON ECONOMY AND WORK LO-4

Functionalist Perspectives on the Economic System

Functionalists view the economy as the means by which needed goods and services are produced and distributed. When the economy runs smoothly, other parts of society function more effectively. However, if the system becomes unbalanced, such as when demand does not keep up with production, a maladjustment occurs (in this case, a surplus). Some problems may be easily remedied in the marketplace (by cutting prices to get rid of the surplus) or through government intervention (such as buying and storing surpluses). Other problems, such as periodic peaks and troughs in the business cycle, are more difficult to resolve. The *business cycle* is the rise and fall of economic activity relative to long-term growth in the economy (McEachern, 1994).

From this perspective, peaks occur when "business" has confidence in the country's economic future. During a peak period, the economy thrives. Plants are built, materials are ordered, workers are hired, and production increases. Upward social mobility for workers and their families becomes possible. For example, some workers hope their children will not have to follow their footsteps into the factory. Ben Hamper describes how GM workers felt:

> Being a factory worker in Flint, Michigan, wasn't something purposely passed on from generation to generation. To grow up believing that you were brought into this world to follow in your daddy's footsteps, just another chip-off-the-old-shoprat, was to engage in the lowest possible form of negativism. Working the line for GM was something fathers did so that their offspring wouldn't have to. (1992:13)

The possibility of upward mobility is greatest during peaks in the business cycle. Once the peak is reached, however, the economy turns down because too large a surplus of goods has been produced. In part, this downturn is due to *inflation*—a sustained and continuous increase in prices (McEachern, 1994). Inflation erodes the value of people's money, and they are no longer able to purchase as much. Because of lower demand, fewer goods are produced, workers are laid off, credit becomes difficult to obtain, and people cut back on their purchases even more, fearing unemployment. Eventually, this produces a *recession*—a decline in an economy's total production that lasts six months or longer. To combat a recession, the government lowers interest rates (to make borrowing easier and to get more money back into circulation), trying to spur the beginning of the next expansion period. This process occurred globally in 2008 and 2009, driven by factors including a speculative bubble in housing prices and a lack of financial regulation in the United States. In many countries, particularly in Europe, the resulting recession continued through 2012.

Conflict Perspectives on the Economic System

Conflict theorists view the economic system differently. From a conflict perspective, business cycles are the result of capitalist greed. To maximize profits, capitalists suppress the wages of workers. As prices increase, the workers are not able to purchase them in the quantities that have been produced. The resulting surpluses cause capitalists to reduce production, close factories, and lay off workers, thus contributing to the growth of the reserve army of the unemployed, whose presence helps reduce the wages of the remaining workers. For example, many businesses have forced wages down by hiring large numbers of part-time workers and by negotiating pay cuts for full-time employees. Companies justify this on the grounds of meeting the lower wages paid by competitors. The practice of contracting out—governments and corporations hiring outside workers to do some jobs rather than using existing staff—has become a favourite cost-cutting technique. In today's economy, it is easy to find someone who will do the work more cheaply than existing employees whose seniority and wages have increased over time.

Much of the pressure to reduce costs has come from shareholders, who want their profits to increase. Conflict theorists view the firing or deskilling of workers as class warfare in which the rich benefit at the expense of the poor. The rich have indeed thrived; those with large amounts of capital have seen their fortunes increase dramatically and the gap between rich and poor has increased over the past two decades.

Alienation occurs when work is done strictly for material gain, with no accompanying sense of personal satisfaction. According to Marx, workers have little power and no opportunities to make workplace decisions. This lack of control contributes to an ongoing struggle between workers and employers. Contemporary pressures to reduce the labour force and cut payroll costs have likely increased the alienation levels of Canadian workers, as remaining workers often work harder and get fewer rewards from their jobs.

Symbolic Interactionist Perspectives

THE MEANING OF WORK Symbolic interactionists have examined the meaning of work and the factors that contribute to job satisfaction. Does work play a role in defining us, or is it just something we have to do to put bread on the table? Some critics view work as dehumanizing, oppressive, and alienating. Others take the view that people find both moral meaning and a sense of personal identity through their work. Robert Wuthnow (1996) found that when people were asked about their most important reason for working, the most common response was "the money." However, when asked what they most preferred in a job, 48 percent chose "a feeling of accomplishment" and only 21 percent chose "high income." Even for many lower-level employees, work is not just a source of money, but also a vital part of their identity. Work connects people to their communities, they share personal friendships in their work settings, and work gives them a sense of accomplishment.

Murial Johnson, one of Wuthnow's interview subjects, had three jobs but spent most of her work time as a security guard at a city convention centre. She took pride in the job because she was able to do it well:

> Johnson says she has earned the "respect and liking" of other employees to the point that she is often called on to serve in a supervisory capacity. She takes pride in having organizational skills. When a big event takes place, or when there is a special crisis . . . she can be counted on to make things work. (Wuthnow, 1996:219)

William Julius Wilson (1996) studied inner-city neighbourhoods to see what happens when work disappears. He found that the impact has been devastating to individuals and to the community. To Wilson, a person without work is incomplete and lacks the concrete goals and expectations, as well as the daily discipline and regularities that work provides. Without work, it is difficult for the urban poor to take control of their lives.

However, even proponents of the view that work has moral meaning recognize that not all jobs allow the same degree of satisfaction and personal fulfillment. Assembly line work can be particularly alienating:

> Basically, I stand there all day and slash the necks of chickens. You make one slash up on the skin of the neck and then you cut around the base of the neck so the next person beside you can crop it . . . The chickens go in front of you on the line and you do every other chicken or whatever. And you stand there for eight hours on one spot and do it. (Armstrong and Armstrong, 1983:128)

JOB SATISFACTION According to symbolic interactionists, work is an important source of self-identity for many people. It can help people feel positive about themselves or it can cause them to feel alienated. A Canadian study found that men and women who enjoyed their work reported a much higher quality of life than those who disliked their jobs (Frederick and Fast, 2001). Worker satisfaction is highest when employees have some degree of control over their work, when they are part of the decision-making process, when they are not too closely supervised, and when they feel that they play an important part in the outcome (Kohn et al., 1990). The reasons contract administrator Beth McEwen gives for liking her job bear this out:

> I've worked for employers who couldn't care if you were gone tomorrow—who let you think your job could be done by anyone because 100,000 people out there are looking for work. But here, there's always someone to help you if you need assistance, and they're open to letting you set out your own job plan that suits what they're after and what you're trying to accomplish. They know every person goes about a job in a different way. (quoted in Maynard, 1987:121)

Feminist Perspectives on Work and Labour

All societies assign some tasks to people based on their gender and their age. In hunting and gathering societies, women typically care for young children and men look after the hunting. In industrial economies, working-age men are involved in wage labour, while women and males who are too young or too old for paid jobs look after household tasks. This situation has been changing slowly, and "Much political activity of the last 100 years has been aimed at overcoming the gender specificity of these definitions" (Wallerstein, 2004:34).

Feminist researchers have studied the relationship between gender and work. According to Amy Wharton, feminist theory "implies that work and the social practices that compose it are organized in ways that create and reproduce gender distinctions and inequalities" (2000:179). She has identified the three major themes of this research: "(1) characteristics of housework and so-called women's work more generally; (2) economic inequality between men and women; and (3) structural and institutional bases of gender in the workplace" (2000:167).

WOMEN'S WORK Early feminist scholars drew attention to the fact that the home was a workplace in which women did a great deal of unpaid work. This research was done at a time when many women were full-time housewives and when the prevailing career model was a male who worked steadily from graduation until retirement to support his family. Society assigned women the tasks of staying at home, caring for children, and supporting the husband's career. This research found that while homemakers were full-time workers, they were often in a financially precarious position because their contribution was not recognized when their husbands died or when they were divorced. Programs, such as Employment Insurance and the Canada Pension Plan, do not provide support for women who have not been in the paid labour force. Other research found that women typically worked in stereotypical "women's" fields, such as nursing and office and clerical work. Women rarely held high-level positions, even in female-dominated occupations. For example, most elementary school teachers were women, but most principals were men. Women were greatly underrepresented in professions such as medicine, law, and dentistry.

When women did work, they arranged their jobs and work hours to ensure that their work did not interfere with their husbands' careers and that they could care for their children (Nelson, 2006). An important study by Hochschild (1989) showed that working women faced a "second shift" when they got home because they were also primarily responsible for household tasks and child-rearing. Because of family demands, many women chose to work part time and are still much more likely than men to hold part-time jobs (Krahn, Lowe, and Hughes, 2011).

GENDER INEQUALITY IN WAGES Women in the paid labour force also faced discrimination. Men were seen as the primary family breadwinners, so the financial needs of women were not recognized. Women were predominantly in low-wage jobs, they were often paid less than men doing the same work, and a "glass ceiling" limited their access to managerial positions. Structural factors, such as the segregation of women into lower-income segments of the labour force, mean that it is very difficult for them to achieve equality. While labour force segregation and the gender wage gap have declined, their persistence led to campaigns by feminist scholars and activists to ensure pay equity and affirmative action hiring. Canada's *Charter of Rights and Freedoms* and provincial pay equity legislation have provided legal support for these actions.

THE STRUCTURAL SOURCES OF GENDER BIAS The work of Rosabeth Kanter (1977) raised important concerns about the impact of structural factors in the workplace. Kanter found that employees whose gender or race made them a minority in their workplace faced difficulties because of their status as "tokens." They were often singled out as representatives of their gender or race, excluded from formal and informal work groups, and lacked support from their peers. In many situations, such as police and fire departments, male colleagues felt women lacked basic job-related qualities, such as strength and courage. As a result, many of the women who were among the first to move into formerly "male" jobs had a difficult time. According to Kanter, once the proportion of minorities reached a "tipping point" of 15 or 20 percent, the pressures on the minority would be reduced and the work environment would be normalized.

Subsequent research has supported Kanter's work but has suggested that women suffer from more than just their token status. Williams (1989) found that women in traditionally male jobs face far more hostility than do men entering female-dominated occupations. A female police officer was more likely to hear derogatory comments from male officers than a male nurse heard from female nurses. While the situation has improved over the past few decades, male hostility toward women in nontraditional jobs still persists. In 2005, Neil French, one of the world's most successful advertising executives, resigned his job because of the controversy created by a speech he made in Toronto. In it, he said that there were few successful women creative directors in the advertising business because they couldn't commit themselves to the job:

> You can't be a great creative director and have a baby and keep spending time off every time your kids are ill. You can't do the job. Somebody has to do it and the guy has to do it the same way that I've had to spend months and months flying around the world and not seeing my kid. You think that's not a sacrifice? Of course it's a

sacrifice. I hate it. But that's the job and that's what I do in order to keep my family fed. (McArthur, 2005)

Thus, social structure is not gender neutral. Rather, "gender is embodied in social structures and other forms of social organization" (Wharton, 2000:175). Occupational gender assignments have almost always reflected male superiority. For example, nurses (almost exclusively female until recently) were subordinate to doctors (who were almost always male), and the role of paralegals (female) was to provide support to lawyers (male). Just as in households, women were assigned the caretaker roles in the occupational world and men were in charge (Pierce, 1995). These structures and practices have become an integral part of the society, so once an occupation has been defined as "male" or "female," it is very difficult to change. Change is resisted by those who benefit from the gender bias. If women had equal access to male-dominated occupations and to high-paying, high-status managerial positions, fewer of these jobs would be available to men. Some men's self-image is also threatened by the presence of women in traditionally male-dominated occupations

The area of gender and work is an area where feminist scholarship has made a major contribution to social change over the past 30 years. Most occupations and professions are now much more open to women and, while the glass ceiling still persists, women are now much more likely to hold managerial positions than they did in the past. Progress has been made in equalizing wages, though again some differences still remain.

TIME TO REVIEW

- How do functionalists view the operation of the business cycle?
- Describe how current efforts by business and government to reduce labour costs fit the conflict perspective on the economy.
- According to symbolic interactionists, how does the work we do affect our self-identity?
- How do feminist theorists analyze the labour market?

CONCEPT SNAPSHOT

FUNCTIONALIST PERSPECTIVES	Functionalists view the economy as the means by which needed goods and services are produced and distributed. When the economy runs smoothly, other parts of society function more effectively. The business cycle involves the rise and fall of economic activity relative to long-term growth in the economy. This system is largely self-correcting, though government intervention may be necessary.
SYMBOLIC INTERACTIONIST PERSPECTIVES **Key thinker:** Robert Wuthnow	Even for many lower-level employees, work is not just a source of money, but also a vital part of their identity. Work connects people to their communities, they share personal friendships in their work settings, and work gives them a sense of accomplishment. However, not all jobs are equally satisfying.
CONFLICT PERSPECTIVES **Key thinker:** Karl Marx	Work in capitalist societies is characterized by conflict between workers and employers. Employers seek to maximize their profits by exploiting workers. Work is alienating when workers' needs for self-identity and meaning are not met and when work is done strictly for material gain, with no accompanying sense of personal satisfaction.
FEMINIST PERSPECTIVES **Key thinkers:** Arlie Hochschild, Rosabeth Kanter, Amy Wharton	Feminist scholars have found that work is gendered and that these gender biases persist because they are an integral part of a patriarchal society. Women are not paid as highly as men and women often work a "second shift" because work in the home is typically assigned to women. Structural factors in the workplace, such as the "token" status of women, also have a negative impact on women in the workplace.

THE SOCIAL ORGANIZATION OF WORK

Occupations

occupations Categories of jobs that involve similar activities at different work sites

Occupations are categories of jobs that involve similar activities at different work sites (Reskin and Padavic, 1994). Historically, occupations have been classified as blue collar and white collar. Blue-collar workers were primarily factory and craftsworkers who did manual labour; white-collar workers were office workers and professionals. However, contemporary workers in the service sector do not easily fit into either of these categories; neither do the so-called pink-collar workers, primarily women, who are employed in occupations such as preschool teacher, dental assistant, secretary, and clerk (Hodson and Sullivan, 2002).

Professions

What occupations are professions? Athletes who are paid for playing sports are referred to as "professional athletes." Dog groomers, automobile mechanics, and nail technicians (manicurists) also refer to themselves as professionals. Although sociologists do not always agree on exactly which occupations are professions, most do agree that the term *professional* includes most doctors, scientists, engineers, accountants, economists, lawyers, professors, and some clergy. What criteria do they use to define the term *professional*?

professions High-status, knowledge-based occupations.

CHARACTERISTICS OF PROFESSIONS **Professions** are high-status, knowledge-based occupations. Sociologists define occupations as professions if they have these characteristics:

1. *Abstract, specialized knowledge.* Professionals have abstract, specialized knowledge of their field, based on formal education and interaction with colleagues.
2. *Autonomy.* Professionals are autonomous in that they can rely on their own judgment in making decisions about their work.
3. *Self-regulation.* In exchange for autonomy, professionals regulate their members. All professions have licensing, accreditation, and regulatory associations that set professional standards and require members to adhere to a code of ethics.
4. *Authority.* Professionals expect compliance with their directions and advice. Their authority is based on mastery of the body of specialized knowledge and on their profession's autonomy.
5. *Altruism.*The term *altruism* implies some degree of self-sacrifice whereby professionals go beyond self-interest or personal comfort so that they can help a patient or client (Hodson and Sullivan, 2002).

Job satisfaction among professionals has generally been high because of relatively high levels of income, autonomy, and authority.

Legislation gives members of many professions a monopoly on the provision of particular services, and these professions use their power to resist attempts by others to provide these services—in fact, power might be considered another characteristic of a profession. Doctors have used their professional associations to protect their right to control the practice of medicine. Chiropractors, midwives, and other alternative healthcare practitioners have been fighting for decades to have governments recognize their right to practise and be paid under provincial healthcare legislation. Similarly, lawyers have actively opposed the attempt by companies of nonlawyers to represent people accused of traffic offences.

Women have made significant gains in most traditionally male-dominated professions in Canada, and women continue to increase their representation in professional schools. In 1971, women received 9 percent of law degrees and 13 percent of medical degrees (see Figure 19.2 on page 556). By 2000, more than half the graduates in law and medicine were women. By 2006, females made up 38 percent of the lawyers in Ontario (Ornstein, 2010). In 2011, 57 percent of medical

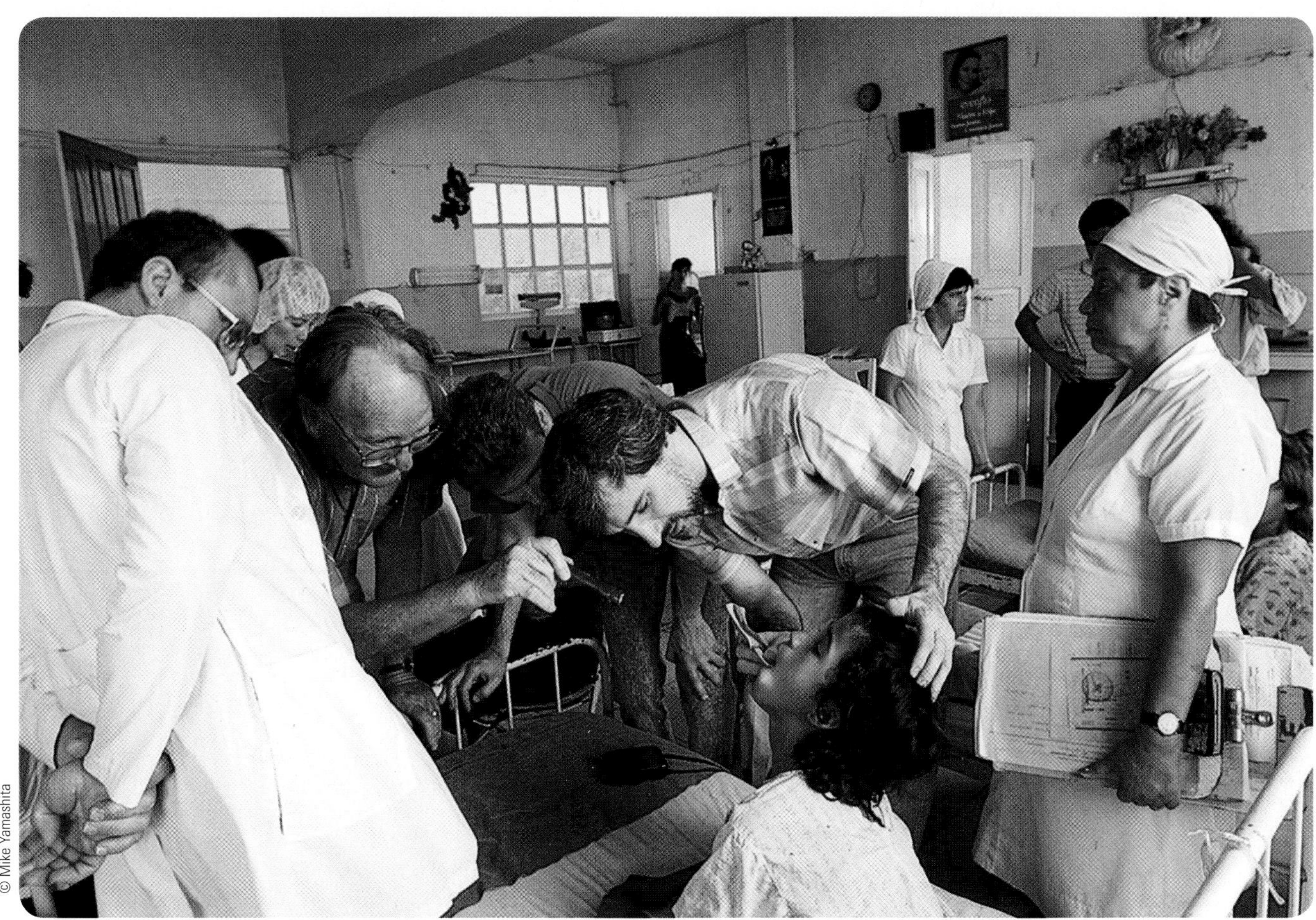
© Mike Yamashita

Professionals are expected to share their knowledge and display concern for others. These surgeons have volunteered their services to people in Ecuador.

graduates were female (Association of Faculties of Medicine of Canada, 2011), and in 2007, 34 percent of all physicians in Canada were women (Canadian Institute for Health Information, 2009) (see Figure 19.2).

Upper-Tier Jobs: Managers and Supervisors

A wide variety of occupations are classified as "management." The term *manager* is used to refer to executives, managers, and administrators (Hodson and Sullivan, 2002). Women are steadily increasing their presence in managerial jobs. In 2009, 37 percent of those working in managerial positions were women, compared with 6 percent in 1971 (Statistics Canada, 1994, 2011e). However, only 32 percent of senior managers were women

MANAGEMENT IN BUREAUCRACIES Upper-level managers are typically responsible for coordination of activities and control of workers. Loss of worker control over the labour process was built into the earliest factory systems through techniques known as scientific management (Taylorism) and mass production (Fordism).

SCIENTIFIC MANAGEMENT (TAYLORISM) Early in the 20th century, industrial engineer Frederick Winslow Taylor revolutionized management with a system he called *scientific management*. To increase productivity in factories, Taylor conducted *time-and-motion* studies of

FIGURE 19.2 GENDER DIFFERENCES IN MEDICAL SCHOOL ENROLLMENT

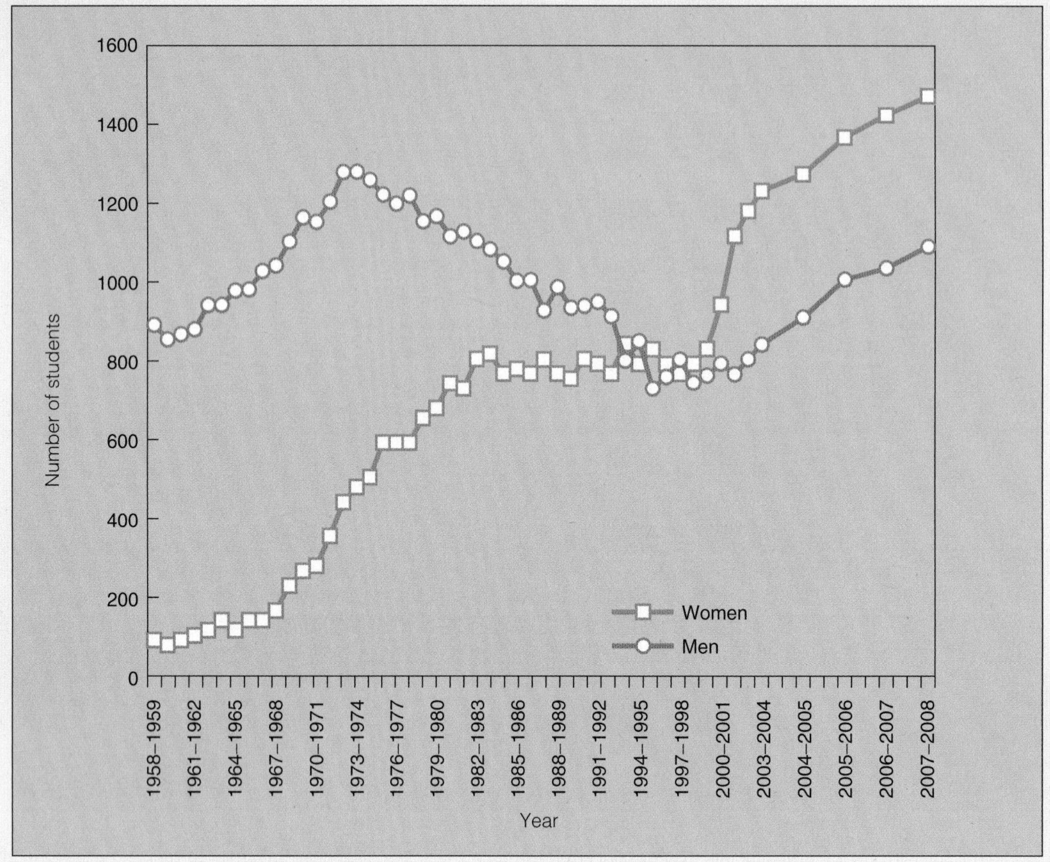

In 1993-1994, women outnumbered men in first-year medical school enrollment for the first time.

Source: Association of Faculties of Medicine of Canada, Canadian Medical Education Statistics 2004.

workers he considered efficient. He then broke down each task into its smallest components to determine the "one best way" of doing that task. Workers were then taught to perform the tasks in a concise series of steps. Skilled workers became less essential, since unskilled workers could be trained to follow routinized procedures. The process of breaking up work into specialized tasks and minute operations contributed to the *deskilling* of work and shifted much of the control of knowledge from workers to management (Braverman, 1974). This greatly reduced the power of workers.

Taylor favoured the incentives provided by the piece-rate system. In this system, workers were paid for the number of units they produced, but estrangement developed between workers and managers. Workers felt distrustful and overworked because managers often increased the number of pieces required when workers met their quotas. Overall, management became more removed from workers with the advent of mass production.

MASS PRODUCTION THROUGH AUTOMATION (FORDISM) *Fordism,* named for Henry Ford, founder of the Ford Motor Company, incorporated hierarchical management structures and scientific management techniques into the manufacturing process (Collier and Horowitz, 1987). Assembly lines and machines provided *technical control* over the work process (Edwards,

1979). The *assembly line,* a system in which workers perform a specialized operation on an unfinished product as it is moved by conveyor past their workstation, increased efficiency and productivity. On Ford's assembly line, a Model T automobile could be assembled in one-eighth the time formerly required. Ford broke the production process of the Model T into 7882 specific tasks (Toffler, 1980).

© George Steinmetz/Corbis

Robots at this Honda factory exemplify the deskilling of jobs through automation. What are managers' responsibilities in workplaces such as this?

This fragmentation of the labour process meant that individual workers had little to do with the final product. There is a huge difference between a craftsperson helping to build a complete automobile and an assembly line worker repeating the same task hundreds of times each shift on hundreds of vehicles. The assembly line allowed managers to control the pace of work by speeding up the line when they wanted to increase productivity. As productivity increased, workers began to grow increasingly alienated as they saw themselves becoming robot-like labourers (Collier and Horowitz, 1987).

Working conditions on the assembly line were so bad that 71 percent of the workers first hired by Ford quit within their first week on the job (Volti, 2008). However, the dramatically increased productivity allowed Ford to give pay raises to $5 a day, about double the usual wage in 1914 (Volti, 2008). The wage kept workers relatively content, while Ford's own profits steadily rose. The difficult working conditions on the assembly line were described in a letter written by a worker's wife to Henry Ford:

> The chain system that you have is a *slave driver. My God!,* Mr. Ford. My husband has come home & thrown himself down & won't eat his supper—so done out! Can't it be remedied? That $5 a day is a blessing—a bigger one than you know, but *oh* they earn it. (Hounshell, 1984:259)

Without mass consumers, there could be no mass production; Ford recognized that better wages would allow the workers to buy his products.

According to Ritzer (2000), assembly line technology even dominates work settings such as fast-food restaurants. Some food chains use conveyor belts to cook hamburgers and pizzas, and food is produced in assembly line fashion. McDonald's has a soft drink dispenser with a sensor that shuts off when the cup is full so that the employee does not have to make this decision (Ritzer, 2000). The task of managers is limited because the restaurant's system is designed to be error free. George Cohon, the former president of McDonald's of Canada, describes how the system works:

> A McDonald's outlet is a machine that produces, with the help of unskilled machine attendants, a highly polished product. Through painstaking attention to total design and facilities planning, everything is built integrally into the technology of the system. The only choice open to the attendant is to operate it exactly as the designers intended. (*Globe and Mail,* 1990:B80)

Of course, managers also hire workers, settle disputes, and take care of other tasks, but in many work settings, automation has also dramatically deskilled managerial jobs.

Lower-Tier and Marginal Jobs

Typical lower-tier positions include janitor, server, salesclerk, farm labourer, and textile worker. Many of these jobs do not provide adequate pay, benefits, opportunity for advancement, or job security and are therefore marginal.

© Reza Estakhrian/Stone/Getty

Occupational segregation by race and gender is clearly visible in personal service industries. Women and visible minorities are disproportionately represented in marginal jobs, such as server, fast-food employee, or cleaner—jobs that do not meet societal norms for minimum pay, benefits, or security.

Marginal jobs differ from the employment norms of the society in which they are located. Examples are service and household workers. Women are more likely than men to be employed in this sector. Younger workers are also more likely than older people to work in this sector, as they pay for their studies with part-time work or use these low-level positions as a means of entering the labour force.

Household service work has shifted. Once done by domestics who worked full time with one employer, it is now usually performed by part-time workers who may work several hours a week in many different homes. Household work lacks regularity, stability, and adequate pay. The jobs are excluded from most labour legislation, the workers are not unionized, and employers sometimes break the rules and regulations that do apply. The jobs typically have no benefits.

Contingent Work

Contingent work is part-time or temporary work that offers advantages to employers but can be detrimental to the welfare of workers. Contingent work is found in every segment of the workforce, including colleges and universities, where tenure-track positions are fewer in number than in the past and a series of one-year, non–tenure-track appointments at the lecturer or instructor level is the only option for many faculty members. In the healthcare field, nurses, personal care homeworkers, and others are increasingly employed through temporary agencies as their jobs are contracted out. Supermarkets have replaced full-time workers with part-timers. Employers benefit by hiring workers on a part-time or temporary basis. They are able to cut wage and benefits costs, maximize profits, and have workers available only when they need them. Kathy Sayers, the co-owner of a Vancouver technical writing company that relies heavily on temporary employees, told a researcher:

marginal job A position that differs from the employment norms of the society in which it is located.

contingent work Part-time or temporary work.

> When the [economic] downturn hits, International Wordsmith will be ready and able to retrench quickly and wait out the storm. It won't have a big payroll to cut, nor high overhead costs. "It takes a load off your mind and lets you sleep easier," says Sayers, "when your company has a plan to deal with a change in the economic weather." When the economy perks up . . . the partners will quickly hire more temporary employees for stints lasting weeks or months. (Zeidenberg, 1990:31)

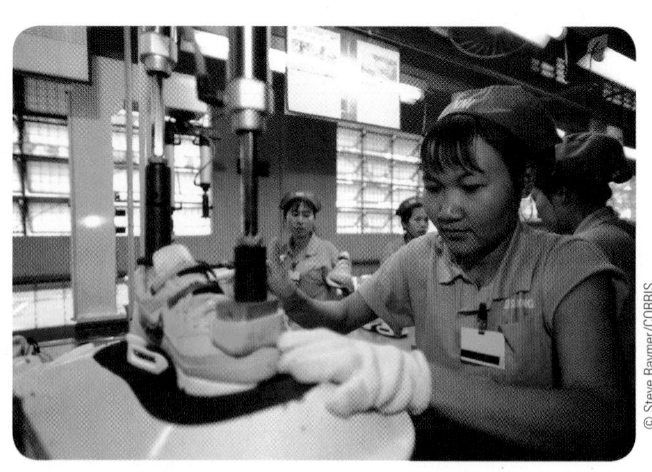

© Steve Raymer/CORBIS

Workers in developing nations—often women or young girls—make or assemble a number of products sold in North America and other developed nations. Workers in Vietnam make many Nike products; in the United States, Nike employees are primarily involved in nonmanufacturing work, including research, design, and retailing.

While employers find it easier to cope with changes in the economy using such methods, their temporary employees earn less than full-time employees, have no economic security, and can find themselves quickly unemployed during economic hard times. And, while some people voluntarily work part time, many people do so because they lack opportunities for full-time employment. Most part-time workers are young people, many of whom are working while attending school. Women are much more likely to hold part-time jobs than men are. In 2009, women accounted for about 70 percent of part-time workers (Statistics Canada, 2009e), a figure that has remained constant for many decades.

A new form of contingent work is crowdsourcing. Some sites, such as Wikipedia, use volunteer labour, but others, such as Amazon's Mechanical Turk and Crowdflower, enable companies to break large jobs involving data entry, tagging Twitter messages, or writing programming code into microtasks and to pay a small amount of money per task to anyone who wants to log on and do the work. Crowdsourcing can be even cheaper for companies than using part-time or casual help (Silverman, 2012) and typically pays the workers very little.

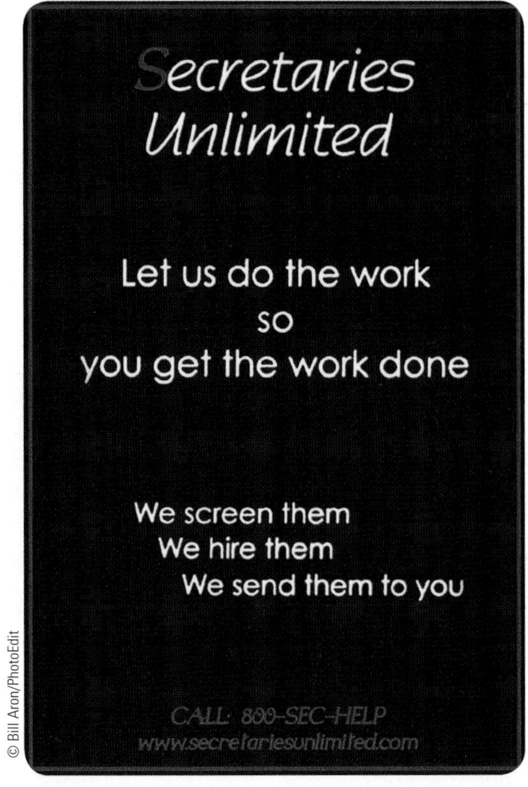

© Bill Aron/PhotoEdit

Hiring contingent workers can increase the profitability of many corporations. Other companies make their profits by furnishing these contingent workers to the corporations. What message does this ad convey to corporate employees?

Unemployment

To many Canadians, unemployment rates are just numbers we see in the news every month. However, behind the statistics lie countless individual tragedies. In the chapter introduction, Wilfred Popoff describes the personal devastation of losing his job. When an entire community is affected, the consequences can be far-reaching. A newspaper article on unemployment in Port Hardy, British Columbia, began with the statement "This picturesque Vancouver Island coastal town is on a deathwatch" (Howard, 1998:A4). The suicide rate increased dramatically in the town following the closing of a copper mine, a reduction in logging activity, and a sharp decline in salmon stocks. With a population of only 5500, Port Hardy had five suicides and 24 attempted suicides in a nine-month period. Those who killed themselves were young to middle-aged adults—the people whose prospects were most affected by the community's poor employment prospects. While suicide is the most serious consequence of a community's loss of jobs, hundreds of communities, particularly in the Atlantic provinces, are in danger of disappearing due to the loss of so many of their young people to other provinces, as traditional resource-related jobs in the fishery and mining industries have disappeared.

The **unemployment rate** is the percentage of unemployed persons in the labour force actively seeking jobs. The unemployment rate is not a complete measure of unemployment because it does not include those who have become discouraged and have stopped looking for work, nor does it count students, even if they are looking for jobs. Unemployment rates vary over several dimensions:

unemployment rate
The percentage of unemployed persons in the labour force actively seeking jobs.

- *Yearly variations.* The Canadian unemployment rate reached a post–World War II high in the early 1980s, when it climbed above 11 percent. After a decline to below 6 percent by 2008, unemployment rose to 8.5 percent in 2009, showing the impact of a global recession. By May 2012, the rate had improved to 7.3 percent (Statistics Canada, 2012b).
- *Regional differences.* Canada's regions have widely different rates of unemployment. Rates in the Atlantic provinces and in Quebec are usually higher than the Canadian average and the Prairie provinces are usually lower. See Figure 19.3.
- *Gender.* In May 2012, the unemployment rate for adult males was 6.2 percent, compared with 5.9 percent for adult women. Females have had lower unemployment rates than men since 1990.
- *Race.* Most immigrants are members of visible minority groups. Despite the fact that immigrants have higher levels of education than nonimmigrants, they are not employed in the same level of jobs. Over one-third of immigrants with university degrees are working in low-skill jobs, compared with 10 percent of native-born Canadians (Krahn, Lowe, and Hughes, 2011). In the 1970s, immigrants' incomes caught up with those of native-born Canadians after 10 years in Canada, but by 2000 this had declined so immigrants made only 80 percent of native-born incomes (Krahn, Lowe, and Hughes, 2011). Some of the problem is due to the fact that immigrants have difficulty getting professional associations and employers to recognize their foreign qualifications, language barriers, a lack of contacts in the labour market, and racial discrimination (Houle and Yssaad, 2010; Krahn, Lowe, and Hughes, 2011).

FIGURE 19.3 UNEMPLOYMENT RATES BY PROVINCE AND TERRITORY

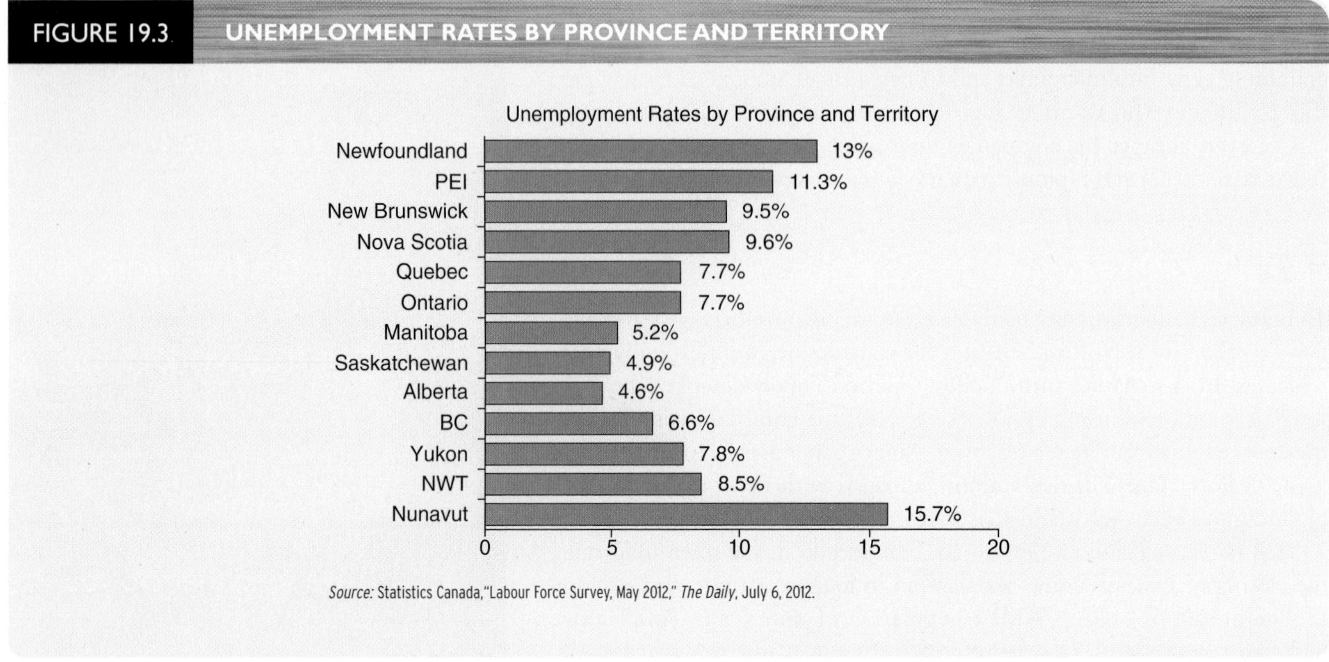

Source: Statistics Canada, "Labour Force Survey, May 2012," *The Daily*, July 6, 2012.

In 2006, Aboriginal Canadians living off-reserve had rates of unemployment that were over twice as high as the national average and Aboriginal Canadians living on reserves had rates of unemployment that were over four times higher than other Canadians (Khran, Lowe, and Hughes, 2012). As a result, incomes for Aboriginal people are far lower than the national average. There is some good news, however, as employment rates for Aboriginal people have been increasing, particularly for those who have postsecondary education (Statistics Canada, 2008c).

- *Age.* Youth have higher rates of unemployment than older persons. Unemployment rates for people age 15 to 24 are double the overall unemployment rate (Statistics Canada, 2012b). The gap between youth and other workers has grown since 1990.
- *Presence of a disability.* People with disabilities are much less likely to be employed than other Canadians. Less than half are seeking work, and those in the labour force have an unemployment rate about 50 percent higher than that of people without disabilities, while those with jobs are often in jobs below their qualifications. As a result, people with disabilities are more likely to be poor (Crompton, 2011).
- *Chronic unemployment.* While many people are occasionally out of work, about 10 percent of labour force members are chronically unemployed. These people were more likely to be from the Atlantic provinces, to have less than high school educations, to be members of visible minority groups, to be female, and to be older (Statistics Canada, 2005i).

LO-5 Labour Unions

labour union A group of employees who join together to bargain with an employer or a group of employers over wages, benefits, and working conditions.

Workers have formed labour unions to improve their work environment and gain some control over their work-related activities. A **labour union** is a group of employees who join together to bargain with an employer or a group of employers over wages, benefits, and working conditions.

During the period of monopoly capitalism, as industries shifted to mass production, workers realized that they needed more power to improve their working conditions. The suppression of the Winnipeg General Strike in 1919 and the employment crisis during the Depression of the 1930s had devastated unions. One of the most important events in Canadian labour history was the United Automobile Workers (UAW) strike against General Motors in 1937 in Oshawa, Ontario (Abella, 1974). At the beginning of 1937, there was no union at the Oshawa plant and workers had suffered their fifth consecutive wage cut while General Motors had announced record profits. When the company announced that the assembly line would be speeded up to produce 32 cars per hour instead of the 27 it had been producing, the men stopped work and organizers started a Canadian chapter of the UAW.

An unusual feature of the strike was the involvement of the premier of Ontario, Mitchell Hepburn. He hoped to crush the strike and stop the spread of industrial unions in Ontario. His fear of unions is shown in this statement made at a press conference:

> We now know what these [union] agitators are up to. We are advised only a few hours ago that they are working their way into the lumber camps and pulp mills and our mines. Well, that has got to stop and we are going to stop it! If necessary we'll raise an army to do it. (Abella, 1974:106)

Hepburn did raise an army. He recruited hundreds of men into the provincial police; the newcomers were irreverently called "Hepburn Hussars" and "Sons of Mitches."

Despite the premier's efforts, the union won the strike and received a contract that became a model for unions throughout Canada. This marked the beginning of *industrial unionism* in Canada, in which all workers in a particular industry, covering a wide variety of different trades, belonged to a single union. This gave the workers a great deal of bargaining power, because a strike could shut down an entire industry.

Industrial unions faced a long struggle to organize. Relations between workers and managers were difficult, and violence against workers was often used to fight unionization. Ultimately, organizers were successful and unions helped to gain an eight-hour workday and a five-day work week, health and retirement benefits, sick leave and unemployment insurance, and workplace health and safety standards for many employees.

Union membership grew, particularly during the two world wars, when labour shortages and economic growth made union expansion easy, and during the 1970s, when governments allowed public servants to unionize (Krahn, Lowe, and Hughes, 2011). However, union membership declined during the 1980s and 1990s as economic recessions and massive layoffs in government and industry reduced the numbers of unionized workers and severely weakened the bargaining power of unions. Between 1981 and 2011, the percentage of workers who belonged to unions declined from 38 percent to 30 percent (Statistics Canada, 2007m; Uppal, 2011). Jobs have shifted from manufacturing and manual work to the service sector, where employees have been less able to unionize. While white-collar workers in the public sector, such as teachers and civil servants, have successfully organized, white-collar workers in the private sector remain largely unorganized. Women now make up over half of all union membership and have accounted for most of the growth in union membership over the past two decades. In 2009, 31 percent of all female paid workers were unionized, compared with 28 percent for male paid workers (Uppal, 2011).The rate of union membership among workers in Canada is higher than in the United States, but far lower than in many Western European countries, though rates in most of these countries have declined as well. Thirty years ago, the union membership rate in the United States was the same as in Canada, but at 12 percent it is now far less than half (U.S. Bureau of Labor Statistics, 2012). American industry has been very anti-union, and state and federal laws such as "right to work" legislation have made it difficult for workers to unionize.

Difficult times may lie ahead for unions: The increase in temporary and part-time work, the ease with which jobs can be moved from one country to another, the replacement of jobs with technology, and the increasing popularity of new patterns of work (such as telecommuting) where workers have little contact with one another are just a few of the challenges that lie ahead. Governments are contracting out unionized jobs. For example, many cities have replaced unionized garbage collectors with private companies whose employees are not likely to be union members and who are paid much lower wages for picking up our garbage. As our economy becomes increasingly service-based, an important challenge for unions will be organizing the lower tier of service sector workers. McDonald's and Walmart, for example, have strongly resisted attempts to organize unions. Both companies have shut down operations where staff have sought to unionize. In 2005, Walmart closed a store in Jonquière, Quebec, in which staff had obtained union certification. The closure put 176 employees out of work. Ironically, high-status workers have profited most from union activities in recent years.Professional athletes' unions such as the NHL Players' Association have been very successful in ensuring that their members are well paid, and provincial medical associations have also done a good job of increasing doctors' salaries at a time when governments have been trying to cut rising medical costs.

The next decade will be a critical time for the labour movement. Unions have to deal with the reality that in a global economy, work can quickly be moved to areas where wages are low. Unions must find ways to recruit knowledge workers and workers engaged in nontraditional forms of work, such as telecommuting, if they are to become involved in the new economy.

How do you think union leaders can change their organizations to meet the new realities of the world of work?

TIME TO REVIEW

- How has the gender structure of some occupations and professions affected the way women are treated in those organizations?
- In what ways would you distinguish between occupations and professions? What are the characteristics of a profession?
- How did the development of scientific management and the assembly line change the nature of work?
- How has the increase in contingent work affected workers and their employers?
- Discuss the history of labour unions in Canada and try to predict how unions will change in the future.

LO-6 THE GLOBAL ECONOMY IN THE FUTURE

How will the nature of work change during your lifetime? What are Canada's future economic prospects? What about the global economy? We cannot predict the future, but some general trends can be suggested.

The End of Work?

Corporations around the world eliminated millions of jobs in 2009 because of a global recession that dramatically reduced the demand for goods and services. Also, some employers have cut jobs because of the impact of globalization, and the increasing use of technology has meant that many workers can be replaced with machines. We live in a post-industrial, information-based economy in which factory work, clerical work, middle management, and many other traditional jobs are falling victim to technology. Bank machines and Internet banking are replacing tellers, robots are replacing factory workers, and electronic scanners are replacing cashiers. Even jobs associated with the post-industrial economy, such as computer programming and working in call centres, are being lost to workers in low-wage countries, such as India. When agriculture became mechanized, displaced workers found jobs in industry, and when industry turned to computers, service jobs were available. However, the information age does not hold the same potential for jobs. Some knowledge workers—the engineers, technicians, and scientists who are leading us into the information age—will gain, but there may be little work for the rest of us. We will have an elite, not a mass, workforce. The elites will be well paid. Microsoft's Bill Gates is just one of a number of people who have made astonishing fortunes in the computer industry. However, most people have not received the benefits of the post-industrial society. Many people do not have jobs, and those with jobs have seen declines in their purchasing power. Nathan Gardels fears that the unemployed face economic irrelevance: "We don't need what they have and they can't buy what we sell" (quoted in Rifkin, 1995:215).

Without adequate incomes, people will not be able to purchase the goods and services created by our new technology. Henry Ford was no great friend of the worker and was strongly opposed to unionization, but he paid his employees very well. However, service economy employers, such as Walmart and McDonald's, keep their prices down and their profits up by paying their employees very low wages. While Henry Ford wanted his employees to be able to buy his cars, the Walton family (which runs Walmart and some of whose members are four of the 20 richest people in the world) pays wages so low that its employees can shop only at low-cost stores—such as Walmart.

Riots in 2011 in countries such as Greece that have been forced to implement severe austerity measures that have cut jobs, wages, and pensions demonstrate that increased inequality can be destabilizing. As British journalist Victor Keegan has observed, "A world in which the majority of people are disenfranchised will not be a pleasant or safe place for the rich minority" (1996:D4). The United States, which has the greatest disparity between rich and poor in the industrialized world, now incarcerates about 2 percent of its adult male population, yet still has a much higher crime rate than most other industrialized countries

Not everyone is poorly paid in today's economy—in 2009, many executives received bonuses even after driving their companies into bankruptcy and ruining the global financial system. It remains to be seen if efforts to raise awareness of this growing income disparity, such as the Occupy movement in 2011, will have an impact on social policy.

The Impact of Communications Technology

In a knowledge-based economy, many workers are not tied to a fixed work location, such as a factory or farm. Computer programmers, accountants, writers, and people in many other occupations can do their work from home, a coffee shop, or any other place with Internet access; iChat and other videoconferencing programs even allow for "face-to-face" meetings of people scattered around the globe.

Modern communications technology brings many benefits. People who work from home avoid wasting time commuting and they are able to respond quickly to the needs of their children. Mobile phones enable people to stay in contact with the office if urgent situations arise. However, this also means that some people are never free of their work, as their employers or their clients expect an immediate response to their requests. This stress is part of a broader problem of work–life balance faced by many workers.

Technology has also had a negative impact on many lower-tier workers. In a return to Taylor's scientific management, companies that are focused on minimizing labour costs to maximize short-term profits use technology to micromanage their employees to ensure that they are not wasting any time. Mac McClelland describes her time working at a large warehouse that filled orders for an Internet sales company. The warehouse employed thousands of people, despite low wages ($7.25 an hour) and appalling working conditions. The workers are continually monitored by an electronic scanner that calculates how long each item should take them to retrieve:

© CP/Jacques Boissinot

Immediately after the employees of this Walmart store in Jonquière, Quebec, obtained certification as a union, Walmart officials closed it down. Such actions have discouraged Walmart employees in other communities from attempting to unionize.

> That afternoon, we are turned loose in the warehouse, scanners in hand. And that's when I realize that for whatever relative youth and regular exercise and overachievement complexes I have brought to this job, I will never be able to keep up with the goals I've been given.
>
> The place is immense. Cold, cavernous. Silent, despite thousands of people quietly doing their picking, or standing along the conveyors quietly packing or box-taping, nothing noisy but the occasional whir of a passing forklift. My scanner tells me in what exact section—there are nine merchandise sections, so sprawling that there's a map attached to my ID badge—of vast shelving systems the item I'm supposed to find resides. It also tells me how many seconds it thinks I should take to get there. Dallas sector, section yellow, row H34, bin 22, level D: wearable blanket. Battery-operated flour sifter. Twenty seconds. I count how many steps it takes me to speed-walk to my destination: 20. At 5-foot-9, I've got a decently long stride, and I only cover the 20 steps *and* locate the exact shelving unit in the allotted time if I don't hesitate for one second or get lost or take a drink of water before heading in the right direction as fast as I can walk or even occasionally jog. Olive oil mister . . . Fairy calendar. Neoprene lunch bag. Often as not, I miss my time target. (2012:6)

These jobs will soon disappear—Amazon has recently purchased Kiva Systems, a company that manufactures robots that will do this task—but McClelland's experience shows the impact that new technology can have on the workforce.

The Underground Economy

> The Bougons are a French-Canadian family that has achieved notoriety not only in their home province of Quebec but also across Canada. The father, Paul Bougon, bribed a Canada Post letter carrier to deliver fraudulent welfare cheques to the Bougon house. His wife, Rita, is a self-employed phone sex operator. Their eldest son, Paul Jr., engages in car theft, among other illegal activities, and their daughter, Dolorès, is an exotic dancer/prostitute. The family also adopted a Chinese child, Mao, to help the family with computer scams. Not a penny of the income earned through any of these activities is reported to the appropriate tax collecting agency. (Tedds, 2005:157)

While the Bougons are a fictional family portrayed in a very popular Quebec television comedy series, their activities represent the *underground economy*. The underground economy is "legal and illegal market-based transactions not reported to the revenue gathering agency"—that is, the Canada Revenue Agency (Tedds, 2005:158). In addition to illegal behaviour, the underground economy also includes legal activities such as making cash payments for home renovations so the contractor can avoid paying taxes on the money. While the size of the underground economy can never be known, Tedds (2005) estimates that between 1976 and 2001, it increased from 7.5 to 15.3 percent of gross domestic product (GDP), or over

$150 billion per year. Governments do not collect tax revenue on this money, so the rest of us pay to make up for this revenue loss.

Global Economic Interdependence and Competition

Global markets and industries do not follow political boundaries. Japanese cars, for example, are assembled in Canada and the United States using components that can be made virtually anywhere in the world. Capital and jobs can move rapidly, so governments have much less power to intervene in markets.

Most futurists predict that multinational corporations will become even more powerful. As they continue to compete for world market share, these corporations will become even less aligned with the values of any one nation. Those who favour increased globalization typically focus on its potential impact on high-income countries, not on the effect it may have on the 80 percent of the world's population that resides in middle- and low-income countries. The gap between rich and poor nations may continue to widen. In recent years, the average worker in Canada and other developed countries has benefited from global economic growth, more than have workers in less developed and developing countries. More than a billion of the world's people live in abject poverty, which, for many, means trying to survive on less than a dollar a day.

There is no consensus about the impact of globalization on Canada. Has our economy benefited from agreements, such as the North American Free Trade Agreement (NAFTA), which involves Canada, the United States, and Mexico? We know that the economies of Canada and the United States are becoming more closely linked. The amount of trade has increased and the border has become almost irrelevant to business. Those looking for opportunities to expand business are increasingly looking south rather than within Canada.

The economic consequences of NAFTA will not be known for decades. Critics complained that NAFTA would bring an end to medicare and our social safety net and would dramatically reduce environmental standards. During the first few years following the 1989 implementation of the agreement with the United States that preceded NAFTA, a great number of manufacturing jobs were lost, just as opponents of the deal had predicted. However, these were also years when Canada's economy was in a recession and high interest rates and the high value of the Canadian dollar made our exports uncompetitive. More recently, Canada has exported more to the United States than we have imported, though this trend ended during the 2009 recession. We do not know whether the future will bring increased prosperity to all three countries or whether factors such as the low wages paid to workers in Mexico and the Southern United States will result in jobs permanently moving out of Canada.

More broadly, competition with low-wage countries has had an impact on all Canadians. By threatening to close plants and move elsewhere, many corporations have forced drastic wage cuts. Governments have also been pressured to adjust taxation and social policies so business remains competitive. Business leaders argue that if Canada's tax rates are higher than those of other countries, particularly the United States, corporations will not locate here and we will steadily lose jobs and people. This international pressure limits the ability of the Canadian government to significantly raise taxes on business or on wealthy Canadians to redistribute income to the poor; doing so would make us less competitive with the low tax rates of the United States. Governments are steadily losing the ability to set national policies in the face of global market forces and multinational corporations that operate without concern for national boundaries.

There are some signs that at least some manufacturing jobs are being repatriated from offshore. Increased costs of transporting manufactured goods, increased wages in lower-income countries, and disruptions to global supply chains such as the one that occurred following the Japanese earthquake and tsunami in 2011 have led some companies to reconsider the value of moving jobs to low-wage countries offshore.

19

VISUAL SUMMARY

KEY TERMS

capitalism An economic system characterized by private ownership of the means of production, from which personal profits can be derived through market competition and without government intervention (p. 544).

contingent work Part-time or temporary work (p. 558).

corporations Large-scale organizations that have legal powers, such as the ability to enter into contracts and buy and sell property, separate from their individual owners (p. 544).

democratic socialism An economic and political system that combines private ownership of some of the means of production, governmental distribution of some essential goods and services, and free elections (p. 548).

economy The social institution that ensures the maintenance of society through the production, distribution, and consumption of goods and services (p. 538).

labour union A group of employees who join together to bargain with an employer or a group of employers over wages, benefits, and working conditions (p. 560).

marginal job A position that differs from the employment norms of the society in which it is located (p. 558).

mixed economy An economic system that combines elements of a market economy (capitalism) with elements of a command economy (socialism) (p. 548).

LO-1 Understand the primary function of the economy.

The economy is the social institution that ensures the maintenance of society through the production, distribution, and consumption of goods and services.

© George Steinmetz/Corbis

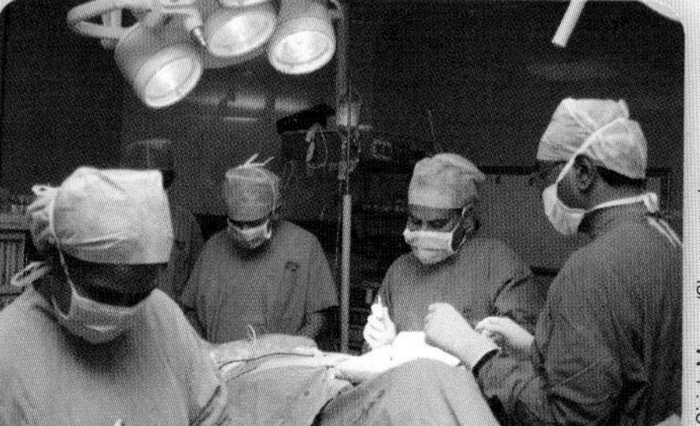

© Girish Menon/Shutterstock.com

LO-2 Describe the differences between the primary, secondary, and tertiary sectors of economic production.

In primary sector production, workers extract raw materials and natural resources from the environment. Industrial societies engage in secondary sector production, which is based on the processing of raw materials (from the primary sector) into finished goods. Post-industrial societies engage in tertiary sector production by providing services rather than goods.

LO-3 Discuss the differences between the three major contemporary economic systems—capitalism, socialism, and mixed economies.

Capitalism is characterized by ownership of the means of production, pursuit of personal profit, competition, and limited government intervention. Socialism is characterized by public ownership of the means of production, the pursuit of collective goals, and centralized decision making. In mixed economies, elements of a capitalist market economy are combined with elements of a command socialist economy.

© CP/AP

LO-4 Understand the functionalist, conflict, symbolic interactionist, and feminist perspectives on the economy and work.

© CP/Jacques Boissinot

According to functionalists, the economy is a vital social institution because it is the means by which needed goods and services are produced and distributed. Business cycles represent the necessary rise and fall of economic activity relative to long-term economic growth. Conflict theorists view business cycles as the result of capitalist greed. To maximize profits, capitalists suppress the wages of workers, who, in turn, cannot purchase products, making it necessary for capitalists to reduce production, close factories, lay off workers, and adopt other remedies that are detrimental to workers and society. Symbolic interactionists focus on issues such as the social organization of work and its effects on workers' attitudes and behaviour. Feminist researchers have documented the ways in which women are discriminated against in the world of work.

© AP Photo/The Canadian Press, Dave Chidley

LO-5 Understand the role of labour unions and identify the challenges currently faced by the union movement.

A labour union is a group of employees who join together to bargain with an employer or a group of employers over wages, benefits, and working conditions. Union membership is declining and facing the pressures of globalization and the desire of employers in the private and public sectors to reduce labour costs.

LO-6 Consider how globalization has affected Canadian workers.

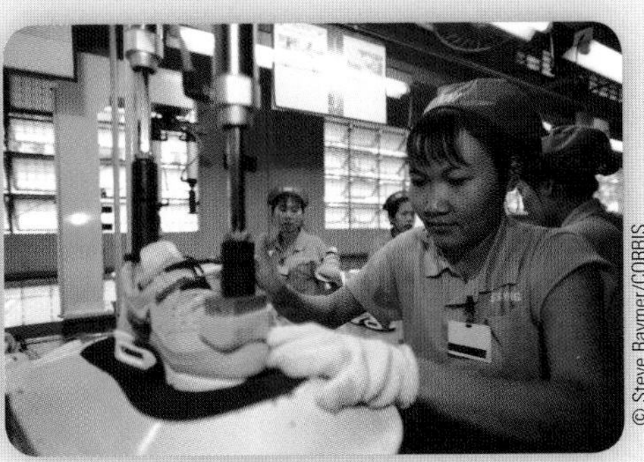
© Steve Raymer/CORBIS

The need to stay competitive with low-wage countries has kept wages down. If workers insist on higher wages, companies can simply close their factories and move production to another country. On the positive side, increased trade has created jobs in Canada.

multinational corporations Large companies that are headquartered in one country and have subsidiaries or branches in other countries (p. 544).

occupations Categories of jobs that involve similar activities at different work sites (p. 554).

oligopoly The situation that exists when several companies overwhelmingly control an entire industry (p. 546).

post-industrial economy An economy that is based on the provision of services rather than goods (p. 542).

primary sector production The sector of the economy that extracts raw materials and natural resources from the environment (p. 538).

professions High-status, knowledge-based occupations (p. 554).

secondary sector production The sector of the economy that processes raw materials (from the primary sector) into finished goods (p. 540).

socialism An economic system characterized by public ownership of the means of production, the pursuit of collective goals, and centralized decision making (p. 547).

unemployment rate The percentage of unemployed persons in the labour force actively seeking jobs (p. 559).

APPLICATION QUESTIONS

1. If you were the manager of a fast-food restaurant, how might you increase job satisfaction and decrease job alienation among your employees? How do you think work differs between a fast-food restaurant and a luxury restaurant? What are the consequences of these differences for employees?
2. What actions could governments and individuals take to ensure that women are fairly treated in the labour market?
3. In what ways do you think new communications technology will affect employment? Do you think it will make work life better or worse?
4. Many occupations will change or disappear in the future. Think of a specific occupation or profession and consider its future. For example, what will be the role of the librarian when books, journals, and abstracts are all instantly accessible on the Internet?

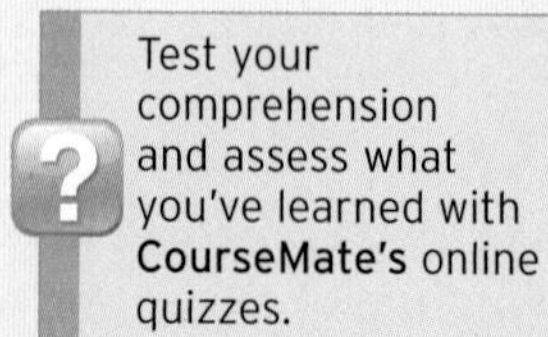

Test your comprehension and assess what you've learned with **CourseMate's** online quizzes.

For other interesting Lived Experiences, watch the video clips on **CourseMate.**

Practise what you've learned with flashcards containing key terms and definitions on **CourseMate.**

CHAPTER

20 Power, Politics, and Government

Canadians have usually been able to settle their political differences through the electoral process. However, some groups have tried to accomplish their goals through political violence.

During the 1960s and early 1970s, the Front de Libération du Québec (FLQ) committed several terrorist acts, culminating in the kidnapping of a British diplomat and the murder of a Quebec cabinet minister. One of the intellectual leaders of the FLQ was Pierre Vallières. In *White Niggers of America,* written in prison following his arrest for the murder of a woman who died in an FLQ bomb attack, Vallières outlined the grievances of the Quebec separatists:

> *In writing this book I claim to do no more than bear witness to the determination of the workers of Quebec to put an end to three centuries of exploitation, of injustices borne in silence, of sacrifices accepted in vain, of insecurity endured with resignation; to bear witness to their new and increasingly energetic determination to take control of their economic, political, and social affairs and to transform into a more just and fraternal society this country, Quebec, which is theirs, this country where they have always been the overwhelming majority of citizens and producers of the "national" wealth, yet where they never have enjoyed the economic power and social freedom to which their numbers and labor entitle them.* (1971:17)

While this sounds like the rhetoric of present-day separatists, the FLQ was different because its members also believed in a revolutionary Marxist ideology that justified violence. Vallières, who saw himself as a political prisoner rather than as a "common criminal," described the movement's goals:

CP/Peter Bregg

> *The FLQ is . . . the armed avant-garde of the exploited classes of Quebec: the workers, the farmers, the petty white-collar workers, the students, the unemployed, and those on welfare—that is, at least 90 percent of the population. The FLQ is struggling not only for the political independence of Quebec, but also and inseparably for the revolution, a total revolution which will give all power to the workers and students in a free, self-administering, and fraternal society.* (1971:258–259)

Many Quebeckers still dream of independence, though few now seek a violent revolution. Feeling their culture threatened by the influence of English-speaking North America, separatists believe they can fulfill their destiny only as a distinct "people" through political independence. While the separatists lost the October 1995 referendum by the narrowest of margins and were supported by a large majority of French-speaking voters, the feelings of Quebeckers remain ambivalent. For example, a poll conducted after the referendum found that two-thirds of Quebeckers wanted their province to remain part of Canada; however, the same poll showed that 55 percent would vote for separation. These data reflect the perception of Quebec comedian Yvon Deschamps that what many Quebeckers really want is an independent Quebec within a strong and united Canada. The data also suggest that some flexibility from the other provinces concerning Quebec's place in Canada would ensure that our country stays together, as most Quebeckers would clearly prefer constitutional reform to separation.

Interestingly, Vallières reflected these two different strains of Quebec political thought. After his release from prison, he disavowed violence and became a member of the separatist Parti Québécois. Prior to his death in 1998, however, he rejected separatism, fearing that it would lead to ethnic and linguistic apartheid. Late in his life, Vallières had been horrified by the ethnic violence in the former Yugoslavia (For other examples of terrorism in Canada, see Box 20.3 on page 592) and did not want to see the same thing happen in Quebec.

This chapter is about politics, and politics is about power. Our political and state institutions are the means through which that power is exercised. Those who control these institutions can implement policies that reflect their interests and values. There are constant tensions as different groups compete to gain the power they need to transform their particular agendas into social policy.

Modern nations face tremendous political challenges. Resolving the future of Quebec is just one of the political issues facing Canadians. In this chapter, we will discuss some of these issues and describe the political system through which Canadians will deal with them. We will also examine other systems of government. Before reading on, test your knowledge about political issues and state institutions by taking the quiz in Box 20.1 on page 573.

Critical Thinking Questions

1. In 2012, Quebec students protesting tuition fee increases vandalized the offices of cabinet ministers, threw Molotov cocktails, and disrupted subway service in Montreal. Do you think that violence is ever justified in protesting the actions of democratically elected governments? Why or why not?
2. Young people in Canada have very low rates of voting. Why do you think young people are not interested in electoral politics? What could be done to increase their involvement and sense of connection to the political process?
3. What action (or lack of action) by the government most interests you? In what ways do you agree or disagree with the government's position on this issue?

CHAPTER FOCUS QUESTION Can the aspirations of Aboriginal people and French-speaking Quebeckers be accommodated within the Canadian political system?

LEARNING OBJECTIVES

AFTER READING THIS CHAPTER, YOU SHOULD BE ABLE TO

- **LO-1** Discuss the meaning of power.
- **LO-2** Understand the relationship between power and politics.
- **LO-3** Explain the three different types of authority that leaders can possess.
- **LO-4** Identify the four main types of political systems.
- **LO-5** Consider the main political issues facing Canadians.

© Ted Wright

Tension between anglophone and francophone Montrealers increased after the 1995 referendum. Many separatists were angry at the English and ethnic voters who refused to support independence.

LO-1 POLITICS, POWER, AND AUTHORITY

Political participation, measured by indicators such as the percentage of people who vote in elections, has been steadily declining. Many Canadians, particularly young people, seem to feel that politics is irrelevant to their lives. However, politics is vitally important to all of us, and many things about your future will be affected by political decisions. At the extreme, we can look at "failed states," such as Somalia and Haiti, where politics has failed and people live miserable lives on the edge of starvation. Even in Canada, political decisions affect all of us:

> The taxes and prices we pay and the jobs available to us, the chances that we will live in peace or perish in war, the costs of education and the availability of scholarships, the safety of the airliner or highway we travel on, the quality of the food we eat and the air we breathe, the availability of affordable housing and medical care, the legal protections against racial and sexual discrimination—all the things that directly affect the quality of our lives are influenced in some measure by politics. (Parenti, 1996:7–8)

Politics is the social institution through which power is acquired and exercised by some people and groups. In contemporary societies, the government is the primary political system. **Government** is the formal organization that has the legal and political authority to regulate the relationships among members of a society and between the society and those outside its borders. Some social scientists refer to government as the **state**—the political entity that possesses a legitimate monopoly over the use of force within its territory to achieve its goals.

politics The social institution through which power is acquired and exercised by some people and groups.

government The formal organization that has the legal and political authority to regulate the relationships among members of a society and between the society and those outside its borders.

state The political entity that possesses a legitimate monopoly over the use of force within its territory to achieve its goals.

authority Power that people accept as legitimate rather than coercive.

LO-2 Power and Authority

Power is the ability of persons or groups to carry out their will despite opposition from others (Weber, 1968/1922). Through the use of persuasion, authority, or force, some people are able to get others to acquiesce to their demands. Thus, power is a *social relationship* that involves both leaders and followers. Power also affects our system of social stratification. People with power control valuable resources of society and are able to influence others by awarding or withholding those resources (Dye and Zeigler, 2006).

The most basic form of power is force. Initially, force may be used to seize and hold power. Max Weber suggested, however, that force is not an effective long-term means of gaining compliance because those who are being ruled do not accept as legitimate those who are doing the ruling. Consequently, most leaders do not want to base their power on force alone; they seek to legitimize their power by turning it into **authority**—power that people accept as legitimate rather than coercive.

LO-3 Ideal Types of Authority

Under what circumstances are people most likely to accept authority as legitimate and submit to it? People have a greater tendency to accept authority as legitimate if it reflects their own beliefs and values. They also accept authority more readily if they are economically or politically dependent on those who hold power (Turner, Beeghley, and Powers, 1995). *Legitimation* refers to the process by which power is institutionalized and given a moral foundation to justify its existence.

BOX 20.1 **SOCIOLOGY AND EVERYDAY LIFE**

How Much Do You Know About Political Issues and State Institutions?

True	False	
T	F	1. A higher proportion of Canadians vote in federal elections than do the citizens of most other industrialized countries.
T	F	2. In Canada, our constitutional right to freedom of speech means that any kind of pornography or hate literature can be legally distributed.
T	F	3. While authoritarian governments still exist in many countries, democratic government has become more widespread throughout the world during the past 25 years.
T	F	4. In Canada, members of the governing party are free to vote against the government in Parliament whenever they wish.
T	F	5. Canada's Aboriginal peoples have been able to vote in federal elections since 1867, the year of Confederation.

For answers to the quiz about political issues and state institutions, go to **www.nelson.com/sociologyinourtimes6e.**

Weber outlined three *ideal types* of authority—charismatic, traditional, and rational-legal—each of which has a different basis of legitimacy and a different means of administration.

charismatic authority
Power legitimized on the basis of a leader's exceptional personal qualities or accomplishments.

CHARISMATIC AUTHORITY **Charismatic authority** is power legitimized on the basis of a leader's exceptional personal qualities or accomplishments, which inspire loyalty and obedience from followers. Charismatic leaders inspire through the force of their personalities and their ability to articulate the feelings of the people they lead.

A charismatic leader may be either a tyrant or a hero. Thus, charismatic authority has been attributed to such diverse historical figures as Jesus Christ, Napoleon, Julius Caesar, Adolf Hitler, Winston Churchill, and Martin Luther King, Jr. Former prime minister Pierre Trudeau was one of the most charismatic leaders in Canadian politics; however, few of our current leaders are known for their charismatic qualities.

Since women are seldom permitted to assume positions of leadership in patriarchal political and social structures, they have been less likely to become charismatic leaders. Famous women who had charismatic appeal include Joan of Arc, Mother Teresa, Indira Gandhi of India, and Margaret Thatcher of the United Kingdom. Kim Campbell's strong performance as Minister of Justice and her personality gave her a charismatic appeal that helped her win the leadership of the Progressive Conservative Party and become Canada's first woman prime minister. However, the fleeting nature of charismatic appeal was illustrated in the 1993 election, when the campaign of Campbell and her party could not overcome the negative feelings Canadians held about the government of her predecessor, Brian Mulroney, and her party was reduced to only two seats in Parliament.

THE CANADIAN PRESS/Jake Wright

U.S. President Barack Obama is a much more charismatic political figure than Canadian Prime Minister Stephen Harper.

Charismatic authority generally tends to be unstable; it derives primarily from individual leaders (who may lose their appeal, leave, or die) and from an administrative structure usually limited to a small

AP Photo/CP, Adrian Wyld

Pierre Trudeau was one of Canada's most charismatic politicians. When he died, 16 years after retiring from the prime minister's office, hundreds of thousands of people paid their respects to him and his family. Shown here is his son Justin Trudeau (now himself a member of Parliament) on the train carrying his father's body from Ottawa to Montreal.

number of faithful followers. For this reason, charismatic authority often becomes routinized. The **routinization of charisma** occurs when charismatic authority is succeeded by a bureaucracy controlled by a rationally established authority or by a combination of traditional and bureaucratic authority (Turner, Beeghley, and Powers, 1995). However, charisma cannot always be successfully transferred to organizations. Many organizations fail when the charismatic leader departs.

TRADITIONAL AUTHORITY **Traditional authority** is power that is legitimized by respect for long-standing custom. In preindustrial societies, the authority of traditional leaders, such as kings, queens, and religious dignitaries, was usually grounded in religious beliefs and established practices. For example, British royalty have historically traced their authority from God. Subordinate classes obey a traditional leader's edicts out of economic and political dependency and sometimes personal loyalty. However, custom and religious beliefs are sufficient to maintain traditional authority only as long as people share similar backgrounds and accept this authority as legitimate.

As societies industrialize, traditional authority is challenged by a more complex division of labour. In industrialized societies, people do not share the same viewpoint on many issues and tend to openly question traditional authority. Weber felt that traditional authority inhibited the development of capitalism, which he felt worked best in systems of rational-legal authority (Weber, 1968/1922).

Gender, race, and class relations are closely intertwined with traditional authority, which is often based on a system of patriarchy in which men have authority in the household and in other small groups. Eisenstein (1994) suggests that *racialized patriarchy*—the continual interplay of race and gender—reinforces traditional structures of power in contemporary societies.

routinization of charisma A term for the process by which charismatic authority is succeeded by a bureaucracy controlled by a rationally established authority or by a combination of traditional and bureaucratic authority.

traditional authority Power that is legitimized by respect for long-standing custom.

Rational-Legal Authority **Rational-legal authority** is power legitimized by law or written rules and regulations. Rational-legal authority is also called *bureaucratic authority* (Chapter 6). Bureaucracies are characterized by a division of labour, hierarchy of authority, formal rules, impersonal enforcement of rules, and job security based on a person's technical qualifications. In rational-legal authority, power is legitimized by procedures; if leaders obtain their positions in a procedurally correct manner (such as by election or appointment), they have the right to act.

Canada's political system gives rational-legal authority to the office of the prime minister, for example, by specifying the procedures by which persons hold the office, as well as its duties and limitations. Rational-legal authority is also held by other elected or appointed government officials and by officers in a formal organization. Authority, however, is invested in the *office,* not in the *person* who holds the office. When the Liberals lost the 2006 federal election, Paul Martin passed on the power of the office of prime minister to Stephen Harper and became an opposition member of Parliament.

Weber's three types of authority are summarized in Table 20.1.

LO-4 GLOBAL POLITICAL SYSTEMS

rational-legal authority Power legitimized by law or written rules and regulations.

In early societies, politics was not separated from other aspects of life. However, all groups have some means of legitimizing power. Hunting and gathering societies do not have political institutions because they have minimal division of labour. Leadership and authority

TABLE 20.1 WEBER'S THREE TYPES OF AUTHORITY

Max Weber's three types of authority are shown here in global perspective. Charismatic authority is exemplified by Indira Gandhi, former prime minister of India. Sultan Qaboos of Oman is an example of traditional authority sanctioned by custom. Canadian members of Parliament represent rational-legal authority, which depends on established rules and procedures.

	DESCRIPTION	EXAMPLES
CHARISMATIC	Based on leaders' personal qualities	Napoleon Bonaparte
	Temporary and unstable	Adolf Hitler
		Indira Gandhi
TRADITIONAL	Legitimized by long-standing custom	Authority resides in traditional leader supported by larger social structures, as in the old British monarchy
	Subject to erosion as traditions weaken	Patriarchy (rule by men occupying traditional positions of authority, as in the family)
RATIONAL-LEGAL	Legitimized by rationally established rules and procedures	Modern British Parliament
	Authority resides in the office, not the person	Canadian prime minister, Parliament, federal bureaucracy

CP/AP

© AP Images/Hamid Al Qasmi

THE CANADIAN PRESS/Tom Hanson

are centred in the family and clan. Individuals acquire leadership roles through personal attributes, such as great physical strength, exceptional skills, or charisma (Lenski, Lenski, and Nolan, 1991).

Political institutions first emerged in agrarian societies as societies acquired surpluses and developed greater social inequality. Elites took control of politics and used traditional authority to justify their position. When cities developed, the *city-state*—a city whose power extended to adjacent areas—became the centre of political power. Both the Roman and Persian empires comprised a number of city-states, each with its own monarchy. Thus, in these societies, political authority was decentralized. After these empires fell, the individual city-states lived on.

AP Photo/David Cheskin, Pool

Former Governor General Michaëlle Jean and her daughter meet with Queen Elizabeth II. Queen Elizabeth is Canada's head of state, but related duties are performed by the governor general, who is appointed by the Queen on the recommendation of the prime minister.

Nation-states began to develop in Spain, France, and England between the 12th and 15th centuries (Tilly, 1975). A *nation-state* is a unit of political organization that has recognizable national boundaries and citizens who possess legal rights and obligations. Nation-states emerge as countries develop specific geographic territories and acquire greater ability to defend their borders. Improvements in communication and transportation make it possible for people in a larger geographic area to share a common language and culture. As charismatic and traditional types of authority are superseded by rational-legal authority, legal standards come to prevail in all areas of life and the nation-state claims a monopoly over the legitimate use of force (Kennedy, 1993).

There are currently about 196 nation-states in the world. The four main types of political systems found in nation-states are monarchies, authoritarian systems, totalitarian systems, and democracies.

Monarchies

monarchy A political system in which power resides in one person or family and is passed from generation to generation through lines of inheritance.

A **monarchy** is a political system in which power resides in one person or family and is passed from generation to generation through lines of inheritance. Monarchies are most common in agrarian societies and are associated with traditional authority patterns. The power of monarchs has varied. *Absolute monarchs* claim a hereditary right to rule (based on family membership) or a divine (God-given) right to rule. In *limited monarchies,* rulers depend on powerful members of the nobility to retain their thrones. Unlike absolute monarchs, limited monarchs are not considered to be above the law. In *constitutional monarchies,* the royalty serve as symbolic rulers or heads of state while actual authority is held by elected officials in the national parliaments. In such present-day monarchies as the United Kingdom, Sweden, Japan, and the Netherlands, members of royal families primarily perform ceremonial functions.

Authoritarian Systems

authoritarian political system A political system controlled by rulers who deny popular participation in government.

An **authoritarian political system** is one controlled by rulers who deny popular participation in government. Some authoritarian regimes are absolute monarchies in which rulers claim a hereditary right to their position. Today, Saudi Arabia and Kuwait are examples of authoritarian absolute monarchies. *Dictatorships,* in which power is gained and held by a single individual, are also authoritarian. Pure dictatorships are rare: All rulers need the support of the military and the backing of business elites to maintain their position. *Military juntas* result when military officers seize power from the government.

Totalitarian Systems

totalitarian political system A political system in which the state seeks to regulate all aspects of people's public and private lives.

A **totalitarian political system** is one in which the state seeks to regulate all aspects of people's public and private lives. The National Socialist (Nazi) party in Germany was a totalitarian regime before and during World War II, as leaders sought to control all aspects of national life, not just government operations.

To keep people from rebelling, totalitarian governments enforce conformity. People are denied the right to assemble for political purposes; access to information is strictly controlled; and secret police enforce compliance, creating an environment of constant fear and suspicion. North Korea is one contemporary example of a totalitarian regime. All aspects of life are controlled by the state and no dissent or contacts with the world outside North Korea are tolerated by the regime.

Democracies

A **democracy** is a political system in which the people hold the ruling power, either directly or through elected representatives. *Direct participatory democracy* requires that citizens be able to meet regularly to debate and decide the issues of the day. Historical examples of direct democracy might include ancient Athens or a town meeting in colonial New England. This type of democracy is not feasible in a large-scale society, and in most democratic countries people have a voice in the government through *representative democracy,* whereby citizens elect representatives to run the government. Elected representatives are supposed to convey the concerns and interests of those they represent, and the government is expected to be responsive to the wishes of the people. Representatives are held accountable to the people through elections.

democracy A political system in which the people hold the ruling power, either directly or through elected representatives.

Canada is a *constitutional monarchy* whose head of state is the Queen, a hereditary ruler who is represented in Canada by the governor general. The governor general, appointed by the Queen but recommended by the prime minister, plays a role that is largely ceremonial—our elected Parliament governs the country. By contrast, the United States and France are *republics,* whose heads of state are elected and share governing power with the legislature.

Another major difference between Canada and the United States is that our system is a *parliamentary* one in which the prime minister is the leader of the party that wins the most seats in the House of Commons. This system is based on parliamentary discipline, which ensures that the policies favoured by the prime minister will become law. If government members oppose these policies, they have the opportunity to debate them in private caucus meetings, but they are normally bound to support the government. Party discipline can be harsh; in 2007, Prime Minister Stephen Harper expelled Nova Scotia member of Parliament Bill Casey from the Conservative Party for voting against the budget. By contrast, U.S. legislators often oppose their party's program.

When Canada adopted the British parliamentary system, the Fathers of Confederation also implemented an important feature of the American system—both Canada and the United States are *federations,* with a division of power between the central government and provincial or state governments. Many other countries, including Israel and Italy, are *unitary states,* or states with a single central political authority. While John A. Macdonald, our first prime minister, would have preferred a centralized unitary state, this structure was opposed by Quebec and the Maritimes, which wished to protect their distinctive identities. *The British North America Act* of 1867 established the distribution of powers between federal and provincial governments and gave a broad range of powers to the provinces.

Some countries appear to be democratic because they hold periodic elections, but they are not. The outcome of these elections is a foregone conclusion because voters get to select from candidates belonging to only one party.

Democracy has spread very rapidly, particularly in formerly communist states. Communism was a one-party system that often maintained its power through repressive means. Since the fall of the Berlin Wall in 1989, the countries of the former Soviet bloc in Eastern Europe, as well as other countries, such as Nicaragua and Zambia, have established democratic governments. While communist governments remain in a number of countries, including China and Cuba, pressures for democratization have been strong around the globe. Between 1990 and 2003, the number of countries that were considered free based on their human rights and civil liberties increased from 65 to 89, and 119 countries are electoral democracies—however, this number did not increase between 2003 and 2009 (Freedom House, 2009).

Some new democracies have been fragile. Zimbabwe has become a "pseudo" democracy as President Robert Mugabe has turned to authoritarian rule in order to maintain power. In 2005, Freedom House reclassified Russia from Partly Free to Not Free because of governmental interference in elections and control of the media.

TIME TO REVIEW

- What is the difference between the terms *politics* and *government*?
- What is the difference between power and force?
- What are the three types of authority outlined by Weber? Give examples of each.
- Describe the four different political systems outlined in the text. How do people become leaders in each of these systems?

PERSPECTIVES ON POWER AND POLITICAL SYSTEMS

Is political power in Canada concentrated in the hands of the few or distributed among the many? Sociologists and political scientists have suggested two models of power to answer this question: pluralist and elite.

Functionalist Perspectives: The Pluralist Model

The pluralist model is rooted in functionalism, which assumes that people share a consensus on central concerns, such as freedom and protection from harm, and that the government serves important functions in society that no other institution can fulfill. Functionalists see the main functions of government as (1) maintaining law and order, (2) planning and directing society, (3) meeting social needs, and (4) handling international relations, including warfare.

What role do people play in the political system? What keeps the government from becoming all-powerful? What happens when people do not agree on specific issues? Functionalists suggest that divergent viewpoints lead to a system of political pluralism in which the government functions as an arbiter between competing interests and viewpoints. According to the **pluralist model**, power in political systems is widely dispersed throughout many competing interest groups (Dahl, 1961). Many of these are **special interest groups**—political coalitions made up of individuals or groups that share a specific interest they wish to protect or advance with the help of the political system (Greenberg and Page, 1996). Examples of special interest groups include the Business Council on National Issues, the Canadian Labour Congress, and the Assembly of First Nations.

pluralist model An analysis of political systems that views power as widely dispersed throughout many competing interest groups.

special interest groups Political coalitions made up of individuals or groups that share a specific interest they wish to protect or advance with the help of the political system.

From a pluralist perspective, representative democracy and the constitutional protections provided by the legal system ensure that no one group can overpower the others and that individual rights are protected.

SPECIAL INTEREST GROUPS Of the thousands of special interest groups in Canada, some (such as consumer groups) seek a collective good, while others (such as the cigarette manufacturers' lobby) have a relatively narrow focus. Categories of special interest groups include banking, business, education, energy, the environment, health, labour, persons with a disability, religious groups, retired persons, and women; obviously, many groups overlap in interests and membership.

Advocates of the pluralist model point out that special interest groups provide a voice for people who otherwise might not be heard by elected officials. However, many special interest groups (such as the Canadian Bankers Association) represent very powerful interests and are part of Canada's elite.

Many people are choosing to work through pressure groups rather than through the normal political party system. Our country is so large and diverse that we have always had a highly pluralistic society, and pluralism will likely become even more important in the future. Our ethnic diversity is growing (see Chapter 10), and groups representing women, French-speaking Quebeckers, Aboriginal peoples, ethnic Canadians, and many others are challenging the elitism of the past. Interest groups are now part of our political culture.

While a pluralistic system ensures that the voice of many groups will be heard, it does not always work as fairly as political theorists might wish. For example, there are many more groups representing business interests than there are groups representing the interests of the lower class (Dyck, 2004). While this does not mean that government actions always reflect the interests of the powerful, it does mean that the weak must work much harder to be heard.

Another potential problem with a highly pluralistic system is that if people turn away from broad social issues to those of particular economic, cultural, racial, and gender groups—a process known as *identity politics*—society may become fragmented. *Single-issue politics* means that political candidates are supported or rejected solely on the basis of their views on a single issue—such as abortion, gun control, tax cuts, or the environment. Single-issue groups derive their strength from the intensity of their beliefs; leaders have little room to compromise on issues.

CP/Tom Hanson

In addition to direct contact with legislators, special interest groups, such as the "gun lobby," try to influence policymaking by mobilizing constituents and stirring up public opinion. Recent years have seen a proliferation of single-issue groups like those on both sides of the gun-control issue. The strong feelings of gun owners are shown in this Ottawa rally.

Conflict Perspectives: Elite Models

Although conflict theorists acknowledge that the government serves important purposes for everyone, they assert that it exists for the benefit of wealthy or politically powerful elites who use it to impose their will on the masses. According to the **elite model**, power in political systems is concentrated in the hands of a small group of elites and the masses are relatively powerless.

elite model A view of society in which power in political systems is concentrated in the hands of a small group of elites and the masses are relatively powerless.

Early Italian sociologists Vilfredo Pareto (1848–1923) and Gaetano Mosca (1858–1941) advanced the view that concentration of power may be inevitable within societies. Pareto first used the term *elite* to refer to "the few who rule the many" (Marshall, 1998). Similarly, Karl Marx claimed that under capitalism, the government serves the interests of the ruling (or capitalist) class that controls the means of production.

The pluralist and elite models are compared in Figure 20.1.

C. WRIGHT MILLS AND THE POWER ELITE C. Wright Mills (1959a) was among the first to formulate and test ideas concerning power elites. The **power elite** is composed of leaders at the top of business, the executive branch of the federal government, and the military. Of these three, Mills speculated that the "corporate rich" (the highest-paid officers of the biggest corporations) were the most powerful because of their unique ability to turn the vast economic resources at their disposal into political power. The legislative branch of government, special

power elite A term devised by C. Wright Mills for a structure composed of leaders at the top of business, the executive branch of the federal government, and the military.

interest groups, and local opinion leaders were at the middle level of the pyramid. The bottom (and widest layer) of the pyramid is occupied by the unorganized masses, who are relatively powerless and vulnerable to economic and political exploitation.

Mills emphasized that individuals who make up the power elite have similar class backgrounds and interests; many of them also interact on a regular basis. Members of the power elite are able to influence many important decisions, including government policies.

G. WILLIAM DOMHOFF AND THE RULING CLASS The term *ruling class* signifies a small group of privileged people who wield sufficient power to constrain political processes and serve underlying capitalist interests. By contrast, *governing power* refers to the everyday operation of the political system; who *governs* is much less important than who *rules*. According to Domhoff (1978), the ruling class is made up of the corporate rich, who make up less than 1 percent of the population.

Like Mills, Domhoff believed that the upper echelon consists of members of a business class that owns and controls large corporations (Domhoff, 1983). The intertwining of the upper class and the corporate community produces economic and social cohesion. Members of the ruling class have business ties and are also socially linked with one another. They attend the same schools, belong to the same clubs, and frequently socialize together. Consider Power Corp., which is controlled by Paul Desmarais, a close friend of former prime ministers Brian Mulroney and Jean Chrétien—in fact, Desmarais' son is married to Chrétien's daughter. Another former prime minister, Paul Martin, used to work for Power Corp., and many politicians and government bureaucrats move back and forth between senior Power Corp. positions and government service. With these contacts, Desmarais has no difficulty in having his views

FIGURE 20.1 **PLURALIST AND ELITE MODELS**

PLURALIST MODEL

- Decisions are made on behalf of the people by leaders who engage in bargaining, accommodation, and compromise.
- Competition among leadership groups makes abuse of power by any one group difficult.
- Power is widely dispersed and people can influence public policy by voting.
- Public policy reflects a balance among competing interest groups.

ELITE MODEL

- Decisions are made by a small elite group.
- Consensus exists among the elite on the basic values and goals of society.
- Power is concentrated at the top of a pyramid-shaped social hierarchy.
- Public policy reflects the values and preferences of the elite.

heard by government leaders. Fox and Ornstein (1986) have documented an extensive network of links between large corporations and the federal cabinet, the Senate, and the federal bureaucracy. These links grew over the three decades they studied.

According to Domhoff (1983), the corporate rich influence the political process in three ways. First, they help finance campaigns and provide favours to political candidates. Second, through participation in the special interest process, the corporate rich are able to obtain favours, tax breaks, and favourable regulatory rulings. Finally, the corporate rich in Canada may gain access to the policymaking process through their appointments to governmental bodies, such as the Senate. While the economic elites do not agree on all issues, they do agree on the need to ensure an economic climate that favours their continuing accumulation of wealth. Fox and Ornstein (1986) conclude that the state is not simply an instrument or tool of the capitalists, but that there are important structural connections between the state and corporations that often help capitalists shape legislation to their benefit.

CLASS CONFLICT PERSPECTIVES Most contemporary elite models are based on the work of Karl Marx. However, there are different viewpoints about the role of the state within the Marxist (or class conflict) perspective. On the one hand, *instrumental Marxists* argue that the state always acts to perpetuate the capitalist class. Capitalists control the government through special interest groups, lobbying, campaign financing, and other types of "influence peddling" to get legislatures and the courts to make decisions favourable to their class (Domhoff, 1970; Miliband, 1969). From this perspective, the state exists only to support the interests of the dominant class (Marger, 1987).

On the other hand, *structural Marxists* contend that the state is not simply a passive instrument of the capitalist class. The state must simultaneously preserve order and maintain a positive climate for the accumulation of capital, so not all decisions can favour the immediate wishes of the dominant class (Marger, 1987; Quadagno, 1984). For example, at various points in Canada's history, the state has had to institute social welfare programs, regulate business, and enact policies that favour unions in order to placate people and maintain "law and order." Ultimately, however, such actions serve the long-range interests of the capitalists by keeping members of subordinate groups from rebelling against the dominant group (O'Connor, 1973).

Critique of Pluralist and Elite Models

Pluralist and elite models each contribute to our understanding of power. The pluralist model emphasizes that many different groups compete for power and advantage in society. This model also shows how coalitions may shift over time and how elected officials may be responsive to public opinion on some occasions. However, critics counter that our system has only the appearance of pluralism and that it is, in reality, elitist. A wide disparity exists between the resources and political clout of big business and those of interest groups representing those with little power. According to critics, consensus is difficult, if not impossible, in populations consisting of people from different classes, religions, and racial–ethnic and age groups.

Mills's power elite model highlights that elites from different sectors may be a relatively cohesive group, while Domhoff's ruling class model emphasizes how elites set and implement policies that benefit the capitalist class. These models call our attention to the important issue of the ability of democratic ideals to survive in the face of the increasingly concentrated power held by capitalist oligarchies.

One important critique of elite models is that social change does not always favour the dominant groups in our society. For example, women have won many battles over the past three decades despite the degree of control that males have had over the corporate and political spheres. The success of the women's movement supports the pluralist claim that non-elites can organize to force change.

TABLE 20.2 PERCENTAGE OF WOMEN IN PARLIAMENT, SELECTED COUNTRIES, 2012

Country	Percentage
Rwanda	56.3%
Sweden	44.7%
Netherlands	40.7%
Spain	36.0%
Algeria	31.6%
New Zealand	32.2%
Ethiopia	27.8%
Australia	24.7%
Canada	**24.7%**
Phillippines	22.9%
United Kingdom	22.3%
United States	16.9%
Japan	10.8%

Note: Data correspond to women in lower or single house.

Source: Inter-Parliamentary Union. 2012. "Women in National Parliaments, Situation as of 31 May 2012." Retrieved 20 June 2012. Available: http://www.ipu.org/wmn-e/classif.htm

Feminist Perspectives

Mary McIntosh (1978) was among the first political theorists to highlight the importance of gender. McIntosh felt that the state supported a system in which women were controlled in the household, where they performed unpaid labour that helped supply a cheap workforce for the capitalist system. Until they achieved some political power, women would inevitably be subordinated by the patriarchal state.

Women have long faced political discrimination. The *Elections Act* of 1903 said that "No woman, criminal, or lunatic can vote," and Canadian women could not vote in federal elections until 1918. Most provinces began allowing women to vote at around this time, though in Quebec women could not vote until 1940. With the vote, women also received the right to run for election. However, few ran, and even fewer were successful. Only 27 women were elected to the federal Parliament between 1921 and 1968. As late as 1980, only 5 percent of members of Parliament were women. Since that time, significant progress has been made; 24.7 percent of the members of Parliament elected in 2011 were women (see Table 20.2). This proportion is similar to that of most provincial legislatures (one exception being Manitoba, where about 30 percent of legislators were women; in Quebec, half the members of the cabinet are women). And women have been slow in reaching the highest political positions. Canada has had one woman prime minister (Kim Campbell) but in 2012 four provinces and 1 territory had female premiers. Women have been more successful at the municipal level; many of Canada's mayors are women. Women have also been successful politicians in First Nations communities as 19 percent of elected chiefs and 30 percent of councillors are female (Voyageur, 2011).

The low representation of women in Canadian political office is typical of most Western countries. The major exceptions are the Scandinavian countries, where women make up over 35 percent of the membership of the national parliaments. The absence of women in our legislatures has meant that many gender-related issues have not received sufficient attention. Issues such as daycare policy, pay equity, the feminization of poverty, and violence against women and children have only recently begun to receive the attention they deserve. Male legislators, whose constituents are more than 50 percent women, could have pursued these issues. But for many years they did not.

Some research has shown that women's participation in the electoral process makes a difference in social policy. In the United States, women received the right to vote in various states between 1869 and 1920. Economist Grant Miller (2008) looked at legislation passed immediately after women received the right to vote in each state. He found that within a year of women receiving the right to vote, public health spending increased by about 35 percent, which had a significant impact on children. The improvement in hygienic conditions and the subsequent decline in infectious diseases meant that child mortality decreased by 8 to 15 percent. Miller attributes this change to the fact that candidates were forced to respond to the concerns of women.

Interactionist Perspectives on the Political Process

The symbolic interactionist perspective is useful because politics is very much a human process and the insights of interactionism can help us understand why people behave the way they do in the political arena. Gusfield's work on the importance of symbolic action in politics provides an example of these insights.

GUSFIELD AND THE SYMBOLIC CRUSADES In 2005, many interest groups, including the Roman Catholic Church and several family organizations, committed time and money to trying to defeat the federal Liberal government's legislation allowing same-sex marriage. At the same time, in the United States, the National Rifle Association was fighting proposed laws that would prevent people whose names were listed on terrorist watch lists from buying weapons. To many of us, these battles might not seem worth the effort. Allowing gays and lesbians to marry should not affect other Canadians, especially because at the time the legislation was being considered, same-sex marriage was already permitted in eight provinces and territories and could not be regulated by the federal government without invoking the notwithstanding clause in the *Charter of Rights and Freedoms.* In the security-conscious United States, denying suspected terrorists access to weapons would seem prudent and it is difficult to see any social benefit in allowing them to legally purchase guns. For many North Americans, however, these issues were vitally important.

Why do interest groups spend so much time and energy on issues such as same-sex marriage and gun control?

Gusfield (1963) was interested in learning why people became involved in the temperance movement. In the early part of the 20th century, this movement convinced governments to prohibit alcohol sales for several years in the United States and in most Canadian provinces. Gusfield concluded that the movement was a *symbolic crusade* in which the recognition of the crusaders' values by the government was at least as important as achieving the instrumental goal of prohibiting alcohol use. During a period of rapid urbanization in the U.S., many of those involved in the temperance movement were rural Protestants who felt that their importance in American society was declining and that their values were being replaced with a more indulgent, urban-oriented value system. This change threatened their place in American society as well as their religious and moral values.

> In response, many in [the Protestant group] fought to reassert the dominance of their lifestyle by pressing for adherence to its values regarding alcohol consumption. However, the movement's alcohol orientation did not simply highlight preferences regarding liquid refreshment; more important, it provided the symbolic means for proclaiming one's membership in a status group that valued self-control and industriousness. Furthermore, the inability to enforce Prohibition was of small consequence . . . What these crusaders defined as important was that other rival status groups had to modify their drinking habits according to "our" law. (Snow, 2003:141)

Gusfield's work highlights the dynamics of the legislative process. Many of our laws have a symbolic component, and passage of these laws reassures various groups that their views are important and have been recognized by the government. For example, faced with rising gang violence in British Columbia in 2009, the federal government announced modest changes in the *Criminal Code* that could not possibly have any impact on gang crime. Nonetheless, the "get tough" rhetoric communicated the symbolic message that the government was responding to public concerns by doing something about the gang problem. Political parties rely heavily on symbolism to appeal emotionally to voters because these symbols have the power to bring people together and unite them behind a political movement (Hall, 1972). Can you think of other political positions or laws that are primarily symbolic?

Postmodern Perspectives on Government

Postmodern scholars have contributed to our understanding of government by broadening the concept to include the means by which the state, along with organizations working above and below the interests of the state, influences the behaviour of the citizenry. They refer to this as *governmentality,* or *governance.* Rather than taking the traditional view that governments and other organizations rule through top-down commands, postmodernists propose that the state controls people in a less repressive fashion by providing them with incentives and by enlisting other members of the community to encourage conforming behaviour. Ideally, conformity becomes part of each individual's self-identity, so people essentially govern themselves.

This concept of governance has been applied in a wide variety of contexts. Tannis Peikoff (2000) used Foucault's (1991) framework to analyze the non-state techniques of governance used to control Aboriginal people in the Red River settlement during the mid-1800s. Her research focused on Anglican missionaries who were not part of the government but who played a significant role in the colonization of Aboriginal people. The missionaries sought to convert the Aboriginal people to Christianity and to a Christian way of life, and to establish an indigenous Anglican clergy who would lead their own congregations. This required a break with traditional forms of Aboriginal spirituality and profound changes in existing practices in areas such as family life and education.

The missionaries were surprised to find strong resistance to their attempts to convert Aboriginal people to Christianity and to convince them to shift to European values and practices in other parts of their lives. While the missionaries had no direct power over Aboriginal people, they tried to overcome this resistance by breaking down Aboriginal people's traditional way of life, spirituality, and sense of self in order to change them from "barbarous Indians" into good Christians. Some of the methods they used included trying to discredit Aboriginal spiritual leaders and trying to convince parents that their children were at risk unless parents agreed to religious conversion. This latter approach is illustrated by the comments of missionary William Cockran to the parents of a child who had just died: "Trifle not with the Master of Life, or He will touch you again. You have more children; you have an only son; perhaps he shall be next, who shall be taken if your reformation is not effected by the present warning" (Peikoff, 2000:105).

Ultimately, the efforts of the missionaries were not successful and they decided that they should focus on educating the children. When this tactic also failed, they began to establish residential schools where they could isolate children from their families and from their cultural traditions in order to resocialize them. The legacy of these residential schools still negatively affects Aboriginal people today.

We have examined functionalist, interactionist, conflict, feminist, and postmodern perspectives on politics (see the Concept Snapshot). These explanations help us understand the causes and consequences of political behaviour.

When people move from one country to another, they learn the political attitudes, values, and behaviour of their new country.

CONCEPT SNAPSHOT

FUNCTIONALIST PERSPECTIVES **Key thinker:** Robert Dahl	The functionalist perspective assumes that people share a consensus on central concerns, such as freedom and protection from harm, and that the government serves important functions in society that no other institution can fulfill. According to the pluralist model power in political systems is widely dispersed through many competing interest groups.
CONFLICT PERSPECTIVES **Key thinkers:** Karl Marx, C. Wright Mills, William Domhoff	Conflict theorists believe that the government serves the interests of the ruling (or capitalist class). Even democratic societies are ruled by a small, interconnected group of people who have power over the politicians who formally run the country.
INTERACTIONIST PERSPECTIVES **Key thinker:** Joseph Gusfield	Interactionists study why people behave the way they do in the political arena. For example, some political initiatives can be explained by the notion of symbolic crusades. Some political groups engage in symbolic crusades in which the recognition of the crusaders' values by the government is at least as important as achieving the instrumental goals of the movement. Political parties rely heavily on symbolism to appeal emotionally to voters because these symbols have the power to bring people together and to unite them behind a political movement.
FEMINIST PERSPECTIVES **Key thinker:** Mary McIntosh	Feminist scholars have highlighted the way in which the state has excluded women from the political process. This exclusion has contributed to the subordination of women in society, a subordination which will continue until women achieve political equality with men.
POSTMODERN PERSPECTIVES **Key thinker:** Michel Foucault	The state does not just control by directing through top-down commands but also by making conformity part of each individual's self-identity. People essentially govern themselves. Governance is also achieved through the actions of non-state actors such as the church and schools.

TIME TO REVIEW

- According to Dahl's pluralist theory, what keeps democratic governments from becoming too powerful?
- Discuss the links between Marx's political theories and power elite theory. In what ways do instrumental and structural Marxists differ in their understanding of the role of the state in maintaining capitalism?
- What did Gusfield mean by the term *symbolic crusade*? Give an example of a symbolic crusade.
- Describe some of the ways in which Canada's political system has discriminated against women.
- Explain how Foucault's term *governmentality* expands the meaning of government.

POLITICS AND GOVERNMENT IN CANADA LO-5

The Canadian political process consists of formal elements, such as the duties of the prime minister and the legislative process, and informal elements, such as the role of political parties in the election process. We will examine these informal elements, including political parties, political socialization, and political participation.

Political Parties

political party An organization whose purpose is to gain and hold legitimate control of government.

A **political party** is an organization whose purpose is to gain and hold legitimate control of government. A political party (1) develops policy positions; (2) educates voters about issues and simplifies the choices for them; and (3) recruits candidates who agree with those policies, helps those candidates win office, and holds the candidates responsible for implementing the party's policy positions. The party that wins the most seats in an election forms the government; the party with the next largest number of seats becomes the official Opposition.

Politics and the People

Why do some people vote and others do not? How do people come to think of themselves as being conservative, moderate, or liberal? Key factors include individuals' political socialization, attitudes, and participation.

political socialization The process by which people learn political attitudes, values, and behaviour.

POLITICAL SOCIALIZATION **Political socialization** is the process by which people learn political attitudes, values, and behaviour. The family is the primary agent of political socialization, and young children tend to learn and hold many of the same opinions as their parents (Burnham, 1983). As they grow older, other agents of socialization, including peers, teachers, and the media, begin to affect children's political beliefs. These other agents may cause political attitudes and values to change, and people may cease to identify with the political party of their parents. Even for adults, political socialization continues through the media, friends, neighbours, and colleagues in the workplace.

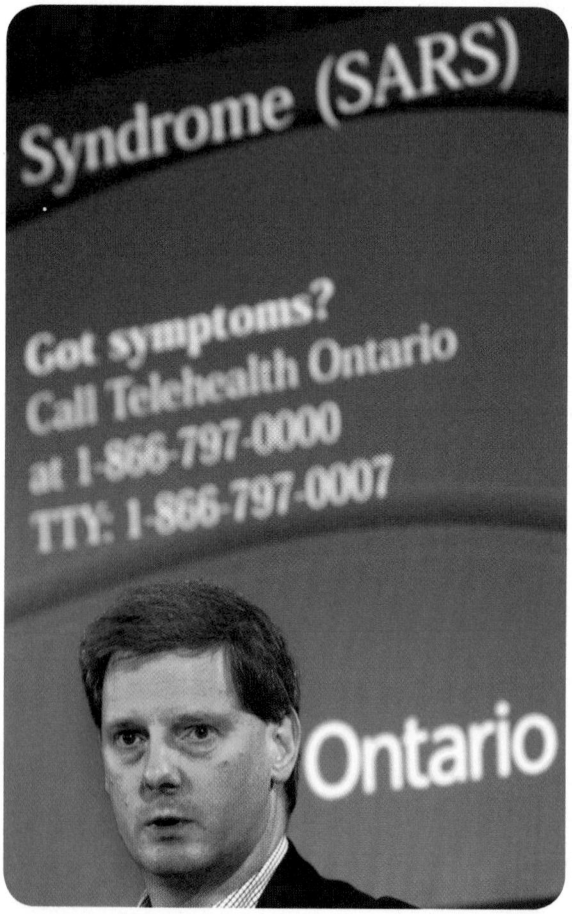

CP/Aaron Harris

The need for federal assistance following the 2003 SARS outbreak in Ontario demonstrates the role that a strong central government can play in our complex society.

POLITICAL ATTITUDES People's socioeconomic status affects their political attitudes, beliefs, and behaviour. For example, individuals who are poor or unable to find employment tend to believe that society has failed them and are therefore often indifferent toward the political system (Zipp, 1985). They tend not to vote because they do not feel that casting a ballot would make any difference in their lives.

Voters tend to select candidates and political parties based on social and economic issues they consider important. *Social issues* are those relating to moral judgments or civil rights, ranging from abortion rights to equal rights for homosexuals. *Economic issues* fall into two broad categories: (1) the amount that should be spent on government programs and (2) the extent to which these programs should redistribute income and assets. Those holding liberal political views believe that governments should intervene to prevent income and assets from becoming concentrated in the hands of even fewer people. The government must redistribute wealth to ensure that everyone gets a fair share. To accomplish this, government raises money through taxes and spends it on social programs. Economic conservatives contend that such programs are unnecessary and counterproductive. They believe that programs financed by tax increases decrease people's incentive to work and to be innovative, and make people dependent on the government.

Social class is correlated with political attitudes. Upper-class people tend to be more conservative on economic issues and more liberal on social issues. They generally favour equality of opportunity but do not want their own income taxed heavily to abolish poverty or to address societal problems that they believe some people bring upon themselves. Most of Canada's social programs, including pensions and medicare, faced opposition from corporate and upper-class interests, and some of these groups led the call for cuts to these programs in the 1990s and more recently for extending the age of qualification. By contrast, Canadians in the lower classes tend to be conservative on social issues, such as capital punishment or abortion rights, but liberal on economic issues, such as increasing the minimum wage and expanding social programs.

Despite these broad tendencies, there is probably less of a connection between voting behaviour and social class in Canada than in many other industrialized countries. The Liberal Party has typically attracted voters from all classes. While the left-wing NDP gets a high proportion of its support from skilled and unskilled labour, more of these workers usually vote for other parties than they do for the New Democrats. And Canadian voters tend to switch parties frequently (Pammett, 1993).

Why is the association between class and voting so low in Canada? Canadian voters appear to be influenced more by individual leaders or particular issues and events than by loyalties to a particular party's philosophy. Also, the mainstream parties have been able to incorporate many of the reforms suggested by more class-based parties into their own platforms. For example, government-funded medical care—which was introduced in Saskatchewan by what is now the New Democratic Party—was subsequently adopted by the Liberals, who implemented it at the national level. The NDP are currently the federal Opposition, so at least in the 2011 election, they were able to move beyond their class-based support.

Finally, politics in Canada is often driven by *regional* interests rather than by class interests. The federal government has given up many of its powers to the provinces over the years, and is under constant pressure to decentralize even further. The separatist movement in Quebec is an obvious example of this pressure, but even federalist governments in Quebec are constantly trying to increase provincial powers. Some Albertans have also been dissatisfied with their role in Confederation. Along with other western Canadians, many Albertans have felt that their region has become economically powerful but that Quebec and Ontario still dominate the federal agenda. Prior to becoming prime minister, Stephen Harper and five colleagues demanded that the premier of Alberta create a "firewall" around Alberta. This Alberta Agenda would remove Alberta from the Canada Pension Plan, set up a system to directly collect Alberta's share of personal income tax, withdraw from RCMP policing contracts and establish an Alberta Provincial Police Force, gain more control over healthcare policy, and reduce the amount of money that oil-rich Alberta contributed to other provinces. This agenda was renewed by the Wildrose Party in the 2012 Alberta election.

Other regions have also expressed dissatisfaction with the federal government. In 2009, George Baker, a Liberal Senate member from Newfoundland and Labrador, raised the idea of forming a separatist party in that province because of a dispute over federal equalization payments. While it is highly unlikely that either Alberta or Newfoundland and Labrador will move toward separation, these examples do show how regional issues are important to many of us.

POLITICAL PARTICIPATION People can actively participate in their government by (1) voting, (2) attending and taking part in political meetings, (3) actively participating in political campaigns, and (4) running for or holding political office.

The voting rate for federal elections declined from 75 percent in 1988 to a record low of 59 percent in 2008 before rising slightly to 61 percent in 2011. The rate is usually slightly higher for provincial elections and much lower for municipal elections. While our 61 percent participation rate means that most Canadians do get involved in the electoral process, in many Western European countries voting rates are normally 80 to 90 percent. On the other hand, the United States has one of the lowest voter participation rates of all Western nations and is usually lower than Canada's. Rates of voting in the United States are slowly increasing, though, and the participation rate was 61 percent in the 2008 U.S. presidential election.

Why do many eligible voters stay away from the polls? Some people do not vote because of illness or lack of transportation. However, most people do not have these reasons. They may be satisfied with the status quo or apathetic and uninformed. Surveys typically show that most Canadians have little knowledge of the candidates or the issues. This makes it difficult for many people to cast a meaningful ballot, so they stay away.

People also do not vote because they feel alienated from politics. Some Canadians believe that government does not care about their views on issues and that only the elites or special interest groups have any influence.

Nevitte (2000) has studied the decline in political participation and concluded that the way in which Canadians relate to their structures of governance has changed over the past three decades. Nevitte believes that the institutions of democratic governance designed in the industrial age no longer reflect the way in which citizens are connected to the state. In addition to low rates of voting, signs of stress in the political systems of some Western democracies include lower levels of attachment to and shifting patterns of support for political parties. In Canada, public confidence in political institutions, particularly in the federal Parliament, has eroded. A majority of people (53 percent) feel that they have little say in the actions of the government (Nevitte, 2000).

Voting rates are particularly low among young Canadians. About 50 percent of people between 18 and 24 voted in the 2011 election, compared with 82 percent for those 65 to 74. Education was also strongly related to voting, particularly among young people. For people age 25 to 34, people with at least a bachelor's degree were more than twice as likely to vote than those with less than high school educations (Uppal and LaRochelle-Côté, 2012).

Why is participation so low among young people? Gidengil and her colleagues have studied this question. Perhaps surprisingly, they found that young people were the most satisfied with democracy in Canada and were less likely than older people to have a negative view of politics and politicians (Gidengil et al., 2004). However, young people paid less attention to politics and were less knowledgeable about political matters. They were also much less likely than older Canadians to feel that they had a duty to vote. An Elections Canada (2012) survey found that young people who did not vote were not interested in politics and felt that political parties did not address their needs and interests. Canada's newest federal political party, the Greens, have particularly targeted young voters who might be attracted to their platform of environmental sustainability.

As their attachment to government declines, citizens are becoming more involved in alternative forms of political behaviour, such as demonstrations and boycotts. The antiglobalization movement is an example of political action outside the regular political system. Many people have become frustrated by the determination of most Western governments to pursue an agenda of globalized free trade through agreements, such as the North American Free Trade Agreement (NAFTA), and through the rules of the World Trade Organization (WTO). These agreements limit the power of individual countries to control many of their own industrial and trade policies, and citizens have little control over the globalized organizations that now have this power. In response, thousands of activists from around the globe have organized major protests during meetings of world leaders. In Canada, we have seen these demonstrations during global political summit meetings in Toronto, Quebec City, Ottawa, and Calgary.

These demonstrations and other protests, such as the Occupy movement in 2011, show that many people are still interested in political issues but feel that the political system does not respond to their concerns. Political parties face the challenge of finding ways of reconnecting people to the political process. Statistics Canada has found that while young adults were less likely than other Canadians to vote, they were more likely than older people to engage in other forms of political behaviour, such as looking for information about a political issue, volunteering for a political party, signing a petition or boycotting a product, attending a public meeting, or participating in a protest or march (Milan, 2005). To find out more about the political impact of new media, see Box 20.2 at **www.nelson.com/sociologyinourtimes6e**.

TIME TO REVIEW

- What role is played by political parties in our system of government?
- What are the most important forms of political socialization?
- Discuss some of the factors that are correlated with Canadians' voting behaviour.
- How have social media affected politics?

THE CANADIAN PRESS/Jacques Boissinot

Many young people have rejected the formal political process because they do not believe that politicians respond to their concerns. Some have turned to alternative forms of political action. These demonstrators marched the streets of Toronto to protest against the G20 meeting in 2010.

MAJOR POLITICAL ISSUES IN CANADA: SEPARATISM AND ABORIGINAL SELF-GOVERNMENT

Quebec separatism and the role of Aboriginal governments are long-standing issues in Canada. In 2012, the possibility of separatism was a major issue in the Quebec provincial election and Aboriginal governments were refusing to allow pipelines and resource companies on their traditional territories.

The Quiet Revolution and Quebec Nationalism

Because of the dissatisfaction of Quebec nationalists, constitutional matters have been prominent in Canada. Events from the early 1960s onward set the stage for the very close results of the 1995 referendum on separation. Nearly two decades after the referendum, these factors still play a major role in Canada's political, economic, and social life

Constitutional crises in the 1980s and 1990s were set in motion by Quebec's Quiet Revolution. Before 1960, Quebec had been a very traditional society. The Roman Catholic Church and the family were at the core of French Canadian society, while economic power in the province was in the hands of English Canadians. However, in a brief time, Quebec dramatically transformed itself into a secular, urban society with a modern educational system and strong health and welfare programs. A new sense of nationalism was used as a core ideology to justify the expanded role of the state. This nationalism was clearly expressed in the 1962 Quebec Liberal campaign slogan *maîtres chez nous* ("masters in our own house"). Economic and social reform would strengthen French culture. The state would replace the Church at the heart of Quebec society. The Quebec government began demanding, and receiving, more control over matters traditionally managed by the federal government.

During this period, language became increasingly important. English was the language of business in the province, and French Canadian owners and managers were rare. In a series of legislative steps beginning in the 1960s, the provincial government moved to ensure that French became the language of business. The goal was stated clearly in the White Paper (a government policy document) that preceded a major piece of language legislation, Bill 101, which was adopted in 1977:

> The Quebec that we wish to build will be essentially French. The fact that the majority of the population is French will be distinctly visible: at work, in communications, in the country . . . . the use of French will not be generalized simply to hide the predominance of foreign powers over Francophones; this usage will accompany, will symbolize a reconquest by the Francophone majority of Quebec of the hold which returns to it on the levers of the economy. (cited in Cook, 1995:133)

By any measure, the Quiet Revolution was a success. Legislation now protects the French language in Quebec. Regulations requiring immigrant children to attend French language schools and restrictions on the use of English on commercial signs have reinforced the dominant role of the French language in Quebec. French-speaking Quebeckers have gained control over the economy and other major social institutions, including culture, politics, and government.

While the transformation of Quebec was remarkably rapid, it was not quick enough for some. Nationalist groups, which began to emerge in the 1960s, saw independence as the only way Quebec could fulfill its destiny. At the same time, another vision was offered by Quebeckers, including Pierre Trudeau, who felt that Quebec's aspirations could best be fulfilled within Canada. For Trudeau, cultural survival did not depend on political sovereignty. A strong federal government that actively promoted bilingualism was the best guarantee that French would survive in a predominantly English North America. As prime minister, Trudeau, in 1969, was instrumental in passing the *Official Languages Act,* which made the federal public service bilingual. This provided opportunities for francophones and ensured that Canadians in all parts of the country could receive services in either language. The government also encouraged French immersion schools in English Canada.

These changes were resisted by some English Canadians. Consider matters from the perspective of those opposed to bilingualism. As Quebec was becoming more autonomous and less bilingual, the need for bilingualism was being promoted throughout the rest of the country (Dyck, 2004). Unilingual anglophone civil servants had to learn French if they wished to be promoted, and bilingualism was a major focus of the federal political agenda. Many felt that Quebec was blackmailing the federal government at the expense of the other provinces. With extreme Quebec nationalists on one side and English-speaking Canadians who were tired of "having French forced down their throats" on the other, the stage was set for several decades of constitutional debate.

After the 1995 referendum, which the separatists lost by a narrow margin of 50.6 percent to 49.4 percent, separatist sentiment gradually waned in Quebec. In a gesture to Quebeckers in 2006, the

Conservatives under Prime Minister Stephen Harper passed a motion in Parliament stating that the Québécois constitute a nation within a united Canada. However, separatist sentiment remains fairly strong in Quebec and rises and falls depending on the political issues of the day.

According to the 2011 Census, Quebecers now make up 23.6 percent of Canada's population, down from 28.9 percent in 1951 and 35.9 percent in 1867. This population shift means that other regions, particularly the West, will have more members in Parliament and Quebec will have less political influence. These changes mean that the future of Quebec will continue to be a major political issue.

Aboriginal Self-Government

Canada's constitutional debate has largely focused on the role of our "two founding peoples"—the English and the French. Aboriginal peoples have objected to this view of Canadian history. Anthropologist Olive Dickason, a Métis, has pointed out that when the Europeans first came to North America, 55 First Nations were already on the continent. Each First Nation had its own government, territory, culture, and language. But Aboriginal objections to the notion of two founding peoples do not focus only on the historical issue of which groups were here first. The more important concern is which groups will have political power in the future. Quebec claims a special status that entitles it to certain powers to govern its own people, and also certain rights within the federation, such as having three Quebec members of the Supreme Court. Aboriginal peoples also claim a unique status based on their position as Canada's First Nations and have pursued their own right to self-government.

The self-government issue is complex and requires some background knowledge. In 1763, the British government issued a royal proclamation that formed the basis for the negotiation of treaties with Aboriginal groups. Without a background in European law, Aboriginal peoples did not realize that title to the land had passed to the Crown. They were, however, still entitled to the use and benefit of that land through their "aboriginal title" (Boldt, 1993). Following Confederation, Aboriginal peoples came under the control of the federal government. The mechanism for this control, the *Indian Act,* was passed in 1876 and gave government bureaucrats almost total control over Aboriginal peoples. The act even went so far as to define a "person" as "an individual other than an Indian" (Hamilton and Sinclair, 1991).

The consequences of the *Indian Act* were profound: Aboriginal children were forced to attend residential schools (which meant that generations of children were not raised by their families); traditional religious practices were restricted; Aboriginal people did not fully control their own land; and the government imposed a "pass system" that restricted the right of Aboriginal peoples to travel off their reserves. Status Indians did not have full voting rights in federal elections until 1960. As Menno Boldt has observed, contemporary "Indian powerlessness has its roots in Canada's Indian policies" (1993:xvii).

In the 1960s, the federal government began to review its policies concerning Aboriginal peoples. A White Paper, tabled in 1969, proposed assimilation of Aboriginal peoples. Treaties were to be dropped, reserves were to become like neighbouring non-Aboriginal communities, and Aboriginal rights and Aboriginal land titles were to be discarded. The "Aboriginal problem" would disappear if Aboriginal people became, in Pierre Trudeau's words, "Canadians as all other Canadians" (Boldt, 1993). Reaction to this paper marked a watershed in Aboriginal politics. A national campaign, which ultimately forced the government to drop its proposals, became a countrywide movement and several national organizations, including the Assembly of First Nations, were formed (Hamilton and Sinclair, 1991). Rather than accepting the federal government's assimilationist model, Aboriginal leaders embraced nationalism. Self-government, Aboriginal rights, and land claims became the rallying points of the movement.

Although some Aboriginal leaders, particularly among the Mohawks, view their bands as separate nations that have sovereign control over their lands, most proponents of Aboriginal self-government take a more limited view. They understand that their First Nations status

Two of Canada's most influential Aboriginal leaders are Shawn Atleo, Chief of the Assembly of First Nations, and Justice Murray Sinclair, Chair of the Indian Residential Schools Truth and Reconciliation Commission.

gives them the "inherent" right to self-government within the Canadian federation (Boldt, 1993). They feel that their status as Canada's first people, who were never conquered and who signed voluntary treaties with the Crown, entitles them to the right of self-determination and to protection of their culture and customs. These rights are not *granted* by the Canadian government but are inherently theirs. On the other hand, the federal and the provincial governments have insisted that the right to self-determination could be extended only as powers delegated to Aboriginal people by government through legislation or constitutional change. Further, governments would only grant the same powers that are now held by municipal governments, rather than the much broader powers sought by Aboriginal peoples.

It is difficult to predict where the current process of ending the colonial rule over Aboriginals will lead. One major change occurred in 1999, when Inuit took over government of the newly created Nunavut Territory, encompassing more than 350,000 square km of land in the Eastern Arctic. Another major move toward self-government came in 1999 with the signing of a treaty with the Nisga'a people, who had been seeking recognition of Aboriginal title to their land for more than a hundred years. This treaty gave the Nisga'a a large land settlement in northwestern British Columbia and significant powers of self-government similar to those of municipal governments.

While the federal government accepted the inherent nature of Aboriginals' right to self-government in 1995, the future form of self-government is not at all clear—not even among Aboriginal peoples. Many problems must also be solved along the way, including decisions about how the growing number of urban Aboriginals will be included and the applicability of the *Canadian Charter of Rights and Freedoms* to Aboriginal communities. The possible separation of Quebec also creates some interesting issues. While the separatists argue strongly for their right to self-determination and their recognition as a "people," they do not accept that Aboriginal people in the resource-rich northern part of Quebec have the same right to separate.

BOX 20.3 SOCIOLOGY IN GLOBAL PERSPECTIVE

Terrorism in Canada

Some of you may have been surprised to read about political terrorism in Canada in the chapter introduction. While most Canadians rightly feel that Canada is a very peaceful country, there have been a significant number of terrorist incidents here.

Kellett (2004) studied acts of terrorism that occurred in Canada between 1960 and 1992. Defining terrorism as "comprising acts of serious violence, planned and executed clandestinely, and committed with clear intention to achieve political ends" (2004:286), Kellett found more than 400 incidents and 13 deaths during this period. While this might seem like a large number, it is much lower than in many European countries, where groups like the Irish Republican Army and the Basque separatist group ETA have been active for many years.

Almost 85 percent of the incidents involved Canadian-based groups attacking domestic targets, while the remainder involved either foreign terrorists or foreign targets in Canada. Incidents such as the Air India bombing, in which an explosive was put on a plane in Canada but detonated outside the country, were excluded from the database. Terrorism incidents peaked in the 1960s, when several secessionist groups were active in Quebec and the Sons of Freedom Doukhobor sect was engaged in bombings and other acts of terrorism in British Columbia. These groups accounted for most of the terrorist attacks in the database.

You read earlier about the role played by Pierre Vallières in events in Quebec. Terrorist acts began in the early 1960s and ended about a decade later. Kellett estimates that only about a hundred people were ever members of the FLQ. Most FLQ members were young and single, and many were students. Like many contemporary terrorist groups, members financed their political activities by engaging in crimes, such as credit card fraud and robbery.

While the FLQ had similarities to other terrorist organizations, the Sons of Freedom Doukhobors were unique. Members of the Sons of Freedom, one branch of the pacifist Christian Doukhobor group that came to Canada in the late 19th century, rejected any government involvement in their lives. They refused to send their children to school, pay taxes, or register births and deaths. While most other Doukhobors eventually accepted the role of government, some members of the Sons of Freedom sect did not. There were many clashes between sect members and the government, and in the 1950s the B.C. government took children away from their communities and forced them to live in residential schools until they were 15 years of age. The protests of the sect against the government and against other Doukhobors between 1960 and 1962 resulted in 107 incidents of arson and bombings of public facilities, such as schools, power lines, bridges, and the property of other Doukhobors. The terrorist acts ended when many of the perpetrators were imprisoned.

The only other category that had a substantial number of terrorist incidents between 1960 and 1989 was that of emigré groups. These included attacks by anti-Castro Cubans on Cuban targets in Canada, attacks on Turks in Canada by Armenian groups, and several attacks by Sikh militants supporting the formation of an independent Sikh state in India.

While Kellett's research did not include terrorist attacks that were supported in Canada but took place elsewhere, several of these have occurred. For example, a disaster was narrowly averted in 1999 when a U.S. customs agent apprehended Ahmed Ressam as he attempted to cross into the United States from Canada with a car loaded with explosives. Ressam, allegedly a member of a Montreal-based al-Qaeda cell, intended to mark the millennium by detonating a car bomb at the Los Angeles airport on January 1, 2000. And a number of terrorist groups, including the Sri Lankan Tamil Tigers, have collected funds in Canada from supporters who have emigrated from their home countries.

In 2006, 18 men were arrested in the Toronto area on charges of planning terrorist attacks in Canada. They allegedly planned to detonate several truck bombs, storm the Parliament Buildings, and behead Prime Minister Harper. They held training camps north of Toronto (which featured the uniquely Canadian touch of visits to Tim Hortons along with lessons in using firearms and discussions of jihad) and tried to order several tonnes of ammonium nitrate to use in their truck bombs. They were arrested before they could put any of their plans into action. Several have been convicted and the group's leader received a life sentence.

Jacques Rose, Paul Rose, Francis Simard, and Bernard Lortie were the members of the Chénier cell of the FLQ who kidnapped and murdered Quebec cabinet minister Pierre Laporte in 1970.

POLITICAL ISSUES FOR THE FUTURE

Economic agreements, such as the North American Free Trade Agreement and the European Union, are helping to create a single market and will inevitably lead to closer relationships between the countries involved. At the same time, budget cuts have reduced the role of governments in providing services to their citizens and globalization of financial markets has dramatically reduced the ability of governments to control their own economic destinies. Many economic decisions are made by international organizations, such as the World Trade Organization and the World Intellectual Property Organization, rather than by national governments. Multinational corporations, some of which are larger economic entities than many of the world's countries, also have an impact on global economic policy that may not reflect the interests of any nation-state. These developments have led many people to ask if the governments of modern nation-states will become obsolete. People have little influence over multinational corporations and international trade agreements. People can vote only within their own countries, yet many of the decisions that affect their lives and their futures are made outside their borders.

The nature of the new challenges facing many governments makes it increasingly difficult for them to control events. For example, how do nations deal with terrorism within their borders, such as the 2001 attacks on the World Trade Center and the Pentagon? In the aftermath of these tragedies, governments' responsibility for protecting citizens but not violating their basic freedoms has been widely examined in national debates that inevitably will continue into the future.

Likewise, how are nations to deal with the proliferation of arms and nuclear weapons in other countries? Will some of the missiles and warheads fall into the hands of terrorists? What should be done with the masses of nuclear waste being produced? Who can control global pollution? No easy answers are forthcoming, but without some form of effective international control, it will be impossible to ensure that future generations are protected from environmental threats, such as global warming and water and air pollution.

While international agreements are necessary, it is possible that these agreements will be reached in different ways and will involve different participants from those in the past. The way in which hundreds of groups came together with governments to create the treaty banning land mines provides a model for involving more grassroots organizations in such negotiations. The Internet has made it much easier for widely scattered organizations to work effectively together.

Another issue that will continue to trouble many countries is nationalism. Can Canada make an accommodation with Quebec? How will European countries adapt to the loss of national powers within the European Community? Will groups continue to make war to support their nationalistic aspirations (Box 20.4)? The issues surrounding nationalism must be resolved if the world is to become more peaceful.

Finally, Canadians, particularly young people, have been losing interest in the traditional political process. Many of us are more concerned with special interests and regional concerns than with broader national questions. What will result from this fragmentation of political activity? Are leaders like Prime Minister Stephen Harper, who wanted to build a firewall around Alberta, or former Newfoundland and Labrador Premier Danny Williams, who took down Canadian flags because of a financial dispute he was having with the federal government, helping to build a society where people can work together to face issues such as global warming and globalization? Will we be able to face the dramatic challenges that lie ahead if we identify as Quebeckers or as Albertans rather than as Canadians, or if our ethnic or religious identities are more important to us than our common bonds as Canadians?

BOX 20.4 SOCIOLOGY IN GLOBAL PERSPECTIVE

Nationalism Around the World

Historian Ramsay Cook has observed, "Everyone belongs somewhere. Yet much of the conflict in the history . . . of mankind has been about who belongs where" (1995:9). Nationalism, he says, is a "doctrine asserting that humanity is naturally divided into groups with common characteristics and that by virtue of those collective traits they have a right to exercise control—sovereignty—over the particular place" (1995:9). Quebec separatists hold that the Québécois constitute a "people" who must have sovereignty over their territory if their destiny is to be fulfilled. The desire for separation from Canada in Quebec is a manifestation of nationalism.

Quebec nationalists are not the only people trying to take control of what they see as their territory. Punjabis in India, Basque separatists in Spain, and Palestinians in the Middle East are some of the hundreds of nationalist groups. Justification for their claims is based upon God, language, culture, or history. However, what ultimately decides things is power. This power may be political—the Czech Republic and Slovakia separated after a democratic vote—but more typically it is military, as with the Iraqis and the Turks who have forcefully prevented the Kurds from establishing a separate homeland.

Nationalism can be a unifying force. Many countries, including Germany and Italy, were formed in the late 19th century through the unification of smaller states with similar language and cultural backgrounds. Diverse groups were brought together under a common flag.

However, nationalism can be divisive—and often deadly. Societies based on national identity can become intolerant of those who do not share the same ethnicity, religion, or culture. Millions have died at the hands of oppressive nationalists. Historically, most wars were fought between countries; today, they are almost all fought within countries. Wars, such as the American-led invasion of Iraq, are the exception, while internal conflicts, such as the genocides in Sudan and Eastern Congo, are much more common and much more deadly in terms of lives lost (www.genocidewatch.org).

Successful nationalist movements often carry with them the seeds of their own destruction. Yugoslavia is a case in point. Prior to 1989, the country had been held together by the communist regime. However, when the communist domination of Eastern Europe ended, the Croats and Muslims in Yugoslavia decided to break away from the Serb-dominated communist government and created the independent states of Croatia and Bosnia-Herzegovina. After years of living within the common boundaries of Yugoslavia, each of the new countries had significant ethnic minorities within its borders. These minorities, in turn, claimed their independence and the ensuing carnage cost hundreds of thousands of lives through *ethnic cleansing*, which is a chilling solution to the minority problem—you kill or expel every man, woman, and child of a different religious or cultural background who has the misfortune of remaining within your territory. Internal conflicts such as these can be extremely complex. In the former Yugoslavia, each of the major groups—Serbs, Croats, and the Muslims of Bosnia-Herzegovina—participated in ethnic cleansing in the areas under its control.

As large nation-states become less relevant in an era of globalization, they lose their ability to unify. People search for a collective identity at the local level. Unfortunately, this identity is often grounded on exclusion—those who are not "like us" are not tolerated. Where this will lead is uncertain. It is difficult to imagine the nationalist process continuing indefinitely. Fewer than 200 countries now exist; if every linguistic group became a nation, there would be about 8000 countries.

TIME TO REVIEW

- Explain how the relationship between Quebec and the rest of Canada has evolved over the past two centuries.
- What are some of the political issues that have affected the lives of Canada's Aboriginal people?
- How has terrorism affected Canadians?
- Discuss how nationalism has led to conflict over the past two decades.

20 VISUAL SUMMARY

KEY TERMS

authoritarian political system A political system controlled by rulers who deny popular participation in government (p. 576).

authority Power that people accept as legitimate rather than coercive (p. 572).

charismatic authority Power legitimized on the basis of a leader's exceptional personal qualities or accomplishments (p. 573).

democracy A political system in which the people hold the ruling power, either directly or through elected representatives (p. 577).

elite model A view of society in which power in political systems is concentrated in the hands of a small group of elites and the masses are relatively powerless (p. 579).

government The formal organization that has the legal and political authority to regulate the relationships among members of a society and between the society and those outside its borders (p. 572).

monarchy A political system in which power resides in one person or family and is passed from generation to generation through lines of inheritance (p. 576).

pluralist model An analysis of political systems that views power as widely dispersed throughout many competing interest groups (p. 578).

political party An organization whose purpose is to gain and hold legitimate control of government (p. 586).

LO-1 Discuss the meaning of power.

Power is the ability of persons or groups to carry out their will even when opposed by others.

THE CANADIAN PRESS/Jake Wright

THE CANADIAN PRESS/Tom Hanson

LO-2 Understand the relationship between power and politics.

Politics is the social institution through which power is acquired and exercised by some people or groups. Government is the formal organization that has the legal and political authority to regulate the relationships among members in a society.

LO-3 Explain the three types of authority that leaders can possess.

Max Weber identified three types of authority. Charismatic authority is based on a leader's exceptional personal qualities. Traditional authority is based on respect for custom. Rational-legal authority is based on law or written rules and regulations.

AP Photo/CP, Adrian Wyld

LO-4 Identify the four main types of political systems.

AP Photo/David Cheskin, Pool

There are four main types of contemporary political systems. In a monarchy, one person is the ruler of the nation based on heredity. In authoritarian systems, rulers tolerate little or no public opposition and generally cannot be removed from office by legal means. In totalitarian systems, the state seeks to regulate all aspects of society and monopolize all societal resources in order to control completely both public and private life. In a democracy, the powers of the government are derived from the consent of all the people.

Courtesy of Shawn Atleo

LO-5 Consider the main political issues facing Canadians.

Some of these issues include the powers of the provinces (particularly Quebec) within the federation, the evolution of First Nations power and governance, and the reluctance of many Canadians to participate in the political process.

APPLICATION QUESTIONS

1. Who is ultimately responsible for decisions and policies that are made in a democracy such as Canada—the people or their elected representatives? Discuss.
2. In Canada's parliamentary system, politicians are elected by the people but normally must follow the policies of their party. Discuss how this affects the democratic system. What are the advantages and disadvantages of this party discipline? Do you think this system needs to change? Why or why not?
3. In what ways does your school (or workplace) reflect a pluralist or elite model of power and decision making?
4. Do you locate yourself politically on the left or on the right? How does this affect the way you look at political issues?
5. In what ways has a recent political decision affected your current life or your future? How do you see politics reflected in your everyday life?
6. Go to the Genocide Watch website (www.genocidewatch.org). What do you think the world community could do to intervene in these tragic situations?

political socialization The process by which people learn political attitudes, values, and behaviour (p. 586).

politics The social institution through which power is acquired and exercised by some people and groups (p. 572).

power elite A term devised by C. Wright Mills for a structure composed of leaders at the top of business, the executive branch of the federal government, and the military (p. 579).

rational-legal authority Power legitimized by law or written rules and regulations. (p. 574).

routinization of charisma A term for the process by which charismatic authority is succeeded by a bureaucracy controlled by a rationally established authority or by a combination of traditional and bureaucratic authority (p. 574).

special interest groups Political coalitions made up of individuals or groups that share a specific interest they wish to protect or advance with the help of the political system (p. 578).

state The political entity that possesses a legitimate monopoly over the use of force within its territory to achieve its goals (p. 572).

totalitarian political system A political system in which the state seeks to regulate all aspects of people's public and private lives (p. 576).

traditional authority Power that is legitimized by respect for long-standing custom (p. 574).

KEY FIGURES

Archive Photos/Getty Images

C. Wright Mills (1916–1962) Mills was one of the most important 20th century U.S. social theorists. Perhaps his best-known work described how the United States was governed by a power elite made up of business, political, and military leaders. This work challenged the view that America was a society in which people from all classes influenced government policy.

Courtesy of G. William Domhoff

G. William Domhoff (b. 1936) Domhoff's 1967 book *Who Rules America?*—which has been revised and updated several times, including in 2010 and 2013—was an important contribution to the literature on power and politics. Domhoff concluded that America was led by a ruling class of business owners who financed political campaigns and were able to have their interests reflected in education and policy.

Joseph Gusfield (b. 1923) Gusfield contributed the insight that political legislation may serve a symbolic function. That is, it was not necessarily passed to change people's behaviour but rather to show some groups that their views were recognized as being important to the government.

absolute poverty A level of economic deprivation in which people do not have the means to secure the basic necessities of life. *(p. 227)*

achieved status A social position a person assumes voluntarily as a result of personal choice, merit, or direct effort. *(p. 120)*

activity theory The proposition that people tend to shift gears in late middle age and find substitutes for previous statuses, roles, and activities. *(p. 524)*

age stratification The inequalities, differences, segregation, or conflict between age groups. *(p. 523)*

ageism Prejudice and discrimination against people on the basis of age, particularly when they are older. *(p. 518)*

agents of socialization The persons, groups, or institutions that teach us what we need to know to participate in society. *(p. 96)*

aggregate A collection of people who happen to be in the same place at the same time but have little else in common. *(p. 144)*

aging The physical, psychological, and social processes associated with growing older. *(p. 510)*

alienation A feeling of powerlessness and estrangement from other people and from oneself. *(p. 13)*

altruism Behaviour intended to help others and done without any expectation of personal benefit. *(p. 31)*

analysis The process through which data are organized so that comparisons can be made and conclusions drawn. *(p. 37)*

animism The belief that plants, animals, or other elements of the natural world are endowed with spirits or life forces that have an impact on events in society. *(p. 424)*

anomie Émile Durkheim's term for a condition in which social control becomes ineffective as a result of the loss of shared values and a sense of purpose in society. *(p. 12)*

anticipatory socialization The process by which knowledge and skills are learned for future roles. *(p. 108)*

ascribed status A social position conferred on a person at birth or received involuntarily later in life. *(p. 120)*

asexual An absence of sexual desire toward either sex. *(p. 340)*

assimilation A process by which members of subordinate racial and ethnic groups become absorbed into the dominant culture. *(p. 283)*

authoritarian personality A personality type characterized by excessive conformity, submissiveness to authority, intolerance, insecurity, a high level of superstition, and rigid, stereotypic thinking. *(p. 278)*

authoritarian political system A political system controlled by rulers who deny popular participation in government. *(p. 576)*

authority Power that people accept as legitimate rather than coercive. *(p. 572)*

bilateral descent A system of tracing descent through both the mother's and father's sides of the family. *(p. 375)*

bourgeoisie Karl Marx's term for the class comprised of those who own and control the means of production. *(p. 12)*

bureaucracy An organizational model characterized by a hierarchy of authority, a clear division of labour, explicit rules and procedures, and impersonality in personnel matters. *(p. 155)*

bureaucratic personality A psychological construct that describes those workers who are more concerned with following correct procedures than they are with doing the job correctly. *(p. 160)*

capitalism An economic system characterized by private ownership of the means of production, from which personal profits can be derived through market competition and without government intervention. *(p. 544)*

capitalist class (bourgeoisie) Karl Marx's term for those who own the means of production. *(p. 214)*

caste system A system of social inequality in which people's status is permanently determined at birth based on their parents' ascribed characteristics. *(p. 209)*

category A number of people who may never have met one another but who share a similar characteristic. *(p. 144)*

central city The densely populated centre of a metropolis. *(p. 21-19)*

charismatic authority Power legitimized on the basis of a leader's exceptional personal qualities or accomplishments. *(p. 573)*

chronological age A person's age based on date of birth. *(p. 510)*

church A large, bureaucratically organized religious body that tends to seek accommodation with the larger society in order to maintain some degree of control over it. *(p. 434)*

civil disobedience Nonviolent action that seeks to change a policy or law by refusing to comply with it. *(p. 22-6)*

class conflict Karl Marx's term for the struggle between the capitalist class and the working class. *(p. 12)*

class system A type of stratification based on the ownership and control of resources and on the type of work people do. *(p. 210)*

cohabitation The sharing of a household by a couple who live together without being legally married. *(p. 380)*

cohort A category of people born within a specified period in time or who share some specified characteristic. *(p. 512)*

collective behaviour Voluntary, often spontaneous activity that is engaged in by a large number of people and typically violates dominant-group norms and values. *(p. 22-4)*

commonsense knowledge A form of knowing that guides ordinary conduct in everyday life. *(p. 4)*

complete observation Research in which the investigator systematically observes a social process, but does not take part in it. *(p. 46)*

conflict perspectives The sociological approach that views groups in society as engaged in a continuous power struggle for control of scarce resources. *(p. 18)*

conformity The process of maintaining or changing behaviour to comply with the norms established by a society, subculture, or other group. *(p. 150)*

contingent work Part-time or temporary work. *(p. 558)*

control group Subjects in an experiment who are not exposed to the independent variable, but later are compared to subjects in the experimental group. *(p. 39)*

core nations According to world-systems analysis, dominant capitalist centres characterized by high levels of industrialization and urbanization, as well as a high degree of control over the world economy. *(p. 261)*

corporate crime An illegal act committed by corporate employees on behalf of the corporation and with its support. *(p. 187)*

corporations Large-scale organizations that have legal powers, such as the ability to enter into contracts and buy and sell property, separate from their individual owners. *(p. 544)*

counterculture A group that strongly rejects dominant societal values and norms and seeks alternative lifestyles. *(p. 78)*

credentialism A process of social selection in which class advantage and social status are linked to the possession of academic qualifications. *(p. 407)*

crime An act that violates criminal law and is punishable by fines, jail terms, and other sanctions. *(p. 175)*

crowd A relatively large number of people who are in one another's immediate vicinity. *(p. 22-4)*

crude birth rate The number of live births per 1000 people in a population in a given year. *(p. 21-4)*

crude death rate The number of deaths per 1000 people in a population in a given year. *(p. 21-4)*

cult A religious group with practices and teachings outside the dominant cultural and religious traditions of a society. *(p. 435)*

cultural capital Pierre Bourdieu's term for people's social assets, including their values, beliefs, attitudes, and competencies in language and culture. *(p. 404)*

cultural imperialism The extensive infusion of one nation's culture into other nations. *(p. 81)* A process whereby powerful countries use the media to spread values and ideas that dominate and even destroy other cultures, and local cultural values are replaced by the cultural values of the dominant country. *(p. 501)*

cultural lag William Ogburn's term for a gap between the technical development of a society (material culture) and its moral and legal institutions (nonmaterial culture). *(p. 74)*

cultural relativism The belief that the behaviours and customs of any culture must be viewed and analyzed by the culture's own standards. *(p. 80)*

cultural transmission The process by which children and recent immigrants become acquainted with the dominant cultural beliefs, values, norms, and accumulated knowledge of a society. *(p. 400)*

cultural universals Customs and practices that occur across all societies. *(p. 66)*

culture The knowledge, language, values, customs, and material objects that are passed from person to person and from one generation to the next in a human group or society. *(p. 61)*

culture shock The disorientation that people feel when they encounter cultures radically different from their own. *(p. 78)*

cybercrime Offences where a computer is the object of a crime or the tool used to commit a crime. *(p. 186)*

date rape Acts in which a date or boyfriend forced or attempted to force any type of sexual activity through threats or use of violence. *(p. 357)*

dating violence A term used for various forms of sexually and nonsexually assaultive behaviours that occur within dating relationships. *(p. 357)*

deductive approach Research in which the investigator begins with a theory and then collects information and data to test the theory. *(p. 34)*

democracy A political system in which the people hold the ruling power, either directly or through elected representatives. *(p. 577)*

democratic socialism An economic and political system that combines private ownership of some of the means of production, governmental distribution of some essential goods and services, and free elections. *(p. 548)*

demographic transition The process by which some societies have moved from high birth and death rates to relatively low birth and death rates as a result of technological development. *(p. 21-17)*

demography The subfield of sociology that examines population size, composition, and distribution. *(p. 21-3)*

dependency theory The perspective that global poverty can at least partially be attributed to the fact that low-income countries have been exploited by high-income countries. *(p. 260)*

dependent variable A variable that is assumed to depend on or be caused by one or more other (independent) variables. *(p. 35)*

descriptive study Research that attempts to describe social reality or provide facts about some group, practice, or event. *(p. 33)*

deviance Any behaviour, belief, or condition that violates cultural norms in the society or group in which it occurs. *(p. 174)*

differential association theory The proposition that individuals have a greater tendency to deviate from societal norms when they frequently associate with persons who favour deviance over conformity. *(p. 177)*

diffusion The transmission of cultural items or social practices from one group or society to another. *(p. 74)*

disability A physical or health condition that reduces a person's ability to perform tasks he or she would normally do at a given stage of life and that may result in stigmatization or discrimination against the person. *(p. 465)*

discovery The process of learning about something previously unknown or unrecognized. *(p. 74)*

discrimination Actions or practices of dominant group members (or their representatives) that have a harmful impact on members of a subordinate group. *(p. 278)*

disengagement theory The proposition that older persons make a normal and healthy adjustment to aging when they detach themselves from their social roles and prepare for their eventual death. *(p. 523)*

dramaturgical analysis The study of social interaction that compares everyday life to a theatrical presentation. *(p. 132)*

dual-earner families Families in which both partners are in the labour force. *(p. 387)*

dyad A group consisting of two members. *(p. 149)*

dysfunctions A term referring to the undesirable consequences of any element of a society. *(p. 17)*

economy The social institution that ensures the maintenance of society through the production, distribution, and consumption of goods and services. *(p. 538)*

education The social institution responsible for the systematic transmission of knowledge, skills, and cultural values within a formally organized structure. *(p. 400)*

egalitarian family A family structure in which both partners share power and authority equally. *(p. 375)*

ego According to Sigmund Freud, the rational, reality-oriented component of personality that imposes restrictions on the innate pleasure-seeking drives of the id. *(p. 105)*

elder abuse A term used to describe physical abuse, psychological abuse, financial exploitation, and medical abuse or neglect of people age 65 or older. *(p. 521)*

elite model A view of society in which power in political systems is concentrated in the hands of a small group of elites and the masses are relatively powerless. *(p. 579)*

emigration The movement of people out of a geographic area to take up residency elsewhere. *(p. 21-5)*

employment equity A strategy to eliminate the effects of discrimination and to make employment opportunities available to groups who have been excluded. *(p. 321)*

environmental racism The belief that a disproportionate number of hazardous facilities (including industries such as waste disposal and treatment and chemical plants) are placed in low-income areas populated largely by people of colour. *(p. 22-17)*

epidemics Sudden, significant increases in the numbers of people contracting a disease. *(p. 461)*

ethnic group A collection of people distinguished, by others or by themselves, primarily on the basis of cultural or nationality characteristics. *(p. 274)*

ethnic pluralism The coexistence of a variety of distinct racial and ethnic groups within one society. *(p. 284)*

ethnocentrism The tendency to regard one's own culture and group as the standard—and thus superior—whereas all other groups are seen as inferior. *(p. 80)*

ethnomethodology The study of the commonsense knowledge that people use to understand the situations in which they find themselves. *(p. 131)*

experiment A research method involving a carefully designed test in which the researcher studies the impact of certain variables on subjects' attitudes or behaviour. *(p. 39)*

experimental group Subjects in an experiment who are exposed to the independent variable. *(p. 39)*

explanatory study Research that attempts to explain relationships and to provide information on why certain events do or do not occur. *(p. 33)*

extended family A family unit composed of relatives in addition to parents and children who live in the same household. *(p. 372)*

fad A temporary but widely copied activity enthusiastically followed by large numbers of people. *(p. 22-10)*

faith Unquestioning belief that does not require proof or scientific evidence. *(p. 422)*

families we choose Social arrangements that include intimate relationships between couples and close familial relationships with other couples, as well as with other adults and children. *(p. 370)*

family A relationship in which people live together with commitment, form an economic unit and care for any young, and consider their identity to be significantly attached to the group. *(p. 371)*

family of orientation The family into which a person is born and in which early socialization usually takes place. *(p. 372)*

family of procreation The family that a person forms by having or adopting children. *(p. 372)*

fashion A currently valued style of behaviour, thinking, or appearance. *(p. 22-10)*

feminism The belief that women and men are equal and that they should be valued equally and have equal rights. *(p. 326)*

feminist perspectives The sociological approach that focuses on the significance of gender in understanding and explaining inequalities that exist between men and women in the household, in the paid labour force, and in the realms of politics, law, and culture. *(p. 20)*

feminization of poverty The trend in which women are disproportionately represented among individuals living in poverty. *(p. 230)*

fertility The actual level of childbearing for an individual or a population. *(p. 21-3)*

field research The study of social life in its natural setting: observing and interviewing people where they live, work, and play. *(p. 46)*

folkways Informal norms or everyday customs that may be violated without serious consequences within a particular culture. *(p. 72)*

formal education Learning that takes place within an academic setting, such as a school, that has a planned instructional process and teachers who convey specific knowledge, skills, and thinking processes to students. *(p. 400)*

formal organization A highly structured group formed for the purpose of completing certain tasks or achieving specific goals. *(p. 125)*

functional age A term used to describe observable individual attributes—such as physical appearance, mobility, strength, coordination, and mental capacity—that are used to assign people to age categories. *(p. 510)*

functionalist perspectives The sociological approach that views society as a stable, orderly system. *(p. 15)*

***Gemeinschaft* (guh-MINE-shoft)** A traditional society in which social relationships are based on personal bonds of friendship and kinship and on intergenerational stability. *(p. 127)*

gender The culturally and socially constructed differences between females and males found in the meanings, beliefs, and practices associated with "femininity" and "masculinity." *(p. 306)*

gender bias Behaviour that shows favouritism toward one gender over the other. *(p. 314)*

gender identity A person's perception of the self as female or male. *(p. 306)*

gender role Attitudes, behaviour, and activities that are socially defined as appropriate for each sex and are learned through the socialization process. *(p. 306)*

gender socialization The aspect of socialization that contains specific messages and practices concerning the nature of being female or male in a specific group or society. *(p. 108)*

generalized other George Herbert Mead's term for the child's awareness of the demands and expectations of the society as a whole or of the child's subculture. *(p. 103)*

gentrification The process by which members of the middle and upper-middle classes move into the central city area and renovate existing properties. *(p. 21-21)*

gerontology The study of aging and older people. *(p. 513)*

***Gesellschaft* (guh-ZELL-shoft)** A large, urban society in which social bonds are based on impersonal and specialized relationships, with little long-term commitment to the group or consensus on values. *(p. 127)*

global interdependence A relationship in which the lives of all people are intertwined closely and any one nation's problems are part of a larger global problem. *(p. 4)*

goal displacement A process that occurs in organizations when the rules become an end in themselves rather than a means to an end. *(p. 159)*

global village A world in which distances have been shrunk by modern communications technology so that everyone is socially and economically interdependent. *(p. 501)*

gossip Rumours about the personal lives of individuals. *(p. 22-10)*

government The formal organization that has the legal and political authority to regulate the relationships among members of a society and between the society and those outside its borders. *(p. 572)*

gross national income (GNI) All the goods and services produced in a country in a given year, plus the income earned outside the country by individuals or corporations. *(p. 246)*

groupthink The process by which members of a cohesive group arrive at a decision that many individual members privately believe is unwise. *(p. 153)*

health The state of complete physical, mental, and social well-being. *(p. 451)*

healthcare Any activity intended to improve health. *(p. 451)*

hermaphrodite An individual born with male testes and a female ovary. *(p. 337)*

heterosexism An attitude in which heterosexuality is considered the only valid form of sexual behaviour, and gay men, lesbians, and bisexuals are considered inferior to heterosexual people. *(p. 392)*

hidden curriculum The transmission of cultural values and attitudes, such as conformity and obedience to authority, through implied demands found in the rules, routines, and regulations of schools. *(p. 406)*

high-income countries Nations with highly industrialized economies; technologically advanced industrial, administrative, and service occupations; and relatively high levels of national and personal income. *(p. 6)*

high-income economies Countries with an annual per capita gross national income of $US12,275 or more. *(p. 246)*

homogamy The pattern of individuals marrying those who have similar characteristics, such as race/ethnicity, religious background, age, education, or social class. *(p. 381)*

homophobia Extreme prejudice directed at gays, lesbians, bisexuals, and others who are perceived as not being heterosexual. *(p. 342)*

hospice A homelike facility that provides supportive care for patients with terminal illnesses. *(p. 532)*

hyperreality A situation in which the distinction between reality and simulation has become blurred. *(p. 491)*

hypotheses Tentative statements of the relationship between two or more concepts or variables. *(p. 33)*

id Sigmund Freud's term for the component of personality that includes all of the individual's basic biological drives and needs that demand immediate gratification. *(p. 105)*

ideal culture The values and standards of behaviour that people in a society profess to hold. *(p. 72)*

illegitimate opportunity structures Circumstances that provide an opportunity for people to acquire through illegitimate activities what they cannot achieve through legitimate channels. *(p. 176)*

immigration The movement of people into a geographic area to take up residency. *(p. 21-5)*

impression management (or presentation of self) A term for people's efforts to present themselves to others in ways that are most favourable to their own interests or image. *(p. 132)*

income The economic gain derived from wages, salaries, income transfers (governmental aid), and ownership of property. *(p. 212)*

independent variable A variable that is presumed to cause or determine a dependent variable. *(p. 35)*

inductive approach Research in which the investigator collects information or data (facts or evidence) and then generates theories from the analysis of that data. *(p. 34)*

industrialization The process by which societies are transformed from dependence on agriculture and handmade products to an emphasis on manufacturing and related industries. *(p. 8)*

infant mortality rate The number of deaths of infants under one year of age per 1000 live births in a given year. *(p. 21-4)*

infertility An inability to conceive after one year of unprotected sexual relations. *(p. 383)*

informal education Learning that occurs in a spontaneous, unplanned way. *(p. 400)*

informal structure Those aspects of participants' day-to-day activities and interactions ignore, bypass, or do not correspond with the official rules and procedures of the bureaucracy. *(p. 157)*

ingroup A group to which a person belongs and with which the person feels a sense of identity. *(p. 146)*

institutionalized racism A situation where the established rules, policies, and practices within an institution or organization produce differential treatment of various groups based on race. *(p. 281)*

intergenerational mobility The social movement (upward or downward) experienced by family members from one generation to the next. *(p. 208)*

internal colonialism According to conflict theorists, a situation in which members of a racial or ethnic group are conquered or colonized and forcibly placed under the economic and political control of the dominant group. *(p. 286)*

Internet The network infrastructure that links together the world's millions of computers. *(p. 479)*

intersexed individuals Persons whose sexual differentiation is ambiguous or incomplete. *(p. 337)*

interview A research method using a data collection encounter in which an interviewer asks the respondent questions and records the answers. *(p. 43)*

intimate partner violence The physical and nonphysical violence experienced by women and men at the hands of current or former partners. *(p. 356)*

intragenerational mobility The social movement (upward or downward) experienced by individuals within their own lifetime. *(p. 208)*

invasion The process by which a new category of people or type of land use arrives in an area previously occupied by another group or land use. *(p. 21-21)*

invention The process of reshaping existing cultural items into a new form. *(p. 74)*

job deskilling A reduction in the proficiency needed to perform a specific job, which leads to a corresponding reduction in the wages paid for that job. *(p. 232)*

kinship A social network of people based on common ancestry, marriage, or adoption. *(p. 371)*

labelling theory The proposition that deviants are those people who have been successfully labelled as such by others. *(p. 179)*

labour union A group of employees who join together to bargain with an employer or a group of employers over wages, benefits, and working conditions. *(p. 560)*

language A system of symbols that expresses ideas and enables people to think and communicate with one another. *(p. 67)*

latent functions Unintended functions that are hidden and remain unacknowledged by participants. *(p. 17)*

laws Formal, standardized norms that have been enacted by legislatures and are enforced by formal sanctions. *(p. 73)*

life chances Max Weber's term for the extent to which individuals have access to important societal resources, such as food, clothing, shelter, education, and healthcare. *(p. 208)*

life expectancy The average length of time a group of individuals of the same age will live. *(p. 510)*

looking-glass self Charles Horton Cooley's term for the way in which a person's sense of self is derived from the perceptions of others. *(p. 102)*

low-income countries Countries that are primarily agrarian, with little industrialization and low levels of national and personal income. *(p. 7)*

low-income cutoff The income level at which a family may be in "straitened circumstances" because it spends considerably more on the basic necessities of life (food, shelter, and clothing) than the average family. *(p. 226)*

low-income economies Countries with an annual per capita gross national income of $US1005 or less. *(p. 246)*

lower-middle-income economies Countries with an annual per capita gross national income between $US1005 and $US3975. *(p. 246)*

macrolevel analysis Sociological theory and research that focuses on whole societies, large-scale social structures, and social systems. *(p. 21)*

majority (dominant) group A group that is advantaged and has superior resources and rights in a society. *(p. 276)*

manifest functions Open, stated, and intended goals or consequences of activities within an organization or institution. *(p. 17)*

marginal job A position that differs from the employment norms of the society in which it is located. *(p. 558)*

marriage A legally recognized and/or socially approved arrangement between two or more individuals that carries certain rights and obligations and usually involves sexual activity. *(p. 342)*

mass A large number of people who share an interest in a specific idea or issue but are not in another's immediate physical vicinity. *(p. 22-4)*

mass behaviour Collective behaviour that takes place when people (who are often geographically separated from one another) respond to the same event in much the same way. *(p. 22-9)*

mass education Free, public schooling for wide segments of a nation's population. *(p. 401)*

mass hysteria A form of dispersed collective behaviour that occurs when a large number of people react with strong emotions and self-destructive behaviour to a real or perceived threat. *(p. 22-10)*

mass media Any technologically based means of communicating between large numbers of people distributed widely over space or time. *(p. 478)*

master status A term used to describe the most important status a person occupies. *(p. 120)*

material culture A component of culture that consists of the physical or tangible creations—such as clothing, shelter, and art—that members of a society make, use, and share. *(p. 64)*

matriarchal family A family structure in which authority is held by the eldest female (usually the mother). *(p. 375)*

matriarchy A hierarchical system of social organization in which cultural, political, and economic structures are controlled by women. *(p. 308)*

matrilineal descent A system of tracing descent through the mother's side of the family. *(p. 374)*

means of production Karl Marx's term for tools, land, factories, and money for investment that form the economic basis of a society. *(p. 13)*

mechanical solidarity Émile Durkheim's term for the social cohesion that exists in preindustrial societies, in which there is a minimal division of labour and people feel united by shared values and common social bonds. *(p. 127)*

media literacy The ability to access, analyze, evaluate, and create media in a varity of forms. *(p. 479)*

medicalization The process whereby an object or a condition becomes defined by society as a physical or psychological illness. *(p. 454)*

medicine An institutionalized system for the scientific diagnosis, treatment, and prevention of illness. *(p. 451)*

meritocracy A hierarchy in which all positions are rewarded based on people's ability and credentials. *(p. 233)*

metropolis One or more central cities and their surrounding suburbs that dominate the economic and cultural life of a region. *(p. 21-19)*

microlevel analysis Sociological theory and research that focus on small groups rather than on large-scale social structures. *(p. 21)*

middle-income countries Nations with industrializing economies, particularly in urban areas, and moderate levels of national and personal income. *(p. 7)*

migration The movement of people from one geographic area to another for the purpose of changing residency. *(p. 21-5)*

minority (subordinate) group A group whose members, because of physical or cultural characteristics, are disadvantaged and subjected to unequal treatment by the dominant group and who regard themselves as objects of collective discrimination. *(p. 276)*

mixed economy An economic system that combines elements of a market economy (capitalism) with elements of a command economy (socialism). *(p. 548)*

mob A highly emotional crowd whose members engage in, or are ready to engage in, violence against a specific target, which may be a person, a category of people, or physical property. *(p. 22-6)*

modernization theory A perspective that links global inequality to different levels of economic development and that suggests that low-income economies can move to middle- and high-income economies by achieving self-sustained economic growth. *(p. 257)*

monarchy A political system in which power resides in one person or family and is passed from generation to generation through lines of inheritance. *(p. 576)*

monogamy An intimate relationship with one person at a time. *(p. 343)*

monotheism A belief in a single, supreme being or god who is responsible for significant events, such as the creation of the world. *(p. 424)*

moral crusades Public and media awareness campaigns that help generate public and political support for moral entrepreneurs' causes. *(p. 181)*

moral entrepreneurs People or groups who take an active role in trying to have particular behaviours defined as deviant. *(p. 181)*

mores Strongly held norms with moral and ethical connotations that may not be violated without serious consequences in a particular culture. (p. 73)

mortality The incidence of death in a population. *(p. 21-4)*

multinational corporations Large companies that are headquartered in one country and have subsidiaries or branches in other countries. *(p. 544)*

network A web of social relationships that link one person with other people and, through them, with more people that those people know. *(p. 146)*

network enterprise Separate businesses, which may be companies or parts of companies, join together for specific projects that become the focus of the network. *(p. 167)*

new international division of labour theory The perspective that commodity production is being split into fragments that can be assigned to whichever part of the world can provide the most profitable combination of capital and labour. *(p. 262)*

nonmaterial culture A component of culture that consists of the abstract or intangible human creations of society—such as attitudes, beliefs, and values—that influence people's behaviour. *(p. 65)*

nontheistic religion A religion based on a belief in divine spiritual forces, such as sacred principles of thought and conduct, rather than on a god or gods. *(p. 424)*

nonverbal communication The transfer of information between persons without the use of speech. *(p. 134)*

norms Established rules of behaviour or standards of conduct. *(p. 72)*

nuclear family A family made up of one or two parents and their dependent children, all of whom live apart from other relatives. *(p. 373)*

objective Free from distorted subjective (personal or emotional) bias. *(p. 33)*

occupations Categories of jobs that involve similar activities at different work sites. *(p. 554)*

occupational, or white-collar, crime A term used to describe illegal activities committed by people in the course of their employment or in dealing with their financial affairs. *(p. 187)*

oligopoly The situation that exists when several companies overwhelmingly control an entire industry. *(p. 546)*

organic solidarity Émile Durkheim's term for the social cohesion that exists in industrial (and perhaps post-industrial) societies, in which people perform specialized tasks and feel united by their mutual dependence. *(p. 127)*

organized crime A business operation that supplies illegal goods and/or services for profit. *(p. 188)*

outgroup A group to which a person does not belong and toward which the person may feel a sense of competitiveness or hostility. *(p. 146)*

overt racism (or redneck or hate racism) Racism that may take the form of deliberate and highly personal attacks, including derogatory slurs and name-calling toward members of a racial or ethnic group who are perceived to be "inferior." *(p. 279)*

panic A form of crowd behaviour that occurs when a large number of people react to a real or perceived threat with strong emotions and self-destructive behaviour. *(p. 22-6)*

participant observation A research method in which researchers collect systematic observations while being part of the activities of the group they are studying. *(p. 467)*

patriarchal family A family structure in which authority is held by the eldest male (usually the father). *(p. 375)*

patriarchy A hierarchical system of social organization in which cultural, political, and economic structures are controlled by men. *(p. 308)*

patrilineal descent A system of tracing descent through the father's side of the family. *(p. 374)*

pay equity (comparable worth) The belief that wages ought to reflect the worth of a job, not the gender or race of the worker. *(p. 321)*

peer group A group of people who are linked by common interests, equal social position, and (usually) similar age. *(p. 98)*

peripheral nations According to world-systems analysis, nations that are dependent on core nations for capital, have little or no industrialization, and have uneven patterns of urbanization. *(p. 261)*

personal space The immediate area surrounding a person that the person claims as private. *(p. 136)*

perspective An overall approach to or viewpoint on some subject. *(p. 15)*

pink-collar occupation Relatively low-paying, nonmanual, semiskilled positions primarily held by women. *(p. 220)*

pluralist model An analysis of political systems that views power as widely dispersed throughout many competing interest groups. *(p. 578)*

polite racism A term used to describe an attempt to disguise a dislike of others through behaviour that is outwardly nonprejudicial. *(p. 279)*

political crime Illegal or unethical acts involving the usurpation of power by government officials, or illegal or unethical acts perpetrated against a government by outsiders seeking to make a political statement or to undermine or overthrow the government. *(p. 189)*

political party An organization whose purpose is to gain and hold legitimate control of government. *(p. 586)*

political socialization The process by which people learn political attitudes, values, and behaviour. *(p. 586)*

politics The social institution through which power is acquired and exercised by some people and groups. *(p. 572)*

polyamory Intimate relationships that involve mutually acknowledged emotional, sexual, or romantic relationships with multiple partners. *(p. 344)*

polyandry The concurrent marriage of one woman with two or more men. *(p. 345)*

polygamy The concurrent marriage of a person of one sex with two or more members of the opposite sex. *(p. 345)*

polygyny The concurrent marriage of one man with two or more women. *(p. 345)*

polytheism A belief in more than one god. *(p. 424)*

population In a research study, those persons about whom we want to be able to draw conclusions. *(p. 43)*

population composition In demography, the biological and social characteristics of a population. *(p. 21-10)*

population pyramid A graphic representation of the distribution of a population by sex and age. *(p. 21-10)*

positivism A belief that the world can best be understood through scientific inquiry. *(p. 9)*

post-industrial economy An economy that is based on the provision of services rather than goods. *(p. 542)*

postmodern perspectives The sociological approach that attempts to explain social life in modern societies that are characterized by post-industrialization, consumerism, and global communications. *(p. 23)*

power According to Max Weber, the ability of people or groups to achieve their goals despite opposition from others. *(p. 217)*

power elite A term devised by C. Wright Mills for a structure composed of leaders at the top of business, the executive branch of the federal government, and the military. *(p. 579)*

prejudice A negative attitude based on preconceived notions about members of selected groups. *(p. 277)*

prestige The respect or regard with which a person or status position is regarded by others. *(p. 217)*

preventive medicine Medicine that emphasizes a healthy lifestyle in order to prevent poor health before it occurs. *(p. 451)*

primary deviance A term used to describe the initial act of rule breaking. *(p. 179)*

primary group A small, less specialized group in which members engage in face-to-face, emotion-based interactions over an extended time. *(p. 124)*

primary sector production The sector of the economy that extracts raw materials and natural resources from the environment. *(p. 538)*

primary sex characteristics The genitalia used in the reproductive process. *(p. 336)*

profane A term used to describe the everyday, secular, or "worldly" aspects of life. *(p. 422)*

professions High-status, knowledge-based occupations. *(p. 555)*

proletariat Karl Marx's term for those who must sell their labour because they have no other means to earn a livelihood. *(p. 13)*

propaganda Information provided by individuals or groups that have a vested interest in furthering their own cause or damaging an opposing one. *(p. 22-11)*

public opinion The political attitudes and beliefs communicated by ordinary citizens to decision makers. *(p. 22-11)*

questionnaire A research instrument containing a series of items to which subjects respond. *(p. 43)*

race A term used by many people to specify groups of people distinguished by physical characteristics, such as skin colour; also, a category of people who have been singled out as inferior or superior, often on the basis of real or alleged physical characteristics, such as skin colour, hair texture, eye shape, or other subjectively selected attributes. *(p. 274)*

racial prejudice Beliefs that certain racial groups are innately inferior to others or have a disproportionate number of negative traits. *(p. 277)*

racism A set of ideas that implies the superiority of one social group over another on the basis of biological or cultural characteristics, together with the power to put these beliefs into practice in a way that denies or excludes minority women and men. *(p. 279)*

rationality The process by which traditional methods of social organization, characterized by informality and spontaneity, are gradually replaced by efficiently administered formal rules and procedures (bureaucracy). *(p. 163)*

rational-legal authority Power legitimized by law or written rules and regulations. *(p. 574)*

reactivity The tendency of experiment participants to change their behaviour in response to the presence of the researcher or to the fact that they know they are being studied. *(p. 42)*

real culture The values and standards of behaviour that people actually follow (as contrasted with *ideal culture*). *(p. 72)*

reference group A group that strongly influences a person's behaviour and social attitudes, regardless of whether that individual is a member. *(p. 146)*

relative poverty A level of economic deprivation in which people may be able to afford basic necessities but still are unable to maintain an average standard of living. *(p. 227)*

reliability In sociological research, the extent to which a study or research instrument yields consistent results. *(p. 37)*

religion A system of beliefs, symbols, and rituals, based on some sacred or supernatural realm, that guides human behaviour, gives meaning to life, and unites believers into a community. *(p. 422)*

replication In sociological research, the repetition of the investigation in substantially the same way that it originally was conducted. *(p. 37)*

representative sample A selection where the sample has the essential characteristics of the total population. *(p. 43)*

research methods Specific strategies or techniques for conducting research. *(p. 38)*

resocialization The process of learning a new and different set of attitudes, values, and behaviours from those in one's previous background and experience. *(p. 110)*

respondent A person who provides data for analysis through an interview or questionnaire. *(p. 42)*

riot Violent crowd behaviour that is fuelled by deep-seated emotions but not directed at one specific target. *(p. 22-6)*

rituals Regularly repeated and carefully prescribed forms of behaviour that symbolize a cherished value or belief. *(p. 422)*

role A set of behavioural expectations associated with a given status. *(p. 121)*

role conflict A situation in which incompatible role demands are placed on a person by two or more statuses held at the same time. *(p. 122)*

role exit A situation in which people disengage from social roles that have been central to their self-identity. *(p. 123)*

role expectation A group's or society's definition of the way a specific role ought to be played. *(p. 121)*

role performance How a person plays a role. *(p. 121)*

role strain The strain experienced by a person when incompatible demands are built into a single status that the person occupies. *(p. 122)*

role-taking The process by which a person mentally assumes the role of another person in order to understand the world from that person's point of view. *(p. 103)*

routinization of charisma A term for the process by which charismatic authority is succeeded by a bureaucracy controlled by a rationally established authority or by a combination of traditional and bureaucratic authority. *(p. 574)*

rumour An unsubstantiated report on an issue or subject. *(p. 22-9)*

sacred A term used to describe those aspects of life that are extraordinary or supernatural. *(p. 422)*

sample The people who are selected from the population to be studied. *(p. 43)*

sanctions Rewards for appropriate behaviour or penalties for inappropriate behaviour. *(p. 72)*

Sapir–Whorf hypothesis The proposition that language shapes its speakers' view of reality. *(p. 68)*

scapegoat A person or group that is incapable of offering resistance to the hostility or aggression of others. *(p. 278)*

second shift Arlie Hochschild's term for the domestic work that employed women perform at home after they complete their workday on the job. *(p. 387)*

secondary analysis A research method in which researchers use existing material and analyze data that originally was collected by others. *(p. 49)*

secondary deviance A term used to describe the process whereby a person who has been labelled deviant accepts that new identity and continues the deviant behaviour. *(p. 179)*

secondary group A larger, more specialized group in which the members engage in more impersonal, goal-oriented relationships for a limited time. *(p. 124)*

secondary sector production The sector of the economy that processes raw materials (from the primary sector) into finished goods. *(p. 540)*

secondary sex characteristics The physical traits (other than reproductive organs) that identify an individual's sex. *(p. 336)*

sect A relatively small religious group that has broken away from another religious organization to renew what it views as the original version of the faith. *(p. 434)*

segregation A term used to describe the spatial and social separation of categories of people by race/ethnicity, class, gender, and/or religion. *(p. 285)*

self-concept The totality of our beliefs and feelings about ourselves. *(p. 101)*

self-fulfilling prophecy A situation in which a false belief or prediction produces behaviour that makes the originally false belief come true. *(p. 130)*

semiperipheral nations According to world-systems analysis, nations that are more developed than peripheral nations but less developed than core nations. *(p. 261)*

sex A term used to describe the biological and anatomical differences between females and males. *(p. 336)*

sexism The subordination of one sex, usually female, based on the assumed superiority of the other sex. *(p. 308)*

sexual double standard The belief that men and women are expected to conform to different standards of sexual conduct. *(p. 359)*

sexual harassment Unwanted sexual advances, requests for sexual favours, or other verbal or physical conduct of a sexual nature. *(p. 315)*

sexual orientation A person's preference for emotional–sexual relationships with members of the opposite sex (heterosexuality), the same sex (homosexuality), or both (bisexuality). *(p. 339)*

sexual revolution A term used for the dramatic changes that occurred regarding sexual attitudes, behaviours, and values during the 1960s. *(p. 359)*

sexual scripts Culturally created guidelines that define how, where, with whom, and under what conditions a person is to behave as a sexual being. *(p. 337)*

sexuality (sexual) The range of human activities designed to produce erotic response and pleasure. *(p. 337)*

sick role Patterns of behaviour defined as appropriate for people who are sick. *(p. 451)*

significant others Those persons whose care, affection, and approval are especially desired and who are most important in the development of the self. *(p. 103)*

simple random sample A selection in which everyone in the target population has an equal chance of being chosen; in other words, choice occurs by chance. *(p. 43)*

simple supernaturalism The belief that supernatural forces affect people's lives either positively or negatively. *(p. 424)*

slavery An extreme form of stratification in which some people are owned by others. *(p. 209)*

small group A collectivity small enough for all members to be acquainted with one another and to interact simultaneously. *(p. 149)*

social bond theory The proposition that the likelihood of deviant behaviour increases when a person's ties to society are weakened or broken. *(p. 177)*

social change The alteration, modification, or transformation of public policy, culture, or social institutions over time. *(p. 22-3)*

social construction of reality The process by which our perception of reality is shaped largely by the subjective meaning that we give to an experience. *(p. 130)*

social control Systematic practices developed by social groups to encourage conformity and discourage deviance. *(p. 174)*

social Darwinism The belief that those species of animals (including human beings) best adapted to their environment survive and prosper, whereas those poorly adapted die out. *(p. 11)*

social determinants of health The conditions in which people are born, grow, live, work and age, including the health system. *(p. 463)*

social devaluation A situation in which a person or group is considered to have less social value than other individuals or groups. *(p. 110)*

social facts Émile Durkheim's term for patterned ways of acting, thinking, and feeling that exist outside any one individual. *(p. 11)*

social group A group that consists of two or more people who interact frequently and share a common identity and a feeling of interdependence. *(p. 124)*

social institution A set of organized beliefs and rules that establish how a society will attempt to meet its basic social needs. *(p. 125)*

social interaction The process by which people act toward or respond to other people. *(p. 118)*

social marginality The state of being part insider and part outsider in the social structure. *(p. 118)*

social mobility The movement of individuals or groups from one level in a stratification system to another. *(p. 208)*

social movement An organized group that acts consciously to promote or resist change through collective action. *(p. 22-12)*

social network A series of social relationships that link an individual to others. *(p. 125)*

social solidarity The state of having shared beliefs and values among members of a social group, along with intense and frequent interaction among group members. *(p. 17)*

social stratification The hierarchical arrangement of large social groups based on their control over basic resources. *(p. 208)*

social structure The stable pattern of social relationships that exist within a particular group or society. *(p. 118)*

socialism An economic system characterized by public ownership of the means of production, the pursuit of collective goals, and centralized decision making. *(p. 547)*

socialization The lifelong process of social interaction through which individuals acquire a self-identity and the physical, mental, and social skills needed for survival in society. *(p. 93)*

societal consensus A situation whereby the majority of members share a common set of values, beliefs, and behavioural expectations. *(p. 15)*

society A large social grouping that shares the same geographical territory and is subject to the same political authority and dominant cultural expectations. *(p. 4)*

sociobiology The systematic study of how biology affects social behaviour. *(p. 94)*

socioeconomic status (SES) A combined measure that attempts to classify individuals, families, or households in terms of indicators, such as income, occupation, and education, to determine class location. *(p. 217)*

sociological imagination C. Wright Mills's term for the ability to see the relationship between individual experiences and the larger society. *(p. 5)*

sociology The systematic study of human society and social interaction. *(p. 4)*

sociology of family The subdiscipline of sociology that attempts to describe and explain patterns of family life and variations in family structure. *(p. 376)*

special interest groups Political coalitions made up of individuals or groups that share a specific interest they wish to protect or advance with the help of the political system. *(p. 578)*

split labour market A term used to describe the division of the economy into two areas of employment: a primary sector, or upper tier, composed of higher-paid (usually dominant group) workers in more secure jobs; and a secondary sector, or lower tier, composed of lower-paid (often subordinate group) workers in jobs with little security and hazardous working conditions. *(p. 287)*

state The political entity that possesses a legitimate monopoly over the use of force within its territory to achieve its goals. *(p. 572)*

status A socially defined position in a group or society characterized by certain expectations, rights, and duties. *(p. 119)*

status conferral The process of giving prominence to particular individuals by focusing media attention on them. *(p. 482)*

status set A term used to describe all the statuses that a person occupies at a given time. *(p. 120)*

status symbol A material sign that informs others of a person's specific status. *(p. 121)*

stereotype An overgeneralization about the appearance, behaviour, or other characteristics of members of particular groups. *(p. 277)*

stigma According to Erving Goffman, any physical or social attribute or sign that so devalues a person's social identity that it disqualifies that person from full social acceptance. *(p. 119)*

strain theory The proposition that people feel strain when they are exposed to cultural goals that they are unable to obtain because they do not have access to culturally approved means of achieving these goals. *(p. 176)*

street crime All violent crime, certain property crimes, and certain morals crimes. *(p. 186)*

subculture A group of people who share a distinctive set of cultural beliefs and behaviours that differ in some significant way from those of the larger society. *(p. 76)*

subliminal racism A term used to describe an unconscious racism that occurs when there is a conflict of values. *(p. 280)*

succession The process by which a new category of people or type of land use gradually predominates in an area formerly dominated by another group or activity. *(p. 21-21)*

superego Sigmund Freud's term for the human conscience, consisting of the moral and ethical aspects of personality. *(p. 105)*

survey A research method in which a number of respondents are asked identical questions through a systematic questionnaire or interview. *(p. 42)*

symbol Anything that meaningfully represents something else. *(p. 22)*

symbolic interactionist perspectives The sociological approach that views society as the sum of the interactions of individuals and groups. *(p. 22)*

taboos Mores so strong that their violation is considered extremely offensive and even unmentionable. *(p. 73)*

technology The knowledge, techniques, and tools that make it possible for people to transform resources into usable forms, as well as the knowledge and skills required to use them after they are developed. *(p. 64)*

terrorism Acts of serious violence, planned and executed clandestinely and committed to achieve political ends. *(p. 22-13)*

theism A belief in a god or gods. *(p. 424)*

theory A set of logically interrelated statements that attempts to describe, explain, and (occasionally) predict social events. *(p. 15)*

total institution Erving Goffman's term for a place where people are isolated from the rest of society for a set period of time and come under the control of the officials who run the institution. *(p. 111)*

totalitarian political system A political system in which the state seeks to regulate all aspects of people's public and private lives. *(p. 576)*

tracking The assignment of students to specific courses and educational programs based on their test scores, previous grades, or both. *(p. 405)*

traditional authority Power that is legitimized by respect for long-standing custom. *(p. 574)*

transsexual A person who believes that he or she was born with the body of the wrong sex. *(p. 338)*

transvestite A male who lives as a woman or a female who lives as a man but does not alter the genitalia. *(p. 338)*

triad A group composed of three members. *(p. 149)*

triangulation Using several different research methods, data sources, investigators, and/or theoretical perspectives in the same study. *(p. 51)*

unemployment rate The percentage of unemployed persons in the labour force actively seeking jobs. *(p. 559)*

universal healthcare system System in which all citizens receive medical services paid for through taxation revenues. *(p. 468)*

unstructured interview A research method involving an extended, open-ended interaction between an interviewer and an interviewee. *(p. 48)*

upper-middle-income economies Countries with an annual per capita gross national income between $US3976 and $US12,274. *(p. 246)*

urban sociology A subfield of sociology that examines social relationships and political and economic structures in the city. *(p. 21-18)*

urbanization The process by which an increasing proportion of a population lives in cities rather than in rural areas. *(p. 8)*

validity In sociological research, the extent to which a study or research instrument accurately measures what it is supposed to measure. *(p. 37)*

value contradiction Values that conflict with one another or are mutually exclusive. *(p. 71)*

values Collective ideas about what is right or wrong, good or bad, and desirable or undesirable in a particular culture. *(p. 71)*

variable In sociological research, any concept with measurable traits or characteristics that can change or vary from one person, time, situation, or society to another. *(p. 35)*

visible minority An official government category of non-white, non-Caucasian individuals. *(p. 276)*

wage gap A term used to describe the disparity between women's and men's earnings. *(p. 320)*

wealth The value of all of a person's or family's economic assets, including income and property, such as buildings, land, farms, houses, factories, and cars, as well as other assets, such as money in bank accounts, corporate stocks, bonds, and insurance policies. *(p. 213)*

working class (proletariat) Karl Marx's term for those who must sell their labour in order to earn enough money to survive. *(p. 214)*

world-systems analysis The perspective that the capitalist world economy is a global system divided into a hierarchy of three major types of nations—core, semiperipheral, and peripheral—in which upward or downward mobility is conditioned by the resources and obstacles that characterize the international system. *(p. 261)*

World Wide Web The computer language that allows us to access information on the Internet. *(p. 479)*

REFERENCES

AAUW (American Association of University Women). 1995. *How Schools Shortchange Girls/The AAUW Report: A Study of Major Findings on Girls and Education.* New York: Marlowe.

Abadie, Alberto, and Sebastien Gay. 2006. "The Impact of Presumed Consent Legislation on Cadaveric Organ Donation: A Cross-Country Study." *Journal of Health Economics* 25 (July): 599–620.

ABC Canada Literacy Foundation. 2001. "Who Wants to Learn." Available: http://www.abc-canada.org.

Abella, Irving. 1974. *On Strike: Six Key Labour Struggles in Canada 1919–1949.* Toronto: James Lewis and Samuel.

———, and Harold Troper. 1982. *None Is Too Many.* Toronto: Lester and Orpen Dennys.

Aberle, D.F., A.K. Cohen, A.K. Davis, M.J. Leng Jr., and F.N. Sutton. 1950. "The Functional Prerequisites of Society." *Ethics* 60 (January): 100–111.

Aberle, David F. 1966. *The Peyote Religion Among the Navaho.* Chicago: Aldine.

Aboujaoude, Elias. 2010. "Problematic Internet Use: An Overview." *World Psychiatry* 9 (2): 85–90.

Abraham, Carolyn. 2012. "Unnatural Selection: Is Evolving Reproductive Technology Ushering in a New Age of Eugenics?" *Globe and Mail* (January 10). Available: http://www.theglobeandmail.com/life/parenting/pregnancy/pregnancy-trends/unnatural-selection-is-evolving-reproductive-technology-ushering-in-a-new-age-of-eugenics/article2294636/?service=mobile.

Abu-Laban, Sharon McIrvin, and Susan A. McDaniel. 2001. "Beauty, Status and Aging." In N. Mandell (ed.), *Feminist Issues* (3rd ed.). Scarborough, Ont.: Prentice-Hall.

Achenbaum, W. Andrew. 1978. *Old Age in the New Land: The American Experience Since 1870.* Baltimore: John Hopkins University Press.

Achilles, Rona. 1996. "Assisted Reproduction: The Social Issues." In E.D. Nelson and B.W. Robinson (eds.), *Gender in the 1990s.* Toronto: Thomson Nelson, 346–364.

ACS/Environics. 2002. "Public Opinion Poll in 30 Years of Multiculturalism." *Canadian Issues* (February): 4–5.

Adam, B., and E. Maticka-Tyndale. 2011. "Emerging Directions in Sociological Research on Sexuality." *Canadian Review of Sociology*, 48 (3): 217–220. doi:10.1111/j.1755-618.

Adams, Michael. 1998. *Sex in the Snow: Canadian Social Values at the End of the Millennium.* Toronto: Penguin.

Adams, Tom. 1991. *Grass Roots: How Ordinary People Are Changing America.* New York: Citadel Press.

Adler, Patricia A., and Peter Adler. 1994. *Constructions of Deviance: Social Power, Context, and Interaction.* Belmont, Cal.: Wadsworth.

———. 1998. *Peer Power: Preadolescent Culture and Identity.* New Brunswick, N.J.: Rutgers University Press.

Adler, Patricia A., Steven J. Kless, and Peter Adler. 1995. "Socialization to Gender Roles: Popularity Among Elementary School Boys and Girls." In E.D. Nelson and B.W. Robinson (eds.), *Gender in the 1990s.* Toronto: Nelson.

Adorno, Theodor W., Else Frenkel-Brunswik, Daniel Levinson, and Nevitt Sanford. 1950. *The Authoritarian Personality.* New York: Harper & Row.

Africentric Alternative School Support Committee. 2009. *Africentric Education: Commonly Asked Questions.* Retrieved May 10, 2012. Available: http://www.tdsb.on.ca/boardroom/bd_agenda/uploads/generalinfo/080516%20africentric%20q&as.pdf.

Agger, Ben. 1993. *Gender, Culture, and Power: Toward a Feminist Postmodern Critical Theory.* Westport, Conn.: Praeger.

Aggleton, P. 1999. *Men Who Sell Sex.* Philadelphia: Temple University Press.

Ahn, Sun Joo, and Jeremy Bailenson. 2011. "Self-Endorsing Versus Other-Endorsing in Virtual Environments: The Effect on Brand Attitude and Purchase Intention." *Journal of Advertising* 40 (Summer): 93–106.

Aiello, John R., and S.E. Jones. 1971. "Field Study of Proxemic Behavior of Young School Children in Three Subcultural Groups." *Journal of Personality and Social Psychology* 19: 351–356.

Albanese, Catherine L. 1992. *America, Religions and Religion.* Belmont, Cal.: Wadsworth.

Albas, Cheryl, and Daniel Albas. 1988. "Emotion Work and Emotion Rules: The Case of Exams." *Qualitative Sociology* 11 (4): 259–275.

———. 1989. "Aligning Actions: The Case of Subcultural Proxemics." *Canadian Ethnic Studies* 21 (2): 74–81.

Albrecht, Gary L. 1992. *The Disability Business: Rehabilitation in America.* Newbury Park, Cal.: Sage.

Alexander, Jeffrey C. 1985. *Neofunctionalism.* Beverly Hills, Cal.: Sage.

Alexander, Peter, and Roger Gill (eds.). 1984. *Utopias.* London: Duckworth.

Alireza, Marianne. 1990. "Lifting the Veil of Tradition." *Austin American-Statesman* (September 23): C1, C7.

Alix, Ernest K. 1995. *Sociology: An Everyday Life Approach.* Minneapolis: West Publishing.

Allahar, Anton. 1989. *Sociology and the Periphery: Theories and Issues.* Toronto: Garamond.

Allport, Gordon. 1958. *The Nature of Prejudice* (abridged ed.). New York: Doubleday/Anchor.

Altemeyer, Bob. 1981. *Right-Wing Authoritarianism.* Winnipeg: University of Manitoba Press.

———. 1988. *Enemies of Freedom: Understanding Right-Wing Authoritarianism.* San Francisco: Jossey-Bass.

Alter, Jonathan. 1999. "Bridging the Digital Divide." *Newsweek* (September 20): 55.

Alwin, Duane, Philip Converse, and Steven Martin. 1985. "Living Arrangements and Social Integration." *Journal of Marriage and the Family* 47: 319–334.

Alzheimer Society of Canada. 2009. *Rising Tide: The Impact of Dementia on Canadian Society.* Ottawa: Alzheimer Society of Canada. Available: http://www.alzheimer.ca/english/media/putyourmind09-RisingTide.htm.

Ambert, Anne-Marie. 1992. *The Effect of Children on Parents.* New York: Haworth.

———. 2001. *Families in the New Millennium.* Toronto: Allyn and Bacon.

———. 2003. "Same-Sex Couples and Same-Sex Families: Relationships, Parenting, and Issues of Marriage." Vanier Institute of the Family. Retrieved August 21, 2003. Available: http://vifamily.ca/library/cft/samesex.html.

———. 2005a. *Divorce: Facts, Figures, and Consequences.* Ottawa: Vanier Institute for the Family. Retrieved May 20, 2009. Available: http://www.vifamily.ca/library/cft/divorce_05.pdf.

———. 2005b. *Same Sex Couples and Same Sex Families: Relationships, Parenting and Issues of Marriage.* Vanier Institute of the Family. Retrieved August 21, 2005. Available: http://www.vifamily.ca/library/cft/samesex_05.html.

———. 2006a. *Changing Families: Relationships in Context* (Canadian ed.). Toronto: Pearson.

———. 2006b. "One-Parent Families: Characteristics, Causes, Consequences, and Issues." Ottawa: Vanier Institute for the Family. Retrieved May 20, 2009. Available: http://www.vifamily.ca/library/cft/oneparent.html.

———. 2009. *Divorce: Facts, Causes and Consequences* (3rd ed.). Ottawa: Vanier Institute of the Family. Retrieved January 17, 2012. Available: http://www.vifamily.ca/sites/default/files/divorce_facts_causes_consequences.pdf

American Sociological Association. 2005. "The Future of Sociology."

Aminzade, Ronald. 1973. "Revolution and Collective Political Violence: The Case of the Working Class of Marseille, France, 1830–1871." Working Paper #86, Center for Research on Social Organization. Ann Arbor: University of Michigan.

Amiri, Rina. 2001. "Muslim Women as Symbols—and Pawns." *New York Times* (Nov. 27): A21.

Amnesty International. 2004. *Stolen Sisters: Discrimination and Violence Against Indigenous Women in Canada.* Online: Amnesty International. Retrieved May 20, 2009. Available: http://www.amnesty.org/en/library/info/AMR20/001/2004.

Amott, Teresa, and Julie Matthaei. 1991. *Race, Gender, and Work: A Multicultural Economic History of Women in the United States.* Boston: South End Press.

———. 1996. *Race, Gender, and Work: A Multicultural Economic History of Women in the United States* (rev. ed.). Boston: South End.

Ananova News Service. 2005. "Cosmetic Surgery Is Teenagers' Reward for Passing Exams." Retrieved March 16, 2005. Available: http://www.ananova.com/news/story/sm_791290.html.

Andersen, Margaret, L. 2006. *Thinking About Women: Sociological Perspectives on Sex and Gender* (7th ed.). Boston: Pearson.

———, and Patricia Hill Collins, eds. 1998. *Race, Class, and Gender: An Anthology* (3rd ed.). Belmont, Cal.: Wadsworth.

Anderson, Elijah. 1990. *Streetwise: Race, Class, and Change in an Urban Community.* Chicago: University of Chicago Press.

———. 1999. *The Code of the Streets: Decency, Violence, and the Moral Life of the Inner City.* New York: Norton.

Anderson, Eric. 2010. "At Least with Cheating There Is an Attempt at Monogamy": Cheating and Monogamism Among Undergraduate Heterosexual Men." *Journal Of Social & Personal Relationships* 27 (7): 851–872. doi:10.1177/0265407510373908.

———. 2012. *The Monogamy Gap: Men, Love and the Reality of Cheating.* New York: Oxford University Press.

Anderson, Karen. 1996. *Sociology: A Critical Introduction.* Toronto: Thomson Nelson.

Anderssen, Gerald F. 1998. *Highlights of the 1998 Multinational Comparisons of Health Care.* New York: The Commonwealth Fund.

Andreatta, David. 2007. "Census 2006: The New Household." *Globe and Mail* (September 13): A8.

Andrews, Lori. 2012. *I Know Who You Are and I Saw What You Did: Social Networks and the Death of Privacy.* New York: The Free Press.

Angier, Natalie. 1993. "'Stopit!' She Said. 'Nomore!'" *New York Times Book Review* (April 25): 12.

Angus Reid. 1991. *Multiculturalism and Canadians: Attitude Study, 1991.* National Survey Report submitted to the Department of Multiculturalism and Citizenship.

———. 2009. *Gender Shapes Views on Debate Over Prostitution in Canada.* Toronto. Retrieved July 27, 2012. Available: http://www.angus-reid.com/wp-content/uploads/2009/11/2009.11.27_Prostitution.pdf.

Annesi, Nicole. 1993. "Like Mother, Like Daughter." In Leslea Newman (ed.), *Eating Our Hearts Out: Personal Accounts of Women's Relationship to Food.* Freedom, Cal.: Crossing Press, 91–95.

Anyon, Jean. 1997. *Ghetto Schooling: A Political Economy of Urban Educational Reform.* New York: Teachers College Press.

———. 1980. "Social Class and the Hidden Curriculum of Work." *Journal of Education* 162: 67–92.

APA Online. 2000. "Psychiatric Effects of Violence." Public Information. APA

Fact Sheet Series. Washington D.C.: American Psychological Association. Retrieved April 5, 2000. Available: http://www.psych.org/psych/htdocs/public_info/media_violence.html.

Appelbaum, R.P., and W.P. Chambliss. 1997. *Sociology* (2nd ed.). New York: Addison-Wesley Longman.

Apple, Michael W. 1980. "Analyzing Determinations: Understanding and Evaluating the Production of Social Outcomes in Schools." *Curriculum Inquiry* 10: 55–76.

Appleton, Lynn M. 1995. "The Gender Regimes in American Cities." In Judith A. Garber and Robyne S. Turner (eds.), *Gender in Urban Research.* Thousand Oaks, Cal.: Sage, 44–59.

Arat-Koc, Sedef. 1999. "Foreign Domestic Workers and the Law." In Elizabeth Comack (ed.), *Locating Law: Race, Class, and Gender Connections.* Halifax: Fernwood Publishing, 125–151.

Arendt, Hannah. 1973. *On Revolution.* London: Penguin.

Armstrong, Elizabeth, Laura Hamilton, and Paula England. 2010. "Is Hooking Up Bad for Young Women? *Contexts* (July 1): 22–27. Retrieved March 27, 2012. Available: http://www.proquest.com.libproxy.uwinnipeg.ca.

Armstrong, Pat. 1993. "Work and Family Life: Changing Patterns." In G.N. Ramu (ed.), *Marriage and the Family in Canada Today* (2nd ed.). Scarborough, Ont.: Prentice-Hall, 127–145.

———. 1994. *The Double Ghetto: Canadian Women and Their Segregated Work.* Toronto: McClelland and Stewart.

———, and Hugh Armstrong. 1983. *A Working Majority: What Women Must Do for Pay.* Ottawa: Canadian Government Publishing Centre.

Arnold, Regina A. 1990. "Processes of Victimization and Criminalization of Black Women." *Social Justice* 17 (3): 153–166.

Arnup, Katherine. 1995a. *Lesbian Parenting: Living with Pride and Prejudice.* Charlottetown, P.E.I.: Gynergy Books.

———. 1995b. "We Are Family: Lesbian Mothers in Canada." In E.D. Nelson and B.W. Robinson (eds.), *Gender in the 1990s.* Toronto: Thomson Nelson, 330–345.

Arquilla, John, and David Ronfeldt. 2001. *Networks and Netwars.* Santa Monica: RAND Corporation.

Asch, Adrienne. 1986. "Will Populism Empower Disabled People?" In Harry G. Boyle and Frank Reissman (eds.), *The New Populism: The Power of Empowerment.* Philadelphia: Temple University Press, 213–228.

———. 2004. "Critical Race Theory, Feminism, and Disability." In Bonnie G. Smith and Beth Hutchison (eds.), *Gendering Disability.* New Brunswick, N.J.: Rutgers University Press, 9–44.

Asch, Solomon E. 1955. "Opinions and Social Pressure." *Scientific American* 193 (5): 31–35.

———. 1956. "Studies of Independence and Conformity: A Minority of One Against a Unanimous Majority." *Psychological Monographs* 70 (9) (Whole no. 416).

Ashkenaz, Marissa. 2008. "You Mean You Chose to Be Fat? Body Image in a Virtual World." Retrieved January 2, 2012. Available: http://marissaracecourse.com/2008/06/03/you-mean-you-chose-to-be-fat-body-image-in-a-virtual-world.

Assembly of First Nations. 2008. "Sexual Exploitation/Abuse of First Nations Children." Retrieved May 22, 2009. Available: http://www.afn.ca/cmslib/general/Sex-Ex.pdf.

Association for Canadian Studies. 2012. *In God We Canadians Trust?* Retrieved May 8, 2012. Available: https://docs.google.com/viewer?url=http%3A%2F%2Fwww.acs-aec.ca%2Fpdf%2Fpolls%2FIn%2520God%2520Canadians%2520Trust%2520II.pdf.

Association of Faculties of Medicine of Canada. 2005. *Canadian Medical Education Statistics 2004.* Ottawa: Association of Faculties of Medicine of Canada.

———. 2011. *Trends in Graduates of Canadian Faculties of Medicine, 1940–2010.* Retrieved June 28, 2012. Available: http://www.afmc.ca/pdf/gradssection2011cmes.pdf.

Associated Press. 2006. "Companies Cross Borders for Immigrants." *New York Times* (March 16). Retrieved March 16, 2006. Available: http://www.nytimes.com/-aponline/business/AP-Cross-Border-Buying-Bizspotlight.html?_r=1&oref =slogin.

Atchley, Robert C., ed. 1997. *Social Forces and Aging* (2nd ed.). Belmont, Cal.: Wadsworth.

———, and Amanda Barusch. 2004. *Social Forces and Aging: An Introduction to Social Gerontology* (10th ed.). Belmont, Cal.: Wadsworth.

Atkins, Rebecca. 2005. "Teenagers Opt for Cosmetic Surgery." *Manchester News.* Retrieved March 16, 2005. Available: http://www.manchesteronline.co.uk/news/s/141/141788_teenagers_opt_for_cosmetic_surgery.html.

Atkinson, M. 2008. "Exploring Male Femininity in the 'Crisis': Men and Cosmetic Surgery." *Body & Society* 14 (1): 67–87. doi:10.1177/1357034X07087531.

Attwood, F. 2006. "Sexed Up: Theorizing the Sexualization of Culture." *Sexualities* 9 (1): 77–94.

AuCoin, Kathy, ed. 2005. *Family Violence in Canada: A Statistical Profile, 2005.* Statistics Canada Cat. no. 85-224XIE. Retrieved May 20, 2009. Available: http://dsp-psd.tpsgc.gc.ca/Collection/Statcan/85-224-X/85-224-XIE2005000.pdf.

Auger, Nathalie, Denis Hamel, Jerome Martinez, and Nancy Ross. 2011. "Mitigating Effect of Immigration on the Relation Between Income Inequality and Mortality: A Prospective Study of 2 Million Canadians." *Journal of Epidemiology & Community Health* (March 30). Retrieved January 12, 2012.Available: http://www.medsp.umontreal.ca/IRSPUM_DB/pdf/26138.pdf.

Aulette, Judy Root. 1994. *Changing Families.* Belmont, Cal.: Wadsworth.

Avert. 2005. "HIV and AIDS in Uganda." Retrieved July 22, 2005. Available: http://www.avert.org/aidsuganda.htm.

Aw, Dr. James. 2011. "Paging Dr. Smartphone: How Medical Apps are Changing Diagnoses and Treatments." *National Post* (November 8).

Aylward, Carol A. 1999. *Canadian Critical Race Theory: Racism and the Law.* Halifax: Fernwood Publishing.

Axtell, Roger E. 1991. *Gestures: The Do's and Taboos of Body Language Around the World.* New York: Wiley.

Baber, K. M., and Murray, C. I. 2001. "A Postmodern Feminist Approach to Teaching Human Sexuality." *Family Relations* 50 (1): 23–33.

Babbie, Earl. 2004. *The Practice of Social Research* (10th ed.). Belmont, Cal.: Wadsworth.

Backstrom, Lars, Paolo Boldi, Marco Rosa, Johan Ugander, and Sebastiano Vigna. 2011. "Four Degrees of Separation." CoRR, abs/1111.4570.

Bahr, Howard M., and Theodore Caplow. 1991. "Middletown as an Urban Case Study." In Joe R. Feagin, Anthony M. Orum, and Gideon Sjoberg (eds.), *A Case for the Case Study.* Chapel Hill: University of North Carolina Press, 80–120.

Bailey, Katie. 2010. "Internet Beats TV in Hours Spent." *Media in Canada.* Retrieved January 16, 2010. Available: http://mediaincanada.com/2010/03/22/ipsos_inter-nettv-20100322.

Bailyn, Bernard. 1960. *Education in the Forming of American Society.* New York: Random House.

Baker, Maureen. 2005. *Families: Changing Trends in Canada* (5th ed.). Toronto: McGraw-Hill Ryerson.

———. 2009. *Families: Changing Trends in Canada* (6th ed). Toronto: McGraw-Hill.

Baker, Robert. 1993. "'Pricks' and 'Chicks': A Plea for 'Persons.'" In Anne Minas (ed.), *Gender Basics: Feminist Perspectives on Women and Men.* Belmont, Cal.: Wadsworth, 66–68.

Ballantine, Jeanne H. 2001. *The Sociology of Education: A Systematic Analysis* (5th ed.). Englewood Cliffs, N.J.: Prentice-Hall.

Ballara, Marcela. 1992. *Women and Literacy.* Prepared for the UN/NGO Group on Women and Development. Atlantic Highlands, N.J.: Zed Books.

Bane, Mary Jo. 1986. "Household Composition and Poverty: Which Comes First?" In Sheldon H. Danzinger and Daniel H. Weinberg (eds.), *Fighting Poverty: What Works and What Doesn't.* Cambridge, Mass.: Harvard University Press.

Banner, Lois W. 1993. *In Full Flower: Aging Women, Power, and Sexuality.* New York: Vintage.

Barboza, David. 2001. "From Golden Arches to Lightning Rod." *International Herald Tribune* (Oct. 15). Retrieved Oct. 22, 2001. Available: http://www.iht.com

———. 2005. "China, New Land of Shoppers, Builds Malls on Gigantic Scale." *New York Times* (May 25): A1.

Bardwell, Jill R., Samuel W. Cochran, and Sharon Walker. 1986. "Relationship of Parental Education, Race, and Gender to Sex Role Stereotyping in Five-Year-Old Kindergarteners." *Sex Roles* 15: 275–281.

Barlow, Maude, and Heather-Jane Robertson. 1994. *Class Warfare: The Assault on Canada's Schools.* Toronto: Key Porter Books.

Barnard, Chester. 1938. *The Functions of the Executive.* Cambridge, Mass.: Harvard University Press.

Baron, Dennis. 1986. *Grammar and Gender.* New Haven, Conn.: Yale University Press.

Baron, Stephen. 1997. "Canadian Male Skinhead: Street Gang or Street Terrorists." *Canadian Review of Sociology and Anthropology* 34 (2): 125–154.

Barraket, Jo, and Millsom S. Henry-Warin. 2008. "Getting It On(line): Sociological Perspectives on E-dating." *Journal of Sociology* 44 (2): 149–165. Retrieved May 19, 2009. Available: http://jos.sagepub.com/cgi/content/abstract/44/2/149.

Barrett, David V. 2001. *The New Believers.* London: Cassell and Company.

Barrett, Stanley R. 1987. *Is God a Racist? The Right Wing in Canada.* Toronto: University of Toronto Press.

Barrette, Jacques. 2009. *Work/Family Balance: What Do We Really Know?* Ottawa: Vanier Institute of the Family. Retrieved May 25, 2009. Available: http://www.vifamily.ca/library/cft/barrette/work_family_balance.pdf.

Bascaramurty, Dakshana. 2012. "Ethnic-focused Nursing Homes Put a Canadian Face on Filial Piety." *Globe and Mail* (January 27). Retrieved May 8, 2012. Available: http://www.theglobeandmail.com/news/national/ethnic-focused-nursing-homes-put-a-canadian-face-on-filial-piety/article1359997/?page=all.

Basham, Patrick, John Merrifield, and Claudia R. Hepburn. 2007. *Home Schooling: From Extreme to Mainstream* (2nd ed.). Studies in Education Policy. Ottawa: The Fraser Institute. Retrieved April 24, 2009. Available: http://www.fraserinstitute.org/commerce.web/product_files/Homeschooling2.pdf.

Basow, Susan A. 1992. *Gender Stereotypes and Roles* (3rd ed.). Pacific Grove, Cal.: Brooks/Cole.

Baudrillard, Jean. 1983. *Simulations.* New York: Semiotext.

———. 1995. *Simulacra and Simulation.* Ann Arbor: University of Michigan Press.

Baym, Nancy. 2010. *Personal Connections in the Digital Age.* Cambridge, U.K.: Polity.

Baxter, J. 1970. "Interpersonal Spacing in Natural Settings." *Sociology* 36 (3): 444–456.

BBC News. 2004. "'More Extended Families' in Homes." (April 29). Retrieved March 16, 2006. Available: http://news.bbc.co.uk/go/pr/fr/-/1/hi/uk/3668579stm.

———. 2012. "FBI Probes Anonymous Intercept of US-UK Hacking Call" (February 3). Retrieved February 4, 2012. Available: http://www.bbc.co.uk/news/world-us-canada-16881582.

Beare, Margaret. 1996a. *Criminal Conspiracies: Organized Crime in Canada.* Toronto: Thomson Nelson.

———. 1996b. "Organized Crime and Money Laundering." In Robert A. Silverman, James J. Teevan, and Vincent F. Sacco (eds.), *Crime in Canadian Society* (5th ed.). Toronto: Harcourt Brace, 187–245.

Beasley, Rob. 1999. "On the Streets." *Amnesty Magazine* (April). In Youth Advocacy Program International, 2009, "Street Children and Homelessness." Retrieved March 6, 2009. Available: http://www.yapi.org/street/.

Beattie, Karen. 2005a. "Adult Correctional Services in Canada, 2003/04." *Juristat* 25 (8). Ottawa: Statistics Canada.

———. 2005b. "Family Violence Against Children and Youth." In Kathy AuCoin (ed.), *Family Violence in Canada: A Statistical Profile, 2005.* Statistics Canada Cat. no. 85-224XIE. Retrieved May 20, 2009. Available: http://dsp-psd.tpsgc.gc.ca/Collection/Statcan/85-224-X/85-224-XIE2005000.pdf.

Beaujot, Roderic. 1991. *Population Change in Canada: The Challenges of Policy Adaptation.* Toronto: McClelland and Stewart.

———, and Robert Anderson. 2007. "Time-Crunch: Impact of Time Spent in Paid and Unpaid Work, and Its Division in Families." *The Canadian Journal of Sociology / Cahiers canadiens de sociologie* 32 (3): 295–315.

———, and Kevin McQuillan. 1982. *Growth and Dualism: The Demographic Development of Canadian Society.* Toronto: Gage.

———, K.G. Basavarajappa, and Ravi B.P. Verma. 1988. *Current Demographic Analysis: Income and Immigrants in Canada.* Cat. no. 91-527. Ottawa: Minister of Supply and Services.

Beaupré, Pascale, Pierre Turcotte, and Anne Milan. 2008. "Junior Comes Back Home: Trends and Predictors of Returning to the Parental Home." *Canadian Social Trends.* Statistics Canada Cat. no. 11-008. Retrieved May 21, 2009. Available: http://www.statcan.gc.ca/pub/11-008-x/2006003/pdf/9480-eng.pdf.

Becker, Howard S. 1963. *Outsiders: Studies in the Sociology of Deviance.* New York: Free Press.

Beech, Hannah. 2001. "China's Lifestyle Choice." *Time* (August 6): 32.

Beeghley, Leonard. 1996. *The Structure of Social Stratification in the United States* (2nd ed.). Boston: Allyn & Bacon.

———. 2000. *The Structure of Social Stratification in the United States* (3rd ed.). Boston: Allyn & Bacon.

Belkin, Lisa. 1994. "Kill for Life?" *New York Times Magazine* (October 30): 47–51, 62–64, 76, 80.

Bell, Inge Powell. 1989. "The Double Standard: Age." In Jo Freeman, *Women: A Feminist Perspective* (4th ed.). Mountain View, Cal.: Mayfield, 236–244.

Bellan, Ruben. 1978. *Winnipeg First Century: An Economic History.* Winnipeg: Queenston House Publishing.

Belsky, Janet. 1990. *The Psychology of Aging: Theory, Research, and Interventions* (2nd ed.). Pacific Grove, Cal.: Brooks/Cole.

Benford, Robert D. 1993. "'You Could Be the Hundredth Monkey': Collective Action Frames and Vocabularies of Motive Within the Nuclear Disarmament Movement." *Sociological Quarterly* 34: 195–216.

Bennahum, David S. 1999. "For Kosovars, an On-Line Phone Directory of People in Exile." *New York Times* (July 15): D7.

Bennett, Holly. 1997. "A Good Spanking or a Bad Habit?" *Today's Parent* (June 1997): 51–52. Retrieved November 20, 2002. Available: http://www.todaysparent.com/behaviour/article.jsp?cId=51.

Benokraitis, Nijole V. 2002. *Marriages and Families: Changes, Choices, and Constraints* (4th ed.). Englewood Cliffs, N.J.: Prentice-Hall.

———. 2005. *Marriages and Families: Changes, Choices, and Constraints* (5th ed.). Englewood Cliffs, N.J.: Prentice-Hall.

———, and Joe R. Feagin. 1986. *Modern Sexism: Blatant, Subtle, and Covert Discrimination.* Englewood Cliffs, N.J.: Prentice-Hall.

Benson, Susan Porter. 1983. "The Customers Ain't God: The Work Culture of Department Store Saleswomen, 1890–1940." In Michael H. Frisch and Daniel J. Walkowitz, *Working Class America: Essays on Labor, Community, and American Society.* Urbana: University of Illinois Press, 185–211.

Benzie, Robert. 2002. "Flaherty Vows to Make Homelessness a Crime: 'Call It Tough Love If You Will.'" *National Post* (February 15). Available: http://www.nationalpost.com.

Bergen, Raquel Kennedy. 1993. "Interviewing Survivors of Marital Rape." In Claire M. Renzetti and Raymond M. Lee (eds.), *Researching Sensitive Topics.* Newbury Park: Sage, 97–211.

Berger, Bennett M. 1988. "Utopia and Its Environment." *Society* (January/February): 37–41.

Berger, Peter. 1963. *Invitation to Sociology: A Humanistic Perspective.* New York: Anchor.

———. 1967. *The Sacred Canopy: Elements of a Sociological Theory of Religion.* New York: Doubleday.

———, and Hansfried Kellner. 1964. "Marriage and the Construction of Reality." *Diogenes* 46: 1–32.

———, and Thomas Luckmann. 1967. *The Social Construction of Reality: A Treatise in the Sociology of Knowledge.* Garden City, N.Y.: Anchor Books.

Berman, H. 2002. "Sexual Harassment: The Unacknowledged Face of Violence in the Lives of Girls." In Helene Berman and Jiwani Y. (eds.), *In the Best Interest of the Girl Child: Phase II Report.* Research funded by the Status of Women Canada.

Bernard, Jessie. 1982. *The Future of Marriage.* New Haven, Conn.: Yale University Press (orig. pub. 1973).

Betschwar, Karl. 2002. "Role Reversal: The Stay-at-Home Dad's Perspective." Retrieved June 30, 2003. Available: http://www.homedad.org.uk/feature_twins.html.

Beyerstein, Barry. 1997. "Alternative Medicine: Where's the Evidence?" *Canadian Journal of Public Health* 88 (May/June): 149–150.

Bibby, Reginald W. 1987. *Fragmented Gods: The Poverty and Potential of Religion in Canada.* Toronto: Irwin.

———. 1993. *Unknown Gods: The Ongoing Story of Religion in Canada.* Toronto: Stoddart.

———. 1995a. *The Bibby Report: Social Trends Canadian Style.* Toronto: Stoddart.

———. 1995b. *Mosaic Madness: The Potential and Poverty of Canadian Life.* Toronto: Stoddart.

———. 1998. "Religion." In Robert J. Brym (ed.), *New Society: Sociology for the 21st Century* (2nd ed.). Toronto: Harcourt Brace Canada, 128–152.

———. 2001. *Canada's Teens: Today, Yesterday, and Tomorrow.* Toronto: Stoddart.

———. 2004. "The Future Families Project: A Survey of Hopes and Dreams." Vanier Institute of the Family. Retrieved September 13, 2005. Available: http://www.vifamily.ca/library/future/future.html.

———. 2012. "Why Bother with Organized Religion?" *Canadian Review of Sociology* 49: 91–101.

Bibby, R., and D.C. Posterski. 1992. *Teen Trends: A Nation in Motion.* Toronto: Stoddart.

Bielski, Zosia. 2010. "Canada's Teen Birth and Abortion Rate Drops by 36.9 per cent." *Globe and Mail* (May 26). Retrieved April 21, 2011. Available: http://www.theglobeandmail.com/life/parenting/canadas-teen-birth-and-abortion-rate-drops-by-369-per-cent/article571685.

Biles, John, Meyer Burstein, and James Frideres. 2008. *Immigration and Integration in Canada in the Twenty-First Century.* Kingston: McGill-Queen's University Press.

Binks, Georgie. 2003. "Are Older Women Invisible?" CBC News Viewpoint. www.cbc.ca.

Bissoondath, Neil. 1994. *Selling Illusions: The Cult of Multiculturalism in Canada.* Toronto: Penguin.

———. 1998. "No Place Like Home." *New Internationalist* Issue 305 (September). Retrieved June 3, 2009. Available: http://www.geocities.com/frankie_meehan/NoPlaceLikeHome.html.

Bittner, Egon. 1980. *Popular Interests in Psychiatric Remedies: A Study in Social Control.* New York: Ayer.

Black, William K. 2012. "Apple's Ethical Blindness Selects for Criminal Suppliers in Fraud-Friendly Nations." *Huffington Post* (January 31). Retrieved June 26, 2012. Available: http://www.huffingtonpost.com/william-k-black/apples-ethical-blindness-_b_1244410.html.

Blackford, Karen A. 1996. "Families and Parental Disability." In Marion Lynn (ed.), *Voices: Essays on Canadian Families.* Toronto: Thomson Nelson, 161–163.

Blascovich, Jim, and Jeremy Bailenson. 2011. *Reality: Avatars, Eternal Life, New Worlds, and the Dawn of the Virtual Revolution.* New York: HarperCollins.

Blau, Peter M., and Otis Dudley Duncan. 1967. *The American Occupational Structure.* New York: Wiley.

———, and Marshall W. Meyer. 1987. *Bureaucracy in Modern Society* (3rd ed.). New York: Random House.

Blauner, Robert. 1972. *Racial Oppression in America.* New York: Harper & Row.

Bluestone, Barry, and Bennett Harrison. 1982. *The Deindustrialization of America.* New York: Basic Books.

Blumberg, Leonard. 1977. "The Ideology of a Therapeutic Social Movement: Alcoholics Anonymous." *Journal of Studies on Alcohol* 38: 2122–2143.

Blumer, Herbert G. 1946. "Collective Behavior." In Alfred McClung Lee (ed.), *A New Outline of the Principles of Sociology.* New York: Barnes & Noble, 167–219.

———. 1969. *Symbolic Interactionism: Perspective and Method.* Englewood Cliffs, N.J.: Prentice-Hall.

———. 1974. "Social Movements." In R. Serge Denisoff (ed.), *The Sociology of Dissent.* New York: Harcourt Brace Jovanovich, 74–90.

Bogardus, Emory S. 1925. "Measuring Social Distance." *Journal of Applied Sociology* 9: 299–308.

———. 1968. "Comparing Racial Distance in Ethiopia, South Africa, and the United States." *Sociology and Social Research* 52 (2): 149–156.

Bogle, Kathleen. 2008. *Hooking Up: Sex, Dating and Relationships on Campus.* New York: New York University Press.

Bolaria, B. Singh, and Rosemary Bolaria. 1994. "Inequality and Differential Health Risks of Environmental Degradation." In Bolaria and Bolaria (eds.), *Racial Minorities, Medicine and Health.* Halifax, N.S.: Fernwood, 85–97.

———, and P. Li. 1988. *Racial Oppression in Canada* (2nd ed.). Toronto: Garamond.

———, and T. Wotherspoon. 1991. "Income, Inequality, Poverty, and Hunger." In B. Singh Bolaria (ed.), *Social Issues and Contradictions in Canadian Society.* Toronto: Harcourt Brace.

Boldt, Menno. 1993. *Surviving as Indians: The Challenge of Self-Government.* Toronto: University of Toronto Press.

Bologh, Roslyn Wallach. 1992. "The Promise and Failure of Ethnomethodology from a Feminist Perspective: Comment on Rogers." *Gender & Society* 6 (2): 199–206.

Bolton, M. Anne. 1995. "Who Can Let You Die?" In Mark Novak (ed.), *Aging in Society: A Canadian Reader.* Toronto: Thomson Nelson, 385–392.

Bonacich, Edna. 1972. "A Theory of Ethnic Antagonism: The Split Labor Market." *American Sociological Review* 37: 547–549.

———. 1976. "Advanced Capitalism and Black–White Relations in the United States: A Split Labor Market Interpretation." *American Sociological Review* 41: 34–51.

Bonger, Willem. 1969. *Criminality and Economic Conditions* (abridged ed.). Bloomington: Indiana University Press (orig. pub. 1916).

Bonvillain, Nancy. 2001. *Women & Men: Cultural Constructs of Gender* (3rd ed.). Upper Saddle River, N.J.: Prentice-Hall.

Boodman, Sandra G. 2004. "For More Teenager Girls, Adult Plastic Surgery." *Washington Post.* Retrieved March 16, 2005. Available: http://www.washingtonpost.com/ac2/-wp-dyn/A61540-2004 Oct25.html.

Bookman, Sonia. 2011. "Media, Consumption, and Everyday Life." In Will Straw, Sandra Gabrielle, and Ira Wagman (eds.). *Intersection of Media and Communications.* Toronto: Emond Montgomery, 267–287.

Borchorst, A., and B. Siim. 1987. "Women and the Advanced Welfare State—A New Kind of Patriarchal Power?" In A. Showstack-Sasson (ed.), *Women and the State.* London: Hutchinson, 128–157.

Bordo, Susan. 1993. *Unbearable Weight: Feminism, Western Culture, and the Body.* Berkeley: University of California Press.

Bougie, Evelyn. 2010. "Family, Community, and Aboriginal Language among Young First Nations Children Living Off Reserve in Canada." Statistics Canada, *Canadian Social Trends,* Cat. no. 11-008-X. Retrieved April 22, 2102. Available: http://www.statcan.gc.ca/pub/11-008-x/2010002/article/11336-eng.pdf.

Bourdieu, Pierre. 1984. *Distinction: A Social Critique of the Judgement of Taste.* Trans. Richard Nice. Cambridge, Mass.: Harvard University Press.

Bourdieu, Pierre, and Jean-Claude Passeron. 1990. *Reproduction in Education, Society and Culture.* Newbury Park, Cal.: Sage.

Bowlby, Geoff. 2005. "Provincial Drop-out Rates—Trends and Consequences." *Statistics Canada Labour Force Survey.* Retrieved April 22, 2009. Available: http://www.statcan.gc.ca/pub/81-004-x/2005004/8984-eng.htm.

Bowles, Samuel. 1977. "Unequal Education and the Reproduction of the Social Division of Labor." In Jerome Karabel and A.H. Halsey (eds.), *Power and Ideology in Education.* New York: Oxford University Press, 137–153.

———, and Herbert Gintis. 1976. *Schooling in Capitalist America: Education and the Contradictions of Economic Life.* New York: Basic Books.

Boyce, W., M. Doherty-Poirier, D. MacKinnon, C. Fortin, H. Saab, M. King, and O. Gallupe. 2006. "Sexual Health of Canadian Youth: Findings from the Canadian Youth, Sexual Health and HIV/AIDS Study." *Canadian Journal of Human Sexuality* 15 (2): 59–68.

Boyd, Monica. 1995. "Gender Inequality: Economic and Political Aspects." In Robert J. Brym, *New Sociology: Sociology for the 21st Century.* Toronto: Harcourt Brace and Company.

———, and Doug Norris. 1999. "The Crowded Nest: Young Adults at Home." *Canadian Social Trends* (Spring). Ottawa: Statistics Canada, 2–5.

Boyes, William, and Michael Melvin. 1994. *Economics* (2nd ed.). Boston: Houghton Mifflin.

Boyko, Ian. 2002. "Low Income Families Excluded from Universities: Report." (December 7). Ottawa: Canadian Federation of Students.

Bozett, Frederick. 1988. "Gay Fatherhood." In Phyllis Bronstein and Carolyn Pape Cowan (eds.), *Fatherhood Today: Men's Changing Role in the Family.* New York: Wiley, 60–71.

Bradbury, Bettina. 1996. "The Social and Economic Origins of Contemporary Families." In Maureen Baker (ed.), *Families: Changing Trends in Canada.* Toronto: McGraw-Hill Ryerson, 55–103.

Bradsher, Keith. 2006. "Ending Tariffs Is Only the Start; In Poorest Lands Like Laos, Limited Markets, Skilled Labor and Banks." *New York Times* (February 28): C1.

Bramlett, Matthew D., and William D. Mosher. 2001. "First Marriage Dissolution, Divorce, and Remarriage: United States." DHHS publication no. 2001–1250 01–0384 (5/01). Hyattsville, MD: Department of Health and Human Services.

Brand, Pamela A., Esther D. Rothblum, and L.J. Solomon. 1992. "A Comparison of Lesbians, Gay Men, and Heterosexuals on Weight and Restrained Eating." *International Journal of Eating Disorders* 11: 253–259.

Brannigan, Augustine. 2003. "The Rise and Fall of Social Psychology." Unpublished manuscript.

———. 2004. *The Rise and Fall of Social Psychology: The Use and Misuse of the Experimental Method.* Hawthorne, N.Y.: Aldine.

Brantingham, Paul J., Shihing Mu, and Aruind Verma. 1995. "Patterns in Canadian Crime." In Margaret A. Jackson and Curt T. Griffiths (eds.), *Canadian Criminology.* Toronto: Harcourt Brace and Company, 187–245.

Braun, Denny. 1991. *The Rich Get Richer: The Rise of Income Inequality in the United States and the World.* Chicago: Nelson-Hall.

Braverman, Harry. 1974. *Labor and Monopoly Capital: The Degradation of Work in the Twentieth Century.* New York: Monthly Review Press.

Brazeau, Robyn, and Jodi-Anne Brzozowski. 2008. "Violent Victimization in Canada." General Social Survey. *Matter of Fact* Issue 1. Statistics Canada Cat. no. 89-630-X. Retrieved June 10, 2009. Available: http://www.statcan.gc.ca/pub/89-630-x/2008001/article/10643-eng.pdf.

Brenner, Susan. 2010. *Cybercrime: Threats from Cyberspace.* Santa Barbara, Cal.: ABC-CLIO.

Breton, Raymond. 1988. "French–English Relations." In James Curtis and Lorne Tepperman (eds.), *Understanding Canadian Society.* Toronto: McGraw-Hill, 557–585.

Briggs, Sheila. 1987. "Women and Religion." In Beth B. Hess and Myra Marx Ferree (eds.), *Analyzing Gender: A Handbook of Social Science Research.* Newbury Park, Cal.: Sage, 408–441.

Brint, Steven. 1994. *In an Age of Experts: The Changing Role of Professionals in Politics and Public Life.* Princeton, N.J.: Princeton University Press.

Britt, Lory. 1993. "From Shame to Pride: Social Movements and Individual Affect." Paper presented at the 88th Annual Meeting of the American Sociological Association, Miami (August).

Broad, William, John Markoff, and David Sanger. 2011. "Israeli Test on Worm Called Crucial in Iran Nuclear Delay." *New York Times* (January 15). Retrieved: February 4, 2012. Available: http://www.nytimes.com/2011/01/16/world/middleeast/16stuxnet.html?pagewanted=all.

Brod, Harry, ed. 1987. *The Making of Masculinities.* Boston: Allen & Unwin.

Bronfenbrenner, Urie. 1990. "Five Critical Processes for Positive Development." From "Discovering What Families Do" in *Rebuilding the Nest: A New Commitment to the American Family.* Retrieved June 29, 1999. Available: http://www.montana.edu/wwwctf/process.html.

Brooks Gardner, Carol. 1989. "Analyzing Gender in Public Places: Rethinking Goffman's Vision of Everyday Life." *American Sociologist* 20 (Spring): 42–56.

Brotman, S., B. Ryan, Y. Jalbert, and B. Rowe. 2002. "Reclaiming Space—Regaining Health: The Health Care Experiences of Two-Spirit People in Canada." *Journal of Gay and Lesbian Social Services* 14: 67–87.

Brooks-Gunn, Jeanne. 1986. "The Relationship of Maternal Beliefs About Sex Typing to Maternal and Young Children's Behavior." *Sex Roles* 14: 21–35.

Brown, Andrew. 2012. *The Sphere of Seduction: How One-Dimensional Seduction Emerges from the Two-Dimensional Screen.* Unpublished bachelor's thesis, University of British Columbia

Brown, Robert W. 1954. "Mass Phenomena." In Gardner Lindzey (ed.), *Handbook of Social Psychology,* vol. 2. Reading, Mass.: Addison-Wesley, 833–873.

Brown, Russell. 2003. "Illusions of Choice: The Selling of *American Idol* and *The Matrix Reloaded."* Retrieved June 21, 2003. Available: http://www.thesimon.com/article_of_week/281.

Brownlee, Jamie. 2005. *Ruling Canada: Corporate Cohesion and Democracy.* Halifax: Fernwood Publishing.

Bruce, Steve. 1996. *Religion in the Modern World.* New York: Oxford University Press.

Brumberg, Joan Jacobs. 1988. *Fasting Girls: The Emergence of Anorexia Nervosa as a Modern Disease.* Cambridge, Mass.: Harvard University Press.

Brunvand, Jan Harold. 2001. *Too Good to Be True: The Colossal Book of Urban Legends.* New York: W.W. Norton and Co.

Brustad, Robert J. 1996. "Attraction to Physical Activity in Urban Schoolchildren: Parental Socialization and Gender Influence." *Research Quarterly for Exercise and Sport* 67: 316–324.

Brym, Robert, and Bonnie Fox. 1989. *From Culture to Power: The Sociology of English Canada.* Toronto: Oxford University Press.

———, and Rhonda L. Lenton. 2001. "Love Online: A Report on Digital Dating in Canada." A Report on Surveys. Funded by MSN.ca. Retrieved August 26, 2003. Available: http://www.soc-canada.com/loveonline.pdf.

Brzozowski, Jodi-Anne, Andrea Taylor-Butts, and Sara Johnson. 2006. "Victimization and Offending Among the Aboriginal Population in Canada." *Juristat* 26 (3). Ottawa: Statistics Canada.

Buchanan, C.M., E.E. Maccoby, and S.M. Dornbusch. 1996. *Adolescents After Divorce.* Cambridge, Mass.: Harvard University Press.

Buchignani, Norman. 1991. "Some Comments on the Elimination of Racism in Canada." In Ormond McKague (ed.), *Racism in Canada.* Saskatoon: Fifth House, 199–205.

———, Doreen M. Indra, and Ram Srivastiva. 1985. *Continuous Journey: A Social History of South Asians in Canada.* Toronto: McClelland and Stewart.

Buechler, Steven M. 2000. *Social Movements in Advanced Capitalism: The Political Economy and Cultural Construction of Social Activism.* New York: Oxford University Press.

Bullard, Robert B., and Beverly H. Wright. 1992. "The Quest for Environmental Equity: Mobilizing the African-American Community for Social Change." In Riley E. Dunlap and Angela G. Mertig (eds.), *American Environmentalism: The U.S. Environmental Movement, 1970–1990.* New York: Taylor & Francis, 39–49.

Buntain-Ricklefs, J.J., K.J. Kemper, M. Bell, and T. Babonis. 1994. "Punishments: What Predicts Adult Approval." *Child Abuse and Neglect* 18: 945–955.

Burciaga, Jose Antonio. 1993. *Drink Cultura.* Santa Barbara, Cal.: Capra.

Burawoy, Michael. 1991. "Introduction." In Michael Burawoy, Alice Burton, Ann Arnett Ferguson et al. (eds.), *Ethnography Unbounded: Power and Resistance in the Modern Metropolis.* Berkeley: University of California Press, 1–7.

Burger, Jerry M. 2009. "Replicating Milgram: Would People Still Obey Today?" *American Psychologist* 64: 1–11.

Burgess, Ernest W. 1925. "The Growth of the City." In Robert E. Park and Ernest W. Burgess (eds.), *The City.* Chicago: University of Chicago Press, 47–62.

Burman, Patrick. 1998. *Killing Time, Losing Ground: Experiences of Unemployment.* Toronto: Wall and Thompson.

Burnham, Walter Dean. 1983. *Democracy in the Making: American Government and Politics.* Englewood Cliffs, N.J.: Prentice-Hall.

Burns, Tom. 1992. *Erving Goffman.* New York: Routledge.

Burros, Marian. 1994. "Despite Awareness of Risks, More in U.S. Are Getting Fat." *New York Times* (July 17): 1, 8.

Busch, Ruth C. 1990. *Family Systems: Comparative Study of the Family.* New York: P. Lang.

Bushnik, Tracey. 2006. "Child Care in Canada." Statistics Canada Cat. no. 89-599-MIE no. 003.

Butler, J. 1999. *Gender Trouble: Feminism and the Subversion of Identity.* New York: Routledge.

———. 2004. *Undoing Gender.* New York: Routledge.

Butler, Robert N. 1975. *Why Survive? Being Old in America.* New York: Harper & Row.

———. 1987. "Future Trends." In George L. Maddox, Robert C. Atchley, and Raymond J. Corsini (eds.), *The Encyclopedia of Aging.* New York: Springer, 265–267.

Buvinić, Mayra. 1997. "Women in Poverty: A New Global Underclass." *Foreign Policy* (Fall): 38–53.

Cable News Network. 1997. "Study: Despair Increases Health Risks in Middle-Aged Men." CNN Website: August 26, 1997. Available: http://www.cnn.com.

Cable, Sherry, and Charles Cable. 1995. *Environmental Problems, Grassroots Solutions: The Politics of Grassroots Environmental Conflict.* New York: St. Martin's Press.

Cain, P.A. 1993. "Feminism and the Limits of Equality." In D.K. Weisberg (ed.), *Feminist Legal Theory: Foundations.* Philadelphia: Temple University Press, 237–247.

California State Auditor. 2010. "California Department of Corrections and Rehabilitation: Inmates Sentence Under the Three Strikes Law and a Small Number of Inmates Receiving Specialty Health Care Represent Significant Costs." *Report 2009-107.2* (May). Retrieved June 7, 2011. Available: www.bsa.ca.gov/reports/summary/2009-107.2.

Callahan, Daniel. 1987. *Setting Limits: Medical Goals in an Aging Society.* New York: Simon and Schuster.

Calliste, Agnes. 1987. "Sleeping Car Porters in Canada: An Ethically Submerged Split Labour Market." *Canadian Ethnic Studies* 19: 1–20.

———. 1993/94. "Race, Gender, and Canadian Immigration Policy: Blacks from the Caribbean, 1900–1932." *Journal of Canadian Studies* 28 (4): 131–148.

Callwood, June. 1995. *Trial Without End.* Toronto: Albert A. Knopf.

———. 2005. "On Turning 80." *Chatelaine* (May): 56.

Campaign 2000. 2002a. "Breaking the Cycle of Poverty for Higher Risk Populations." In *Putting Promises into Action: A Report on a Decade of Child and Family Poverty in Canada.* Retrieved November 21, 2002. Available: http://campaign2000.ca/rc/unsscMAY02/un8.html.

———. 2002b. "Canada Falling Behind on International Stage." Retrieved August 7, 2002. Available: http://www.campaign2000.ca/rc/unsscMAY02/un10.html.

———. 2002c. "A Decade of Decline." In *Putting Promises into Action: A Report on a Decade of Child and Family Poverty in Canada.* Retrieved November 21, 2002. Available: http://campaign2000.ca/rc/unsscMAY02/un8.html.

———. 2002d. "Developing a National Plan of Action for Canada's Children." Retrieved August 8, 2002. Available: http://campaign2000.ca/rc/unss-cMAY02/unplan.html.

———. 2003. *Honouring Our Promises: Meeting the Challenge to End Child and Family Poverty—2003 Report Card on Child Poverty in Canada.* Retrieved August 20, 2005. Available: http://www.campaign2000.ca/rc/rc03/NOV03ReportCard.pdf.

———. 2006. *Oh Canada! Too Many Children in Poverty for Too Long—2006 Report Card on Child and Family Poverty.* Retrieved May 24, 2009. Available: http://www.campaign2000.ca/rc/rc06/06_C2000NationalReportCard.pdf.

———. 2010. *Reduced Poverty = Better Health for All—2010 Report Card on Child and Family Poverty in Canada.* Retrieved August 6, 2012. Available: http://www.campaign2000.ca/reportCards/national/2010EnglishC2000NationalReportCard.pdf.

Campbell, Marie, and Frances Gregor. 2004. "Theory 'in' Everyday Life." In William K. Carroll (ed.), *Critical Strategies for Social Research.* Toronto: Canadian Scholars' Press, 170–180.

Campenni, C. Estelle. 1999. "Gender Stereotyping of Children's Toys: A Comparison of Parents and Non-Parents." *Sex Roles* 40 (January): 121–138.

Canada Centre for Global Security Studies. 2011. *Casting a Wider Net.* Toronto: Munk School of Global Affairs, University of Toronto.

Canadian Council on Learning. 2007. "Canada Slow to Overcome Limits for Disabled Learners." *Lessons in Learning* (February 27). Retrieved May 6, 2009. Available: http://www.ccl-cca.ca/pdfs/LessonsIn-Learning/Feb-26-07-Canada-slow-to-ov.pdf.

CanadaGlobalWarming.com. 2007. "Canada and Climate Change." Retrieved March 12, 2009. Available: http://www.canadaglobalwarming.com/.

Canada Mortgage and Housing Corporation. 1998. "Survey of Canadians' Attitudes Toward Homelessness." Available: http://www.cmhc-schl.gc.ca/Research/Homeless/F_public.html.

Canadian Association of Food Banks. 2005. Retrieved August 22, 2005. Available: http://www.cafb-acba.ca/english/GetInvolved.html.

———. 2009. "About Hunger in Canada." Retrieved June 18, 2009. Available: http://foodbankscanada.ca/main2.cfm?id=10718629-B6A7-8AA0-6D9B9CE378DE06DA.

Canadian Business. 2004. "The Rich 100: 2003–2004 Edition." Retrieved August 12, 2005. Available: http://www.canadianbusiness.com/rich100/index.htm.

———. 2011. "The Rich 100." Retrieved August 2, 2012. Available: http://list.canadianbusiness.com/rankings/rich100/2011/Default.aspx?sp2=1&d1=a&sc1=0.

Canadian Cancer Society. 2005. *Canadian Cancer Statistics, 2005.* Retrieved July 21, 2005. Available: http://www.cancer.ca/vgn/images/portal/cit_86751114/48/28/401594768cw_2005stats_en.pdf.

———. 2011. "Breast Cancer Statistics at a Glance." *About Cancer.* Retrieved February 19, 2012. Available: http://www.cancer.ca/canada-wide/about%20cancer/cancer%20statistics/stats%20at%20a%20glance/breast%20cancer.aspx.

Canadian Centre for Policy Alternatives. 2006. "Growing Gap, Growing Concerns: Canadian Attitudes Toward Income Inequality." November.

Canadian Council on Social Development. 1996. *The Progress of Canada's Children 1996.* Ottawa: Canadian Council on Children Development.

———. 1998. *The Progress of Canada's Children: 1998 Highlights.* Ottawa: Canadian Council on Social Development.

———. 2001. "Children and Youth with Special Needs." November. Ottawa: Canadian Council on Social Development.

———. 2002a. "Disability Information Sheet: Number 5." Retrieved August 8, 2002. Available: http://www.ccsd.ca/drip/research/dis5/dis5.pdf.

———. 2002b. "Percentage and Numbers of Persons in Poverty: Canada, 1990 and 1999." Ottawa: Canadian Council on Social Development.

———. 2002c. "Percentage and Number of Persons in Low Income/Poverty, by Age, Sex and Family Characteristics, Canada, 1990 and 1999." Ottawa: Canadian Council on Social Development. Retrieved June 25, 2002. Available: http://www.ccsd.ca/factsheets/fs_pov9099.htm.

———. 2003. "How the Poverty Line is Calculated." Retrieved May 20, 2003. Available: http://www.ccsd.ca/facts.html.

———. 2009. "A Profile of Economic Security in Canada." Stats and Facts Retrieved June 17, 2009. Available: http://www.ccsd.ca/factsheets/economic_security/poverty/index.htm.

Canadian Criminal Justice Association. 2005. "Aboriginal Peoples and the Criminal Justice System." Retrieved September 14, 2005. Available: http://www.ccja-acjp.ca/en/aborit.html.

Canadian Education Association. 1999. "Educational Trends in Canada." Available: http://www.acea.ca/trends.html.

Canadian Federation of Students. 2012. "Student Debt in Canada: Education Shouldn't Be a Debt Sentence." The Facts About Post-Secondary Education (Spring 2012). Available: http://www.cfs-fcee.ca/html/english/research/factsheets/Factsheet-2012-Student%20debt-En-8x11-Bleed.pdf

Canadian Institute of Child Health. 1994. *The Health of Canada's Children* (2nd ed.). Ottawa: Canadian Institute of Child Health.

Canadian Institute for Health Information. 2004a. *Health Care in Canada, 2004.* Retrieved July 21, 2005. Available: http://www.cihi.ca.

———. 2004b. *Improving the Health of Canadians.* Retrieved July 22, 2005. Available: http://www.cihi.ca.

———. 2004c. *Full-Time Equivalent Physicians, Canada, 2002–2003.* Retrieved July 23, 2005. Available: http://www.cihi.cahttp://secure.cihi.ca/cihiweb/dispPage.jsp?cw_page=AR_17_E.

———. 2004d. *Health Research—Investing in Canada's Future, 2003–2004.* Retrieved February 15, 2012. Available: http://www.cihr-irsc.gc.ca/e/24936.html.

———. 2008a. *Canada's Health Care Providers, 2007.* Ottawa: Canadian Institute for Health Information.

———. 2008b. *National Health Expenditure Trends, 1975–2008.* Retrieved April 21, 2009. Available: http://secure.cihi.ca/ews/en/index.jsp.

———. 2009. *Health Human Resources—Physicians.* Retrieved April 19, 2009. Available: http://secure.cihi.ca/cihiweb/dispPage.jsp?cw_page=statistics_results_topic_physicians_e&cw_topic=Health%20Human%20Resources&cw_subtopic=Physicians.

———. 2011a. *Health Care Cost Drivers: The Facts.* Ottawa: Canadian Institute for Health Information.

———. 2011b. *National Health Expenditure Trends, 1975 to 2011.* Ottawa: Canadian Institute for Health Information.

Canadian Internet Project. 2004. Retrieved November 25, 2005. Available: http://www.canadianinternetproject.ca/en/documents/Canada%20Online%20Final%20English%20Version%2010302005.pdf.

Canadian Labour Congress, 2008. *Women in the Workforce: Still a Long Way from Equality.* Retrieved February 16, 2012. Available: http://www.canadianlabour.ca/sites/default/files/pdfs/womensequalityreportEn.pd.

Canadian Medical Association. 2010. "Health Care System: Canadians Fear Effect of the 'Silver Tsunami.'" Retrieved May 13, 2012. Available: http://www.cma.ca/advocacy/silver-tsunami.

Canadian Public Health Association. 1997. "Position Paper on Homelessness and Health." Available: http://www.cpha.ca/cpha.docs/homeless.eng.html.

Canadian Safe Schools Network. 2012. "Programs and Resources." Retrieved May 10, 2012. Available: http://www.canadiansafeschools.com/programs/overview.htm.

Canadian Society of Plastic Surgeons. 2009. "Code of Ethics." Retrieved June 11, 2009. Available: http://www.plasticsurgery.ca/content.aspx?catID=757&subcatID=467.

Cancian, Francesca M. 1990. "The Feminization of Love." In C. Carlson (ed.), *Perspectives on the Family: History, Class, and Feminism.* Belmont, Cal.: Wadsworth, 171–185.

Canetto, S.S., and Isaac Sakinofsky. 1998. "The Gender Paradox in Suicide." *Suicide and Life-Threatening Behavior* 28: 1–22.

Cannon, M. 1998. "The Regulation of First Nations Sexuality." *Canadian Journal of Native Studies* 18 (1): 1–18.

Canter, R.J., and S.S. Ageton. 1984. "The Epidemiology of Adolescent Sex-Role Attitudes." *Sex Roles* 11: 657–676.

Cantor, Muriel G. 1980. *Prime-Time Television: Content and Control.* Newbury Park, Cal.: Sage.

———. 1987. "Popular Culture and the Portrayal of Women: Content and Control." In Beth B. Hess and Myra Marx Ferree, *Analyzing Gender: A Handbook of Social Science Research.* Newbury Park, Cal.: Sage, 190–214.

Cantril, Hadley. 1941. *The Psychology of Social Movements.* New York: Wiley.

Capek, Stella M. 1993. "The 'Environmental Justice' Frame: A Conceptual Discussion and Application." *Social Problems* 40 (1): 5–23.

Carlson, Kathryn Blaze. 2010. "Baby By Stealth: Reproduction Law Forcing 'Dangerous Alternatives.'" National Post (March 12). Retrieved January 25, 2012. Available: http://www.proudparenting.com/node/15104.

Carmichael, Amy. 2005. "And the Booby Prize Goes to . . ." Retrieved January 13, 2006. Available: http://www.theglobe.ca/servlet/story/RTGAM.20050724.wimplants0724/BNStory/National/.

Carrier, James G. 1986. *Social Class and the Construction of Inequality in American Education.* New York: Greenwood.

Carrington, Peter, and Robin Fitzgerald. 2012. "Do Police Discriminate Against Minority Youth in Canada?" In Julian Roberts and Michelle Grossman (eds.), *Criminal Justice in Canada* (4th ed.). Toronto: Nelson, 187–198.

Carroll, John B., ed. 1956. *Language, Thought, and Reality: Selected Writings of Benjamin Lee Whorf.* Cambridge, Mass.: MIT Press.

Carroll, William K. 2004. *Critical Strategies for Social Research.* Toronto: Canadian Scholars' Press.

Carter, Stephen L. 1994. *The Culture of Disbelief: How American Law and Politics Trivializes Religious Devotion.* New York: Anchor/Doubleday.

Carter, Tom, Anita Friesen, Chesya Polevychok, and John Osborne. 2007. "Panhandling in Winnipeg: Legislation vs. Support Services." Winnipeg: Public Interest Law Centre.

Cashmore, E. Ellis. 1996. *Dictionary of Race and Ethnic Relations* (4th ed.). London: Routledge.

Cassidy, B., R. Lord, and N. Mandell. 2001. "Silenced and Forgotten Women: Race, Poverty, and Disability." In Nancy Mandell (ed.), *Feminist Issues: Race, Class, and Society* (3rd ed.). Toronto: Prentice-Hall, 75–107.

Castellano, Marlene. 2002. "Aboriginal Family Trends: Extended Families, Nuclear Families, Families of the Heart." Ottawa: Vanier Institute of the Family. Retrieved May 12, 2009. Available: http://www.vifamily.ca/library/cft/aboriginal.html.

———. 2007. "Healing Narrative: Recovery from Residential School Trauma." *Transitions* 36 (Winter 2006–2007). Ottawa: Vanier Institute of the Family. Retrieved April 7, 2009. Available: http://www.vifamily.ca/library/transition/364/364.pdf.

Castells, Manuel. 1977. *The Urban Question.* London: Edward Arnold (orig. pub. 1972 as *La Question Urbaine,* Paris).

———. 1998. *End of Millennium.* Malden, Mass.: Blackwell.

———. 2000a. *The Rise of the Network Society* (2nd ed.). Oxford: Blackwell Publishers.

———. 2000b. "Materials for an Exploratory Theory of the Network Society." *British Journal of Sociology* (January/March): 5–24.

———. 2004. "Informationalism and the Network Society." In Manuel Castells (ed.), *The Network Society.* Cheltenham: Edward Elgar, 3–45.

Castles, Stephen. 1995. "Trois Siècles de Dépopulation Amerindienne." In L. Normandeau and V. Piche (eds.), *Les Populations Amerindienne et Inuit du Canada.* Montreal: Presse de l'Université de Montréal.

Catalyst Canada. 2005. "2004 Catalyst Census of Women Corporate Officers and Top Earners of Canada." Retrieved September 22, 2005. Available: http://www.catalystwomen.org/bookstore/files/fact/2004%20Canadian%20COTE%20Census%20Fact%20Sheet.pdf.

———. 2012. "Women CEOs and Heads of the Financial Post 500." Retrieved February 6, 2012. Available: http://www.catalyst.org/publication/322/women-ceos-and-heads-of-the-financial-post-500.

Catholic News Agency. 2009. "Benedict XVI Says Church Needs to Proclaim Gospel on the "Digital Continent."" Retrieved May 8, 2012. Available: http://www.catholicnewsagency.com/news/benedict_xvi_says_church_needs_to_proclaim_gospel_on_the_digital_continent.

Caukin, Jennifer. 2011. "A Day in the Life of Skype." *The Big Blog* (September). Retrieved December 27, 2011. Available: http://blogs.skype.com/en/2011/09/a_day_in_the_life_of_skype_inf.html.

Cavender, Gray. 1995. "Alternative Theory: Labeling and Critical Perspectives." In Joseph F. Sheley (ed.), *Criminology: A Contemporary Handbook* (2nd ed.). Belmont, Cal.: Wadsworth, 349–371.

Cavender, Nick. 2001. "It's a Dad's Life." Retrieved June 20, 2003. Available: http://www.homedad.org.uk/feature_dadslife.html.

CBC News. 1997. *The National* (December 18).

———. 2004. "Firefighter Claims Union Turning Members Against Her." Retrieved February 4, 2005. Available: http://www.cbc.ca/story/news/national/2004/11/04/firefighter041104.html.

———. 2006a. "Day Care in Canada." CBC News Indepth. Retrieved December 1, 2008. Available: http://www.canadiancrc.com/Newspaper_Articles/CBC_INDEPTH_Day_Care_in_Canada_09FEB05.aspx.

———. 2006b. "In Depth: The Hutterites." CBC News Indepth. Retrieved January 20, 2009. Available: http://www.cbc.ca/news/background/hutterites/.

———. 2007. "Almost 4 out of 5 Canadians Believe in Global Warming: Poll." CBC News Online. Retrieved March 15, 2009. Available: http://www.cbc.ca/canada/story/2007/03/22/environment-poll.html.

———. 2008a. "Tuition Fees: The Higher Cost of Higher Education." CBC News Indepth. Retrieved April 9, 2009. Available: http://www.cbc.ca/news/background/higher-education.

———. 2008b. "PM Cites 'Sad Chapter" in Apology for Residential Schools." Retrieved April 9, 2012. Available: http://www.cbc.ca/news/canada/story/2008/06/11/aboriginal-apology.html.

———. 2009. "Assisted Human Reproduction: Regulating and Treating Conception Problems." February 5. Retrieved May 19, 2009. Available: http://www.cbc.ca/health/story/2009/02/05/f-reprotech.html.

———. 2010a. "Four in 10 First Marriages End in Divorce: Report." Retrieved February 3, 2012. Available: http://www.cbc.ca/news/canada/story/2010/10/04/vanier-study004.html.

———. 2010b. "Marriage: Is It Still Important?" Retrieved February 21, 2012. Available http://www.cbc.ca/news/pointofview/2010/10/marriage-is-it-still-important.html.

Center for Media Literacy. 2011. "What Is Media Literacy? A Definition . . . and More." Retrieved January 30, 2012. Available: http://www.medialit.org/reading-room/what-media-literacy-definitionand-more.

Chafetz, Janet Saltzman. 1984. *Sex and Advantage: A Comparative, Macro-Structural Theory of Sex Stratification.* Totowa, N.J.: Rowman & Allanheld.

———. 1989. "Marital Intimacy and Conflict: The Irony of Spousal Equality." In Jo Freeman (ed.), *Women: A Feminist Perspective* (4th ed.). Mountain View, Cal.: Mayfield, 149–156.

Chagnon, Napoleon A. 1992. *Yanomamö: The Last Days of Eden.* New York: Harcourt Brace Jovanovich (rev. from

4th ed., *Yanomamö: The Fierce People,* by Holt, Rinehart & Winston).

Chalfant, H. Paul, Robert E. Beckley, and C. Eddie Palmer. 1994. *Religion in Contemporary Society* (3rd. ed.). Ithaca, Ill.: Peacock.

Chambliss, William J. 1973. "The Saints and the Roughnecks." *Society* 11: 24–31.

Chandler, Tertius, and Gerald Fox. 1974. *3000 Years of Urban History.* New York: Academic Press.

Chandler, M. J., and C.E. Lalonde. 2008. "Cultural Continuity as a Protective Factor Against Suicide in First Nations Youth." *Horizons.* A Special Issue on Aboriginal Youth, Hope or Heartbreak: Aboriginal Youth and Canada's Future. 10 (1): 68–72.

Chang, Jen, Bethany Or, Eloginy Tharmendran, Emmie Tsumura, Steve Daniels, and Darryl Leroux, compilers. 2001. *RESIST! A Grassroots Collection of Stories, Poetry, Photos and Analysis from the FTAA Protests in Québec City and Beyond.* Halifax: Fernwood Publishing.

Chapkis, W. 2000. "Power and Control in the Commercial Sex Trade." In Ronald Weitzer (ed.), *Sex for Sale: Prostitution, Pornography and the Sex Industry.* New York: Routledge, 181–201.

Chapman, Amanda. 2003. "Gender Bias in Education." *Multicultural Pavilion: Exchange Research Room.* Retrieved September 20, 2003. Available: http://www.edchange.org/multicultural/papers/genderbias.html.

Charlton, Angela. 1999. "Natalya Gracheva Is Giving McDonald's Heartburn." Associated Press (June 23). Retrieved Sept. 7, 1999. Available: http://www.mcspotlight.org/media/press/apny_23june99.html.

Chawla, Raj K. 2008. "Changes in Family Wealth." *Perspectives on Labour and Income* 9 (6). Retrieved June 16, 2009. Available: http://www.statcan.gc.ca/pub/75-001-x/2008106/pdf/10640-eng.pdf.

Cheal, David, ed. 2007. *Canadian Families Today: New Perspectives.* Toronto: Oxford University Press.

Chen, Elsa. 2008. "Impacts of 'Three Strikes and You're Out' on Crime Trends in California and Throughout the United States." *Journal of Contemporary Criminal Justice* 24: 345–370.

Cheney, Peter. 2004. "They'll Bop Till They Drop." *Globe and Mail* (February 28): F4–F5.

———, Robert Matas, and David Roberts. 1998. "Abuse Claims Against Churches Surge." *Globe and Mail* (June 9): A1, A5.

Cherlin, Andrew J. 1992. *Marriage, Divorce, Remarriage.* Cambridge, Mass.: Harvard University Press.

Chernin, Kim. 1981. *The Obsession: Reflections on the Tyranny of Slenderness.* New York: Harper & Row.

Chidley, Joe. 1995. "Spreading Hate on the Internet." *Maclean's* (May 8): 3.

Chipungu, Joel. 1999. "Polygamy Is Alive and Well in Zambia." African News Service (July 22). Retrieved September 11, 1999. Available: http://www.comtexnews.com.

Chisholm, Patricia. 1995. "Schooling for the Disabled." *Maclean's* (March 27): 52–54.

———, Sharon Doyle Driedger, and Susan McClelland. 1999. "The Mother Load." *Maclean's* (March 1). Available: http://www.macleans.ca/pub-doc/1999/03/01.

Cho, Kyong. 2011. "New Media and Religion: Observations on Research." *Communication Research Trends* (March). Retrieved May 11, 2012. Available: http://findarticles.com/p/articles/mi_7081/is_1_30/ai_n57221190/?tag=content;col1.

Cho, Sumi K. 1993. "Korean Americans vs. African Americans: Conflict and Construction." In Robert Gooding-Williams (ed.), *Reading Rodney King, Reading Urban Uprising.* New York: Routledge, 196–211.

Chon, Margaret. 1995. "The Truth About Asian Americans." In Russell Jacoby and Naomi Glauberman (eds.), *The Bell Curve Debate: History, Documents, Opinions.* New York: Times Books, 238–240.

Chossudovsky, Michel. 1997. *The Globalization of Poverty.* Penang: Third World Network.

Christ, Carol P. 1987. *Laughter of Aphrodite: Reflections on a Journey to the Goddess.* San Francisco: Harper & Row.

Christians, Clifford G.G., Kim B. Rotzoll, and Mark Fackler. 1987. *Media Ethics.* New York: Longman.

Christie, B. 2001. "Attack Hoax Makes Rounds on the Web." *The Bakersfield Californian* (September 18): A1.

Chui, Tina, Kelly Tran, and Hélène Maheux. 2007. "Immigration in Canada: A Portrait of the Foreign-Born Population, 2006 Census." Statistics Canada Cat. no. 97-557-XIE. Available: http://www12.statcan.ca/census-recensement/2006/as-sa/97-557/pdf/97-557-XIE2006001.pdf.

Chunn, Dorothy E. 2000. "Politicizing the Personal: Feminism, Law, and Public Policy." In Nancy Mandell and Ann Duffy (eds.), *Canadian Families: Diversity, Conflict, and Change* (2nd ed.). Toronto: Harcourt, 225–259.

Church Council on Justice and Corrections. 1996. *Satisfying Justice.* Ottawa: Church Council on Justice and Corrections.

Church, Elizabeth. 1996. "Kinship and Stepfamilies." In Marion Lynn (ed.), *Voices: Essays on Canadian Families.* Toronto: Thomson Nelson, 81–106.

———. 2003. "Kinship and Stepfamilies." In Marion M. Lynn (ed.), *Voices: Essays on Canadian Families* (2nd ed.). Toronto: Thomson Nelson, 55–75.

Churchill, Ward. 1994. *Indians Are Us? Culture and Genocide in Native North America.* Monroe, Maine: Common Courage Press.

CIA (Central Intelligence Agency). 2001. *The World Factbook 2001.* Washington, D.C.: Office of Public Affairs.

———. 2004. *The World Factbook 2004.* Washington D.C.: Office of Public Affairs.

———. 2005. *The World Factbook 2005.* Washington D.C.: Office of Public Affairs. Available: http://www.cia.gov/cia/publications/factbook/index.html.

———. 2009. *The World Factbook 2009.* Washington, D.C.: Office of Public Affairs. Retrieved February 22, 2009. Available: https://www.cia.gov/library/publications/the-world-factbook.

———. 2012. *The World Factbook 2012.* Washington, D.C.: Office of Public Affairs. Retrieved June 4, 2012. Available: https://www.cia.gov/library/publications/the-world-factbook/rankorder/2054rank.html.

Citizen's Forum on Canada's Future. *Report to the People and Government of Canada.* 1991. Ottawa: Privy Council Office.

Citizenship and Immigration Canada. 2005. *Facts and Figures: Immigration Overview.* Ottawa: Citizenship and Immigration Canada. Retrieved July 14, 2005. Available: http://www.cic.gc.ca/english/pub/facts2003/overview/1.html.

———. 2008. *Facts and Figures 2007—Immigration Overview.* Ottawa: Citizenship and Immigration Canada. Retrieved April 10, 2009. Available: http://www.cic.gc.ca/english/resources/statistics/facts2007/index.asp.

———. 2010. *Facts and Figures 2010.* Ottawa: Citizenship and Immigration Canada. Retrieved June 4, 2012. Available: http://www.cic.gc.ca/english/pdf/research-stats/facts2010.pdf.

Clairmont, D.H., and F.C. Wein. 1980. "Race Relations in Canada." In Jay E. Goldstein and Rita Bienvenue (eds.), *Ethnicity and Ethnic Relations in Canada.* Toronto: Butterworths, 313–315.

Clark, Lorenne, and Debra Lewis. 1977. *Rape: the Price of Coercive Sexuality.* Toronto: Women's Press.

Clark, Warren. 1998. "Religious Observance: Marriage and Family." *Canadian Social Trends* (Autumn): 2–7. Ottawa: Statistics Canada.

———. 2003. "Pockets of Belief: Religious Attendance in Canada." *Canadian Social Trends* (Spring): 2–5.

———, and Susan Crompton. 2006. "Till Death Do Us Part? The Risk of First and Second Marriage Dissolution." *Canadian Social Trends.* Statistics Canada Cat. no. 11-008. Retrieved May 6, 2009. Available: http://www.statcan.gc.ca/pub/11-008-x/2006001/pdf/9198-eng.pdf.

———, and Grant Schellenberg. 2006. "Who's Religious?" *Canadian Social Trends* (Summer): 2–9. Ottawa: Statistics Canada.

Clarke, Harold D., Jane Jenson, Lawrence LeDuc, and John H. Pammett. 1991. *Absent Mandate: The Politics of Discontent in Canada* (2nd ed.). Toronto: Gage.

Clayman, Steven E. 1993. "Booing: The Anatomy of a Disaffiliative Response." *American Sociological Review* 58 (1): 110–131.

Clement, Wallace. 1975. *The Canadian Corporate Elite.* Toronto: McClelland and Stewart.

———, and John Myles. 1994. *Relations of Ruling: Class and Gender in Postindustrial Societies.* Montreal: McGill-Queen's University Press.

Cleveland, Gordon, and Michael Krashinsky. 2003. "Eight Myths about Early Childhood Education and Care." Retrieved June 14, 2005. Available: http://www.childcarecanada.org/pubs/other/FF/FactandFantasy.pdf.

Clifford, Pat. 2005. "CYBER Kids." *Education Canada* 45 (Spring): 14.

Cloward, Richard A., and Lloyd E. Ohlin. 1960. *Delinquency and Opportunity: A Theory of Delinquent Gangs.* New York: Free Press.

CNN. 1994. "Both Sides: School Prayer." November 26.

———. 1999. Chatpage "Jan Harold Brunvand." Retrieved September 27, 2002. Available: http://www.cnn.com/COMMUNITY/transcripts/jan.harold.brunvand.html.

———. 2005. "Leadership Vacuum Stymied Aid Offers." CNN.com. Retrieved September 16, 2005. Available: http://edition.cnn.com/2005/US/09/15/katrina.response/index.html.

Coakley, Jay J. 2004. *Sport in Society: Issues and Controversies* (8th ed.). New York: McGraw-Hill.

Cohen, Leah Hager. 1994. *Train Go Sorry: Inside a Deaf World.* Boston: Houghton Mifflin.

Cohen, Marjorie Griffin. 1993. "Capitalist Development, Industrialization, and Women's Work." In Graham S. Lowe and Harvey J. Krahn (eds.), *Work in Canada.* Toronto: Thomson Nelson, 142–144.

Cohen, Theodore, ed. 2001. *Men and Masculinity: A Text Reader.* Belmont, Cal.: Wadsworth.

Colapinto, John. 2001. *As Nature Made Him: The Boy Who Was Raised as a Girl.* New York: HarperCollins.

Colby, David C., and Timothy E. Cook. 1991. "Epidemics and Agendas: The Politics of Nightly News Coverage of AIDS." *Journal of Health Politics, Policy and Law* 16 (2): 215–249.

Coles, Gerald. 1987. *The Learning Mystique: A Critical Look at "Learning Disabilities."* New York: Pantheon.

Collier, Peter, and David Horowitz. 1987. *The Fords: An American Epic.* New York: Summit Books.

Collin, Chantal, and Hillary Jensen, 2009. *A Statistical Profile of Poverty in Canada.* Ottawa: Library of Parliament. Retrieved April 12, 2010. Available: http://www.parl.gc.ca/Content/LOP/ResearchPublications/prb0917-e.pdf.

Collins, Catherine, and Douglas Frantz. 1993. *Teachers: Talking out of School.* Boston: Little, Brown.

Collins, Patricia Hill. 1990. *Black Feminist Thought: Knowledge, Consciousness, and the Politics of Empowerment.* London: HarperCollins Academic.

———. 1991. "The Meaning of Motherhood in Black Culture." In Robert Staples (ed.), *The Black Family: Essays and Studies.* Belmont, Cal.: Wadsworth, 169–178. Orig. pub. in *SAGE: A Scholarly Journal on Black Women* 4 (Fall 1987): 3–10.

———. 1998. *Fighting Words: Black Women and the Search for Justice.* Minneapolis: University of Minnesota Press.

Collins, Randall. 1971. "A Conflict Theory of Sexual Stratification." *Social Problems* 19 (1): 3–21.

———. 1979. *The Credential Society: An Historical Sociology of Education.* New York: Academic Press.

———. 1982. *Sociological Insight: An Introduction to Non-Obvious Sociology.* New York: Oxford University Press.

———. 1994. *Four Sociological Traditions.* New York: Oxford University Press.

———. 1997. "An Asian Route to Capitalism: Religious Economy and the Origins of Self-Transforming Growth in Japan." *American Sociological Review* 62: 843–865.

Coltrane, Scott. 1992. "The Micropolitics of Gender in Nonindustrial Societies." *Gender and Society* 6: 86–107.

Collison, Robert. 2006. "Men and the Pursuit of Youthfulness." *Financial Post* (September 30).

Comack, Elizabeth. 1996a. "Women and Crime." In R. Linden (ed.), *Criminology: A Canadian Perspective* (3rd ed.). Toronto: Harcourt Brace, 139–175.

———. 1996b. *Women in Trouble.* Halifax: Fernwood Publishing.

———. 2000. "Women and Crime." In R. Linden (ed.), *Criminology: A Canadian Perspective* (4th ed.). Toronto: Harcourt Brace.

———. 2004. "Feminism and Criminology." In Rick Linden (ed.), *Criminology: A Canadian Perspective* (5th ed.) Toronto: Thomson Nelson, 164–195.

———. 2012. "Feminism and Criminology." In Rick Linden (ed.), *Criminology: A Canadian Perspective* (7th ed.) Toronto: Nelson, 179–216.

———, and Evan Bowness. 2010. "Dealing the Race Card: Public Discourse on the Policing of Winnipeg's Inner-city Communities." *Canadian Journal of Urban Research* 19: 34–50.

Comfort, Alex. 1976. "Age Prejudice in America." *Social Policy* 7 (3): 3–8.

Commission of Inquiry into the Investigation of the Bombing of Air India Flight 182. 2010. *Air India Flight 182: A Canadian Tragedy. Volume One: The Overview.* Ottawa: Public Works and Government Services Canada.

Commission on Systemic Racism in the Ontario Criminal Justice System. 1995. *Report of the Commission on Systemic Racism in the Ontario Criminal Justice System.* Toronto: Queen's Printer for Ontario.

Commonwealth Fund. 2002. "Canadian Adults' Health Care System Views and Experiences." *Commonwealth Fund 2001 International Health Policy Survey.* New York: Commonwealth Fund. Retrieved December 17, 2002. Available: http://www.cmwf.org/programs/international/can_sb_552.pdf.

———. 2007. *2007 International Health Policy Survey in Seven Countries.* New York: Commonwealth Fund. Retrieved April 21, 2009. Available: http://www.commonwealthfund.org/Content/Surveys/2007/2007-International-Health-Policy-Survey-in-Seven-Countries.aspx.

Condry, Sandra McConnell, John C. Condry Jr., and Lee Wolfram Pogatshnik. 1983. "Sex Differences: A Study of the Ear of the Beholder." *Sex Roles* 9: 697–704.

Congregatio Pro Doctrina Fidei (Congregation for the Doctrine of the Faith). 2012. Doctrinal Assessment of the Leadership Conference of Women Religious. United States Conference of Catholic Bishops. Retrieved April 18, 2012. Available: http://www.usccb.org/loader.cfm?csModule=security/getfile&pageid=55544.

Connidis, Ingrid. 1989. *Family Ties and Aging.* Toronto: Butterworths.

Conrad, Peter. 1975. "The Discovery of Hyperkinesis." *Social Problems* 23 (October): 12–21.

Conrad, Peter, and Joseph W. Schneider. 1980. "The Medical Control of Deviance: Conquests and Consequences." In Julius A. Roth (ed.), *Research in the Sociology of Health Care: A Research Annual,* vol. 1. Greenwich, Conn.: Jai Press, 1–53.

———. 1992. *Deviance and Medicalization: From Badness to Sickness.* Philadelphia: Temple University Press.

Cook, Ramsay. 1995. *Canada, Quebec and the Uses of Nationalism* (2nd ed.). Toronto: McClelland and Stewart.

Cook, Sherburn F. 1973. "The Significance of Disease in the Extinction of the New England Indians." *Human Biology* 45: 485–508.

Cook, Shirley J. 1969. "Canadian Narcotics Legislation, 1908–1923: A Conflict Model Interpretation." *Canadian Review of Sociology and Anthropology* 6 (1): 36–46.

Cooke, Lynn Prince. 2004. "The Gendered Division of Labor and Family Outcomes in Germany." *Journal of Marriage and the Family* 66 (December): 1246–1259.

Cooke, Martin, Daniel Beavon, and Mindy McHardy. 2004. *Measuring the Well-Being of Aboriginal People: An Application of the United Nations' Human Development Index to Registered Indians in Canada, 1981–2001.* Ottawa: Indian and Northern Affairs Canada.

Cookson, Peter W., Jr., and Caroline Hodges Persell. 1985. *Preparing for Power: America's Elite Boarding Schools.* New York: Basic Books.

Cool, Julie, 2010. *Wage Gap Between Women and Men.* Background Paper: Library of Parliament Publication No 2010-30-E (July 29). Retrieved June 1, 2012. Available: http://www.parl.gc.ca/Content/LOP/ResearchPublications/2010-30-e.pdf.

Cooley, Charles Horton. 1922. *Human Nature and Social Order.* New York: Scribner (orig. pub. 1902).

———. 1926. *Human Nature and Social Order.* New York: Scribner (orig. pub. 1902).

———. 1962. *Social Organization.* New York: Schocken Books (orig. pub. 1909).

———. 1998. "The Social Self—The Meaning of 'I.'" In Hans-Joachim Schubert (ed.), *On Self and Social Organization—Charles Horton Cooley.* Chicago: University of Chicago Press, 155–175. Reprinted from *Charles Horton Cooley, Human Nature and the Social Order.* New York: Schocken, 1902.

Coontz, Stephanie. 1992. *The Way We Never Were: American Families and the Nostalgia Trap.* New York: Basic Books.

Cooper, A., McLoughlin, I. P., and Campbell, K. M. 2000. "Sexuality in Cyberspace: Update for the 21st Century." *Cyberpsychology & Behavior,* 3 (4)L 521—536. doi:10.1089/109493100420142.

Coppel, Jonathan, Jean-Christophe Dumond, and Ignazio Visco. 2001. "Trends in Immigration and Economic Consequences." OECD Economics Department Working Papers 284, OECD Economics Department. Paris: OECD.

Corrado, Raymond R. 1996. "Political Crime in Canada." In Rick Linden (ed.), *Criminology: A Canadian Perspective* (3rd ed.). Toronto: Harcourt Brace and Company, 459–493.

Corsaro, William A. 1985. *Friendship and Peer Culture in the Early Years.* Norwood: N.J.: Ablex.

———. 1992. "Interpretive Reproduction in Children's Peer Cultures." *Social Psychology Quarterly* 55 (2): 160–177.

———. 1997. *Sociology of Childhood.* Thousand Oaks, Cal.: Pine Forge.

Cortese, Anthony. 1999. *Provocateur: Images of Women and Minorities in Advertising.* Latham, Md.: Rowman and Littlefield.

———. 2004. *Provocateur: Images of Women and Minorities in Advertising* (2nd ed.). Latham, Md: Rowman and Littlefield.

Cose, Ellis. 1993. *The Rage of a Privileged Class.* New York: HarperCollins.

Coughlin, Ellen K. 1993. "Author of Noted Study on Black Ghetto Life Returns with a Portrait of Homeless Women." *The Chronicle of Higher Education* (March 31): A7–A8.

Council of Ministers of Education. 2002. *Education Indicators in Canada: Report of the Pan-Canadian Education Indicators Program, 1999.* Toronto: Council of Ministers of Education.

Cowgill, Donald O. 1986. *Aging Around the World.* Belmont, Cal.: Wadsworth.

Craig, Steve. 1992. "Considering Men and the Media." In Steve Craig (ed.), *Men, Masculinity, and the Media.* Newbury Park, Cal.: Sage, 1–7.

Crane, B., and Crane-Seeber, J. 2003. "The Four Boxes of Gendered Sexuality: Good Girl/Bad Girl and Tough Guy/Sweet Guy." In Robert Heasley and Betsy Crane, *Sexual Lives: A Reader on the Theories and Realities of Human Sexualities.* New York: McGraw-Hill, 196–216.

Cranswick, Kelly. 1999. "At Work Despite a Chronic Health Problem." *Canadian Social Trends* (Spring): 11–15. Ottawa: Statistics Canada.

———. 2003. *General Social Survey Cycle 16: Caring for an Aging Society.* Ottawa: Statistics Canada.

Crawford, Elizabeth. 2003. "Campus Castoffs." *Chronicle of Higher Education* (June 20): A6.

Creese, Gillian, and Brenda Beagan. 1999. "Gender at Work: Seeking Solutions for Women's Equality." In James Curtis, Edward Grabb, and Neil Guppy (eds.), *Social Inequality in Canada: Patterns, Problems, and Policies.* Scarborough, Ont.: Prentice-Hall, 199–221.

———. 2008. "Gender at Work: Strategies for Equality in Neo-liberal Times." In Edward Grabb and Neil Guppy (eds.), *Social Inequality in Canada: Patterns, Problems, and Policies* (5th ed.). Toronto: Pearson.

Creswell, John W. 1998. *Qualitative Inquiry and Research Design: Choosing Among Five Traditions.* Thousand Oaks, Cal.: Sage.

Crichton, Anne, Ann Robertson, Christine Gordon, and Wendy Farrant. 1997. Health *Care: A Community Concern?* Calgary: University of Calgary Press.

Crompton, Susan. 2005. *Always a Bridesmaid: People Who Don't Intend to Marry.* Canadian Social Trends, Statistics Canada. Cat. no. 11-008. Retrieved January 26, 2012. Available: http://thesurvey.womenshealthdata.ca/pdf_files/7961.pdf.

———. 2011. "Women with Activity Limitations." Statistics Canada. Cat. no. 89-502-X. Retrieved September 13, 2011. Available: http://www.statcan.gc.ca/pub/89-503-x/2010001/article/11545-eng.htm.

CRTC. 2011. "Frequently Asked Questions." Ottawa: CRTC. Retrieved September 23, 2011. Available: http://www.crtc.gc.ca/eng/faqs.htm.

CTV. 2005. "Blacks Stopped More Often by Police, Study Finds." Retrieved July 12, 2005. Available: http://www.ctv.ca/servlet/ArticleNews/story/CTVNews/1117145635847_112554835?s_name=&no_ads=.

Cumming, Elaine C., and William E. Henry. 1961. *Growing Old: The Process of Disengagement.* New York: Basic Books.

Cunningham, J., and J.K. Antill. 1995. "Current Trends in Non-Marital Cohabitation: In Search of the POSSLQ." In J.T. Wood and S. Duck (eds.), *Under-Studied Relationships: Off the Beaten Track*. Thousand Oaks, Cal.: Sage, 148–172.

Currie, Raymond, and John Stackhouse. 1996. "Religious Institutions." In L. Tepperman, J.E. Curtis, and R.J. Richardson (eds.), *Sociology*. Toronto: McGraw-Hill Ryerson, 482–519.

Curtis, James, and Edward Grabb. 1999. "Social Status and Beliefs About What's Important for Getting Ahead." In James Curtis, Edward Grabb, and Neil Guppy (eds.), *Social Inequality in Canada: Patterns, Problems and Policies* (3rd ed.). Scarborough, Ont.: Prentice-Hall, 330–346.

———, and Ronald D. Lambert. 1994. "Culture." In R. Hagedorn (ed.), *Sociology* (5th ed.). Toronto: Holt Rinehart and Winston, 57–86.

———, Edward Grabb, and Neil Guppy, eds. 1999. *Social Inequality in Canada: Patterns, Problems, Policies* (3rd ed.). Scarborough, Ont.: Prentice-Hall.

Curtiss, Susan. 1977. *Genie: A Psycholinguistic Study of a Modern Day "Wild Child."* New York: Academic Press.

Cyrus, Virginia. 1993. *Experiencing Race, Class, and Gender in the United States.* Mountain View, Cal.: Mayfield.

Czitrom, D. 1982. *Media and the American Mind: From Morse to McLuhan*. Chapel Hill: University of North Carolina Press.

Dagg, Alexandra, and Judy Fudge. 1992. "Sewing Pains: Homeworkers in the Garment Trade." *Our Times* (June): 22–25.

Dahl, Robert A. 1961. *Who Governs?* New Haven, Conn.: Yale University Press.

Dahrendorf, Ralph. 1959. *Class and Class Conflict in an Industrial Society.* Stanford, Cal.: Stanford University Press.

Daly, Kerry. 2000. *It Keeps Getting Faster: Changing Patterns of Time in Families.* Ottawa: Vanier Institute of the Family.

Darley, John M., and Thomas R. Shultz. 1990. "Moral Rules: Their Content and Acquisition." *Annual Review of Psychology* 41: 525–556.

Dart, Bob. 1999. "Kids Get More Screen Time Than School Time." *Austin American-Statesman* (June 28): A1, A5.

Das Gupta, Tania. 1995. "Families of Native Peoples, Immigrants, and People of Colour." In Nancy Mandell and Ann Duffy (eds.), *Canadian Families: Diversity, Conflict and Change*. Toronto: Harcourt Brace, 141–174.

———. 2000. "Families of Native People, Immigrants, and People of Colour." In Nancy Mandell and Ann Duffy (eds.), *Canadian Families: Diversity, Conflict, and Change* (2nd ed.). Toronto: Harcourt, 146–187.

Dauvergne, Mia. 2003. "Family Violence Against Seniors." *Canadian Social Trends* (Spring): 10–14. Ottawa: Statistics Canada.

———. 2004. "Homicide in Canada, 2003." *Juristat* 24 (8). Ottawa: Statistics Canada.

———, and Holly Johnson. 2001. "Children Witnessing Family Violence." *Juristat* 21 (6). Cat. no. 85-002-XPE Ottawa: Statistics Canada.

———, and John Turner. 2010. "Police-Reported Crime Statistics in Canada, 2009." *Juristat* 30 (2).

DaVanzo, Julie, and David Adamson. 1997. "Russia's Demographic 'Crisis': How Real Is It?" *Rand Issue Paper.* Rand Corporation: Center for Russian and Eurasian Studies. Available: http://www.rand.org/publications/IP/IP162.

Davies, Scott. 1999. "Stubborn Disparities: Explaining Class Irregularities in Schooling." In James Curtis, Edward Grabb, and Neil Guppy (eds.), *Social Inequality in Canada: Patterns, Problems and Policies.* Scarborough, Ont.: Prentice Hall, 138–150.

———, and Neil Guppy. 2006. *The Schooled Society: An Introduction to the Sociology of Education.* Don Mills: Oxford University Press.

Davis, K. 1937. "The Sociology of Prostitution." *American Sociological Review* 2 (5): 744–755.

Davis, Fred. 1992. *Fashion, Culture, and Identity.* Chicago: University of Chicago Press.

Davis, Kingsley. 1937. "The Sociology of Prostitution." *American Sociological Review* 2 (5): 744–755.

———. 1940. "Extreme Social Isolation of a Child." *American Journal of Sociology* 45 (4): 554–565.

———. 1949. *Human Society.* New York: Macmillan.

———, and Judith Blake. 1956. "Social Structure and Fertility: An Analytical Framework." *Economic Development and Cultural Change* 4 (April): 211–235.

———, and Wilbert Moore. 1945. "Some Principles of Stratification." *American Sociological Review* 7 (April): 242–249.

Dawson, Lorne L. 1998. *Comprehending Cults: The Sociology of New Religious Movements*. Toronto: Oxford University Press.

Dean, L.M., F.N. Willis, and J.N. la Rocco. 1976. "Invasion of Personal Space as a Function of Age, Sex and Race." *Psychological Reports* 38 (3) (pt. 1): 959–965.

Dear, Michael, and Steven Flusty. 1998. "Postmodern Urbanism." *Annals of the Association of American Geographers* 88 (1): 50–72.

De Broucker, Patrice. 2005. *Without a Paddle: What to Do About Canada's Young Drop-outs?* Ottawa: Canadian Policy Research Networks. Retrieved April 22, 2009. Available: http://www.cprn.org/documents/39460_en.pdf.

———, and Laval Lavalleé. 2000. "Getting Ahead in Life: Does Your Parents' Education Count?" *Canadian Social Trends* 3: 143–147.

Deegan, Mary Jo. 1988. *Jane Addams and the Men of the Chicago School, 1892–1918.* New Brunswick, N.J.: Transaction.

DeGroot-Maggetti, Greg. 2002. *A Measure of Poverty in Canada: A Guide to the Debate About Poverty Lines.* Toronto: Public Justice Resource Centre.

DeKeseredy, Walter S. 1996. "Patterns of Family Violence." In Maureen Baker (ed.), *Families: Changing Trends in Canada.* Whitby, Ont.: McGraw-Hill Ryerson, 249–272.

———, and Katherine Kelly. 1995. "Sexual Abuse in Canadian University and College Dating Relationships: The Contribution of Male Peer Support." *Journal of Family Violence* 10 (1): 41–53.

Delgado, Richard. 1995. "Introduction." In Richard Delgado (ed.), *Critical Race Theory: The Cutting Edge.* Philadelphia: Temple University Press, xiii–xvi.

Denton, Margaret A., and Alfred A. Hunter. 1995. "What Is Sociology?" In Lorne Tepperman and R.J. Richardson (eds.), *The Social World* (3rd ed.). Toronto: McGraw-Hill Ryerson, 1–32.

Denzin, Norman K. 1989. *The Research Act* (3rd ed.). Englewood Cliffs, N.J.: Prentice-Hall.

Department of Justice. 1994. "Minister of Justice Introduces Sentencing Reform Bill." Ottawa: Press Release (June 13).

———. 2002. "Child Abuse: A Fact Sheet from the Department of Justice." Ottawa: Author.

———. 2002a. "Spousal Abuse: A Fact Sheet from the Department of Justice Canada." Ottawa: Department of Justice. Retrieved May 16, 2002. Available: http://canada.justice.gc.ca/en/ps/fm/spouseafs.html.

———. 2002b. "Family Violence." Ottawa: Department of Justice. Retrieved May 16, 2002. Available: http://canada.justice.gc.ca/en/ps/fm/overview.html.

———. 2002c. "Child Abuse: A Fact Sheet from the Department of Justice Canada." Ottawa: Department of Justice Canada.

———. 2002d. "Marriage and Legal Recognition of Same-Sex Unions." Ottawa: Department of Justice.

———. 2009a. *Assisted Human Reproduction Act.* Retrieved May 25, 2009. Available: http://laws.justice.gc.ca/en/A-13.4/.

———. 2009b. "Family Violence: A Fact Sheet." Retrieved May 20, 2009. Available: http://www.justice.gc.ca/eng/pi/fv-vf/facts-info/fv-vf.html.

———. 2011. "About Family Violence in Canada." Retrieved January 23, 2012. Available: http://www.justice.gc.ca/eng/pi/fv-vf/about-aprop.

Derber, Charles. 1983. *The Pursuit of Attention: Power and Individualism in Everyday Life.* New York: Oxford University Press.

Desai, Sabra. 2001. "But You Are Different." In Carl E. James and Adrianne Shadd (eds.), *Talking About Identity: Encounters in Race, Ethnicity, and Language* (2nd ed.). Toronto: Between the Lines, 241–249.

Desjardins, B. 1993. *Population Ageing and the Elderly.* Cat. no. 91-533E. Ottawa: Minister of Industry, Science and Technology.

Desrosier, Heather Juby, and Celine LeBourdais. 1999a. "Female Family Paths." In Peron et al., *Canadian Families Approach the Year 2000.* Ottawa: Statistics Canada, 124.

———. 1999b. "Male Family Paths." In Peron et al., *Canadian Families Approach the Year 2000.* Ottawa: Statistics Canada, 180.

Deutschmann, Linda B. 2002. *Deviance and Social Control* (3rd ed). Toronto: Thomson Nelson.

Dikotter, Frank. 1996. "'Race' and Nation: The Formation of Identity in Twentieth-Century China." *Journal of International Affairs* (Winter): 590–605.

DiMaggio, Paul. 1987. "Classification in Art." *American Sociological Review* 52: 440–455.

———, and Michael Useem. 1978. "Social Class and Arts Consumption: The Origins and Consequences of Class Differences in Exposure to the Arts in America." *Theory and Society* 5 (2): 141–161.

Ditchburn, Jennifer. 1988. "Info-Poor Nations Lose Out, Group Told." *Globe and Mail* (August 19): A7.

Dobbin, Murray. 2011. "Wake Up and Listen to Occcupiers" *The Tyee* (November 21). Retrieved June 2, 2012. Available: http://thetyee.ca/Opinion/2011/11/21/Listen-To-Occupy.

Dodds, Peter Sheridan, Roby Muhamad, and Duncan J. Watts. 2003. "An Experimental Study of Search in Global Networks." *Science* 301: 827–829.

Dollard, John, Leonard W. Doob, Neil E. Miller, O.H. Mowrer, and Robert R. Sears. 1939. *Frustration and Aggression.* New Haven, Conn.: Yale University Press.

Domhoff, G. William. 1974. *The Bohemian Grove and Other Retreats.* New York: Harper and Row.

———. 1978. *The Powers That Be: Processes of Ruling Class Domination in America.* New York: Random House.

———. 1983. *Who Rules America Now? A View for the '80s.* Englewood Cliffs, N.J.: Prentice-Hall.

———. 1990. *The Power Elite and the State: How Policy Is Made in America.* New York: Aldine De Gruyter.

———. 2002. *Who Rules America? Power and Politics* (4th ed.). New York: McGraw-Hill.

Doob, Anthony, and Julian V. Roberts. 1983. *An Analysis of the Public's View of Sentencing.* Ottawa: Department of Justice Canada.

Dooley, Stephen, and B. Gail Frankel. 1990. "Improving Attitudes Toward

Elderly People: Evaluation of an Intervention Program for Adolescents." *Canadian Journal on Aging* 9: 400–409.

Doucet, Andrea. 2009. "Can Men Mother? Or Is Mothering Essentially Female?" *Transitions Magazine* 39 (Spring). Ottawa: Vanier Institute for the Family. Retrieved May 20, 2009. Available: http://www.vifamily.ca/library/transition/391/391.pdf.

Douglas, Shirley. 2000. "A Politician Who Gave People Hope." *Maclean's* (January 1): 195.

Downey, Alana. 2009. "Daycare Crisis? A Single-Parent Speaks Out." Citizen Bytes, CBC News (February 2). Retrieved February 3, 2009. Available: http://action.web.ca/home/crru/rsrcs_crru_full.shtml?x=123681&AA_EX_Session=c781c9c8ef01ec07bcfbb8f4116ee7a0.

Driedger, Sharon Doyle. 1997. "Radical Responses." *Maclean's* (July 28): 46–47.

———. 1998. "Divorce." *Maclean's* (April 20): 39–44.

Drolet, Marie. 2001a. "The Male–Female Wage Gap." *Perspectives on Labour and Income: The Online Edition* 2 (December). Cat. no. 75-001-X1E. Ottawa: Statistics Canada. Retrieved Oct. 15, 2002. Available: http://www.statcan.ca/english/indepth/75-001/online/01201/hi-fs_200112_01_a.html.

———. 2001b. "The Persistent Gap: New Evidence on the Canadian Gender Wage Gap." Cat. no. 11F0019MPE-157. Ottawa: Statistics Canada.

———. 2002. "Can the Workplace Explain Canadian Gender Pay Differentials?" *Canadian Public Policy,* Special Issue 2002.

———. 2005. *Participation in Post-Secondary Education in Canada: Has the Role of Parental Income and Education Changed over the 1990s?* Ottawa: Statistics Canada. Retrieved April 9, 2009. Available: http://www.statcan.gc.ca/pub/11f0019m/11f0019m2005243-eng.pdf.

———. 2011. *Why Has the Gender Wage Gap Narrowed?* Cat no. 75-001-X. Ottawa: Statistics Canada. Retrieved February 6, 2012. Available: http://www.statcan.gc.ca/pub/75-001-x/2011001/pdf/11394-eng.pdf.

Drucker, Peter. 1994. "The Age of Social Transformation." *The Atlantic Monthly* (November): 53–80.

———. 2005. "Trading Places." *The National Interest* (Spring): 1–13. Retrieved March 25, 2005. Available: www.nationalinterest.org.

D'Sousa, Dinesh. 1996. *The End of Racism: Principles for a Multicultural Society.* New York: Free Press.

Du Bois, W.E.B. 1967. *The Philadelphia Negro: A Social Study.* New York: Schocken Books (orig. pub. 1899).

Dube, Francine. 1999. "One in 10 Canadians Plan to Retire on Lottery Winnings." *National Post* (January 15): A1.

Duchesne, D. 1995. *Street Prostitution in Canada.* Ottawa: Juristat.

Duffy, Ann, Nancy Mandell, and Norene Pupo, eds. 1989. *Few Choices: Women, Work and Family.* Toronto: Garamond Press.

Duhigg, Charles, and Keith Bradsher. 2012. "How the U.S. Lost Out on iPhone Work." *New York Times* (January 22): A1.

Dumas, Jean. 1990. *Rapport sur l'état de la population du Canada.* Cat. no. 91-209. Ottawa: Minister of Supply and Services.

———. 1997. "Report on the Demographic Situation in Canada, 1996." Cat. no. 91-209-XPE, 121–186. Ottawa: Minister of Industry.

Duncan, Otis Dudley. 1968. "Social Stratification and Mobility: Problems in Measurement of Trend." In E.B. Sheldon and W.E. Moore (eds.), *Indicators of Social Change.* New York: Russell Sage Foundation.

Dunlap, Riley E. 1992. "Trends in Public Opinion Toward Environmental Issues: 1965–1990." In Riley E. Dunlap and Angela G. Mertig (eds.), *American Environmentalism: The U.S. Environmental Movement, 1970–1990.* New York: Taylor & Francis, 89–113.

Dunning, Paula. 1997. *Education in Canada: An Overview.* Toronto: Canadian Education Association.

Durkheim, Émile. 1933. *Division of Labor in Society.* Trans. George Simpson. New York: Free Press (orig. pub. 1893).

———. 1956. *Education and Sociology.* Trans. Sherwood D. Fox. Glencoe, Ill.: Free Press.

———. 1964a. *The Rules of Sociological Method.* Trans. Sarah A. Solovay and John H. Mueller. New York: Free Press (orig. pub. 1895).

———. 1964b. *Suicide.* Trans. John A. Sparkling and George Simpson. New York: Free Press (orig. pub. 1897).

———. 1995. *The Elementary Forms of Religious Life.* Trans. Karen E. Fields. New York: Free Press (orig. pub. 1912).

Durlauf, Steven, and Daniel Nagin. 2011. *The Deterrent Effect of Imprisonment.* Retrieved June 9, 2011. Available: www.nber.org/chapters/c12078.pdf.

Durning, Alan. 1993. "Life on the Brink." In William Dan Perdue (ed.), *Systemic Crisis: Problems in Society, Politics, and World Order.* Fort Worth: Harcourt Brace, 274–282.

Durrant, Joan. 2002. "Physical Punishment and Physical Abuse." *B.C. Institute Against Family Violence Newsletter* (Winter): 1–7.

———, Anders G. Broberg, Linda Rose-Krasnor. 2000. "Predicting Mothers' Use of Physical Punishment During Mother–Child Conflicts in Sweden and Canada." In Paul D. Hastings and Caroline C. Piotrowski, *Conflict as a Context for Understanding Maternal Beliefs About Child Rearing and Children's Misbehavior: New Directions for Child and Adolescent Development.* Hoboken, N.J.: Jossey-Bass.

Duster, Troy. 1995. "Symposium: The Bell Curve." *Contemporary Sociology: A Journal of Reviews* 24 (2): 158–161.

Dworkin, Andrea. 1974. *Woman Hating.* New York: Dutton.

Dyck, Rand. 2004. *Canadian Politics: Critical Approaches* (4th ed.). Toronto: Thomson Nelson.

———. 2008. *Canadian Politics: Critical Approaches* (5th ed.). Toronto: Nelson.

———. 2010. *Canadian Politics: Critical Approaches* (6th ed.). Toronto: Nelson

Dye, Thomas R., and Harmon Zeigler. 2006. *The Irony of Democracy: An Uncommon Introduction to American Politics* (13th ed.). Belmont, Cal.: Wadsworth.

Eagle, David. 2011. "Changing Patterns of Attendance at Religious Services in Canada, 1986–2008. *Journal for the Scientific Study of Religion* 50: 187–200.

Ebaugh, Helen Rose Fuchs. 1988. *Becoming an EX: The Process of Role Exit.* Chicago: University of Chicago Press.

Eberstadt, Nicholas. 2004. "Power and Population in Asia." *Policy Review Online.* Retrieved December 24, 2004. Available: http://www.policyreview.org/feb04/eberstadt.html.

Eccles, Jacquelynne S., Janis E. Jacobs, and Rena D. Harold. 1990. "Gender Role Stereotypes, Expectancy Effects, and Parents' Socialization of Gender Difference." *Journal of Social Issues* 46: 183–201.

Economic Council of Canada. 1991. *New Faces in the Crowd: Economic and Social Impacts, Immigration.* Ottawa: Economic Council of Canada.

The Economist. 1997. "The Anti-Management Guru." May 4.

Eder, Donna. 1985. "The Cycle of Popularity: Interpersonal Relations Among Female Adolescents." *Sociology of Education* 58 (July): 154–165.

———. 1995. *School Talk: Gender and Adolescent Culture* (with Catherine Colleen Evans and Stephen Parker). New Brunswick, N.J.: Rutgers University Press.

Edgerton, Robert B. 1992. *Sick Societies: Challenging the Myth of Primitive Harmony.* New York: Free Press.

Edmonston, B., S. M. Lee, and Z. Wu. 2008. *Childless Canadian Couples.* Victoria: Department of Sociology and Population Research Group, University of Victoria. Retrieved January 20, 2012. Available: http://www.horizons.gc.ca/doclib/PA-pwfc2008-Edmonston-eng.pdf.

Edsall, Thomas Byrne, with Mary D. Edsall. 1992. *Chain Reaction: The Impact of Race, Rights, and Taxes on American Politics.* New York: Norton.

Edwards, Harry. 1973. *Sociology of Sport.* Homewood, Ill.: Dorsey.

Edwards, Richard. 1979. *Contested Terrain.* New York: Basic Books.

———. 1993. "An Education in Interviewing." In C.M. Renzetti and R.M. Lee (eds.), *Researching Sensitive Topics.* Newbury Park: Sage, 181–196.

Eggertson, Laura. 2008. "Despite Federal Promises, First Nations' Water Problems Persist." *Canadian Medical Association Journal* 178 (April 8).

Ehrenreich, Barbara. 2001. *Nickel and Dimed: On (Not) Getting By in America.* New York: Metropolitan.

Ehrlich, Paul R., and Anne H. Ehrlich. 1991. *The Population Explosion.* New York: Touchstone/Simon & Schuster.

———, Anne H. Ehrlich, and Gretchen C. Daily. 1995. *The Stork and the Plow: An Equity Answer to the Human Dilemma.* New Haven, Conn.: Yale University Press.

Eichler, Margrit. 1981. "The Inadequacy of the Monolithic Model of the Family." *Canadian Journal of Sociology* 6: 367–388.

———. 1988a. *Families in Canada Today* (2nd ed.). Toronto: Gage.

———. 1988b. *Nonsexist Research Methods: A Practical Guide.* Boston: Allen & Unwin.

———. 1996. "The Impact of New Reproductive and Genetic Technologies on Families." In Maureen Baker (ed.), *Families: Changing Trends in Canada.* Toronto: McGraw-Hill Ryerson, 104–108.

———. 1997. *Family Shifts: Families, Policies, and Gender Equality.* Don Mills, Ont.: Oxford University Press.

Eighner, Lars. 1993. *Travels with Lizbeth.* New York: St. Martin's Press.

Eisenberg, Mark, Kristian Filion, Arik Azoulay, Anya Brox, Seema Haider, and Louise Pilote. 2005. *Archives of Internal Medicine* 165: 1506–1513.

Eisenstein, Zillah R. 1994. *The Color of Gender: Reimaging Democracy.* Berkeley: University of California Press.

EKOS Research Associates. 2003. *Making Ends Meet: The 2001–2002 Student Financial Survey.* Montreal, Que.: Canadian Millennium Scholarship Foundation.

Elections Canada. 2009. "Young Voters: Election Basics: Frequently Asked Questions." Retrieved March 15, 2009. Available: http://www.elections.ca/content_youth.asp?section=yth&dir=bas/faq&document=index&lang=e#q15.

———. 2012. *National Youth Survey Report.* Retrieved April 30, 2012. Available: http://www.elections.ca/content.aspx?section=res&dir=rec/part/nysr&document=bkr&lang=e.

Elifson, Kirk W., David M. Petersen, and C. Kirk Hadaway. 1983. "Religiosity and Delinquency: A Contextual Analysis." *Criminology* 21: 505–527.

Elkin, Frederick, and Gerald Handel. 1989. *The Child and Society: The Process of Socialization* (5th ed.). New York: Random House.

Elkind, David. 1995. "School and Family in the Postmodern World." *Phi Delta Kappan* (September): 8–21.

Elliott, D.S., and A. Ageton. 1980. "Reconciling Differences in Estimates of Delinquency." *American Sociological Review* 45 (1): 95–110.

Emling, Shelley. 1997. "Haiti Held in Grip of Another Drought." *Austin American-Statesman* (September 19): A17, A18.

Engels, Friedrich. 1972. *The Origins of the Family, Private Property, and the States.* Ed. Eleanor Burke Leacock. New York: International (orig. pub. 1884).

Engerman, Stanley L. 1995. "The Extent of Slavery and Freedom Throughout the World as a Whole and in Major Subareas." In Julian L. Simon (ed.), *The State of Humanity.* Cambridge, Mass.: Blackwell, 171–177.

Environics Institute. 2010. *Focus Canada 2010.* Toronto: Environics Institute. Accessed June 1, 2012. Available: http://www.queensu.ca/cora/_files/fc2010report.pdf.

Epstein, Cynthia Fuchs. 1988. *Deceptive Distinctions: Sex, Gender, and the Social Order.* New Haven, Conn.: Yale University Press.

Epstein, Ethan B. 1996. "Workers and the World Economy." *Foreign Affairs* 75 (May/June): 16–37.

Epstein, Rachel. 1996. "Lesbian Families." In Marion Lynn (ed.), *Voices: Essays on Canadian Families.* Toronto: Thomson Nelson.

———. 2003. "Lesbian Families." In Marion Lynn (ed.), *Voices: Essays on Canadian Families* (2nd ed.). Toronto: Thomson Nelson, 76–102.

Equal Voice. 2005. "The Facts Ma'am: Some Facts About Women in Politics in Canada." Retrieved June 9, 2005. Available: http://www.equalvoice.ca/research.html.

Ericson, Richard, and Aaron Doyle. 1999. "Globalization and the Policing of Protest: The Case of APEC 1997." *British Journal of Sociology* 50 (December): 589–609.

Erikson, Eric H. 1963. *Childhood and Society.* New York: Norton.

Erikson, Kai T. 1962. "Notes on the Sociology of Deviance." *Social Problems* 9: 307–314.

———. 1976. *Everything in Its Path: Destruction of Community in the Buffalo Creek Flood.* New York: Simon & Schuster.

———. 1991. "A New Species of Trouble." In Stephen Robert Couch and J. Stephen Kroll-Smith (eds.), *Communities at Risk: Collective Responses to Technological Hazards.* New York: Peter Land, 11–29.

———. 1994. *A New Species of Trouble: Explorations in Disaster, Trauma, and Community.* New York: Norton.

Esbensen, Finn-Aage, and David Huizinga. 1993. "Gangs, Drugs, and Delinquency in a Survey of Urban Youth." *Criminology* 31 (4): 565–589.

Esping Anderson, Gosta. 2000. "Two Societies, One Sociology, and No Theory." *British Journal of Sociology* (January/March): 59–77.

Essed, Philomena. 1991. *Understanding Everyday Racism.* Newbury Park, Cal.: Sage.

Esterberg, Kristen G. 1997. *Lesbians and Bisexuals: Constructing Communities, Constructing Self.* Philadelphia: Temple University Press.

Etter, Commander Barbara. 2002. "Critical Issues in Hi-Tech Crime." Paper presented to the "Embracing the Future Together" Commonwealth Investigations Conference.

Evans, Glen, and Norman L. Farberow. 1988. *The Encyclopedia of Suicide.* New York: Facts on File.

Evans, John, and Alexander Himelfarb. 2012. "Counting Crime." In Rick Linden (ed.), *Criminology: A Canadian Perspective* (7th ed.). Toronto: Nelson, 101–132.

Evans, Peter B., and John D. Stephens. 1988. "Development and the World Economy." In Neil J. Smelser (ed.), *Handbook of Sociology.* Newbury Park, Cal.: Sage, 739–773.

Ex, Carine, and Jan Janssens. 1998. "Maternal Influences on Daughters' Gender Role Attitudes." *Sex Roles* 38 (February): 171–186.

Eyre, Linda. 1992. "Gender Relations in the Classroom: A Fresh Look at Coeducation." In J. Gaskell and A. McLaren (eds.), *Women and Education.* Calgary: Detselig.

Fabes, Richard A., and Carol L. Martin. 1991. "Gender and Age Stereotypes of Emotionality." *Personality and Social Psychology Bulletin* 17: 532–540.

Fagot, Beverly I. 1984. "Teacher and Peer Reactions to Boys' and Girls' Play Styles." *Sex Roles* 11: 691–702.

Fahmi, Wael Salah. 2001. " 'Honey, I Shrunk the Space': Planning in the Information Age." Paper presented at the 37th International Planning Congress. Utrecht: The Netherlands.

Fallon, Patricia, Melanie A. Katzman, and Susan C. Wooley. 1994. *Feminist Perspectives on Eating Disorders.* New York: Guilford Press.

Farb, Peter. 1973. *Word Play: What Happens When People Talk.* New York: Knopf.

Farley, John E. 1992. *Sociology* (2nd ed.). Englewood Cliffs, N.J.: Prentice-Hall.

Farren, Sandra. 1998. "Money Matters." *The Maclean's Guide to Canadian Universities, 1998,* 44–47.

Fatah, Natasha. 2012. "Allah in the Cafeteria: Inside the School Prayer Scandal at Valley Park Middle School." *Toronto Life* (March 12). Retrieved May 8, 2012. Available: http://www.torontolife.com/daily/informer/from-print-edition-informer/2012/03/21/allah-in-the-cafeteria.

Fausto-Sterling, Anne. 1985. *Myths of Gender: Biological Theories About Women and Men.* New York: Basic Books.

———. 2002. "The Five Sexes: Why Male and Female Are Not Enough." In C. Williams and A. Stein (eds.), *Sexuality and Gender.* London: Blackwell, 489–473.

"The Favoured Infants." 1976. *Human Behaviour* (June): 49–50.

Fawcett, Gail. 1996. *Living with Disability in Canada: An Economic Portrait,* Cat. no. SDDP-020-10-96-E. Ottawa: Canadian Council on Social Development.

———. 2000. *Bringing Down the Barriers: The Labour Market and Women with Disabilities in Ontario.* Ottawa: Canadian Council on Social Development. Retrieved June 27, 2002. Available: http://www.ccsd.ca/pubs/2000/wd/intro.htm.

Feagin, Joe R. 2003. *Racial and Ethnic Relations.* (7th ed.). Upper Saddle River, N.J.: Prentice Hall.

———. 2008. *Racial and Ethnic Relations* (8th ed.). Upper Saddle River, N.J.: Prentice-Hall.

———, and Clairece Booher Feagin. 1997. *Social Problems : A Critical Power-Conflict Perspective.* (5th ed). Englewood Cliffs, N.J.: Prentice Hall.

———, and Robert Parker. 1990. *Building American Cities: The Urban Real Estate Game* (2nd ed.). Englewood Cliffs, N.J.: Prentice-Hall.

———, and Melvin P. Sikes. 1994. *Living with Racism: The Black Middle-Class Experience.* Boston: Beacon.

———, and Hernán Vera. 1995. *White Racism: The Basics.* New York: Routledge.

———, David B. Baker, and Clairece B. Feagin. 2006. *Social Problems: A Critical Power–Conflict Perspective* (6th.). Englewood Cliffs, N.J.: Prentice-Hall.

———, Anthony M. Orum, and Gideon Sjoberg, eds. 1991. *A Case for the Case Study.* Chapel Hill: University of North Carolina Press.

Featherstone, Mike, and Mike Hepworth. 1998. "Aging, the Lifecourse and the Sociology of Embodiment." In Graham Scamble and Paul Higgs (eds.), *Community, Medicine and Health.* New York: Routledge, 147–175.

Fennema, Elizabeth, and Gilah C. Leder, eds. 1990. *Mathematics and Gender.* New York: Teachers College Press.

Ferguson, Sue. 2004. "Stressed Out." *Maclean's* 117 (47): 30–33.

Ferrao, Vincent. 2010. "Paid Work." In Statistics Canada, 2011, *Women in Canada: A Gender-Based Statistical Report* (6th ed.). Cat. no. 89-503-X. Retrieved February 6, 2012. Available: http://www.statcan.gc.ca/pub/89-503-x/2010001/article/11387-eng.pdf.

Ferrell, Keith. 1997. *Truth, Lies, and the Internet.* CNET (October 9). Available: www.cnet.com/content/Features/Dlife/Truth/index.html.

Financial Post. 2011. "Women in Power: Canadian Women Seek the Way Up." Retrieved February 6, 2012. Available: http://business.financialpost.com/2011/12/22/canadian-women-seek-the-way-up.

Findlay, Deborah A., and Leslie J. Miller. 1994. "Through Medical Eyes: The Medicalization of Women's Bodies and Women's Lives." In B. Singh Bolaria and Harley D. Dickinson (eds.), *Health, Illness and Health Care in Canada.* (2nd ed.). Toronto: Harcourt Brace, 276–306.

———. 2002. "Through Medical Eyes: The Medicalization of Women's Bodies and Women's Lives." In B. Singh Bolaria and Harley D. Dickinson (eds.), *Health, Illness, and Health Care in Canada* (3rd ed.). Toronto: Nelson,185–210.

Findlay-Kaneko, Beverly. 1997. "In a Breakthrough for Japan, a Woman Takes Over at a National University." *Chronicle of Higher Education* (June 20): A41–A42.

Fine, Michelle. 1987. "Silencing and Nurturing Voice in an Improbable Context: Urban Adolescents in Public Schools." In Henry A. Giroux and Peter McLaren (eds.), *Schooling and the Politics of Culture.* Albany: SUNY Press.

———. 1989. "Coping with Rape: Critical Perspectives on Consciousness." In Rhoda Kesler Unger (ed.), *Representations: Social Constructions of Gender.* Amityville, N.Y.: Baywood, 186–200.

———, and Lois Weis. 1998. *The Unknown City: The Lives of the Poor and Working Class Young People.* Boston: Beacon.

Finley, M.I. 1980. *Ancient Slavery and Modern Ideology.* New York: Viking.

Firestone, Shulamith. 1970. *The Dialectic of Sex.* New York: Morrow.

Fisher, Luke. 1994. "A Holy War Over Holidays." *Maclean's* (August 12): 26.

Fisher, M., N. Golden, D. Katzman, R.E. Kreipe, J. Rees, J. Schebendach, G. Sigman, S. Ammerman, and H.M. Hoberman. 1995. "Eating Disorders in Adolescents: A Background Paper." *Journal of Adolescent Health* 16: 420–437.

Fisher, Mary. 1993. "Tap Moral Courage to Mold Opinions." *Masthead* 45 (3): 27–30.

Fisher-Thompson, Donna. 1990. "Adult Sex-Typing of Children's Toys." *Sex Roles* 23: 291–303.

Fiske, J (1994) *Media Matters: Everyday Culture and Political Change.* Minneapolis: University of Minnesota Press.

Fjellman, Stephen M. 1992. *Vinyl Leaves: Walt Disney World and America.* Boulder, Col.: Westview.

Flanagan, William G. 1999. *Urban Sociology: Images and Structure* (3rd ed.). Needham Heights, Mass.: Allyn & Bacon.

Fleming, Jim. 2000. "Barbie Super Sports." Retrieved July 13, 2003. Available: http://www.gradingthe-movies.com/html/games/barbie_sports.shtml.

Fleras, Augie, and Jean Leonard Elliott. 1992. *Multiculturalism in Canada.* Toronto: Nelson.

———. 1996. *Unequal Relations: An Introduction to Race, Ethnic and Aboriginal Dynamics in Canada* (2nd. ed.). Scarborough, Ont.: Prentice-Hall Canada.

———. 1999. *Unequal Relations: An Introduction to Race, Ethnic and Aboriginal Dynamics in Canada* (3rd ed.). Scarborough, Ont.: Prentice-Hall Canada.

———. 2003. *Unequal Relations: An Introduction to Race, Ethnic and Aboriginal Dynamics in Canada* (4th ed.). Scarborough, Ont.: Prentice-Hall Canada.

Fleras, Augie, and Jean Lock Kunz. 2001. *Media and Minorities: Representing Diversity in a Multicultural Canada.* Toronto: Thompson Educational.

Foderaro, Lisa. W. 2007. "Child Wants Cellphone: Reception Is Mixed." *New York Times* (Mar. 29): E1–E2.

Forbes. 2002. "The World's Richest People." Retrieved June 25, 2002. Available: http://www.forbes.com.

Forcese, Dennis. 1986. *The Canadian Class Structure.* Toronto: McGraw-Hill Ryerson.

Ford, Clyde W. 1994. *We Can All Get Along: 50 Steps You Can Take to Help End Racism.* New York: Dell.

Forsey, Caitlin. 2009. "Postmodernism." Unpublished paper.

Foucault, Michel. 1978. *The History of Sexuality, Volume 1: An Introduction.* New York: Pantheon.

———. 1979. *Discipline and Punish: The Birth of the Prison.* New York: Vintage.

———. 1991. "Governmentality." In Buchell et al. (eds.). *The Foucault Effect.* Hemel Hempstead: Harvester Wheatsheaf.

———. 1994. *The Birth of the Clinic: An Archaeology of Medica Perception.* New York: Vintage (orig. pub. 1963).

Fournier, S., and F. Crey. 1997. *Stolen from Our Embrace: The Abduction of First Nations Children and the Restoration of Aboriginal Communities.* Vancouver: Douglas & McIntyre, cited in Ambert, Anne-Marie. *Changing Families: Relationships in Context* (Canadian ed.). Toronto: Pearson.

Fox, John, and Michael Ornstein. 1986. "The Canadian State and Corporate Elites in the Post-War Period." *Canadian Review of Sociology and Anthropology* 23: 481–506.

Fox, Mary Frank. 1989. "Women and Higher Education: Gender Differences in the Status of Students and Scholars." In Jo Freeman (ed.), *Women: A Feminist Perspective.* Mountain View, Cal.: Mayfield, 217–235.

Fox, Susannah. 2011. "The Social Life of Health Information, 2011." Pew Internet and American Life Project. Retrieved February 18, 2012. Available: http://pewinternet.org/Reports/2011/Social-Life-of-Health-Info/Part-1/Section-1.aspx.

Frank, Andre Gunder. 1969. *Latin America: Underdevelopment or Revolution?* New York: Monthly Review Press.

———. 1981. *Reflections on the World Economic Crisis.* New York: Monthly Review Press.

Frankenberg, Ruth. 1993. *White Women, Race Matters: The Social Construction of Whiteness.* Minneapolis: University of Minnesota Press.

Frederick, Judith A., and Janet E. Fast. 2001. "Enjoying Work: An Effective Strategy in the Struggle to Juggle." *Canadian Social Trends* (Summer): 8–11.

Freedom House. 2009. *Map of Freedom in the World.* Retrieved August 24, 2009. Available: http://www.freedomhouse.org/template/cfm?page=363&year=2009.

Freeland, Chrystia. 2012. "Social Media Statecraft: A Multiplatform Strategy." *Globe and Mail* (April 5). Retrieved April 27, 2012. Available: http://www.theglobeandmail.com/report-on-business/commentary/chrystia-freeland/social-media-statecraft-a-multiplatform-strategy/article2393250.

Freidson, Eliot. 1965. "Disability as Social Deviance." In Marvin B. Sussman (ed.), *Sociology and Rehabilitation.* Washington, D.C.: American Sociology Association, 71–99.

———. 1970. *Profession of Medicine.* New York: Dodd, Mead.

———. 1986. *Professional Powers.* Chicago: University of Chicago Press.

French, Howard W. 2003. "Japan's Neglected Resource: Female Workers." *New York Times* (July 25): A3.

Freud, Sigmund. 1924. *A General Introduction to Psychoanalysis* (2nd ed.). New York: Boni & Liveright.

Freudenberg, Nicholas, and Carl Steinsapir. 1992. "Not in Our Backyards: The Grassroots Environmental Movement." In Riley Dunlap and Angela G. Mertig (eds.), *American Environmentalism: The U.S. Environmental Movement, 1970–1990.* New York: Taylor and Francis, 27–37.

Frideres, James. 1994. "The Future of Our Past: Native Elderly in Canadian Society." In National Advisory Council on Aging, *Aboriginal Seniors' Issues,* 17–37. Cat. no. H71-2/1-15-1994E. Ottawa: Minister of Supply and Services.

———. 1998. *Aboriginal Peoples in Canada: Contemporary Conflicts* (5th ed.). Scarborough, Ont.: Prentice-Hall.

———. 2007. "Building Bridges: Aboriginal, Immigrant, and Visible Minority Families in the Twenty-First Century." In David Cheal (ed.), *Canadian Families Today: New Perspectives.* Don Mills: Oxford University Press, 195–212.

———, and René R. Gadacz. 2001. *Aboriginal Peoples in Canada: Contemporary Conflicts* (6th ed.). Scarborough, Ont.: Prentice-Hall.

———. 2005. *Aboriginal Peoples in Canada* (7th ed.). Scarborough, Ont.: Prentice-Hall.

Friedan, Betty. 1993. *The Fountain of Age.* New York: Simon & Schuster.

Friedman, Milton. 1970. "The Social Responsibility of Business Is to Increase Its Profits." *New York Times Magazine* (September 13): 33.

Friedman, Thomas L. 2005. *The World Is Flat.* New York: Farrar, Straus and Giroux.

Friendly, Martha. 2006a. *Early Learning and Child Care: How Does Canada Measure Up? International Comparisons Using Data from Starting Strong II.* Briefing Note. Toronto: Childcare Resource and Research Unit.

———. 2006b. "Looking Beyond Our Borders." Toronto: Childcare Resource and Research Unit. Retrieved February 28, 2009. Available: http://www.childcarecanada.org/ECEC2006/pdf/ECEC06_LookingBeyondBorders.pdf.

———, and Jane Beach. 2005. *Early Childhood Education and Care in Canada 2004* (6th ed.). Retrieved January 20, 2009. Available: http://www.childcarecanada.org/ECEC2004/#toc.

———, and Susan Prentice. 2009. *About Canada: Child Care.* Halifax: Fernwood.

———, Jane Beach, and Michelle Turiano. 2002. *Early Childhood Education and Care in Canada 2001.* Childcare Resource and Research Unit, December 2002. Retrieved September 14, 2005. Available: http://www.childcarecanada.org/ECEC2001.

Fries, Christopher. 2008. "Governing the Health of the Hybrid Self: Integrative Medicine, Neoliberalism, and the Shifting Biopolitics of Subjectivity." *Health Sociology Review* 17 (December): 353–367.

Fukuyama, Francis. 2005. "The Calvinist Manifesto." *The New York Times Review of Books.* Retrieved March 13, 2005. Available: www.nytimes.com/200/03/13/books/review/013/FUKUYA.

Fulton, E. Kaye, and Ian Mather. 1993. "A Forest Fable." *Maclean's* (August 16): 0.

Fuse, Toyama. 1997. *Suicide, Individuality, and Society.* Toronto: Canadian Scholars' Press.

Gabor, Thomas. 1994. *Everybody Does It! Crime by the Public.* Toronto: University of Toronto Press.

Gabriel, Trip. 1996. "High-Tech Pregnancies Test Hope's Limit." *New York Times* (January 7): 1, 10–11.

Gadd, Jane. 1998. "Young Men Across Canada Earning Less, Report Says." *Globe and Mail* (July 29): A5.

Gagnon, John H., and *William* Simon. 1973. *Sexual Conduct: The Social Sources of Human Sexuality* (paperback ed.). Chicago: Aldine.

Gailey, Christine Ward. 1987. "Evolutionary Perspectives on Gender Hierarchy." In Beth B. Hess and Myra Marx Ferree (eds.), *Analyzing Gender: A Handbook of Social Science Research.* Newbury Park, Cal.: Sage, 32–67.

Galarneau, Diane. 2005. "Earnings of Temporary Versus Permanent Employees." *Perspectives on Labour and Income* 6 (January): 5.

———, and Marian Radulescu. 2009. "Employment Among the Disabled." *Perspectives on Labour and Income* 19 (5). Retrieved June 18, 2009. Available: http://www.statcan.gc.ca/pub/75-001-x/2009105/pdf/10865-eng.pdf.

Galbi, Douglas. 2002. "Rapid Development of Communications Capabilities in Low-Income Countries." Presentation at the World Bank. Retrieved August 14, 2005. Available: http://www.galbithink.org/wbp2_files/v3_document.htm.

Gale, Richard P., Christopher P. Gale, T.A. Roper, and Graham P. Mulley. 2003. "Depiction of Elderly and Disabled People on Road Traffic Signs: International Comparisons." *British Medical Journal* 327: 1456–1457.

Galloway, Gloria. 1999. "Number of Racist Canadians Falling." *National Post.* Online. Retrieved March 1, 1999.

Gamson, William. 1990. *The Strategy of Social Protest* (2nd ed.). Belmont, Cal.: Wadsworth.

———. 1995. "Constructing Social Protest." In Hank Johnston and Bert Klandermans (eds.), *Social Movements and Culture.* Minneapolis: University of Minnesota Press, 85–106.

Gann, R. 2000. "Postmodern Perspectives on Race and Racism: Help or Hindrance?" Retrieved September 2, 2005. Paper for the Political Studies Association-UK, 10–13 April 2000. Ebsco host database.

Gans, Herbert. 1974. *Popular Culture and High Culture: An Analysis and Evaluation of Tastes.* New York: Basic Books.

———. 1982. *The Urban Villagers: Group and Class in the Life of Italian Americans* (updated and expanded ed.; orig. pub. 1962). New York: Free Press.

Garber, Judith A., and Robyne S. Turner. 1995. "Introduction." In Judith A. Garber and Robyne S. Turner (eds.), *Gender in Urban Research.* Thousand Oaks, Cal.: Sage, x–xxvi.

Garcia Coll, Cynthia T. 1990. "A Message to a Future Child About the Danger of Gangs." *Austin American-Statesman* (August 17): A6.

Garfinkel, Harold. 1967. *Studies in Ethnomethodology.* Englewood Cliffs, N.J.: Prentice-Hall.

Gargan, Edward A. 1996. "An Indonesian Asset Is Also a Liability." *New York Times* (March 16): 17, 18.

Garlick, S. 2011. "A New Sexual Revolution? Critical Theory, Pornography, and the Internet." *Canadian Review of Sociology* 48 (3): 221–239. doi:10.1111/j.1755-618X.2011.01264.x.

Garreau, Joel. 1993. "GAK Attack." *Austin American-Statesman* (January 9): D1, D6.

Garson, Barbara. 1989. *The Electronic Sweatshop: How Computers Are Transforming the Office of the Future into the Factory of the Past.* New York: Penguin.

Gaskell, Jane. 2009. "Feminist Approaches to the Sociology of Education in Canada." In Cynthia

Levine-Rasky (ed.), *Canadian Perspectives on the Sociology of Education.* Toronto: Oxford University Press, 17–29.

———, Arlene McLaren, and Myra Novogradsky. 1995. "What Is Worth Knowing? Defining the Feminist Curriculum." In E. D. Nelson and B. W. Robinson (eds.), *Gender in the 1990s: Images, Realities and Issues.* Toronto: Thomson Nelson, 100–118.

Gaylin, Willard. 1992. *The Male Ego.* New York: Viking/Penguin.

Gecas, Viktor. 1982. "The Self-Concept." In Ralph H. Turner and James F. Short Jr. (eds.), *Annual Review of Sociology, 1982.* Palo Alto, Cal.: Annual Reviews, 1–33.

Gee, Ellen. 1994. "What Is Family?" In R. Hagedorn (ed.), *Sociology.* Toronto: Harcourt Brace, 369–398.

———. 2000. "Voodoo Demography, Population Aging, and Social Policy." In E.M. Gee and G.M. Guttman (eds.), *The Overselling of Population Aging: Apocalyptic Demography, Intergenerational Challenges, and Social Policy.* Don Mills, Ont.: Oxford University Press.

Geertz, Clifford. 1966. "Religion as a Cultural System." In Michael Banton (ed.), *Anthropological Approaches to the Study of Religion.* London: Tavistock, 1–46.

Gelfand, Donald E. 1994. *Aging and Ethnicity: Knowledge and Services.* New York: Springer.

Gelles, Richard J., and Murray A. Straus. 1988. *Intimate Violence: The Definitive Study of the Causes and Consequences of Abuse in the American Family.* New York: Simon & Schuster.

"General Facts on Sweden." 2005. Retrieved July 23, 2005. Available: http://www.finansforbundet.se/Resource.phx/plaza/content/material/internationellteu.htx.pdf.material.3.pdf.

George, Molly. 2005. "Making Sense of Muscle: The Body Experiences of Collegiate Women Athletes." *Sociological Inquiry* 75 (3): 317–345.

Gerber, Linda. 1990. "Multiple Jeopardy: A Socioeconomic Comparison of Women Among the Indian, Metis, and Inuit Peoples of Canada." *Canadian Ethnic Studies* 22 (3): 22–34.

Gerbner, George, Larry Gross, Michael Morton, and Nancy Signorielli. 1987. "Charting the Mainstream: Television's Contributions to Political Orientations." In Donald Lazere (ed.), *American Media and Mass Culture: Left Perspectives.* Berkeley: University of California Press, 441–464.

Gerds, Jenna. 2011. "Famous for Being Famous: Celebrity Socialites and the Framework of Fame." In Robin DeRosa (ed.), *Simulation in Media and Culture: Believing the Hype.* Lanham, Md.: Lexington Books, 8–24.

Gereffi, Gary. 1994. "The International Economy and Economic Development." In Neil J. Smelser and Richard Swedberg (eds.), *The Handbook of Economic Sociology.* Princeton, N.J.: Princeton University Press, 206–233.

Gergen, Kenneth J. 1991. *The Saturated Self: Dilemmas of Identity in Contemporary Life.* New York: Basic Books.

Gerschenkron, Alexander. 1962. *Economic Backwardness in Historical Perspective.* Cambridge, Mass.: Harvard University Press.

Gerson, Kathleen. 1993. *No Man's Land: Men's Changing Commitment to Family and Work.* New York: Basic Books.

Ghosh, Ratna, and Rabindra Kanungo. 1992. *South Asian Canadians: Current Issues in the Politics of Culture.* Montreal: Shastri Indo-Canadian Institute.

Gibbs, Jennifer, Nicole Ellison, and Chih-Hui Lai. 2011. "First Comes Love, Then Comes Google: An Investigation of Uncertainty Reduction Strategies and Self-Disclosure in Online Dating." *Communication Research* 38 (1): 70–100.

Gibbs, Lois Marie, as told to Murray Levine. 1982. *Love Canal: My Story.* Albany: SUNY Press.

Giddens, Anthony, 1992. "Intimacy Transformed? A Critical Look at the 'Pure Relationship.'" In Christine L. Williams and Arlene Stein (eds.), *Sexuality and Gender.* Malden, Mass.: Blackwell Readers in Sociology, 456–467.

———. 1996. *Introduction to Sociology* (2nd ed.). New York: W.W. Norton & Co.

Gidengil, Elisabeth, Neil Nevitte, Andre Blais, Patrick Fournier, and Joanna Everitt. 2004. "Why Johnny Won't Vote." *Globe and Mail* (August 4): A11.

Gideonse, Ted. 1998. "Review: Author Sees Distortion in Marketing of Gays." *Salon.* Available: http://www.salonmagazine.com.

Gilbert, Dennis L. 2003. *The American Class Structure in an Age of Growing Inequality* (6th ed.). Belmont, Cal.: Wadsworth.

———, and Joseph A. Kahl. 1998. *The American Class Structure: A New Synthesis* (5th ed.). Belmont, Cal.: Wadsworth.

Gilbert, S.N. 1989. "The Forgotten Purpose and Future of University Education." *Canadian Journal of Community Mental Health* 8 (2): 103–122.

Gilder, George F. 1986. *Men and Marriage.* New York: Pelican.

Gill, Indermit, and Homi Kharas. 2007. *An East Asian Renaissance: Ideas for Economic Growth.* Washington: The World Bank.

Gilligan, Carol. 1982. *In a Different Voice: Psychological Theory and Women's Development.* Cambridge, Mass.: Harvard University Press.

Gillis, A.R. 1995. "Urbanization." In Robert J. Brym (ed.), *New Society: Sociology for the 21st Century.* Toronto: Harcourt Brace and Company, 13.1–13.40.

Ginsberg, Jeremy, Matthew Mohebbi, Rajan Patel, Lynnette Brammer, Mark Smolinski, and Larry Brilliant. 2009. "Detecting Flu Epidemics Using Search Engine Query Data." *Nature* 457 (February 19): 1012–1014.

Gionet, Linda. 2009. "First Nations People: Selected Findings of the 2006 Census." *Canadian Social Trends* 87 (Summer). Catalogue no. 11-008-X. Retrieved May 11, 2009. Available: http://www.statcan.gc.ca/pub/11-008-x/2009001/article/10864-eng.pdf.

Glascock, A.P., and S.L. Feinman. 1981. "Social Asset or Social Burden: Treatment of the Aged in Non-industrial Societies." In C.L. Fry (ed.), *Dimensions: Aging, Culture, and Health.* New York: Praeger.

Glaser, Barney, and Anselm Strauss. 1967. *The Discovery of Grounded Theory.* Chicago: Aldine.

———. 1968. *Time for Dying.* Chicago: Aldine.

Glazer, Nona. 1990. "The Home as Workshop: Women as Amateur Nurses and Medical Care Providers." *Gender & Society* 4: 479–499.

Glenny, Misha. 2011. *DarkMarket: Cyberthieves, Cybercops and You.* New York: Albert A. Knopf.

Global Health Council. 2002. *Health: A Key to Prosperity. Success Stories in Developing Countries.* Retrieved July 22, 2005. Available: http://www.globalhealth.org/sources/view.php3?id=390.

Global Media Monitoring Project. 2010. *Who Makes the News.* London: World Association for Christian Communication. Retrieved January 12, 2012. Available: http://www.whomakesthenews.org.

Globe and Mail, Report on Business Magazine. 1990. October: B80.

Godin-Beers, Monique, and Cinderina Williams. 1994. "Report of the Spallumcheen Child Welfare Program." Research study prepared for the Royal Commission on Aboriginal Peoples (unpublished), cited in Castellano, Marlene. 2002. "Aboriginal Family Trends: Extended Families, Nuclear Families, Families of the Heart." Ottawa: Vanier Institute of the Family. Retrieved May 12, 2009. Available: http://www.vifamily.ca/library/cft/aboriginal.html.

Goffman, Erving. 1956. "The Nature of Deference and Demeanor." *American Anthropologist* 58: 473–502.

———. 1959. *The Presentation of Self in Everyday Life.* New York, N.Y.: Doubleday.

———. 1961a. *Asylums: Essays on the Social Situation of Mental Patients and Other Inmates.* Chicago: Aldine.

———. 1961b. *Encounters: Two Studies in the Sociology of Interaction.* Indianapolis, Ind.: Bobbs-Merrill.

———. 1963a. *Behavior in Public Places: Notes on the Social Structure of Gatherings.* New York: Free Press.

———. 1963b. *Stigma: Notes on the Management of Spoiled Identity.* Englewood Cliffs, N.J.: Prentice-Hall.

———. 1967. *Interaction Ritual: Essays on Face to Face Behavior.* Garden City, N.Y.: Anchor Books.

———. 1971. *Relations in Public.* New York: Basic Books.

———. 1974. *Frame Analysis: An Essay on the Organization of Experience.* Boston: Northeastern University Press.

———. 1979. *Gender Advertisements.* Cambridge, Mass.: Harvard University Press.

Gold, Rachel Benson, and Cory L. Richards. 1994. "Securing American Women's Reproductive Health." In Cynthia Costello and Anne J. Stone (eds.), *The American Woman 1994–95.* New York: Norton.

Goldberg, Robert A. 1991. *Grassroots Resistance: Social Movements in Twentieth Century America.* Belmont, Cal.: Wadsworth.

Golden, Anne. 1999. *Taking Responsibility for Homelessness: An Action Plan for Toronto.* Report to the Mayor's Homelessness Action Task Force. Toronto: City of Toronto.

Golden, Stephanie. 1992. *The Women Outside: Meanings and Myths of Homelessness.* Berkeley: University of California Press.

Gonzales, David. 1994. "Frenzied Passengers, Their Hair and Clothes in Flames, Flee Burning Train." *New York Times* (December 22): A12.

Goode, William J. 1960. "A Theory of Role Strain." *American Sociological Review* 25: 483–496.

Goodman, Peter S. 1996. "The High Cost of Sneakers." *Austin American-Statesman* (July 7): F1, F6.

Gordon, David. 1973. "Capitalism, Class, and Crime in America." *Crime and Delinquency* 19: 163–186.

Gordon, Milton. 1964. *Assimilation in American Life: The Role of Race, Religion, and National Origins.* New York: Oxford University Press.

Gordon, Robert M., and Jacquelyne Nelson. 1993. *Census '93: The Report of the 1993 Census of Provincial Correctional Centres in British Columbia.* Victoria: Ministry of the Solicitor General.

Gorey, Kevin, Eric J. Holowaty, Gordon Fehringer, Ethan Laukkanen, Agnes Moskowitz, David J. Webster, and Nancy L. Richter. 1997. "An International Comparison of Cancer Survival: Toronto, Ontario, and Detroit, Michigan, Metropolitan Areas." *American Journal of Public Health* 87: 1156–1163.

Gotham, Kevin Fox. 1999. "Political Opportunity, Community Identity, and the Emergence of a Local Anti-Expressway Movement." *Social Problems* 46: 332–254.

Gottdiener, Mark. 1985. *The Social Production of Urban Space.* Austin: University of Texas Press.

———. 1997. *The Theming of America.* Boulder, Col.: Westview.

Gough, K. 1975. "The Origin of the Family." In Rayna R. Reiter (ed.),

Toward an Anthropology of Women. New York: Monthly Review Press, 69–70.

Gouldner, Alvin W. 1970. *The Coming Crisis of Western Sociology.* New York: Basic Books.

Grahame, Peter. 2004. "Ethnography, Institutions, and the Problematic of the Everyday World." In William K. Carroll (ed.), *Critical Strategies for Social Research.* Toronto: Canadian Scholars' Press, 181–190.

Grameen Bank. 2005. "Grameen Bank." Retrieved December 30, 2005. Available: http://www.grameen-info.org/bank/index.html.

Granovetter, Mark. 1994. *Getting a Job: A Study in Contacts and Careers.* Cambridge, Mass.: Harvard University Press.

Grant, Karen. 1993. "Health and Health Care." In Peter S. Li and B. Singh Bolaria (eds.), *Contemporary Sociology: Critical Perspectives.* Toronto: Copp-Clark Pitman, 394–409.

Gratton, Bruce. 1986. "The New History of the Aged." In David Van Tassel and Paul N. Stearns (eds.), *Old Age in a Bureaucratic Society.* Westport, Conn.: Greenwood Press, 3–29.

Gray, John, Megan Harman, Lauren McKeon, Zena Olijnyk, and Regan Ray. 2007. "The Rich 100: Canada's Wealthiest People." *Canadian Business Magazine Online.* Retrieved June 16, 2009. Available: http://www.canadian-business.com/after_hours/article.jsp?content=20071128_205745_2952.

Gray, Paul. 1993. "Camp for Crusaders." *Time* (April 19): 40.

Green, Donald E. 1977. *The Politics of Indian Removal: Creek Government and Society in Crisis.* Lincoln: University of Nebraska Press.

Greenberg, Edward S., and Benjamin I. Page. 1996. *The Struggle for Democracy* (2nd ed.). New York: HarperCollins.

Greenemeier, L. 2009. "Caster Semenya and the Issue of Gender Ambiguity." *Scientific American* (August 21). Retrieved July 31, 2012. Available: http://blogs.scientificamerican.com/observations/2009/08/21/caster-semenya-and-the-issue-of-gender-ambiguity.

Greenfeld, Karl Taro. 1999. "What Glass Ceiling?" *Time* (August 2): 72.

Greenpeace. 2005. "You Can Make a Difference." Retrieved July 18, 2005. Available: http://www.greenpeace.org.au/getactive/difference/people_t.html#Solomon.

Greenspan, Edward. 1982. "The Role of the Defence Lawyer in Sentencing." In Craig L. Boydell and Ingrid Connidis (eds.), *The Canadian Criminal Justice System.* Toronto: Holt, Rinehart and Winston, 200–210.

Gregg, Allan. 2006. "Identity Crisis." *The Walrus* (March).

Griggs, Brandon. 2010. "Twitter Hoax Spreads Rumors of Airlines' Free Flights to Haiti." CNN.com (Jan. 14). Retrieved April 18, 2010. Available: http://edition.cnn.com/2010/TECH01/14/twitter.hoax.haiti.

Grint, Keith, and Steve Woolgar. 1997. *The Machine at Work: Technology, Work, and Organization.* Cambridge: Polity.

GSMA.com. 2011. "New Report Shows Africa is World's Second Largest Mobile Market." Retrieved June 26, 2012. Available: http://www.gsma.com/publicpolicy/new-report-shows-africa-is-worlds-second-largest-mobile-market.

Guglani, Sacha, Peter G. Coleman, and Edmund J.S. Sonuga-Barke. 2000. "Mental Health of Elderly Asians in Britain: A Comparison of Hindus from Nuclear and Extended Families of Differing Cultural Identity." *International Journal of Geriatric Psychiatry* 15: 1046–1099.

Guppy, Neil. 1995. "Education and Schooling." In L. Tepperman, J.E. Curtis, and R.J. Richardson (eds.), *Sociology.* Toronto: McGraw-Hill Ryerson, 450–478.

———, and Scott Davies. 1998. *Education in Canada: Recent Trends and Future Challenges.* Ottawa: Statistics Canada.

———, Sabrina Freeman, and Shari Buchan. 1987. "Representing Canadians: Changes in the Economic Backgrounds of Federal Politicians, 1965–1984." *Canadian Review of Sociology and Anthropology* 24: 417–430.

Gusfield, Joseph. 1963. *Symbolic Crusade: Status Politics and the American Temperance Movement.* Urbana: University of Illinois Press.

Haas, Jack. 1977. "Learning Real Feelings: A Study of High Steel Ironworkers' Reactions to Fear and Danger." *Sociology of Work and Occupations* 4 (May): 147–170.

———, and W. Shaffir. 1995. "Giving Medical Students a Cloak of Competence." In L. Tepperman and James Curtis (eds.), *Everyday Life.* Toronto: McGraw-Hill Ryerson.

Hackler, James C. 1994. *Crime and Canadian Public Policy.* Scarborough, Ont.: Prentice Hall.

Hadden, Jeffrey. 1987. "Toward Desacralizing Secularization Theory." *Social Forces* 65: 587–611.

Hadden, Richard W. 1997. *Sociological Theory: An Introduction to the Classical Tradition.* Peterborough, Ont.: Broadview.

Hagan, John. 2004. "Corporate and White-Collar Crime." In Rick Linden (ed.), *Criminology: A Canadian Perspective* (5th ed.). Toronto: Thomson Nelson, 480–515.

———, and Bill McCarthy. 1992. "Streetlife and Delinquency." *British Journal of Sociology* 43 (4): 533–561.

Hahn, Harlan. 1987. "Civil Rights for Disabled Americans: The Foundation of a Political Agenda." In Alan Gartner and Tom Joe (eds.), *Images of the Disabled, Disabling Images.* New York: Praeger, 181–203.

Haines, Valerie A. 1997. "Spencer and His Critics." In Charles Camic (ed.), *Reclaiming the Sociological Classics: The State of the Scholarship.* Malden, Mass.: Blackwell, 81–111.

Halberstadt, Amy G., and Martha B. Saitta. 1987. "Gender, Nonverbal Behavior, and Perceived Dominance: A Test of the Theory." *Journal of Personality and Social Psychology* 53: 257–272.

Hale-Benson, Janice E. 1986. *Black Children: Their Roots, Culture, and Learning Styles* (rev. ed.). Provo, Utah: Brigham Young University Press.

Hall, Edward. 1966. *The Hidden Dimension.* New York: Anchor/Doubleday.

Hall, Emily. 2011. "Planting Crops in the Hyperreal: Farmville and Simulated Work." In Robin DeRosa (ed.), *Simulation in Media and Culture: Believing the Hype.* Lanham, Md.: Lexington Books, 106–112.

Hall, Michael, David Lasby, Glenn Gumulka, and Catherine Tryon. 2006. *Caring Canadians, Involved Canadians: Highlights from the 2004 Canada Survey of Giving, Volunteering and Participating.* Ottawa: Statistics Canada.

Hall, Peter M. 1972. "A Symbolic Interactionist Analysis of Politics." *Sociological Inquiry* 42: 35–75.

Hall, Stuart. 1982. "The Rediscovery of 'Ideology': Return of the Repressed in Media Studies." In Michael Gurevitch, Trevor Bennett, James Curran, and J. Woollacott (eds.), *Culture, Society, and the Media.* London: Methuen, 56–90.

Halle, David. 1993. *Inside Culture: Art and Class in the American Home.* Chicago, Ill.: University of Chicago Press.

Hamilton, Allen C., and C. Murray Sinclair. 1991. *Report of the Aboriginal Justice Inquiry of Manitoba,* vol. 1. Winnipeg: Queen's Printer.

Hamilton, L., and E. Armstrong. 2009. "Gendered Sexuality in Young Adulthood: Double Binds and Flawed Options." *Gender & Society* 23 (5): 589. Retrieved March 27, 2012. Available: http://www.proquest.com.libproxy.uwinnipeg.ca.

Hamper, Ben. 1992. *Rivethead: Tales from the Assembly Line.* New York: Warner Books.

Hannigan, John. 1998. *Fantasy City: Pleasure and Profit in the Postmodern Metropolis.* London: Routledge.

Hartnagel, Timothy. 2004. "Correlates of Criminal Behaviour." In Rick Linden (ed.), *Criminology: A Canadian Perspective* (5th ed.). Toronto: Thomson Nelson, 120–163.

Haraway, Donna. 1994. "A Cyborg Manifesto: Science, Technology, and Socialist-Feminism in the Late Twentieth Century." In Anne C. Herrmann and Abigail J. Stewart (eds.), *Theorizing Feminism: Parallel Trends in the Humanities and Social Sciences.* Boulder, Colo.: Westview, 427–457.

Harding, Sandra. 1986. *The Science Question in Feminism.* Ithaca, N.Y.: Cornell University Press.

Hardy, Melissa A., and Lawrence E. Hazelrigg. 1993. "The Gender of Poverty in an Aging Population." *Research on Aging* 15 (3): 243–278.

Hargrave, Connie. 2005. "Homelessness in Canada: From Housing to Shelters to Blankets." SHARE International Archives. Retrieved June 1, 2005. Available: http://www.shareintl.org/archives/homelessness/hl-ch_ Canada.htm.

Harlow, Harry F., and Margaret Kuenne Harlow. 1962. "Social Deprivation in Monkeys." *Scientific American* 207 (5): 137–146.

———. 1977. "Effects of Various Mother–Infant Relationships on Rhesus Monkey Behaviors." In Brian M. Foss (ed.), *Determinants of Infant Behavior,* vol. 4. London: Methuen, 15–36.

Harman, Lesley. 1989. *When a Hostel Becomes a Home: Experiences of Women.* Toronto: Garamond Press.

Harper, Miheala, and Andrew Ploeg. 2011. "Drafting the Hyperreal: Ownership, Agency, Responsibility in Fantasy Sports." In Robin DeRosa (ed.), *Simulation in Media and Culture: Believing the Hype.* Lanham, Md.: Lexington Books, 151–161.

Harrington Meyer, Madonna. 1990. "Family Status and Poverty Among Older Women: The Gendered Distribution of Retirement Income in the United States." *Social Problems* 37: 551–563.

———. 1994. "Gender, Race, and the Distribution of Social Assistance: Medicaid Use Among the Frail Elderly." *Gender & Society* 8 (1): 8–28.

Harris, Chauncey D., and Edward L. Ullman. 1945. "The Nature of Cities." *Annals of the Academy of Political and Social Sciences* (November): 7–17.

Harris, Marvin. 1974. *Cows, Pigs, Wars, and Witches.* New York: Random House.

———. 1985. *Good to Eat: Riddles of Food and Culture.* New York: Simon & Schuster.

Harrison, Algea O., Melvin N. Wilson, Charles J. Pine, Samuel Q. Chan, and Raymond Buriel. 1990. "Family Ecologies of Ethnic Minority Children." *Child Development* 61 (2): 347–362.

Harrison, Janine. 2001. "Welfare Reports Document Increasing Homelessness in Australia." *World Socialist Web Site.* Retrieved September 11, 2001. Available: http://wsws.orgarticles/2001/jun2001/home-j07_prn.shtml.

Hartmann, Heidi. 1976. "Capitalism, Patriarchy, and Job Segregation by Sex." *Signs: Journal of Women in Culture and Society* 1 (Spring): 137–169.

———. 1981. "The Unhappy Marriage of Marxism and Feminism." In Lydia Sargent (ed.), *Women and Revolution.* Boston: South End Press.

Hartnagel, Timothy F. 2000. "Correlates of Crime." In Rick Linden (ed.), *Criminology: A Canadian Perspective* (4th ed.). Toronto: Harcourt Brace.

———. 2012. "Correlates of Criminal Behaviour." In Rick Linden (ed.),

Criminology: A Canadian Perspective (7th ed.) Toronto: Nelson, 133–178.

Harvey, Frank P. 2004. *Smoke and Mirrors: Globalized Terrorism and the Illusion of Multilateral Security.* Toronto: University of Toronto Press.

HateWatch. 2000. "Hate on the Internet." Retrieved December 18, 2002. Available: http://www.hatewatch.org/hate_internet/index.jsp.

Hauchler, Ingomar, and Paul M. Kennedy (eds.). 1994. *Global Trends: The World Almanac of Development and Peace.* New York: Continuum.

Hauser, Robert M. 1995. "Symposium: The Bell Curve." *Contemporary Sociology: A Journal of Reviews* 24 (2): 149–153.

———, and David L. Featherman. 1976. "Equality of Schooling: Trends and Prospects." *Sociology of Education* 49: 99–120.

Havighurst, Robert J., Bernice L. Neugarten, and Sheldon S. Tobin. 1968. "Disengagement and Patterns of Aging." In Bernice L. Neugarten (ed.), *Middle Age and Aging.* Chicago: University of Chicago Press, 161–172.

Haviland, William A. 1993. *Cultural Anthropology* (7th ed.). Orlando, Fla.: Harcourt Brace Jovanovich.

Haynes, Jeff. 1997. "Religion, Secularisation and Politics: A Postmodern Conspectus." *Third World Quarterly* 18: 709–728.

Health Canada. 1997. *For the Safety of Canadian Children and Youth: From Injury Data to Preventative Measures.* Cat. no. H39-412/1997E. Ottawa: Health Programs and Services Branch.

———. 1999. "Social Inequality in the Health of Canadians." In James Curtis, Edward Grabb, and Neil Guppy (eds.), *Social Inequality in Canada: Patterns, Problems and Policies* (3rd ed.). Scarborough, Ont.: Prentice-Hall, 300–314.

———. 2002a. *Adult Survivors of Child Sexual Abuse.* National Clearinghouse on Family Violence. Ottawa: Health Canada. Available: http://www.hc-sc.gc.ca/hppb/familyviolence/pdfs/adsurexa.pdf.

———. 2002b. *HIV and AIDS in Canada: Surveillance Report to June 30, 2002.* Ottawa: Health Canada, Centre for Infectious Disease Prevention and Control.

———. 2005. *A Statistical Profile on the Health of First Nations in Canada: Highlights.* Ottawa: Health Canada.

Health and Welfare Canada. 1998. *Active Health Report: The Active Health Report on Seniors.* Ottawa: Minister of Supply and Services.

Hébert, Benoît-Paul, and May Luong. 2008. "Bridge Employment." *Perspectives on Labour and Income* (November): 5–12.

Hedges, Chris. 1997. "In Bosnia's Schools, 3 Ways Never to Learn from History." *New York Times* (November 25): A1, A4.

Hefley, James C. 1976. *Textbooks on Trial.* Wheaton, Ill.: Victor Books.

Heilbron, Johan. 1995. *The Rise of Social Theory.* Trans. Sheila Gogol. Minneapolis: University of Minnesota Press.

Henley, Nancy. 1977. *Body Politics: Power, Sex, and Nonverbal Communication.* Englewood Cliffs, N.J.: Prentice-Hall.

Henry, Frances, and Effie Ginzberg. 1984. *Who Gets Work: A Test of Racial Discrimination in Employment.* Toronto: Urban Alliance on Race Relations and the Social Planning Council of Toronto.

———, and Carol Tator. 2000. *The Colour of Democracy: Racism in Canadian Society* (2nd ed). Toronto: Harcourt Canada.

———, and Carol Tator. 2006. *The Colour of Democracy: Racism in Canadian Society* (3rd ed.). Toronto: Thomson Nelson.

———, Carol Tator, Winston Mattis, and Tim Rees. 1996. "The Victimization of Racial Minorities in Canada." In Robert J. Brym (ed.), *Society in Question: Sociological Readings for the 21st Century.* Toronto: Harcourt Brace and Company, 133–144.

Heritage, John. 1984. *Garfinkel and Ethnomethodology.* Cambridge, Mass.: Polity.

Herman, Nancy. 1996. "'Mixed Nutters,' 'Looney Tuners,' and 'Daffy Ducks.'" In Earl Rubington and Martin S. Weinberg (eds.), *Deviance: The Interactionist Perspective* (6th ed.). Boston: Allyn & Bacon, 254–266.

Herman, Norman, and Noam Chomsky. 1998. *Manufacturing Consent.* London: Vintage.

Hernandez, Debra Gersh. 1994. "AIDS Fades: The Epidemic Swells But Reporters Complain Editors Have Lost Interest." *Editor & Publisher* 127 (34): 16–18.

Herrnstein, Richard J., and Charles Murray. 1994. *The Bell Curve: Intelligence and Class Structure in American Life.* New York: Free Press.

Herz, J.C. 1998a. "New Title on the Cutlass Edge of Software." *New York Times* (September 3): D4.

———. 1998b. "Puzzling Over the Allure of Virtual Barbie." *New York Times* (March 19): D4.

Herzog, David B., K.L. Newman, Christine J. Yeh, and M. Warshaw. 1992. "Body Image Satisfaction in Homosexual and Heterosexual Women." *International Journal of Eating Disorders* 11: 391–396.

Heshka, Stanley, and Yona Nelson. 1972. "Interpersonal Speaking Distances as a Function of Age, Sex, and Relationship." *Sociometry* 35 (4): 491–498.

Hesse-Biber, Sharlene. 1996. *Am I Thin Enough Yet? The Cult of Thinness and the Commercialization of Identity.* New York: Oxford University Press.

———. 2010. *The Cult of Thinness* (2nd ed.). New York: Oxford University Press

Hettne, Bjorn. 1995. *Development Theory and the Three Worlds* (2nd ed.). Essex: Longman.

Heywood, Leslie. 1998. *Pretty Good for a Girl.* New York: The Free Press.

———, and Shari L. Dworkin. 2003. *Built to Win: The Female Athlete as Cultural Icon.* Minneapolis: University of Minnesota Press.

Hier, Sean P., and B. Singh Bolaria (eds.). 2006. *Identity and Belonging: Rethinking Race & Ethnicity in Canadian Society.* Toronto: Canadian Scholars' Press.

———. 2007. *Race & Racism in 21st Century Canada: Continuity, Complexity, and Change.* Peterborough: Broadview.

Hill, Darryl. 2005. "Coming to Terms: Using Technology to Know Identity." *Social Problems* 9 (3): 24–52.

Himmelstein, David, Elizabeth Warren, Deborah Thorne, and Steffie Woolhandler. 2005. "Marketwatch: Illness and Injury as Contributors to Bankruptcy." *Health Affairs* 24 (March/April): 570.

The Hindu. 1998. "The Idea of Human Development." (October 25): 25.

Hirschi, Travis. 1969. *Causes of Delinquency.* Berkeley: University of California Press.

———, and Michael Gottfredson. 1983. "Age and the Explanation of Crime." *American Journal of Sociology* 89 (3): 552–584.

Hoban, Phoebe. 2002. "Single Girls: Sex But Still No Respect." *New York Times* (Oct. 12): A19, A21.

Hochschild, Arlie Russell. 1983. *The Managed Heart: Commercialization of Human Feeling.* Berkeley: University of California Press.

———. 1989. *The Second Shift: Working Parents and the Revolution at Home.* New York: Viking/Penguin.

———. 1997. *The Time Bind: When Work Becomes Home and Home Becomes Work.* New York: Metropolitan Books.

———. 2003. *The Commercialization of Intimate Life: Notes from Home and Work.* Berkeley: University of California Press.

Hodge, Robert W., Paul Siegel, and Peter Rossi. 1964. "Occupational Prestige in the United States, 1925–63." *American Journal of Sociology* 70 (November): 286–302.

Hodgetts, Darrin, Kerry Chamberlain, and Graeme Bassett. 2003. "Between Television and the Audience: Negotiating Representations of Ageing." *Health: An Interdisciplinary Journal for the Social Study of Health, Illness and Medicine* 7 (4): 417–438.

Hodgson, Doug. 1989. "The Legal and Public Policy Implications of Human Immunodeficiency Virus Antibody Testing in New Zealand." In *Legal Implications of AIDS.* Auckland: Legal Research Foundation, 39–95.

Hodkinson, Paul. 2011. *Media, Culture and Society: An Introduction.* London: Sage.

Hodson, Randy, and Robert E. Parker. 1988. "Work in High Techology Settings: A Review of the Empirical Literature." *Research in the Sociology of Work* 4: 1–29.

———, and Teresa A. Sullivan. 2002. *The Social Organization of Work* (3rd ed.). Belmont, Cal.: Wadsworth.

Hoecker-Drysdale, Susan. 1992. *Harriet Martineau: First Woman Sociologist.* Oxford, England: Berg.

Hoffman, Bruce. 1995. "'Holy Terror': The Implications of Terrorism Motivated by a Religious Imperative." *Studies in Conflict and Terrorism* 18: 271–284.

———. 2003. "Al Qaeda, Trends in Terrorism, and Future Potentialities: An Assessment." *Studies in Conflict and Terrorism* 26: 429–442.

Holland, Dorothy C., and Margaret A. Eisenhart. 1981. *Women's Peer Groups and Choice of Career.* Final Report for the National Institute of Education. ERIC ED 199 328. Washington, D.C.

———. 1990. *Educated in Romance: Women, Achievement, and College Culture.* Chicago: University of Chicago Press.

Holmes, Mark. 1998. *The Reformation of Canada's Schools: Breaking the Barriers to Parental Choice.* Montreal: McGill-Queen's University Press.

Holmes, Morgan. 2002. "Rethinking the Meaning and Management of Intersexuality." *Sexualities* 5 (2): 159–180.

Homer-Dixon, Thomas. 1993. *Environmental Scarcity and Global Security.* Foreign Policy Association, Headline Series, Number 300. Ephrata, Penn.: Science Press.

Hook, Jennifer L., and Chalasani, Satvika, 2008. "Gendered Expectations? Reconsidering Single Fathers' Child-Care Time." *Journal of Marriage and Family* 70 (4): 978–990. doi: 10.1111/j.1741-3737.2008.00540.x.

Hooyman, Nancy R.R., and H. Asuman Kiyak. 1996. *Social Gerontology: A Multidisciplinary Perspective* (4th ed.). Boston: Allyn & Bacon.

Horan, Patrick M. 1978. "Is Status Attainment Research Atheoretical?" *American Sociological Review* 43: 534–541.

Horkheimer, Max, and Theodor W. Adorno. 1972. *Dialectic of Enlightenment.* New York: Herder and Herder.

Horsburgh, Susan. 2003. "Daddy Day Care." *People* (June 23): 79–81.

Hou, Feng, and T.R. Balakrishnan. 1999. *The Economic Integration of Visible Minorities in Contemporary Canadian Society.* 214–225.

Houle, René, and LahouraiaYssaad. 2010. "Recognition of Newcomers' Foreign Credentials and Work Experience." *Perspectives* (September): 18–33. Ottawa: Statistics Canada.

Hounshell, David. 1984. *From the American System to Mass Production, 1800–1932: The Development of*

Manufacturing Technology in the United States. Baltimore: Johns Hopkins University Press.

Howard, Michael E. 1990. "On Fighting a Nuclear War." In Francesca M. Cancian and James William Gibson (eds.), *Making War, Making Peace: The Social Foundations of Violent Conflict.* Belmont, Cal.: Wadsworth, 314–322.

Howard, Ross. 1998. "No Way Out for Despairing Port Hardy." *Globe and Mail* (June 15): A4.

Hoyt, Homer. 1939. *The Structure and Growth of Residential Neighborhoods in American Cities.* Washington, D.C.: Federal Housing Administration.

HRSDC (Human Resources and Skills Development Canada). 2003. "Winnipeg Annual Labour Market Perspectives, 2003." Retrieved June 14, 2005. Available: http://www.hrsdc.gc.ca/asp/gateway.asp?hr=/en/mb/lmireports/perspectives2003-3.shtml&hs=mb0.

———. 2006. "Advancing the Inclusion of People with Disabilities, 2006." Retrieved May 6, 2009. Available: http://www.hrsdc.gc.ca/eng/disability_issues/reports/fdr/2006/advancinginclusion.pdf.

Hugill, David. 2010. *Missing Women, Missing News: Covering Crisis in Vancouver's Downtown Eastside.* Halifax/Winnipeg: Fernwood.

Hughes, Everett C. 1945. "Dilemmas and Contradictions of Status." *American Journal of Sociology* 50: 353–359.

Hulchanski, David. 2009. *Homelessness in Canada: Past, Present, and Future.* Retrieved April 21, 2012. Available: http://www.cprn.org/documents/51110_EN.pdf.

Hull, Gloria T., Patricia Bell-Scott, and Barbara Smith. 1982. *All the Women Are White, All the Blacks Are Men, But Some of Us Are Brave.* Old Westbury, N.Y.: Feminist.

Humphreys, Laud. 1970. *Tearoom Trade: Impersonal Sex in Public Places.* Chicago: Aldine.

Hunt, Charles W. 1989. "Migrant Labor and Sexually Transmitted Diseases: AIDS in Africa." *Journal of Health and Social Behaviour* 30: 353–73.

Hunter, Floyd. 1953. *Community Power Structure.* Chapel Hill, N.C.: University of North Carolina Press.

Hurst, Charles E. 1998. *Social Inequality: Forms, Causes, and Consequences* (3rd ed.). Boston: Allyn & Bacon.

———. 2007. *Social Inequality: Forms, Causes, and Consequences* (6th ed.). Boston: Allyn & Bacon.

Huston, Aletha C. 1985. "The Development of Sex Typing: Themes from Recent Research." *Developmental Review* 5: 2–17.

Huyssen, Andreas. 1984. *After the Great Divide.* Bloomington: Indiana University Press.

Hyde, Mary, and Carol La Prairie. 1987. "American Police Crime Prevention." Working paper. Ottawa: Solicitor General.

Ibrahim, Youseff M. 1990. "Saudi Tradition: Edicts from Koran Produce Curbs on Women." *New York Times* (November 6): A6.

IGN Entertainment. 2003. "Review of Red Jack: Revenge of the Brethren." Retrieved July 19, 2003. Available: http://pc.ign.com/articles/160/160369p1.html.

Ikegami, Naoki. 1998. "Growing Old in Japan." *Age and Ageing* (May): 277–283.

Indian and Northern Affairs Canada. 2000. *Comparison of Social Conditions, 1991 and 1996.* Ottawa: Indian and Northern Affairs Canada.

———. 2005. "Some Fast Fasts on the Funding of Aboriginal Programs." Retrieved September 8, 2005. Available: http://www.ainc-inac.gc.ca/nr/prs/j-a2000/mar7_e.html.

Innis, Harold. 1984. *The Fur Trade in Canada.* Toronto: University of Toronto Press (orig. pub. 1930).

Interfaith Social Assistance Reform Coalition. 1998. *Our Neighbours' Voices: Will We Listen?* Toronto: James Lorimer & Company.

Inter-Parliamentary Union. 2009. "Women in National Parliaments." Retrieved March 4, 2009. Available: http://www.ipu.org/wmn-e/classif.htm.

———. 2012. "Women in National Parliaments." Retrieved June 20, 2012. Available: http://www.ipu.org/wmn-e/classif.htm.

Institute for Social Research. Centre for Research in Higher Education. 1995. "York Student Experience Study: Do Private High Schools Make A Difference." *Bulletin 8* (October 15). Available: http: www.isr.yorku.ca.isr/bulletins/bullet8.asp.

Institut National d'Études Demographiques. 1995. From Julie DaVanzo and David Adamson. 1997. "Russia's Demographic 'Crisis': How Real Is It?" *Rand Issue Paper,* July 1997. Santa Monica, Cal.: Rand Center for Russian and Eurasian Studies.

International Longevity Center Japan. 2012. *Aging in Japan: A Profile of Older Japanese.* Retrieved May 21, 2012. Available: http://www.ilcjapan.org/agingE/POJ12.html.

Internet World Stats. 2005. "Internet Usage Statistics: The Big Picture." Retrieved August 14, 2005. Available: http://www.internetworldstats.com/stats.htm.

———. 2009. "The Internet Big Picture." Retrieved April 30, 2009. Available: http://www.internetworldstats.com/stats.htm.

———. 2012a. "Usage and Population Statistics." Retrieved January 31, 2021. Available: http://www.internetworld-stats.com/stats.htm.

———. 2012b. "Internet Users in the World." Retrieved June 26, 2012. Available: http://www.internetworld-stats.com/stats.htm.

Ip, Greg. 1996. "Shareholders vs. Job Holders." *Globe and Mail* (March 23): B1.

Isajiw, Wsevolod W. 1999. *Understanding Diversity: Ethnicity and Race in the Canadian Context.* Toronto: Thompson Educational Publishing.

ITAR/TASS News Agency. 1999. "Polygamy Allowed in Southern Russia" (July 21). Retrieved September 11, 1999. Available: http://www.comtexnews.com.

IVF.ca. 2012. "Frequently Asked Questions." Retrieved January 24, 2012. Availble: http://www.ivf.ca/faq.htm.

Jackman, Philip. 1999. "The Greying of Canada's Sisters and Brothers." *Globe and Mail* (February 23): A24.

Jackson, Beth E. 1993. "Constructing Adoptive Identities: The Accounts of Adopted Adults." Unpublished masters thesis, University of Manitoba.

Jackson, John D., Greg Nielsen, and Yon Hsu. 2011. *Mediated Society: A Critical Sociology of Media.* Toronto: Oxford University Press.

Jacobs, Gloria. 1994. "Where Do We Go from Here? An Interview with Ann Jones." *Ms.* (September/October): 56–63.

Jaffer, M., and P. Brazeau. 2011. *The Sexual Exploitation of Children in Canada: The Need for National Action.* Ottawa: Government of Canada.

James, Carl E. 1998. "'Up to No Good': Black on the Streets and Encountering the Police." In Vic Satzewich (ed.), *Racism and Social Inequality in Canada.* Toronto: Thompson Educational Publishing, 157–176.

———. 1999. *Seeing Ourselves: Exploring Ethnicity, Race and Culture.* Toronto: Thompson Educational Publishing.

———. 2001. *Seeing Ourselves: Exploring Ethnicity, Race and Culture* (2nd ed.). Toronto: Thompson Educational Publishing.

———. 2005. *Possibilities and Limitations: Multicultural Policies and Programs in Canada.* Halifax: Fernwood.

———. 2006. "Race, Ethnicity, and Cultural Identity." In Sean P. Hier and B. Singh Bolaria (eds.), *Identity and Belonging: Rethinking Race and Ethnicity in Canadian Society.* Toronto: Canadian Scholars' Press, 43–55.

———. 2010. *Seeing Ourselves: Exploring Race, Ethnicity and Culture* (4th ed.). Toronto: Thompson Educational.

Jameson, Fredric. 1984. "Postmodernism, or, the Cultural Logic of Late Capitalism." *New Left Review* 146: 59–92.

Jamieson, L. 1999. "Intimacy Transformed? A Critical Look at the "Pure Relationship.'" *Sociology* 33 (3): 477–494.

———. 2004. "Intimacy, Negotiated Non-Monogamy and the Limits of the Couple." In J. Duncombe, K. Harrison, G. Allan, and D. Marsden (eds.), *The State of Affairs,* pp. 35–57. Mahwah, N.J.: Lawrence Erlbaum.

Janigan, Mary. 2000. "The Wealth Gap." *Maclean's* (August 28): 42–46.

Janis, Irving. 1972. *Victims of Groupthink.* Boston: Houghton Mifflin.

———. 1989. *Crucial Decisions: Leadership in Policymaking and Crisis Management.* New York: Free Press.

Jankowski, Martin Sanchez. 1991. *Islands in the Street: Gangs and American Urban Society.* Berkeley: University of California Press.

Jary, David, and Julia Jary. 1991. *The Harper Collins Dictionary of Sociology.* New York: HarperPerennial.

Jenkinson, Edward B. 1979. *Censors in the Classroom: The Mind Benders.* Carbondale: Southern Illinois University Press.

Jensen, Mike. 2002. "The African Internet: A Status Report." Retrieved August 14, 2005. Available: http://www3.sn.apc.org/africa/afstat.htm.

Jewell, K. Sue. 1993. *From Mammy to Miss America and Beyond: Cultural Images and the Shaping of US Social Policy.* New York: Routledge.

Jha, Prabhat, Richard Peto, Witold Zatroski, Jillian Boreham, Martin Jarvis, and Alan Lopez. 2006. "Social Inequalities in Male Mortality, and in Male Mortality from Smoking: Indirect Estimation from National Death Rates in England and Wales, Poland, and North America." *Lancet* 368: 367–370.

Jiwani, J., and M. Young. 2006. "Missing and Murdered Women: Reproducing Marginality in News Discourse." *Canadian Journal of Communication* 31 (4): 895–917.

Johns Hopkins. 1998. "Can Religion be Good Medicine?" *The Johns Hopkins Medical Letter* (November 3).

Johnson, Allan. 1995. *The Blackwell Dictionary of Sociology.* Malden, Mass.: Blackwell.

———. 2005. "The Perspective of Sociology." In Bruce Ravelli (ed.), *Exploring Canadian Sociology: A Reader.* Toronto: Pearson, 8–13.

Johnson, Claudia. 1994. *Stifled Laughter: One Woman's Story About Fighting Censorship.* Golden, Col.: Fulcrum.

Johnson, Earvin "Magic," with William Novak. 1992. *My Life.* New York: Fawcett Crest.

Johnson, Holly. 1995 "Violence Against Women: A Special Topic Survey." In R. Silverman, J. Teevan, and V. Sacco (eds.), *Crime in Canadian Society* (5th ed.). Toronto: Harcourt Brace, 210–221.

———. 1996. *Dangerous Domains: Violence Against Women in Canada.* Toronto: Thomson Nelson.

———, and Myrna Dawson. 2011. *Violence Against Women in Canada: Research and Policy Perspectives.* Toronto: Oxford University Press.

Johnson, L.A. 1974. *Poverty in Wealth.* Toronto: New Hogtown Press.

Johnstone, Ronald L. 1997. *Religion in Society: A Sociology of Religion* (5th ed.). Saddle River, N.J.: Prentice-Hall.

Jolis, Alan. 1996. "The Good Banker." *Independent on Sunday.* (May 5): 15–16.

Jones, Jennifer M., Susan Bennett, Marion P. Olmsted, Margaret L. Lawson, and Gary Rodin. 2001. "Disordered Eating Attitudes and Behaviours in Teenaged Girls: A School-Based Study." *Canadian Medical Association Journal* 165: 547–552.

Jones, Meredith. 2004. "Architecture of the Body: Cosmetic Surgery and Postmodern Space." *Space and Culture* 7 (1): 90–101.

Juergensmeyer, Mark. 1993. *The New Cold War? Religious Nationalism Confronts the Secular State.* Berkeley: University of California Press.

———. 2003. *Terror in the Mind of God.* Berkeley: University of California Press.

Jung, John. 1994. *Under the Influence: Alcohol and Human Behavior.* Pacific Grove, Cal.: Brooks/Cole.

Kahneman, Daniel, Alan Krueger, David Schkade, Norbert Schwartz, and Arthur Stone. 2006. "Would You Be Happier if You Were Richer? A Focusing Illusion." *Science* 312 (June 30): 1908–1910.

Kahney, Leander. 2003. "E-mail Mobs Materialize All Over." Wired News. Retrieved August 11, 2003. Available: http://www.wired.com/news/culture/0,1284,59518,00.html.

Kakuchi, Suvendrini. 1998. "Population: Japan Desperate for a Baby Boom." World News: InterPress Service. Retrieved September 21, 1999. Available: http://www.oneworld.org/ips2/nov/japan.html.

Kanter, Rosabeth Moss. 1977. *Men and Women of the Corporation.* New York: Basic Books.

———. 1983. *The Change Masters: Innovation and Entrepreneurship in the American Corporation.* New York: Simon & Schuster.

Kantrowitz, Barbara. 2003. "Hoping for the Best, Ready for the Worst." *Newsweek* (May 12): 50–51.

Kapadia, Kamal. 2008. *Developments After a Disaster: The Tsunami, Poverty, Conflict and Reconstruction in Sri Lanka.* Unpublished PhD Dissertation, University of California at Berkeley.

Karabanow, Jeff. 2008. "Getting off the Street: Exploring the Processes of Young People's Street Exits" *American Behavioral Scientist* 51: 772.

Karmona, Laurie Krever. 2001. "Who Me, Disabled?" *Globe and Mail* (October 18): A16.

Karp, David A., and William C. Yoels. 1976. "The College Classroom: Some Observations on the Meanings of Student Participation." *Sociology and Social Research* 60: 421–439.

Kaspar, Anne S. 1986. "Consciousness Re-evaluated: Interpretive Theory and Feminist Scholarship." *Sociological Inquiry* 56 (1): 30-49.

Kata, Anna. 2011. "Anti-Vaccine Activists, Web 2.0, and the Postmodern Paradigm—An Overview of Tactics and Tropes Used Online by the Anti-Vaccination Movement." *Vaccine Special Issue.* Online (December 13).

Katz, Michael B. 1989. *The Undeserving Poor: From the War on Poverty to the War on Welfare.* New York: Pantheon.

Katz, Stephen. 1999. *Old Age as Lifestyle in an Active Society.* Doreen B. Townsend Center Occasional Papers. Berkeley: University of California. Retrieved May 30, 2005. Available: http://townsendcenter.berkeley.edu/pubs/OP19_Katz.pdf.

Katzer, Jeffrey, Kenneth H. Cook, and Wayne W. Crouch. 1991. *Evaluating Information: A Guide for Users of Social Science Research.* New York: McGraw-Hill.

Kaufert, S.R., and M. Lock. 1997. "Medicalization of Women's Third Age." *Journal of Psychosomatic Obstetrics and Gynaecology* 18: 81–86.

Kaufman, Gayle. 1999. "The Portrayal of Men's Family Roles in Television Commercials." *Sex Roles* 313: 439–451.

Kauppinen-Toropainen, Kaisa, and Johanna Lammi. 1993. "Men in Female-Dominated Occupations: A Cross-Cultural Comparison." In Christine L. Williams (ed.), *Doing "Women's Work": Men in Nontraditional Occupations.* Newbury Park, Cal.: Sage, 91–112.

Kazemipur, Abdolmohammad, and Shiva Halli. 2001. "The Changing Colour of Poverty in Canada." *Canadian Review of Sociology and Anthropology* 38 (2): 217–238.

Kedrowski, Karen. 2010. "Women's Health Activism in Canada: The Cases of Breast Cancer and Breastfeeding." Paper presented to the Canadian Political Science Association Meeting, Montreal.

Keegan, Victor. 1996. "A World Without Bosses—Or Workers." *Globe and Mail* (August 24): D4.

Keister, Lisa A. 2000. *Wealth in America: Trends in Wealth Inequality.* Cambridge, U.K.: Cambridge University Press.

Keller, James. 1994. "I Treasure Each Moment." *Parade Magazine* (September 4): 4–5.

Kellner, Douglas. 2011. "Cultural Studies, Multiculturalism, and Media Culture." In Gail Hines and Jean Humez (eds.), *Gender, Race, and Class in Media.* Los Angeles: Sage.

Kelman, Steven. 1991. "Sweden Sour? Downsizing the 'Third Way.'" *New Republic* (July 29): 19–23.

Kellett, Anthony. 2004. "Terrorism in Canada, 1960–1992." In Jeffrey Ian Ross (ed.), *Violence in Canada: Sociopolitical Perspectives* (2nd ed.). New Brunswick, N.J.: Transaction Press, 284–312.

Kelly, John, and David Stark. 2002. "Crisis, Recovery, Innovation: Responsive Organization After September 11." Paper presented at the Reginald H. Jones Center's 3rd Annual Conference on the Internet and Strategy "The Internet and the 21st Century Firm." Philadelphia: The Wharton School.

Kemp, Alice Abel. 1994. *Women's Work: Degraded and Devalued.* Englewood Cliffs, N.J.: Prentice-Hall.

Kennedy, Leslie W. 1983. *The Urban Kaleidoscope: Canadian Perspectives.* Toronto: McGraw-Hill Ryerson.

Kennedy, Paul. 1993. *Preparing for the Twenty-First Century.* New York: Random House.

Kenny, Charles. 2003. "Development's False Divide." *Foreign Policy* (January/February): 76–77.

Kephart, William M. 1982. *Extraordinary Groups.* New York: St. Martin's Press.

Kerbo, Harold. 2000. *Social Stratification and Inequality: Class Conflict in Historical, Comparative, and Global Perspective* (4th ed.). New York: McGraw-Hill.

Kerstetter, Steve. 2002. *Rags and Riches: Wealth Inequality in Canada.* Ottawa: Canadian Centre for Policy Alternatives.

Kessler, Suzanne. 1998. *Lessons Learned from the Intersexed.* New Brunswick, N.J.: Rutgers University Press.

Kettle, John. 1998. "Death Still Looks Like a Healthy Business." *Globe and Mail* (May 7): B15.

Khayatt, Didi. 1994. "The Boundaries of Identity at the Intersection of Race, Class and Gender." *Canadian Woman Studies* 14 (Spring).

Kidron, Michael, and Ronald Segal. 1995. *The State of the World Atlas.* New York: Penguin.

Kilbourne, Jean. 1994. "Still Killing Us Softly: Advertising and the Obsession with Thinness." In Patricia Fallon, Melanie A. Katzman, and Susan C. Wooley (eds.), *Feminist Perspectives on Eating Disorders.* New York: Guilford, 395–454.

———. 1999. *Deadly Persuasion: The Addictive Power of Advertising.* New York: Simon & Schuster.

———. 2000. *Killing Us Softly 3: Advertising's Image of Women.* Film. Northampton, Mass.: Media Education Foundation.

Killian, Lewis. 1984. "Organization, Rationality, and Spontaneity in the Civil Rights Movement." *American Sociological Review* 49: 770–783.

Kim, Ryan. 2006. "The World's a Cell-Phone Stage." *San Francisco Chronicle* (February 27). Retrieved Mar. 30, 2007. Available: http://www.sfgate.com/cgi-in/article.cgi?file=/chronicle/archive/2006/02/27/BUG2IHECTO1.DTL&type=printable.

Kimmel, Michael S., and Michael A. Messner (eds.). 1992. *Men's Lives* (2nd ed.). New York: Macmillan.

King, Gary, Robert O. Keohane, and Sidney Verba. 1994. *Designing Social Inquiry: Scientific Inference in Qualitative Research.* Princeton, N.J.: Princeton University Press.

King, Leslie, and Madonna Harrington Meyer. 1997. "The Politics of Reproductive Benefits: U.S. Insurance Coverage of Contraceptive and Infertility Treatments." *Gender and Society* 11 (1): 8–30.

King, Samantha. 2006. Pink *Ribbons, Inc.: Breast Cancer and the Culture of Philanthropy.* Minneapolis, Minn: University of Minnesota Press.

Kinsey, A. , C. Pomeroy, and C. Martin. 1948. *Sexual Behavior in the Human Male.* Philadelphia: W.B. Sanders.

Kinsey, A., C. Pomeroy, W. Gebhard, and C. Marin. 1953. *Sexual Behaviour in the Human Female.* Philadelphia: W.B. Sanders.

Kinsey Institute. 2012. "Kinsey's Homosexual-Heterosexual Rating Scale." Retrieved August 1, 2012. Available: http://www.iub.edu/~kinsey/research/ak-hhscale.html.

Kinsley, Michael. 2008. "Mine is Longer Than Yours: The Last Boomer Game." *The New Yorker* (April 7). Retrieved May 14, 2012. Available: http://www.newyorker.com/reporting/2008/04/07/080407fa_fact_kinsley.

Kirby, S.L., and A. Robinson. 1998. *Lesbian Struggles for Human Rights in Canada: Report to the Secretary of State on the Status of Women.* Ottawa.

Kirby, Sandra, and Kate McKenna. 1989. *Experience Research Social Change: Methods from the Margins.* Toronto: Garamond.

Kirmayer, Laurence J. 1994. "Suicide Among Canadian Aboriginal Peoples." *Transcultural Psychiatric Research Review* 31: 7.

———, Gregory M. Brass, Tara Holton, Ken Paul, Cori Simpson, and Caroline Tait. 2007. *Suicide Among Aboriginal People in Canada.* Ottawa: Aboriginal Healing Foundation.

Kitano, Harry, Iris Chi, Siyon Rhee, C.K. Law, and James E. Lubben. 1992. "Norms and Alcohol Consumption: Japanese in Japan, Hawaii, and California." *Journal of Studies on Alcohol* 53 (1): 33–39.

Klein, Alan M. 1993. *Little Big Men: Bodybuilding Subculture and Gender Construction.* Albany: SUNY Press.

Klein, Naomi. 2000. *No Logo.* Toronto: Vintage Canada.

Kleinfeld, Judith S. 2002. "The Small World Problem." *Society* (January/February): 61–66.

Klesse, C. 2005. 'Bisexual Women, Non-Monogamy, and Differentialist Anti-Promiscuity Discourses." *Sexualities* 8 (4): 445–464.

Klockars, Carl B. 1979. "The Contemporary Crises of Marxist Criminology." *Criminology* 16: 477–515.

Kluckhohn, Clyde. 1961. "The Study of Values." In Donald N. Barrett (ed.), *Values in America.* South Bend, Ind.: University of Notre Dame Press, 17–46.

Knox, Paul L., and Peter J. Taylor, eds. 1995. *World Cities in a World-System.* Cambridge, England: Cambridge University Press.

Knudsen, Dean D. 1992. *Child Maltreatment: Emerging Perspectives.* Dix Hills, N.Y.: General Hall.

Kohen, Dafna, Sharanjit Uppal, Anne Guevremont, and Fernando Cartwright. 2007. "Children with Disabilities and the Educational System—A Provincial Perspective." *Education Matters: Insights on Education, Learning and Training in Canada* 4 (1). Health Analysis and Measurement Group, Statistics Canada. Retrieved April 24, 2009. Available: http://www.statcan.gc.ca/pub/81-004-x/2007001/9631-eng.htm.

Kohlberg, Lawrence. 1969. "Stage and Sequence: The Cognitive-Developmental Approach to Socialization." In David A. Goslin, *Handbook of Socialization Theory and Research.* Chicago: Rand McNally, 347–480.

Kohn, Melvin L. 1977. *Class and Conformity: A Study in Values* (2nd ed.). Homewood, Ill.: Dorsey Press.

———, Atsushi Naoi, Carrie Schoenbach, Carmi Schooler, and Kazimierz M. Slomczynski. 1990. "Position in the Class Structure and Psychological Functioning in the United States, Japan, and Poland." *American Journal of Sociology* 95: 964–1008.

Kolata, Gina. 1993. "Fear of Fatness: Living Large in a Slimfast World." *Austin American-Statesman* (January 3): C1, C6.

———. 2006. "Old But Not Frail: A Matter of Heart and Head." *The New York Times* (October 5).

Kome, Penney. 2002. "Canada Court Tells Parliament to OK Gay Marriages." Women's eNews. Retrieved August 23, 2003. Available: http://www.womensnews.org/article/cfm/dyn/aid/987/context/archive.

Korkeila, Jyrki. 2010. "Problematic Use in Context." *World Psychiatry* 9 (2): 94–95.

Kornblum, Janet. 2004. "There's a Risk to the Beauty of Surgery." Retrieved March 17, 2005. Available: http://www.usatoday.com/news/health/2004-01-21-plastic--surgery-risks_x.htm.

Korsmeyer, Carolyn. 1981. "The Hidden Joke: Generic Uses of Masculine Terminology." In Mary Vetterling-Braggin (ed.), *Sexist Language: A Modern Philosophical Analysis.* Totowa, N.J.: Littlefield, Adams, 116–131.

Korte, Charles and Stanley Milgram. 1970. "Acquaintance Networks Between Racial Groups: Application of the Small World Method." *Journal of Personality and Social Psychology* 15: 101–108.

Korten, David C. 1996. *When Corporations Rule the World.* West Hartford, Conn.: Kumarian Press.

Koskela, Hille. 1997. "Bold Walk and Breakings: Women's Spatial Confidence versus Fear of Violence." *Gender, Place and Culture* 4 (3): 301–320.

Kowinski, William Severini. 2002. *The Malling of America: Travels in the United States of Shopping.* New York: Xlibis.

Kozol, Jonathan. 1988. *Rachael and Her Children: Homeless Families in America.* New York: Fawcett Columbine.

———. 1991. *Savage Inequalities: Children in America's Schools.* New York: Crown.

Krahn, Harvey J., and Graham S. Lowe. 1998. *Work, Industry, and Canadian Society* (3rd ed.). Toronto: Thomson Nelson.

———. 2002. *Work, Industry and Canadian Society* (4th ed.). Toronto: Nelson Thomson Learning.

Krahn, Harvey J., and Alison Taylor. 2007. "Streaming in the 10th Grade in Four Canadian Provinces in 2000." *Education Matters.* Statistics Canada Cat. no. 81-004-XIE. Retrieved April 14, 2009. Available: http://www.statcan.gc.ca/pub/81-004-x/2007002/9994-eng.htm.

———, Graham Lowe, and Karen Hughes. 2008. *Work, Industry and Canadian Society* (5th ed.). Toronto: Nelson.

———. 2011. *Work, Industry and Canadian Society* (6th ed.). Toronto: Nelson.

Kramnick, Isaac, ed. 1995. *The Portable Enlightenment Reader.* New York: Penguin.

Krashinsky, Susan. 2009. "Click by Click, Greeting Cards Get Licked." *Globe and Mail* (December 24): B3.

Krebs, Valdis E. 2002. "Mapping Networks of Terrorist Cells." *Connections* 24 (3): 43–52.

Kristof, Nicholas D. 2006. "Looking for Islam's Luthers." *New York Times* (Oct. 15): A22.

———. 2012a. "After Recess: Change the World." *New York Times* (February 4).

———. 2012b. "Africa on the Rise." *New York Times* (July 1): SR11.

Kshetri, Nir. 2010. *The Global Cybercrime Industry.* Berlin: Springer-Verlag.

Kumar, K. 1997. "The Post-Modern Condition." In A.H. Halsey, H. Lauder, P. Brown, and A.S. Wells (eds). *Education: Culture, Economy, and Society.* Don Mills: Oxford University Press.

Kunz, Jean L., Anne Milan, and Sylvain Schetagne. 2000. *Unequal Access: A Canadian Profile of Racial Differences in Education, Employment and Income.* Ottawa: Canadian Race Relations Foundation.

Kurian, George. 1991. "Socialization in South Asian Immigrant Youth." In S.P. Sharma, A.M. Erwin, and D. Meintel (eds.), *Immigrants and Refugees in Canada.* Saskatoon: University of Saskatchewan.

Kurtz, Lester. 1995. *Gods in the Global Village: The World's Religions in Sociological Perspective.* Thousand Oaks, Cal.: Sage.

Kutcher, Stanley P., and Magdalena Szumilas. 2008. "Youth Suicide Prevention." *Canadian Medical Association Journal* 178 (3).

Kvale, Steinar. 1996. *Interviews: An Introduction to Qualitative Research Interviewing.* Thousand Oaks, Cal.: Sage.

Kymlicka, W. 2010. *The Current State of Multiculturalism in Canada and Research Themes on Multiculturalism, 2008–2010.* Citizenship and Immigration Cat. no. Ci96-112/201E-PDF. Retrieved June 2, 2012. Available: http://www.cic.gc.ca/english/pdf/pub/multi-state.pdf.

Laberge, Danielle. 1991. "Women's Criminality, Criminal Women, Criminalized Women?: Questions in and for a Feminist Perspective." *Journal of Human Justice* 2 (2): 37–56.

Lacayo, Richard. 2001. "About Face: An Inside Look at How Women Fared Under Taliban Oppression and What the Future Holds for Them Now." *Time* (Dec. 5): 36–49.

Ladd, E.C., Jr. 1966. *Negro Political Leadership in the South.* Ithaca, N.Y.: Cornell University Press.

Lafreniere, Sylvie A., Yves Carriere, Laurent Martel, and Alain Belanger. 2003. "Dependent Seniors at Home: Formal and Informal Help." *Health Reports* 14 (August): 31–39.

Lamanna, Mary Ann, and Agnes Riedmann. 2003. *Marriages and Families: Making Choices and Facing Change* (8th ed.). Belmont, Cal.: Wadsworth.

———. 2011. *Marriages and Families: Making Choices and Facing Change* (11th ed.). Belmont, Cal.: Wadsworth.

Lancet. 2012. "Living with Grief." Volume 379 (February 18): 589.

Landry, Laura, and Maire Sinha. 2008. "Adult Correctional Services in Canada, 2005/2006." *Juristat* 28 (6). Ottawa: Statistics Canada.

Lane, Harlan. 1992. *The Mask of Benevolence: Disabling the Deaf Community.* New York: Vintage Books.

Langdon, Steven. 1999. *Global Poverty, Democracy and North-South Change.* Toronto: Garamond Press.

Lankenau, S.E. 1999. "Panhandling Repertoires and Routines for Overcoming the Non-Person Treatment." *Deviant Behaviour: An Interdisciplinary Journal* 20: 183–206.

Lapchick, Richard E. 1991. *Five Minutes to Midnight: Race and Sport in the 1990s.* Lanham, Md.: Madison Books.

Lapsley, Daniel K. 1990. "Continuity and Discontinuity in Adolescent Social Cognitive Development." In Raymond Montemayor, Gerald R. Adams, and Thomas P. Gullota (eds.), *From Childhood to Adolescence: A Transitional Period? (Advances in Adolescent Development,* vol. 2). Newbury Park, Cal.: Sage.

Larimer, Tim. 1999. "The Japan Syndrome." *Time* (October 11): 50–51.

Larson, Magali Sarfatti. 1977. *The Rise of Professionalism: A Sociological Analysis.* Berkeley: University of California Press.

Lasch, Christopher. 1977. *Haven in a Heartless World.* New York: Basic Books.

Lash, Scott, and John Urry. 1994. *Economies of Signs and Space.* London: Sage.

Lashmar, Paul. 2004. "It's All for Your Own Good." *The Guardian* (September 25).

Latané, Bibb, and John M. Darley. 1970. *The Unresponsive Bystander: Why Doesn't He Help?* New York: Appleton Century Crofts.

Latouche, Serge. 1992. "Standard of Living." In Wolfgang Sachs (ed.), *The Development Dictionary.* Atlantic Highlands, N.J.: Zed Books, 250–263.

Laird, Kristin. 2009. "TD's Old Men Are Grumpy About Mortgages." *Marketer News* (April 1). Available: http://www.marketingmag.ca/english/news/marketer/article.jsp?content=20090331_173938_7252.

Lavigne, Yves. 1987. *Hell's Angels: Taking Care of Business.* Toronto: Ballantine Books.

Lavizzo-Mourey, Risa, William Richardson, Robert Ross, and John Rowe. 2005. "A Tale of Two Cities." *Health Affairs* 24: 313–315.

Law Reform Commission of Canada. 1974. *The Native Offender and the Law.* Ottawa: Information Canada.

Laxer, Gordon. 1989. *Open for Business: The Roots of Foreign Ownership in Canada.* Don Mills: Oxford University Press.

Layton, Jack. 2008. *Homelessnes: How to End the National Crisis.* Toronto: Penguin.

Lazar, Shira. 2012. "How the White House Became a Social-Media Powerhouse." *The Daily Dose* (February 8).

Lazarsfeld, Paul, and Robert Merton. 1948. "Mass Communication, Popular Taste and Organized Social Action." In L. Bryson (ed.), *The Communication of Ideas.* New York: Harper and Brothers, 95–118.

Lebenkoff, S. 2011. *"Being Labeled as a Bride. . . It Makes You Want to Punch Them in the Face": An Exploratory Study of Queer Weddings in Vancouver, Canada.* Unpublished master's thesis, University Of British Columbia.

LeBlanc, Cathie. 2011. "Fear and Loathing in *Second Life*: Body Surveillance in the Online Community." In Robin DeRosa (ed.), *Simulation in Media and Culture: Believing the Hype.* Lanham, Md.: Lexington Books, 113–119.

Le Bon, Gustave. 1960. *The Crowd: A Study of the Popular Mind.* New York: Viking (orig. pub. 1895).

Lee, Kevin K. 2000. "Urban Poverty in Canada: A Statistical Profile." Ottawa: Canadian Council on Social Development.

Leenaars, Antoon A., Susan Wenckstern, Isaac Sakinofsky, Ronald J. Dyck,

Michael J. Kral, and Roger C. Bland. 1998. *Suicide in Canada.* Toronto: University of Toronto Press.

Lefrançois, Guy R. 1999. *The Lifespan* (6th ed.). Belmont, Cal.: Wadsworth.

Lehmann, Jennifer M. 1994. *Durkheim and Women.* Lincoln: University of Nebraska Press.

Leidner, Robin. 1993. *Fast Food, Fast Talk: Service Work and the Routinization of Everyday Life.* Berkeley: University of California Press.

Leiss, William, Stephen Kline, Sut Jhally, and Jacqueline Botterill. 2006. *Social Communication in Advertising: Consumption in the Mediated Marketplace* (3rd ed.) New York: Routledge.

Lele, J., G.C. Perlin, and H.G. Thorburn. 1979. "The National Party Convention." In H.G. Thorburn (ed.), *Political Parties in Canada.* Scarborough, Ont.: Prentice-Hall, 89–97.

Lemann, Nicholas. 1997. "Let's Guarantee the Key Ingredients." *Time* (October 27): 96.

Lemert, Charles. 1997. *Postmodernism Is Not What You Think.* Malden, Mass.: Blackwell.

Lemert, Edwin M. 1951. *Social Pathology.* New York: McGraw-Hill.

Lengermann, Patricia Madoo, and Jill Niebrugge-Brantley. 1998. *The Women Founders: Sociology and Social Theory, 1830–1930.* New York: McGraw-Hill.

———, and Ruth A. Wallace. 1985. *Gender in America: Social Control and Social Change.* Englewood Cliffs, N.J.: Prentice-Hall.

Lenski, Gerhard. 1966. *Power and Privilege: A Theory of Social Stratification.* New York: McGraw-Hill.

———, Jean Lenski, and Patrick Nolan. 1991. *Human Societies: An Introduction to Macrosociology* (6th ed.). New York: McGraw-Hill.

Lenzer, Gertrud, ed. 1998. *The Essential Writings: Auguste Comte and Positivism.* New Brunswick, N.J.: Transaction.

Leonard, Andrew. 1999. "We've Got Mail—Always." *Newsweek* (September 20): 58–61.

Lerner, Gerda. 1986. *The Creation of Patriarchy.* New York: Oxford University Press.

LeShan, Eda. 1994. *I Want More of Everything.* New York: New Market Press.

LeVay, Simon. 2000. "As Nature Made Him: The Boy Who Was Raised as a Girl. Book Review" *Psychology Today* (May). Retrieved September 25, 2003. Available: http://findarticles.com/m1175/3_33/62215090/pl/article.

Leventman, Paula Goldman. 1981. *Professionals Out of Work.* New York: Free Press.

Leviathan, U., and J. Cohen. 1985. "Gender Differences in Life Expectancy Among Kibbutz Members." *Social Science and Medicine* 21: 545–551.

Levin, William C. 1988. "Age Stereotyping: College Student Evaluations." *Research on Aging* 10 (1): 134–148.

Levine, Adeline Gordon. 1982. *Love Canal: Science, Politics, and People.* Lexington, Mass.: Lexington Books.

Levine, Arthur. 1993. "Student Expectations of College." *Change* (September/October): 4.

Levine, Nancy E., and Joan B. Silk. 1997. "Why Polyandry Fails: Sources of Instability in Polyandrous Marriages." *Current Anthropology* (June): 375–399.

Lewis, Kevin, Marco Gonzalez, and Jason Kaufman. 2012. "Social Selection and Peer Influence in an Online Social Network." *Proceedings of the National Academy of Sciences of the United States of America* 109: 68–72.

Lewis, Paul. 1998. "Marx's Stock Resurges on a 150-Year Tip." *New York Times* (June 27): A17, A19.

Lewis-Thornton, Rae. 1994. "Facing AIDS." *Essence* (December): 63–130.

Levitt, Kari. 1970. *Silent Surrender: The Multinational Corporation in Canada.* Toronto: Macmillan of Canada.

Leyton, Elliott. 1979. *The Myth of Delinquency: An Anatomy of Juvenile Nihilism.* Toronto: McClelland and Stewart.

———. 1997. *Dying Hard: The Ravages of Industrial Carnage.* Toronto: Oxford University Press.

Li, Geoffrey. 2008. "Homicide in Canada, 2007." *Juristat* 28 (9). Ottawa: Statistics Canada.

Liberty. 2001. "You Could See the Shame on Their Faces." In *RESIST! A Grassroots Collection of Stories, Poetry, Photos and Analysis from the FTAA Protests in Québec City and Beyond.* Compiled by Jen Chang, Bethany Or, Eloginy Tharmendran, Emmie Tsumura, Steve Daniels, and Darryl Leroux. Halifax: Fernwood, 103–107.

Liebow, Elliot. 1993. *Tell Them Who I Am: The Lives of Homeless Women.* New York: Free Press.

Lin, J. 2003. "A New Look: Retail Clothing Sales in Canada." *Statistics Canada Analytical Paper.* Ottawa: Statistics Canada.

Linden, Greg, Kenneth Kraemer, and Jason Dedrick. 2007. "Who Captures Value in a Global Innovation System? The Case of Apple's iPod." Irvine, Cal.: Personal Computing Industry Center. Retrieved June 21, 2010. Available: http://www.escholarship.org/uc/item/1770046n.

Linden, Rick. 1994. "Deviance and Crime." In Lorne Tepperman, James E. Curtis, and R.J. Richardson (eds.), *The Social World* (3rd ed.). Whitby, Ont.: McGraw-Hill Ryerson, 188–226.

———. 2000. *Criminology: A Canadian Perspective* (4th ed.) Toronto: Harcourt Brace.

———. 2004. *Criminology: A Canadian Perspective* (5th ed.). Toronto: Nelson.

———. 2009. *Criminology: A Canadian Perspective* (6th ed.). Toronto: Nelson.

———. 2012. *Criminology: A Canadian Perspective* (7th ed.). Toronto: Nelson.

———, and Raymond C. Currie. 1977. "Religiosity and Drug Use: A Test of Social Control Theory." *Canadian Journal of Criminology and Corrections* 19: 346–355.

———, and Cathy Fillmore. 1981. "A Comparative Study of Delinquency Involvement." *Canadian Review of Sociology and Anthropology* 18: 343–361.

———, and Dan Koenig. 2012. "Deterrence, Routine Activity, and Rational Choice Theories." In Rick Linden (ed.), *Criminology: A Canadian Perspective* (7th ed.). Toronto: Nelson, 463–490.

———, David Last, and Christopher Murphy. 2007. "Obstacles on the Road to Peace and Justice: The Role of Civilian Police in Peacekeeping." In Andrew Goldsmith and James Sheptycki (eds.), *Crafting Transnational Policing: Police Capacity-Building and Global Policing Reform.* Oxford: Hart Publishing, 149–175.

Lindsay, Colin. 2002. *Poverty Profile, 1999.* Ottawa: Statistics Canada.

———. 2007. "Census Snapshot on Canada: Families." *Canadian Social Trends* (Winter). Retrieved May 14, 2009. Available: http://www.statcan.gc.ca/pub/11-008-x/2007006/article/10380-eng.pdf.

———. 2008. "Are Women Spending More Time on Unpaid Domestic Work Than Men in Canada?" *Matter of Fact* (September). Statistics Canada Cat. no. 89-630-X. Retrieved June 1, 2009. Available: http://www.statcan.gc.ca/pub/89-630-x/2008001/article/10705-eng.pdf.

———, and Marcia Almey. 2006. *Women in Canada* (5th ed.). Ottawa: Statistics Canada.

Linton, Ralph. 1936. *The Study of Man.* New York: Appleton-Century-Crofts.

Lipovenko, Dorothy. 1997. "Older People Looking for Work Often Face Frowns, Study Says." *Globe and Mail* (November 19): A6.

Lippa, Richard A. 1994. *Introduction to Social Psychology.* Pacific Grove, Cal.: Brooks/Cole.

Lips, Hilary M. 1989. "Gender-Role Socialization: Lessons in Femininity." In Jo Freeman (ed.), *Women: A Feminist Perspective* (4th ed.). Mountain View, Cal.: Mayfield, 197–216.

———. 1993. *Sex and Gender: An Introduction* (2nd ed.). Mountain View, Cal.: Mayfield.

———. 2001. *Sex and Gender: An Introduction* (4th ed.). New York: McGraw-Hill.

———. 2007. *Sex and Gender: An Introduction* (6th ed). New York McGraw-Hill.

Lipton, Eric, Christopher Drew, Scott Shane, and David Rohde. 2005. "Breakdowns Marked Path from Hurricane to Anarchy." NYTimes.com (September 11). Retrieved September 12, 2005. Available: http://www.nytimes.com/2005/09/11/national/nationalspecial/11response.html?pagewanted=1&ei=5070&en=b1231d972456e252&ex=1126670400.

Liskiewicz, Patrick, A.J. 2010. "Cultivated Play: FarmVille." *Media Commons: A Digital Scholarly Network.* Retrieved December 26, 2011. Available: http://mediacommons.futureofthebook.org/content/cultivated-play-farmville.

Livingston, D.W. 2002. "Universities and the Left." *Canadian Dimension* 36 (May/June). Lorber, Judith (ed.). 2001. *Gender Inequality: Feminist Theories and Politics* (2nd ed.). Los Angeles: Roxbury.

———, and Meg Luxton. 1995. "Gender Consciousness at Work: Modification of the Male Breadwinner Norm Among Steelworkers and Their Spouses." In E.D. Nelson and B.W. Robinson (eds.), *Gender in the 1990s.* Toronto: Thomson Nelson, 172–200.

Lochhead, Clarence, and Vivian Shalla. 1996. "Delivering the Goods: Income Distribution and the Precarious Middle Classes." *Perception* 20 (1). Canadian Council on Social Development. Retrieved June 27, 2002. Available: http://www.ccsd.ca/deliver.html.

Lock, Ineke, and Satoshi Ikeda. 2005. "Clothes Encounters: Consumption, Culture, Ecology, and Economy." In Debra Davidson and Kierstin Hatt (eds.), *Consuming Sustainability.* Halifax: Fernwood Publishing, 20–46.

Lofland, Lyn. 1973. *A World of Strangers: Order and Action in Urban Public Space.* New York: Basic Books.

Lofland, John. 1993. "Collective Behavior: The Elementary Forms." In Russell L. Curtis, Jr., and Benigno E. Aguirre (eds.), *Collective Behavior and Social Movements.* Boston: Allyn & Bacon, 70–75.

———, and Rodney Stark. 1965. "Becoming a World-Saver: A Theory of Conversion to a Deviant Perspective." *American Sociological Review* 30 (6): 862–875.

Lombardo, William K., Gary A. Cretser, Barbara Lombardo, and Sharon L. Mathis. 1983. "For Cryin' Out Loud—There Is a Sex Difference." *Sex Roles* 9: 987–995.

Lorber, Judith. 1994. *Paradoxes of Gender.* New Haven, Conn.: Yale University Press.

———. 2001. *Gender Inequality: Feminist Theories and Politics* (2nd. ed.), Los Angeles: Roxbury.

———. 2001. "Night to His Day": The Social Construction of Gender." In Theodore Cohen (ed.), *Men and Masculinity: A Text Reader.* California: Wadsworth,19–28.

Loseke, Donileen. 1992. *The Battered Woman and Shelters: The Social Construction of Wife Abuse.* Albany: SUNY Press.

Lothian, Jane. 1990. *Status Offenders in Manitoba: Hidden Systems of Social Control.* Unpublished master's thesis, University of Manitoba.

Lott, Bernice. 1994. *Women's Lives: Themes and Variations in Gender Learning* (2nd ed.). Pacific Grove, Cal.: Brooks/Cole.

Low, Setha. 2003. *Behind the Gates: Life, Security, and the Pursuit of Happiness in Fortress America.* New York: Routledge.

Lowe, Graham S. 1999. "Labour Markets, Inequality, and the Future of Work." In James Curtis, Edward Grabb, and Neil Guppy (eds.), *Social Inequality in Canada: Patterns, Problems, and Policies.* Scarborough, Ont.: Prentice-Hall, 113–128.

Lowe, Maria R. 1998. *Women of Steel: Female Bodybuilders and the Struggle for Self-Definition.* New York: New York University Press.

Lowe, Mick. 2002. "It Takes a Moment to Change the World: Reflections on Quebec City and Beyond." *Straight Goods* (March 18).

Lowman, J., and L. Fraser. 1995. *Violence Against Persons Who Prostitute: The Experience in British Columbia.* Ottawa: Department Of Justice.

Luciw, Roma. 2002. "Dropout Rate Falls to 12% as Students Focus on Future." *Globe and Mail* (January 24). Available: http://www.globeandmail.com.

Lummis, C. Douglas. 1992. "Equality." In Wolfgang Sachs (ed.), *The Development Dictionary.* Atlantic Highlands, N.J.: Zed Books, 38–52.

Luong, May. 2010. *The Financial Impact of Student Loans.* Statistics Canada Cat. no. 75-001.X. Retrieved June 21, 2012. Available: http://www5.statcan.gc.ca/access_acces/alternative_alternatif.action?l=eng&loc=../pdf/11073-eng.pdf.

Lupton, Deborah. 1997. "Foucault and the Medicalization Critique." In Alan Petersen and Robin Bunton (eds.), *Foucault: Health and Medicine.* London: Routledge, 94–110.

Lupul, M.R. 1988. "Ukrainians: The Fifth Cultural Wheel in Canada." In Ian H. Angus (ed.), *Ethnicity in a Technological Age.* Edmonton: Canadian Institute of Ukrainian Studies, University of Alberta, 177–192.

Luttrell, Wendy. 1997. *School-Smart and Mother-Wise: Working-Class Women's Identity and Schooling.* New York: Routledge.

Luttwak, Eugene. 1996. Quoted in Kenneth Kidd, "Social Contracts." *Globe and Mail Report on Business Magazine* (September): 24.

Luxton, Meg. 1980. *More Than a Labour of Love.* Toronto: Women's Press.

———. 1995. "Two Hands for the Clock: Changing Patterns of Gendered Division of Labour in the Home." In E.D. Nelson and B.W. Robinson (eds.), *Gender in the 1990s.* Toronto: Thomson Nelson, 288–301.

———. 1999. *Work, Family, and Community: Key Issues and Directions for Future Research.* Ottawa: Canadian Council on Social Development.

———, and J. Corman. 2001. *Getting By in Hard Times: Gendered Labour at Home and on the Job.* Toronto: University of Toronto Press.

Lynd, Robert S., and Helen M. Lynd. 1929. *Middletown.* New York: Harcourt.

———. 1937. *Middletown in Transition.* New York: Harcourt.

Lynn, Marion, ed. 1996. *Voices: Essays on Canadian Families.* Toronto: Thomson Nelson.

———, and Eimear O'Neill. 1995. "Families, Power and Violence." In Nancy Mandell and Ann Duffy (eds.), *Canadian Families: Diversity, Conflict and Change.* Toronto: Harcourt Brace, 271–305.

Lyons, John. 1998. "The Way We Live: Central Plains." *Winnipeg Free Press* (June 7): B3.

Maass, Peter, and Megha Rajagopalan. 2012. "That's No Phone. That's My Tracker." *New York Times* (July 13). Retrieved July 23, 2012. Available: http://www.nytimes.com/2012/07/15/sunday-review/thats-not-my-phone-its-my-tracker.html.

Maccoby, Eleanor E., and Carol Nagy Jacklin. 1987. "Gender Segregation in Childhood." *Advances in Child Development and Behavior* 20: 239–287.

MacDonald, Kevin, and Ross D. Parke. 1986. "Parental-Child Physical Play: The Effects of Sex and Age of Children and Parents." *Sex Roles* 15: 367–378.

MacDonald, Marci. 1996. "The New Spirituality." *Maclean's* (October 10): 44–48.

MacGregor, Roy. 2002. "Questioning the Value of an Education." *National Post* (April 25). Available: http://www.nationalpost.com.

Mack, Raymond W., and Calvin P. Bradford. 1979. *Transforming America: Patterns of Social Change* (2nd ed.). New York: Random House.

Mackie, Marlene. 1995. "Gender in the Family: Changing Patterns." In Nancy Mandell and Ann Duffy (eds.), *Canadian Families: Diversity, Conflict, and Change* (2nd ed.). Toronto: Harcourt Brace, 17–43.

MacKinnon, Catherine. 1982. "Feminism, Marxism, Method and the State: An Agenda for Theory." In N.O. Keohane et al. (eds), *Feminist Theory: A Critique of Ideology.* Chicago: University of Chicago Press, 1–30.

MacLean, M.J., and R. Bonar. 1983. "The Normalization Principle and the Institutionalization of the Elderly." *Canada's Mental Health* 31: 16–18.

MacLeod, Calum. 2012. "China Strikes at West through Pop Culture Wars." *USA Today* (January 10). Retrieved January 12, 2012. Available: http://www.usatoday.com/news/world/story/2012-01-10/china-video-games/52483442/1.

MacLeod, Linda. 1980. *Wife Battering in Canada: The Vicious Circle.* Ottawa: Canadian Council on the Status of Women.

———. 1987. *Battered But NOT Beaten: Preventing Wife Battering in Canada.* Ottawa: Canadian Advisory Council on the Status of Women.

Macmillan, Ross, Annette Nierobisz, and Sandy Welsh. 2000. "Experiencing the Streets: Harassment and Perceptions of Safety Among Women." *Journal of Research in Crime and Delinquency* 37 (3).

Maggio, Rosalie. 1988. *The Non-Sexist Word Finder: A Dictionary of Gender-Free Usage.* Boston: Beacon Press.

Magid, Larry. 2004. "Talk to Your Kids About Cell Phone Use." Retrieved March 30, 2007. Available: http//www.safekids.com/cellphone.htm.

Mahony, Tina. 2011. *Homicide in Canada, 2010.* Juristat (October). Ottawa: Canadian Centre for Justice Statistics.

Malenfant, Eric, André Lebel, and Laurent Martel. 2010. *Projections of the Diversity of the Canadian Population, 2006–2031.* Ottawa: Statistics Canada.

Malinowski, Bronislaw. 1922. *Argonauts of the Western Pacific.* New York: Dutton.

———. 1964. "The Principle of Legitimacy: Parenthood, the Basis of Social Structure." In Rose Laub Coser (ed.), *The Family: Its Structure and Functions.* New York: St. Martin's Press (orig. pub. 1929).

Man, Guida. 1996. "The Experience of Middle-Class Women in Recent Hong Kong Chinese Immigrant Families in Canada." In Marion Lynn (ed.), *Voices: Essays on Canadian Families.* Toronto: Nelson Canada, 271–300.

Mancini, Chantal. 2012. *Still Not Laughing: Challenging Sexual Harassment in Our Schools.* Toronto: Ontario Secondary Schools Teachers' Federation.

Mandell, Nancy, ed. 2001. *Feminist Issues: Race, Class, and Sexuality* (3rd ed.). Toronto, Ont.: Prentice-Hall.

———. 2005. *Canadian Families: Diversity, Conflict, and Change* (3rd ed.). Toronto: Oxford University Press.

———, and Julianne Momirov. 1999. "Family Histories." In Nancy Mandell and Ann Duffy (eds.), *Canadian Families: Diversity, Conflict, and Change* (2nd ed.). Toronto: Harcourt Brace, 17–43.

Mann, Patricia S. 1994. *Micro-Politics: Agency in Postfeminist Era.* Minneapolis: University of Minnesota Press.

Mansfield, Alan, and Barbara McGinn. 1993. "Pumping Irony: The Muscular and the Feminine." In Sue Scott and David Morgan (eds.), *Body Matters: Essays on the Sociology of the Body.* London: Falmer Press, 49–58.

Mantell, David Mark. 1971. "The Potential for Violence in Germany." *Journal of Social Issues* 27 (4): 101–112.

Mao, Y., B.W. Moloughney, R. Semenciw, and H. Morrison. 1992. "Indian Reserve and Registered Indian Mortality in Canada." *Canadian Journal of Public Health* 83: 350–353.

Marchak, Patricia. 1975. *Ideological Perspectives on Canadian Society.* Toronto: McGraw-Hill.

Marger, Martin N. 1987. *Elites and Masses: An Introduction to Political Sociology* (2nd ed.). Belmont, Cal.: Wadsworth.

———. 2000. *Race and Ethnic Relations: American and Global Perspectives* (5th ed.). Belmont, Cal.: Wadsworth.

———. 2003. *Race and Ethnic Relations: American and Global Perspectives* (6th ed.). Belmont, Cal.: Wadsworth.

Marion, Russ, and Mary Uhl-Bien. 2003. "Complexity Theory and Al-Qaeda: Examining Complex Leadership." *Emergence* 5 (1): 54–76.

Mark, Kristen P., Erick Janssen, and Robin R. Milhausen. 2011. "Infidelity in Heterosexual Couples: Demographic, Interpersonal, and Personality-Related Predictors of Extradyadic Sex." *Archives of Sexual Behavior* 40 (5): 971–982.

Markoff, John. 2000. "Napster Debate About More Than Music." *Globe and Mail* (May 9): B14.

Marquardt, Elizabeth. 2006. "The Revolution in Parenthood: The Emerging Global Clash Between Adult Rights and Children's Needs." Institute for American Values. Retrieved May 22, 2009. Available: http://www.american-values.org/pdfs/parenthood.pdf.

Marquart, James W., Sheldon Ekland-Olson, and Jonathan R. Sorensen. 1994. *The Rope, the Chair, and the Needle.* Austin: University of Texas Press.

Marquis, Christopher. 2001. "An American Report Finds the Taliban's Violation of Religious Rights 'Particularly Severe.'" *New York Times* (Oct. 27): B3.

Marshall, Gordon, ed. 1998. *The Concise Oxford Dictionary of Sociology* (2nd ed.). New York: Oxford University Press.

Marshall, Katherine. 1995. "Dual Earners: Who's Responsible for Housework?" In E.D. Nelson and B.W. Robinson, *Gender in the 1990s.* Toronto: Thomson Nelson, 302–308.

———. 2006. "Converging Gender Roles." *Perspectives on Labour and Income,* 7 (7). Statistics Canada Cat. no. 750001-XIE. Retrieved May 20, 2009. Available: http://www.statcan.gc.ca/pub/75-001-x/75-001-x2006107-eng.pdf.

———. 2009a. "Stay-at-Home Fathers, 2007." Unpublished figures obtained from Statistics Canada, Labour and Household Surveys Analysis Division.

———. 2009b. "The Family Work Week." *Perspectives on Labour and Income* (April). Statistics Canada Cat. no. 75001-XIE.

———. 2011. "Generational Change in Paid and Unpaid Work." *Canadian Social Trends 82.* Statistics Canada Cat. no. 11-008-X. Retrieved January 20, 2011. Available: http://www.statcan.gc.ca/pub/11-008-x/2011002/article/11520-eng.pdf.

Marshall, S.L.A. 1947. *Men Against Fire.* New York: Morrow.

Martel, Laurent, Alain Belanger, Jean-Marie Berthelot, and Yves Carriere. *Healthy Today, Healthy Tomorrow? Findings From the National Population Health Survey*. Ottawa: Statistics Canada.

Martin, Carol L. 1989. "Children's Use of Gender-Related Information in Making Social Judgments." *Developmental Psychology* 25: 80–88.

Martin, Michael T., and Howard Cohen. 1980. "Race and Class Consciousness: A Critique of the Marxist Concept of Race Relations." *Western Journal of Black Studies* 4 (2): 84–91.

Martin, Nick. 1996. "Aboriginal Speech Dying." *Winnipeg Free Press* (March 29): A8.

Martin, Vivian B. 2008. "Media Bias: Going Beyond Fair and Balanced." *Scientific American*. Retrieved October 17, 2011. Available: http://www.scientificamerican.com/article.cfm?id=media-bias-presidential-election.

Martineau, Harriet. 1962. *Society in America* (edited, abridged). Garden City, N.Y.: Doubleday (orig. pub. 1837).

———. *How to Observe Morals and Manners*. In Michael R. Hill (ed.). New Brunswick, N.J.: Transaction (orig. pub. 1838).

Martinussen, John. 1997. *Society, State and Market: A Guide to Competing Theories of Development*. Halifax: Fernwood Books.

Marvell, Thomas, and Calisle Moody. 2001. "The Lethal Effects of Three Strikes Laws." *Journal of Legal Studies* 30 (1): 89–106.

Marx, Gary, and Douglas McAdam. 1994. *Collective Behavior and Social Movements: Process and Structure*. Englewood Cliffs, N.J.: Pearson Education.

Marx, Karl. 1967. *Capital: A Critique of Political Economy*. Friedrich Engels (ed.). New York: International Publishers (orig. pub. 1867).

———. 1970. *The German Ideology*, Part 1. C.J. Arthur (ed). New York: International (orig. pub. 1845–1846).

———, and Friedrich Engels. 1967. *The Communist Manifesto*. New York: Pantheon (orig. pub. 1848).

Mason Lee, Robert. 1991. *Death and Deliverance*. Toronto: Macfarlane Walter and Ross.

———. 1998. "I'll Be Home for Christmas." *Globe and Mail* (December 24).

Mastro, Dana, and Susanah Stern. 2006. "Race and Gender in Advertising: A Look at Sexualized Images in Prime-Time Commercials." In Tom Reichert and Jacqueline Lambiase (eds.), *Sex in Consumer Culture: The Erotic Content of Media and Marketing*. Mahwah, N.J.: Lawrence Erlbaum, 281–299.

Maticka-Tyndale, E. 2008. "Sexuality and Sexual Health of Canadian Adolescents: Yesterday, Today and Tomorrow." *Canadian Journal of Human Sexuality*, 17 (3): 85–95.

Matthews, Beverly J. 2001. "The Body Beautiful: Adolescent Girls and Images of Beauty." In Lori G. Beaman (ed.), *New Perspectives on Deviance: The Construction of Deviance in Everyday Life*. Scarborough, Ont.: Prentice-Hall, 208–219.

Mawhinney, J. 2002. "Gay Unions Garner Public Support." *Toronto Star* (September 28): K4.

Maynard, Rona. 1987. "How Do You Like Your Job?" *Globe and Mail Report on Business Magazine* (November): 120–25.

McAdam, Doug. 1996. "Conceptual Origins, Current Problems, Future Directions." In Doug McAdam, John McCarthy, and Meyer N. Zald (eds.), *Comparative Perspectives on Social Movements*. New York: Cambridge University Press, 23–40.

McArthur, Keith. 2005. "Criticism of Women's Fitness for Top Jobs Causes International Stir." *Globe and Mail* (October 21): A1.

McCall, George J., and Jerry L. Simmons, 1978. *Identities and Interactions: An Explanation of Human Associations in Everyday Life*. New York: Free Press.

McCarthy, Terry. 2001. "Stirrings of a Woman's Movement." *Time* (Dec. 3): 46.

McCarthy, John D., and Mayer N. Zald. 1977. "Resource Mobilization and Social Movements: A Partial Theory." *American Journal of Sociology* 82: 1212–1241.

McClelland, Mac. 2012. "I Was a Warehouse Wage Slave." *Mother Jones* (March/April).

McCormick, Chris. 1995. *Constructing Danger: The Mis/Representation of Crime in the News*. Halifax: Fernwood Publishing.

McDonald's. 2004. *2004 Summary Annual Report*. Retrieved July 24, 2005. Available: http://www.mcdonalds.com/corp/invest/pub/2004_Summary_Annual_Report.html.

———. 2008. *2007 Annual Report*. Retrieved March 17, 2009. Available: http://www.mcdonalds.com/corp/invest/pub/2007_annual_report.html.

———. 2012. "Frequently Asked Questions." Retrieved July 5, 2012. Available: http://www.mcdonalds.ca/ca/en/contact_us/faq.html.

McEachern, William A. 1994. *Economics: A Contemporary Introduction*. Cincinnati: South-Western.

McGee, Reece. 1975. *Points of Departure*. Hinsdale, Ill.: Dryden Press.

McGovern, Celeste. 1995. "Dr. Death Speaks." *Alberta Report/Western Report* 22 (January 9): 33.

McGuire, Meredith B. 1997. *Religion: The Social Context* (4th ed.). Belmont, Cal.: Wadsworth.

McIntosh, Mary. 1968. "The Homosexual Role." *Social Problems* 16 (2): 182–192.

———. 1978. "The State and the Oppression of Women." In Annette Kuhn and Ann Marie Wolpe (eds.), *Feminism and Materialism*. London: Routledge and Kegan Paul.

McIntyre, M. 2011. "Rape Victim Inviting: So No Jail." *Winnipeg Free Press* (February 24). Retrieved July 9, 2012. Available: http://www.winnipegfreepress.com/breakingnews/rape-victim-inviting-so-no-jail--rape-victim-inviting-so-no-jail-116801578.html.

McIsaac, Elizabeth. 2003. "Immigrants in Canadian Cities: Census 2001—What Do the Data Tell Us?" *Policy Options* (May): 58–63.

McKay, Alexander. 2006. "Trends in Teen Pregnancy in Canada with Comparisons to U.S.A. and England/Wales." *Canadian Journal of Human Sexuality* 15 (3–4): 157–161.

McKenzie, Roderick D. 1925. "The Ecological Approach to the Study of the Human Community." In Robert Park, Ernest Burgess, and Roderick D. McKenzie, *The City*. Chicago: University of Chicago Press.

McKeown, Larry, and Cathy Underhill. 2007. "Learning Online Factors Associated with Use of the Internet for Education Purposes." *Education Matters: Insights on Education, Learning and Training in Canada*. Cat. no. 81-004-XIE. Retrieved May 8, 2009. Available: http://www.statcan.gc.ca/pub/81-004-x/2007004/10375-eng.htm.

McKie, Craig. 1994. "Population Aging: Baby Boomers into the 21st Century." *Canadian Social Trends*. Toronto: Thompson Educational Publishing, 3–7.

McKnight, Peter. 2012. "The Funhouse Mirror: Media Representations of Crime and Justice." In Julian Roberts and Michelle Grossman (eds.). *Criminal Justice in Canada*. Toronto: Nelson, 44–54.

McLanahan, Sara, and Karen Booth. 1991. "Mother-Only Families." In Alan Booth (ed.), *Contemporary Families: Looking Forward, Looking Backward*. Minneapolis: National Council on Family Relations, 405–428.

McLuhan, Marshall. 1964. *Understanding Media: The Extensions of Man*. New York: McGraw-Hill.

———, Quentin Fiore, and Shepard Fairey. 1967. *The Medium Is the Massage*. New York: Bantam Books.

McMellon, C.A., and L.G. Schiffman. 2002. "Cybersenior Empowerment: How Some Older Individuals are Taking Control of Their Lives." *Journal of Applied Gerontology* 21 (2): 157–75.

McMullen, Katherine. 2005. "Early Indicators of Students at Risk of Dropping out of High School." *Education Matters*. Cat. no. 81-001-XIE. Available: http://www.statcan.gc.ca/pub/81-004-x/2004006/7781-eng.htm.

McNish, Jacquie, and Sinclair Stewart. 2004. *Wrong Way: The Fall of Conrad Black*. Toronto: Viking Canada.

McPhail, Clark. 1971. "Civil Disorder Participation: A Critical Examination of Recent Research." *American Sociological Review* 36: 1058–1073.

———. 1991. *The Myth of the Maddening Crowd*. New York: Aldine de Gruyter.

McPhail, Clark, and Ronald T. Wohlstein. 1983. "Individual and Collective Behavior within Gatherings, Demonstrations, and Riots." In Ralph H. Turner and James F. Short, Jr. (eds.), *Annual Review of Sociology* 9. Palo Alto, Cal.: Annual Reviews, 579–600.

McPherson, Barry D. 1998. *Aging as a Social Process: An Introduction to Individual and Population Aging*. Toronto: Harcourt Brace.

McPherson, J. Miller, and Lynn Smith-Lovin. 1982. "Women and Weak Ties: Differences by Sex in the Size of Voluntary Organizations." *American Journal of Sociology* 87 (January): 883–904.

———. 1986. "Sex Segregation in Voluntary Associations." *American Sociological Review* 51 (February): 61–79.

McQuillan, Kevin. 2006. *Canada's Changing Families: Implications for Individuals and Society*. Toronto: University of Toronto Press.

———, and Marilyn Belle. 1999. "Who Does What? Gender and the Division of Labour in Canadian Households." In James E. Curtis, Edward Grabb, and Neil Guppy (eds.), *Social Inequality in Canada: Patterns, Problems, Policies* (3rd ed.). Scarborough, Ont.: Prentice-Hall, 186–198.

McSpotlight. 1999. "McDonald's and Employment." Retrieved September 7, 1999. Available: http://www.mcspotlight.org/issues/rants/employment.html.

McVey, Wayne W., and Warren E. Kalbach. 1995. *Canadian Population*. Toronto: Thomson Nelson.

Mead, George Herbert. 1962. *Mind, Self, and Society*. Chicago: University of Chicago Press (orig. pub. 1934).

Medved, Michael. 1992. *Hollywood vs. America: Popular Culture and the War on Traditional Values*. New York: HarperPerennial.

Mehrotra, Santosh, and Richard Jolly. 2000. *Development with a Human Face: Experiences in Social Achievement and Economic Growth*. Oxford: Clarendon Press.

Meisel, Dr. Zachary. 2011. "Googling Symptoms Helps Patients and Doctors." *Time Health* (January 19). Retrieved May 14, 2012. Available: http://www.time.com/time/health/article/0,8599,2043125,00.html.

Melchers, Ronald. 2003. "Do Toronto Police Engage in Racial Profiling?" *Canadian Journal of Criminology and Criminal Justice* 45 (July): 347–366.

Merchant, Carolyn. 1983. *The Death of Nature: Women, Ecology, and the Scientific Revolution*. San Francisco: Harper & Row.

———. 1992. *Radical Ecology: The Search for a Livable World*. New York: Routledge.

Merkle, Erich R., and Rhonda A. Richardson. 2000. "Digital Dating and Virtual Relating: Conceptualizing Computer-Mediated Romantic Relationships." *Family Relations* 49 (April): 187–211.

Merton, Robert King. 1938. "Social Structure and Anomie." *American Sociological Review* 3 (6): 672–682.

———. 1949. "Discrimination and the American Creed." In Robert M. MacIver (ed.), *Discrimination and National Welfare.* New York: Harper & Row, 99–126.

———. 1968. *Social Theory and Social Structure* (enlarged ed.). New York: Free Press.

Messner, Michael A. 2000. "Barbie Girls Versus Sea Monsters: Children Constructing Gender." In Margaret L. Andersen (ed.), *Thinking About Women: Sociological Perspectives on Sex and Gender* (7th ed.). Boston: Pearson, 765–784.

———. 2002. *Taking the Field: Women, Men and Sports.* Minneapolis: University of Minnesota Press.

Meyer, David S., and Suzanne Staggenborg. 1996. "Movements, Countermovements, and the Structure of Political Opportunity." *American Journal of Sociology* 101: 1628–1660.

Miall, Charlene. 1986. "The Stigma of Involuntary Childlessness." *Social Problems* 33 (4): 268–282.

Michael, Robert T., John H. Gagnon, Edward O. Laumann, and Gina Kolata. 1994. *Sex in America.* Boston: Little, Brown.

Michelson, William H. 1994. "Cities and Urbanization." In Lorne Tepperman, James Curtis, and R.J. Richardson (eds.), *The Social World* (3rd ed.). Toronto: McGraw-Hill, 672–709.

Mick, Hayley. 2009. "At the Science Fair, Girls Dominate the Class." *Globe and Mail* (May 15). Available: http://www.scwist.ca/index.php/main/entry/at-the-science-fair-girls-dominate-the-class/.

Mickleburgh, Rod. 2011. "Anti–Wall Street Protests Take Off Thanks to a Canadian Idea." *Globe and Mail* (October 4). Retrieved January 11, 2012. Available: http://www.theglobeandmail.com/news/world/americas/article2191364.ece.

Mies, Maria, and Vandana Shiva. 1993. *Ecofeminism.* Highlands, N.J.: Zed Books.

Mihorean, Steve, and Stan Lipinski. 1992. "International Incarceration Patterns, 1980–1990." *Juristat* 12 (3). Ottawa: Statistics Canada.

Miki, Roy, and Cassandra Kobayashi. 1991.*Justice in Our Own Time: The Japanese Canadian Redress Settlement.* Vancouver: Talonbooks.

Milan, Anne. 2005. "Willing to Participate: Political Engagement of Young Adults." *Canadian Social Trends* (Winter): 2–7.

———, and Brian Homm. 2003. "Across the Generations: Grandparents and Grandchildren." *Canadian Social Trends* (Winter). Retrieved May 14, 2009. Available: http://www.statcan.gc.ca/pub/11-008-x/2003003/article/6619-eng.pdf.

———, Leslie-Anne Keown, and Covadonga Robles Urquijo. 2011. "Families, Living Arrangements and Unpaid Work." In *Women in Canada: A Gender-Based Statistical Report,* Statistics Canada Cat. no. 89-503X.

Milgram, Stanley. 1963. "Behavioral Study of Obedience." *Journal of Abnormal and Social Psychology* 67: 371–378.

———. 1967. "The Small World Problem." *Psychology Today* 2: 60–67.

———. 1974. *Obedience to Authority.* New York: Harper & Row.

Milhausen, Robin R., and Kristen P. Mark. 2009. "Infidelity in Committed Relationships." In Harry T. Reis and Susan Sprecher (eds.), *Encyclopedia of Human Relationships.* Thousand Oaks, CA: Sage.

Miliband, Ralph. 1969. *The State in Capitalist Society.* New York: Basic Books.

Miller, Casey, and Kate Swift. 1991. *Words and Women: New Language in New Times* (updated). New York: HarperCollins.

———. 1993. "Who Is Man?" In Anne Minas, *Gender Basics: Feminist Perspectives on Women and Men.* Belmont, Cal.: Wadsworth, 68–75.

Miller, Dan E. 1986. "Milgram Redux: Obedience and Disobedience in Authority Relations." In Norman K. Denzin (ed.), *Studies in Symbolic Interaction.* Greenwich, Conn.: JAI Press, 77–106.

Miller, Grant. 2008. "Women's Suffrage, Political Responsiveness, and Child Survival in American History." *The Quarterly Journal of Economics* 123 (3): 1287–1327.

Miller, James. 2003. "Out Family Values." In Marion Lynn (ed.), *Voices: Essays on Canadian Families* (2nd ed.). Toronto: Thomson Nelson, 103–130.

Miller, L. Scott. 1995. *An American Imperative: Accelerating Minority Educational Advancement.* New Haven, Conn: Yale University Press.

Mills, C. Wright. 1956. *White Collar.* New York: Oxford University Press.

———. 1959a. *The Sociological Imagination.* London: Oxford University Press.

———. 1959b. *The Power Elite.* Fair Lawn, N.J.: Oxford University Press.

Minister of Indian Affairs and Northern Development. 2000. "Comparison of Social Conditions, 1991 and 1996: Registered Indians, Registered Indians Living on Reserve and the Total Population in Canada." Ottawa: Minister of Indian Affairs and Northern Development.

Misztal, Barbara A. 1993. "Understanding Political Change in Eastern Europe: A Sociological Perspective." *Sociology* 27 (3): 451–471.

Mitchell, Alanna. 1997. "Native Life in Canada: Seed Money for Grassroots Entrepreneurs." *Globe and Mail* (July 22).

———. 1999. "Home Schooling Goes AWOL." *Globe and Mail* (February 2): A1, A7.

Molotch, Harvey, and Marilyn Lester. 1974. "News as Purposive Behavior: On the Strategic Use of Routine Events, Accidents and Scandals." *American Sociological Review* 39: 101–112.

Money, John, and Anke A. Ehrhardt. 1972. *Man and Woman, Boy and Girl.* Baltimore: Johns Hopkins University Press.

Monsebraaten, Laurie. 2008. "Child-Care Report Card: Canada Fails." (December 11). Retrieved February 3, 2009. Available: http://www.parentcentral.ca/parent/article/552007.

Moore, Patricia, with C.P. Conn. 1985. *Disguised.* Waco, Tex.: Word Books.

Moore, Wilbert E. 1968. "Occupational Socialization." In David A. Goslin (ed.), *Handbook on Socialization Theory and Research.* Chicago: Rand McNally, 861–883.

Morgan, Steven, and Colleen Cunningham. 2011. "Population Aging and the Determinants of Hospital, Medical and Pharmaceutical Care in British Columbia, 1996 to 2006." *Healthcare Policy* 7 (1): 68–79.

Morris, David B. 1998. *Illness and Culture in the Postmodern Age.* Berkeley: University of California Press.

Morrissette, Rene, and Xuelin Zhang. 2006. "Revisiting Wealth Inequality." *Perspectives on Labour and Income* (December). Statistics Canada Cat. no. 75-001-XIE. Retrieved June 17, 2009. Available: http://www.statcan.gc.ca/pub/75-001-x/11206/9543-eng.pdf.

———, Grant Schellenberg, and Anick Johnson. 2005. "Diverging Trends in Unionization." *Perspectives on Labour and Income* 6 (April): 5–12. Statistics Canada Cat. no. 75-001-XIE. Ottawa: Statistics Canada.

Morselli, Henry. 1975. *Suicide: An Essay on Comparative Moral Statistics.* New York: Arno Press (orig. pub. 1881).

Moscovitch, Arlene. 1998. "Electronic Media and the Family." *Contemporary Family Trends.* Ottawa: Vanier Institute of the Family. Retrieved November 20, 2002. Available: http://www.vifamily.ca/cft/media/media.htm.

———. 2007. *Good Servant, Bad Master? Electronic Media and the Family.* Ottawa: Vanier Institute of the Family. Retrieved May 14, 2009. Available: http://www.vifamily.ca/library/cft/media07.html.

MTV. 2005. "MTV: I Want a Famous Face." Retrieved March 17, 2005. Available: http://www.mtv.com/onair/dyn/i_want_a_-famous_face-2/meet_cast.jhtml.

Mucciolo, Louis. 1992. *Eighty something: Interviews with Octogenarians Who Stay Involved.* New York: Birch Lane Press.

Mukerji, Chandra, and Michael Schudson. 1991. *Rethinking Popular Culture: Contemporary Perspectives in Cultural Studies.* Berkeley: University of California Press.

Murdie, Robert. 1999. "The Housing Careers of Polish and Somali Newcomers in Toronto's Rental Market." Paper presented at the 4th International Metropolis Conference (October), Washington, D.C. Retrieved November 27, 2002. Available: http://www.library.utoronto.ca/hnc/publish/careers.pdf.

Murdock, George P. 1945. "The Common Denominator of Cultures." In Ralph Linton (ed.), *The Science of Man in the World Crisis.* New York: Columbia University Press, 123–142.

Murphy, Barbara. 2000. *On the Street: How We Created the Homeless.* Winnipeg: J. Gordon Shillingford Publishing.

Murphy, Brian, Paul Roberts, and Michael Wolfson. 2007. "High Income Canadians." *Perspectives on Labour and Income* 8 (9). Statistics Canada Catalogue no. 75-001-XWE. Retrieved June 16, 2009. Available: http://www.statcan.gc.ca/pub/75-001-x/75-001-x2007109-eng.pdf.

Murphy, Christopher, and Curtis Clarke. 2005. "Policing Communities and Communities of Policing: A Comparative Study of Policing and Security in Two Canadian Communities." In Dennis Cooley (ed.), *Re-Imagining Policing in Canada.* Toronto: University of Toronto Press, 209–259.

Murphy, Emily F. 1922. *The Black Candle.* Toronto: Thomas Allen.

Murphy, Robert E., Jessica Scheer, Yolanda Murphy, and Richard Mack. 1988. "Physical Disability and Social Liminality: A Study in Rituals of Adversity." *Social Science and Medicine* 26: 235–242.

My dans, Seth. 1997. "Its Mood Dark as the Haze, Southeast Asia Aches." *New York Times* (October 26): 3.

Myles, John. 1999. "Demography or Democracy? The 'Crisis' of Old-Age Security." In Curtis, James E., Edward Grabb, and Neil Guppy (eds.), *Social Inequality in Canada: Patterns, Problems, Policies* (3rd ed.). Scarborough, Ont.: Prentice Hall.

Myrdal, Gunnar. 1970. *The Challenge of World Poverty: A World Anti-Poverty Program in Outline.* New York: Pantheon/Random House.

Nader, George A. 1976. *Cities of Canada,* vol. 2. Profiles of Fifteen Metropolitan Centres. Toronto: Macmillan of Canada.

Naeyaert, Kathleen. 1990. *Living with Sensory Loss: Vision.* Ottawa: National Advisory Council on Aging.

Nagler, Mark. 1997. *Yes You Can: A Guide for Parents of Children with Disabilities.* Toronto: Stoddart.

Naiman, Joanne. 2000. *How Societies Work: Class, Power, and Change in a Canadian Context.* Concord, Ont.: Irwin.

———. 2008. *How Societies Work: Class, Power, and Change in a Canadian Context* (4th ed.). Halifax: Fernwood.
Nairne, Doug. 1998. "Good Samaritan Feels That He Was Victimized Twice." *Winnipeg Free Press* (June 4): A4.
Nakhaie, M. Reza, and Robert Arnold. 1996. "Class Position, Class Ideology, and Class Voting: Mobilization of Support for the New Democratic Party in the Canadian Election of 1984." *Canadian Review of Sociology and Anthropology* 33 (2): 181–212.
Nancarrow Clarke, Juanne. 1996. *Health, Illness and Medicine in Canada* (2nd ed.). Toronto: Oxford University Press.
Nanda, Serena. 2000. *Gender Diversity: Cross Cultural Variations.* Prospect Heights. Ill.: Waveland.
NAPO (National Anti-Poverty Association). 2002. "Governments Targeting Poor People Instead of Poverty." October 17, 2002. Retrieved December 14, 2002. Available: http://www.napo-onap.ca/media_room.htm.
———. 2005. "Towards a National Poverty Elimination Strategy." Retrieved September 12, 2005. Available: http://www.napo-nap.ca/en/issues/NAPO%202005%20finance%20committee%20submission.pdf.
Nason-Clark, Nancy. 1993. "Gender Relations in Contemporary Christian Organizations." In W.E. Hewitt (ed.), *The Sociology of Religion: A Canadian Focus.* Toronto: Butterworths, 215–234.
Natanson, Maurice. 1963. "A Study in Philosophy and the Social Sciences." In Maurice Natanson (ed.), *Philosophy of the Social Science: A Reader.* New York: Random House, 271–285.
National Aboriginal Economic Development Board. 2012. *The Aboriginal Economic Benchmarking Report.* Retrieved June 10, 2012. Available: http://www.naedb-cndea.com/wp-content/uploads/TheAboriginal EconomicBenchmarkingReport2.pdf
National Advisory Council on Aging. 1992. *The NACA Position on Canada's Oldest Seniors: Maintaining the Quality of Their Lives.* Ottawa: National Advisory Council on Aging, 54–55.
———. 2005. *Aging and Poverty in Canada.* Ottawa: Minister of Public Works and Government Services Canada.
National Council of Welfare. 2002. *Poverty Profile 1999.* Ottawa: National Council of Welfare.
National Opinion Research Center. 1989. *General Social Survey.* Chicago: National Opinion Research Center.
———. 1996. *General Social Surveys, 1972–1996: Cumulative Codebook.* Chicago: National Opinion Research Center.
National Post. 2003. "Quality of Life and Quality of Service." *National Post* (A8).
Navarrette, Ruben, Jr. 1997. "A Darker Shade of Crimson." In Diana Kendall (ed.), *Race, Class, and Gender in a Diverse Society.* Boston, Mass.: Allyn & Bacon, 274–279. Reprinted from Ruben Navarrette Jr., *A Darker Shade of Crimson.* New York: Bantam, 1993.
nbc.com. 2007. *The Banker's Blog* (February 4). Retrieved March 17, 2007. Available: http://blog.nbc.com/dealornodeal/2007/02/04-week.
Neal, Lainie, ed. 2004. *Voices of Survivors.* Winnipeg: North End Women's Centre.
Neal, Rusty. 2004. "Voices: Women, Poverty and Homelessness in Canada." Ottawa: National Anti-Poverty Organization. Retrieved March 6, 2009. Available: http://intraspec.ca/WomenPovertyAndHomelessness InCanada.pdf.
Negroponte, Nicholas. 1995. *Being Digital.* New York: Alfred A. Knopf.
Nelson, Adie. 2006. *Gender in Canada* (3rd ed.). Toronto: Pearson.
Nelson, Margaret K., and Joan Smith. 1999. *Working Hard and Making Do: Surviving in Small Town America.* Berkeley: University of California Press.
Nemeth, Mary, Nora Underwood, and John Howse. 1993. "God Is Alive." *Maclean's* (April 12): 32–36.
Nett, Emily M. 1993. *Canadian Families: Past and Present* (2nd ed.). Toronto: Butterworths.
Nettler, Gwynn. 1984. *Explaining Crime* (3rd ed.). Toronto: McGraw-Hill.
Nevitte, Neil. 2000. "Value Change and Reorientations in Citizen-State Relations." *Canadian Public Policy* 26 (Supplement): 73–94.
Newman, Katherine S. 1988. *Falling from Grace: The Experience of Downward Mobility in the American Middle Class.* New York: Free Press.
———. 1993. *Declining Fortunes: The Withering of the American Dream.* New York: Basic Books.
———. 1999. *No Shame in My Game: The Working Poor in the Inner City.* New York: Knopf and the Russell Sage Foundation.
New York Times. 2002. "Text: Senate Judiciary Committee Hearing, June 6, 2002." Retrieved June 9, 2002. Available: http://www.nytimes.com/2002/06/06../06TEXT-INQ2.html.
———. 2005. "The Missing Condoms." Retrieved September 4, 2005. Available: http://www.nytimes.com/2005/09/04/opinion/04sun2.html.
Ng, Edward. 1994. "Children and Elderly People: Sharing Public Income Resources." In Craig McKie (ed.), *Canadian Social Trends.* Toronto: Thompson Educational, 249–252.
Niebuhr, H. Richard. 1929. *The Social Sources of Denominationalism.* New York: Meridian.
Nielsen. 2010. "U.S. Teen Mobile Report: Calling Yesterday, Texting Today, Using Apps Tomorrow." *NielsenWire* (October 14). Retrieved December 14, 2011. Available: http://blog.nielsen.com/nielsenwire/online_mobile/u-s-teen-mobile-report-calling-yesterday-texting-today-using-apps-tomorrow.
Nielsen, Joyce McCarl. 1990. *Sex and Gender in Society: Perspectives on Stratification* (2nd ed.). Prospects Heights, Ill.: Waveland Press.
Nielsen, T.M. 2005. "Streets, Strangers, and Solidarity." In Bruce Ravelli (ed.), *Exploring Canadian Sociology: A Reader.* Toronto: Pearson, 89–98.
Nisbet, Robert. 1979. "Conservatism." In Tom Bottomore and Robert Nisbet (eds.), *A History of Sociological Analysis.* London: Heineman, 81–117.
Noel, Donald L. 1972. *The Origins of American Slavery and Racism.* Columbus, OH: Merrill.
Nolen, Stephanie. 2007. "Swaziland: The Economics of an Epidemic." *Globe and Mail* (December 22): A15.
Norland, J.A. 1994. *Profile of Canada's Seniors.* Cat. no. 96–312E. Scarborough, Ont.: Statistics Canada and Prentice-Hall.
Norris, Mary Jane. 1998. "Canada's Aborginal Languages." *Canadian Social Trends* (Winter): 8–16.
———. 2007. "Aboriginal Languages in Canada: Emerging Trends and Perspectives on Second Language Acquisition." *Canadian Social Trends* (Spring). Cat. no. 11-008, 19–27. Retrieved January 19, 2009. Available: http://www.statcan.gc.ca/pub/11-008-x/2007001/pdf/9628-eng.pdf.
Norris, Pippa, and Ronald Inglehart. 2004. *Sacred and Secular: Religion and Politics Worldwide.* Cambridge: Cambridge University Press.
Norris, Sonya. 2001. "Reproductive Infertility: Prevalence, Causes, Trends and Treatments." *In Brief.* PRB-0032-E. Parliamentary Research Branch, Government of Canada. Retrieved May 20, 2009. Available: http://dsp-psd.pwgsc.gc.ca/Collection-R/LoPBdP/EB-e/prb0032-e.pdf.
Northcott, Herbert, C. 1982. "The Best Years of Your Life." *Canadian Journal on Aging* 1: 72–78.
Novak, Mark. 1993. *Aging and Society: A Canadian Perspective.* Toronto: Thomson Nelson.
———. 1995. "Successful Aging." In *Aging and Society: A Canadian Reader.* Toronto: Thomson Nelson.
———. 1997. *Aging and Society* (3rd ed.). Toronto: Thomson Nelson.
———, and Lori Campbell. 2001. *Aging and Society: A Canadian Perspective* (4th ed.). Toronto: Nelson Thomson Learning.
———. 2006. *Aging and Society: A Canadian Perspective* (5th ed.). Toronto: Nelson.
NOW (National Organization for Women). 2002. "Stop the Abuse of Women and Girls in Afghanistan!" Retrieved July 14, 2002. Available: http://www.nowfoundation.org/_global/taliban.html.
Nussbaum, Emily. 2003. "Nature vs. Nurture." Retrieved October 6, 2003. Available: http://btosearch.barnesandnoble.com/booksearch.
Nyhan, Brendan. 2010. "Why the 'Death Panel' Myth Wouldn't Die: Misinformation in the Health Care Reform Debate." *Forum* 8 (1). Retrieved January 3, 2012. Available: http://www.bepress.com/forum/vol8/iss1/art5.
Oakes, Jeannie. 2005. *Keeping Track: How Schools Structure Inequality.* New Haven: Yale University Press.
Oberschall, Anthony. 1973. *Social Conflict and Social Movements.* Englewood Cliffs, N.J.: Prentice-Hall.
Obomsawin, Alanis. 1993. *Kanehsatake: 270 Years of Resistance* [motion picture]. Montreal: National Film Board of Canada.
O'Brien, Carol-Anne, and Lorna Weir. 1995. "Lesbians and Gay Men Inside and Outside Families." In Nancy Mandell and Ann Duffy (eds.), *Canadian Families.* Toronto: Harcourt Brace, 111–139.
O'Connell, Helen. 1994. *Women and the Family.* Prepared for the UN-NGO Group on Women and Development. Atlantic Highlands, N.J.: Zed Books.
O'Connor, James. 1973. *The Fiscal Crisis of the State.* New York: St. Martin's Press.
Odendahl, Teresa. 1990. *Charity Begins at Home: Generosity and Self-Interest Among the Philanthropic Elite.* New York: Basic.
OECD (Organisation for Economic Co-operation and Development). 2004. "Trends in International Migration Reflect Increasing Labour-Related Immigration and Persistent Integration Problems." Paris: OECD. Retrieved April 9, 2009. Available: http://www.oecd.org/document/50 / 0,2340,en_2649_201185_24968882_1_1_1_1,00.html
———. 2005. *OECD Health Data 2005.* Paris: OECD. Retrieved July 21, 2005. Available: http://www.oecd.org/document/30/0,2340,en_2649_34631_12968734_1_1_1_1,00.html.
———. 2008. *OECD Health Data 2008.* Paris: OECD. Retrieved April 21, 2009. Available: http://www.oecd.org/document/16/0,3343,en_2649_34631_2085200_1_1_1_1,00.htmlRe.
———. 2009. *Education Today: The OECD Perspective.* Paris: OECD. Retrieved April 9, 2009. Available: http://www.oecd.org/document/57/0,3343,en_2649_ 33723_42440761_1_1_1_1,00.html#3.
———. 2011. *OECD Health Data 2011.* Paris: OECD. Retrieved February 13, 2012. Available: http://www.oecd.org/document/16/0,3746,en_2649_37407_2085200_1_1_1_37407,00.html.
———, and Statistics Canada. 2000. *Literacy in the Information Age: Final Report of the International Adult Literacy Survey.* Ottawa: Statistics Canada.
Ogburn, William F. 1966. *Social Change with Respect to Culture and Original*

Nature. New York: Dell (orig. pub. 1922).

Ogden, Russel D. 1994. *Euthanasia and Assisted Suicide in Persons with Acquired Immunodeficiency Syndrome (AIDS) or Human Immunodeficiency Virus (HIV)*. Pitt Meadows, B.C.: Perreault Goedman.

Ogmundson, Rick. 1975. "Party Class Images and the Class Vote in Canada." *American Sociological Review* 40: 506–512.

———, and M. Ng. 1982. "On the Inference of Voter Motivation: A Comparison of the Subjective Class Vote in Canada and the United Kingdom." *Canadian Journal of Sociology* 7: 41–59.

Ogrodnik, Lucie. 2007. *Seniors as Victims of Crime: 2004 and 2005*. Ottawa: Canadian Centre for Justice Statistics.

———. 2008. *Family Violence in Canada: A Statistical Profile, 2008*. Statistics Canada Cat. no. 85-224-XIE. Retrieved May 20, 2009. Available: http://dsp-psd.pwgsc.gc.ca/collection_2008/statcan/85-224-X/85-224-XIE2008000.pdf.

Oliver, Michael. 1990. *The Politics of Disablement: A Sociological Approach*. New York: St. Martin's Press.

Ontario Human Rights Commission. 2005. "Policy on Height and Weight Requirements." Retrieved September 17, 2005. Available: http://www.ohrc.on.ca/en_text/publications/height-weight-policy.shtml.

Ontario Secondary School Teachers' Federation. 1995. "The Joke's Over: Student to Student Sexual Harassment in Secondary Schools." Toronto: OSSTF.

Opinion Canada. 2004. "Fewer Canadians Believe Religious Practice Is Important." *Facts and Figures* 6 (September 16): 27.

Orbach, Susie. 1978. *Fat Is a Feminist Issue*. New York: Paddington.

O'Reilly, Terry. 2011. *The Age of Persuasion*, Season 5, Episode 10. Podcast. 2011.

O'Reilly-Fleming, Thomas. 1993. *Down and Out in Canada: Homeless Canadians*. Toronto: Canadian Scholars' Press.

Orenstein, Peggy, in association with the American Association of University Women. 1995. *School Girls: Young Women, Self-Esteem, and the Confidence Gap*. New York: Anchor/Doubleday.

Oreopoulis, Philip, 2009. *Why Do Skilled Immigrants Struggle in the Labor Market? A Field Experiment with 6000 Résumés*. Metropolis British Columbia. Centre of Excellence for Research on Immigration and Diversity Working Paper Series No. 09-03 (May). Retrieved June 19, 2012. Available: http://mbc.metropolis.net/assets/uploads/files/wp/2009/WP09-03.pdf.

Ornstein, Michael. 2010. *Racialization and Gender of Lawyers in Ontario*. Toronto: Law Society of Upper Canada.

Ortner, Sherry B. 1974. "Is Female to Male as Nature Is to Culture?" In Michelle Rosaldo and Louise Lamphere (eds.), *Women, Culture, and Society*. Stanford, Cal.: Stanford University Press.

———, and Harriet Whitehead, eds. 1981. *Sexual Meanings: The Cultural Construction of Gender and Sexuality*. Cambridge, Mass.: Cambridge University Press.

Orum, Anthony M. 1974. "On Participation in Political Protest Movements." *Journal of Applied Behavioral Science* 10: 181–207.

———, and Amy W. Orum. 1968. "The Class and Status Bases of Negro Student Protest." *Social Science Quarterly* 49 (December): 521–533.

Osborne, Ken. 1999. *Education: A Guide to the Canadian School Debate—Or, Who Wants What and Why*. Toronto: Penguin Books.

Ostrower, Francie. 1997. *Why the Wealthy Give: The Culture of Elite Philanthropy*. Princeton, N.J.: Princeton University Press.

Osuh, Chris. 2011. "Jailed: Knife Killer Who Stole to Play 'Farmville' Game on Facebook. *Manchester Evening News* (August 31). Retrieved December 23, 2011. Available: http://menmedia.co.uk/manchestereveningnews/news/crime/s/1457399_jailed-knife-killer-who-stole-to-play-farmville-game-on-facebook.

O'Sullivan, Chris. 1993. "Fraternities and the Rape Culture." In Emile Buchwald et al. (eds.), *Transforming a Rape Culture*. Minn.: Milkweed Ltd.

Otnes, C.C., and E.H. Pleck. 2003. *Cinderella Dreams: The Allure of the Lavish Wedding*. Berkeley: University Of California Press.

Overall, Christine. 1991. "Reproductive Technology and the Future of the Family." In Jean E. Veevers (ed.), *Continuity and Change in Marriage and the Family*. Toronto: Holt, Rinehart and Winston, 466–477.

Oxfam. 2001. *Rigged Trade and Not Much Aid: How Rich Countries Help to Keep the Least Developed Countries Poor*. London: Oxfam.

Page, Charles H. 1946. "Bureaucracy's Other Face." *Social Forces* 25 (October): 89–94.

Palmore, Erdman. 1981. *Social Patterns in Normal Aging: Findings from the Duke Longitudinal Study*. Durham, N.C.: Duke University Press.

Palys, Ted. 1997. *Research Decisions: Quantitative and Qualitative Perspectives*. Toronto: Harcourt Brace.

Pammett, Jon H. 1993. "Tracking the Votes." In Alan Frizell et al. (eds.), *The Canadian General Election of 1993*. Ottawa: Carleton University Press.

Panitch, Leo, and Donald Swartz. 1993. *Assault on Trade Union Freedoms* (2nd ed.). Toronto: Garamond.

Panzarino, Connie. 1994. *The Me in the Mirror*. Seattle, Wash.: Seal Press.

Parenti, Michael. 1994. *Land of Idols: Political Mythology in America*. New York: St. Martin's Press.

———. 1996. *Democracy for the Few* (5th ed.). New York: St. Martin's.

———. 2001. "Monopoly Media Manipulation." *Michael Parenti Political Archive*. Retrieved October 17, 2011. Available: http://www.michael-parenti.org/MonopolyMedia.html.

Park, Jungwee. 2011. "Retirement, Health and Employment Among Those 55 Plus." *Perspectives on Labour and Income* 31 (January): 3–12.

Park, Robert E. 1915. "The City: Suggestions for the Investigation of Human Behavior in the City." *American Journal of Sociology* 20: 577–612.

———. 1928. "Human Migration and the Marginal Man." *American Journal of Sociology* 33.

———. 1936. "Human Ecology." *American Journal of Sociology* 42: 1–15.

———, and Ernest W. Burgess. 1921. *Human Ecology*. Chicago: University of Chicago Press.

Parker, Robert Nash. 1995. "Violent Crime." In Joseph F. Sheley, *Criminology: A Contemporary Handbook* (2nd. ed.). Belmont, Cal.: Wadsworth, 169–185.

Parliament of Canada. 2006. *Final Report on the Canadian News Media*. Ottawa: Standing Senate Committee on Transportation and Communications.

Parrish, Dee Anna. 1990. *Abused: A Guide to Recovery for Adult Survivors of Emotional/Physical Child Abuse*. Barrytown, N.Y.: Station Hill Press.

Parsons, Lee. 2003. "Food Bank Use Continues to Rise." Retrieved August 12, 2003. Available: http://www.wsws.org/articles/2003/oct2003/food-o22.shtml.

Parsons, Talcott. 1951. *The Social System*. Glencoe, Ill.: Free Press.

———. 1955. "The American Family: Its Relations to Personality and to the Social Structure." In Talcott Parsons and Robert F. Bales (eds.), *Family, Socialization and Interaction Process*. Glencoe, Ill.: Free Press, 3–33.

———. 1960. "Toward a Healthy Maturity." *Journal of Health and Social Behavior* 1: 163–173.

———, and Edward A. Shils, eds. 1951. *Toward a General Theory of Action*. Cambridge, Mass.: Harvard University Press.

Patterson, Christopher, and Elizabeth Podnieks. 1995. "A Guide to the Diagnosis and Treatment of Elder Abuse." In Mark Novak (ed.), *Aging and Society: A Canadian Reader*. Toronto: Thomson Nelson.

Pavlik, John V., and Shawn McIntosh. 2011. *Converging Media: A New Introduction to Mass Communication* (2nd ed.). New York: Oxford University Press.

PBS. 1992. "Sex, Power and the Workplace."

———. 2001. "Crossing Borders: How Terrorists Use Fake Passports, Visas, and Other Identity Documents." Retrieved July 12, 2005. Available: http://www.pbs.org/wgbh/pages/frontline/shows/trail/etc/fake.html.

Pearce, Diana. 1978. "The Feminization of Poverty: Women, Work, and Welfare." *Urban and Social Change Review* 11 (1/2): 28–36.

Pearson, Judy C. 1985. *Gender and Communication*. Dubuque, Iowa: Brown.

Peikoff, Tannis. 2000. *Anglican Missionaries and Governing the Self: An Encounter with Aboriginal Peoples in Western Canada*. Unpublished Ph.D. dissertation, University of Manitoba.

Pepler, D.J., W.M. Craig, and P. O'Connell. 2010. "Peer Processes in Bullying: Informing Prevention and Intervention Strategies." In S.R. Jimerson, S.M. Swearer, and D.L. Espelage (eds.), *The International Handbook of School Bullying*. Mahwah, N.J.: Lawrence Erlbaum, 469–480.

Perreault, Samuel, and Shannon Brennan. 2010. "Criminal Victimization in Canada 2009." *Juristat* 30. Ottawa: Statistics Canada.

Perrow, Charles. 1984. *Normal Accidents*. New York: Basic Books.

———. 1986. *Complex Organizations: A Critical Essay* (3rd ed.). New York: Random House.

Perrucci, Robert, and Earl Wysong. 1999. *The New Class Society*. Lanham, Md: Rowman and Littlefield.

Perry, David C., and Alfred J. Watkins, eds. 1977. *The Rise of the Sunbelt Cities*. Beverly Hills, Cal.: Sage.

Peter, Karl A. 1987. *The Dynamics of Hutterite Society*. Edmonton: University of Alberta Press.

Peters, John F. 1985. "Adolescents as Socialization Agents to Parents." *Adolescence* 20 (Winter): 921–933.

Peters, Linda, and Patricia Fallon. 1994. "The Journey of Recovery: Dimensions of Change." In Patricia Fallon, Melanie A. Katzman, and Susan C. Wooley (eds.), *Feminist Perspectives on Eating Disorders*. New York: Guilford Press, 339–354.

Petersen, John L. 1994. *The Road to 2015: Profiles of the Future*. Corte Madera, Cal.: Waite Group Press.

Peterson's Educational Center. 1996. "Report on Private Secondary Education 1996–97." Retrieved November 23, 1997. Available: http://www.peterson.com/research/reports/privateschools.html.

Pew Research Center. 2007. *The Pew Global Attitudes Project*. Washington: Pew Research Center.

Pheonix, A. and A.Woollett. 1991. "Motherhood, Social Construction, Politics, and Psychology." In A. Pheonix, A Woollett, and E. Lloyd (eds.), *Motherhood: Meanings, Practices and Ideologies*. London: Sage.

Philbeck, Joyce. 1997. "Seniors and the Internet." *Cybersociology*, 2. Available: http://www.socio.demon.co.uk/magazine/magazine.html.

Phillips, Sarah. 2009. "Ivy Bean: The Oldest Tweeter in Town."

The Guardian (October 23). Retrieved May 14, 2012. Available: http://www.guardian.co.uk/technology/2009/oct/23/ivy-bean-oldest-tweeter.

———. 2010. "Ivy Bean Obituary." *The Guardian* (July 30). Retrieved May 14, 2012. Available: http://www.guardian.co.uk/technology/2010/jul/30/ivy-bean-obituary.

Philp, Margaret. 1997. "Poverty Crusade Gets Personality." *Globe and Mail* (September 20): A1.

Piaget, Jean. 1932. *The Moral Judgment of the Child.* London: Routledge and Kegan Paul.

———. 1954. *The Construction of Reality in the Child.* Trans. Margaret Cook. New York: Basic Books.

Picot, Garnett, and John Myles. 2004. "Income Inequality and Low Income in Canada." *Horizons* 7 (December): 9–18.

Pierce, Jennifer. 1995. *Gender Trials: Emotional Lives in Contemporary Law Firms.* Berkeley: University of California Press.

Pietilä, Hilkka, and Jeanne Vickers. 1994. *Making Women Matter: The Role of the United Nations.* Atlantic Highlands, N.J.: Zed Books.

Pinderhughes, Dianne M. 1986. "Political Choices: A Realignment in Partisanship Among Black Voters?" In James D. Williams (ed.), *The State of Black America 1986.* New York: National Urban League, 85–113.

Pinderhughes, Howard. 1997. *Race in the Hood: Conflict and Violence Among Urban Youth.* Minneapolis: University of Minnesota Press.

Pines, Maya. 1981. "The Civilizing of Genie." *Psychology Today* 15 (September): 28–29, 31–32, 34.

Plante, Johanne, and David Beattie. 2004. *Connectivity and ICT Integration in Canadian Elementary and Secondary Schools: First Results from the Information and Communications Technologies in Schools Survey 2003–2004.* Culture, Tourism and the Centre for Education Statistics—Research Papers. Statistics Canada Cat. no. 81-595-MIE20040017.

Plummer, Ken. 2003. "Queers, Bodies, and Postmodern Sexualities: A Note on Revisiting the 'Sexual' in Symbolic Interactionism." *Qualitative Sociology* 26 (4): 515–530.

Pohl, Rudy. 2002. "Poverty in Canada." Ottawa: Ottawa Innercity Ministries. Retrieved June 25, 2002. Available: http://www.ottawainnercityministries.ca/homepage/homelessness2InCanada_Part2.htm.

Polakow, Valerie. 1993. *Lives on the Edge: Single Mothers and Their Children in the Other America.* Chicago: University of Chicago Press.

Polanyi, Karl. 1944. *The Great Transformation: The Political and Economic Origins of Our Time.* New York: Beacon.

Polivka, Larry. 2000. "Postmodern Aging and the Loss of Meaning." *Journal of Aging and Identity* 5: 225–235.

Pomice, Eva. 1990. "Madison Avenue's Blind Spot." In Karin Swisher (ed.), *The Elderly: Opposing Viewpoints.* San Diego: Greenhaven Press, 42–45.

Ponse, B. 1978. *Identities in the Lesbian World: The Social Construction of Self.* Westport, Conn.: Greenwood.

Ponting, J.R. 1997. *First Nations in Canada: Perspectives on Opportunity, Empowerment and Self-Determination.* Toronto: McGraw-Hill Ryerson.

Popenoe, David. 1993. "American Family Decline, 1960–1990: A Review and Appraisal." *Journal of Marriage and the Family* 55 (3): 527–543.

Popoff, Wilfred. 1996. "One Day You're Family; the Next Day You're Fired." *Globe and Mail* (March 14): A22.

Porter, John. 1965. *The Vertical Mosaic: An Analysis of Social Class and Power in Canada.* Toronto: University of Toronto Press.

Postone, Moishe. 1997. "Rethinking Marx (in a Post-Marxist World)." In Charles Camic (ed.), *Reclaiming the Sociological Classics: The State of the Scholarship.* Malden, Mass.: Blackwell, 45–80.

Pratt, Courtney. 1997. "Business Accountability: Shareholders, Stakeholders or Society?" Address to the Canadian Club of Toronto (September 29).

Preece, Melady. 2004. "When Lone Parents Marry: The Challenge of Stepfamily Relationships." *Transition* (Winter 2003–2004). Ottawa: Vanier Institute of the Family. Available: http://www.vifamily.ca/library/transition/334/334.htm.

President's Commission. 1986. *Report of the President's Commission on the Space Shuttle Challenger Accident.* Washington: U.S. Government Printing Office.

Prensky, Marc. 2001. "Digital Natives: Digital Immigrants." *On the Horizon* 9 (October). Retrieved May 11, 2009. Available: http://www.marcprensky.com/writing/Prensky%20-%20Digital%20Natives,%20Digital%20Immigrants%20-%20Part1.pdf.

Prestage, G. 1994. "Male and Transsexual Prostitution." In Roberta Perkins, *Sex Work and Sex Workers in Australia.* Sydney: University of New South Wales Press, 177.

PrevNet.ca. 2012. "Are Bullying and Victimization on the Rise in Canada?" Retrieved May 12, 2012. Available: http://prevnet.ca/BullyingFacts/BullyingStatistics/tabid/122/Default.aspx.

Prochner, Larry, and Nina Howe. 2000. *Early Childhood Education in Canada: Past, Present, and Future.* Vancouver: University of British Columbia Press.

Prose, Francine. 2010. "The Original Sin." *Lapham's Quarterly* (Winter). Retrieved May 7, 2012. Available: http://www.laphamsquarterly.org/magazine/religion.php.

Prus, Robert. 1996. *Symbolic Interaction and Ethnographic Research: Intersubjectivity and the Study of Human Lived Experience.* Albany: State University of New York Press.

Pryor, John, and Kathleen McKinney (eds.). 1991. "Sexual Harassment." *Basic and Applied Social Psychology* 17 (4).

———. 1995. "Research Advances in Sexual Harassment: Introduction and Overview." *Basic and Applied Social Psychology* 17: 421–424.

Public Health Agency of Canada. 2004. *Epi Update 2004.* Ottawa: Public Health Agency of Canada. Retrieved July 20, 2005. Available: http://www.phac-aspc.gc.ca/publicat/epiu-aepi/epi_update_may_04/10_e.html.

———. 2005. "Understanding the HIV/AIDS Epidemic Among Aboriginal Peoples in Canada: The Community at a Glance." Ottawa: Public Health Agency of Canada. Retrieved April 27, 2009. Available: http://www.phac-aspc.gc.ca/publicat/epiu-aepi/epi-note/.

———. 2007. *HIV/AIDS Epi Update.* Ottawa: Public Health Agency of Canada. Retrieved April 17, 2009. Available: www.phac-aspc.gc.ca/aids-sida/publication/epi/pdf/epi2007_e.pdf.

———. 2010. *HIV/AIDS Epi Updates – July 2010.* Retrieved February 19, 2012. Available: http://www.phac-aspc.gc.ca/aids-sida/publication/epi/2010/8-eng.php.

Public Safety and Emergency Preparedness Canada. 2004. *Corrections and Conditional Release Statistical Overview.* Ottawa: Author.

Public Safety Canada. 2010. *Corrections and Conditional Release: Statistical Overview 2010.* Ottawa: Public Safety Canada.

Pue, W. Wesley, ed. 2000. *Pepper in Our Eyes: The APEC Affair.* Vancouver: UBC Press, 77–84.

Quadagno, Jill S. 1984. "Welfare Capitalism and the Social Security Act of 1935." *American Sociological Review* 49: 632–647.

Quart, Alissa. 2003. *Branded: The Buying and Selling of Teenagers.* New York: Basic.

Quebec Population Health Research Network (QPHRN). 2008. "Aboriginal Youth and Social Inequalities in Health." *PopHealth Notes* 4 (November). Retrieved April 12, 2012. Available: http://www.santepop.qc.ca/fichier.php/114.

Queen, Stuart A., and David B. Carpenter. 1953. *The American City.* New York: McGraw-Hill.

Quigley, Tim. 1994. "Some Issues in the Sentencing of Aboriginal Offenders." Cited in Royal Commission on Aboriginal Peoples Report, 1996, *Bridging the Cultural Divide.* Ottawa: Minister of Supply and Services Canada.

Quinney, Richard. 1979. *Class, State, and Crime.* New York: McKay.

———. 1980. *Class, State, and Crime* (2nd ed.). New York: Longman.

Quinton, Rhonda. 1989. "Liability of Search and Rescuers." Unpublished paper, Faculty of Law, University of Victoria.

Qvortrup, Jens. 1990. *Childhood as a Social Phenomemon.* Vienna: European Centre for Social Welfare Policy and Research.

Raag, Tarja. 1999. "Influences of Social Expectations of Gender, Gender Stereotypes, and Situational Constraints on Children's Toy Choices." *Sex Roles* 41 (December): 800–831.

Rabinowitz, Fredric E., and Sam V. Cochran. 1994. *Man Alive: A Primer of Men's Issues.* Pacific Grove, Cal.: Brooks/Cole.

Radcliffe-Brown, A.R. 1952. *Structure and Function in Primitive Society.* New York: Free Press.

Raising the Roof. 2009. "Our Achievements." Retrieved March 3, 2009. Available: http://www.raising-theroof.org/au-our-index.cfm.

Rankin, Jim, and Betsy Powell. 2008. "Why the Difference for 'Non-Whites'?" *Toronto Star* (July 21): A6.

Ranson, Dave. 2008. "ADISQ vs. Heri: Can the CRTC Control Internet Radio Content?" *Alberta Law Review Online Supplement* (October 28). Retrieved September 23, 2011. Available: http://ualbertalaw.typepad.com/alr_supplement/2008/10/index.html.

Raphael, Dennis. 2001. *Inequality Is Bad for Our Hearts: Why Low Income and Social Exclusion Are Major Causes of Heart Disease in Canada.* Toronto: North York Heart Health Network.

Razack, Sherene H. 1998. *Looking White People in the Eye.* Toronto: University of Toronto Press.

Reckless, Walter C. 1967. *The Crime Problem.* New York: Meredith.

Reed, Christopher. 1998. "No Fingerprints Puts Man Under Society's Thumb." *Globe and Mail* (April 23): A11.

Rees, T. 1991. "Racial Discrimination and Employment Agencies." *Currents: Readings in Race Relations* 7 (2): 16–19.

Reich, Robert. 1993. "Why the Rich Are Getting Richer and the Poor Poorer." In Paul J. Baker, Louis E. Anderson, and Dean S. Dorn (eds.), *Social Problems: A Critical Thinking Approach* (2nd ed.). Belmont, Cal.: Wadsworth, 145–149. Adapted from *The New Republic,* May 1, 1989.

Reid, Julie A., Sinikka Elliott, and Gretchen R. Webber. 2011. "Casual Hookups to Formal Dates: Refining the Boundaries of the Sexual Double Standard." *Gender & Society* 25: 545–568.

Reiman, Jeffrey H. 1979. *The Rich Get Richer and the Poor Get Prison.* New York: Wiley.

———. 1984. *The Rich Get Richer and the Poor Get Prison* (2nd ed.). New York: Wiley.

Reinharz, Shulamit. 1992. *Feminist Methods in Social Research.* New York: Oxford University Press.

Reinisch, June. 1990. *The Kinsey Institute New Report on Sex: What You Must*

Know to Be Sexually Literate. New York: St. Martin's Press.

Reitz, Jeffrey G. 2001. "Immigrant Skill Utilization in the Canadian Labour Market: Implications for Human Capital Research." *Journal of International Migration and Integration* 2 (3): 347–378.

———. 2011. *Pro-Immigration Canada: Social and Economic Roots of Popular Views.*" IRRP Study 20, Oct. 2011. Retrieved June 1, 2012. Available: http://www.irpp.org/pubs/irppstudy/irpp_study_no20.pdf.

———, and Raymond Breton. 1994. *The Illusion of Difference: Realities of Ethnicity in Canada and the United States.* Toronto: C.D. Howe Institute.

Renzetti, Claire M., and Daniel J. Curran. 1995. *Women, Men, and Society* (3rd ed.). Boston: Allyn & Bacon.

———. 1998. *Living Sociology.* Boston: Allyn & Bacon.

Reskin, Barbara F., and Irene Padavic. 1994. *Women and Men at Work.* Thousand Oaks, Cal.: Pine Forge Press.

———. 2002. *Women and Men at Work* (2nd ed.). Thousand Oaks, Cal.: Pine Forge Press.

Ressler, A. 1998. "'A Body to Die For': Eating Disorders and Body-Image Distortion in Women." *International Journal of Fertility and Women's Medicine* 43: 133–138.

Rheingold, Howard. 2003. *Smart Mobs: The Next Social Revolution.* New York: Perseus.

Rhoten, Diana, and Wayne Lutters. 2009. "Virtual Worlds for Virtual Organizing." In W.S. Bainbridge (ed.), *Online Worlds: Convergence of the Real and the Virtual.* London: Springer-Verlag, 175–186.

Rich, A. 1980. "Compulsory Heterosexuality and Lesbian Existence." *Signs* 5 (4): 631–660.

Richard, Justice K. Peter. 1997. *The Westray Story: A Predictable Path to Disaster*, Executive Summary. Halifax: Government of Nova Scotia.

Richardson, John G., and Carl H. Simpson. 1982. "Children, Gender and Social Structure: An Analysis of the Content of Letters to Santa Claus." *Child Development* 53: 429–436.

Richardson, Laurel. 1993. "Inequalities of Power, Property, and Prestige." In Virginia Cyrus (ed.), *Experiencing Race, Class, and Gender in the United States.* Mountain View, Cal.: Mayfield, 229–236.

Richardson, R. Jack. 1992. "Free Trade: Why Did It Happen?" *Canadian Review of Sociology and Anthropology* 29: 307–328.

Richer, Stephen. 1988. "Equality to Benefit from Schooling: The Issue of Educational Opportunity." In D. Forcese and S. Richer (eds.), *Social Issues: Sociological Views of Canada.* Toronto: Prentice Hall, 262–86.

Richler, Mordecai. 1992. *Oh Canada! Oh Quebec!* Toronto and New York: Knopf.

Rifkin, Jeremy. 1995. *The End of Work.* New York: G.P. Putnam's Sons.

Rigler, David. 1993. "Letters: A Psychologist Portrayed in a Book About an Abused Child Speaks Out for the First Time in 22 Years." *New York Times Book Review* (June 13): 35.

Riley, Matilda White, and John W. Riley, Jr. 1994. "Age Integration and the Lives of Older People." *The Gerontologist* 34 (1): 110–115.

Rinehart, James W. 1996. *The Tyranny of Work: Alienation and the Labour Process* (3rd ed.). Toronto: Harcourt Brace.

Risman, Barbara J. 1987. "Intimate Relationships from a Microstructural Perspective: Men Who Mother." *Gender & Society* 1: 6–32.

Ritzer, George. 1993. *The McDonaldization of Society: An Investigation into the Changing Character of Contemporary Social Life.* Thousand Oaks, Cal.: Pine Forge Press.

———. 1996. *Sociological Theory* (4th ed.). New York: McGraw-Hill.

———. 1997. *Postmodern Society Theory.* New York: McGraw-Hill.

———. 1998. *The McDonaldization Thesis.* London: Sage.

———. 2000. *The McDonaldization of Society.* Thousand Oaks, Cal.: Pine Forge.

Roberts, Keith A. 1995b. *Religion in Sociological Perspective.* Belmont, Cal.: Wadsworth.

Roberts, Lance W., and Rodney A. Clifton. 1999. "Multiculturalism in Canada: A Sociological Perspective." In Peter S. Li (ed.), *Race and Ethnic Relations in Canada* (2nd ed.). Toronto: Oxford University Press.

———, Rodney A. Clifton, Barry Ferguson, Karen M. Kampen, and Simon Langlois. 2005. *Recent Social Trends in Canada, 1960–2000.* Montreal: McGill–Queen's University Press.

Robertshaw, Corinne. 2003. "Strike Down S.43." *Law Times.* June 16, 2003. Retrieved June 16, 2005. Available: http://www.repeal43.org/constitution.html#scchearing.

Robertson, Ian. 1977. *Sociology.* New York: Worth Publishers.

Robinson, David, Frank J. Porporino, William A. Millson, Shelley Trevethan, and Barry McKillop. 1998. "A One-Day Snapshot of Inmates in Canada's Adult Correctional Facilities." *Juristat* 18 (8). Ottawa: Statistics Canada.

Rodgers, Kain, and Rebecca Kong. 1996. "Crimes Against Women and Children in the Family." In Leslie Kennedy and Vincent Sacco (eds.), *Crime Counts: A Criminal Event Analysis.* Toronto: Thomson Nelson, 115–132.

Rodriguez, Havidan, and Russell Dynes. 2006. *Finding and Framing Katrina: The Social Construction of Disaster.* Understanding Katrina. Social Science Research Council. Retrieved February 1, 2009. Available: http://understandingkatrina.ssrc.org/Dynes_Rodriguez/.

———, Joseph Trainor, and Enrico Quarantelli. 2006. "Rising to the Challenges of a Catastrophe: The Emergent and Prosocial Behavior Following Hurricane Katrina." *Annals of the American Academy of Political and Social Sciences* 604 (March): 82–101.

Roethlisberger, Fritz J., and William J. Dickson. 1939. *Management and the Worker.* Cambridge, Mass.: Harvard University Press.

Rogers, Deborah D. 1995. "Daze of Our Lives: The Soap Opera as Feminine Text." In Gail Dines and Jean M. Humez (eds.), *Gender, Race, and Class in Media: A Text-Reader.* Thousand Oaks, Cal.: Sage, 325–331.

Rollins, Judith. 1985. *Between Women: Domestics and Their Employers.* Philadelphia: Temple University Press.

Romaniuc, Anatole. 1994. "Fertility in Canada: Retrospective and Prospective." In Frank Trovato and Carl F. Grindstaff (eds.), *Perspectives on Canada's Population.* Toronto: Oxford University Press, 214–229.

Roof, Wade Clark. 1993. *A Generation of Seekers: The Spiritual Journeys of the Baby Boom Generation.* San Francisco: HarperSanFrancisco.

Roos, Leslie, Elliott Fisher, Ruth Brazauskas, Sandra Sharp, and Evelyn Shapiro. 1992. "Health and Surgical Outcomes in Canada and the United States." *Health Affairs* 11: 56–73.

Roos, Noralou, Evelyn Forget, and Gerard Beirne. 2004. "Health Care User Fees: Clinic Charges are Wrong Way to Go." *Winnipeg Free Press* (January 20): A11.

Root, Maria P.P. 1990. "Disordered Eating in Women of Color." *Sex Roles* 22 (7/8): 525–536.

Rose, Jerry D. 1982. *Outbreaks.* New York: Free Press.

Rosenbloom, Stephanie. 2011. "Love, Lies and What They Learned." *The New York Times* (November 13): ST1.

Rosenburg, Michael. 1995. "Ethnic and Race Relations." In L. Tepperman, J.E. Curtis, and R.J. Richardson (eds.), *Sociology.* Toronto: McGraw-Hill Ryerson, 302–344.

Rosenfeld, Alvin, and Nicole Wise. 2000. *The Over-Scheduled Child: Avoiding the Hyper-Parenting Trap.* New York: St. Martin's Griffin.

Rosenfeld, Michael J., and Reuben J. Thomas. 2012. "Searching for a Mate: The Rise of the Internet as a Social Intermediary." *American Sociological Review,* 77 (4): 523–547.

Rosenthal, Naomi, Meryl Fingrutd, Michele Ethier, Roberta Karant, and David McDonald. 1985. "Social Movements and Network Analysis: A Case Study of Nineteenth-Century Women's Reform in New York State." *American Journal of Sociology* 90: 1022–1054.

Rosenthal, Robert, and Lenore Jacobson. 1968. *Pygmalion in the Classroom: Teacher Expectation and Student's Intellectual Development.* New York: Holt, Rinehart, and Winston.

Rosnow, Ralph L., and Gary Alan Fine. 1976. *Rumor and Gossip: The Social Psychology of Hearsay.* New York: Elsevier.

Ross, Becki. 2010. "Sex and (Evacuation from) the City: The Moral and Legal Regulation of Sex Workers in Vancouver's West End, 1975–1985." *Sexualities* 13 (2): 197–218.

Ross, David P., and Paul Roberts. 1997. "Does Family Income Affect the Healthy Development of Children?" *Perception* 21 (Summer): 1–5. Ottawa: Canadian Council on Social Development.

———, Katherine Scott, and M.A. Kelly. 1996. *Growing Up in Canada: National Longitudinal Survey of Children and Youth.* Ottawa: Human Resources Development Canada and Statistics Canada.

———, Katherine Scott, and Peter Smith. 2000. *The Canadian Fact Book on Poverty, 2000.* Ottawa: Canadian Council on Social Development.

———, E. Richard Shillington, and Clarence Lochhead. 1994. *The Canadian Fact Book on Poverty.* Ottawa: Canadian Council on Social Development.

Ross, Rupert. 1996. *Returning to the Teachings: Exploring Aborginal Justice.* Toronto: Penguin Books.

Rossi, Alice S. 1980. "Life-Span Theories and Women's Lives." *Signs* 6 (1): 4–32.

Rossides, Daniel W. 1986. *The American Class System: An Introduction to Social Stratification.* Boston: Houghton Mifflin.

Rostow, Walt W. 1971. *The Stages of Economic Growth: A Non-Communist Manifesto* (2nd ed.). Cambridge: Cambridge University Press (orig. pub. 1960).

———. 1978. *The World Economy: History and Prospect.* Austin, Tex.: University of Texas Press.

Rotermann, Michelle. 2008. *Trends in Teen Sexual Behaviour and Condom Use.* Statistics Canada Cat. no. 82-003-X. Retrieved April 21, 2012. Available: http://www.statcan.gc.ca/pub/82-003-x/2008003/article/10664-eng.pdf.

Roth, Guenther. 1988. "Marianne Weber and Her Circle." In Marianne Weber, *Max Weber: A Biography.* New Brunswick, N.J.: Transaction.

Rothman, Robert A. 2001. *Inequality and Stratification: Class, Color, and Gender* (4th ed.). Upper Saddle River, N.J.: Prentice-Hall.

Royal Commission on Aboriginal Peoples. 1995. *Choosing Life: Special Report on Suicide Among Aboriginal Peoples.* Ottawa: Canada. Communications Group Publishing.

Royal Commission on Learning. 1994. *For the Love of Learning: Report of the Royal Commission on Learning,* vol. 4. Toronto: Queen's Printer, 4–5.

Rubin, Lillian B. 1994. *Families on the Fault Line.* New York: HarperCollins.

Ruiz-Duremdes, Sharon. n.d. "An Open Letter to My Children (On the National Situation)." Anglican Church of Canada. Unpublished.

Rushkoff, Douglas. 2010. *Program or Be Programmed: Ten Commands for a Digital Age.* New York: OR Books.

Rutherford, Leanna. 1998. "An Anorexic's Recovery." *Canadian Living* (October): 107–110.

Ruthven, Malise. 2004. *Fundamentalism: The Search for Meaning.* Oxford: Oxford University Press.

Rutstein, Nathan. 1993. *Healing in America.* Spring-field, Mass.: Whitcomb.

Rymer, Russ. 1993. *Genie: An Abused Child's Flight from Silence.* New York: HarperCollins.

Sacks, Nancy E., and Catherine Marrone. 2004. *Gender and Work in Today's World.* Cambridge, Mass.: Westview Press.

Sadker, Myra, and David Sadker. 1994. *Failing at Fairness: How America's Schools Cheat Girls.* New York: Scribner.

Safilios-Rothschild, Constantina. 1969. "Family Sociology or Wives' Family Sociology? A Cross-Cultural Examination of Decision-Making." *Journal of Marriage and the Family* 31 (2): 290–301.

Samovar, Larry A., and Richard E. Porter. 1991a. *Communication Between Cultures.* Belmont, Cal.: Wadsworth.

———. 1991b. *Intercultural Communication: A Reader* (6th ed.). Belmont, Cal.: Wadsworth.

Samuelson, Paul A., and William D. Nordhaus. 1989. *Economics* (13th ed.). New York: McGraw-Hill.

Sandals, Leah. 2007. "'Public Space Protection'—But for Which 'Public'?" Retrieved February 24, 2007. Available: http://spacing.ca/wire/?p=1466.

Sanders, D. 1972. "The Bill of Rights and Indian Status." *University of British Columbia Law Review* 7 (1): 81–105.

Sanmartin, Claudia, Edward Ng, Debra Blackwell, Jane Gentleman, Michael Martinez, and Catherine Simile. 2004. *Joint Canada/United States Survey of Health, 2002–03.* Ottawa: Statistics Canada.

Sapir, Edward. 1961. *Culture, Language and Personality.* Berkeley: University of California Press.

Sargent, Margaret. 1987. *Sociology for Australians* (2nd ed.). Melbourne, Australia: Longman Cheshire.

Sarick, Lila. 1999. "Record Numbers Turn to Food Banks to Cope, National Survey Shows." *Globe and Mail* (September 29): A3.

Sassen, Saskia. 1991. *The Global City: New York, London, Tokyo.* Princeton, N.J.: Princeton University Press.

Satzewich, Vic, ed. 1998. *Racism and Social Inequality in Canada: Concepts, Controversies and Strategies for Resistance.* Toronto: Thompson Educational Publishing.

Satzewich, V., and N. Liodakis. 2007. *Race and Ethnicity in Canada.* Toronto: Oxford University Press.

Saunders, Eileen. 1999. "Theoretical Approaches to the Study of Women." In James Curtis, Edward Grabb, and Neil Guppy (eds.), *Social Inequality in Canada: Patterns and Policies.* Scarborough, Ont.: Prentice-Hall, 168–185.

Sauvé, Roger. 2001. *Wealth: How Many Millionaires Does It Take to Buy "Everything" and More?* Ottawa: Vanier Institute of the Family. Retrieved June 25, 2002. Available: http:// www .vifamily.ca/wealth/four.htm.

———. 2002. "The Dreams and Reality: Assets, Debts, and Net Worth." People Patterns Consulting. Retrieved August 16, 2005. Available http://www .vifamily.ca.

———. 2003. "Rich Canadians, Poor Canadians, and Everyone in Between." *Transition Magazine* 32 (4).

———. 2003b. "The Current State of Family Finances—2003 Report." People Patterns Consulting. Retrieved August 12, 2005. Available http:// www.vifamily.ca/library/cft/state03 .html#3_million.

———. 2008. "The Current State of Canadian Family Finances, 2007 Report." Ottawa: Vanier Institute for the Family. Retrieved June 17, 2009. Available: http://www.vifamily.ca/ library/cft/famfin07.pdf.

———. 2012. "The Current State of Canadian Family Finances, 2011 Report." Ottawa: Vanier Institute for the Family. Retrieved April 12, 2012. Available: http://www.vanierinstitute .ca/include/get.php?nodeid=1779.

Savin-Williams, Ritch C. 2004. "Memories of Same-Sex Attractions." In Michael S. Kimmel and Michael A. Messner (eds.), *Men's Lives* (6th ed.). Boston: Allyn & Bacon, 116–132.

Scelfo, Julie. 2011. "Video Chat Reshapes Domestic Rituals." *New York Times* (December 21). Retrieved December 27, 2011. Available: http:// www.nytimes.com/2011/12/22/garden/ video-chat-reshapes-domestic-rituals .html?pagewanted=all.

Schaefer, Richard T. 1993. *Racial and Ethnic Groups.* New York: HarperCollins.

———. 1995. *Race and Ethnicity in the United States.* New York: HarperCollins.

Schafer, A. 1998. *Down and Out in Winnipeg and Toronto: The Ethics of Legislating Against Panhandling.* Ottawa: Institute of Social Policy.

Schama, Simon. 1989. *Citizens: A Chronicle of the French Revolution.* New York: Knopf.

Schellenberg, Grant, and Helene Maheux. 2007. "Immigrants' Perspectives on Their First Four Years in Canada: Highlights from Three Waves of the Longitudinal Survey of Immigrants to Canada." *Canadian Social Trends* (April): 1–35.

———, and David P. Ross. 1997. *Left Poor by the Market: A Look at Family Poverty and Earnings.* Ottawa: Canadian Council on Social Development.

———, and Cynthia Silver. 2004. "You Can't Always Get What You Want: Retirement Preferences and Experiences." *Canadian Social Trends* (Winter): 2–7.

Schemo, Diana Jean. 1996. "Indians in Brazil, Estranged from Their Land, Suffer an Epidemic of Suicide." *New York Times* (August 25): 7.

Schiller, Herbert. 1992. "A Quarter Century Retrospective." In Herbert Schiller (ed.), *Mass Communications and American Empire* (2nd ed.). Boulder, Colo.: Westview Press.

Schlesinger, Ben. 1998. *Strengths in Families: Accentuating the Positive Contemporary Family Trends.* Ottawa: Vanier Institute of the Family.

Schmidt, Sara. 2008. "Brain Cancer Linked to Youngsteres Using Cell Phone." Canwest News Service. Retrieved August 20, 2009. Available: http://www.canada.com/story_print .html?id=1398135&sponsor=.

Schneider, Keith. 1993. "The Regulatory Thickets of Environmental Racism." *New York Times* (December 19): E5.

Schneider, Stephen. "Organized Crime." In Rick Linden (ed.), *Criminology: A Canadian Perspective* (7th ed.). Toronto: Nelson, 493–531.

Scholastic Parent & Child. 2007. "How and When to Praise." Retrieved January 3, 2008. Available: http://content.scholastic.com/browse/article.jsp?id=2064.

Schrock, Douglas, Daphne Holden, and Lori Reid. 2004. "Creating Emotional Resonance: Interpersonal Emotion Work and Motivational Framing in a Transgender Community." *Social Problems* 51 (1): 61–81.

Schur, Edwin M. 1965. *Crimes Without Victims: Deviant Behavior and Public Policy.* Englewood Cliffs, N.J.: Prentice-Hall.

———. 1983. *Labeling Women Deviant: Gender, Stigma, and Social Control.* Philadelphia: Temple University Press.

Schutz, Alfred. 1967. *The Phenomenology of the Modern World.* Evanston: Northwestern University Press (originally published in 1932).

Sciadas, G. 2006. "Our Lives in Digital Times." Statistics Canada Connectedness Series Cat. no. 56F0004MIE—no. 014. Retrieved May 8, 2009. Available: http://www.statcan.gc.ca/ pub/56f0004m/56f0004m2006014-eng .pdf.

Scott, Robert A. 1969. *The Making of Blind Men: A Study of Adult Socialization.* New York: Russell Sage Foundation.

Scully, Diana. 1990. *Understanding Sexual Violence: A Study of Convicted Rapists.* Boston: Unwin Hyman.

Seccombe, Karen. 1991. "Assessing the Costs and Benefits of Children: Gender Comparisons Among Childfree Husbands and Wives." *Journal of Marriage and the Family* 53 (1): 191–202.

Seegmiller, B.R., B. Suter, and N. Duviant. 1980. *Personal, Socioeconomic, and Sibling Influences on Sex-Role Differentiation.* Urbana: ERIC Clearinghouse of Elementary and Early Childhood Education, ED 176 895, College of Education, University of Illinois.

Segall, Alexander, and Christopher Fries. 2011. *Pursuing Health and Wellness.* Toronto: Oxford University Press.

Seid, Roberta P. 1994. "Too 'Close to the Bone': The Historical Context for Women's Obsession with Slenderness." In Patricia Fallon, Melanie A. Katzman, and Susan C. Wooley (eds.), *Feminist Perspectives on Eating Disorders.* New York: Guilford Press, 3–16.

Senate Committee on Legal and Constitutional Affairs. 2006. "Evidence." (December 4).

Serazio, Michael. 2008. "Virtual Sports Consumption, Authentic Brotherhood: The Reality of Fantasy Football." In Lawrence W. Hugengerg, Paul Haridakis, and Adam Earnheardt (eds.), *Sports Mania: Essays on Fandom and the Media in the 21st Century.* Jefferson, N.C.: McFarland, 229–242.

Serbin, Lisa A., Phyllis Zelkowitz, Anna-Beth Doyle, Dolores Gold, and Bill Wheaton. 1990. "The Socialization of Sex-Differentiated Skills and Academic Performance: A Mediational Model." *Sex Roles* 23: 613–628.

Sex Information and Education Council of Canada (SIECCAN). 2011. *Sexting: Considerations for Canadian Youth.* Retrieved June 21, 20120. Available: http://sexualityandu.ca/uploads/files/ CTRsextingEnglishApril2011.pdf.

Shadd, Adrienne. 1991. "Institutionalized Racism and Canadian History: Notes of a Black Canadian." In Ormond McKague (ed.), *Racism in Canada.* Saskatoon: Fifth House, 1–5.

———. 1994. "Where Are You Really From?" In Carl E. James and Adrienne Shadd (eds.), *Talking About Difference.* Toronto: Between the Lines Press, 9–15.

Shapiro, Ari, and Melissa Block. 2009. "U.S. Busts Largest-Ever ID-Theft Scheme." National Public Radio (August 17). Retrieved February 4, 2012. Available: http://www.npr .org/templates/story/story.php? storyId=111964002.

Shapiro, Eve. 2010. *Gender Circuits: Bodies and Identities in a Technological Age.* New York: Routledge.

Shapiro, Joseph P. 1993. *No Pity: People with Disabilities Forging a New Civil Rights Movement.* Toronto: Time Books/Random House.

Shapiro, Susan P. 1990. "Collaring the Crime, Not the Criminal: Reconsidering the Concept of White-collar Crime." *American Sociological Review* 55: 346–365.

Sharell, Janine. 1996. "Exercise Bulimia: Too Much of a Good Thing." *CNN Interactive: Food and Health* (May 20). Retrieved November 22, 2002. Available: http://www.cnn.com/ HEALTH/9605/20/exercise.bulimia.

Sharif, Iman, and James D. Sargent. 2006. "Association Between Television, Movie, and Video Game Exposure and School." *Pediatrics* 118 (October 1). Retrieved April 21, 2012. Available: http://www.pediatricsdigest.mobi/content/118/4/e1061.full.pdf+html.

Sharma, Monica, and James Tulloch. 1997. "Commentary: Unfinished Business." *Progress of Nations 1996.* New York: The United Nations. Retrieved December 7, 2002. Available: http://www.unicef.org/pon96/heunfini.htm.

Shaughnessy, K., S. Byers, and S. Thornton. 2011. "What is Cybersex? Heterosexual Students' Definitions." *International Journal of Sexual Health,* 23 (2): 79–89. doi:10.1080/19317611.2010.546945.

Shaw, Randy. 1999. *Reclaiming America: Nike, Clean Air, and the New National Activism.* Berkeley: University of California Press.

Shawver, Lois. 1998. "Notes on Reading Foucault's *The Birth of the Clinic.*" Retrieved October 2, 1999. Available: http://www.california.com/~rathbone/foucbc.htm.

Sheen, Fulton J. 1995. *From the Angel's Blackboard: The Best of Fulton J. Sheen.* Ligouri, Miss.: Triumph.

Sheley, Joseph F. 1991. *Criminology: A Contemporary Handbook.* Belmont, Cal.: Wadsworth.

Shenon, Philip. 1994. "China's Mania for Baby Boys Creates Surplus of Bachelors." *New York Times* (August 16): A1, A4.

Sheptycki, James. 1998. "Policing, Postmodernism, and Transnationalism." *British Journal of Criminology* 38 (3): 485–503.

Sher, Julian, and William Marsden. 2003. *How the Biker Gangs Are Conquering Canada.* Toronto: Alfred A. Knopf.

Shilts, Randy. 1988. *And the Band Played On: Politics, People, and the AIDS Epidemic.* New York: Penguin.

Shirpak, K., E. Maticka-Tyndale, and M. Chinichian. 2007. "Iranian Immigrants' Perceptions of Sexuality in Canada: A symbolic Interactionist Approach." *Canadian Journal of Human Sexuality* 16 (3–4): 113–128.

Shisslak, Catherine M., and Marjorie Crago. 1992. "Eating Disorders Among Athletes." In Raymond Lemberg (ed.), *Controlling Eating Disorders with Facts, Advice, and Resources.* Phoenix: Oryx Press, 29–36.

Shkilnyk, Anastasia M. 1985. *A Poison Stronger Than Love: The Destruction of an Ojibwa Community.* New Haven, Conn.: Yale University Press.

Shmueli, Sandra. 2003. "'Flash Mob' Craze Spreads." CNN.com. Retrieved August 11, 2003. Available: http://www.cnn.com/2003/TECH/internet/08/ 04/flash.mob.

Shor, Ira. 1986. *Culture Wars: School and Society in the Conservative Restoration 1969–1984.* Boston: Routledge & Kegan Paul.

Sikorsky, Robert. 1990. "Highway Robbery: Canada's Auto Repair Scandal." *Reader's Digest* (February): 55–63.

Silver, Cynthia. 2001. "Older Surfers." *Canadian Social Trends* (Winter): 9–12.

Silverman, Rachel. 2012. "Big Firms Try Crowdsourcing." *Wall Street Journal* (January 17).

Silverman, Robert, and Leslie Kennedy. 1993. *Deadly Deeds: Murder in Canada.* Toronto: Thomson Nelson.

Simon, W., and J. Gagnon. 1986. "Sexual Scripts: Permanence and Change." *Archives of Sexual Behavior* 15 (2): 97–120.

Simmel, Georg. 1904. "Fashion." *American Journal of Sociology* 62 (May 1957): 541–558.

———. 1950. *The Sociology of Georg Simmel.* Trans. Kurt Wolff. Glencoe, Ill.: Free Press (orig. written 1902–1917).

———. 1990. *The Philosophy of Money.* Ed. David Frisby. New York: Routledge (orig. pub. 1907).

Simon, David R., and D. Stanley Eitzen. 1993. *Elite Deviance* (4th ed.). Boston: Allyn & Bacon.

Simons, Marlise. 1993a. "Homeless Find a Spot in France's Heart." *New York Times* (December 9): A4.

———. 1993b. "Prosecutor Fighting Girl-Mutilation." *New York Times* (November 23): A4.

Simpson, George Eaton, and Milton Yinger. 1972. *Racial and Cultural Minorities: An Analysis of Prejudice and Discrimination* (4th ed.). New York: Harper & Row.

Sjoberg, Gideon. 1960. *The Preindustrial City: Past and Present.* New York: The Free Press.

Sloan, R.P., E. Bagiella, and T. Powell. 1999. "Religion, Spirituality, and Medicine." *The Lancet* 353: 664–667.

Smandych, Russell. 1985. "Marxism and the Creation of Law: Re-Examining the Origins of Canadian Anti-Combines Legislation." In Thomas Fleming (ed.), *The New Criminologies in Canada: State, Crime and Control.* Toronto: Oxford University Press, 87–99.

Smelser, Neil J. 1963. *Theory of Collective Behaviour.* New York: Free Press.

———. 1988. "Social Structure." In Neil J. Smelser (ed.), *Handbook of Sociology.* Newbury Park, Cal.: Sage, 103–129.

Smith, Adam. 1976. *An Inquiry into the Nature and Causes of the Wealth of Nations.* Ed. Roy H. Campbell and Andrew S. Skinner. Oxford, England: Clarendon Press (orig. pub. 1776).

Smith, Allen C., III, and Sheryl Kleinman. 1989. "Managing Emotions in Medical School: Students' Contacts with the Living and the Dead." *Social Science Quarterly* 52 (1): 56–69.

Smith, Dorothy. 1974. "Women's Perspective as a Radical Critique of Sociology." *Sociological Inquiry* 44: 7–13.

———. 1985. "Women, Class and Family." In Varda Burstyn and Dorothy Smith (eds.), *Women, Class and the State.* Toronto: Garamond.

———. 1987. *The Everyday World as Problematic: A Feminist Sociology.* Toronto: University of Toronto Press.

Smith, Michael D. 1996. "Patriarchal Ideology and Wife Beating." In Robert J. Brym (ed.), *Society in Question: Sociological Readings for the 21st Century.* Toronto: Harcourt Brace, and Company.

Smith, Paula, Paul Gendreau, and Kristin Swartz. 2009. "Validating the Principles of Effective Intervention: A Systematic Review of the Contributions of Meta-Analysis in the Field of Corrections." *Victims and Offenders* 4: 148–169.

Smith, R. Jeffrey. 2003. "Mistakes of NASA Toted Up." *The Washington Post* (July 13): A1.

Smyke, Patricia. 1991. *Women and Health.* Atlantic Highlands, N.J.: Zed Books.

Smylie, Janet, and Paul Adomako. 2009. *Indigenous Children's Health Report: Health Assessment in Action.* Toronto: St. Michael's Hospital.

Smyth, Julie. 2001. "Prepare Them for Work and Create Good Citizens, Too." *State of Education Quarterly Report.* Edition 2. *National Post* (September 8). Available: http://quarterlyreport.nationalpost.com/stateofeducation/edupoll.html.

Snider, Laureen. 1988. "Commercial Crime." In Vincent F. Sacco (ed.), *Deviance, Conformity and Control in Canadian Society.* Scarborough, Ont.: Prentice-Hall, 231–283.

Snow, David A. 2003. "Observations and Comments on Gusfield's Journey." *Symbolic Interaction* 26: 141–149.

———, and Leon Anderson. 1991. "Researching the Homeless: The Characteristic Features and Virtues of the Case Study." In Joe R. Feagin, Anthony M. Orum, and Gideon Sjoberg (eds.), *A Case for the Case Study.* Chapel Hill: University of North Carolina Press, 148–173.

———. 1993a. "Researching the Homeless: The Characteristic Features and Virtues of the Case Study." In Joe R. Feagin, Anthony M. Orum, and Gideon Sjoberg (eds.), *A Case for the Case Study.* Chapel Hill: University of North Carolina Press, 148–173.

———. 1993b. *Down on Their Luck: A Case Study of Homeless Street People.* Berkeley: University of California Press.

———, and Robert Benford. 1988. "Ideology, Frame Resonance, and Participant Mobilization." In Bert Klandermans, Hanspeter Kriesi, and Sidney Tarrow (eds.), *International Social Movement Research,* vol. 1: *From Structure to Action.* Greenwich, Conn.: JAI, 133–155.

———, E. Burke Rochford, Jr., Steven K. Worden, and Robert D. Benford. 1986. "Frame Alignment Processes, Micromobilization, and Movement Participation." *American Sociological Review* 51: 464–481.

———, Louis A. Zurcher, and Robert Peters. 1981. "Victory Celebrations as Theater: A Dramaturgical Approach to Crowd Behavior." *Symbolic Interaction* 4 (1): 21–41.

Snowdon, Anne. 2012. "Strengthening Communities for Canadian Children with Disabilities." Paper Presented at the Annual Conference of the Sandbox Project.

Snyder, Benson R. 1971. *The Hidden Curriculum.* New York: Knopf.

Snyder, Trish, and Terri Foxman. 1998. "The Global Marketing Hall of Shame." *Canadian Inflight Magazine* (July): 42–560.

Sokoloff, Natalie. 1992. *Black Women and White Women in the Professions.* New York: Routledge.

Solyom, Catherine. 2012. "Debate over Interview Material Could Be Key to Luka Rocco Magnotta Murder Trial." *Montreal Gazette* (August 1).

Sommers, C.H. 2000. "The War Against Boys: How Misguided Feminism Is Harming Our Young Men." *Atlantic Monthly* 285 (5): 59–74.

Sorokin, Pitirim. 1950. *Altruistic Love.* Boston: The Boston Press.

South, Scott J., Charles M. Bonjean, Judy Corder, and William T. Markham. 1982. "Sex and Power in the Federal Bureaucracy." *Work and Occupations* 9 (2): 233–254.

Sowell, Thomas. 1981. *Ethnic America.* New York: Basic.

Spain, Daphne. 2002. "What Happened to Gender Relations on the Way from Chicago to Los Angeles?" *City & Community* 1 (June): 155–169.

Spence, Jan. 1997. "Homeless in Russia: A Visit with Valery Sokolov." Share International. Retrieved September 15, 2001. Available: http://www.shareintl.org/archives/homelessness/hl-jsRussia.htm.

Spencer, Metta. 1993. *Foundations of Modern Sociology* (6th ed.). Scarborough, Ont.: Prentice-Hall.

Stackhouse, John. 1998. "Village Phones Ring Up Profit." *Globe and Mail* (July 6): A1, A8.

———. 1999. "Foreign Aid Cuts Assailed for Harming Children." *Globe and Mail* (February 23): A1, A12.

Stamler, Rodney T. 2004. "Organized Crime." In Rick Linden (ed.), *Criminology: A Canadian Perspective* (5th ed.). Toronto: Thomson Nelson, 444–479.

Stanley, Alessandra. 2004. "Old-Time Sexism Suffuses New Season." *New York Times* (Oct. 1): B1–B22.

Stannard, David E. 1992. *American Holocaust: Columbus and the Conquest of the New World.* New York: Oxford University Press.

Stark, Rodney. 1999. "Secularization: R.I.P." *Sociology of Religion* 60: 249–273.

———. 2004. *Exploring the Religious Life.* Baltimore: The Johns Hopkins Press.

———, and William Sims Bainbridge. 1981. "American-Born Sects: Initial Findings." *Journal for the Scientific Study of Religion* 20: 130–149.

———, Daniel P. Doyle, and Lori Kent. 1982. "Religion and Delinquency: The Ecology of a 'Lost' Relationship." *Journal of Research in Crime and Delinquency* 19: 4–24.

Statham, Anne, Laurel Richardson, and Judith A. Cook. 1991. *Gender and University Teaching: A Negotiated Difference.* Albany: SUNY Press.

Statistics Canada. 1961. *1961 Census Bulletin* 1.2-2.

———. 1985. *Population Projections for Canada, Provinces and Territories 1984–2006.* Cat no. 91-520. Ottawa: Statistics Canada.

———. 1993. *Canadian Social Trends.* Ottawa: Statistics Canada.

———. 1994. *Women in the Labour Force.* Ottawa: Ministry of Industry, Science, and Technology.

———. 1996a. *Canada's Retirement Income Programs: A Statistical Overview.* Ottawa: Ministry of Industry.

———. 1996b. *General Social Survey.* Cat. no. 11–612.

———. 1997a. "1996 Census: Marital Status, Common-law Unions and Families." *The Daily* (October 14). Cat. no. 11-001E.

———. 1997b. "1996 Census: Mother Tongue, Home Language and Knowledge of Languages." *The Daily* (December 2). Ottawa: Minister of Supply and Services. Available: http://www.statcan.ca/Daily/English/971202/d971202.htm.

———. 1997c. "Breast Cancer Mortality and Mammography." *The Daily* (July 28). Ottawa: Minister of Supply and Services.

———. 1997d. "Family Income After Separatism." *The Daily* (April 9).

———. 1997e. "1996 Census: Immigration and Citizenship." *The Daily* (November 4). Cat. no. 11-001E.

———. 1997f. "The Social Context of Young Children." *Canadian Social Trends* (Winter). Cat. no. 11-008-XPE.

———. 1998a. "Canadian Crime Statistics, 1997." *Juristat* 18 (11): 12. Cat. no. 85-002-XPE. Ottawa: Statistics Canada.

———. 1998b. "Deaths, 1996." *The Daily* (April 16).

———. 1999a. "Computer Technology in Schools." *The Daily* (October 1). Retrieved December 10, 1999. Available: http://www.statcan.ca: 80/Daily/English/991012/d991012a.htm.

———. 1999b. "National Longitudinal Survey of Children and Youth." Ottawa: Special Surveys Division and Human Resources Development Canada.

———. 1999c. "National Longitudinal Survey of Children and Youth: School Component." *The Daily* (October 14). Retrieved June 3, 2005. Available: http://www.statcan.ca: 80/Daily/English/991014/d99104a.htm.

———. 2000a. "Criminal Victimization." *The Daily* (November 2). Retrieved January 14, 2005. Available: http://www.statcan.ca/Daily/English/001102/d001102a.htm.

———. 2000b. "Divorces." *The Daily* (September 28).

———. 2000c. "Enrolment in Elementary and Secondary Schools." Cat. no. 81-229-X1B. Ottawa: Statistics Canada.

———. 2001a. *2001 Census.* Available: http://www.12.statcan.ca/english/census01/products/analytic/companion/age/pyramid.cfm.

———. 2001b. "Alternative Health Care Practitioners." *The Daily* (December 13).

———. 2001c. "General Social Survey: Internet Use." *The Daily* (March 26). Retrieved December 15, 2002. Available: http://www.statcan.ca/Daily/English/010326/d010 326a.htm.

———. 2001d. "Homicide Statistics." *The Daily* (October 31). Ottawa: Statistics Canada.

———. 2001e. "Measuring Student Knowledge and Skills: The Performance of Canada's Youth in Reading, Mathematics, and Science." *The Daily* (December 4).

———. 2001f. "Number of Earners Who Worked Full Year, Full-Time in 1995 in the 25 Highest-Paying and 25 Lowest-Paying Occupations and Their Average Earnings by Sex." Retrieved March 10, 2003. Available: http://www.statcan.ca/english/census96/may12/t2.htm.

———. 2001g. "Participation in Postsecondary Education and Family Income." *The Daily* (December 7).

———. 2002a. "Aboriginal Peoples of Canada: A Demographic Profile." *2001 Census Analysis Series.* Cat. no. 96F0030X1E200107.

———. 2002b. "Births." *The Daily* (September 26).

———. 2002c. "Canada's Ethnocultural Portrait: The Changing Mosaic." *2001 Census Analysis Series.* Cat. no. 96F0030X1E200108.

———. 2002d. "Census: Families, Number and Average Size." Cat. no. 91-213-XPB.

———. 2002e. "Changing Conjugal Life in Canada." *The Daily* (July 11). Available: http://www.statcan.ca/Daily/English/020711/d020711a.htm.

———. 2002f. "Crime and Statistics in Canada, 2001." Cat. no. 85-00XPE. *Juristat* 22 (6). Ottawa: Statistics Canada.

———. 2002g. "Crime Statistics, 2001." *The Daily* (July 17).

———. 2002h. "Deaths." *The Daily* (May 7).

———. 2002i. "Divorces." *The Daily* (December 2). Retrieved March 15, 2003. Available: http://www.statcan.ca/Daily/English/021202/d021202f.htm.

———. 2002j. "Family Income." *The Daily* (October 30). Retrieved October 30, 2002. Available: http://www.statcan.ca/Daily/English/021030/d021030a.htm.

———. 2002k. "Geographic Units: Census Metropolitan Area and Census Agglomeration." Retrieved July 15, 2005. Available: http://www12.statcan.ca/english/census01/Products/Reference/dict/geo009.htm.

———. 2002l. "Health of the Off-Reserve Aboriginal Population." *The Daily* (August 27). Retrieved February 21, 2003. Available: http://www.statcan.ca/Daily/English/020827/d020827a.htm.

———. 2002m. "Impact of Income and Mortality in Urban Canada." *The Daily* (September 26).

———. 2002n. "Participation and Activity Limitation Survey: A Profile of Disability in Canada." *The Daily* (December 3).

———. 2002o. *Profile of Canadian Families and Households: Diversification Continues.* Cat. no. 96F0030X1E2001003. Retrieved December 13, 2002. Available: http://www12.statcan.ca/english/census01/products/analytic/companion/fam/canada.cfm.

———. 2002p. *Profile of the Canadian Population by Age and Sex: Canada Ages.* Cat. no. 96 F0030XIE2001002. Retrieved May 5, 2003. Available: http://www.12.statcan.ca/english/census01/products/analytic/companion/age/contents.cfm.

———. 2002q. "Profile of Languages in Canada: English, French, and Many Others." *2001 Census: Analysis Series.* Cat. no. 96F0030XIE2001005.

———. 2002r. *Women in Canada: Work Chapter Updates.* Cat. no. 89F0133XIE.

———. 2002s. "Youth in Transition Survey." *The Daily* (January 23).

———. 2002t. "Uniform Crime Reporting Survey." *Juristat* Cat. no. 85-00.

———. 2002u. "Homicide Survey." Policing Services Program, Canadian Centre for Justice Statistics. *Juristat* Cat. no. 85-00.

———. 2003a. "2001 Census: Ethic Origins, 2001." Cat. no. 96F0030XIE200108.

———. 2003b. "Census of Population: Immigration, Birthplace and Birthplace of Parents, Citizenship, Ethnic Origin, Visible Minorities and Aboriginal Peoples." *The Daily* (January 21). Retrieved February 20, 2003. Available: http://www.statcan.ca/Daily/English/030121/do30121a/htm.

———. 2003c. "The Changing Profile of Canada's Labour Force." *2001 Census Analysis Series.* Cat. no. 96F0030XIE200109. Retrieved March 15, 2003. Available: http://www.statcan.ca/english/IPS/Data/96F003XIE200109.htm.

———. 2003d. "Earnings of Canadians: Making a Living in the New Economy." Cat. no. 96F0030XIE2001013. Retrieved March 8, 2003. Available: http://www12.statcan.ca/english/census01/products/analytic/companion/earn/contents.cfm.

———. 2003e. "Education in Canada: Raising the Standard." *2001 Census: Analysis Series.* Cat. no. 96F0030XIE2001012. Retrieved March 11, 2003. Available: http://www.statcan.ca/English/census01/Products/Analytic/companion/educ/pdf/96F0030XIE2001012.pdf.

———. 2003f. "Ethnic Origin, Sex, and Single and Multiple Responses for Population Canada." Catalogue 97F00101XCB01001. Retrieved February 20, 2003. Available: http://www.statcan.ca/english/census01/products/standard/themes/ListProducts.cfm?Temporal=2001&APATH=3&THEME=44&FREE=0.

———. 2003g. "Income of Canadian Families." *2001 Census: Analysis Series.* Cat. no. 96F0030XIE2001014. Ottawa: Ministry of Industry.

———. 2003h. "Marriages." *The Daily* (February 6). Retrieved March 3, 2003. Available: http://www.statcan.ca/Daily/English/030206/d030206c.htm.

———. 2003i. "Population by Mother Tongue, Provinces, and Territories." Retrieved February 19, 2003. Available: http://www.statcan.ca/english/Pgdb/demo18a.htm.

———. 2003j. "Religions in Canada." *2001 Census: Analysis Series.* Cat. no. 96F0030XIE2001015. Ottawa: Ministry of Industry.

———. 2003k. "University Qualifications Granted by Field of Study, by Sex." CANSIM cross-classified table 00580602. Retrieved May 5, 2003. Available: http://www.statcan.ca/english/Pgdb/healtheduc.21.htm.

———. 2003l. "Census of Population: Income of Individuals, Families, and Households; Religion." *The Daily* (May 13). Retrieved May 26, 2003. Available: http://www.statcan.ca/Daily/English/030513/d030513a.htm.

———. 2003m. *Income of Individuals, Families, and Households Highlight Tables.* Cat. no. 97F0024XIE2001014 Retrieved August 20, 2005. Available: http://www12.statcan.ca/english/census01/products/highlight/Income/Index.cfm?Lang=E.

———. 2003n. "Marriages." *The Daily* (November 20). Retrieved September 13, 2005. Available: http://www.statcan.ca/Daily/English/031120/d031120c.htm.

———. 2003o. *Report on the Demographic Situation in Canada 2002.* Cat. no. 91-209-XPE. Ottawa: Ministry of Industry.

———. 2003p. "Satisfaction with Life, by Age Group and Sex, Household Population Aged 15 and Over, Canada Excluding Territories, 2002." *Canadian Community Health Survey: Mental Health and Well-Being* 2002, Table 21. Cat. no. 82-617-X1I. Ottawa: Ministry of Industry.

———. 2003q. "Study: Finances in the Golden Years." *The Daily* (November 17).

———. 2003r. "Women in Canada: Work Chapter Updates 2003." Cat. no. 89F0133XIE. Retrieved July 23, 2005. Available: http://www.statcan.ca/english/freepub/89F0133XIE/89F0133XIE2003000.pdf.

———. 2003s. "Crime Statistics, 2003." *Juristat* 24 (6).

———. 2003t. "Study: Knowledge Workers in Canada's Workforce." *The Daily* (October 30).

———. 2004a. "Adult Correctional Services in Canada, 2002/03." *Juristat.* Ottawa: Canadian Centre for Justice Statistics.

———. 2004b. "Crime Statistics." *The Daily* (July 28). Retrieved February 3, 2005. Available: http://www.statcan.ca/Daily/English/040728/d040728a.htm.

———. 2004c. "Deaths." *The Daily* (September 27).

———. 2004d. "Family Income." *The Daily* (May 20). Retrieved August 18, 2005. Available: http://www.statcan.ca/Daily/English/040520/d040520b.htm.

———. 2004e. "Foreign Control in the Canadian Economy." *The Daily* (November 2).

———. 2004f. "Low-income in Census Metropolitan Areas." *The Daily* (April 7). Retrieved August 18, 2005. Available: http://www.statcan.ca/Daily/English/040407/d040407a.htm.

———. 2004g. "Marriages." *The Daily* (December 21). Retrieved September 13, 2005. Available: http://www.statcan.ca/Daily/English/041221/d041221d.htm.

———. 2004h. "Profile of Disability in 2001." *Canadian Social Trends* (Spring): 16–20. Ottawa: Statistics Canada.

———. 2004i. "Seniors at Work: An Update." *The Daily* (February 25).

———. 2004j. "Computers in the Classroom." *Education Matters: Insights on Education, Learning and Training in Canada.* Cat. no. 81-004-XE. Retrieved May 8, 2009. Available: http://www.statcan.gc.ca/pub/81-004-x/200409/7017-eng.htm.

———. 2004k. "Paying for Higher Education." *Education Matters.* Cat. no. 81-004-XIE. Retrieved March 26, 2009. Available: http://www.statcan.gc.ca/bsolc/olc-cel/olc-cel?lang=eng&catno=81-004-X20040037018.

———. 2005a. "Births." *The Daily* (July 12).

———. 2005b. "Canadian Community Health Survey: Obesity Among Children and Adults." *The Daily* (July 6).

———. 2005c. "Crime Statistics in Canada, 2004." *Juristat* 25 (5).

———. 2005d. "Divorces." *The Daily* (March 9). Retrieved November 12, 2008. Available: http://www.statcan.ca/Daily/English/050309/d050309b.htm.

———. 2005e. "Health Reports: The Use of Alternative Health Care." *The Daily* (March 15).

———. 2005f. "Labour Force Survey: Western Canada's Off-Reserve Aboriginal Population." *The Daily* (June 13).

———. 2005g. "Study: Are Good Jobs Disappearing in Canada?" *The Daily* (January 26).

———. 2005h. "General Social Survey: Criminal Victimization." *The Daily.* Retrieved November 12, 2008. Available: http://www.statcan.ca/Daily/English/051124/d051124b.htm.

———. 2005i. "Study: Chronic Unemployment." *The Daily* (September 6). Ottawa: Statistics Canada.

———. 2005j. *Population Projections for Canada, Provinces, and Territories, 2005–2031.* Catalogue no. 91-520-X1E.

———. 2006a. 2006 Census of the Population. Retrieved November 12, 2008. Available: http://www12.statcan.ca/english/census06/analysis/education/tables.cfm.

———. 2006b. "2006 Census: Mother Tongue, Knowledge of Official Languages." Statistics Canada Cat. no. 97-555-XCB2006015. Retrieved January 18, 2009. Available: http://www12.statcan.ca/english/census06/data/topics/Print.cfm?PID=89201&GID=837928&D1=0&D2=0&D3=0&D4=0&D5=0&D6=0.

———. 2006c. "Aboriginal Identity, Highest Certificate, Diploma or Degree." 2006 Census Highlight Tables. Retrieved April 22, 2009. Available: http://www12.statcan.gc.ca/english/-census06/data/topics/RetrieveProductTable.cfm?ALEVEL=3&APATH=3&CATNO=97-560-XCB2006036&DETAIL=0&DIM=&DS=99&FL=0&FREE=0&GAL=&GC=99&GK=NA&GRP=0&IPS=97-560-XCB2006036&METH=0&ORDER=&PID=97686&PTYPE=88971&RL=0&S=1&ShowAll=&StartRow=&SUB=&Temporal=2006&Theme=75&VID=&VNAMEE=&VNAMEF=.

———. 2006d. "Study: The Death of a Spouse and the Impact on Income." *The Daily* (July 10).

———. 2006e. *Women in Canada: A Gender-Based Statistical Report* (5th ed.). Cat. no. 89-503-XIE. Retrieved June 10, 2009. Available: http://www.statcan.gc.ca/pub/89-503-x/89-503-x2005001-eng.pdf.

———. 2006f. *Women in Canada: Work Chapter Updates.* Ottawa: Statistics Canada.

———. 2006g. "2006 Census: Earnings, Income and Shelter Costs." *The Daily* (May 1).

———. 2007a. "2006 Census: Immigration, Citizenship, Language, Mobility, and Migration." *The Daily* (December 4).

———. 2007b. "A Portrait of Seniors." *The Daily* (February 27).

———. 2007c. *Family Portrait: Continuity and Change in Canadian Families and Households in 2006, 2006 Census.* Cat. no. 97-553-XIE. Retrieved May 12, 2009. Available: http://www12.statcan.ca/census-recensement/2006/as-sa/97-553/pdf/97-553-XIE2006001.pdf.

———. 2007d. "Homicides." *The Daily* (October 17). Retrieved November 12, 2008. Available: http://www.statcan.ca/Daily/English/071017/d071017b.htm.

———. 2007e. "Household Size, by Province and Territory (2006 Census)." Retrieved May 12, 2009. Available: http://www40.statcan.ca/l01/cst01/famil53a-eng.htm.

———. 2007f. "Immigration in Canada: A Portrait of the Foreign-Born Population, 2006 Census: Driver of Population Growth." Ottawa: Statistics Canada. Retrieved April 9, 2009. Available: http://www12.statcan.ca/english/census06/analysis/immcit/canada_foreign.cfm.

———. 2007g. "Marriages." *The Daily.* Retrieved May 12, 2009. Available: http://www.statcan.gc.ca/daily-quotidien/070117/dq070117a-eng.htm.

———. 2007h. "Participation and Activity Limitation Survey 2001." *The Daily* (December 3).

———. 2007i. "Population by Language Spoken Most Often at Home and Age Groups, Percentage Distribution (2006), for Canada, Provinces and Territories—20% Sample Data (table)." Language Highlight Tables, 2006 Census. Statistics Canada Cat. no. 97-555-XWE2006002. Retrieved January 18, 2009. Available: http://www12.statcan.ca/english/census06/data/highlights/Language/Table402.cfm?Lang=E&T=402&GH=4&SC=9&S=99&O=A.

———. 2007j. "Portrait of the Canadian Population in 2006, by Age and Sex, 2006 Census." Ottawa: Statistics Canada.

———. 2007k. "Study: Using the Internet for Education Purposes." Retrieved May 8, 2009. Available: http://www.statcan.gc.ca/daily-quotidien/071030/dq071030b-eng.htm.

———. 2007l. "The Evolving Linguistic Portrait, 2006 Census." Statistics Canada Cat. no. 97-555-XIE. Retrieved June 2, 2009. Available: http://www12.statcan.ca/census-recensement/2006/as-sa/97-555/pdf/97-555-XIE2006001.pdf.

———. 2007m. "Unionization." *Perspectives on Labour and Income* (August). Ottawa: Statistics Canada.

———. 2007n. CANSIM table 179-0004. Corporations Return Act, Major Financial Variables.

———. 2007o. *The Canadian Labour Market at a Glance.* Cat. no. 71-222-XWE. Retrieved May 13, 2009. Available: http://www.statcan.gc.ca/pub/71-222-x/71-222-x2008001-eng.pdf.

———. 2008a. "2006 Census: Ethnic Origin, Visible Minorities, Place of Work and Mode of Transportation." *The Daily* (April 2). Retrieved June 27, 2008. Available: http://www.statcan.ca/Daily/English/080402/d080402a.htm.

———. 2008b. "Aboriginal Peoples in Canada in 2006: Inuit, Métis and First Nations, 2006 Census." Cat. no. 97-558-XIE. Retrieved May 29, 2009. Available: http://www12.statcan.ca/census-recensement/2006/as-sa/97-558/pdf/97-558-XIE2006001.pdf.

———. 2008c. "Aboriginal Peoples Living Off-Reserve and the Labour Market." *The Daily* (December 15).

———. 2008d. "Births, 2006." Ottawa: Statistics Canada.

———. 2008e. "Canada's Ethnocultural Mosaic, 2006 Census." Cat. no. 97-562-X. Retrieved May 27, 2009. Available: http://www12.statcan.gc.ca/english/census06/analysis/ethnicorigin/index.cfm.

———. 2008f. "Canadian Internet Use Survey." *The Daily* (June 12) Ottawa: Statistics Canada.

———. 2008g. "Earnings and Incomes of Canadians over the Past Quarter Century, 2006 Census Findings." Retrieved August 24, 2008. Available: http://www12.statcan.ca/english/census06/analysis/income/pdf/97-563-XIE2006001.pdf.

———. 2008h. "Educational Portrait of Canada: 2006 Census." Cat. no. 97-560-X. Retrieved April 8, 2009. Available: http://www12.statcan.ca/english/census06/analysis/education/pdf/97-560-XIE2006001.pdf.

———. 2008i. *Participation and Activity Limitation Survey of 2006: Labour Force Experience of People with Disabilities in Canada.* Ottawa: Statistics Canada.

———. 2008j. "Public Education Indicators." *The Daily* (July 28). Retrieved April 21, 2009. Available: http://www.statcan.gc.ca/daily-quotidien/080728/dq080728b-eng.htm.

———. 2008k. "The Canadian Labour Market at a Glance." Cat. no. 71-222-XWE. Retrieved June 11, 2009. Available: http://www.statcan.gc.ca/pub/71-222-x/2008001/sectionj/j-gap-ecart-eng.htm.

———. 2008l. "University Tuition Fees." *The Daily* (October 8). Retrieved May 6, 2009. Available: http://www.statcan.gc.ca/daily-quotidien/081009/dq081009a-eng.htm.

———. 2008m. "Violent Victimization in Canada." General Social Survey. *Matter of Fact.* Cat. no. 89-630-X. Retrieved May 16, 2009. Available: http://www.statcan.gc.ca/pub/89-630-x/2008001/article/10643-eng.pdf.

———. 2008n. *Income and Earnings Highlights Tables, 2006 Census.* Retrieved August 24, 2008. Available: http://www12.statcan.ca/english/-census06/data/highlights/income/index.cfm?Lang=E.

———. 2008o. *Report of the Demographic Situation in Canada, 2005 and 2006.* Catalogue no. 91-209-X. Retrieved January 23, 2012, Available: http://publications.gc.ca/collections/collection_2008/statcan/91-209-X/91-209-XIE2004000.pdf.

———. 2009a. "Births and Birth Rate, by Province and Territory." Retrieved April 8, 2009. Available: http://www40.statcan.ca/l01/cst01/demo04b-eng.htm.

———. 2009b. "Deaths: 2006." Ottawa: Statistics Canada.

———. 2009c. "Deaths and Death Rate, by Province and Territory." Retrieved April 8, 2009. Available: http://www40.statcan.gc.ca/l01/cst01/demo07b-eng.htm.

———. 2009d. "Income in Canada, 2007." Statistics Canada Cat. no. 75-202-X. Retrieved June 2, 2009. Available: http://www.statcan.gc.ca/pub/75-202-x/75-202-x2007000-eng.pdf.

———. 2009e. "Labour Force Information: February 15 to February 21, 2009." Cat. no. 71-001-X. Ottawa: Statistics Canada.

———. 2009f. "Labour Force Survey, July 2009." Ottawa: Statistics Canada.

———. 2009g. "Life Expectancy." CANSIM Table 102-0511.

———. 2009h. "Table 101-6501. Divorces and Crude Divorce Rates, Canada, Provinces and Territories, Annual." CANSIM (database). Retrieved May 20, 2009. Available: http://cansim2.statcan.gc.ca/cgi-win/cnsmcgi.exe?Lang=E&CNSM-Fi=CII/CII_1-eng.htm.

———. 2009i. "Infant Mortality Rates, by Province and Territory." Ottawa: Statistics Canada. Retrieved August 25, 2009. Available: http://www40.statcan.go.ca/101/cst01/health21a-eng.htm.

———. 2009j. "University Enrolments by Registration Status and Sex." Retrieved August 26, 2009. Available: http://www40.statcan.ca/l01/cst01/educ53a-eng.htm.

———. 2009k. *Population Projections for Canada, Provinces and Territories, 2005–2031.* Cat. no. 91-520-XIE2005001. Retrieved November 21, 2009: Available: http://www.statcan.gc.ca/ads-annonces/91-520-x/index-eng.htm.

———. 2010a. "Study: Projections of the Diversity of the Canadian Population." *The Daily* (March 9). Retrieved June 24, 2012. Available: http://www.statcan.gc.ca/daily-quotidien/100309/dq100309a-eng.htm.

———. 2010b. "University Degrees, Diplomas and Certificates Awarded." *The Daily* (July 14). Retrieved February 3, 2012. Available: http://www.statcan.gc.ca/daily-quotidien/100714/dq100714b-eng.htm.

———. 2011a. "Births and Total Fertility Rate, by Province and Territory." Retrieved June 3, 2012. Available: http://www.statcan.gc.ca/tables-tableaux/sum-som/l01/cst01/hlth85b-eng.htm.

———. 2011b. "Canadian Internet Use Survey." *The Daily* (May 25).

———. 2011c. "Crude Birth Rate, Age-Specific and Total Fertility Rates (Live Births), Canada, Provinces and Territories." CANSIM Table 102-4505. Ottawa: Statistics Canada.

———. 2011d. "Deaths." *The Daily* (September 27).

———. 2011e. "Women in Canada: A Gender-Based Statistical Report," 6th ed. Statistics Canada Cat. no. 89-503-XIE2010001.

———. 2011f. "Ethnic Diversity and Immigration." Statistics Canada Cat. no. 11-402-X. Retrieved June 27, 2012. Available: http://www.statcan.gc.ca/pub/11-402-x/2011000/chap/imm/imm-eng.htm.

———. 2011g. "Individual Internet Use and E-Commerce." *The Daily* (October 12).

———. 2012a. "Deaths, 2009." *The Daily* (May 31).

———. 2012b. "Labour Force Survey, May 2012." *The Daily* (June 6).

———. 2012c. *The Canadian Population in 2011: Population Counts and Growth.* Ottawa: Statistics Canada.

———. 2012d. "University Tuition Fees, 2012–13" *The Daily* (September 12).

Steele, Tracey. 2005. *Sex, Self, and Society: The Social Construction of Sexuality.* Belmont, Cal: Wadsworth.

Stein, Joel. 2003. "The Singin', Dancin' American Idyll. Time.com. Retrieved June 21, 2003. Available: http://www.time.com/time/magazine/printout/0.8816,458781,00.html.

Stein, Peter J. 1976. *Single.* Englewood Cliffs, N.J.: Prentice-Hall.

———, ed. 1981. *Single Life: Unmarried Adults in Social Context.* New York: St. Martin's Press.

Steinbacher, Roberta, and Helen Bequaert Holmes. 1987. "Sex Choice: Survival and Sisterhood." In Gena Corea et al. (eds.), *Man-made Women: How New Reproductive Technologies Affect Women.* Bloomington: Indiana University Press, 52–63.

Steinem, Gloria. 2011. "Sex, Lies, and Advertising." In Gail Dines and Jean Humez (eds.). *Gender, Race, and Class in Media: A Critical Reader* (3rd ed.). Los Angeles: Sage, 235–241 (orig. pub. in *Ms.* Magazine, July/August 1990).

Stevens, Angi Becker. 2012. "Polyamory: Rebooting Our Definitions of Love and Family." *Role/Reboot* (February 7). Retrieved August 1, 2012. Available: http://www.rolereboot.org/family/details/2012-02-polyamory-rebooting-our-definitions-of-love-and-fami.

Stevenson, Mary Huff. 1988. "Some Economic Approaches to the Persistence of Wage Differences Between Men and Women." In Ann H. Stromberg and Shirley Harkess (eds.), *Women Working: Theories and Facts in Perspective* (2nd ed.). Mountain View, Cal.: Mayfield, 87–100.

Stewart, Abigail J. 1994. "Toward a Feminist Strategy for Studying Women's Lives." In Carol E. Franz and Abigail J. Stewart (eds.), *Women Creating Lives: Identities, Resilience, and Resistance.* Boulder, Col.: Westview, 11–35.

Stier, Deborah S., and Judith A. Hall. 1984. "Gender Differences in Touch: An Empirical and Theoretical Review." *Journal of Personality and Social Psychology* 47 (2): 440–459.

Stine, Mara. 2009. "Thow to Remain in Jail Until Extradition Hearing Tomorrow." *The Vancouver Sun* (February 19): A2.

Stobert, Susan, and Kelly Cranswick. 2004. "Looking After Seniors: Who Does What for Whom?" *Canadian Social Trends* (Autumn): 2–6.

———, and Anna Kemeny. 2003. "Child Free by Choice." *Canadian Social Trends.* Statistics Canada Cat. no. 11-008. Retrieved May 19, 2009. Available: http://www.statcan.gc.ca/pub/11-008-x/2003001/article/6528-eng.pdf.

Stoller, Eleanor Palo, and Rose Campbell Gibson. 1997. *Worlds of Difference: Inequality in the Aging Experience* (2nd ed.). Thousand Oaks, Cal.: Sage.

Stone, Brad. 2001. "Love Online." *Newsweek Magazine* (February 19): 46–51.

Stone, Leroy O. 1967. *Urban Development in Canada: 1961 Census Monograph.* Ottawa: Queen's Printer.

Stout, Cam. 1994. "Common Law: A Growing Alternative." In C. McKie (ed.), *Canadian Social Trends,* vol. 2. Toronto: Thompson Educational Publishing, 179–182.

Straus, M.A. and C. Smith. 1992. "Family Patterns and Child Abuse." In M.A. Straus and R.J. Gelles (eds.), *Physical Violence in American Families: Risk Factors and Adaptations to Violence in 8145 Families.* New Brunswick, N.J.: Transaction.

———, and I. Luis Ramirez. 2004. "Criminal History and Assault of Dating Partners: The Role of Type of Prior Crime, Age of Onset, and Gender." *Violence and Victims* 19 (4): 414–434. Retrieved September 10, 2005. Available: http://pubpages.unh.edu/~mas2/ID03-PR13.pdf.

Strauss, Neil. 2005. *The Game: Penetrating the Secret Society of Pickup Artists.* New York: HarperCollins.

Straw, Will. 2011. "Dimensions of Media: Time and Space, Storage and Transmission." In Will Straw, Sandra Gabrielle, and Ira Wagman (eds.), *Intersection of Media and Communications.* Toronto: Emond Montgomery, 37–52.

Strogatz, Steven H., and Duncan J. Watts. 1998. "Collective Dynamics of 'Small-World' Networks." *Nature* 393: 440–442.

Stross, Randall. 2006. "Cellphone as Tracker: X Marks Your Doubts." *New York Times* (Nov. 19). Retrieved March 30, 2007. Available: http://select.nytimes.com/search/restricted/article?res=F30F1FF63F5A0C7A8DDDA80994DE404482.

Suicide Information & Education Centre. 2002. "About Suicide: Frequently Asked Questions." Retrieved September 7, 2002. Available: http://www.suicideinfo.ca/faq/suicide/faq.asp?faqID=2.

Sumner, William G. 1959. *Folkways.* New York: Dover (orig. pub. 1906).

Sutherland, Anne. 2008. "Montreal Man's $50 M Disappearance 'Shatters' Friends." *Montreal Gazette* (July 13). Retrieved August 16, 1009. Available: http://www.canada.com/news/Montreal+disappearance+shatters+friends/1787353/story.html.

Sutherland, Edwin H. 1939. *Principles of Criminology.* Philadelphia: Lippincott.

———. 1949. *White Collar Crime.* New York: Dryden.

Sutin, Laura. 2002. "At Home with the Kids: Balancing the Child Care Equation," *Transition* (Winter 2001–2002): 14.

Swidler, Ann. 1986. "Culture in Action: Symbols and Strategies." *American Sociological Review* 51 (April): 273–286.

Synge, Jane. 1980. "Work and Family Support Patterns of the Aged in the Early Twentieth Century." In Victor Marshall (ed.), *Aging in Canada: Social Perspectives.* Toronto: Fitzhenry and Whiteside.

Takaki, Ronald. 1993. *A Different Mirror: A History of Multicultural America.* Boston: Little, Brown.

Tamburri, Rosanna. 2008. "Indebted to Higher Education." *University Affairs* (January).

Tannen, Deborah. 1990. *You Just Don't Understand: Women and Men in Conversation.* New York: Morrow.

———. 1993. "Commencement Address, State University of New York at Binghamton." Reprinted in *Chronicle of Higher Education* (June 9): B5.

———. 1995. "Wears Jump Suit. Sensible Shoes. Uses Husband's Last Name." In E.D. Nelson, and B.W. Robinson (eds.), *Gender in the 1990s: Images, Realities, and Issues.* Toronto: Thomson Nelson, 3–7.

Tanner, Julian. 2001. *Teenage Troubles: Youth and Deviance in Canada.* Toronto: ITP Nelson.

Tanofsky, M.B., et al. 1997. "Comparison of Men and Women with Binge Eating Disorder." *International Journal of Eating Disorders* 21 (1): 49.

Tapscott, Don. 1998. *Growing Up Digital: The Rise of the Net Generation.* New York: McGraw-Hill.

Tator, Carol, and Frances Henry. 1999. "South Pacific Perspective Based on Denigrating Stereotypes." *Toronto Star* (January 3).

Tavris, Carol. 1993. *The Mismeasure of Woman.* New York: Touchstone.

Taylor, Charles. 1989. *Sources of the Self.* Cambridge: Cambridge University Press.

Taylor, C., and T. Peter. 2011. "'We Are Not Aliens, We're People, and We Have Rights.' Canadian Human Rights Discourse and High School Climate for LGBTQ Students." *Canadian Review of Sociology* 48 (3): 275–312. doi:10.1111/j.1755-618X.2011.01266.x.

Taylor, Peter Shawn. 1995. "Grandma! Grandpa! Back to Work." *Saturday Night* (June): 18–23, 96.

Tedds, Lindsay. 2005. "The Underground Economy in Canada." In Chris Bajada and Friedrich Schneider (eds.), *Size, Causes and Consequences of the Underground Economy*. Farnham, U.K.: Ashgate, 157–178.

Tepperman, Lorne. 1994. *Choices and Chances: Sociology for Everyday Life* (2nd ed.). Toronto: Harcourt Brace and Company.

Terkel, Studs. 1996. *Coming of Age: The Story of Our Century by Those Who've Lived It*. New York: St. Martin's Griffin.

theadventuresofiman.com. 2007. "The Adventures of Iman." Retrieved March 18, 2007. Available: http://www.theadventuresofiman.com/AboutIman.asp.

Thomas, D. 1992. *Criminality Among the Foreign Born: Analysis of Federal Prison Population*. Ottawa: Immigration and Employment Canada.

Thomas, William I., and Dorothy Swaine Thomas. 1928. *The Child in America*. New York: Knopf.

Thompson, Becky W. 1992. "'A Way Outa No Way': Eating Problems Among African-American, Latina, and White Women." *Gender & Society* 6 (4): 546–561. Revised article, "Food, Bodies, and Growing Up Female: Childhood Lessons About Culture, Race, and Class." In Patricia Fallon, Melanie A. Katzman, and Susan C. Wooley (eds.), *Feminist Perspectives on Eating Disorders*. New York: Guilford Press, 1994, 355–378.

———. 1994. *A Hunger So Wide and So Deep: American Women Speak Out on Eating Problems*. Minneapolis: University of Minnesota.

Thompson, Paul. 1983. *The Nature of Work*. London: Macmillan.

Thornberry, T.P., and M. Farnworth. 1982. "Social Correlates of Criminal Involvement." *American Sociological Review* 47 (4): 505–518.

Thorne, Barrie. 1993. *Gender Play: Girls and Boys in School*. New Brunswick, N.J.: Rutgers University Press.

———. 1995. "Girls and Boys Together . . . But Mostly Apart: Gender Arrangements in Elementary Schools." In Michael S. Kimmel and Michael A. Messner (eds.), *Men's Lives* (3rd ed.). Boston: Allyn & Bacon, 61–73.

———, Cheris Kramarae, and Nancy Henley. 1983. *Language, Gender, and Society*. Rowley, Mass.: Newbury House.

Thornton, Russell. 1984. "Cherokee Population Losses During the Trail of Tears: A New Perspective and a New Estimate." *Ethnohistory* 31: 289–300.

Tieffer, L. 2004. "In Pursuit of the Perfect Penis." In T. L. Steele (ed), *Sex, Self, and Society: The Social Context of Sexuality*. Belmont, Cal.: Wadsworth.

Tilly, Charles. 1973. "Collective Action and Conflict in Large-Scale Social Change: Research Plans, 1974–78." Center for Research on Social Organization. Ann Arbor: University of Michigan, October.

———, ed. 1975. *The Formation of National States in Western Europe*. Princeton, N.J.: Princeton University Press.

———. 1978. *From Mobilization to Revolution*. Reading, Mass.: Addison-Wesley.

Timpson, Joyce. 1995. "Four Decades of Literature on Native Canadian Child Welfare: Changing Themes." *Child Welfare* 74: 525.

Tirrito, Terry. 2003. *Aging in the New Millennium*. Columbia: University of South Carolina Press.

Tiryakian, Edward A. 1978. "Émile Durkheim." In Tom Bottomore and Robert Nisbet (eds.), *A History of Sociological Analysis*. New York: Basic Books, 187–236.

Titchkosky, Tanya. 2003. *Disability, Self and Society*. Toronto: University of Toronto Press.

Titmuss, Richard. 1971. *The Gift Relationship: From Human Blood to Social Policy*. New York: Vintage Books.

Tittle, Charles W., William J. Villemez, and Douglas A. Smith. 1978. "The Myth of Social Class and Criminality." *American Sociological Review* 43 (5): 643–656.

Tjepkema, Michael. 2002. "The Health of the Off-Reserve Aboriginal Population." Statistics Canada. Retrieved August 2, 2005. Available: http://www.statcan.ca/english/freepub/82-003-SIE/2002001/pdf/82-003-SIE2002004.pdf.

Toffler, Alvin. 1980. *The Third Wave*. New York: Bantam.

Tokunaga, Robert, and Stephen Rains. 2010. "An Evaluation of Two Characterizations of the Relationships between Problematic Internet Use, Time Spent Using the Internet, and Psychosocial Problems." *Human Communication Research* 36 (October): 512–545.

Toma, Catalina, and Jeffrey Hancock. 2010. "Looks and Lies: The Role of Physical Attractiveness in Online Dating Self-Presentation and Deception." *Communication Research* 37 (93): 335–351.

Tong, Rosemarie. 1989. *Feminist Thought: A Comprehensive Introduction*. Boulder, Col.: Westview Press.

Tönnies, Ferdinand. 1940. *Fundamental Concepts of Sociology (Gemeinschaft und Gesellschaft)*. Trans. Charles P. Loomis. New York: American Book Company (orig. pub. 1887).

Tonry, Michael. 2009. "The Mostly Unintended Effects of Mandatory Minimum Penalties: Two Centuries of Consistent Findings." In Michael Tonry (ed.), *Crime and Justice: A Review of Research, Volume 38*. Chicago: University of Chicago Press, 65–114.

Toronto Disaster Relief Committee. 2004. "Homelessness is a National Disaster." Retrieved July 3, 2005. Available: http://www.tdrc.net/1aboutTDRC.htm.

Toronto Healthy City Office. 1998. *Homeless Voices*. Toronto: City of Toronto.

Touraine, Alain. 1971. *Post Industrial Society*. New York: Random House.

Transport Canada. 2002. "Urbanization by Province/Territory." Retrieved July 13, 2005. Available: http://www.tc.gc.ca/pol/en/T-Facts3/main.asp?id=10&table=05-Table10&file=economy&Lang=&title=ECONOMY%20%20-%20Demography#graph.

Trevithick, Alan. 1997. "On a Panhuman Preference for Moandry: Is Polyandry an Exception?" *Journal of Comparative Family Studies* (September): 154–184.

Trocmé, Nico, Bruce MacLaurin, Barbara Fallon, Joanne Daciuk, Diane Billingsley, Marc Tourigny, Micheline Mayer, John Wright, Ken Barter, Gale Burford, Joe Hornick, Richard Sullivan, and Brad McKenzie. 2001. *Canadian Incidence Study of Reported Child Abuse and Neglect: Final Report*. Ottawa: Health Canada.

Tran, Kelly. 2004. "Visible Minorities in the Labour Force: 20 Years of Change." *Canadian Social Trends* (Summer): 7–11. Ottawa: Statistics Canada.

Troeltsch, Ernst. 1960. *The Social Teachings of the Christian Churches*, vols. 1 and 2. Trans. O. Wyon. New York: Harper & Row (orig. pub. 1931).

Trotter, E. C., and K.G. Alderson. 2007. "University Students' Definitions of Having Sex, Sexual Partner, and Virginity Loss: The Influence of Participant Gender, Sexual Experience, and Contextual Factors." *Canadian Journal of Human Sexuality* 16: 11–29.

Trottier, Helen, Laurent Martel, Christian Houle, Jean-Marie Berthelot, and Jacques Legare. 2000. "Living at Home or in an Institution: What Makes the Difference for Seniors?" *Health Reports* 11 (Spring): 49–61.

Tryhorn, Chris. 2009. "Nice Talking to You .... Mobile Phone Use Passes Milestone." *The Guardian*. Retrieved January 31, 2012. Available: http://www.guardian.co.uk/technology/2009/mar/03/mobile-phones1?intcmp=239.

Tuggle, Justin L. and Malcolm D. Holmes. 2000. "Blowing Smoke: Status Politics and the Smoking Ban." In Patricia A. Adler and Peter Adler (eds.), *Constructions of Deviance*. Belmont, Cal.: Wadsworth, 159–168.

Tumin, Melvin. 1953. "Some Principles of Stratification: A Critical Analysis." *American Sociological Review* 18 (August): 387–393.

Turcotte, Martin. 2006. "Parents with Adult Children Living at Home." *Canadian Social Trends* (Spring). Statistics Canada Cat. no. 11-008. Available: http://www.statcan.gc.ca/pub/11-008-x/2005004/article/9124-eng.pdf.

Turcotte, Peter, and Alain Bélanger. 1997. "Moving in Together." *Canadian Social Trends* (Winter). Cat. no. 11-008-XPE, 7–10. Ottawa: Statistics Canada.

Turkle, Sherry. 2011. *Alone Together: Why We Expect More from Technology and Less from Each Other*. New York: Basic Books.

Turner, Jonathan, Leonard Beeghley, and Charles H. Powers. 1995. *The Emergence of Sociological Theory* (3rd ed.). Belmont, Cal.: Wadsworth.

———. 1998. *The Emergence of Sociological Theory* (4th ed.). Belmont, Cal.: Wadsworth.

Turner, Jonathan H., Royce Singleton, Jr., and David Musick. 1984. *Oppression: A Socio-History of Black–White Relations in America*. Chicago: Nelson-Hall (reprinted 1987).

Turner, Ralph H., and Lewis M. Killian. 1993. "The Field of Collective Behavior." In Russell L. Curtis, Jr., and Benigno E. Aguirre (eds.), *Collective Behavior and Social Movements*. Boston: Allyn & Bacon, 5–20.

Twenhofel, Karen. 1993. "Do You Diet?" In Leslea Newman (ed.), *Eating Our Hearts Out: Personal Accounts of Women's Relationship to Food*. Freedom, Cal.: Crossing Press.

Tyre, Peg, and Daniel McGinn. 2003. "She Works, He Doesn't." *Newsweek* (May 12): 45–52.

UNAIDS. 2002. *AIDS Epidemic Update 2002*. Geneva: Joint United Nations Program on HIV/AIDS and World Health Organization.

———. 2004. *Global Summary of the HIV and AIDS Epidemic*. New York: United Nations. Retrieved July 20, 2005. Available: http://www.unaids.org/en/resources/epidemiology/epicore.asp.

———. 2008. *2008 Report on the Global AIDS Epidemic*. New York: United Nations. Retrieved April 17, 2009. Available: http://www.unaids.org/en/KnowledgeCentre/HIVData/GlobalReport/2008/2008_Global_report.asp.

———. 2011. *UNAIDS World AIDS Day Report, 2011*. Geneva: UNAIDS. Retrieved: June 20, 2012. Available: http://www.unaids.org/en/media/unaids/contentassets/documents/unaidspublication/2011/JC2216_WorldAIDSday_report_2011_en.pdf.

Underhill, Susan, Victor Marshall, and Sylvie Deliencourt. 1997. *Options 45+: HRCC Survey Final Report*. Ottawa: One Voice.

UNICEF. 2002. *The State of the World's Children*. New York: UNICEF.

———. 2005. "Fertility and Contraceptive Use." UNICEF Statistics. Retrieved July 15, 2005. Available: http://www.childinfo.org/eddb/fertility.

UNICEF Innocenti Research Centre. 2000. "A League Table of Child Poverty in Rich Nations." (Innocenti Report Card No. 1, June). Florence, Italy: UNICEF Innocenti Research Centre.

UNICEF. 2007. "Child Poverty in Perspective: An Overview of Child Well-Being in Rich Countries." Innocenti Report Card 7. Florence: UNICEF Innocenti Research Centre. Retrieved June 18, 2009. Available: http://www.unicef.org/media/files/ChildPovertyReport.pdf.

———. 2008a. "A League Table of Early Childhood Education and Care in Economically Advanced Countries." Retrieved March 1, 2009. Available: http://www.unicef.ca/portal/SmartDefault.aspx?at=2250.

———. 2008b. *State of the World's Children 2008*. New York: UNICEF. Retrieved April 22, 2009. Available: http://www.unicef.org/sowc08/index.php.

———. 2008c. *The Child Care Transition.* (Innocenti Report Card 8). Florence, Italy: UNICEF Innocenti Research Centre. Retrieved February 3, 2009. Available: http://www.unicef.ca/portal/-Secure/Community/502/WCM/HELP/take_action/Advocacy/rc8.pdf.

———. 2009. *State of the World's Children 2009*. New York: UNICEF. Retrieved April 22, 2009. Available: http://www.unicef.org/sowc09/.

———. 2010. "Child Survival and Development'. Retrieved February 20, 2012. Available: http://www.unicef.org/media/media_45485.html.

United Nations. 1997. *Report of the Workshop on Managing the Social Consequences of Structural Change*. New York: Economic and Social Council.

———. 2000. *Report of the Panel on United Nations Peace Operations.* New York: Author.

———. 2001a. "A World Fit for Children." Preparatory Committee for the Special Session of the General Assembly on Children. Revised draft outcome document A/AC-256/CRP.6/Rev. 3 (June). New York: United Nations.

———. 2001b. "We the Children: End-Decade Review of the Follow-up to the World Summit for Children." Report of the Secretary General. A/S-27/3 (May 4). New York: United Nations.

———. 2002. *World Population Ageing 1950–2050*. New York: United Nations Population Division. Retrieved May 23, 2005. Available: http://www.un.org/esa/population/publications/worldageing19502050/countriesorareas.htm.

———. 2008. *The Millennium Goals Report, 2008*. New York: United Nations Population Division.

———. 2009. *World Population Prospects: The 2008 Revision.* New York: United Nations Population Division.

———. 2011. *World Population Prospects: The 2010 Revision.* New York: United Nations Population Division.

United Nations Department for Policy Coordination and Sustainable Development (DPCSD). 1997. "Report of Commission on Sustainable Development, April 1997." New York: United Nations Department for Policy Coordination and Sustainable Development. Online.

United Nations Development Programme. 1996. *Human Development Report, 1996.* New York: Oxford University Press.

———. 1997. *Human Development Report, 1997.* New York: Oxford University Press.

———. 1998. *Human Development Report, 1998.* New York: Oxford University Press.

———. 1999. *Human Development Report 1999: Globalization with a Human Face.* New York: Oxford University Press. Available: http://hdr.undp.org.

———. 2001. *Human Development Report 2001: Making Technologies Work for Development.* New York: Oxford University Press. Available: http://hdr.undp.org.

———. 2003. *Human Development Report, 2003.* New York: Oxford University Press. Retrieved July 20, 2005. Available: http://hdr.undp.org/reports/global/2003/.

———. 2004. *Human Development Report, 2004.* New York: Oxford University Press. Retrieved August 10, 2005. Available: http://hdr.undp.org/reports/global/2004/.

———. 2005. *Human Development Report, 2005.* New York: Oxford University Press. Retrieved December 30, 2005. Available: http://hdr.undp.org/reports/global/2005/.

———. 2008. *Human Development Index, 2008.* New York: United Nations. Retrieved May 4, 2009. Available: http://hdr.undp.org/en/statistics/data/hdi2008.

———. 2010. *Human Development Report, 2010.* New York: Palgrave Macmillan.

———. 2011a. *Human Development Report, 2011.* New York: Palgrave Macmillan.

———. 2011b. *Human Development Index Covers Record 187 Countries, Puts Norway at Top, DR Congo Last.* New York: United Nations Development Programme. Retrieved January 25, 2012. Available: hdr.undp.org/en/media/PR2-HDI-2011HDR-English.pdf.

United Nations Platform for Action Committee. 2005. "Women and the Economy: The Wage Gap." Retrieved September 22, 2005. Available: http://unpac.ca/economy/wagegap3.html.

———. 2011. "Women and the Economy: The Wage Gap." Retrieved February 6, 2012. Available: http://www.unpac.ca/economy/wagegap3.html.

University of Winnipeg. 2002. "Careers in Sociology." Department of Sociology.

Uppal, Sharanjit. 2010. "Labour Market Activity Among Seniors". *Perspectives on Labour and Income* (July): 5–18.

———. 2011. "Unionization 2011." *Perspectives on Labour and Income* (Winter): 3–12.

———, and Sébastien LaRochelle-Côté. 2012. "Factors Associated with Voting." *Perspectives on Labour and Income* (Spring): 4–15.

———, Dafna Kohen, and Saeeda Khan. 2007. "Educational Services and the Disabled Child." *Education Matters: Insights on Education, Learning and Training in Canada* 3 (5). Health Analysis and Measurement Group, Statistics Canada. Retrieved April 24, 2009. Available: http://www.statcan.gc.ca/pub/81-004-x/2006005/9588-eng.htm.

Ursel, Jane. 1996. *Submission to the Commission of Inquiry into the Deaths of Rhonds LaVoie and Roy Lavoie.* Winnipeg.

U.S. Bureau of Labor Statistics. 2012. *Union Members Summary*. Retrieved July 5, 2012. Available: http://www.mcdonalds.ca/ca/en/contact_us/faq.html.

U.S. Census Bureau. 2000. *World Population Profile 2000.* Washington, U.S. Census Bureau.

———. 2005a. *World Population Information.* Washington: U.S. Census Bureau. Retrieved July 14, 2005. Available: http://www.census.gov/ipc/www/world.html.

———. 2005b. "IDB Population Pyramids." Retrieved July 15, 2005. Available: http://www.census.gov/ipc/www/idbpyr.html.

———. 2008. *Income, Poverty, and Health Insurance Coverage in the United States: 2007.* Washington: U.S. Census Bureau.

———. 2009. *World Population Information.* Washington: U.S. Census Bureau. Retrieved April 8, 2009. Available: http://www.census.gov/ipc/www/idb/worldpopgraph.html.

———. 2012. *World Population Information.* Washington: U.S. Census Bureau. Retrieved June 8, 2012. Available: http://www.census.gov/population/international/data/idb/informationGateway.php.

U.S. Congress, Office of Technology Assessment. 1979. "The Effects of Nuclear War." Report quoted in Michael E. Howard, 1990, "On Fighting a Nuclear War." In Francesca M. Cancian and James William Gibson (eds.), *Making War, Making Peace: The Social Foundations of Violent Conflict.* Belmont, Cal.: Wadsworth, 314–322.

Valiquet, Dominique. 2011. *Cybercrime: Issues.* Ottawa: Library of Parliament.

Vallières, Pierre. 1971. *White Niggers of America.* Toronto: McClelland and Stewart.

Valpy, Michael. 2007. "Churches Come Tumbling Down." *Globe and Mail.* December 22: A 17.

Van Biema, David. 1993. "But Will It End the Abortion Debate?" *Time* (June 14): 52–54.

Vander Ploeg, Casey. 2008. *Big Cities and the Census.* Calgary: Canada West Foundation.

Vanier Institute of the Family. 1998. *Families: Change and Continuity.* Available: http://www.cfc-efc.ca/docs/00000329.htm.

———. 2000. *Profiling Canada's Families II.* Retrieved March 3, 2003. Available: http://www.vifamiliy.ca/profiling/p2introe.htm.

———. 2002. *Family Facts.* Ottawa: Vanier Institute of the Family.

———. 2008a. *Family Facts.* Retrieved May 12, 2009. Available: http://www.vifamily.ca/library/facts/facts.html.

———. 2008b. "Finding a Forever Family." *Fascinating Families* 12.Retrieved January 8, 2012. Available: http://www.vifamily.ca/media/node/262/attachments/ff12.pdf.

———. 2009a. "Fathers Matter." *Fascinating Families* 8. Retrieved May 10, 2009. Available: http://www.vifamily.ca/families/issue8.pdf.

———. 2009b. "Paid Work and Housework Combined . . . Lone-Parents Do the Most." *Fascinating Families* 4. Retrieved May 25, 2009. Available: http://www.vifamily.ca/families/issue4.pdf.

———. 2009c. "Raised by a Village." *Fascinating Families* 17. Retrieved January 8, 2012. Available: http://www.vifamily.ca/node/252.

———. 2010. "Children Growing Up in Stepfamilies." *Fascinating Families* 31. Retrieved January 20, 2012. Available: http://www.vifamily.ca/node/513.

———. 2011a. "Four in Ten Marriages End In Divorce." *Fascinating Families* 41. Retrieved January 12 ,2012. Available: http://www.vifamily.ca/media/node/945/attachments/2011-09-15_FASFAM_4-in-10-marriages-end-in-divorce_ENG.pdf.

———. 2011b. *Fathers in Canada.* Retrieved January 12, 2012. Available: http://www.vifamily.ca/media/node/852/attachments/06-13-2011_Tweet_one.pdf.

Vanneman, Reeve, and Lynn Weber Cannon. 1987. *The American Perception of Class.* Philadelphia: Temple University Press.

Vaughan, Diane. 1985. "Uncoupling: The Social Construction of Divorce." In James M. Henslin (ed.), *Marriage and Family in a Changing Society* (2nd ed.). New York: Free Press, 429–439.

Vaughan, Ted R., Gideon Sjoberg, and Larry T. Reynolds, eds. 1993. *A Critique of Contemporary American Sociology.* Dix Hills, N.Y.: General Hall.

Veblen, Thorstein. 1967. *The Theory of the Leisure Class.* New York: Viking (orig. pub. 1899).

Veenhof, Ben, and Peter Timusk. 2009. "Online Activities of Canadian Boomers and Seniors." *Canadian Social Trends* (August): 25–32. Ottawa: Statistics Canada.

Vetter, Harold J., and Gary R. Perlstein. 1991. *Perspectives on Terrorism.* Pacific Grove, Cal.: Brooks/Cole.

Volti, Rudi. 2008. *An Introduction to the Sociology of Work and Occupations.* Los Angeles: Pine Forge Press.
Voyageur, Cora. 2011. "Out in the Open: Elected Female Leadership in Canada's First Nations Community." *Canadian Review of Sociology* 48 (February): 67–85.
Voynick, Steve. 1999. "Living with Ozone." *The World* 1 (July): 192–199.
Wadud, Amina. 2002. "A'ishah's Legacy: Amina Wadud Looks at the Struggle for Women's Rights Within Islam." *New Internationalist* (May). Retrieved March 18, 2007. Available: http://newint.org/-features/2002/05/01/aishahs-legacy.
Wagner, Elvin, and Allen E. Stearn. 1945. *The Effects of Smallpox on the Destiny of the American Indian.* Boston: Bruce Humphries.
Wake, Bev. 2000. "Home Schooling Gets Top Marks." *Ottawa Citizen* (September 7).
Waldman, Amy. 2001. "Behind the Burka: Women Subtly Fought Taliban." *New York Times* (November 19): A1, B4.
Waldram, James B., D. Ann Herring, and T. Kue Young. 1995. *Aboriginal Health in Canada: Historical, Cultural, and Epidemiological Perspectives.* Toronto: University of Toronto Press.
Waldron, Ingrid. 1994. "What Do We Know About the Causes of Sex Differences in Mortality? A Review of the Literature." In Peter Conrad and Rochelle Kern (eds.), *The Sociology of Health and Illness: Critical Perspectives.* New York: St. Martin's Press, 42–54.
Walker, Danna L. 2007. "The Longest Day: Could a Class of College Students Survive Without iPods, Cellphones, Computers and TV from One Sunrise to the Next?" *Washington Post Magazine* (August 5): W20. Retrieved December 29, 2011. Available: http://www.washingtonpost.com/wp-dyn/content/article/2007/08/01/AR2007080101720.html.
Walker, James W. St. G. 1997. *"Race": Rights and the Law in the Supreme Court of Canada.* Waterloo: Wilfrid Laurier Press.
Walker, Lenore. 1979. *The Battered Woman.* New York: Harper & Row.
Wallace, Marnie, 2009. "Police-Reported Crime Statistics in Canada, 2008." *Juristat* 29 (3). Ottawa: Statistics Canada.
Wallace, Walter L. 1971. *The Logic of Science in Sociology.* New York: Aldine de Gruyter.
Wallerstein, Immanuel. 1979. *The Capitalist World-Economy.* Cambridge, England: Cambridge University Press.
———. 1984. *The Politics of the World Economy.* Cambridge, England: Cambridge University Press.
———. 1991. *Unthinking Social Science: The Limits of Nineteenth-Century Paradigms.* Cambridge, England: Polity Press.
———. 2004. *World Systems Analysis: An Introduction.* Durham: Duke University Press.
Wannell, Ted, and Nathalie Caron. 1994. "A Look at Employment Equity Groups Among Recent Postsecondary Graduates: Visible Minorities, Aboriginal Peoples and the Activity Limited." Cat. 11F0019MPE, no. 69. Ottawa: Statistics Canada.
Ward, Margaret. 1998. *The Family Dynamic: A Canadian Perspective* (2nd ed.). Toronto: ITP Nelson.
———. 2005. *The Family Dynamic: A Canadian Perspective* (4th ed.). Toronto: Nelson.
———, and Marc Belanger. 2011. *The Family Dynamic: A Canadian Perspective* (5th ed). Toronto: Nelson.
Ward, Mike. 1996. "Firm Fined $6,000 After Man Killed in Unsafe Workplace." *Winnipeg Free Press* (March 7).
Warner, W. Lloyd, and Paul S. Lunt. 1941. *The Social Life of a Modern Community.* New Haven, Conn.: Yale University Press.
Warr, Mark. 1995. "America's Perceptions of Crime and Punishment." In Joseph F. Sheley, *Criminology: A Contemporary Handbook* (2nd ed.). Belmont, Cal.: Wadsworth, 15–31.
Waters, Malcolm. 1995. *Globalization.* London and New York: Routledge.
Watson, Tracey. 1987. "Women Athletes and Athletic Women: The Dilemmas and Contradictions of Managing Incongruent Identities." *Sociological Inquiry* 57 (Fall): 431–446.
Weaver, A.D., K.L. MacKeigan, and H.A. MacDonald. 2011. "Experiences and Perceptions of Young Adults in Friends with Benefits Relationships: A Qualitative Study." *Canadian Journal of Human Sexuality* 20 (1/2): 41–53.
Webb, Eugene. 1966. *Unobtrusive Measures: Nonreactive Research in the Social Sciences.* Chicago: Rand McNally.
Weber, Max. 1947. *The Theory of Social and Economic Organization.* Trans. A.M. Henderson and Talcott Parsons; ed. Talcott Parsons. New York: Oxford University Press.
———. 1963. *The Sociology of Religion.* Trans. E. Fischoff. Boston: Beacon Press (orig. pub. 1922).
———. 1968. *Economy and Society: An Outline of Interpretive Sociology.* Trans. G. Roth and G. Wittich. New York: Bedminster Press (orig. pub. 1922).
———. 1976. *The Protestant Ethic and the Spirit of Capitalism.* Trans. Talcott Parsons. Introduction by Anthony Giddens. New York: Scribner (orig. pub. 1904–1905).
Weeks, John R. 2002. *Population: An Introduction to Concepts and Issues* (8th edition). Belmont, Cal.: Wadsworth/Thomson Learning.
Weigel, Russell, and P.W. Howes. 1985. "Conceptions of Racial Prejudice: Symbolic Racism Revisited." *Journal of Social Issues* 41: 124–132.
Weinfeld, Morton. 1995. "Ethnic and Race Relations." In R. Brym (ed.), *New Society: Sociology for the 21st Century.* Toronto: Harcourt Brace and Company, 4.1–4.29.
Weinstein, Michael M. 1997. "'The Bell Curve,' Revisited by Scholars." *New York Times* (October 11): A20.
Weintraub, J. 2000. "Where's Bill Cosby When You Need Him?" *National Post* (July 24).
Weiskel, Timothy. 1994. "Vicious Circles." *Harvard International Review* 16: 12–20.
Weisner, Thomas S., Helen Garnier, and James Loucky. 1994. "Domestic Tasks, Gender Egalitarian Values and Children's Gender Typing in Conventional and Nonconventional Families." *Sex Roles* (January): 23–55.
Weiss, Meira. 1994. *Conditional Love: Parents' Attitudes Toward Handicapped Children.* Westport, Conn.: Bergin & Garvey.
Weitz, Rose. 1993. "Living with the Stigma of AIDS." In Delos H. Kelly (ed.), *Deviant Behavior: A Text-Reader in the Sociology of Deviance* (4th ed.). New York: St. Martin's Press, 222–236.
———. 1995. *A Sociology of Health, Illness, and Health Care.* Belmont, Cal.: Wadsworth.
———. 1996. *The Sociology of Health, Illness, and Health Care: A Critical Approach.* Belmont, Cal.: Wadsworth.
Weitzer, R. 2005. "New Directions in Research on Prostitution." *Crime, Law and Social Change* 43: 211–235.
Weitzman, Lenore. 1999. "Poverty After Divorce—The Divorce Revolution: The Unexpected Social and Economic Consequences for Women and Children in America." In M. Reza Nakhaie (ed.), *Debates on Social Inequality: Class, Gender, and Ethnicity.* Toronto: Harcourt Canada, 204–213.
Wekerle, Gerda. 2005. "Gender and the City: Urban Restructuring, Social Exclusion, and Gender Claims." In Harry Hiller (ed.), *Urban Canada: Sociological Perspectives.* Toronto: Oxford University Press, 225–245.
Wellhousen, Karyn, and Zenong Yin. 1997. "Peter Pan Isn't a Girls' Part: An Investigation of Gender Bias in a Kindergarten Classroom." *Women and Language,* 20: 35–40.
Welner, Kevin Grant, and Jeannie Oakes. 2000. *Navigating the Politics of Detracking.* Arlington Heights, Ill.: Skylight.
Wendell, Susan. 1995. "Toward a Feminist Theory of Disability." In E.D. Nelson and B.W. Robinson (eds.), *Gender in the 1990s.* Toronto: Thomson Nelson, 455–465.
Wente, Margaret. 2005. "The Footprint of My Future." *Globe and Mail.* (June 4): A19.
———. 2006. "In the Best Interests of the Child?" *Globe and Mail* (September 30): A21.
———. 2011. "Andy Rooney had the Right Idea About Retirement." *Globe and Mail* (November 8). Retrieved May 12, 2012. Available: http://www.theglobeandmail.com/news/opinions/margaret-wente/andy-rooney-had-the-right-idea-about-retirement/article2228480.
West, Candice, and Don H. Zimmerman. 1991. "Doing Gender." In J. Lorber and Susan A. Farrell (eds.), *The Social Construction of Gender.* London: Sage Publications, 13–37.
West, D. 1993. *Male Prostitution.* New York: Routledge.
Weston, Kath. 1991. *Families We Choose: Lesbians, Gays, Kinship.* New York: Columbia University Press.
Westrum, Ron. 1991. *Technologies and Society: The Shaping of People and Things.* Belmont, Cal.: Wadsworth.
Wharton, Amy. 2000. "Feminism at Work." *The Annals of the American Academy of Political and Social Science* 571 (September): 167–182.
———. 2004. *The Sociology of Gender: An Introduction to Theory and Research.* London: Blackwell.
Whitaker, Barbara. 1997. "Earning It; If You Can't Beat Dilbert, Hire Him." *New York Times* (June 29): C12.
Whitaker, Reg. 1991. *Double Standard: The Secret Story of Canadian Immigration.* Toronto: Lester and Orpen Dennys.
White, Merry. 1994. *The Material Child: Coming of Age in Japan and America.* Berkeley: University of California Press.
———. *Perfectly Japanese: Making Families in an Era of Upheaval.* Berkeley: University of California Press.
White, Richard W. 1992. *Rude Awakening: What the Homeless Crisis Tells Us.* San Francisco: ICS Press.
Whiting, Dominic. 2005. "Taubman Targets Shopping Mall 'Cash Cows' in China." Boston.com. Retrieved Jan. 15, 2006. Available: http://www.boston.com/business/articles/2005/06/20/-taubman_targets_asian_retail_cash_cow.
Whittington, Les. 2012. "Visible Minorities Increasing in Canada." *Toronto Star* (May 17). Retrieved June 1, 2012. Available: http://www.thestar.com/news/canada/politics/article/1180164--visible-minorities-increasing-in-canada.
Whorf, Benjamin Lee. 1956. *Language, Thought and Reality.* John B. Carroll (ed.). Cambridge, Mass.: MIT Press.
Whyte, William Foote. 1988. *Street Corner Society: Social Structure of an Italian Slum.* Chicago: University of Chicago Press (orig. pub. 1943).
———. 1989. "Advancing Scientific Knowledge Through Participatory Action Research." *Sociological Forum* 4: 367–386.
Whyte, William H., Jr. 1957. *The Organization Man.* Garden City, N.Y.: Anchor.
Wieler, Joseph M. 1986. "The Role of Law in Labour Relations." In Ivan Bernier and Andree Lojoie (eds.), *Labour Law and Urban Law in Canada.* Toronto: University of Toronto Press.
Williams, Cara. 2006. "Disability in the Workplace." *Perspectives on Labour and*

Income (February): 16–24. Ottawa: Statistics Canada.
———. 2011. "Economic Well-being." In Statistics Canada, 2011, *Women in Canada: A Gender-Based Statistical Report* (6th ed.). Cat. no, 89-503-XIE2010001. Available: http://www.statcan.gc.ca/pub/75-001-x/2011001/pdf/11394-eng.pdf.
Williams, Christine L. 1989. *Gender Differences at Work.* Berkeley: University of California Press.
Williams, Robin M., Jr. 1970. *American Society: A Sociological Interpretation* (3rd ed.). New York: Knopf.
Williamson, Robert C., Alice Duffy Rinehart, and Thomas O. Blank. 1992. *Early Retirement: Promises and Pitfalls.* New York: Plenum Press.
Wilson, Beth, and Carly Steinman. 2000. *Hunger Count 2000: A Surplus of Hunger*. Toronto: Canadian Association of Food Banks.
Wilson, David, ed. 1997. "Globalization and the Changing U.S. City." *Annals of the American Academy of Political and Social Sciences,* special issue, 551 (May).
Wilson, Edward O. 1975. *Sociobiology: A New Synthesis.* Cambridge, Mass.: Harvard University Press.
Wilson, Elizabeth. 1991. *The Sphinx in the City: Urban Life, the Control of Disorder, and Women.* Berkeley: University of California Press.
Wilson, William Julius. 1996. *When Work Disappears: The World of the New Urban Poor.* New York: Knopf.
Winn, Maria. 1985. *The Plug-in Drug: Television, Children, and the Family.* New York: Viking.
Winnipeg Free Press. 2012. "Student Suspended for Wearing a T-Shirt That Says 'Life is Wasted Without Jesus.'" May 3. Retrieved May 3, 2012.Available: http://www.winnipegfreepress.com/canada/student-suspended-for-wearing-t-shirt-that-says-life-is-wasted-without-jesus-150040515.html.
Wirth, Louis. 1938. "Urbanism as a Way of Life." *American Journal of Sociology* 40: 1–24.
———. 1945. "The Problem of Minority Groups." In Ralph Linton (ed.), *The Science of Man in the World Crisis.* New York: Columbia University Press, 38.
Wiseman, Jacqueline. 1970. *Stations of the Lost: The Treatment of Skid Row Alcoholics.* Chicago: University of Chicago Press.
Wolf, Daniel. 1996. "A Bloody Biker War." *Maclean's* (January 15): 10–11.
Wolf, Robert M., and Lisa K. Sharp. 2005. "Vaccination or Immunization? The Impact of Search Terms on the Internet." *Journal of Health Communication* (September): 537–551.
Wolfe, Jeanne M. 1992. "Canada's Livable Cities." *Social Policy* 23: 56–63.
Wolfe, Robert, and Lisa Sharp. 2005. "Vaccination or Immunization? The Impact of Search Terms on the Internet." *Journal of Health Communication* 10: 539–553.
Wollstonecraft, Mary 1974. *A Vindication of the Rights of Woman.* New York: Garland (orig pub. 1797).
Wong, Sandra L. 1991. "Evaluating the Content of Textbooks: Public Interests and Professional Authority." *Sociology of Education* 64: 11–18.
Wood, Darryl S., and Curt T. Griffiths. 1996. "Patterns of Aboriginal Crime." In Robert A. Silverman, James J. Teevan, and Vincent F. Sacco (eds.), *Crime in Canadian Society* (5th ed.). Toronto: Harcourt Brace and Company, 222–223.
Wood, Julia T. 1999. *Gendered Lives: Communication, Gender, and Culture* (3rd ed.). Belmont, Cal.: Wadsworth.
Wooden, Wayne S. 1995. *Renegade Kids, Suburban Outlaws: From Youth Culture to Delinquency.* Belmont, Cal.: Wadsworth.
Woodward, Kathleen. 1991. *Aging and Its Discontents: Freud and Other Fictions.* Bloomington: Indiana University Press.
Woolley, Frances. 1998. "Work and Household Transactions." Ottawa: Canadian Policy Research Networks.
WordSpy.com. 2003. "Flash Mob." Retrieved August 11, 2003. Available: http://www.wordspy.com/words/flashmob.asp.
World Bank. 2002. "Suicide Rates (per 100,000), by Gender, Canada, 1950–1997." Retrieved October 5, 2002. Available: http://www5.who.int/-mental_health/download.cfm?id=000000029.
———. 2003a. *World Health Report 2003.* Retrieved July 20, 2005. Available: http://www.who.int/whr/2003/overview/en/.
———. 2003b. *World Development Indicators 2003.* Retrieved August 8, 2005. Available: http://www.worldbank.org/data/wdi2003.
———. 2004a. *World Health Report 2004.* Retrieved August 10, 2005. Available: http://www.who.int/whr/2004/en/.
———. 2004b. "Millennium Development Goals: Global Data Monitoring System. Promote Gender Equality and Empower Women." Retrieved August 12, 2005. Available: http://ddp-ext.worldbank.org/ext/MDG/gdmis.do.
———. 2005a. *World Development Indicators 2005.* Retrieved July 22, 2005. Available: http://www.worldbank.org/data/wdi2005.
———. 2005b. "Data and Statistics: Country Classification." Retrieved August 9, 2005. Available: http://www.worldbank.org/data/countryclass/countryclass.html.
———. 2005c. *World Health Report 2005.* Retrieved July 20, 2005. Available: http://www.who.int/whr/2005/en/index.html.
———. 2006. *World Development Report 2006.* New York: World Bank.
———. 2008a. *On-Line Atlas of the Millennium Development Goals.* Retrieved May 4, 2009. Available: http://devdata.worldbank.org/atlas-mdg/.
———. 2008b. *The Role of Mobile Phones in Sustainable Rural Poverty Reduction.* Washington: ICT Policy Division, World Bank.
———. 2008c. *World Development Indicators 2008.* Retrieved May 9, 2009. Available: http://siteresources.worldbank.org/DATASTATISTICS/Resources/front.pdf.
———. 2010. *World Development Report 2010.* Washington: World Bank.
———. 2011. *World Development Report 2011.* Washington: World Bank.
World Food Program. 2009. *Hunger Stats.* Rome: World Food Program. Retrieved May 4, 2009. Available: http://www.wfp.org/hunger/stats.
World Health Organization. 1998. *Fifty Facts from the World Health Report 1998.* Available: www.who.int/whr/1998/factse.htm.
———. 2009. *World Health Statistics, 2008.* Retrieved April 27, 2008. Available: http://www.who.int/whosis/whostat/2008/en/index.html.
———. 2012a. *World Health Statistics 2012.* Geneva: World Health Organization.
———. 2012b. "Social Determinants of Health". Retrieved February 22, 2012. Available: http://www.who.int/social_determinants/en.
World Literacy of Canada. 2005a. "Facts and Figures." Retrieved September 15, 2005. Available: http://www.worldlit.ca/facts.html.
———. 2005b. "Learning About Literacy." Retrieved November 15, 2005. Available: http://www.worldlit.ca/literacy.html.
Worster, Donald. 1985. *Nature's Economy: A History of Ecological Ideas.* New York: Cambridge University Press.
Wortley, Scott, and Julian Tanner. 2003. "Data, Denials, and Confusion: The Racial Profiling Debate in Toronto." *Canadian Journal of Criminology and Criminal Justice* 45 (July): 367–390.
———. 2004. "Discrimination or 'Good' Policing? The Racial Profiling Debate in Canada." *Our Diverse Cities* 1: 197–201. Retrieved May 27, 2009. Available: http://canada.metropolis.net/pdfs/WortleyTanner_e.pdf.
Wotherspoon, Terry. 1994. "Colonization, Self-Determination, and the Health of Canada's First Nations Peoples." In B. Singh Bolaria and Rosemary Bolaria (eds.), *Racial Minorities, Medicine and Health.* Halifax, N.S.: Fernwood, 247–267.
———. 2009. *The Sociology of Education in Canada.* Toronto: Oxford University Press.
Wouters, Cas. 1989. "The Sociology of Emotions and Flight Attendants: Hochschild's Managed Heart." *Theory, Culture & Society* 6: 95–123.
Wresch, William. 1996. *Disconnected: Haves and Have-Nots in the Information Age.* New Brunswick, N.J.: Rutgers University Press.
Wright, Erik Olin. 1978. "Race, Class, and Income Inequality." *American Journal of Sociology* 83 (6): 1397.
———. 1979. *Class Structure and Income Determination.* New York: Academic Press.
———. 1985. *Class.* London: Verso.
———. 1997. *Class Counts: Comparative Studies in Class Analysis.* Cambridge, U.K.: Cambridge University Press.
Wright, Charles. 1959. *Mass Communication: A Sociological Perspective.* New York: Random House.
Wright, Erik Olin, Karen Shire, Shu-Ling Hwang, Maureen Dolan, and Janeen Baxter. 1992. "The Non-Effects of Class on the Gender Division of Labor in the Home: A Comparative Study of Sweden and the U.S." *Gender & Society* 6 (2): 252–282.
Wuthnow, Robert. 1996. *Poor Richard's Principle: Recovering the American Dream Through the Moral Dimension of Work, Business, and Money.* Princeton, N.J.: Princeton University Press.
Yee, Nick, and Jeremy Bailenson. 2007. "The Proteus Effect: the Effect of Transformed Self-Representation on Behavior." *Human Communication Research* 33 (July): 271–290.
———, Jeremy Bailenson, and Nicolas Duchenault. 2009. "The Proteus Effect: Implications of Transformed Digital Self-Representation on Online and Offline Behavior." *Communication Research* 36 (March): 285–312.
Yinger, J. Milton. 1960. "Contraculture and Subculture." *American Sociological Review* 25 (October): 625–635.
———. 1982. *Countercultures: The Promise and Peril of a World Turned Upside Down.* New York: Free Press.
Yong, Ed. 2011. "New Evidence That IQ Is Not Set in Stone." cbsnews.com (April 26). Retrieved April 28, 2011. Available: www.cbsnews.com/stories/2011/04/26/scitech/main20057536.shtml.
Young, A. 2008. "The State Is Still in the Bedrooms of the Nation: The Control and Regulation of Sexuality in Canadian Criminal Law." *Canadian Journal of Human Sexuality* 17 (4): 203–220.
Young, K., and L. Curry. 1997. "Beyond White Pride: Identity, Meaning, and Contradiction in the Canadian Skinhead Subculture." *Canadian Review of Sociology and Anthropology* 34 (2): 176–206.
Young, Michael Dunlap. 1994. *The Rise of the Meritocracy.* New Brunswick, N.J.: Transaction (orig. pub. 1958).
Youth Advocacy Program International. 2009. "Street Children and Homelessness." Retrieved March 6, 2009. Available: http://www.yapi.org/street/.
Yunus, Muhammad. 1997. "Empowerment of the Poor: Eliminating the Apartheid Practiced by Financial Institutions." Paper presented to the State of the World Forum, San Francisco.

———. 2009. "Creating a New World: A Dream or a Reality?" 7th Nelson Mandela Annual Lecture. Retrieved 25 March 2012. Available: http://muhammadyunus.org/Speeches/7th-nelson-mandela-annual-lecture.

Zakaria, Fareed. 2011. "Fareed's Take: The Role of Social Media in Revolutions." CNN. Retrieved October 12, 2011. Available: http://globalpublicsquare.blogs.cnn.com/2011/03/27/the-role-of-social-media-in-revolutions.

Zavella, Patricia. 1987. *Women's Work and Chicano Families: Cannery Workers of the Santa Clara Valley.* Ithaca, N.Y.: Cornell University Press.

Zehr, Mary Ann. 2006. "Public Schools Fare Well Against Private Schools in Study." *Education Week.* Retrieved April 22, 2009. Available: http://www.edweek.org/login.html?source=http://www.edweek.org/ew/articles/2006/07/26/43private.h25.html&destination=http://www.edweek.org/ew/articles/2006/07/26/43private.h25.html&levelId=2100.

Zeidenberg, Jerry. 1990. "The Just-in-Time Workforce." *Small Business* (May): 31–34.

Zeitlin, Irving M. 1997. *Ideology and Development of Sociological Theory* (6th ed.). Upper Saddle River, N.J.: Prentice-Hall.

Zelizer, Viviana. 1985. *Pricing the Priceless Child: The Changing Social Value of Children.* New Haven, Conn.: Yale University Press.

Zgodzinski, Rose. 1996. "Where Immigrants Come From." *Globe and Mail* (June 20).

Zhang, Xuelin. 2010. *Low Income Measurement in Canada: What Do Different Lines and Indexes Tell Us?* Statistics Canada, Income Research Series, Cat. no. 75F0002M—No. 3. Retrieved April 12, 2012. Available: http://www.statcan.gc.ca/pub/75f0002m/75f0002m2010003-eng.pdf.

Zhu, Wei Xing, Li Lu, and Therese Hesketh. 2009. "China's Excess Males, Sex Selective Abortion, and One Child Policy: Analysis of Data from 2005 Intercensus Survey. *British Medical Journal* (April): 920–923.

Zimmerman, Don H. 1992. "They Were All Doing Gender, But They Weren't All Passing: Comment on Rogers." *Gender & Society* 6 (2): 192–198.

Zimring, Franklin. 2012. *The City That Became Safe: New York's Lesson for Urban Crime and Its Control.* New York: Oxford University Press.

Zipp, John F. 1985. "Perceived Representativeness and Voting: An Assessment of the Impact of 'Choices' vs. 'Echoes.'" *American Political Science Review* 60 (3): 738–759.

Zuboff, Shoshana. 1988. *In the Age of the Smart Machine.* New York: Basic Books.

Zuckerman, Ethan. 2011. "Cute Cats and the Arab Spring: The 2011 Vancouver Human Rights Lecture." *Ideas.* CBC Radio (December 9, 2011). Available: http://www.cbc.ca/ideas/episodes/2012/02/24/the-vancouver-human-rights-lecture---cute-cats-and-the-arab-spring.

Zurcher, Louis. 1983. *Social Roles: Conformity, Conflict, and Creativity.* Beverly Hills, Cal.: Sage.

NAME INDEX

Note: Page numbers that begin with "21" and "22" (e.g., 21-11, 22-15–22-16) refer to Chapters 21 and 22, the online chapters.

SUBJECT INDEX

Note: Page numbers that begin with "21" and "22" (e.g., 21-11, 22-15–22-16) refer to Chapters 21 and 22, the online chapters.